Economics

Economics

David King

Emeritus Professor of Public Economics,
University of Stirling

OXFORD
UNIVERSITY PRESS

Great Clarendon Street, Oxford OX2 6DP

Oxford University Press is a department of the University of Oxford.
It furthers the University's objective of excellence in research, scholarship,
and education by publishing worldwide in

Oxford New York

Auckland Cape Town Dar es Salaam Hong Kong Karachi
Kuala Lumpur Madrid Melbourne Mexico City Nairobi
New Delhi Shanghai Taipei Toronto

With offices in

Argentina Austria Brazil Chile Czech Republic France Greece
Guatemala Hungary Italy Japan Poland Portugal Singapore
South Korea Switzerland Thailand Turkey Ukraine Vietnam

Oxford is a registered trade mark of Oxford University Press
in the UK and in certain other countries

Published in the United States
by Oxford University Press Inc., New York

British Library Cataloguing in Publication Data
Data available

Library of Congress Cataloging in Publication Data
Data available

Typeset by Techset Composition Ltd, Salisbury, UK
Printed in Italy
on acid-free paper by
L.E.G.O. S.p.A.—Lavis TN

ISBN 978-0-19-954302-1

10 9 8 7 6 5 4 3 2 1

Brief contents

Detailed contents

Part III Macroeconomics

Preface for students

Why study economics?

This book is written for students who are studying economics for the first time. So let's begin by considering why it is a rewarding subject to study.

One reason is that it concerns some major issues that will affect you throughout your life. Here is merely a small selection.

- How do producers decide on the prices you must pay?
- Are producers who offer discounts to some buyers, such as students and senior citizens, doing so simply to be nice to those customers?
- We all need food to live and we all need health care when we are ill. Why do governments leave food production to firms but often provide hospitals themselves?
- Why do some jobs attract higher wages than others? Will the jobs that have relatively high wages today always have relatively high wages?
- How might a young person weigh up the pros and cons of undertaking further full-time education rather than seeking a full-time job?
- Will the world run out of non-renewable resources such as oil?
- Why do governments struggle so hard to reduce the number of people in poverty?
- How safe are banks?
- Why do countries sometimes go into recessions, which lead to high unemployment? Why do governments often struggle to reduce unemployment?
- Will incomes and living standards in rich countries continue to grow? Will incomes and living standards in poor countries ever catch up with those in rich countries?
- Why do many governments want to spend less, despite the effects on government services?
- Why are so many of the things that you buy produced abroad, when they could perfectly well be produced in your own country?

Another reason for studying economics is that, on average, employers pay economics graduates who enter graduate jobs more than they pay almost any other new graduates. This is shown in the table on p. 335. The main exceptions are graduates who have studied medicine, but they have to study for longer to achieve their advantage.

The reason that a study of economics is so beneficial is doubtless that it imparts a wide range of transferable skills. These include:

- an ability to analyse problems by identifying the key issues and by thinking logically about them;
- an ability to devise and develop theories about how people behave, and to use statistical techniques to test and apply these theories;
- an ability to devise policies while understanding that all options will have pros and cons that must be looked at from different viewpoints, without any initial prejudices, before a choice is made.

A book for students

In writing this book, I tried constantly to have the needs of students in mind, most particularly in the following ways:

- by showing that economics covers interesting and important issues;
- by showing that economists look at problems in a logical and interesting way;
- by showing that economics is a body of principles to be understood and applied to the world in which you live—not a huge body of knowledge that you have to learn;
- by keeping the book as short as possible—I know you have other calls on your time, both earning money and leisure activities;
- by having short paragraphs and sentences, and a minimum of jargon;
- by being thorough, to help you to understand as much as possible and to misunderstand as little as possible.

As an aid to understanding, there are several features that I hope you will find useful. More on these can be found in the walk-through of the textbook features on page xviii.

Preface for instructors

A key principle of this book

The key principle of this text is to present economics as a subject that must be understood and applied, not merely learned. Accordingly, I probably devote a larger proportion of the text than is usual to applying the models given.

For example, in Part II on Microeconomics, rather than hoping the student will simply learn the short-run equilibrium condition for a perfect competitor, I hope the student will see how understanding this condition can show why the firm might react differently to changes in the prices of fixed inputs and variable inputs. And in Part III on Macroeconomics, I hope students can see how the *AS–AD* model, once properly understood, throws light on a wide array of issues.

Building a course

The adjacent table of contents lists the chapters in this book. Those shown in bold are generally necessary prerequisites for understanding the material of the later chapters, while those shown in italics are not. Accordingly, it would generally be advisable to cover the bold chapters in the order in which they are given, while the chapters shown in italics could be left until later than they appear in the text.

Unusual pedagogical points

There are a few cases in which my exposition has a minor departure from the conventional treatment, and these are as follows.

- **Chapter 1: The Nature of Economics**. In the circular flow, I refer under factor incomes to wages and trading profits, without separating out interest and

TABLE OF CONTENTS

Chapters including material needed for some later chapters are shown in **bold type**. Chapters including material that can be left until later are shown in *italics*.

rent from other profits. This brings the treatment into line with the official presentation of the national income statistics, which are discussed in Chapter 18. It also allows the term 'profit' on its own to be used throughout the book to mean economic profit.

- **Chapter 8: Costs and Production Methods**. For my exposition of production functions with two inputs, I do not use a typical agricultural example of crops. This is partly because it is hard to claim that only two inputs are needed to produce crops, namely land and labour, as there must also be some seeds or trees; and it is partly because I prefer an example that uses labour and capital. So I hope my example of a ferry firm that uses rowing boats and rowers will be found at least acceptable.
- **Chapter 19: GDP and the Multiplier Model**. My circular flow figures replace the box usually labelled 'firms' with one labelled 'firms and government departments'. The conventional approach often seems to imply that governments raise taxes and then pay firms to provide services—but it seems to me to stretch the term 'firms' too far, and certainly way beyond what is assumed in the theory of the firm, to include among them producers such as the armed forces, the police, and state schools.
- **Chapter 21: GDP and Prices—the AS-AD model**. I have derived the short-run aggregate supply curve more thoroughly than usual. It is sometimes implied that this curve slopes upwards throughout its length because wages are sticky in both directions. However, it is hard to persuade students that wages could be so sticky upwards that an inflationary gap might last for a significant period. So I give additional explanations for the slope. Incidentally, we expect students to be familiar with a fairly rigorous derivation of the supply curve in perfect competition, and the aggregate supply curve surely deserves at least as rigorous treatment.
- **Chapter 27: International Trade**. I have explored how far countries that trade will specialize in the production of the products that they export. It is very easy for students to conclude from simple examples of comparative advantage theory that each country will specialize wholly in the production of one good.
- **Chapter 28: International Finance**. I have kept to a minimum the analysis of countries that severely restrict capital flows or which use fixed exchange rates. The UK and the eurozone have done neither during the lifetime of any students—except some mature students—and they are unlikely to do so in future; I am not sure that a first-year course is the right place to discuss what are now hypothetical alternatives.

Acknowledgements

Publisher's acknowledgements

I would like to join the publishers in thanking the following people for their invaluable comments and helpful reviews throughout the process of developing the text and the Online Resource Centre:

- Dr Fiona Atkins, *Economics Department, Birkbeck College*
- Professor Steve Cook, *Swansea University*
- Joe Cox, *University of Portsmouth*
- Mr Marco Faravelli, *University of Queensland*
- Dr Ian Jackson, *Staffordshire University Business School*
- Professor Colin Jones, *Heriot-Watt University*
- Dr Jassodra Maharaj, *University of East London*
- Dr James Reade, *University of Birmingham*
- Gonzalo Varela, *University of Sussex*
- Ms Peri Yavash, *Coventry University*

We are also most grateful to those reviewers who chose to remain anonymous.

Author's acknowledgements

On a personal level, I would like to express my gratitude to the very many students I have taught for what I have learned from their help and suggestions. I would also like to thank my former and current colleagues at the University of Stirling for discussing many issues with me. I am greatly indebted to many people at Oxford University Press, particularly Kirsty Reade, Jo Hardern, and Helen Cook, for their support and encouragement, and also to Vanessa Plaister for her painstaking help with the proofreading. Finally, and most importantly, I would like to thank my wife Susan for her understanding and patience over the entire project.

Walk-through of the textbook features

Remember Boxes... alert you to key points from earlier chapters that will be built on in the chapter you are about to read.

Remember from Chapter 1 that the world has only a limited amount of resources of labour, land, and capital. The economic problem is that these scarce resources can produce only a limited amount of goods and services, yet there is no limit to the amount that we would like to consume.

Learning Objectives... outline the main concepts and ideas, and indicate what you can expect to learn from each chapter.

This chapter shows you how to answer questions like these, by understanding:

* How the economic problem of scarcity can be illustrated with a diagram.
* The varying extents to which governments intervene in their economies.
* How governments can intervene in an effort to ease the economic problem.

Section Summaries... regularly allow you to see if there are key points that you have missed or misunderstood.

3.2 Summary

- A demand curve shows the quantity that would be demanded at each price or wage, and a supply curve shows the quantity that would be supplied at each price or wage. The price or wage will settle at its equilibrium level, which is the level at which the two curves intersect.
- At that equilibrium price or wage, there is no excess demand or excess supply, so the quantity demanded equals the quantity supplied, and this is the equilibrium quantity.

In-text Questions... enable you to check your understanding regularly, with answers given at the end of each chapter.

Question 3.1 In Figure 3.6, would producers know that the new equilibrium price would be 20p immediately after the demand curve shifted?

Everyday Economics Boxes... show global real-world examples of the material discussed in the chapters.

2.3 Everyday economics

A planned economy that works poorly

North Korea has regular food shortages and the World Food Programme has just announced that it will send in aid worth $200m to help 3.5 million people who are on government rations that meet only about half their needs.

'UN body starts emergency food aid to North Korea', *Reuters*, 29 April 2011
'WFP begins emergency food aid to N. Korea', *Arirang*, 30 April 2011

Comment There had recently been poor crops in North Korea, but there is no food shortage in neighbouring South Korea. Admittedly, it is hard to say exactly how far the problems in the North stem from planning in principle, or from bad planning.

Glossary... includes all of the key terms in the chapter you have just read, and allows you to check your understanding of these terms.

abc Glossary

Command economy: another term for a planned economy.

Free market: a market with no government intervention over price or quantity.

Planned economy: an econom determines how, for what, for resources are used.

Positive statement: a statemen

Questions for Review... help you to check if you have understood the chapter, with answers provided on the Online Resource Centre.

Question for review

2.1 Consider the country with the production possibility frontier shown in Figure 2.2. What if anything will happen to this frontier in each of the following circumstances?

(a) The country acquires new machines which can be used

(c) The country improves its e who are entering the workforce can produce more than people v of their careers.

Questions for Discussion... encourage you to think about the issues which lead on from the chapter.

Questions for discussion

2.1 Suppose a government stimulates immigration to increase the amount of labour available to firms. What might be the effects of this on the country's economic problem?

ers. What might be the effects economic problem?

2.3 Suppose a government enc tion of a country's resources to b

Common Student Errors... highlight those mistakes which are easily made, enabling you to recognize them and so avoid losing marks in essays and exam questions.

Common student errors

Students often assume that a production possibility frontier applies to a firm or to a government. Instead, it must apply to an economy, that is an area with producers and consumers. Usually when we talk of production possibility

take yourself as an example. Sup ing curtains. You sell the curtai buy other items like food and c tains are the only thing you pro

Walk-through of the Online Resource Centre features

www.oxfordtextbooks.co.uk/orc/king/

The Online Resource Centre (ORC) comprises resources for both lecturers and students, which include:

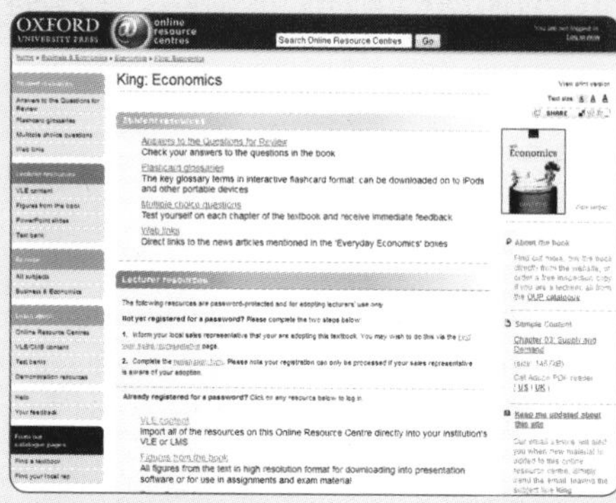

For Students

Multiple choice questions... are ideal in helping you test your understanding of a topic before progressing to the next stage. These are available for each chapter, and provide instant feedback and page references.

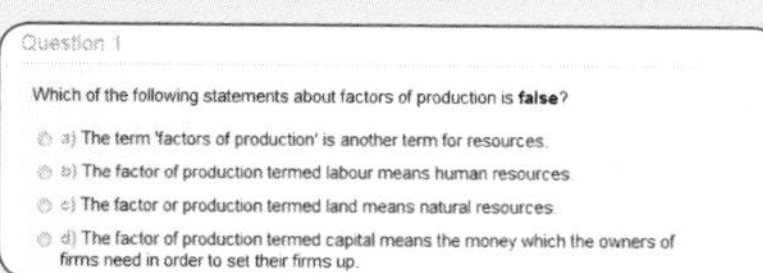
Question 1

Which of the following statements about factors of production is **false**?

a) The term 'factors of production' is another term for resources.

b) The factor of production termed labour means human resources.

c) The factor or production termed land means natural resources.

d) The factor of production termed capital means the money which the owners of firms need in order to set their firms up.

Flashcard glossary... which can be downloaded to an MP3 player allows you to check your understanding of important key concepts on the go.

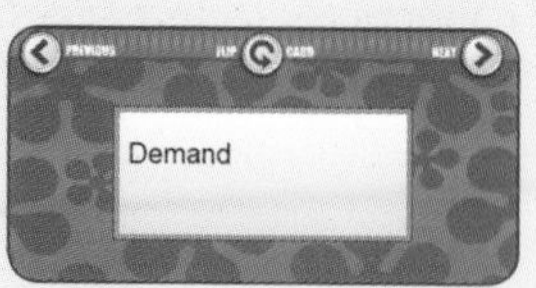

Answers to the Questions for Review... for you to check against your own and identify how well you are progressing in your learning.

Answers to Questions for Review

2.1 (a) The end of the production possibility frontier (*PPF*) on the vertical axis shift upwards. (b) The end of the *PPF* on the horizontal axis shifts to the right. (c) Wit more highly trained labour, the *PPF* shifts outwards; (d) The *PPF* would not move nut production would move from a point inside the *PPF* to a point closer to the *PPF*

Direct web links... to the articles mentioned in the 'Everyday Economics' boxes show you the relevance of economics in real life situations.

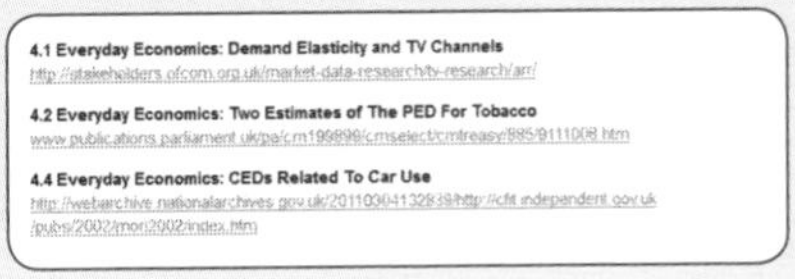

4.1 Everyday Economics: Demand Elasticity and TV Channels
http://stakeholders.ofcom.org.uk/market-data-research/tv-research/arr/

4.2 Everyday Economics: Two Estimates of The PED For Tobacco
www.publications.parliament.uk/pa/cm199899/cmselect/cmtreasy/885/9111008.htm

4.4 Everyday Economics: CEDs Related To Car Use
http://webarchive.nationalarchives.gov.uk/20110304132839/http://cfit.independent.gov.uk/pubs/2002/mori2002/index.htm

For Adopting Lecturers

Customizable PowerPoint slides... accompany each chapter for use in your lecture presentations.

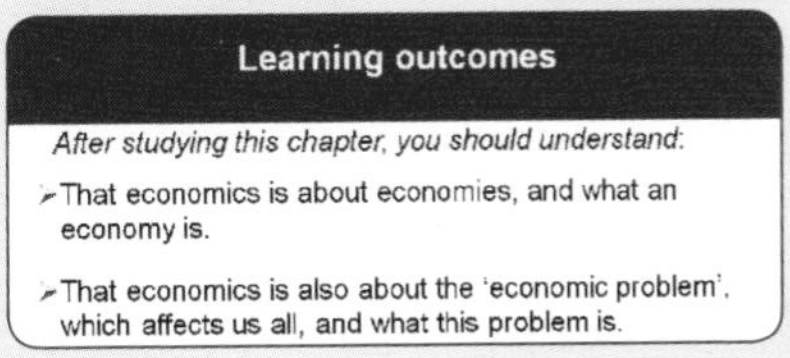

Learning outcomes

After studying this chapter, you should understand:

- That economics is about economies, and what an economy is.
- That economics is also about the 'economic problem', which affects us all, and what this problem is.

Test bank... provides you with a ready-made electronic testing resource to help you to save time creating assessments. This is fully customizable and contains feedback for students.

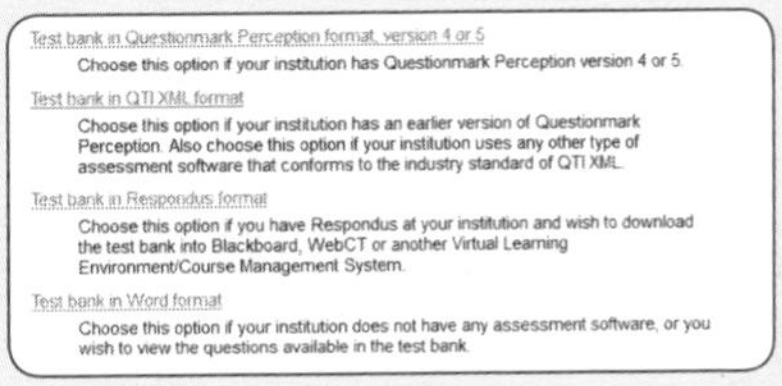

Test bank in Questionmark Perception format, version 4 or 5

Choose this option if your institution has Questionmark Perception version 4 or 5.

Test bank in QTI XML format

Choose this option if your institution has an earlier version of Questionmark Perception. Also choose this option if your institution uses any other type of assessment software that conforms to the industry standard of QTI XML.

Test bank in Respondus format

Choose this option if you have Respondus at your institution and wish to download the test bank into Blackboard, WebCT or another Virtual Learning Environment/Course Management System.

Test bank in Word format

Choose this option if your institution does not have any assessment software, or you wish to view the questions available in the test bank.

A **VLE cartridge** is provided, enabling quick and easy import of the resources into a VLE or LMS.

Figures from the book are available in electronic format to download and use in handouts or lecture slides.

Part I

Introduction to Economics

1

The Nature of Economics

If unemployment rises, it will be harder for you and other people to get jobs: why does unemployment often rise? If interest rates rise, it will cost you more to borrow to study, and more to have a mortgage: why do interest rates often rise? Why does the EU adopt policies that raise the price you pay for many foodstuffs? Why does the UK regulate the price you pay for energy, but not the price you pay for clothes? If the number of people in poverty rises, more people will have financial problems: why does the number of people in poverty often rise?

These economic issues, and many others that affect us all, are discussed in this book. This first chapter sets the scene. After reading this chapter, you will understand:

* that economics is about economies, and what an economy is;
* that economics is also about the 'economic problem', which affects us all, and what this problem is;
* how the key issues discussed in economics fit together;
* that economics has two main branches—microeconomics and macroeconomics;
* what is meant by an economic model.

1.1 Introduction to economics

Welcome to economics. But maybe you wonder exactly what you are being welcomed to, for you may have only a vague idea of what economics is about, and only a vague idea of why we study it.

In contrast, students who study other sciences may start with less vague ideas. For example, they may be studying computer science: everyone knows that this is about computers, and that we study it to help us to make and use computers. Or they may be studying medicine: everyone knows that this is about the human body, and that we study it to know how to keep people fit and how to treat them when they are ill.

We can actually give equally short answers to the questions of what economics is about and why we study it: it is about economies, and we study it to help us to find ways of easing the economic problem from which we all suffer. But these short answers are of limited use, because you may have little idea of what is meant by an economy, and you may not have heard of the economic problem.

So this section explains briefly what is meant by an economy and what the economic problem is. The remaining sections of this chapter give a fuller description of economies, and Chapter 2 gives a fuller description of the economic problem.

Economies and what happens on them

An **economy** is an area in which people do two things.

- **They produce products**. Products come in the form of goods, such as bread and iPads, and services, such as haircuts and public transport.
- **They consume products**. By consuming products, we mean using them, and this includes eating bread, operating an iPad, having one's hair cut, and travelling by bus or train.

Sometimes we study the economies of large areas: so we might talk about the global economy, or the European Union (EU) economy, or the United Kingdom (UK) economy. At other times we study the economies of smaller areas, such as a region or town.

Goods and services cannot be produced out of nothing. For example, suppose you buy a cup of coffee in the college coffee bar. That cup of coffee needed a field for the coffee beans to grow in, and people to harvest the beans. It also needed a ship to take the beans to the coffee factory and some grinding machinery in the factory. Then it needed a lorry to take the ground coffee to the coffee bar, and some hot water and milk in the bar.

We use the terms **resources**, or **factors of production**, for the things that are used to produce goods and services. The coffee example indicates that there are many different resources. However, economists group all resources under three broad headings: labour, capital, and land.

- **Labour** is the time, effort, and skills that people use in production. It includes the work of the coffee harvesters, the ship's crew, the factory workers, and the coffee bar staff. **Human resources** is another term for labour.
- **Capital** is equipment that has been made to be used in production. It includes buildings, such as the barn where freshly picked beans are kept and the coffee bar itself. It includes vehicles, such as the ship and the lorry. It includes machines, such as the coffee-making equipment in the bar. And it includes industrial plant, such as the coffee-grinding factory and the oil refineries that supplied fuel for the harvesting machine, the ship, and the lorry.
- **Land** is defined by economists in a wider way than you might expect, and covers all the gifts of nature. These gifts obviously include the land where the beans are grown and the land where the coffee grinding plant is built. But the gifts of nature also include the rain and sunshine that helped the beans to grow, the crude oil that was converted into fuel

for the harvesting machine, the ship and the lorry, and the natural gas that was supplied to the bar to use for heating the water and the milk. These gifts of nature are often also referred to as **natural resources**.

The economic problem

To understand the economic problem, let's consider four people.

Alan is a poor student who shares a room in a dismal flat and takes the bus to college. Barbara is a rich student who rents a room in a nice flat and has a second-hand car. Charles has left college and now has a job that has enabled him to buy a small house and a small car. Debbie is his boss, and her better paid job allows her to have a luxury home and a smart 4 x 4 car.

Why can't we all be like Debbie? Why are some people poor like Alan? Why are some people in the UK even poorer, living homeless in the streets? Why do some people in other countries struggle even to find enough to eat?

The answer is that the world has only a limited quantity of resources of labour, capital, and land. So the world can produce only a limited amount of goods and services. Indeed, it can produce only a small fraction of the goods and services that people would like to consume. Because there are not enough resources to produce everything that people want to consume, economists say there is a **scarcity** of resources. And the fact that we cannot produce as much as we would like to consume is called the **economic problem**. This problem lies behind all economics.

More about the economic problem

One feature of the economic problem is that because there are too few resources to produce everything we want, people compete for the use of resources. At the national level, for example, if UK citizens want a better health service, then the resources used will not be available for producing other products, such as defence, perhaps. At a personal level, you may soon be like Charles, with a higher income than you have now, so you will buy more products. So more resources will be used to meet your wants, and these resources will not be available to meet other people's wants.

Because there are too few resources to meet everyone's wants, it is important that we make good use of our resources. Economists use the term **allocation of resources** to refer to the way in which we use our resources. Ultimately, economics can be seen as studying the use, or allocation, of scarce resources in a situation of competing wants that are effectively unlimited.

It would be great if the study of economics would eventually lead to a solution to the economic problem, but the economic problem will never disappear. For example, even if we could wave a magic wand and get everyone enough to eat and a room of their own, they might want a home of their own and a car. If we were to wave the wand again to sort that out, they might aspire to nicer homes and nicer cars. And if we were to wave the wand yet again to sort that out, then they would have yet further wants, such as private jets and holiday homes on tropical islands. So we can never produce as much as we would all like to have. But what economics can do is to show us how to make the best use of our scarce resources.

The four key issues raised by scarcity

In studying how we use our scarce resources, economists focus on four key questions about their use. We call these questions the 'How?', 'For what?', 'For whom?', and 'How many?' questions.

- **How are resources used?** To make the best use of our scarce resources, we should use them efficiently and not waste them. When producers are inefficient and waste resources, the economy produces fewer goods and services with its scarce resources than it could produce, so the economy suffers from **productive inefficiency**. How can we promote **productive efficiency**, which is a situation where producers do not waste resources?

- **For what are resources used?** To make the best use of our scarce resources, we should try to produce the goods and services that people value the most. Do we manage this? Or should we try to change what is produced, and perhaps reduce the amount of resources used to produce cigarettes and increase the amount of resources used for healthcare services?
- **For whom are resources used?** When you buy something, you ensure that some resources are used to satisfy your wants instead of someone else's wants. So rich people, who spend much, have many resources used to satisfy their wants. In contrast, poor people, who spend little, have few resources used to satisfy their wants. Why are some people richer than others? And how can we raise the incomes of poor people so that they can buy more, and so in turn have more resources used to satisfy their wants?
- **How many resources are being used?** As our resources are scarce, we want to use and have as many as possible. So we don't want idle fields, unused factories, and millions of unemployed people, and we want to acquire more capital. What determines the extent to which the economy has some unused resources? And how can we acquire more capital?

Two types of productive inefficiency

There are actually two ways in which a productively inefficient producer might waste resources. We will illustrate these using the college coffee bar.

- **A producer may use more resources than it needs**. For example, you may find that even in the busiest periods, the coffee bar staff have plenty of time to spare. If so, the bar is wasting some of the economy's resources of labour, because it is using more than it needs.
- **A producer might use resources that are more valuable than it needs**. For example, your coffee bar might use electricity to boil water. However, gas is cheaper in most areas, because the resources needed to produce gas are less valuable than those needed to produce electricity. So, if the coffee bar uses electricity, then it is probably using more valuable resources than it needs to use.

Note, though, that despite the problem of scarcity, we do not always want producers to use the most efficient production methods. Sometimes, other considerations come into play. For example, free-range chickens use more land than battery chickens, but people concerned with animal welfare prefer us to buy free-range eggs, even though more land is then used for egg production. Also, timber from forests where new trees are planted to replace those that are felled costs more than timber from forests where replanting does not occur, but people concerned about the environment prefer us to use the more costly timber.

The economic problem and population growth

The world's population is growing relentlessly, and this increases the quantity of goods and services that people want. So it seems inevitable that population growth puts downward pressure on living standards. But the following three points show that population growth actually has diverse effects on living standards.

- **Population growth means that land or natural resources are spread over more people**. This does put downward pressure on living standards.
- **Population growth increases the amount of labour we can use**. And with more labour, we can also produce more capital. If labour and capital

grow as quickly as population, this will help us to maintain our living standards.

- **Population growth might lead to more ideas for better products and better production methods**. The reason for this is that the more people there are, the more good ideas people may come up with between them. These ideas will help to increase living standards.

Question 1.1 Suppose the government printed millions of new banknotes and give them out, would this ease the economic problem by allowing people to buy more products and so satisfy more of their wants?

1.1 Everyday economics

Water becomes increasingly scarce

Perhaps the most serious problem of scarcity facing the world over the present century will be fresh water. The world's population was around 6 billion in 2010 and it might almost double by 2050. Shortages are appearing in dry countries where it might be expected, including the Middle East and parts of Africa, but it is also a problem in many other areas, including India, China, the south-western US, and parts of the UK. There is a risk that in some places the shortage might lead to political instability. And in all areas there will be a pressing need to consider how it is used, for what it is used, and for whom it is used.

1.1 Summary

- An economy is an area in which goods and services are produced and consumed. They are produced by using three groups of resources: labour or human resources; capital; and land or natural resources.
- We study economies to see how we can ease the economic problem of scarcity. This problem is that the world has a limited quantity of scarce resources, which cannot produce nearly as many goods and services as people want to consume. People compete for the output or use of these scarce resources.
- Economists are interested in how efficiently scarce resources are used, in what they are used to produce, in why some people have more resources used to meet their wants than other people have, and in whether the total quantity of resources in use can be increased.
- Population growth increases the strain on natural resources, but it also means there is more labour, and this can supply more capital. Also, with population growth, there will be more people who may have ideas for new products and new production methods from which we can all benefit.

1.2 The five sectors of an economy

We saw in the last section that economics is the study of economies, and that an economy is an area in which there is both production and consumption. We now ask two questions.

- **Who produces the goods and services that are consumed in an economy?**
- **Who consumes the goods and services that are produced in an economy?**

We cannot answer these questions by looking at people, and trying to divide them into producers and consumers. This is because everyone consumes and, as we shall see, almost everyone produces as well. Instead, we will explain who the producers and the consumers are by seeing what institutions people are concerned with when they produce and consume.

We divide an economy's institutions into five groups or **sectors**, as follows:

- **households**;
- **firms**;
- **government departments**;
- **non-profit producers**;
- **the foreign sector**.

We will now take all these five sectors in turn and explain how they are all involved in production. We will then see that only two of these sectors are involved in consumption.

Households as producers

Economists say that everyone is a member of an institution called a **household**. In practice, while many people do actually live in houses, many others do not: for example, some people live in flats, student residences, caravans, prisons, and cardboard boxes. For simplicity, however, economists regard everyone as living in a household, no matter what type of accommodation they actually have.

Although it seems reasonable to talk abut households as institutions in which people live, it may seem surprising to regard households also as institutions in which production occurs. Nevertheless, a large proportion of the goods and services that people consume are produced by members of their own households.

For example, in the last 24 hours, you may have provided yourself with cleaning services, washing services, cooking services, and some entertainment. If you work out how much it would cost you to pay someone else to clean your room, shave you or put on your make-up, cook your tea, and entertain you, then you can see that your services are valuable. You can also see why we said that almost everyone is a producer: even a baby produces some services by smiling at its parents and entertaining them!

Firms as producers

People do not produce in their own households all the goods and services that they want to consume. Instead, they set up various other institutions to do much of the economy's production. One type of institution that they set up is called a **firm**: firms make and sell products, and aim to earn profits for the owners. Some firms are owned by just one household, or by just a few, while others are huge concerns owned by many households scattered across the globe.

It is interesting to consider why people who buy products from firms do not instead try to produce those products in their own households. One important reason is that people buy from firms many products that they do not have the knowledge or equipment to produce themselves. Examples include textbooks and medicines.

However, many people could produce some of the other products that they buy from firms, such as simple furniture, woollen clothes, and vegetables. Even so, there are good reasons for having these items produced by specialist firms. Having specialist firms allows their workers to spend their working time producing a narrow range of products that suit their individual skills, and it also allows for large-scale production, which is often more efficient. So having firms helps us to make the best of our scarce resources.

Government departments as producers

As well as setting up firms, people set up governments, and then tell them to raise taxes and see that certain goods and services are produced. The reason that people want governments to organize the production of some goods and services is that there may be problems with allowing these products to be produced by households or firms. We explore this issue in Chapter 13.

In this book, we will suppose that governments do not actually supply goods and services themselves, but rather that they in turn set up and pay **government departments**, or ministries, to do the production. In the UK, for example, the central government has set up a health ministry to provide health care services, which it does with the National Health Service, and it has set up a defence ministry to produce defence services, which it does with the armed forces. Also, local authorities have set up education departments to provide education, which they do with state schools, and they have set up law and order departments, which seek to maintain law and order with police officers.

Non-profit institutions as producers

People also set up **non-profit institutions**, which, like firms, produce goods and services, but which, unlike firms, pay no profits to their owners. Instead, they simply try to cover their costs through fees and voluntary donations. There are many organizations like this, including charities, churches, many colleges, hospices, and mosques.

Different types of non-profit institution are set up for different reasons. For example, some are charities, like Oxfam, which are set up to raise funds to supply goods and services to people who could not afford to pay for them. And others are religious bodies and educational establishments, which are set up by households who believe that these provide desirable services, but they do not want to make a profit from them.

The foreign sector as producers

It might seem that all the goods and services consumed in an economy must be produced by the households, firms, government departments, and non-profit institutions that are there. However, many of the goods and services that are consumed in any area, such as the UK, are produced by institutions outside the area, chiefly firms. The term 'the **foreign sector**' is used to cover the institutions outside an economy that, among other things, produce the products that it imports.

The two sectors involved in consumption

We have seen that all five sectors contribute to the production of the goods and services in an economy like the UK's. However, these products are produced for the benefit of only two sectors.

The chief beneficiaries of the goods and services produced in the UK are the people who live in its households. The other beneficiaries are people who live in the foreign sector and who buy products made in the UK. Some products have to be sold as exports to them in order to earn the money that is needed to buy imports from them.

Of course, some products, like hospitals and warplanes, are bought and used by government departments, and other products, like factories and white vans, are bought and used by firms. But for whose benefit are they used? Ultimately, they are used to produce goods and services to benefit households and people who buy exports.

International trade and scarce resources

Many of the products that people in the UK import from foreign firms could be made by UK firms. Examples include imported cars and televisions. Likewise, many of the products produced in the UK and exported to foreign consumers could be produced abroad. Examples include plastics and financial services.

We explore the reasons for international trade like this in Chapter 27. But the basic idea is that we import products that foreign firms are relatively good at making, and we export products that we are relatively good at making. The world will make the best use of its scarce resources if each country specializes in producing those goods and services that it is relatively good at making.

Globalization

A country like the UK has huge imports. But you should not imagine that all the products you buy here are made *either* in the UK *or* in a particular foreign country. If you buy a computer, it is likely that the software was devised in one country, the screen made in a second, other components in others, and that the final assembly was done somewhere else.

Integration of the economies of different countries has existed for centuries, but it has increased greatly in the last 50 years in a process called **globalization**. There are many reasons for this. For example, large container ships have reduced transport costs, the Internet has made it easier for firms to get information about costs in different countries, and many restrictions on trade have been eased, as occurred, for example, when the communist regimes in Eastern Europe collapsed.

1.2 Everyday economics

The importance of household production

For the year 2000, the estimated value of production by households in the UK of housing, transport, nutrition, clothing, laundry services, childcare, adult care and voluntary activity, was £693bn.

'Household Satellite Account', National Statistics Online

Comment This figure comes from an experimental project to try to value household production. The same source estimated the production by other sectors in the economy as £892bn. Adding household production gives a total of £1,585bn, with household production accounting for 43%.

1.2 Summary

- Everyone living in an economy belongs to a sector called households. Households produce some of the goods and services that they consume.
- The remaining goods and services are produced by four other sectors: firms; government departments; non-profit institutions; and the foreign sector.
- Although most of the goods and service produced in an economy are consumed by its households, some are exported and consumed by people in the foreign sector.
- International trade allows countries to specialize in producing goods and services that they are relatively good at making, and this helps the world to make the best use of its scarce resources.
- In recent years, the world's economies have become more specialized and more integrated in a process called globalization.

1.3 A diagram that illustrates a simple economy

We will now build up a diagram that will give us a picture of what happens in an economy. We could build up a diagram for an economy with five sectors, but to keep our diagram simple, we will consider an economy that has only two sectors: households and firms. So we will assume that the households here have not set up any governments or non-profit institutions, and that they do not buy or sell anything abroad.

To keep things even simpler, we will assume that the households have set up only three firms, which we will call Aco, Bco, and Cco.

A table for a two-sector economy

To see how Aco, Bco, and Cco interact with each other and with households, we will refer to their accounts for a particular week, as shown in Table 1.1. In the top

Table 1.1 **Accounts for the three firms in a simple economy in one week (£m)**

Revenue	**Aco**	**Bco**	**Cco**	**Total**
Sales of consumer goods and services to households	5	10	85	**100**
Sales of capital goods to other firms	0	30	0	**30**
Sales of intermediate goods and services to other firms	45	60	15	**120**
Total revenue	**50**	**100**	**100**	**250**
Expenditure				
Intermediate goods and services bought from other firms	5	50	65	**120**
Wages	40	30	20	**90**
Trading profit	5	20	15	**40**
Total expenditure	**50**	**100**	**100**	**250**

part of this table, we can see that each firm gets some revenue during this week by selling some output. Each firm's sales are divided in the table into three groups.

- **Sales of consumer goods and services.** Products sold to households are called **consumer goods and services**. Household spending on them is called **consumer spending**.
- **Sales of capital goods to other firms.** These arise only with Bco. Presumably Aco and Cco do not produce plant, buildings, vehicles, or machinery.
- **Sales of intermediate goods and services to other firms.** Most firms sell to other firms some goods and services, which those other firms then use up in their own production. For example, one firm may sell to others raw materials, energy, insurance services, advertising, or transport services. These items are called **intermediate goods and services**.

It is important to distinguish between capital goods and intermediate goods and services. Suppose a delivery firm buys and runs a white van. The van is a capital good, which the firm will keep and use over a long period of time. But any fuel that is put into the van is an intermediate good, which the firm will expect to use up very quickly.

Between them, the three firms in the table receive £100 million from their sales of consumer goods, £30 million from their sales of capital goods, and £120 million from their sales of intermediate goods and services. So they have a total revenue of £250 million.

The lower part of the table show what happens to each firm's revenue in the week concerned. It is used in three ways.

- **Purchase of intermediate goods and services.** Each firm buys some intermediate goods and services from other firms.
- **Wages.** These are paid to the firm's workers who, like everyone, belong to households.
- **Trading profits.** This is any money left over from sales after allowing for purchases of intermediate goods and services and wages. We will suppose that all this money is paid to the firm's owners, who belong to households. Very possibly, the owners will use some of this profit to buy new capital for their firm.

A simple diagram for a two-sector economy

The information given in Table 1.1 can be used to build up a simple diagram for this economy, as shown in Figure 1.1. This has two rectangular boxes: one for households and one for firms.

Look first at the three arrows flowing into the bottom of the 'firms' box. These arrows show the 'firms' total revenues for the week. This revenue comprises £100 million from sales of consumer goods and services, £30 million from sales of capital goods, and £120 million from sales of intermediate goods and services.

Next, look at the two arrows flowing out of the 'firms' box at the top. One of these arrows shows their spending of £120 million on intermediate goods and services. The other shows all their payments to households of wages and trading profits: the total value of these payments to households is £130 million.

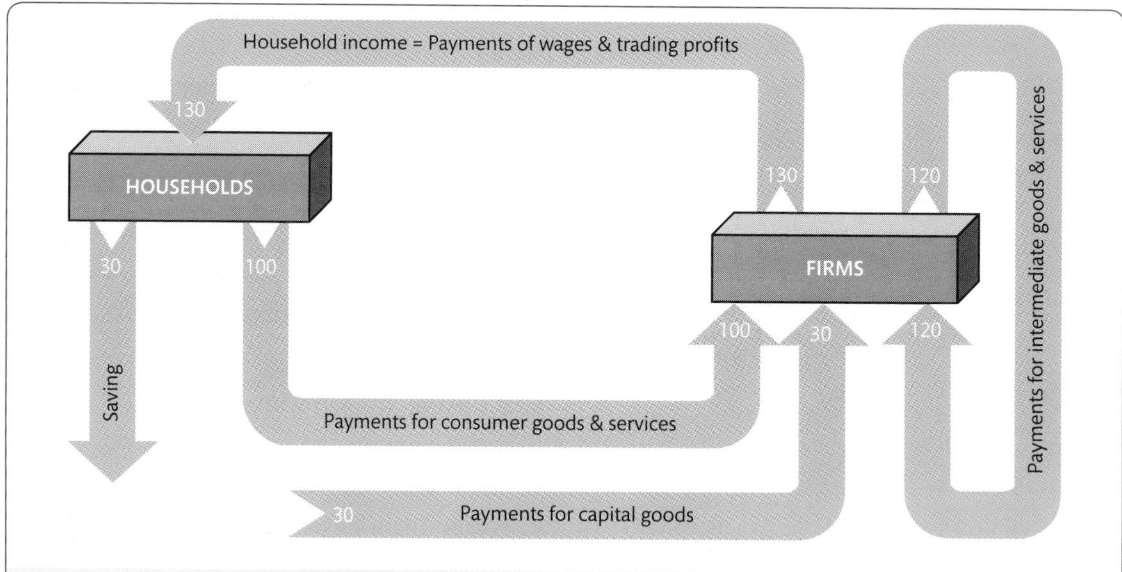

Figure 1.1 **The principal income and expenditure flows in a two-sector economy**

This figure includes all the flows noted in Table 1.1. For simplicity, the flows from firms to households of wages and trading profits are all combined in a single arrow.

Now look at the 'households' box. At the top, there is just one arrow. This shows the income of £130 million that households receive from wages and trading profits. There are two arrows at the bottom. One of these shows that £100 million of this week's income is used to purchase consumer goods and services. The gap between household income and consumer spending income is called **saving**: so saving this week is £30 million and is shown by the other arrow.

A final diagram for a two-sector economy

We will now make two changes to Figure 1.1 to produce the final figure for this economy, which is shown in Figure 1.2. The first change, made purely for simplicity, is to omit the arrows for payments for intermediate goods and services. This change removes £120 million flowing into the 'firms' box and an identical £120 million flowing out. Instead of showing these payments with arrows, we imagine in Figure 1.2 that these payments occur inside the 'firms' box.

The second change made by Figure 1.2 is to show several groups of markets. To understand what economists mean by markets, consider, for example, your purchases of bread, paper, and soap. Although you pay your money directly to firms, usually shops, economists say that all these transactions occur in markets; so they regard you as making your purchases in the bread market, the paper market, and the soap market. You can think of every shop that sells these items as being a part of the market concerned. These three markets form part of an almost countless number of markets, with one market for each good and service.

Figure 1.2 divides the markets in the economy into five groups.

- **Markets for final goods and services**. These are markets in which firms sell goods and services to households and in which they sell capital goods to other firms. These products are called final goods and services because they are finished products as far as the economy is concerned. They include products like bread and tractors.

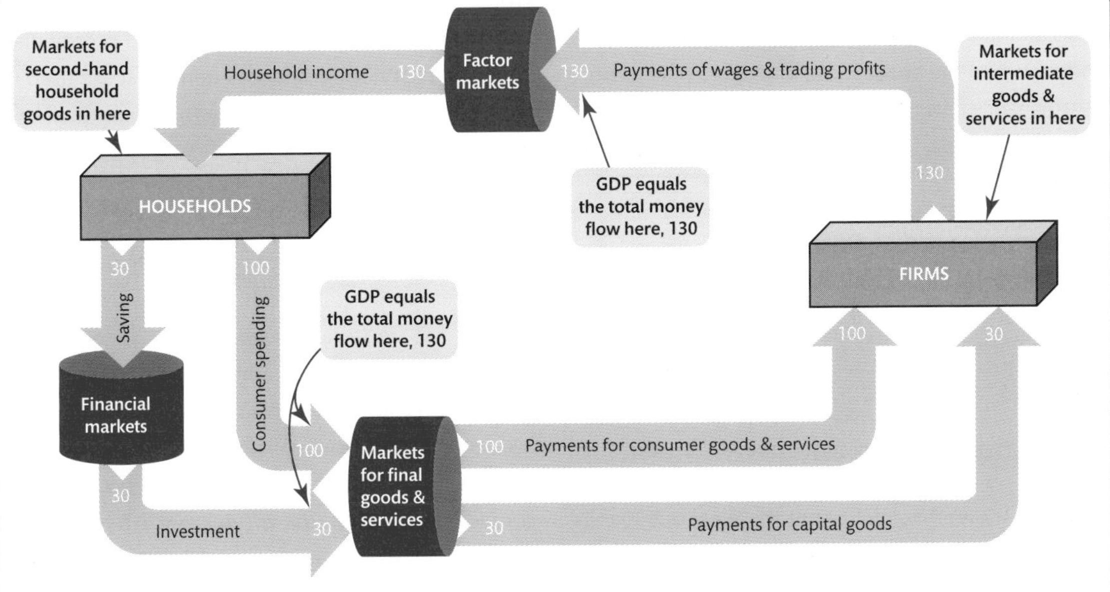

Figure 1.2 **The circular flow of income between households and firms in a two-sector economy**

This figure builds on Figure 1.1 by adding in the main groups of markets in an economy. It also shows two points in the circular flow where GDP is often measured: these are the total flow of spending paid into the markets for final goods and services, and the equal total flow paid into factor markets.

- **Markets for intermediate goods and services**. These are markets in which firms sell products like raw materials to other firms. We do not regard these products as final products, because the buying firms use them up in their own products. Figure 1.2 supposes that all purchases and sales of intermediate goods and services take place inside the 'firms' box, and it indicates that that is where the markets are.
- **Factor markets**. Wages and trading profits are said to flow to households through factor markets. That is partly because wages are paid to workers in return for supplying a factor of production in the form of labour, and it is partly because trading profits are paid to the people who own firms in return for setting the firms up and for ensuring that they have factors of production in the form of land and capital.
- **Markets for second-hand goods**. These include houses and used cars. We can regard these markets as inside the 'households' box, because the money spent in these markets simply flows from one household to another.
- **Financial markets**. To understand these, note first that purchases of capital goods are called **investment**. Figure 1.2 shows at the bottom that the value of investment this week is £30 million. The figure also shows on the left that the value of saving this week is £30 million. In fact, the value of saving *must* equal the value of investment in any week, or any other period. You could easily prove this for yourself by putting any numbers you like on the arrows, provided that you ensure that the total amount flowing out of each box exactly equals the total amount flowing in, which must be the case.

Saving and investment are closely linked. Any households that do not want to spend all this week's income on consumer goods and services can use their saving to help firms to finance their investment. For example, these households can take their saving to what are termed financial markets, which have institutions like banks and the stock exchange. There, households can lend money to the firms whose managers wish to borrow to finance investment, or buy shares in those firms and so become part-owners of them.

Question 1.2 Suppose that, in the week after that shown in Figure 1.2, payments for consumer goods and services rise to £110 million, while payments for capital goods rise to £35 million. What will saving and investment be?

More about saving and investment

Figure 1.2 shows that investment this week is £30 million and that it is financed by flows worth £30 million from the financial markets. But suppose some of this week's £30 million worth of saving is kept by households at home in cash and does not flow into the financial markets. How would the flow into the financial markets have been 'topped up' to finance the £30 million worth of investment?

Some of the top-up might have come from other households who had saved cash in previous weeks and who this week took their savings to the capital markets. Another source of top-up is the banks, which, as we shall see in Chapter 20, can create money and so inject new money into the financial markets when needed.

The circular flow of income

In Figure 1.2, all the money flows between firms and households move anti-clockwise in a roughly circular way. This figure is called the **circular flow of income** because it shows this circular flow between households and firms.

Gross domestic product

Table 1.1 and Figure 1.1 divided the goods and services sold by firms into three groups: consumer goods and services; capital goods; and intermediate goods and services. Figure 1.2 shows only the first two of these groups. These two groups represent finished or **final goods and services**. The third group, intermediate goods and services, comprises items that are used up by the firms that buy them when they make their own output.

Ultimately, what matters in terms of the economic problem is the output by firms of final goods and services, that is their output of consumer goods and services and of capital goods. Consumer goods and services are important because they directly satisfy some consumer wants. Capital goods are important because they form extra resources of capital that can be used to make more consumer goods in future.

The value of the total sales of final goods and services is called **gross domestic product**, or **GDP**. The GDP for the week covered by Figure 1.2 is £130 million. Note that GDP does not actually measure the total value of all the finished goods and services produced, even in this simple two-sector economy, because it ignores those that households produce for themselves.

Aside from products produced by households, GDP actually measures the total value of the goods and services produced in the economy. This may seem odd, because it ignores intermediate goods and services. However, in assessing the value of the goods and services produced in an economy, we do not want to add in the value of intermediate goods and services. For example, when you buy a cup of coffee, the price you pay for this final good includes the value of the ground coffee, the milk, water and the gas that were used in its production. We would overestimate the value of the economy's production if we were to add in the value of the coffee bar's purchases of milk, ground coffee, water, and gas as well as your expenditure on the final good.

Figure 1.2 shows at the bottom how GDP equals the value of the spending on the two types of final good. This is the total value of the money flowing into the 'firms' box, so it also equals the total value of the money flowing out of that box to households. So we can also estimate GDP by adding together the value of wages and trading profits, as shown at the top of the circular flow. We refer to this later in Chapter 18.

1.3 Summary

- A simple economy can be illustrated by a figure called the circular flow of income. This shows the income flowing from firms to households in the form of wages and trading profits, and it shows the income flowing from households to firms for consumer spending.
- Households spend much of their income on consumer spending and save the rest: saving flows to financial markets in which firms obtain funds for investment, that is for purchasing capital goods.
- The total value of consumer spending plus investment measures the total output of finished goods and services and is called gross domestic product (GDP).

1.4 Two branches of economics: microeconomics and macroeconomics

We can use the picture of an economy in Figure 1.2 to outline the main topics that concern economists. These topics fall under two broad headings: microeconomics and macroeconomics.

The nature of microeconomics

Microeconomics is concerned chiefly with individual markets. We saw in Figure 1.2 that there are five main groups of market, and within each group there are many individual markets. For example, markets for final goods and services include markets for sugar, trainers, and lorries. And factor markets include markets for sugar refiners, shoemakers, and lorry drivers.

When we study microeconomics, we look at individual markets. In each market, we are chiefly concerned about three things, as follows.

- **The price at which the items traded there are sold**. So we might study the price of sugar or the wages of lorry drivers.
- **The quantity traded in a period of time**. So we might study the quantity of sugar traded in a day, or the total number of hours worked by lorry drivers in a week.
- **The expenditure in a period of time**. So we might study how much is spent on sugar in a day, and how much is paid in wages to lorry drivers in a week.

It is important to appreciate what we mean by 'study'. It is not the aim of microeconomics to discover what prices, quantities, and expenditures actually are. Collecting information like this is merely collecting facts. What economists try to do is to understand prices, quantities, and expenditures. For example, we ask *why* the price of trainers, *why* the quantity of sugar sold, and *why* the total wages paid to lorry drivers are what they are, and we ask why they might change.

Microeconomics helps us to answer many interesting questions. For example, why are the wages of many footballers higher than those of farmhands, when we could survive much more easily without the footballers? Why is the price of diamonds so high in relation to water, when water is essential and diamonds are not?

Also, when we understand the quantities of different final products that are produced, we will understand how the economy determines 'What?' products its resources will be used to produce. And when we understand how much firms buy of various inputs, we will understand 'How?' things are produced. And when we understand why different workers are paid different wage rates, and so understand what income and spending power different people will have, we will be able to say a great deal about how the economy decides 'For whom?' things are produced.

More about microeconomics

In our study of microeconomics, we will discover that the price, quantity, and expenditure in any market are determined by the interaction of the people who are buying the item concerned—or demanding it—and the people who are selling it—or supplying it. So it becomes important to look at the behaviour of individual households and individual firms to understand the factors that determine how much they want to buy and sell.

In microeconomics, we will also consider the government and foreign sectors, which we omitted in Figure 1.2. We will not have time to discuss non-profit-making institutions, which form a much smaller sector.

Regarding the government sector, we will see how governments can affect individual markets. For instance, if the government imposes taxes of about 60p on each litre of petrol, do pump prices rise by 60p, or by more or by less? How are food prices affected by the EU's agricultural policies?

Regarding the foreign sector, we will look at markets in which goods and services are sold between countries, that is markets for imports and exports. And we will see why a country like the UK imports products such as televisions and cars, which it could produce for itself.

The nature of macroeconomics

Macroeconomics is concerned with the economy as a whole. So, for example, instead of being interested in the quantity of different types of worker that get hired in different individual labour markets, it looks at employment as a whole, and then in turn at the total level of unemployment. This is important to our study of 'How many?' resources we are using. Unemployment is serious, not only because it means that we are not producing as much as we could, but also because it brings distress to those concerned.

Also, instead of being interested in the price of different individual goods and services, macroeconomics is interested in the overall level of prices, and whether this is rising. We will see in our study of macroeconomics what determines the rate of inflation and why inflation is important.

Again, instead of being interested in spending on sugar or lorries, macroeconomics is interested in the total spending on consumer goods and services and in the total spending on capital goods, that is investment. These are important, because consumer spending tells us how far households can satisfy their wants, and investment tells us how much extra capital we will have in future to meet more of our wants. And once macroeconomics has explained what determines consumer spending and investment, it also explains what determines GDP, which—at least in a two-sector economy—equals these two items added together.

More about macroeconomics

Macroeconomics also considers the implications of introducing the two main sectors that are omitted in Figure 1.2. In the case of the government sector, though, macroeconomics is not interested in the effects of the tax on fuel or of the Common Agricultural Policy on butter. Instead, it is more interested in the total level of taxation and in the total level of government spending. And in the case of exports and imports, it is not interested in the markets for individual traded goods and services, but rather in the total level of exports and the total level of imports.

1.4 Summary

- There are two main branches of economics: microeconomics and macroeconomics.
- Microeconomics studies individual markets, and analyses why in each market the price, the quantity traded, and the spending are what they are, and why they might change.
- Macroeconomics studies the economy as a whole, including topics such as unemployment and inflation.

1.5 Economic models

We have seen that economists try to understand the production and consumption that occurs in an economy. For example, some economists might try to understand the level of spending on electricity each day. One problem these economists would face is that the UK has about 60 million people who consume electricity, and electricity spending depends on each of them. So spending today depends in part on whether you overslept and turned the lights on late.

Economists cannot contact every consumer, so they cannot fully understand today's electricity spending. Indeed, they can rarely fully understand anything. Instead, they act as follows.

- **They make some assumptions about what the key factors or variables are**. For today's electricity spending, these might be the weather, the day of the week, the time of year, the prices of electricity, gas and oil, and people's incomes.

- **They make some assumptions about the effects of these key variables to develop a theory**. To be more precise, they build an **economic model**, that is a theory that is based on key variables and presented in formal terms. For example, a model might suggest how each of the key variables that are believed to affect electricity spending actually does affect it. Economic models may be described entirely in words, or with the help of graphs, or with the use of mathematical notation. In this book, they are chiefly described with words and graphs.

- **They use the model to make some predictions**. For example, they might use a model of electricity spending to predict the level of spending on electricity each day next week.

- **They collect some data so that they can test the model by seeing if its predictions are reasonably accurate**. For example, they might in due course ask the electricity suppliers how much people actually spent each day next week. Of course, the model has not included everything, such as the time at which you wake up each day, so it cannot make precise predictions about spending. But if the predictions were reasonably accurate, then the economists might accept the model as useful. If the predictions were poor, then they would alter the model, either by adding in extra variables, or by discarding some of the existing variables, or by suggesting other ways in which the existing variables affect spending.

One problem for economists is that testing economic models to see if they make correct predictions is often very tricky. To see why, let's compare an economist with a chemist.

If a chemist devises a theory to predict what will happen if two chemicals are mixed, then the chemist can conduct an experiment by mixing the chemicals and seeing if the predictions are correct. But if an economist develops a theory to predict what will happen to spending on electricity when gas prices rise, then the economist will not be allowed to raise gas prices to conduct an experiment to see if the predictions are correct! One possibility is to wait until gas prices do rise, and then see what happens to electricity spending—but a problem here is that other things, such as incomes and the weather, may change at the same time, so it is hard to isolate the effect of the higher gas prices. Another possibility is to ask a sample of people what they would do if gas prices were to rise, but what people say they would do is not always a reliable predictor of what they would actually do.

In this book, once we have presented a model, we will often use it to predict what will happen if one factor changes and all the others stay the same. Economists often describe this procedure with the Latin words *ceteris paribus*, which means 'other things staying the same'.

1.5 Summary

- To try to understand what happens in an economy, economists construct theories or models. Because the real world is so complex, these models are based on assumptions about what the key variables are.
- Once an economic model has been used to make predictions, it can be tested by seeing if its predictions are reasonably consistent with observed behaviour.

In the next chapter we will see how the main issues that concern economists all arise from scarcity. We will also see what actions might be taken by the government to alleviate the problem of scarcity.

abc Glossary

Allocation of resources: how resources are used.

Capital: equipment that has been made to be used in production, including plant buildings, machinery, and vehicles.

Circular flow of income: the circular flow of income from households to firms and from firms to households.

Consumer goods and services: products sold to households.

Consumer spending: spending by households on consumer goods and services.

Economic model: a theory based on key variables and presented in formal terms.

Economic problem: the fact that we cannot produce as much as we would like to consume.

Economy: an area in which people produce and consume goods and services.

Factors of production: another term for resources.

Final goods and services: finished goods and services, including consumer goods and services bought by households and capital goods.

Firms: institutions set up by households to produce goods and service for sale in order to earn a profit for the households that own them.

Foreign sector: people outside an economy who, for example, supply imports and purchase exports.

Globalization: the increasing integration of different economies across the globe.

Government departments: institutions set up by governments to provide certain services.

Gross domestic product (GDP): the total value of the final goods and services produced in the economy, excluding those produced by households for themselves.

Households: institutions in which consumers live and in which they also produce some goods and services for themselves.

Human resources: another term for labour.

Intermediate goods and services: products like raw materials that are bought by one producer off another and then used up by the purchaser in its own production.

Investment: purchases of capital goods (we will see in Chapter 19 that it also includes additions to stocks of raw materials and additions to stocks of unsold finished goods).

Labour: the time, effort, and skills that people use in production.

Land: the gifts of nature, or natural resources.

Macroeconomics: the study of an economy as a whole.

Microeconomics: the study of individual markets and the people who take part in them.

Natural resources: the gifts of nature, often simply called land by economists.

Non-profit institutions: institutions set up by households to produce goods and services without making profits.

Productive efficiency: when producers waste no resources, so that the economy produces as goods and services from its resources as it can.

Productive inefficiency: when producers waste resources, so that the economy produces fewer goods and services from its resources than it could.

Resources: the land, labour, and capital that are used to produce goods and services.

Saving: the gap between household incomes and household spending on consumer goods and services.

Scarcity: the fact that there are too few resources to produce as much as we would like to consume.

Sector: a group of institutions. (*See* households, firms, government departments, non-profit institutions, and the foreign sector.)

= Answers to in-text questions

1.1 There might be little or no effect on how much we can consume. The economic problem arises because there are too few resources of labour, capital, and land to produce as much as we all want. Printing banknotes does not of itself create one extra worker, one extra machine, or any more natural resources. The main effect will be huge increases in prices as people armed with more money try to buy the same quantity of goods and services as before. But we study the full effects of creating more money in more detail in later chapters.

1.2 All the figures in this answer are in £ million. Investment equals spending on capital goods, that is 35. The total flow into the firms box is 110 + 35, or 145, so the total flow from that box to the households box must also be 145. With household income at 145 and consumer spending at 110, saving is 35, the same as investment.

? Questions for review

1.1 Which of the following complaints are caused by the economic problem?

(a) The student who says 'I want to work hard and get a good job, but the result is that I can go swimming less often than I would like'.

(b) The new graduate who says 'at last I can afford to buy a flat, but I wish I could also afford a car'.

(c) The parent who says 'I give part of my income to my student child, and so I have less money for travel than I would like'.

1.2 Which of the following issues would come under microeconomics, and which would come under macroeconomics?

(a) The price of this textbook.

(b) The rate of inflation in the US last year.

(c) The number of nurses in Ireland.

(d) The number of unemployed people in France.

(e) The earnings of pop stars.

(f) The gap between the value of UK exports and the value of UK imports.

? Questions for discussion

1.1 Think back on your last big meal, your last lecture, and your last dental appointment. What sort of institutions produced these? Think of two intermediate products that each of these producers used.

1.2 If households were to become more self-sufficient and buy less, would that ease the problem of scarcity?

2

Scarcity, Governments, and Economists

Remember from Chapter 1 that the world has only a limited amount of resources of labour, land, and capital. The economic problem is that these scarce resources can produce only a limited amount of goods and services, yet there is no limit to the amount that we would like to consume.

What can you do about the economic problem? What can firms and governments do about it? And economists who study the problem, what can they do about it?

This chapter shows you how to answer questions like these, by understanding:

* how the economic problem of scarcity can be illustrated with a diagram;
* the varying extents to which governments intervene in their economies;
* how governments can intervene in an effort to ease the economic problem;
* the extent to which economists can help governments when they intervene;
* the important concept of opportunity cost.

2.1 The production possibility frontier

Economists often use diagrams, and we will now develop a diagram to illustrate the economic problem. We want this diagram to show that there is a limit to how much an economy can produce. To do this simply, we will look at the economy of an imaginary country that produces only two goods: bread and bricks. We will assume there are just two products because it allows us to use a two-dimensional diagram. Fortunately, this diagram illustrates issues that arise no matter how many different products are produced.

We will make three further assumptions.

- **The economy is using all of its resources of labour, land, and capital**. So there is no unemployed labour, which means that everyone who wants to work has a job. Also, there is no idle land and no unused capital.
- **There is full productive efficiency**. **Productive efficiency** means that each producer produces as much output as it is possible to produce from the resources that it uses. In other words, no producer uses more resources than are needed to produce its output. Chapter 1 noted that an inefficient producer might use more resources than it needs, either by wasting some inputs, or by using costly inputs when cheap ones are available.
- **All producers are using the latest technologies**.

Starting the diagram

Given these assumptions, let's consider how many loaves of bread and how many bricks this economy can produce each day. This depends on what proportion of its resources it uses for each item. Suppose that it currently uses half of its resources for bread and half for bricks, and suppose it finds that each day it produces 70,000 loaves of bread and 35,000 bricks. We illustrate this in Figure 2.1, which measures the quantity of bricks on the horizontal axis. The economy is producing 35,000 bricks each day, so it must be somewhere above the point on this axis that represents 35,000. If it were at a point to the right of this point, then it would be producing more than 35,000, and if it were at a point to the left, it would be producing fewer than 35,000. So it must be on the dashed vertical line drawn above this point.

Figure 2.1 marks the quantity of bread on the vertical axis. The economy is producing 70,000 loaves each day, so it must be somewhere to the right of the point on the vertical axis that represents 70,000. If it were at a point higher than this, then it would be producing more than 70,000, and if it were at a point lower than this, it would be producing fewer than 70,000. So it must be on the dashed horizontal line drawn to the right of this point.

So the economy is at a point on the vertical dashed line above the mark on the horizontal axis for 35,000

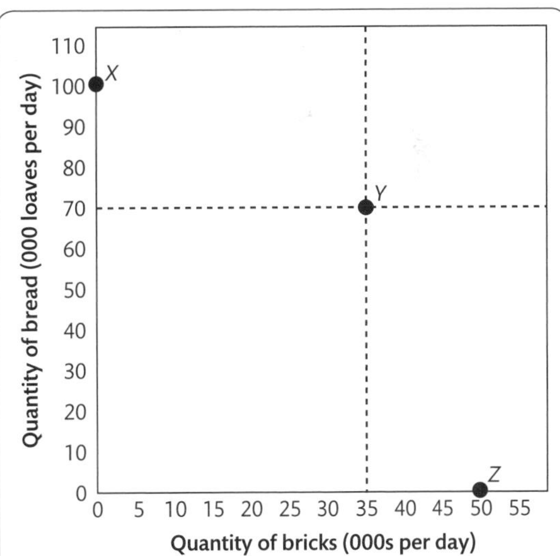

Figure 2.1 **Some possible output combinations**

With half its resources used for each product, the economy is at *Y*, and each day it produces 35,000 bricks and 70,000 loaves of bread. If it put all its resources into bread, it would go to *X*. If it put all its resources into bricks, it would go to *Z*.

bricks. It is also at a point on the horizontal dashed line to the right of the mark on the vertical axis for 70,000 loaves of bread. The only point that meets both these requirements is *Y*, where the lines cross. So *Y* represents what the economy is producing.

If the economy were to switch some of its resources from bricks to bread, then brick output would fall and bread output would rise. So production would rise to a point higher than *Y* and to the left of it. To consider where the economy might go, take an extreme case in which it put all its resources into producing bread. With no resources used for bricks, the output of bricks would fall to zero. And with twice as many resources as before used for bread, it might seem that bread output would rise from 70,000 loaves a day to 140,000.

However, it is most unlikely that bread output would double. In the initial position, *Y*, half the resources of labour, land, and capital are used for each product. But the economy will use for making bread the half of its resources that are most suited for making bread, and it will use for making bricks the half of its resources that are most suited for making bricks. So if it were to shift all the resources that are now used for bricks into bread, then these shifted resources would not produce 70,000 more loaves of bread a day, because they are not as good at making bread as the resources that are currently used for bread. Suppose the shifted resources would produce just 30,000 loaves a day. Then the economy would be at the point marked X, with bread output at a total of 100,000 loaves a day and brick output at zero.

If, instead, the economy were to switch some of its resources from bread to bricks, then bread output would fall and brick output would rise. So production would go to a point lower than *Y* and to the right of it. To see where the economy might go, take an extreme case in which it put all its resources into making bricks. With no resources used for bread, the output of bread would be zero. With twice as many resources as before used for bricks, it might seem that brick output would double from 35,000 a day to 70,000. However, the resources that are currently used for bread will not be as good at making bricks as the resources that are currently used for making bricks. So if all the resources now used for bread were shifted into bricks, they would not make an extra 35,000 bricks a day. Suppose the shifted resources would produce just 15,000 bricks a day. Then the economy would be at the point marked *Z*, with brick output at 50,000 a day and bread output at zero.

Finishing the diagram

Figure 2.1 shows that, with half the economy's resources devoted to bread and half to bricks, the pattern of output each day will be at *Y*, with 35,000 bricks and 70,000 loaves. If all resources were used for bread, the pattern of output would be at *X*, with no bricks and 100,000 loaves of bread. And if all resources were used for bricks, the pattern of output would be as shown at *Z*, with 50,000 bricks and no bread.

These three points, *X*, *Y*, and *Z* are reproduced in Figure 2.2. But this figure adds a curve through them, to show all the other output patterns that the country

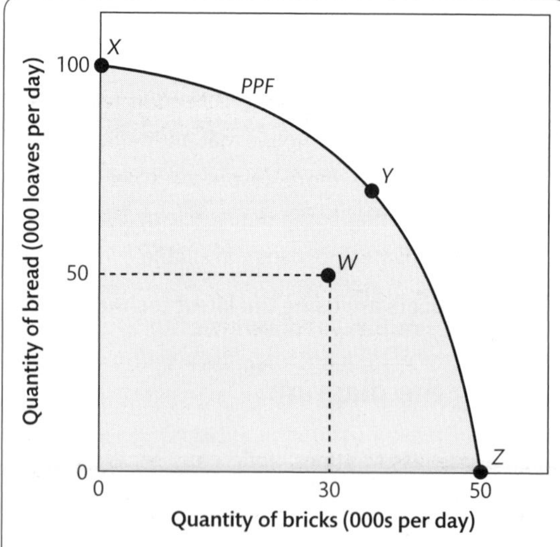

Figure 2.2 **The production possibility frontier**

If the economy uses all its resources with productive efficiency, then it will produce at a point somewhere on *PPF*. If some resources are unused, or used inefficiently, then it will produce at a point like *W*, which is inside *PPF*. It can never produce at a point outside *PPF*.

could have if it were to allocate varying proportions of its resources to bricks and bread. So this curve shows the various output patterns that it is possible for the country to produce—assuming it has full employment and full efficiency—and it is called the **production possibility frontier**. It is labelled *PPF*.

The production possibility frontier and scarcity

We have assumed that the country uses all its resources and has full efficiency. And we have seen that, in this case, it can produce at any point it chooses on *PPF*. The production possibility frontier shows us the limits to its production. These limits arise because the country has limited or scarce resources. If the country has any unemployment or any inefficiency, then it cannot reach *PPF*. Instead, it will produce at a point somewhere in the grey area inside *PPF* in Figure 2.2. For example, it might be at point *W*, and produce 30,000 bricks and 50,000 loaves each day.

In practice, a country always has some inefficiency and some unemployment, so it is always producing at a point inside its frontier. The economic problem is that its citizens would like to consume at a point well outside the frontier, with virtually limitless bread and bricks.

2.1 Everyday economics

A shortage of rice

The world market for rice is facing a serious shortage. This has been triggered by a combination of factors: poor harvests in Russia and the US caused by draughts; disruption to supplies in Pakistan and China from flooding; and a typhoon in the Philippines. But against this, India is expecting an exceptionally good crop. And in the aftermath of previous shortages, governments have built up stocks, which can be used to alleviate food shortages.

'Philippines may lose 600,000 tons rice from typhoon', *Business Week*, 18 October 2010
'Asia continues to face rice scarcity, higher prices', *Commodity Online*, 18 October 2010
'Rice yields down, prices up in Asia', *Asia News*, 27 October 2010

Comment The potential output of rice has fallen because of adverse weather, which can be seen as a hopefully temporary deterioration in the gifts of nature.

2.1 Summary

- A country's production possibility frontier shows the various combinations of goods and services that it can produce with its scarce resources, assuming it has no unemployment and uses resources efficiently.
- If there is any unemployment or any inefficiency, then a country will produce at a combination of products represented by a point inside its production possibility frontier.

2.2 Firms and households and the economic problem

There is no 'solution' to the economic problem. But the different sectors of the economy can try to ease it. In this section we will look briefly at what firms and households could do about it. In the following sections we will look more closely at what governments could do about it.

Firms and the economic problem

Firms can do two things to ease the economic problem.

- **Reduce any inefficiency in their production**. The more efficient they are, the closer the combination of products that are produced will be to the country's production possibility frontier.

- **Shift the production possibility frontier outwards.** They can try to do this by introducing new improved technology, or by buying extra capital.

Shifts in the production possibility frontier are shown in Figure 2.3, where PPF_0 reproduces the original frontier *PPF* from Figure 2.2. Suppose that firms introduce a new technology that reduces the baking time for bread, so that they can produce more bread from their existing ovens. Or suppose they acquire more capital that can be used for bread, like ovens. In either case, if the economy now puts all its resources into bread, it will be able to make more bread than before. Say it can make 110,000 loaves a day instead of 100,000. Then the top end of the frontier will shift up to 110,000. The other end will be unaffected because there is no change in the amount of bricks that could be produced if all resources were used for bricks. So the frontier would now be like PPF_1.

If the new technology or capital had been concerned with brick-making, then the other end of the frontier would have shifted out to the right. In practice, firms often manage to introduce new technology and buy new capital that aids production in a range of industries. If they can do this with both bread and bricks, then the frontier might shift from PPF_0 to a position like PPF_2. Then, if the economy were to use all its resources efficiently, it could produce at any point on PPF_2; otherwise, it would produce at a point somewhere in the pink grid inside PPF_2.

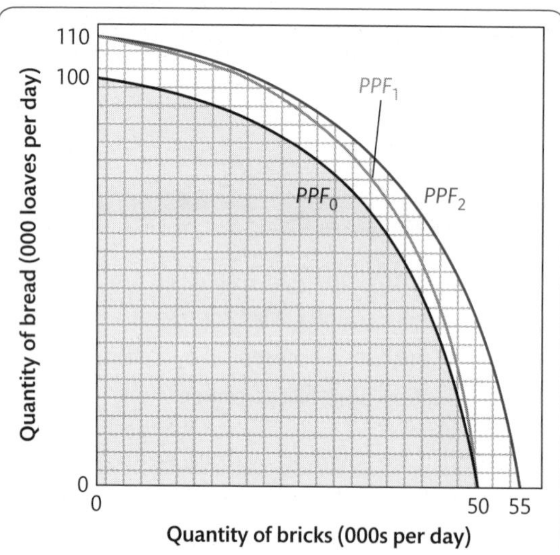

Figure 2.3 **New technology or extra capital**

If there is new technology or extra capital in the bread industry, then at any level of brick output, the economy can now produce more bread; so PPF_0 is replaced by PPF_1. If there is new technology or extra capital in both industries, then PPF_0 is replaced by PPF_2. When PPF_2 applies, the economy can produce at any point on it or at any point in the pink grid.

Households and the economic problem

At first, it might seem that households cannot do anything about the fact that output is limited by scarce resources. But remember that households undertake a lot of production themselves. Perhaps they produce some of the bread in the economy illustrated in Figures 2.2 and 2.3. If so, they could try to remove any inefficiency in their own production, to help production in the economy to get closer to whichever frontier applies. Or they could introduce new technology and buy new capital, to allow them to produce more bread, and so help to shift the frontier from PPF_0 to a position like PPF_1.

There is more that households can do to increase the resources available to the economy and so shift the frontier from PPF_0 to a position like PPF_2. For instance, they can lend more money to firms, or give more money to any firms that they own, to help firms to buy extra capital. Also, households can increase the labour available to the economy by working longer hours or retiring at a later age.

Finally, households can in principle help to ease the problem of scarcity by wanting less!

2.2 Everyday economics

Green energy

Advances are being made that allow household waste to be converted into energy. This can be done by capturing the gases emitted by decomposing rubbish and using them to generate electricity. For example, a recent plant installed in Aberdeen can provide electricity for 2,400 homes.

'£1 million investment creates green energy at Aberdeen landfill', SITA press release, *13 April 2010*
'Landfill gas energy for 2,400 Aberdeen homes', *Building4Change*, 28 April 2010

Comment Effectively, this technology means that the resources that were used to produce the products that ended up as waste are now being exploited further by being used also to generate electricity instead of being wasted. There is also an environmental spin-off as the gases that are no longer released to the atmosphere might have been harmful.

2.2 Summary

- Firms and households can help to ease the problem of scarcity by producing more efficiently, shifting production closer to the possibility frontier. They can also buy more capital and perhaps use improved technologies to shift the frontier outwards.
- Households could also ease the problem of scarcity by offering more labour and reducing their wants.

2.3 Governments and the economic problem

All governments intervene with the economies of their countries. Indeed, they intervene with 'How?' resources are used, 'For what?' they are used, 'For whom?' they are used, and 'How many?' are used. They intervene because they believe they can ease the economic problem. This section explores the different types of intervention that governments undertake. But before we explore them, we will explain that the extent to which governments intervene varies between countries.

A market economy and a command economy

To explain how much government intervention can vary, we will consider first two extreme positions that a government might in principle take.

- **The government makes no intervention**. In this case, all decisions over how, for what, for whom, and how many resources were used would depend entirely on what happened in the various markets in the country. For example, if people bought shoes from an inefficient firm, than that inefficiency would persist. If people decided to buy more bicycles and fewer burgers, then cycle-makers would expand while burger-makers would contract. If people were willing to pay high prices for concerts by certain singers, then those singers would earn high wages and be able to consume a lot. And if the owners of firms wanted them to expand, they could buy more capital and so use extra resources. A market in which there is no government intervention is called a **free market**; a country in which all the markets are free has what is called a **free market economy**, or, more simply, a **market economy**.
- **The government takes complete control**. In this case, a government might make all the decisions over how, for what, for whom, and how many resources were used. So it would tell producers

how to produce, what to produce, how much to pay different workers, and how many resources to use. Its country would have what is termed a **command economy**, or a **planned economy**.

A mixed economy

In practice, all governments adopt a position in between these two extremes, and influence rather than control how, what, for whom, and how many resources are used: so all countries actually have what is called a **mixed economy**.

To see how a mixed economy differs from a market economy and a planned economy, consider how prices are set. A government in a market economy will allow all prices to be set freely in markets. A government in a planned economy will determine all prices itself. A government in a mixed economy will let some prices be set in free markets, but it will influence other prices, and it may set a few prices itself. In the UK, for instance, the government allows the prices of children's clothes to be set in free markets, but it taxes petrol to push petrol prices up, and it sets the prices that people must pay for prescriptions.

Although all economies are mixed, some governments get their economies very close to the planned economy extreme. The governments in communist countries have often done so, and Cuba and North Korea are probably the two that are closest to it today. Conversely, some governments intervene very little: important examples are Switzerland and the United States.

Governments intervene to varying extents chiefly because they disagree over how effective intervention is at easing the economic problem. But even if they were to agree about the effects, it is possible that some countries would benefit from more intervention than others, and that any given country might benefit from more intervention at some times than at others. But we will not explore these issues here. Instead, we will consider how government intervention might ease the economic problem.

A raft of government policies

In their efforts to ease the economic problem, most governments operate a raft of policies simultaneously. To illustrate these policies, we will assume that an economy starts off as a market economy, with no intervention, and that its government then introduces a raft of policies. But we will assume that it introduces these policies one at a time. Taking them one at a time helps us to see the effects of each individual policy. We could take the policies in any order, but we will start with policies that concern the issue of 'How?', and then move on to policies that concern 'For what?', 'For whom?', and 'How many?'

For simplicity, we will continue to look at a country that produces only bread and bricks. And to begin with we will assume that the country undertakes no trade with foreign countries. We will also assume that its government is very successful with the policies that it introduces.

Governments and 'How?'

Suppose the country concerned initially has the production possibility frontier PPF_0 shown in Figure 2.4. And suppose that each day it initially produces 35,000 bricks and 25,000 loaves of bread. So it is at point *A*, which is well inside PPF_0. The country's production may be at a point inside PPF_0 because there is some inefficiency, or because there is some unemployment, or because there is some of both. We will suppose that there is some of both, and that the government first tackles the inefficiency.

The inefficiency means that the answer to the question 'How are resources used?' is 'With some inefficiency'. The government may try to improve how resources are used by increasing the degree of competition between firms. In a competitive environment, inefficient firms will have their prices undercut by efficient ones. So the inefficient firms will either have to become efficient or else go out of business; either way, the economy will end up with all of its firms efficient. Some of the ways in which

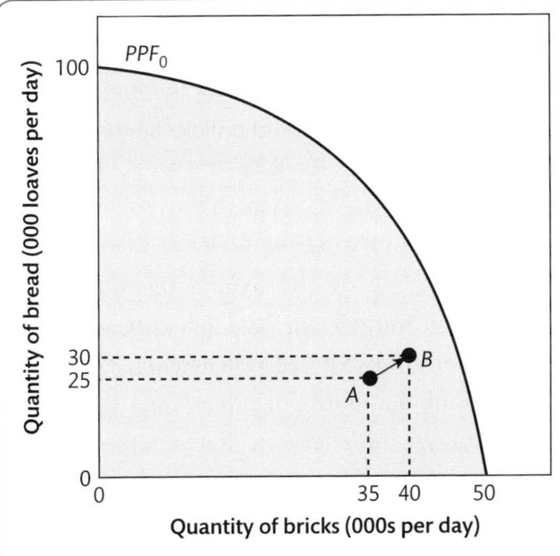

Figure 2.4 **Changes in 'How?' resources are used**

The government removes inefficiency, perhaps by having more competition between firms. The pattern of production moves closer to the production possibility frontier, PPF_0.

governments try to promote competition are discussed in Chapter 12.

Once efficiency has improved, production will increase. In Figure 2.4, we assume that the pattern of output shifts along the arrow from point *A* to point *B*. At *B*, the output of both goods is higher than it was at *A*, with 40,000 bricks and 30,000 loaves produced each day. Suppose for simplicity that the government has actually managed to remove all inefficiency. Then the reason why output has not moved all the way to PPF_0 is because the government has not yet tackled the unemployment; this is a 'How many?' issue, which we will look at shortly.

Governments and 'For what?'

For the moment, though, suppose the government has tackled only the 'How?' problem and has moved the country to point *B* in Figure 2.4. This point is reproduced in Figure 2.5. Now suppose that the government would like more bread to be produced. Perhaps it feels that if people eat more bread, then they will be stronger and fitter. At present, people may not eat more than 30,000 loaves a day because they underestimate the benefits that eating more bread would bring.

In this situation, the government believes that the answer to the question 'For what are resources used?' is 'Too few are used for bread'. So it may decide to shift resources from bricks to bread. Suppose it does this by imposing a tax on bricks and introducing a subsidy on bread. The tax on bricks should raise the price of bricks, so that people will buy fewer, causing the output of bricks to fall. And the subsidy on bread should reduce the price of bread, so that people will buy more, causing the output of bread to rise.

In Figure 2.5, the tax and the subsidy shift the pattern of output along the arrow from point *B* to point *C*. The output of bread has risen to 45,000 loaves a day, and the output of bricks has fallen to 37,000 day. *C* is no closer to PPF_0 than *B* because the government has still not tackled the unemployment that is holding output inside the frontier.

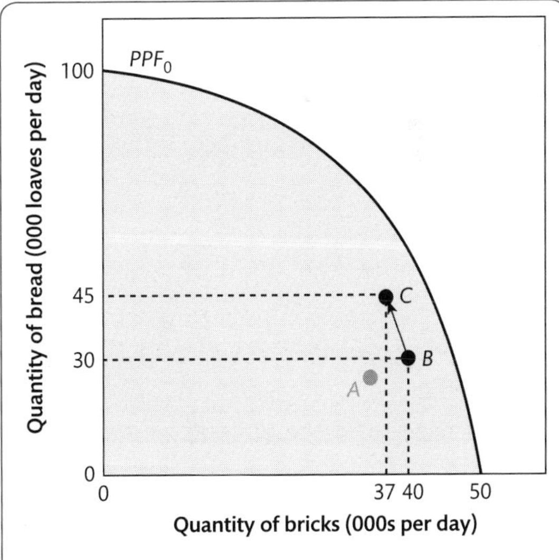

Figure 2.5 **Changes in 'For what?' are resources used**

The government changes the pattern of output by making a deliberate attempt to reduce the output of bricks, perhaps by taxing them, and to increase the output of bread, perhaps by subsidizing it.

Governments and 'For whom?'

Suppose the government has tackled both the 'How?' and the 'For what?' questions, and has moved the country to point *C* in Figure 2.5. This point is reproduced in Figure 2.6. The government may now decide that there are too many people on low incomes who are unable to buy much of anything. So it believes that the answer to the question 'For whom are resources used?' is 'Too few resources are used for the poor'.

Suppose the government helps the poor by paying them benefits, which it finances by taxing the rich. So rich people now buy fewer loaves and fewer bricks, while poor people buy more loaves and more bricks. It is possible that the fall in the number of loaves bought by the rich exactly offsets the rise in the number of loaves bought by the poor, and that the fall in the number of bricks bought by the rich exactly offsets the rise in the number of bricks bought by the poor. If so, the pattern of output will stay at point *C*.

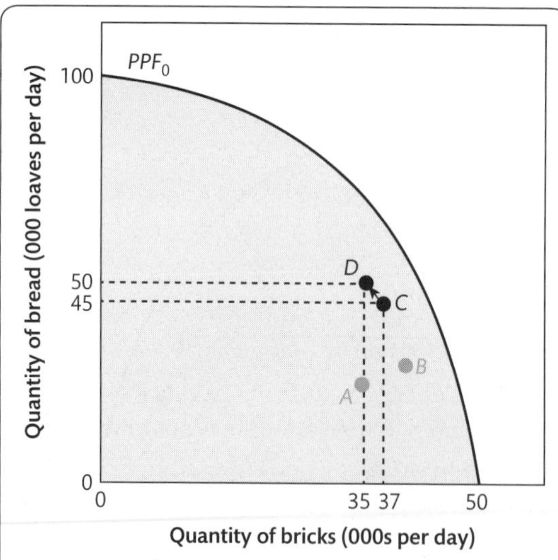

Figure 2.6 **Changes in 'For whom?' resources are used**

The government taxes the rich to fund benefits for the poor. Then the rich buy far fewer bricks and the poor buy a few more, so brick output falls. Also, the rich buy a little less bread and the poor buy far more, so bread output rises.

However, exact offsets are unlikely. Let's suppose that the rise in the number of loaves bought by the poor slightly exceeds the fall in the number of loaves bought by the rich, so the output of bread rises slightly. Let's also suppose that the fall in the number of bricks bought by the rich slightly exceeds the rise in the number of bricks bought by the poor, so the output of bricks falls slightly. So the pattern of output shifts along the short arrow in Figure 2.6 from point *C* to point *D*. The output of bread has risen to 50,000 loaves a day, and the output of bricks has fallen to 35,000 a day. Of course, the effect on the pattern of output shown here is simply a side-effect of helping the poor and taxing the rich.

Notice that *D* is still no closer to PPF_0 than *B* or *C* were. This is because the government has still not tackled the unemployment, which is still holding output inside the frontier.

Governments and 'How many?'

Suppose the government has tackled the 'How?', 'What?', and 'For whom?' problems, and has moved the country to point *D* in Figure 2.6. This point is reproduced in Figure 2.7. The government now considers the question 'How many resources are used?' It may well have two answers, as follows:

- **'Not enough resources are being used, because too many are unemployed;' and**
- **'Firms could buy some extra capital, such as new plant, buildings, vehicles and machinery'.**

The unemployment problem may extend beyond people who want to work but cannot find jobs. There may also be idle or unemployed land and unemployed capital, such as empty buildings and unused plant, vehicles, and machinery. To reduce all this unemployment, the government must increase the amount of goods that firms sell each day. Then firms will produce more, and so hire extra workers and use more land and capital.

The government can increase the amount that firms sell in various ways. For instance, it could get its government departments to buy more from firms.

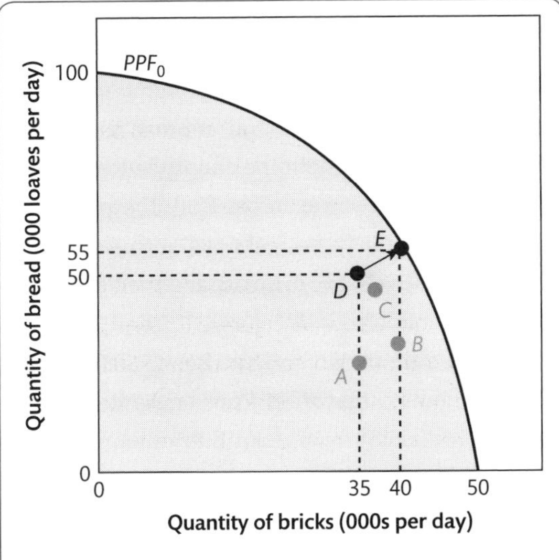

Figure 2.7 **One change in 'How many?' resources are used**

The government manages in various ways to remove all unemployment. As all inefficiency has already been removed, production moves to a point on the production possibility frontier, PPF_0.

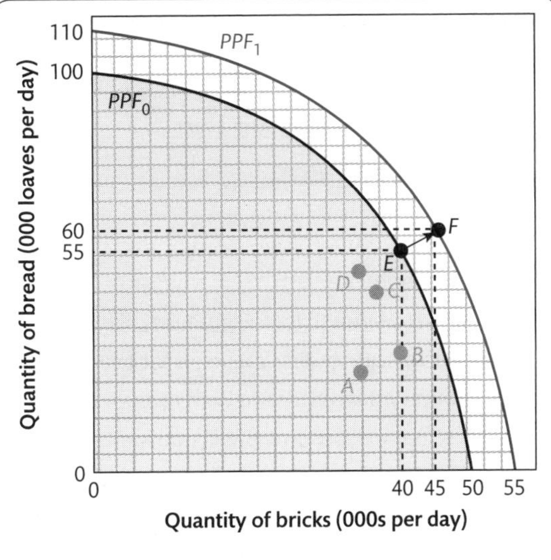

Figure 2.8 **Another change in 'How many?' resources are used**

The government cuts interest rates to encourage firms to buy more capital. So the frontier shifts to PPF_1. If full efficiency and full unemployment persist, production will be at a point on PPF_1, here *F*. Otherwise production will be somewhere in the pink grid.

Let's suppose that, in its various ways, the government removes all unemployment. Then, in Figure 2.7, the pattern of output will shift along the arrow from point *D* to point *E*. At *E*, the output of both goods is higher than it was at *D*, with 40,000 bricks and 55,000 loaves produced each day. And at *E* output is at last on PPF_0. This is because there is now no unemployment, and all inefficiency has already been removed.

Now suppose that the government tries to encourage firms to acquire more capital. It might do so by reducing interest rates, to make it cheaper for firms to borrow money to finance the purchase of extra capital. When firms acquire more capital, the country will have more resources, so it can produce more bread and more bricks. This means that the production possibility frontier shifts, as illustrated in Figure 2.8, where PPF_0 and point *E* are reproduced from Figure 2.7.

The new frontier is PPF_1. This shows, for example, that if the country were to use all its resources for bricks, then it could now produce 55,000 a day, not 50,000 as applied on PPF_0. And if it were to use all its resources to produce bread, it could now produce 110,000 loaves a day, not 100,000 as applied on PPF_0. Of course, the country is unlikely to produce just one good. It will instead produce some of both and so be at a point somewhere along PPF_1.

To ensure that the country produces at a point on PPF_1, the government must maintain full efficiency and full employment. In Figure 2.8, we assume that it does so, and that the pattern of output moves along the arrow from point *E* on PPF_0 to point *F* on PPF_1. At *F*, the output of both goods is higher than it was at *E*, with 45,000 bricks and 60,000 loaves produced each day. If inefficiency or unemployment were to reappear, production would end up somewhere in the pink grid inside PPF_1.

In Figure 2.8, the frontier shifted outwards because firms acquired more capital. We saw in Figure 2.3 that the frontier can also shift outwards if firms introduce new technologies. Governments could help here by encouraging research and development of new technology.

Another way of easing the economic problem

Suppose the government has tackled the 'How?', 'For what?', 'For whom?', and 'How many?' problems, and the country is at point *F* in Figure 2.8. This point is reproduced in Figure 2.9. So far, we have assumed that this country does no trade with foreign countries. This means that its consumers will consume whatever pattern of output its producers produce. For example, at the initial point *A*, the country's producers produced 35,000 bricks and 25,000 loaves of bread each day, and these were also the amounts that its consumers then consumed. Likewise, at point *F*, the country's producers now produce 45,000 bricks and 60,000 loaves each day, and that is what its consumers now consume.

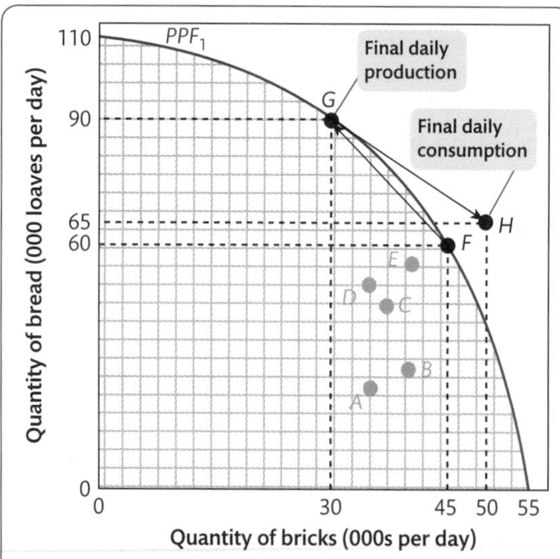

Figure 2.9 **Specialization and trade**

The government encourages the country to produce more bread, which it is relatively good at making, and fewer bricks, which it is relatively bad at making. So the pattern of production moves along PPF_1 from *F* to *G*. But the country also exports some loaves and imports some bricks, so its final pattern of consumption, at *H*, differs from its final pattern of production, at *G*.

But suppose the government opens up trade with a foreign country. And suppose that the foreign country is relatively poor at making one product—say bread—and relatively good at making the other—bricks. Then it will benefit the country we have been considering to move resources from the product at which it is relatively poor, bricks, into the one at which it is relatively good, bread, and then trade with the foreign country.

The results are shown in Figure 2.9, where the country shifts enough resources from bricks to bread to take its production from point *F* to point *G*. Here, it produces 30,000 bricks a day and 90,000 loaves. Its consumers would prefer to consume more bricks than it produces and less bread, and this is easily arranged. The country exports 25,000 loaves each day, leaving 65,000 of the 90,000 produced for its own citizens to consume. It uses the money received from its exports of bread to import 20,000 bricks each day, which, along with the 30,000 it produces, allows its citizens to consume 50,000. So while the country's pattern of production ends up at point *G*, its pattern of consumption ends up at point *H*.

The key attraction of this trade is that it allows this country to consume at a point outside its current production possibility frontier, PPF_1, even though it cannot produce at a point outside its frontier. You might wonder if this means that the foreign country ends up consuming inside its production possibility frontier, but we will see in Chapter 27 that trade actually allows all countries to consume outside their frontiers. So most governments try to promote trade in various ways, for example by joining trading blocks like the EU.

Question 2.1 In Figure 2.9, consumers end up consuming the pattern of products shown at point *H*, having initially consumed the pattern at point *A*. Has this move from *A* to *H* solved the economic problem?

Three groups of government policies

We have now explored a wide range of government policies for easing the economic problem. Economists often divide these policies into three groups, as follows.

- **Resource allocation policies**. These aim to change the way in which resources are used. They include policies that aim to increase the efficiency with which resources are used, as illustrated in Figure 2.4, and policies that aim to change the output of some products, and so change the amount of resources used for them, as illustrated in Figure 2.5. Although all the other policies we looked at also changed the way in which the country used its resources, these changes were side-effects of the policies and not their aims. So those policies come under the two other groups.
- **Redistribution policies**. These aim to make some people better off and other people worse off. They generally end up changing the amount of resources used for different products, as occurred in Figure 2.6.
- **Stabilization policies**. These aim to stabilize the overall performance of the economy in a satisfactory way. They include policies like those illustrated in Figure 2.7, where the government aimed to stabilize unemployment at zero; in practice, governments simply try to keep unemployment low. Stabilization policies also include policies like those illustrated in Figure 2.8, where the government aimed to increase the level of output that the economy could produce; in practice, governments try to keep the production possibility frontier moving constantly outwards at a stable rate. Stabilization policies also include attempts to stabilize exports and imports to secure major benefits from trade; so these policies relate to trade, which was illustrated in Figure 2.9.

Governments pursue one more stabilization policy, aiming to stabilize the rate at which prices on average rise, that is the rate of inflation. They aim to stabilize it at a low level. This policy cannot be related to the production possibility frontier because that concerns outputs of goods rather than their prices. The reasons why governments are, nevertheless, interested in stabilizing prices are explored in Chapter 17.

2.3 Everyday economics

A planned economy that works poorly

North Korea has regular food shortages and the World Food Programme has just announced that it will send in aid worth $200m to help 3.5 million people who are on government rations that meet only about half their needs.

'UN body starts emergency food aid to North Korea', *Reuters*, 29 April 2011
'WFP begins emergency food aid to N. Korea', *Arirang*, 30 April 2011

Comment There had recently been poor crops in North Korea, but there is no food shortage in neighbouring South Korea. Admittedly, it is hard to say exactly how far the problems in the North stem from planning in principle, or from bad planning.

2.3 Summary

- To try to ease the economic problem, all governments intervene with their economies, so all economies are mixed economies. But some governments intervene much more than others.
- Some government policies, called resource allocation polices, aim to affect 'How?' resources are used, by promoting efficiency, and 'For what?' they are used, by changing the output of some products.
- Governments also use redistribution policies. These aim to affect 'For whom?' resources are used by taxing the rich, who can then buy less, and paying benefits to the poor, who can then buy more.
- Governments also use stabilization policies. Some of these tackle 'How many?' resources are used by promoting low unemployment, and also by encouraging purchases of new capital. Stabilization policies also promote, the development of new technologies, international trade, and low rates of inflation.

2.4 The economic problem, economists, and opportunity costs

We have seen various ways in which governments try to ease the economic problem. To help them to devise policies, governments often seek advice from economists. In this section, we consider what sort of advice economists can give. We also meet the important concept of opportunity cost.

Positive statements

To see what sort of advice a study of economics allows economists to give, and also to see what sort of advice it does not allow them to give, we must distinguish between two types of statement: positive statements and normative statements.

Positive statements are statements of fact about what was, what is, or what will be. These statements can be about any facts, but five examples about economic facts are given below. The first three are statements about what was, the fourth is a statement about what is, and the fifth is a statement about what will be.

- **Statement A**. Since 2000, UK governments have spent more on the National Health Service.
- **Statement B**. In 2010, UK prices increased by an average of 21%.
- **Statement C**. In 1700, there were 15,259 unemployed people in London.
- **Statement D**. Value added tax (VAT) is not imposed on books.
- **Statement E**. Higher university tuition fees will reduce the number of students going to university.

Notice three key points about positive statements.

- **Positive statements may include the word 'not'.** For example, statement D includes the word 'not', but D is still a positive statement, because it is a statement of fact.
- **Positive statements may not be true**. Indeed, statement B is not true because inflation in 2010 was about 3%, not 21%. But B is still a positive statement, because it is a statement of fact, even though the fact is untrue.
- **To see whether a positive statement is true, it is often but not always possible to make a test**. For instance, it is possible to test statement A by looking at figures of spending on the National Health Service. It is possible to test statement B by looking at figures of price rises in 2010. It is possible to test statement D by looking at the legislation on VAT. And it will be possible in time to test statement E by looking at the numbers of students. However, statement C cannot be tested because there are no figures on unemployment for 1700.

Economics is a science, and like any other science, economics tries to establish facts. So economists can make positive statements like those listed above. Of course, their positive statements may sometimes be false!

Normative statements

Normative statements are statements of opinion about what should be. Here are three economic examples.

- **Statement F**. Spending on the National Health Service should rise still more.
- **Statement G**. All major cities should have congestion charges.
- **Statement H**. Universities should receive more government money so that tuition fees can be abolished.

Economics is a science and, like any other science, it can never prove what should or ought to be done. So, although individual economists often hold strong opinions about what governments should do, they cannot use their study of economics to prove whether their opinions are right or wrong. In turn, they cannot use their studies to tell governments what they ought to do.

For example, suppose the government wants to increase the top rate of income tax to raise £2 billion to spend on pensions. Two economists may well agree about how far the tax rate would have to be raised to produce the extra £2 billion, but their economics will not tell them whether the government should put the tax rate up. One may believe that it should, to help pensioners. The other may believe that it should not, because it will encourage people on high wages to move abroad. There is nothing in economics to say that one is right and one is wrong, because they are disagreeing on opinions, not about scientific facts.

Similar situations occur in other sciences. For example, two doctors may agree from their medical studies that a terminally ill patient who is in pain would be killed by a large dose of morphine. But their studies will not tell them whether the morphine should be given. One may believe that it should be given, to end the pain. The other may prefer to 'let nature take its course'. There is nothing in medical science to say that one is right and one is wrong, because they are disagreeing on opinions, not on facts.

The uses and limitations of economics

You may wonder what use economics is if it cannot tell a government what it ought to do. Its value is that it can often tell a government what the effects of various policies will be, and this will help the government to choose what it will do. For example, if economists show that even high university fees have little effect on the number of students going into higher education, then the government may persist with them. On the other hand, if economists show that even small fees have a big effect, then governments may decide to end them.

Opportunity cost

We end this chapter by discussing an important economic concept. To understand this concept, suppose that an economy produces only bread and bricks, and suppose that it wants to produce some more bricks. Extra resources will have to be used to produce the extra bricks, and these resources could instead have been used to make bread. So, to get the extra bricks, the economy must sacrifice, or forgo, the bread that it could have had instead. We say that the forgone bread represents the true cost of the extra bricks, because the forgone bread is what is sacrificed to get the extra bricks.

Question 2.2 Suppose a country can produce only bread and bricks, and suppose its production possibility frontier is the same as the one in Figure 2.9. Currently it is at the bottom end, producing 55,000 bricks a day and no bread. (**a**) Suppose it wants in future to produce 60,000 loaves of bread a day: what would be the opportunity cost? (**b**) Suppose at a later date, it wants to raise bread production once again to 90,000 loaves a day: what would be the opportunity cost?

In reality, economies produce many products. Suppose the UK economy starts to produce more bricks. The resources being used for the extra bricks could instead have been used for, say, extra bread, or extra books, or extra cars. So, to produce the extra bricks, the UK had to forgo some bread, or some books, or some cars.

The **opportunity cost** of any action is the forgone alternative that the people taking the action would most have preferred. So if, after bricks, we would have most preferred the resources to be used for books, then it is those books that we would have had instead, and it is those books that we will sacrifice to get the extra bricks. So the opportunity cost of the bricks is the forgone books.

Opportunity costs and governments

Let's look at an example of opportunity cost from the government's point of view. Suppose the government has £1 billion, which it could spend on a hospital, a road, or a submarine. Suppose its first preference is the road, its second preference is the hospital, and its third preference is the submarine. Then it will choose the road because that is what it most prefers. The opportunity cost of the road is the hospital, because that is what the government preferred most apart from the road, and it would have built the hospital if the road had not been built. The opportunity cost is not the submarine, because that is not what it preferred most apart from the road. Incidentally, the opportunity cost of the road is not £1 billion either. Opportunity costs are measured as something we sacrifice to get something else; they are not measured as monetary costs.

Opportunity costs and you

Now let's look at an example of opportunity cost from your point of view. Suppose you have £5 that you could spend on a film, a magazine, or a burger. Suppose your first preference is the film, your second preference is the magazine, and your third preference is the burger. You will choose the film because that is what you most prefer. The opportunity cost will be the magazine, because that is what you prefer most apart from the film. The opportunity cost is not the burger, because that is not what you want most apart from the film. Incidentally, the opportunity cost is not £5 either. As before, opportunity costs are measured as something we sacrifice to get something else; they are not measured as monetary costs.

Here is another example that does not involve money, so it helps to show that opportunity cost is not about money. Suppose you have an evening that you could spend reading this book, or in the company of your partner, or in the gym. Suppose your first preference is time with this book, your second preference is time with your partner, and your third preference is time in the gym. Then you will choose time with this book because it is what you most prefer. The opportunity cost will be the time with your partner, because that is what you prefer most apart from the book. The opportunity cost is not time in the gym, because that is not what you prefer most apart from the book. As before, opportunity costs are measured as something you sacrifice—here, time with your partner—to get something else.

Question 2.3 In 2011, the UK had millions of unemployed people and some unused capital. So it could have produced some extra homes without producing less of anything else. Does that mean the homes would have had no opportunity cost?

2.4 Summary

- Positive statements are statements of fact. Normative statements are statements of opinion. As a science, economics attempts to establish facts, not opinions.
- The opportunity cost of any action is the most preferred alternative that is forgone in order to take the action. Opportunity costs are not measured in money.

In the next chapter we look at an economic model that explains how many prices are determined. It also explains how the quantities produced of many goods and services are determined. So it is central to understanding why the pattern of goods and services produced is what it is.

abc Glossary

Command economy: another term for a planned economy.

Free market: a market with no government intervention over price or quantity.

Free market economy: an economy in which all markets are free markets, so the government has no influence over how, for what, for whom, or how many resources are used.

Market economy: another term for a free market economy.

Mixed economy: an economy with government influence rather than control over how, for what, for whom, and how many resources are used.

Normative statement: a statement of opinion about what should be.

Opportunity cost: the most preferred alternative that is forgone in order to take an action.

Planned economy: an economy in which the government determines how, for what, for whom, and how many resources are used.

Positive statement: a statement of fact about what was, what is, or what will be.

Production possibility frontier: a curve showing the various output patterns that it is possible for a country to produce, assuming there is full employment and full efficiency.

Redistribution policy: a policy that aims to make some people better off and others worse off.

Resource allocation policy: a policy that aims to change the way in which resources are used.

Stabilization policy: a policy that aims to stabilize the overall performance of the economy in a satisfactory way.

= Answers to in-text questions

2.1 No. Consumers are certainly much better off at *H* than *A*, but even at this higher level of consumption, their consumption is likely to be well below their wants. The economic problem has been eased, but not solved.

2.2 **(a)** 10,000 bricks a day. **(b)** 15,000 bricks a day. Note how the opportunity cost increases.

2.3 It is tempting to suppose that the homes would have no opportunity cost. However, the unemployed resources that might have been used for them could instead have been used for many other products. The opportunity cost of the homes would be whatever people would most like those resources to be have been used for after homes.

? Questions for review

2.1 Consider the country with the production possibility frontier shown in Figure 2.2. What, if anything, will happen to this frontier in each of the following circumstances?

(a) The country acquires new machines that can be used only for making bread.

(b) The country acquires new machines that can be used only for making bricks.

(c) The country improves its education so that people who are entering the workforce at the start of their careers can produce more than people who are retiring at the end of their careers.

(d) The country reduces the level of unemployment.

2.2 Suppose a government undertakes the following policies. For each policy say whether it is a resource allocation policy, a redistribution policy, a stabilization policy, or perhaps a combination of these.

(a) The government helps train companies to buy new coaches.

(b) The government raises the age at which people can claim the winter fuel allowance.

(c) The government helps workers who have been made redundant to retrain, and so helps them in time to find different sorts of jobs.

(d) The government introduces new grants paid to students.

2.3 Which of the following are positive statements? In the case of those that you think are positive statements, say whether they are true.

(a) Economics is a science.

(b) Economics is not a science.

(c) Economics ought to be a science.

(d) Opportunity costs are always measured in money terms.

? Questions for discussion

2.1 Suppose a government stimulates immigration to increase the amount of labour available to firms. What might be the effects of this on the country's economic problem?

2.2 Suppose a government raises the age at which people can retire and get pensions, so making many people work more years and increasing the labour available to producers. What might be the effects of this on the country's economic problem?

2.3 Suppose a government encourages a larger proportion of a country's resources to be used for making capital goods, so that a smaller proportion is available for making consumer goods and services. Will consumers be worse off indefinitely?

Common student errors

Students often assume that a production possibility frontier applies to a firm or to a government. Instead, it must apply to an economy, that is an area with producers and consumers. Usually when we talk of production possibility frontiers, we refer to the ones that apply to countries.

Students sometimes find it difficult to grasp that the basket of goods and services that is consumed in an economy can differ from the basket of goods and services that is produced there. This does happen, though, because of trade, as shown in Figure 2.9. To help you to understand how this happens, consider yourself as an example. Suppose you have a job making curtains. You sell the curtains and use the money to buy other items like food and clothes. Just because curtains are the only thing you produce does not mean they must be the only thing you consume. And just because you don't produce food or clothes does not mean you cannot consume them. What is true for you is also true for countries—they can consume a different basket of goods and services from the basket they produce.

Part II

Microeconomics

3

Supply and Demand

Remember from Chapter 1 that markets fall into several groups. For example, consumers buy new products in markets for final goods and services, and firms hire labour in factor markets. For each market, microeconomics tries to explain what determines the price and the quantity traded in a period of time, and in turn the expenditure in a period of time. It also considers why prices, quantities, and spending often change.

Why do you have to pay about 30p for a free-range egg, rather than more or less? Why are some 15 million of them sold each day, rather than more or fewer? Why do the price and the quantity of eggs and other products often change? Why are DJs often paid about £12 an hour? Why do their wages, and the wages in many other occupations, change over time?

This chapter shows you how to answer questions like these, by understanding:

* what determines the price and the quantity traded in the markets for many goods and services;
* what determines the wage rate and the total hours worked in the markets for many types of labour;
* how changes in behaviour by buyers can alter the price or wage and the quantity traded in these markets;
* how changes in behaviour by sellers can alter the price or wage and the quantity traded in these markets.

3.1 The supply and demand model

Markets in which the supply and demand model applies

Economists are interested in the price, the quantity traded, and the expenditure in all markets. But we cannot use a single model to cover every market, because markets vary so much. In this chapter, we will study a model called the supply and demand model. This model applies to markets that meet these three conditions:

- there are many sellers;
- there are many buyers;
- all these people buy and sell an identical item.

These conditions are met in many markets. One example is the UK market for free-range eggs, which is a final goods market. Another example is the market for the services of DJs in a large city, which is a factor market. And another example is the market for steel, which is a market for intermediate goods. In this chapter, we will chiefly use as examples the UK market for free-range eggs and the market for DJs in a large city.

Throughout this chapter, we will assume that the markets we are discussing are free markets, so that the government does not intervene to affect the price, the quantity, or the spending. In Chapter 5, we will relax this assumption and see what happens if the government does intervene.

The supply and demand model applies only if all the three conditions that we have listed apply. There are many markets in which at least one of these three conditions is not met, so the supply and demand model does not apply to them. Here are some cases in which it does not apply.

- **Some markets do not have many sellers**. For example, this applies in the UK markets for gas and rail travel. We will study markets like this in Chapters 10 and 11.
- **Some markets do not have many buyers**. For example, this applies in the UK markets for train drivers and doctors: drivers are hired by only a few train companies, and most doctors are hired by the National Health Service. We will study markets like this in Chapter 14.
- **Some markets have many buyers and sellers, but they buy and sell items that are not identical**. For example, a city may have many student flats to rent, but the flats will vary in size, quality, and location, so they will have different rents. We will study markets like this in Chapter 10.

Supply and demand schedules

We will begin our study of the supply and demand model by applying it to the market for free-range eggs. For simplicity, we will assume that all these eggs are exactly the same and have exactly the same price. We want to know what factors determine this price, and the quantity of eggs that is traded each day, and the amount that people spend on them each day.

In principle, the price of these eggs could be anything, but we will begin by considering seven possible prices: 0p, 10p, 20p, 30p, 40p, 50p, and 60p. These are shown in the first column of Table 3.1. At each of

Table 3.1 **Demand and supply schedules for eggs**

Price of eggs (p)	Quantity demanded per day (million)	Quantity supplied per day (million)
0	30	0
10	24	0
20	19	8
30	15	15
40	12	21
50	10	26
60	8	30

these prices, the table shows two different quantities, as follows.

- The **quantity demanded**. This is the quantity that consumers between them would be willing to buy at that price in a period of time, here a day.
- The **quantity supplied**. This is the quantity that sellers between them would be willing to sell at that price in a period of time, here a day.

The column about the quantity demanded is called the **demand schedule**. It is called a schedule because it is given in the form of a table, just as a bus schedule gives information about bus times in a table. The column about the quantity supplied is called the **supply schedule**.

Of course, the quantity of eggs that buyers wish to buy depends on many factors other than the price of eggs. For example, it depends on the number of buyers and their incomes. Also, the quantity of eggs that sellers wish to sell depends on many factors other than the price of eggs. For example, it depends on the number of sellers and the cost of chicken food. However, the schedules assume that every factor except the price is held constant. So, in Table 3.1, it is only the different prices that cause people to wish to buy and sell different quantities.

The demand schedule in Table 3.1 shows that buyers would demand fewer eggs at high prices than at low prices. The reason is that if egg prices rise, then people will buy fewer eggs and more of other foods instead.

The supply schedule in Table 3.1 shows that sellers would supply fewer eggs at low prices than at high prices. The reason is that at low prices, suppliers will make less profit from eggs, so they will be less interested in supplying them. Indeed, the table shows that if the price were 10p or less, then egg production would not be worthwhile, and producers would supply no eggs.

Excess supply

Suppose that the price of an egg is currently 50p. Then Table 3.1 shows that buyers want to buy 10 million eggs each day, while sellers want to sell 26 million. When the quantity supplied exceeds the quantity demanded, there is an **excess supply**. The excess supply is the difference between the quantity supplied and the quantity demanded, so each day it is 26 million eggs minus 10 million, that is 16 million eggs.

When there is an excess supply, economists expect the price to fall. Just why the price falls depends a little on the market. In this case, egg producers will see that people are willing to buy far fewer eggs than they want to sell, and this will tempt them to reduce the price. How far will they reduce it? We cannot say how far they will reduce it initially, but we can say how far they will reduce it eventually.

To see this, suppose they initially reduce the price to 40p. This lower price decreases the quantity of eggs that sellers want to supply to 21 million a day, and it increases the quantity of eggs that buyers demand to 12 million a day. So there is still an excess supply. Admittedly the excess supply is now only 9 million eggs a day, that is the gap between 21 million and 12 million, but because there is still an excess supply, we expect the price to fall again below 40p.

Indeed, we expect the price to continue to fall until there is no excess supply. The table shows that this will happen when the price reaches 30p. At that price, the quantity of eggs supplied will have decreased to 15 million eggs a day, and the quantity demanded will have increased to 15 million. So there will now be no excess supply, and so no pressure for any further fall in the price.

Excess demand

Now suppose that the price of an egg is currently 10p. Then Table 3.1 shows that buyers want to buy 24 million each day, while sellers want to sell no eggs at all. When the quantity demanded exceeds the quantity supplied, there is an **excess demand**. The excess demand is the difference between the quantity demanded and the quantity supplied, so each day it is 24 million eggs.

When there is an excess demand, economists expect the price to rise. Just why the price rises depends a little on the market. In this case, egg producers will see that people want to buy far more eggs than they want to sell, and this will tempt them to raise the price. How far will they raise it? We cannot say how far they will raise it initially, but we can say how far they will raise it eventually.

To see this, suppose they initially raise the price to 20p. This higher price increases the quantity of eggs that sellers will supply to 8 million a day, and it decreases the quantity of eggs that buyers demand to 19 million a day. So there is still an excess demand. Admittedly the excess supply is now only 11 million eggs a day, that is the gap between 19 million and 8 million, but because there is still an excess supply, we expect the price to rise again to above 20p.

Indeed, we expect the price to continue to rise until there is no excess demand. The table shows that this will happen when the price reaches 30p. At that price, the quantity of eggs supplied will have increased to 15 million eggs a day, and the quantity demanded will have decreased to 15 million. So there will now be no excess supply, and so no pressure for any further fall in the price.

Equilibrium in the egg market

We have seen that if the price of eggs is below 30p, there will be an excess demand. So the price will rise, and it will continue to rise until it reaches 30p. And if the price of eggs is above 30p, there will be an excess supply. So the price will fall, and it will continue to fall until it reaches 30p.

So if the price is not 30p, there will be forces at work changing it. Only when it reaches 30p will there be no forces changing it, so only then will it settle down. A situation in which there are no forces for change is called an **equilibrium**. So we call 30p the **equilibrium price**. When the market has settled down with the equilibrium price, buyers and sellers will settle down to trading 15 million eggs a day. So we call this the **equilibrium quantity**.

We can also work out how much money will be spent in the market when it reaches equilibrium. 15 million eggs will be sold each day for 30p each. So total spending will be 450 million pence or £4.5 million. This is the **equilibrium expenditure**.

The laws of demand and supply

Economists sometimes mention a 'law' of demand. This claims that buyers *always* want to buy less at higher prices, if other things are held constant. This law applies to most markets. But in some markets the law does not apply because buyers demand the same quantity at all prices. For example, diabetics do not want less insulin at higher prices, for fear of their lives.

There *may* even be some markets in which the law does not apply because buyers demand more at higher prices. For example, people who like showing off fine jewels *may* buy more if the price rises, because the jewels will then be more impressive. However, no-one has yet found a market in which it can be proved that buyers demand more at higher prices.

Economists also sometimes mention a 'law' of supply. This claims that sellers *always* want to sell more at higher prices, if other things are held constant. This law applies in most markets. But in some markets the law does not apply because sellers will supply the same quantity at higher prices. For example, this applies to land, where the amount that landowners can supply to land users is fixed by nature.

Actually, there may well be some markets in which the law does not apply because suppliers will supply less at higher prices. For example, suppose there were a rise in the wage rate paid to dentists, that is a rise in the price of a day's labour. Maybe most dentists would then supply less labour. By working fewer hours, they would enjoy more leisure, and yet they might still manage to earn more because of the higher wage rate.

Fortunately, the supply and demand model will work whether or not the laws of demand and supply apply. In each case, there should still be one price at which the quantity demanded equals the quantity supplied, and that will give us the equilibrium price and the equilibrium quantity.

3.1 Everyday economics

Cotton prices continuing to slip

The price of cotton fell sharply over a period of several weeks in April and May 2011, and it was unclear when the fall would stop.

'Raw cotton prices slip sharply', *The News*, 10 May 2011
'Cotton further plunges to Rs 8,500 per maund', *Pakistan Observer*, 15 May 2011

Comment A continuing fall in cotton prices shows that the market was moving towards a new equilibrium.

3.1 Summary

- The supply and demand model discussed in this chapter applies only to markets in which many buyers and many sellers trade an identical item. This includes many product markets and many labour markets.
- Demand and supply schedules are tables that show the quantity demanded and the quantity supplied at a selection of possible prices.
- The price settles at its equilibrium level, which is where there is no excess demand or excess supply, so that the quantity demanded equals the quantity supplied: this quantity is the equilibrium quantity.

3.2 Supply and demand curves

In the last section, we discovered the equilibrium price in the egg market by using a table with schedules. However, there is a problem with schedules: they show the quantity demanded and the quantity supplied at only a selection of possible prices. Our schedules considered just seven possible prices.

It was lucky that the equilibrium price happened to be one of these prices, 30p, because we were able check that the quantity demanded equalled the quantity supplied at that price. If the equilibrium price had instead been one that was not shown on the table, such as 27p, then we could not have used the table to check that the quantity demanded and the quantity supplied were equal at that price.

To avoid this problem with schedules, we will not use them again. Instead we will use graphs, like Figure 3.1. On this graph, we measure the quantity of eggs per day on the horizontal axis, and we measure the price of eggs on the vertical axis. Some black points have been plotted on the graph, along with two curves, and these we will now explain.

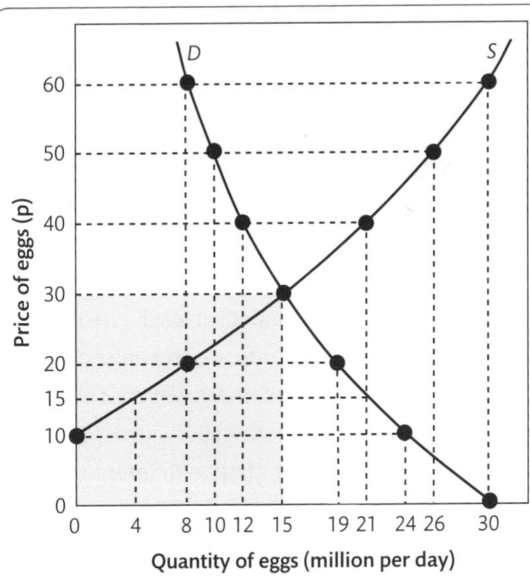

Figure 3.1 **Equilibrium in the egg market**

Equilibrium occurs at a price of 30p and a quantity of 15 million eggs a day. The equilibrium level of expenditure is £4.5 million a day, as indicated by the shaded rectangle.

Drawing the supply and demand curves

On Figure 3.1, the curve labelled *D* goes though seven points, which repeat the information given in the 'quantity demanded' column of Table 3.1. For example, the second highest point on *D* shows that if the price—shown on the vertical axis—were 50p, then the quantity demanded—shown on the horizontal axis—would be 10 million eggs a day. Unlike the demand schedule, however, this curve also shows the quantity that would be demanded at all prices between 0p and 60p. For instance, it shows that if the price were 15p, then the quantity demanded would be 21 million eggs a day. This curve is called a **demand curve** because it shows the quantity that would be demanded at each possible price.

Also in Figure 3.1, the curve labelled *S* goes though seven points, which repeat the information in the 'quantity supplied' column of Table 3.1. For example, the second highest point on *S* shows that if the price were 50p, then the quantity supplied would be 26 million eggs a day. Unlike the supply schedule, however, this curve also shows the quantity that would be demanded at all prices between 0p and 60p. For instance, it shows that if the price were 15p, then the quantity supplied would be 4 million eggs a day. This curve is called a **supply curve** because it shows the quantity that would be supplied at each possible price.

The demand curve shows clearly that a different quantity would be demanded at each price. When economists discuss **demand**, they mean the quantities that would be demanded at each possible price, as shown by the whole demand curve. Likewise, the supply curve shows that a different quantity would be supplied at each price. When economists discuss **supply**, they mean the quantities that would be supplied at each possible price, as shown by the whole supply curve.

The equilibrium position on a graph

Figure 3.1 shows that *S* and *D* intersect at a price of 30p and a quantity of 15 million eggs a day. These are the equilibrium price and quantity that we discovered earlier, so the intersection point shows the equilibrium position. This point can also be used to show the equilibrium expenditure. To see this, look at the grey rectangle between this point and the origin: that is the point on the graph at which the value on each axis is zero. This rectangle has a length of 15 million eggs and a height of 30p, so its area represents the total expenditure of £4.5 million per day.

But *why* is the equilibrium position in the market at the intersection point? To answer this, we will use Figures 3.2 and 3.3. These repeat the curves from Figure 3.1, but for simplicity they omit the black points that were used to plot those curves.

Graphs and an excess supply

Suppose for a moment that the price of eggs is currently above the level where *S* and *D* intersect, at 40p. Then, in Figure 3.2, we can see from *D* that buyers will buy 12 million eggs a day, and we can see from *S* that

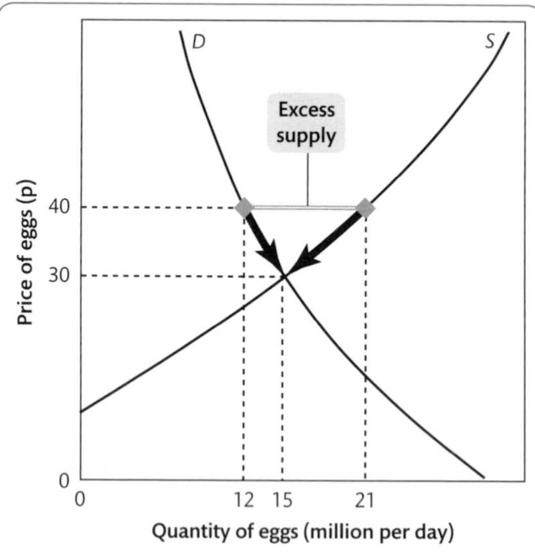

Figure 3.2 **The egg price won't stay above 30p**

If the price were 40p, there would be an excess supply, shown by the double line, and the price would fall. As it fell, the thick arrows show that the quantity demanded would rise and the quantity supplied would fall. The price would fall to 30p, where the quantities demanded and supplied are equal.

sellers want to sell 21 million eggs. So there is an excess supply of 9 million eggs a day, as shown by the double line.

We know that an excess supply causes the price to fall. As it falls, producers will gradually supply smaller quantities. So they will 'move along' the part of *S* where there is a thick arrow. Also, as the price falls, buyers will demand larger quantities. So they will 'move along' the part of *D* where there is a thick arrow.

The price will continue to fall to 30p where *D* and *S* intersect. At that price, the quantity that buyers will demand and the quantity that sellers will supply will be equal, at 15 million eggs a day. So there will be no excess supply.

Graphs and an excess demand

Suppose instead that the price of eggs is currently below the level at which *S* and *D* intersect, at 20p. Then, in Figure 3.3, we can see from *S* that sellers will sell only 8 million eggs a day, and we can see from *D* that buyers want to buy 19 million eggs. So there is an excess demand of 11 million eggs a day, as shown by the double line.

We know that an excess demand causes the price to rise. As it rises, producers will supply larger quantities. So they will 'move along' the part of *S* with a thick arrow. Also, as the price gradually rises, buyers demand smaller quantities, so they will 'move along' the part of *D* with a thick arrow.

The price will continue to rise until 30p where *D* and *S* intersect. At that price the quantity that buyers will demand and the quantity that sellers will supply will be equal, at 15 million eggs a day. So there will be no excess demand.

In short, the price will not settle at any price above the intersection of *D* and *S*, for then there would be an excess supply. Nor will the price settle at any price below the intersection, for then there would be an excess demand. So the price will settle at the intersection, and this point shows the equilibrium position for the market.

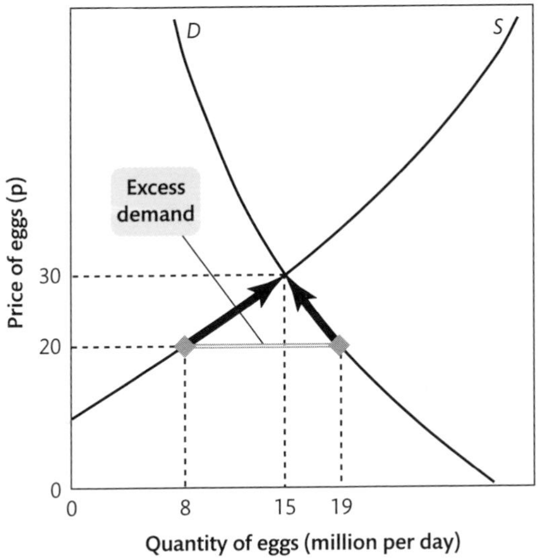

Figure 3.3 **The egg price won't stay below 30p**

If the price were 20p, there would be an excess demand, shown by the double line, so the price would rise. As it rose, the thick arrows show that the quantity demanded would fall and the quantity supplied would rise. The price would rise to 30p, where the quantities demanded and supplied are equal.

Supply and demand in a labour market

We said earlier that the supply and demand model applies to any market in which many buyers and sellers trade the same item. This occurs in many factor markets, especially the markets for some types of labour. Figure 3.4 shows how the model can be applied to a labour market.

The figure uses as an example the market for DJs in a large city. Many pubs and clubs want to hire DJs, and many people, including some students, want to work as DJs. Like the earlier figures, this has the quantity on the horizontal axis and the price on the vertical axis. Here, the quantity is measured in hours of labour per week, and the price is measured in pounds paid per hour. As the price for labour is usually called a wage, the graph uses the word 'wage' instead of 'price'.

In Figure 3.4, the supply curve, *S*, shows the quantity of DJ labour that will be supplied at each wage. As the wage rises, more people will want to work more hours as a DJ, so the quantity of hours supplied rises.

So the supply curve slopes upwards, as did the one for eggs. Also, the demand curve, *D*, shows the quantity of DJ labour that will be demanded at each wage. As the wage falls, pubs and clubs will want to use DJs more often, so the quantity of hours demanded rises. So the demand curve slopes downwards, as did the one for eggs.

In Figure 3.4, the market will settle at the equilibrium wage rate of £12 per hour. We can find this rate by seeing where *D* and *S* intersect.

At any wage above £12, the quantity of hours that people would like to supply as DJs would be more than the quantity of hours that would be demanded. So there would be an excess supply. This would put downward pressure on the wage rate. For instance, when employers found that people wanted to work more hours as DJs than were needed, they would tend to reduce the wage. As the wage fell, the quantity of labour supplied would fall, and the quantity of labour demanded would rise. So the wage would fall until there was no excess demand, which happens at £12 an hour.

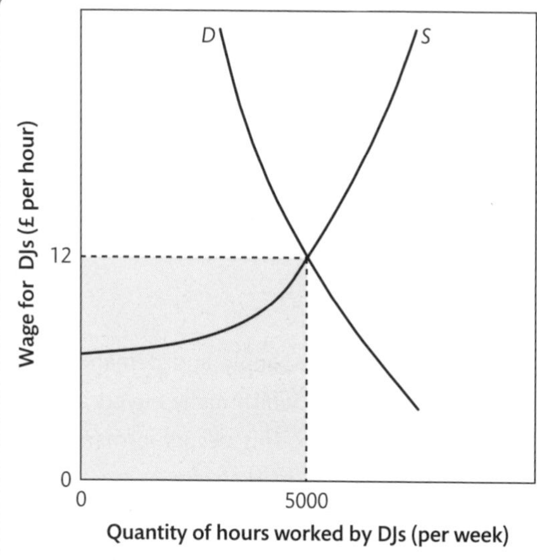

Figure 3.4 **Equilibrium in the DJ market in a city**
The market settles where *D* intersects *S*, at a wage of £12 an hour and a quantity of 5,000 hours a week. Expenditure will be £60,000 a week, as indicated by the shaded rectangle.

At any wage below £12, the quantity of hours demanded would be more than the quantity of hours that DJs would like to supply. So there would be an excess demand. This would put upward pressure on the wage rate. For instance, employers would find that they could not employ as many hours of DJ labour as they wanted, so they would tend to offer a higher wage. As the wage rose, the quantity of labour demanded would fall, and the quantity supplied would rise. So the wage would rise until there was no excess demand, which happens at £12 an hour.

The intersection of *S* and *D* in Figure 3.4 also shows the equilibrium quantity, which is 5,000 hours a week. So the total equilibrium expenditure on DJs in this city is £12 times 5,000, which is £60,000, and this is shown by the area of the grey rectangle.

3.2 Summary

- A demand curve shows the quantity that would be demanded at each price or wage, and a supply curve shows the quantity that would be supplied at each price or wage. The price or wage will settle at its equilibrium level, which is the level at which the two curves intersect.
- At that equilibrium price or wage, there is no excess demand or excess supply, so the quantity demanded equals the quantity supplied, and this is the equilibrium quantity.

3.3 How the buyers in a market can change the equilibrium

Let's return to the egg market. We saw that this would settle with a price of 30p and a quantity of 15 million eggs traded a day. However, the price and quantity won't stay at 30p and 15 million for ever. From time to time, they will change. But why will they change, if they have reached the equilibrium levels? The answer is that, from time to time, the demand curve will shift and the supply curve will shift. And, as we shall now see, when either curve shifts, the point at which they intersect—that is the equilibrium position—changes.

The effects of a decrease in demand

Consider, first, a shift in the demand curve. Suppose the demand curve is initially the same as *D* in Figures 3.1, 3.2, and 3.3. This curve is repeated in Figure 3.5, where it is labelled D_0. It shows the quantity of eggs that people would initially demand at each possible price.

Now suppose that a report is published proving that many eggs contain the bacteria salmonella, which can cause food poisoning. Then people will want to consume fewer eggs. So the whole demand curve will shift to the left, perhaps to the position of the demand curve D_1 in Figure 3.5.

D_1 tells us, for instance, that if the price were 50p, then buyers would now demand 3 million eggs a day instead of 10 million; if the price were 30p, they would now demand 6 million eggs instead of 15 million; and

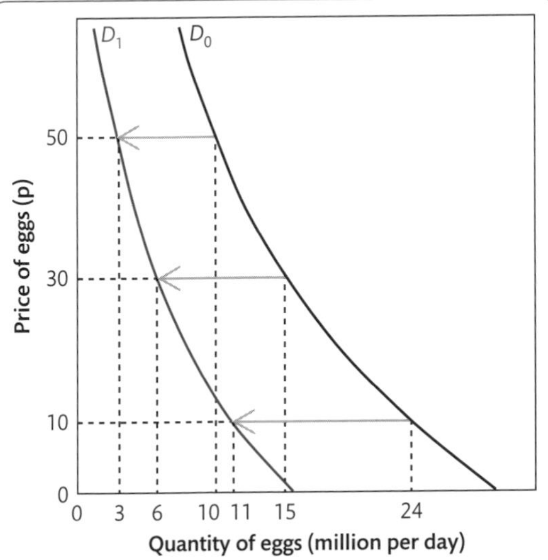

Figure 3.5 **A decrease in demand shifts *D* left**

At each price, the quantity demanded falls. This effect is shown at three prices by the arrows.

if the price were 10p, they would now demand 11 million eggs instead of 24 million. The changes in quantity demanded at these three prices are shown by arrows. We could add similar arrows at any other prices.

To see what happens to the market, we must add in the supply curve, *S*. This is done in Figure 3.6. The initial equilibrium was where D_0 intersected *S*. This was at a price of 30p, a quantity of 15 million eggs a day, and an expenditure of £4.5 million a day, as shown by the grey rectangle. But now the demand curve shifts left to D_1. This shift triggers a sequence of events. It is important to see the order in which these events occur.

- **Initially, the price stays at 30p**. At this price, the quantity supplied is still 15 million eggs a day, but the quantity demanded is now 6 million. So there is now an excess supply of 9 million eggs a day, as shown by the double line.

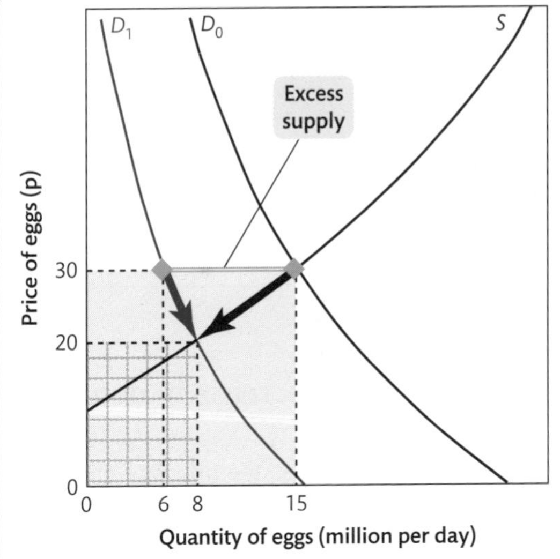

Figure 3.6 **The effects of a decrease in demand**

The price starts at 30p, where the quantities demanded and supplied are equal, at 15 million eggs a day. Then demand decreases. The quantity demanded falls to 6 million to create the excess supply shown by the double line. So the price falls, and this increases the quantity demanded and decreases the quantity supplied, as the thick arrows show. The price falls to 20p, where the quantities demanded and supplied become equal again, at 8 million a day. Expenditure falls, as shown by the pink grid.

- **The excess supply puts downward pressure on the price**. We saw this in section 3.1 and in Figure 3.2. So the price will fall. Note that it falls only because the shift in demand has created an excess supply at the original price.
- **As the price falls, the quantity supplied falls and the quantity demanded rises**. These movements along *S* and D_1 are shown by thick arrows.
- **Eventually, the price settles at 20p where *S* intersects the new demand curve D_1**. Here, the quantity demanded once again equals the quantity supplied, but now at 8 million eggs a day. So the new equilibrium is a price of 20p and the new equilibrium quantity is 8 million eggs a day. The new equilibrium expenditure is 20p × 8 million, which is 160 million pence, or £1.6 million per day, as shown by the pink grid that overlays part of the grey rectangle.

So a decrease in demand leads to a lower price, or a lower wage in a labour market, a lower quantity, and a lower expenditure.

Question 3.1 In Figure 3.6, would producers know that the new equilibrium price would be 20p immediately after the demand curve shifted?

The effects of an increase in demand

An increase in demand has the opposite effects. We can show these with the market for DJs in a large city. Suppose the demand curve is initially as shown by D_0 in Figure 3.7. This shows the number of hours of DJs labour that employers initially wish to hire at each possible wage.

Now suppose that more clubs open up in the city, so that employers now want to hire more DJ labour. Then the whole demand curve shifts right, perhaps to the position shown by D_1. The arrows show how much more labour would be demanded at three possible wages, £24, £16, and £8. For instance, if the wage were £24, employers would now demand 4,750 hours a week instead of 3,050. We could add similar arrows at any other wages.

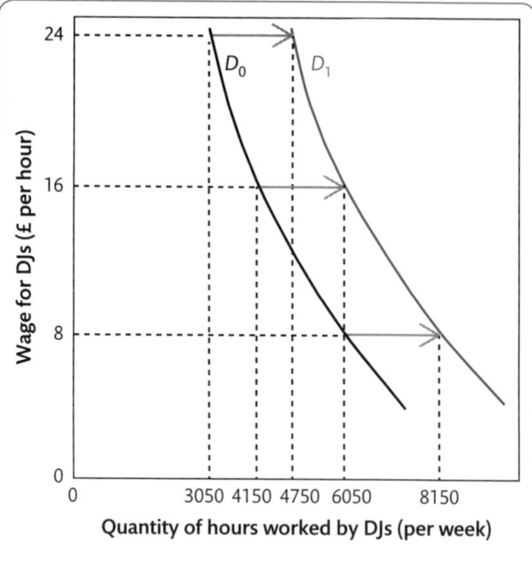

Figure 3.7 **An increase in demand shifts *D* right**
At each wage, the quantity demanded rises. This effect is shown at three wage rates by the arrows.

To see what happens to the market, we must add in the supply curve, *S*. This is done in Figure 3.8. The market was initially in equilibrium where D_0 intersected *S*, at a wage of £12 and a quantity of 5,000 hours a week. Expenditure was £60,000 a week, as shown by the grey rectangle. Now the demand curve shifts right to D_1 and the following sequence of events occurs.

- **Initially the wage stays at £12**. The quantity supplied is still 5,000 hours a week, but the quantity demanded is now 7,000. So there is an excess demand of 2,000 hours, as shown by the double line.
- **The excess demand puts upward pressure on the wage**. We saw the effects of an excess demand on prices in section 3.1 and in Figure 3.3. So, in Figure 3.8, the wage will rise. Note that it rises only because the shift in demand has created an excess demand at the original wage.
- **As the wage rises, the quantity supplied rises and the quantity demanded falls**. These movements along *S* and D_1 are shown by thick arrows.

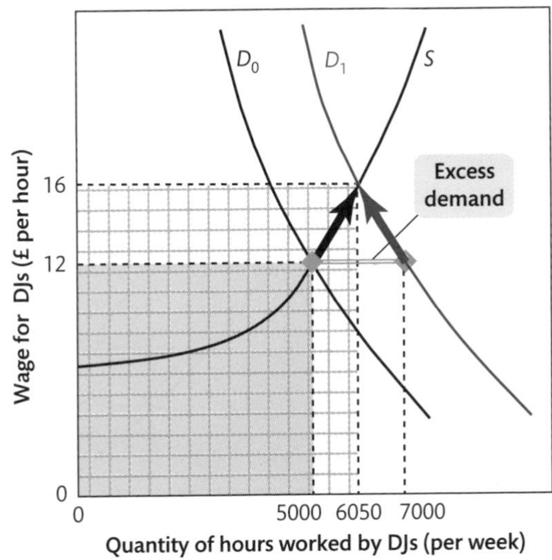

Figure 3.8 The effects of an increase in demand

The wage starts at £12, where the quantity demanded and quantity supplied are equal at 5,000 hours a week. Then demand increases. The quantity demanded rises to 7,000 to create the excess demand shown by the double line. So the wage rises. This reduces the quantity demanded and raises the quantity supplied, as the thick arrows show. The wage rises to £16, where the quantities become equal again, at 6,050 hours. Expenditure rises, as shown by the pink grid.

- **Eventually, the wage settles at £16 where *S* intersects the new demand curve D_1.** Here, the quantity demanded once again equals the quantity supplied, but now at 6,050 hours a week. So the new equilibrium is a wage of £16 and the new equilibrium quantity is 6,050 hours a week. The new equilibrium expenditure is £16 × 6,050, which is £96,800, as shown by the pink grid that overlays part of the grey rectangle.

So an increase in demand leads to a higher wage, or a higher price in a product market, a higher quantity, and a higher expenditure.

3.2 Everyday economics

Rising beef prices in the US

Beef prices rose sharply in the US following a large increase in demand.

'Beef-buying Koreans fuel record meat rally in U.S. groceries', *Bloomberg*, 13 May 2011
'Supermarket milk prices rise by most in three years, beef, pork also up', *Drovers Cattle Network*, 13 May 2011

Comment The US is just part of the global beef market, and its price rise merely reflected an international trend for higher prices following a global increase in demand.

3.3 Summary

- If demand decreases, buyers will demand a smaller quantity at each possible price. So the demand curve shifts left, and the equilibrium price or wage, quantity, and expenditure all fall.
- If demand increases, buyers will demand a higher quantity at each possible price. So the demand curve shifts right, and the equilibrium price or wage, quantity, and expenditure all rise.

3.4 How the sellers in a market can change the equilibrium

We have seen how the equilibrium in a market changes if the demand curve shifts. The equilibrium also changes if the supply curve shifts.

The effects of a decrease in supply

To see this, we will first return to the egg market. Suppose that the supply curve starts in the same position in which it started before, as repeated by S_0 in Figure 3.9. Here, S_0 shows the quantity of eggs that producers would initially supply at each possible price.

Now suppose a law is passed that increases the amount of space that free-range chickens must have. This law will raise egg producers' costs and make their industry less profitable. So they will be less inclined to supply eggs. So the whole supply curve will shift left, perhaps to the position of S_1. The arrows in Figure 3.9 show how much less would be supplied at prices of 20p, 30p, and 40p. We could add similar arrows at any other prices.

To see what happens to the market, we must add in the demand curve, *D*. This is done in Figure 3.10. Initially, the market was in equilibrium where *D* intersected the supply curve. This was at a price of 30p, a quantity of 15 million eggs a day, and an expenditure of £3 million a day shown by the grey rectangle. But now supply shifts left to S_1. This shift triggers a sequence of events.

- **Initially, the price stays at 30p**. At this price, the quantity demanded is still 15 million eggs a day, but the quantity supplied is now 9 million. So there is now an excess demand of 6 million eggs a day, as shown by the double line.
- **The excess demand puts upward pressure on the price**. So the price will rise. Note that it rises only because the shift in supply has created an excess demand at the original price.

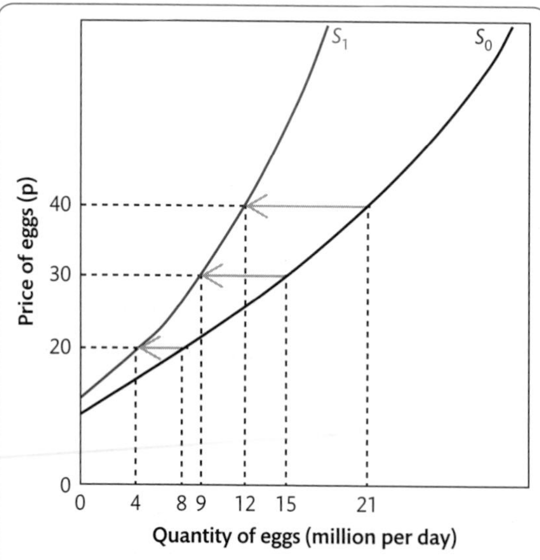

Figure 3.9 **A decrease in supply shifts *S* left**

At each possible price, suppliers would supply a smaller quantity. This effect is shown at three prices by the arrows.

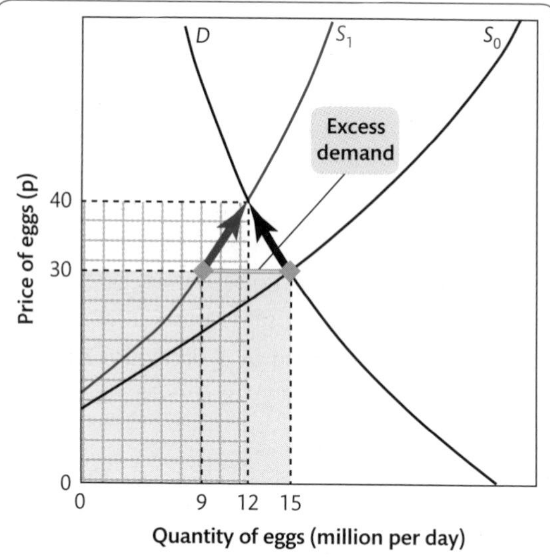

Figure 3.10 **The effects of a decrease in supply**

The price starts at 30p, where the quantity demanded equals the quantity supplied, at 15 million eggs a day. Then supply decreases. The quantity supplied falls to 9 million to create the excess demand shown by the double line. So the price rises. The thick arrows show how this rise increases the quantity supplied and decreases the quantity demanded. The price rises to 30p, where both quantities become equal again, at 12 million a day. Expenditure is now shown by the pink grid.

- **As the price rises, the quantity supplied rises and the quantity demanded falls**. These movements along S_1 and *D* are shown by thick arrows.
- **Eventually, the price settles at 40p where *D* intersects the new supply curve S_1**. Here, the quantity demanded once again equals the quantity supplied, but now at 12 million eggs a day. So the new equilibrium is a price of 40p and a quantity of 12 million eggs a day. The new equilibrium expenditure is 40p times 12 million, which is 480 million pence, or £4.8 million per day, as shown by the pink grid.

So a decrease in supply leads to a higher price and a lower quantity. The higher price tends to push expenditure up, while the lower quantity tends to push it down. In some cases, the rise in price is more marked than the fall in quantity, so expenditure ends up increasing, as it does here from £4.5 million to £4.8 million. But in other cases expenditure may fall.

The effects of an increase in supply

An increase in supply has the opposite effects. We can illustrate these with the market for DJs in a city. Suppose that initially it is term time at colleges and the supply curve starts in the same position in which it started before, as repeated by S_0 in Figure 3.11. This shows the quantity of hours that DJs will initially supply at each possible wage.

Now suppose college terms finish. So students want to supply more hours of labour as DJs than before. So the whole supply curve will shift right, perhaps to the position of S_1. The arrows show how much more labour will be supplied at three possible wage rates, £24, £16, and £8. We could add in similar arrows at any other wages.

To see what happens to the market, we must add in the demand curve, *D*. This is done in Figure 3.12. Initially, the market was in equilibrium where *D* intersected the supply curve S_0, at a wage of £12 and a quantity of 5,000

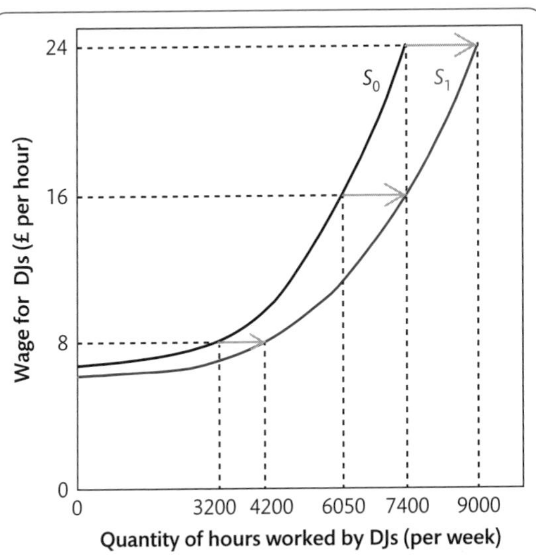

Figure 3.11 **An increase in supply shifts S right**

At each price, the quantity supplied rises. This effect is shown at three prices by the arrows.

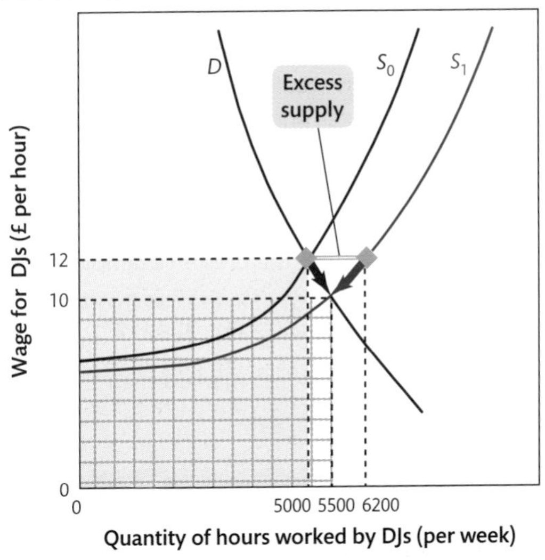

Figure 3.12 **The effects of an increase in supply**

The wage starts at £12, where the quantity demanded equals the quantity supplied at 5,000 hours a week. Then supply increases. The quantity supplied rises to 6,200 to create the excess supply shown by the double line, so the wage falls. The thick arrows show how this fall decreases the quantity demanded and increases the quantity supplied. The wage falls to £10, where the quantities become equal again at 5,500. Spending is now as shown by the pink grid.

hours a week. Expenditure was £60,000 a week, as shown by the grey rectangle. But now supply shifts right to S_1 and the following sequence of events occurs.

- **Initially the wage stays at £12**. The quantity demanded is still 5,000 hours a week, but the quantity supplied is now 6,200 hours. So there is an excess supply of 1,200 hours, as shown by the double line.
- **The excess supply puts downward pressure on the wage**. So the wage will fall. Note that it falls only because the shift in supply has created an excess demand at the original wage.
- **As the wage falls, the quantity supplied falls and the quantity demanded rises**. These movements along S_1 and *D* are shown by thick arrows.
- **Eventually, the wage settles at £10 where *D* intersects the new supply curve S_1**. Here, the quantity demanded once again equals the quantity supplied,

but now at 5,500 hours a week. So the new equilibrium is a wage of £10 and a quantity of 5,500 hours a week. The new equilibrium expenditure is £10 times 5,500, or £55,000 a week, as shown by the pink grid.

So an increase in supply leads to a lower wage or price and a higher quantity. In the present example, the fall in price was more marked than the rise in quantity, so expenditure fell from £60,000 to £55,000. But sometimes the fall in price is less marked than the rise in quantity, so expenditure rises.

3.3 Everyday economics

Falling supply leads to soaring sugar prices

The price of sugar is expected to rise to new heights. The supply of sugar is still falling owing to adverse weather conditions in all the major supplying countries, so there is still an excess demand. And the measures taken to increase its production are having limited success.

'Prices of sugar to increase due to deficit in supply', *Topnews*, 13 October 2010
'Still higher prices possible for sugar', *ABC Rural*, 13 October 2010

Comment The main problem with trying to expand sugar production is that there are a limited number of places where both the land and the climate are suitable.

3.4 Summary

- If supply decreases, sellers will supply less at each possible price. So the supply curve shifts left, the equilibrium price or wage rises, the equilibrium quantity falls, and expenditure may rise or fall.
- If supply increases, sellers will supply more at each possible price. So the supply curve shifts right, the equilibrium price or wage falls, the equilibrium quantity rises, and expenditure may rise or fall.

3.5 Why do demand curves shift?

We know that if a demand curve shifts, then the equilibrium in the market changes. But why do demand curves shift? We will consider first why there may be shifts in the demand curves by households, or consumers, for the various goods and services that they buy. We will merely outline the main reasons for these shifts here, using free-range eggs as an example. Chapter 6 discusses the reasons more fully.

A change in the number of buyers

The demand curve for a product such as eggs shows the total quantity that all buyers between them would demand at each possible price. If the number of buyers increases, then buyers will demand more at each possible price, so demand will increase and the demand curve will shift to the right, and vice versa.

For many products, including eggs, the main factor affecting the number of buyers is the total population. But this is not always the case. For example, suppose the total population remains the same, but the number of people aged 17–22 falls while the number aged over 85 rises. Then fewer people will demand driving lessons and more people will demand walking sticks. So the demand for these products will change.

A change in consumer preferences

Demand can change even if the number of buyers is constant. One reason is that buyers' preferences may change. For example, if eating eggs were found to be unhealthy, then buyers would demand fewer eggs at each possible price, so the demand curve would shift to the left.

A change in the price of complements and substitutes

Many people eat eggs with bacon. When two products are consumed together, they are called **complements**, so bacon is a complement for eggs. If the price of bacon rises, then people will eat eggs and bacon less often, and so demand fewer eggs. So a rise in the price of a complement for a product shifts the demand curve for the product itself to the left, and vice versa.

Some people who eat eggs sometimes eat kippers instead. When two products are seen as alternatives, they are called **substitutes**, so kippers are a substitute for eggs. If the price of kippers falls, then some people will eat more kippers and fewer eggs. So a fall in the price of a substitute for a product shifts the demand curve for the product to the left, and vice versa.

A change in household incomes

Suppose that consumers' incomes rise. They will buy more of most products. The products of which they buy more are called **normal goods**. These include services like pedicures and foreign holidays, as well as goods like beef and large cars. So a rise in incomes leads to an increase in the demand for normal goods, and vice versa.

However, there are some items of which consumers will buy less when their incomes rise. This is because these items have more expensive substitutes that consumers prefer, and which they can now more readily afford. Products of which people demand less when their incomes rise are called **inferior goods**. Apples and sausages are examples. When incomes rise, people instead buy more costly fruit and better cuts of meat. So rises in incomes decrease the demand for inferior goods, and vice versa.

There are also some items of which the quantities that consumers buy are scarcely affected by changes in income. Examples might include pepper and paper clips, for which changes in income will have little or no effect on demand.

A product may be normal at low incomes and inferior at high incomes. For example, suppose a low income household buys no wine. Then its income rises and it starts to buy cheap wines, so here it regards cheap wines as normal goods. But if its income rises again and it switches from cheap wines to expensive wines, then it now regards cheap wines as inferior goods.

In fact, if a household had zero income, it could not buy anything at all. So a rise in its income could not lead to it buying less of anything! So households with very low incomes will not regard any products as inferior goods.

An expected change in price

Suppose the demand curve for eggs is the initial one shown on the figures. So, if the price is 40p, people will buy 12 million a day, and if it is 30p, they will buy 15 million. Suppose the price is now 30p, so people do buy 15 million a day.

Now suppose there is a rumour that the price may rise to 40p next week. Then, even while the price is still 30p, people may buy more than 15 million eggs each day, and store some in the fridge ahead of the price rise. As they now buy more than 15 million eggs a day at the original price of 30p, the demand curve has shifted to the right.

This shift is only temporary. It lasts only while people wait to see what happens. If the price does not rise, then people will eventually revert to buying 15 million a day at 30p, so they will return to the original point on the original demand curve. If the price does rise to 40p, then people will eventually buy 12 million a day and so be at a higher point on the original demand curve than the point at which they started.

Government intervention

Sometimes governments intervene with the demand in a market, for example by making it illegal to buy certain drugs. We will explore the effects of various types of government intervention in Chapter 5.

Shifts in demand curves by firms

We saw in Chapter 1 that there are several groups of markets. In many of these, the people doing the buying or demanding are firms. For example, they buy capital goods and intermediate goods and services, and they hire labour. There are five main reasons why their demand curve for any of these inputs may shift. We will note these reasons very briefly here and discuss them more fully in Chapters 14 and 15.

In our present discussion, we will use as an example the demand by firms for a type of labour, but will use their demand for lorry drivers rather than DJs. The reasons why the demand curve for these drivers may shift are as follows.

- **The number of firms using the input may change**. If the number of firms using lorries rises, then the demand curve for lorry drivers will shift to the right.
- **The demand for the output of the firms that use lorries may change**. Suppose, for instance, that the economy booms and all firms produce more. Then firms will want to use more lorries to move their extra output around. So the demand for lorry drivers will increase, and the demand curve will shift to the right.
- **The price of complementary inputs may change**. Lorry drivers are used with lorries, so lorries are a complementary input to drivers. If the price of lorries falls, then firms will buy more lorries and so want more drivers, so the demand curve for drivers will shift to the right.
- **The price of substitute inputs may change**. Rail transport is a substitute input for lorry transport. If rail transport prices rise, then firms will use trains less and lorries more. So they will want more lorry drivers and the demand curve for drivers will shift to the right.
- **There may be a change in the productivity of the input**. Suppose, for instance, that the law changes to allow larger lorries to take to the road. This has two effects on the demand for drivers. One effect is that each driver can now move more goods, so firms can move the same amount of goods by road as before with fewer drivers: this effect *decreases* the demand for drivers. The other effect is that road transport is now cheaper, so firms may use more road transport and less rail transport: this effect *increases* the demand for road transport and increases the demand for lorry drivers. If the first effect is stronger than the second, then the demand curve for lorry drivers will shift to the left; if the second effect is stronger than the first, then the demand curve will shift to the right.

Workers always worry when firms find ways in which to improve their productivity, in case it reduces the demand for their labour and so leads to lower wages. But sometimes, as we have just seen, improved productivity can lead to a higher demand and higher wages.

Question 3.2 What happened to the demand for farm labourers in the early 20th century when their productivity greatly increased because horse-drawn equipment was replaced by faster tractor-drawn equipment? What happened to the demand for car assemblers in the early 20th century when their productivity greatly increased because they were set to work on assembly lines?

3.5 Summary

- The demand curve by households for a product shifts if (a) the number of buyers changes, (b) consumer preferences change, (c) the price of a complement changes, (d) the price of a substitute changes, or (e) there is a change in incomes. Also, an expected change in price can cause a temporary shift in a demand curve. Note that a rise in incomes might increase the demand for the product, or decrease it.

- The demand curves by firms for an input shifts if (a) the number of firms changes, (b) there is a change in the demand for the output of the firms using the input, (c) the price of a complementary input changes, (d) the price of a substitute input changes, or (e) there is a change in the productivity of the input. Note that an increase in productivity might reduce the demand for the input, or increase it.

3.6 Why do supply curves shift?

We know that if a supply curve shifts, then the equilibrium in the market changes. But why do supply curves shift? We will consider first why the supply curves by firms for products may shift. We will merely outline the main reasons for these shifts here, using free-range eggs as an example.

The reasons are discussed more fully in Chapter 9.

A change in the number of firms

If more farms start to supply eggs, then more eggs will be supplied at each possible price. So the supply curve will shift to the right.

A change in the price of an input

Suppose the price of chicken food rises. Then the costs of egg producers rise and their industry becomes less profitable. So egg producers will be less keen to supply eggs and the supply will decrease, shifting the supply curve to the left. (It is tempting to suppose that producers will try to improve their profits by supplying more output, but Chapter 9 explains that they won't.)

A change in the productivity of an input

Suppose it is found that a new chicken food causes hens to lay more eggs and so be more productive. Then the cost of producing each egg falls, so the egg industry is more profitable. So egg producers will be more keen to supply eggs, so the supply will increase, shifting the supply curve to the right. This reason for a shift is often called a change in technology. But productivity can change for many other reasons. For example, adverse weather can change the productivity of farmland.

An expected change in the product price

If producers expect the price of their product to rise, they may temporarily supply less and store the unsold output ready to sell at a higher price. They will stop doing this either when the price does rise, or when they decide that it will not rise.

A change in demand for a joint product

A few producers produce two or more products in the same process: such products are called **joint products**. For instance, when oil refineries refine crude oil to produce petrol, the refining process simultaneously produces several other products, including asphalt. If there is an increase in the demand for one joint product, then its price will rise and suppliers will supply more. As a result, the supply of the other joint product will increase. For example, if the demand for petrol increases, then refineries will refine more oil to produce more petrol, and so increase the supply of asphalt.

Government intervention

Sometimes governments intervene with the supply in a market, for example with taxes or price controls. We will explore the effects of various types of government intervention in Chapter 5.

Shifts in supply curves by households

We will now consider why the supply curve by households for a particular type of labour may shift. We will outline here the four main reasons for these shifts, using the labour supplied for driving lorries as an example. We will discuss the reasons more fully in Chapter 6.

- **The number of people of working age may change**. If the number falls, then fewer people will want to drive lorries, so the supply curve of labour by lorry drivers will shift to the left.
- **Household preferences may change**. In this context, this means a change in worker preferences. For instance, if lorry hijacks become common, then fewer people will want to drive lorries. So the supply curve of labour by lorry drivers will shift to the left.
- **Wages in related occupations may change**. For example, if the wages of bus drivers rise, then some lorry drivers will choose to drive buses instead. So the supply curve of labour by lorry drivers will shift to the left.
- **The financial rewards that drivers actually get at any given wage may change**. Suppose that lorry drivers earn £20 an hour, but that after income tax this is £16. Then suppose income tax rates rise, so that drivers instead get only £15 after tax. This will affect different drivers in different ways. Some drivers may drive more: they may have mortgages to service, and must do more overtime to earn more income before tax, so that they can have the same amount of income after tax and still service their mortgages. Other drivers may drive less: they may decide it is no longer worth working overtime if the reward is just £15 an hour. Depending on which type of driver is more common, those who will drive more or those who will drive less, the net effect will be to shift the supply curve of lorry driving labour to the right or to the left.

3.6 Summary

- The supply curve by firms for a product shifts if (a) the number of firms changes, (b) the price of an input changes, (c) the productivity of an input changes, (d) firms expect the price of the product to change, and (e) for any product that has a joint product, a change in the demand for the joint product.
- The supply curves by households for a given type of labour shifts if (a) the number of people of working age changes, (b) worker preferences change, (c) wages in related occupations change, or (d) there is a change in the financial rewards that workers actually get at any given wage change. Regarding (d), note for example that a rise in income tax rates might increase the supply of labour, or decrease it.

3.7 Simultaneous changes in supply and demand

Occasionally, both the demand and supply curves shift at once. Sometimes they shift in the same direction, and sometimes in opposite directions. We will now consider the effects of both possibilities, using free-range eggs as an example.

The curves shift in the same direction

Suppose the supply and demand curves for eggs are initially as shown by S_0 and D_0 in Figure 3.13. So the initial equilibrium is at the point where they intersect,

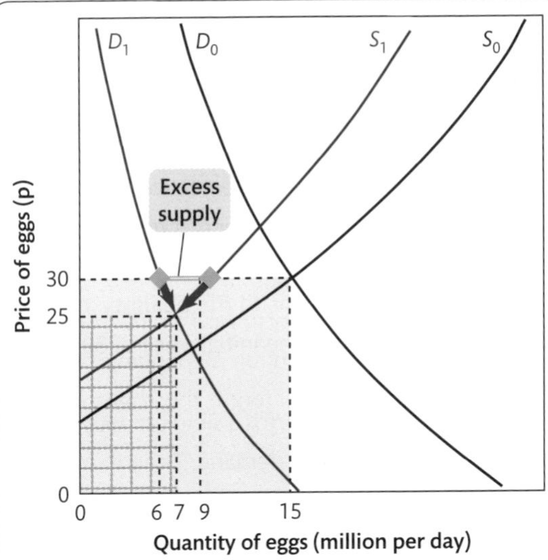

Figure 3.13 **The possible effects of a simultaneous decrease in supply and demand**

The price and quantity start at 30p and 15 million eggs a day, where D_0 intersects S_0. Then demand decreases and the quantity demanded falls to 6 million. Also supply decreases and the quantity supplied falls to 9 million. There is an excess supply, as shown by the double line, so the price falls. This raises the quantity demanded and reduces the quantity supplied, as shown by the thick arrows. The price falls to 25p, where the new equilibrium quantity is 7 million. Expenditure falls, as shown by the pink grid.

with a price of 30p and with 15 million eggs traded each day. Then suppose that a health scare with eggs decreases the demand for eggs to D_1, and, at the same time, the price of chicken feed rises, so that the supply of eggs decreases to S_1. In this example, notice that the demand curve has the bigger shift at the initial price. The following events will occur.

- **The price initially stays at 30p**. However, the quantity demanded is now 6 million eggs a day, while the quantity supplied is 9 million. So there is an excess supply, as shown by the double line.
- **This excess supply will put downward pressure on the price**. As it falls, the quantity demanded rises and the quantity supplied falls, as shown by the thick arrows on D_1 and S_1.
- **The price ends up at 25p where the quantity demanded equals the quantity supplied, here at 7 million eggs a day**. The new equilibrium expenditure per day is 25p × 7 million, which is £1.75 million. This is shown by the pink grid.

Note that if the supply curve had instead shifted more than the demand curve at the initial price, then at that price there would have been an excess demand, so the price would have risen. But again there would have been a fall in quantity.

Occasionally, the two curves shift by exactly the same amount. Suppose this happens and that, at the initial price of 30p, both the quantity demanded and the quantity supplied fall to 10 million. Then there will be no excess demand or excess supply, so the price will stay at 30p. But the quantity will fall to 10 million, the quantity where the new curves intersect at this same price.

Finally, suppose there is a simultaneous increase in both supply and demand. Depending on which curve shifts more, there might, at the initial price of 30p, be an excess supply, or an excess demand, or perhaps neither. So the price might fall, or rise, or stay at 30p. But in all cases there will be a rise in the quantity as both curves shift to the right.

The curves shift in opposite directions

Suppose the supply and demand curves for eggs are initially as shown by S_0 and D_0 in Figure 3.14. So the initial equilibrium is at the point where they intersect, with a price of 30p and with 15 million eggs traded each day. Also, suppose that some egg farms close, so that the supply decreases to S_1, and suppose that, at the same time, a new study suggests eating eggs is beneficial, so the demand increases to D_1. The following events will occur.

- **The price initially stays at 30p**. However, the quantity demanded is now 25 million eggs a day while the quantity supplied is 9 million. So there is an excess demand, as shown by the double line.

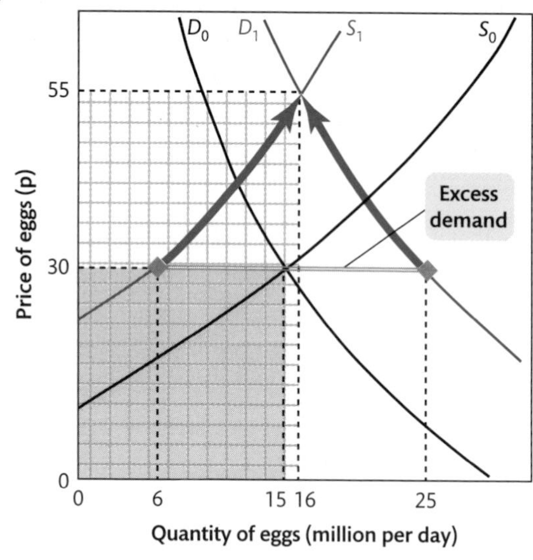

Figure 3.14 **The possible effects of a simultaneous decrease in supply and increase in demand**

The price starts at 30p, where the quantity demanded equals the quantity supplied at 15 million eggs a day. Then demand increases and the quantity demanded rises to 25 million. Also, supply decreases and the quantity supplied falls to 6 million. There is an excess demand, as shown by the double line. So the price rises. This reduces the quantity demanded and raises the quantity supplied, as shown by the thick arrows. The price rises to 55p, where the quantities demanded and supplied are equal again, here at 16 million. Spending rises to £8.8 million a day, as shown by the pink grid.

- **This excess demand will put upward pressure on the price**. As it rises, the quantity demanded falls and the quantity supplied rises, as shown by the thick arrows.
- **The price ends up at 55p where the quantity demanded equals the quantity supplied, here at 16 million eggs a day**. The new equilibrium expenditure is 55p × 16 million, which is £8.8 million. This is shown by the pink grid.

If the supply curve had shifted more, or the demand curve less, then their new intersection would be at fewer than 16 million eggs. Indeed, it might even be at fewer than the initial equilibrium quantity of 15 million. But whatever happens to the quantity, there will be an excess demand at the initial price of 30p, so the price will rise.

Conversely, suppose there is a simultaneous increase in supply and decrease in demand. Then there will be an excess supply at the initial price of 30p, so the price will fall. But the quantity might end up higher than, equal to, or lower than the original quantity, depending on the shapes of the curves and how far each one shifts.

3.7 Summary

- If both supply and demand decrease, then the equilibrium quantity falls, but the equilibrium price may rise, fall, or stay the same. Likewise, if both supply and demand increase, then the equilibrium quantity rises, but the equilibrium price may rise, fall, or stay the same.
- If supply decreases and demand increases, then the equilibrium price rises, but the equilibrium quantity may rise, fall, or stay the same. Likewise, if supply increases and demand decreases, then the equilibrium price falls, but the equilibrium quantity may rise, fall, or stay the same.

In the next chapter we look more closely at the effects of shifts in the supply and demand curves, and we consider why sometimes shifts have a large effect on quantity and little effect on price, and vice versa.

abc Glossary

Complements: two products that are often consumed together.

Demand: the quantity that would be demanded at each possible price, as shown by a demand curve.

Demand curve: a curve showing the quantity that would be demanded at each possible price.

Demand schedule: a table showing the quantity demanded at each of a selection of prices.

Equilibrium: a situation in which there are no forces for change.

Equilibrium expenditure: the amount that will be spent in a market in a period of time when the price is the equilibrium price.

Equilibrium price: the price at which a market settles, where the quantity demanded equals the quantity supplied.

Equilibrium quantity: the quantity that is demanded and supplied in a market in a period of time when the price is the equilibrium price.

Excess demand: the amount by which the quantity demanded exceeds the quantity supplied at a given price.

Excess supply: the amount by which the quantity supplied exceeds the quantity demanded at a given price.

Inferior good: a product of which households buy less when their incomes increase, because it is inferior to a more expensive substitute that they can now better afford.

Joint products: two or more products that are produced in the same process.

Normal good: a product of which households buy more when their incomes increase.

Quantity demanded: the quantity that buyers are willing to buy at a particular price in a period of time.

Quantity supplied: the quantity that sellers are willing to produce for sale at a particular price in a period of time.

Substitutes: two products that are seen as alternatives for each other.

Supply: the quantity that would be supplied at each possible price, as shown by a supply curve.

Supply curve: a curve showing the quantity that would be supplied at each possible price.

Supply schedule: a table showing the quantity supplied at each of a selection of prices.

Answers to in-text questions

3.1 No. Although supply and demand curves explain to economists what is going on, producers do not have them to hand. All producers know is that there has been a change in demand that has caused an excess supply. They will not know that the market has reached its new equilibrium until they find that the quantity they eventually wish to supply equals the quantity that consumers eventually wish to buy.

3.2 These two classic examples may help to clarify the points at issue here. The increased productivity of each type of worker meant that the products they helped to produce—food and cars—were cheaper. But although food became cheaper, people didn't eat much more, so farm output was pretty static, and farms needed fewer labourers. In contrast, when cars became cheaper, far more people wanted them, so far more car assemblers were needed, despite the fact that they were more productive than before.

? Questions for review

3.1 Suppose the market for Cheddar cheese is in equilibrium where the demand and supply curves intersect. Take each of the following events (a)–(f) separately. For each event say: (i) which curve or curves will shift, and why, and if they will shift to the left or right; (ii) if, at the initial price, there will now be an excess demand or an excess supply;

(iii) if the price of Cheddar cheese will then rise or fall; and (iv) if, at the new price, the quantity traded each week will be more or less than it was before.

(a) The price of Wensleydale cheese rises.

(b) The price of milk rises.

(c) The price of cream crackers rises.

(d) Several new Cheddar cheese factories open up.

(e) The price of Wensleydale cheese rises and, simultaneously, the price of milk rises.

(f) The price of cream crackers rises and, simultaneously, several new Cheddar cheese factories close down.

3.2 Consider the town where your college is, and suppose the market for bar staff there is in equilibrium where the demand and supply curves intersect. Take each of the following events (a)–(d) separately. For each event say: (i) which curve or curves will shift, and why, and if they will shift to the left or right; (ii) if, at the initial wage, there will now be an excess demand or an excess supply; (iii) if the wage will then rise or fall; and (iv) if, at the new wage, the quantity of hours worked by bar staff each week will be higher or lower than it was before.

(a) Several new bars open.

(b) New slot machines are introduced that can prepare and dispense cocktails.

(c) The wages paid to checkout staff in the town rise.

(d) Your college undergoes a rapid expansion in student numbers.

? Questions for discussion

3.1 Consider three products for which prices have changed in the last year or so. Do you think their changes were the result of changes in supply, or demand, or both? What factors caused the supply or demand to change?

3.2 Consider a wage rate that has risen lately. Do you think it rose because of a change in demand, or supply, or both? Why did the demand or supply change?

Common student errors

Consider this essay title: 'If drinking tea were found to be harmful, explain what would happen to the price of tea.'

A student may think: 'My intuition tells me that the price of tea would fall, because people would want to drink less. If the price falls, then demand will increase, so the demand curve will shift to the right. Also, if the price falls, then supply will decrease, so the supply curve will shift to the left.' So the student draws a figure similar to Figure 3.14. This shows the two new curves intersecting at a higher price than the initial one, even though the student believes that the price will fall! This student has made *three* errors.

The first error was to start with intuition. Economists use models *instead of* intuition, because intuition is not always reliable. The essay should start by saying: 'When people want to drink less tea, then demand will decrease, so the demand curve shifts to the left.' So this essay actually needs a diagram similar to Figure 3.6. The essay should continue: 'At the initial price there now is an excess supply. So the price will fall. It will fall until there is no excess supply, which is at the price at which the new demand curve intersects the unchanged supply curve.'

The second error was to confuse 'demand' with 'quantity demanded'. It was wrong to say that 'if the price falls, then demand will increase', and then shift the demand curve. We already have a new demand curve that has *caused* the price to fall. As the price falls, we move along this new demand curve and the quantity demanded rises, as shown by the thick arrow on part of D_1 in Figure 3.6.

The third error was to confuse 'supply' with 'quantity supplied'. It was wrong to say that 'if the price falls, then supply will decrease', and then shift the supply curve. Instead, as the price falls, the quantity supplied falls, and we move along the unchanged supply curve, as shown by the thick arrow on part of the supply curve in Figure 3.6.

4

Elasticity of Demand and Supply

Remember from Chapter 3 that a change in supply in a market, that is a shift of the whole supply curve, tends to change the price and, in turn, the quantity demanded. Remember, too, that a change in demand, that is a shift of the whole demand curve, tends to change the price and, in turn, the quantity supplied.

Why does a fall in air fares cause a surge in air travel, while a rise in rush-hour bus fares has almost no effect on rush-hour bus travel? Why has growing car use caused small rises in tyre prices and big rises in parking prices? If the wages of checkout staff and dental nurses rise by similar amounts, why do employers cut back more on checkout staff than on dental nurses? If your income trebles in the next ten years, why may you spend much less on some products and much more on others?

This chapter shows you how to answer questions like these, by understanding:

* what price elasticity of demand and price elasticity of supply mean;
* what income elasticity of demand and cross elasticity of demand mean;
* why all these elasticities matter;
* how all these elasticities are measured;
* why all these elasticities vary between markets.

4.1 Price elasticity of demand: its meaning and importance

Price changes and expenditure

Suppose that, a year ago, the market for air travel in a country was as shown in the left-hand part of Figure 4.1, with the supply and demand curves S_0 and D. The market was in equilibrium at point ***v*** where S_0 and D intersect, with the price at 21p a mile, and consumers demanding 600 million miles a week.

Suppose that, since then, demand has not changed, but new airlines have been set up, so the supply curve has shifted to the right to S_1. Then the equilibrium is now at point ***w*** where S_1 intersects D, so the price has fallen modestly, from 21p a mile to 19p. Yet despite this modest fall in the price, the quantity of miles demanded has risen greatly, from 600 million a week to 1,000 million.

Because the quantity demanded has risen greatly while the price has fallen only a little, total spending on air travel has risen. Last year, people bought 600 million miles per week at 21p a mile, and so spent £126 million a week; this is shown by the grey rectangle, whose length indicates 600 million miles and whose height indicates 21p, as shown by the pink grid. So, in this example, a fall in price has increased spending. And if supply ever shift to the left and the price rises, spending will fall.

Suppose also that, a year ago, the market for rush-hour bus travel in the same country was as shown in the right-hand part of Figure 4.1, with the supply and demand curves S_0 and D. The market was in equilibrium at point ***x*** where S_0 and D intersect, with the price at 40p a mile, and consumers demanding 525 million miles a week.

Suppose that, since then, demand has not changed, but bus drivers' wages and fuel costs have risen, so the supply curve has shifted to the left to S_1. Then the equilibrium is now at point ***y*** where S_1 intersects D. The price has risen greatly, from 40p a mile to 60p. Yet despite this

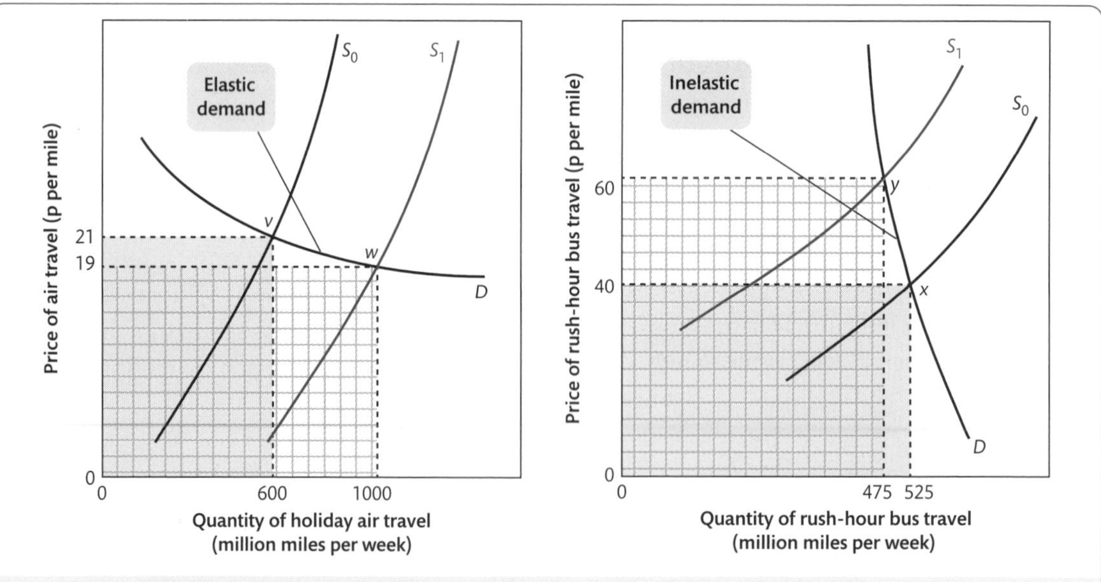

Figure 4.1 **The importance of price elasticity of demand**

In each market here, the supply curve shifts, so the price changes. In the left-hand figure, the price changes only a little, yet the quantity demanded changes a lot; so here, demand is elastic and a fall in price increases spending. In the right-hand figure, the price changes a lot, yet the quantity demanded changes only a little; so here demand is inelastic and a rise in price increases spending.

large rise in price, the quantity of miles demanded has fallen modestly, from 525 million a week to 475 million.

Because the quantity demanded has fallen only modestly while the price has risen greatly, total spending on rush-hour bus travel has risen. Last year, people spent £210 million a week, buying 525 million miles at 40p a mile, as shown by the grey rectangle. This year, people are spending £285 million a week, buying 475 million miles at 60p a mile, as shown by the pink grid. So, in this example, a rise in price has increased spending. And if supply were ever to shift to the right and the price to fall, spending would fall.

So with the demand curve in the left part of Figure 4.1, the quantity demanded responds greatly to a small change in price. In contrast, with the demand curve in the right part, the quantity demanded responds very little to a large change in price.

The responsiveness of quantity demanded to changes in price is called the **price elasticity of demand**, or *PED*. Between ***v*** and ***w*** on the left-hand demand curve, the quantity demanded responds so much to price changes that a price fall leads to more spending, and vice versa; in cases like this, we say demand is price elastic. Between ***x*** and ***y*** on the right-hand demand curve, the quantity demanded responds so little to price changes that a price rise leads to more spending, and vice versa; in cases like that, we say demand is price inelastic.

Why price elasticity of demand matters

Differences in *PED* matter. Here is just one example of why they matter to you. What sort of industry would it be better for you to work in: one that produces products for which the demand is price elastic, or one that produces products for which the demand is price inelastic? This depends on what happens in future to costs in the industry.

- **If costs fall, so that supply increases, it is better to work in an industry whose products have price elastic demand**: then, as in the left-hand part of Figure 4.1, output will rise greatly, so job opportunities and wages may improve greatly. If, instead, demand were inelastic, output would rise very little, so workers would be less likely to benefit.
- **If costs rise, so that supply decreases, it is better to work in an industry whose products have price inelastic demand**: then, as in the right-hand part of Figure 4.1, the quantity sold will fall modestly, so that few jobs will be lost. If, instead, demand were elastic, the quantity sold would fall greatly, so that many jobs would be lost.

The following sections explain how *PED* can be measured and also why it varies for different items. We will then look at some other elasticities.

4.1 Everyday economics

Demand elasticity and TV channels

The demand for advertising slots on television channels Channel 4 and Channel 5 is price elastic: so if they make slots chapter, their advertising revenue rises. But the demand for slots on ITV1 is slightly price inelastic: so if it makes slots cheaper, its revenue falls slightly, and if it makes slots dearer, its revenue rises slightly.

Advertising Regulation Review: Publication of Econometric Analysis, and Next Steps, Ofcom, May 2010

Comment If Channels 4 and 5 can readily raise their advertising revenue by cutting slot prices, while ITV1 can only slightly raise its revenue by raising slot prices, then it will be easier for Channels 4 and 5 to expand.

4.1 Summary

- Price elasticity of demand, *PED*, means the responsiveness of quantity demanded to a change in price that is caused by a shift in the supply curve. The responsiveness varies from market to market.
- If the quantity demanded responds sufficiently to a change in price that a price fall leads to higher spending and a price rise leads to lower spending, then demand is price elastic.
- If the quantity demanded responds so little to a change in price that a price fall leads to lower spending and a price rise leads to higher spending, then demand is price inelastic.

4.2 Price elasticity of demand: its measurement

In Figure 4.1, we saw that the quantity demanded was more responsive to changes in price in the left-hand part than in the right. We defined the responsiveness of quantity demanded to changes in price as the price elasticity of demand, or *PED*. This section explains how *PED* is measured.

If you look back to Figure 4.1, you will see that the demand curve in the left-hand part is much flatter than the one on the right, so you might think that we would measure the *PED* in each case by using the slopes of the demand curves. But we don't refer to the slopes for the following two reasons.

- **Demand curves are rarely straight**. If you look at the demand curves in each part of Figure 4.1, you will see that their slopes vary all along. So it wouldn't make sense to say that we should measure 'the' slope of either curve.
- **Slopes are measured in units**. Even if a demand curve were straight, we would not want to use its slope to measure *PED*. For example, suppose the demand curve in the left-hand part were straight, and that all along it a 1p fall in price led to 200 million more miles being demanded. Then its slope would be –1p divided by 200 million miles. But if we were to use this slope to measure the *PED* of air travel, and then compare that *PED* with, say, the *PED* for aviation fuel, we would compare it with a *PED* measured in pence divided by litres. This would be a meaningless comparison. We prefer to measure *PED* in a way that does not refer to units such as pence, miles, or litres.

A formula for price elasticity of demand

To avoid units, we measure *PED* with *percentage* changes in price and quantity, using this formula:

$$PED = \frac{\text{\% change in quantity demanded}}{\text{\% change in price}}$$

Here are two examples to illustrate this formula.

- **Suppose a 10% rise in the price of lamb decreases the quantity demanded by 19%**. Then the quantity demanded changes by –19% and the price changes by +10%, so the *PED* of lamb is –19/10, or –1.9.
- **Suppose a 10% fall in the price of sugar increases the quantity demanded by 8%**. Then the quantity demanded changes by +8% and the price changes by –10%, so the *PED* of sugar is 8/–10, or –0.8.

Most *PED*s are negative. This is because a rise or positive change in price leads to a fall or negative change in quantity, and vice versa. So the two percentages in the formula have different signs.

Now that we know how to measure *PED*s, there are three terms we need to define sharply.

- **Unit price elasticity of demand**. This applies if the percentage changes in quantity demanded and price happen to be of equal size, such as a 10% fall in price and a 10% rise in quantity. In this case, the *PED* is exactly –1.0.
- **Price elastic demand**. This applies if the percentage change in quantity demanded is more sizeable than the percentage change in price, as with lamb. This means that the *PED* is a number that is lower than –1.0; for lamb, it is –1.9.
- **Price inelastic demand**. This applies if the percentage change in quantity demanded is less sizeable than the percentage change in price, as with sugar. This means that the *PED* is a number that is higher than –1.0; for sugar, it is –0.8.

A problem with using percentage changes

It is easy to work out a *PED* from the percentage changes. However, there is a problem with working out these changes. To see the problem, suppose the

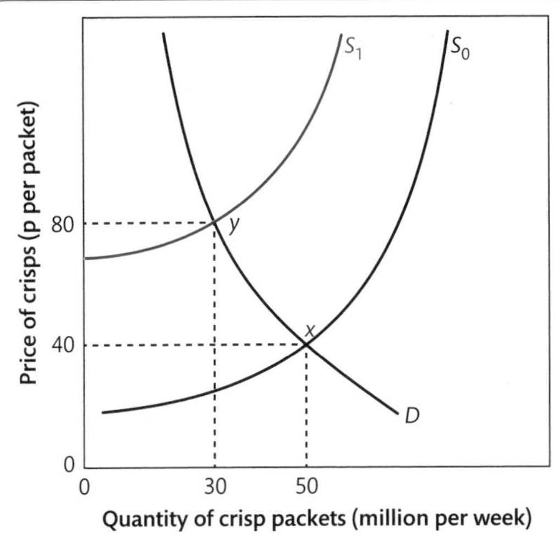

Figure 4.2 **Calculating a price elasticity of demand**

To calculate the *PED* between points **x** and **y**, economists first work out that the change in quantity of –20 million is –50% of the average quantity of 40 million. They then work out that the change in price of 40p is 66⅔% of the average price of 60p. So the *PED* is –50/66⅔, which is –0.75.

demand curve for packets of crisps is as shown by *D* in Figure 4.2.

The market here starts at point **x** where *D* intersects the original supply curve, S_0. The price is 40p a packet, and 50 million packets are traded each week. Now we will consider two events.

- **Event A: supply decreases, and the supply curve shifts to the left from S_0 to S_1.** Then the market equilibrium moves from point **x** to point **y**, so the price rises by 40p from 40p to 80p, and the quantity demanded responds with a decrease of 20 million packets from 50 million to 30 million.
- **Event B: at a much later time, the supply curve shifts to the right from S_1 to S_0.** Then the market equilibrium moves from point **y** to point **x**, so the price falls by 40p from 80p to 40p, and the quantity demanded responds with an increase of 20 million packets from 30 million to 50 million.

Each event moves the market equilibrium between points **x** and **y**. So in each event the price changes by 40p, and the quantity demanded is equally responsive and changes by 20 million. So we naturally want a measure of *PED* that will give the same *PED* for each event. However, we will now see that if we calculated the percentages in the normal mathematical way, we would get a different *PED* for each event, which is unsatisfactory. We will then see how economists use a different way of calculating percentages that gives the same *PED* for each event.

Calculating percentages like mathematicians

The figures for *PED* that would be obtained if we calculated percentages in the mathematicians' way are shown in Table 4.1. To calculate a percentage change, mathematicians work out the actual change as a percentage of the *initial* value. The top half of the table shows that in event A, where the initial quantity was 50 million and the change was –20 million, they would give the percentage change as –20 as a percentage of 50, which is –40%. On the same approach, the table shows that they would give the percentage change in price as 100%. So they would give the *PED* as –40/100, or –0.40.

Table 4.1 **Estimates of *PED* that use percentage changes calculated in the mathematicians' way**

Event A: the supply curve shifts from S_0 to S_1		
	Quantity	**Price**
Initial value	50 million	40p
Final value	30 million	80p
Change	-20 million	40p
% change	100(–20/50) = –40	100(40/40) = 100
So *PED* is measured as -40/100 = -0.40.		
Event B: the supply curve shifts from S_1 to S_0		
	Quantity	**Price**
Initial value	30 million	80p
Final value	50 million	40p
Change	20 million	-40p
% change	100(20/30) = 66⅔	100(–40/80) = –50
So *PED* is measured as 66⅔/-50 = -1.33.		

The lower part of the table shows that, in event B, mathematicians would work out the change in quantity of 20 million as a percentage of the initial value in event B, which is 30 million, to get 66⅔%. On the same approach, they would give the percentage change in price as -50%. So they would give the *PED* as (66⅔)/–50, or 1.33.

So the mathematicians' approach to percentages would give two very different figures for the *PED* between points ***x*** and ***y*** in Figure 4.2, simply depending on which way the equilibrium moved. Therefore it is unsatisfactory to base measures of *PED* on percentages that are calculated in this way.

Calculating percentages like economists

The figures for *PED* that are obtained when we calculate percentages in the economists' way are shown in Table 4.2. The key point to note is that to work out a percentage change, economists work out the actual change as a percentage of the *average* value. For example, the top half of the table shows that, in event A, where the initial quantity was 50 million and the final quantity was 30 million, the average quantity was 40 million. The change in quantity was –20 million, so the percentage change is –20 as a percentage of 40, which is –50%. On the same approach, the table shows that the percentage change in price is 66⅔%, so the *PED* is –50/(66⅔) or –0.75.

The lower part of the table shows that, in event B, the quantity changes from 30 million to 50 million, so the average is again 40 million. The change is 20 million, so the percentage change is 50%. Also, the table shows that the percentage change in price is –66⅔%, so the *PED* is 50/(–66⅔), which is again –0.75. So this way of calculating percentages gets the same *PED*, no matter which way the equilibrium moves between points ***x*** and ***y***, and we will use it in all of our elasticity calculations.

Table 4.2 **Estimates of *PED* that use percentage changes calculated in the economists' way**

Event A: the supply curve shifts from S_0 to S_1		
	Quantity	**Price**
Initial value	50 million	40p
Final value	30 million	80p
Average value	40 million	60p
Change	-20 million	40p
% change	100(-20/40) = -50	100(40/60) = 66⅔
So *PED* is measured as -50/66⅔ = -0.75		
Event B: the supply curve shifts from S_1 to S_0		
	Quantity	**Price**
Initial value	30 million	80p
Final value	50 million	40p
Average value	40 million	60p
Change	20 million	-40p
% change	100(20/40) = 50	100(-40/60) = -66⅔
So *PED* is measured as 50/-66⅔ = -0.75		

Arc elasticity of demand

We now know that, in Figure 4.2, the *PED* on the part of the demand curve between points ***x*** and ***y*** is –0.75. A part of a curve is called an arc. So, as this elasticity of –0.75 applies to an arc of the curve, we call it an **arc elasticity of demand**.

Question 4.1 Use the method of calculating *PED* that is given in Table 4.2 to find the arc elasticity of demand along the arcs ***vw*** and ***xy*** shown in Figure 4.1.

PED usually varies all along a demand curve

On most demand curves, the *PED* actually varies from one arc to another, even if the curve happens to be a straight line. To see this, look at Figure 4.3. Suppose that supply here shifts from S_0 to S_1, taking the equilibrium from point ***w*** to point ***x***. And suppose that supply later shifts again to S_2, taking the equilibrium to point ***y***. We can easily show that arcs ***wx*** and ***xy*** have different *PED*s.

- **On arc *wx***. The change in quantity is 10 and the average quantity is 15, so the percentage change is

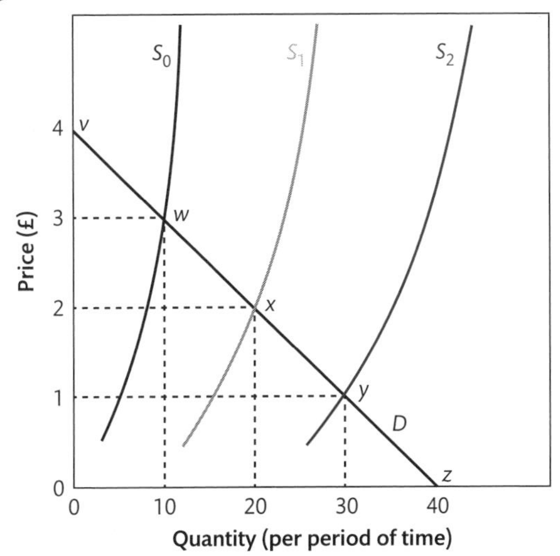

Figure 4.3 **Varying price elasticity of demand along a curve**

PED usually varies along a demand curve, even if it is straight. Here, *PED* is –1.67 along ***wx*** and –0.60 along ***xy***. In fact, *PED* here is less than –1.00 all along ***vx***, and more than –1.00 all along ***xz***. So demand is elastic along ***vx*** and inelastic along ***xz***. On any straight demand curve like this, the *PED* is –1.00 at the mid-point, here ***x***.

100(10/15), or 66⅔%. The change in price is –1 and the average price is 2.5, so the percentage change is 100(–1/2.5), or –40%. So the *PED* is (66⅔)/– 40, or –1.67.

- **On arc *xy*.** The change in quantity is 10 and the average quantity is 25, so the percentage change is 100(10/25), or 40%. The change in price is –1 and the average price is 1.5, so the percentage change is 100(–1/1.5), or –66⅔%. So the *PED* is 40/(–66⅔), or –0.60.

So the *PED* is –1.67 along ***wx*** and –0.60 along ***xy***, and you could easily calculate that the *PED* between prices of £4 and £3, along ***vw***, is –7.0, while the *PED* between prices of £1 and £0, along ***yz***, is –0.14. In fact, along any straight demand curve, the *PED* is below –1.0 on any arc between the price axis and the midpoint, ***x***, so demand there is price elastic; the *PED* is above –1.0 on any arc between the midpoint, ***x***, and the quantity axis, so demand there is price inelastic.

You can check that demand is elastic at prices above £2 by working out that spending will rise if the price falls from £4 to £3, or from £3 to £2. You can check that demand is inelastic at prices below £2 by working out that spending will fall if the price falls from £2 to £1 or from £1 to £0.

Point elasticity of demand

Instead of dividing a demand curve up into arcs, we could split it into a series of points. We could then work out the *PED* at any one of these points to get a **point elasticity of demand** instead of an arc elasticity. However, we will not work out point elasticities in this book, because we can work them out only if we know the equation of the demand curve and use calculus. But we will note that, on a straight-line demand curve like the one in Figure 4.3, where the *PED* is below –1.0 above the midpoint and above –1.0 below the midpoint, the *PED* must equal –1.0 at the midpoint.

Constant price elasticity of demand

Figure 4.3 illustrated a straight-line demand curve, and we found that even though it was straight, the *PED* varied from one arc to another. The *PED* usually does vary all along a demand curve, but sometimes it is the same all the way along.

Actually, we could construct a demand curve along which the *PED* was constant at any number we chose, say –0.8 or –1.9. But there are only three cases of demand curves with constant elasticities that we need to know about.

- ***PED* is minus infinity all along any horizontal demand curve**. For example, look at the left-hand part of Figure 4.4; this concerns the market for the tiny amount of oil produced in Germany on a day when the price of oil on the world oil market is €80 a barrel. The demand curve for German oil is horizontal because people will be willing to buy all the German oil that is produced if its price equals the

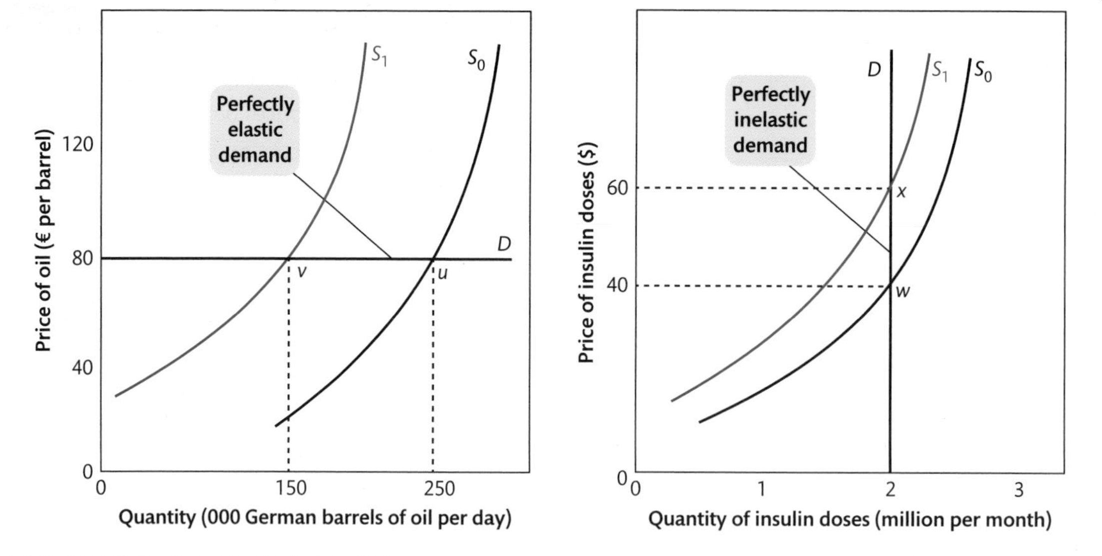

Figure 4.4 **Demand curves with extreme elasticities**

On the left, shifts in supply have no effect on price at all, yet quantity demanded still changes; here, demand is always perfectly elastic. On the right, shifts in supply do have an effect on price, but the quantity demanded remains the same; here, demand is always perfectly inelastic.

world price of €80, but will buy none if its price is higher. So if, for instance, some German wells were to dry up and Germany's supply to shift to the left from S_0 to S_1, the price would still not go above €80. However, the quantity demanded would fall from the initial 250,000 barrels a day to 150,000, to match the decrease in supply. So the quantity demanded would fall without any change in price. Quantity demanded cannot be more responsive than that, so here we have **perfectly elastic demand**. The *PED* along any arc, such as ***uv***, is minus infinity because the percentage change in quantity along this arc must be divided by a 0% change in price.

- ***PED* is zero all along any vertical demand curve**. For example, look at the right-hand part of Figure 4.4, which concerns the insulin market in the United States. Diabetics need insulin to survive, and the demand curve here is vertical to show that the quantity of doses demanded would not respond to changes in price. Quantity demanded cannot be less responsive than that, so here we have **perfectly inelastic demand**. The *PED* along any arc, such as ***wx***, is zero, because there is a 0% change in quantity demanded to be divided by the percentage change in price.
- ***PED* is –1.0 all along any demand curve where spending would be the same at each price**. Look at the demand curve in Figure 4.5. At first sight, this may appear like any typical demand curve, but it has been very carefully drawn so that the expenditure would be the same at each price. For example, if S_0 applied, then the price would be £6 and the quantity 20 per week, so spending would be £120 a week, as shown by the grey rectangle. If S_1 were to apply, then the price would be £4 and the quantity 30 per week, so spending would still be £120 a week, as shown by the pink grid. You can see, too, that if the price were £8, the quantity would be 15, and if the price were £2 the quantity would be 60; in each case, spending would still be £120. As spending here never changes when the price changes, demand is neither elastic nor inelastic, but unit elastic.

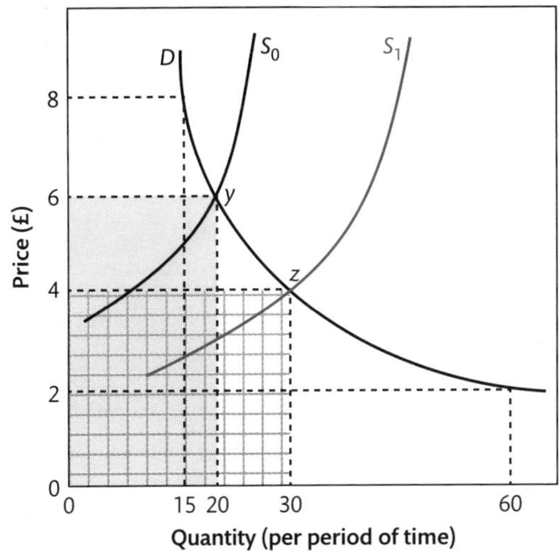

Figure 4.5 **A demand curve where price elasticity of demand always equals minus one**

Along this curve, spending per period will be £120, whether the price is £8, £6, £4, or £2. With constant spending, demand is neither elastic nor inelastic, but unit elastic.

Question 4.2 Use the method of calculating *PED* that is given in Table 4.2 to check that the arc elasticity of demand along the arc **yz** in Figure 4.5 is -1.0.

4.2 Everyday economics

Two estimates of the *PED* for tobacco

It was found that the price elasticity of demand for tobacco was –0.77 for a price increase and –0.37 for a price decrease.

Treasury select committee quoting the Tobacco Manufacturers' Association, November 1999

Comment These differing estimates may be largely due to the *PED* being different in different price ranges. For example, suppose the price of the product in Figure 4.3 started at £2. Then if the price were to increase to £3, the estimated *PED* would be –1.67; but if the price were instead to decrease to £1, the estimated *PED* would be –0.60.

4.2 Summary

- A *PED* equals the percentage change in quantity demanded divided by the percentage change in price.
- *PED*s are negative. If demand is price elastic, or very responsive, then the *PED* is a number lower than –1.0. If demand is price inelastic, or not very responsive, then the *PED* is between –1.0 and 0.
- To find a percentage change in quantity demanded, we work out the change in quantity as a percentage of the average of the initial and final quantities. To find a percentage change in price, we work out the change in price as a percentage of the average of the initial and final prices.
- An arc elasticity applies to a particular arc along a demand curve. A point elasticity applies to a particular point on a demand curve.
- The *PED* usually varies along a demand curve, even if it happens to be a straight line.
- Some demand curves have a constant *PED*: a horizontal demand has a constant *PED* of minus infinity, a vertical demand curve has a constant *PED* of 0, and a demand curve where expenditure would be the same at each price has a constant *PED* of - 1.0.

4.3 Estimating price elasticities of demand, and why they vary

Estimating *PEDs*

It is hard to estimate actual *PEDs* in the real world. To see why, suppose your college has a coffee machine and you want to discover the *PED* for coffee at that machine. So one day you sit by the machine all day, note that the price is 60p, and count 230 people buying coffee. A few months later, the price rises to 90p, so you sit by the machine for another day and count 170 people buying coffee. If you were sure that it was *only* the 30p rise in price that had reduced the number of people by 60, then you could work out that the demand was price inelastic with a *PED* of −0.75.

Unfortunately, you cannot be sure that the change in price was the only factor at work. Maybe the demand is price elastic, and it was only because there were more students about on the second day that the quantity demanded fell so modestly. Or maybe the demand is almost perfectly inelastic, and the quantity demanded fell as much as it did only because the second day was in a heatwave.

To estimate actual *PEDs*, economists always watch out for problems like this, but they may make mistakes. So their figures really are just *estimates*, not necessarily the truth. With this warning, Table 4.3 presents estimates of the *PED* for a selection of final products, and is based on several sources. The *PEDs* here range from −0.12 for potatoes to −2.01 for pork. When the *PED* is well above −1.0, as it is with potatoes, demand is very price inelastic; when it is well below −1.0, as it is with pork, demand is very price elastic.

Variations in the *PED* for final products

We will now explain why price elasticities of demand vary between different final products. There are three main factors that affect the *PED* of any given product, and we will discuss them in turn, using the products in Table 4.3 as the main examples. These factors are as follows:

- **the price and availability of substitutes**;
- **the percentage of consumer income that is spent on the product**;
- **the time that consumers have to respond to changes in price**.

The price and availability of substitutes

Suppose that non-vegetarians like to eat roast lamb with potatoes, and suppose the prices of both of these products rise. Then consumers can easily switch out of lamb into substitutes such as beef or pork, which have similar prices. So the quantity of lamb demanded is very responsive to changes in price, and its *PED* is well below −1.0 at −1.86. The demand for lamb would be

Table 4.3 **Some estimated price elasticities of demand for the UK**

Product	*PED*	Period	Source
Inelastic demand			
Potatoes	−0.12	1990s	***a***
Motor fuel	−0.23	1990s	***b***
Eggs	−0.28	1990s	***a***
Prescriptions	−0.35	1990s	***c***
Bread	−0.40	1990s	***a***
Beer	−0.76	2000s	***d***
Sugar	−0.79	1990s	***a***
Elastic demand			
Long-haul leisure flights	−1.50	1980s	***e***
Beef	−1.45	1980s	***f***
Lamb	−1.86	1980s	***f***
Pork	−2.01	1980s	***f***

Sources: ***a*** Department for Environment, Food & Rural Affairs; ***b*** Department of Trade and Industry; ***c*** T Hitiris, University of York; ***d*** Institute for Fiscal Studies; ***e*** R Doganis, *Flying Off Course*, 1985; ***f*** National Food Survey Committee.

less elastic if the substitutes had much higher prices, so that people were less willing to switch into them.

It is harder to find a substitute for potatoes, at any price. Roast meat with, say, rice, would be a very different sort of meal. So the quantity of potatoes demanded is much less sensitive to changes in price, and its *PED* is well above –1.0 at –0.12.

Other products in Table 4.3 with inelastic demand include motor fuel, eggs, and prescriptions. In each case, it is hard to switch into a substitute if the price rises. There is no close substitute for fuel because most car users are reluctant to switch to public transport, or cycle, or walk. Eggs are used in many dishes, and switching out of eggs would make some people face very different menus. Switching out of prescriptions might be fatal for some people and painful for others.

The percentage of consumer income spent on the product

If the price and availability of substitutes were the only factor affecting *PED*s, we would expect the demand for long-haul leisure flights to be inelastic. If you want a holiday in Australia, there is no real alternative to flying. Yet Table 4.3 shows that the demand here is elastic. This is because a second factor that affects *PED* is the percentage of income that people spend on the product. If the price of flights to Australia goes up, then many people simply cannot afford to go at all, and this causes a big drop in the quantity demanded.

The time that buyers have to respond to price changes

In some markets, a third factor that affects the *PED* is how much time consumers need to respond fully to a price change. For example, consider rush-hour bus travel. If the supply decreases and fares rise, commuters will want to use buses in the rush hour less. But how much less they will use them depends on how long they have to respond. For a year or two, they may be able to respond very little, perhaps working occasionally at home, or negotiating lifts with car owners, or walking or cycling if their journeys are short. But after that time, they can respond more, by moving home or job, or by buying a car and learning to drive.

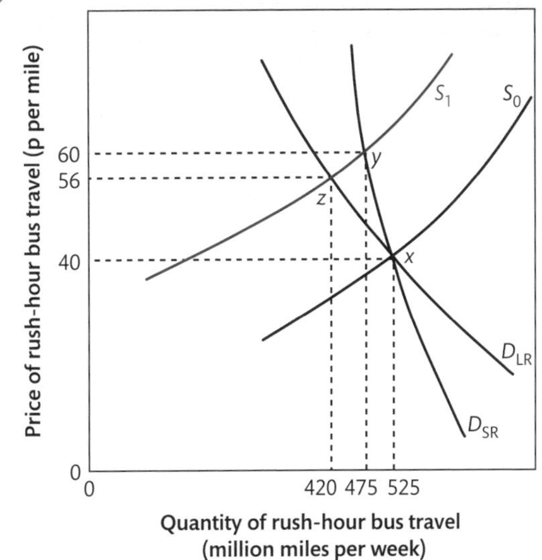

Figure 4.6 **Short-run and long-run demand curves**

If the supply of bus travel falls, the equilibrium in the short run moves up D_{SR}; the *PED* along ***xy*** is –0.25. In the long run, the more elastic D_{LR} applies instead. The *PED* along ***xz*** is –0.67.

This means that commuters actually have two demand curves, as shown in Figure 4.6. Suppose the market starts at point ***x*** where both of these intersect the supply curve, S_0, with a price of 40p a mile and 525 million miles travelled each week. Then supply decreases to S_1. To see exactly what happens, we need to consider two time frames.

- **The short run**. For a year or two, commuters cannot vary their use very much, and can move only along the demand curve labelled D_{SR}. This is a short-run demand curve, which shows how much buyers will demand at each price when they cannot react fully to price changes. Over this time, the market will be at point ***y*** where D_{SR} intersects S_1, with the price at 60p and the quantity demanded at 475 million miles a week. The *PED* along ***xy*** on D_{SR}, is –0.25.
- **The long run**. After a year or two, commuters can respond fully to price changes, and so move along

the demand curve labelled D_{LR}. This is a long-run demand curve: it shows how much buyers will demand at each price when they can respond fully to price changes. The market ends up at **z** where D_{LR} intersects S_1, with the price at 56p and the quantity demanded at 420 million miles a week. Of course, the market started at **x**, and the *PED* along arc **xz** on D_{LR} is –0.67.

So this market has a short-run demand curve and a long-run demand curve, and demand is more elastic, or at any rate less inelastic, in the long run than in the short run. This situation applies to relatively few products. Another example is gas: here, a price rise may lead to only a small fall in quantity demanded in the short run, but a much bigger fall in the long run when people have time to switch from gas heating to oil heating.

However, for most products, like eggs and lamb, there is just one demand curve, because people can react fully to a price change on the day that it occurs. Even if there are two curves, economists are often interested in either the short run or the long run, so they may show only one demand curve, and add no subscript to say which it is. We did just that for rush-hour bus travel in Figure 4.1.

Variations in *PED* between labour markets

The *PED* for different types of labour also varies. The reasons are similar to those with products, as follows.

- **The price and availability of substitutes**. For example, if the wages of checkout staff rise, more shops will introduce self-service checkouts and use fewer staff; so the demand for these staff may be elastic. But if the wages of dental nurses rise, there is no real substitute input, so the number employed may hardly fall; the demand for these nurses is therefore inelastic.
- **The percentage of employers' costs accounted for by the labour concerned**. For example, suppose the Royal Mail faces a rise in the wages of postmen and women. These wages account for a large part of its costs, so it will have to raise the price of stamps. In turn, fewer people will post letters, so the Royal Mail will lay off some postmen and post-women, and therefore the demand for them may be elastic. In contrast, suppose the Royal Mail faces a rise in the wages of the painters who keep the letter boxes red. These wages account for only a tiny part of its costs, so it may well employ almost as many painters as before, and therefore the demand for them may be inelastic.
- **The *PED* of the products that the labour helps to produce**. For example, suppose the wages of petrol tanker drivers and shepherds rise. Their employers will raise the prices of motor fuel and lamb. The demand for fuel is inelastic, so sales will not fall much; in turn, few tanker drivers will be laid off, so the demand for them is inelastic. But the demand for lamb is elastic, so sales will fall greatly; in turn, many shepherds may be laid off, so the demand for them is elastic.
- **The time employers have to respond to wage changes**. For example, suppose a firm with an assembly line faces a wage rise for the workers on that line. In the short run, it may have little option other than to employ as many as before, so demand may be inelastic. But in the long run it may be able to replace many staff with robots, and then the demand for workers may prove very elastic.

4.3 Summary

- The *PED* for a final product depends on how far substitutes are available at a reasonable price and on the proportion of consumers' incomes for which it accounts. Demand is most elastic where substitutes are available at a reasonable price, and where the percentage of income spent on the product is low.
- For products where buyers need time to respond fully to a price change, demand is more elastic in the long run than in the short run.

- The *PED* for a type of labour depends on the price and availability of substitutes for that labour, the percentage of employers' costs accounted for by that labour, and the *PED* of the products that the labour helps to make. In some cases, it also depends on how long employers need to respond fully to wage changes.

4.4 Income elasticity of demand and cross elasticity of demand

We have seen that price elasticity of demand concerns the responsiveness of the quantity of a product demanded to changes in its price. We will now explore two other reasons why the quantity of a product demanded may change.

Income elasticity of demand

One of these reasons why the quantity demanded may change is that consumers' incomes may change. We saw in Chapter 3 that with most products, which we call normal goods, a rise in incomes increases the quantity bought. But with products that we call inferior goods, rises in income reduce the quantity bought; this happens when a rise in incomes means that consumers can now afford to switch out of these inferior goods into better, but pricier, substitutes.

The responsiveness of the quantity of a product demanded to changes in consumer incomes is called its **income elasticity of demand**, *IED*. As with other elasticities, we use percentages to calculate *IED*s. The formula is as follows:

$$IED = \frac{\%\text{ change in quantity demanded}}{\%\text{ change in income}}$$

For example, if a 10% rise in incomes leads to a 2.5% rise in the quantity of beef demanded, then the *IED* for beef is 2.5/10, or 0.25. The *IED* is actually positive for all normal goods, because a rise or positive change in income leads to a rise or positive change in quantity demanded, and vice versa, so both the percentages in the formula have the same sign.

But suppose a 10% rise in incomes also leads to a 3.7% fall in the quantity of margarine demanded; then the *IED* for margarine is –3.7/10, or –0.37. The *IED* is actually negative for all inferior goods, because a rise or positive change in income leads to a fall or negative change in quantity, so we always have one positive percentage in the formula and one negative percentage.

Some *IED* estimates

Table 4.4 shows estimates of the *IED* for a number of products. The first four have negative *IED*s, so they are inferior goods. One of them, margarine, does indeed have an *IED* of –0.37.

All the other products in Table 4.4 have positive *IED*s, so they are all normal goods. But we divide these products into two groups.

- **Products with income inelastic demand**. This applies if a change in income of any percentage, say 10%, changes the quantity of the product demanded by less than 10%, so that its *IED* is less than 1.0. This applies to many foods, and the table gives five examples. The reason is that when people's incomes rise, they do not want to eat much more in total, so the quantity they demand of many foods responds very little.
- **Products with income elastic demand**. This applies if a change in income of any percentage, say 10%, changes the quantity of the product demanded by more than 10%, so that its *IED* is greater than 1.0. The table shows that these products include home space and garden space. When people's incomes rise, they often want more space, so the quantity they demand is very responsive to changes in income.

Table 4.4 **Some estimated income elasticities of demand for the UK**

Product	*IED*	Period	Source
Inferior goods			
Bus travel	−0.75	1990s	*g*
Margarine	−0.37	1990s	*a*
Apples	−0.07	1990s	*a*
Eggs	−0.01	1990s	*a*
Normal goods - income inelastic			
Milk	0.05	1990s	*a*
Pork	0.13	1980s	*a*
Lamb	0.15	1980s	*a*
Oranges	0.23	1990s	*a*
Beef	0.25	1980s	*a*
Normal goods - income elastic			
Motor fuel	1.14	1990s	*h*
Home space	2.00	1980s	*i*
Garden space	2.40	1980s	*i*

Sources: ***a*** Department for Environment, Food & Rural Affairs; ***g*** Transport Research Laboratory; ***h*** S Glaister & D Graham, *Utilities Journal*, 2001; ***i*** P Cheshire & S Sheppard, London School of Economics.

Table 4.4 also hints at the importance of *IED*s. If incomes continue to rise over your lifetime, then people will demand much bigger homes, little more meat, and fewer apples. Employment and profitability in the building, livestock, and orchard sectors of industry may move in similar ways. Also, it may be smart to try and acquire some home and garden space before the increases in demand push prices up even higher than they are today.

4.3 **Everyday economics**

*IED*s and different income ranges

J. Dargay and P. Vythoulkas (*Journal of Transport Economics and Policy*, 1999) have estimated the *IED* for car ownership as 0.80 for low-income households and 0.65 for high-income households. Probably low-income households have a high *IED* because they are keen to buy their first or second car, while high-income households are closer to having all the cars they want, so they have a lower *IED*.

Cross elasticity of demand

Another reason why the quantity demanded of an item may change, even when its price is constant, is if the prices of related products change. We saw in Chapter 3 that with substitutes, like beef and lamb, a rise in the price of one increases the quantity demanded of the other; with complements, which are products that are consumed together like fish and chips, a rise in the price of one decreases the quantity demanded of the other.

We call the responsiveness of the quantity demanded of one product to changes in the price of another product the **cross elasticity of demand**, *CED*, of the first product with respect to the second. As with other elasticities, we use percentages to calculate *CED*s. The formula is:

$$CED = \frac{\text{\% change in quantity demanded of one product}}{\text{\% change in the price of another product}}$$

So if, for example, a 10% rise in the price of beef leads to a 2.8% rise in the quantity demanded of lamb, then the *CED* of lamb with respect to beef is 2.8/10, or 0.28. All *CED*s between substitutes are positive, because a rise or positive change in the price of one leads to a rise or positive change in the quantity demanded of the other, so the percentages have the same sign.

On the other hand, if a 10% rise in the price of frozen fish leads to a 3.1% fall in the quantity of processed vegetables demanded, then the *CED* of processed vegetables with respect to frozen fish is −0.31. All *CED*s between complements are negative, because a rise or positive change in the price of one leads to a fall or negative change in the quantity demanded of the other, so one percentage is positive and the other is negative.

Some *CED* estimates

Table 4.5 shows estimates of the *CED*s for four pairs of products. The first two pairs are substitutes, so the *CED*s are all positive. For example, the *CED* of

Table 4.5 **Some estimated cross elasticities of demand for the UK**

QD of	on *P* of	*CED*	Period	Source
Inferior goods				
Beef	Lamb	0.11	2000s	*f*
Lamb	Beef	0.28	2000s	*f*
Spirits	Wine	0.77	1980s	*d*
Wine	Spirits	0.66	1980s	*d*
Complements				
Processed vegetables	Frozen fish	−0.31	1990s	*a*
Frozen fish	Processed vegetables	−0.07	1990s	*a*
Unrelated products				
Beverages	Fresh fish	0.00	1990s	*a*
Fresh fish	Beverages	0.00	1990s	*a*

Sources: ***a*** Department for Environment, Food & Rural Affairs; ***d*** Institute for Fiscal Studies; ***f*** National Food Survey Committee.

lamb with respect to beef is indeed 0.28, while the *CED* of beef with respect to lamb is smaller, at 0.11. These different figures mean that the switch into lamb when the price of beef rises is larger than the switch into beef when the price of lamb rises. The table then shows much larger *CED*s between wine and spirits.

The middle part of Table 4.5 concerns frozen fish and vegetables. Because these are complements, the *CED*s between them are negative. The *CED* of processed vegetables with respect to frozen fish is indeed −0.31. The *CED* for frozen fish with respect to processed vegetables is much smaller at −0.07.

Of course, many products are unrelated, so that changes in the price of one have no impact on the quantity demanded of the other. This is the case with fresh fish and beverages, and Table 4.5 ends by showing that the *CED*s between them are zero.

Table 4.5 hints at the importance of *CED*s. If you work for a firm and the price of a substitute rises, you will hope the *CED* is well over 0.0, so that many of the substitute's purchasers now switch to your product. But if the price of the substitute falls, you will hope the *CED* is close to 0.0, so that few of your customers switch to the substitute.

Also, if the price of a complement rises, you will hope that the *CED* is only a little below 0.0, so that consumers do not buy much less of your product. But if the price of a complement falls, you will hope that the *CED* is well below 0.0, so that consumers buy much more of your product.

4.4 Everyday economics

*CED*s related to car use

The *CED* for car use with respect to the price of park-and-ride schemes has been estimated as –0.10, and the *CED* of car use with respect to the fares for inter-urban bus travel as –0.01.

'The CiFT Report 2002', *The National Archives*, 22 February 2002

Comment The *CED* of -0.10 suggests that some motorists who visit town centres, where traffic is slow and parking slots are scarce, can be tempted to switch to park-and-ride schemes if their prices are cut. The *CED* of -0.01 suggests that virtually no motorists can be tempted to use buses for inter-urban travel if their fares are cut, presumably because they need to get to and from the bus stops, and the buses may be much slower than a car.

4.4 Summary

- Income elasticity of demand (*IED*) measures the responsiveness of the quantity of a product demanded to changes in consumers' incomes.
- *IED* is negative for inferior goods, and positive for normal goods. It is above 1.0 for products with income elastic demand, and between 0.0 and 1.0 for products with income inelastic demand.
- Cross elasticity of demand (*CED*) measures the responsiveness of the quantity of one product demanded to changes in the price of another product.
- *CED* is positive between substitutes and negative between complements.

4.5 Price elasticity of supply: its meaning and importance

Different effects of increases in demand

In recent years, the use of cars in the UK has grown enormously. This has led to increases in the demand for the goods and services that motorists require, including tyres and parking slots. But the effects of the increases in demand on price and quantity are very different in the markets for these two items.

The left-hand part of Figure 4.7 illustrates the market for car tyres. The supply curve is *S*, and the 1990 demand curve is D_0. The 1990 equilibrium was where these two curves intersect, at point **w**, with the price of a tyre at £76 and 40 million tyres traded in a year.

The demand curve D_1 shows what the demand for tyres may be in 2030. This curve is well to the right of D_0 because of the large rise in car use. The new equilibrium in 2030 is shown at point **x**, where D_1 intersects *S*. This intersection suggests that, in 2030, the price of tyres may be £84. This is a modest rise compared with the £76 in 1990. Yet despite this modest rise in the price, the quantity of tyres supplied is shown rising greatly, from 40 million in 1990 to 56 million in 2030.

The right-hand part of Figure 4.7 illustrates the market for parking slots in the centre of a large city. The supply curve is *S*, and the 1990 demand curve is D_0. The 1990 equilibrium was at point **y** where these curves intersect, with the price of a slot at £0.90 an hour and 19 million hours used per year.

The demand curve D_1 shows what the demand for parking slots may be in 2030. This curve is well to the right of D_0 because of the large rise in car use. The new equilibrium in 2030 is shown at point **z** where D_1 intersects *S*. This intersection suggests that, in 2030, the price of a slot may be £1.50 an hour. Yet despite this large rise in the price, the quantity of slots supplied is shown as rising only modestly, from 19 million hours in 1990 to 21 million in 2030.

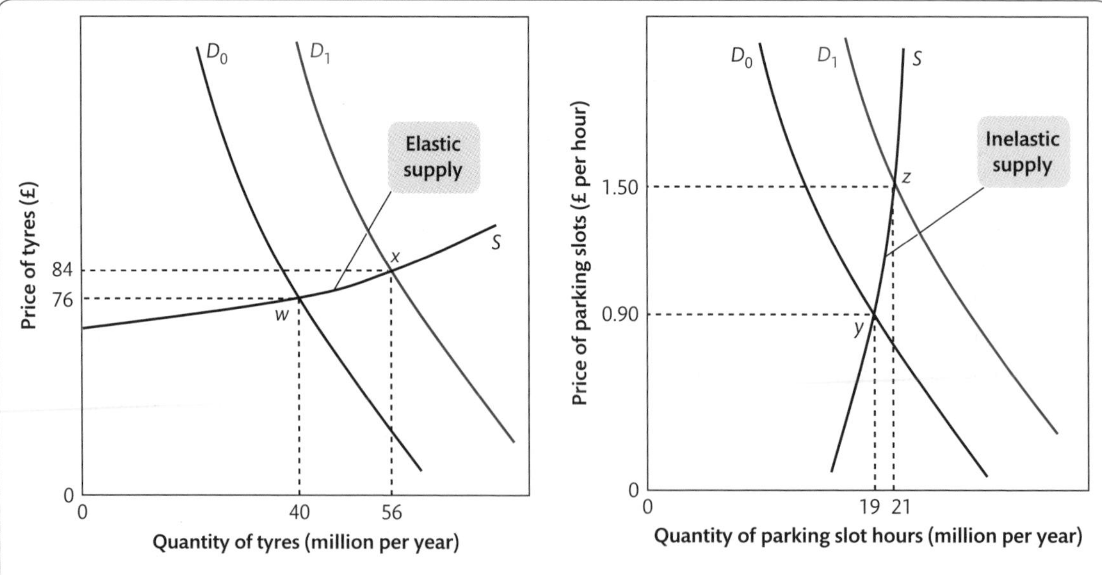

Figure 4.7 **The importance of price elasticity of supply**

In each market here, the demand curve shifts, so the price changes. In the left-hand figure, the price changes only a little, yet the quantity supplied responds by changing a lot; so here supply is elastic. In the right-hand figure, the price changes a lot, yet the quantity supplied responds by changing only a little; so here supply is inelastic.

Elastic and inelastic supply

So with the supply curve on the left side of Figure 4.7, the quantity supplied responds greatly to a small change in price, and with the supply curve on the right, the quantity supplied responds very little to a large change in price. The responsiveness of quantity supplied to changes in price is called **price elasticity of supply**, or *PES*. Supply is very responsive, and so elastic, along arc ***wx*** on the left, but supply is very unresponsive, and so inelastic, along arc ***yz*** on the right.

Differences in *PES* are important to consumers. For example, some of the items that you want are in inelastic supply: home space is an example. If the demand for these items increases in future, then you may soon pay much higher prices than you pay now. On the other hand, you also demand some items that are in elastic supply: phone calls are an example. If the demand for these items increases in future, then you may find that you never have to pay a price much above the price that you pay now. The responsiveness of quantity supplied to changes in price varies from market to market. The following two sections explain how *PES* is measured and why it varies.

4.5 Everyday economics

Inelastic supply and volatile prices

The *PES* of crude oil seems to be very low. This means that demand changes cause large changes in price, as in the right-hand part of Figure 4.7. This in turn leads to volatile prices. However, the price of petrol at the pumps is much less volatile. This is because only a little of what motorists pay goes on crude oil; most of it goes on refining costs, retailing costs, and tax. So large changes in crude oil prices lead to only small percentage changes in pump prices for petrol.

4.5 Summary

- Price elasticity of supply, *PES*, means the responsiveness of quantity supplied to a change in price that is caused by a shift in the demand curve. The responsiveness varies from market to market.
- If a shift in demand causes a small change in price, which leads to a large change in quantity supplied, then supply is price elastic. If a shift in demand causes a large change in price, which leads to a small change in quantity supplied, then supply is price inelastic.

4.6 Price elasticity of supply: its measurement

We have seen that the responsiveness of quantity supplied to changes in price is called price elasticity of supply, or *PES*. If you look back to Figure 4.7, you will see that the supply curve in the left-hand part is much flatter than the one in the right-hand part, so you might think that we would measure the *PES* in each case by using the slopes of the supply curves. But we don't refer to the slopes for the same reasons that applied with *PED*.

- **Supply curves are rarely straight**. For example, the slope of each supply curve in Figure 4.7 varies throughout its length. So it wouldn't make sense to say that we should measure 'the' slope of either curve.
- **Slopes are measured in units**. Even if a supply curve were straight, we would not want to use its slope to measure *PES*, because its slope would refer to units. For example, the *PES* for tyres would refer to units such as pounds and numbers of tyres, while the *PES* for parking slots would refer to pounds and hours of slots. So we could not meaningfully compare these two elasticities.

A formula for *PES*

To avoid units, we measure *PES* with *percentage* changes in price and quantity, using this formula:

$$PES = \frac{\text{\% change in quantity supplied}}{\text{\% change in price}}$$

When we use this formula, we calculate percentage changes in the same way that we use for all elasticities. We can use it to estimate the *PES* along **wx** and **yz** in Figure 4.7, as follows.

- **Arc *wx***. The quantity supplied rose from 40 million tyres to 56 million, a change of 16 million. The average quantity, which is the average of 40 and 56, is 48. So the percentage change in quantity supplied is 16 as a percentage of 48, which is 100(16/48), or 33⅓%. The price rose from £76 to £84, a change of £8, and the average price is £80. So the percentage change in price is 100(8/80), or 10%. So the *PES* equals (33⅓)/10, or 3.3.
- **Arc *yz***. The quantity supplied rose from 19 million hours to 21 million, a change of 2 million. The average quantity was 20 million. So the percentage change in quantity supplied is 2 as a percentage of 20, which is 100(2/20), or 10%. The price rose from £0.90 to £1.50, a change of £0.60. The average price was £1.20, so the percentage change in price is 100(0.6/1.20), or 50%. So the *PES* equals 10/50, or 0.2.

Figures for *PES* are usually positive. This is because a rise or positive change in price usually leads to a rise or positive changes in the quantity supplied, and vice versa. So the two percentages in the formula usually have the same sign.

Now that we know how to measure *PES*, there are three terms we need to define sharply.

- **Unit price elasticity of supply**. This applies if the percentage changes in quantity supplied and price happen to be of equal size, such as a 5% rise in price and a 5% rise in quantity. In this case, the *PES* is exactly 1.0.
- **Price elastic supply**. This applies if the percentage change in quantity supplied is bigger than the percentage change in price, as with tyres. This means the *PES* is bigger than 1.0: for tyres, it is 3.3.
- **Price inelastic supply**. This applies if the percentage change in quantity supplied is smaller than the percentage change in price, as with parking slots. This means the *PES* is smaller than 1.0; for parking slots, it is 0.2.

Arc elasticity of supply

In Figure 4.7, we found that the *PES* along **wx** in the left-hand part was 3.3, and that the *PES* along **yz** in the right-hand part was 0.2. Because each elasticity figure applies to part of a supply curve, or an arc, each is called an **arc elasticity of supply**.

On most supply curves, the *PES* varies from one arc to another, even if the curve happens to be a straight line. To see this, look at Figure 4.8. This figure concerns a labour market, specifically the labour market for checkout staff in a city where we will suppose that there is no minimum wage.

Suppose that demand here shifts from D_0 to D_1, so that the equilibrium moves from point **x** to point **y**. And suppose that demand later shifts again to D_2, moving the equilibrium from **y** to **z**. We will now show that arcs **xy** and **yz** have different *PES*s.

- **Arc *xy***. The change in quantity is 8,000 hours and the average is 12,000, so the percentage change is

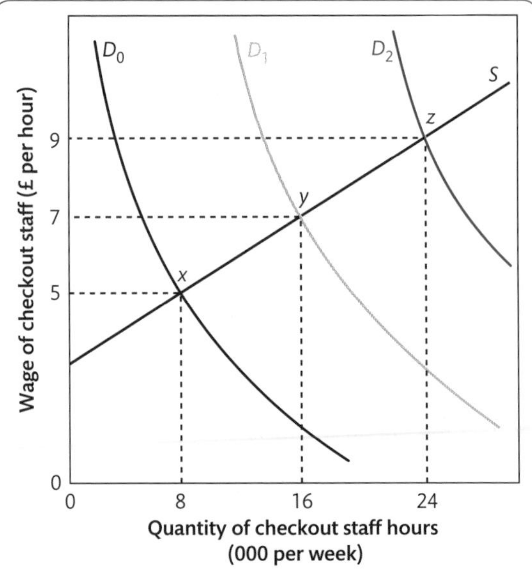

Figure 4.8 **Varying price elasticity of supply along a curve**

Price elasticity of supply usually varies along a supply curve, even if the curve is straight. Here, the *PES* is 2.0 along arc **xy** and 1.6 along arc **yz**.

100(8,000/12,000), or 66⅔%. The change in the price or wage is £2 and the average is £6, so the percentage change is 100(2/6), or 33⅓%. So the *PES* is (66⅔)/(33⅓), or 2.0.

- **Arc *yz***. The change in quantity is 8,000 hours and the average is 20,000, so the percentage change is 100(8,000/20,000), or 40%. The change in the price or wage is £2, and the average is £8, so the percentage change is 100(2/8), or 25%. So the *PES* is 40/25, or 1.6.

So the *PES* is 2.0 along one arc and 1.6 along the other. If we were to extend the curve, then we could work out the *PES* along more arcs and we would get different numbers again. We could also divide each of our two arcs up into smaller arcs and find that the *PES* were different yet again along these smaller arcs. For instance, if we divided the arc ***yz*** into two halves, then we would find that the *PES* were 1.67 along the left-hand arc, from a wage of £7 to a wage of £8, and 1.55 along the right-hand arc, from a wage of £8 to a wage of £9.

Point elasticity of supply

Instead of dividing a supply curve up into small arcs, we could split it into a series of points. We could work out the *PES* at any one of these points and so get a **point elasticity of supply** instead of an arc elasticity. However, to work out point elasticities, we need to know the equation of the supply curve and then use calculus. So we will not work out point elasticities in this book.

Constant price elasticity of supply

Figure 4.8 illustrated a straight-line supply curve, and we found that, even though it was straight, the *PES* varied from one arc to another. The *PES* usually does vary all along a supply curve, but sometimes the *PES* is exactly the same all the way along. Actually, we could construct a supply curve where the *PES* was constant at any number we chose, say 3.3 or 0.2. But there are only three cases of supply curves with constant elasticities that we need to know about.

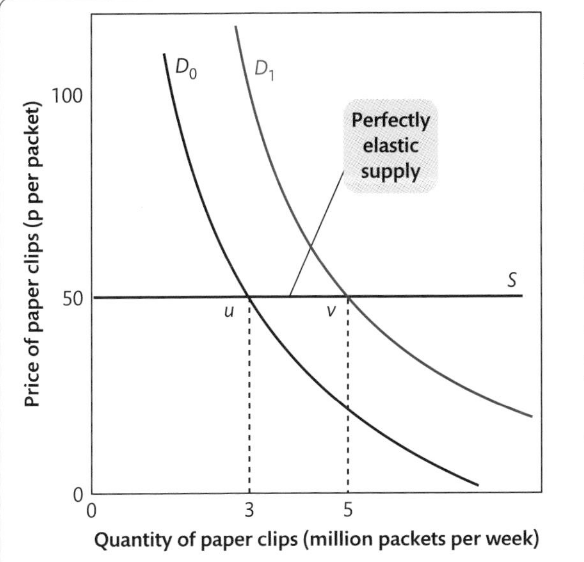

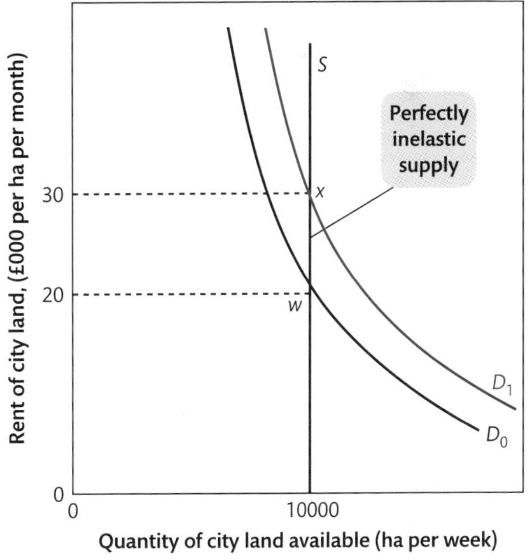

Figure 4.9 **Supply curves with extreme elasticities**

On the left, shifts in demand have no effect on price at all, yet quantity supplied still changes; here, supply is always perfectly elastic. On the right, shifts in demand do have an effect on price, but the quantity supplied remains the same; here, supply is always perfectly inelastic.

- ***PES* is infinity all along any horizontal supply curve.** For example, look at the left-hand part of Figure 4.9, which concerns the market for paper clips. The supply curve here has been drawn horizontal on the assumption that manufacturers are willing to produce any quantity of clips at 50p per packet. Here, a shift in demand will not alter the price at all. For instance, if demand were to shift from D_0 to D_1, the price would stay at 50p, but the quantity supplied would rise from 3 million packets a week to 5 million, to match the increase in demand. So the quantity supplied would rise without any change in price. Quantity supplied cannot be more responsive than that, so here we have **perfectly elastic supply**. The *PES* along any arc, such as ***uv***, is infinity because the percentage change in quantity along the arc must be divided by a 0% change in price.

- ***PES* is zero all along any vertical supply curve.** For example, look at the right-hand part of Figure 4.9, which concerns the market for land available for use by owner-occupiers and tenants in a city. This supply curve is vertical because the quantity of land is fixed, so the quantity supplied cannot respond to changes in the price or rent. Quantity supplied cannot be less responsive than that, so here we have **perfectly inelastic supply**. The *PES* along any arc, such as ***wx***, is zero, because there is a 0% change in quantity supplied to be divided by the percentage change in price.

- ***PES* is 1.0 all along any supply curve that is straight and which also passes through the origin.** This applies no matter how steep the curve is. For example, the *PES* equals 1.0 all along both the supply curves shown in Figure 4.10. This case is called the unit elasticity of supply.

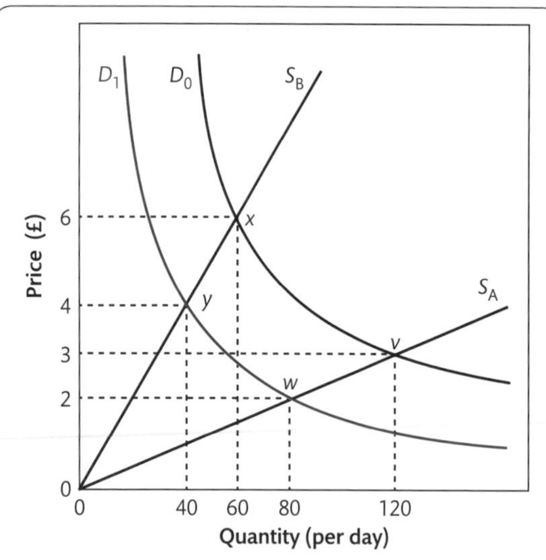

Figure 4.10 **Two supply curves where price elasticity of supply is always one**

Along any straight-line supply curve through the origin, the change in quantity supplied is always proportional to the change in price. So each supply curve here has unit price elasticity of supply.

Question 4.3 Use the formula for *PES* to show that it is 1.0 along both arcs ***vw*** and ***xy*** shown in Figure 4.10. Remember to calculate each percentage change in quantity supplied and price as the actual change as a percentage of the average quantity supplied or price.

4.6 Summary

- Price elasticity of supply, *PES*, is measured as the percentage change in quantity supplied divided by the percentage change in price.
- If the percentage change in quantity supplied is greater than the percentage change in price, then the *PES* is greater than one and supply is price elastic. If the percentage change in quantity supplied is smaller than the percentage change in price, then the *PES* is less than one and supply is price inelastic.
- We can find arc elasticities that apply to arcs along a curve, and point elasticities for particular points.
- Price elasticity of supply usually varies all along a supply curve, even if the curve is a straight line.
- Some supply curves have a constant *PES*: a vertical one has a constant *PES* of zero, a horizontal one has a constant *PES* of infinity, and a straight-line supply curve through the origin has a constant *PES* of one.

4.7 Why price elasticities of supply vary

PES variations in product markets

We will now explain why price elasticities of supply vary between different products. There are three main factors that affect the *PES* of any given product, and we will discuss them in turn. These factors are:

- **how close the industry making the product is to its maximum possible output, that is to its full capacity**;
- **the price elasticity of supply of the key inputs that are needed to produce the product**;
- **the time that the producers of the product have to respond to changes in its price**.

The *PES* for products and industry capacity

To see how industry capacity affects the *PES* for a product, consider two examples. Suppose, first, that you run a salt mine and that you and other mines are using your equipment around the clock. Then suppose that the demand for salt for use on the roads increases in a bad winter. The price of salt will rise, but you and other mines cannot offer much more salt in response to the higher price. So the *PES* is low for products supplied by industries that are running close to full capacity.

In contrast, suppose that you run a rural bus company and that your buses are rarely if ever full. Then suppose that the demand for travel on your buses increases so that fares go up. You can readily offer more seats in response to the higher fares. So the *PES* is high for products supplied by industries that are running well below full capacity.

The *PES* for products and the *PES* of inputs

The *PES* of a product is affected by the *PES* of the key inputs that are used to make it. This is shown in the following two cases.

- **The *PES* of a product tends to be inelastic if the *PES* of key inputs is inelastic**. To see this, suppose that you make diamond earrings, and that the demand for them increases. Then you raise their price and so you want to supply more. The key input that you need is diamonds. As the price of earrings has risen, you can offer a higher price for diamonds. Unfortunately, the *PES* of diamonds is very low, because no matter how much their price rises, their suppliers cannot find many more. So, even if you offer a much higher price for diamonds, you will be unable to buy many more. In turn, you will be unable to supply many more earrings. So the quantity of earrings that you supply will be very unresponsive to changes in their price. In short, the supply of diamond earrings is very inelastic because the supply of diamonds is very inelastic.
- **The *PES* of a product tends to be elastic if the *PES* of key inputs is elastic**. To see this, suppose that you make razor blades, and that the demand for them increases. Then you raise their price and so you want to supply more. The key input you need is steel. Fortunately, the *PES* of steel is very high because it is easy for steel makers to get more iron ore and supply more steel. So even if you offer only a slightly higher price for steel, you will be able to gets much more. In turn, you can produce many more blades. So the quantity of blades that you supply will be very responsive to changes in their price. In short, the supply of blades is very elastic, because the supply of steel is very elastic.

The *PES* for products and the time producers have to respond

When the price of a product rises, its producers like to supply more. So they need more inputs. Usually they find that there are some inputs of which they can quickly acquire more, and others of which it takes a while to acquire more. So the extent to which they can respond to a rise in price by increasing their output depends on how much time they have to get more inputs.

For example, consider milk farmers. If the demand for milk increases and the price of milk rises, then these farmers will want to supply more milk. For a few days, however, they will be unable to get any more key inputs like cows, so they cannot supply any more milk. Within a week or two, they can buy some more cows, from abroad if necessary, and buy more cattle feed, and then supply some more milk. But they may not be able to increase their milk production as much as they would like, because to do that they would need more milking parlours, and it might take a year or two to get these designed and built.

What this means is that milk farmers actually have three supply curves, as shown in Figure 4.11. Suppose that the market starts at point ***w*** where all of these supply curves intersect the demand curve, D_0. So the price is 60p a litre and 12 million litres are sold each day. Then demand increases to D_1. So the price rises, and farmers want to supply more milk each day. But just how much more they can supply depends on how long they have to alter their production. We need to consider three time frames.

- **The very short run**. For a few days, farmers cannot get any more cows and can still supply only 12 million litres a day. So they are 'stuck' on the vertical supply curve labelled S_{VSR}. This is the **very short-run supply curve**: it shows how much producers will supply at each price when they have too little time to alter the quantity they use of one or more key inputs. While farmers are stuck on S_{VSR}, the market will settle where S_{VSR} intersects D_1. So the price will rise to 180p while the quantity supplied stays at 12 million litres a day. The *PES* on the arc ***wx*** on S_{VSR} is zero because, as we saw in the right-hand part of Figure 4.9, the *PES* is zero on a vertical supply curve.

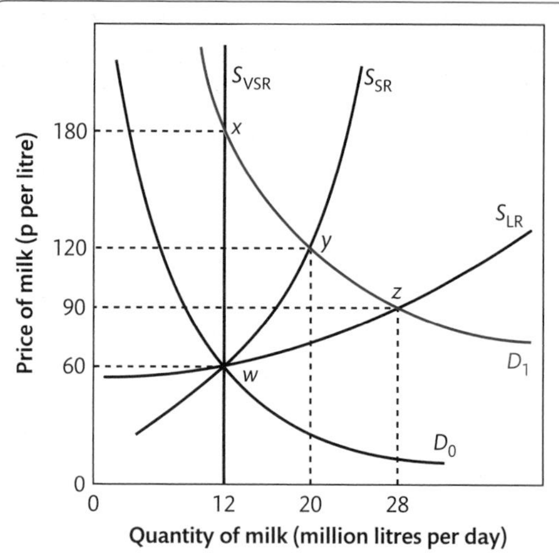

Figure 4.11 **Three supply curves for milk**

Each supply curve intersects the initial demand curve, D_0, at the initial equilibrium. If demand rises to D_1, S_{VSR} shows how much farmers will produce at each price before they can get any more inputs. S_{SR} shows how much they will produce when they can get more of some inputs. S_{LR} shows how much they will produce when they can get more of all inputs.

- **The short run**. After a few days, farmers can acquire more cows and cattle feed, so they can supply more milk. They can now move along the sloping supply curve labelled S_{SR}. This is the **short-run supply curve**: it shows how much producers will supply at each price when they can alter the quantity of some inputs, but not all. Farmers may be 'stuck' on this for a year or two until they can get more milking parlours. For all this time, the price will settle where S_{SR} intersects D_1. So the price will be 120p, and the quantity supplied will be 20 million litres each day. You could work out that the *PES* on the arc ***wy*** on S_{SR}, between the initial equilibrium and the new equilibrium, is 0.75.

- **The long run**. After a year or two, farmers can alter the amount they use of every input, including milking parlours. So they can respond more to changes in the price of milk, and can move along the sloping supply curve labelled S_{LR}. This is the

long-run supply curve: it shows how much producers will supply at each price when they can alter the quantity they use of all inputs. Once they have acquired the extra parlours, the market will settle where S_{LR} intersects D_1. So the price will be 90p and the quantity supplied will be 28 million litres each day. You could work out that the *PES* on the arc ***wz*** on S_{LR}, between the initial equilibrium and the final equilibrium, is 2.00.

More about the three time frames

This milk example shows us that to give a full description of what will happen in the milk market if demand changes, we need three supply curves. For most products, however, we can dispense with the very short-run supply curve. This is because most producers can vary the amounts they use of all inputs right away. For example, if a car maker wants to produce more cars today, it can probably just keep its assembly lines working a little longer and use parts from its stores.

However, most products do have a short-run supply curve and a long-run supply curve. So, to give a full description of what happens in each case when demand changes, we should consider two time frames and refer to both the supply curves. However, economists are usually concerned chiefly with short-run supply curves. So usually our diagrams have only one supply curve, and we do not add a subscript to say that it is the short-run curve.

PES variations in labour markets

Finally, we will consider why the *PES* of labour may vary between labour markets for different types of labour. Consider, first, the labour market for waiting staff. If the wage for such staff rises, then we expect many people to want to switch into this job from jobs such as stackers and dishwashers. So we expect the hours supplied to respond greatly to the higher wage, and we therefore expect a high *PES*. For the same reason, we expect a high *PES* in many other labour markets.

There are exceptions. These arise most frequently for types of labour that need rare skills that people cannot easily acquire. For instance, consider the labour market for dentists. Suppose the wages of dentists rise. Many people might now like to become dentists, but they cannot do so because they do not have the necessary skills. So, in this labour market, the number of workers will not respond much to wage increases, so there will be an inelastic supply with a low *PES*.

4.7 Summary

- The price elasticity of supply for a product depends on how close the industry is to full capacity, on the *PES* of the key inputs needed, and on the time that producers have to respond to price changes.
- Most products have two supply curves: a short-run supply curve, which shows how the quantity supplied varies with price when only some inputs can be varied, and a long-run supply curve, which shows how the quantity supplied varies with price when all inputs can be varied.
- The *PES* in a labour market depends chiefly on how far workers need skills that are hard to acquire.

In the next chapter we see how the equilibrium position in many markets is influenced by governments. In passing, we will see that elasticities often greatly affect this influence.

Glossary

Arc elasticity of demand: the *PED* along an arc of a demand curve.

Arc elasticity of supply: the *PES* along an arc of a supply curve.

Cross elasticity of demand (*CED*): the responsiveness of the quantity demanded of one product to changes in the price of another product; the *CED* equals the percentage change in the quantity demanded of the first product divided by the percentage change in the price of the other.

Income elastic demand: when a rise or fall in income of any percentage leads to a greater percentage rise or fall in quantity demanded, so the *IED* is greater than one.

Income elasticity of demand (*IED*): the responsiveness of the quantity of a product demanded to changes in consumer incomes; *IED* equals the percentage change in the quantity demanded divided by the percentage change in consumer incomes.

Income inelastic demand: when a rise or fall in income of any percentage leads to a smaller percentage rise or fall in quantity demanded, so the *IED* is less than one.

Long-run supply curve: the supply curve when suppliers can vary the quantity of all inputs.

Perfectly elastic demand: when the quantity demanded may change without any change in price, so the *PED* equals minus infinity.

Perfectly elastic supply: when the quantity supplied may change without any change in its price, so the *PES* equals infinity.

Perfectly inelastic demand: when the quantity demanded does not respond at all to changes in price, so the *PED* equals zero.

Perfectly inelastic supply: when the quantity supplied does not respond at all to changes in price, so the *PES* equals zero.

Point elasticity of demand: the *PED* at a point on a demand curve.

Point elasticity of supply: the *PES* at a point on a supply curve.

Price elastic demand: when the percentage change in quantity demanded is more sizeable than the percentage change in price, so the *PED* is below minus one; a rise in price leads to less spending, and a fall in price leads to more spending.

Price elasticity of demand (*PED*): the responsiveness of the quantity of an item demanded to changes in its price; *PED* equals the percentage change in quantity demanded divided by the percentage change in price.

Price elasticity of supply (*PES*): the responsiveness of the quantity of an item supplied to changes in its price; *PES* equals the percentage change in quantity supplied divided by the percentage change in price.

Price elastic supply: when the percentage change in quantity supplied exceeds the percentage change in price, so the *PES* is greater than one.

Price inelastic demand: when the percentage change in quantity demanded is less sizeable than the percentage change in price, so the *PED* is between minus one and zero; a rise in price leads to more spending, and a fall in price leads to less spending.

Price inelastic supply: when the percentage change in quantity supplied is smaller than the percentage change in price, so the *PES* is between zero and one.

Short-run supply curve: the supply curve that applies for as long as suppliers can vary the quantities they use of some inputs, but not all inputs.

Unit price elasticity of demand: when demand is neither price elastic nor price inelastic, so the *PED* equals minus one.

Unit price elasticity of supply: when supply is neither price elastic nor price inelastic, so the *PES* equals one.

Very short-run supply curve: the vertical supply curve that applies while suppliers cannot acquire more of some key inputs and so cannot supply more output; it is not applicable for most products.

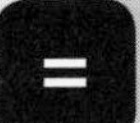

Answers to in-text questions

Note that in these answers, P = price and Q = quantity.

4.1 Arc ***vw*** in Figure 4.1 left: change in *Q* is 400 million and average *Q* is 800 million, so percentage change is 100(400/800), or 50%; change in *P* is –2p and average *P* is 20p, so percentage change is 100(–2/20), or –10%; so *PED* is 50/–10, or –5. Arc ***xy*** in Figure 4.1 right: change in *Q* is –50 million and average is 500 million, so percentage change is 100(–50/500), or –10%; change in *P* is 20p and average is 50p, so percentage change is 100(20/50), or 40%; so *PED* is –10/40, or –0.25.

4.2 Arc ***yz*** in Figure 4.5: change in *Q* is 10 million and average is 25 million, so percentage change is 40%; change in *P* is –£2 and average is £5, so percentage change is –40%; so *PED* is 40/–40, which is –1.0.

4.3 Arc ***vw*** in Figure 4.10: change in *Q* is –40 and average is 100, so percentage change is –40%; change in *P* is –£1 and average is £2.50, so percentage change is –40%; so *PES* is –40/–40, or 1.0. Arc ***xy***: change in *Q* is –20 and average is 50, so percentage change is –40%; change in *P* is –£2 and average is £5, so percentage change is –40%; so *PES* is –40/–40, or 1.0.

? Questions for review

4.1 When, if ever, do we expect to get a negative value for (**a**) a *PED*, (**b**) an *IED*, (**c**) a *CED*, and (**d**) a *PES*?

4.2 When, if ever, do we expect to get a positive value for (**a**) a *PED*, (**b**) an *IED*, (**c**) a *CED*, and (**d**) a *PES*?

4.3 Say the quantity demanded of a product would be 50 at a price of £2, 30 at a price of £4, 20 at a price of £6, and 10 at a price of £10. What would be the expenditure at each of these four prices? What is the *PED* for this product along the demand curve on (**a**) the arc between £2 and £4, (**b**) the arc between £4 and £6, and (**c**) the arc between £6 and £10?

4.4 Which of the following would you expect to have a high *PES* and which would you expect to have a low *PES*? Give brief reasons for your answers.

(**a**) Petrol, if oil refineries have spare capacity.

(**b**) Gold jewellery.

(**c**) Potatoes, if producers are given one week to respond to the change in price.

(**d**) Potatoes if producers have two years to respond.

4.5 Which of the following types of labour would you expect to have a high *PES* and which would you expect to have a low *PES*? Give brief reasons for your answers.

(**a**) Footballers good enough for a top team.

(**b**) Heavy goods vehicle drivers.

? Questions for discussion

4.1 (a) Think of three products for which your demand is price elastic. In each case say why it is elastic.

(b) Think of three products for which your demand is price inelastic. In each case say why it is inelastic.

4.2 Think of three types of labour employed in higher education. Which do you think has the highest *PES* and which do you think has the lowest? Why?

4.3 Think of two products for which you have income elastic demand, two for which you have income inelastic demand, and two for which your *IED* is negative. Suppose that in five years' time your income has trebled. Would your *IED* for any of these products be very different from what it is today?

Common student errors

Some students are reluctant to accept that *PED* and *PES* generally vary along straight supply and demand curves, but Figures 4.3 and 4.8 show that this is the case. Because *PED* and *PES* can vary greatly along a curve, it is best not to talk about 'an elastic curve' or 'an inelastic curve'. It is also best not to talk about elastic or inelastic products: it is their supply and demand that may be elastic or inelastic.

Some students argue that demand is price elastic for luxuries and price inelastic for necessities, but these terms are not used in this book because very few products are necessary except water. Students who use these terms should beware that, while some economists do define necessities as products with price inelastic demand and luxuries as products with price elastic demand, others define necessities as products with income inelastic demand and luxuries as products with income elastic demand. But both these definitions seem odd, because the first makes beer a necessity and the second makes oranges a necessity!

5

Governments and Markets

Remember from Chapter 3 that, in many markets, the forces of supply and demand determine the price of the item traded, the quantity traded in a period of time, and the expenditure in a period of time.

Does a law that imposes a minimum wage raise unemployment, and make it harder for people to find low-paid jobs? Does a tax of 40p on a pint of beer add 40p to the price paid by buyers? Why does the EU run a Common Agricultural Policy that increases the price of many foods for EU consumers? How does making it illegal to trade a drug affect its price? How else do governments affect markets?

This chapter shows you how to answer questions like these, by understanding:

* the main ways in which governments change the prices and quantities in different markets;
* who loses and who gains when governments intervene in markets.

5.1 An argument against government intervention

In Chapter 3, we saw how the forces of supply and demand determine the price and the quantity traded in many markets. In that chapter, we assumed that the markets were free, so that there was no government intervention. In practice, though, governments intervene in many markets. They intervene in a variety of ways which we will study in the following sections of this chapter. But, in this first section, we will briefly note an argument that suggests that governments should be wary about intervening.

To see this argument, consider Figure 5.1, which concerns the market for mineral water. If this market is free, it will settle where the demand curve, *D*, intersects the supply curve, *S*, with 30 million litres of water traded each week at a price of 15p a litre. Let's consider what this equilibrium means for buyers and sellers.

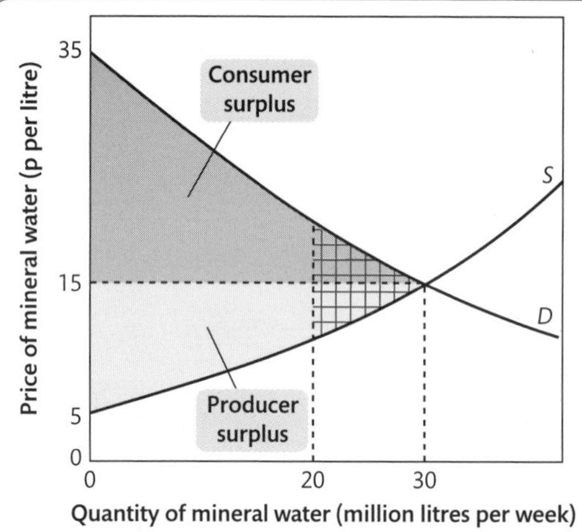

Figure 5.1 **The advantage of a free market**

If the market is free, consumers enjoy a surplus shown by the dark grey area: the value they place on water, shown by the prices they are willing to pay, is above the price they do pay. Also, producers enjoy a surplus shown by the light grey area: the cost of producing water is below the price they are paid. The grid shows how much the surpluses would fall if government intervention were to cut the quantity traded to 20 million.

Note: The price refers to water alone and excludes bottling.

- **Buyers**. *D* shows how much water buyers would be willing to buy at each possible price. It meets the price axis at a price of 35p. This means that at least one buyer places a value of 35p on a litre of water and would be willing to pay 35p for it, if that were indeed the price. Yet that buyer can in fact buy that litre at the market price of 15p. The gap between the price that a buyer would be willing to pay, that is the value to the buyer, and the price that the buyer does pay is called **consumer surplus**, so this buyer has a consumer surplus of 20p. Now *D* is above the price level of 15p at every quantity up to 30 million litres, so all buyers, except the one who buys the 30 millionth litre, value water at more than the 15p they pay, so every buyer except that one enjoys some consumer surplus. The total consumer surplus for all consumers is shown by a dark grey area.
- **Sellers**. *S* shows how much water sellers would be willing to sell at each possible price. It meets the price axis at a price of 5p. This means that at least one seller could produce a litre for 5p and would be willing to sell it for 5p, if that were indeed the price. Yet that seller can in fact sell that litre at the market price of 15p. The gap between the price that a seller would be willing to accept, that is the cost to the seller, and the price that the seller actually receives is called **producer surplus**, so this seller has a producer surplus of 10p. Now *S* is below the price level of 15p at every quantity up to 30 million litres; this means that every seller, except the one who sells the 30 millionth litre, has a cost below 15p, so every seller except that seller enjoys some producer surplus. The total producer surplus for all producers is shown by a light grey area.

So, if there is no government intervention and the quantity traded each week is 30 million litres, then the total surplus for consumers and producers is as shown by the grey areas. But now suppose the government intervenes in this market and forces the quantity to settle at a different level from 30 million litres a week. There are two possibilities.

- **The quantity is forced below the free market quantity, say to 20 million litres a week.** In this case, the consumer surplus falls by the amount covered by the upper part of the grid in Figure 5.1, because consumers no longer enjoy a surplus by buying between 20 and 30 million litres of water a week at a price below the value they put on it. Also, the producer surplus falls by the amount covered by the lower part of the grid, because producers no longer enjoy a surplus by selling between 20 and 30 million litres of water a week at a price above the cost they face in producing it. Governments should be wary about reducing the surpluses that consumers and producers enjoy.
- **The quantity is forced above the free market quantity.** The supply curve in Figure 5.1 shows that producers would want more than 15p to supply each litre above 30 million, because each would cost more than 15p to produce. The demand curve shows that consumers would value each litre above 30 million at less than 15p, which is why they would pay less than 15p for it. Governments should be wary about forcing the output of a product to a level at which its cost exceeds the value placed on it by consumers, because this seems a poor use of resources.

It follows that governments should be wary about intervening in markets and causing the quantity to differ from what it would be if the market were free. However, there is a case for government intervention in some markets, in which issues arise that we have so far ignored. In this chapter, we will look mostly at *how* governments intervene. We will also say a little about *why* they intervene, but we say much more about that in Chapter 13.

5.1 Summary

- In a free market, most buyers get some consumer surplus because the value they place on the product exceeds its price, and most sellers get some producer surplus because their costs are less than its price.
- If a government forces the output below the free market quantity, then consumers and producers lose some of their surpluses. If a government forces output above the free market quantity, then some units of output will be produced at a cost that exceeds the value placed on them by consumers.
- Nevertheless, governments often intervene in markets. They do so in various ways for many reasons.

5.2 Price controls

One way in which governments can intervene in markets is with laws or controls that require suppliers to set a price that is different from the free market price. There are two types of price control, called price ceilings and price floors, and we will take each in turn.

Price ceilings

Figure 5.2 shows the market in a city for rented accommodation. The market settles where the demand and supply curves, *D* and *S*, intersect. So Q_0 square metres are let each year at a price or rent of R_0 per square metre for the year. Now suppose the city council feels that current rents stretch the finances of many tenants unacceptably. It may simply impose a maximum rent, R_{MAX}, that is below R_0. An imposed price that is below the free market price is called a **price ceiling**.

If landlords are law-abiding, then the rent will fall to R_{MAX}. This fall in the rent has two effects.

- **It reduces the quantity of accommodation supplied from Q_0 to Q_S.** For example, some landlords

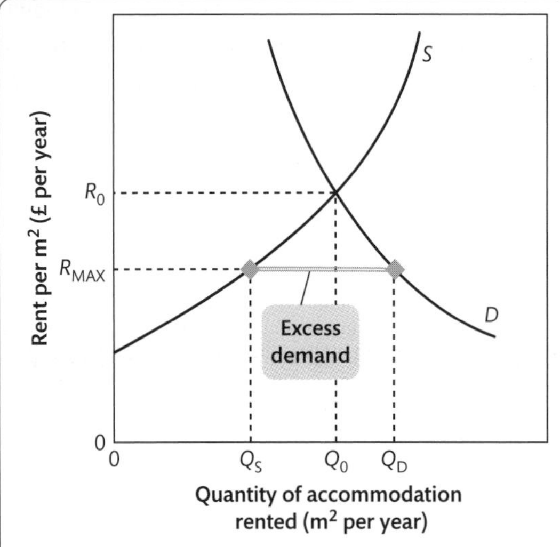

Figure 5.2 **The effects of a price ceiling**

If the market were free, the rent would be R_0, where *D* intersects *S*. If a price ceiling equal to R_{MAX} is imposed, making higher rents illegal, the rent is forced down to R_{MAX}. At this rent, only Q_S space is supplied while Q_D is demanded, so there is an excess demand, as shown by the double line.

who used to let out spare rooms may feel that doing so is no longer worth the bother.

- **It increases the quantity of accommodation demanded from Q_0 to Q_D.** This is partly because some tenants now want to rent more space, and partly because some people who previously could not afford to rent at all now wish to do so.

These effects combine to create an excess demand, as shown in Figure 5.2 by a double line. This excess demand means that many people will want to secure each property that becomes available. So landlords would like to raise their rents, but they cannot because doing so is illegal.

The rent ceiling creates gainers and losers. To see this, consider four groups of people.

- **The people who rent the Q_S square metres that are still available.** These people gain, because they now pay only R_{MAX} instead of R_0.
- **The people who would have rented the space between Q_S and Q_0.** These people lose because this space is no longer available to rent.
- **Landlords.** They lose because rents are lower.
- **The people who now want to rent the space between Q_0 and Q_D.** At the old R_0 these people did not want to rent this space. Yet at the new lower R_{MAX} they do, but they cannot find any space available. So both before and now these people do not rent this space. But the new situation is more frustrating for them, because before they did not bother to look for it, while now they waste time looking in vain.

Price floors

Sometimes governments impose a **price floor**, which is a price that is above the free market price. Figure 5.3 shows the market for waiting staff in a city. The market settles where the demand and supply curves, *D* and *S*, intersect, with Q_0 hours worked each week at a wage of W_0 per hour.

Now suppose the government feels that W_0 is so low that waiting staff are in financial hardship. It may impose a price floor at a higher wage. A price floor in a labour market is called a **minimum wage**. Suppose the price floor or minimum wage here is W_{MIN}. If the employers are law-abiding, then the wage will rise to W_{MIN}. This rise in the wage has two effects.

- **It reduces the quantity of hours that employers demand from Q_0 to Q_D.** For example, it may make some restaurants decide to move from waiting service to self-service.
- **It increases the quantity of hours that people want to work as waiting staff from Q_0 to Q_S.**

These effects combine to create an excess supply, as shown in Figure 5.3 by a double line. People will queue up to apply for jobs, and employers will want to cut the wage, but they cannot because doing so is illegal.

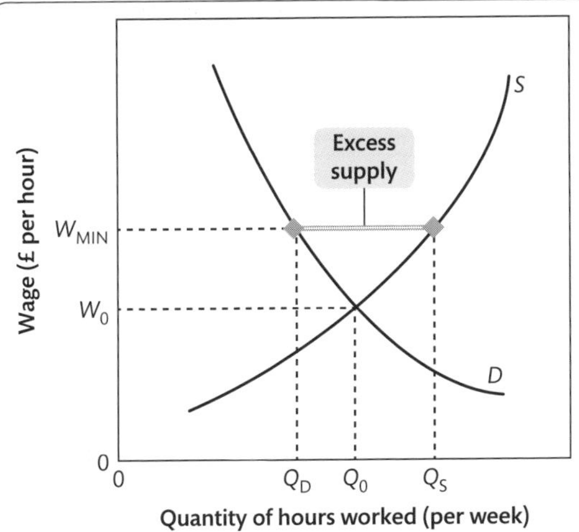

Figure 5.3 **The effects of a price floor**

If the market were free, the wage would be W_0, where *D* intersects *S*. If a price floor equal to W_{MIN} is imposed, making lower wages illegal, the wage is forced up to W_{MIN}. So employers pay for only Q_D hours work while workers want to work Q_S hours, so there is an excess supply, as shown by the double line.

The minimum wage creates gainers and losers. To see this, consider five groups of people.

- **The people who work the Q_D hours that are still available**. These people gain, because they are now paid W_{MIN} instead of W_0.
- **The people who would have worked the hours between Q_D and Q_0**. These people used to do waiting work, but cannot now find any waiting work to do. In turn, unemployment rises. It is because minimum wages pose this threat to raise unemployment that governments keep them low; then wages will not rise by much and unemployment will not rise by much.
- **Restaurant owners**. They lose because they have to pay higher wages.
- **People who eat in restaurants**. They lose because restaurant owners will raise their prices.
- **The people who now want to work the hours between Q_0 and Q_S**. At the old W_0 these people did not want to work as waiting staff. At the new higher W_{MIN} they do, but there are no jobs on offer. So both before and now these people do not work as waiting staff. But the new situation is more frustrating for them, because before they did not bother to look for waiting jobs, but now they waste time looking in vain.

5.1 Everyday economics

The UK National Minimum Wage and unemployment

When the UK's National Minimum Wage was introduced in 1999, people feared that employers would hire fewer workers, but it is very hard to see whether the minimum wage had this effect. To see why, note that Figure 5.3, like all economic models, considers what happens if the only change is the one under discussion, here the imposition of a minimum wage, while all else stays constant. But other things do not stay constant. So, while there is little evidence that the minimum wage increased unemployment, it is possible that other factors offset its effects. For example, workers may have become more productive so that the demand curve for labour shifted to the right, or people may have worked shorter working weeks, so that a fall in hours worked did not reduce the number of people with jobs. It must also be noted that the National Minimum Wage was set at a low level.

5.2 Summary

- Governments can force a price to go below the free market price by having a legal price ceiling set at a lower price. Price ceilings create excess demand and lead to some people gaining and others losing.
- Governments can force a price to go above the free market price by having a legal price floor set at a higher price. Price ceilings create excess supply and lead to some people gaining and others losing.

5.3 Quantity controls

Another way in which governments can intervene in markets is to act directly on the quantity traded. They can do this by regulating either the quantity that is supplied or the quantity that is demanded. We will take each case in turn.

Supply-side quantity controls

Figure 5.4 shows the market for taxi rides in a small city. Suppose the city council will grant taxi licences to any vehicles that are in good order, but otherwise leaves the market alone. Then the market settles where the demand and supply curves, D and S_0, intersect, with 12,000 miles travelled each day at a price or fare of £2 a mile. Suppose that, to supply this quantity, taxi firms need 80 cabs.

Now suppose that the council decides to restrict the number of cabs it will license to 60, and suppose that this limits the quantity of miles that can be supplied each day to 9,000. Then the supply curve becomes vertical at this quantity, as shown by S_1: suppliers cannot supply more than 9,000 miles of rides, no matter how high the price might be. The market will now settle where S_1 intersects D, at a fare of £3 per mile and 9,000 miles a day.

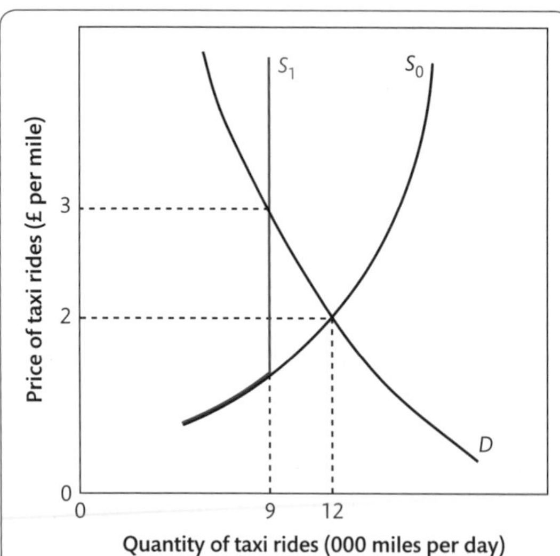

Figure 5.4 **Supply-side quantity controls**

With a free market for taxi rides, 12,000 miles would be travelled each day at £2 a mile. If the quantity supplied is restricted to 9,000 miles per day, the supply curve becomes vertical at that quantity. The price will rise, unless the price is also regulated to hold it at the original £2 a mile.

Most local authorities do restrict the number of cabs and so, as in Figure 5.4, put upward pressure on the price. However, many authorities prevent high prices by also imposing price ceilings close to what might arise in a free market. Suppose the authority concerned in Figure 5.4 imposes a ceiling of £2 per mile. Then restricting cab numbers to 60 will not raise the fare above the free market price of £2. But, at £2, there will be an excess demand, because consumers will want to travel 12,000 miles a day and only 9,000 will be available. So instead of facing high fares, consumers will face long waits for cabs.

In this example, output was limited indirectly by restricting the number of cabs. Sometimes, governments limit output directly by giving each firm a limit on its actual output. The effects are the same, but limits like these are called **quotas**.

Demand-side quantity controls

Figure 5.5 shows the market for free-range eggs. It settles where D_0 and S intersect, with 15 million eggs sold per day at a price of 30p. Now suppose a long war starts, so the government wants to have more resources available for defence. One way of doing this is to use fewer resources for producing eggs. To reduce the resources used for eggs, suppose the government makes it illegal for people to buy eggs unless they produce some ration tickets, which the government will give them. And suppose that each person is given enough tickets to buy only 60 eggs a year.

Suppose that the result is that buyers between them cannot buy more than 8 million eggs a day. Then the

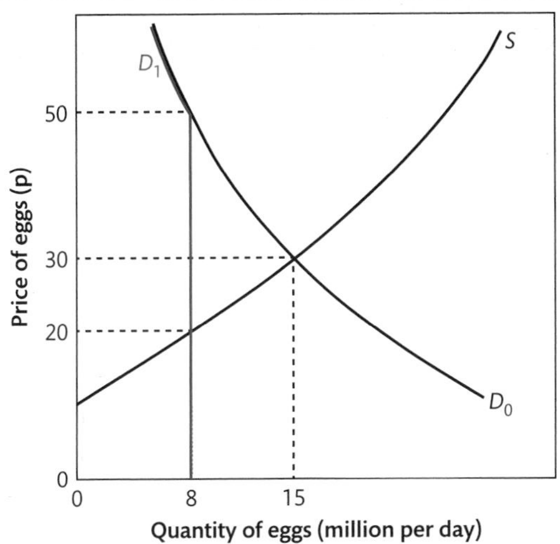

Figure 5.5 **Demand-side quantity controls**

If the quantity demanded is held below the free market quantity of 15 million eggs a day, the demand curve becomes vertical at that quantity. The price in this market will fall to 20p. However, frustrated buyers may offer higher prices up to 50p in an illegal second-hand black market.

demand curve becomes vertical at this quantity, as shown by D_1. The market will settle where D_1 intersects *S*, with 8 million eggs per day sold at a price of 20p.

However, *D* shows that, at this quantity, some people will be willing to pay up to 50p for extra eggs that they cannot buy legally.

These people may offer to pay well over 20p to buy eggs from other people who do not much care for eggs, but who have used their tickets to buy some. So a second-hand market may develop in which buyers and sellers ignore the legal controls over how many eggs individuals are meant to buy each year. A market that ignores legal limits on prices or quantities is called a **black market**.

5.3 Summary

- A government can force the quantity traded below the free market quantity by restricting the amount that suppliers can supply. This will raise the price, unless that is also subject to regulation.
- A government can force the quantity traded below the free market quantity by limiting the amount that buyers can buy. This should reduce the price, but it may lead to high prices on an illegal black market.

5.4 Taxes on expenditure

We now turn to a very common form of government intervention, which is to impose **taxes on expenditure**; these taxes are taxes on individual products, and they come in two forms.

- **Specific taxes**: with these, the amount of tax paid depends on the quantity of the product that is sold. The UK has major specific taxes on beer, wine, and oil, all of which are levied at set amounts per litre, and on tobacco products.
- ***Ad valorem* taxes**: with these, the amount of tax paid depends on the price or value of the product that is sold; the term *ad valorem* is Latin for 'according to value'. The UK's main *ad valorem* tax is value added tax (VAT). This is levied at 20% on most products, but to see exactly what this rate means, suppose you buy a ream of printer paper for £4.80. Your receipt will say the VAT is 80p, so this leaves £4 to be kept and divided among the people whom we will call the sellers; these are the people who produced it and sold it. Now 80p is actually only 16⅔% of £4.80, but the tax rate is called 20% because the law requires sellers to pay a tax equal to 20% of what they keep, that is £4, not 20% of what you pay, and 80p is 20% of £4.

We will now study the effects of both types of tax.

The effects of a specific tax

To explain the effects of a specific tax, Figure 5.6 gives an example. Suppose the supply curve for a product is as shown by *S* in part (a), and suppose that initially there is no tax. Then *S* shows the quantity that sellers will supply for each price they might receive from buyers. For example, if sellers were to receive a price of £6, they would supply 70 units a day, and if they were to receive a price of £10, they would supply 100 units a day.

Now suppose a specific tax of £8 per unit is imposed. In this case, if the price paid by buyers were, say, £14, then sellers would have to pay £8 tax to the government, and so keep only £6 for themselves, and we have seen that they would then supply 70 units a day. If the price paid by buyers were £18, then sellers would still have to pay £8 tax to the government, but would now keep £10 for themselves, and we have seen that they would then supply 100 units a day.

In Figure 5.6, the curve *S* + *tax* shows the quantity that sellers will supply at each possible price that might be paid by buyers, after the tax is imposed. For example, it shows that if buyers pay £14, sellers will supply 70 units a day, and if buyers pay £18, sellers will supply 100. The £8 vertical gap between *S* and *S* + *tax*, which is shown by arrows, equals the amount of the tax.

To see the effect of the tax, we add in the demand curve, *D*, as in part (b). Initially, the market settles where *D* intersects *S* at a price of £10, with 100 units sold each day. When the £8 tax is imposed, the market settles where *D* intersects *S* + *tax*, at a price for buyers of £14 and with 70 units sold a day. Although buyers pay £14, sellers pay the government £8 in tax and keep just £6 for themselves. We can read this figure of £6 off the graph from the point on *S* below where *S* + *tax* intersects *D*. The double line shows that the £6 price here is £8 less than the buyer price,

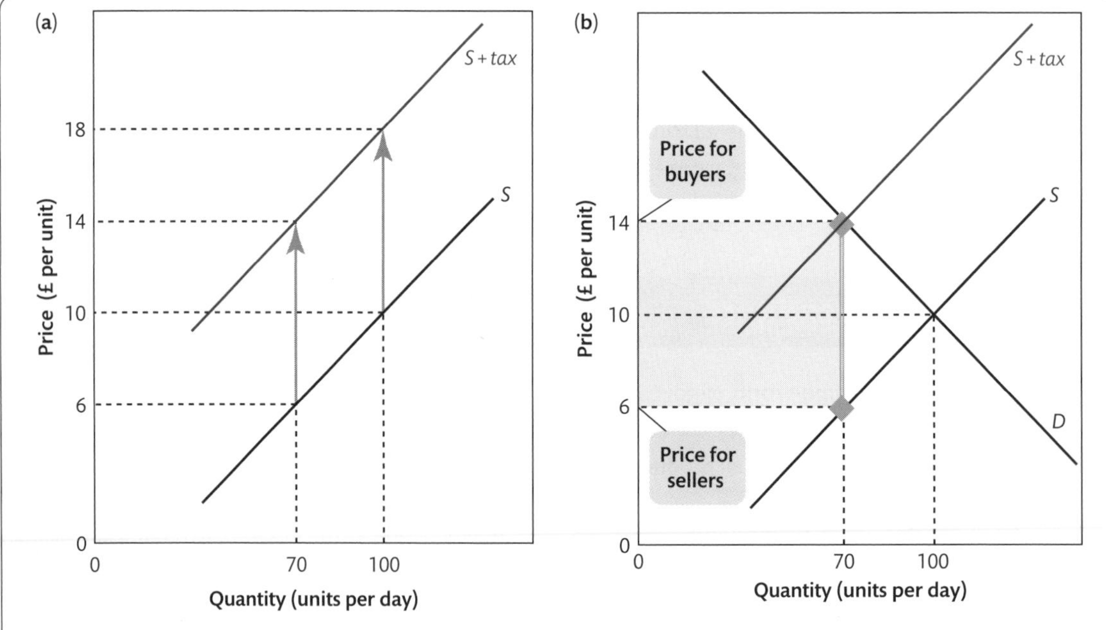

Figure 5.6 **The effects of a specific tax**

In part (a), *S* shows how much sellers will supply at each possible price for buyers, if there is no tax. *S* + *tax* shows how much sellers will supply at each price for buyers if there is a tax of £8; it is £8 above *S*, as shown by the arrows, because to supply any quantity, sellers want £8 more than before so that they can pay the tax and keep as much as before. Part (b) adds *D*. The price for buyers is £14, where *D* intersects *S* + *tax*. Sellers get £8 less, as shown by the double line. The revenue equals the shaded area.

because the £8 tax creates an £8 gap between *S* and *S + tax*.

Many people assume that a tax of, say, £8 must raise the price paid by buyers by £8, but this is unlikely, and in Figure 5.6 it raises the price for buyers by only £4. The reason that the price paid by buyers rises by less than the tax can be seen in the figure. When the tax is imposed, sellers pay £8 per unit to the government in tax, but they charge consumers only £4 more than before, that is £14 instead of £10. Sellers manage to do this because they now keep less for themselves, here £6 compared with £10 before. So the £8 tax here raises the price that buyers pay by £4, and it cuts the price that sellers keep by £4. The effect of a tax on expenditure on the buyer and seller prices is called its **incidence**, and in Figure 5.6 the incidence is £4 on both sellers and buyers.

We complete Figure 5.6 by adding a shaded area to show the tax revenue. This area has a length of 70 units a day, that is the quantity now sold each day, and a height of £8, the tax per unit. So the tax revenue is £560 per day.

The effects of an *ad valorem* tax

Figure 5.7 shows the effects of an *ad valorem* tax. Suppose the supply curve for reams of printer paper is as shown by *S* in part (a), and suppose there is initially no tax. Then *S* shows the quantity that sellers will supply at each price that they might receive from buyers. For example, if sellers were to receive a price of £4, they would supply 12 million reams a week, and if they were to receive a price of £6, they would supply 22 million.

Now suppose an *ad valorem* tax like VAT is imposed with a rate of 20%. In this case, if buyers paid a price of £4.80, then sellers could keep £4 for themselves and pay a tax equal to 20% of this £4, which is 80p; by keeping £4, they would be willing to supply 12 million

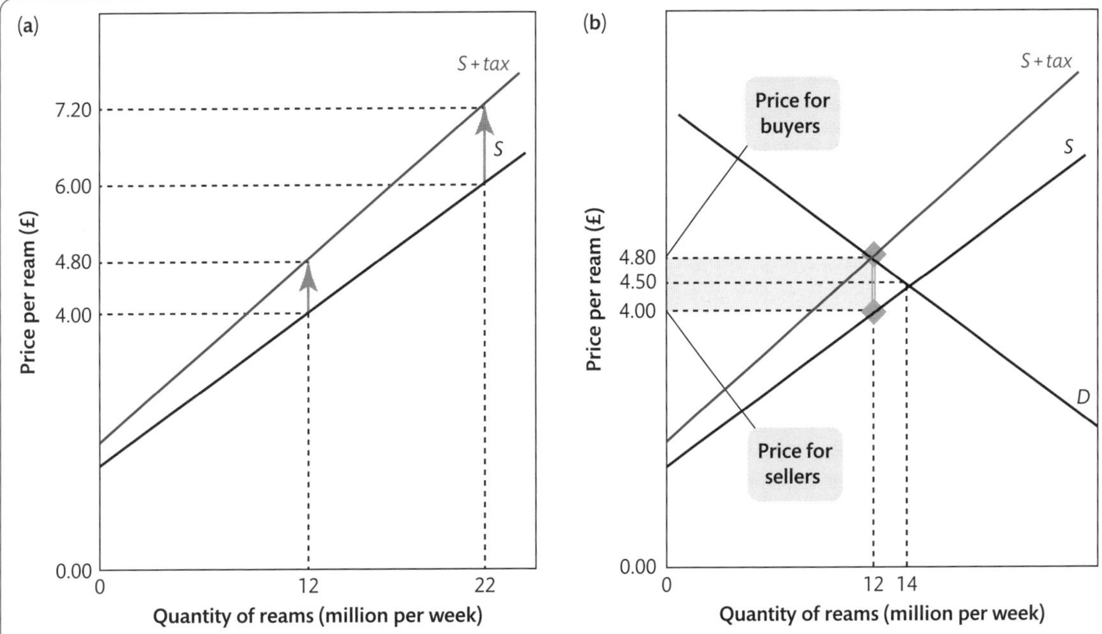

Figure 5.7 **The effects of an *ad valorem* tax**

In part (a), the quantity that sellers will supply at each possible price paid by buyers is shown by *S* if there is no tax, and by *S + tax* if there is a 20% tax. *S + tax* is 20% above *S*, as shown by the arrows, because to supply any quantity, sellers want 20% more than before so that they can keep as much as before. Part (b) adds *D*. With no tax, the price is £4.40 where *S* intersects *D*. With the tax, buyers pay £4.80, and sellers get £4. The tax is 80p per ream, and the tax revenue equals the shaded area.

reams a week. If buyers paid a price of £7.20, then sellers could keep £6 for themselves and pay a tax equal to 20% of this £6, which is £1.20; by keeping £6, they would be willing to supply 22 million reams a week.

In Figure 5.7, the curve *S + tax* shows the quantity that sellers will supply at each possible price paid by buyers when this tax is imposed. It is 20% above *S*, because to supply any particular quantity, like 12 million reams a week, sellers want 20% more from buyers than before. As the tax per ream is bigger at high prices, the gap between *S + tax* and *S* is bigger at high prices, so *S + tax* is not parallel to *S*.

To see the effect of the tax, we add in the demand curve, *D*, as in part (b). Initially, the market settles where *D* intersects *S* at a price of £4.50 and 14 million reams sold each week. When the 20% VAT is imposed, the market settles where *D* intersects *S + tax*, at a price for buyers of £4.80 and 12 million reams sold a week. Although buyers pay £4.80, sellers pay the government 80p in tax and keep just £4 for themselves. We can read this figure of £4 off the graph from the point on *S* below where *S + tax* intersects *D*. The double line shows that the £4 price here is 80p less than the buyer price because the 20% tax creates an 80p gap between *S* and *S + tax*.

The shaded area in Figure 5.6 shows the tax revenue. This area has a length of 12 million reams a week, the quantity now sold each day, and a height of 80p, the tax per unit. So the tax revenue is £9.6 million per week.

In this example, the price paid by buyers rose from £4.50 to £4.80, that is by 30p, while the price received by sellers fell from £4.50 to £4, that is by 50p. So buyers bore just under half the total incidence of 80p while sellers bore just over half.

The incidence on sellers and buyers

In Figure 5.6, the tax incidence was shared equally between buyers and sellers. In Figure 5.7, it fell a little more heavily on sellers than buyers. The division of the incidence between buyers and sellers depends on the slopes of the demand and supply curves. In Figure 5.6, the curves had the same slope and the burden was shared equally. In Figure 5.7, the supply curve was actually a little steeper than the demand curve, and sellers were hit slightly more.

The relationship between the slopes and how the incidence is shared is shown more clearly in the two examples in Figure 5.8. In case (a), the demand curve is much steeper than the supply curve, *S*, while in case (b), the demand curve is flatter than the supply curve. In each case, we assume the following.

- **There is initially no tax**. So the equilibrium is where *D* intersects *S* at a price of £10 a unit and 100 units sold each day.
- **Then a specific tax of £8 per unit is imposed**. This creates a curve *S + tax* that is £8 above *S*, as shown by arrows.
- **The price for buyers ends up where *S + tax* intersects *D***. So in case (a) buyers pay a price of £17 and in case (b) they pay a price of £12.
- **The price received by sellers is below that paid by buyers by the amount of the tax, which is £8**. So sellers receive £9 in case (a) and £4 in case (b). In each case we can read the value from *S*, at the quantity where *S + tax* intersects *D*.

If *D* is steeper than *S*, as in case (a), the incidence falls more on buyers; here, buyers pay £7 more than before while sellers receive only £1 less. If *D* is flatter than *S*, as in case (b), the incidence falls more on sellers; here, buyers pay £2 more than before while sellers receive £6 less. Of course, the exact division of the incidence, and also the final quantity, depend on the exact shape and position of the two curves.

Tax incidence: four extreme cases

There are four extreme cases in which the incidence of a tax falls wholly on buyers or wholly on sellers; they are shown on Figure 5.9. In each case here, the market begins where *D* intersects *S* at a price of £6 and a quantity of 100 per day. Then a specific tax of £4 per unit is imposed, to create a new *S + tax* curve £4 above

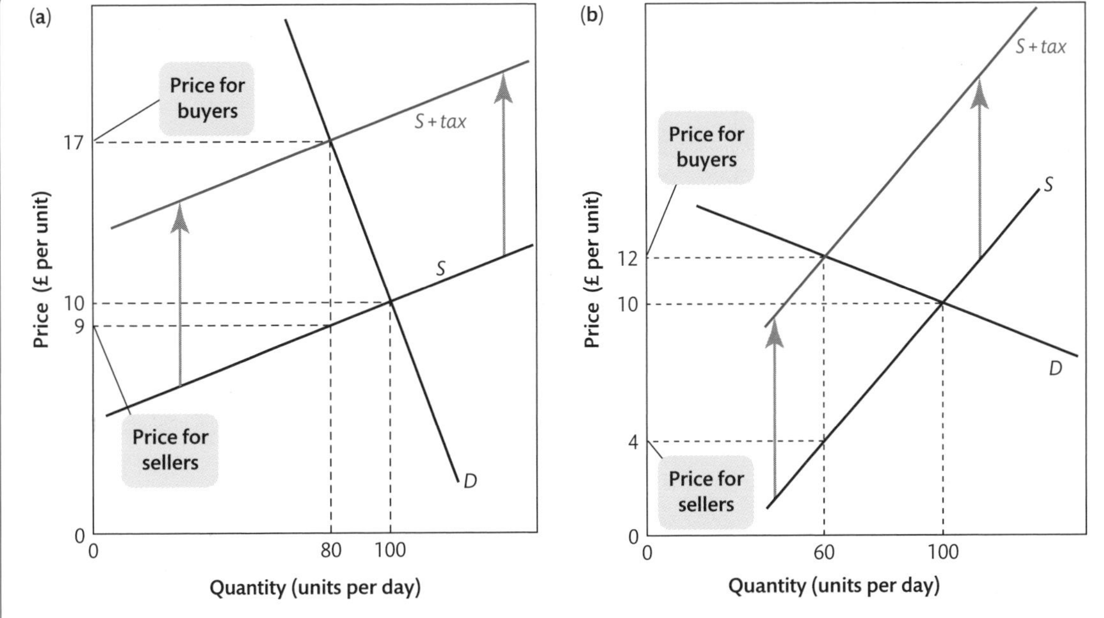

Figure 5.8 **Tax incidence and the slopes of *S* and *D***

In each case, the pre-tax price for buyers is £10, where *S* cuts *D*, and sellers keep all £10. An £8 tax creates the curve *S* + *tax*, £8 above *S*, as shown by arrows. Buyers now pay the price where *S* + *tax* cuts *D*: this is £17 in case (a) and £12 in (b). Sellers now keep £8 less than buyers pay, as shown by the point on *S* below where *S* + *tax* cuts *D*; so they keep £9 in case (a) and £4 in (b). So the tax falls more on buyers than sellers if *D* is steeper than *S*, and vice versa.

S, so the new price for buyers is found where *S* + *tax* intersects *D*. The new price for sellers is £4 less than this. The four cases are as follows.

- **Case (a): demand is perfectly inelastic so that *D* is vertical**. Here, the buyer price rises by the full £4 of the tax, and the seller price remains at £6, so buyers bear the full incidence.
- **Case (b): supply is perfectly elastic, so that *S* is horizontal**. Here, too, the buyer price rises by the full £4 of the tax, and the seller price remains at £6, so buyers bear the full incidence.
- **Case (c): demand is perfectly elastic, so that *D* is horizontal**. Here, the buyer price remains at £6 and the seller price falls by the full £4 of the tax, so sellers bear the full incidence.
- **Case (d): supply is perfectly inelastic, so that *S* is vertical**. It is tricky to draw *S* + *tax* here, because *S* is vertical, so *S* + *tax*, which is vertically above it, overlaps it. However, *S* + *tax* is drawn starting at £4 rather than £0 to show that it is £4 above *S*. Here, the buyer price remains at £6. However, we cannot find the seller price by looking for 'the' point on *S* below the intersection *D* and *S* + *tax* because *S* is vertical, so every point on *S* is below this intersection. We just note that because the buyer price is the same as before, sellers must receive £4 less than before, £2, and we mark in this price for the sellers. As the seller price falls by the full £4 of the tax, sellers bear the full incidence.

Incidence and elasticities

We have seen that the extent to which the incidence of a tax is shared between buyers and sellers depends on the slopes of the demand and supply curves. These slopes are related to the responsiveness of changes in

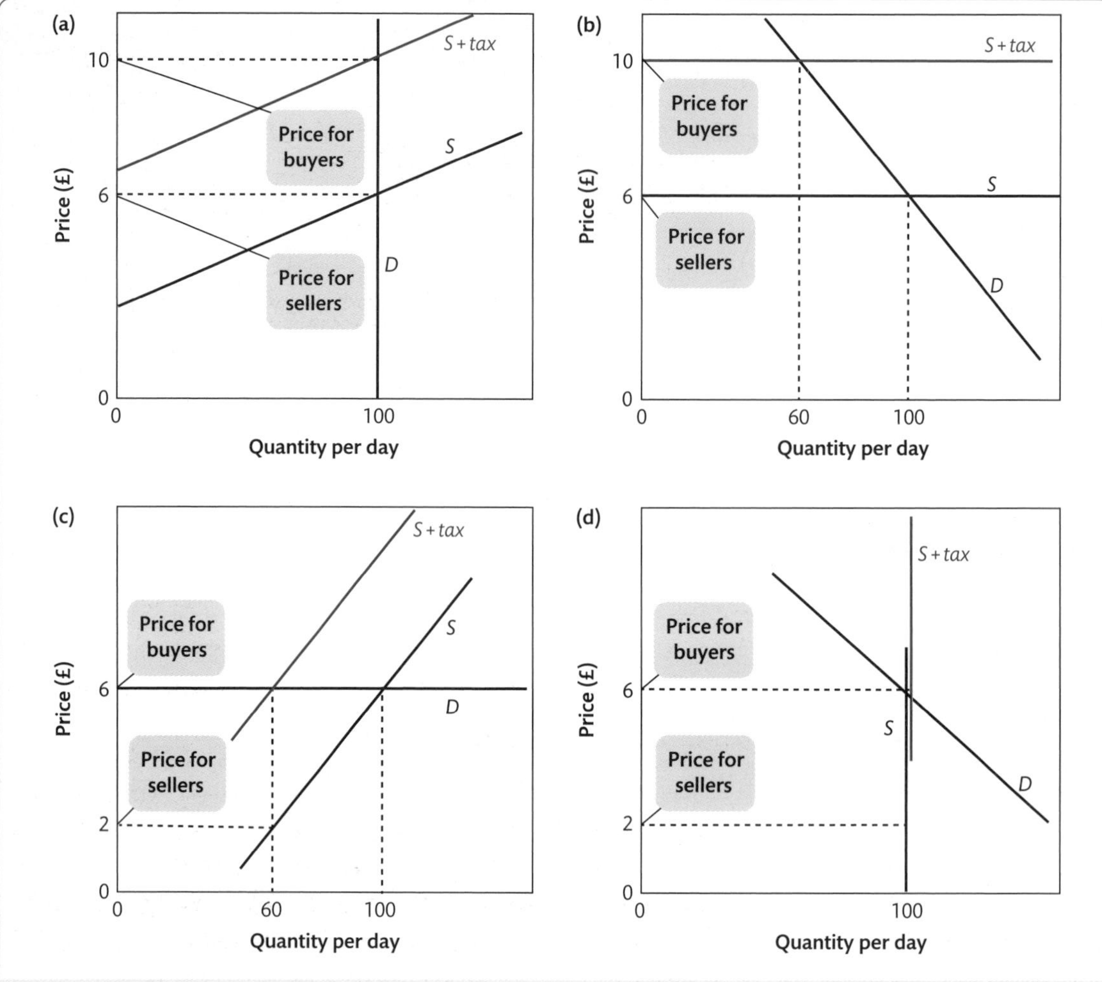

Figure 5.9 **Tax incidence with extreme elasticities**

In each case, the price is initially £6 where *S* cuts *D*. Then a tax of £4 per unit sold is imposed, creating the curve *S* + *tax*, which is £4 above *S*. The final buyer price is where *S* + *tax* cuts *D*, and the final seller price is £4 less. In case (a), demand is perfectly inelastic, and in case (b) supply is perfectly elastic. In these two cases, buyers end up paying £10, £4 more than before, while sellers receive the same price as before. So the incidence of the tax in these two cases falls wholly on buyers. In case (c), demand is perfectly elastic, and in case (d), supply is perfectly inelastic. In these two cases, buyers end up paying £6, the same as before, while sellers receive £4 less than before. So the incidence of the tax in these two cases falls wholly on sellers. Note that, in (d), *S* + *tax* overlaps part of *S*, and the post-tax seller price of £2 is found simply by subtracting the tax of £4 from the post-tax buyer price of £6.

the quantities demanded and supplied to changes in price, so they are related to the price elasticity of demand and the elasticity of supply.

However, there is no simple rule for relating the incidence of a tax to elasticities. For example, if the price elasticities of supply and demand are the same—ignoring the minus sign that we always get in demand elasticities—then the incidence falls more on buyers than on sellers. This is shown by the example in Figure 5.10. Here, the demand curve, *D*, has a *PED* of –1.0 throughout its length because, like the demand curve back in Figure 4.5, it has been carefully drawn so that total spending would be the same at each price, in this case £180 per day. Likewise the supply curve in

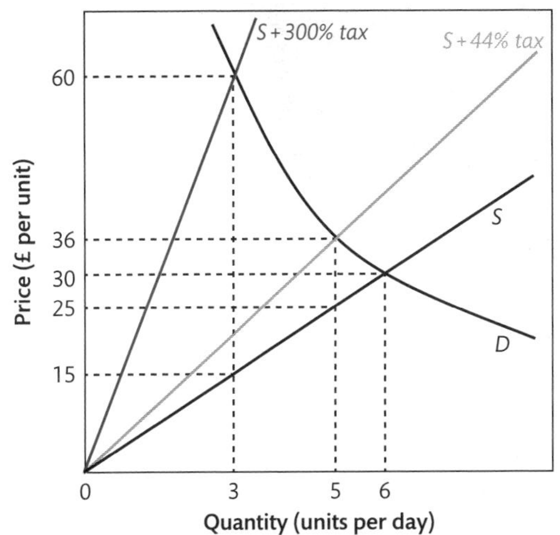

Figure 5.10 **Taxes when supply and demand have equal elasticity, here unity**

If there is no tax, the price is £30 for buyers and sellers. A 44% tax would create the curve *S + 44% tax*, raising the buyer price by £6 to £36, while reducing the seller price by £5 to £25. A 300% tax would create the curve *S + 300% tax*, raising the buyer price by £30 to £60, while reducing the seller price by £15 to £15.

Figure 5.10, *S*, has a *PES* of 1.0 throughout its length because, like the both supply curves back in Figure 4.10, it is a straight line through the origin.

In Figure 5.10, the intersection of *S* and *D* shows that if there is initially no tax, then the price for both buyers and sellers will be £30. If a 44% *ad valorem* tax is imposed, then the curve *S + 44% tax* shows that the buyer price will rise by £6 to £36 while the seller price will fall by slightly less, £5, to £25. If there were instead a 300% *ad valorem* tax, then the curve *S + 300% tax* shows that the buyer price would rise by £30 to £60, while the seller price would fall by much less, £15, to £15.

Generally, though, if in the pre-tax position demand is inelastic and supply is elastic, then the demand curve is steeper than the supply curve and the incidence falls chiefly on buyers. And if demand is elastic and supply is inelastic, then the demand curve is flatter than the supply curve, and the incidence falls chiefly on sellers.

Question 5.1 In Table 4.3 we saw that the demand for beer is price inelastic. Because beer uses readily available inputs, its supply is likely to be fairly elastic. So will the 40p excise duty on a pint raise the price to buyers by 40p? If not, will it have more effect on the buyers' price or the sellers' price?

5.2 Everyday economics

A tax on expenditure that saves lives

In 1999, the World Health Organization issued a Factsheet entitled *Tobacco – Health Facts*, which estimated that by 2030 some 10 million people a year would die from tobacco smoking.

Tobacco - Health Facts: Factsheet No 221, World Health Organization, April 1999

Comment Every 1% increase in the price of tobacco caused through higher taxes would reduce smoking and so save many thousands of lives. The people most likely to benefit would be young people, because for older people a reduction in smoking may already be too late.

5.4 Summary

- Taxes on expenditure create a curve, *S + tax* that is above the original supply curve, *S*. The gap between *S* and *S + tax* equals the amount of the tax. The point at which *S + tax* intersects *D* gives the new price for buyers and the new quantity traded. The point on *S* below this intersection gives the new price for sellers.
- The new buyer price is usually above the initial price, but the buyer price rises by the full amount of the tax only in exceptional cases. Sellers keep a price equal to the new buyer price minus the tax.
- The incidence of a tax falls more heavily on buyers than sellers if the demand curve is steeper than the supply curve, and more on sellers than buyers if the supply curve is steeper than the demand curve.

5.5 The EU's Common Agricultural Policy (CAP)

Although people often talk about 'the' Common Agricultural Policy (CAP), the European Union (EU) has never had just one policy. It has used slightly different policies for different foodstuffs, and these policies have changed as time has passed by. However, the EU's policies have mostly hinged around a simple core principle, and this section focuses on that principle. This principle has not been affected by the changing number of EU members, or by the general rise in prices over the years, so we will keep the analysis simple by ignoring those factors.

The core CAP principle

Figure 5.11 shows the EU market for one foodstuff, butter. The figure concerns the butter market in the year 1960, in the early days of the EU. S_{60} was the supply curve for farmers in the EU, and *D* was the demand curve by EU consumers. If the market had been free, with no intervention, you might suppose that it would have settled with price P^* where the curves intersect, but it wouldn't. This is because farmers in the rest of the world, that is outside the EU, had low costs, and could supply butter at price, P_R, well below P^*.

If the EU had not intervened, EU consumers would have refused to pay more than P_R, and at that price they would have bought Q_D. EU producers would have been unable to sell anything at a price above P_R, and S_{60} shows that, at that price, they would have supplied Q_A. The gap between Q_D and Q_A would have been bridged by imports, shown by the long double line. The income of EU farmers from butter would have been as shown by the grey rectangle: its length is the quantity of butter they would have produced, Q_A, and its height is the price for which they would have sold it, P_R.

However, the EU members did not want the market to settle here for two main reasons.

- **They did not want such large imports for food.** They had relied greatly on food imports from outside Europe before World War II and suffered when imports were reduced by shipping losses.
- **The incomes that would arise in a free market would have left farm workers on low wages.** About 18% of EU workers worked in agriculture.

In response, to fix these concerns, the CAP put a tax on food imported from the rest of the world. A tax on imports is called a **tariff**. So anyone buying butter from outside the EU had to pay a price of P_R *plus* the tariff, *T*, that is $P_R + T$, and Figure 5.11 shows the effects.

It was now impossible to buy non-EU butter at a price below $P_R + T$. This means EU farmers could charge this price for their own butter because it was

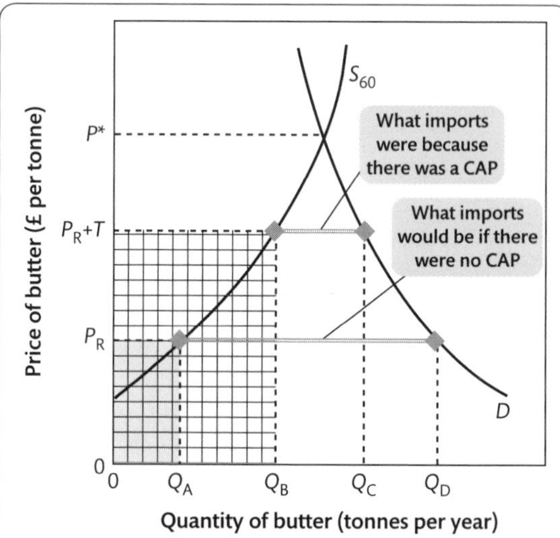

Figure 5.11 **The core principle of CAP**

D is the demand by EU consumers. S_{60} is the 1960 supply by EU farmers. If the market were free, the price would *not* have been P^*, where *D* cuts S_0, because farmers in the rest of the world could supply butter at P_R. So EU consumers would have bought Q_D, EU farmers would have supplied Q_A, imports would have been ($Q_D - Q_A$), and EU farm incomes would have equalled the grey rectangle. In fact, the CAP put a tariff, *T*, on imports, so they sold butter in the EU for $P_R + T$. So EU consumers bought Q_C, EU farmers supplied Q_B, imports were ($Q_C - Q_B$), and EU farm incomes equalled the black grid.

not subject to the tariff. At this price, EU farmers supplied Q_B and EU consumers bought Q_C. The gap between Q_C and Q_B was bridged by imports, shown by the short double line. The black grid shows the income of EU farmers from butter. Its length is their new output, Q_B, and its height is the new price for which their butter sells, $P_R + T$.

Although this core principle reduced imports and raised farm incomes, it had several drawbacks, including the following.

- **It raised food prices for EU consumers.**
- **It reduced sales of food to the EU by farmers in the rest of the world, who are often poor.**
- **It redistributed income within the EU to countries with the largest agricultural sectors.** To see this, suppose there were only two EU countries, one with no farmers and one with many. Consumers in both countries would lose by paying higher prices for butter, but the only people who would be financially better off would be the farmers in the second country. So, overall, the first country would be worse off, while the second country would be better off. The UK loses a lot here, because only 2% of its workers are in agriculture; in contrast, Poland gains a lot, because 18% of its workers are in agriculture.

The biggest drawback of the CAP

However, the biggest drawback of the CAP was that it generally promised farmers that they could sell as much as they wished to supply at $P_R + T$. This wasn't a problem in 1960, but it became a growing problem from the 1970s onwards. The reason is that, over time, the costs of supplying food in the EU fell, so that the supply curve of EU farmers shifted to the right. Costs fell for many reasons. For example, new machinery was invented, improved fertilizers were developed, and more productive animals were created by selective breeding.

Figure 5.12 repeats S_{60} and D from Figure 5.11, and it adds the EU's 1990 supply curve, S_{90}. The EU told its farmers that they could sell as much butter as they wanted at $P_R + T$, and in 1990 this amount was Q_E. So EU output rose from Q_B to Q_E, and the income of EU farmers from butter rose by the area of the pink grid. But EU consumers still wanted to buy only Q_C. So the EU itself had to buy the surplus output between Q_E and Q_C, as shown by the double line. This food was initially stored in 'food mountains' and then often sold later to the rest of the world. But it had to be sold there at the price that applied in the rest of the world, P_R. So the CAP became very expensive, because the EU bought some food at $P_R + T$ and sold it at P_R.

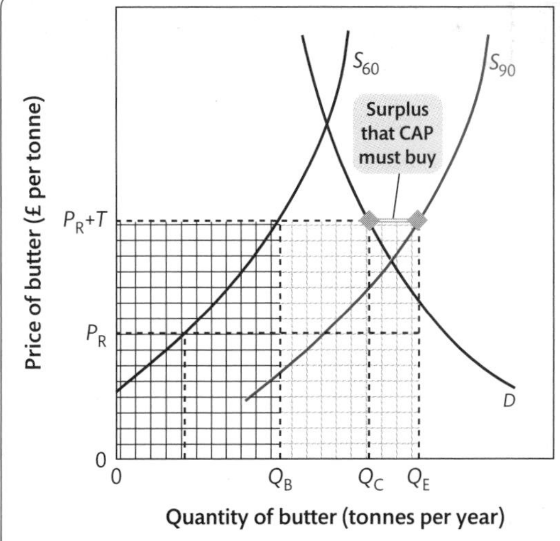

Figure 5.12 **CAP and the problem of surpluses**

By 1990, supply by EU farmers rose to S_{90}. At $P_R + T$, they wanted to sell Q_E and the CAP guaranteed that they could. But EU consumers wanted to buy only Q_C. So the EU itself had to buy the surplus output ($Q_E - Q_C$) at $P_R + T$. It could sell this to the rest of the world for the lower price P_R. EU farm incomes now equal the black grid plus the pink grid.

The big issue for the CAP for the last 30 or so years has been trying to reduce this problem of surpluses. Various ideas have been used. For example, farmers have been given output limits or quotas for some products. Also, they have been required to leave some arable land idle under a set-aside policy, albeit being given financial compensation for the lost output. In addition, farmers have been given financial incentives to use less-intensive farming methods.

Another strategy has been to reduce the tariffs. When T falls, $P_R + T$ falls, so EU farmers want to supply less and EU consumers want to buy more. This reduces the surpluses. However, the EU agricultural lobby dislikes cuts in T, because if $P_R + T$ falls and, in turn, EU output falls, then EU farm incomes will be much reduced. To soften the fall in EU farm incomes, tariff cuts have been coupled with many direct payments to farmers, to prevent their incomes falling far.

These various policies have led to substantial aid being paid to farmers under various schemes. Since 2003, individual EU members have decided how to allocate these payments to their own farmers. Different members use different methods. For example, the UK's payments encourage environmental improvements. A key theme of the current arrangements is to ensure that no individual farm would receive a higher payment if its output were to increase. This ensures that the payments do not encourage a higher output. Breaking any link between financial aid and output is called 'decoupling'.

Question 5.2 In Figure 5.12, the grids suggest that farm incomes roughly doubled between 1960 and 1990. Why might this underestimate the extent to which the incomes of people supplying butter rose?

5.5 Summary

- The CAP has placed many tariffs on food imports into the EU from the rest of the world.
- The chief aims of the CAP are to raise the income of EU farmers and to reduce EU dependence on food imports.
- The CAP has often guaranteed high prices for EU farmers, and so caused them to supply more than EU consumers want to buy. To reduce these surpluses, the EU has used a variety of policies, including reducing some tariffs.

5.6 Government regulation, prohibition, and supply

This final section briefly mentions three more ways in which governments can intervene in markets.

Government regulation

One type of intervention is the use of regulation or legislation. For example, governments may impose high hygiene standards on restaurants, or high safety standards on factories. These policies raise production costs, so production becomes less profitable. In turn, supply curves shift to the left, so the prices rise and the quantities traded fall.

Government prohibition

An extreme form of regulation is **prohibition** under which trading a product is made illegal. Consider cocaine. In Figure 5.13, D_F and S_F show the demand and supply curves that would arise in a free market. The market would settle where D_F and S_F intersect, with a price of P_F per kilogram and a quantity of Q_F kilograms per day. Now suppose that the government makes trading in cocaine illegal. If everyone were law-abiding, then no producers would supply it, and no consumers would buy it, so this market would disappear.

In practice, the prohibition reduces both supply and demand, but they do not vanish, and the market operates underground, or illegally. Let's suppose that supply is greatly affected and shifts to S_P, far to the left of S_F. And let's suppose demand is less affected, and shifts to D_P, which is not as far to the left of D_F. Then the price rises well above the free market price to P_P, and the quantity falls below the free market quantity to Q_P.

An alternative way of raising the price and reducing the quantity would be to tax cocaine, just like the products in Figures 5.6 and 5.7 were taxed. A tax has

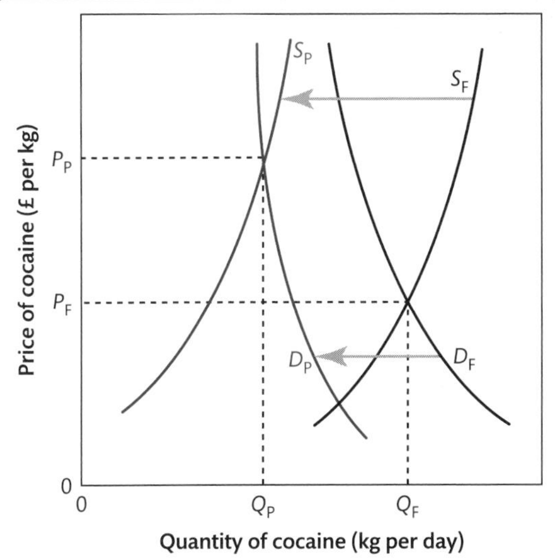

Figure 5.13 **A possible effect of prohibition**

If cocaine were legal, with a free market, the market would settle where D_F intersects S_F, with price P_F and quantity Q_F. In practice, prohibition reduces both supply and demand to S_P and D_P. In this figure, prohibition restricts supply more than demand, so it leads to a price way above P_F at P_P.

the advantages over prohibition of raising revenue for the government and of not criminalizing buyers and sellers. However, the government believes that prohibition sends a signal that cocaine is unacceptable rather than undesirable. Also, it would need a very high tax to reduce output as much as occurs with prohibition. And with a high tax, the market might still go underground as buyers and sellers seek to avoid the incidence of this high tax.

Government supply

While governments may prohibit products that they believe are undesirable, they also provide some products that they believe are desirable, and this affects the market for those products.

Suppose that, at present, a country has no hospitals provided by the government out of tax revenue. So all hospitals are privately owned, and they charge fees, which patients have to pay. Suppose the supply and demand for nights in these private hospitals are as shown by D_0 and S in Figure 5.14. Then the market will settle with Q_0 nights a year taken by patients, at a price of P_0 per night.

Now suppose the government builds its own hospitals where patients can stay at no charge, the costs being met out of taxes. Then the demand for nights in the fee-charging private hospitals will plummet. In principle, this demand might wholly disappear, but in practice some patients may still prefer private hospitals on account of comfort or convenience. Suppose the demand curve shifts sharply to the left to D_1. Then the number of nights spent in private hospitals will fall greatly to Q_1, and the price will fall to P_1. So the market for these hospitals is much affected.

Similar effects occur in any markets in which governments produce substitute goods or services at a zero price. For example, the introduction of tax-financed schools in 19th-century Britain greatly reduced the number of places that parents were willing to pay for at private schools.

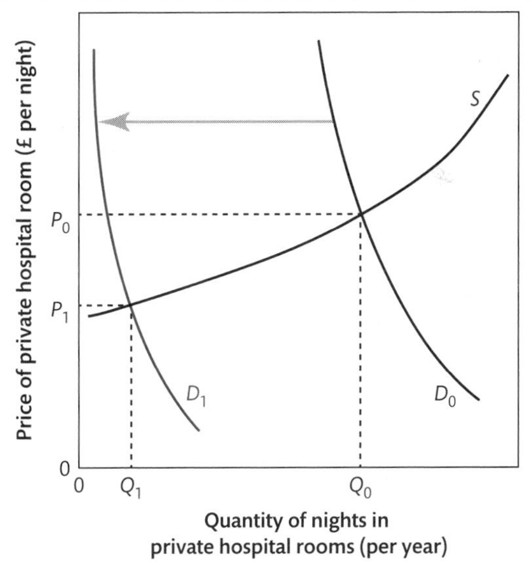

Figure 5.14 **The effects of a tax-financed service**

If there were no government hospitals, the demand for private hospitals would be D_0, so patients would spend Q_0 nights a year in them at a price P_0. The existence of government hospitals with no fees cuts the demand for private hospitals to D_1, so the quantity is Q_1 and the price is P_1.

5.3 Everyday economics

Cannabis: a UK growth industry

The criminalization of cannabis production drives production underground. A 2007 DrugScope press release entitled 'DrugScope reveals child victims of UK cannabis farm boom' suggests that over two-thirds of the farms that are discovered by the police and shut down are operated by criminal Vietnamese gangs, whose labour often includes people illegally trafficked from Vietnam, including some children as young as 14. In spite of police raids on the farms, it is generally believed that UK production has grown in recent years, although this has certainly not led to any fall in the price. Possibly the supply from abroad has diminished, or demand has risen, or both.

'DrugScope reveals child victims of UK cannabis farm boom', *DrugScope*, 6 September 2007

5.6 Summary

- Governments intervene in some markets with regulations. If these raise costs, then prices will rise.
- Governments intervene in some markets with prohibition. This may lead to illegal underground markets, in which, if prohibition reduces supply more than demand, prices will be higher than in a free market.
- Governments intervene in some markets by providing the product themselves. If their product is supplied at no charge to the consumer, the private market for the product may largely disappear.

In the next chapter we look more closely at household demand curves. We then have several chapters in which we look more closely at producer supply.

abc Glossary

***Ad valorem* tax:** a tax on a product for which the tax paid depends on the price at which it is sold.

Black market: a market in which legal limits on quantities or prices are ignored.

Consumer surplus: the gap between the price a buyer would be willing to pay, that is the value to the buyer, and the price the buyer does pay.

Incidence: with a tax on expenditure, the changes in the buyer and seller prices that it causes.

Minimum wage: a legal minimum wage that can be paid in a labour market.

Price ceiling: a legal maximum price that can be set in a given market.

Price floor: a legal minimum price that can be set in a given market.

Producer surplus: the gap between the price that a seller would be willing to accept, that is the cost to the seller, and the price the seller actually receives.

Prohibition: making the trade in a product illegal.

Quota: a legal limit to the amount that a supplier can supply.

Specific tax: a tax on a product for which the tax paid depends on the quantity sold.

Tariff: a tax on imports.

Tax on expenditure: a tax levied on an individual product.

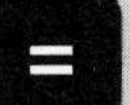

Answers to in-text questions

5.1 The situation will be similar to case (a) in Figure 5.8. The buyer price will not rise by the full 40p, but it will rise by far more than the seller price falls.

5.2 One of the reasons why supply has increased in agriculture is that labour has become more productive. So, even if output and incomes roughly doubled, the number of people involved in production probably fell. So incomes per worker in the industry probably more than doubled. However, incomes in other industries also increased, so the relative incomes of butter suppliers may not have increased in relation to average wages.

? Questions for review

5.1 Suppose the government wishes the price of a given product to rise above the free market price. List the policies covered in this chapter that it could use.

5.2 Suppose the government wants to have some specific taxes, and it wants their incidence to fall more heavily on buyers than sellers. What can be said about the demand and supply curves of the products it should choose?

5.3 Suppose that quantities demanded and supplied for a give product at various prices are as shown in the table below.

(a) Draw the supply and demand curves. What are the free market equilibrium price and quantity?

(b) Suppose a specific tax of 4 per unit is imposed. Draw the appropriate *S + tax* curve. What will the buyer price, the quantity traded, and the seller price be?

(c) Suppose instead an *ad valorem tax* of 50% is imposed. Draw the appropriate *S + tax* curve. What will the buyer price, the quantity traded, and the seller price be?

Price	0	1	2	3	4	5	6	7	8	9
Q_D	90	80	70	60	50	40	30	20	10	0
Q_S	0	0	10	20	30	40	50	60	70	80

? Questions for discussion

5.1 Return to question 5.1 for review. What are the relative advantages and disadvantages of the different possible policies?

5.2 Return to question 5.2 for review. The main specific taxes in the UK fall on alcohol, motor fuel, and tobacco. Would you expect their incidence to fall more on consumers or producers?

5.3 If the EU were to abandon the CAP and have a free market for all foodstuffs, who inside the EU would gain and who would lose? Who outside it would gain and who would lose?

Common student errors

In spite of the analysis in section 5.4, many students instinctively feel that a tax of, say, 30p must raise the price paid by buyers by 30p. So, asked to illustrate the effects of a 30p tax, many students simply draw *S + tax* in the position needed to get it to intersect *D* at a price that is 30p above the initial price. It is important to see that a 30p tax creates an *S + tax* curve that is *exactly* 30p above *S*, as shown in part (a) of Figure 5.6. Once the *S + tax* curve is correctly drawn, it is easy to show that the price paid by buyers is likely to rise by less than 30p, as shown in part (b) of Figure 5.6. The only cases in which the price paid by buyers will rise by the full amount of the tax are when demand is perfectly inelastic or supply is perfectly elastic, as shown in the extreme cases (a) and (b) of Figure 5.9.

Many students also feel uncomfortable about finding the new price that is received by sellers. This should be found by looking at the point on *S* below the point at which *D* intersects *S + tax*. This discomfort may arise because, at this point on *S*, *S* does not intersect any other curve. But in spite of the absence of an intersection, this point *does* show the price kept by sellers.

6

Household Behaviour

Remember from Chapter 3 that the price and quantity traded in a market for a consumer product change when the demand curve by households for that product shifts. Remember, also, that the wage and quantity of work done in a labour market change when the supply curve by households for that type of labour shifts.

You consume many different products. How do you decide what quantity of each to buy? Might you benefit if you bought different quantities? If you have a job, how do you choose how many hours to work each week? How might your choice change if your wage rate increased, or if income tax rates were to rise?

This chapter shows you how to answer questions like these, by understanding:

* how consumers make their purchasing decisions;
* how these purchasing decisions are affected by changes in prices and incomes;
* how workers decide on their hours of work;
* how these work decisions are affected by income tax.

6.1 Individual and market demand curves for products

In Chapter 3, we saw how, in many markets, the price and quantity traded are determined by the forces of supply and demand. We also saw that if the demand curve or the supply curve shifts, then the price and quantity change. So to understand these markets fully, we need to explain why supply and demand curves may shift.

This chapter looks at the demand curves by households for final products and at the supply curves by households of labour. Later chapters look at the supply curves by firms of their outputs and at the demand curves by firms for their inputs.

We begin with household demand curves for final products. The market demand curve for any final product shows the total quantity that households would demand at each possible price. For example, part (c) of Figure 6.1 repeats as D_{MARKET} the market demand curve for free-range eggs that we used in Chapter 3; it shows that households would demand 15 million eggs a day at a price of 30p, and 10 million at a price of 50p.

Of course, all households make different decisions, and Figure 6.1 explains how all the varied individual households are linked to the market. Parts (a) and (b) show as D_A and D_B the demand curves for eggs by two households, called A and B. If the price were, say, 30p, then A would demand five eggs a day and B four. These households would make different choices at other prices. For example, if the price were 50p, A would demand two eggs a day and B three.

The market demand curve, D_{MARKET}, includes this information about households A and B, and it includes similar information about all other households. So at a price of 30p, the figure of 15 million means that if we add up the five eggs that A would demand, the four B would demand, and how many all other households would demand, then the total would be 15 million a day. D_{MARKET} also shows that, at a price of 50p, the total quantity demanded would be 10 million a day.

As D_{MARKET} includes the demand of every household that buys eggs, it will shift if the number of these households changes. It will also shift if individual households change their behaviour so that their own demand curves shift. For example, suppose household A now decides to buy twice as many eggs at each possible price. Then D_A will shift to the right, and

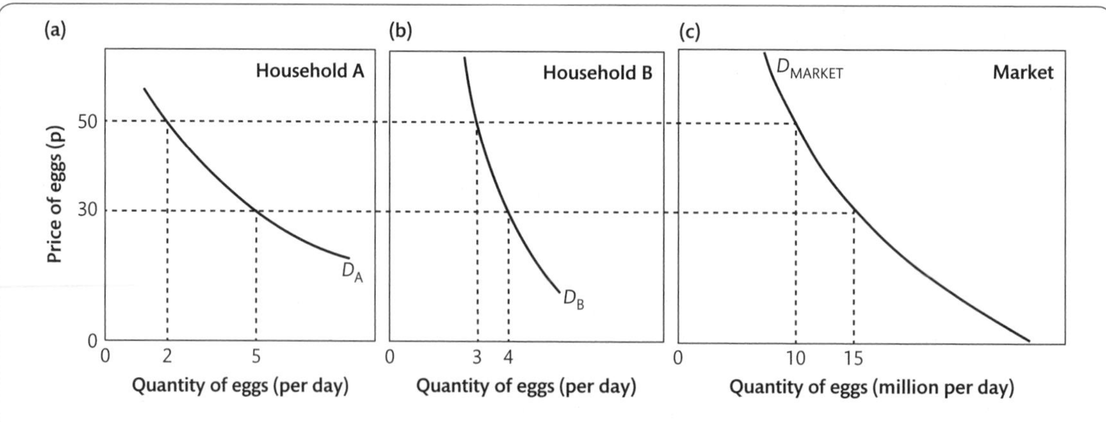

Figure 6.1 **Individual demand curves and a market demand curve**

Parts (a) and (b) give the demand curves for eggs of two individual households, A and B. At a price of 30p, for example, A would demand 5 eggs a day and B would demand 4. Part (c) gives the market demand curve. This shows how many eggs all households between them would demand at each price. At 30p, it includes the 5 demanded by A, the 4 demanded by B, and those demanded by all other households; the total is 15 million.

D_{MARKET} will also shift to the right because 15,000,005 eggs would now be demanded at 30p, and 10,000,002 at 50p.

It follows from this discussion that, to understand fully why market demand curves for final products may shift, we need to understand why the behaviour of households as consumers may change. The following three sections develop a model that explains why this behaviour may change.

6.1 **Summary**

- The market demand curve for a final product represents the individual demand curves of all households added together. To understand why a market demand curve may shift, we need to understand how individual households behave as consumers and why their individual demand curves may shift.

6.2 Utility

We will now study the behaviour of households as consumers, by using as an example the demand curve for visits to a club by a student, Tom. We will consider how many evenings a month Tom will go to the club at various possible entry prices.

The more often Tom goes to the club, the less money he has for other items. So when he chooses how often to go, he is also choosing how many other products he can afford. We will assume that he makes the choices which give him the most total satisfaction that he could possibly get from his income. Economists use the word **utility** instead of satisfaction, and they call a person who makes the choices that lead to the maximum possible utility a **rational consumer**.

To make his choices, Tom must consider how much utility he would get from varying numbers of visits to the club and varying amounts of other products. Utility cannot be accurately measured, but economists can reach some important conclusions by assuming that it can be measured. We assume that it can be measured in units called **utils**. For each possible number of visits that Tom might make to the club each month, the second column of Table 6.1 shows the total number of utils, or **total utility** (*TU*), that he would get from these visits. For example, if he went twice a month, then his visits to the club would give him a total of 275 utils a month. The more often he goes, the more *TU* he will get from his visits.

Marginal utility

The third column in Table 6.1 is headed *MU*: this stands for **marginal utility**, which shows how much a consumer's *TU* per period of time from consuming a product would change if consumption in that period were to change by one unit. For example, if Tom changes from no club visits a month to one, his *TU* per month

Table 6.1 **A consumer's total and marginal utilty from club visits and train trips home**

Club visits per month			Home visits per month		
Quantity	*TU*	*MU*	Quantity	*TU*	*MU*
0	0		0	0	
		154			140
1	154		1	140	
		121			113
2	275		2	253	
		92			92
3	367		3	345	
		67			73
4	434		4	418	
		46			57
5	480		5	475	
		29			44
6	509		6	519	
		16			34
7	525		7	553	
		7			27
8	532		8	580	
		2			23
9	534		9	603	
		1			22
10	535		10	625	

from club visits will rise by 154 utils from 0 to 154, giving a *MU* of 154. If he later changes from one visit a month to two, his *TU* from visits will rise by 121 utils from 154 to 275, giving a *MU* of 121. The *MU* column prints the 154 on a level between the lines for no visits and one visit, and the 121 on a level between the lines for one visit and two, because these figures show what happens if the number of visits changes from zero to one, and from one to two. The other *MU* figures are found and printed in a similar way.

The table shows that Tom's *MU* falls as the number of club visits rises. This does *not* mean that he gets 154 utils from the first club visit each month, 121 from the second, 92 from the third, and so on. If he goes three times each month, why should he enjoy the first visit any more than the second or third? Indeed, if he goes three times a month to get 367 utils a month, we would expect each visit to create a third of the 367, that is about 122.

What the decreasing *MU does* mean is that if Tom increases the number of visits a month from, say, two to three, then his *TU* per month will rise by less than the 121 utils that arose when he increased the number from one to two. It will actually rise by 92. And if he later increases visits from three to four, then his *TU* will rise by even less than 92 utils. It will rise by 67.

Economists assume that the *MU* falls for all consumers for all products. This is called the principle of **diminishing marginal utility**. Because we can't measure utility, we can't prove that this assumption is correct, but households do behave in ways consistent with this.

The rate at which *MU* falls for any product varies between households. Also, the rate at which *MU* falls for a given household varies between the different products it buys. Table 6.1 shows this by looking also at another product consumed by Tom, namely return train tickets to make visits to his family home. Again, his *TU* rises with the number of visits, while his *MU* diminishes with increasing numbers of visits. But his *MU* here diminishes less rapidly than his *MU* for club visits.

Marginal utility and rational consumers

Let's briefly take another student, Liz. Among the products that Liz consumes are electricity and telephone calls. Suppose for simplicity that the price of electricity, P_E, is 12p a unit and the price of phone calls, P_T, is 12p a minute.

Suppose Liz reckons that her marginal utilities from these two products are as follows.

- **Electricity**: if she consumed one more or less unit a day, her total utility from electricity would change by about 8 utils, so her marginal utility from electricity, MU_E, is about 8 utils.
- **Telephone calls**: if she rang for one more or less minute a day, her total utility from calls would change by about 4 utils, so her marginal utility from telephone calls, MU_T, is about 4 utils.

If Liz reckons this, then she is not a rational consumer! This is because she is not getting the maximum possible utility from her income. She could get more utility by spending one less minute on the phone each day, so losing 4 utils, and spending the 12p saved to buy one more unit of electricity, so gaining 8 utils.

Now suppose Liz buys more electricity and makes fewer calls. Then her MU_E will fall, just as Tom's *MU* for either product in Table 6.1 would fall if he consumed more; and her MU_T will rise, just as Tom's *MU* for either product would rise if he consumed less. Suppose her MU_E falls to 6 utils and her MU_T rises to 6 utils. Now she *is* a rational consumer, because she cannot now change her pattern of consumption to get more utility overall. For example, if she now buys one unit less of either product, then she will save 12p and lose 6 utils, but she could buy only one more unit of the other product and gain 6 utils from it.

Liz became rational when the *MU* of each product was the same. But rationality requires equal *MU*s only in the simple case in which the prices are the same. More generally, maximizing utility requires consumers to adjust their consumption of all products so that each has the same *MU/P*. To begin with, Liz's MU_E/P_E was $8/12 = 0.67$, while her MU_T/P_T was $4/12 = 0.33$. Later, her MU_E/P_E was $6/12 = 0.50$ and her MU_T/P_T was also $6/12 = 0.50$.

Like Liz, all rational consumers will maximize their total utility only if they adjust their consumption of all products so that they end up with the same *MU/P* for each product. If your *MU/P* varies between products, then you are irrational: you could get more total utility if you consume more of those products for which your *MU* is relatively high in relation to its price, and less of those for which your *MU* is relatively low in relation to its price.

Question 6.1 In his 1776 book *The Wealth of Nations*, the economist Adam Smith wondered why water, which is essential and so has a high total utility, has a much lower price than diamonds, which we can well live without. What do these prices tell us about the relative *MU*s of water and diamonds?

6.2 **Summary**

- Utility is a term used to describe satisfaction. Every time a consumer consumes more of a product in a period of time, the consumer's total utility (*TU*) from the product rises. However, the extra–or marginal–utility (*MU*), which the consumer gets by consuming more, diminishes with each extra unit.
- A rational consumer maximizes total utility. The consumer can do this by adjusting the consumption of all products until the consumer finds that the *MU/P* is the same for each product.

6.3 Illustrating preferences with indifference curves

We have seen that a rational consumer adjusts the quantities of all the products consumed until the consumer's *MU/P* for each is the same. To relate this insight to the factors that affect individuals' demand curves, we will now build up a diagram for a consumer. To keep the diagram simple, we will suppose that the consumer buys only two products. We will return to Tom, and suppose that the only two products he buys are club visits and train tickets for home visits. We will also suppose that Tom has an income of £60 a month to divide between these two products.

How Tom allocates this £60 depends in part on the price of each item, P_C for club visits and P_H for home visits. It also depends on the utility he gets from each, that is on his preferences or tastes. Figure 6.2 illustrates his preferences. This figure measures the quantity of his club visits per month, Q_C, on the horizontal axis and the quantity of his home visits per month, Q_H, on the vertical axis.

Figure 6.2 has three curves labelled *IC*′, *IC*″, and *IC*‴. To understand these curves, consider three points on *IC*′ and the total utility they would bring.

- **Two club visits and three home visits**. Table 6.1 shows this would give Tom 275 + 345 = 620 utils.
- **Three club visits and two home visits**. Table 6.1 shows this would give Tom 367 + 253 = 620 utils.
- **Five club visits and one home visit**. Table 6.1 shows this would give Tom 480 + 120 = 620 utils.

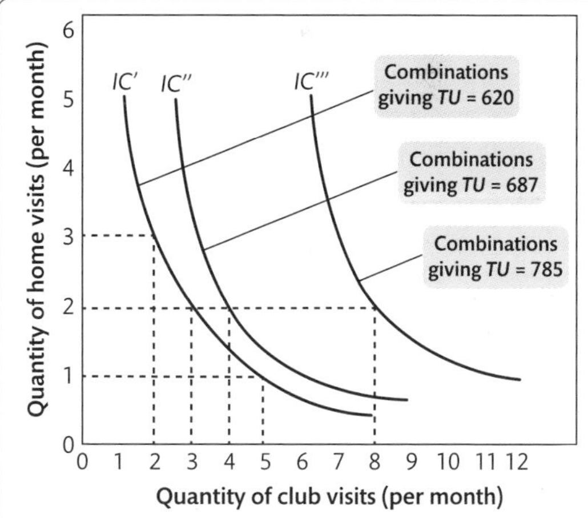

Figure 6.2 **Indifference curves**

On any individual indifference curve, such as *IC*′, all the combinations of home and club visits that the curve passes through give the consumer the same total utility. However, the combinations on *IC*′ give less total utility than those on *IC*″, which is further from the origin, and these give less total utility than those on *IC*‴, which is still further from the origin.

In fact, all the combinations of the two products that lie on *IC′* would give Tom a total utility of 620 utils, so Tom would be indifferent between these combinations. A curve like this, which shows combinations of items between which a consumer is indifferent, is called an **indifference curve**.

The slope of an indifference curve

IC′ slopes down all the way from left to right. This is because we assume that Tom likes both items. So if he makes fewer home visits, say two rather than three, then his utility from them falls. To keep his overall utility at 620, he needs more utility from club visits, and this means making more visits to the club. So every time the quantity of the product on the vertical axis falls, the quantity on the horizontal axis must rise.

IC′ also gets flatter to the right. This arises from diminishing *marginal utility*. To see why, suppose Tom initially makes three home visits and two club visits a month to get 620 utils a month. Then he progressively makes fewer home visits, as follows.

- **He cuts home visits by one from three to two**. This reduces his *TU* by 92 utils. He can offset this with one more club visit, three instead of two, as that will raise his *TU* by 92 utils.
- **He cuts home visits by one from two to one**. Because *MU* falls when consumption rises, it rises when consumption falls, so this cut reduces his *TU* by more than 92 utils—in fact by 113. Also, because *MU* falls when consumption rises, one more club visit would raise his *TU* by less than 92 utils. So offsetting this fall in home visits requires more than one extra club visit, so *IC′* is flatter along this stretch than it is between three home visits and two home visits.

Indifference maps

IC′ shows combinations that give Tom 620 utils. We could add more curves to show combinations that give other levels of overall utility. A figure with more than one indifference curve is called an **indifference map**. For simplicity, indifference maps are usually drawn with only two or three curves, and Figure 6.2 has just three. *IC″* passes the point for four club visits and two home visits. Table 6.1 shows that this gives a *TU* of $434 + 253 = 687$ utils, so all the other combinations on *IC″* must do the same. *IC‴* passes the point for eight club visits and two home visits. Table 6.1 shows that this gives a *TU* of $532 + 253 = 785$ utils, so all the other combinations on *IC‴* must do the same. Notice that the further an indifference curve is from the origin, the more *TU* it represents.

Three features of indifference curves

We will now note three features of indifference curves. These are illustrated in Figure 6.3.

- **Indifference curves cannot intersect if both products are desirable**. To see why, look at part (a) of Figure 6.3, and suppose that Tom had the two intersecting indifference curves shown there. *IC′* tells us that he gets the same utility from the combination of visits shown at point ***a*** and the combination shown at point ***b***. *IC″* tells us that he gets the same utility from the combinations of visits shown by points ***a*** and ***c***. If both these intersecting curves were to apply, then Tom would get the same utility from the combinations of visits shown by points ***b*** and ***c***. However, ***c*** involves one more home visit a month than ***b***, and the same number of club visits. If both products are desirable, ***c*** *must* give more *TU* than ***b***, so the indifference curves cannot intersect like this.
- **Indifference curves are straight if the two products are perfect substitutes**. To see this, look at part (b) of Figure 6.3. This shows an indifference map for a consumer between two brands of bottled water, 'Valley Water' and 'Hill Water'. This consumer is just as happy with one brand as the other. So, for example, the consumer will be indifferent between six litres of either and none of the other, or five litres of either and one of the other, or four

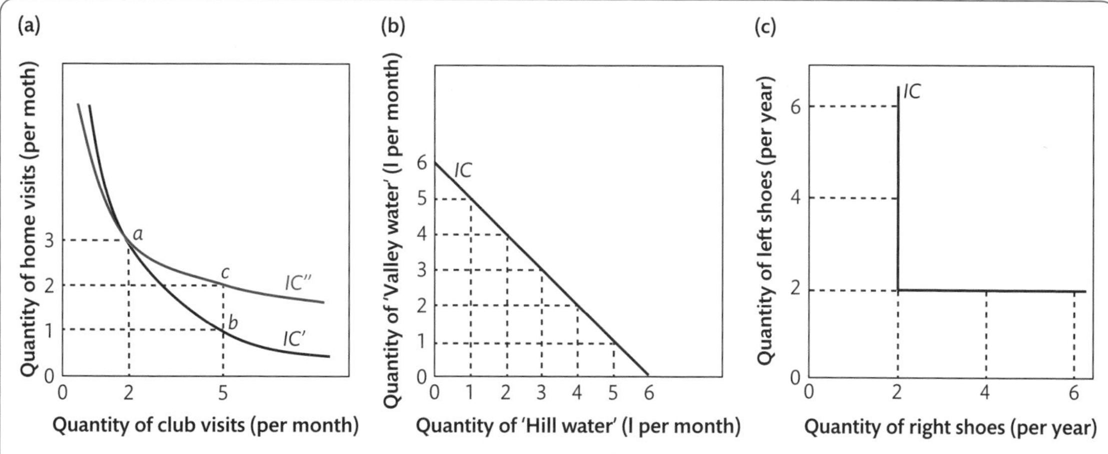

Figure 6.3 **Features of indifference curves**

If both products are desirable, indifference curves cannot intersect like those in part (a): these curves imply that ***b*** and ***c*** both give the same utility as ***a***, so that ***b*** and ***c*** would give the same utility as each other, yet ***c*** has more home visits than ***b*** and the same club visits, so ***c*** must give more utility. Part (b) shows a straight curve, which arises with products that are perfect substitutes. Part (c) shows an L-shaped curve, which arises with two products that are perfect complements.

litres of either and two of the other, or three litres of each. This information is conveyed by curve *IC*, which passes through all of those combinations.

- **Indifference curves are kinked and L-shaped if the two products are perfect complements**. To see this, look at part (c) of Figure 6.3. This shows an indifference map between left shoes and right shoes for a two-legged consumer. This consumer would get a certain amount of utility from a combination of two left shoes and two right shoes. But there would be no increase in utility from two left shoes and, say, four or six right shoes, or from two right shoes and, say, four or six left shoes. This information is conveyed by curve *IC*, which passes through all of those combinations.

6.3 Summary

- Indifference curves, *IC*s, are drawn for individual consumers. Each point on an *IC* represents a different combination of two products consumed, but each combination on a given *IC* gives the consumer the same total utility. The further an *IC* is from the origin, the more total utility it represents.
- If both products are desirable, then a consumer's *IC*s slope down and do not intersect.

6.4 Indifference maps and product demand

Budget lines and maximum utility

We will now develop the example of Tom to show how rational households make their consumption decisions. Figure 6.4 repeats from Figure 6.2 his indifference map between club visits and home visits, and this gives us some information about his preferences. But his decisions will also depend on his income and the prices of the two products, and all of this is represented by the line *BL*.

BL is a **budget line**: this is a line that shows the limits of what a consumer can buy at current prices. In our example, we are supposing that Tom has £60 a month to spend on the two products. Suppose also that the return fare home is £10. Then, if he never visits the club, the most home visits he can afford is six a month. This is shown by the top point of *BL*. Suppose too that the price of club visits is also £10. Then, if he never visits home, the most club visits he can afford is six a month. This is shown by the bottom point of *BL*. Tom can afford to make some visits to both home and the club. For example, he could use £40 to make four visits home, and use the remaining £20 to make two visits to the club. Or he could use £20 to make two visits home, and use the remaining £40 to make four visits to the club. *BL* passes both these combinations, and also all the other combinations that he can just afford.

We assume that Tom is rational, so he wants to maximize his utility. This means he will choose the combination of club and home visits on *BL* that will give him the most total utility. This is the combination where *BL* just touches *IC″*, because *IC″* is the furthest indifference curve from the origin that he can attain from *BL*. So each month he will make four club visits and two home visits.

Figure 6.4 shows an economic model of the behaviour of households as consumers. We will now use this model to study the three reasons why the behaviour of consumers like Tom may change: these reasons are a change in preferences, a change in prices, and a change in income.

A change in preferences

One factor that may change Tom's behaviour is a change in his preferences. As his preferences are illustrated by an indifference map, so a change in his preferences creates a new map. Say that, in a few months, his preferences move away from club visits towards home visits; perhaps an exam is due, so he wants to spend less time socializing at the club and more time revising quietly at home.

Figure 6.5 illustrates this change in preferences. Here, *BL* and IC_0 repeat from Figure 6.4 his budget line and the indifference curve that he was on there. To keep Figure 6.5 simple, no other curves from his original map are shown. Tom's new preferences create a new indifference map. Again, for simplicity, only one curve from this map is shown, IC_1. This one was chosen because Tom now maximizes utility at the point where *BL* just touches it. With his new preferences, he

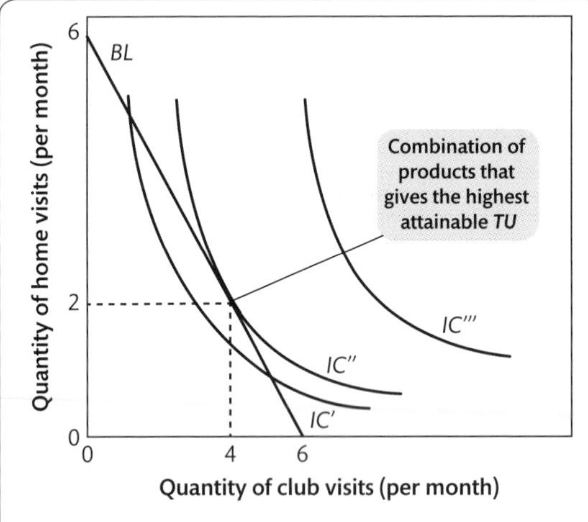

Figure 6.4 **Maximizing utility**

A rational consumer maximizes utility by choosing the combination of products that gets the consumer onto the highest possible indifference curve. Here, the consumer pays for two home visits and four club visits each month.

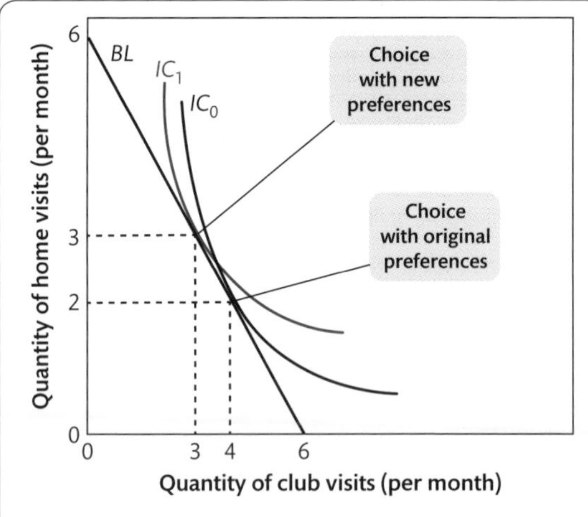

Figure 6.5 **A change in preferences**

A change in preferences changes a consumer's indifference map. IC_0 is the curve from the original map, which just touches *BL*, and IC_1 is the curve from the new map, which just touches it. The consumer now makes different choices.

cuts club visits from four per month to three, and he raises home visits from two a month to three.

A change in prices

Another factor that may change Tom's behaviour is a change in prices. We will assume that the ticket price for home visits remains at £10, while the price for the club changes. The top part of Figure 6.6 repeats Tom's indifference curves from Figure 6.4, and it also repeats his budget line as BL_0. This relates to the initial club price of £10. Tom maximizes his utility by choosing the combination of four club visits and two home visits a month, where BL_0 touches the highest attainable indifference curve, *IC″*.

Now consider two other possible prices that the club might charge.

- **A club price of £15**. In this case, the most club visits Tom could make each month with his £60 income is four, but he could still make six home visits. So his budget line would pivot about its top end to become BL_1. He would maximize his utility by choosing the point where BL_1 touches *IC′*, which is now his highest attainable indifference curve. He would make two club visits and three home visits each month.
- **A club price of £5**. In this case, the most club visits Tom could make each month with his £60 income is 12, but he could still make six home visits. So his budget line would pivot about its top end to become BL_2. He would maximize his utility by choosing the point where BL_1 touches *IC‴*, which is now his highest attainable indifference curve. He would make eight club visits and two home visits each month.

The top part of Figure 6.6 is completed with a dashed black arrow labelled *PCC*. This is a **price consumption curve**, and it is drawn through the various positions that the consumer chooses when the price of one product changes.

The bottom part of Figure 6.6 uses the results obtained in the top part to trace out Tom's individual demand curve for club visits. It shows that as the price of club visits changes between £15, £10, and £5, his consumption changes between two, four, and eight.

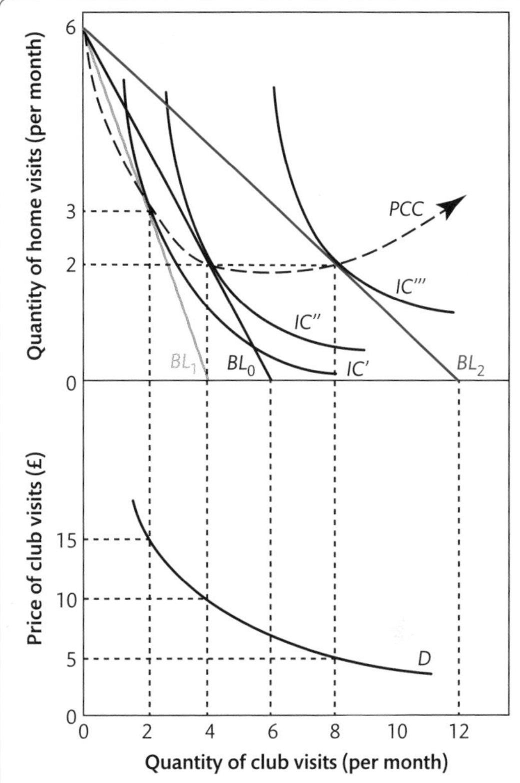

Figure 6.6 **Deriving an individual demand curve**

In the top part, *IC′*, *IC″*, and *IC‴* are indifference curves for a student. If the price of club visits is £15, BL_1 applies and the student pays for 2 per month. If the price is £10, BL_0 applies and the student pays for 4. If the price is £5, BL_2 applies and the student pays for 8. This information is used to plot a price consumption curve (*PCC*) in the top part, and also the student's demand curve for club visits in the bottom part.

A change in income

Household behaviour is also affected by changes in income. We saw in Chapter 3 that a rise in incomes leads households to buy more of most products, called normal goods, and less of other products, called inferior goods. Figure 6.7 contrasts the indifference maps for the two cases. Part (a) concerns a

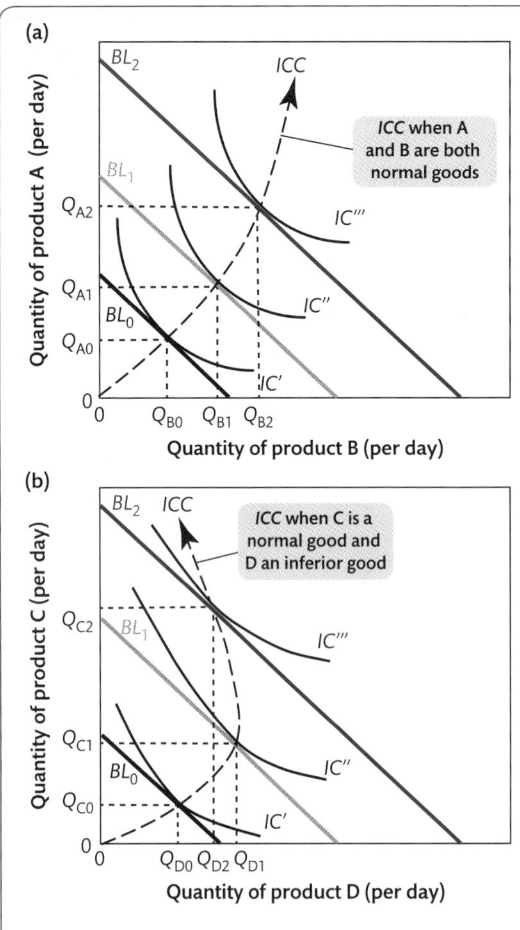

Figure 6.7 **Changes in income**

Each part shows how income rises affect the budget lines and, in turn, household choices. For the household in part (a), products A and B are always normal. For the household in part (b), C is always normal, but D becomes inferior at high income levels.

household for which income is divided between products A and B. Part (b) concerns a household for which income is divided between products C and D. Each part shows an indifference map with three curves for the household concerned. Each part also shows, the initial budget line of the household concerned, BL_0. The household in part (a) initially buys Q_{A0} of A and Q_{B0} of B, and the household in part (b) initially buys Q_{C0} of C and Q_{D0} of D.

Let's now see what happens if each household has two successive rises in its income. Each rise shifts its budget line further from the origin, because the household can now buy larger quantities. But there is no change in the slope of the budget line, which depends on the prices of the two products.

- **A first rise in income that takes it to budget line BL_1.** The part (a) household now buys Q_{A1} and Q_{B1}; these are higher than Q_{A0} and Q_{B0}, so this household regards both products as normal. The part (b) household now buys Q_{C1} and Q_{D1}; these are higher than Q_{C0} and Q_{D0}, so this household also regards both products as normal.
- **A second rise in income that takes it to budget line BL_2.** The part (a) household now buys Q_{A2} and Q_{B2}; these are higher than Q_{A1} and Q_{B1}, so this household still regards both products as normal. The part (b) household now buys Q_{C2} and Q_{D2}; Q_{C2} is higher than Q_{C1}, so the household still regards C as normal. But Q_{D2} is lower than Q_{D1}, so this household regards D as inferior at high incomes.

Each part of Figure 6.7 is completed with a dashed black arrow labelled *ICC*. This is an **income consumption curve**, which passes through the various positions that the household chooses when its income rises. Each *ICC* passes the origin, for if incomes were zero, neither household could buy either product. The *ICC* in part (a) then always slopes upwards to the right, because this household always buys more of both products if its income rises. The *ICC* in part (b) eventually slopes backwards to the left, because this household eventually regards D as inferior.

Question 6.2 Suppose the product on the horizontal axis was always normal and the product on the vertical axis became interior at high incomes. Then how would the slope of *ICC* vary along its length?

Income and substitution effects: normal good

We can now look more closely at why households demand different quantities of a product when its

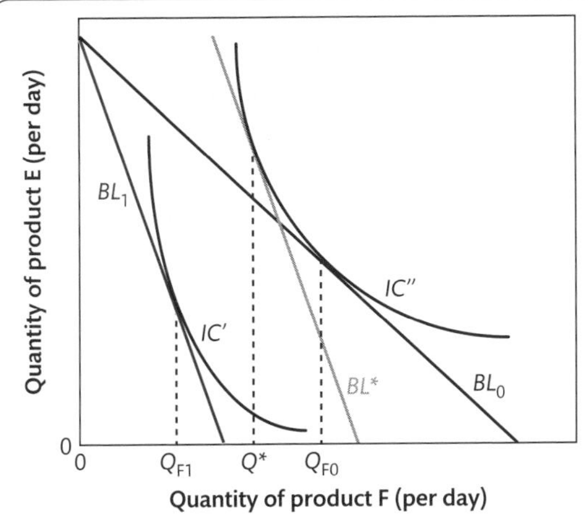

Figure 6.8 **Income and substitution effects for a normal good**

A rise in F's price pivots the budget line from BL_0 to BL_1. Purchases of F fall from Q_{F0} to Q_{F1}. One reason for the fall is the substitution effect: F is now dearer in relation to E. Another is the income effect: the household has less purchasing power. Budget line BL^* allows us to separate these effects. The fall from Q_{F0} to Q^* is the substitution effect. The fall from Q^* to Q_{F1} is the income effect.

price changes. Figure 6.8 considers a household that divides its income between products E and F. It regards both of them as normal. It starts on BL_0 and chooses the point where this touches the highest attainable indifference curve, IC'', so it buys Q_{F0} of F. Then the price of F rises. The budget line is now BL_1, and the household chooses the point where this touches IC', to buy Q_{F1} of F.

The household's decision to buy less F stems from *two* effects of the price rise, as follows.

- **The substitution effect**: this means that a change in relative prices encourages households to buy more of the products that become relatively cheaper, and fewer of those that become relatively dearer. In this example, F becomes dearer compared to E, and this inclines the household to buy less F.
- **The income effect**: this means that a price change alters the household's total purchasing power, and this affects its choices in a similar way to a change in incomes. In this example, a price rise reduces the household's purchasing power, and this effect also inclines it to buy less F, assuming that it regards F as a normal good.

It is possible to see how much of the household's reduced purchases of F are due to each effect. To do this, we add the grey budget line BL^*. This is the budget line that the household would be on if it were to enjoy its initial purchasing power, but face the final prices. BL^* reflects the original purchasing power because, like BL_0, it touches IC''. So if the household were on BL^*, it could buy as much utility as it bought on BL_0. BL^* reflects the final prices because it is parallel to BL_1. Like the parallel budget lines in Figure 6.7, BL_1 and BL^* show what would happen if income changed while prices stayed the same. If the household were on BL^*, it would choose the point where it touches IC'' and buy Q^* of F.

Now recall that the rise in price of F reduced the household's purchases from Q_{F0} to Q_{F1}. This fall can be split up into two parts, as follows.

- **The change from Q_{F0} to Q^***. This is the substitution effect, and it reflects a rise in the price of F in relation to the price of E, while keeping purchasing power at the initial level.
- **The change from Q^* to Q_{F1}**. This is the income effect, and it reflects a fall in purchasing power with no change in prices.

Income and substitution effects: inferior good

Figure 6.9 concerns a rise in the price of an inferior good, and shows how the resulting fall in quantity demanded can be divided between the substitution effect and the income effect. The household here divides its income between product G, which it regards as normal, and product H, which it regards as inferior.

The household starts on BL_0 and chooses the point where this touches IC'', so it buys Q_{H0} of H. Then the price of H rises, so the budget line becomes BL_1 and the household chooses the point where this touches

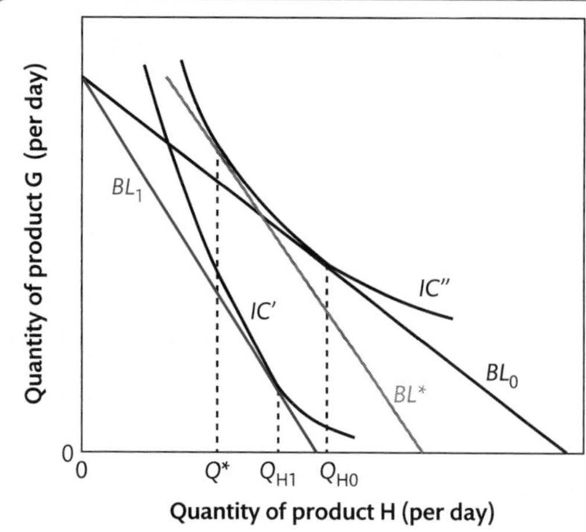

Figure 6.9 **Income and substitution effects for an inferior good**

A rise in H's price pivots the budget line from BL_0 to BL_1. Purchases of H fall from Q_{H0} to Q_{H1}. One reason for this is the substitution effect: H is now dearer in relation to G. Another is the income effect: the household has less purchasing power. Budget line BL^* allows us to separate these effects. The fall from Q_{H0} to Q^* is the substitution effect. The rise from Q^* to Q_{H1} is the income effect. With inferior goods, the effects work in opposite directions.

IC', and so buys Q_{H1} of H. To separate the substitution and income effects of this price change, we add the grey budget line BL^*. Like BL^* in Figure 6.8, this touches *IC''*, but is parallel to BL_1. So it is the budget line on which the household would be if it were to enjoy its initial purchasing power, but face the final prices. If the household were on BL^*, it would choose the point where it touches *IC''* and buy Q^* of H.

Now recall that the rise in price of H reduced the household's purchases from Q_{H0} to Q_{H1}. This fall can be split up into two parts, as follows.

- **The change from Q_{H0} to Q^*.** This is the substitution effect, and it reflects a rise in the price of H in relation to the price of G, while keeping purchasing power at the initial level. This effect leads the household to buy less H.
- **The change from Q^* to Q_{H1}.** This is the income effect, and it reflects a fall in purchasing power with no change in prices. Because H is inferior, this effect leads the household to buy more H, so here the income and substitution effects work in opposite directions. But the substitution effect is stronger, so it ends up buying less H than Q_{H0}.

In principle, the income effect with a deeply inferior good could be stronger than the substitution effect. In this case, a rise in price would *increase* the quantity demanded, so the individual's demand curve would slope upwards! No one has ever found a product for which it is certain that this is the case. But economists sometimes use the term 'Giffen goods' for them because Sir Robert Giffen, in the 19th century, seems to have suggested the possibility.

6.1 Everyday economics

Size zero models banned

Victoria Beckham has denied 12 models from appearing in her New York fashion show under a new rule in which models have to be at least UK size 6—this excludes models of UK size 4, which is about the same as the US size 0. The idea is to prevent teenage girls from being tempted into eating disorders in pursuit of an unrealistic size zero.

'Victoria Beckham bans size zero models from her show', *Deccan Herald*, 12 September 2010
'Skinny Victoria Beckham bans size zero models in New York Fashion Week show', *MailOnline*, 13 September 2010

Comment Preferences can be influenced in many ways, and the idea of this ban is to influence the dietary preferences of young teenage girls.

6.4 Summary

- An indifference map is a set of indifference curves for a consumer. The consumer's purchasing possibilities are shown by a budget line, *BL*. The consumer maximizes utility by buying the combination of products at the point where *BL* touches the highest attainable indifference curve.
- Consumer choices change if preferences change, or if incomes change, or if prices change.

- A change in a product's price changes the quantity bought partly because of a substitution effect, which means that the price of that product changes relative to other prices, and partly because of an income effect, which means there is a change in the consumer's purchasing power.

6.5 Individual and market supply curves for labour

So far, we have developed a theory of household behaviour to explain how households behave when they demand final products. We will now use the same theory to explain how households behave when they supply labour, to see why the supply curves in individual labour markets may shift.

The supply curve in any labour market shows the total quantity of hours that households would supply at each possible wage. For example, part (c) of Figure 6.10 repeats, as S_{MARKET}, the market supply curve for DJ labour in a city that we used in Chapter 3; it shows that if the wage were, say, £12 an hour, then households there would supply a total of 5,000 hours of DJ labour per week. S_{MARKET} also shows that these households would supply different amounts of DJ labour at other wages.

Of course, all households make different decisions, and Figure 6.10 shows how these varied households are linked to the market. Parts (a) and (b) show as S_A and S_B the supply curves of DJ labour by two households, A and B. If, for example, the wage were £12, A would supply 10 hours a week and B would supply 15. S_A and S_B show that these households would supply different hours of DJ labour at other wages.

The market supply curve, S_{MARKET}, includes this information about these two households, and also includes similar information about all other households that supply DJ labour in the city. The figure of 5,000 at a wage of £12 means that if we add up the 10 hours of DJ labour that A would supply, the 15 that

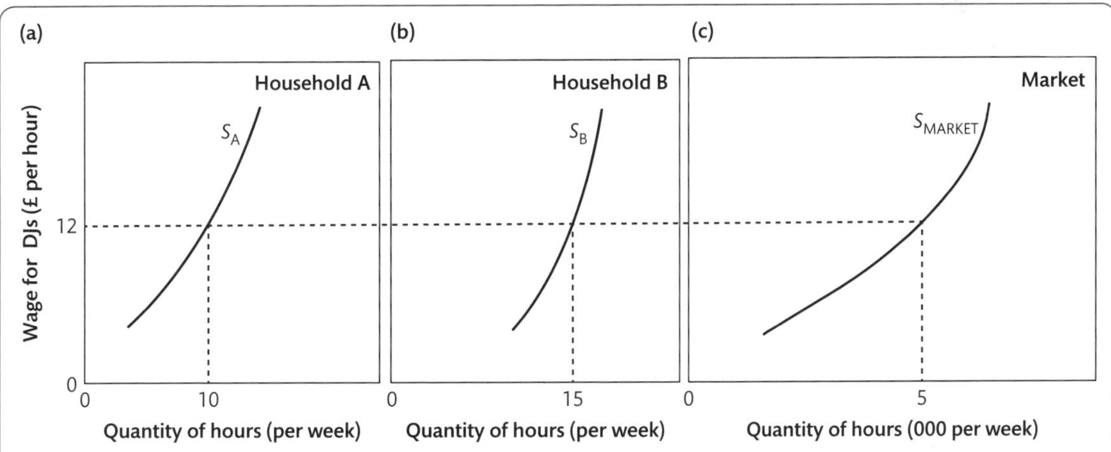

Figure 6.10 **Individual supply curves and a market supply curve**

Parts (a) and (b) give the supply curves of DJ labour for two individual households, A and B. At a wage of £12, for example, A would supply 10 hours a week while B would supply 15. Part (c) gives the market supply curve. This shows how many hours all households between them would supply at each wage. At £12, it includes the 10 supplied by A, the 15 supplied by B, and also the hours supplied by all other households; the total is 5,000.

B would supply, and the hours all other households would supply, then the total would be 5,000.

Because S_{MARKET} includes the supply of every household that supplies DJ labour in the city, it will shift if the number of these households changes. It will also shift if individual households change their behaviour so that their own supply curves shift. We will now use the theory of household behaviour to see why these individual curves may shift.

6.5 Summary

- The market supply curve for any type of labour represents the individual supply curves of all households that supply labour in that market added together.
- To understand why a market supply curve may shift, we need to understand how individual households behave as workers and why their individual supply curves may shift.

6.6 Indifference maps and labour supply

Figure 6.11 applies the principles of indifference maps to labour supply. It concerns the supply of DJ labour by Pat, who is the only person in her household. We assume that Pat spends 68 hours a week on sleep and other life-preserving activities. The figure concerns her remaining 100 hours. She fills these with a mixture of DJ work and leisure. The key to understanding this figure is to recall that indifference maps assume that both axes concern something that is desirable. In Figure 6.11, the vertical axis measures the earnings that Pat takes home from her work, and the horizontal axis measures her hours of leisure. She regards both earnings and leisure as desirable.

Suppose that, at present, the wage of DJs is £5 an hour. Suppose, too, that there is no income tax, so Pat can take home £5 for each hour she works. Then if she spends all 100 hours as a DJ, her take-home earnings will be £500 per week, but she will have no leisure. On the other hand, if she does no work, she will earn £0 and have 100 hours of leisure. These possibilities are shown by the ends of the line labelled EL_0. This is an **earnings–leisure line**, which also shows every other possible combination of take-home earnings and leisure that Pat could choose, such as working 30 hours to earn £150 and having 70 hours of leisure, and so on.

Figure 6.11 also shows three of Pat's indifference curves, IC', IC'', and IC'''. On any curve, all the

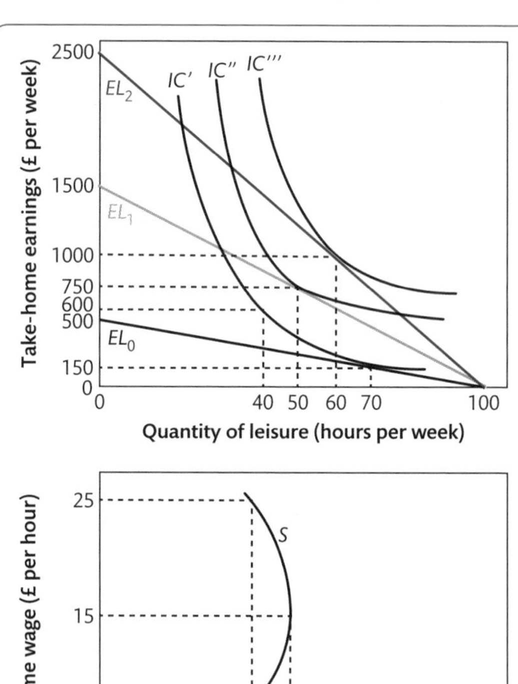

Figure 6.11 **Labour supply**

The top part shows how a worker decides how many hours to work at three different wage rates, each with its own earnings–leisure line, *EL*. The bottom part uses this information to derive the individual's labour supply curve. This slopes backwards at high wage rates.

combinations of earnings and leisure through which the curve passes would give Pat the same total utility. For example, *IC′*, shows that she would be indifferent between 40 hours of leisure plus £600 of earnings, and 70 hours of leisure plus £150.

Each indifference curve slopes downwards because both earnings and leisure are desirable. To see this, look again at the point on *IC′* where Pat would combine 40 hours of leisure with £600 of earnings. This combination gives her a certain overall utility. Now suppose that, instead of having 40 hours of leisure, she has 70. Her utility from leisure will be higher, so she will need less utility from earnings to keep her overall utility the same. This means that she will need less than £600 of earnings. The point on *IC′* above 70 hours of leisure is at £150 of earnings, which shows that she will actually need £150. This point is lower than the point on *IC′* above 40 hours, and also to the right of it. So *IC′* slopes downwards.

We also assume that Pat has diminishing marginal utility of income and leisure, just as Tom in Table 6.1 had diminishing marginal utility of home visits and club visits. So, for example, every fall of £1 in earnings for Pat leads to ever larger falls in her total utility from earnings, while every extra hour of leisure leads to ever smaller rises in her total utility from leisure. So every time her earnings fall by £1, she needs more and more extra leisure to maintain constant overall utility. In turn, all her indifference curves get flatter as earnings fall.

At present, Pat is on EL_0, so she will maximize her utility by choosing the point on EL_0 at which she can get the highest utility. This is where EL_0 touches the highest attainable indifference curve, *IC′*. There, she will indeed take 70 hours of leisure, and so work for the other 30 hours to earn £150.

An individual labour supply curve

Suppose the wage for DJs rises to £15. Then Pat can move on to EL_1. One end of this shows that she could now choose to have no leisure and work for 100 hours a week to take home £1,500. The other end shows that she could still choose to take 100 hours of leisure and have no earnings. She could also choose any of the intermediate positions shown along EL_1. She will now maximize her utility by choosing the point where EL_1 touches the highest attainable indifference curve, *IC″*. There, she will take 50 hours of leisure, and so work for the other 50 hours to earn £750.

Now suppose the wage for DJs rises again to £25. Then, Pat can move on to EL_2. One end of this shows that she could now choose to have no leisure and work for 100 hours a week to take home £2,500. The other end shows that she could still choose to take 100 hours of leisure and have no earnings. She could also choose any of the intermediate positions along EL_2. She will now maximize her utility by choosing the point where EL_2 touches the highest attainable indifference curve, *IC‴*. There, she will take 60 hours of leisure and work for the other 40 hours to earn £1,000.

So, as the wage rises from £5 to £15 and then £25, Pat will take 70, 50, and 60 hours of leisure. So, she initially takes less leisure, and then takes more again. The reason for this concerns the substitution and income effects of a wage rise.

- **Substitution effect**. A rise in the wage means that Pat sacrifices more money when she takes an hour of leisure. We can look at this in another way and say that it raises the price of leisure, from £5 an hour to £15 and then to £25. As leisure becomes more expensive relative to items, the substitution effect encourages her to have less leisure.
- **Income effect**. A rise in the wage rate means that Pat can secure more purchasing power, and this encourages her to consume more normal goods. Suppose that she regards leisure as a normal good, which simply means that she would take more leisure if her income rose. Then the income effect encourages her to take more leisure.

Taking the two effects together, we can deduce that when the wage rises from £5 to £15, the substitution effect is stronger than the income effect, so Pat takes less leisure. But when the wage rises from £15 to £25, the income effect is stronger than the substitution effect, so she takes more leisure.

We have now seen that, at wages of £5, £15, and £25, she will supply 30, 50, and 40 hours of work. This information is used in the bottom part of Figure 6.11 to show Pat's supply curve of labour, *S*. This curve initially slopes upwards, and then slopes backwards, to show that as the take-home wage rises from £5 to £25, Pat will initially work more, and later work less.

Work effort and income taxes

Let's now consider what effect the introduction of an income tax would have on Pat's chosen hours of work. Suppose initially there is no tax, and then a simple one is introduced that taxes all income at 20%. The effect on Pat's hours of work will depend on what her wage is. The effects if she earns £15 or £25 are as follows.

- **A wage of £15**. Before the tax is introduced, Pat can take home £15 an hour, and the supply curve, *S*, in the bottom part of Figure 6.11 shows that she will work 50 hours a week. After the tax is introduced, she must pay £3 an hour in tax, that is 20% of £15, so her take-home wage is now just £12 an hour. So she will move down the supply curve, *S*, from a take-home wage of £15 to £12, and she will work fewer hours.
- **A wage of £25**. Before the tax is introduced, Pat can take home £25 an hour, and the supply curve, *S*, in the bottom part of Figure 6.11 shows that she will work 40 hours a week. After the tax is introduced, she must pay £5 an hour in tax, that is 20% of £25, so her take-home wage is now just £20 an hour. So she will move down the supply curve, *S*, from a take-home wage of £25 to £20, and she will work more hours.

Of course, the supply curve in Figure 6.11 is just the supply curve of labour for Pat. All other DJs will have their own individual labour supply curves, and so do all workers in all other occupations. Many of these individual supply curves will slope back at some wage, but the wage rate at which this happens will be different for everyone, depending on their individual preferences.

If most of these individual supply curves slope backwards at the wages that people currently earn, then an increase in income tax rates will make most people work harder. However, most governments believe that few workers in the economy are on labour supply curves that bend backwards at their current wages. Instead, most governments believe that an increase in income tax will make most people work less. It is hard to prove whether they are right in holding this belief.

Individual and market supply curves

Suppose most DJs have individual labour supply curves that eventually slope backwards. Then you might suppose that the market supply curve for DJs must also slope backwards once a certain wage is reached. In fact, the market supply curve for this type of labour, or indeed any type, probably slopes forwards all along. This is because if the wage for DJs rose, while other wages stayed the same, then even if existing DJs chose to work fewer hours, almost certainly other people would now start to work as DJs. So the market supply curve would now cover the supplies of more individuals.

6.2 **Everyday economics**

Incentives: Australia versus the Netherlands

Income taxes can have different incentives on different groups. An Australian study (L. Cai, G. Kalb, Y. Tseng, and H. Vu 'The effect of financial incentives on labour supply: evidence for sole parents from microsimulation and quasi-experimental evaluation', *Melbourne Institute Working Paper Series*, 10/05) found that the 2000 cut in Australia's tax rates encouraged single parents to work longer hours. But a Dutch study (N. Bosch, B. van der Klaauw, J. van Ours 'Female part-time work in the Netherlands', *Vox*, 5 September 2009) found that the 2001 cut in the Netherlands' income tax rates encouraged part-time female workers to work fewer hours. It is possible that many single parents in Australia have low incomes and are on forward-sloping parts of their labour supply curves, while many Dutch women working part-time may have well-paid partners and live in high-income households in which both parties may react to lower tax rates by taking more leisure, and so be on backward-bending parts of their supply curves.

6.6 Summary

- An indifference map between leisure and earnings can be used to see how changes in an individual worker's wage rate affect the amount of labour that the worker will supply.
- As wages rise, a worker may initially choose to work more hours, and then choose to work fewer. A rise in income tax rates may lead some workers to work more hours and others to work fewer.

In the next chapter and also in the five that follow it, we leave households and instead study the behaviour of firms. We will see that while some firms have supply curves, others do not.

abc Glossary

Budget line: a line showing the limits to what a consumer can afford at current prices, with the consumer's current income.

Diminishing marginal utility: the fact that the marginal utility from consumption (or income or leisure) falls when consumption (or income or leisure) rise.

Earnings-leisure line: a line showing a worker's possible combinations of take-home earnings and leisure at the current wage rate.

Income consumption curve: a curve showing how the combination of two products demanded by a consumer changes when the consumer's income changes.

Income effect: the effect on a consumer's consumption of a product (or leisure) that would arise if its price was constant, but the consumer's income or purchasing power changed.

Indifference curve: a curve showing combinations of two items (e.g. two products or earnings and leisure) that give an individual equal overall utility, so that the individual is indifferent between the combinations.

Indifference map: a group of indifference curves for two items for the same individual.

Marginal utility: the change in total utility in a period of time if consumption (or income or leisure) in the period changes by one unit.

Price consumption curve: a curve showing how the combination of two products demanded by a consumer changes when the price of one of them changes.

Rational consumer: a consumer who makes the choices that maximize his or her total utility.

Substitution effect: the effect on a consumer's consumption of a product (or leisure) that would arise if income or purchasing power stayed the same, but the relative price of the product (or leisure) changed.

Total utility: the total satisfaction from varying choices about consumption (or income and leisure).

Util: a unit in which economists imagine that they can measure utility.

Utility: the satisfaction that arises from consumption, income, or leisure.

Answers to in-text questions

6.1 Using W for water and D for diamonds, people adjust their purchases until $MU_W/P_W = MU_D/P_D$. So, as P_W is well below P_D, MU_W must be well below MU_D. And MU_W certainly is well below MU_D, because people consume water in such huge quantities that their MU_W is almost zero.

6.2 *ICC* would slope upwards to the right along the income range when both products were normal, and then slope down to the right when the one on the vertical axis became inferior.

? Questions for review

6.1 Four students regularly use machines that dispense coffee for 60p and crisps for 40p. Their preferences vary. The marginal utilities of coffee and crisps are for 12 and 8 for Andy, 8 and 12 for Joe, 18 and 12 for Mary, and 20 each for Pam. Which students are not maximizing their utility, and how could they alter their consumption to get more utility?

6.2 Ann likes strawberries and tomatoes, and draws an indifference curve for herself with strawberries on the vertical axis and tomatoes on the horizontal axis. At which end of the curve will her marginal utility of strawberries be lowest in relation to that for tomatoes, and at which end will it be highest? She then adds in a budget line. What, if anything, will happen to this budget line if **(a)** her income rises, **(b)** the price of strawberries rises, **(c)** she 'goes off' tomatoes?

6.3 Zoe draws an indifference curve for herself with earnings on the vertical axis and leisure on the horizontal axis. At which end of the curve will her marginal utility of earnings be highest in relation to that for leisure, and at which end will it be lowest?

? Questions for discussion

6.1 Among the products you buy, think of one that gives you a high *TU* and a high *MU*, one that gives you a high *TU* and a low *MU*, one that gives you a low *TU* and a high *MU*, and one that gives you a low *TU* and a low *MU*.

6.2 Consider the effects on the hours worked by existing graduates, and the incentives for young people to go to university, of **(a)** an increase in income tax rates for all workers, and **(b)** an increase in income tax rates for only graduates.

Common student errors

Some students think diminishing marginal utility means, for example, that tea drinkers find each successive cup of tea during a day less enjoyable than the one before. But it actually means that if they raise their consumption each day by one cup, say from five to six, and later from six to seven, then their total utility per day will rise more with the rise from five to six than with the rise from six to seven.

Also, many students are a little careless about drawing indifference curves. If both items concerned are desirable, then the curves must slope down all the way, like this: ⟍. But often in essays they slope suspiciously upwards at each end, like this: ◡.

7

Introducing the Theory of the Firm

Suppose you own a firm: what would happen to you if the firm was unable to repay its debts? Suppose there are other firms that make a similar product to your own: how would this limit the freedom of your firm to decide what price it sets? How would you discover if your firm was making a profit?

This chapter shows you how to answer questions like these, by understanding:

- sole proprietorships, partnerships, and companies;
- limited liability and unlimited liability;
- four different market structures;
- explicit costs and implicit costs;
- accounting profits and economic profits.

7.1 The profit-maximizing assumption

We saw in Chapter 1 that many of the goods and services that we consume are produced by firms. So economists are very interested in firms, and we now turn to what is called the theory of the firm, which seeks to explain how firms behave. We will introduce the theory in this chapter, and develop it in the five chapters that follow.

Consider a firm Icecool, which makes fridges. Icecool's managers have to make many choices or decisions for their firm, but the theory of the firm focuses on the four most important choices concerning their output, which are as follows.

- **Their production method**. For example, should their assembly line be handled chiefly by robots or by humans?
- **Their output level**. How many fridges should they make in a period of time, say each day?
- **Their price**. What price should they set for their fridges?
- **Their marketing**. For example, how much should they spend on advertising?

We cannot explain what choices Icecool's managers will make unless we know what the owners of Icecool want its managers to achieve. Most economic theory assumes that firms' owners want their firms to make as much profit as possible, so that firms are **profit-maximizers**. A firm's **profit** is the gap between the income or revenue that it receives from selling its products and the cost of producing them.

Suppose Icecool's owners want it to maximize its profit. And suppose that each day Icecool receives £10 million from selling fridges and has production costs of £9 million, so its profit is £1 million a day. Then we can say that the managers will be meeting the owners' aim of profit maximization if there is no change in production method, output, price, or marketing that would raise the profit above £1 million a day.

There is no law that says that a firm must aim to maximize its profit. So Icecool's owners could tell the managers to pursue a different aim in future, such as selling as many fridges as possible without making a loss: if Icecool's owners were to do this, then the managers would cut their price until they only just covered their production costs; with a lower price, they would sell more fridges than they sell now. Economists have developed detailed theories about how firms will behave if they adopt a range of aims other than profit-maximization. But in this book we will stick to that aim, because most economists believe it is the most common.

In this chapter, we look at three basic issues:

- **the main types of firm**;
- **the main types of industry in which firms operate**;
- **the precise meaning of costs and profits**;

7.1 Summary

- Most theories about firms assume that each firm is a profit-maximizer.
- So firms are taken to make choices that give them the largest possible gap between revenue and cost.

7.2 Types of firm

In 2009, there were about 4.8 million businesses in the UK. These varied greatly in size, as shown in Table 7.1: 99.3% were small firms with fewer than 50 employees, and only 0.1% were large firms with 250 or more

Table 7.1 **Some data on firm sizes in the UK, 2009**

Size (no. of employees)	% of firms	% of employees	% of turnover
Small (0–49)	99.3	48.2	35.7
Medium (50–249)	0.6	11.5	13.3
Large (250+)	0.1	40.2	51.0
Total	**100.0**	**100.0**	**100.0**

Source: Department for Business, Innovation and Skills. http://stats.berr.gov.uk/ed/sme/

Table 7.2 **Types of firm in the UK, 2009**

Type	Number (millions)	% with employees	Liability
Sole proprietorships	3.1	10	Unlimited
Partnerships	0.4	38	Unlimited
Companies	1.3	57	Limited
Total	**4.8**	**27**	–

Source: Department for Business, Innovation and Skills. http://stats.berr.gov.uk/ed/sme/

employees. However, these large firms accounted for 40.2% of total employment and for 51.0% of total turnover, that is the value of total sales.

Depending on how they are owned, these businesses can be divided into three groups, which we will now explain. These groups are called sole proprietorships, partnerships, and companies.

Sole proprietorships

Suppose, in a few years' time, you give up an office job and become a self-employed driving instructor. You need some capital, chiefly a car and maybe a computer. Say that altogether these goods cost £15,000, which you fund as follows:

- **You use £1,000 of your savings.**
- **You borrow £14,000 from a bank.**

Anything of value that is owned is called an **asset**. So the firm's car and computer are assets to the firm. Also, the firm is an asset to you, because you own the firm. A firm owned by one person is a **sole proprietorship**. Table 7.2 shows that in 2009 there were 3.1 million sole proprietors in the UK. Although each of these firms has only one owner, the table shows that 10% of those owners hired one or more employees to work with them.

Suppose that after, some months, the number of pupils you attract falls and you decide to close the firm down. You sell the car and the computer and find they are now worth only £10,000. You give this to the bank, but of course it wants £14,000. It points out that, by law, the owner of a sole proprietorship has **unlimited liability**: this means that the firm's liability to anyone who lends it money is not limited to the value of the firm's assets. So if selling the firm's assets raises too little, in your case £4,000 too little, then you as its owner must raise the other £4,000 by selling some of your other assets, even your home if necessary.

Partnerships

Suppose that instead of setting up as a sole proprietor, you want to set up a larger driving school. To do this, you could persuade some other people to become joint owners, so that you all combine to form a **partnership**. Some of these partners will probably agree to work more hours for the firm than others. Suppose, also, that you plan to hire some additional instructors, and that your firm wants eight cars. And say that to buy these cars, and a few other assets, the partnership needs £120,000, which it funds as follows.

- **It uses £30,000 of the partners' savings**. The partners will probably put up varying amounts.
- **It borrows £90,000 from a bank**.

Table 7.2 shows that in 2009 there were 400,000 partnerships in the UK, with 38% of them hiring one or more employees to work with the working partners. Partnerships can have many partners, and their profits are divided between the partners on an agreed basis that reflects how much money each partner has put up and how much work each does for the firm.

Partnerships also face unlimited liability. Suppose that, a few months after your partnership is set up, it starts to attract fewer pupils, so the partners decide to close it down. They sell off all its cars and its other assets for a total of, say, £70,000 and give this to the bank. But the bank wants another £20,000. As the liability of the owners is not limited to the value of the firm's assets, the partners must raise this £20,000 by selling off some of their private possessions.

Companies

As an alternative to a partnership, you might agree with some other people to set up a **company**. Suppose the company needs £100,000 to buy its assets. It might fund this as follows.

- **It sells 30,000 shares each for £1**. It could sell these to anyone who would buy some, including you. The shareholders would use some of their savings to pay for them, and they would *all* be joint owners of the firm. They would appoint directors to run it. The directors, and all other workers, would be paid a wage or salary.
- **It borrows £70,000, say from a bank**.

Suppose that the company makes a profit. It will probably pay much of this to the shareholders as a **dividend**, paying the same amount for each of the 30,000 shares. But the company may retain some of its profit to help it to fund future expansion. So, over time, companies raise funds in three ways.

- **Selling shares**: this is called using **equity**.
- **Borrowing**: this is called using **debt**.
- **Internal finance**: this is using retained profits.

If your company flourishes, then its dividends may increase over time. This will make its shares more attractive, so if any shareholders want to sell their shares, they may be able to sell them for more than the £1 they initially paid. If, instead, your company does badly and its dividends fall over time, then its shares will become less attractive, and may fetch less than £1 if they are sold.

Suppose in fact that your company closes down after a few months, and that its assets are sold for £50,000, which is paid to the bank. The bank wants £20,000 more, but by law companies have **limited liability**: this means that the firm's liability to people who lend it money is limited to the value of the firm's assets. If selling the firm's assets does not raise enough to meet all the firm's debts, that is unfortunate for the lenders; the owners, or shareholders, never have to sell any of their private possessions. But in return for protecting companies with this law, the government takes 26% of their profits with a tax called corporation tax.

Table 7.2 shows that there were 1.3 million companies in the UK in 2009, and 57% of these hired employees. There are two types of company, as follows.

- **Private limited companies**. These put 'Ltd' after their names. They have a small number of shareholders. Shareholders who wish to sell their shares must find buyers privately; they often agree not to sell shares to anyone without the approval of the other shareholders.
- **Public limited companies**. These put 'plc' after their names. They may have many shareholders. Shareholders who wish to sell their shares sell them publicly on a stock exchange to anyone who will buy them.

The largest companies have thousands of shareholders and thousands of employees, with little overlap between the two groups. Some companies operate in more than one country, and these are often called **multinational enterprises** (MNEs), or **transnational companies** (TNCs).

The principal-agent problem

Consider a plc owned by thousands of shareholders. They will appoint some directors to run the company. The shareholders want the company to maximize its profit, but the directors will be paid salaries and may have little personal interest in the company making large profits. This separation of ownership and control creates a principal–agent problem.

A **principal** is someone who hires or employs an **agent** to perform a task. For example, you are a principal when you visit the hairdresser or the dentist, while the hairdresser and dentist are your agents. The **principal–agent problem** is that principals take the risk that the task may be done poorly. The degree of risk varies from case to case. Your risk is more serious with the dentist than the hairdresser, because you have too little knowledge to know whether the dentist has provided the right treatment or done it well. In general, the risk is greatest when the agent has more information than the principal, so that the parties have **asymmetric information**.

Shareholders take a big risk with directors, because directors usually know far more about the firm than shareholders. So if the directors enjoy their salaries, but do not try hard to maximize profits, then the shareholders might not know. Yet if the directors fail to maximize profits, then the shareholders will have lower dividends than they could have; also, the theory of the firm that we will develop here will not apply, because this theory assumes that firms do maximize profits.

In practice, most directors face financial incentives, which encourage them to maximize profits. For example, in addition to paying the directors' salaries, the shareholders may pay them bonuses the size of which depends on the amount of profit the company makes. Also, shareholders may give share options to the directors. This means giving them the right to buy shares in future at a price agreed today. Directors then have an incentive to maximize profits, because large profits mean the price of the company's shares should rise, and then the directors may be able to buy shares at the agreed price and at once sell them for more.

Directors face a further incentive: the risk of losing their jobs. If they run the firm poorly so that it makes low profits and pays low dividends, then the firm's shares will be unattractive and their price will fall. Then another firm may write to the shareholders and offer to buy their shares for slightly more than their current low value. This other firm will aim to run the original one more profitably, and in the process decide to fire the original directors! If one firm tries to buy the shares of another from its shareholders, there is said to be a **competition for corporate control**.

7.1 Everyday economics

Chief executives' pay soars by 55%

Figures issued by Income Data Services (*Directors' Pay Report 2010/11*, Incomes Data, 22 October 2010) show that the average earnings of the chief executives of the UK's 100 largest companies rose by 55% between 2009 and 2010 to an average of £4.9m. These rises were widely criticized, because they came at a time when many people lost their jobs and most wages and salaries hardly rose. However, the higher earnings of chief executives did not arise chiefly from increases in their basic salaries: these rose by just 3.6%. Instead, they came from shares options, bonuses, and other incentive payments linked to company performance. It may seem odd that these rewards were so lucrative in a recession, but they were, and this is because many companies shed employees in successful moves to cut costs and raise profits. However, shareholders may try to limit the earnings of all directors in future.

7.2 Summary

- The owners of sole proprietorships and partnerships have unlimited liability, so they may have to sell their private possessions if selling the firm's assets raises too little to repay the firm's debts.
- The shareholders who own companies have limited liability, so they need never sell anything except the company's assets, even if doing so raises too little to pay the firm's debts.
- The directors who run companies often face substantial financial incentives to maximize profits.

7.3 Types of market or industry

To understand how any individual firm behaves, we need to understand the structure of the market—or industry—in which it operates. In particular, we must understand how much competition there is in that industry. Economists divide industries into four main groups: those with perfect competition; those with monopolistic competition; those with an oligopoly; and those with a monopoly. These four structures are discussed below, and their main characteristics are summarized in Table 7.3.

An industry with perfect competition

An industry with **perfect competition** has a structure with three characteristics.

- **There are many firms**. Each of these firms is assumed to be small relative to the industry.
- **These firms all sell identical products**.
- **There are no barriers to entry**. This means that it is easy for new firms to enter the industry.

The firms in these industries are called **perfect competitors**, and their identical products are sometimes called **undifferentiated** or **homogeneous**. The most common perfectly competitive industries are those for unbranded food products, such as fish, meat, fruit, and vegetables. Other examples are those for unbranded raw materials such as iron ore.

Firms in these industries have two major features.

- **No firm has any influence over the market price**. For example, if you supply peas and raise your price when no one else raises theirs, then you will sell nothing, because there are plenty of other suppliers for people to buy peas from.
- **Firms must keep their costs as low as possible**. Otherwise new more efficient firms may start up and enter the industry, and underprice the existing ones, forcing them out of business.

An industry with monopolistic competition

An industry with **monopolistic competition** has a structure with three characteristics.

- **There are many firms**. Again, each of these is assumed to be small relative to the industry.
- **These firms all sell slightly different products**.
- **There are no barriers to entry**.

In any industry like this, the firms are called **monopolistic competitors**, and their varying products are

Table 7.3 **Types or structures of industries in which firms operate**

Structure	Number of firms	Products	Barriers to entry?	Examples
Perfect competition	Many	Homogeneous (i.e. identical)	No	Many food products and raw materials, e.g. apples, beef, cod, potatoes, iron ore
Monopolistic competition	Many	Heterogeneous (i.e. varied)	No	Clothes, footwear, furniture, and many firms in a big town, e.g. filling stations, hairdressers, hotels, restaurants
Oligopoly	Few	Homogeneous or heterogeneous	Yes	*Homogeneous:* electricity, gas, sugar *Heterogeneous:* beer, cigarettes, confectionery, soft drinks
Monopoly	One	Unique to firm and no close substitute	Yes	*Large firms:* National Grid, Network Rail *Small firms:* many bus routes and ferry routes

sometimes called **differentiated** or **heterogeneous**. However, the fact that the firms are in the same industry means that their products are similar, so they compete for customers. Good examples include clothing, footwear, and furniture. Also, there is monopolistic competition between many firms in any large town. For example, there will be many hairdressers, hotels, and restaurants that vary in their location and quality.

Firms in these industries have four major features.

- **Each firm has some control over its price**. For example, if you run a filling station, you could raise your price a little without losing all your customers, because some will prefer your location or your garage shop to those of your competitors. But you could not raise your price greatly without losing a lot of business. Also, as each firm is small, none has a significant impact on the general level of prices in the market.
- **Firms must keep their costs as low as possible**. Otherwise new, more efficient firms may start up and enter the industry, and underprice the existing ones, forcing them out of business.
- **The firms engage in price competition**. Each firm tries to attract customers with its prices.
- **The firms engage in non-price competition. Non-price competition** means trying to attract customers in ways other than with prices. For example, a firm might undertake marketing and tell potential customers about its products, often using advertisements. Or it might undertake product development, and try to design products that are better or more stylish. Or it might try to appeal to customers in other ways. For example, a manufacturer might offer better guarantees, while a retailer might try a more friendly approach to customers, or move to a better location, or open up a cafe in its shop.

A market with an oligopoly

A market or industry with an **oligopoly** has a structure with just one characteristic: there are few firms. These firms are called **oligopolists**.

Some oligopolists sell identical products, such as electricity, gas, or sugar. Others sell differentiated products, such as beer, cigarettes, and daily newspapers. In a small town, firms such as hairdressers, hotels, and restaurants are also oligopolists with differentiated products.

When we say that an oligopoly has a 'few' firms, we do not mean that the number is below a set figure, say 12. We mean that the number is low enough for each firm to do two things:

- **monitor all of its competitors' prices and products**;
- **supply a sufficiently large share of the market to be able to influence prices in the market**.

Oligopolists generally engage in price competition and non-price competition, although price competition may be limited where the products are homogeneous. The fact that their industries have few firms suggests that there are some **barriers to entry**, that is some factors that make it hard to establish new firms in the industry. The most common types of barrier are the following.

- **Firm size**. In some cases, such as car making, a firm must be very big to run a competitive production line, and it is hard to set up a firm that will be big right away.
- **Market size**. Suppose you want to set up a pub in a small town that already has two. There is too little demand to sustain three, so one will soon have to close. The risk that it might be yours is a barrier to entry. In contrast, there is no such barrier to setting up a pub in a large city.
- **'Know-how'**. It is difficult to set up firms making products like drugs or aeroplanes for which a lot of knowledge is required.
- **Patents**. Even if a new firm can acquire the know-how it needs, it may not be possible to use this know-how if it is protected by patents.
- **Brand names**. Even if you had the know-how to make a product similar to, say, Coca-Cola or Pepsi-Cola, you would find it hard to enter the industry

because everyone has heard of your competitors and no one has heard of you.

- **Economies of scope**. Suppose you develop a new shampoo. You need to transport it to wholesalers, and send sales representatives to retailers. But other firms may make a wide range of shampoos and other toiletries, and be able to get lorries and representatives to transport and sell them all. So their costs per shampoo carton will be lower than yours. A multi-product firm that can reduce its total costs by sharing some costs between its different products is said to have **economies of scope.**
- **Licensing**. In some industries, entrants need a licence before they can trade legally. For example, banks must get licences from the Financial Services Authority, which is a central government body, and taxis must get them from local authorities. Sometimes it is hard to get a licence.
- **Fears of sunk costs**. Suppose you set up a firm and, to get it going, you spend money on research, machinery, and vehicles. Then, your firm makes a loss and you close it down. You may get some money back for the vehicles, a little for the machinery, and nothing for the research. The costs that you cannot recover are called **sunk costs**. Fear of these deters entry to industries in which they would be large. So this forms a barrier to, say, setting up a firm that will make a new drug, but not to, say, setting up a taxi firm.
- **Existing firms' tactics**. If existing firms have saved some past profits, they can afford to make it hard for new firms to enter the industry by cutting their prices for a while, and selling at a loss. They can also afford big advertising campaigns.

A market with a monopoly

A market or industry with a **monopoly** has a structure with just one characteristic: there is only one firm. This firm is called a **monopolist**. It does not make sense to ask whether the monopolist's product is the same or different from that of its competitors, because there are none.

It is tempting to think that monopolists must be big firms, because they supply an entire market. But their size depends on the size of their market. Some monopolists are big firms, such as the National Grid and Network Rail, and they supply the big markets for electricity and railway lines. But many monopolists are small firms, such as many rural bus firms that supply the small markets for travel on some rural routes.

The fact that there is only one firm in a monopoly is evidence of barriers to entry. All the barriers we noted with oligopolies may apply to monopolies, and there is yet another. In some cases, it would simply be wasteful to have more than one firm, which is why a monopoly emerges. For example, it would be wasteful to have two or more railways tracks between many cities, or to have two or more networks of gas pipes within any town.

> **Question 7.1** Suppose you own four firms: a sheep farm producing wool; a clothes firm making woollen sweaters; a major football club; and a football club shop, which is the only outlet for the club's strip. What type of firm is each of these?

Contestable markets

We have seen that there are barriers to entry in oligopolistic and monopolistic industries, so it is hard for new firms to enter them and compete or contest with the existing firms. But in perfectly or monopolistically competitive industries there are no barriers, so new entrants can come in and compete or contest; these industries or markets are called **contestable markets.**

Concentration ratios

In both perfect competition and monopolistic competition, there are many firms, and we argued that if all these many firms are relatively small, then none will be able to influence the price level in its industry. In practice, though, industries with many firms often have firms that vary greatly in size, and some of them may be large enough to influence the price level. One way of indicating whether some firms in an industry may be large enough to influence the price level is to look at the industry's **five-firm concentration ratio**, which shows the percentage of the industry's output that is accounted for by the five largest firms.

Table 7.4 shows the concentration ratios in the UK for a range of industries in 2004, the last year for which official figures are available. These ratios range from 99% in tobacco products and over 75% in soft drinks, man-made fibres, and confectionery, to under 15% in clothes, publishing, and furniture. It is the biggest firms in the industries with the highest ratios that potentially are most able to affect price levels.

The impact of globalization

However, even if a UK industry has a high concentration ratio such as 80%, its biggest firms sometimes still have very limited influence over price levels. The reason is that concentration ratios like those in Table 7.4 show only how concentrated manufacturing in that industry is in the UK. The largest firms in an industry often face stiff competition from foreign firms, and so supply well under 80% of the UK consumers who buy the product, and this reduces their power over prices.

Table 7.4 **Examples of five-firm concentration ratios, UK 2004**

Industry	Ratio	Industry	Ratio
Tobacco products	99	Alcoholic drinks	50
Confectionery	81	Domestic appliances	44
Man-made fibres	79	Accounting firms	36
Soft drinks	75	Motor vehicles	34
Fertilizers	72	Meat processing	17
Cement	71	Bread, biscuits, etc.	16
Telecommunications	61	Clothes	14
Oil & gas extraction	57	Publishing	12
Pharmaceuticals	57	Law firms	9
Electricity supply	55	Furniture	5

Source: Office for National Statistics, *Economic Trends*, October 2006, pp. 42–44.

7.2 **Everyday economics**

Changing supermarket fortunes

The UK supermarket industry is highly concentrated, with Tesco, Asda, Sainsbury's, and Morrisons having about 75% of the market between them in 2010. But in early 2011 all of these saw a slight fall in their market shares, except Morrisons. In contrast, there was slight growth for the smaller discount traders Aldi and Lidl, as well as for Waitrose. The discount traders have benefited from the recession making consumers more cost conscious. All these changing fortunes reveal an important truth: there is no guarantee that a firm that is in the top five one day will forever stay there.

Data from Kantar Worldpanel published in 'WM Morrison market share rises for second consecutive period', *Wall Street Journal*, 27 April 2011 and 'Tesco, Asda and Sainsbury feel the squeeze as budget stores make gains', *The Telegraph*, 27 April 2011

7.3 **Summary**

The main types of market structure or industry are as follows:

- perfect competition, in which many firms sell identical products and there are no barriers to entry;
- monopolistic competition, in which many firms sell differentiated products, and there are no barriers to entry;
- oligopolies, in which there are only a few firms, and there are barriers to entry;
- monopolies, in which there is just one firm, and there are barriers to entry.

7.4 Profits and costs

We said at the start of the chapter that, in this book, we will develop the theory of the firm on the assumption that each firm tries to maximize its profit, that is the gap between its revenue and its costs. Before we develop this theory, though, we need to see precisely how we will measure revenue, costs, and profits.

To see how we do this, suppose again that you give up your job in a few years' time and set up a driving school, which you call U-Pass. We will suppose that U-Pass is larger than the sole proprietorship we met before. To set it up, you take out £15,000 of your own savings and borrow £30,000 at a garage to buy three cars and a computer. You hire instructors to teach in two of the cars, and you teach in the third car yourself. We will now work out this firm's revenue, costs, and profit for one week, as shown in Table 7.5.

We will begin with total revenue. Suppose you and the other drivers give a total of 100 driving lessons a week and charge £30 for each lesson. Then U-Pass's revenue for the week is £3,000.

Table 7.5 **Profit and loss account for U-Pass Driving School, 15–21 January 2012**

Total revenue	**3,000**
Explicit costs	
Wages	1,200
Intermediate goods & services	150
Taxes (vehicle duty)	500
Interest to bank	50
Total explicit costs	**1,900**
Implicit costs	
Depreciation	180
Your lost wages	700
Your lost savings income	20
Total implicit costs	**900**
Total costs	**2,800**
Profit (i.e. economic profit)	**200**

To measure U-Pass's costs, we use the concept of opportunity cost. This means that we list everything that you give up so that your firm can earn this revenue. We divide the items on our list into two groups: explicit costs and implicit costs.

Explicit costs and implicit costs

Explicit costs are costs for which you actually pay out money. Table 7.5 lists these costs as follows.

- **Wages**. You pay these to your employees.
- **Intermediate goods and services**. You pay other firms for many goods and services that you 'use up', such as fuel and car maintenance.
- **Taxes**. This includes value added tax (VAT) and vehicle excise duty.
- **Interest**. You have to pay this on your loan.

Implicit costs are costs for which you do not pay money. Although you pay no money, you will want U-Pass to earn enough revenue to cover them. The table lists these costs as follows.

- **Depreciation**. You spent £45,000 on three cars and a computer, and they will fall in value over the week through wear and tear and obsolescence; this fall in value is called **depreciation**. You could instead have kept the £45,000 in a bank, where it would not fall in value. So you will want U- Pass to earn enough revenue each week to offset this fall in value.
- **Your lost wages**. You left your old job, so you will want U-Pass to earn enough revenue to offset the wage that you gave up by leaving. This lost wage is the opportunity cost of your work for U-Pass. Incidentally, this cost does not arise for companies because all of their workers are paid wages, which are covered by explicit costs.
- **Your lost savings income**. You took out £15,000 of your savings. So you will want U-Pass to earn

enough revenue to offset the income that you could have earned on that sum if you had instead invested it in another company with a level of risk similar to that of U-Pass. This forgone income is the opportunity cost of the savings that you put into U-Pass.

Economic profit

Table 7.5 gives the total value of U-Pass's explicit costs as £1,900 and the total value of its implicit costs as £900. The combined total of these costs is £2,800. The gap between U-Pass's revenue of £3,000 and its total explicit and implicit costs is £200. Economists define this gap as a firm's **economic profit**, but often they simply call it 'profit', and that is what we will do in this book.

So U-Pass's profit for the week in the table is £200. This means that U-Pass's revenue is £200 more than is needed to cover all the costs that you would want its revenue to cover in order to feel that U-Pass were worth setting up. In other words, its revenue is £200 more than is needed to cover the opportunity cost of all its inputs.

Accounting profit

If you were to hire an accountant to draw up U-pass's account for the week in Table 7.5, the account would follow conventions that all accountants use. This account would agree that the revenue was £3,000, but it would allow as costs only the explicit costs of £1,900 and the depreciation of £180; it would not allow your other implicit costs of your lost wages and the lost income on your savings. So this account would show a total cost of £2,080 to give U-Pass a profit of £920; we call this an **accounting profit**, which is a measure of the monetary value of a firm's returns to its owners.

U-Pass's monetary return to you for the week is its revenue of £3,000 *less* its explicit costs of £1,900 and its depreciation of £180, and this is indeed £920. However, £720 of this £920 is really a cost that covers the forgone income from the job that you gave up and from the savings that you used to set up U-Pass. This part of accounting profit, which is really a cost, is called **normal profit**.

Question 7.2 Suppose that, a year after you left your job to set up U-Pass, the wage paid on that job increased. What, if anything, will happen to (**a**) U-Pass's explicit costs, (**b**) its implicit costs, (**c**) its accounting profit, and (**d**) its economic profit?

Profits and resource allocation

Economic profits send out important signals that affect the allocation of a country's resources. To see this, suppose that all the firms in a contestable market are earning economic profits. This means that their revenues are greater than the costs that are needed to run them. These profits act as a signal to people elsewhere that this is a good industry in which to have firms. So this industry is likely to expand, and more resources will be allocated to producing the output of that industry.

Alternatively, suppose that all the firms in another market have revenues that fail to cover their costs, so they are making losses. This acts as a signal to the owners of firms there that this is a bad industry in which to have firms. So this industry is likely to contract, and fewer resources will be allocated to producing the output of that industry.

Transactions costs

We conclude with a final point about costs. To see this, we need to appreciate that a typical firm uses many inputs, so it has to choose which inputs it will produce for itself and which it will buy from suppliers. For example, a restaurant has to offer desserts. It could produce its own desserts or buy desserts from a supplier. Its choice depends in part on which option has the lower **transactions costs**: these are the costs of making a transaction beyond paying for the item bought.

If the restaurant buys its desserts ready-made, it will face transactions costs in trying out samples from different suppliers, in discovering the prices each supplier would set, and in monitoring and dealing with whichever supplier it uses. If it produces the desserts itself, it will face transactions costs in dealing with the people who supply the ingredients. When it makes its choice, the relative transactions costs will be one factor that it considers. It will also bear in mind that producing the desserts itself should make it easier to get them made to its exact specifications, although there will be additional costs of supervising extra chefs.

Changes in technology can affect transactions costs and so affect firms' choices. For example, the introduction of the Internet made it much easier for a firm to find out about possible suppliers of inputs and their prices. So it reduced the transactions costs to firms of using external suppliers and increased their use of them.

7.4 Summary

- In any period of time, a firm's economic profit, which is simply called profit in later chapters, is the difference or gap between the total revenue from its sales and the total cost of producing what it sold.
- A firm's costs include explicit costs, for which it pays money.
- A firm's costs also include implicit costs, for which it does not pay money.
- Implicit costs cover depreciation and also compensation for any lost earnings or investment income made by the owners as a result of working for the firm or using their savings to help to finance it.

In the next chapter we study firms' costs in greater depth than we have done in the present chapter.

abc Glossary

Accounting profit: the gap between revenue from output sold and explicit costs plus depreciation.

Agent: someone who is employed by a principal.

Asset: something of value that is owned.

Asymmetric information: when one party to a contract has more information than the other.

Barrier to entry: anything that makes it hard for a new firm to enter an industry.

Company: a firm owned by shareholders, who enjoy limited liability.

Competition for corporate control: when one company tries to buy the shares of another.

Contestable markets: markets in which potential new firms do not face barriers to entry.

Debt: raising funds by borrowing.

Depreciation: the fall in the value of capital caused by wear and tear and obsolescence.

Differentiated products: differing products.

Dividend: a payment made to a company's shareholders out of its profit.

Economic profit: the gap between total revenue from output sold and explicit costs plus implicit costs.

Economies of scope: the scope for a multi-product firm to reduce its costs by sharing some inputs between the different products.

Equity: shares sold by a company to raise funds.

Explicit cost: a cost for which a firm pays money.

Five-firm concentration ratio: the percentage of an industry's output produced by its five largest firms.

Heterogeneous products: differing products.

Homogeneous products: identical products.

Implicit cost: a cost for which a firm does not pay money, but which it nevertheless wants to cover.

Limited liability: under this, a firm's owners would not have to sell off their private property if selling the firm's assets were to raise too little to repay its debts.

Monopolist: the sole firm in a monopoly.

Monopolistic competition: a market or industry structure in which many firms produce slightly different products and which has no barriers to entry.

Monopolistic competitor: one of the many firms in a market or industry structure with monopolistic competition.

Monopoly: a market structure or industry with one firm.

Multinational enterprise (MNE): a company that operates in more than one country.

Non-price competition: when a firm tries to attract customers in ways other than with its prices.

Normal profit: the part of accounting profit that economists regard as a cost, that is all implicit costs aside from depreciation.

Oligopolist: one of the few firms in an oligopoly.

Oligopoly: a market structure or industry with few firms.

Partnership: a firm with unlimited liability and owned by two or more people.

Perfect competition: a market or industry structure with many firms producing identical products and with no barriers to entry.

Perfect competitor: one of the many firms in a market or industry with perfect competition.

Principal: someone who employs an agent.

Principal–agent problem: the risk that an agent may perform a task poorly for a principal.

Private limited company: a company designated 'Ltd' in which shares are sold privately.

Profit: another term for economic profit.

Profit-maximizer: a firm that tries to make the maximum profit per period of time.

Public limited company: a company designated 'plc' in which shares are sold on a stock exchange.

Sole proprietorship: a firm with unlimited liability owned by one person.

Sunk costs: costs that cannot be recovered.

Transactions costs: the costs of making a transaction beyond paying for the item bought.

Transnational company (TNC): another term for a multinational enterprise.

Undifferentiated products: identical products.

Unlimited liability: under this, a firm's owners would have to sell off their private property if selling the firm's assets were to raise too little to repay its debts.

Answers to in-text questions

7.1 The farm is a perfect competitor. The clothes maker is a monopolistic competitor. There are few major football clubs, so they are oligopolies. The shop is a monopoly because it is the only supplier of the club's strip.

7.2 (**a**) Nothing. (**b**) They will increase by the amount by which the wage you are forgoing increases. (**c**) Nothing. (**d**) It will fall by the amount by which implicit costs have increased.

Questions for review

7.1 (**a**) Does a profit-maximizing firm want to achieve the highest possible total revenue? (**b**) Does it want to produce at the lowest possible cost?

7.2 Claire gives up a £40,000 a year job with a firm of marketing consultants and sets up a sole proprietorship consultancy business. She buys £15,000 worth of computers and other equipment; she pays for this by taking £10,000 from her savings, which previously earned 5% interest, and by borrowing £5,000 from a bank at 10%. Over a year, this equipment falls in value by £2,000. One year, the firm's revenue is £100,000. Its costs include a secretary on £20,000 a year, an office rented for £10,000 a year, and £5,000 spent on all other inputs such as paper and electricity. What are its explicit costs, its implicit costs and its profit if any?

7.3 Gill and Geoff give up their £30,000 a year jobs and, along with their families and friends, buy 100,000 £1 shares in a new company. The company also borrows £100,000 from various lenders. (**a**) If Geoff and Gill are appointed as directors with salaries of £35,000, what is the correct way of measuring the cost of their labour to the firm? (**b**) If the shareholders agree that each year, three-quarters of any profit will be paid in dividend, are the dividends likely to be stable?

7.4 Industry X has seven firms. The five largest account for the following shares of the market: 20%, 18%, 16%, 14%, and 12%. Industry Y has 60 firms. The five largest account for the following shares of the market: 10%, 8%, 6%, 4%, and 2%. Work out the five-firm concentration ratios in each industry. These figures give useful information about the market power of the five largest firms, but do they necessarily help us to understand the power of the remaining firms?

? Questions for discussion

7.1 Think back on some of the products that you have bought recently. Which were produced by firms in perfect competition, which by firms in monopolistic competition, which by firms in an oligopoly, and which by firms with a monopoly or near-monopoly?

7.2 Suppose you run a small grocery shop, and a supermarket is established in your area, threatening your firm's existence. The supermarket says that consumers have the choice, so you can't complain if they desert you for it. How far would you agree?

7.3 Think of three firms that have recently made decisions that they think will raise their profits.

Common student errors

The main error is to assume that monopolists and large firms are one and the same. However, a firm can be huge, like Shell, and still face intense competition from other firms selling identical products. On the other hand, a small company with only one bus might have a monopoly of a bus route in a rural area.

8

Costs and Production Methods

Remember from Chapter 7 that we assume that each firm aims to make the maximum possible profit.

Suppose you run a firm: is it possible that you could reduce the cost of producing each individual unit of output? Suppose you start to produce more each week: will your total costs rise by a lot or by a little? Will your firm's costs be affected by what other firms in your industry do? How could your firm be efficient? How should your firm choose between a production method that uses a lot of labour and little capital, or a method that uses a lot of capital and little labour?

This chapter shows you how to answer questions like these, by understanding:

* the distinction between the short run and the long run;
* fixed costs and variable costs;
* average costs and marginal costs;
* the law of diminishing marginal returns;
* economies of scale and diseconomies of scale;
* production functions and isoquants;
* economic efficiency and technical efficiency.

8.1 Two different profit-maximizing outputs for a single firm

Suppose you run a firm that makes high-quality mobiles, and suppose you want to make as much profit as possible. Then, during any period of time, such as a week, you will want to produce and sell the number of phones that will give you the maximum possible profit for that week.

To find out what this output is, you must first work out how much profit you would get from each possible output, and then see which output would give the most profit. For each output, the profit will equal the gap between your total revenue from selling phones and your total cost in making them. So you need information about two things.

- **Revenue**. You need to know what your total revenue would be at each possible output.
- **Cost**. You need to know what your total cost would be at each possible output.

We will now consider how the total revenue and the total cost of a firm like yours may vary with its output.

Revenue

Your firm will set its output level at the same level as its sales, and they depend on your price. Suppose the effects of three possible prices are as follows.

- **At a price of £120**, you would sell no phones, so your total revenue would be £0.
- **At a price of £115**, you would sell 1,000 phones each week, to get a total revenue of £115,000.
- **At a price of £110**, you would sell 2,000 phones each week, to get a total revenue of £220,000.

Table 8.1 shows the output and revenue that you would get at a range of prices, including these.

Two time frames for costs

Your costs arise because you need inputs. Suppose your inputs are labour, components, and assembly lines. Suppose, too, that you can readily change the quantity of labour and components you use each week, but it takes you six months to change the quantity of assembly lines you use; maybe it takes six months to install a new line or to sell an unwanted line.

In this situation, you, like all other firms, need to make choices about two time frames, as follows.

- **The short run.** This is the period during which a firm has *at least one* input of which quantity is fixed. For your firm, the short run is six months.
- **The long run.** This is the period after which a firm can vary the quantity of all of its inputs. For your firm, it starts after the next six months.

Short-run total costs

Suppose you have four assembly lines at present. Then you will be stuck with them for the next six months. Even if you make no phones, you will still face costs on them, like insurance, depreciation, and the interest on any loans that you used to help to buy them. Say these costs are £80,000 a week. Then, even if you make no phones, your total costs will be £80,000 a week.

If you do make some phones, you will also face costs for labour and components, so your costs will be higher. Table 8.1 shows the lowest total cost at which each output level shown can be produced during the short run, that is while there is at least one input of which quantity is fixed: this is the **short-run total cost**, *STC*.

Long-run total costs

After six months, you can vary the quantity of assembly lines as well as other inputs. Table 8.1 shows also the lowest total cost at which each output level shown can be produced in the long run, that is when the quantity of every input can be varied: this is the **long-run total cost**, *LTC*.

Table 8.1 **Daily costs and daily profits in the short run and in the long run**

Price £ per phone	Output Phones per week	Total revenue £000s per week	Short-run total cost (*STC*) £000s per week	Short-run profit £000s per week	Long-run total cost (*LTC*) £000s per week	Long-run profit £000s per week
120	0	0	80	−80	0	0
115	1,000	115	120	−5	60	55
110	2,000	220	156	64	120	100
105	3,000	315	189	126	180	135
100	4,000	400	240	160	240	160
95	5,000	475	310	**165**	300	175
90	6,000	540	402	138	360	**180**
85	7,000	595	525	70	420	175

Let's compare *STC* and *LTC* at three output levels.

- **Output = 0**. If you were to make no phones, this would cost £80,000 in the short run, but £0 a week in the long run. It is less in the long run, because you have time to sell your four assembly lines.
- **Output = 1,000**. This would cost £120,000 a week in the short run and £60,000 in the long run. Presumably you don't need four assembly lines for a low output like this, and in the long run you can sell some off and reduce your costs.
- **Output = 6,000**. This would cost £402,000 a week in the short run and £360,000 in the long run. Presumably the ideal number of assembly lines for a high output like this is more than four, and in the long run you can get some more.

The two profit-maximizing output levels

For the next six months, you will choose the output that will give you the maximum profit in the short run. For each output, Table 8.1 shows the short-run profit, which is the gap between total revenue and *STC*. The highest figure is £165,000 a week. Your firm will earn this amount of profit if you set a price of £95 to sell 5,000 phones a week. Then, each week, you will have a total revenue of £475,000 and a short-run total cost of £310,000.

After six months, you will choose the output that will give you the maximum profit in the long run. Suppose you expect demand to stay the same, so you think that your sales and total revenue at each price will be the same as they are now. Then, for each output, Table 8.1 shows the long-run profit, which is the gap between total revenue and *LTC*. The highest figure is £180,000 a week. Your firm will earn this amount of profit if you set a price of £90 to sell 6,000 phones a week. Then, each week, you will have a total revenue of £540,000 and a long-run total cost of £360,000.

So you will make these three decisions today.

- **Choose your output for the short run**. For the next six months, you will produce 5,000 phones a week, which you will sell at a price of £95.
- **Choose your output for the long run**. After six months, you will produce 6,000 phones a week, which you will sell at a price of £90.
- **Start changing the quantity of inputs that are fixed in the short run**. At present, with four assembly lines, producing 6,000 phones a week would cost £402,000. You must install extra lines to cut the cost to £360,000 in six months.

To reach these decisions, you needed to know how your revenue, your short-run costs, and your long-run costs would vary with your output level. All firms need to know this. As it happens, the relationship between output and costs is broadly similar for most firms, and the remaining sections of this chapter analyse this relationship in some depth.

In contrast, the relationship between output and revenue depends in large part on whether a firm is a perfect competitor, a monopolistic competitor, an oligopolist, or a monopolist. The following chapters study each of these types of firm.

Question 8.1 These are inputs whose quantity could vary today, and two that it could probably not vary for a year or so.

8.1 Everyday economics

A future for UK car-making?

The firms that own car plants in the UK could instead locate their plants in other countries, such as Eastern Europe, where wages are much lower. So why don't they? It's a matter of fixed and variable costs. The biggest component in the cost of making a car is the assembly line, and these last for perhaps 40 years. So, while a firm actually has a UK plant, it makes more sense to operate it, even if wages are relatively high, than to build a new one elsewhere. In any case, labour costs probably account for only 10–15% of the cost of making a car, so savings in wages don't affect the final price greatly. But when the UK plants wear out, will the companies build new ones here or abroad? When they ponder that decision, one issue they will consider is that high wage costs in the UK will make car plants here relatively costly to build as well as to operate. So the long-term future of car-making in the UK is uncertain.

8.1 Summary

- For each period of time, such as a week, every firm must decide what output level it will produce in the short run, during which it can vary the quantity of some inputs it uses, but not all of its inputs.
- For each period of time, such as a week, every firm must also decide what output level it will produce in the long run, by when it will have had enough time to vary the quantity it uses of all of its inputs.
- Each firm must also think about the inputs the quantity of which it cannot vary in the short run. Should it order more of these inputs for the long run, or should it try to sell some of those that it currently has?

8.2 Short-run costs

We will begin our analysis of costs with short-run costs. To discuss these, we will now assume that you run a bakery that makes bread. We will measure your output in batches of 1,000 loaves, and we will consider your decision about how many batches to produce each day.

Like all firms, you use a range of inputs, which we can divide into two groups.

- **Variable inputs.** These are inputs for which quantity *can* be varied in the short run. In your case, we will assume that these inputs are labour, gas, and ingredients.
- **Fixed inputs.** These are inputs for which quantity *cannot* be varied in the short run. In your case, we will assume these inputs are ovens and the factory space in which the ovens are put.

Suppose it would take you a year to get extra ovens and extra factory space, or to dismantle unwanted ovens and sell off unwanted factory space. Then, for your firm, the short run will apply for one year, and then the long run begins. Your key short-run decision is how many batches to make each day during the next year.

To make this decision, you need information about the short-run costs of producing different numbers of batches. Table 8.2 gives this information. The first column here gives the number of batches per day, that is the quantity of output, *Q*.

Short-run total costs

The second column in Table 8.2 shows the short-run total cost, *STC*, of producing each number of batches. At each output level, we can divide this total into two components, as follows.

- **Total fixed cost**: this is shown in a later column headed *TFC*, and is the total cost of the firm's fixed inputs. For your firm, it is the total cost of the factory space and ovens, so it includes the insurance and depreciation on these, and the interest on any loans that you took out to pay for them. You will see in the table that *TFC* is the same, £420 per day, at each output.

  The reason that *TFC* is the same at each output is that no matter what your output is, you cannot, in the short run, vary the amount of factory space and ovens you have, so you cannot alter the cost of them. For example, even if you set $Q = 0$, and so make no loaves, and so want no factory space or ovens, you will still have total fixed costs of £420 per day, because you cannot get rid of your space and ovens for a year. On the other hand, if you set a high output, say $Q = 7$, and might like more space and ovens than you have now, you will still have total fixed costs of £420 per day, because you cannot get any more space and ovens for a year.

- **Total variable cost**: this is shown in a later column headed *TVC* and is the total cost of the firm's variable inputs. For you, it is the cost of labour, gas, and ingredients. You will see in the table that your *TVC* depends on your output. For example, if you produce no bread, so $Q = 0$, then you may lay off every worker, buy no ingredients, and use no gas, so your *TVC* will be £0. But the more batches you produce, the more of these inputs you will use, and so the higher your *TVC* will be.

  Your short-run total cost at each output equals the *TFC* plus the *TVC*. For example, if $Q = 3$, then *TFC* is £420 per day and *TVC* is £660 per day, so the short-run total cost is £1,080 per day, as shown in the column headed *STC*.

Average short-run costs

As well as looking at total costs, economists are interested in the cost of producing each individual unit of output. In your case, this would be the cost of each batch. We measure these costs per unit with three types of average cost, as explained below. Table 8.2 shows the three average cost figures for each possible output, except for $Q = 0$: we cannot talk about the cost of making an individual batch if no batch is made.

Table 8.2 **Short-run total costs, fixed costs, and variable costs for a range of output levels**

Output, Q Batches per day	*STC* £ per day	*SAC* £ per batch	*SMC* £ per batch	*TFC* £ per batch	*AFC* £ per batch	*MFC* £ per batch	*TVC* £ per batch	*AVC* £ per batch	*MVC* £ per batch
0	420	–		420	–		0	–	
			320			0			320
1	740	740		420	420		320	320	
			200			0			200
2	940	470		420	210		520	260	
			140			0			140
3	1,080	360		420	140		660	220	
			180			0			180
4	1,260	315		420	105		840	210	
			240			0			240
5	1,500	300		420	84		1,080	216	
			360			0			360
6	1,860	310		420	70		1,440	240	
			520			0			520
7	2,380	340		420	60		1,960	280	

- **Short-run average cost**, shown in the column headed *SAC*: this is the total cost for each unit of output, in the short run. For example, suppose $Q = 3$, so *STC* is £1,080 per day for the three batches or units taken together. We cannot be sure how much each individual batch contributes to this. For instance, if the ovens start from cold each day, then the first batch made each day may need more gas than the others. However, if the *STC* for the three batches together is £1,080, we can say that, *on average*, each batch costs £1,080/3, or £360. So at each *Q*, the figure for *SAC* equals *STC/Q*.
- **Average fixed cost**, shown in the column headed *AFC*: this is the fixed cost for each unit of output. At each output, *AFC* equals *TFC/Q*. For example, suppose $Q = 3$. The total fixed cost for the three batches taken together is £420 per day, so we can say that, on average, each batch has a fixed cost of £420/3, which is £140. *AFC* gets smaller as *Q* rises. This is because, as *Q* rises, the constant *TFC* of £420 gets divided by higher *Q*s to produce lower *AFC*s.
- **Average variable cost**, shown in the column headed *AVC*: this is the variable cost for each unit of output. At each output, *AVC* equals *TVC/Q*. For example, suppose $Q = 3$, so that the total variable cost for the three batches taken together is £660 per day. Then we say that, on average, each batch has a variable cost of £220 per day.

Notice that at each *Q*, $SAC = AFC + AVC$. For example, if $Q = 3$, so that $AFC = £140$ and $AVC = £220$, then $SAC = £140 + £220$, which is £360.

Marginal short-run costs

Aside from total costs and average costs, economists also consider how much total costs will change if the output, *Q*, changes. They measure these changes with what are called marginal costs. There are three types of marginal cost, as explained below. Table 8.2 gives all the figures.

- **Short-run marginal cost**, shown in the column headed *SMC*: this is the change in the short-run total cost if output changes by one unit. For example, suppose you currently set $Q = 3$, so that *STC* is £1,080 per day. Then you raise *Q* to four. Table 8.2 shows that *STC* rises to £1,260. This is an increase of £180, so $SMC = £180$.
- **Marginal fixed cost,** shown in the column headed *MFC*: this is the change in the total fixed cost if output changes by one unit. For example, suppose you currently set $Q = 3$, so that *TFC* is £420 per day. Then you raise *Q* to four. *TFC* will stay at £420 because you cannot vary the quantity of your fixed inputs for a year. As *TFC* does not actually change, so $MFC = £0$.
- **Marginal variable cost** shown in the column headed *AVC*: this is the change in the total variable cost if output changes by one unit. For example, suppose you currently set $Q = 3$, so that *TVC* is £660 per day. Then you raise *Q* to four. Table 8.2 shows that *TVC* rises to £840. This is an increase of £180, so $MVC = £180$. Note that *SMC* equals *MVC*. This is always the case, because *SMC* shows how much total short-run costs change when *Q* changes by one, and the only costs that change are variable costs.

In Table 8.2, all these marginal cost figures are printed between the lines for outputs of three and four. This is because these costs do not show what happens *at* outputs of three or four: they show what happens if output rises *between* three and four. All the other marginal cost figures are also printed between the lines for the changes in output concerned.

Graphs of short-run cost curves

Later chapters use many graphs with curves for average costs and marginal costs. It may seem that we will need graphs with six curves to show *AFC*, *AVC*, and *SAC*, and *MFC*, *MVC*, and *SMC*. In practice, we need to use only three curves. Figure 8.1 shows these for the firm in Table 8.1.

This graph has two average cost curves, one for *AVC* and one for *SAC*. The points on the graph show how these curves were plotted. For example, above an output of three, there is a point on *AVC* at £220 and a point on *SAC* at £360.

We could plot a third average cost curve for *AFC*, which is £140 when $Q = 3$. But we do not need a curve for *AFC* because we can work out what *AFC* is at each output without a curve. This is because *AFC* equals the gap between *SAC* and *AVC*. The graph shows, as an example, how we can work out that if $Q = 3$, then *AFC* is £140.

Figure 8.1 has only one marginal cost curve. It shows both *MVC* and *SMC*, which, as we have seen, are always the same. The points on this curve show how it was plotted. For example, halfway between an output of 3 and an output of 4, there is a point at £180, to show that costs change by £180 if output changes from 3 to 4. We could add a marginal cost curve for *MFC* on the figure, but as *MFC* is always £0, this would simply run along the horizontal axis.

Question 8.2 In Figure 8.1, the gap between the *AVC* and *SAC* curves gets smaller as output rises. What does this tell us about *AFC* as output rises?

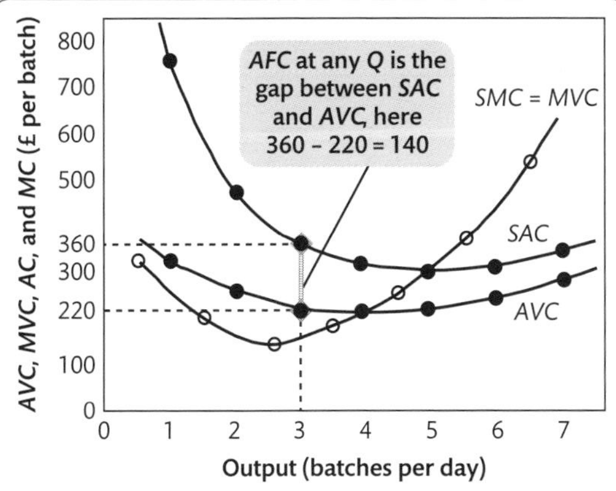

Figure 8.1 **The curves for *AVC*, *SAC*, *SMC*, and *MVC***

There is no need to draw a curve for *AFC*, because the *AFC* at any output level such as three equals the gap between *SAC* and *AVC* at that output. There is also no need to draw a curve for *MFC*, because *MFC* is always zero.

Intersections of short-run cost curves

All the cost curves in Figure 8.1 are U-shaped. We will explain why in a moment. But first note that the curve for *SMC* and *MVC* passes through the bottom points of both the *AVC* and *SAC* curves. We can put this another way, and say the curve for *SMC* passes the bottom point of *SAC*, while the curve for *MVC* passes the bottom point of the curve for *AVC*. It is important to understand why this happens, and to do so we need to understand how average and marginal figures are related.

To understand this relationship, suppose you arrive early for a lecture and reckon that the average height of the students who are there, *AH*, is 1.7 m. Then along come two students, as follows.

- **A student 1.9 m high**. The height of this extra or marginal student, *MH*, is above *AH*. So if you recalculate the average, you will find it has risen.
- **A student 1.5 m high**. The height of this marginal student, *MH*, is below *AH*. So if you recalculate the average, you will find it has fallen.

So, when a marginal figure is above the average, the average rises, and when it is below the average, the average falls. This explains the relationship between the *AVC* and *MVC* curves in Figure 8.1. When *MVC* is above *AVC*, to the right of the point where these curves intersect, *AVC* must be rising; when *MVC* is less than *AVC*, to the left of where they intersect, *AVC* must be falling. So if *AVC* is falling to the left of the intersection and rising to the right, then the intersection must be at its lowest point. Likewise, *SMC* intersects *SAC* at its lowest point.

The law of diminishing marginal returns

We will now consider why the firm in Figure 8.1, and indeed most firms, have U-shaped curves for *MVC* and *MC*, and for *AVC* and *STC*. To understand these U-shapes, we must remember that these curves apply in the short run when a firm cannot vary the quantity it uses of one or more inputs.

To see how having some fixed inputs affect the shape of a firm's short-run cost curves, we will take a simple case of a firm with only one variable input, labour. Suppose this firm varies its number of workers from 0 to 6. The effects on its output are shown in the first three columns of the table at the top of Figure 8.2, as follows.

- **Total product** (*TP*): this is the firm's total output. For example, if it hires three workers, then its total output is 48 tonnes a week.
- **Average product** (*AP*): this is the average output per worker. For example, if it hires three workers who produce a total of 48 tonnes, then on average each worker produces 16 tonnes.
- **Marginal product** (*MP*): this is the change in total product if the number of workers changes by one. For example, if the number rises from three to four, then *TP* rises from 48 tonnes to 68 tonnes, so the *MP* between three and four workers is 20 tonnes. This is printed between the rows for three and four workers, because it shows what happens if the number rises from three to four.

The figures for *MP* here initially increase. For example, if the firm hires one worker, its output is only 8 tonnes a week. If it hires a second, its output rises by 16 tonnes to 24 tonnes, so *MP* is 16. If it then hires a third, its output rises by 24 tonnes to 48 tonnes, so *MP* is bigger, at 24. *MP* initially rises in any firm in which the first few workers benefit from teamwork. For example, consider a dustcart. With one worker, the driver must constantly waste time getting in and out to empty bins, so output or *TP*, measured as tonnes of rubbish collected, is small. Adding a second worker will raise *TP* a lot, and adding a third may raise it even more.

However, the benefits of teamwork are limited. For example, adding yet more workers to the dustcart may raise *TP* very little, because there will be no bins near the cart for them to empty. There is a so-called **law of diminishing marginal returns**, which says that if extra units of one variable input are added to a fixed amount of all other inputs, then sooner or later the marginal returns, or *MP*s, will get smaller. In Figure 8.2, the *MP* falls from the third worker onwards.

Workers Number per week	*TP* Tonnes per week	*AP* Tonnes per worker	*MP* Tonnes per worker	*TVC* £ per week	*AVC* £ per tonne	*MVC* £ per tonne
0	0	-		0	-	
			8			90
1	8	8		720	90	
			16			45
2	24	12		1,440	60	
			24			30
3	48	16		2,160	45	
			20			36
4	68	17		2,880	42	
			12			60
5	80	16		3,600	45	
			4			180
6	84	14		4,320	51	

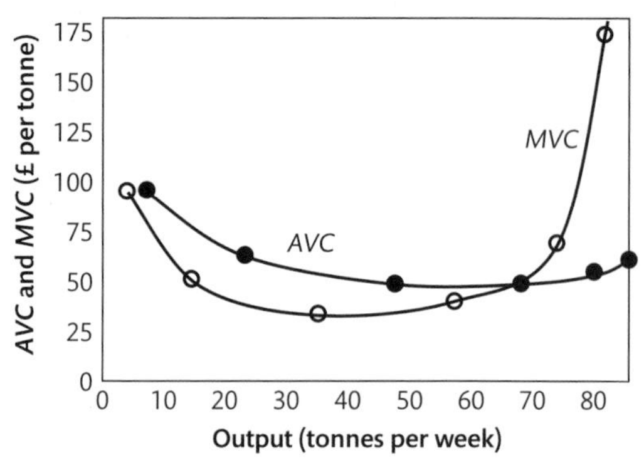

Figure 8.2 **U-shaped *AVC* and *MVC* curves**

The marginal returns here initially rise and then fall, so the *AP* and *MP* curves initially slope up and then slope down. In turn, the *AVC* and *MVC* curves initially slope down and then up.

Curves for average and marginal products

The numbers for *AP* and *MP* in the table in Figure 8.2 were used to plot the points in the graph below it.

Then curves for *AP* and *MP* were plotted through the appropriate points. The *MP* curve has the shape of an upside-down U because, as we have just seen, *MP* initially rises and then falls.

The *AP* curve also has an upside-down U-shape, and it is cut at its highest point by *MP*. The reason is that initially *MP* is above *AP*, so *AP* increases; later *MP* is below *AP*, so *AP* decreases.

Why *MVC* and *AVC* curves are U-shaped

To see why *MVC* and *AVC* curves are U-shaped, consider again the firm in Figure 8.2. Suppose its workers are paid £720 per week. As they are this firm's only variable input, their cost is its only variable cost. So its variable costs depend on how many workers it hires. The final three columns on the table give figures for its variable costs with each number of workers, as explained below.

- **Total variable cost**. Say the firm hires three workers. Its *TVC* is three times £720 at £2,160.
- **Average variable cost**. Say the firm hires three workers. Its *TVC* is £2,160, and the table shows that its output is 48 tonnes. The *AVC* of each of those 48 tonnes is £2,160/48, which is £45.
- **Marginal variable cost**. Say the firm now hires a fourth worker and so pays £720 more in variable costs. Its output rises by 20 tonnes to 68. So we can regard the extra cost of each of these 20 extra tonnes as £720/20, which is £36.

The bottom part of Figure 8.3 plots curves for both *AVC* and *MVC*. The reasons why both these curves have U-shapes are as follows.

- **The *MVC* curve**. This slopes downwards at first because *MP* initially rises. For example, suppose the firm initially hires one worker, then two, and then three. The second worker costs £720 and adds 16 tonnes, so the *MVC* of each of these tonnes is £720/16, or £45. The third worker also costs £720 and adds even more tonnes, 24, so the *MVC* of each of these is £720/24, or £30, which is less than £45. But as soon as *MP* starts to fall, extra workers add fewer tonnes, so the *MVC* of extra tonnes gets bigger, and then *MVC* slopes upwards. So *MVC* is U-shaped.
- **The *AVC* curve**. This slopes downwards initially because *MVC* is below *AVC*. It later slopes upwards because *MVC* is above *AVC*. Note that *MVC* goes through the bottom point of *AVC*.

Why *SMC* and *SAC* curves are U-shaped

To see why *SMC* and *SAC* curves are U-shaped, consider again the firm that we had in Figure 8.1.

- **The *SMC* curve**. Figure 8.1 shows that a firm's *SMC* curve is the same as its *MVC* curve. We have just seen that *MVC* curves are U-shaped, so *SMC* curves must also be U-shaped.
- **The *SAC* curve**. At any output, *SAC* equals the *AFC* at that output plus the *AVC* at that output. We have just seen that *AVC* curves are U-shaped: this means that the *AVC* is high at both low and high outputs. Also, *AFC* is always high at low outputs, because *TFC* is then spread over very few units of output; you can check this from Table 8.2. So, if *AFC* and *AVC* are high at low outputs, *SAC* will be high there; if *AVC* is high at high outputs, *SAC* will be high there. So *SAC* curves are also U-shaped.

Changes in input prices

We know that, in the short run, a firm sets its output at the level at which the gap between its total revenue and its short-run total cost is biggest. But suppose the price of an input changes. This will change the total cost of producing each output level. So the biggest gap between total revenue and total cost may now be at a different output. So the firm may change its output.

To understand firms' output decisions fully, we must see how changes in input prices affect their costs. We will discuss these changes in the case of the bakery firm we met in Table 8.1. The initial cost curves for this firm were shown in Figure 8.1, and are repeated in black in

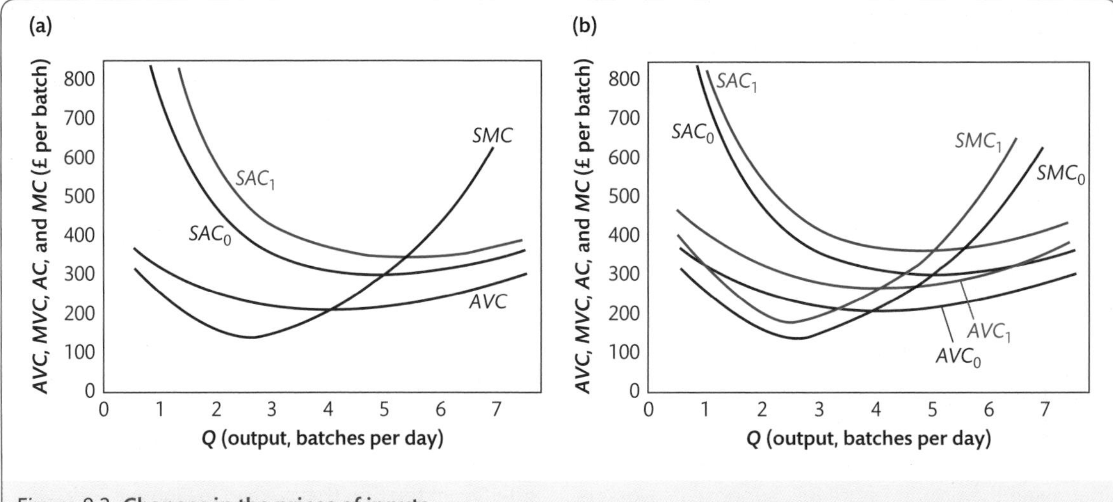

Figure 8.3 **Changes in the prices of inputs**

If the price of one or more fixed inputs rises, only the *SAC* curve shifts up, as in part (a). If the price of one or more variable inputs rises, then all three curves shift up, as in part (b).

each part of Figure 8.3. These parts concern an increase in the price of a fixed input and an increase in the price of a variable input, which we will discuss in turn.

Changes in the price of fixed inputs

Suppose the price of one of the bakery's fixed inputs rises. It may seem odd that anything about a fixed input can change, but remember that the only thing about a fixed input that is fixed is the *quantity* that the firm can use in the short run. The *price* of a fixed input can change. For example, the bakery may face a rise in the interest rate it has to pay on a loan borrowed to buy an oven, or a rise in the premium for insuring it.

Other firms may have other fixed inputs for which prices can rise. For example, the rent they pay on a building for which they have signed a long-term lease may rise. Or they may raise the wages of some staff who have long-term contracts and who cannot, therefore, be fired in the short term. Or they may have signed a long-term contract with a raw material supplier and find that the price has increased.

The effects of the rise in the price of the fixed input on the firm's cost curves are shown in part (a) of Figure 8.3 and are as follows.

- **The *SAC* curve shifts up**. This is because at each output the short-run average cost, *SAC*, equals *STC*/*Q*. Now the rise in the input price increases *STC* at each output, so in turn it increases *SAC* at each output. So the *SAC* curve shifts upwards.
- **The *AVC* curve stays put**. This is because at each output the average variable cost, *AVC*, equals *TVC*/*Q*. Now the rise in the price of a fixed input has no effect on the cost of buying variable inputs, so *TVC* remains the same and in turn *AVC* remains the same.
- **The curve for *MVC* and *SMC* stays put**. This curve shows the change in the firm's total cost when it raises its output by one unit. But when the firm raises its output in the short run, the only extra inputs that it can buy more of are variable inputs. A change in the price of a fixed input has no effect on the cost of buying whatever extra variable inputs it needs, so this curve stays put.

Changes in the price of variable inputs

Suppose that the price of one of the bakery's variable inputs rises. Perhaps there is a rise in the price it pays for one of its ingredients or for gas, or perhaps it pays its workers higher wage rates. The effects of the rise in the price of the variable input on the firm's cost curves are shown in part (b) of Figure 8.3 and are as follows.

- **The *SAC* curve shifts up**. This is because at each output the short-run average cost, *SAC*, equals *STC*/*Q*. Now the rise in the input price increases *STC* at each output, so in turn it increases *SAC* at each output. So the *SAC* curve shifts upwards.
- **The *AVC* curve shifts up**. This is because at each output the average variable cost, *AVC*, equals *TVC*/*Q*. Now the rise in the price of a variable input increases the total cost of the firm's variable inputs, so *TVC* increases and in turn *AVC* increases. So the *AVC* curve shifts upwards.
- **The curve for *MVC* and *SMC* shifts up**. This curve shows the change in the firm's total cost when it raises its output by one unit. When the firm raises its output in the short run, the only inputs it can buy more of are its variable inputs. So if the price of one of these rises, then the cost of buying the extra inputs it needs increases, so the marginal cost curve shifts upwards. Note that the new marginal cost curve passes the bottom points of the new *SMC* and *SAC* curves.

Conclusions on changes in input price

We have now seen that changes in the prices of fixed inputs and variable inputs have different effects on a firm's short-run cost curves. We will see in later chapters that in turn they have different effects on a firm's output. For example, the effect on the bakery's output of a rise in an insurance premium would be different from the effect of a rise in the price of flour.

8.2 Everyday economics

Diminishing marginal returns and aid

In the 1990s, developed countries agreed to double their aid to Africa by 2015. A report by The United Nations conference on Trade and Development (*Economic Development: Doubling Aid, Making the Big Push Work*, UNCTAD, 20 September 2006) noted that sceptics had raised concerns about how much effect the doubling of aid would have on output and incomes in Africa, if the quantity of other inputs such as human capacity and institutions were to remain fixed. It also pointed to divisions between the sceptics, with some suggesting the returns would diminish when aid reached only 4% of GDP, while others thought they would diminish only when it had reached 50%. It should be added that even if the returns do begin to diminish, they could still be very important.

8.2 Summary

- A firm's short-run total costs, *STC*, equal its total fixed cost, *TFC*, plus its total variable cost, *TVC*, where *TFC* is the total cost of the inputs for whose quantity cannot be changed in the short run and *TVC* is the total cost of the inputs for which quantity can be changed in the short run.
- Short-run average costs, *SAC*, average fixed costs, *AFC*, and variable costs, *AVC*, are the relevant total costs per unit of output. The gap between the *SAC* and *AVC* curves shows *AFC* at each output.
- Short-run marginal costs, *SMC*, marginal fixed costs, *MFC*, and marginal variable costs, *MVC*, are the changes in the relevant total costs if output changes by one unit. *MFC* is always zero and *SMC* = *MVC*.
- The curve for *SMC* and *MVC* passes the lowest points of the *AVC* and *SAC* curves.
- The *AVC* and *MVC* (or *SMC*) curves are generally U-shaped because of the law of diminishing marginal returns. This says that if successive units of one variable input are added to fixed quantities of all other inputs, then sooner or later the additions to output, that is the marginal product, *MP*, will diminish.
- The *SAC* curve is U-shaped because *AVC* is U-shaped and also because *AFC* is high if output is low.
- A rise in the price of a fixed input shifts only a firm's *SAC* curve.
- A rise in the price of a variable input shifts a firm's *SAC* curve, its *AVC* curve, and its *SMC* curve.

8.3 Long-run costs

We saw in section 8.1 that the figures for a firm's long-run total costs, *LTC*, show the lowest total cost at which it can produce each output in the long run, when it has had time to vary the quantity it uses of all its inputs. We will now see how these costs vary with output.

In one respect, the analysis of long-run costs is simpler than that of short-term costs. This is because there is no need to distinguish between fixed and variable inputs: in the long run, all inputs are variable. On the other hand, the ways in which total costs vary with output are more varied in the long run than in the short run, and we will now consider several possibilities.

Q Units per week	*LTC* £ per week	*LAC* £ per unit	*LMC* £ per unit
10	2,000	200	200
11	2,200	200	
20	4,000	200	200
21	4,400	200	
30	6,000	200	200
31	6,600	200	
40	8,000	200	200
41	8,800	200	

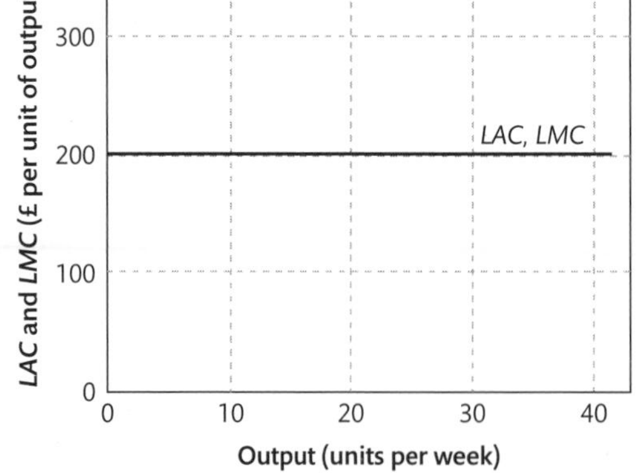

Figure 8.4 **Constant costs**

When this firm's output doubles, its *LTC* also doubles, so *LAC* is constant.

Constant costs

Suppose you run the firm for which the table in Figure 8.4 gives some information. The first column shows the long-run total cost, *LTC*, for a selection of possible weekly outputs. For example, if you were to produce 10 units a week, and had time to adjust the quantity of all your inputs, the lowest total cost you could manage would be £2,000.

The table in Figure 8.4 also gives figures for two more types of long-run cost, as follows.

- **Long-run average cost** (*LAC*) is the cost per unit of output in the long run, that is *LTC/Q*. For example, if you set $Q = 10$, so that *LTC* is £2,000, then *LAC* is £2,000/10, or £200. Now suppose you double your output to 20. For this firm, the cheapest way of producing this new output in the long run is to use twice as many inputs as when $Q = 10$, so *LTC* is twice as much, £4,000, while *LAC* is £4000/20, or £200, the same as before. Now suppose you double your output again to 40. For this firm, the cheapest way of producing this new output is to use twice as many inputs as when $Q = 20$, so *LTC* is twice as much, £8,000, while *LAC* is £8000/40, which is still £200. So this firm has a horizontal *LAC* curve, as shown in Figure 8.4. This means you could produce any number of units per week at £200 each, provided that you had time to vary the quantity you use of all inputs.
- **Long-run marginal cost** (*LMC*) is the change in long-run total cost if output changes by one unit. For example, if you were to raise *Q* from 10 a week to 11, *LTC* here would rise by £200 from £2,000 to £2,200, so *LMC* would be £200. Indeed, with this firm, every time output per week rises by 1, whether from 10 to 11, 20 to 21, or 40 to 41, *LTC* will rise by £200. So this firm has a horizontal *LMC* curve that coincides with its *LAC* curve, as shown in the figure.

If a firm can, in the long run, produce any output at a the same average cost, in this case £200, then it is said to have **constant costs**, and it has a horizontal *LAC* and *LMC* curve. Some firms may well have constant costs, but there are other equally plausible situations, as we will now see.

Economies of scale

Instead of having constant costs, your firm might be like that shown in Figure 8.5. Here, if you set $Q = 10$, then *LTC* is £3,000, but if you then double your output to 20, you find that you do not need to spend twice as much, so *LTC* does not double to £6,000 and instead rises to just £5,320. And if you double your output again to 40, once more your *LTC* does not double, which would make it £10,640, but instead rises to just £8,400.

Q Units per week	*LTC* £ per week	*LAC* £ per unit	*LMC* £ per unit
10	3,000	300	
			261
11	3,261	296	
20	5,320	266	
			199
21	5,519	263	
30	7,080	236	
			150
31	7,230	233	
40	8,400	210	
			112
41	8,512	208	

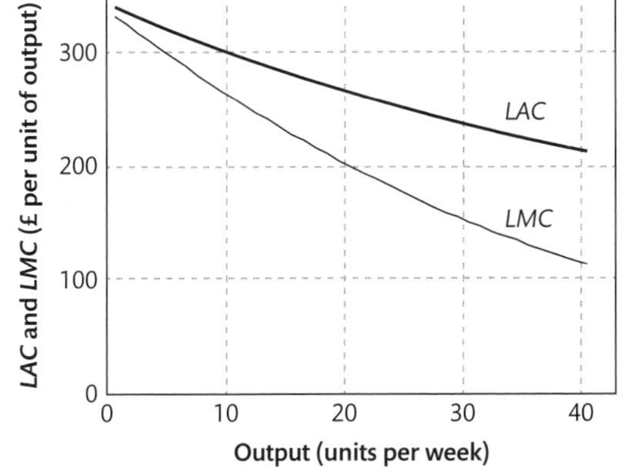

Figure 8.5 **Economies of scale**

When this firm's output doubles, its *LTC* less than doubles, so *LAC* falls.

Here, *LTC* rises more slowly than output, so *LAC* falls. For example, if $Q = 10$, *LAC* is £3,000/10, or £300, and if $Q = 40$, *LAC* is £8,400/40, or £210. In turn, the *LAC* curve slopes down. Because *LAC* falls when the output or scale of production increases, this firm is said to have **economies of scale**.

We know that when an average curve slopes down, the associated marginal curve must be below it, so here the entire *LMC* must be below *LAC*. To check that it is, suppose for example that *Q* rises from 20 to 21. The table shows that *LAC* falls from £266 to £263, but the increase in total cost, or *LMC*, is way below these figures at £199.

Economies of scale can arise for several reasons. These include the following.

- **Increasing returns to scale**. If a firm increased all of its inputs by the same percentage and found that its output rose by a larger percentage, then it would have **increasing returns to scale.** So if it wanted to double its output, then it would not need twice as many inputs, so its average cost would fall. A simple example is a removal firm that expands from one worker plus one lorry to two workers plus two lorries: the scope for teamwork with two workers might enable the firm to move much more than twice as much.
- **One-off costs**. Although many firms have to use more of every input to increase their output, some do not. For example, a firm might spend £10 million developing a new drug. It needs to make this research only once. So it can then double its output without doubling its total cost.
- **Specialized inputs**. When a firm produces more, it expands. It may then be able to afford specialized inputs, which reduce its average costs. For example, if a sole proprietor makes tables and hires no workers, then the proprietor must do all the designing, manufacturing, selling, and accounts. If the firm expands, it can hire specialists in design, manufacture, selling, and accounts. By using specialists, the firm's output might rise faster than its total costs, to give it a lower average cost. Moreover, the firm might now also be able to afford specialist machines that a small firm could not afford.

- **Financial economies**. A large firm may be able to negotiate low input prices from its suppliers.
- **Larger inputs that reduce average costs**. A big firm might simply be able to use bigger inputs that allow it to cut its average cost. A good example arises with containers. Figure 8.6 shows two containers, one a 1 m cube and the other a 2 m cube. The bigger cube needs four times as much material to make it, but it holds eight times as much. So if the firms in an industry need containers, then big firms that use big ones can have lower average costs. This example applies in many situations, including large cargo ships, large aircraft, large lorries, large furnaces, and even large ovens.

Diseconomies of scale

Instead of having a horizontal or downward-sloping *LAC*, your firm might be like the one shown in Figure 8.7. Here, if you set $Q = 10$, then *LTC* is £1,000, but if you then double your output to 20, you need to spend more than twice as much, so *LTC* does not double to £2,000 and instead rises to £2,294. If you double your output again to 40, once more your *LTC* does not double, which would make it £4,588, but instead rises more to £6,940.

Here, *LTC* rises more quickly than output, so *LAC* rises. For example, if $Q = 10$, *LAC* is £1,000/10, or £100, and if $Q = 40$, *LAC* is £6,940/40, or £174. In turn, the *LAC* curve slopes up. Because *LAC* rises when the output or scale of production increases, this firm is said to have **diseconomies of scale**.

We know that when an average curve slopes up, the associated marginal curve must be above it, so here the entire *LMC* must be above *LAC*. To check that it is, suppose for example that *Q* rises from 20 to 21. The table shows that *LAC* rises a little from £115 to £117, but the increase in total cost, or *LMC*, is well above these figures at £157.

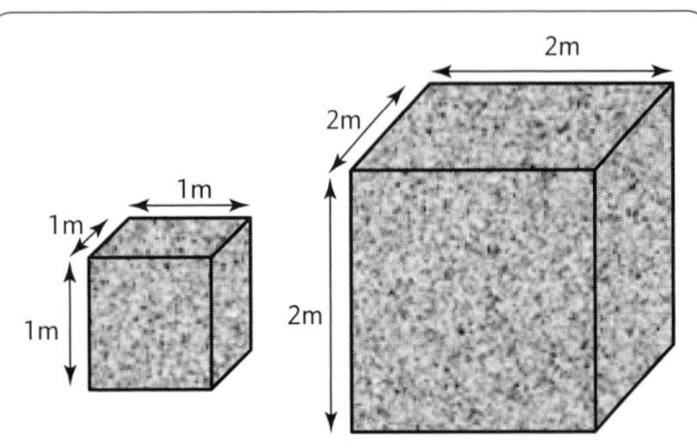

Figure 8.6 **Economies of scale with containers**

The small container has six sides, each with an area of 1 m²; so its total surface area is 6 m². The large one has six sides, each with an area of 4 m²; So its total surface area is 24 m². So the large one will cost four times as much to make. However, the small container holds just 1 m³, while the large one holds 8 m³. So the large one costs four times as much to make, but holds eight times as much. So the cost of 1 m³ storage space in the large one is half that of the small one.

Q Units per week	*LTC* £ per week	*LAC* £ per unit	*LMC* £ per unit
10	1,000	100	
			111
11	1,111	101	
20	2,294	115	
			157
21	2,451	117	
30	4,176	139	
			232
31	4,408	142	
40	6,940	174	
			336
41	7,276	177	

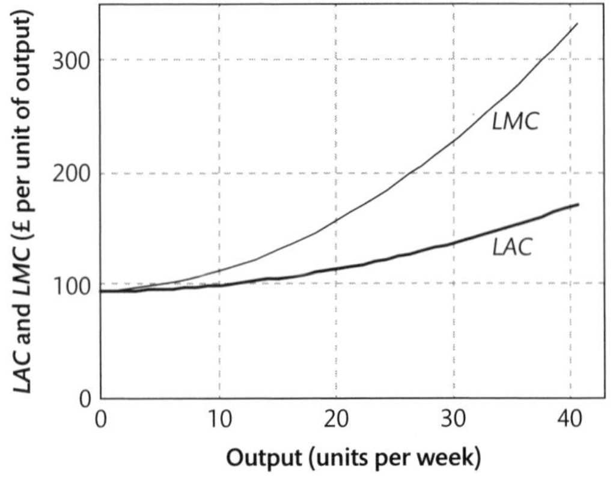

Figure 8.7 **Diseconomies of scale**

When this firm's output doubles, its *LTC* more than doubles, so *LAC* rises.

Diseconomies of scale can arise for several reasons. These include the following.

- **Decreasing returns to scale**. If a firm increased all of its inputs by the same percentage and find that its output rose by a smaller percentage, then it would have **decreasing returns to scale.** Also, if it wanted to double its output, it would need more than twice as many inputs, so its total cost would more than double. A simple example is a smart hotel with, say, 250 bedrooms that finds that two porters are enough. It might then double the number of rooms, but many of these will now be far from the hotel reception, so it might take five porters to give the same level of service as before.
- **Managerial diseconomies**. When a firm increases its output, it may need proportionately more managers. For example, a small firm may employ three sales staff and two design staff who form a closely knit team. If the firm expands to produce ten times as much, it may expect to need 30 sales staff and 20 design staff. But these staff will now form different groups, maybe in distant offices, and extra managers may be needed to coordinate them.
- **Staff motivation problems**. If a firm expands, its employees may begin to feel very distant from the management. So they may have less motivation and work less hard, causing costs per unit of output to rise; moreover, the remote management may not notice the problem and check it. However, some firms overcome this problem with incentives and promotion schemes.

Q Units per week	*LTC* £ per week	*LAC* £ per unit	*LMC* £ per unit
10	1,520	152	130
11	1,650	150	
20	3,000	150	150
21	3,150	150	
30	4,500	150	155
31	4,655	150	
40	6,640	166	304
41	6,944	169	

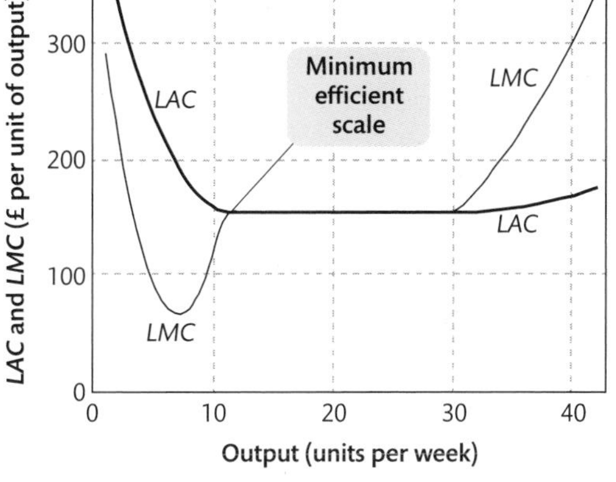

Figure 8.8 **A *LAC* with economies of scale, then constant costs, then diseconomies of scale**

The minimum efficient scale is at the start of the flat part of *LAC*.

Other possible shapes for *LAC* curves

Many firms enjoy economies of scale as they expand from small to medium-sized, so their *LAC* curves slope downwards at low levels of output. Then their economies of scale disappear to give them a horizontal *LAC*. This situation is shown in Figure 8.8. But in this example, *LAC* does not remain horizontal, because diseconomies of scale set in at very high outputs. This firm would have the lowest possible average cost, and so be most efficient, if it were to produce an output on the horizontal part of its *LAC* curve; the lowest output on this part is the level at its left-hand end and is called the **minimum efficient scale**. Notice that the *LMC* is below *LAC* when *LAC* slopes down, coincides with *LAC* when *LAC* is horizontal, and is above *LAC* when *LAC* slopes up.

An alternative is for diseconomies of scale to set in as soon as the economies are exhausted. This creates a U-shaped *LAC* and *LMC*, as shown in Figure 8.9. Again *LMC* is below *LAC* when *LAC* slopes down and above it when *LAC* slopes up.

LAC and types of industry

In Chapter 7, we divided industries into four types: perfect competition; monopolistic competition; oligopoly;

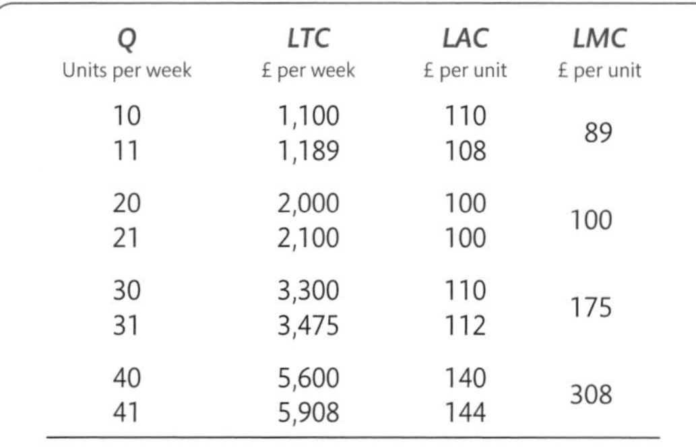

Q Units per week	LTC £ per week	LAC £ per unit	LMC £ per unit
10	1,100	110	89
11	1,189	108	
20	2,000	100	100
21	2,100	100	
30	3,300	110	175
31	3,475	112	
40	5,600	140	308
41	5,908	144	

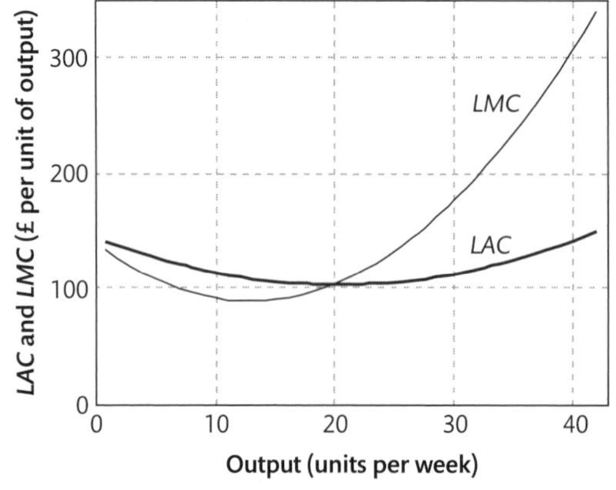

Figure 8.9 **A U-shaped *LAC* curve**

Initially, this firm has economies of scale; then it has diseconomies of scale.

and monopoly. The type that arises in any given industry is related to the shape of the *LAC* curves that firms in the industry have. Here are some examples.

- **An industry in which economies of scale persist up to output levels that would supply the whole market**. In this case, the average cost of supplying the market will be lower with one big firm than with two or more smaller ones. The result is likely to be a monopoly, because any smaller firms can cut their average costs by merging; in turn, they will have a lower combined total cost and so make more profit. A monopoly that arises for this reason is called a **natural monopoly**. Examples include firms that produce electricity or gas supply networks. It is cheaper to have one firm install a single grid that supplies each building in a town than to have two or more firms with separate grids.
- **An industry in which economies of scale are exhausted at outputs that are less than the whole market, but still relatively large**. Here, there may be only a few firms and so an oligopoly.
- **An industry in which economies of scale are exhausted at relatively low outputs and then remain constant over a wide efficient scale**. Here, many firms of widely ranging size may compete on level terms in respect of costs.
- **An industry in which economies of scale are exhausted at relatively low outputs and then diseconomies of scale set in quickly**. Here, the result is likely to be many small firms.

There are two further points to note. First, oligopolies and monopolies can arise, irrespective of the shape of firms' *LAC* curves, if there are barriers to entry, as discussed in Chapter 7.

Secondly, small firms can arise even in industries with appreciable economies of scale and no barriers to entry. This may occur in monopolistic competition. Here, the firms all have different products, and while a firm that expands might reduce its average cost, it might also exhaust the demand for its particular product. Indeed, we will see in Chapter 10 that, in the long run, monopolistic competitors produce outputs that are lower than their minimum efficient scales.

8.3 Everyday economics

Water, sewage, and scale

The water and sewerage industries in the UK are regulated by Ofwat. In 2004, Ofwat published a report (*An Investigation into Opex Productivity Trends and Causes in the Water Industry in England & Wales 1992–93 to 2002–03*, Ofwat, May 2004), which found significant diseconomies of scale for firms handling both water supply and sewage. It also found that water-only firms probably had constant returns to scale. The reason that the largest existing firms do not have economies of scale is that water is heavy and expensive to move around. The findings disappointed the existing firms, which hoped significant economies of scale would be found, in which case they hoped they would be allowed to merge, reduce their combined costs, and so make more profit.

Shifts in long-run cost curves

We know that a firm will set its output in the long run at the level that gives it the biggest gap between its total revenue and its long-run total cost. Suppose the price of an input changes. This will change the cost of producing each possible output. So it may cause the firm to set a different level of output in the long run, because the biggest gap between total revenue and total long-run cost may now be at a different output.

So to understand firms' output decisions more fully, we need to see what effect changes in input prices have on their costs. In the long run, all inputs are variable, so we do not need to distinguish between fixed and variable inputs.

Suppose a firm starts with the U-shaped LAC_0 shown in Figure 8.10. Then, the effects of a change in input prices on its long-run costs are as follows.

- **A rise in input prices.** If the prices of one or more inputs rise, then the total cost of each output increases, so the long-run average cost curve shifts up, say to LAC_1.
- **A fall in input prices.** If the prices of one or more inputs fall, then the total cost of each output decreases, so the long-run average cost curve shifts down, say to LAC_2.

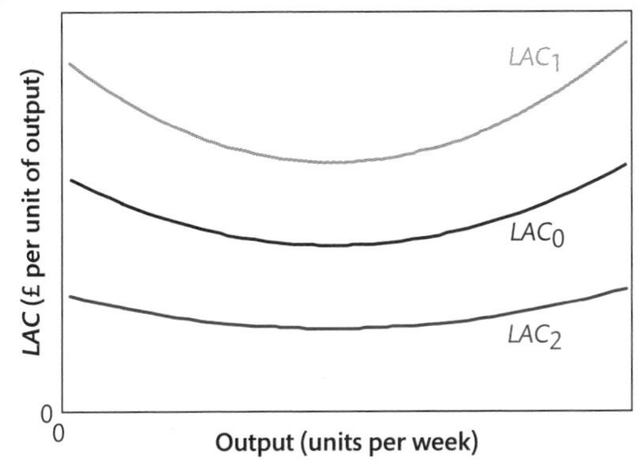

Figure 8.10 **Changes in input prices**

Changes in input prices alter the average cost of each possible output. LAC_1 shows the effect of a rise in the price of one or more inputs, while LAC_2 shows the effect of a fall.

External economies and diseconomies of scale

Input prices can change for many reasons. For example, wages for most types of labour rise each year. So, in turn, do the prices of many other inputs for which production involves a lot of labour.

Occasionally, a firm finds that the price of an input changes as a direct result of a change in the size of its industry. For example, suppose that more tour operators enter the industry of providing holidays on a remote island. The expansion of the industry could affect the input prices of the existing tour operators in two ways.

- **Some input prices may rise.** For example, increased tourism on the island will increase the demand for hotel accommodation, so the existing operators may face a higher price for each room they book. So these firms face a rise in costs, or a diseconomy, which is caused by a change in the scale of the industry, that is by the scale of something external to the firms themselves. Cost increases like this are called **external diseconomies of scale**.
- **Some input prices may fall.** For example, airlines flying to the island may now be able to justify more economical, bigger planes, so the existing operators may face a lower price for each ticket they buy. So these firms face a fall in costs, or an economy, which is caused by a change in the scale of the industry, that is by the scale of something external to the firms themselves. Cost decreases like this are called **external economies of scale**.

For any actual firm, a change in the industry size will shift its *LAC* upwards if any external diseconomies of scale outweigh any external economies of scale, and vice versa.

8.3 Summary

- In the long run, when all inputs can be varied, firms' *LAC* curves have varying shapes.
- A firm may have constant costs, which means it could double its output by using exactly twice as many inputs. If so, it would have a horizontal *LAC* curve that coincided with a horizontal *LMC* curve.
- A firm may instead have economies of scale and find that a rise in its output leads to lower long-run average costs. So its *LAC* curve would slope down, and its *LMC* curve would be below its *LAC* curve.
- A firm may instead have diseconomies of scale and find that a rise in its output leads to higher long-run average costs. So its *LAC* curve would slope upwards, and its *LMC* curve would be above its *LAC* curve.
- A firm's *LAC* curve may also slope downwards at low outputs and upwards at high outputs. In between, there may be a horizontal part of the curve; the outputs along this part are called the efficient scale.
- A firm's *LAC* shifts up if input prices rise and it shifts down if they fall.
- If a firm's industry expands, then its input prices will rise if there are external diseconomies of scale and fall if there are external economies of scale.

8.4 Relating the short run, the long run, and the very long run

We have so far explored short-run average costs curves and long-run average cost curves. But we now need to see how these are related for an individual firm. Figure 8.11 shows the relationship for a typical firm, say a bakery. The curves shown here are as follows.

- **The long-run average cost curve**. This curve, *LAC*, shows the lowest average cost at which the firm could produce each output, if it were given time to vary the quantity of all its inputs.
- **Several short-run average cost curves**. Each of these shows the lowest average cost at which the firm could produce each output in the short run, while it was stuck with its current quantity of fixed inputs. Maybe SAC_1 would apply if it had five ovens and the space for them, SAC_2 if it had ten, and so on. We could easily add more *SAC* curves between and beyond those shown.

Each *SAC* curve touches the *LAC* curve at just one point. This point is at the one output level for which the quantity of fixed inputs relating to that *SAC* is the quantity that the firm would choose even in the long run.

For example, suppose the firm currently has 10 ovens, so that SAC_2 applies at present. This touches *LAC* at the output where 10 ovens is the best number. At higher outputs, the firm would prefer more ovens, and it could in the long run produce at a lower total cost and a lower average cost than it can manage while it has 10. At lower outputs, the firm would prefer fewer ovens, and could in the long run produce at a lower total cost and a lower average cost than it can manage while it has 10.

Maybe in a few years the firm will have 15 ovens and so be on SAC_3. With more ovens, the costs of high outputs will be lower than they are now. But the costs of low outputs will be higher than they are now, because the firm would be facing costs for more ovens and factory space than it needed for low outputs. So SAC_3 is below SAC_2 at high outputs and above SAC_2 at low outputs.

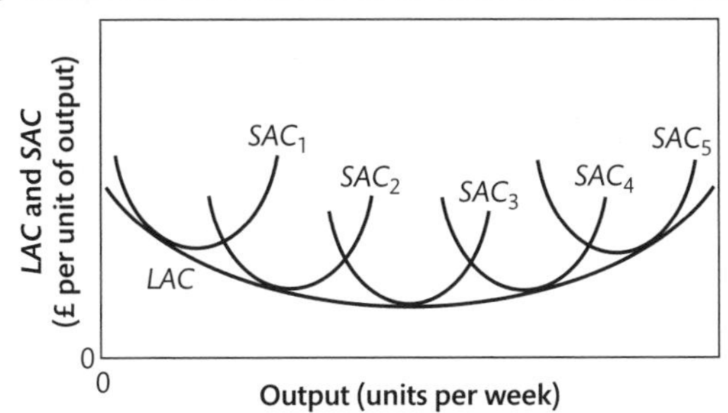

Figure 8.11 **Relating a firm's *LAC* curve and *SAC* curves**

A firm has one *LAC* curve: it shows the lowest average cost at which it could produce each output in the long-run, when it has time to alter the amount it uses of all inputs. In the short-run, a firm does not have time to alter the amount it uses of one or more inputs, so the average cost for each output depends on how many of these fixed inputs it has. The curves SAC_1 to SAC_5 show the short-run average costs that apply with five different levels of fixed inputs. SAC_1 applies if there is a low level of fixed inputs: here, it is very costly—even perhaps impossible—to produce a high output. SAC_5 applies if there is a high level of fixed inputs: here, there is a high average cost if output is low, because the firm then faces costs for fixed inputs that get little or no use.

Question 8.3 If the price of an input used by the firm in Figure 8.11 were to rise, what would happen to its cost curves?

The very long run

The long run is the period after which a firm can vary the quantity of all the inputs it uses. So it can get to any point on its *LAC*. Therefore, it may seem that it cannot do any more to reduce its costs.

However, if the firm is given even longer, then it may be able to reduce costs in further ways. For example, it might devise better work practices and training programmes for its employees. Or it might do research and development that allows it to develop better capital.

The **very long run** is the period after which a firm can begin to alter the *quality* of its inputs as well as their *quantity*. It may seem interesting to ask how long a firm needs to make all these improvements. In practice, though, improvements can continue almost indefinitely. Sometimes, government agencies try to help firms to develop new technologies and, even, new products.

8.4 Summary

- In the short run, a firm has some fixed inputs, and its costs depend on how many of these it has. So it has a different *SAC* curve for each possible level of fixed inputs that it could have. Each of these *SAC* curves touches its *LAC* at the output where the quantity of fixed inputs for that *SAC* curve is the best quantity.
- In the very long run, a firm can usually vary the quality of some of its inputs as well as their quality.

8.5 Choosing a production method

Each firm has to choose a **production method**: this means that it must choose what inputs it will use and choose the proportions in which it will use them. For example, a security firm protecting an airport could use guards, CCTV cameras, dogs, and security lights in many different proportions.

In order to maximize profits, firms aim to use the cheapest available method. This section explores this issue in more depth, but you need not study it in order to understand the rest of the book.

Production functions

To explain fully how a firm chooses its production method, we need to consider its production function. A **production function** shows the highest output that a firm could produce from every possible combination of available inputs.

To keep the discussion simple, it helps to take as an example a firm that uses just two inputs. Very few firms do that, but we will consider a firm that ferries people across a river in rowing boats. One input is labour in the form of rowers, who work eight hours in a full day; the other input is capital in the form of boats. We will assume that the proportion of boats to rowers can be varied: for example, one rower could use more than one boat, by rowing one boat and towing others; and one boat could be used by more than one rower, if they rowed together or worked in shifts.

The table in Figure 8.12 gives this firm's production function. It shows its maximum output, in passengers per day, for every combination of rowers, from 1 to 18, and boats, from 1 to 6. For example, with 6 rowers and 3 boats, its maximum output is 300 passengers.

Of course, with 6 rowers and 3 boats, the ferry might be unable to have an output of 300: this could happen if it were to leave some inputs idle some of the time, or if it were to use its inputs wastefully, perhaps allowing the rowers to take roundabout routes. The output of 300 will arise only if no inputs are idle and none are used wastefully, which means the firm is **technically efficient**. All the numbers in the table show the technically efficient or maximum output for each combination of inputs.

No. of rowers	1 boat	2 boats	3 boats	4 boats	5 boats	6 boats
1	71	100	122	141	158	173
2	100	141	173	200	224	245
3	122	173	212	245	274	**300**
4	141	200	245	283	316	346
5	158	224	274	316	354	387
6	173	245	**300**	346	387	424
7	187	265	324	374	418	458
8	200	283	346	400	447	490
9	212	**300**	367	424	474	520
10	224	316	387	447	500	548
11	235	332	406	469	524	574
12	245	346	424	490	548	600
13	255	361	442	510	570	624
14	265	374	458	529	592	648
15	274	387	474	548	612	671
16	283	400	490	566	632	693
17	292	412	505	583	642	714
18	**300**	424	520	600	671	735

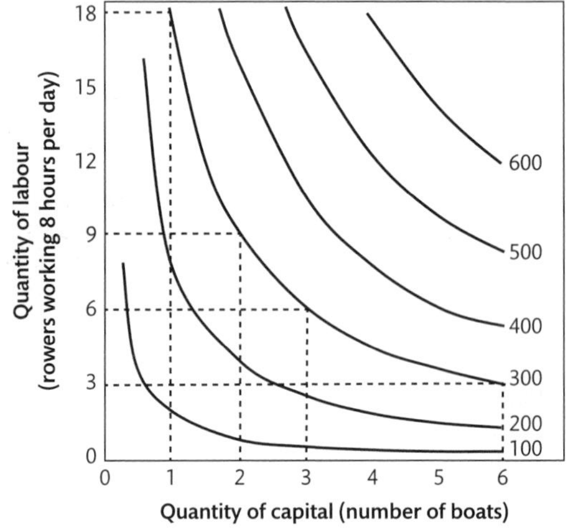

Figure 8.12 **A production function**

The table shows the maximum output that can be produced from varying combinations of inputs. The graph uses this information to plot some isoquants. For example, the 300 isoquant passes all the combinations of inputs that can produce an output of 300. These include 1 boat and 18 rowers, 2 boats and 9 rowers, 3 boats and 6 rowers, and 6 boats and 3 rowers.

Isoquants

Figure 8.12 shows the firm's production function in another way. This graph has the number of boats on the horizontal axis and the number of rowers on the vertical axis.

The graph has six curves. Each curve refers to a particular output. For example, the one labelled 300 refers to an output of 300 passengers a day. This curve passes through every combination of inputs that would give an output of 300. For reference, these combinations are shown in bold in the table: they include 1 boat with 18 rowers, 2 boats with 9 rowers, 3 boats with 6 rowers, and 6 boats with 3 rowers.

A curve like this, which shows various combinations of inputs that could all produce the same output level, is called an **isoquant**. Figure 8.12 also has isoquants for outputs of 100, 200, 400, 500, and 600 passengers. The isoquants that are furthest from the origin reflect the use of the most inputs, so they relate to the highest output levels.

You will see that the isoquants slope downwards. To see why, suppose the firm wants an output of 300 and is initially at the point on the 300 isoquant where it uses 2 boats and 9 rowers. Then suppose it gets a third boat. If it sticks with 9 rowers, its output will rise. So if it wants to use 3 boats, but keep its output at 300, then it must use fewer rowers, and the 300 isoquant shows that it must use 6. The downward slope of the isoquant simply shows that the firm's output can be kept at 300 whenever it uses extra boats, provided that it also uses fewer rowers.

You will also see that the isoquants are curved, and get flatter from left to right. This curvature arises because each input has diminishing marginal returns. To see this, suppose the firm wants an output of 300, and suppose it initially has 9 rowers and 2 boats. Then it considers two possible changes to the number of boats.

- **Adding a third boat**. The table shows that if this were the firm's only change, then its output would rise by 67 to 367. To reduce its output by 67, back to 300, while using three boats, the firm must hire 6 rowers, 3 fewer than at present.
- **Removing the second boat**. The table shows that if this were the firm's only change, then its output would fall by 88 to 212. To raise its output by 88, back to 300, while using one boat, the firm must hire 18 rowers, 9 more than at present.

There are two reasons why the number of rowers has to change more when a boat is added than when a boat is removed.

- **Boats have diminishing marginal returns**. This means that output initially changes less when one boat is added than when one is removed. The number of passengers here rises by 67 when a boat is added, but falls by 88 when a boat is removed.
- **Rowers have diminishing marginal returns**. This means that output changes less when a rower is added than when a rower is removed. Here, it actually needs 9 more rowers to increase output by 88, but only 3 fewer to reduce output by 67.

So a fall in the number of boats by one has to be offset by a change of 9 rowers, while a rise in the number of boats by one can be offset by a change of just 3 rowers. This means that the 300 isoquant is steeper to the left of the point with 2 boats and 9 rowers than it is to the right of this point. For similar reasons, all isoquants become flatter towards the right throughout their lengths.

Expansion paths

Figure 8.13 repeats the production function given in Figure 8.12. Take any isoquant, say the 200 one. This shows how an output of 200 can be produced using different combinations of labour and capital. In other words, it shows how 200 can be produced using a

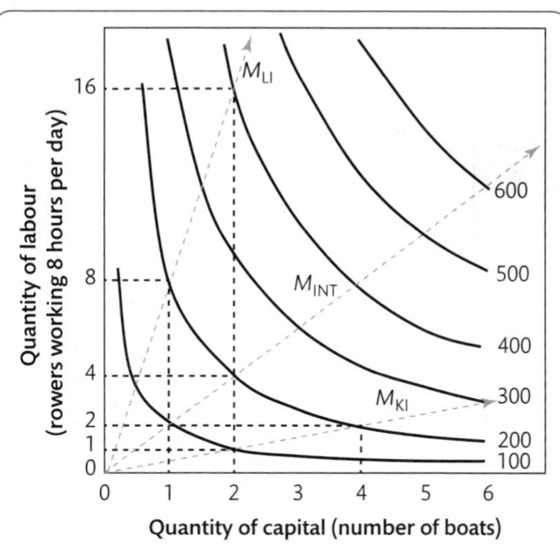

Figure 8.13 **Illustrating production methods**

A firm's production method depends on the inputs it uses and on the proportions it uses them in. Input combinations on M_{LI} involve a labour-intensive method that uses much labour in relation to capital. Combinations on M_{KI} involve a capital-intensive method that uses much capital in relation to labour. Combinations on M_{INT} involve an intermediate method.

range of different production methods. Let's consider three of these methods.

- **A labour-intensive method**. Suppose the firm produced 200 with 1 boat and 8 rowers. It would use a lot of labour in relation to capital and so have a **labour-intensive** method. It could, of course, combine its inputs in these proportions, and so use the same method, but use more or fewer inputs to produce more or less output. For example, it could double the number of boats and rowers to 2 and 16 and produce an output of 400. The various outputs that can be secured with this particular labour-intensive method, combining inputs in these combinations, are shown by the grey dashed arrow M_{LI}.
- **A capital-intensive method**. Suppose the firm produced 200 with 4 boats and 2 rowers. It would use a lot of capital in relation to labour and so have a **capital-intensive** production method. It could, of course, combine its inputs in the same proportions, and so use the same method, but use more or fewer inputs to produce more or less output. For example, it could halve the number of boats and rowers to 2 and 1 and produce 100. The various outputs that can be used with this particular capital-intensive method, combining inputs in these combinations, are shown by the grey dashed arrow M_{KI}.
- **An intermediate method**. We could add further arrows through the origin, at different slopes, to show the outputs that are possible with different methods. For example, the arrow M_{INT} shows the outputs with one intermediate method, which uses rowers and boats in the ratio 2 to 1.

Each dashed arrow in Figure 8.13 is called an **expansion path**. This is because it shows how output would expand if the firm were to stick to one method, but increase the number of all inputs.

Isocost lines

A profit-maximizing firm will choose the cheapest available production method. Which method this is depends on the prices of its inputs. Let's suppose these are as follows.

- **The price or cost of labour**. Suppose it costs £80 to employ a rower for an 8-hour day.
- **The price or cost of capital**. Suppose it costs £160 to use a boat for a day: this covers items such as its depreciation, maintenance, and insurance, and any fee for using it on the river.

Now suppose that the firm decides to spend £640 a day. Then it could, for example, use 8 rowers and no boats, or 4 rowers and 2 boats, or no rowers and 4 boats. In Figure 8.14, which repeats in grey the production function from earlier figures, the line C_{640} passes all these three combinations. Indeed, every combination of inputs on C_{640} would cost £640. A line that shows input combinations with the same total cost is called an **isocost line**.

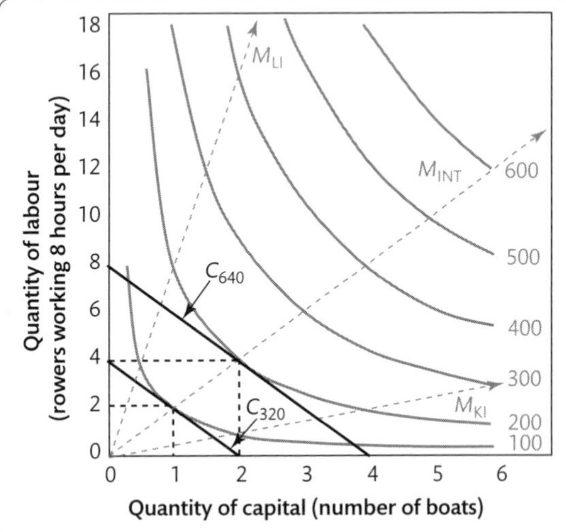

Figure 8.14 **Choosing a production method**

C_{320} and C_{640} show the input combinations that can be bought at current prices for total outlays of £320 and £640. The firm wants to produce as much output as it can for any outlay; so if it spends £640 it will produce an output of 200 using 2 boats and 4 workers. If it spends £320 it will produce 100 using 1 boat and 2 workers. However much it spends, it will go to a point on M_{INT} and use the intermediate method.

If it spends £640, the firm will want to produce and sell the most amount of output that it can manage. We can see from Figure 8.14 that this output is 200, because the highest isoquant that the £640 isocost line reaches is the 200 one. This point is on M_{INT}, so to get here the firm must use the intermediate technology, and actually use 2 boats and 4 rowers.

If the firm were to spend less, say £320, then it could buy only half as many inputs, including 4 rowers and no boats, or 2 boats and no rowers. So it would be able to buy any combination of inputs shown on the parallel isocost line C_{320}. The highest output it could now produce is 100, because the highest output that C_{320} reaches is at a point on the 100 isoquant. This point is also on M_{INT}, so to get here the firm must again use the intermediate technology, and use 1 boat and 2 rowers.

In fact, no matter how much the firm spends, it will face an isocost line parallel to C_{320} and C_{640}. And to produce as much as possible for that cost, it will go where that isocost line just touches the highest possible isoquant, which will be at a point on M_{INT}, so it will use the intermediate method.

The production method with the lowest cost

The 200 isoquant shows all the input combinations that will result in an output of 200. But aside from the combination of 2 boats and 4 rowers, these all lie outside the £640 isocost line and would cost more. So that combination is the cheapest way to produce 200. Likewise, the 100 isoquant shows all the input combinations that will result in an output of 100. But aside from the combination of 1 boat and 2 rowers, these all lie outside the £320 isocost line and would cost more. So this combination is the cheapest way of producing 100. So no matter how much it produces, the firm will use the intermediate method because it is the cheapest.

A change in the price of an input

Suppose the ferry spends £320 a day to carry 100 passengers with 1 boat and 2 rowers. Then suppose the price of labour falls. For simplicity, say it falls greatly from £80 a day to £20. Then the isocost line for £320 will pivot to be like C_{320} in Figure 8.15. This figure also repeats the production function given in earlier figures.

At one end of C_{320} the firm could hire 16 rowers and use no boats, and at the other end it could hire no rowers and use 2 boats. The highest output that it can produce for £320 is now 200, because C_{320} just touches the 200 isoquant. But to produce 200 for £320, the firm would now have to use the labour-intensive method, as the expansion path that passes this point is M_{LI}.

Of course, the firm may not end up spending the same as it did before, £320. Say it instead ended up spending £640. Then it would be on the parallel isocost line C_{640} in Figure 8.15, which just touches the 400 isoquant. So the firm would end up producing 400 with 16 rowers and 2 boats. Again it would use the labour-intensive method, as the expansion path that passes this point is M_{LI}.

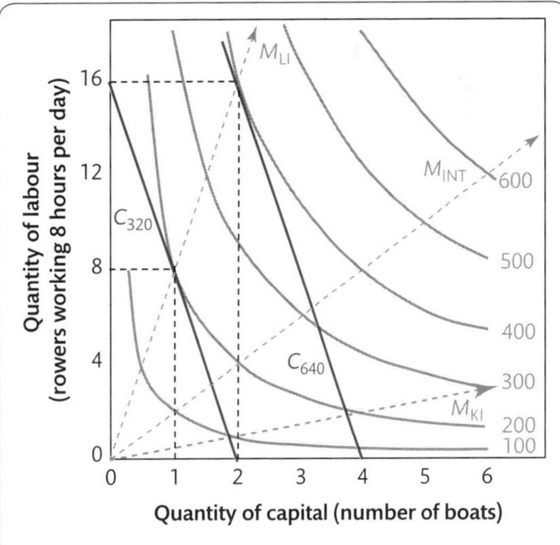

Figure 8.15 **Changing the production method**

If the price of labour is lower than in Figure 8.3, at £20, while the price of capital stays at £160, then the firm faces steeper isocost lines, like those shown in purple for £320 and £640. It will now use the more labour-intensive method on M_{LI}.

Indeed, no matter how much it spends, the firm will now face an isocost line parallel to those in Figure 8.15 and will produce where that line touches the highest possible isoquant. This will be at a point on M_{LI}, so it will use the labour-intensive method.

So a fall in the price of labour in relation to the price of capital makes the isocost lines steeper, and then the firm switches to a more labour-intensive method. So it uses less capital, and substitutes it with more labour. The effect of a change in relative input prices, which leads to a switch to a different production method that uses the now relatively cheaper input more intensively, is called the **principle of substitution**.

Production functions and efficiency

The term **economic efficiency** is used when a firm produces its output at the lowest possible cost. In contrast, the term economic inefficiency is used when a firm does not produce its output at the lowest possible cost. Each profit-maximizing form aims to secure economic efficiency, and to do so it must do two things.

- **It must have technical efficiency**. It should not have any idle or wastefully used inputs. This actually means that it should produce its chosen output with a combination of inputs that lies on the relevant isoquant. For example, if the firm has an output of 200, but uses 2 boats and 6 rowers or 3 boats and 4 rowers, then it will be technically inefficient, because these combinations lie outside the 200 isoquant and could produce more than 200. The table in Figure 8.12 shows that each could actually produce 245; so if the output were only 200, then some inputs would be idle or wastefully used.
- **It must choose the cheapest method**. Every combination of inputs on the 200 isoquant is a technically efficient way of producing 200 because this isoquant shows that the most that can be produced with all those combinations is 200. To be economically efficient, however, the firm must go beyond technical efficiency and choose the cheapest combination on the isoquant. This is the combination at the point where the isoquant is just touched by an isocost line, and it is the only technically efficient combination that is also economically efficient.

8.5 Summary

- A production function shows the maximum output that a firm can get from each possible combination of inputs, assuming no inputs are idle or used wastefully, so that the firm is technically efficient.
- Each isoquant shows the combinations of inputs that would secure a particular level of output.
- Isoquants slope down because when a firm uses more of one input, it must use less of the other to maintain a constant output. Isoquants are curved because of diminishing marginal returns.
- A firm will choose the production method with the lowest cost for its chosen output. It is the method the expansion path of which passes the point on the isoquant for which output that is touched by an isocost line.
- Input prices determine which production method is the cheapest. If the price of one input falls in relation to the others, then firms will switch to methods that use the cheaper input more intensively.

8.6 Production functions and costs

In this final section, we build on our understanding of production functions to relate them to long-run and short-run average cost curves, and also to changes in technology.

We will continue to use the example of the ferry, but we will add a further assumption. This is that, in the short run, the firm can vary only the amount of labour it uses, simply by hiring more or fewer rowers or by altering their hours of work. In the short run, though, it cannot alter the number of boats. If it wants an extra boat, it may take time to build one or find a suitable one to buy. If it wants one fewer boat, it may take time to sell one, and meanwhile it will be saddled with costs such as depreciation and insurance on the unwanted boat.

Suppose it would take six months to acquire a new boat or to sell an existing one. Then for this firm the short run lasts six months, and for that time it is stuck with however many boats it has today.

Long-run average costs

Let's consider first the long-run costs for this firm. They depend on the prices of its inputs, and we will suppose that it costs £80 to hire a rower for an 8-hour day, and that it costs £160 to use a boat for a day.

In this case, as we saw in Figure 8.14, the cheapest way for the firm to produce an output of 100 would be to use 2 rowers and 1 boat. This is shown in the top line of Table 8.3, which works out that the total cost would be £320 a day. And it shows that the cost of each of the 100 individual passengers could be seen as £320/100, or 320p. This is the *LAC* for 100 passengers.

We also saw in Figure 8.14 that the cheapest way for the firm to produce 200 would be to use 4 rowers and 2 boats. This is shown in the second line of Table 8.3. The total cost here is £640, so the cost of each of the 200 individual passengers could be seen as £640/200, or 320p. This is the *LAC* for 200 passengers.

The remaining lines of Table 8.3 work out the costs of using the same method to produce outputs of 300, 400, 500, and 600. In each case, the *LAC* is 320p. So the long-run average cost curve for this firm is horizontal, as shown in Figure 8.16. This firm has constant costs, or constant returns to scale.

Short-run average costs

Now let's consider the firm's short-run average costs. These depend on how many boats it is stuck with for the next six months. We will consider two possibilities.

- **One boat**: in this case, Table 8.4 uses the information in Figure 8.12 to show, for example, that it would need 2 rowers for an output of 100, 8 for an output of 200, and 18 for an output of 300. The

Table 8.3 **Calculating total and average costs for the long run, when all inputs can be varied**

Passengers per day	Number of rowers per day	Number of boats per day	Cost of labour per day	Cost of capital per day	Total cost per day	Average cost per passenger
100	2	1	£160	£160	£320	320p
200	4	2	£320	£320	£640	320p
300	6	3	£480	£480	£960	320p
400	8	4	£640	£640	£1,280	320p
500	10	5	£800	£800	£1,600	320p
600	12	6	£960	£960	£1,920	320p

Table 8.4 **Calculating total and average costs for the short run, when only some inputs can be varied**

	Output per day	Number of rowers per day	Cost of labour per day	Cost of boats per day	Total cost per day	Average cost per passenger
Suppose firm has 1 boat:	100	2	£160	£160	£320	320p
	200	8	£640	£160	£800	400p
	300	18	£1,440	£160	£1,600	533p
Suppose firm has 2 boats:	100	1	£8	£320	£400	400p
	200	4	£320	£320	£640	320p
	300	9	£720	£320	£1,040	347p

top part of Table 8.4 works out the average cost in each case. This allows us to plot the curve SAC_1 in Figure 8.16.

- **Two boats**: in this case, Table 8.4 shows for example that it would need 1 rower for an output of 100, 4 for an output of 200, and 9 for an output of 300.

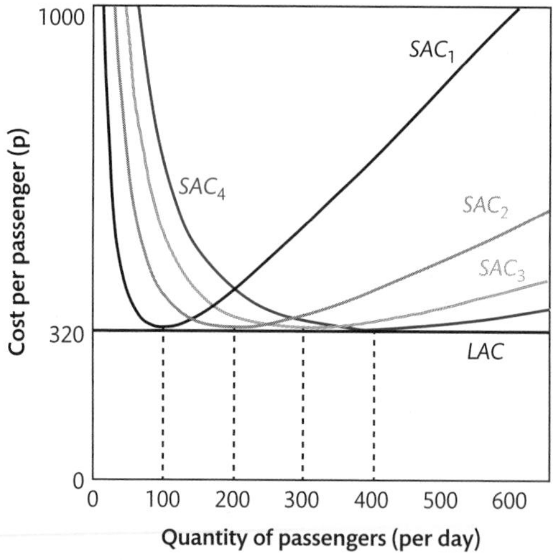

Figure 8.16 **The *LAC* curve and three *SAC* curves**

The *LAC* shows the lowest average cost for each output level, if the firm is given time to change the quantity it uses of all inputs. If it does not have time to change the number of boats, the four *SAC* curves show what the lowest average costs was be while it was stuck with 1, 2, 3, or 4 boats.

The bottom part of Table 8.4 works out the average cost in each case. This allows us to plot the curve SAC_2 in Figure 8.16.

It is possible to work out *SAC* curves for other numbers of boats in a similar way, and Figure 8.16 adds SAC_3 for 3 boats and SAC_4 for 4 boats. You will see how, as in Figure 8.11, each *SAC* curve touches the *LAC* curve at one point. This is the output for which the number of boats concerned is the number that the firm would most like to have.

Production functions and technology

In a production function, the isoquants show how much output would be produced from different combinations of inputs, using current technology. So the *LAC* curve in Figure 8.16 assumes that technology will be the same in the long run as it is now. But, over time, technology improves. This changes the production function and the cost curves. Technology improves in two main ways.

- **New inputs are developed and made available.** In the present case, for example, motor boats might be introduced, which would result in lower costs than arise with rowing boats. To illustrate the effects of this, we would need a completely new production function that would have motor boats on one axis and boat drivers on the other.

- **Better ways are found for using existing inputs**. For example, the firm might devise a training scheme that enables its rowers to row faster. To show the effects of this, we would have to shift each isoquant. In fact, the isoquant for any number of passengers, such as 200, would now be nearer the origin because 200 passengers could now be shifted with fewer inputs.

However, for most of the theory of the firm in later chapters, we will assume for simplicity that technology stays constant.

8.6 Summary

- It is possible to derive a firm's long-run average cost curve, and all its short-run average cost curves, from its production function.
- The production function and the cost curves will change if technology changes. If new and better inputs are introduced, or better ways found of using existing inputs, all cost curve should shift downwards.

In the next chapter we use our knowledge of costs to explain the behaviour of the firms in an industry in which there is perfect competition. The subsequent chapters look at the other types of industry.

abc Glossary

Average fixed cost (*AFC*): the fixed cost for each unit of output, that is *TFC/Q*.

Average product (*AP*): the average amount of product for each worker, that is *TP* divided by the number of workers.

Average variable cost (*AVC*): the variable cost for each unit of output, that is *TVC/Q*.

Capital-intensive: a production method that uses a high amount of capital in relation to labour.

Constant costs: a case in which a firm can produce any output for the same *LAC*.

Decreasing returns to scale: when a firm that increases its use of all inputs by a certain percentage finds its output rises by a smaller percentage.

Diseconomies of scale: a case in which *LAC* increases when a firm increases its scale of production.

Economic efficiency: producing a given output at the lowest possible cost.

Economic inefficiency: not producing a given output at the lowest possible cost.

Economies of scale: a case in which *LAC* decreases when a firm increases its scale of production.

Expansion path: a line showing how a firm's output would expand if it were to use one production method, but increase the quantity of all inputs.

External diseconomy of scale: an upward shift in a firm's *LAC* curve caused by an increase in the scale of the industry of which it is part.

External economy of scale: a downward shift in a firm's *LAC* curve caused by an increase in the scale of the industry of which it is part.

Fixed inputs: inputs whose quantity a firm cannot change in the short run.

Increasing returns to scale: when a firm that increases its use of all inputs by a certain percentage finds its output rises by a larger percentage.

Isocost line: a line showing various combinations of inputs that have the same total cost.

Isoquant: a curve showing various combinations of inputs that could all produce the same output.

Labour-intensive: a production method that uses a high amount of labour in relation to capital.

Law of diminishing marginal returns: the fact that that when extra units of one variable input are added to a fixed amount of all other inputs, sooner or later the marginal returns or *MP*s get smaller.

Long run: the future period that begins when a firm has had enough time to vary the quantity it uses of all of its inputs.

Long-run average cost (*LAC*): the lowest cost for each unit of output in the long run, that is *LTC*/*Q*.

Long-run marginal cost (*LMC*): the change in *LTC* if output changes by one unit.

Long-run total cost (*LTC*): the lowest total cost at which output can be produced in the long run.

Marginal fixed cost (*MFC*): the change in *TFC* if output changes by one unit; *MFC* is always zero.

Marginal product (*MP*): the change in *TP* if the amount of one variable input changes by one unit while the amounts of all other inputs stay the same.

Marginal variable cost (*MVC*): the change in *TVC* if output changes by one unit.

Minimum efficient scale: the lowest output on the horizontal part of any *LAC* with a horizontal part.

Natural monopoly: a monopolist that can supply a market at a lower total cost than any number of smaller firms could manage between them.

Principle of substitution: the effect of a change in relative input prices, which leads firms to switch to a different production method that uses the now relatively cheaper input more intensively.

Production function: the maximum output that a firm could produce from every possible combination of available inputs, assuming that it uses its inputs in the most productive way that is currently known.

Production method: a method defined by the proportion of inputs used to produce a product.

Short run: the future period during which a firm has at least one input the quantity of which it cannot vary.

Short-run average cost (*SAC*): the lowest cost for each unit of output in the short run, that is *STC*/*Q*; *SAC* also equals *AFC* + *AVC*.

Short-run marginal cost (*SMC*): the change in *STC* if *Q* changes by one unit.

Short-run total cost (*STC*): the lowest total cost at which output can be produced in the short run.

Total fixed cost (*TFC*): the total cost of a firm's fixed inputs.

Total product (*TP*): the quantity of output that a firm produces.

Total variable cost (*TVC*): the total cost of a firm's variable inputs.

Variable inputs: inputs whose quantity a firm can change in the short run.

Very long run: the period after which a firm can begin to alter the quality of its inputs.

Answers to in-text questions

8.1 The easiest inputs to vary would include items like electricity, stationery, library books, and telephone calls. Many staff costs could probably be varied fairly quickly, except for staff with long-term contracts. Fixed inputs would notably include buildings of all sorts, plus capital such as computer networks and heating plant.

8.2 The gap gets smaller because it represents *AFC*, and we saw in Table 8.2 that *AFC* gets smaller as *Q* rises.

8.3 All the curves would shift up. But they would shift up in such a way that each new *SAC* curve touched the new *LAC* at one point.

? Questions for review

8.1 A firm for which labour is the only variable input in the short run finds that its *TP* is 0 units a week with no workers, 20 units with 1, 120 units with 2, 270 with 3, 320 units with 4, 350 units with 5, and 360 units with 6. Construct a table to show its *AP* and *MP* figures on the same basis as the table in Figure 8.3. Use the figures in your table to plots curves for *AP* and *MP*, and check that *MP* cuts the highest point of *AP*. Where do diminishing marginal returns set in?

8.2 Suppose the firm in Table 8.2 faced a 50% rise in the prices of all its fixed inputs, so that its *TFC* increased to £630 per day. For each *Q* from 1 to 7, calculate the new figures for *AFC* and *SAC*.

8.3 Suppose the firm in Table 8.2 faced a 25% rise in the prices of all its variable inputs, so the figures for *TVC* now read 0, 400, 650, 825, 1,050, 1,350, 1,800, and 2,450. For each *Q* from 1 to 7 work out the new figures for *AVC* and *SAC*. Also work out the new figures for *MVC* and *SMC*.

8.4 Suppose an industry has an output of 600 units a day and each firm finds that it has an efficient scale running from 30 units to 40. What can be said about the number of firms? Suppose a new technology was introduced that led to efficient scales running from 200 units to 300. What might happen in the industry?

8.5 A firm puts the quantity of labour on the vertical axis of its production function. It then finds that it has to pay its workers a higher wage. What, if anything, will happen to **(a)** its isoquants, **(b)** its isocost lines, **(c)** its production method, and **(d)** its average cost curves?

? Questions for discussion

8.1 Look at the bullet points on page 154, which show why different industries may have firms of various sizes. Think of examples of industries that come under each of these bullet points.

8.2 Suggest some industries in which firms may suffer from external diseconomies of scale, and suggest others in which firms may enjoy external economies of scale.

8.3 Suggest some industries that have responded to higher wage rates by switching into more capital-intensive methods of production. Suggests some industries that may continue to do so in future or which may start to do so in future.

Common student errors

Some students assume that the long run refers to how much a firm will produce over a long period of time. But it refers to how much a firm will produce in a short period, such as a day or a week, after a long period has elapsed, which will allow the firm to alter the quantity it uses of all inputs.

Students also find marginal costs a slippery concept. These costs show how much total costs change if there is a change in output by one unit. So a point on a marginal cost curve measures a change in total cost, even though there is no curve labelled total cost on the same graph.

Diminishing marginal returns are often confused with decreasing returns to scale. Diminishing marginal returns arise when more of *one* variable input is added to fixed amounts of other inputs, and output rises by less and less; decreasing returns to scale arise if *all* inputs increase by the same percentage, and output rises by a smaller percentage.

9

Perfect Competition

Remember from Chapter 3 that if many buyers and sellers trade an identical item, then both the quantity traded and the price are determined by supply and demand. Remember from Chapter 7 that when many firms produce an identical product, they are perfect competitors, and remember that we assume all firms want to get the maximum possible profit. Also remember from Chapter 8 that, in the long run, a firm can vary the quantity it uses of all of its inputs; in the short run, however, there are some inputs whose quantity it cannot vary.

Suppose you run one of many firms that produce identical printer paper. Could you choose the price at which you sell your paper? How would you decide how much to produce each day at the moment? How would you plan how much to produce each day in a year's time? Would you change your output if you had to pay higher wages, or if the prices of your raw materials were to rise? Would you react in the same way if the cost of insuring your factory were to rise? Would you ever be willing to produce at a loss?

This chapter shows you how to answer questions like these, by understanding:

* the distinction between price-takers and price-setters;
* the relationship between marginal cost, marginal revenue, and profit maximization;
* a perfect competitor's short-run supply curve and its shutdown point;
* the effect on a perfect competitor's output of changes in the prices of its fixed and variable inputs;
* the long run in perfect competition.

9.1 Individual and market supply curves for products

When many firms sell an identical product, they are called perfect competitors. We will now study the theory of perfect competition, which explains the behaviour of these firms and their industries.

Think first about the price of the product that any firm like this sells. Assuming there are many buyers of the product, as well as many sellers, then the price is determined in the market for the product by the demand and supply curves.

The market or industry supply curve shows how much will be supplied by all the perfect competitors between them at each possible price. For example, consider the industry supply curve for free-range eggs shown in the last part of Figure 9.1, S_{IND}. This curve shows that if the price of these eggs is 20p, then all the firms will between them supply 8 million eggs a day.

However, individual firms will produce different quantities, and Figure 9.1 shows how these varied firms are related to their market. The first two parts of the figure show, as S_A and S_B, the supply curves for two individual firms, A and B. At a price of 20p, A will supply 3,000 eggs a day and B, 4,000. These firms would make different decisions at other prices. For example, if the price were 50p, A would supply 7,000 eggs a day and B, 6,000.

The industry supply curve, S_{IND}, represents all the individual firms' supply curves added together. For example, the point on S_{IND} at a price of 20p shows that if we add the 3,000 eggs a day that A would supply, the 4,000 that B would supply, and the eggs that all the other firms would supply, we get a total of 8 million. S_{IND} also shows that at a price of, say, 50p, the total would be 26 million.

All of these curves are short-run supply curves. This means that they show how much will be supplied at each price today, and for however long it is that firms find they have some inputs whose quantity they cannot vary. In this chapter, we use the letters *SS* for short-run supply curves, and we will see that, in the long run, firms and industries may supply different quantities at each price.

If the industry supply curve shifts, then the price and quantity traded in the market will change. The industry supply curve will shift if the number of firms changes or

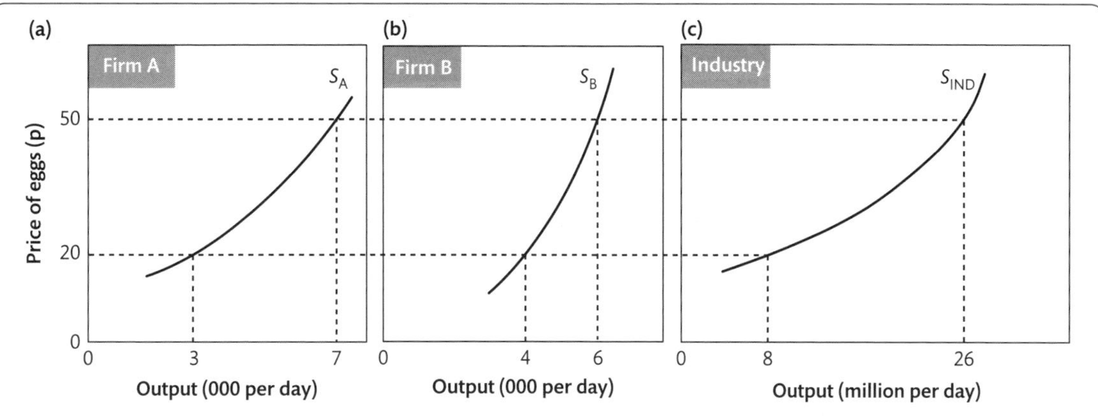

Figure 9.1 **Individual supply curves and the market or industry supply curve**

The first two graphs show supply curves for two individual firms, A and B. At a price of 20p an egg, for example, A would supply 3,000 eggs a day and B 4,000. The last graph shows the industry supply curve. This shows how much all firms between them would supply. At 20p, it includes the 3,000 supplied by A, the 4,000 supplied by B, and the quantities supplied by the many other firms; the total is 8 million eggs.

if the supply curves of individual firms shift. For example, suppose firm A decided to supply twice as many eggs at each possible price. Then S_A would shift to the right. In turn, S_{IND} would shift a little to the right, to show that a total of 8,003,000 eggs would now be supplied at a price of 10p, and a total of 26,007,000 eggs at 50p. So to understand shifts in S_{IND}, we must see why individual supply curves shift. To do that, we must study the economic behaviour of individual perfect competitors.

9.1 Summary

The supply curve for a perfectly competitive industry represents the individual supply curves of all the firms in the industry added together. To understand the industry's supply curve, we need to understand the behaviour of individual firms, and to understand why their individual supply curves may shift.

9.2 Perfect competitors as price-takers

To understand how perfect competitors behave, suppose that you run the bakery that we met in Chapter 8, and that many other bakeries make identical bread. Suppose that all these firms bake loaves in batches of up to 1,000, and sell them to wholesalers. The price of a batch of loaves is fixed in the market in which bakers are sellers and wholesalers are buyers.

The left-hand part of Figure 9.2 shows the supply and demand curves in this market. The supply curve, SS, is the short-run supply curve; this shows the quantity of bread that bakeries would supply each day at each possible price for the next year or so, while they cannot vary the quantity they use of some inputs, like factory space and ovens. The demand curve shows the quantity of bread that buyers would demand at each price. The current market price is £440, where the curves intersect.

Because your firm is one of many bakeries that produce identical bread, you will have to sell your

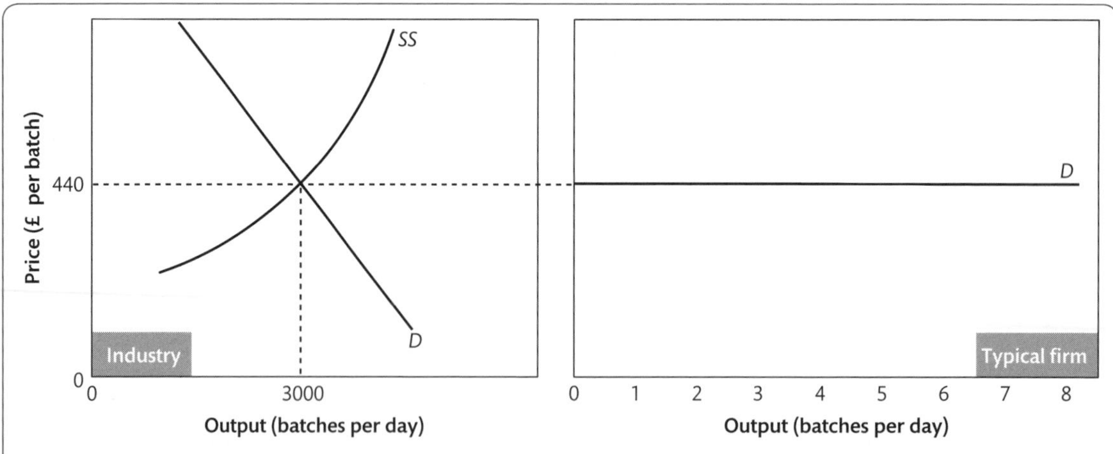

Figure 9.2 **The demand curve faced by a typical price-taker**

The left-hand graph shows how the current price of £440 is determined by the market demand curve and the short-run market or industry supply curve. The right-hand graph shows the demand curve faced by a typical firm. If it were to charge over £440 it would sell nothing. If it were to charge less, it would be deluged with orders.

bread at the current market price of £440. To see why, suppose that you set a price that is only slightly different, as follows.

- **A slightly higher price of £441 a batch**. In this case, buyers will buy no bread from you; instead, they will buy identical bread for £440 a batch from your many competitors.
- **A slightly lower price of £439 a batch**. Then every buyer will want to buy bread from you rather than from your competitors, who charge £440 for identical bread. Unfortunately, you cannot possibly supply all the bread that all these buyers want, because you are one of many firms and produce only a fraction of what the buyers want. So if you charge £439, then buyers will queue up to buy more bread from you than you can possibly produce, and you will decide it makes more sense to sell your bread at £440.

The result is that a typical firm like yours must set, or take, the current market price, here £440, and firms like this are called **price-takers**. Also, each individual firm faces a horizontal demand curve for its own bread, like *D* in the right-hand part of Figure 9.2. This curve shows how much bread buyers will demand from a typical firm at any price it might set, whilst the market price is £440. If this firm charges more than £440, buyers will demand no bread from it. If this firm charges less than £440, buyers will demand a huge quantity from it, far to the right of the figure.

Two exceptional situations

Occasionally, a firm that is one of many supplying an identical product does have some control over its price. For example, if your firm were huge and all your competitors were small, then you might be able to raise your price a little. Buyers would then prefer to go elsewhere, but the other firms might be unable between them to supply as much as buyers want, so they might still buy some bread from you.

Also, even if all the firms are small, you might be able to raise your price if the buyers were not well informed about prices. They might pay you £441 if they were unaware that other firms were charging £440. But in this chapter we will assume that all the firms are relatively small, and that all buyers are fully informed about prices. So we will assume that all firms face demand curves that are horizontal at the current market price.

9.1 Everyday economics

Dairy firms take rising market prices

The farm gate price for milk in August 2010 was 24.7p a litre, 1.4p more than a year ago. The response has been a 6.6% increase in output.

Farming and Food Brie. Department for Environment, Food and Rural Affairs, October 2010

Comment Many farms supply identical milk. In November 2010, each farm could sell as much as it wished at 24.7p a litre, so it faced a horizontal demand curve at that price. But the market price often changes, and in turn the demand curves that farms face often shift up or down. A year earlier, farms faced demand curves that were horizontal at a price of 23.3p. Interestingly, the increased output occurred despite a fall in the size of dairy herds, owing to cows having higher yields.

9.2 Summary

- If a perfect competitor were to charge more than the current market price, then it would sell nothing.
- If it were to charge less than the current market price, it would face far more orders than it could produce.
- So each perfect competitor has to accept, or take, the current price set in the market.
- So each perfect competitor faces a demand curve that is horizontal at the current market price.

9.3 Perfect competitors as profit-maximizers in the short run

Although a perfect competitor cannot choose its own price, it can, and indeed must, choose its own output level. It must actually make two decisions.

- **How much should it produce in each period of time, say per day or week, in the short run?** This covers a period of maybe a year or more during which it cannot vary the quantity it uses of some inputs. Sometimes a firm decides to produce nothing in the short run, and so **shut down**. But it must still pay for those fixed inputs the quantity of which it cannot vary, so it will still exist.
- **How much should it produce in each period of time, say per day or week, in the long run?** This covers the period starting after maybe a year or more, by when it can vary the quantity it uses of all of its inputs. Sometimes a firm decides to produce nothing in the long run, and so **close down**. In this case, it will have time to get rid of all of its inputs, so it will no longer exist.

This section and the next section consider firms' short-run output decisions, while later sections consider their long-run output decisions.

So let's now see how much your bakery will produce in the short run. We will assume that you want to choose the output that will give you the maximum possible profit. To find this, you must consider two things:

- **how much revenue you would get from each possible output level**;
- **how much it would cost you to produce each possible output level**;

Revenues

Suppose the market price of £440 per batch of loaves, so that your firm faces the demand curve shown in the right-hand part of Figure 9.2. Then we can work out three sorts of information about your revenues, as shown in the table in Figure 9.3.

- **Total revenue** (*TR*). This is your total sales receipts. The table in Figure 9.3 gives your *TR* figures for eight possible outputs. For example, if you sell one batch a day, your *TR* will be just £440, and if you sell four batches, your *TR* will be £1,760.
- **Average revenue** (*AR*). This is the revenue from each individual unit of output sold. For example, suppose your output per day, *Q*, is 4, so that *TR* is £1,760. Then your revenue from each batch is *TR*/*Q*, that is £1,760/4, or £440. The table shows that *AR* would equal the price of £440 at every output except zero. No *AR* is shown if $Q = 0$, because we cannot talk about the revenue from each unit sold if none are sold.
- **Marginal revenue** (*MR*). This is how much total revenue changes if output changes by one unit. For example, if you were to raise your output from 4 batches a day to 5, your *TR* would rise by £440 from £1,760 to £2,200, so *MR* would be £440. In the table, this figure is put between the lines for a quantity of 4 and a quantity of 5 because it concerns a change in output between 4 and 5. The table shows that *MR* would equal the price of £440 for any change in output by one unit. This is because each extra batch sold always raises *TR* by £440 a day.

The graph in Figure 9.3 plots curves for both *AR* and *MR*. To plot *AR*, we first put in the points marked as filled circles. These are plotted at £440 above each number for *Q*, for 1, 2, 3, and so on. We then draw the *AR* curve through these points. *AR* is a horizontal line at £440.

To plot *MR*, we first put in the points marked as rings. These are plotted at £440 between the various numbers for *Q*, for example between 2 and 3 and between 4 and 5. We then draw the *MR* curve through

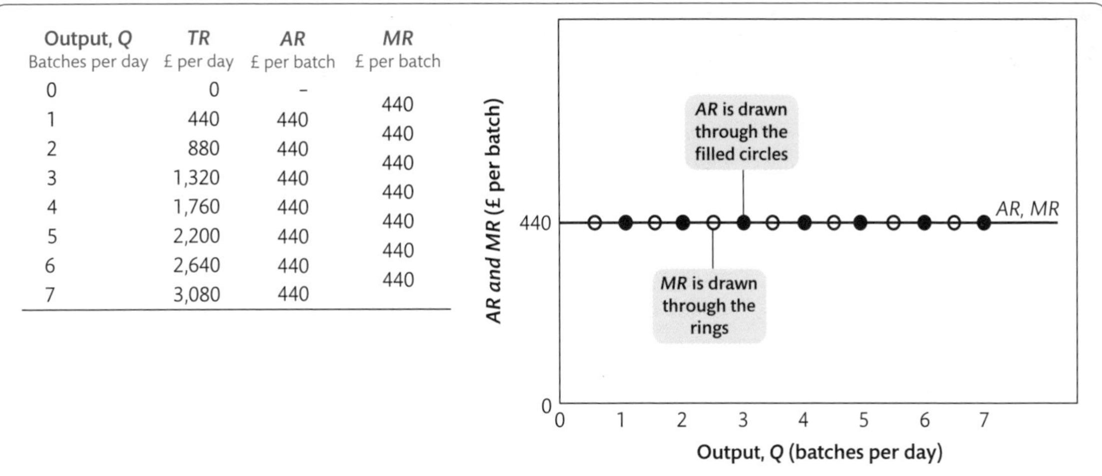

Output, *Q* Batches per day	*TR* £ per day	*AR* £ per batch	*MR* £ per batch
0	0	-	
1	440	440	440
2	880	440	440
3	1,320	440	440
4	1,760	440	440
5	2,200	440	440
6	2,640	440	440
7	3,080	440	440

Figure 9.3 **Average and marginal revenue for a firm**

AR shows the revenue from each unit of output; with a price of £440, *AR* is always £440. *MR* shows the change in total revenue when output changes by 1. With a price of £440, *MR* is always £440. So the *AR* and *MR* curves are both horizontal lines at the current price.

these points. *MR* is also a horizontal line at £440, so it coincides with *AR*.

We saw in Figure 9.2 that this firm faces a demand curve, *D*, which is also a horizontal line at £440. Many later figures for a firm have a horizontal line labelled *D,AR,MR* to show that it is the firm's demand curve, *and* its AR curve, *and* its *MR* curve. Each time it is drawn at the current market price.

Costs

We actually studied this firm's costs in Table 8.2 and Figure 8.1 of Chapter 8. Figure 9.4 sums up the information that was given. This information covers three types of cost.

- **Total costs**: *TFC* and *TVC* show the total fixed cost and the total variable cost for each level of output, *Q*; *TFC* is constant, because it is the total cost of those inputs whose quantity the firm cannot vary in the short run. *STC* shows the short-run total cost, that is *TFC* + *TVC*.
- **Average costs**: *AFC*, *AVC*, and *SAC* show the costs for each unit of output at each output level. They are found as *TFC*/*Q*, *TVC*/*Q*, and *STC*/*Q*.
- **Marginal costs**: *MFC*, *MVC*, and *SMC* show the change in *TFC*, *TVC*, and *STC* if output changes by one unit.

The question facing a profit-maximizer

We are imagining that your bakery makes loaves in batches of up to 1,000 and sells them at the current price of £440 for a batch of 1,000. It faces the revenue situation shown in Figure 9.3 and the cost situation shown in Figure 9.4. We will now explain three methods by which we could try to find out which output will give you the maximum possible profit, that is the biggest possible gap between total revenue and total cost. We will also see why the third method is the best.

Using a schedule for *TR* and *STC*

The first method for trying to find out your profit-maximizing output is to use a table or schedule. Look at the table in the top part of Figure 9.5. This lists eight possible levels for your output, or *Q*. For each of these, it gives the total revenue, *TR*, copied from Figure 9.3,

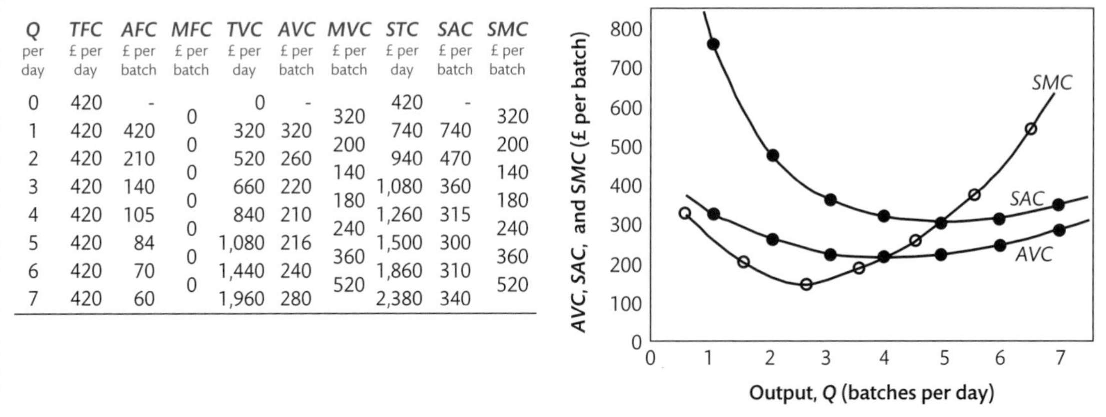

Q per day	TFC £ per day	AFC £ per batch	MFC £ per batch	TVC £ per day	AVC £ per batch	MVC £ per batch	STC £ per day	SAC £ per batch	SMC £ per batch
0	420	-		0	-		420	-	
			0			320			320
1	420	420		320	320		740	740	
			0			200			200
2	420	210		520	260		940	470	
			0			140			140
3	420	140		660	220		1,080	360	
			0			180			180
4	420	105		840	210		1,260	315	
			0			240			240
5	420	84		1,080	216		1,500	300	
			0			360			360
6	420	70		1,440	240		1,860	310	
			0			520			520
7	420	60		1,960	280		2,380	340	

Figure 9.4 **Costs for one firm**

For each *Q*, *TFC*, *TVC*, and *STC* give the total fixed cost, the total variable cost and the short-run total cost; *STC* = *TFC* + *TVC*. *AFC*, *AVC*, and *SAC* give average costs per unit of output. The marginal costs, *MFC*, *MVC*, and *SMC* give the change in total costs if output changes by one unit.

and the short-run total cost, *STC*, copied from Figure 9.4, and it then works out the profit. Here are two examples.

- **Q = 3**. If your output is 3 batches a day, then the table shows that your *TR* is £1,320 and your STC is £1,080. So your profit each day will be £1,320 – £1,080, which is £240.
- **Q = 1**. If your output is 1 batch a day, then the table shows that your *TR* is £440 and your *STC* is £740. So your profit each day is £440 – £740, which is –£300. In other words, you will actually be making a loss of £300 each day.

In the profit column, the highest figure is £780. This would arise if your output were 6 batches a day. However, you cannot be sure from the schedule if your best output is *exactly* 6 batches, that is 6,000 loaves. You might make more profit with, say, 5.9 batches or 5,900 loaves; you cannot tell this from the schedule, because it has only a limited number of rows and so covers only a limited number of outputs. Because we cannot be sure from a schedule what the *exact* profit-maximizing output is, we do not use this method.

Using a graph of *TR* and *STC*

A second method for trying to find the profit-maximizing output is to use a graph with curves for *TR* and *STC*, as in the middle part of Figure 9.5. Each of these curves is plotted from a series of points shown as solid circles. For example, at an output of 6, the point for *STC* is at £1,860 and the point for *TR* is at £2,640, both numbers being taken from the table. Because the curves that have been plotted through these points are continuous, they show the total revenue and total cost at every output level, not only at the output levels given in the table.

At each output, the profit or loss is shown by the gap between *TR* and *STC*. For example, take *Q* = 6. Here *TR* = £2,640 and *STC* =£1,860. So the profit each day would be £2,640 – £1,860, which is £780.

To find the output that gives the maximum profit, you need to find the output where the *TR* curve is furthest above *STC*. This is certainly close to 6. But is it *exactly* 6, or could it be say 5.9?

You could answer that question from the graph by taking careful measurements at all output levels close to 6, to see which gives the maximum profit. So this method is better than using a schedule, because you

Q Batches per day	*TR* £ per day	*STC* £ per day	Profit £ per day	*MR* £ per batch	*SMC* £ per batch
0	0	420	-420		
				440	320
1	440	740	-300		
				440	200
2	880	940	-60		
				440	140
3	1,320	1,080	240		
				440	180
4	1,760	1,260	500		
				440	240
5	2,200	1,500	700		
				440	360
6	2,640	1,860	780		
				440	520
7	3,080	2,380	700		

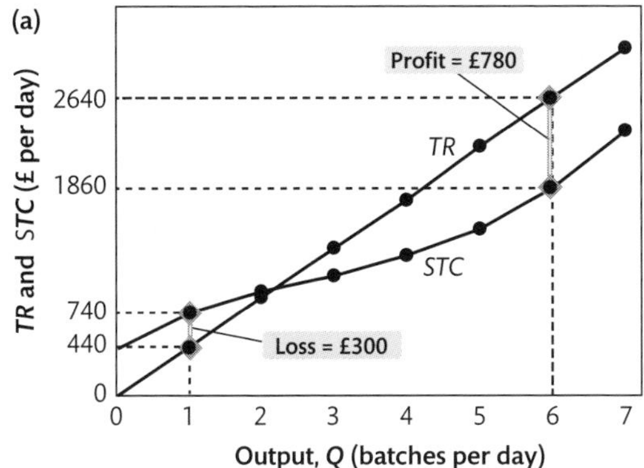

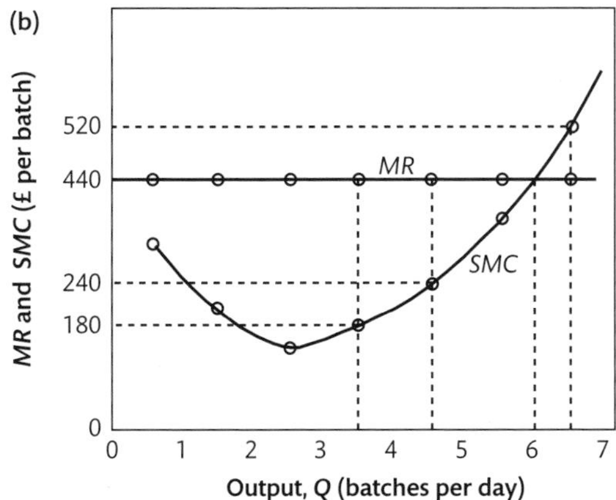

Figure 9.5 **Finding the profit-maximizing output**

To consider every possible output, we use a graph, because the table covers only a few outputs. Using a graph with *TR* and *STC* means finding the output where the gap is biggest: this is time-consuming. Using a graph with *MR* and *SMC* is better, because the profit-maximizing output is the level where they cross—here, 6—and this can be seen instantly.

could find exactly the best output. But making measurements is time-consuming, so we don't use this method either.

Using a graph of *MR* and *SMC*

The third and best method for finding the profit-maximizing output is to use a graph with two curves that intersect at that output. By using curves, we can consider every output level, and by looking for an intersection we avoid time-consuming measurements. The two curves that are needed for this purpose are *MR* and *SMC*. They are plotted in the bottom part of Figure 9.5, using the numbers given in the table at the top, which are copied from Figures 9.3 and 9.4?

To plot these curves, we begin with the points shown as circles. These points are placed between the various output levels. For example, if output rises from 3 to 4, then total revenue rises by £440 and total cost rises by £180, so between outputs of 3 and 4 there is a point at £440 for *MR* and another point at £180 for *SMC*.

These curves intersect at an output of 6. To see why this output is best, consider what you would find if you set a lower output or a higher output.

- **Suppose *Q* is less than the level at which *MR* and *SMC* intersect**. Say, for example, that, at present, your *Q* is 4. The *MR* of £440 between outputs of 4 and 5 tells you that if you were to raise your output by one batch a day to 5, then your *TR* would rise by £440; and the *SMC* of £240 between outputs of 4 and 5 tells you that if you were to raise your output by one batch a day to 5, then your *STC* would rise by £240.

  So if you were to raise your output by one batch a day, you would raise your revenue by £440 and raise your costs by £240, which is less. This means that you would add £440 – £240 to your profit, that is £200. The profit column in the table in Figure 9.5 confirms this: if *Q* rises from 4 to 5, the profit rises by £200 from £500 to £700.

- **Suppose Q is higher than the level at which *MR* and *SMC* intersect**. Say, for example, that, at present, your *Q* is 7. The *MR* of £440 between outputs of 7 and 6 tells you that if you were to reduce your output by one batch a day to 6, then your *TR* would fall by £440; the *SMC* between outputs of 7 and 6 tells you that if you were to reduce your output to 6, then your *STC* would fall by £520.

So if you were to produce one fewer batch each day, then each day you would reduce your costs by £520 and reduce your revenue by £440, which is less. This means that you would add £520 – £440 to profit, that is £80. The profit column in the table in Figure 9.5 confirms: For if *Q* falls from 7 to 6, the profit rises by £80 from £700 to £780.

Question 9.1 Using the approach used in the text, explain why you would not be maximizing your profit if your output were 5, where *MR* is greater than *SMC*.

So, if your output is at a point to the left of the level at which *MR* intersects *SMC*, then *MR* is greater than *SMC* and your profit will rise if you raise *Q*. But if your output is at a point to the right of the level at which *MR* intersects *SMC*, then *MR* is less than *SMC* and your profit will rise if you cut *Q*. So the profit-maximizing output must be the one where the curves intersect. This is indeed 6, so this third method shows us the *exact* output level needed to maximize your profit, and it shows this output *at a glance*. So it is the best method.

The profit at the profit-maximizing output

Although the graph at the bottom of Figure 9.5 shows the profit-maximizing output at a glance, it has some major shortcomings: it does not show us what the *TR* or *STC* will be at that output; nor does it show us what the profit will be; nor does it show us how the total cost will be divided between fixed costs and variable costs.

Figure 9.6 shows how we can find out all this extra information. It begins by copying *MR* and *SMC* from the bottom of Figure 9.5. However, it labels the *MR* curve as *D,AR,MR*, because Figures 9.2 and 9.3 showed that the demand curve, *D*, and the *AR* curve both coincide with *MR* curve. We can then find out the extra information as follows.

- **To find the total revenue, *TR*, when Q = 6**, we look at the point on *AR* at this output: this point is at £440, so each of the 6 batches brings in a revenue of £440. So the total revenue is £2,640. This is represented by the three shaded areas taken together: these areas are 6 batches long and, between them, £440 high, so they represent £2,640.
- **To find the short-run total cost, *STC*, when Q = 6**, we copy the curve *SAC* from Figure 9.4 and look at the point on *SAC* at this output: this point is at £310. So each of the 6 batches costs £310, making a total cost of £1,860. This is shown by the wavy shading plus the brick-like shading. These areas are 6 batches long and, between them, £310 high, so they represent £1,860.
- **To find the profit when Q = 6**. Each of the 6 batches brings in £440 and costs £310, so each batch gives a

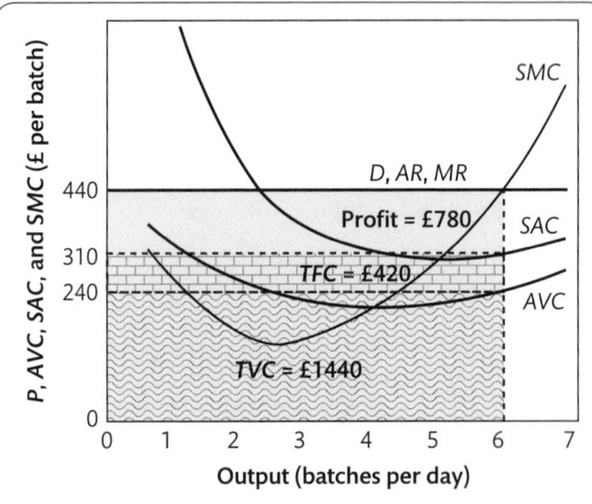

Figure 9.6 **Revenue, cost, and profit**

At an output of 6, *AVC* is £240, so *TVC* is 6 times this or £1,440, as shown by wavy shading. *AFC* equals the gap between *SAC* of £310 and *AVC* of £240, which is £70, so *TFC* is 6 times this or £420, as shown by brick-like shading. The profit per unit is the gap between *AR* of £440 and *SAC* of £310, that is £130, so the total profit is 6 times this or £780, as shown by plain shading. The total value of the shaded areas is 6 times the *AR* of £440, or £2,640: this equals the *TR*.

profit of £130. This gives a total profit of £780, as represented by the plain grey area, which is 6 batches long and £130 high.

- **To find total variable cost, *TVC*, when $Q = 6$**, we copy the curve *AVC* from Figure 9.4 and look at the point on it at this output: this point is at £240. So each of the 6 batches has a variable cost of £240, giving a total variable cost of £1,440. This is shown by the area with wavy shading, which is 6 batches long and £240 high.
- **To find the total fixed cost, *TFC*, when $Q = 6$**. The *AFC* at this output is the gap of £70 between the *SAC* and *AVC* here. So each of the 6 batches has a fixed cost of £70, making a total fixed cost of £420. This is shown by the brick-like shading.

9.3 **Summary**

- The best way to find the profit-maximizing output for a perfect competitor is to draw a graph with *MR* and *SMC* curves; the profit-maximizing output is the output level at which these curves intersect.
- At any lower output, *MR* is above *SMC*: so a rise in output would raise profit by adding more to revenue than it added to costs. At any higher output, *SMC* is above *MR*: so a fall in output would raise profit by reducing costs by more than it reduced revenue.
- Adding curves for *AR* and *SAC* lets us see the total revenue, the total cost, and the profit at the profit-maximizing output. Adding a curve for *AVC* lets us divide total costs into variable costs and fixed costs.

9.4 The short-run supply curve for a perfect competitor

We have seen how to find the short-run profit-maximizing output for your perfectly competitive bakery at a given market price. We will now derive the firm's short-run supply curve, *SS*. This curve will show how much it would produce in the short run at every possible market price. We will build *SS* up by considering the output you would set at six possible prices. We will look first at three prices at which you could cover all your costs.

Output if a firm can cover all of its costs

The top part of Figure 9.7 assumes the price starts at £440. Then we suppose that the demand for bread falls in two stages, so the price falls to £360 in the middle part and to £300 in the bottom part. In each part, the demand curve is a horizontal line at the current price, so in the top part it is shown by D_0,AR_0,MR_0 at a price of £440, in the middle by D_1, AR_1, MR_1 at a price of £360, and at the bottom by D_2,AR_2,MR_2 at a price of £300.

In each part, the profit-maximizing output is the one where *MR* and *SMC* intersect; if they intersect at two outputs, as in the bottom part, then the profit-maximizing output is the higher one. In each part, your profit would fall if you were to move from the output at the relevant intersection, as follows:

- **If you were to raise your output**, then *SMC* would be above *MR*, so your costs would rise by more than your revenue, so your profit would fall.
- **If you were to reduce your output**, then *MR* would be more than *SMC*, so your revenue would fall by more than your costs, so your profit would fall.

Question 9.2 Can you explain why it would not make sense to produce the lower of the two outputs where *MR* intersects *SMC* in the bottom part of Figure 9.7?

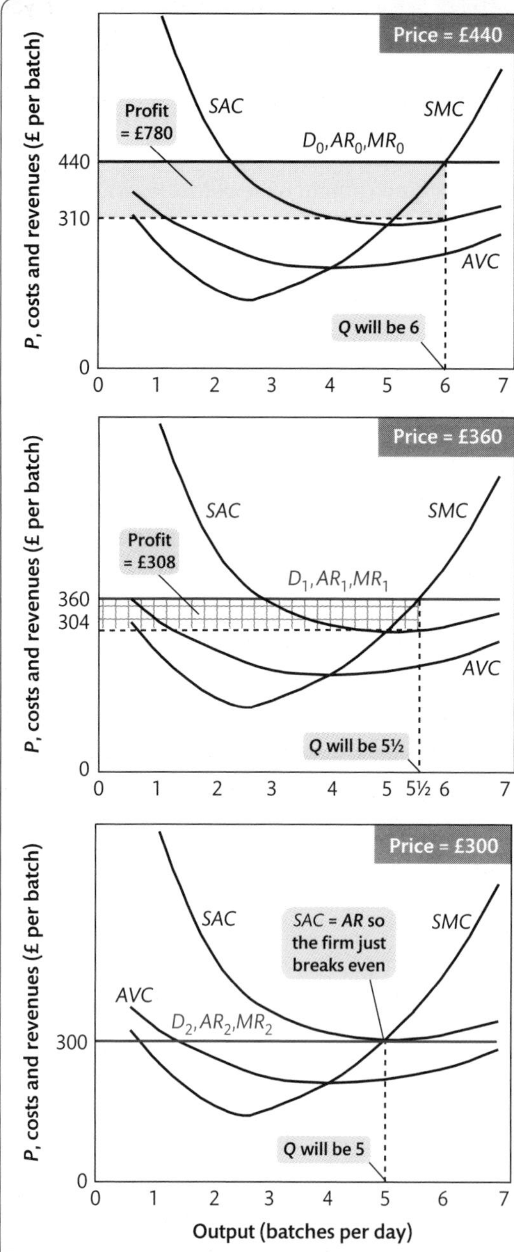

Figure 9.7 **Output at three prices where the firm can cover its costs**

In each case, the firm's *D*,*AR*,*MR* curve is a horizontal line at the price concerned. At a price of £440, it sets *Q* = 6 per day and earns a profit. At £360, it sets *Q* = 5½ and earns less profit. At £300, it sets *Q* = 5 and breaks even.

Let's now look more closely at each price.

- **Price = £440**. Here, MR_0 intersects *SMC* at an output of 6, so, as we have already seen in Figure 9.6, you will set *Q* = 6. The profit per batch will equal the *AR* of £440 minus the *SAC* of £310. This is £130 per batch, making a total of £780 with 6 batches, as shown by the grey area.
- **Price = £360**. Here, MR_1 intersects *SMC* at an output of 5.5, so you will set *Q* = 5½. The profit per batch will equal the *AR* of £360 minus the *SAC* of £304, that is £56, making a total of £308 with 5½ batches, as shown by the pink grid. So the lower price leads to a lower profit.
- **Price = £300**. Here, MR_2 intersects *SMC* at an output of 5, so you will set *Q* = 5. Here, you will make no profit, because the revenue per batch, *AR*, and the cost per batch, *SAC*, both equal £300. So you merely break even. You would obviously prefer to make a profit, but there is no output where you can. To check this, notice that, at every output except 5, *SAC* is above *AR*, so each batch would cost more to make than the £300 for which it would sell, so you would make a loss.

Output if a firm can only make a loss

We now turn to Figure 9.8, which concerns three lower prices at which you could not cover all your costs. This figure supposes that the demand for bread falls in three further stages, so that the price is £250 in the top part, £210 in the middle part, and £180 in the bottom part.

In each part, the demand curve is a horizontal line at the current price, so in the top it is shown by D_3,AR_3,MR_3 at a price of £250, in the middle by D_4,AR_4,MR_4 at a price of £210, and in the bottom by D_5,AR_5,MR_5 at a price of £180. In each case, *SAC* is above *AR* at every output. So whatever output you set, the cost per batch will exceed the revenue per batch, so you will make a loss.

Even so, in each part there is a case for setting the higher of the two outputs where *SMC* and *MR*

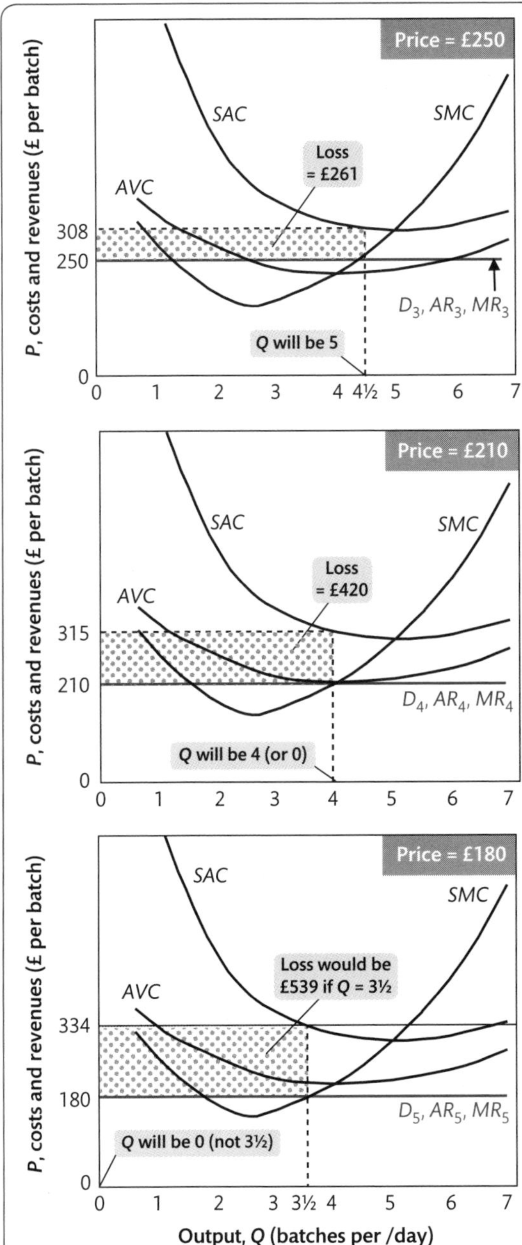

Figure 9.8 **Output at three prices where the firm cannot cover its costs**

Each *D,AR,MR* curve is a horizontal line at the price concerned. At £250, the firm sets $Q = 4\frac{1}{2}$ and has a loss less than its *TFC* of £420. At £210, it may set $Q = 4$ and just cover its variable costs, or shut down with $Q = 0$; either way, its loss will equal its *TFC*. At £180, it will certainly shut down with $Q = 0$ and a loss equal to *TFC*.

intersect, because your loss would increase if you were to move from the output at that intersection.

- **If you were to raise your output**, then *SMC* would be above *MR*, so your costs would rise by more than your revenue, so your loss would increase.
- **If you were to reduce your output**, then *SMC* would be less than *MR*, so your revenue would fall by more than your costs, so your loss would increase.

However, because in each part you would end up with a loss at this output, you might wonder if you should instead shut down and produce nothing. But beware: if you do shut down, you will still make a loss! Your revenue will be £0, and you can cut your total variable cost to £0 by buying no variable inputs. But in the short run, maybe for a year or so, you cannot get rid of your fixed inputs, so you will still face a total fixed cost of £420 a day for them. So you will make a daily loss equal to your *TFC* of £420, as shown in the table in Figure 9.5.

So if the loss at the output where *MR* intersects *SMC* would be less than your *TFC*, then you should produce that output and have this smaller loss. In contrast, if the loss here would be bigger than your *TFC*, then you should shut down and have a loss equal to your *TFC*. Let's now look more closely at each price in Figure 9.8.

- **Price = £250**. Here, *MR* intersects *SMC* at an output of 4½, where *SAC* is £308 and *AR* is £250. So you would lose £58 per batch, which, with 4½ batches, is £261 a day, as shown by the pink dots. But notice that, at this output, *AR* is higher than *AVC*, so the revenue from each batch you sold would more than cover its variable cost. Therefore, you could use the rest of your revenue to help to pay your fixed costs of £420. So your loss would be less than the loss of £420 that would arise if you were to shut down. So it is best to set $Q = 4\frac{1}{2}$.
- **Price = £210**. Here, *MR* intersects *SMC* at an output of 4, where both *AR* and *AVC* are £210. So the revenue from any batches sold would cover only their variable costs, and so your loss would equal *TFC*. To check this, note that *SAC* is £315 and *AR* is £210: so you would lose £105 per batch, which,

with 4 batches, is £420 a day, as shown by the pink dots. At this price, you will be indifferent between setting $Q = 4$ or shutting down with $Q = 0$: either way you lose £420 a day.

- **Price = £180**. Here, *MR* intersects *SMC* at an output of 3½. Notice that, at this output, *AR* is less than *AVC*, so any batches sold would not even cover their variable costs, therefore your loss would be higher than your fixed costs. Indeed, *SAC* would be £334 and *AR*, £180. So you would lose £154 per batch, which, with 3½ batches, is £539, as shown by the pink dots. It would be better to shut down and produce nothing and just lose the £420 per day spent on your fixed inputs.

The perfect competitor's supply curve

Figure 9.9 repeats each price from Figures 9.7 and 9.8, except £180 at which you would shut down. At each of these five prices, Figure 9.9 shows how much you would produce, assuming you would set $Q = 4$ at a price of £210.

We can then draw the thick black curve through these price and output combinations to show your short-run supply curve, *SS*. *SS* follows your *SMC* above the point at which *SMC* intersects *AVC*. This point is called the **shutdown point** because at any price below £210 you will definitely shut down and produce nothing. Notice that *SS* extends below *SAC*. The point at which *SS* intersects *SAC* is called the **break-even point** because at this price, £300, you will break even.

We saw in Figure 9.1 that we can add the equivalent short-run supply curves for all firms to get the short-run market or industry supply curve.

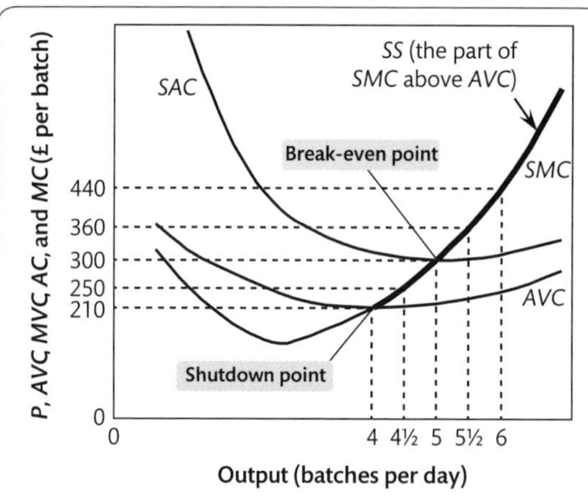

Figure 9.9 **A perfect competitor's short-run supply curve**

At each price, the firm sets its output at the level where its short-run marginal cost equals the price, *provided* that the price covers its variable costs; if the price is below *AVC*, then producing would give it a loss greater than *TFC*, so it would shut down with $Q = 0$ and a loss equal to *TFC*. So *SS* follows *SMC* above where it cuts *AVC*. If the price is the one at the bottom of *SAC*, then the firm just breaks even.

9.2 Everyday economics

Zambia's copper output soars

'Zambia's copper output rose by 17% in 2010, from under 700,000 tonnes to over 800,000.'
The Bulletin & Record, February 2011
'Zambia's 2010 preliminary copper output beats forecast', *Bloomberg Business Week*, 24 January 2011

Comment Many firms supply identical copper, and, like all perfect competitors, they have upward-sloping supply curves. So when the copper price rose in 2010, following soaring demand from China, Zambian mines produced more. Zambian mines had actually produced around 700,000 tonnes a year back in the 1960s, but many old Zambian mines became exhausted, and output fell until transport links to new deposits were improved.

9.4 Summary

- The best output for a perfect competitor is usually the one where its *D,AR,MR* curve intersects its *SMC* curve.
- At lower outputs, *MR* is above *SMC*: so raising *Q* would raise profit by raising revenue more than costs.
- At higher outputs, *SMC* is above *MR*: so reducing *Q* would raise profit by cutting costs more than revenue.

- If D,AR,MR is above SAC at this output, the firm will make a profit. If D,AR,MR just touches SAC at this output, the firm will break even. And if D,AR,MR is below SAC at this output, the firm will make a loss.
- If D,AR,MR is below AVC at this output, then the firm cannot even cover its variable costs. So it should instead shut down and have a loss equal to its total fixed costs.
- The firm's short-run supply curve, SS, follows the part of its SMC that lies above AVC.

9.5 Why the short-run equilibrium might change

The left-hand part of Figure 9.10 shows, as D_0 and SS_0, the initial demand and short-run supply curves in a perfectly competitive industry. Their intersection gives the initial market price and output, P_0 and Q_0. The right-hand part of the figure shows a typical firm for which the initial demand, average revenue, and marginal revenue curve, D_0,AR_0,MR_0, is horizontal at P_0. The firm sets its initial output at Q_0, where this curve intersects its short-run supply curve, SS, which is part of its short-run marginal cost curve, SMC. At Q_0, the firm's average revenue is above its average cost, so it makes a profit on each unit sold, and a total profit shown by the grey rectangle.

We will now consider why this equilibrium position for the industry and typical firm may change.

A change in demand

One event that will alter this equilibrium is a change in market demand. For example, suppose in Figure 9.10 that the market demand decreases to D_1, so the price falls to P_1. Then the firm will face at P_1 a new demand, average revenue, and marginal revenue curve, D_1,AR_1,MR_1, and set its new output at Q_1, where this curve intersects its supply curve, SS. At Q_1, AR is still above SAC, so the firm still makes a profit, but its total profit is smaller, and is shown by the pink grid.

If demand had fallen so much that D_1,AR_1,MR_1 intersected the firm's SS at a point between SAC and AVC, then the firm would make a loss, like the firm in the top part of Figure 9.8. And if demand had fallen so much that D_1, AR_1, MR_1 intersected the firm's SMC at a point below AVC, and so below its SS curve, then the firm would shut down, like the one in the bottom part of Figure 9.8.

A change in the number of firms

Another event that will alter the equilibrium is a change in the number of firms in the industry. Look again at Figure 9.10 and suppose the market and the firm are back in their initial positions shown by the black curves, with the market price and output at P_0 and Q_0, and with the firm facing D_0,AR_0,MR_0 and setting its output at Q_0.

Now suppose new competing firms enter the industry. Each has its own supply curve, and these must be allowed for by the market supply curve because, as we saw in Figure 9.1, this represents the supply curve of all individual firms added together. So the industry supply curve in Figure 9.10 will shift to the right to SS_1, and the market output will rise to Q_2. However, the price falls, and for simplicity it is shown as falling once again to P_1.

So the firm will again face the demand, average revenue, and marginal revenue curve labelled D_1,AR_1,MR_1 and sets its new output at Q_1. Again, at this output, average revenue is still above average cost, so the firm will make the profit shown by the pink grid. It may seem surprising that the typical firm's output falls while the market output rises, but remember that there are now more firms in the industry.

If the number of firms were to increase so much that D_1,AR_1,MR_1 intersected the firm's SS at a point between

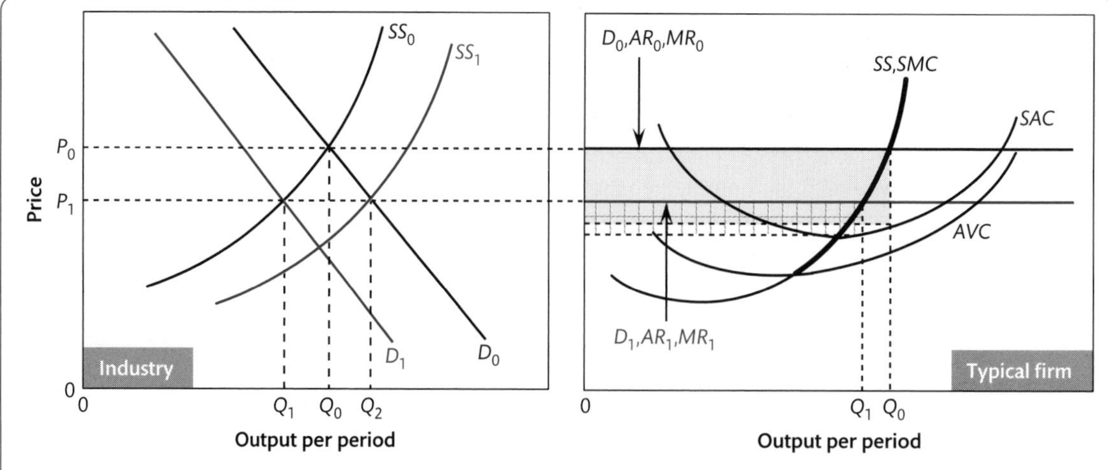

Figure 9.10 **A fall in demand and the entry of new firms**

If market demand falls from D_0 to D_1, then the industry output falls from Q_0 to Q_1, the price falls from P_0 to P_1, and the typical firm faces D_1,AR_1,MR_1 instead of D_0,AR_0,MR_0. So the firm moves along its supply curve and cuts output from Q_0 to Q_1. If, instead, new firms enter the industry, then the industry supply curve shifts from SS_0 to SS_1 and output rises to Q_2, but again the price falls from P_0 to P_1 with the same effect on the typical firm. In each case, the firm's profit falls from the grey area to the pink grid.

SAC and *AVC*, then the firm would make a loss. And if the number of firms were to increase so much that D_1,AR_1,MR_1 intersected the firm's *SMC* at a point below *AVC*, and so below its *SS* curve, then the firm would shut down.

A change in the price of a fixed input

The equilibrium in perfect competition is also affected by changes in the prices of inputs. Consider first a change in the price of a fixed input.

Suppose the industry and typical firm start in the position shown by the black curves in Figure 9.11. So the market price and output start at P_0 and Q_0, and the typical firm faces *D,AR,MR* and sets its output at Q_0 where this curve intersects its *SS*, and it makes a profit as shown by the grey rectangle.

Now suppose the price of a fixed input rises. Perhaps there is a rise in the interest rate on a loan that the firm used to buy some plant, or a rise in the annual premium it pays to insure its buildings, or a rise in the rent on a building for which it has a long-term tenancy, or a rise in the wage rate of some staff on long-term contracts.

In Chapter 8, we saw in the left-hand part of Figure 8.3 that a rise in the price of a fixed input increases the cost of producing each unit. So, in Figure 9.10, the firm's average cost curve shifts up from SAC_0 to SAC_1. However, its *AVC* curve stays put because there is no change in the price of any variable inputs. Its *SMC* curve also stays put, because there is no change in its marginal costs. Remember that marginal cost is the cost of producing extra units of output, and in the short run the only inputs that a firm can get more of in order to increase its output are variable inputs for which prices have stayed the same.

As the *AVC* and *SMC* curves stay put, so does the firm's supply curve, *SS*, because this follows *SMC* above its intersection with *AVC*. And as the typical firm's supply curve stays put, so does the market supply curve. And as market demand has not changed, there is no change at all in the industry figure. So the market price and output stay the same, and the firm faces the same demand, average revenue, and marginal revenue curve, *D,AR,MR*. So its new output, Q_1, where this curve intersects *SS*, equals its initial output, Q_0.

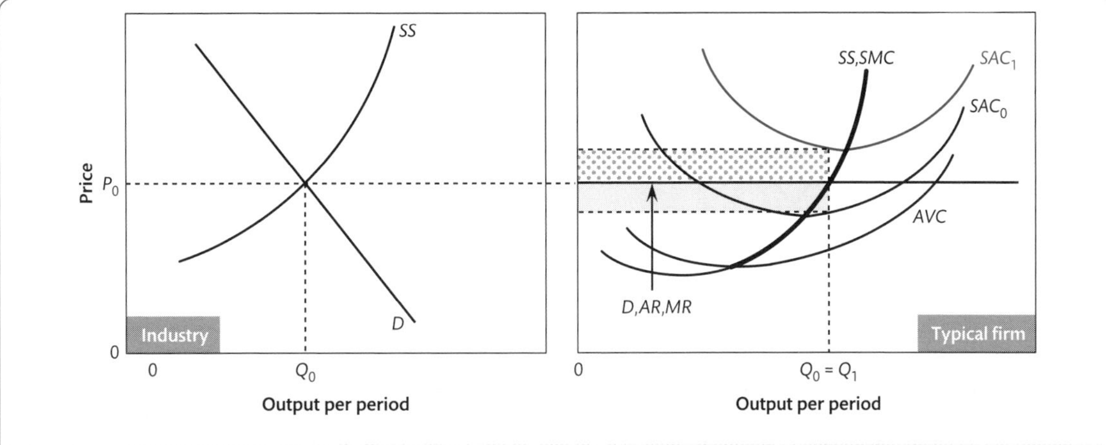

Figure 9.11 **A rise in the price of a fixed input**

If the price of a fixed input rises, then the only cost curve to shift is *SAC*. So the firm produces the same output, but makes a lower profit or, as shown here, a loss. The market is unaffected.

So a change in the price of a fixed input does not affect the market output or price, or the firm's output. But it does affect the firm's profit. In Figure 9.11, the firm's average cost curve shifts up so much that, at its unchanged output, the average cost is now above the average revenue, leaving the firm with a total loss shown by the pink dots. However, if the rise in the input price were so small that the new average cost intersected *SS* at a price below P_0, then the firm would instead have ended up with less profit.

A change in the price of a variable input

The effects of a change in the price of a variable input are shown in Figure 9.12. Suppose the initial situation is as shown by the black curves. So the market price and output are P_0 and Q_0, and the typical firm faces D_0, AR_0,MR_0 and sets its output at Q_0 where this intersects its SS_0. Also, the firm makes a profit shown by the grey rectangle.

Now suppose the price of a variable input rises. Perhaps the wage rate paid to employees who do not have long-term contracts rises, or the price of a raw material rises. This increases the average variable cost and the short-run average cost of each unit of output. It also increases the firm's short-run marginal costs: these are the costs of producing extra units, and the only extra inputs that can be used in the short run to increase output are variable inputs, one of which now has a higher price. So, as noted in the right-hand part of Figure 8.3 in Chapter 8, all three cost curves shift upwards. Figure 9.12 shows the new curves as AVC_1, SAC_1, and SMC_1.

These shifts give the firm a new supply curve, SS_1, which follows SMC_1 above where it intersects AVC_1. No doubt the other firms in the industry use similar inputs and face the same rise in the price of one of them, so their supply curves also shift. In turn, the market supply curve shifts to the left to SS_1, so the market price rises to P_1. This shifts the demand, average, and marginal revenue curve faced by the firm to D_1,AR_1,MR_1, and the firm reduces its output to Q_1, where D_1,AR_1,MR_1 intersects its new SS_1.

The firm's profit is also affected. In Figure 9.12, at the firm's new output Q_1, its new average revenue is greater than its new average cost. So it still makes a profit, as shown by the pink grid, but its profit is smaller than before. If the cost curves had risen so much that D_1,AR_1,MR_1 intersected SMC_1 at a point between SAC_1 and AVC_1, then the firm would make a loss. And if the cost curves had risen so much that D_1,AR_1,MR_1 intersected SMC_1 at a point below AVC_1, that is below SS_1, then it would shut down.

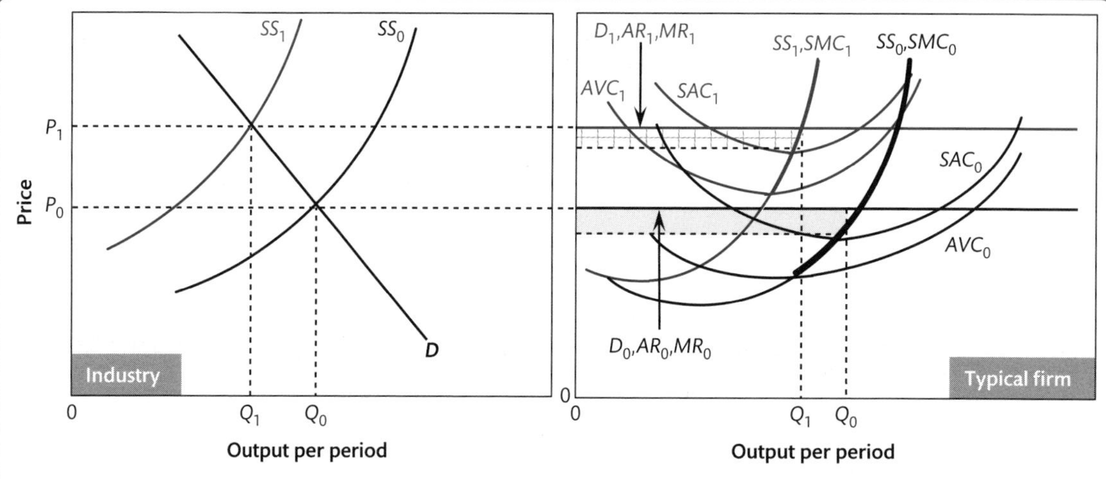

Figure 9.12 **A rise in the price of a variable input**

If the price of a variable input rises, all the firm's cost curves shift. So its supply curve shifts and the industry supply curve shifts. So the price rises and the firm faces the new D_1,AR_1,MR_1 curve. It produces where this intersects its new supply curve SS_1. So it will either make less profit, as shown, or in some cases a loss.

9.3 Everyday economics

Corn price rise causes farm to shut down

Mallorie's, a dairy farm in Oregon with a reputation for being well run, has said that it will cease operation. Its problems stem from a low price for milk combined with rising costs of animal feed. It is feared that other dairy farms may also close.

'Oregon dairy closure worries other farmers', *The Register-Guard*, 11 January 2011
'Mallorie's closure rattles an industry', *Statesman Journal*, 10 January 2011

Comment Cattle feed is a variable input for farmers. One important type of feed is corn, and its price rose 53% in the previous year, partly because government subsidies to firms using bio-fuels raised the market demand for corn and drove up its price. For this farm, the input price rose so much that it faced a *D,AR,MR* curve that intersected its *SMC* curve at a point below its *SS* curve. When a firm shuts down, its owners may keep it idle in the hope that the situation improves, or put it up for sale, or plan to use it to produce something else—in this case, corn perhaps!

9.5 Summary

- If the market demand decreases for the output of a perfectly competitive industry, then the market price and output both fall. Also, the typical firm faces a lower price and produces less, and it makes less profit or a loss; it might even shut down. The opposite effects occur if market demand increases.
- If the number of firms in the industry rises, then the market price falls and market output rises. Also, the typical firm faces a lower price and produces less, and it makes less profit or a loss; it might even shut down. The opposite effects occur if the number of firms falls.
- If the price of a fixed input increases, then there is no effect on the market. The typical firm faces the same price and sets the same output, but its *SAC* curve shifts up and it makes less profit or a loss. The opposite effects occur if the price of a fixed input falls.

- If the price of a variable input rises, then a firm's *SMC*, *SAC*, and *AVC* curves shift up, so its supply curve shifts. Other firms' supply curves also shift, so the market supply curve shifts left, and the market price rises and market output falls. The typical firm faces a higher price, and sets its output at the level at which its new *D,AR,MR* curve intersects its new supply curve. It makes less profit and may make a loss; it might even shut down. The opposite effects occur if the price of a variable input falls.

9.6 The long run in perfect competition

Two time frames for decisions by firms

We saw in section 9.3 that a perfect competitor has to make two major decisions:

- **how much it should produce in each period of time, say per day or week, in the short run;**
- **how much it should produce in each period of time, say per day or week, in the long run.**

We have seen how firms make the first decision, and we now turn to the second. Here, we must recall from Chapter 8 that a perfectly competitive industry has three characteristics: there are many firms; they produce identical products; and there is freedom of entry for new firms along with freedom of exit for existing ones. This third characteristic is central to the long-run analysis.

The firm's long-run cost curves

A perfect competitor's long-run output depends in part on the shape of its long-run average cost curve, *LAC*. In Chapter 8, we saw in Figures 8.4–8.9 that *LAC* curves can have various shapes. For simplicity, we will assume here that the typical firm has a U-shaped curve, as shown in the right-hand part of Figure 9.13.

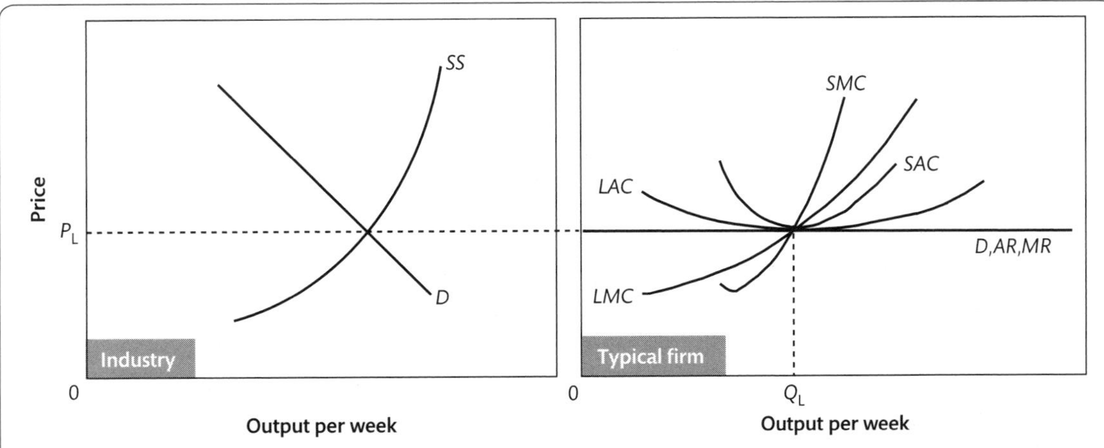

Figure 9.13 **The long-run equilibrium price**

In the long run, firms enter or leave the industry, shifting its *SS* right or left, until the price is P_L. At P_L, the *D,AR,MR* curve for a typical firm touches the lowest point of its *LAC*, and the firm will just break even at output Q_L. In the long run, the firm also has the *SAC* curve that touches its *LAC* at Q_L.

This curve shows the lowest average cost at which the firm could produce each possible weekly output level, if it was given time to adjust the quantity it uses of every input.

Figure 9.13 also shows the firm's long-run marginal cost curve, *LMC*, which passes the lowest point of its *LAC*. *LMC* shows how much its total weekly cost would change if it were to change its weekly output by one unit, and were given time to vary the quantity it used of every input.

The long-run equilibrium price

The price faced by this firm is set in the market. At any moment in time, the market price is determined by the current market *short-run* supply curve, *SS*, and the market demand curve, *D*, which are shown in the left-hand part of Figure 9.13.

You might imagine that *SS* and *D* could intersect at any price, but in the long run they can intersect at only one price. This price, marked P_L, is the one that results in the firm facing the demand, average revenue, and marginal revenue curve shown in the right-hand part by *D,AR,MR*. The special feature of this *D,AR,MR* curve is that it just touches the lowest point on the firm's *LAC* curve.

We will see shortly that the firm will set its output in the long run at the level Q_L where these curves touch. Here, it just breaks even because its average revenue and average cost, read off *AR* and *LAC*, are equal. But first we must see why the price in the long run cannot be above or below P_L.

- **The price in the long run cannot be above P_L.** If it were, then the firm's *D,AR,MR* curve would be above its *LAC* over a range of outputs. So there would be a range of outputs where *AR* was above *LAC* so that the firm could make a profit. But if it were possible to make a profit over a range of outputs, new profit-seeking firms would enter the industry and produce in that range. So the industry *SS* would shift to the right, and the price would continue to fall until, in the long run, it reached P_L. Then firms can only just break even, so no one is tempted to set up new ones.
- **The price in the long run cannot be below P_L in Figure 9.13.** If it were, then the typical firm would face a *D,AR,MR* curve that was below its *LAC* at every output. So, no matter how much it produced, its *AR* would be less than its *LAC* and it would make a loss. In this case, some firms would exit the industry, shifting the market *SS* to the left until, in the long run, the price was at P_L so that, once again, firms can just break even.

The long-run equilibrium for a firm

We have seen how, in the long run, firms enter or exit a perfectly competitive industry, and so shift the market supply curve, until the price is P_L, as shown in Figure 9.13. The typical firm then faces a *D,AR,MR* curve that touches the lowest point of its *LAC* at output Q_L, and this is the output that any profit-maximizing firm will set. This is because it can break even at this output, whereas it would make a loss at any other output because *AR* is less than *LAC* at every other output.

Once the firm has decided that, in the long run, its output will be Q_L per week, it will want to be sure that it can produce Q_L at the lowest possible cost, which is shown by the point on *LAC* at this output. To be able to produce Q_L at this cost, the firm may first need to change the quantities of those inputs that are fixed in the short run, but which can be changed in the long run.

After it has made these changes, the firm will be able to produce Q_L at this cost, even in the short run. So it will be on the *SAC* curve shown, which touches *LAC* at Q_L. It will now have more fixed inputs than is ideal for lower outputs than Q_L, and fewer than is ideal for higher outputs, so its *SAC* curve will be above its *LAC* curve at every output except Q_L. Associated with *SAC* is the short-run marginal cost curve, *SMC*, which passes through the bottom point of *SAC*. You can see that, when the firm settles at Q_L, it also settles where *MR* intersects *SMC*, as it usually does in the short run.

You can also see from Figure 9.13 that, at Q_L, the firm will be setting the output where *MR* equals *LMC*. Let's look a little more closely at why this is the profit-maximizing output in the long run.

- **At lower outputs, *LMC* is less than *MR*, so the firm's profit would rise if it were to produce more.** This is because a rise in output would, in the long run, raise costs by less than it raised revenue.
- **At higher outputs, *LMC* is more than *MR*, so the firm's profit would rise if it were to produce less.** This is because a fall in output would, in the long run, reduce costs by more than it reduced revenue.

Incidentally, a perfectly competitive firm does not have a long-run supply curve showing what output it would produce in the long run at each possible price. This is because there is only one possible price in the long run, P_L, at which it will produce Q_L. However, the *industry* does have a long-run supply curve, as we will see in the next section.

Outputs for firms and for their industry

We have argued that, in the long run, firms will enter or exit a perfectly competitive industry until the typical firm faces a *D,AR,MR* curve that allows it only to break even. In Figure 9.13, the firm had a U-shaped *LAC* curve and the only output at which its *D,AR,MR* curve allowed it to break even was Q_L. If all the firms in its industry have similar *LAC* curves, then they will all have similar long-run outputs.

However, not all firms have a U-shaped *LAC* curve. For example, Figure 8.8 (on p. 153) shows an *LAC* curve the lowest part of which is horizontal over a range of output levels. If a perfect competitor had an *LAC* curve like that, and in the long run faced a *D,AR,MR* curve that coincided with this lowest part of its *LAC* curve, then it could break even at any output in that range. If all the firms in its industry had similar *LAC* curves, then they could end up all breaking even and yet have very different outputs in this range.

In either case, though, each firm's output must be small in relation to the market. Then no firm will be able to influence the market price by changing its output, so each will be a price-taker, as assumed in perfect competition.

9.6 Summary

- In the long run, firms enter or exit a perfectly competitive industry until typical firms just break even.
- So the industry settles with demand and supply curves that intersect at the one price at which this occurs.
- Because only one price is possible in the long run, it does not make sense to ask what output a firm would set at other prices; in turn it does not make sense to look for a long-run supply curve for a firm.
- The long-run output for a perfect competitor with a U-shaped *LAC* is the output at the lowest point on it.
- The long-run output of a perfect competitor with an *LAC* that is horizontal over a range of outputs will be in that range.

9.7 A perfectly competitive industry's long-run supply curve

In Figure 9.13, we saw the long-run equilibrium position for an industry and a typical firm in perfect competition. We will now see how these positions change if the demand for the product changes. We will also derive a long-run supply curve for a perfectly competitive industry.

Changes in demand if costs are constant

Look at Figure 9.14. The black curves here show the initial long-run equilibrium for an industry on the left and a typical firm on the right. The short-run market supply curve, SS_0, and the market demand curve, D_0, determine the price P_0. At this price, the firm faces D_0,AR_0, MR_0, which touches the lowest point on its long run average cost curve, *LAC*, at output Q_0. In the long-run, the firm will produce output Q_0 and break even. It will also adjust any inputs that are fixed in the short run, so that it will face *SAC*, which also touches *LAC* at Q_0.

Now suppose market demand increases to D_1. In the short run, the price rises to P_1 where D_1 intersects SS_0. So the firm now faces D_1,AR_1,MR_1 and raises its output to its Q_1 where MR_1 intersects *SMC*. At Q_1, its average revenue, which is shown by AR_1, exceeds its short-run average cost, which is shown by *SAC*, so it makes a profit.

With the typical firm making a profit, new firms will enter the industry, shifting the short-run industry supply curve to the right. Firms will continue to enter the industry until this curve has shifted to SS_1, so that the price has been driven down to P_2, which equals P_0. Then the typical firm will face D_2,AR_2,MR_2, which is the same as D_0,AR_0,MR_0. So it will again produce Q_0 and break even. Then no more firms will enter the industry.

By now, the extra firms will have raised the industry output to Q_2, as shown in the left-hand part of the figure. So initially the industry was in long-run equilibrium, with the price at P_0 and output at Q_0. It then moves to a new long-run equilibrium, with the same price and output at Q_2. The industry long-run supply curve, *LS*, which is shown in grey, passes these two long-run positions. *LS* shows that the industry could, in the long run, supply either Q_0 or Q_2 at the same price.

Because P_0 and P_2 are the same, *LS* here is horizontal. This implies that, in the long run, this industry could supply *any* desired output at that same price. However, an industry's *LS* will be horizontal only if the entry of new firms into the industry does not affect the costs of the existing firms. We must now see what happens if their costs are affected.

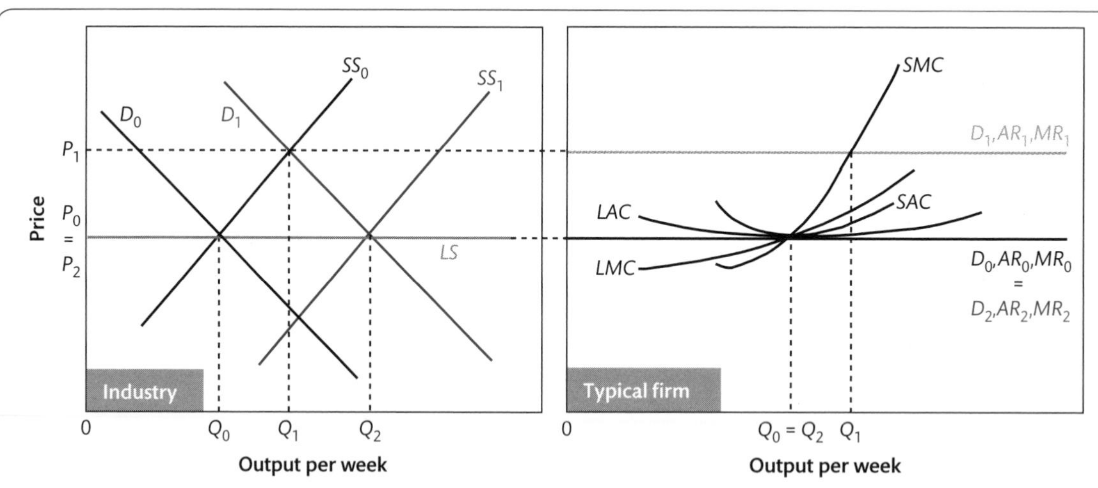

Figure 9.14 **The long-run supply curve, *LS*, for a perfectly competitive industry with constant costs**

The industry starts in long-run equilibrium with price P_0 and output Q_0. Then demand increases. In the short run, the price rises to P_1 and industry output rises to Q_1. The firm now faces D_1,AR_1,MR_1 and produces its Q_1 where MR_1 cuts *SMC*. But here its average revenue, given by AR_1, is above its short-run average costs, given by SAC_0, so it makes a profit. So new firms enter the industry. This shifts the short-run supply curve to SS_1. In the long run, the industry settles with price P_2 and output Q_2. *LS* passes the original and new industry equilibria. In this case, P_2 equals P_0, so *LS* is horizontal.

Changes in demand with increasing costs and decreasing costs

In some industries, the costs of existing firms are affected when the industry expands. Their costs can be affected in two different ways, and these are shown in Figure 9.15 as case (a) and case (b). In each case, the numerous black curves show the initial long-run equilibrium. The industry starts in long-run equilibrium where SS_0 intersects D_0 with output Q_0 and price P_0. The firm faces D_0,AR_0,MR_0 and is in long-run equilibrium with its output at Q_0, where D_0,AR_0,MR_0 touches its LAC_0 and where MR_0 intersects its SMC_0. It is also breaking even.

Then, in each case, demand increases to D_1. Demand is shown increasing more in case (a) than in case (b)

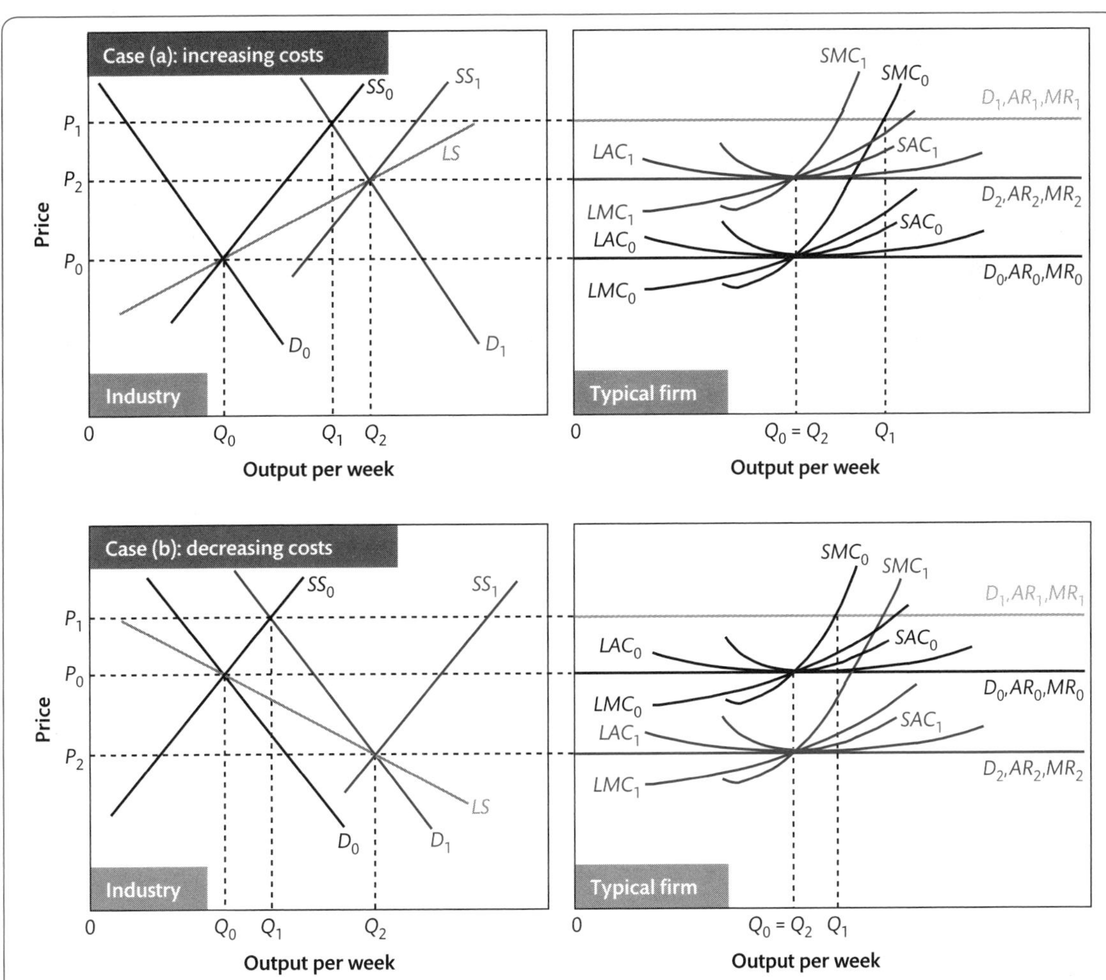

Figure 9.15 **The long-run supply curve, *LS*, for industries with increasing and decreasing costs**

In each part, the industry starts in long-run equilibrium with price P_0 and output Q_0. Then demand increases. In the short run, the price rises to P_1. The typical firm now faces D_1, AR_1, MR_1 and produces its Q_1 where MR_1 cuts SMC_0. Here, its average revenue, given by AR_1, is above its short-run average cost, given by SAC_0, so it makes a profit. So new firms enter the industry and shift the short-run industry supply curve to SS_1. In case (a), a larger industry raises existing firms' costs, shifting their cost curves up; here, the final P_2 is above P_0 and LS slopes upwards. In case (b), a larger industry reduces firms' costs, shifting their cost curves down; here, the final P_2 is below P_0 and LS slopes downwards.

simply for clarity. In the short run, the price rises to P_1, so the firm faces D_1,AR_1,MR_1 and produces Q_1 where MR_1 intersects SMC_0. Here, its average revenue, shown by AR_1, exceeds its short-run average cost, shown by SAC_0, so it makes a profit. As the typical firm now makes a profit, new firms enter the industry, with the following effects.

- **The costs of existing firms change**. In case (a), these firms find that, as the scale of the industry grows, they face external diseconomies of scale or increasing costs, so their cost curves shift up. Probably the new firms increase the demand for inputs and force input prices up. In case (b), the existing firms find that, as the scale of the industry grows, they face external economies of scale or decreasing costs, so their cost curves shift down. Perhaps input suppliers expand and can now afford research into cheaper ways of making inputs. Or perhaps banks and other lenders take more interest in the larger industry and offer better advice. Or perhaps the extra demand by the industry for skilled labour encourages colleges to put on relevant courses and so reduce the training costs borne by firms.
- **The short-run market supply curve shifts**. This curve represents the short-run supply curves of all the firms in the industry added together, so the entry of new firms shifts it to the right. However, the existing firms' short-run supply curves will shift because these follow part of their short-run marginal cost curves. In case (a), these firms have a new SMC_1 to the left of SMC_0, so their supply curves shift to the left and this reduces the extent to which the market supply curve shifts to the right; in case (b), the existing firms have a new SMC_1 to the right of SMC_0, so their supply curves shift to the right, and this increases the extent to which the market supply curve shifts to the right.
- **The market price changes**. New firms will stop entering the industry when the short-run market supply curve is in each case as shown by SS_1, so that the price is P_2. Then firms face D_2,AR_2,MR_2, which touches the bottom points of their new long-run average cost curves, LAC_1. They now produce output Q_2 at this point, because it is also where MR_2 intersects SMC_1. For simplicity, in each case, Q_2 is shown equal to Q_0. Once again, the firms break even, so this is the new long-run equilibrium. But P_2 is above P_0 in case (a) in which there are increasing costs, and P_2 is below P_0 in case (b) in which there are decreasing costs.
- **The industry's long-run supply curve slopes**. In each case, the industry's long-run supply curve, LS, passes the initial market equilibrium of P_0 and Q_0, and the final one of P_2 and Q_2. In case (a), LS slopes upwards because increasing costs mean that P_2 exceeds P_0; in case (b), LS slopes downwards because decreasing costs mean that P_2 is less than P_0.

Cost changes when demand is constant

In the left-hand parts of Figures 9.14 and 9.15, the industry was initially in equilibrium with price P_0, where the industry's long-run supply curve, LS, intersected the market demand curve, D_0. Each firm faced P_0 and was in equilibrium, breaking even with its output at Q_0. And we have seen that these equilibrium positions will change if demand changes.

The equilibrium positions will also change if firms face a change in their costs. There are two quite separate reasons why their costs may change in the long run.

- **Changes in input prices**. Input prices often rise over time. This shifts firms' cost curves up.
- **A change in technology**. Technological improvements lead to lower production costs and shift firms' cost curves down.

We saw in Figure 9.14 and 9.15 that, no matter what the shape of an industry's LS curve, it is derived from the lowest point of the LAC of the typical firm. If firms' cost curves move up, then the industry LS will move up. At the new long-run equilibrium, where the higher *LS* intersects *D*, there will be a higher price. But there will also be a lower output, so probably some firms will leave the industry. Those that remain will end up at the lowest point on their new higher *LAC* curves and so break even.

If firms' cost curves move down, then the industry *LS* will move down. At the new long-run equilibrium where the lower *LS* intersects *D*, there will be a lower price. But there will also be a higher output, so probably some new firms will enter the industry. The original firms will end up at the lowest point on their new lower *LAC* curves and so break even.

If the lower costs result from new technology, and some existing firms fail to adopt this new technology, then their *LAC* curves will not shift down. However, they will face the lower market price. So instead of breaking even, they will make losses and will be forced out of the industry. It follows that perfect competitors must keep up with changes in technology in order to survive.

9.7 Summary

- For a perfectly competitive industry, the long-run supply curve *LS* shows the combinations of price and output at which the industry can settle in the long run.
- If the entry of new firms has no effect on the cost curves of existing firms, then *LS* is horizontal.
- If the entry of new firms increases the costs of existing firms through external diseconomies of scale, then *LS* slopes upwards. If the entry of new firms decreases the costs of existing firms through external economies of scale, then *LS* slopes downwards.
- If input prices rise, the industry's *LS* curve shifts up, so the price rises, some firms leave the industry and market output falls. If input prices fall, or technology improves, the industry's *LS* curve shifts down, so the price falls, some firms enter the industry and market output rises.

In the next chapter we will look at the behaviour of firms in industries that have a monopoly or monopolistic competition. The subsequent chapter looks at the fourth market structure: oligopoly.

abc Glossary

Average revenue (*AR*): the revenue per unit of output, that is *TR*/*Q*.

Break-even point: the price at which a firm breaks even, and so has neither a profit nor a loss; it is the price in which its average revenue equals its short-run average cost.

Close down: when a firm decides to produce nothing in the long run, and will no longer exist.

Marginal revenue (*MR*): the change in total revenue if output changes by one unit.

Price-taker: a firm that has to accept the market price for its product and cannot set its own price.

Shut down: when a firm decides to produce nothing in the short run; it will have zero variable costs and zero revenue, and so have a loss equal to its total fixed cost.

Shutdown point: the price below which a firm will shut down; it is the price at which its average revenue equals its average variable cost.

Total revenue (*TR*): the total revenue from sales in a period of time.

Answers to in-text questions

9.1 Between $Q = 5$ and $Q = 6$, *MR* exceeds *SMC*. So if you were to raise your output from 5 to 6, your revenue would rise by more than your costs rise, so you would make more profit.

9.2 If *MR* were to intersect *SMC* at two different outputs, then the lower of these would actually be the worst output to produce. If you were to produce at this output, you would gain if you raised your output, because *MR* is greater than *SMC*, so your revenue would rise by more than your costs rose. You would also gain if you reduced your output, because *MR* is less than *SMC* so your revenue would fall by less than your costs fall.

? Questions for review

9.1 A firm finds that its total revenue and short-run total cost per day at various levels of output are as follows.

Output per day	0	1	2	3	4	5	6
***TR* per day**	0	100	200	300	400	500	600
***STC* per day**	40	110	160	225	320	450	660

Construct a table like the one in Figure 9.5 and calculate the figures for *MR* and *SMC*. Suppose the firm has at present an output of 1 per day. Using these *MR* and *SMC* figures, explain what it should raise its output to. Add a row for profit to your table to check that you get the right output. Why can't we be certain this is exactly the profit-maximizing output?

9.2 What is the *TFC* of the firm in question 9.1? If the price of all this firm's fixed inputs were to double, would its profit-maximizing output change?

9.3 Which of the following events could cause a perfect competitor to increase its output in the short run? Which of these events could cause it to move from making a loss to a profit? **(a)**: A rise in the market demand for its product. **(b)**: A fall in the price of a fixed input. **(c)**: A fall in the price of a variable input.

9.4 Suppose that, as a perfectly competitive industry expands, there are initially external economies of scale and then external diseconomies of scale. What shape will the *LS* curve for the industry be?

? Questions for discussion

9.1 Many food products are produced by firms in perfect competition. Consider any two food products and explain the likely effect in their markets, and on typical firms, of continued growth in the world's population. Can you suggest any other factors that might help to offset the effect on prices that population growth on its own would cause?

9.2 Suppose you run a perfectly competitive firm. Using the theory covered in this chapter, summarize how you would decide on **(a)** your output in the short run, **(b)** your output in the long run, and **(c)** whether in the long run, to increase or decrease the quantity of those inputs you use for which quantities are fixed in the short run.

Common student errors

Students sometimes blur the distinction between the short run and the long run. Asked what will happen in a perfectly competitive industry if demand rises, they sometimes make two statements called here (a) and (b). (a) 'The rise in demand causes a rise in price, so firms face a higher *D*, *AR*, *MR* curve and make profits.' (b) 'So new firms enter the industry, shifting the market supply curve right, so the price drops to the level where all firms break even.'

Both statements are broadly correct. The error is not saying clearly that the events in (a) occur in the short run, while those in (b) will not take place until the long-run. So the price may rise for some time.

Aside from this, a more polished answer would say in (a) that a firm might go from breaking even to a profit, or from a small profit to a large one, or from a small loss to a small profit, or from a large loss to a small loss; if the typical firm ends up making a loss despite the price rise, then new firms will not enter the industry, rather, some existing ones will leave.

Also, in (b), a polished answer would note that if external economies or diseconomies of scale were to arise, then the price might end up as lower or higher than the one that would have allowed all firms to break even initially.

10

Monopoly and Monopolistic Competition

Remember from Chapter 7 that we assume each firm wants the maximum possible profit. Also, in the short run, each firm can vary the quantity it uses of some of its inputs, but not others, while in the long run it can vary the quantity it uses of all inputs.

Suppose you run the only hotel in a remote town, or one of many hotels in a busy resort. How would you decide your current price per night for a room? How would you decide what price to set in a few years' time? Would you ever keep your hotel open if the best you could do were to make a loss? How would a change in staff wage rates affect your price? Would a change in the cost of insuring your hotel have the same effect? Would you vary your price between customers? Suppose a tourist tax of £5 a night were introduced: why might you raise your price by more than £5?

This chapter shows you how to answer questions like these, by understanding:

- what it means to be a price-setter;
- the relationship between marginal cost, marginal revenue, and profit maximization;
- the effect on a price-setter's price of changes in the prices of its fixed and variable inputs;
- price discrimination;
- taxes on price-setters;
- the long run in monopoly and monopolistic competition.

10.1 Price-setters compared with price-takers

In Chapter 9, we studied industries with perfect competition. In a perfectly competitive industry, many firms sell an identical product for which price is determined by the market demand and supply curves. Each firm is a price-taker, which means that it has to accept the current market price. As it cannot decide its own price, the main decision it has to make is the quantity to sell.

This chapter looks at industries with a monopoly, in which there is only one firm, and industries with monopolistic competition, in which many firms sell differentiated products. Supply and demand analysis does not apply to these industries, so we will have no graphs with market demand curves and market supply curves. All we will have are graphs for the individual firms under discussion.

In both monopoly and monopolistic competition, each firm sets its own price, so it is called a **price-setter**. To see why these firms can choose their own prices, let's contrast them with perfect competitors, which cannot.

- **A perfect competitor**. Suppose you run one of many firms producing identical potatoes for which the current market price is £150 a tonne. Then you could not sensibly set any other price for your potatoes. If you were to set a slightly higher price, say £151, you would lose all your customers to other firms who supply identical potatoes for £150. And if you were to set a slightly lower price, say £149, all the customers of all the other firms would like to buy from you, rather than pay those firms £150 for identical potatoes, so you would actually be swamped with orders that you could not meet. So the only sensible choice for you is to set the market price.
- **A monopolist**. Suppose you run the only bus service between two towns, and your current fare is £7. You could perfectly well change this. If you raise it to £8, you will no doubt lose some passengers, but you will not lose all your passengers because there are no other buses they can use. If you cut your price to £6, you will no doubt attract more passengers. But you will not be swamped by people who currently use other buses, because there are no other buses that they could use.
- **Monopolistic competitor**. Suppose you run one of many firms that make slightly different shirts, and your current price is £20. You could perfectly well change this. If you raise it to £22, no doubt some people will now buy shirts from your competitors instead of you, but you will not lose all your customers, because some of them will prefer the style or fabric of your shirts. If you cut your price to £18, no doubt some people will now buy shirts from you instead of from your competitors, but you will not be swamped with orders, because most people who buy from them will prefer the style or fabric of their shirts.

Key decisions for price-setters

As with all firms, we will assume that each monopolist and monopolistic competitor aims to maximize its profit in the short run and also in the long run. To do so, it must decide the following.

- **Its short-run output**. How much output it should produce in the short run, in each period of time, say per day? The short run is the period lasting from now for maybe a year or more during which it cannot vary the quantity it uses of some inputs. Some firms decide to shut down and produce nothing in the short run, but then they must still pay for their fixed inputs, the quantity of which they cannot vary, so they still exist.
- **Its short-run price**. What price should it set now to ensure that, in the short run, it sells the quantity it wants to produce each day?
- **Its long-run output**. How much should it produce each period of time, say per day, in the long run? The long run is the period starting after maybe a year or more by when it can vary the quantity it

uses of all inputs. Some firms decide to close down and produce nothing in the long run. These firms will have time to get rid of all of their inputs, so they will no longer exist.

- **Its long-run price**. What price should it set in the long run, to ensure that each day it will sell the quantity that it then wants to produce?

Sections 10.2–10.4 study the two short-run decisions made by monopolists, and section 10.5 studies the two long-run decisions. Sections 10.6 and 10.7 study the short-run and long-run decisions made by monopolistic competitors. Almost everything that applies to monopolists applies also to monopolistic competitors, so sections 10.6 and 10.7 focus on the few differences.

10.1 Summary

- Monopolists and monopolistic competitors set their own prices instead of accepting a going market price.
- In the short run, these firms set the price that will result in them selling the quantity of output that will lead to the maximum profit in the short run. In the long run, they set the price that will result in them selling the quantity of output that will lead to the maximum profit in the long run.
- The analysis for both monopolists and monopolistic competitors is for the most part very similar.

10.2 Monopolists as profit-maximizers in the short run

Suppose you run a monopoly. To discover which output will give you the maximum profit in the short run, you need to know what your cost and revenue would be at each possible output. We will assume that the relationship between your output and your costs is shown by U-shaped cost curves like those we met in Chapter 8. But the relationship between your output and your revenue depends on the prices you might set, and we must now study this relationship.

Revenue curves for a monopolist

Suppose the quantity of output, *Q*, which your monopoly would sell each day at various prices is as shown in the first two columns of the table at the top of Figure 10.1. This information is also given in the demand curve, *D*, in the figure below. For example, at a price of £8, you would sell 4 units a day. Unlike a perfect competitor, you face a sloping demand curve, because you can set your own price and sell more at low prices than at high prices. Admittedly, if you were to raise your price as far as £16, then you would lose all of your customers.

From this information, we can work out some information about your revenue.

- **Total revenue**. For each price, the column in the table headed *TR* shows the total revenue you would get. For example, if you were to set a price of £12 and so sell 2 units a day, your *TR* would be £24.
- **Average revenue**. The column headed *AR* shows the revenue you would get from each individual unit of output. For example, suppose your price is £12 so *Q* is 2 per day and *TR* is £24 per day. Then *AR*, the revenue you get from each unit you sell, is *TR*/*Q*, or £12. In fact, because *AR* equals *TR*/*Q*, it must always equal the price, no matter what the price is, as you can see from the table.
- **Marginal revenue**. The column headed *MR* shows how much your total revenue would change if you were to change your output by one unit. For example, suppose your current price is £12, so *Q* is 2 per day and *TR* is £24 per day. Then suppose you raise output by one unit to 3. To sell 3 per day, you must cut the price to £10, so your *TR* will be £30. As your

P £ per unit	*Q* Units per day	*TR* £ per period	*AR* £ per unit	*MR* £ per unit
16	0	0	-	
14	1	14	14	14
12	2	24	12	10
10	3	30	10	6
8	4	32	8	2
6	5	30	6	-2
4	6	24	4	-6
2	7	14	2	-10
0	8	0	0	-14

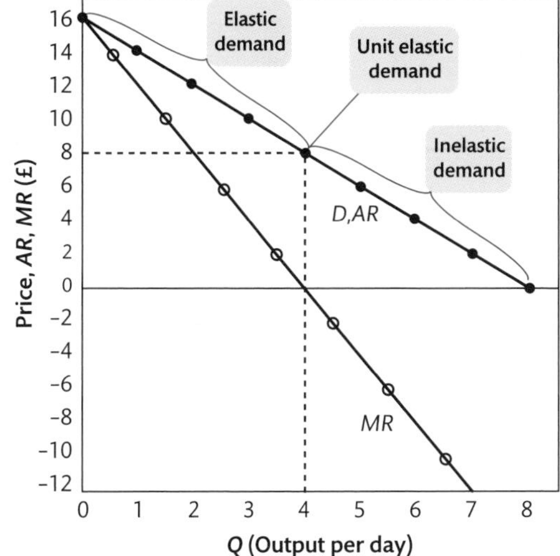

Figure 10.1 A monopolist's demand curve and revenue curves

The sloping *D* curve shows that the firm sells more if it reduces its price. At any *Q*, the *AR* equals the price needed to sell that *Q*. If the price is cut between £16 and £8, *TR* rises so *MR* is positive. But if the price is cut below £8, *TR* falls so *MR* becomes negative.

TR will rise by £6, so your *MR* will be £6. In the table, this figure of £6 is put between the lines for a *Q* of 2 and a *Q* of 3, to show that it concerns a change in output between 2 and 3. The table gives the *MR* figures for all other changes in output.

We can now add two curves to the figure.

- **The average revenue curve**. To plot this, we first put in the points marked as filled circles. These show the *AR* at each output in the table. For example, at an output of 2, there is a point at £12. Then we plot the *AR* curve through these points. As with a price-taker, a monopolist's *AR* curve always coincides with the demand curve it faces, so we label this curve as *D,AR*.
- **The marginal revenue curve**. To plot this, we first put in the points marked as rings. These show the *MR* for each one unit change in output. For example, between outputs of 2 and 3, there is a ring at £6. We then plot the *MR* curve through these points. Unlike a perfect competitor's *MR*, a monopolist's *MR* does *not* coincide with its *D,AR*.

Revenues and the elasticity of demand

You can see from the table in Figure 10.1 that if the price falls in the range above £8, then *TR* rises so that *MR* is positive. For example, if *P* falls from £12 to £10, then *Q* rises from 2 to 3 and *TR* rises from £24 to £30, so *MR* is £6. But if the price falls in the range below £8, then *TR* falls, so *MR* is negative. For example, if *P* falls from £6 to £4, and *Q* rises from 5 to 6, then *TR* falls from £30 to £24, so *MR* is –£6. In fact, *MR* is positive up to a *Q* of 4 and then becomes negative, and this is why the vertical axis in the graph goes below £0.

We saw in Chapter 4 that if a fall in price leads to an increase in revenue, then demand is price elastic, while if a fall in price leads to a decrease in revenue, then demand is price inelastic. So, in Figure 10.1, demand is elastic at prices above £8 and inelastic at prices below £8. At a price of £8, demand is neither elastic nor inelastic, but instead has unit elasticity. All this is marked on the graph.

Although *MR* may be negative at high outputs, a profit-maximizing firm never produces such a high output, so in future we will not show any *MR* curve below the point at which it meets the quantity axis.

Question 10.1 Why wouldn't a profit-maximizing firm want to produce at an output where *MR* was negative?

The relation between *AR* and *MR*

We need to note three points about the relationship between a monopolist's *AR* and *MR* curves.

- **The position of *MR* if *AR* is straight**. In Figure 10.1, *D,AR* is a straight line. When that happens, *MR* is also straight, and it starts at the same point as *D,AR* on the price axis, here £16. But *MR* is steeper than *D,AR*, and at any lower price it is only halfway across to *D,AR*. Here, for example, at a price of £0, the quantity on *D,AR* is 8, while the quantity on *MR* is 4.
- **The position of *MR* if *AR* is curved**. Most firms probably face a curved *D,AR*. With these, however, it is tricky to work out exactly where *MR* should be drawn. So students are generally advised to draw *D,AR* straight. We will follow that advice in this chapter except in the two situations in which curved and straight *D,AR* curves may lead to different outcomes.
- **At any output above zero, *MR* is less than *AR***. This may seem odd. Suppose your price is £12 and you sell 2 units a day. Then you cut the price to £10 and sell 3 units a day. You sell each of these 3 units at the same price, or *AR*, of £10, so your revenue from the third is clearly £10. So it may seem that the *MR* between outputs of 2 and 3 should equal this amount of £10, yet the table and the *MR* curve show it as £6.

  The reason that *MR* is below £10 is that *MR* does not measure your £10 revenue from the last unit. Instead, it measures the *change* in your *TR* when you sell one more. When the price was £12 and you sold 2 units a day, each unit brought in £12 and *TR* was £24. To sell a third unit, you had to cut the price to £10, so each unit brings in £10 and *TR* is £30. This is just £6 more than £24, so *MR* between outputs of 2 and 3 is £6.

  The shaded areas in Figure 10.2 illustrate this change in revenue. At the price of £12, the 2 units sold each day sold for £12 each, so *TR* was £24, as shown by the grey rectangle. At the new price of £10, the 3 units sold each day sell for £10 each, so *TR* is £30, as shown by the pink grid. Although each unit now brings in £10, *TR* rises by only £6 because the first 2 units sold each day sell for £2 less than before.

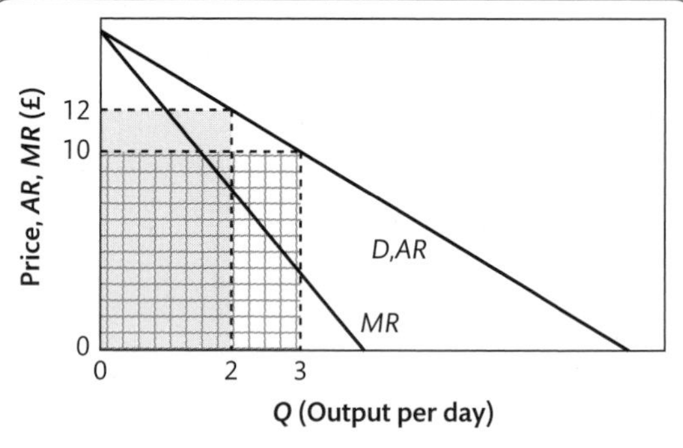

Figure 10.2 **Why the *MR* curve is below *AR***

If the price is £12, the firm sells 2 units a day, so its *TR* is £24, as shown by the grey rectangle. If the price is cut to £10, it sells 3 a day, so its *TR* is £30, as shown by the pink grid. These 3 units each sell for £10, but *TR* rises by only £6, because the first 2 units sold each day now fetch £10 instead of £12.

The profit-maximizing output

Once a monopolist knows what its revenue and cost would be at each possible output, it can find out which output will give it the most profit. Like the perfect competitor we looked at in Chapter 9, it could try to find this output in three ways.

- **Using a schedule**. A monopolist could draw up a schedule or table in which each row concerned a different output level. The table could show for each of these outputs how much total revenue, *TR*, the firm would earn, and also the short-run total cost, *STC*, that it would face. It could also show at each of these outputs how much profit the firm would get, the profit in each case, being equal to *TR* minus *STC*. Finally, the firm could see which of these outputs would give it the highest profit. The problem with this method is that the firm can see only which of the outputs shown on the schedule is best. Its profit might actually be maximized at an output in between two of those shown on the schedule.

- **Using a graph with curves for *TR* and *STC*.** The monopolist could instead plot a graph with two curves to show the *TR* and *STC* at every output. To find the profit-maximizing output, it would look for the output where *TR* was furthest above *STC*. The problem here is that it might take some time to do enough measurements to find the *precise* output that gives the most profit.
- **Using a graph with curves for *MR* and *SMC*.** The third and best method is to draw a graph with curves for marginal revenue, *MR*, and short-run marginal cost, *SMC*. Usually, the best output is the level at which these curves intersect.

To see this, suppose a monopolist faces the *MR* and *SMC* curves shown in Figure 10.3. These intersect at an output of 6. It is easy to explain why it should not produce any other output.

- **It should not set *Q* where *MR* is above *MC*.** For example, suppose its output is 2. If it were to raise this by one unit to 3, then *MR* shows that its total revenue would rise by £30, and *SMC* shows that its short-run total cost would rise by £15. So its profit would rise by £30 – £15, that is £15.
- **It should not set *Q* where *MR* is below *MC*.** For example, suppose its output is 8. If it were to reduce this by one unit to 7, then *MR* shows that its revenue would fall by £10, and *SMC* shows that its short-run total cost would fall by £20. So its profit would rise by £20–£10, that is £10.

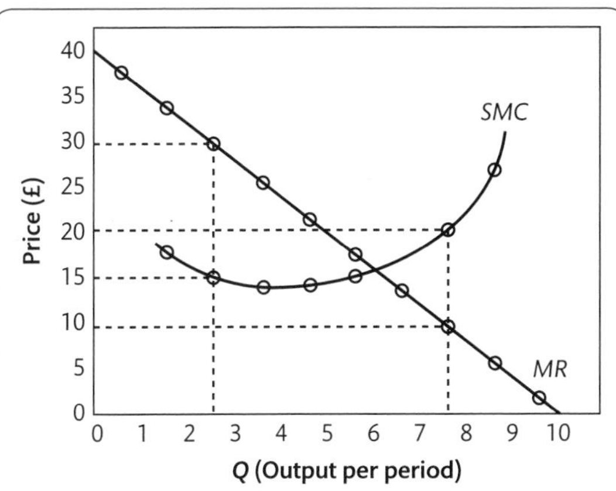

Figure 10.3 **Maximizing profit at the output where *MR* = *SMC***

If the firm has a *Q* such as 2, where *MR* exceeds *SMC*, then a rise in *Q* will raise *TR* more than *TC*. If it has a *Q* such as 8, where *MC* exceeds *MR*, then a fall in *Q* will reduce *TC* more than *TR*. So the *Q* where *MR* = *SMC*, here 6, is usually the best for profit-maximizing firms.

The level of profit

Although Figure 10.3 suggests that the best output is 6, it does not show what price the firm must set to get this output. Nor does it show what the firms' revenue, cost, and profit will be when it has set that price. To fix all of this, we need to add in a demand and average revenue curve, *D,AR*, and a short-run average cost curve, *SAC*. We will also add in a curve for average variable cost, *AVC*, to divide the firm's costs into fixed costs and variable costs. If we add these curves to Figure 10.3, we get the diagram shown in Figure 10.4. We can use this diagram find the following.

- **The price the firm must set.** The output where *MR* intersects *SMC* is 6. To find the price, *P*, at which the firm must sell this output, we look at the point on *D* at this output: it is at a price of £28. Points on *D* to the left of this show that if the firm sets its price above £28, then it will sell fewer than 6 units; points on *D* to the right show that if it sets its price below £28, then it will sell more than 6 units. To sell 6, it must set its price at £28.
- **The firm's total revenue, *TR*.** To find this, we look at the point on *AR* at the output of 6: it is at £28. So each of the 6 units brings in £28, making a total revenue of £168. This is represented by the whole shaded area, which is 6 units long and £28 high, making a total of £168.
- **The firm's short-run total cost, *STC*.** To find this, we look at the point on *SAC* at the output of 6: it is at £25. So each of the 6 units costs £25, making a

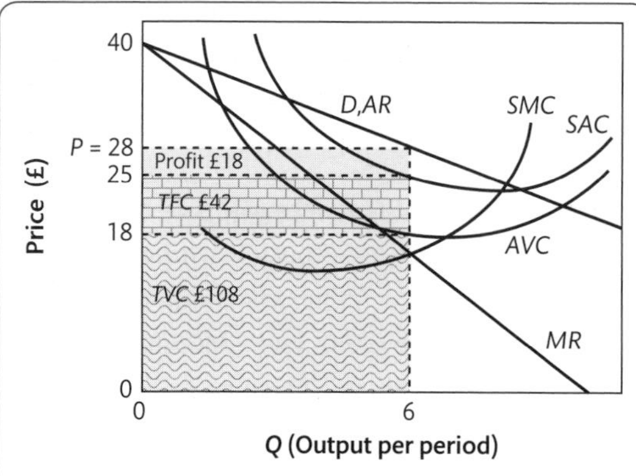

Figure 10.4 **Showing a monopolist's costs and profit**

The profit-maximizing *Q*, 6, is found where *MR* intersects *SMC*. The price, *P*, needed to sell 6 is £28, found from the point on *D* at this output. *AVC* is £18, so *TVC* is £90, shown by wavy shading. *AFC* equals *SAC* - *AVC*, that is £25 - £18 or £7, so *TFC* is £42, shown by brick-like shading. The profit per unit is *AR* - *SAC*, that is £28 - £25, or £3, so the total profit is £18, shown by plain shading. The total value of the shaded areas is £150: this is *TR*, that is *AR* of £25 × 6.

total cost of £150. This is represented by the areas with wavy shading and brick-like shading. These areas are 6 units long and, between them, £25 high, making a total of £150.

- **The firm's profit**. This equals *TR* minus *STC*, that is £168 minus £150, or £15. It is shown by the plain grey shaded area.
- **The firm's total variable cost, *TVC***. To find this, we look at the point on *AVC* at the output of 6: it is at £18. So each of the 6 units has a variable cost of £18, making a total variable cost of £108. This is shown by the wavy shading, which is 6 units long and £18 high, making a total of £108.
- **The firm's total fixed cost, *TFC***. This equals *STC* minus *TVC*, that is £150 minus £108, or £42. It is shown by the brick-like shading.

The possibility of a loss

The firm in Figures 10.3 and 10.4 made a profit, but monopolists can make losses. Figure 10.5 shows two cases of monopolists who make losses. In each case, there is no output where *AR* is greater than *SAC*, so there is no output where either firm could make a profit.

Each of these firms will consider the output *Q** where *MR* intersects *SMC*. Admittedly it would then make a loss on each unit sold because, at *Q**, *SAC* is above *AR*. The total loss would be as shown by the area with grey dots. Despite this loss, each firm might argue as follows.

- If our output were less than *Q**, *MR* would exceed *SMC*, so a rise in output would raise revenue by more than costs and reduce the loss.
- If our output were more than *Q**, *SMC* would exceed *MR*, so a fall in output would reduce costs by more than revenue and reduce the loss.

However, each firm should also consider whether the loss that it would make at *Q** would be bigger than the loss it would get if it were to shut down and produce nothing. If it shuts down and sells nothing, its total revenue will be zero, and it will buy no variable inputs and so have a zero *TVC*. But it will still have to pay for its fixed inputs whose quantity it cannot vary in the short run. So its total cost will equal its *TFC*, and with a zero *TR*, its loss will also equal its *TFC*.

In case (a), the firm will produce *Q**. Here, *AR* is above *AVC*, so the revenue from each unit more than covers its variable costs. So some revenue is left over to help pay the firm's fixed costs, and in turn its loss will be less than its *TFC*. This is better than shutting down and having a loss equal to *TFC*.

In case (b), the firm will shut down and have a zero output. If it instead produces at *Q**, where *AR* is below *AVC*, the revenue from each unit sold will not even cover its variable costs. So the firm's loss will equal its total fixed costs plus part of its variable costs, and so be bigger than the loss of *TFC* that arises with a zero output.

The key difference between these two cases is that the *AR* curve intersects *AVC* in case (a) but not in case (b). So in case (a) there is a range of outputs, including

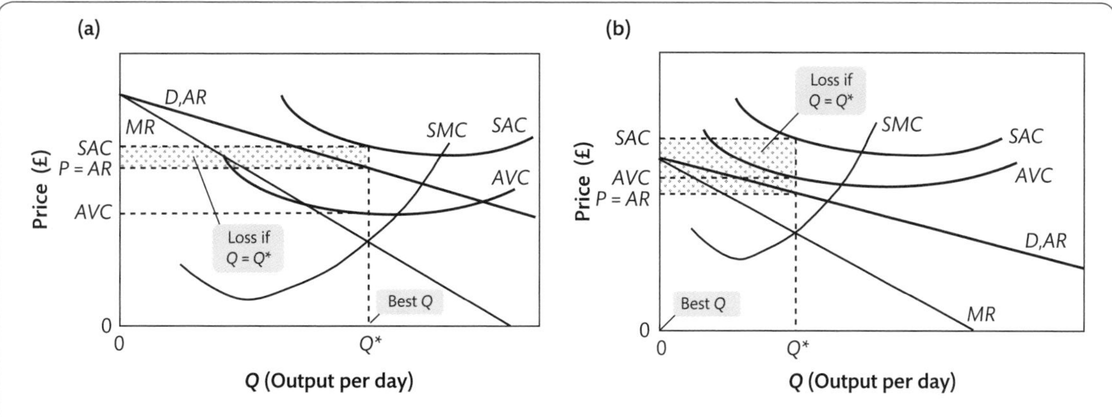

Figure 10.5 **Losses in the short-run**

In each case, at output Q^* where *MR* cuts *MC*, *SAC* exceeds *AR*, so if each firm produces Q^*, it will make a loss shown by the dotted area. But if it shuts down, it will have a loss equal to its total fixed cost. The case (a) firm will produce Q^*: here *AR* exceeds *AVC*, so it will earn enough to cover all of its variable costs and some fixed costs. The case (b) firm will shut down and produce nothing, for at Q^*, *AVC* exceeds *AR*, so it would not even cover its variable costs.

Q^*, where *AR* is above *AVC*, so that the firm can more than cover its variable costs. There is no such range in case (b).

The absence of a supply curve in monopoly

In Figure 9.9, we derived a supply curve for a perfect competitor. This curve showed how much that firm would produce at each possible price. For example, at a price of £440, it would always produce 6 units a day, provided that its cost curves stayed constant. In contrast, at any given price, a monopolist might produce a range of different outputs, even if its cost curves stay constant. Because it might produce different outputs at any given price, we cannot draw a supply curve for it.

The reason that, at any given price, a monopolist might produce different outputs while a perfect competitor will always produce the same output is that a monopolist can face a greater variety of demand curves. A perfect competitor faces a horizontal demand curve that can vary only in height. A monopolist faces a sloping demand curve that can vary in both height and slope.

Figure 10.6 shows how a monopolist might produce different outputs at a given price. This figure concerns a firm which, over time, faces four different demand and average revenue curves, D_0,AR_0, D_1,AR_1, D_2,AR_2, and D_3,AR_3. For the sake of clarity, two of these are given in part (a) and two in part (b); the *SMC* curve is the same in each part. Each *D,AR* curve has an associated marginal revenue curve that is drawn correctly to start at the same price as the related *D,AR* curve and to be halfway across to it at lower prices.

Consider this firm's response to each *D,AR* curve.

- $\mathbf{D_0,AR_0}$. The firm will set its output at 4, found where MR_0 intersects *SMC*, and set a price of £6, found from the point on D_0 at this output.
- $\mathbf{D_1,AR_1}$. The firm will set its output at 8, found where MR_1 intersects *SMC*, and set a price of £6, found from the point on D_1 at this output.
- $\mathbf{D_2,AR_2}$. The firm will set its output at 4, found where MR_2 intersects *SMC*, and set a price of £5, found from the point on D_2 at this output.
- $\mathbf{D_3,AR_3}$. The firm will set its output at 8, found where MR_3 intersects *SMC*, and set a price of £5, found from the point on D_3 at this output.

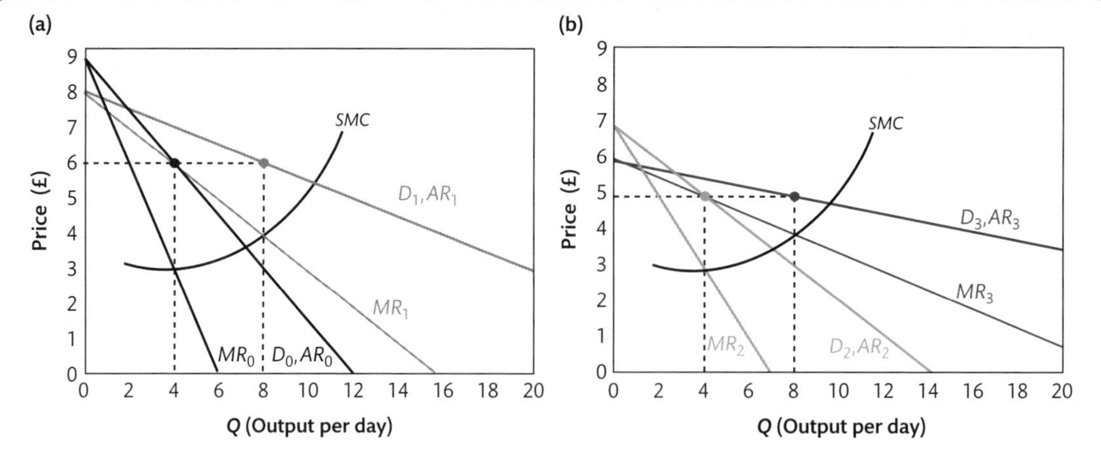

Figure 10.6 **There is no supply curve in monopoly**

This is because, at each price, a monopolist may produce various output levels, even if its *SMC* curve never changes. Its output depends on the height and slope of its *D,AR* and *MR* curves. For example, in part (a), the firm would supply 4 per day at a price of £6 with D_0,AR_0 and MR_0, but 8 at a price of £6 with D_1,AR_1 and MR_1. In part (b), it would supply 4 per day at a price of £5 with D_2,AR_2 and MR_2, but 8 at a price of £5 with D_3,AR_3 and MR_3.

So part (a) shows that, at a price of £6, this firm might set its output at 4 or 8, and part (b) shows that, at a price of £5, it might set its output at 4 or 8. And with different demand curves, it might set yet other outputs at these two prices, or set a range of possible outputs at other prices.

10.2 Summary

- A monopolist will usually maximize its profit by selling the output where *MR* equals *SMC*. The price that it must set to sell this output is found from the point on its demand curve at that output.
- If the firm cannot cover its variable costs at the output where *MR* equals *SMC*, then it should instead shut down and produce nothing. It will then have a zero output and a loss equal to its total fixed costs.
- At any given price, a monopolist might produce different outputs, depending on both the height and the slope of its demand curve; so it is not possible to derive a supply curve for a monopolist.

10.1 Everyday economics

Price of first-class stamps soars past 40p

In April 2010, the price of a first-class stamp rose above 40p for the first time. Royal Mail said that the move reflected the continuing losses made by Royal Mail in collecting and delivering stamped mail. This loss amounted to £250m in 2008–09.

'Stamp prices will rise by 2p in April says Royal Mail', *BBC News*, 22 December 2009
'Businesses blast Royal Mail plans to increase stamp prices yet again', *Mail Online*, 30 September 2009

Comment Royal Mail needs permission to raise prices. Because of its loss, it was given permission to raise the price of a first-class stamp by 3p, but it actually raised it by only 2p. It may seem odd that it did not raise the price as much as possible, but it may have thought that the 2p rise would take it to the position of the loss-making firm in case (a) in Figure 10.5 when it sets price *P*. This price results in output Q^* and the loss shown. But if this firm were to raise its price, then it would sell less than Q^* and so, as we saw, make a bigger loss.

10.3 Why the short-run equilibrium in monopoly might change

We will now see how the short-run output and price chosen by a monopolist may change if there is a change in demand or a change in the price of an input. As examples, we will look at an increase in demand and a rise in the price of an input.

A change in demand

The effects on a monopolist of an increase in the demand for its product are shown in two different cases in Figure 10.7. In case (a), the firm faces the straight demand and average curve D_0,AR_0, with its associated straight marginal revenue curve MR_0. As D_0,AR_0 is straight, MR_0 starts at the same price and is halfway across at any lower price.

In case (b), the firm faces the strongly curved demand and average revenue curve, D_0,AR_0. It is possible to use calculus to show that the associated marginal revenue curve, MR_0, will also curve sharply, and will be as shown in the figure.

Each firm faces the short-run marginal cost curve *SMC*, and will consider setting the output Q_0 where MR_0 intersects *SMC*. The point on D_0 above Q_0 shows that, to sell this output, the firm must set the price P_0. This is also the *AR* that it would earn with that output.

For simplicity, the average cost and average variable cost curves have been omitted in the figure, but let's assume in each case that, at Q_0, *AR* exceeds *AVC* so that the firm would more than cover its variable costs if it were to set that output. Then it would indeed produce Q_0, rather than shut down, and it would sell this output at price P_0.

Now suppose that each firm faces an increase in demand that results in it facing the new demand curve D_1,AR_1, with its associated marginal revenue curve MR_1. Each firm will now raise its output to Q_1, where MR_1 intersects *SMC*. But what will each firm do to its price?

To sell the output Q_1, each firm must set the price at the point on the demand curve at that output. In each

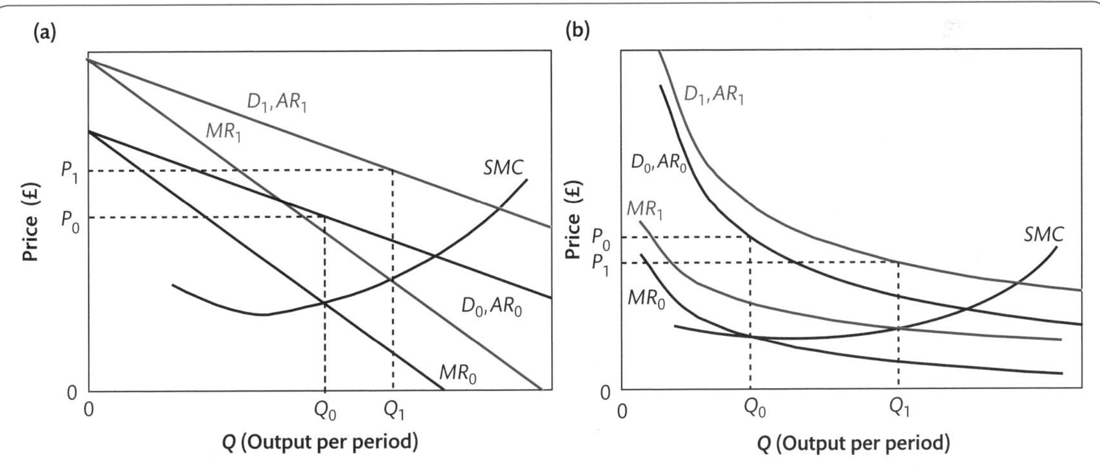

Figure 10.7 **A change in demand**

In each case, if demand increases, then D_0,AR_0 shifts right to D_1,AR_1 and MR_0 shifts right to MR_1. The result is a rise in output from Q_0 to Q_1. In case (a) there is also a rise in price from P_0 to P_1. But if the *D*,*AR* and *MR* curves are sufficiently curved, then the price could actually fall, as in case (b). For simplicity, no *SAC* curves are shown here, but they could be added and used to show that in each case the profit would rise.

case, this price is marked P_1. In case (a), P_1 is higher than the original price, but in case (b), P_1 is *below* the original price.

To sum up, a rise in demand always leads to a rise in output. Also, if the *D,AR* and *MR* curves are straight, as in case (a), or indeed if they are only slightly curved, it leads to an increase in price. But if *D,AR* and *MR* are sufficiently curved, as in case (b), the price will actually fall. In all cases, though, if we were to add in the average cost curves, we would find that the profit increased.

A change in input prices

The effect on a monopolist of a change in input prices depends on whether the input is a fixed one, whose quantity cannot be varied in the short run, or a variable one, whose quantity can be varied in the short run. The effects are compared in the two parts of Figure 10.8. In each case, the firm faces the demand and average revenue curve, *D,AR*, with its associated marginal revenue curve, *MR*. Also, in each case, the firm initially faces the short-run average and marginal cost curves SAC_0 and SMC_0, so it initially sets the output Q_0 where MR_0 intersects SMC_0. The point on the demand curve above Q_0 shows that, to sell this output, it must set the price P_0. This price is also the *AR* at Q_0, and it exceeds the average cost at Q_0, so the firm makes the profit shown by the grey rectangle.

A change in the price of a fixed input

Now suppose that there is a rise in the price of a fixed input. Perhaps there is a rise in the rate of interest on a loan that was used to buy a building, or a rise in the rent on some land for which the firm has a long-term tenancy, or a rise in the annual insurance premium for its vehicles.

As explained in Chapter 8 in connection with part (a) of Figure 8.3, these changes will increase the average cost of production, so the average cost curve rises from SAC_0 to SAC_1. However, there is no change in the firm's marginal cost: remember that marginal cost is the cost of producing extra units of output, and in the short run the only inputs of which a firm can get more in order to increase its output are variable inputs for which prices have stayed the same. So the firm's new short-run marginal cost curve, SMC_1, is the same as the original SMC_0.

As SMC_1 is the same as SMC_0, it intersects *MR* at the same quantity, so the new output Q_1 is the same as Q_0.

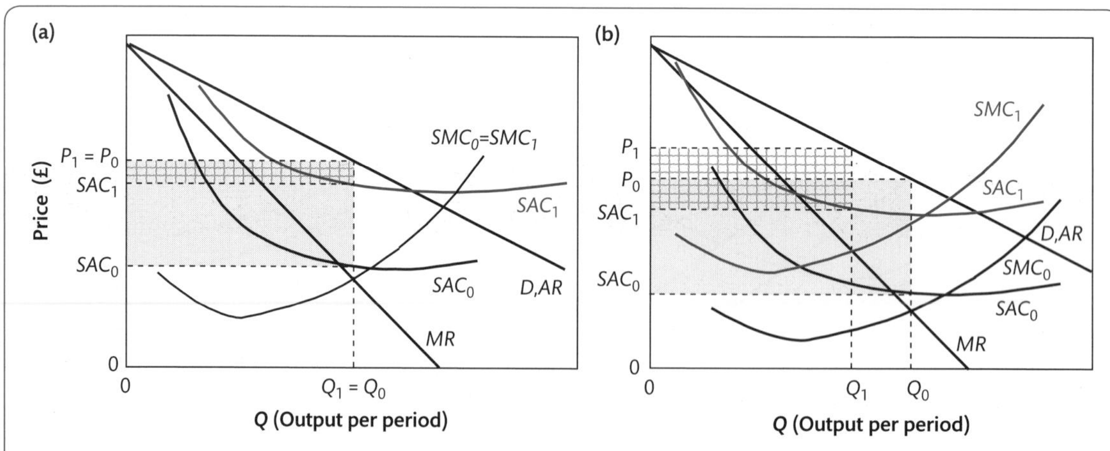

Figure 10.8 A change in the price of an input

Case (a) shows the effect of a rise in the price of a fixed input. Only the *SAC* curve shifts. Output and price both remain the same, but the profit falls from the area of the grey rectangle to that of the pink grid. Case (b) shows the effect of a rise in the price of a variable input. Both the *SMC* and *SAC* curves shift. Output falls and price rises. Again the profit falls from the area of the grey rectangle to that of the pink grid.

The point on *D* above Q_1 shows, not surprisingly, that the price P_1 that must be set to sell the same output is the same as the old price, P_0. So a rise in the price of a fixed input has no effect on the firm's price or output. However, it will reduce its profit. The shift in the average cost curve reduces the gap between *AR* and average cost at the unchanged output, so the profit falls to the area shown by the pink grid. If the new average cost were above the price at this output, then the firm would make a loss.

A change in the price of a variable input

Suppose, instead, that there is a rise in the price of a variable input. Perhaps there is a rise in the price of a raw material or a rise in the wage rate paid to employees who do not have long-term contracts. As explained in Chapter 8 in connection with part (b) of Figure 8.3, this will increase the average cost of production, so in case (b) of Figure 10.8, the average cost curve shifts from SAC_0 to SAC_1. The marginal cost curve also shifts up from SMC_0 to SMC_1. Remember that marginal cost is the cost of producing an extra unit, and increasing output now costs more in the short run because the only extra inputs that can be used are variable inputs, and one of these now has a higher price.

The firm will now set its output where SMC_1 intersects *MR*, that is at Q_1. This is less than Q_0. The point on the demand curve above Q_1 shows the price P_1 that must be set to sell this lower output. This price is above the original price, P_0. So a rise in the price of a variable input reduces the firm's output and increases its price. It also reduces its profit. The profit per unit of output now equals the gap at Q_1 between *AR* and SAC_1, and the total profit falls to the area shown by the pink grid. If the new average cost were above *AR* at output Q_1, the firm would make a loss. And if the prices of one or more variable inputs were to rise so much that at the output where *MR* intersects the new SMC_1 the firm could not cover its variable costs, then it would shut down.

10.3 Summary

- A rise in demand will lead to a higher output and a higher profit. Also, the price will rise if the demand curve is straight or slightly curved, but the price will fall if the demand curve is sufficiently curved.
- A rise in the price of a fixed input has no effect on price or output, but it leads to a lower profit or a loss.
- A rise in the price of a variable input leads to a higher price, a lower output, and to less profit or a loss.

10.4 Two applications of monopoly theory

We now turn to two further aspects of monopoly: price discrimination and taxes on expenditure.

The meaning of price discrimination

Sometimes, monopolists charge different prices to different consumers for the same product. This is called **price discrimination**, and it is possible only if the person who buys the product is also the person who uses it. A monopolist cannot apply price discrimination to products that could be resold, like iPads, for instance, because people who faced high prices could commission people who faced low prices to make purchases on their behalf.

Price discrimination by groups

The most usual type of price discrimination is to charge different prices to different types of consumer. For example, theatres, cinemas, and bus companies often have different prices for children, students, the elderly, and other adults. Airlines and train firms often discriminate even further, with the price depending also on how far ahead the ticket is booked and the terms under which it can be changed.

Of course, airlines and train companies also have different prices for different classes of travel, but this is not price discrimination because the different prices really apply to different products. For example, airlines offer business passengers a faster check-in, more space, and better food.

We will explore price discrimination in a simple case of a bus company that, on a particular route, has just two fares: a low fare for students and a high fare for other passengers. You may imagine that this company is just being nice to students, and making less profit than it would otherwise. To see if this is so, we will first see what happens when it does discriminate, and then see what would happen if it instead were to charge the same fare to all passengers.

The first two parts of Figure 10.9 show how the firm will set its fare for each group, if it adopts price discrimination. The analysis is as follows.

- **The demand by the two groups**. The first part of Figure 10.9 shows the student demand with the curve D,AR_{STU}. The second part shows the demand by other passengers with D,AR_{OTH}. The associated marginal revenue curves are MR_{STU} and MR_{OTH}. Students have the more elastic demand. For example, if the price for each group were to rise from £3 to £5, then the quantity of trips by students would fall from 600 to 200, while the quantity by other passengers would fall by much less, from 600 to 400. Students may have a more elastic demand because they could afford few trips at high fares and might do several trips a day at low fares, while many other passengers may be workers who will do the same number of trips at almost any fare.
- **The costs**. To keep the example simple, we will assume that the firm can always carry an extra passenger from either group at a constant extra or marginal cost of £3. This means that its average cost for any number of passengers is also £3. So each part of Figure 10.9 has a horizontal line at £3 representing *SMC* and *SAC*.
- **The discriminatory price for students**. The profit-maximizing number of student journeys is 300 a day, where MR_{STU} intersects *SMC*. The point on D,AR_{STU} at this output shows that the price needed to sell 300 student tickets is £4.50.
- **The discriminatory price for other passengers**. The profit-maximizing number of journeys for other

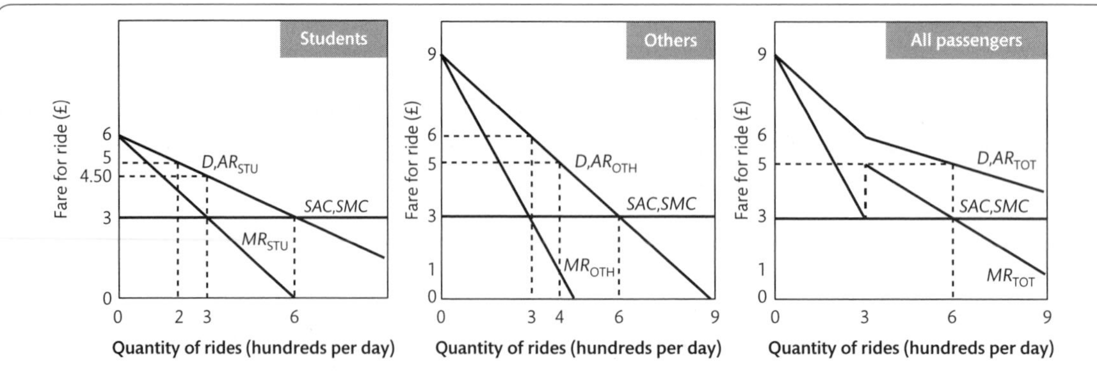

Figure 10.9 **Price discrimination by groups**

On a certain bus route, students have a more elastic demand than other passengers. With price discrimination, the firm takes 300 students for a £4.50 fare, and takes 300 others for a £6 fare. Without discrimination, it would have a uniform fare of £5 and take 200 students and 400 others. Compared to non-discrimination, price discrimination leads to a lower fare and more use by students, a higher fare and less use by others, and more profit for the firm.

passengers is also, by chance, 300 a day, where MR_{OTH} intersects *SMC*. The point on AR_{OTH} at this output shows that the price needed to sell 300 non-student tickets is £6.

- **The student discount**. The profit-maximizing price for students of £4.50 means they will have a 25% discount off the £6 fare for other passengers. Profit-maximizing firms that adopt price discrimination always give the lowest prices to the groups with the most elastic demand.
- **The total profit**. With price discrimination, 300 student journeys are made each day, each at a price of £4.50 and a cost of £3, so the profit from them is £1.50 per journey, or £450 per day in all. Some 300 other journeys are made each day, each at a price of £6 and a cost of £3, so the profit from them is £3 per journey, or £900 per day in all. So the total profit is £450 plus £900, which is £1,350 per day.

The third part of Figure 10.9 shows what would happen if the firm were to set one fare for all types of passenger. The analysis is as follows.

- **Total demand without discrimination**. If the firm had one fare for all passengers, then it would not need to know about the demand by each type of passenger. It would need to know only the total demand, as shown by D,AR_{TOT}. At each price, D,AR_{TOT} shows the quantities demanded by students and others added together. D,AR_{TOT} is kinked because, at prices above £6, where students are priced out, a price fall would lead only to more journeys by other passengers. At lower prices, a price fall would lead to more journeys by passengers of both types.
- **Marginal revenue without discrimination**. Associated with D,AR_{TOT}, there is actually a two-part *MR* curve; its two parts are joined by dashes at the output where D,AR_{TOT} has a kink, but we will be concerned only with outputs to the right of the kink on the second part of MR_{TOT}.
- **The non-discriminatory price**. When there is no discrimination, the profit-maximizing number of journeys is 600 a day, where MR_{TOT} intersects *SMC*. In any example in which all groups have straight demand curves, the total output without discrimination is the same as the total with discrimination, in this example, 600. The point on D,AR_{TOT} at this output shows that the price needed to sell this number of tickets is £5.
- **The total profit without discrimination**. Each day, 600 journeys will be made, each at a price of £5 and a cost of £3, so the profit is £2 each, which is £1,200 per day in total. This is less than the profit of £1,350 made with price discrimination.

This simple example shows that price discrimination has three effects, as follows.

- **It leads to low prices for the groups with the more elastic demand**. These prices are usually called discounted prices.
- **It leads to a high price for the group with the least elastic demand**. This may be called the normal price, but it is really a high price for a group where a high price raises the firm's profit.
- **It leads to a bigger profit for the firm**.

As well as discriminating between different types of passenger, transport firms may discriminate between those who travel at peak times and those who travel off-peak. People who travel at peak times are mostly workers with little choice over whether or when they will travel. So their demand is less elastic than that of other passengers, and therefore discrimination leads to them being charged the higher fares.

10.2 Everyday economics

Rail fares: a maze or price discrimination?

Anyone who travels by train in the UK knows that the train operators offer a bewildering array of fares. It is reasonable to suppose that this is because they are profit-maximizing companies that adopt price discrimination in a way that results in the lowest fares for the groups with the most elastic demand. So, like many public transport firms, they offer concessions to young people and senior citizens, many of whom might otherwise rarely travel by train. Price discrimination also entails charging the highest fares to groups with the most inelastic demand: these include people who travel at peak times, because they may have to travel and have no alternative mode of travel, and people who book at short notice, because they may have some pressing need that obliges them to make a journey.

Price discrimination by individuals

Occasionally, monopolists are able to discriminate between individual buyers. Suppose you are a sports champion, and sports clubs around the country want to hire you for coaching sessions. Suppose you face the *D,AR* curve, and the associated *MR* curve, shown in part (a) of Figure 10.10. And suppose you have the marginal cost curve *SMC*: maybe this slopes upwards because the more clubs you visit, the further from home you have to go, so your travel costs rise.

If you do not engage in price discrimination, you will set your output where *MR* intersects *SMC* at 30 sessions a year. The point on *D* at this output shows that, to sell this number, you must set a price or fee of £500 a session. The slope of *D* means that some clubs are willing to pay you more than others, perhaps because they are richer or keener. Indeed, the intersection of *D* with the price axis at £800 tells us that one club is willing to pay you just about £800. We can also see from *D* that, for example, the club willing to pay the 10th most would be willing to pay you £700, while the club willing to pay the 20th most would be willing to pay you £600.

Suppose you were shrewd enough to work out which these two clubs were, and charge them £700 and £600 instead of your normal £500. Then your revenue from them would rise from £500 by £200 and £100 respectively; your profit would rise by the same amounts, because your costs would not be affected. These extra revenues and profits are measured by the vertical pink lines in part (a) above each quantity.

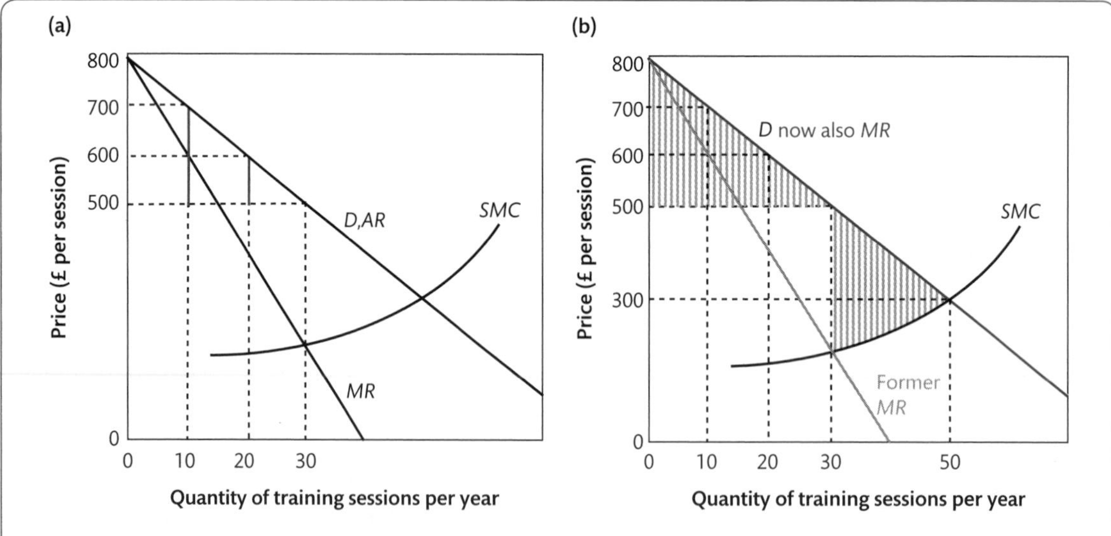

Figure 10.10 **Price discrimination by individuals**

With no discrimination, as in part (a), 30 clubs each pay £500. But 29 would be willing to pay more; e.g. the 10th would pay £700. If the sportsperson could make each pay the most it would be willing to pay, the revenue and profit from them would rise by the area of the triangle with 29 pink stripes at the top of part (b); also, the sportsperson would raise output to 50, with the profit from the extra 20 clubs equal to the pink area with 19 stripes between D and SMC.

Now suppose you were shrewd enough to charge *every* club the most it would pay. Then you would have a pink line for all 30 clubs, as shown in part (b). These lines form a triangle, which shows how much your revenue and profit would rise.

In fact, if you are this shrewd, you may be able to do even better. Part (b) shows that you might raise your output to 50 by charging each of the next 20 clubs as much as they are willing to pay. Your revenue from these extra clubs will rise by the amounts shown for them on *D*, and your cost in each case will rise as shown by *SMC*. So your profit will rise by the pink lines in the output range 30–50. You will not visit the 51st club because the most it would be willing to pay, shown by *D*, is less than your cost of visiting it, shown by *SMC*.

The real reason that you will supply more output with price discrimination is that your marginal revenue curve changes. In part (a), your *MR* curve slopes steeply. This is because to raise your number of visits from, say, 9 to 10, you have to cut your price, perhaps from £710 to £700. So the extra £700 you would get from the 10th club would be partly offset by getting £700 rather than £710 from each of the first 9. But with price discrimination in part (b), you can charge the 10th club the full £700 they are willing to pay, without charging the first 9 any less. So your revenue will rise by the full £700, and in fact you now have a new *MR* curve that coincides with *D*. Your new output of 50 is where this *MR* intersects *SMC*.

Even if a monopolist is not as shrewd as we have imagined you to be, price discrimination of this type can raise its profit appreciably. But this type of discrimination is relatively rare, because few monopolists know individual buyers well enough.

Monopolists and taxes on expenditure

In Chapter 5, we saw how taxes on expenditure affect markets in which supply and demand curves apply. But these markets apply only to products produced in perfect competition. Figure 10.11 shows two cases of a monopolist facing a tax on expenditure. Case (a) concerns a firm with a straight *D,AR*, while case (b) concerns a firm with a strongly curved *D,AR*. Each *D,AR* curve has an associated *MR* curve. In each case, there is initially no tax, and the firm supplies output Q_0 where *MR* intersects the marginal cost curve *SMC*. The

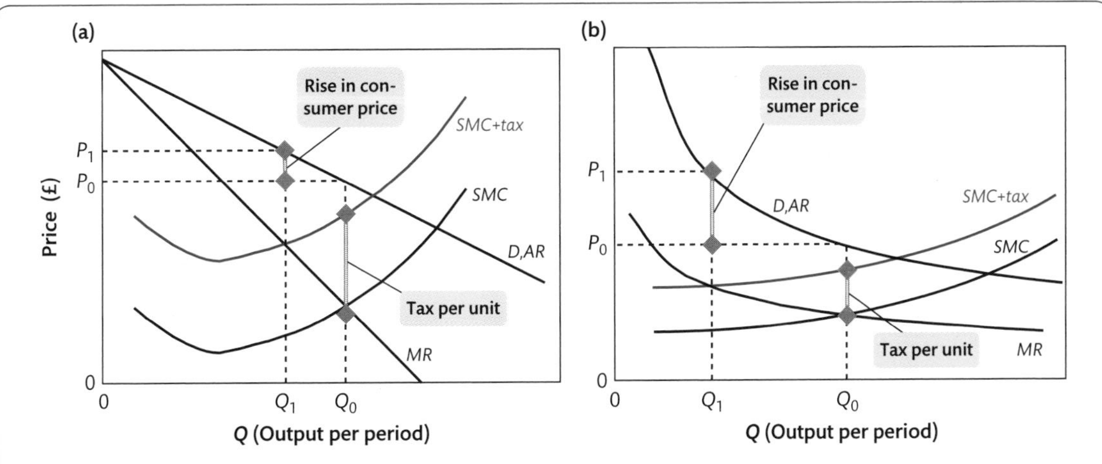

Figure 10.11 **A specific tax with a monopolist**

The effects of the tax can be shown by adding curve *SMC + tax*, which lies above *SMC* by the amount of the tax. In each case, the firm cuts output from the initial Q_0 to Q_1, where *SMC + tax* intersects *MR*. The firm also raises its price to consumers from P_0 to P_1, which is at the point on *D,AR* above Q_1. In case (a) the consumer price rises by less than the tax, but in case (b), with strongly curved *D,AR* and *MR* curves, the consumer price rises by more than the tax.

point on D above Q_0 shows that, to sell this output, the firm must set the price P_0. Consumers will pay P_0 and all their money will go to the firm.

Now suppose the government imposes a specific tax of a certain sum per unit on each firm's product. The effects can be shown in various ways, and in Figure 10.11 we show this by having a new marginal cost curve, $SMC + tax$, which is above SMC by the amount of the tax. In each case, the tax per unit of output is shown by a double line between SMC and $SMC + tax$. To make the figures clear, the tax is bigger in case (a) than in case (b).

The new curve $SMC + tax$ tells us how much the firm's costs will rise if it produces an extra unit, allowing for both its production costs shown by SMC and its tax payment to the government. In each case, the firm will set the new lower output, Q_1, where $SMC + tax$ intersects MR. And in each case, the point on D above Q_1 shows the new price, P_1, which must be charged to consumers to sell this output.

In each case the new consumer price, P_1 is above the original consumer price P_0. However, each case has another double line to show how much the consumer price rises. In case (a), it rises by less than the tax, a result consistent with what we found in Chapter 5 for markets in perfect competition. But in case (b), the price paid by consumers actually rises by *more* than the tax. So a specific tax of, say, £5 a unit could result in a price rise for consumers of *more* than £5!

For simplicity, Figure 10.11 does not show the new price kept by the monopolist. This will equal the new consumer price minus the amount of tax. In case (a), in which the consumer price rises by less than the tax, the producer price will end up below the initial P_0. In case (b), in which the consumer price rises by more than the tax, the producer price will actually end up *above* P_0!

10.4 Summary

- Firms can increase their profits by using price discrimination.
- Typically, firms set lower prices for groups of customers who have the more elastic demand.
- If firms know individual buyers and how much they would be willing to pay, price discrimination by individuals can greatly increase their profits and will also raise their output.
- When a monopolist's product is taxed, the price to consumers may possibly rise by more than the tax.

10.5 The long run in monopoly

In section 10.2, we saw how a monopolist will decide on its price and its output each period of time in the short run. We will now see how it will decide on its price and its output each period of time in the long run.

The long-run cost curves

A monopolist's long-run equilibrium position depends in part on the shape of its long-run cost curves. In Chapter 8, we saw in Figures 8.4–8.9 that LAC curves and LMC curves can have various shapes. For simplicity, we will consider here a monopolist whose LAC and LMC curves are both U-shaped, as in Figure 10.12. LAC here shows the lowest average cost at which the firm could produce each output per period of time, such as a week, if it had time to vary the quantity of each input it uses. LMC shows how much its total costs per period would change if it were to change its output per period by one unit, and have time to vary the quantity it uses

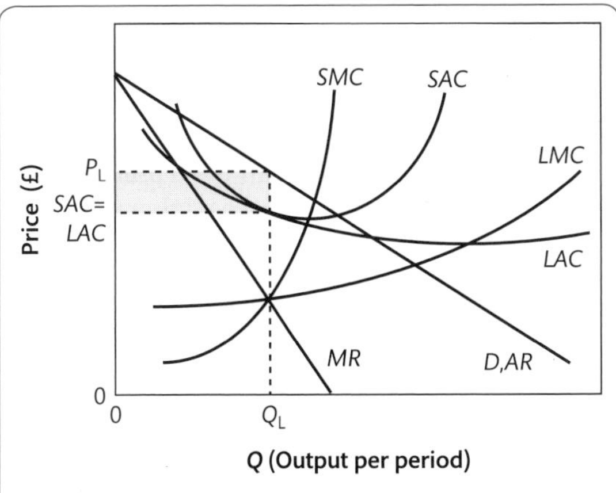

Figure 10.12 **A monopolist's long-run equilibrium**

The firm will set output Q_L in the long-run, where *MR* intersects *LMC*, and sell it at price P_L. It will adjust the quantity it uses of inputs for which quantity can be varied only in the long run so that it ends up on *SAC*, which just touches *LAC* at Q_L.

of each input. Figure 10.12 also shows the firm's demand and average revenue curve, *D,AR*, and its marginal revenue curve, *MR*.

The monopolist's long-run equilibrium

In the long run, the firm in Figure 10.12 will set its output at Q_L where *MR* intersects *LMC*. The point on *D* above Q_L shows that the price it will have to set to sell this output is P_L. The reason that Q_L is the profit-maximizing output is as follows.

- **At any lower output, where *LMC* is less than *MR*, the profit would rise if output were higher.** This is because a rise in output would, in the long run, raise costs by less than it raised revenue.

- **At any higher output, where *LMC* is more than *MR*, the profit would rise if output were lower.** This is because a fall in output would, in the long run, reduce costs by more than it reduced revenue.

Once the firm has decided that, in the long run, its output will be Q_L per period, it will want to be sure that it can produce Q_L at the lowest possible cost, which is shown by the point on *LAC* at this output. To be able to produce Q_L at this cost, the firm may first need to change the quantities of those inputs that are fixed in the short run, but which can be changed in the long run.

After it has made these changes, the firm will be able to produce Q_L at this cost, even in the short run. So it will then be on the *SAC* curve shown, which touches *LAC* at Q_L. It will now have more fixed inputs than is ideal for lower outputs than Q_L, and fewer than is ideal for higher outputs, so its *SAC* curve will be above its *LAC* curve at every output except Q_L. Associated with this *SAC* is a short-run marginal cost curve, *SMC*, which intersects *MR* at the same output, Q_L; it must do so because, once the firm is on *SAC*, Q_L will also be its best output in the short run.

Once it reaches its long-run equilibrium, the firm will make a profit per unit shown by the gap at Q_L between *AR* and *LAC*. Multiplying this by Q_L gives the total profit shown by the grey rectangle.

Question 10.2 What would happen to the monopolist's long-run output, price, and profit if there were **(a)** a rise in the price of an input, or **(b)** a rise in demand?

New entrants and limit pricing

Figure 10.12 shows a monopolist making a profit in the long run, which monopolists usually do. Its profit will certainly tempt other firms to try to enter its industry. If they were to enter it, then the demand for this firm's product would fall, and in turn its output and profit would fall. But there are barriers to entry in monopoly, and if potential new firms cannot overcome these, then the existing firm may make persistent profits in the long run.

However, monopolists know that potential entrant firms might try to overcome the barriers, so they may try to strengthen the barriers. A common strategy is to threaten potential entrants that if they do enter, then the existing firm will cut its price to one so low that the entrants, which would have to set a competitive price to make any sales, would make no profit after all.

This threat is not always credible. If the entrants know that they would have similar costs to the existing firm, then they know that any such price that caused them to make a loss would also cause the exiting firm to make a loss, so they can be sure that it will not actually do as it threatens.

But sometimes a monopolist has a cost advantage over new entrants, perhaps from its know-how, or its scale, or its well-known brand names. If so, it may deter entrants with a credible threat to set a price that would be high enough to give it some profit, but low enough to give them a loss. Some monopolists actually maintain their prices at such a level, and so below the profit-maximizing level, to deter other firms from even considering entry. This practice is called **limit pricing**.

10.3 Everyday economics

Microsoft fined for creating barriers

If monopolists can keep out rival firms, then they can set higher prices and earn more profits than they otherwise would. Microsoft enjoys a large share of the operating systems market, and is widely accused of acting like a monopolist and making it hard for rivals to compete in any of its activities. Both in the US and EU it has been pressured by the authorities to make itself more open to competition, and in 2004 the EU Competition Commission instructed it to give program developers more information to help them to develop software that worked with Windows. Of course, Microsoft has a profit incentive to do no more than the minimum needed to comply with these requirements, or even to ignore them, and in 2008 the EU Competition Commission fined Microsoft €899 m for failing to comply with the 2004 ruling. Microsoft is appealing over this.

10.5 Summary

- In the long run, a profit-maximizing monopolist sets its output where its *MR* and *LMC* curves intersect.
- The monopolist will also adjust the quantities of any inputs the quantity of which can be varied only in the long run so that it will end up on a *SAC* that just touches *LAC* at its long-run output level.
- A monopolist may make a profit indefinitely, and may try to strengthen the entry barriers to its industry, perhaps using limit pricing to keep the price at a level at which new entrants would make a loss.

10.6 Monopolistic competitors in the short run

We now turn to monopolistic competitors. These operate in industries in which many firms produce differentiated products. We saw in section 10.1 that they are price-setters, so they can raise or lower their prices to sell lower or higher quantities. So, like monopolists, they face downward-sloping demand curves. This means that we can analyse them with identical diagrams.

Figure 10.13 shows the short-run equilibrium for a monopolistic competitor. Like a monopolist, it will set its output where its marginal revenue curve, *MR*, intersects its short-run marginal cost curve, *SMC*, here at an output of 5, provided that it will then cover its variable costs. Otherwise, it will shut down. In the figure, the point on the demand and average revenue curve, *D,AR*, at an output of 5 shows that the price needed to sell 5 is £5, and that the average revenue from this output would also be £5. This *AR* is above the average variable cost of £3 at this output, shown by the *AVC* curve, so the firm will more than cover its variable costs, and so it will indeed produce 5 at a price of £5. Its *AR* is also above its average cost of £4 at this out-

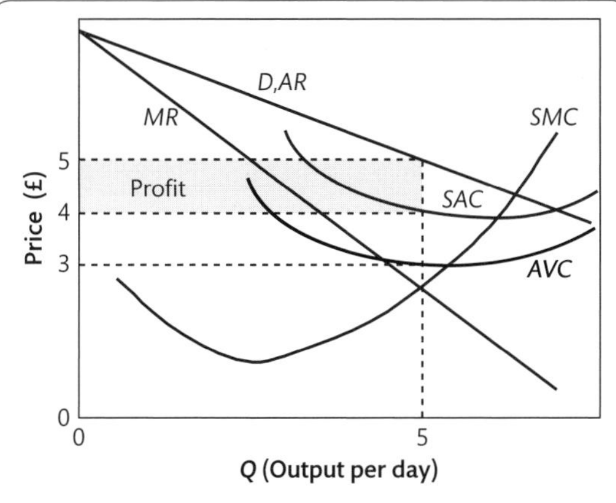

Figure 10.13 **A monopolistic competitor making a short-run profit**

Like a monopolist, a monopolistic competitor sets its short-run output where *SMC* cuts *MR*, and it finds the price it needs to set by looking at the point on *D* above. Its profit per unit of output is the gap between *AR* and *SAC* here. Its total profit is shown by the grey area.

put, shown by the *SAC* curve. So its profit will be £1 a unit, or £5 in all, as shown by the grey rectangle.

One difference from monopoly is that monopolistic competitors less often use price discrimination. They worry that if they set different prices for different customers, then those customers who face high prices may instead buy from competitors who do not discriminate against them.

The effect of product differentiation

As monopolistic competitors produce differentiated products, they face different demand and cost curves, and sometimes make very different decisions. Figure 10.14 shows this for four hotels in a skiing resort. Suppose that it is summer at present, and each hotel faces the black summer demand and average revenue curve D_S,AR_S, with its associated marginal revenue curve MR_S. Also, suppose each faces the black cost curves labelled *SAC*, *SMC*, and *AVC*.

Each hotel will consider setting its output this summer, measured perhaps as rooms filled each night, at Q_A, where MR_S intersects *SMC*. In each case, the price needed to sell this output, P_A, is read off D_S at the point above Q_A; this is also the average revenue each would get, AR_A. In each case, AR_A is less than the short-run average cost at Q_A, which is shown by SAC_A, so each hotel would make a loss shown by the grey area. Finally, note that the average variable cost of Q_A for each hotel is marked as AVC_A.

Although all the hotels will make losses this summer, they will make different decisions about their output this summer, as follows.

- **Hotels (a) and (b), this summer**. These hotels find that, at Q_A, their average revenues, AR_A, exceed their average variable costs, AVC_A. So although producing Q_A leads to a loss, their revenues will more than cover their variable costs and so help them to meet their fixed costs. So their losses are less than their total fixed costs, and so less than the losses they would face if they were to shut down and have zero revenues along with costs equal to their total fixed costs. So these hotels will open this summer with outputs at Q_A and prices at P_A.
- **Hotels (c) and (d), this summer**. They find that if they were to produce Q_A, then their average variable costs, AVC_A, would exceed their average revenues, AR_A. So they would not even cover their variable costs and their losses would exceed their total fixed costs. So they will shut down this summer, to get zero revenues and have costs and losses equal to their total fixed costs.

Each hotel also looks ahead to next winter. Each expects to face a higher demand as shown by the purple demand and revenue curves labelled D_W,AR_W and MR_W. Each hotel will consider setting its output at Q_B where MR_W intersects *SMC*. In each case, the price needed to achieve this output, P_B, is read off D_W above Q_B, and this is also the average revenue they would get at this output, AR_B. However, the hotels will make two different types of plan for next winter, as follows.

- **Hotels (a) and (c), next winter**. They reckon that if they were to produce Q_B, then their average revenue, AR_B, would exceed their average cost, marked

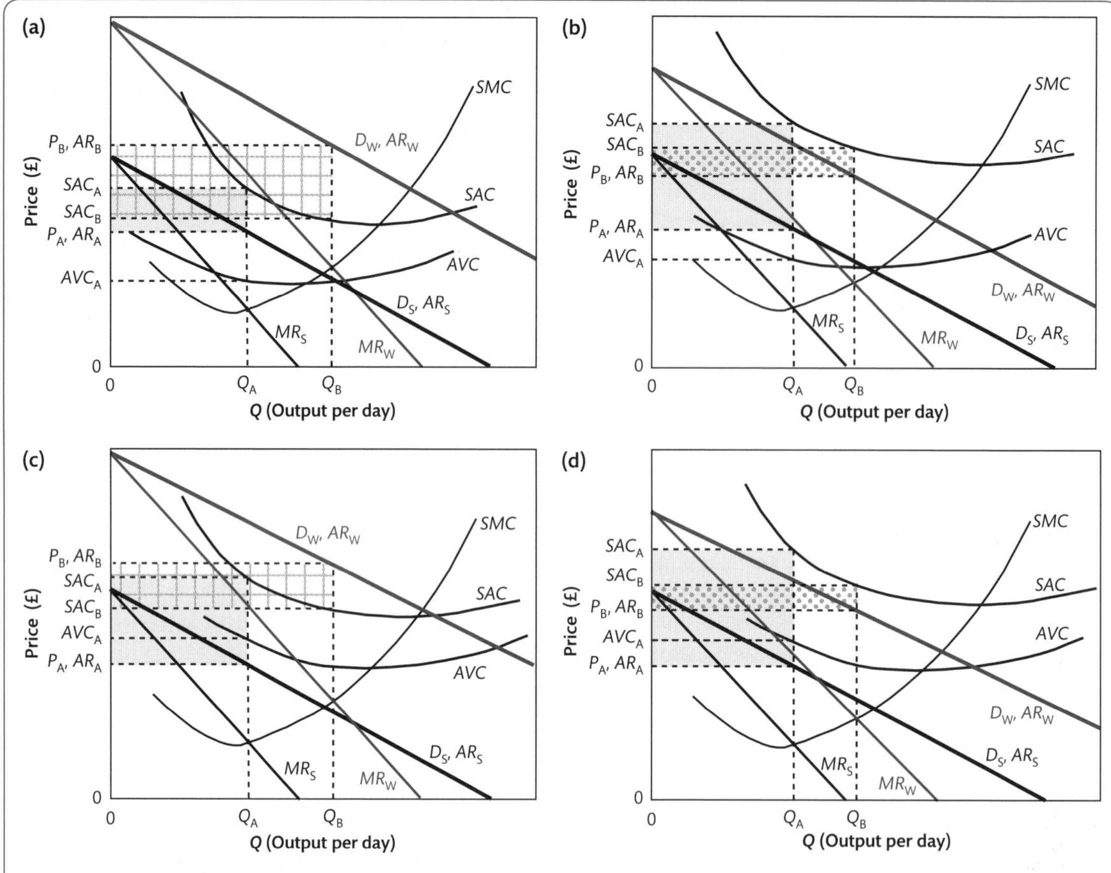

Figure 10.14 **Decisions in summer by ski resort hotels**

For each hotel, the black D_S,AR_S and MR_S curves show the current summer situation. In each case, at Q_A, where MR_S cuts *SMC*, AR_A is below SAC_A, so each hotel would make the loss shaded grey at that output. In cases (c) and (d), though, AVC_A at Q_A exceeds AR_A, so these hotels will actually shut down for the summer, having summer outputs of zero and losses equal to their total fixed costs. The purple D_W, AR_W and MR_W curves show what the hotels expect next winter. In cases (a) and (c), at the output Q_B where MR_W cuts *SMC*, AR_B exceeds SAC_B, so these hotels plan to be open and expect the profits shown by pink grids. But in cases (b) and (d) at output Q_B, SAC_B exceeds AR_B, so these two hotels would expect to make the losses shown by pink dots. With no prospect of profits, they may well be up for sale.

as SAC_B, so they would make the profits shown by the pink grids. So they will plan to set their prices at P_B and have the resulting outputs of Q_B.

- **Hotels (b) and (d), next winter**. They reckon that if they were to produce Q_B, then their average revenue, AR_B, would be less than their average cost, marked as SAC_B, so they would make the losses shown by pink dots. With no prospect of profits this summer or next winter, the owners of these hotels will put them up for sale, unless perhaps they think that in later years they will have lower costs or face higher demand.

So the hotels will make varying decisions about this summer and next winter. They may well display these decisions with the following signs.

- **Hotel (a)**: 'Open now and open next winter'.
- **Hotel (b)**: 'Open now' and also 'For sale'

- **Hotel (c)**: 'Shut now, but open next winter'
- **Hotel (d)**: 'Shut now' and also 'For sale'

Why short-run equilibria may change

As the analysis of monopolistic competitors in the short run is the same as that of monopolists, the same factors can change their short-run equilibrium, as follows.

- **A rise in demand**. As in Figure 10.7, output and the profit rise. The price may fall if *D,AR* is strongly curved, but will otherwise rise.
- **A rise in the price of a fixed input**. As in case (a) in Figure 10.8, output and the price stay the same, but the profit falls and may turn to a loss.
- **A rise in the price of a variable input**. As in case (b) in Figure 10.8, output falls, the price rises, and the profit falls and may turn to a loss. The firm may even shut down.
- **The imposition of a tax on expenditure**. As in Figure 10.11, the price for consumers rises. If *D,AR* is strongly curved, this rise could exceed the amount of the tax.

10.6 Summary

- Monopolistic competitors are price-setters and face downward-sloping demand curves.
- In the short run, they set the output where *MR* intersects *SMC*, unless this would give a loss bigger than total fixed costs, in which case they would shut down and have a loss equal to total fixed costs.
- The price needed for the output where *MR* intersects *SMC* is given by the point on *D,AR* at this output.

10.7 Monopolistic competitors in the long run

The long run in monopolistic competition is different from monopoly because in monopolistic competition there are no barriers to entry. To see the implications of this, consider two possible scenarios for the short run.

- **The typical firm in the industry makes a loss**. In this case, some firms will leave the industry. Their customers will switch to the remaining firms, the *D,AR* and *MR* curves of which therefore shift to the right. In turn, their outputs will rise and their losses will fall. Firms will continue to exit until the typical firm breaks even.

- **The typical firm in the industry makes a profit**. In this case, new firms will enter the industry. They will take some customers away from existing firms, so their *D,AR* and *MR* curves will shift to the left. In turn, their outputs will fall and their profits will fall. New firms will continue to enter until the typical firm only breaks even.

The result is that, in the long run, the typical firm just breaks even, as shown in Figure 10.15. As with all firms, its best output is where *MR* intersects *LMC*, here at Q_L, but here its *D,AR* curve just touches its *LAC* curve; this means that, at Q_L, the firm's price, P_L, and its average revenue just equal its long-run average cost, so it just breaks even.

As *D,AR* slopes downwards, the equilibrium output Q_L where it touches *LAC* is on the downward-sloping part of *LAC*, and so to the left of the lowest point on *LAC*. This means that, in the long run, a monopolistic competitor never produces at its lowest possible long-run average cost and, if it has a minimum efficient scale, it never reaches it.

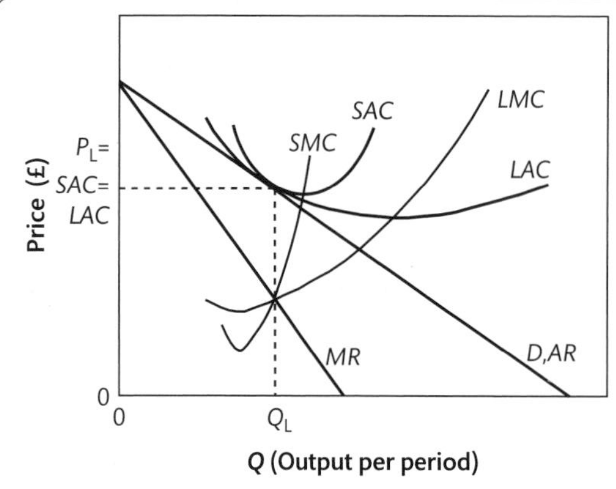

Figure 10.15 **A monopolistic competitor in long-run equilibrium**

In the long run, firms enter or leave a monopolistically competitive industry, altering the demand for existing firms until they can just break even at one output, where their final *D,AR* curve touches *LAC*. The firms adjust the quantity of the inputs for which they can vary quantity only in the long run, until they end up on a *SAC* that touches *D,AR* at the same output. Both *LMC* and *SMC* intersect *MR* at this output, as they always intersect *MR* at the best output.

Once it decides that, in the long run, it will produce output Q_L per period, the firm will make plans to ensure that it will be able to produce Q_L at the lowest possible cost, as shown by the point on *LAC* at this output. So, in the long run, the firm may need to change the quantities it has of those inputs for which quantities are fixed in the short run and can be changed only in the long run.

After it makes these changes, the firm will be able to produce Q_L at this cost, even in the short run. So it will then be on the *SAC* curve shown, which touches *LAC* at Q_L. But it will now have more fixed inputs than is ideal for a lower output, and fewer than is ideal for a higher output, so this *SAC* curve will be above its *LAC* curve at every output except Q_L. The associated short-run marginal cost curve is *SMC*. This must also intersect *MR* at Q_L, because, once the firm has these short-run costs, Q_L will also be its best output in the short run.

Why the long-run equilibrium may change

Two factors can change the long-run equilibrium of firms in a monopolistically competitive industry.

- **A change in input prices**. Suppose input prices rise. Then each firm's cost curves shift up, so each makes a loss. In the long run, some firms will leave the industry, raising the demand for those that remain, and each of these will end up breaking even again at the output where its new *D,AR* curve just touches its new *LAC* curve. This new output may be close to the initial output, but the price will be higher than it was initially,
- **A change in the demand faced by the industry**. Say demand rises. Then each firm's *D,AR* and *MR* curves shift to the right, so it now makes a profit. These profits tempt new firms to enter the industry in the long run. Each original firm will then lose some customers, so its *D,AR* and *MR* curves will shift back to the left. Each firm will end up breaking even at the output where its final *D,AR* curve touches its final *LAC* curve. This *LAC* curve may be the original one, but it will be higher or lower if the industry has external diseconomies of scale or external economies of scale. So while each firm's final output may be close to its initial output, its price may be the same, higher, or lower than it was initially.

10.7 Summary

- In the long run, firms enter or exit a monopolistically competitive industry until the typical firm settles at the one output where it can just break even. At this output, its *D,AR* curve just touches its *LAC* curve.
- Also, the firm will adjust the quantity of those inputs that are fixed in the short run until it ends up on a *SAC* curve that touches *D,AR* at the same output as its *LAC* touches *D,AR*.

In the next chapter we will look at the behaviour of firms in industries with oligopolies.

abc Glossary

Limit pricing: when a firm sets its price below the profit-maximizing level to deter other firms from considering entry to its industry

Price discrimination: charging different prices to different consumers for the same product.

Price-setter: a firm that can set its own price and does not have to accept a going market price.

= Answers to in-text questions

10.1 A firm that has an output where *MR* is negative cannot be maximizing its profit, because its profit would rise if it were to produce less. This is because if *MR* is negative, then a fall in output will increase total revenue (you can see this in the table in Figure 10.1), and it will also decrease total costs as fewer inputs are needed.

10.2 (a) The higher input price will shift *LAC* and *LMC* up. The new *LMC* will intersect *MR* at a lower output, and the firm will sell this output at a higher price. It will also end up with a higher *SAC* and *SMC*. However, its profit will fall, and if the best it could do in the long run were actually to make a loss, it would close down.

(b) If demand increases, then the effects are similar to those in the short run and could be shown on a figure identical to Figure 10.7, but with the short-run cost curves relabelled as long-run ones. So output will rise and the price may well rise, but the price could fall if *D,AR* were sufficiently curved; either way, profit will rise.

? Questions for review

10.1 Draw three diagrams for a monopolist like the one in Figure 10.4, but with the shading for variable and fixed costs omitted. Then **(a)** in one diagram show what happens to the firm's output, price, and profit if demand falls; **(b)** in another show what happens if the price of a fixed input falls; and **(c)** in the third show what happens if the price of a variable input falls.

10.2 Consider a monopolist in long-run equilibrium. **(a)** Could its output be on the upward-sloping part of its *LAC* curve? **(b)** Could it be making a profit?

10.3 A profit-maximizing monopolistic competitor has a short-run output of 10 units per day. Does it follow that it is **(a)** minimizing its total cost, or **(b)** maximizing its total revenue, or **(c)** making a profit?

10.4 Suppose a monopolistic competitor is in long-run equilibrium. **(a)** Could its output be on the upward-sloping part of its *LAC* curve? **(b)** Could it be making a profit?

? Questions for discussion

10.1 Think of three monopolists in three different industries,. Note that some of your firms may be local monopolies, such as the only hairdressing salon in a remote town. What are closest substitutes, if any, for their products? What are the main barriers for new firms hoping to enter their industries?

10.2 Think of three monopolistic competitors in three different industries. How do their products vary? Do you think they make profits that will attract new firms into their industries? How easily could firms enter them?

Common student errors

Many students forget that a monopolist's *AR* and *MR* curves are related. Remember from Figure 10.1 that they both derive from the same *TR* numbers, so they must be related. One result of this error is that *MR* is often shown too close or too far from *AR*. Another result is that, when asked what happens when there is a change in demand, students often shift *D,AR*, but forget to shift *MR* and so conclude wrongly that there is no change in output.

Also, some students struggle to see that output is set where *MR* intersects *SMC*, yet the price is not found at this intersection, but instead from the point on *D* above it.

11

Oligopoly

Remember from Chapter 7 that an oligopoly is an industry with few firms, and that they are profit-maximizers.

Suppose you run a firm, and there are only a few other firms with competing products. How would you decide your price? How would you react if any of your competitors were to change their prices? Would you try to cooperate with your competitors to restrict sales, and so maintain high prices? How would you decide how to market your product, or develop it, or change the way in which it was produced?

This chapter shows you how to answer questions like these, by understanding:

* what it means for firms to interact with each other;
* the various ways in which oligopolists in different industries may set their prices;
* how cooperation between oligopolists may work, and why cooperation may easily collapse;
* how oligopolists may decide on their marketing, new products, and technology.

11.1 Key features of oligopolists

Two special features of oligopoly

An oligopoly is an industry with only a few firms. The fact that there are only a few firms implies that there are some barriers to entry.

By 'few', we do not mean that the number of firms is below a particular level, say 12. Instead, we mean that the number of firms is small enough for two issues to arise that require special economic models. These issues are as follows.

- **The possibility of cooperation**. When an industry has a few firms, these firms may be able to cooperate and act together in ways that benefit them all. Indeed, the 18th-century Scottish economist Adam Smith claimed in his 1776 book *The Wealth of Nations* that 'people of the same trade seldom meet together, even for merriment and diversion, but the conversation ends in a conspiracy against the public, or in some contrivance to raise prices'.
- **Interdependence**. In an oligopoly, each firm affects the others. For example, suppose you run a firm in such an industry and you reduce your price. Then your competitors may face a significant fall in the demand for their products, so they may well react, and their reaction may well affect you. So when you set your price, you must consider their possible reactions. A situation in which people consider other people's reactions is called **interdependence.**

Interdependence arises in many settings. For example, tennis players must consider how their opponents will react to every shot or move. But unlike them, oligopolists often have the additional complexity of playing against several competitors at the same time. However, to present the main ideas of oligopoly simply, this chapter will usually focus on a particular type of oligopoly called a **duopoly**, in which there are only two firms.

The importance of oligopoly

Oligopolies are very common. Many products that you buy are sold by oligopolists who closely watch their competitors. You may shop at one of the big supermarkets: they watch each other. You may buy cereal, soap, frozen chips, or a daily newspaper: their makers watch each other. You may recently have bought a new laptop or mobile, and you will certainly have used some gas or electricity: all their makers watch each other.

Many oligopolists sell differentiated products, such as cars or breakfast cereals. Others sell homogeneous products, such as gas or petrol.

Structure of this chapter

Section 11.2 considers how oligopolists might set their prices and outputs if they do not cooperate with each other. Section 11.3 introduces a theory called game theory; this helps us to see, in section 11.4, how oligopolists might set their outputs and prices if they do cooperate. Game theory also helps in section 11.5, which considers how oligopolists decide on other matters, such as marketing, product development, and technology.

11.1 Summary

- An oligopoly is an industry with a few firms the behaviour of which is interdependent, so that choices by one firm affect the choices made by the others.
- There are some barriers to entry in oligopoly.
- Oligopolists may often find it beneficial to cooperate, rather than to compete independently.
- Oligopoly is a very common form of industry structure.

11.2 Non-cooperative models of oligopoly

This section presents four models that consider how oligopolists might behave if they do not cooperate with one another, but instead act independently. The reason we have so many models is that these firms might behave in various ways, so different models apply in different cases.

The example used

To contrast the models, we will use an example. Suppose it is your first term at college and you decide to produce a student magazine with news and pictures about the college. You plan to produce one issue each term. Another first-year student, Zoe, intends to produce a very similar magazine. We will call your firm Y and hers Z.

We will assume that you and Zoe are profit-maximizers, so your decisions will depend in part on your costs. For simplicity, we will assume that, each term, you must each spend £1,000 on fixed inputs to set your magazine up, and then you have to pay £2 on variable inputs for every copy you produce. This means the cost of an extra copy is always £2, so your short-run marginal cost, *SMC*, is always £2. Table 11.1 shows for a range of output levels your magazine's total fixed cost, *TFC*, total variable cost, *TVC*, short-run total cost, *STC*, and short-run average cost, *SAC*. It also shows *SMC*.

Your decisions will also depend on the demand for magazines. Some oligopoly models assume that the firms have homogeneous products, while other models assume they have differentiated products. To keep using the same example, we will sometimes assume that your magazine is effectively the same as Zoe's, and we will sometimes assume that it is differentiated. But, given the similarity of the two magazines, we will always suppose that they end up with the same price, and that no student will buy both. We will also suppose that the market demand curve for these magazines is as shown by D_{MKT} in Figure 11.1. For example, at a price of £8, you and Zoe would sell 1,200 copies between you each term.

Two alternative market structures

Before we see what you and Zoe might do, it is useful to see what would happen in your industry if, instead of having an oligopoly, it had two other market structures, as follows.

- **Perfect competition**. Here, our assumption that *SMC* is always £2 means that each firm in the industry would have a horizontal *SMC* curve at £2. In turn, each firm's supply curve, and the market supply curve, would be horizontal at £2, as shown in Figure 11.1 by S_{COM}. The equilibrium is where

Table 11.1 **Costs for each duopolist, *Y* and *Z***

Output, *Q* Copies per term	***TFC*** £ per term	***TVC*** £ per term	***STC*** £ per term	***SAC*** £ per copy	***SMC*** £ per copy
0	1,000	0	1,000	–	2.00
200	1,000	400	1,400	7.00	2.00
400	1,000	800	1,800	4.50	2.00
600	1,000	1,200	2,200	3.67	2.00
800	1,000	1,600	2,600	3.25	2.00
1,000	1,000	2,000	3,000	3.00	2.00
1,200	1,000	2,400	3,400	2.83	2.00
1,400	1,000	2,800	3,800	2.71	2.00

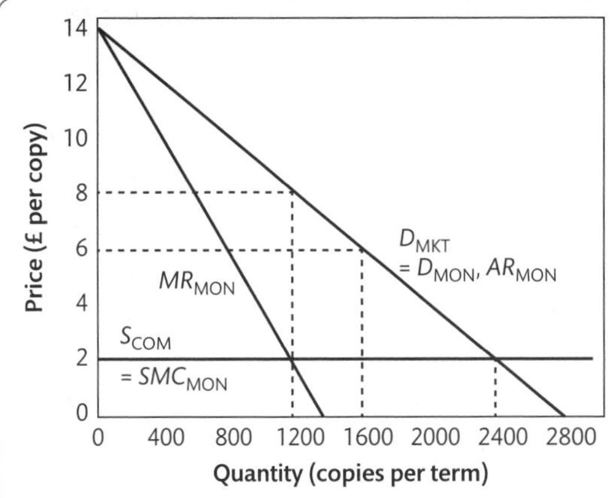

Figure 11.1 **Outcomes with monopoly and perfect competition**

D_{MKT} is the market demand curve. If there were perfect competition, and each firm had a constant *SMC* of £2, the market supply curve would be S_{COM}, so 2,400 copies a term would be sold at £2. If there were a monopolist, its demand curve and average revenue curve would be D_{MON},AR_{MON} and MR_{MON} would be its marginal revenue curve. If the monopolist had a constant marginal cost of £2, as shown by SMC_{MON}, it would set its output at 1,200 a term where this intersects MR_{MON}, and sell them at £8.

S_{COM} intersects *D*, with 2,400 copies of the magazine produced each term at a price of £2.

- **Monopoly**. Here, our assumption that *SMC* is always £2 means the monopolist would have a horizontal *SMC* curve at £2, as shown by SMC_{MON} in Figure 11.1. This firm would face the whole demand curve, now labelled D_{MON}, and this would also be its average revenue curve, AR_{MON}; its marginal revenue curve is MR_{MON}. The firm would produce 1,200 copies a term, where SMC_{MON} intersects MR_{MON}. The point at this output on D_{MON} shows that its price would be £8.

The assumptions of the Cournot model

Our first oligopoly model was put forward in 1838 by the French economist Augustin Cournot. He studied two firms producing a homogeneous product—in his case, mineral water. His model can be adapted for differentiated products, but this makes it more complex, so here we will assume that your magazine and Zoe's are so similar that students are indifferent about which they buy.

The **Cournot model** says that, in each period, each firm sets its output simultaneously, not knowing how much the other firm will produce, but each firm makes an assumption about how much the other will produce, and sets its own output at the level that would give it the highest profit *if* the other were to produce that output. So you will think as follows: 'Zoe must set some output, Q_Z. I don't know what this will be, but I will make an assumption about it. Then I will set my output, Q_Y, at the level that would maximize my profit if Zoe were to set that assumed Q_Z.' You will also set whatever price is needed to sell your chosen Q_Y.

In practice, each Q_Z that you might assume leads to a different Q_Y being best for you. To see this, look at the top part of Figure 11.2, where D_0,AR_0 is the market demand curve, and consider two values for Q_Z that you might assume.

- $\mathbf{Q_Z = 0}$. In this case, you would face the entire demand, as shown by D_0,AR_0, and the associated MR_0. To maximize your profit, you would set $Q_Y = 1{,}200$, where MR_0 intersects your *SMC* curve.
- $\mathbf{Q_Z = 1{,}600}$. In this case, the quantity of your magazine that was demanded at each possible price would be 1,600 lower, so you would face the demand curve D_1,AR_1 and the associated MR_1. To maximize your profit, you would set $Q_Y = 400$ where MR_1 intersects your *SMC* curve.

In a similar way, we can work out your best Q_Y for other possible values of Q_Z and then plot a **reaction curve**, which is a curve that shows one firm's reactions to another firm's behaviour. In the bottom part of Figure 11.2, your output is measured on the horizontal axis and Zoe's on the vertical axis, and CRC_Y is your Cournot reaction curve. This shows your best Q_Y for

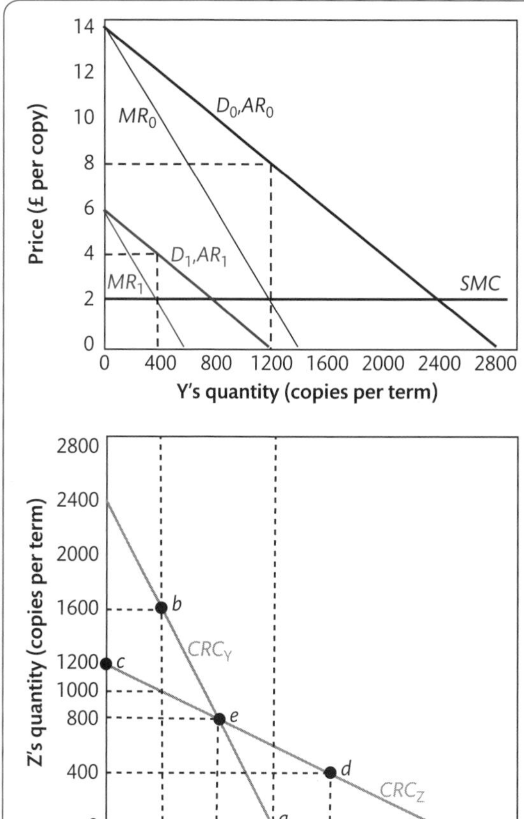

Figure 11.2 **Reaction curves under Cournot**

Y's output is measured on the horizontal axis and Z's on the vertical axis. Y's Cournot reaction curve, CRC_Y, shows the best output for Y at each possible output for Z. Z's Cournot reaction curve, CRC_Z, shows the best output for Z at each possible output for Y. The point ***e*** where the curves intersect is the Cournot equilibrium.

any possible Q_Z. For example, point ***a*** shows that if $Q_Z = 0$, then you will set $Q_Y = 1{,}200$, and point ***b*** shows that if $Q_Z = 1{,}600$, then you will set $Q_Y = 400$.

On the Cournot model, Zoe will behave in the same way, and work out her best Q_Z for each Q_Y you might set. Owing to the similarity of the two firms in our example, she will set $Q_Z = 1{,}200$ if she assumes that $Q_Y = 0$, and $Q_Z = 400$ if she assumes $Q_Y = 1{,}600$. These reactions give us points ***c*** and ***d*** on her Cournot reaction curve, CRC_Z, which is also plotted on Figure 11.2.

Equilibrium in the Cournot model

Equilibrium in the Cournot model arises when the firms end up producing the outputs shown at point ***e*** at which the two reaction curves intersect. At this point, each firm will think: 'The other firm has now set its output at 800 a term, so my best output is 800, and that is what my output is. So I have no incentive to change my output in future.'

At any other point, at least firm a would be off its reaction curve and would want to change its output. For example, if the firms actually produce the combination of outputs at point ***b***, Zoe will think: 'Q_Y is now 400 a term, so CRC_Z shows that my best output is 1,000, but I am producing 1,600, so I should produce less in future.'

Once the market reaches the Cournot equilibrium, the total output is 1,600 a term. We can see from D_{MKT} in Figure 11.1 that the price needed to sell this is £6. This is above the perfect competition price of £2 and below the monopoly price of £8.

The Stackelberg model

The Cournot model assumes that each firm sets its output simultaneously, not knowing what the other will do. The German economist Heinrich von Stackelberg put forward a modified model in 1934. The **Stackelberg model** supposes that one firm is a leader, and sets its output first, and then the other firm reacts and sets its output. The model assumes that the leader expects the follower to react on the basis of its Cournot reaction curve.

Question 11.1 Which do you think it would be best for your firm to be, the leader or the follower?

Suppose you are the leader. The first column of Table 11.2 shows various outputs that you might set. For each of these, it also shows the output with which Zoe will react. It then works out the total output, the price, and each firm's profit. (If you want to see how

Table 11.2 **The Stackelberg solution if Y chooses its output before Z chooses its output**

QY Copies per term	QZ Copies per term	Total Q Copies per term	Price £ per copy	Y's profit £ per term	Z's profit £ per term
2,800	0	2,800	0	–1,000	–1,000
2,400	0	2,400	2	–1,000	–1,000
2,000	200	2,200	3	1,000	–800
1,600	400	2,000	4	2,200	–200
1,200	600	1,800	5	2,600	800
800	800	1,600	6	2,200	2,200
400	1,000	1,400	7	1,000	4,000
0	1,200	1,200	8	–1,000	6,200

Example of calculating the figures in one row. Suppose Q_Y is set at 1,200, as in the fifth row. CRC_Z in Figure 11.2 shows Q_Z will be set at 600. So the industry output, $Q_Y + Q_Z$, will be 1,800. We can deduce from D_{MKT} in Figure 11.1 that, to sell this output, the price must be £5. So Y sells 1,200 copies at £5, to get a total revenue of £6,000, and Y's short-run total cost is £3,400 (from Table 11.1). So Y's profit is £2,600. Z sells 600 copies at £5, to get a total revenue of £3,000; Z's short-run total cost is £2,200 (from Table 11.1). So Z's profit is £800.

the calculations are done, the table shows the arithmetic for the case in which you set Q_Y at 1,200 and get a profit of £2,600, while Zoe gets a profit of £800.)

You care only about your profit. Looking down the 'Y's profit' column, you see that your best strategy is to set $Q_Y = 1{,}200$, leaving Zoe to react with $Q_Z = 600$. So a total of 1,800 copies will be sold at a price of £5, and your profit will be £2,600, while Zoe's will be just £800. This is the Stackelberg equilibrium if you move first. If Zoe had moved first, the total output and price would be the same, but your positions would be reversed. The £5 price is lower than the £6 with Cournot, but still above the perfect competition price of £2.

Disequilibrium in the Stackelberg model

Moving first here was an advantage, because you could set a large output and force Zoe to react with a low one. But Zoe will now know that being leader is best. Next term, she may quickly set a large Q_Z, hoping to force you to react with a low Q_Y, yet you might quickly set a large Q_Y, hoping to force her to set a low Q_Z. So instead of reaching a Stackelberg equilibrium, your firms may be at constant war with a huge joint output that leads to a low price and, possibly, losses for you both. Stackelberg thought this was the most likely outcome. It is called a 'Stackelberg disequilibrium'.

The assumptions of the Bertrand model

The French economist Joseph Bertrand put forward the **Bertrand model** in 1883. This model says that, in each period, each firm makes an assumption about the price that the other will set, and sets its own price at the level that would give it the highest profit if the other one were to set that price. So you will think as follows: 'Zoe must set some price, P_Z. I don't know what this will be, but I will make an assumption about it. Then I will set my price, P_Y, at the level that would maximize my profit if Zoe were to set that assumed P_Z.' You will also set your output at the level that you will be able to sell at your chosen price.

We will use this model twice, first assuming that you and Zoe have homogeneous products, and then assuming that you have differentiated products. These different assumptions give very different results.

Bertrand with homogeneous products

With homogeneous products, the result is easy to determine. If one firm sets a higher price than the other, then it will sell nothing. So competition will drive the price down. It will actually drive it down to the perfect competition price of £2, where the total sales will be 2,000 copies.

To see why the price will fall to £2, suppose you both set a higher price, say £6 for you and £5 for Zoe. Then Zoe will capture the whole market. But then next term you would set maybe £4, and then Zoe would respond with £3, and so on until the price fell to £2. Neither of you would ever set a price below £2, because then you would not cover your variable costs, so it would be better for you to shut down and produce nothing.

Bertrand with differentiated products

Next, suppose there is differentiation between your magazine and Zoe's. In this case, if you set a higher price than Zoe, you will still sell some magazines, because some students will prefer your product. However, your sales, Q_Y, would rise if Zoe were to increase her price, P_Z, and of course they would fall if you were to increase your own price, P_Y. Likewise, her sales, Q_Z, would rise if you were to increase your price, but they would fall if she were to increase her own price. Let's suppose that the quantities you each sell depend on the prices you each set as follows:

$$Q_Y = 1400 + 100.P_Z - 200.P_Y$$
$$Q_Z = 1400 + 100.P_Y - 200.P_Z$$

Suppose, for a moment, that Zoe sets a price of £10. Table 11.3 works out what profit you would make at a number of possible prices with which you might react. For example, if you were to react with a price of £11, then your profit would be £800. (If you want to see how the calculations are done, the table includes the arithmetic for the case in which you react by setting P_Y at £7.)

The last column in Table 11.3 shows that the highest profit you could make if Zoe were to set a price of £10 is £4,000, which you would get if you were to react with a price of £7. We could add in a whole set of extra tables to work out what your best price would be at each other price that Zoe could set.

Table 11.3 **Finding the best price for one firm, Y, when the other firm, Z, has set its price at £10**

Y's price £ per copy	Y's output Copies per term	Y's *TR* £ per term	Y's *STC* £ per term	Y's profit £ per term
12	0	0	1,000	–1,000
11	200	2,200	1,400	800
10	400	4,000	1,800	2,200
9	600	5,400	2,200	3,200
8	800	6,400	2,600	3,800
7	**1,000**	**7,000**	**3,000**	**4,000**
6	1,200	7,200	3,400	3,800
5	1,400	7,000	3,800	3,200

Example of calculating the figures in one row. The whole table supposes that P_Z is set at £10. Suppose that P_Y is set at £7, as in the sixth row. In this example $Q_Y = 1{,}400 + 100.P_Z - 200.P_Y$. So $Q_Y = 1400 + 100.10 - 200.7 = 1{,}000$. By selling 1,000 copies at £7, Y's total revenue would be £7,000. And with a short-run total cost of £3,000 (from Table 11.1), its profit would be £4,000.

We could then use the results to plot your Bertrand reaction curve, BRC_Y, which is shown in Figure 11.3. Here, the horizontal axis shows your price and the vertical axis shows hers. For example, point ***a*** on BRC_Y shows that if Zoe were to set a price of £10, then you would be best to set a price of £7, as we have just found. We could find Zoe's Bertrand reaction curve, BRC_Z, in the same way.

The two reaction curves intersect where you both set a price of £6, and this is the Bertrand equilibrium with product differentiation. This means that if you each set a price of £6, then, on this model, neither of you has an incentive to change in future. For example, you will think: 'Zoe's price is actually £6. So the best price for me is £6, and that is what my price is.'

At any other combination of prices, at least one of you would be off your reaction curve, and so not have the best price you could have, given what the other

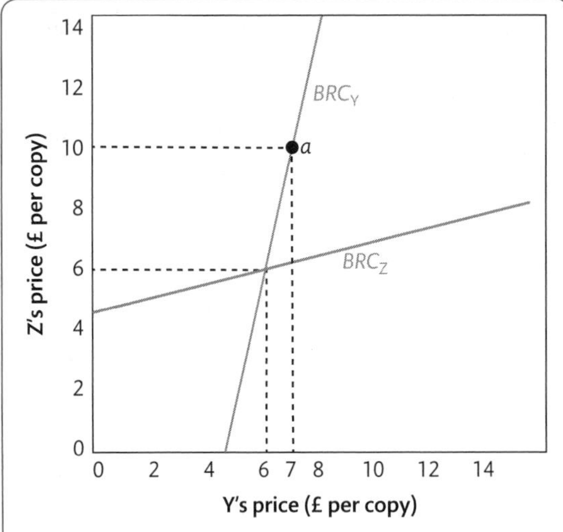

Figure 11.3 **Bertrand reaction curves**

BRC_Y shows the profit-maximizing price for firm Y at any given price set by firm Z. BRC_Z shows the profit-maximizing price for firm Z at any given price set by firm Y. The point where the curves intersect is the Bertrand equilibrium.

one is doing. So at least one of you will want to change your price next period.

So the Bertrand equilibrium price is £6, which, as Figure 11.1 shows, leads to a market output of 1,600 and so 800 for each firm. The Cournot equilibrium price was also £6, but the similarity is not significant, because with Cournot we assumed that you and Zoe had homogeneous products and here we assume you have differentiated products. But, like the Cournot price, the Bertrand price will be between the monopoly price of £8 and the perfect competition one of £2.

In this example, the firms end up with equal prices. But if the products had differed in quality, then the final prices would have been different.

The kinked-demand curve model

The Cournot and Bertrand models both use reaction curves. To derive these curves, in Figure 11.2 and Table 11.3, we referred to the firms' costs. So if the price of an input changes and changes the firms' costs, then their reaction curves will shift. So both models predict that the firms will then change their prices and outputs.

In practice, though, oligopoly outputs and prices do not always change when the prices of inputs alter. To try to explain this, the kinked-demand curve model was devised in 1939 by Paul Sweezy in the US and, independently, by Robert Hall and Charles Hitch in the UK. This model usually envisages duopolists with differentiated products.

Figure 11.4 shows the model from the viewpoint of one firm that currently has the price P_0 and output Q_0. The model argues that if this firm raises its price, then the other will keep its price the same, so this firm will lose many customers to the other and move up along the highly elastic demand curve, D_A, shown in part (a). This will also be its average revenue curve, AR_A, which has the associated marginal revenue curve, MR_A.

The model also argues that if this firm reduces its price, then the other firm will also reduce its price. So this firm will not pick up any customers from the other, although its own customers will buy a little more; so it will move down the much less elastic demand curve, D_B, shown in part (b). This will also be its average revenue curve, AR_B, which has the associated marginal revenue curve, MR_B.

So the curves in part (a) apply at prices above P_0, and so at outputs below Q_0, while those in part (b) apply at prices below P_0, and so at outputs above Q_0. The parts of these curves that do not apply are dashed. Part (c) shows the firm's full demand curve, D,AR, and its full marginal revenue curve, MR. These follow D_A,AR_A and MR_A at outputs below Q_0, and follow D_B,AR_B and MR_B at outputs above Q_0. D,AR has a kink at P_0. MR has two separate parts, one each side of Q_0, but these parts are joined by dashes to show that they both apply at the same time.

Part (c) also gives the firm's initial short-run average marginal cost curve, SMC_0. As we have already said, the firm sets the output Q_0, which it sells at price P_0. It chooses Q_0 because, at lower outputs, MR would be above SMC, so the firm could raise its profit by selling more, and at higher outputs, MR would be below SMC, so it could raise its profit by selling less.

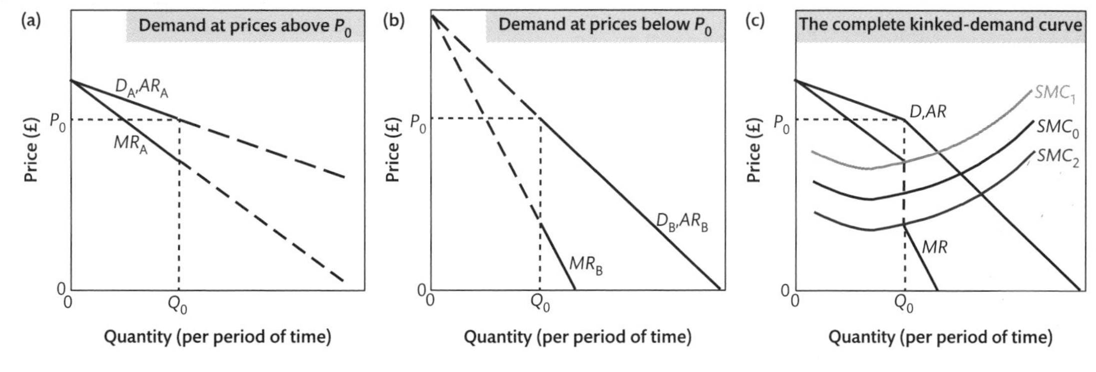

Figure 11.4 **The kinked-demand curve model**

A duopolist currently sells Q_0 per period at a price of P_0. If it were to raise its price, its sales would fall sharply because its competitor would keep its price the same. So it faces the highly elastic D_A,AR_A curve shown in part (a) along with MR_A. If it were to cut its price, its sales would rise modestly because its competitor would also cut its price. So it faces the less elastic D_B,AR_B shown in part (b) along with MR_B. Altogether, it faces the kinked-demand *D,AR* curve shown in part (c), along with the two-part *MR*; these curves copy those in parts (a) and (b), but omit the dashed sections, which don't apply. The firm starts with the short-run marginal cost curve SMC_0 and sets output Q_0, because *MR* is above *SMC* at lower outputs and *MR* is below *SMC* at higher outputs. If the prices of variable inputs change, the firm will not change its output or price unless its short-run marginal cost curve shifts above SMC_1 or below SMC_2 shown in part (c).

Now suppose that the price of a variable input changes. Then the marginal cost curve will shift. But unless it shifts above the curve labelled SMC_1 or below the one labelled SMC_2, the firm will keep its output at Q_0, because *MR* will still be above *SMC* at lower outputs and will still be below it at higher outputs. To sell its unchanged output, it needs to keep the same price, P_0. However, although this model suggests why prices might be stable, it has a major limitation: it does not explain why the current P_0 is what it is.

Comparison of the models

Table 11.4 lists the results of the various models. On the basis of our example, this table shows that if oligopolists act independently, then they will usually set a price between those that would arise with perfect competition and monopoly, and so have an output between those that would arise with monopoly and perfect competition. The only exception is that, in the Bertrand model, the result will be the same as in perfect competition if the firms produce homogeneous products.

The three named oligopoly models may apply to different types of oligopoly, as follows.

- **The Cournot model** may apply in oligopolies in which firms compete chiefly on output levels, and the firms have roughly equal sizes.
- **The Stackelberg model** may apply in oligopolies in which firms compete chiefly on output levels, and one firm is a leader on account of its size.
- **The Bertrand model** may apply in oligopolies in which firms compete chiefly on price and have roughly equal sizes. This may be rare, because Bertrand assumes that firms first set their prices and then set whatever output is demanded at that price; yet in practice, many manufacturing firms

Table 11.4 **A comparison of the different models**

Model	Products	Price £ per copy	Quantity Copies per term
Monopoly	Homogeneous	8	1,200
Cournot	Homogeneous	6	1,600
Bertrand	Differentiated	6	1,600
Stackelberg	Homogeneous	5	1,800
Bertrand	Homogeneous	2	2,400
Perfect competition	Homogeneous	2	2,400

have plants with a limited production capacity in the short run, so there is a limit to how far they can behave as he suggested.

11.1 Everyday economics

Gas prices: volatile or sticky?

The price of natural gas on world markets changes daily. Yet the companies that supply gas to homes and businesses change their prices infrequently. Of course, they cannot change their own prices daily because they would then need to monitor usage by individual consumers on a daily basis. But often they maintain stable prices for long periods. In 2008, the BBC's economics editor Evan Davis suggested that this may be because these firms face kinked-demand curves, which lead to sticky prices. If this model does apply to gas firms, and rising world gas prices shift their short-run marginal cost curves, then, as in Figure 11.4, they may not change their own prices at all until their short-run marginal cost curves move a considerable distance.

'Setting prices', *BBC News*, 8 January 2008

11.2 **Summary**

- The Cournot model assumes that oligopolists act independently and each determines its output in response to the output it expects from the other.
- The Stackelberg model is similar to the Cournot model, but assumes one firm will set its output first.
- The Bertrand model assumes that oligopolists act independently and each determines its price in response to the price it expects from the other.
- All three models predict that the equilibrium price will generally be in between those that would arise if the industry were in perfect competition or in monopoly.
- The kinked-demand curve model explains why a firm's output price may not change when its input prices change, but it does not explain why its price is what it is.

11.3 Game theory

Game theory studies how people behave in situations in which their choices have to allow for the choices that other people make. The first major text on game theory was written in 1944 by John von Neumann and Oskar Morgenstern in the US. The best-known person to work on it since is the US economist John Nash, whose schizophrenia inspired the 2002 film about him, *A Beautiful Mind*.

The term 'game theory' may make the subject matter seem trivial, but it is not. It was developed by economists to help us to understand important issues, such as the behaviour of oligopolists. It has since proved very useful in many other fields, including biology, business, diplomacy, and politics.

Game theory uses three important terms.

- **Players:** these are the people whose behaviour is being studied. In this chapter, we consider only games with two players; game theory can handle more, but is then more complex.
- **Strategies:** each player has a choice of actions called strategies. In this chapter, we consider only games in which each player chooses between two strategies: game theory can handle more, but is then more complex.
- **Pay-offs:** these are the effects on the players of the different combinations of strategies they might adopt. In oligopoly theory, the pay-offs refer to

profits. But in this introductory section we will consider other types of pay-off.

A game with one Nash equilibrium

To introduce game theory, we will first apply it to the choices made one evening by two first-year students, Jo and Max. One evening, shortly after they meet, these students independently consider two strategies: going to a cinema or going to a club. After allowing for admission costs, Jo would get 20 utils from the cinema and 10 from the club, while Max would get 10 from the cinema and 20 from the club. However, each would also get 5 extra utils if the other were at the same place, to help them to get to know each other.

There are four combinations of strategies. The pay-offs from these combinations are shown in the four boxes in Figure 11.5, in which each box is divided into two triangles. For example, the top left-hand box shows that if they both go to the cinema, then Jo gets 20 utils from the cinema plus 5 from being with Max, that is 25, and Max gets 10 from the cinema plus 5 from being with Jo, that is 15.

We assume that the players make their independent decisions at the same time. Jo thinks as follows.

- **If Max goes to the cinema:** 'I would get 25 utils from going there with him, or 10 from going to the club alone, so I should to go to the cinema.'
- **If Max goes to the club:** 'I would get 15 utils from going there with him, or 20 from going to the cinema, so again I should go to the cinema.'

When a player finds that one strategy is best, no matter what the other one chooses, this strategy is called the player's **dominant strategy**, and the player will naturally play it. Going to the cinema is Jo's dominant strategy. It is easy to work out that Max's dominant strategy is going to the club. If Jo goes to the cinema, then he gets more utils from going to the club; if she goes to the club, he again gets more utils from going to the club.

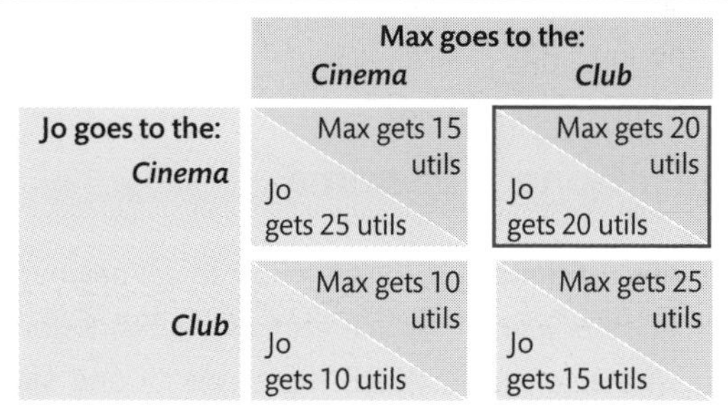

	Max goes to the: *Cinema*	*Club*
Jo goes to the: *Cinema*	Max gets 15 utils / Jo gets 25 utils	Max gets 20 utils / Jo gets 20 utils
Club	Max gets 10 utils / Jo gets 10 utils	Max gets 25 utils / Jo gets 15 utils

Figure 11.5 **A game with two dominant strategies and one Nash equilibrium**

Jo gets 20 utils from going to the cinema or 10 from the club; Max gets 10 from the cinema or 20 from the club. If they are together, each gets 5 more utils. Jo will go to the cinema and Max to the club: this is a Nash equilibrium.

So Jo chooses the cinema and Max the club, and they get the pay-offs in the top right-hand box. This box has been given a dark border, but this is *not* because it shows where the game ends. It is instead because it shows a **Nash equilibrium**: this is a situation in which each player adopts the best strategy for them, given the strategy chosen by the other. Here, Max chooses the club, and Jo has adopted what is then her best strategy, which is to go to the cinema. Likewise Jo chooses the cinema, and Max has adopted what is then his best strategy, which is to go to the club.

No other combination of strategies gives a Nash equilibrium. For example, suppose they both go to the cinema. Then Jo would be doing the best she can, given that Max goes to the cinema—but Max would not be doing the best he can, given that Jo goes to the cinema.

Other possible outcomes

In that game, both players had a dominant strategy, so we could be predict the outcome. This is not always the case. Later, we will see two other possibilities.

- **Only one player has a dominant strategy.** Here, we can be sure only of what that player will do.
- **Neither player has a dominant strategy.** Here, we cannot be sure of what either player will do.

We will also see that some games have no Nash equilibria, while others can have two.

The prisoners' dilemma

We will conclude this introduction to game theory with another game in which each player has a dominant strategy, and in which there is only one Nash equilibrium. To see the special feature of this game, notice first from Figure 11.5 that if Jo and Max both play their dominant strategies, they both get 20 utils and are both better off than if they had both played their other strategies, when they would both have got 10 utils. In our new game, both players actually get a worse pay-off by playing their dominant strategies than they would have got if they had both played the other strategy! We will show this with the best-known example, which is called 'the prisoners' dilemma': this was first presented in the US in the 1950s.

Two players, Abi and Ben, are arrested on suspicion of committing a serious crime, for which the standard sentence is 10 years in prison. However, this is reduced to 8 years for a prisoner who confesses. The prosecutor does not have enough evidence to convict either of them of this crime, but he does have enough to convict each of them for a lesser crime for which the penalty is 2 years in prison. However, he is happy to forget about this lesser crime if he can get at least one of them convicted for the serious crime. So, he visits them each in turn in their separate cells and says:

- '**If both you and the other prisoner confess to the serious crime,** then I will convict you both for it, so you will both get the reduced 8-year sentence.'
- '**If you confess that both of you committed the serious crime, but the other prisoner does not confess,** then I will use your evidence to convict the other who will get 10 years. But I will make no charges against you, to thank you for helping me, so you will go free.'
- '**If the other prisoner confesses that both of you committed the serious crime and you do not confess,** then I will use the other's confession to convict you and you will get 10 years. But I will drop all charges against the other by way of thanks, so the other will go free.'
- '**If neither you nor the other prisoner confess to the serious crime,** then I will convict you both for the lesser crime, so you will both get 2 years.'
- '**I will not tell you what the other prisoner says.**

Figure 11.6 shows the pay-offs. Abi thinks as follows.

- **If Ben confesses:** 'I will get 8 years if I confess and 10 years if I don't. So I should confess.'
- **If Ben does not confess:** 'I will go free if I confess and get 2 years if I don't. So I should confess.'

So confessing is the dominant strategy for Abi, and also for Ben who is in the same situation. So they both confess and get 8 years. Yet if each had played the non-dominant strategy of not confessing, then both would have ended up with better pay-offs of 2 years. In game theory, the term **prisoners' dilemma** is used for any game in which both players get worse pay-offs by playing their dominant strategies than they would have got by playing their non-dominant strategies.

Although the actual outcome here is not the best one for the players, it is a Nash equilibrium, so its box

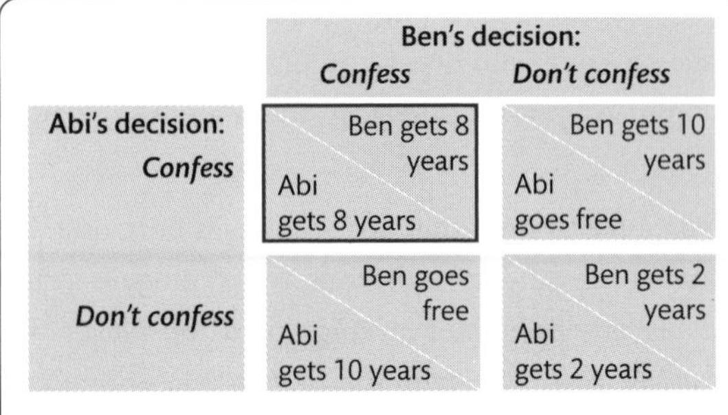

	Ben's decision: *Confess*	Ben's decision: *Don't confess*
Abi's decision: *Confess*	Ben gets 8 years / Abi gets 8 years	Ben gets 10 years / Abi goes free
Don't confess	Ben goes free / Abi gets 10 years	Ben gets 2 years / Abi gets 2 years

Figure 11.6 **The prisoner's dilemma**

Abi and Ben are offered the prison sentences shown for various combinations of confessing or not. The only Nash equilibrium is both confessing. The dilemma is that they will both be better off if neither confesses.

has a dark border: if Ben confesses, the best Abi can do is confess; if Abi confesses, the best Ben can do is confess.

Question 11.2 Suppose one prisoner is allowed to choose *after* being told the first prisoner's choice. Will the outcome be different?

11.3 Summary

- In any game, a number of players choose between different strategies and get varying pay-offs according to the combination of strategies that they play.
- In a Nash equilibrium, each player is doing the best he or she can, given what the other is doing.
- In some games, each player has a dominant strategy and will play it. These games have only one Nash equilibrium. But sometimes—in a prisoners' dilemma situation—both players would have secured higher pay-offs if both had instead played the non-dominant strategy.
- In some games, only one player has a dominant strategy, and in some games neither player has a dominant strategy.

11.4 Cooperative models of oligopoly

We now return to you and Zoe and your student magazines. We will suppose you are at the equilibrium predicted by the Cournot or Bertrand models, each with an output of 800 and a price of £6. If you both have a fair idea of the market demand curve, then you will know that a monopolist would have an output of 1,200 and a price of £8, as shown in Figure 11.1. This is the price and output combination that squeezes the maximum possible profit from the market. So if you and Zoe could somehow cooperate and restrict your sales to 600 copies each, then you could sell them at a price of £8 and share the maximum possible profit.

Methods of cooperation

There are three ways in which oligopolists can cooperate to reduce their sales and raise their price. These are as follows.

- With a **cartel**: here, firms make a *formal* agreement, perhaps in writing, about prices and outputs, or other matters such as marketing, technology, or product development. Cartels are illegal in many countries, including the EU and the US, but it is hard to outlaw cartels between producers in different countries or cartels agreed on behalf of firms by governments. The best known cartel is OPEC, the Organization of the Petroleum Exporting Countries, which is agreed by governments.
- With **collusion**: here, firms make an *informal* agreement, perhaps using only verbal communication, about prices and outputs or other matters. Collusion is also usually illegal.
- With **cooperation without agreement**: here, firms restrict output and raise prices without any agreement, simply because they know that doing so is in their interests.

Arrangements for cartels, or collusion, or cooperation without agreement, are easier to make in the following circumstances.

- **If there are few firms**: then it will be easier for each party to the agreement to know what all the parties are doing.

- **If entry to the industry is hard:** then high profits will not be threatened by new entrants.
- **If the firms produce similar products:** then they will already tend to change their prices and outputs at the same time.
- **If demand and input prices are fairly stable:** then any agreements should last for some time.

You and Zoe could attempt a cartel or collusion, but these are illegal. Admittedly, the authorities may not investigate student magazines, but we are using this example to illustrate what happens more generally. So we will instead assume that you simply set your output at 600, and hope that Zoe cooperates by doing the same, because then the price will settle at £8 and you and she will share the monopoly profit.

The incentive for firms to cooperate

This outcome would benefit you both. Initially, you both set a price of £6 and total output is 1,600 per term, or 800 each. The first line in Table 11.5 uses this information to show that you will each have a profit of £2,200. If you both cooperate to restrict output to 600 each, the total output will be 1,200 per term and the price £8. The second line of Table 11.5 uses this information to show that you will each have a profit of £2,600.

> **11.2 Everyday economics**
>
> **OPEC and the world energy market**
>
> OPEC was set up in 1960 to influence oil prices by controlling supply. It was very successful in forcing up the price of oil between 1973 and 1985. Its power then weakened, largely because its market share fell following increased output from non-OPEC sources in the Gulf of Mexico, the North Sea, and Russia. But BP reckons that OPEC's market share will return to the level of the 1970s by 2030 because it expects most of the growth in the world's oil reserves in the next 20 years to come from OPEC nations. There are often disagreements within OPEC. Some members want to restrain output tightly, to force oil prices up as far as possible. Others, principally Saudi Arabia and Kuwait, have huge reserves and want to supply enough oil to prevent oil prices rising so much that users develop new technologies that will reduce the future demand for oil. Already developments in fuel efficiency and energy from renewables are moderating demand.
>
> 'BP Energy Outlook 2030', BP, January 2011, p 37

The incentive for firms to cheat

Although this cooperation would increase the profits of both firms, it has a major problem: it is unstable.

Table 11.5 **Profits under different scenarios**

	Y's Q Copies per term	Z's Q Copies per term	Total Q Copies per term	Price £ per copy	Y's *TR* £ per term	Y's *STC* £ per term*	Y's profit £ per term	Z's *TR* £ per term	Z's *STC* £ per term*	Z's profit £ per term
Nash Equilibrium	800	800	1,600	6	4,800	2,600	2,200	4,800	2,600	2,200
Both firms restrict Q	600	600	1,200	8	4,800	2,200	2,600	4,800	2,200	2,600
Only Y restricts Q	600	800	1,400	7	4,200	2,200	2,000	5,600	2,600	3,000
Only Z restricts Q	800	600	1,400	7	5,600	2,600	3,000	4,200	2,200	2,000
Neither firm restricts Q	800	800	1,600	6	4,800	2,600	2,200	4,800	2,600	2,200

*The *STC* figures are taken from Table 11.1.

This is because each firm has an incentive to cheat and produce more than its cooperative output of 600.

To see this, suppose first that you restrict your output to the cooperative level of 600, but Zoe 'cheats' and sets her output at the initial equilibrium level of 800. With a total output of 1,400, the price will be £7. The third line of Table 11.5 uses this information to show that your profit will be £2,000, less than the £2,600 you would get if you were both to cooperate, but Zoe's profit will be higher than that at £3,000. If, instead, you cheat with an output of 800 while Zoe restricts her output to the cooperative level of 600, then the outcomes will be reversed, as shown by the fourth line of the table.

Of course, you might both cheat and set an output of 800. In this case, the total output is 1,600, as it was at the initial equilibrium, so the outcome is as shown on the last line of Table 11.5.

Figure 11.7 uses game theory format to show the pay-offs to you and Zoe from the various combinations of cheating and not cheating strategies. The outcome will be both of you cheating, because you will each think as follows.

- **'If the other restricts output to 600,** then I would make more profit with an output of 800 than with 600. So I should cheat and produce 800.'

	Zoe's decision: Q=600	Zoe's decision: Q=800
Your decision: Q=600	Zoe's profit £2,600 Your profit £2,600	Zoe's profit £3,000 Your profit £2,000
Q=800	Zoe's profit £2,000 Your profit £3,000	Zoe's profit £2,200 Your profit £2,200

Figure 11.7 **Output and pricing with monopoly**

The situation is similar to that in the prisoner's dilemma shown in Figure 11.6. The only Nash equilibrium is where neither firm cooperates and each earns a profit of £2,200. The dilemma is that each would earn £2,600 if they were to cooperate to restrict output.

- **'If the other cheats with an output of 800,** then I would make more profit with an output of 800 than with 600. So I should cheat and produce 800.'

So, for each of you, cheating is a dominant strategy. So, like the prisoners in Figure 11.6, you both have an incentive to choose one strategy, here cheating, even though you would both be better off if you were both to choose the other strategy.

Incidentally, the outcome of both cheating is actually a Nash equilibrium, so its box has a dark border. It is a Nash equilibrium because, given that you produce 800, Zoe is adopting her best strategy, which is an output of 800; given that she produces 800, you are adopting your best strategy, which is an output of 800.

Repeated games

Figure 11.7 suggests that players who could cooperate without agreement have a strong incentive to choose the 'wrong' strategy, just like the prisoners. However, we have so far ignored an important difference between the prisoners and oligopolists. The prisoners played their game only once; oligopolists like you and Zoe may play repeated games. In your case, there will be a new game every term with each new issue of your magazines. Could you encourage Zoe not to cheat this term by threatening that, if she does, you will punish her next term by cheating then? Could she threaten to punish you in the same way if you cheat this term? The answer depends on whether you know how many games you will play.

Threats with a known number of games

Suppose you and Zoe are both in the first of nine terms, and you both plan to publish one magazine each term, or nine in all. Now consider your final term 9. Neither of you will be deterred from cheating in term 9 by the threat of a punishment in term 10, because there will be no term 10. So you will both cheat in term 9. Next take term 8. Neither of you will be deterred from cheating in term 8 by the threat of a punishment in term 9, because you both know you will both cheat in term 9 anyway. So you will also both cheat in term 8. Likewise in term 7, neither of you is deterred from cheating by the threat of a punishment in term 8, because you both know you will both cheat in term 8 anyway. So you will also both cheat in term 7.

We could work back in a similar way to term 1 and see that no punishment strategy will deter you both from cheating right away. So with a known number of games, no matter how many there are, threats of punishment will not deter cheating.

Threats with an unknown number of games

Suppose instead that you and Zoe plan to live near your college after graduating, and you both plan to produce an indefinite number of magazines. Then the analysis of the previous paragraph does not hold, because there is no final term to work backwards from. So let's suppose that, in term 1, you and Zoe cooperate and you both set output at 600 to earn £2,600 profit each, and then you wonder whether to cheat in term 2.

You know that if you cheat in term 2 and Zoe does not, then your profit will be £3,000, but hers will be just £2,000. So if you cheat in term 2, Zoe might opt for punishment in term 3 rather than continue with her cooperation output. If your strategy does trigger a response from Zoe, then the strategy she adopts would be called a **trigger strategy**. Zoe could operate a variety of trigger strategies. They each involve her cheating in term 3, but differ in what happens later. For example:

- **she may cooperate again from the next period, hoping that you will too;**
- **she might cooperate again from a later period,** which will be after punishing you for what she deems a sufficient number of terms;
- **she might never cooperate again;**
- **she might operate a tit-for-tat strategy,** which means that if you cheat in one period, then she will cheat in the next, but if you later start to cooperate, then she will cooperate again immediately.

Research suggests that firms generally do best if they all adopt tit-for-tat strategies. For example, suppose you cheat in term 2 to raise your profit from £2,600 to £3,000. Then Zoe will also cheat in term 3, and your profit will fall to £2,200, and it will stay at this low level for as long as you go on cheating. So you have an incentive to stop cheating and hope that Zoe's strategy is indeed tit-for-tat, so that she will then also stop cheating.

Because tit-for-tat strategies give firms an incentive not to cheat, they help cooperation to persist when firms play an unknown number of games, or, in other words, compete over an indefinite period.

Tacit collusion

We have seen that oligopolists make the biggest combined profit if they cooperate to set the same price that a monopolist would have, and in turn have the same total output. However, cooperating to secure the monopoly outcome can prove very hard over time, especially if there is a change in demand or in the price of a variable input. These changes can cause a monopolist to change its price and output, and any oligopolists who operates a cartel or collusion will agree to react in the same way. But how should oligopolists who cooperate without an agreement react?

Oligopolists in this situation sometimes behave *as though* they had some sort of agreement, and so engage in what is called **tacit collusion**. The most common form of tacit collusion arises when the firms in an industry follow a **price leadership** strategy. This means that they allow one firm to set its price and then follow its price. They will hope that the leader's price is not too far from the monopoly price. There are two forms of price leadership:

- **dominant firm price leadership;**
- **barometric price leadership.**

Dominant firm price leadership

In some oligopolies, one firm is much bigger than any of the others, and the small firms may follow the price of the large dominant firm. This is called **dominant price leadership**. As a profit-maximizer, the dominant firm will set its output where its *SMC* and *MR* curves intersect, and then set the price it need to sells that quantity. The followers will then accept that price.

Figure 11.8 shows how dominant price leadership works. It concerns an industry in which 10 equal-sized small firms and one large firm make a homogeneous product. The small firms can be considered to be perfect competitors. The left-hand part of the figure shows the combined supply curve of these 10 following firms, S_{10F}. This part of the figure also shows the market demand curve, D_{MKT}.

Suppose, for a moment, that the price is £2. S_{10F} tells us that the 10 firms will between them supply an output of 10 each period, while D_{MKT} shows that the buyers will want to buy 70. The gap of 60 is measured by a double line. This line tells us how much buyers will want to buy from the dominant firm at a price of £2. So it gives us a point on that firm's demand curve, D_{DOM}, which is shown on the right-hand part of the figure.

We can readily work out two more points on D_{DOM}.

- **At a price of £5**, S_{10F} in the left-hand part shows that the 10 firms would between them supply 40 each period, while D_{MKT} shows that the buyers would want to buy 40. So buyers would not want to buy anything from the dominant firm. So D_{DOM} shows that the quantity demanded from it at £5 would be zero.
- **At a price of £1**, S_{10F} in the left-hand part shows that the 10 firms would supply nothing each period, while D_{MKT} shows that the buyers would want to buy 80. So buyers would want to buy 80 from the dominant firm. So D_{DOM} shows that the quantity demanded from it at £1 would be 80. At lower prices, where the followers continue to sell nothing, D_{DOM} follows D_{MKT}.

The dominant firm's demand curve is also its average revenue curve, AR_{DOM}, which has the associated marginal revenue curve, MR_{DOM}. The dominant firm will

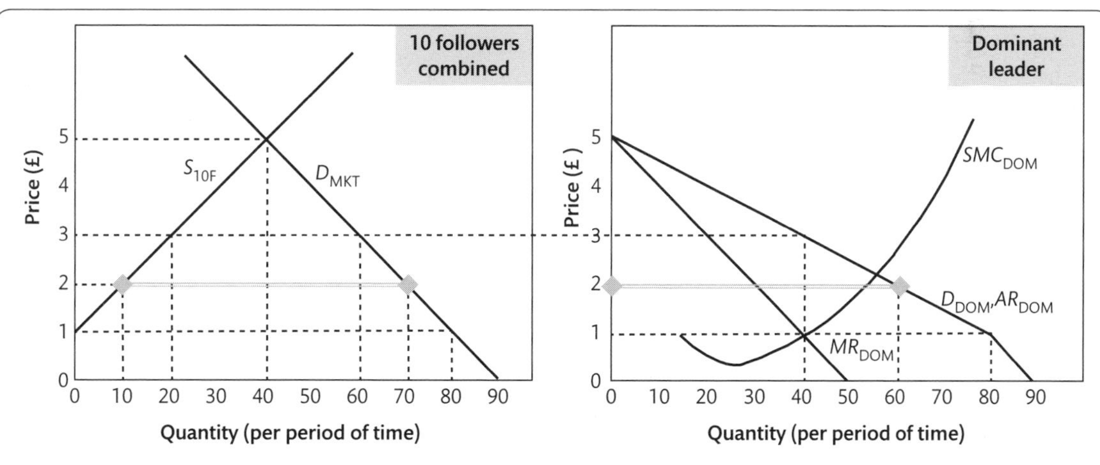

Figure 11.8 **Followers and a dominant leader**

This industry has 10 small following firms, the combined supply curve of which S_{10F}, is shown on the left, and a dominant leader, shown on the right. At any price, such as £2, the gap between S_{10F} and the market demand curve, D_{MKT}, shows how much buyers will demand from the leader at that price. By finding the gap at each price, we can find the leader's demand and average revenue curve, D_{DOM}, AR_{DOM}. Its output is 40, where its associated MR_{DOM} cuts its SMC_{DOM}. D_{DOM} here gives its price as £3. The followers also set this price and have a combined output of 20, as shown by S_{10F}.

maximize its profit by setting its output at 40 where its short-run marginal cost curve, SMC_{DOM}, intersects MR_{DOM}. The point at this output on D_{DOM} shows that it will set a price of £3 to sell this quantity. The followers will then accept this price. On the left, S_{10F} shows that the 10 followers will supply a total of 20 at this price, that is 2 each. And D_{MKT} shows that buyers will want to buy 60, just matching the 20 supplied by the followers plus the 40 supplied by the leader.

If market demand or input prices change, then MR_{DOM} or SMC_{DOM} will shift. So the dominant firm will adjust its output to the level at which these curves now intersect, and set the price needed for this output. The followers will follow its new price.

Barometric price leadership

Sometimes oligopolists follow the price of a firm that is not a dominant one. They may choose a firm that is believed to make the most reliable changes to its output and price when there is a change in market conditions. So this firm is taken to be a good indicator, or barometer, of the market, and this price leadership is called **barometric price leadership**. In industries in which this occurs, the firms may over time make different choices over which of their competitors should be seen to be the barometer.

11.3 Everyday economics

Airline collusion

In recent years, the airline industry has been the subject of repeated heavy fines for collusion. For example, in 2007, British Airways was fined about £270m in the US after it admitted collusion in fixing the prices of fuel surcharges, and £121.5m by the UK's Office of Fair Trading after it held illegal talks with rival Virgin Atlantic; Virgin escaped any penalty because it exposed the talks. In May 2011, Qantas was fined about £3m in New Zealand for fixing cargo prices with other airlines, which the New Zealand authorities are also investigating. Qantas had already faced heavy fines in the US.

'BA's price-fix fine reaches £270m', BBC News, 1 August 2007
'BA fined £270m for price fixing', The Guardian, 1 August 2007
'Qantas coughs up record fine', The National Business Review, 12 May 2011
'$6.5 million cargo fine for Qantas', Radio New Zealand News, 12 May 2011

11.4 Summary

- Oligopolists may cooperate without agreement, or perhaps illegally form cartels or engage in collusion.
- Cooperation that leads to the monopoly price and output raises the firms' combined profits. But, in any given period, each firm would gain by cheating to produce more than its share of the monopoly output.
- If firms make repeated decisions over a number of periods, then cheating may be deterred by punishment. The most effective punishment is usually tit-for-tat, which means that non-cheating firms punish a cheater by also cheating in all later periods until the cheater starts to cooperate again.
- Sometimes oligopolists undertake tacit collusion and follow the price set by a large dominant firm, or else by a smaller firm that is taken as a barometer indicating the best price for the industry to set.

11.5 Further strategic decisions by oligopolists

We have so far considered the output and pricing strategies of oligopolists. But oligopolists make many other types of strategic decision. The following types are among the most important.

- **Deciding on their technology:** this concerns how they make their products.
- **Choosing products to develop:** this includes designing new products and improving old ones.
- **Deciding on their marketing:** this covers issues such as advertising and sponsorship.

Product development and marketing are two ways in which firms can try to achieve more sales without making their products cheaper. So they are called forms of **non-price competition**.

When a firm selects strategies like these, it must allow for the interdependence between itself and its competitors. We will now illustrate this interdependence with three games. To make these particular games more interesting, they have been designed to show cases in which one or more players do not have a dominant strategy.

A game in which only one player has a dominant strategy

In our first game, only one firm has a dominant strategy. This game concerns technology, that is how things are produced. Suppose Billabong and Quiksilver are choosing whether to use the same amount of organic cotton next year as this year, or whether to use more. Organic cotton is grown without insecticides or pesticides, so it costs more to produce. So if both firms use more, both will have a lower profit. However, if only one firm uses more, then it will attract environmentally concerned customers from the other, while its higher price will drive some of its customers to the other. So its profit might rise or fall.

Suppose the various combinations of strategies actually give the profits or pay-offs shown in Figure 11.9. Billabong has a dominant strategy, which is to use the same amount of organic. This is its best strategy, no matter what Quiksilver does. Quiksilver does not have a dominant strategy. If Billabong uses the same amount of organic cotton as before, then Quiksilver should use more, but if Billabong uses more organic cotton, then Quiksilver should use the same as before.

	Quiksilver (QS): *Same organic*	Quiksilver (QS): *More organic*
Billabong (BB): *Same organic*	QS's profit £8m BB's profit £10m	QS's profit £9m BB's profit £9m
More organic	QS's profit £9m BB's profit £9m	QS's profit £7m BB's profit £8m

Figure 11.9 **A game with one dominant strategy**

With these payoffs, Quiksilver has no dominant strategy, but Billabong does: to use the same amount of organic cotton as before. Quiksilver will expect Billabong to use the same amount, and its best response is to use more. With these strategies, the outcome is at the Nash equilibrium shown.

Although Quiksilver has no dominant strategy, it may well expect Billabong to choose its dominant strategy and so use the same amount of organic cotton; if Billabong does that, it is best for Quiksilver to use more than before. So the outcome may be the top right-hand box, with £9 million profit for each. This outcome is a Nash equilibrium, so it has a dark border: when Billabong uses the same amount of organic, Quiksilver should use more, which it does; when Quiksilver uses more, Billabong should use the same amount, which it does.

However, Quiksilver might act differently. This is because it cannot be sure that Billabong will do its sums correctly and so choose the best strategy for itself, which is to use the same amount of organic cotton as before. If Quiksilver is unsure what Billabong will do, it may choose to use the same amount of organic as before. With this strategy, the worst it can do is end up with a £8 million profit if Billabong does use the same as before. If instead Quiksilver uses more than before, it could end up with just £7 million if Billabong mistakenly does so too.

If Quiksilver makes its choice in this way, then it would be choosing its **maximin strategy**, that is the strategy for which the worst possible pay-off is the best. The outcome will be the top left-hand box if

Billabong correctly chooses the same, and the bottom left-hand box if Billabong mistakenly chooses more.

A game in which no player has a dominant strategy and with two Nash equilibria

In our second game, neither firm has a dominant strategy, yet the game has *two* Nash equilibria. This game concerns product development. Suppose two manufacturers of fluorescent lamp bulbs, Osram and Philips, have limited resources for research and must each choose between developing bulbs that use less power, so they are cheaper to run, or bulbs with nicer shapes.

Suppose their various combinations of strategies give the profits or pay-offs shown in Figure 11.10. Neither firm has a dominant strategy. For example, if Osram develops cheaper-to-run bulbs, then Philips hould develop nicer-shaped ones, while if Osram develops nicer-shaped ones, then Philips should develop cheaper-to-run ones.

We cannot predict the outcome here. But we can see that there are two Nash equilibria. Each is shown with dark borders and arises if the firms develop different products. It seems that each firm would be best to develop a product for which it would have no competition from the other. Notice that, in each equilibrium, the firm developing the cheaper-to-run bulb does best. So, in this game, each firm would benefit if it were to manage to choose its strategy first: it would then announce that it was looking into cheaper-to-run bulbs, and leave its competitor deciding to look into nicer shapes.

Question 11.3 Which outcome will arise if each firm plays its maximin strategy?

A game in which no player has a dominant strategy and with no Nash equilibrium

In our final game, no firm has a dominant strategy and there is no Nash equilibrium. This game concerns marketing. Suppose that, in a remote town, only one firm called Old sells electrical appliances. Then a second firm called New is set up. New stocks a wider range of goods and has competitive prices. Each firm plans to advertise either in the local paper or on local radio. Neither firm can afford to advertise with both.

Suppose their various combinations of strategies give the profits or pay-offs shown in Figure 11.11. Here, every combination of strategies gives the firms a combined pay-off of £80,000. A game with the same total

	Philips' bulbs: *Cheaper to run*	Philips' bulbs: *Nicer shape*
Osram's bulbs: *Cheaper to run*	P's profit up £100 m O's profit up £100 m	P's profit up £120 m O's profit up £200 m
Nicer shape	P's profit up £200 m O's profit up £120 m	P's profit up £60 m O's profit up £60 m

Figure 11.10 **A game with no dominant strategies, and two Nash equilibria**

With these payoffs, neither firm has a dominant strategy and there are two Nash equilibria. It is best for the firms to develop different products. Each firm would gain by choosing its product first.

	New's ads: *In local paper*	New's ads: *On local radio*
Old's ads: *In local paper*	New's profit £50k Old's profit £30k	New's profit £30k Old's profit £50k
On local radio	New's profit £30k Old's profit £50k	New's profit £50m Old's profit £30k

Figure 11.11 **A game with no dominant strategies, and also no Nash equilibrium**

With these payoffs, neither firm has a dominant strategy, and there is no Nash equilibrium. Each firm would like the other to move first.

pay-off in each box is called a **constant sum game**. It may arise here because the total demand for appliances in the town is fixed. Incidentally, a constant sum game is not a necessary assumption to get no Nash equilibrium.

If the firms advertise in the same place, then all the people who see or hear their advertisements will get information about both firms, which should indicate that New has the wider range. So New should get more customers and make more profit. But if the firms advertise in different places, then it may be hard for many people to compare them. So most people might shop at Old simply because that is where they have always shopped. So Old would get more customers and make more profit.

In this case, no firm has a dominant strategy. Old finds that whatever strategy New chooses, it should choose the opposite strategy. New finds that whatever strategy Old chooses, it should choose the same strategy. There is also no Nash equilibrium because whichever outcome emerges, one firm will regret its choice. In the top left-hand box, for example, where they both use the paper, Old would wish it were using the radio instead.

We cannot predict the outcome here. Even the maximin approach is no help because each firm finds that the minimum pay-off is the same, £30,000, for each strategy. All we can say is that each firm would like the other to move first so that it could make the best response! This is a rare example of a case in which moving second is best.

11.5 Summary

- Game theory helps us to understand strategic decisions taken by interdependent oligopolists over matters such as marketing, technology, and product development.
- In some games, each firm has a dominant strategy that it will choose. This may give the firms the highest possible combined pay-off, or lead to a prisoners' dilemma outcome in which each is worse off than it would be if they had both played their non-dominant strategy.
- In some games, only one firm has a dominant strategy. Here, the other firm may make its decision on the assumption that its competitor will adopt its dominant strategy, but, if it fears that its competitor will mistakenly choose another strategy, then it may instead choose its maximin strategy, that is the one for which the worst possible outcome is higher than the worst possible outcome from any other strategy.
- In some games, no firm has a dominant strategy. Firms may choose strategies on the maximin basis.

In the next chapter we consider government policies towards firms, and the regulation of firms.

abc Glossary

Barometric price leadership: a case of price leadership in which the leader is not a dominant firm.

Bertrand model: a model of oligopoly in which each firm sets its profit-maximizing price, taking as given assumed prices for its competitors.

Cartel: a formal agreement between firms about prices and outputs and, perhaps, other matters.

Collusion: an informal agreement between firms about prices and outputs or, perhaps, other matters.

Constant sum game: a game in which the total pay-off is the same with each possible outcome.

Cooperation without agreement: a situation in which firms restrict output and raise prices without any communication.

Cournot model: a model of oligopoly in which each firm set its profit-maximizing output, taking as given assumed outputs for its competitors.

Dominant price leadership: a case of price leadership in which a large dominant firm is leader.

Dominant strategy: a strategy that is best for one player, irrespective of other players' strategies.

Duopoly: an oligopoly with only two firms.

Game theory: the study of people's behaviour when they choose strategies that take account of the strategies that other people may adopt.

Interdependence: any situation in which people consider other people's reactions.

Maximin strategy: the strategy for which the worst possible outcome is better than the worst possible outcome of every other strategy.

Nash equilibrium: when each player adopts his or her best strategy, given what the other players do.

Non-price competition: when firms strive for more sales without making their products cheaper.

Pay-off: a term in game theory for the effects on the players from a combination of strategies.

Player: a term in game theory for someone choosing a strategy.

Price leadership: a strategy in which the firms in an industry follow the price set by one particular firm.

Prisoners' dilemma: a game in which all the players would be better off if they were all to adopt non-dominant strategies instead of dominant strategies.

Reaction curve: a curve showing one firm's reactions to another firm's behaviour.

Stackelberg model: a model of oligopoly in which one firm sets its output first, and then the others follow by reacting as on the Cournot model.

Strategy: a term in game theory for any possible action for a player to choose.

Tacit collusion: a situation in which firms that have made no agreement behave as though they had.

Tit-for-tat strategy: a strategy whereby one firm reacts to cheating by another by cheating itself until the first firm stops cheating.

Trigger strategy: any response by one player that is triggered by the strategy chosen by another.

Answers to in-text questions

11.1 You may imagine that it is best to be the follower, but page 224 shows that it is best to be the leader.

11.2 The first prisoner would confess for the reasons explained in the text. If the second were to know the first had confessed, the best choice for the second would still be to confess also.

11.3 Each firm's maximin strategy is to develop bulbs that are cheaper to run.

? Questions for review

11.1 Look at Figure 11.1 and suppose that, in a future term, demand for magazines falls from the level shown there: the new demand curve runs from £10 to 2,000 copies. Work out the new perfect competition output and price and the new monopoly price and output. Which way will the Cournot reaction curves shift?

11.2 Suppose instead that, in a future term, the *SMC* for magazines rises from the level shown in Figure 11.1 to £4. Work out the new perfect competition output and price and the new monopoly price and output. Which way will the Cournot reaction curves shift?

11.3 Table 11.3 shows how to find Y's profit-maximizing price if $P_Z = £10$. Construct a similar table for $P_Z = £14$. Consider only four values for P_Y: £10; £9; £8; and £7. Find Y's profit at each of these prices and so find its profit-maximizing price.

11.4 Suppose in Figure 11.8 that the price of a variable input rises. Its effect on S_{10F} is to shift it to the left. Which other curves will shift and in which direction?

11.5 Look at Figure 11.9. Suppose the pay-off for Quiksilver in the bottom left-hand box changes to £6 million. **(a)** Would each firm have a dominant strategy? **(b)** Would there be any Nash equilibria? **(c)** What would the outcome be, and what could be said about it?

11.6 Look at Figure 11.10. Suppose both the figures in the top left-hand box change to £125 million. **(a)** Would each firm have a dominant strategy? **(b)** Would there be any Nash equilibria? **(c)** Would the outcome make the combined payoffs of the firms as high as it could be?

11.7 Look at Figure 11.11. Suppose each pay-off for New were raised by 10%, to make them all £33,000 or £55,000. **(a)** Would this still be a constant sum game? **(b)** Would either firm now have a dominant strategy? **(c)** Would there now be any Nash equilibria?

? Questions for discussion

11.1 In the prisoners' dilemma in Figure 11.6, Abi and Ben were *suspected* of the serious crime. Suppose they were innocent of it. Would the prosecutor's tactics still persuade them to confess to it?

11.2 Think of two oligopolistic industries in your locality and two for the UK. Have you noticed any pricing behaviour by any firm in any of these industries that is consistent with the kinked-demand curve theory?

11.3 Suppose a country has two tobacco companies. Both companies choose to sponsor sports, even though each would make more profit if neither sponsored sports. Use game theory to discuss this situation.

Common student errors

Many students are attracted to the kinked-demand curve model because it recalls the models for other types of firm. But remember that it is the least satisfying oligopoly model in one respect, which is that it does not actually explain why the current prices set are what they are.

In game theory, students sometimes fail to distinguish between the outcome that we can predict will arise and Nash equilibria. Note, for example, that we can make no predictions about the outcome in Figure 11.10, but we can work out two Nash equilibria here.

12

Governments, Monopolies, and Oligopolies

Remember from Chapter 6 that if you are a rational consumer, you will maximize your total satisfaction by adjusting your pattern of consumption so that, for each product, your marginal utility divided by the price of the product is the same. Remember from Chapter 9 that a perfect competitor sets its short-run output where its price equals its short-run marginal cost, and sets its long-run output where its price equals its long-run marginal cost. Remember from Chapter 10 that a monopolist sets its short-run output where its price exceeds its short-run marginal cost, and sets its long-run output where its price exceeds its long-run marginal cost.

Why do we have national monopolies in key industries like the railway network, postal services, and electricity and gas supply? Why is water supplied by firms that each have a monopoly in their local areas? Suppose you run one of these national or local monopolies: why might you create a range of inefficiencies and so need regulating? How do the regulators that oversee these firms decide on the prices they should set? How do the UK and the EU promote competition in other industries?

This chapter shows you how to answer questions like these, by understanding:

* what types of inefficiency result from monopolies, and also from oligopolies;
* how these inefficiencies affect people's well-being or economic welfare;
* what is meant by a 'natural monopoly';
* how monopolies and oligopolies can be regulated;
* what more general powers governments have to promote competition.

12.1 Introduction to welfare economics

We saw in Chapter 1 that resources are scarce, so we want to make good use of them. And we saw in Chapter 2 that if a country had a market economy, then its government would allow markets to make all decisions about 'How many?' resources are used, 'For what?' they are used, 'For whom?' they are used, and 'How?' they are used.

In practice, all governments intervene with these decisions, believing that they can improve the use of resources. This chapter looks at the question 'How?' resources are used and discusses the concerns that arise when they are used by oligopolies and monopolies.

Pareto-efficiency

This chapter uses a branch of economics called **welfare economics**: this studies people's economic well-being or welfare. Welfare economics is based on a principle suggested by the Italian economist Vilfredo Pareto (1848–1923).

The **Pareto principle** considers the following question: is it possible to change the way in which an economy's resources are used to make at least one person better off, without making anyone else worse off? If it is possible, then resources could be used more efficiently, so their present use is called **Pareto-inefficient**. If it is not possible, then the present use of resources is called **Pareto-efficient**.

A country's resources may be used in a Pareto-inefficient way because of two types of problem:

- **there may be inefficiency in production**;
- **there may be inefficiency in consumption**.

To see this, we will explore a very simple economy with these two characteristics.

- **Only two products are produced: eggs and figs.**
- **There are only two consumers: Gary and Holly.**

Pareto-efficiency and production

Suppose that if this simple economy were to use all of its resources, then the most it could produce is four units of output per day. It might, for example, produce 4 eggs and 0 figs, or 3 eggs and 1 fig, and so on. So its production possibility frontier would be as shown in Figure 12.1.

Suppose this economy produced at a point inside its production possibility frontier, like **x**, where it produces 1 egg and 1 fig. Then its production would be Pareto-inefficient. This is because it would be possible to produce more of both products, and so make at least one person better off without making the other person worse off.

Pareto-efficiency and consumption

Next, suppose the economy has no problems with its production and is producing four units of output each day, so it is somewhere on its production possibility frontier. Even so, its resources may not be being used in a Pareto-efficient way. To discover if they are, we

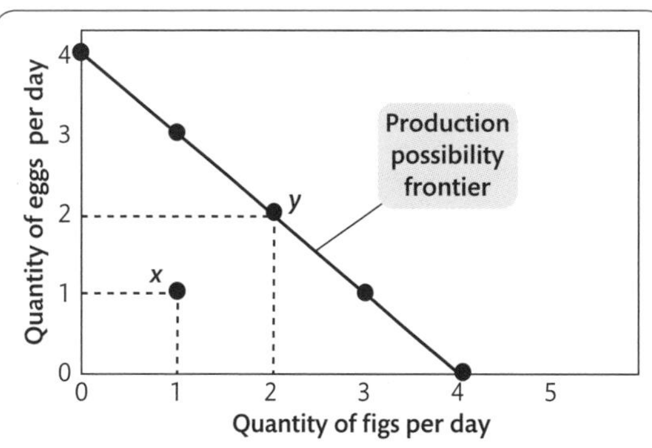

Figure 12.1 **A simple production possibility frontier**

All points inside the frontier, like **x**, are Pareto-inefficient. A point on the frontier, like **y**, may be efficient: it depends how the products are shared between consumers.

need to answer two questions about consumers, as follows.

- **How much of each product does each consumer consume?** This naturally depends on how much of each product Gary and Holly buy, and this in turn depends on their incomes, their preferences, and the prices of eggs and figs.
- **How much satisfaction, or utility, do the consumers receive from the products they consume?** We noted in Chapter 6 that economists cannot actually measure utility, but it often helps to suppose that we can measure it in units called utils. We will assume that Gary gets 10 utils from each egg and 5 from each fig, while Holly gets 5 from each egg and 10 from each fig.

When the economy produces four units of output a day, it could produce various combinations of eggs and figs, and these could be consumed by Gary and Holly in various amounts. Table 12.1 shows just four of the possible outcomes, and calls them A, B, C, and D. It shows how much utility Gary and Holly would get with each. Look first at outcomes A and B. In each of these, the total output is 2 eggs and 2 figs, as at point **y** on Figure 12.1.

Outcome A shows each consumer getting 15 utils from 1 egg and 1 fig. This is Pareto-*inefficient*, because we could make both consumers better off by switching to outcome B; here, they would each get 20 utils, Gary from 2 eggs and Holly from 2 figs. Outcome B is Pareto-*efficient*, because here we could make one consumer better off only by letting them consume more than two units of output a day, but then the other would have to consume fewer than two and so become worse off.

Table 12.1 **Pareto-efficiency and equity**

Outcome	A	B	C	D
Eggs for Gary	1	2	2	4
Figs for Gary	1	0	2	0
Eggs for Holly	1	0	0	0
Figs for Holly	1	2	0	0
*Gary's utils	15	20	30	40
*Holly's utils	15	20	0	0
Is the outcome Pareto-efficient?	No	Yes	Yes	No

* Each egg gives Gary 10 utils and each fig gives him 5. Each egg gives Holly 5 utils and each egg gives her 10.

Pareto-efficiency and equity

In outcomes A and B, each consumer ends up with equal utility. In the real world, consumers end up with different amounts of utility. Some unequal outcomes are Pareto-inefficient and some are efficient.

Consider outcome C at which the output is still 2 eggs and 2 figs, but now Gary consumes them all, so he gets 30 utils and Holly gets 0. This outcome is Pareto-inefficient because we could make Gary even better off, without making Holly worse off, by switching to outcome D at which only 4 eggs are produced and Gary consumes them all to get 40 utils; Holly still has 0 utils, so she is no worse off.

Question 12.1 Look again at outcome C in Table 12.1. How could the situation be changed to make Holly better off without making Gary worse off?

In contrast, outcome D is Pareto-efficient. Here, there is no way to make Gary better off, and there is no way to make Holly better off without switching some resources from satisfying Gary to satisfying Holly, which would make Gary worse off.

This simple example shows three key points.

- **There can be many different Pareto-efficient outcomes.** B and D are examples.
- **Some Pareto-efficient outcomes are very unequal or inequitable.** D is an example.
- **For any inefficient outcome, there is a better outcome at which at least one person is better off while the other is no worse off.** For example, this would occur with a switch from A to B and with a switch from C to D.

Market failure

A market economy would actually fail to produce a Pareto-efficient outcome: this failure is called **market failure**, and it arises for two reasons.

- **There are problems with the types of firm in some markets.** These problems are most severe in markets in which the firms are monopolists or oligopolists. We will see in sections 12.2 and 12.3 how these firms may lead to Pareto-inefficiency in both production and consumption. For simplicity, we will focus chiefly on monopolists. In later sections, we will see how governments can tackle these problems.
- **There are problems with the types of product in some markets.** Chapter 13 discusses this issue.

Market failure explains why governments intervene in their economies: they believe that the outcome will be better if they intervene than if they do not intervene. Of course, a government knows that even if its intervention does result in an efficient outcome, then this may be very inequitable, like D in Table 12.1. If so, it must also redistribute income from the rich to the poor. Chapter 16 discusses this issue.

12.1 Summary

- If it is possible to change the use of a country's resources to make at least one person better off without making anyone else worse off, then those resources are being used in a Pareto-inefficient way.
- If it is not possible to change the use of a country's resources to make at least one person better off without making anyone else worse off, then those resources are being used in a Pareto-efficient way.
- Even if there is great inequality in a country, its use of resources may still be Pareto-efficient.
- Market failure refers to the fact that market economies will not deliver a Pareto-efficient use of resources. Governments intervene in the hoping of securing a better use.

12.2 Welfare economics and problems in production

We have seen that one reason why a country's resources may not be used in a Pareto-efficient way is that the country may be producing at a point inside its production possibility frontier. There are two possible causes of this:

- **some of its resources may be unemployed**;
- **the resources that are employed may not be producing as much as they could**.

The first cause concerns 'How many?' resources are used, which we will leave to later chapters. In this chapter, we will assume that all resources are used, and in this section we will see why they may not produce as much as they could. This can result from three types of inefficiency in production:

- **technical inefficiency**;
- **economic inefficiency**;
- **productive inefficiency**.

We will now look at these, and then see why they may arise chiefly with monopolists and oligopolists.

Technical inefficiency and efficiency

Suppose a firm has resources that are idle or wastefully used. For example, a restaurant might open from

5pm to 7pm when few people want to eat, so its kitchen, tables, and staff might rarely be fully used. These resources would produce more output if the restaurant were to open from 7pm to 9pm when more people wanted to eat. If a firm could produce more output with the same quantities of resources that it currently uses, then it displays **technical inefficiency**; if it could not, then it displays **technical efficiency**.

Economic inefficiency and efficiency

Suppose a firm has no idle or wasteful resources, so it is technically efficient. Even so, it might be able to produce its current output more efficiently by using a cheaper combination of inputs. If it does not produce its output as cheaply as possible, then it displays economic inefficiency; if it does, then it displays economic efficiency.

To explore economic efficiency, take the firm in Table 12.2, which makes a product called alphas. This firm uses just two inputs. For capital, it uses a type of machine that it can hire for £20 an hour, and for labour it uses a type of worker whom it can hire at £10 an hour. So the price of capital, P_K, is £20, and the price of labour, P_L, is £10. The ratio of these prices, P_K/P_L, is 2.

Suppose that if this firm were to hire one more or fewer machine, while keeping the quantity of labour the same, then its output would change by 50 alphas an hour: then its marginal product of capital, MP_K, is 50. And suppose that if it were to hire one more or fewer worker, while keeping the quantity of capital the same, then its output would change by 10 alphas an hour: then its marginal product of labour, MP_L, is 10. The ratio of these *MP* figures, MP_K/MP_L, is 5, as shown in the middle of Table 12.2.

For this firm, MP_K/MP_L and P_K/P_L are unequal. The fact that they are unequal means that it is economically inefficient. To see why, suppose that each hour it:

- **used 1 more machine**, so spending £20 more on capital, and also producing 50 more alphas;
- **used 5 fewer workers**, so spending £50 less on labour, and producing 10 fewer alphas from each of those 5 workers, that is 50 fewer in all.

Then the firm would produce the same quantity as before, but spend £30 less. Because it could produce more cheaply, it is economically inefficient.

Question 12.2 Suppose the firm initially had $MP_K = 15$ and $MP_L = 15$, so that $MP_K/MP_L = 1$, which is less than P_K/P_L. What switch of inputs would result in it producing its current output more cheaply?

How a firm can secure economic efficiency

We have seen that if the firm in Table 12.2 had the marginal product figures shown in the middle of the table, it could cut its costs by switching from labour to capital. Imagine that it makes a large switch. Then its MP_K will fall, because its machines will have fewer people to operate them, while its MP_L will rise, because each worker will have more machines to use.

Suppose it switches from labour to capital until its MP_K was 40 and its MP_L was 20, as shown at the bottom of Table 12.2. Here, MP_K/MP_L is 2. So:

$$MP_K/MP_L = P_K/P_L$$

Table 12.2 **A firm is economically efficient if it adjusts its inputs so that $MP_K/MP_L = P_K/P_L$**

Price of capital, P_K (£ per hour)	20
Price of labour, P_L (£ per hour)	10
P_K/P_L (ratio)	**2**
The following MP figures give economic inefficiency	
Marginal product of capital, MP_K	50
Marginal physical product of labour, MP_L	10
MP_K/MP_L (ratio)	**5**
The following MP figures give economic efficiency	
Marginal product of capital, MP_K	40
Marginal physical product of labour, MP_L	20
MP_K/MP_L (ratio)	**2**

Note: Marginal products here are measured as units of output per hour.

A firm that meets this condition will be economically efficient. To see why, suppose this firm switches even more resources by taking these actions each hour:

- **using 1 more machine**, so spending £20 more on labour, and also producing 40 more alphas.
- **using 2 fewer workers**, so spending £20 less on labour, and producing 20 fewer alphas from each of those 2 workers, that is 40 fewer in all.

Then it would produce the same quantity as before, but its costs would not fall. Because this firm cannot now alter its use of resources to produce its output more cheaply, it is economically efficient.

Table 12.3 **Economic efficiency leads to productive inefficiency if firms face different input prices**

Industry	Alphas	Betas
Price of capital, P_K (£ per hour)	20	15
Price of labour, P_L (£ per hour)	10	15
P_K/P_L (ratio)	**2**	**1**
The following MP figures give economic efficiency, but productive inefficiency		
Marginal product of capital, MP_K	40	30
Marginal product of labour, MP_L	20	30
MP_K/MP_L (ratio)	**2**	**1**

Note: Marginal products here are measured as units of output per hour.

Productive inefficiency

Suppose all firms were both economically and technically efficient. Even then, an economy might not be producing as much as it could. Instead, it might have **productive inefficiency**: this means that, by using the same resources, it could produce more of one product without producing less of any other.

To see this, suppose there is a second product, betas, the makers of which use exactly the same type of machines and labour as the firms that make alphas. But suppose that the firms in each industry face different prices for these inputs. Perhaps the capital is hired out by a monopolist that operates price discrimination. And perhaps the labour is unionized and has negotiated different wage rates in each industry.

Suppose that, for firms in the alpha industry, P_K is £20 and P_L is £10. And suppose that, for firms in the beta industry, both P_K and P_L are £15. These prices are shown in Table 12.3, which concerns a typical firm in each industry. Here, P_K/P_L is 2 for the alpha firm and 1 for the beta firm. When the firms face different ratios for input prices, we can show that there will be productive inefficiency.

To see this, recall that each firm is economically efficient, so it adjusts the amounts it uses of each input until its MP_K/MP_L equals the P_K/P_L that it faces. Suppose the firms end up with the marginal product figures shown at the bottom of Table 12.3, where MP_K/MP_L is 2 for firms in the alpha industry and 1 for firms in the beta industry.

Now suppose we could somehow make the following two changes to this economy.

- **Switch one machine to the alpha-making firm from the beta-making firm**. Then the MP_K figures show that, each hour, the country would make 40 more alphas and 30 fewer betas.
- **Switch one worker from the alpha-making firm to the beta-making firm**. Then the MP_L figures show that, each hour, the country would make 20 fewer alphas and 30 more betas.

So if we were to make both changes, then the same total resources would produce 20 more alphas and no fewer betas. So there is productive inefficiency.

Productive efficiency

Productive efficiency arises when firms face the same prices for the same inputs. To see this, suppose now that the beta-making firms face the same prices for capital and labour as the alpha-making firms. These prices are shown in Table 12.4, and here P_K/P_L is 2 for both firms.

Table 12.4 **Economic efficiency leads to productive efficiency if all firms face the same input prices**

Industry	Alphas	Betas
Price of capital, P_K (£ per hour)	20	20
Price of labour, P_L (£ per hour)	10	10
P_K/P_L (ratio)	**2**	**2**
The following MP figures give economic efficiency and productive efficiency		
Marginal product of capitalm, MP_K	40	30
Marginal product of labour, MP_L	20	15
MP_K/MP_L (ratio)	**2**	**2**

Note: Marginal products here are measured as units of output per hour.

Assuming each firm is economically efficient, each will adjust the quantities it uses of each input so that its MP_K/MP_L is 2. Suppose the firms end up with the marginal product figures shown at the bottom of the table. The figures for the beta-making firm are different from those in Table 12.3 because it now faces different input prices.

The economy will now have **productive efficiency**, which means that, using the same resources, it could not produce more of one product without producing less of the other. To see this, suppose the country wanted to produce more alphas while producing no fewer betas. And suppose it made the following two changes.

- **Switched one machine to the alpha-making firm from the beta-making firm**. The MP_K figures show that, each hour, the country would make 40 more alphas, but 30 fewer betas.
- **Switched two workers from the alpha-making firm to the beta-making firm**. The MP_L figures show that, each hour, the country would make 40 fewer alphas and 30 more betas.

Allowing for both changes, the country would indeed produce no fewer betas, but it would also fail to produce any more alphas. Here, the only way to produce more alphas is to take more resources from betas, and so produce fewer betas. So this economy displays productive efficiency.

Question 12.3 Why would it also be impossible to produce more betas without producing fewer alphas?

How to secure productive efficiency

Productive efficiency will arise if MP_K/MP_L is the same for each firm. This applied in Table 12.4, but not in Table 12.3, where MP_K/MP_L was higher for alphas. This means that, in Table 12.3, extra capital is relatively more useful for alphas than betas, while extra labour is relatively less useful. So output will rise if capital is shifted from betas to alphas, and labour is shifted from alphas to betas.

Efficiency, monopolists, and oligopolists

To produce as much as it can from the resources it uses, an economy needs all firms to be technically efficient and economically efficient. It also needs all firms to face the same input prices in order to secure productive efficiency. Would this happen if there were no government intervention?

It might seem that there is no need to intervene to make firms technically efficient and economically efficient. This is because profit-maximizing firms have an incentive not to pay for idle or wastefully used resources, and they have an incentive to use the cheapest possible production methods. However, this incentive differs in strength between different types of firm.

- **For perfect and monopolistic competitors, the incentive is strong**. If any such firm is technically or economically inefficient, then new efficient firms can enter its industry and have lower prices, and so force it out of business.
- **For oligopolists and monopolists, the incentive is weak**. If any such firm is technically or economically inefficient, then new efficient firms find it hard to enter the industry, because they face barriers to entry. So governments worry about these firms.

As for productive efficiency, the inefficiency in Table 12.3 arose because different firms faced different prices for the same inputs. In the case of capital, this was because capital was supplied by a monopolist that operated price discrimination. Governments can prevent this problem by making price discrimination illegal. In the case of wages, the union negotiated a particularly high wage in the beta industry. Governments can try to tackle this problem by reducing the power of unions to negotiate high wages in any industry.

12.1 Everyday economics

Biscuit factory closures

The biscuit maker Burton's Foods has announced its intention to close its factory in the Wirral, with the loss of 342 jobs. The company defended its decision by saying that it faced significant cost pressures, and planned to invest £7m in its sites in Edinburgh and Llantarnam to ensure a profitable future.

'Staff in tears as Burton's Foods announces Wirral factory to close', *Liverpool Daily Post*, 13 January 2011
'Burton's Foods set to axe 400 jobs', *Belfast Telegraph*, 12 January 2011

Comment Food manufacture is highly competitive. This leads to a fairly ruthless pursuit for efficiency among competing firms anxious to flourish.

12.2 Summary

- Technical inefficiency arises if firms have idle or wastefully used inputs.
- Economic inefficiency arises if firms fail to use the cheapest possible production methods.
- Productive inefficiency arises if different firms face different prices for the same inputs, because it would then be possible for an economy to produce more of one product without producing less of another.
- These inefficiencies cause an economy to produce less than it might from the resources that it uses.
- These inefficiencies are most likely to arise with monopolists and oligopolists.

12.3 Welfare economics and problems in consumption

Consumption inefficiency and efficiency

Suppose a country has tackled all sources of inefficiency in production, and is on its production possibility frontier. Even then, as we saw in section 12.1, the situation might not be Pareto-efficient, because it might be possible to move to a different point on the frontier to make one person better off without making anyone else worse off.

For example, suppose an economy produces only alphas and betas, and all consumers would get more utility if they were to consume fewer alphas and more betas than they do now. Then we could make everyone better off by producing fewer alphas and more betas, so letting everyone consume fewer alphas and more betas.

If it is possible to change the pattern of consumption to make at least one person better off without making anyone else worse off, we say there is **consumption inefficiency**. If it is not possible, there is **consumption efficiency**.

When consumption efficiency arises

An economy will have consumption efficiency, without any government intervention, if the following two conditions are met:

- **Every consumer is rational and maximizes his or her utility**. We will assume this is the case.
- **Every firm has its price equal to its short-run marginal cost and its long-run marginal cost**. This

is not the case because, as we saw in Chapters 9–11, it applies only to perfect competitors. For simplicity, when this section refers to marginal costs, it will not distinguish between short-run and long-run marginal costs.

To see how these conditions lead to consumption efficiency, consider the country in Table 12.5, which produces just two goods: alphas and betas. The price of alphas, P_A, is £4, and the price of betas, P_B, is £8.

Suppose each industry is in perfect competition. Then each firm sets its output at a level at which its marginal cost equals the price that it faces. So the marginal cost for alphas, MC_A, must be £4, and the marginal cost for betas, MC_B, must be £8.

Suppose you buy both products, and you are a rational consumer who maximizes utility. Then, as we saw in Chapter 6, you will adjust the quantity you consume of each product so that:

$$MU_A/P_A = MU_B/P_B$$

where MU_A is your marginal utility from alphas, and MU_B is your marginal utility from betas. Suppose you adjust your consumption so that your MU_A is 24 utils and your MU_B is 48 utils. Then your MU_A/P_A of 24/4 and your MU_B/P_B of 48/8 are the same because they both equal 6.

You cannot now change your consumption to increase your total utility. If, for example, you were to buy one fewer alpha and spend the £4 saved on half a beta, the 24 utils gained from that half beta would be no more than the 24 lost on the alpha.

Also, the country cannot make you better off without making anyone else worse off. For example, if the country were to produce one fewer alpha for you, so you lose 24 utils, the marginal cost of alphas is £4, so £4 worth of resources would be freed up. As the marginal cost of betas is £8, these resources could make an extra half a beta for you, which would give you 24 utils. So this switch would not make you better off overall. To make you better off, the country would have to use more resources for you, and so use fewer for other people, making them worse off.

If all other consumers are also rational, the same result applies to them. So, if every industry is in perfect competition, with its price equal to marginal cost, it is impossible to change the pattern of consumption to make anyone better off without making someone else worse off. So there is consumption efficiency.

Table 12.5 **Consumption efficiency arises if all prices equal MC and consumers are rational**

Price of alphas, P_A	£4
Price of betas, P_B	£8
Marginal cost of alphas, MC_A	£4
Marginal cost of betas, MC_B	£8
The following MU figures are rational for the consumer and lead to consumption efficiency	
Marginal utility of alphas	24
Marginal utility of betas	48

When consumption inefficiency arises

Now let's see what happens if the second condition needed for consumption efficiency does not apply, so that some firms have a price that is not equal to the marginal cost. Suppose, for example, that the beta-making firms merge to form a monopoly. We saw in Chapter 10 that monopolists set a price above *MC*. Say this monopoly sets the price of betas at £12, above the MC_B of £8. Table 12.6 gives these new prices and also repeats the MC_A and MC_B figures from Table 12.5.

As a rational consumer, you must now adjust your pattern of purchases. Otherwise your MU_A/P_A will stay at 24/4, or 6, and so not equal your MU_B/P_B, which would be 48/12, or 4. Suppose you buy more alphas and fewer betas, so that your MU_A falls, say to 20 utils, and your MU_B rises, say to 60 utils, as shown in Table 12.6. So MU_A/P_A is 20/4, or 5, and MU_B/P_B is 60/12, which is also 5.

Here, again, you cannot change your consumption to get more utility. If, for example, you bought one fewer alpha and spent the £4 saved on a third of a

Table 12.6 **Consumption inefficiency arises if some prices differ from *SMC* and consumers are rational**

Price of alphas, P_A	£4
Price of betas, P_B	£12
Marginal cost of alphas, MC_A	£4
Marginal cost of betas, MC_B	£8
The following* MU *figures are rational for the consumer, but lead to consumption efficiency	
Marginal utility of alphas	20
Marginal utility of betas	60

beta, the 20 utils gained from that third of a beta would merely equal the 20 lost on the alpha.

However, the country could make you better off without making anyone else worse off. For example, if it were to produce one fewer alpha for you, so you lose 20 utils, the *MC* of alphas is £4, so £4 worth of resources would be freed up. As the *MC* of betas is £8, these resources could make an extra half a beta for you, which would give you 30 utils. So this switch would make you better off overall without affecting anyone else. So here consumption is inefficient, and this makes governments dislike monopolists and oligopolists that have prices above their marginal costs.

The problem of the second-best

Suppose a country has five perfectly competitive industries with prices equal to their *MC*s, and five monopolies with prices above their *MC*s. As some prices differ from *MC*, consumption is inefficient. If the government could get *all* the monopolies to set their prices equal to their *MC*s, then consumption would be efficient.

But suppose that the government can get only four of the monopolies to have prices equal to their *MC*s. Because prices do not equal *MC*s in all industries, consumption will still be inefficient. You may feel that, with more prices at the correct level, the outcome must be better than the initial situation, but we cannot be sure of this. We will end up with an inefficient allocation, and in principle this might be even worse than the initial one.

A very different example may help you to see this. Suppose two people bake sponge cakes. They get most quantities right, but one person uses half the correct amount of flour, and one person uses half the correct amounts of flour and eggs. Will the first cake taste better? We can't be sure that it will simply by adding up the number of wrong amounts!

If a government could get *all* prices equal to *MC*s, then it would secure consumption efficiency, which we can call the best outcome. But it would be immensely hard to tackle every firm that is not a perfect competitor. So a government can reduce only the number of prices that differ from *MC*s, and it cannot be sure that this limited approach will raise welfare at all; still less can it be sure that it will take society to what might be a second-best outcome. However, governments generally believe that tackling some prices that differ from *MC*s leads to a better outcome than doing nothing.

12.3 Summary

- If the price of each product equals its marginal cost, then the behaviour of rational consumers results in consumption efficiency: so it would not be possible to make one consumer better off without diverting resources from producing products for other consumers and so making them worse off.
- If one or more prices exceed marginal cost, then the behaviour of rational consumers leads to consumption inefficiency: indeed, resources could be reallocated to make all consumers better off.
- Consumption efficiency requires all firms to have a price equal to their marginal cost. Having only a few prices that are unequal may not lead to a better outcome than having many that are unequal.

12.4 A diagrammatic view of the key problems of monopolies

We have seen that consumption efficiency is helped by perfect competitors, because their prices equal their marginal costs, and hindered by monopolies, because their prices don't. We will now use some diagrams to compare a perfectly competitive industry with a monopoly, and see how the former leads to more welfare. These diagrams concern the short run.

Surpluses with perfect competition

Suppose the alpha industry is in perfect competition. And suppose its price and output, which we will now call P_{PC} and Q_{PC}, are determined by the short-run supply curve and the demand curve shown in part (a) of Figure 12.2. So P_{PC} is £4 per kg and Q_{PC} is 10 million per week. We saw in Chapter 9 that, in a perfectly competitive industry, this *SS* is found by adding together the short-run supply curves for each firm, and that their short-run supply curves followed their short-run marginal cost curves.

D shows how many alphas buyers would like to buy at each possible price. *D* meets the price axis at £9. So if the price were just under £9, then at least one buyer would be willing to buy one alpha. The part of *D* above the price of £4 shows that, up to the quantity of 10 million a week, there are always buyers who would be willing to pay more for the next alpha than the £4 that they actually do pay. The excess of how much consumers are willing to pay above what they do pay is called 'consumer surplus'. It is shown here by the dark

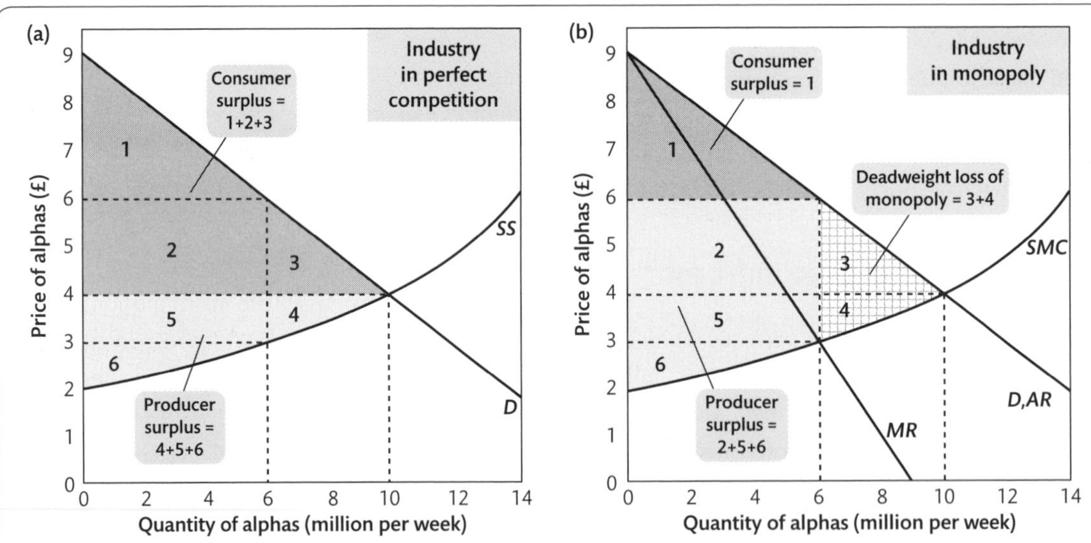

Figure 12.2 **The deadweight loss of monopoly**

If the alpha industry were in perfect competition, as in part (a), 10 million alphas would be traded each week at a price of £4. Consumer surplus would equal areas 1 + 2 + 3 and producer surplus would equal areas 4 + 5 + 6. If the industry were to merge to form a monopoly, it would face the same demand curve, labelled *D,AR* in part (b), with the associated *MR* curve. Its short-run marginal cost curve, *SMC*, would be the same as *SS* in part (a). The price would rise to £6 and the quantity would fall to 6 million. Consumer surplus would equal area 1 and producer surplus would equal areas 2 + 5 + 6. The combined consumer and producer surplus would fall by areas 3 + 4, so they show the deadweight loss of monopoly.

grey triangle, which is divided into three parts labelled 1, 2, and 3.

SS shows how many alphas sellers would like to sell at each possible price. *SS* meets the price axis at £2. So if the price were just over £2, then at least one seller would be willing to supply one alpha. The part of *S* below the price of £4 shows that, up to the quantity of 10 million a week, there are always suppliers who would be willing to take less for the next alpha than the £4 that they actually receive. This means that every alpha except the last must cost under £4 to produce. The excess that producers receive from consumers above their costs is called 'producer surplus'. It is shown here by the light grey triangle, which is divided into three parts labelled 4, 5, and 6.

Surpluses with monopoly

Now suppose all the alpha-making firms merge to form a monopoly. Part (b) of Figure 12.2 shows the effects. The new firm will face the same demand curve from consumers as before, as shown by *D*. With a monopolist, the demand curve is also the firm's average revenue curve, *AR*, and the associated marginal revenue curve is *MR*.

A monopolist does not have a supply curve, but the old *SS* curve, which was based on the perfect competitors' short-run marginal cost curves, will now show the monopolist's short-run marginal cost curve, *SMC*. The profit-maximizing output for the monopolist, called Q_{MON}, is 6 million where *MR* intersects *SMC*. The point on *D* above Q_{MON} shows that the monopolist's price, P_{MON}, will be set at £6.

The effects on the surpluses are as follows.

- **Consumer surplus**. This shrinks to area 1. Area 2 disappears because consumers now pay £6, not £4, and area 3 disappears because consumers do not buy beyond 6 million.
- **Producer surplus**. This equals areas 2 + 5 + 6. Area 4 disappears because producers now sell only 6 million alphas rather than 10 million. Area 2 is added because these 6 million now sell for £2 more than before, £6 instead of £4.

The monopoly is bad for consumers, who pay a higher price and consume less, and it is good for producers, who receive a higher price and save costs by producing less. If that were all that happened, so that producers gained at the expense of consumers, then the formation of the monopoly would not have reduced the welfare of society as a whole. However, it also means that the combined consumer and producer surplus has shrunk by areas 3 and 4, and this means that total welfare has fallen: this fall in surplus or welfare is called the **deadweight loss of a monopoly**.

Moreover, the new situation is Pareto-inefficient. *D* in part (b) shows that one consumer would now be willing to pay just under £6, say £5.99, for another alpha. And *SMC* shows that it would cost the monopoly just over £3 to produce another alpha, say £3.01. If the consumer could give the producer any intermediate amount, say £4, then the producer would be better off by £4 minus £3.01, and the consumer would be better off by £5.99 minus £4. So both would be better off and no one else would be worse off.

12.4 Summary

- If an industry that was in perfect competition were to merge to form a monopoly, then there would be less consumer surplus and more producer surplus. However, the combined surplus would fall.
- The fall in total surplus that would arise from the merger is called the deadweight loss of the monopoly.

12.5 Natural monopolies

Previous sections have shown that monopolies generally lead to inefficient outcomes. But, in this section, we will look at one type of market in which monopolies have a significant advantage.

The meaning of a natural monopoly

In some industries, firms have economies of scale up to very large outputs compared with the size of the market. This means that no matter how much any firm expands, its average cost of producing each unit of output continues to get lower.

This situation chiefly arises if a firm needs to have a costly grid or network, such as the following:

- **electricity cable grids**;
- **gas pipeline grids**;
- **overground and underground railway networks**;
- **mail delivery networks covering all addresses**;
- **water supply and sewerage pipeline grids**;
- **telephone cable networks**.

In these industries, the grid or network is a very costly input that a firm must install before it can get going. Once the grid or network is in place, the firm may see it as an input for which quantity is fixed, even in the long run. Having a fixed input in the long run is unusual; so, for simplicity, when this section refers to costs, it will not distinguish between short-run costs and long-run costs.

Because the cost of the grid or network is fixed, its cost per unit of output becomes smaller when the firm expands and can spread that cost over more units of output. So a firm's average total cost falls when its output rises, and in an industry in which that happens, there tends to be a monopoly called a **natural monopoly**. Let's see why.

Why natural monopolies arise

Consider the water supply industry in a large city where people pay for water according to their use, as measured by meters. Suppose that, for any firm in this industry, the average cost curve, *AC*, would be as shown in Figure 12.3. Suppose, too, that the total industry output is 16 billion litres a week. Let's see what the average production cost in this industry would be with different numbers of firms.

- **Four firms, each producing 4 billion litres a week.** *AC* in Figure 12.3 shows that each firm would have an average cost of 0.25p per litre.
- **Two firms, each producing 8 billion litres a week.** *AC* in Figure 12.3 shows that each firm would have an average cost of 0.15p per litre.

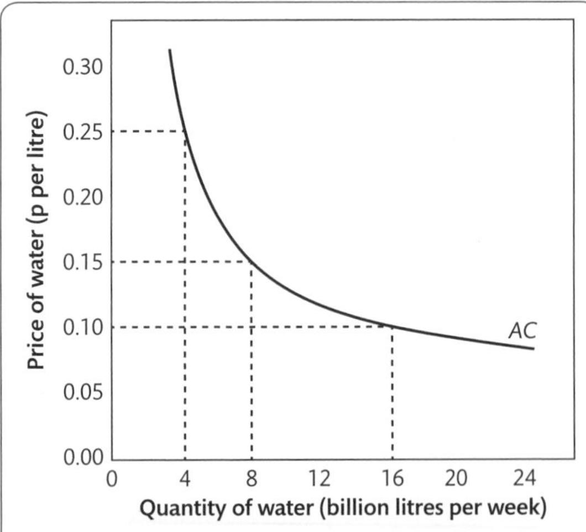

Figure 12.3 **If each firm's *LAC* slopes downwards, costs are lowest with a natural monopoly**

For example, if two firms each were to produce 8 billion litres a week, each would have an average cost of 0.15p per litre. If a monopoly produces 16 billion, its average cost will be 0.10p.

- **One firm producing 16 billion litres a week.** *AC* in Figure 12.3 shows that this firm would have an average cost of 0.10p per litre.

Because the average cost would be lowest with one firm, so the profit would be highest. So if there were more than one firm here, they might well merge to form a natural monopoly. Admittedly not every industry with a grid or network has a natural monopoly. For example, several companies have networks of parcel distribution depots and mobile phone masts. The costs of these networks are apparently not high enough to deter new entrants.

How natural monopolies want to behave

Suppose there is a natural monopoly in the water supply industry for the city concerned in Figure 12.3. Figure 12.4 shows how it might behave. This reproduces the *AC* curve from Figure 12.3. It also adds in a marginal cost curve, *MC*, to show the extra variable costs like wages and energy needed to supply each extra litre. For simplicity, it is assumed that this extra cost is always 0.05p per litre, so *MC* is horizontal.

Figure 12.4 also shows the market demand curve, *D*, which will also be the firm's average revenue curve, *AR*. Associated with this is the firm's marginal revenue curve, *MR*. To maximize its profit, this firm will set its output where *MR* intersects *MC*. This is at an output of 10 billion litres a week, and *D* shows that, to sell this quantity, the firm must set its price at 0.18p. *AC* at this output shows that the average cost of producing each litre is 0.13p per litre, so the firm will make the profit shown by the grey rectangle.

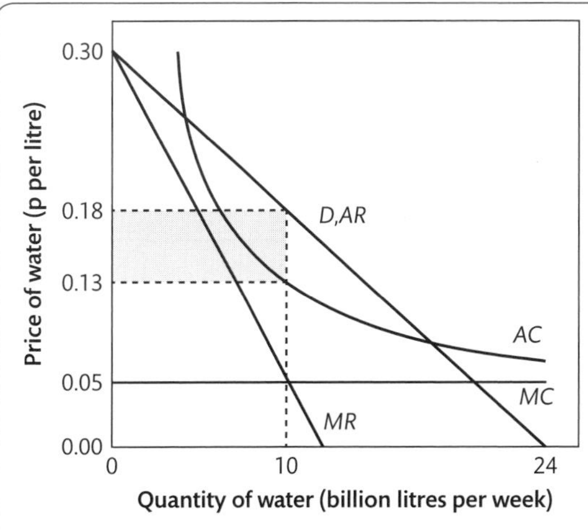

Figure 12.4 **The behaviour of an unregulated natural monopoly**

To maximize its profit, the firm sets its output where *MR* cuts *MC*, that is at 10 million litres per week. The demand curve shows that, to sell this output, it must set its price at 0.18p per litre. This is above its average cost of 0.13p, so it makes the profit shown in grey.

Nationalization, privatization, and regulation

In Figure 12.4, the monopolist's preferred output is 10 billion a week. Here, the marginal cost, read off *MC*, is 0.05p, which is below the price of 0.18p. But we know that consumption efficiency requires all prices to equal marginal cost. So a government may intervene to try to make the price and marginal cost equal.

However, there is a second-best problem here. There are few industries in which prices do equal marginal cost because few industries are in perfect competition; the second-best problem means that tackling the difference between price and marginal cost in natural monopolies, while leaving differences in most other industries, will not necessarily increase total welfare. Nevertheless, most governments believe that it will, and they often intervene in natural monopolies in one of two ways.

- **Buying the firm to bring it into public ownership, that is government ownership.** Then the government can control its price.
- **Leaving the firm in private ownership, but regulating it.** Usually the government will set up a body called a **regulator** to oversee it and control its price as the government wishes.

Table 12.7 **The principal UK regulators whose remit includes some natural monopolies**

Name	Natural monopolies over which it has authority
Ofcom (*The Office of Communications*)	Telecommunications
Ofgem (*The Office of Gas and Electricity Markets*)	Gas and electricity distribution
ORR (*The Office of Rail Regulation*)	The railway network
Ofwat (*The Water Services Regulation Authority*)	Water and sewerage
Postcomm (*The Postal Services Commission*)	Postal services

In the UK, the first approach was adopted from the 1940s to the 1980s. Taking industries into government ownership is called **nationalization**. Since then, almost all government owned natural monopolies have been sold to private shareholders in a process called **privatization**. Several regulatory bodies, called regulators, have been set up to regulate these industries, and Table 12.7 lists the main ones. Each regulator devises rules for the prices that the firms it regulates can set and we will now look at several possible rules.

The marginal cost pricing rule

A regulator might require a natural monopoly to set a price that results in its sales being at a level at which its marginal cost equals the price; this is called a **marginal cost pricing** rule. Figure 12.5 shows how the firm we have been studying would respond to this rule. To find the price it must set, we see where *MC* intersects *D*. This is at a price of 0.05p. With this price, the firm would sell 20 billion litres, and at that output *MC* shows that its marginal cost would also be 0.05p.

Because this pricing rule creates a price equal to marginal cost, there would be consumption efficiency if all other prices were to equal marginal cost. However, imposing this rule would create a problem: at the output of 20 billion litres, the price or *AR* of 0.05p is less than the average cost of 0.08p, read off *AC*, so the firm would make the loss shown by the pink grid.

If a regulator imposes a marginal cost pricing rule, and forces firms to make a loss, they will go out of business, and this will not help welfare. To avoid this, the regulator could ask the government to make up the loss for these firms with a subsidy. However, many governments prefer not to pay a subsidy, partly because they will have to raise taxes to finance the subsidy. Also, if firms know that they will receive a subsidy equal to any loss, they may not try hard to be efficient.

Instead of arranging a subsidy, the regulator may allow a firm to try to avoid a loss by using price discrimination. For example, the water company in Figure 12.5 might be required to adopt marginal cost pricing for domestic consumers, charging them 0.05p, but be allowed to charge business consumers more.

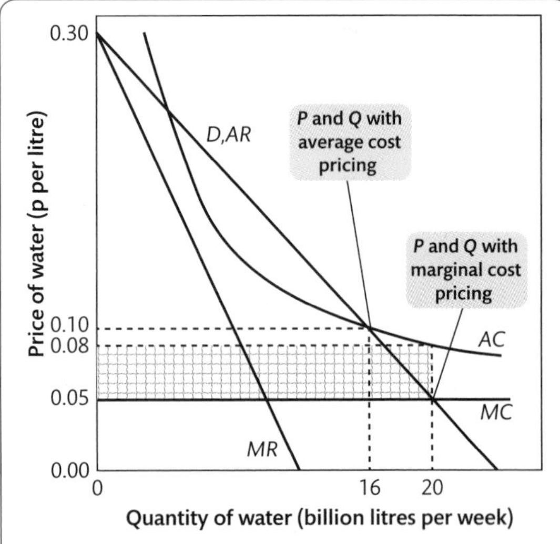

Figure 12.5 **Marginal cost pricing and average cost pricing rules**

With marginal cost pricing, the firm's output is where *MC* cuts *D*, 20 billion litres a week; here *MC* is 0.05p a litre, and the price needed to sell that quantity is also 0.05p. But *AC* is above *AR*, so the firm makes the loss shown by the pink grid. With average cost pricing, the firm's output is where *AC* cuts *D*, 16 billion litres; here *AC* is 0.10p a litre, and the price or *AR* needed to sell that quantity is also 0.10p. Because *AC* equals *AR*, the firm breaks even.

A two-part tariff

There is yet another way in which a regulator could help a firm that would make a loss under marginal cost pricing. This is to allow the firm to operate a **two-part tariff**: here, it will charge a price per litre equal to the marginal cost, but also impose on consumers an additional second charge that does not relate to their usage. For example, the monopoly in Figure 12.5 might send everyone a bill that charges them 0.05p per litre used plus anther sum, say £100 per year, called something like a 'standing charge' or 'network charge'.

This charge is effectively a tax levied by the monopoly. But it has an advantage over a tax levied by the government in that it is paid only by consumers. If the government were to make up the loss with a subsidy financed by general taxes, then even people who were not connected to this company would have to pay taxes for its water.

Note that a two-part tariff is not feasible for all natural monopolies. For example, an underground railway system cannot charge passengers an annual fee on top of their tickets.

The average cost pricing rule

Another pricing rule is to require a natural monopoly to set a price that results in its sales being at a level at which its average cost equals the price; this is called an **average cost pricing** rule. Figure 12.5 also shows how the firm we have been studying would respond to this rule.

To find the price at which it must set, we look where *AC* intersects *D*. This is at a price, or *AR*, of 0.10p. With this price, the firm would sell 16 billion litres, and *AC* shows that its average cost at that output would also be 0.10p. Because *AR* equals *AC*, the firm will break even rather than make a loss.

The price of 0.10p here does not equal the marginal cost of 0.05p, so average cost pricing does not lead to consumption efficiency. But at least it leads to a lower price than the 0.18p that would arise if the firm were allowed to maximize its profit, as in Figure 12.4. Also, unlike marginal cost pricing, it allows natural monopolies to break even instead of make losses.

Peak load pricing

We have so far ignored the fact that the demand for water fluctuates. In practice, there are seasonal variations, and demand can be 30% higher in the summer than in the winter, partly because more water is used in gardens and parks. In some natural monopolies, such as trains and electricity grids, demand fluctuates greatly even during each day.

People who consume when demand is highest impose the highest costs on suppliers. For example, to handle commuters, railway companies need more trains and bigger stations than they need at other times. So some regulators allow prices to fluctuate during the day or season in line with costs. This is why regulators allow rail fares to be relatively high during rush hours, and allow relatively low prices for off-peak electricity. One effect of high peak load prices is that it encourages some people to consume at off-peak times, so reducing the demand at peak times.

Some alternative pricing rules

To impose the rules that we have discussed, a regulator needs to know what the monopolist's costs are and what the market demand curve is. In practice, regulators have only partial information, so their rules are often less sophisticated than those we have looked at.

Three less-sophisticated rules have been used fairly widely in the UK, as follows.

- **Rate of return regulation**. Here, a regulator tells a firm to hold its prices down to ensure that the firm's annual profit does not exceed a given percentage of the value of its capital.
- **Revenue cap regulation**. Here, a regulator tells a firm that it can raise its price each year in line with other retail prices, as measured by the retail prices index (RPI). But the regulator may add that, each year, the firm should try to become more efficient

by a specified amount called X. So if the RPI were to rise by 5%, and the firm were given an X of 2%, then it could raise its prices each year by only (RPI - X), that is 3%. Regulators often set a new X every five years.

- **Price cap regulation**. This is a modified form of revenue cap legislation, which allows slightly larger price rises, given by (RPI - X + K). K is set in a way that allows bigger price rises for any firms that are deemed to need extra capital, in order to help them to finance it.

12.2 Everyday economics

Shorter mobile phone contracts

With the latest smartphones, consumers have often been offered only 18-month or 24-month contracts. But, as from May 2011, Ofcom will enforce EU rules that require mobile phone providers to offer 12-month contracts. The aim of the new ruling is to help to make it easier for consumers to use the latest models and to change to cheaper contracts.

'Mobile operators forced to offer 12-month contracts', *Money Saving Expert*, 27 January 2011
'Ofcom to force mobile operators to offer 12-month contracts', *The Next Web*, 28 January 2011

Comment The rising popularity of smartphones resulted in lengthier contracts that tied users in for up to two years. While shorter terms will give users greater flexibility, it is likely they will be more expensive per month.

Nationalization versus privatization

We have seen that governments may try to control the prices of natural monopolies by nationalizing their industries or by regulating them. In the 1940s, the UK government and many others chose nationalization. The arguments for this approach included the following.

- It was hoped that nationalization would allow the government to appoint managers who would pursue technical and economic efficiency, despite their firms having a monopoly situation.
- It was hoped that public ownership might lead to better informed control than regulation, because it is hard for regulators to acquire first-hand information about the industries.
- It was feared that regulators might be subject to **regulatory capture** by the industries they were meant to regulate; this means that the regulators might work so closely with the regulated industries that they came to work with them rather than control them.
- It was feared that private companies might be deterred from investing in regulated industries, because then companies would never know what regulations would be imposed in future.
- Many people on the political left believed that state control of the economy would improve its performance, and that this control would be easier if the state were to own some key industries.
- It was hoped that, free from the pursuit of profit, the publicly owned industries could take care of loss-making activities, such as railway lines and postal services in remote areas.
- It was hoped that industrial relations would improve if employees were to work for the publicly owned companies rather than private ones.
- It was feared that private companies might put the profit motive ahead of heath and safety.

By the 1980s, there was a reversal of this nationalization process in the UK and many other countries, with a policy of privatization, under which government-owned industries were sold to private shareholders and then usually supervised by regulators. The arguments for this included the following concerns with nationalized industries.

- For political reasons, previous governments sometimes made nationalized industries persist with activities that made high losses.
- Previous governments sometimes interfered with nationalized industries for economic reasons in periods of inflation by freezing prices and reducing invest-

ment, even if the industries needed higher prices and more investment for commercial reasons.

- Governments found it difficult to resist wage demands in the nationalized industries because unions knew these could always be funded in part by taxation.
- It was sometimes suggested that governments ran the industries in ways that would help them secure to votes rather than in the interests of the country as a whole.
- The revenues from selling the industries helped to finance government activities and so, in the years when they were sold, allowed taxes to be lower than they would otherwise have been.
- Shares were sold in a way that encouraged many people to become shareholders for the first time, so increasing the number of people with some ownership in industry. Admittedly, many new shareholders soon sold their shares for a profit.

12.5 Summary

- In an industry with very high fixed costs, average costs will fall up to a very high output.
- If average costs fall up to an output level close to that of the market, the most likely industry structure is a monopoly, called in these circumstances a natural monopoly.
- It would make no sense to break up a natural monopoly because costs would rise. But a government may try to control it by nationalizing it, or placing it under the control of a regulator.
- If a natural monopoly has to follow a marginal cost pricing rule to get $P = MC$, it will make a loss; this could be offset by a subsidy, or by letting it operate price discrimination, or by allowing it to impose a two-part tariff.
- If a natural monopoly has to follow an average cost pricing rule to get $P = AC$, it will break even.
- Regulators may impose other rules, such as limiting the rate of return natural monopolies can make, or linking their permitted price rises to the average level of retail prices in the economy.
- There are pros and cons of having nationalization or private industries under the control of a regulator. In the UK, nationalization was preferred between the 1940s and 1980s, but has since fallen from favour.

12.6 Monopolies, oligopolies, and competition policy

We have seen that monopolies and oligopolies have less incentive than other firms to operate with technical efficiency and economic efficiency. Monopolies may also practice price discrimination and so cause productive inefficiency. Further, both types of firm generally have prices above marginal cost to create consumption inefficiency.

All of these issues concern governments, and this final section looks at the main ways in which the UK and EU address and tackle them.

The UK's Office of Fair Trading (OFT)

In the UK, the government's attempt to tackle these issues is overseen by the Office of Fair Trading (OFT), which was set up in 1973. The OFT has a broad mission, which is to make markets work well for consumers. The OFT regards its work as having four main aspects.

- **Encouraging businesses to comply with EU and UK competition law and consumer law**. It also encourages them to go beyond the law and improve their practices through self-regulation.

- **Acting decisively to stop hardcore or flagrant offenders of the law.**
- **Helping consumers to make informed choices and to get the best value from markets.** It also helps to them resolve problems with suppliers by using Consumer Direct, a government-funded advice service.
- **Studying markets and recommending action where required.**

For the present chapter, we need consider only the OFT's concerns about markets in which some firms have large market shares or restrict competition in other ways. When the OFT gets worried about one of these markets, it refers the matter for a closer look by the Competition Commission.

The UK's Competition Commission (CC)

The Competition Commission (CC) was set up by the government in 1999, although it is essentially a restructuring of an earlier body called the Monopolies and Mergers Commission.

The CC usually studies cases that are referred to it by the OFT, but occasionally it receives a request from the government or a regulator. It undertakes three main types of activity.

- **It examines markets when it appears that competition may be being prevented, distorted, or restricted by any type of business practice.** After its examination, the CC is permitted to consult with the firms concerned, and then require changes to be made.
- **It studies sectors of the economy that have regulators if it is felt that the regulatory system is not working well, or if the regulator and the regulated firms are in dispute.** The CC will try to resolve the issues concerned, which may include the regulator's price controls.
- **It examines proposed or recent mergers under which the merged company's UK sales would exceed £70 million per year, or under which it would have more than a 25% market share and is likely to reduce competition substantially.** The CC has the power to forbid a merger, or to permit it only if certain conditions are met.

The market share issue in this final activity generally refers to a firm that supplies over 25% of the entire UK market, but the CC is empowered to look at firms that supply over 25% of a local market: for example, many dairies supply over 25% of the milk in their local areas.

The CC is also mindful of the global economy. For example, a firm that supplies over 25% of the UK market for gas may hardly need investigation, if it is in fierce competition with other overseas firms who have a foothold in the UK market that they could develop. This issue has become more important in recent years owing to globalization, that is the trend for the markets of different countries to interact and for firms to compete in the world or global economy.

Table 12.8 lists some recent CC decisions.

The European Commission (EC)

The European Union (EU) has always tried to ensure that firms in member countries compete fairly. In pursuit of this aim, it has empowered its executive arm, the European Commission (EC), to act in a variety of areas, which include the following.

- **Antitrust**. This refers to EU laws that forbid firms to make agreements that restrict competition. This covers cartels, which are secret agreement between competitors to fix or raise their prices, or to restrict their output, or to divide up their consumers. Antitrust concerns also cover **predatory pricing**, under which a multi-product firm sets a very low price on one product, either to make it impossible for competitors to survive or to deter new firms entering the industry.

Table 12.8 **Some recent Competition Commission activities in support of competition**

Concern and report date	Summary of CC action
A recent merger 7 May 2010	The OFT referred to the CC the recent merger of Live Nation, which promotes concerts and owns concert venues, with Ticketmaster, which sells tickets on behalf of promoters and venues. The CC concluded that the merger was acceptable.
A proposed merger 8 March 2010	The OFT referred to the CC the proposed acquisition by Brightsolid Group, which sells data to people researching family histories, of Friends Reunited, which makes some historical records available to people who use its social networking website. The CC felt that it would still be easy for other firms to build up and sell genealogical data, and approved the merger.
Anti-competitive practices 19 March 2009	The OFT referred the British Airports Authority (BAA) to the CC believing that, by owning many key UK airports, it reduced competition. The CC ruled that BAA must sell Gatwick and Stansted Airports within two years, as well as Glasgow or Edinburgh airports. Later, BAA successfully challenged the CC's ruling in the courts, but only after it had sold Gatwick.

Source: http://www.Competition-Commission.org.uk

- **Mergers**. If two firms that operate in the EU propose to merge, and their combined sales in either the EU or the world would exceed a stated level, then the EC vets the proposal. It does not matter where the firms have their head offices or factories. The EC can forbid these mergers, or at least restrain their activities in the EU, if it thinks they would seriously affect competition.
- **Liberalization**. This refers to EC support for promoting international competition in services such as transport, energy, postal services, and telecommunications; these industries have not always been highly competitive.
- **State aid control**. The EC does not want some EU governments to give support, such as subsidies, to some of their country's industries that would give them an unfair advantage over competitors in other EU countries. Its permission must be sought by governments wanting to offer state aid.
- **International activity**. Globalization is leading to more international companies and cartels. As a result, the activities of companies based outside the EU may affect competition within the EU. So the EC promotes international cooperation on competition policy, and has made agreements on competition with the EU's main trading partners.

Table 12.9 outlines some recent EC actions.

Deregulation

When many of the UK's nationalized industries were privatized, they became subject to controls by new

Table 12.9 **Some recent EC activities in support of competition**

Concern and date	Summary of CC action
Merger 26 January 2011	The EC prohibited the proposed merger between Aegean Airlines and Olympic Air. The two carriers control more than 90% of Greek domestic air transport, and the EC believed the merger would have led to higher fares for four million out of six million Greek and European consumers flying to and from Athens each year.
Antitrust 8 December 2010	The EC fined five liquid crystal display (LCD) panel producers a total of €649m for operating a cartel, along with Samsung Electronics, which harmed European buyers of television sets, computers, and other products that use the key LCD component. Samsung Electronics was not fined because it was the first to provide information about the cartel.
State aid 23 July 2009	The EC outlined three principles for state aid to banks with financial difficulties. The principles are: aided banks must be made viable in the long term without further state aid; aided banks and their owners must carry a fair burden of the restructuring costs; measures must be taken to protect competition between banks within the EU.

Source: Europa Press Release Archive on http://ec.europa.eu/comm/competition/antitrust/overview_en.html

regulatory bodies like those listed in Table 12.7. However, these regulators have far less control over the industries than the government had before they were privatized. So the privatization process was seen as resulting in less regulation or control, that is in **deregulation**.

However, deregulation has gone beyond privatization, and in the UK, the EU, and the US, and in many other countries, there is now less interference with industries than there was back in the 1980s. One major factor that has encouraged deregulation is a concern that regulation might actually have adverse effects on consumers, for reasons such as these:

- **regulators have only partial information about the industries they regulate**;
- **many more firms compete between countries, so many firms that were once monopolies or oligopolies now face active competition**;
- **technical change and innovation make it hard for regulators to keep pace with the needs of the industries they regulate**.

12.3 Everyday economics

Mining merger abandoned

Two of the world's largest mining companies, Rio Tinto and BHP Billiton, have abandoned their plans to merge. The companies, which have headquarters in-Australia, said the deal would save them $10b in costs. But it was fiercely opposed by regulators around the world, including those in Australia, China and Japan, and also the European Commission.

'BHP Billiton and Rio Tinto end iron ore tie-up', *The Telegraph*, 18 October 2010
'Plan to merge iron-ore mining giants is buried', *The Independent*, 19 October 2010

Comment Australia was the only country that could actually stop these two Australian firms merging. But aside from objections in Australia, those elsewhere suggested that the merged firms would face heavy sanctions, which would remove any financial benefit the merger might have.

12.6 Summary

- The UK's efforts to promote competition are overseen by the Office of Fair Trading (OFT). The OFT refers markets in which it thinks mergers or other practices may be against consumer interest for detailed studies by the Competition Commission (CC). The CC can require firms to change their practices and forbid proposed or recent mergers.
- The EU has given the European Commission (EC) powers to act in a variety of situations in which competition may be restricted.
- In the last two decades, there has been widespread deregulation, partly in the form of replacing state ownership with private firms supervised by a regulator, and partly with fewer other controls over firms.

In the next chapter we look at markets that, in the absence of government intervention, would fail to secure Pareto-efficiency because of the nature of the products traded in those markets.

abc Glossary

Average cost pricing: a firm setting a price that results in its sales being at a level at which its average cost equals its price, so it breaks even.

Consumption efficiency: applies to an economy in which it is not possible with a change in consumption to make one person better off without making anyone else worse off.

Consumption inefficiency: applies to an economy in which it is possible with a change in consumption to make one person better off without making anyone else worse off.

Deadweight loss of a monopoly: the fall in combined consumer surplus plus producer surplus (that is in total welfare) that would arise if a perfectly competitive industry became a monopoly.

Deregulation: a reduction in regulation.

Marginal cost pricing: a firm setting a price that results in its sales being at a level at which its marginal cost equals its price.

Market failure: the fact that a market economy will fail to produce a Pareto-efficient outcome.

Nationalization: taking a firm or industry into government ownership, that is public ownership.

Natural monopoly: the monopoly that tends to arise in an industry in which economies of scale persist up to high outputs in relation to the market.

Pareto-efficient: *see* Pareto principle.

Pareto-inefficient: *see* Pareto principle.

Pareto principle: the idea that resources are used Pareto-efficiently if no change in their use could make one person better off without making another worse off, but Pareto-inefficiently if a change in their use could make one person better off without making another person worse off.

Predatory pricing: arises when a firm sets a very low price on a product, to make it impossible for competitors to survive, or to deter new firms entering the industry.

Price cap regulation: when a regulator adjusts revenue cap regulation to allow bigger price rises for firms that need more profit to finance extra capital.

Privatization: selling a government-owned firm, that is a publicly owned firm, to private owners.

Productive efficiency: applies to an economy that, while using the same resources that it currently uses, could not produce more of one product without producing less of any other.

Productive inefficiency: applies to an economy that, while using the same resources that it currently uses, could produce more of one product without producing less of any other.

Rate of return regulation: when a regulator tells a firm that its prices must be held down to a level at which the firm's annual profit does not exceed a given percentage of the value of its capital.

Regulator: a regulatory body set up by the government to oversee and regulate an industry.

Regulatory capture: arises if a regulator works so closely with a regulated industry that it comes to work with them rather than to control them.

Revenue cap regulation: when a regulator allows a firm to raise its prices in line with retail prices or with retail prices minus a fixed percentage.

Technical efficiency: this applies to a firm that could not produce more output than it does with the level of resources that it currently uses.

Technical inefficiency: this applies to a firm that could produce more output than it does with the level of resources that it currently uses.

Two-part tariff: when a firm imposes two charges, only one of which is based on a customer's usage.

Welfare economics: the branch of economics that studies people's economic well-being or welfare.

Answers to in-text questions

12.1 The economy could produce 3 eggs and 1 fig, and allow Holly to consume 1 fig and 0 eggs, to get 10 utils, and allow Gary to consume 3 eggs and 0 figs, to get 30 utils. So Holly is better off and Gary is no worse off.

12.2 The firm could hire one fewer machine, and so save £20, and spend £10 on one more worker. It would lose 15 alphas from having one fewer machine, but gain 15 from having one more worker, so its output would remain the same while its costs fell by £10.

12.3 The economy might switch one machine to the beta-making firm from the alpha-making firm, and so make 30 more betas and 40 fewer alphas. It could make up the lost alphas by switching two workers from betas to alphas, but would lose 15 betas from each, that is a combined loss of 30. So taking both steps together, it would produce no more betas. So, to produce more beta, the economy must settle for having fewer alpha.

Questions for review

12.1 The text assumed that consumers are all rational. Can you think of some consumers who might not be rational? Would their behaviour prevent an economy from securing Pareto-efficiency in consumption?

12.2 A natural monopoly has a downward-sloping *AC* curve. Explain why its *MC* curve must be below this. Does this mean it would necessarily make a loss with a marginal cost pricing rule? Will it necessarily produce less if it faces an average cost pricing rule, and less still if it faces no rules at all?

12.3 Estimate the consumer surplus that arises from the unregulated natural monopoly in Figure 12.4. Use Figure 12.5 to find the consumer surplus with both marginal cost pricing and average cost pricing. (Note that the area of a triangle is equal to half of its length times its height.)

Questions for discussion

12.1 Like monopolists, monopolistic competitors set prices above marginal cost, yet the economics literature and the Competition Commission seem largely to ignore them. Should they be ignored?

12.2 Think of any producers who levy a two-part tariff on you. To what extent do you think that the part that relates to your usage reflects their marginal costs?

12.3 Look at the Competition Commission's website and look at its reports over the last three months. Do the majority of these seem concerned or unconcerned about the activities it has studied? Repeat this exercise with the European Commission.

12.4 Appraise the different possible pricing rules that a regulator might lay down for Royal Mail.

Common student errors

It is easy to confuse the different types of efficiency. For a country to have productive efficiency, and so be on its production possibility frontier, each firm must be technically efficient, with no idle or wastefully used resources, and economically efficient, and so produce at the lowest possible cost. Also, all firms must face the same input prices. To have consumption efficiency, each firm must set its output at a level at which its marginal cost equals its price. If all these efficiencies were to apply, there would be Pareto-efficiency, so it would be impossible to make one person better off without making another worse off. However, people's incomes might be very unequal.

13

Governments and Resource Allocation

Remember from Chapter 12 that if resources are used in what is termed a Pareto-inefficient way, then it is possible to alter the way in which they are used to make one person better off without making anyone else worse off. In a world in which resources are scarce, it is unsatisfactory to use them in a Pareto-inefficient way.

We hear about pollution almost daily, especially greenhouse gases. What sort of policies can be used to reduce pollution? Should we aim to have no pollution? In the UK, why are most schools and hospitals government-owned, while universities and doctors' surgeries are not? Why does the EU limit fishing in the North Sea? Does the democratic process lead to an efficient use of resources?

This chapter shows you how to answer questions like these, by understanding:

* what externalities are and how governments can try to tackle them;
* why is it efficient for society to have some pollution;
* what is meant by a public good and why most public goods, but not all, are provided by governments;
* why there could be overfishing unless governments intervene;
* how governments help to tackle situations in which consumers or producers lack some key information;
* many reasons why governments intervene in the provision of education and health care.

13.1 Externalities from consumption and production

In Chapter 12, we said that a market economy will fail to secure a Pareto-efficient allocation of resources, a result known as market failure. We also saw that one cause of market failure is that some firms are oligopolists or monopolists.

However, even if all firms were perfect competitors, there would still be market failure. This is because some types of product cause problems. In this chapter, we will discuss the following problem products:

- products that generate externalities;
- products known as public goods;
- products the suppliers of which use common resources;
- products for which there is asymmetric information between buyers and sellers;
- products known as merit goods or demerit goods;
- products for which there might be no market, that is to say a missing market;
- health care and education, in which many problems arise.

Governments often intervene in their economies to tackle the problems with these products, but we will see later that they, too, may fail to secure Pareto-efficiency. We will begin by looking at the problem with products that generate externalities.

The concept of externalities

Suppose you buy a T-shirt with a witty slogan. You are the consumer and benefit from wearing it. Several producers were involved in producing it and shared the production costs: these are the people who make the fabric, the people who used the fabric to make the T-shirt, and the shop that stored it until you bought it.

It may seem that the only consumer whose utility is affected by your T-shirt is you; it may seem that the only producers whose use of resources was affected by it were those directly involved producing it. In fact, though, your T-shirt may affect the utility of other consumers and the use of resources by other producers.

If your T-shirt causes other consumers to gain utility, or other producers to use fewer resources for their current output, then we say these people receive an **external benefit** or a **positive externality**. If your T-shirt causes other consumers to lose utility, or other producers to use more resources for their current output, then we say these people receive a **negative externality** or **external cost**.

Both the consumption and the production of your T-shirt could create externalities. Let's see how.

Externalities from consumption

Here are some ways in which your consumption of your T-shirt might generate externalities.

- **External benefit on other consumers**: people who find the slogan on your T-shirt amusing gain utility from seeing it.
- **External cost on other consumers**: people who find the slogan on your T-shirt tasteless or offensive lose utility from seeing it.
- **External benefit on producers not directly involved**: if you wear your T-shirt at work and make other workers happier, they may work harder, so your employer needs fewer workers.
- **External cost on producers not directly involved**: if you wear your T-shirt at work and offend other workers, they may work less hard, so your employer needs more workers.

Externalities from production

Here are some ways in which the production of your T-shirt might generate externalities.

- **External benefit on consumers not directly involved**: the farmer who grew the cotton for your

T-shirt might have attractive fields, which increase the utility of people living nearby.

- **External cost on consumers not directly involved**: the factory that wove the cotton into cloth might create a lot of noise, which reduces the utility of people living nearby.
- **External benefit on other producers**: the cotton farmer might have used an insecticide that killed insects that could have destroyed the crops of other farmers. So other farmers may need to use less insecticide themselves.
- **External cost on other producers**: the firm that made the dye for your T-shirt might have dumped its waste in a nearby river and killed many fish, so firms that fish in the river had to spend more hours finding fish to catch.

The importance of externalities

Our T-shirt example hints at how consumption and production can lead to many externalities. Among all externalities, the one that causes the most concern is the emission of greenhouse gases by producers and consumers who burn fossil fuels. These gases are widely accepted as the chief cause of climate change, and this could have serious consequences, including:

- **biodiversity effects**, because many plant and animal species may become extinct;
- **rising sea levels**, because the polar ice caps are melting; as a result, low-level land will flood more often, or in some cases be lost to the sea;
- **water supply problems**, because some areas may become more prone to droughts;
- **food supply problems**, because some fertile areas may become infertile;
- **disease problems**, because hotter weather may cause more food poisoning and malaria; admittedly, hotter weather may also reduce illnesses like the common cold and pneumonia.

Other external costs that attract much publicity include noise from roads and aircraft, litter, and the effects of 'neighbours from hell'.

Marginal private cost

To see how externalities can prevent a Pareto-efficient allocation of resources, we will now consider the potato market in a country. Suppose many firms supply identical potatoes, so the industry is in perfect competition. In Figure 13.1, *D* is the market demand curve and *S* is the short-run supply curve. In the absence of government intervention, the market settles where these curves intersect, with a price of 70p per kg and an output of 100 million kg per week.

We saw in Chapter 9 that the market supply curve in perfect competition is based on the short-run marginal cost curves of the firms in the industry, so it shows the extra cost that producers would incur if they were to produce an extra kg. For example, if

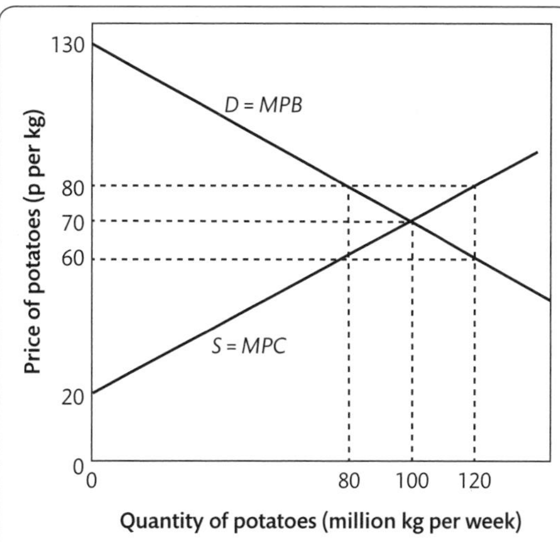

Figure 13.1 **Perfect competition is efficient if there are no externalities**

Perfect competition gives an output of 100 million kg a week, which is efficient here. At a lower output, like 80 million, extra kgs would benefit consumers more than they cost producers. At a higher output like 120 kg, cutting back would reduce costs by more than benefits.

output is 80 million kg a week, then *S* shows that it will cost 60p to produce one more kg.

The cost to the producers of a product is called its **private cost**, and the extra private cost of an extra unit of output is the **marginal private cost** (*MPC*). Because *S* in Figure 13.1 shows the *MPC* at each quantity, it is also labelled *MPC*.

Marginal private benefit

The benefit to the consumers of a product is called its **private benefit**, and the extra private benefit that consumers get from consuming an extra unit is the **marginal private benefit** (*MPB*). The demand curve in Figure 13.1, *D*, indicates the *MPB* of potatoes at each quantity, so it is also labelled *MPB*. For example, if output is 80 million kg a week, then *D* shows that someone will be willing to pay 80p for an extra potato, so the *MPB* is 80p.

Efficiency if there are no externalities

We will now use the concepts of marginal private benefits and costs to show why the perfectly competitive potato market would give Pareto-efficiency, *if there were no externalities.*

- **If output were below the market equilibrium** of 100 million kg a week at, say, 80 million, then the *MPB* would exceed the *MPC*, so society would be better off producing more potatoes; this is because society values extra potatoes more highly than the resources they would use.
- **If output were above the market equilibrium** at, say, 120 million a week, then the *MPC* would exceed the *MPB*, so society would be better off by producing fewer potatoes; this is because society would value the resources saved more highly than the potatoes lost.

Marginal social cost

We will now see why externalities would make this market outcome Pareto-inefficient. We will explain the effect using Figure 13.2. Part (a) here shows what happens if there are external costs, and part (b) shows what happens if there are instead external benefits. Each part repeats *MPB* and *MPC* from Figure 13.1.

In part (a) of Figure 13.2, we suppose that, before harvesting potatoes, farmers spray defoliant chemicals on them; these smell foul to people living nearby, and may spread by air, damaging the health of people at a distance. So producing potatoes has an external cost on consumers, because each potato affects many consumers, not only the one who eats it. The total cost to society of any product is its private cost plus its external cost and is called its **social cost**.

When an extra unit of a product with externalities is produced, the increase in the amount of externalities it generates is called its **marginal external cost** (*MEC*). And the extra total or social cost, which equals *MPC* plus *MEC*, is called its **marginal social cost** (*MSC*). Suppose we can somehow value external costs, and find that the *MEC* of the 80 millionth kg of potatoes is 20p. Then the *MSC* of that kg is 80p, which equals its *MPC* of 60p plus its *MEC* of 20p.

The *MEC* might be a constant 20p for every extra kg, but it need not be constant. We will suppose that *MEC* rises each time an extra kg is produced; this would happen if, as output rises, farmers were to grow potatoes on fields closer to towns, so that more people were affected by the defoliant. So if output were above 80 million kg, say 100 million, then the *MEC* would be above 20p, say 25p. So the *MSC* would be the *MPC* here of 70p plus the *MEC* of 25p, that is 95p.

In part (a) of Figure 13.2, the curve *MSC* plots the marginal social cost at each output level. The gap between *MSC* and *MPC* at each output level equals the *MEC* there, and is 20p at an output of 80 million kg and 25p at 100 million kg. In part (b) of the figure, we assume there are no external costs, so here *MSC* equals *MPC*.

Marginal social benefit

In part (b) of Figure 13.2, we suppose that potato farmers use pesticides. As a result, other farmers who grow other crops that are attacked by the same pests need

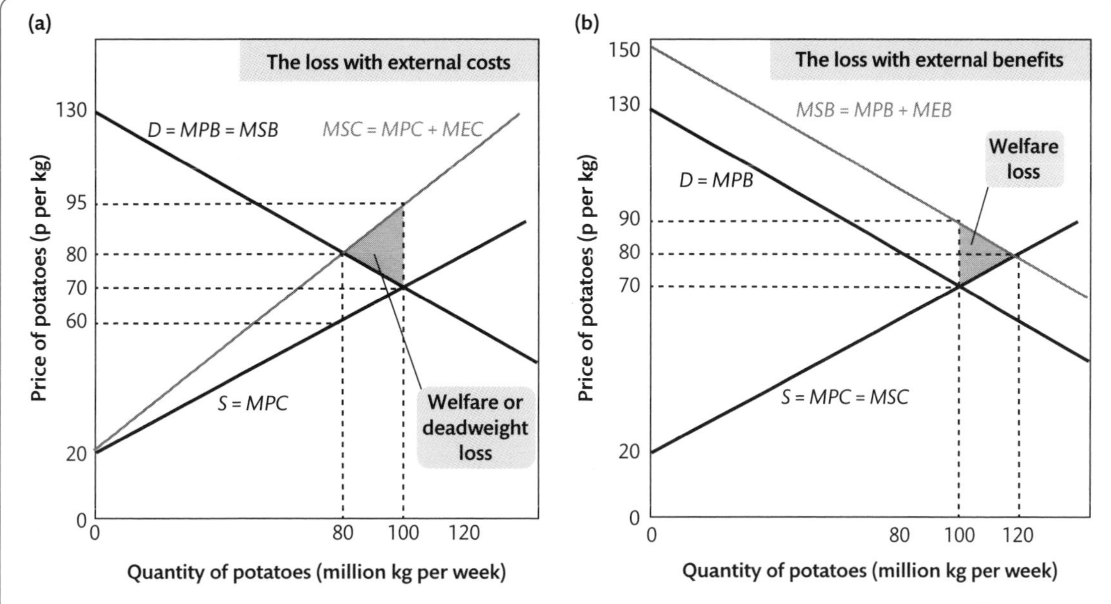

Figure 13.2 **Welfare losses in perfect competition from externalities**

In each part, a competitive market would give an output of 100 million kg of potatoes a week at a price of 70p. In part (a), external costs create an *MSC* curve above *MPC*; the efficient output is 80 million, where this *MSC* cuts *MSB*. Each kg between 80 and 100 million creates more cost than benefit, and so generates the welfare (or deadweight) loss shaded grey. In part (b), external benefits create an *MSB* curve above *MPB*; the efficient output is 120 million, where this *MSB* cuts *MSC*. Each kg between 100 million and 120 million would create more benefit than cost, giving to society the net welfare shaded grey—but this welfare is lost with perfect competition.

to use less pesticide because potato farmers have already killed many of the pests. So producing potatoes has an external benefit on producers, because producing a potato affects other producers, not only the one that grows it. The total benefit of any product to society equals its private benefit plus its external benefit and is called its **social benefit**.

Suppose an extra unit of output is produced and leads to more external benefit. The extra external benefit is called the **marginal external benefit** (*MEB*). And the extra total or social benefit, that is *MPB* plus *MEB*, is called the **marginal social benefit** (*MSB*). Suppose we can somehow value external benefits, and suppose the *MEB* of the 100 millionth kg of these potatoes is 20p. Then the *MSB* of that kg is 70p for its *MPB* plus 20p for its *MEB*, that is 90p.

Suppose for simplicity that the *MEB* is a constant 20p for each extra kg. Then the *MSB* at each output level will be as shown in part (b) of Figure 13.2 by the curve *MSB*. The gap between *MSB* and *MPB* at each output level equals the *MEB* at that output, which is always 20p. In part (a) of the figure, we assume there are no external benefits. So here *MSB* equals *MPB*.

The efficient outcome with external costs

In part (a) of Figure 13.2, the market output of 100 million kg is inefficient. This is because each kg beyond 80 million kg would have a total cost, as shown by *MSC*, that exceeded its total benefit, as shown by *MSB*. So these units create a welfare loss for society equal to the gap between *MSC* and *MPB*. The total loss that arises from units beyond 80 million kg is called a deadweight loss, and is shown by a grey triangle.

The efficient output is 80 million kg, where *MSC* = *MSB*. Up to this level, each extra unit generates more social benefits than social costs. Admittedly, each of these 80 million kg has generated an extra external cost shown by the gap between *MSC* and *MPB*, and given the adverse media coverage of externalities, you may think it seems wrong that the efficient output is one for which there are any external costs. But it *is* efficient to produce 80 million kg, despite the external costs, because each unit produced up to that level creates for society more extra benefit than extra cost.

In part (a) of Figure 13.2, the *MSC* curve was above the *MPC* curve because production created external costs for consumers. But the *MSC* curve will be above the *MPC* curve for all products with external costs, whether the external costs are created by consumption or production, and whether they are felt by producers or consumers. So, for every product with external costs, the efficient output is less than a perfectly competitive market would produce.

The efficient outcome with external benefits

In part (b) of Figure 13.2, as in Part (a), the market output of 100 million kg is inefficient. In part (b), this is because, up to an output of 120 million kg, each extra kg would generate a total benefit, as shown by *MSB*, that exceeded its total cost, as shown by *MSC*. So each unit up to 120 million would create a welfare gain for society equal to the gap between *MSB* and *MPC*. So the efficient output level is 120 million kg, and the perfectly competitive market's output of 100 million kg means that society never gains the potential welfare shown by the grey triangle.

In part (b) of Figure 13.2, the *MSB* curve was above the *MPB* curve because production created external costs for producers. But the *MSB* curve is above the *MPB* curve for all products with external benefits, whether the external benefits are created by consumption or production, and whether they are felt by producers or consumers.

So, for every product with external benefits, the efficient output is less than a perfectly competitive market would produce.

13.1 Everyday economics

The 20 largest emitters of CO_2 in 2009

Country	Total million tonnes	Tonnes per head	Country	Total million tonnes	Tonnes per head
Australia	418	19.6	UK	520	8.4
Saudi Arabia	470	18.6	Spain	330	7.1
US	5,425	17.7	Italy	408	7.0
Canada	541	16.2	Iran	527	6.9
Taiwan	291	12.7	France	397	6.3
Russia	1,572	11.2	China	7,711	5.8
South Korea	528	10.9	Mexico	444	4.0
Germany	766	9.3	Brazil	420	2.1
South Africa	450	9.2	Indonesia	413	1.7
Japan	1,098	8.6	India	1,602	1.4

Source: International Energy Statistics, US Energy Information Administration, 2009

Comment It is easy enough to provide estimates like these to show how much each country emits in greenhouse gases. But valuing the effect, or external cost, of these emissions is very hard, and some people dispute the general view that they are causing climate change with severe consequences. China produces the most greenhouse gases, but many countries far exceed it in relation to population.

13.1 Summary

- There are many types of product for which a perfectly competitive market would supply a pareto-inefficient output level.
- One type is products the production or consumption of which affects producers and consumers other than those who have produced it or consumed it: these effects are called externalities.
- If producing or consuming a product creates external costs, then the marginal social cost of the product exceeds its marginal private cost, and a perfectly competitive market will produce too much.

- If producing or consuming a product creates external benefits, then the marginal social benefit of the product exceeds its marginal private benefit, and a perfectly competitive market will produce too little.

13.2 Government policies for externalities

We have seen that if consumption or production create externalities, then even markets in perfect competition will fail to secure a Pareto-efficient allocation of resources. However, governments can then intervene, and in principle they can even ensure that the outcome is efficient, but to do that they will need to know the value of each externality, and unfortunately these can rarely be estimated accurately.

Governments tackle external costs by trying to reduce them, and in this section we will see how they do this; we will also see briefly how they may tackle external benefits.

Regulations

One way of reducing external costs is with regulations. For example, the UK government has regulations limiting many emissions from vehicles and factories. But regulations have two problems.

- **Emissions must be monitored to check that they are at legal levels, but this can be difficult and costly.**
- **To seem fair, the government may let firms with the same output have the same emissions, but there might be cheaper ways of securing any desired total fall in emissions.**

To illustrate this second problem, suppose the government wants potato farms to use 30,000 tonnes less of defoliant. Suppose, too, that we can divide potato farms into hill farms and lowland farms. And suppose that each group has the same total output and uses the same amount of defoliant to create the same amount of pollution.

Now suppose the government imposes a regulation that, to seem fair, results in each group of farms having to use 15,000 tonnes less of defoliant. And suppose each individual farm switches some of its land to a new type of potato that has less foliage, and so needs less defoliant. But suppose this new type of potato needs more fertilizer, especially on hill farms. Then it would cost hill farms more than lowland ones to maintain their current total potato output, and so cost them more to reduce pollution.

In Figure 13.3, the horizontal axes measure the amounts by which farms in each group reduce their pollution. The extra cost of using one fewer unit of a pollutant is the **marginal cost of reducing pollution**, and is shown by the curves labelled *MCRP*; these curves slope upwards because cutting pollution usually becomes more costly with every tonne that is cut. For example, each time a farm uses 1 tonne less of defoliant, it may switch slightly less suitable land to the new potatoes and so spend even more on extra fertilizer. The *MCRP* curves show, for example, that if each group of farms were to cut pollution by 15,000 tonnes, the cost of cutting the last tonne would be £800 for hill farms and £100 for lowland farms. Allowing for the cost of cutting each of the 15,000 tonnes, the total cost of this cut for each group would be as shown by the grey areas.

However, it would cost the economy less to let hill farms cut back by only 10,000 tonnes, and make lowland farms cut back by 20,000. Hill farms would then save the amount shown by the pink grid in part (a); this is much more than the extra cost for the lowland farms shown by the pink grid in part (b). But lowland farmers

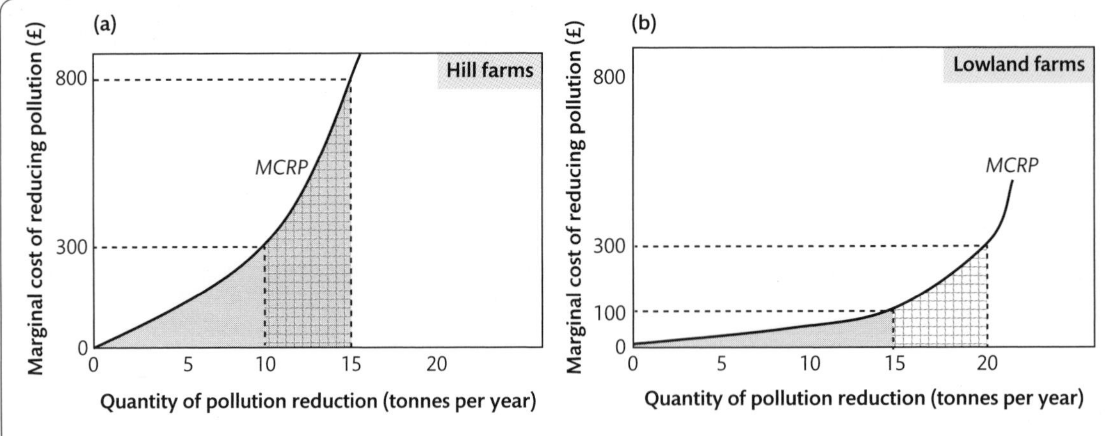

Figure 13.3 **The least cost way to cut pollution**

The *MCRP* curves show the extra cost of cutting pollution by another tonne; *MCRP* is highest for hill farms. If each type of farm had to cut back by 15,000 tonnes, the total cost for each type would be as shown by the grey areas. But if hill farms were to cut back by just 10,000 tonnes, they would save the costs shown by the pink grid in part (a); if lowland farms were to cut back by 20,000 tonnes, they would incur the extra costs shown by the pink grid in part (b). As the pink grid in part (a) is bigger than the pink grid in Part (b), the total cost of cutting back by 30,000 tonnes would be less.

might object if they were to face tougher regulations than hill farmers.

Taxes on products

Another way of reducing external costs is to tax the products that lead to them. To show this, Figure 13.4 repeats the example in part (a) of Figure 13.2. Without intervention, the output here will be 100 million kg of potatoes a week, but the efficient output is 80 million. The government could secure this with a specific tax of 20p per kg.

We saw in Chapter 5 that a tax on expenditure creates a new curve, *S + tax*, which is above the original one by the amount of the tax. So, in Figure 13.4, the new curve *S + tax* is 20p above the original supply curve *S*. The market settles where S + tax intersects *D*, at the desired efficient output of 80 million kg. Consumers will pay a price of 80p, where *S + tax* intersects *D*, but 20p will go to the government, leaving 60p for producers.

The government could instead impose an *ad valorem* tax of 33%. This would create an *S + tax* curve that is one third higher than *S* at each quantity. This curve is not shown in Figure 13.4, but at an output of 80 million it would be one third above *S* at 80p and intersect *D* there. So the market would again settle at an output of 80 million kg and a consumer price of 80p.

A problem with these taxes is that they do not hit most of the farms for which it costs least to switch to the new potatoes. So they do not achieve a given cut in pollution at the lowest possible cost.

Emissions or Pigovian taxes

A government can use a tax to cut pollution at the lowest possible cost, but to do so it must tax pollution, and not use a tax on products as it did in Figure 13.4. Taxes on pollution have two names:

- **emission taxes**, because they tax emissions of pollutants;
- **Pigovian taxes**, after the British economist Arthur Pigou, who first proposed them in 1920.

To illustrate these taxes, we will continue with our example. What is needed is a tax on each unit of pollutant, in our case defoliant, that is set to equal the

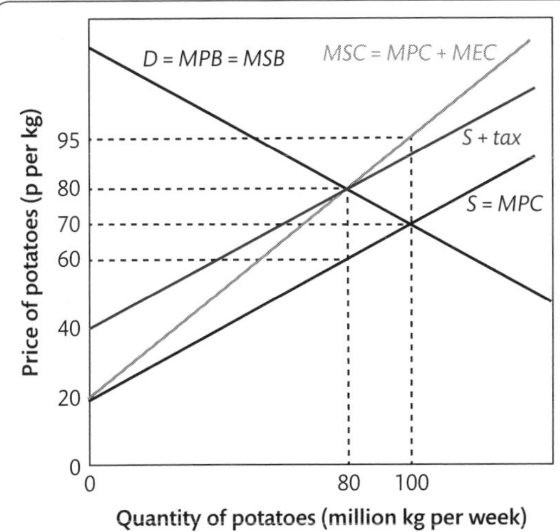

Figure 13.4 **Tackling an external cost with taxes**

A specific tax of 20p per unit of output would create the curve *S* + *tax* and reduce output from the initial level of 100 million kg per week to the efficient level of 80 million. A 33% *ad valorem* tax would result in the same output by producing a *S* + *tax* curve that is one third above the *S* curve.

marginal external cost of that unit of pollutant. Then farmers that consider producing an extra tonne of potatoes will face two marginal costs:

- **the marginal production cost of those potatoes**, which they pay in the cost of their extra inputs;
- **the marginal external cost of those potatoes**, which they pay in the tax on the defoliant.

So the marginal cost of potatoes to farms, and in turn their individual supply curves, now allow for both the *MPC* and the *MEC* of the potatoes, that is their marginal social cost, *MSC*. So the market supply curve will now be as shown by the *MSC* curve in Figure 13.4. Then the market will secure the efficient output of 80 million kg a week.

Suppose that, at this output, the *MEC* of a tonne of defoliant is £300. Then the tax should be £300 a tonne. This tax will encourage firms to cut back on defoliant. To maintain their output, they will switch some production to new potatoes and spend more on fertilizer. They will switch as long as the cost of switching, that is their *MCRP*, is less than the tax of £300. Looking at Figure 13.3, we can see that hill farms will reduce their pollution by 10,000 tonnes; after that, their *MRCP* is above £300, so it will be cheaper to pay the tax than cut back any more. Likewise, lowland farms will reduce their pollution by 20,000 tonnes, because after that their *MCRP* is above £300. We have seen that these reductions will reduce pollution at the lowest possible cost.

Tradable permits

Another way to reduce pollution is with emission permits. Suppose, in Figure 13.3, that the government wants to cut pollution by a total of 30,000 tonnes a week. It could legislate that, in future, each farm needs a permit for each tonne of defoliant it uses, and it could issue enough permits to let them use 30,000 tonnes less than they use now. It could allocate these permits in various ways: for example, it could divide them between farms in proportion to their current potato crops.

Suppose the government allocates permits to hill farms that mean that, between them, they could in future use 15,000 tonnes less of defoliant than before. And suppose it does the same for the lowland farms. Then it may seem that each type of farm must reduce its pollution by 15,000 tonnes, even though it is more efficient for pollution to be cut chiefly by lowland farms.

This problem can be solved by having **tradable permits** that firms may buy and sell. Farms that buy permits can then reduce their defoliant use by less, while farms that sell them must reduce their use by more. In the example of Figure 13.3, hill farms will buy permits for 5,000 tonnes from lowland farms, at a price of £300 a permit. To see why, consider each type of farm.

- **Hill farms**. Buying 5,000 permits allows them to cut their pollutant use by 10,000 tonnes instead of 15,000. For each tonne between 10,000 and 15,000 that they no longer cut back, they must buy a permit for £300, but they gain because this is less than the cost of cutting back, which they would otherwise face, as shown by *MCRP*.

- **Lowland farms**. Selling 5,000 permits forces them to cut their pollutant use by 20,000 tonnes instead of 15,000. So they face the extra costs shown by *MCRP* between 15,000 and 20,000 tonnes, but they gain because the total amount of these costs is less than they get by selling 5,000 permits at £300 each.

Establishing property rights

There is another way of reducing pollution that works only in cases in which few people are affected by the emission. To see this, suppose that one isolated farm affects only 20 households.

The government could make a law that gave people the property right to the air by their homes: a **property right** to something means owning it and so having the rights over it. In this case, the households would be able to let the farm use defoliant only if it were to pay them compensation for the pollution. Alternatively, the government could give the property rights to the farm, and allow it to use the defoliant unless the affected households paid it a sum sufficient to persuade it not to.

Whoever has the rights, the pollution will end up at the efficient level. This is where the *MCRP* with a pollutant equals its *MEC*: there is no point cutting back more, because the cost of doing so would exceed the value of the external cost that would be avoided. In our example, we will suppose the *MEC* is £300. Let's see why the *MCRP* will end up also at £300.

- **Householders are given the property rights**. With *MEC* at £300, households would have to be paid at least £300 for every tonne of pollution they permitted. The farm would actually cut back its pollution as long as *MCRP* was less than £300, because it would cost less to cut back its pollution than to pay households £300. But the farm would not cut back its pollution any more, because it would be cheaper to pay households £300 for each extra tonne of pollution than to cut back on pollution.
- **The firm is given the property rights**. With *MEC* at £300, households would offer to pay the farm £300 a tonne to reduce its pollution. The farm would then be willing to cut back its pollution as long as the *MCRP* were less than £300, because the payments from households would cover its costs in reducing pollution, but it would not cut back its pollution any more when the *MCRP* was more than £300.

The fact that compensation agreements regarding pollution will lead to the efficient level of pollution, no matter which party has the property rights, was first shown in 1960 by the British economist Ronald Coase and is called the **Coase theorem**.

The advantage of the property rights approach is that the government does not have to measure pollution. The disadvantage of it is that, in practice, pollution usually affects many people. For example, a factory might emit pollutants that affect millions of people over a wide area. In this case, the costs to the polluter of contacting all the affected people, or vice versa, would be prohibitively high. These costs of making a deal are called **transactions costs**.

Government provision

Suppose we had a market economy. Then people would have to hire private firms to empty their dustbins and dispose of the rubbish. This would encourage people to have smoky or dangerous bonfires, or to indulge in fly-tipping, or to allow their rubbish to rot, encouraging vermin and disease. In short, there would be huge external costs.

The government largely avoids these externalities by using a different policy from those we have considered so far. It arranges for local authorities to provide a rubbish collection and disposal service, which is paid for out of tax revenue.

Policies for external benefits

When the production or consumption of a product results in external benefits, the government wants output to expand. To see how it could do this, Figure 13.5 repeats part (b) of Figure 13.3. Here, the only externality generated by potato farms is an external benefit; this arises from their use of pesticides that benefit other farms. The government would like to raise output from the 100 million kg week that would arise with a market economy up to 120 million, because each kg of potatoes generates 20p worth of external benefits, that is the gap between *MSB* and *MPB*.

To secure this output, the government could pay a subsidy of 20p per kg to potato farms. This subsidy can be seen as a negative tax, which creates the new curve *S-sub* that is 20p below the original supply curve, *S*. The market settles where *S-sub* intersects *D*, with the efficient output of 120 million and a price of 60p for consumers. But producers also collect 20p from the subsidy, to get 80p in all, which their initial supply curve *S* shows is the amount they need to produce 120 million.

One example of such a subsidy is that paid to UK bus firms. Buses create external benefits because they reduce congestion on the roads, by encouraging some people not to use their cars.

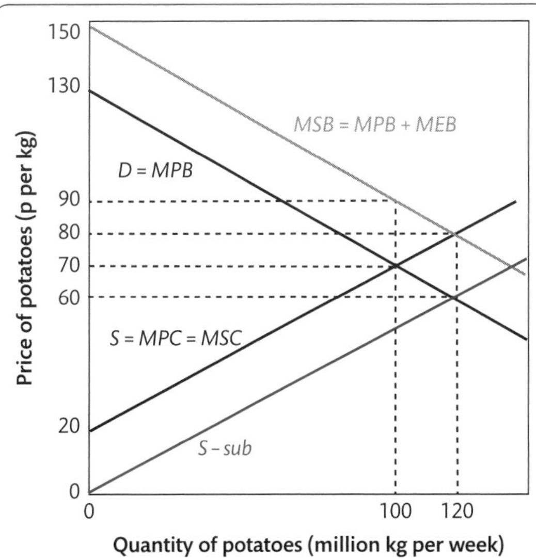

Figure 13.5 **Tackling an external benefit with a subsidy**

A subsidy of 20p per unit of output would create the curve *S - sub* and raise output from the initial level of 100 million kg per week to the efficient level of 120 million.

13.2 Everyday economics

Disappointment and hope in Copenhagen

In 2009, the UN held a climate change conference in Copenhagen that was attended by over 190 countries. Many people hoped that the countries would agree to legally binding targets for the emission of greenhouse gases. Instead, they merely pledged to ensure that temperatures do not rise by more than 2°C, and although some countries volunteered targets, these were not sufficient to achieve that. More positively, developed nations pledged aid to developing countries to help them to reduce their emissions, and some people saw the conference as a useful step towards future global agreements.

'Copenhagen accounting: what countries are currently offering on climate', *The Economist*, 16 February 2010
'Low targets, goals dropped: Copenhagen ends in failure', *The Guardian*, 19 December 2009

Comment Since the conference, many more countries have set targets for the emission of greenhouse gases. Efforts to reduce these emissions are sure to intensify, and will use many measures. For example, there will be tighter regulations over emissions so that new homes will be better insulated and coal-fired power stations will be replaced by ones using the tides, wind, and nuclear power. There will also be more taxes on products that generate externalities, such as fuel and large cars. And some countries may have a 'carbon tax', which is an emissions tax on CO_2. All this will stimulate research into new technologies, like hydrogen cars and solar power.

13.2 Summary

- External costs can be tackled in many ways.
- A problem with many policies is that they might not secure a given reduction in pollution at the lowest possible cost. This applies to regulations about the level of external cost that each firm may generate and to taxes on products the production or consumption of which generates external costs.

- This problem can be avoided with taxes on emissions, which tax the actual amount of pollution, and with tradable emission permits that firms would be required to have in order to be allowed to pollute.
- If the number of parties affected by an externality is small, an efficient outcome may be possible if the government confines itself simply to determining which party has the relevant property rights and allowing the parties to negotiate.
- The output of products that generate external benefits can be stimulated with subsidies.

13.3 Public goods

Economists use the term 'public good' for a specific type of product for which perfect competition is unlikely to secure a Pareto-efficient output. To understand what this type of product is, we need to study the concepts of rivalry and excludability.

Rivalry and non-rivalry

Imagine you are consuming a product: could an extra person come along and also consume it at the same time? If not, then the product is called **rival**, because the extra person and you would be rivals for it. Rival products fall into three groups.

- **Some can be consumed by only one person**. Examples include your last haircut or appointment with a doctor.
- **Some can be consumed by more than one person, but not at the same time**. Examples include your bicycle or your computer.
- **Some can be consumed by more than one person at the same time, but it is impossible for an extra person to come and consume them at the same time**. Examples include a school lesson and a movie if the classroom or cinema is full.

Now imagine you are consuming a product and an extra person could come along and consume it at the same time. Then the product would be **non-rival**. The following are some examples.

- A school lesson and a movie if the classroom or cinema is not full.
- The music provided by a busker, the light from a streetlamp, and the use of a road. You might benefit from one of these at, say 11pm tonight, but no doubt an extra person could also benefit.
- The defence provided by the armed forces, and the law and order provided by the police, courts, and prisons. You constantly benefit from the country being defended and many criminals being locked up, yet babies and immigrants can arrive and also get the same benefits.

The concepts of rivalry and non-rivalry also apply to natural resources. Here are some examples.

- **Rival natural resources**: these include nectar that bees gather for honey, fishes in the open sea, and mineral water. If one person's bees take nectar from a certain plant, then no one else's bees can take it. And if you eat a fish from the open sea or drink some mineral water, then no one else can come and consume that fish or water.
- **Non-rival natural resources**: these include beautiful waterfalls and sunsets. If you are enjoying one of

these, extra people can come along and enjoy them too.

Excludability and non-excludability

Imagine you want to consume a product or a natural resource, and you could be excluded from consuming it if you were to refuse to pay: then we say the product or resource is **excludable**. Excludable items fall into two groups:

- products and resources from which non-payers *could be* excluded and *are* excluded, like haircuts, bicycles, computers, movies, and mineral water;
- products and resources from which non-payers *could be* excluded, but *are not* excluded. Examples include lessons in UK state schools, doctors' appointments in the UK, and most waterfalls.

Now imagine you want to consume a product or resource, and you could not be excluded from consuming it if you were to refuse to pay: then the product or resources would be **non-excludable**. Here are some examples.

- The music provided by a busker and the lighting provided by a streetlamp. Their suppliers cannot supply the music and lighting only when people who have paid are in the vicinity.
- The defence provided by the armed forces, and the law and order services provided by the police, courts, and prisons. If any of these suppliers keep out an invader or lock up a criminal, they cannot confine the benefits only to people who pay.
- Nectar taken by bees, fishes in the open sea, and beautiful sunsets. People with plants cannot confine the nectar only to beekeepers who pay, and there is no one to charge for taking fish from the open sea or for looking at sunsets.

Sometimes, it is hard to decide if a product is excludable. For example, could people be excluded from using roads if they were to refuse to pay? The answer is 'no' for minor roads, where having tollbooths at each entrance would cost too much, and 'yes' for motorways, where having tollbooths at each entrance would be affordable. Note that motorways are excludable because non-payers *could be* excluded; so they are excludable, even if there is no toll so that non-payers are allowed.

Sometimes, a change in technology can transform a non-excludable product into an excludable one. For example, it might become feasible to levy charges for using minor roads if satellite technology were used to record car movements.

Four types of good

Table 13.1 lists all the products and resources that we have just mentioned, and it divides them into four groups with the following names.

- **Private goods**: these are products or resources that are both rival and excludable.
- **Common goods or common resources**: these are products or resources that are rival, but non-excludable.
- **Club goods**: these are products or resources that are non-rival, but are excludable.
- **Public goods**: these are products or resources that are non-rival and also non-excludable.

Note that a public good is *not* defined as a product supplied by the government or public sector. Some of their products are *not* public goods, for example state school education and NHS health care. And some public goods have nothing to do with the public sector, like sunsets and music from buskers.

Question 13.1 What types of good are (**a**) lectures for your economics course and (**b**) TV broadcasts?

Table 13.1 **The definitions of four types of good**

Private goods	**Club goods**
Rival *and* excludable	**Non-rival *and* excludable**
Haircut Doctor's appointments Bicycles Computers School lessons *(if full)* Movies *(if full)* Mineral water	School lessons *(if not full)* Movies *(if not full)* Minor roads *(when satellite technology becomes possible)* Motorways Waterfalls
Common goods or common resources	**Public goods**
Rival *and* non-excludable	**Non-rival *and* non-excludable**
Nectar Fishes in the open sea	Music from buskers Streetlighting Defence Law and order Minor roads *(until satellite technology is possible)* Beautiful sunsets

The economic problem with public goods

Suppose you live in a market economy, with no government intervention. Suppose, too, that at present no firms are offering haircuts, screening movies, or supplying streetlights. In time, firms will discover that people would like these products. But firms will not want to supply them unless they can cover their costs by selling them.

Firms will have little problem supplying haircuts or movies. People who want these will be willing to pay, and the products are excludable, so producers can exclude people who don't pay.

However, firms will have a big problem supplying products that are public goods, like streetlighting, because people cannot be excluded from the benefits even if they refuse to pay. A firm's only hope will be to ask for voluntary donations, and some public goods, like music from buskers, are indeed financed by voluntary donations.

However, there is a snag with financing products with voluntary donations. Everyone is tempted to think like this: 'I would like firms to provide streetlighting, but my donation will make negligible difference to the level of service, so it is in my interest not to make any donations, and rely on other people to pay enough for a good service.' People who consume a non-excludable product without paying for it are called **freeriders**.

Some public goods, like busking, need modest funds, and voluntary donations raise enough for their suppliers, so governments do not intervene. But other pubic goods, like streetlighting, defence, and law and order, need huge funds, so relying on voluntary contributions could well lead to very poor services: this result of freeriding is called the **freerider problem**. To ensure that adequate services are provided, governments usually provide these services themselves. Unlike firms, they can force people to pay for them with taxes.

Although governments raise taxes to pay for these public goods, they do not have to do all the production involved. Instead, they can pay private firms to do some of the production. For example, a government may pay private firms to operate streetlamps, run prisons, and build warships.

The efficient quantity of a public good

If a government provides a public good, it must decide how much to provide. As with all products, the efficient output level is the one at which the marginal social benefit, *MSB*, equals the marginal social cost, *MSC*. For example, suppose you value the benefit of the government building another prison at £5 a year. The *MSB* of the prison is your £5 added to the value that all other people would place on it, say a total of £200 million a year. If the government reckons that the *MSC* of another prison would be less than its *MSB* at, say £180 million, then it would be efficient to have an extra prison.

Common resources

We have seen that the key problem with public goods for a market economy is that they are non-excludable, so firms may be reluctant to supply them. Common resources are also non-excludable, but they do get supplied because they aren't supplied by firms. However, they can lead to a very different sort of problem, which we will explore in the next section.

13.3 Summary

- A public good is both non-rival and non-excludable. Non-rival means it cannot be consumed by an extra person, at least not at the same time as the person or people who are currently consuming it. Non-excludable means it is not possible for a supplier to refuse to supply any consumer who refuses to pay.
- The non-excludability feature means any firms supplying these goods would have to rely on voluntary donations from consumers, yet many might opt to be freeriders. So, in a market economy, output could be well below the efficient level at which the marginal social benefit equals the marginal social cost.
- Governments can fix the problem of under-provision by financing public goods out of tax revenue, which they can compel people to pay. They can then do some of the production and pay firms to do the rest.

13.4 The problem with common resources

'The Tragedy of the Commons'

Another type of market failure may arise with products the producers of which use a common resource for which they do not pay. We will see that these producers will use the common resource more than is efficient, and in turn they may harm it.

The analysis of this topic derives from an article written by the American ecologist Garrett Hardin in 1968 called 'The Tragedy of the Commons'. He argued that if ordinary people were allowed to graze animals on common land for which they did not have to pay, there would be overgrazing, and the common land could be seriously damaged.

We will illustrate the problem using the case of fishing by fishing boats. Often, crews have access to a sea or large lake, and do not have to pay for that access. We will see that too many people will then go fishing, so that some species may become extinct.

The social benefits from fishing

Consider a lake with only one species of fish and suppose this species is caught in many other places, and that the lake's output is too small to affect its price. Also, suppose there are no external benefits from catching or consuming fish, and assume that the total social benefit, *TSB*, equals the total revenue that the crews get from selling their fish.

The *TSB* on any given day, say today, depends in part on how many boats go fishing today and on the stock of fish. The stock depends on how many boats have been fishing in the past; the stock may be very low if there have always been many boats fishing before. Suppose, for simplicity, that the number of boats has always been constant.

In Figure 13.6, the first column of the table shows various numbers of boats that might have gone out every day. The next column shows the *TSB*, that is the value of today's catch, if the same number go out today. For example, if there has always been one boat, and one goes today, today's catch will be worth £2,500. If there have always been two boats and two go today, the catch will be worth £4,400. Two boats will not land twice as many fish as one, because they will have to go beyond the richest parts of the lake.

The *TSB* continues to rise up to five boats, and then falls. The problem with many boats is that they reduce the fish stock, so fish get harder to find. The *TSB* is shown on the graph in the figure by a curve. This graph plots the number of boats on the horizontal axis. The yield with five boats is the highest that this resource can sustain, and this is called the **maximum sustainable yield**.

The marginal social benefit, *MSB*, is shown in the next column of the table and in the graph. The numbers in the table are printed between the lines for boat numbers. For example, the *MSB* number on the line between one boat and two shows that using a second boat raises the *TSB* by £1,900.

No. of boats	Total social benefit (*TSB*) £ per day	Marginal social benefit (*MSB*) £ per day	Total social cost (*TSC*) £ per day	Marginal social cost (*MSC*) £ per day	Benefit per crew £ per day
0	0		0		-
		2,500		990	
1	2,500		990		2,500
		1,900		990	
2	4,400		1,980		2,000
		1,300		990	
3	5,700		2,970		1,900
		700		990	
4	6,400		3,960		1,600
		100		990	
5	6,500		4,950		1,300
		-500		990	
6	6,000		5,940		1,000
		-1,100		990	
7	4,900		6,930		700
		-1,700		990	
8	3,200		7,920		400

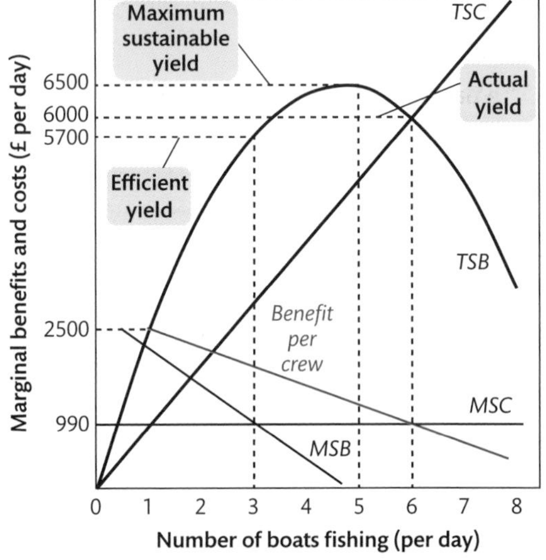

Figure 13.6 **Overfishing a fishing ground**

The efficient fishery yield is £5,700 from 3 boats where the *MSB* equals the *MSC*. The maximum sustainable yield is £6,500 from 5 boats. The actual yield is £6,000 from 6 boats, where the benefit per crew equals the *MSC*.

The efficient use of the common resource

Suppose the private daily cost of fishing is a constant £990 per boat, and suppose there are no external costs. Then the total social cost, *TSC*, will equal the total private cost and be as shown in the column headed *TSC* in the table in Figure 13.6. *TSC* is shown in the graph with a line.

The marginal social cost, *MSC*, is shown in the next column of the table and in the graph. Again the numbers in the table are printed between the lines for the number of boats. In each case, the number is the £990 needed for the next boat.

It is efficient to use the resource more for as long as its *MSB* exceeds its *MSC*. So the intersection of the *MSC* and *MSB* curves shows that the efficient use is three boats, and their *TSB* of £5,700 is the efficient yield. The third boat is worth using, because it adds £1,300 to *TSB* and only £990 to *TSC*. The fourth boat is not worth using, because it adds only £700 to *TSB*, but adds £990 to *TSC*.

The efficient yield is always below the maximum sustainable yield. This is because the *MSB* approaches zero as the maximum sustainable yield is reached, so the *MSB* here must be below the *MSC*. If the number of boats used were to exceed three, so that the *MSB* were below the *MSC*, it would make economic sense to use fewer boats and reduce the yield.

The actual use of the common resource

We have seen what is efficient; now we must see what will happen. This depends on the decisions of the boat crews, so we must look at things from their viewpoint. They will reason as follows.

- **The first boat crew will say**: 'If we are always the only boat to fish, then each day our catch would be worth £2,500 and our costs would be £990. So we should go fishing.'
- **The second boat crew will say**: 'If we also go fishing every day, the total catch will be worth £4,400, and we will get half, worth £2,200. Our costs will be £990. So we should go fishing.'

The last column in the table, headed 'Benefit per crew', shows the £2,500 worked out by the first crew, the £2,200 worked out by the second, and the equivalent figures that the other crews will work out. These figures are plotted on the graph with a pink line.

Extra boats will go out every day provided that their crews expect a benefit of more than the £990 it costs them to go. The figure shows that this applies up to the sixth boat: its crew expect a catch worth £1,000 at a cost of £990. A seventh boat will not put out: its crew will expect a catch worth £700 at a cost of £990. The actual yield from the six boats that do go out is £6,000.

We can draw two important conclusions.

- **More boats will use the resource than are needed for the efficient yield**. This is because the benefit per crew is greater than the *MSB*. In other words, each crew thinks only about its catch and its costs, and ignores the fact that its catch reduces the catch of the other boats.
- **More boats may use the resource than are needed for the maximum sustainable yield**. This happens in our example, in which the effects on the fish stock cause the actual yield to be below the maximum sustainable yield. The situation will get worse if the price of fish rises. Then the pink curve showing the benefits per crew will shift upwards, so more boats will go out, reducing the stock further. In time, the total catch could become very low, or fall to zero if the fish become extinct.

The EU wants the use of EU waters for fishing to be at what it believes to be the efficient levels. It also wants to stop fish stocks there falling. So for each of 150 species of fish, it sets a daily quota that may be caught. It also decides how much can be caught by boats from each country, but it allows each country to apportion its share between its own boats. By imposing quotas, the EU effectively claims that it has the property rights to the common resource and can regulate its use.

Another example of an overused common resource, which lasted in the UK until the 19th century, was grazing on common land. This land was always owned by local landowners, but the law gave ordinary people the right to use it, and it became overused. The government sorted this out with a series of enclosure acts. These gave the owners the additional property right to enclose the commons and deny other people grazing rights. Overgrazing disappeared, but those who lost the right to graze often became impoverished.

13.4 **Summary**

- The efficient yield from a common resource is less than the maximum yield that it could sustain.
- The actual use of a common resource in a competitive market will exceed the efficient use, and may also exceed the use needed for the maximum sustainable yield; so, in a fishing ground, some species may become extinct. In response to such overuse, governments may limit access to the resource.

13.5 Asymmetric information

Suppose a private good is produced by perfect competitors that use no common resources, and suppose there are no issues with externalities. Even then, a market would fail to produce the efficient output if the buyers or the sellers were to lack some information about each other or about the product; the term **asymmetric information** is used for this situation, because one party usually lacks more information that the other.

Asymmetric information can actually cause problems in many situations, and this section looks at four groups of people whom it affects:

- **buyers of new products;**
- **buyers and sellers of second-hand goods;**
- **lenders;**
- **insurers.**

Asymmetric information and new products

Look back at Figure 13.1, which shows a perfectly competitive market. We said that if there were no externalities, then the equilibrium quantity of 100 million kg a week would also be the efficient quantity. At lower outputs, the marginal benefit to consumers would exceed the marginal cost, so it would be efficient to produce more, and at higher outputs, the marginal cost would exceed the marginal benefit, so it would be efficient to produce less.

However, the demand curve here, like all demand curves, shows what consumers are willing to pay, and that reflects what they *believe* the benefits of the product to them are. If the *true* benefits were very different, they might actually be better off buying far more or far less than 100 million kg.

Here are some products for which the true benefit to you may be different from what you believe.

- **A meal in a restaurant that, unknown to you but known by its staff, has a filthy kitchen.** You believe the meal will benefit you: the truth is that it will give you food poisoning!
- **Some cream advertised as 'clinically proven' to keep skin soft; however, unknown to you, but known by the makers, this cream has only a trivial effect.** You may believe it will greatly benefit you: the truth is that it will not.
- **Some fuel in a garage where the pumps, unknown to you, but known by the garage, have faulty gauges.** You believe you have bought, say, 30 litres: the truth is that you have bought only 28.

In cases like these, you will be buying products that you would not buy if you were to know the true benefit to you. To handle these problems, a government often uses legislation. For example:

- it may impose hygiene standards on restaurant kitchens and send inspectors unannounced to ensure the standards are maintained;
- it may have strict laws on advertising and make misleading advertisements illegal;
- it may legislate that all retail outlets must use accurate measuring equipment.

Asymmetric information and used goods

Suppose you want to buy a second-hand car or home. The seller may know about problems that are not observable to you. For example, the car's body might suffer from severe rust, which the seller has hidden with fresh paint that will soon wear off. Or the home may seem to be quiet when you visit it, but the sellers do not tell you that their neighbours from hell are away on holiday.

When a seller knows of a serious fault of which the buyer is unaware, the product is called a **lemon**. This term was used by the American economist George Akerlof in 1970.

Lemons create problems for market efficiency. For example, suppose someone wants to sell a used car that, if it were sound, would be worth £5,000. However, potential buyers cannot be sure it is sound, and if it is a lemon, they know it will be worth much less than £5,000. They are unwilling to pay £5,000 for something that might be worth less, so the most they will offer is, say, £4,000.

So, if the car is sound, the situation is bad for sellers and good for buyers, because the price of £4,000 is less than the real value of £5,000. But if the car is a lemon, the situation may well be good for sellers and bad for buyers, because the price of £4,000 may well be above the real value. So we can draw two conclusions:

- **people with sound cars that they would like to sell may, nevertheless, be reluctant to sell them, because the price will be below the true value;**
- **people with lemons that they would like to sell will be very keen to sell them, because the price may be above the true value**.

Taken together, these problems mean that the selection of used cars for sale becomes adversely affected. But both buyers and sellers can try to improve the situation as follows.

- **With signalling**: this occurs if sellers who claim their products are sound take action to make the claim credible. For example, if a garage offers guarantees on second-hand cars, then buyers know that it is unlikely to sell lemons because it would have to fix them.
- **With screening**: this occurs if buyers get information about the seller. For example, you could ask friends who have bought used cars what they think about various garages.

Also, governments may intervene. For example, with housing, the UK government requires the vendor of any home with three or more bedrooms to prepare a Home Information Pack (HIP), which gives much information to buyers.

Asymmetric information for lenders

Our next example of problems with asymmetric information concerns banks and other firms that lend money for interest. If they know that a borrower is risky, then they will charge a high interest rate, to reduce their loss if the loan is not repaid. If they know that a borrower is safe, then they will be willing to charge a low rate.

But often lenders do not know how risky borrowers are. For example, a bank that lends money to students does not know which of them will study hard and get well-paid jobs, and which will not. Of course, the students have a much better idea about how risky they are: so there is asymmetric information.

Because the bank cannot assess the riskiness of individual students, it may charge them all the same rate of interest. This means that 'safe' students may pay higher rates than is appropriate for their risk, while 'risky' students pay less.

In turn, safe students may borrow less than they would, while risky ones borrow more. This is the exact opposite of what a bank wants: it wants to lend as much as possible to safe borrowers and as little as possible to risky ones. So the bank faces an adverse selection of borrower. But there is little a government can do to help here, except lend money to students itself.

Insurers and missing markets

Insurers often face similar problems. For example, they insure the contents of many people's homes, not knowing which people carelessly leave the windows open when they are away. The premiums they set are 'too high' for careful people and 'too low' for careless people.

With some types of insurance policy that consumers would like to buy, the information problems for insurers are so serious that they refuse to sell them. If firms are so reluctant to supply a product that little or none is traded, then we say the product has a **missing market**, and the government may have to meet consumer demand by supplying the product itself.

An important missing market is insurance cover for unemployment. Insurers are reluctant to offer policies that cover this, because some people might buy a policy and then try to get laid off, aiming to live indefinitely at the insurer's expense.

To fix this missing market, the UK government runs its own insurance scheme called National Insurance. With this, people pay contributions to the government when they are working and receive benefits from the government if they are made redundant, and also if they are ill or retired. Of course, the government knows that some insured people might want to be laid off and live at the government's expense. But, unlike private firms, it can tackle this with legislation.

13.3 Everyday economics

Alert over teeth whitening

In the East Riding of Yorkshire, council officials have warned the public to take extra care after finding excessive levels of hydrogen peroxide in some teeth-whitening products. The legal limit for hydrogen peroxide is 0.1%, but the council's trading standards team found that some products used by beauticians and dentists contain 360 times as much at 36%.

'Teeth-whitening warning issued in East Yorkshire', *BBC News*, 15 January
'Alert over tooth whitening gels', *The York Press*, 13 January 2011

Comment Hydrogen peroxide can damage tooth enamel. This news item shows that consumer protection requires not only laws but also officials to monitor what actually happens.

13.5 Summary

- Asymmetric information arises if one party to a transaction lacks information about the other party or the product. Lacking information, people may trade different amounts from what they would otherwise.
- To help to overcome this problem, sellers may use signalling, buyers may use screening, and governments may introduce various laws and controls.
- Asymmetric information may lead to some desirable products being offered inadequately, if at all, such as insurance for unemployment. Governments may tackle this by offering insurance themselves.

13.6 Merit goods and demerit goods

Suppose a perfectly competitive industry uses no common resources and provides a private good that has no problems of externalities or even asymmetric information. Even then, a government might believe that the output is inefficient, because it believes that consumers make poor choices, and do not buy the quantity that, at the current price, would maximize their utility. There are two types of product concerned, and we will look at both, as follows.

- **Merit goods**: with these, the government believes that people choose to consume less than they should to maximize their utility.
- **Demerit goods**: with these, the government believes that people choose to consume more than they should to maximize their utility.

Merit goods

One reason why consumers may consume too little of a product to maximize their utility is if the person who actually consumes the product is not the person who pays for it. For example, in a market economy, children might consume very little education or health care if their parents were to cut back on school fees or on health care insurance for their children. Accordingly, children's education and health care are seen as merit goods, and most governments intervene to ensure that far more of these products are supplied than would apply in market economy.

Some parents might also cut back on other items, such as food and clothes. Fortunately, this is rare, so governments do not see children's food and clothes as merit goods and do not intervene in the markets for them. Instead, when poor parenting occurs, the government tries to sort out the problems by using social workers or by taking children into care.

Even when the consumers *are* the people who pay, they may consume too little of some items if they have learning or age difficulties that prevent them making rational choices. However, the general approach to this problem is not to intervene in the markets for the many products that they might underconsume, but to have social workers and carers to help these people to make better choices, or else to take them into care and make choices on their behalf.

Sometimes, though, so many people would buy too little of a product that the government does intervene with the product. The best example is investing in pension schemes as a preparation for retirement. Many people are very short-sighted about pension planning and, in a market economy, would invest far too little. To fix this, governments often run their own schemes, as discussed in Chapter 16.

Demerit goods

Sometimes, governments believe that consumers consume too much of a product to maximize their utility. The classic examples are alcohol and tobacco products, which attract high taxes, and 'controlled substances' of which both possession and supply are illegal.

The main reason why some people consume too much of these products is that they develop an addiction and find it hard to cut back, even though they know the damage being done. Taxes and laws may help them to make better choices. However, intervention like this does have some undertones of paternalism.

13.6 Summary

- A merit good is one of which the government believes consumers buy less than they need to maximize their utility. This may arise if the purchasers differ from the ultimate consumers, as with education and health insurance bought by parents for children, or if people are short-sighted and save too little for retirement. Governments often intervene to increase the consumption of these products.
- A demerit good is one of which the government believes consumers buy more than they need to maximize their utility, such as alcohol and tobacco products and illegal drugs. Governments tackle these with taxes and laws.

13.7 Two important government services: health care and education

Two types of government provision

The three most costly government services in the UK are defence, education, and health care. We have seen that defence is a public good, which makes a good case for government provision, but education and health care are not public goods. In this section, we discuss why, nevertheless, UK governments provide them. We will see that this is because of concerns with equity, or fairness, as well as concerns with various types of market failure.

Our discussion will refer at times to two types of government provision, as follows.

- **Using government funds to reimburse privately owned facilities**. The UK essentially uses this approach for most colleges and universities, and for most general practitioners and dentists.
- **Using government funds to finance government-owned facilities**. The UK uses this approach with state schools and hospitals.

We will see that very few of the arguments for government provision of education and health care actually require the provision to be supplied by government-owned facilities, and there is a disadvantage in this type of provision. This is that facilities like state schools and hospitals may secure business from the government no matter how poorly they perform, so they may become inefficient and unfriendly.

Equity arguments for government provision

If education and health care were left to the market, then the outcome might seem inequitable, or unfair for reasons such as the following.

- **Some people are poor**. Poor parents might be unable to pay school fees, and poor people might be unable to pay the high premiums needed for health insurance that would cover all medical needs. Arguably, however, this is a weak argument for government provision of education and health care; the government could instead use its tax revenues to give more money to poor people to help them to purchase education and health care, or it could subsidize private providers.
- **Rich people could afford better education and health care than the poor**. This is also a weak argument for government provision, because this on its own will not remove expensive private schools and healthcare facilities. Solving this problem might instead require limits on the fees that private schools and health care providers may charge, or making private education and health care illegal, but these policies might be challenged as infringing liberty.
- **Unhealthy people would have to pay more for health care than healthy people**. This problem would clearly arise if everyone were to pay their own medical bills, but it might seem that it would be avoided if people were to take out health care insurance and let insurers meet more claims for unhealthy people than for healthy people. In fact, the problem would still arise. Let's see why.

To see why unhealthy people would still pay the most, even with healthcare insurance, suppose two insurance firms, A and B, are set up as follows.

- Firm A sets different premiums for different people, according to the chances of them making claims. So it sets low premiums for low-risk healthy people, and high premiums for high-risk people, such as diabetics.
- Firm B has the same medium premium for everyone.

When choosing between these two firms, all low-risk people will prefer firm A and all high-risk people will prefer firm B. But when firm B is left only with high-risk people, its uniform premium will have to be high. And when firm A ends up only with low-risk people, it will be able to offer them all low premiums. So the high-risk people will pay the most. This unfairness can be avoided with government provision, although it does not require the government to use its own facilities.

Let's now turn to look at some market failure arguments for government provision.

Monopoly problems

A market economy would probably have many schools and healthcare providers, so it might seem that monopolies in education and health care would be of no concern. In sparsely populated areas, though, schools and healthcare providers might face little competition, and might exploit the lack of competition by setting high prices. However, having tax-financed services everywhere seems a dramatic response; perhaps these monopolies could be treated like others, and be subject to scrutiny by the Competition Commission.

Merit good problems

In a market economy, parents might choose to buy too little healthcare insurance and education for their children. However, this problem does not justify government provision. All it needs is laws that require parents to purchase adequate healthcare insurance for their children, and to educate their children up to the school-leaving age.

Externalities

The main externality with health care concerns transmittable diseases. Treating people with these benefits not only them, but also those to whom they might otherwise give the disease. However, these diseases account for only a small part of the healthcare budget; even then, this point hardly justifies intervention, because people with these diseases have a strong incentive to seek treatment and be cured.

The main externalities with education are that people who have been educated not only get benefits themselves, in terms of more rewarding and better paid jobs, but also confer benefits on others. This is because we all benefit from a society in which everyone has been educated to a reasonable level and some people to a high level.

This externality issue is a further argument for making education compulsory up to a certain age, and it would justify subsidies to colleges and universities to hold down their fees and encourage a high take-up. But this issue scarcely seems to justify government provision of schools.

Asymmetric information

A market economy would create several problems with asymmetric information concerning education and health care, including the following.

- **Ignorance about quality**. Parents and students would not know how good the education is at different institutions, and ill people might not know how good different suppliers are. Unfortunately, government provision cannot fix this, even if government-owned facilities are used, because the government cannot guarantee that all its facilities are good. Maybe the best policies are regulations and league tables covering all suppliers.
- **Ignorance about the need for medical treatment**. Doctors in private hospitals may be paid for each treatment they give, and so have an incentive to do too much treatment. Government hospitals might fix that, but might instead pay their doctors salaries that do not depend on how much treatment they undertake, so they might have an incentive to offer too little treatment.

Further issues in an education market

We have seen several arguments for government intervention in education, but none seems to require provision by state schools. These schools were first established in the 1870s to ensure that even the poorest parents could have their children educated, but, as we have seen, there are alternatives, such as giving more money to poor people to help them to purchase education, or subsidizing private providers.

The main arguments for government schools may go beyond economics. If the government were merely to reimburse private schools, would some fail to promote social cohesion? Would some indoctrinate rather than teach, or give one side to many-sided issues? In principle, governments could legislate about what schools might do, but the legislation might well be so complex that government schools seem a better option.

A further problem with health care

A market economy could have a further problem with health care, resulting from the need for people to take out healthcare insurance. This is that some people might simply not bother to insure, and will then want help with their bills when they are ill. This would impose an external cost on other people who would not like to see these ill people being untreated. A government might tackle this by making insurance compulsory, but it might regard forcing people to pay for government provision through taxes as simpler.

A problem with tax finance

We have seen many arguments in favour of government provision of education and health care, but one problem with government provision should be noted: that is that some people will be reluctant to vote for a government that promises better education and health care financed by higher taxes. The reluctance arises because voters cannot be sure that the extra taxes will find their way to their local healthcare providers and schools, yet they can be sure their taxes will rise.

13.7 Summary

- Education and health care are the two most costly government services, but they are not public goods.
- Governments provide some education and health care by using government-owned facilities like state schools and hospitals; they provide some by reimbursing private facilities.
- Government-owned facilities may lack a competitive drive to efficiency.
- Many equity arguments and market failure arguments are sometimes used to justify government provision, but in some cases these may be weaker than they initially sound.
- There may be arguments for state health care that arise from problems with healthcare insurance, and other arguments for state education that arise from considerations beyond economics.
- Some people might be reluctant to vote for more spending on services provided by governments.

13.8 Government failure and public choices

We know that the Pareto-efficient output level for a product is where the marginal social cost, *MSC*, equals the marginal social benefit, *MSB*. And we have seen many reasons why the market for a product may fail to secure this output level. It is this market failure that lies behind much government intervention with the economy.

Unfortunately, though, government intervention is most unlikely to lead to an efficient output level, and its failure to do so is called **government failure**. A government must simply hope that the failure of its intervention will be less serious than the market failure that would otherwise occur.

The main cause of government failure is that governments may have limited information about two important matters, as follows.

- **The *MSC* of government services.** Of course, a government knows how much it actually pays to its own facilities and to any private suppliers that it reimburses. But it does not know how efficient these producers are, so it does not know what the true costs are.
- **The *MSB* of government services.** The main source of information comes from how people vote, but people vote at elections on a raft of issues, so voting gives little precise information.

A government may well react to these problems by abandoning any effort to set its service levels at the efficient levels where *MSB* equals *MSC*. Instead, it may set them at the levels that it thinks will secure the most votes. To see what these levels may be, we need to study **public choice theory**, which is the theory about how government choices are made in a democracy.

How parties compete for votes

Suppose a country has only two political parties, the Hawks and the Doves, and suppose an election is due in four months. Each party tells voters what policies it will implement if it wins. To see how the parties choose their policies, we will consider an example: the number of aircraft carriers and the taxes needed to finance them.

Suppose that, four months before the election, the Hawks declare that it wants 7 carriers while the Doves wants 2, so the Hawks will have higher taxes. Then the parties look at the opinion polls to see what the election outcome may be.

The opinion poll findings reflect voters' preferences. Suppose there are seven voters, A, B, C, D, E, F, and G, whose preferences on this issue are as shown at the top of Table 13.2. For example, B wants 2 carriers with fairly low taxes.

When the parties announce their proposals, we suppose that voters prefer the party with the number closest to their own preferences. So A, B, C, and D, who want 1, 2, 3, and 4 carriers respectively, prefer the Doves' proposal of 2 to the Hawks' proposal of 7. But E, F, and G, who want 5, 6, and 7 respectively, prefer the Hawks' proposal of 7 to the Doves' proposal of 2.

With a majority of voters behind the Doves, opinion polls predict that the Doves will win, as shown in the first line of the bottom part of Table 13.2. So the Hawks will probably revise its proposal. Say that, three months before the election, it announces a new policy for 5 carriers. Now D will prefer the Hawks' proposal to the 2 proposed by the Doves. So now four of the seven voters, D, E, F, and G, support the Hawks, and opinion polls predict a victory for that party.

The Doves will probably now revise its proposal, say to 4. So polls taken two months before the election predict a Dove victory, because A, B, C, and D support that party, while only E, F, and G support the Hawks.

The Hawks will then probably cut its proposal to 4, so that it has the same policy as the Doves. A, B, and C will support the Doves, while E, F, and G will support the Hawks; D will be undecided, because both parties promise what D wants. One month before the election, opinion polls say the result is too close to call, and there is no revised policy available to either party that will prove more popular.

The median voter theorem

Notice that three people want more carriers than D and three want fewer, so D is in the middle as far as preferences on this issue go. The voter whose preferences are in the middle is called the **median voter**, and a theorem called the **median voter theorem** says that, on any issue, competing political parties choose the policy preferred by the median voter on that issue, as we saw happening here.

According to the median voter theorem, the parties will choose their polices on health, education, and all

Table 13.2 **The preferences and voting intentions of five voters, A, B, C, D, and E**

Number of aircraft carriers preferred by voters:

A:1	B:2	C:3	D:4	E:5	F:6	G:7

Months to election	**Doves' proposal**	**Hawks'proposal**	**Opinion poll predictions**
Four	2	7	Doves will win
Three	2	5	Hawks will win
Two	4	5	Doves will win
One	4	4	Too close to call

other issues in line with the preferences of the median voters on each of those issues. For example, A may the median voter on education and F on health. So each party will end proposing the education policy desired by A and the health policy desired by F, along with the aircraft carrier policy desired by D.

Government failure

Because the parties end up with similar policy proposals, we would expect the winning party to apply A's education policies, F's health policies, and D's aircraft carrier policies. Unfortunately, there is no reason why these individuals will prefer the efficient levels of spending on those services. So there is every reason to expect the government to fail to provide the efficient levels.

Rational ignorance

There is another issue. At the next election, will you work out which number of carriers, hospitals, or schools is best for you, allowing also for the tax implications of different numbers? Almost certainly you will not, and nor will other voters.

It may seem that you and other voters are irresponsible. But almost all voters think as follows: 'My vote is unlikely to affect the outcome, so why should I make a huge effort to work out the implications for me of the parties' alternative policies?' In economic terms, we say that although each voter is ignorant about the effects of different policies, it is a **rational ignorance** because the cost of acquiring the information would outweigh any benefits. But the result is that median voters are unlikely even to choose the best policies for themselves.

Pressure for overspending by governments

We have used public choice theory to show that government spending on any service is unlikely to be at the efficient level. Public choice theory goes on to argue that the spending is most likely to be above the efficient level, because politicians come under pressure from two groups of people with vested interests in high spending.

- **Bureaucrats**: these are the people who deliver public services, so, in the case of aircraft carriers, they include officials in the ministry of defence and people in the navy. If they can persuade the government to spend more on their service, their ministry and the navy will grow and become more prestigious, and there will be more promotion opportunities.
- **Rent-seekers**: this term is used for any other people who will make more income if government spending rises. In the case of aircraft carriers, they include the workers and owners of the shipyards that might build them.

These two groups may persuade parties like the Hawks and Doves to start off proposing more carriers than they would otherwise have proposed; they may also persuade median voters to accept more carriers than they would accept if they were not rationally ignorant.

Question 13.2 Can you suggest some groups of people who would be bureaucrats and rent-seekers in the case of state education and health care?

13.8 Summary

- When a government intervenes with the provision of products, it is unlikely to ensure that the output is at the efficient level. So there will be government failure. Government failure arises because governments have insufficient information about the costs and benefits of different services.
- The median voter theorem argues that the actual quantity of a service subject to government intervention will reflect the preferences of the median voter on that service.

- Governments and voters may be pressurized by bureaucrats who want bigger and more prestigious departments, and by rent-seekers who want higher incomes, to secure service levels above efficient levels.

In the next chapter we move away from markets for products and look at markets for labour.

abc Glossary

Asymmetric information: when the buyers or sellers of a product lack some information about each other or about the product.

Bureaucrats: people who deliver public services.

Club good: a product or natural resource that is non-rival and excludable.

Coase theorem: the fact that the efficient level of pollution will arise from compensation agreements about it, whichever party has the property right.

Common good: a product or natural resource that is rival and non-excludable.

Demerit good: a product of which the government believes consumers choose to consume too much to maximize their utility.

Emission tax: a tax on the emission of pollutants.

Excludable: applies to a product or natural resource for which non-payers can be excluded from consumption.

External benefit: when the production or consumption of a product causes other consumers to gain utility, or causes other producers to use fewer resources for their current output.

External cost: when the production or consumption of a product causes other consumers to lose utility, or causes other producers to use more resources for their current output.

Externality: *see* external costs (or negative externalities) *and* external benefits (or positive externalities).

Freerider: someone who consumes a non-excludable product without paying for it.

Freerider problem: the fact that, in a market economy, the output of some public goods might be low because many people will be freeriders.

Government failure: the failure of government intervention to secure a Pareto-efficient outcome.

Lemon: a product with a serious fault known to the seller, but of which the buyer is unaware.

Marginal cost of reducing pollution (*MCRP*)**:** the extra cost to producers of using one fewer unit of a pollutant.

Marginal external benefit (*MEB*)**:** the rise in social benefit when an extra unit of a product is produced or consumed.

Marginal external cost (*MEC*)**:** the rise in social cost when an extra unit of a product is produced or consumed.

Marginal private benefit (*MPB*)**:** the rise in private benefit when an extra unit of a product is consumed.

Marginal private cost (*MPC*)**:** the rise in private cost when an extra unit of output is produced.

Marginal social benefit (*MSB*)**:** *MPB* plus *MEB*.

Marginal social cost (*MSC*)**:** *MPC* plus *MEC*.

Maximum sustainable yield: the highest yield from a resource that can be sustained.

Median voter: the voter whose preferences are in the middle, so that the number of voters who want more equals the number who want less.

Median voter theorem: the theorem that, on any issue, competing political parties will choose the policy preferred by the median voter on that issue.

Merit good: a product of which the government believes consumers choose to consume too little to maximize their utility.

Missing market: the small or non-existent market for a product that firms are reluctant to supply.

Negative externality: the same as external cost.

Non-excludable: applies to a product or natural resource for which non-payers cannot be excluded from consumption.

Non-rival: applies to a product or natural resource that an extra person could come and consume at the same time.

Pigovian tax: the same as an emissions tax.

Positive externality: the same as external benefit.

Private benefit: the benefit that the consumers of a product get from consuming it.

Private cost: the costs incurred by the producers of a product.

Private good: a product or natural resource that is both rival and excludable.

Property right: the legal ownership of something, and so the right to decide what can be done with it.

Public choice theory : the theory about how government choices are made in a democracy .

Public good: a product or natural resource that is both non-rival and non-excludable.

Rational ignorance: ignorance that arises when the costs of acquiring information would outweigh the benefits from it.

Rent-seekers: people (other than bureaucrats) who hope to earn more income when the government provides more services.

Rival: applies to a product or natural resource that an extra person could not come and consume at the same time.

Social benefit: the total benefit to society of a product, that is its private benefit plus its external benefit.

Social cost: the total cost to society of a product, that is its private cost plus its external cost.

Tradable permit: a permit to emit pollutants that may be bought and sold between firms.

Transactions costs: the costs of making a deal.

Answers to in-text questions

13.1 (**a**) Like school lessons, your economics lectures are excludable, because non-payers could be excluded. So, if there is space for more people, making them non-rival, they are a club good; otherwise they are a private good. (**b**) TV broadcasts are non-rival. With satellite and cable broadcasts, price exclusion is possible and used, so they are club goods. In the UK, terrestrial broadcasts are also arguably excludable because people are fined if they don't have licences, so they too can be seen as club goods.

13.2 Bureaucrats include officials in the central and local government departments concerned with education and health care; they also include teachers and doctors and other people who directly provide the services. Rent-seekers include firms who build schools and hospitals, or who produce drugs, textbooks, and all other items used in hospitals and education. They would all hope to gain if state education and health care were to expand.

Questions for review

13.1 Which government policies for reducing pollution should manage to do so at the minimum cost?

13.2 Which, if any, government policies for reducing pollution to the efficient level would not require the government to estimate the external cost of pollution?

13.3 Explain the principal reason that public goods might be underproduced in a market economy.

13.4 Look back at the example in Figure 13.6. Suppose the cost of taking a boat out increases to £1,500 per day, so that all the *MSC* figures in the table become £1,500. Work out (**a**) what the efficient number of boats to use the lake would now be, (**b**) what the actual number would now be, and (**c**) whether the actual yield would still exceed the maximum sustainable yield.

13.5 At a general election in the UK, explain (**a**) whether you would you expect the main parties to have similar policies on many issues, and (**b**) what might happen if they generally had very different policies.

? Questions for discussion

13.1 Aside from your education, can you think of any products you consume for which the production or the consumption has external benefits?

13.2 What sorts of help will poor countries most want from rich ones if they are to limit their emissions of CO_2?

13.3 Suggest some products of which you might have bought **(a)** a smaller quantity and **(b)** a larger quantity if you had possessed more information.

13.4 Some people addicted to gambling may spend more on it than they should to maximize their utility. Does this imply that the government should try to reduce gambling? How does it actually encourage it?

13.5 Does it make sense for the government to own most of the schools and hospitals in the UK, but to reimburse non-government facilities for university education and for the services of general practitioners?

Common student errors

Many students find it surprising that the efficient level of pollution is greater than zero; but the efficient level arises when the extra cost of making any further reduction exceeds the extra benefit that would arise.

Some students also get confused by the term 'public good', forgetting that this applies to a service that is non-rival and non-excludable, and does not depend on whether the service is actually provided by the government. Further, students sometimes forget that non-excludability is a matter of whether exclusion *could* occur, not whether it *does* occur.

14

Markets for Labour

Remember from Chapter 3 that in the markets for many types of labour, there are many buyers and sellers. In each of these markets, the wage rate and quantity of labour are determined by the supply and demand for that type of labour, and the wage and quantity of labour change if the demand curve or supply curve shifts.

When your friends leave college, they will embark on different careers that pay very different wages. Why do wages vary so much? Suppose you run a firm: why might you actually employ more workers if their union were to negotiate a higher wage rate, or if you were forced to raise the wage because of minimum wage laws? Does it make sense for employers to discriminate between workers of different genders or races, if it means paying relatively high wages to their preferred groups?

This chapter shows you how to answer questions like these, by understanding:

* the factors that determine the demand for labour in different occupations;
* why wage rates vary so much between occupations;
* how trade unions and minimum wage laws can affect wages and employment;
* the different ways in which employers may discriminate between races and genders.

14.1 The demand for labour

In an economy, there is a labour market for each type of labour. In some labour markets, the labour is hired by many firms and is supplied by many households: a labour market like this is called a **competitive labour market**. We saw in Chapter 3 that the wage rate and the total hours worked in such a labour market are determined by the supply and demand for that labour.

We studied the supply of labour to labour markets in Chapter 6. In this present chapter, we look first at the demand for labour by firms in competitive labour markets. We then discuss why wage rates vary widely between different labour markets. We also look at labour markets that are not competitive, and at the effects of trade unions, minimum wage laws, and discrimination.

Derived demand

Consider a large suburb with thousands of similarly sized houses, and suppose that many households like their windows to be cleaned by window-cleaning firms. These firms hire workers in the labour market for window cleaners in that suburb. Of course, these firms wouldn't demand any labour unless some households had demanded to have their windows cleaned. So we call the demand for labour, and indeed the demand for all inputs used by firms, a **derived demand**, because it derives from the demand for the product that the input helps to produce.

The demand curve in this labour market is given by D_{MARKET} in the final part of Figure 14.1. This shows, for example, that if the wage were £160 a day, 100 window cleaners would be demanded, while if the wage were £80 a day, 400 would be demanded. D_{MARKET}, would shift if the number of firms were to change. It would also shift if, for any reason, firms individual were to demand more or fewer window cleaners at any given wage. So, to understand shifts in D_{MARKET}, we must see why individual firms may demand more or fewer workers.

All firms are run by different people who often make different decisions. Figure 14.1 shows the link between these varied individual firms and the market. The first

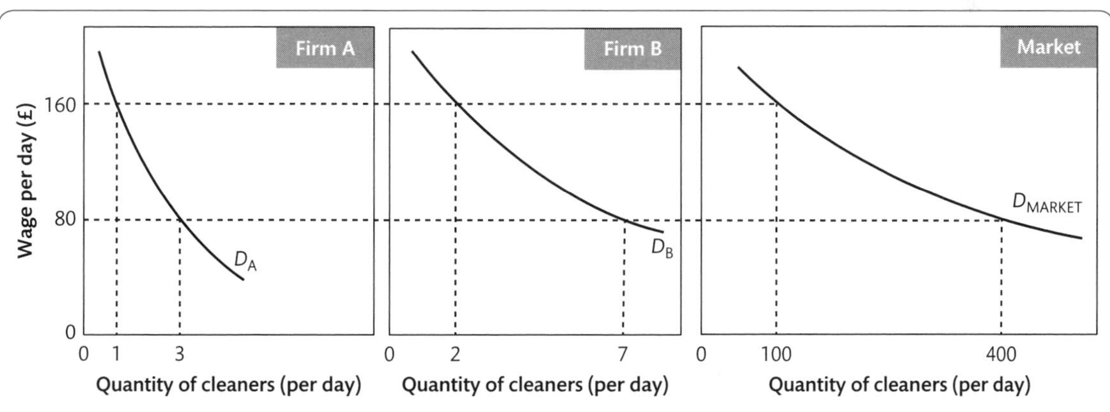

Figure 14.1 **Individual demand curves and the market demand curve**

The figure relates to the market for cleaners hired by window-cleaning firms in a large suburb. The first two figures give the individual demand curves for two window-cleaning firms, A and B. At a wage of £80 per day, for example, A would hire 3 cleaners while B would hire 7. The last figure gives the market demand curve. This shows how much all firms between them would hire. At £80, it includes the 3 demanded by A, the 7 demanded by B, and the quantities demanded by all the other firms in the market; the total is 400.

two parts of the figure show, as D_A and D_B, the demand curves for cleaners by two firms called A and B. For example, if the price were £160, A would demand one cleaner and B two. And if the wage were £80, A would demand three cleaners per day and B seven.

D_{MARKET} includes this information about firms A and B, and it includes similar information about all the other firms in this labour market. For example, the figure of 400 at a wage of £80 means that if we add up the three cleaners that A would demand at that wage, the seven that B would demand, and however many all the other firms would demand, then the total is 400.

The demand by an individual firm

To understand the demand curve of an individual firm, let's suppose that, one summer, you set up a firm to clean windows in this large suburb. You find that there are already many other window-cleaning firms there, and that the market price for cleaning a home is currently £10. Your output of window cleaning will be small relative to the market, so you will be a price-taker in that market. If you charge more than £10, no one will ask your firm to clean their windows; if you charge less, you will be swamped with customers.

Suppose that the wage for workers is currently very high at £160 a day. Your demand for workers will be small relative to the labour market for cleaners, so you will be a price-taker in that market also. If you pay less than £160, no one will work for you; if you pay more, you will be swamped by people wanting to work for you.

Suppose, finally, that you hire one van, and buy two ladders, two buckets, and two sponges. With this information, let's consider how many workers you would hire at each possible wage, in order to discover your demand curve for labour.

Two initial simplifying assumptions

To find your demand curve, we will initially keep the analysis simple by making two assumptions that are not realistic. We will relax them later. They are as follows.

- **No matter what the wage rate is, other firms will always hire the same number of workers.** This means that a change in the wage rate has no significant impact on the supply of window-cleaning services in the market, so the price will stay at £10 per home.
- **No matter what the wage rate is, and no matter how many workers you hire, you will always use the same quantity of other inputs.** So you will always use one van, two ladders, two buckets, and two sponges.

The marginal revenue product of an input

To find your demand curve in this situation, consider first how many homes your firm could handle each day with different numbers of workers up to, say, six. Table 14.1 shows this information in the column headed total product, *TP*.

The next column shows the marginal product, *MP*, that is the change in *TP* when the number of workers changes by one. For example, if you were to go from two workers to three, the number of homes cleaned each day would rise from 39 to 53, that is a rise of 14. So the *MP* of 14 is shown in between the lines for two and three workers.

The *MP* figures get smaller as the number of workers rises, according to the law of diminishing marginal returns that we met in Chapter 8. With one van, two ladders, buckets, and sponges, your firm will be able to clean many more homes if you raise the number of workers from one to two, but it will clean very few extra homes if you increase the number from five to six.

The market price for window cleaning is £10 per home. So each time your firm produces an extra unit of output by cleaning one more home, your revenue rises by £10. So your marginal revenue from each extra unit of output, *MR*, is £10.

Table 14.1 **Calculating the *MRP* and *MCL* for an input when the price and *MR* for the output are constant at £10, and the price of the input is £160**

No. of workers Hired per day	*TP* Houses cleaned per day	*MP* Houses cleaned per day	*MRP* £ per day	*TCL* £ per day	*MCL* £ per day
0	0			0	
		21	210		160
1	21			160	
		18	180		160
2	39			320	
		14	140		160
3	53			480	
		10	100		160
4	63			640	
		6	60		160
5	69			800	
		1	10		160
6	70			690	

Suppose you raise the number of workers by one, while still holding constant the quantity you use of all other inputs: then your total revenue would rise by an amount called the **marginal revenue product**, *MRP*. For each increase by one in the number of workers, your *MRP* equals the number of extra homes cleaned, *MP*, times the *MR* of £10 from each of these extra homes. For example, if you raise the number of workers from three to four, the *MP* is 14, so 14 more homes are cleaned, and each of these gives you an *MR* of £10, so your total revenue rises by £140, and this is your *MRP*.

Table 14.1 gives the *MRP* for each rise by one in the number of workers. These *MRP* figures are plotted as black circles on Figure 14.2, and a curve for *MRP* is drawn through them.

The marginal cost of an input

For each number of workers, Table 14.1 shows the total cost of labour, *TCL*. As workers are paid £160 a day, each *TCL* figure equals the number of workers times £160. Table 14.1 also shows the **marginal cost of labour**, *MCL*, that is the change in *TCL* when the number of workers changes by one. *MCL* here always equals the £160 paid to the extra worker. The *MCL* figures are plotted on Figure 14.2 by black circles, and a curve, MCL_{160}, is drawn through them to show the marginal cost of labour when the wage is £160.

The labour quantity that maximizes profit

To maximize its profit, your firm should hire more workers until the number at which MCL_{160} intersects

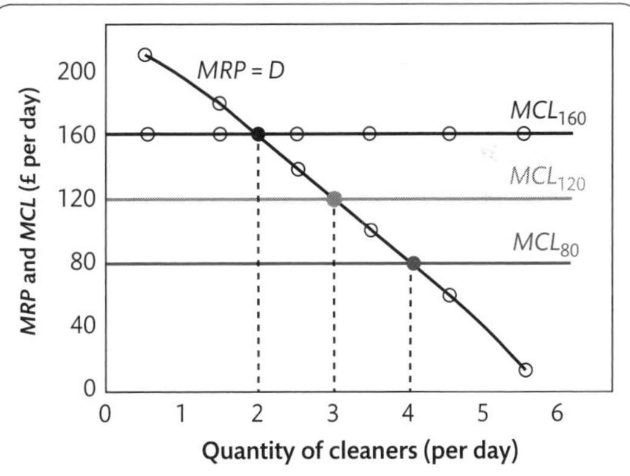

Figure 14.2 **The demand curve by a firm for an input under two simplifying assumptions**

If the wage falls from £160 to £120, and then to £80, the *MCL* curve shifts down. If this firm uses a constant amount of all other inputs, and if other firms don't react to wage changes, then the *MRP* curve stays in the same position and it shows the firm's demand curve for the input. This is because, at each wage, the firm will maximize its profit by hiring extra workers so as long as *MRP* exceeds *MCL*, so it will hire 2 at a wage of £160, 3 at a wage of £120, and 4 at a wage of £80.

MRP, which is two workers. It is easy to show why the firm wouldn't want any other number.

- **Suppose it had a number, like one worker, at which *MRP* is more than *MCL*.** Then hiring another worker would add more to revenue than to costs, so the profit would rise. In fact, *MRP* shows that adding a second worker would add £180 to revenue, while *MCL* shows that it would add just £160 to costs.
- **Suppose it had a number, like three workers, at which *MCL* is more than *MRP*.** Then laying off a worker would reduce costs by more than it reduced revenue, so the profit would rise. In fact, *MCL* shows that laying off a third worker would reduce costs by £160, while *MRP* shows that it would reduce revenue by just £140.

Under the simplifying assumptions, the *MRP* curve is the firm's demand curve for labour

So, if the wage is £160, you face MCL_{160} and hire two workers. This gives us a point on your demand curve, as shown in Figure 14.2 by a black dot.

Suppose the wage falls to £120 a day. Each extra worker now costs you £120, so you now face MCL_{120}, as shown in Figure 14.2. You will now hire a third worker, because the *MRP* curve shows that this worker adds £140 to your revenue, while adding only £120 to your cost. This gives us another point on your demand curve, shown in the figure by a grey dot.

Suppose the wage falls again to £80 a day. Each extra worker will now cost you £80, so you now face MCL_{80}. You will now hire a fourth worker, because the *MRP* curve shows that this worker adds £100 to your revenue, while adding only £80 to your cost. This gives us a third point on your demand curve, shown in the figure by a pink dot.

Your demand curve must pass through all three dots, and you can see that it is given by your *MRP* curve. But remember that we have simplified the analysis by making two unrealistic assumptions.

Relaxing the simplifying assumptions

If we relax these assumptions, then a fall in the wage will actually shift your *MRP* curve, and it may shift it down or up. These possibilities are shown respectively in cases (a) and (b) of Figure 14.3. In each case, the initial wage is £160, so the initial *MCL* curve is MCL_{160}. You hire two workers, where this intersects the initial black *MRP* curve, which is labelled MRP_{160}.

Now suppose the wage falls to £80. To see what happens to the *MRP* curve, consider one point on it, say the point between three and four workers. The *MRP* here is the *MP* of the fourth worker times the *MR*. So far we have said that the *MP* is 10 and the *MR* is £10, giving an *MRP* of £100. This is shown in each part of the figure by a black circle on MRP_{160}.

However, we will get different figures for *MP* and *MR* if we relax the simplifying assumptions, as explained below.

- **At a lower wage, we will now allow that other firms will hire more workers.** In turn, they will increase the supply of window-cleaning services. So the price of cleaning will fall below £10 per home and the *MR* you would get from each extra home will fall below £10. On its own, this factor will reduce the *MRP* of the fourth worker.
- **At lower wage, when you hire more workers, we will now allow that you will get more other inputs for them to use**. With more equipment, they will be more productive, so the number of extra homes cleaned by a fourth worker will now be more than ten. On its own, this factor will increase the *MRP* of the fourth worker.

So will the *MRP* of the fourth worker be less than £100 or more than £100? This depends on which factor is stronger, the fall in *MR* caused by an increase in supply of window cleaning, or the rise in *MP* caused by you having more other inputs. Figure 14.3 illustrates each possibility as follows.

- **Case (a) assumes the fall in *MR* is stronger**. Say *MR* falls from £10 to £5 and *MP* rises from 10 to 12.

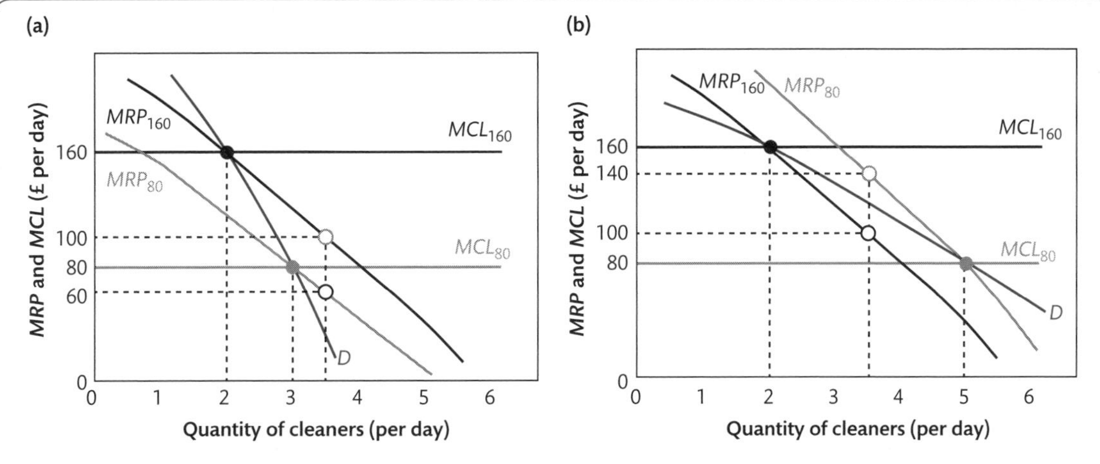

Figure 14.3 **Deriving the true demand curve for an input**

If the wage is £160, then the firm's *MRP* curve is given by MRP_{160}, and its marginal cost of labour is given by MCL_{160}. In each case, the profit-maximizing number of workers, 2, is shown by the black dot where these curves intersect. If the wage falls to £80, then in each case the *MCL* curve shifts to MCL_{80}. Also, the industry output rises, which reduces the price of window cleaning and the *MR* from it, pushing *MRP* down, and the firm uses more other inputs, raising its *MP* of labour, so pushing *MRP* up. In case (a) the effect on *MR* is stronger, so the net result is a lower *MRP*. In case (b) the effect on *MP* is stronger, so the net result is a higher *MRP*. In each case the firm settles at the grey dots where MRP_{80} cuts MCL_{80}, with 3 workers in (a) and 5 in (b). In each case, the true demand curve, *D*, passes both the dots.

Then the *MRP* is £60, as shown by a grey circle. Your *MRP* curve must shift *down* to pass this point, and the new one is labelled MRP_{80}.

- **Case (b) assumes the rise in *MP* is stronger**. Say *MP* rises from 10 to 20 and *MR* falls from £10 to £7. Then the *MRP* is £140, as shown by a grey circle. Your *MRP* curve here shifts *up* to pass this point, and the new one is labelled MRP_{80}.

Deriving the demand curve for an input

We can now use Figure 14.3 to find your demand curve. In each case, the wage is initially £160 and you hire two workers, as shown by a black dot. This is a point on your demand curve, because it shows that at a wage of £160 you hire two workers.

Now the wage falls to £80. In case (a), the main effect of this is the fall in *MR* caused by other firms producing more, so your *MRP* curve shifts down to the MRP_{80} here. In case (b), the main effect is the rise in *MP* when you use more other inputs, so your *MRP* curve shifts up to the MRP_{80} here. In each case, the *MCL* is now MCL_{80}, and the number of workers you hire is given by the intersections of MCL_{80} with the new MRP_{80}. This is three workers in case (a) and five in case (b).

The grey dots at these intersections give us second points on your demand curve for labour, because they show how many workers you will hire at a wage of £80. So your demand curve is as shown in each case by the purple curve labelled *D*, because this shows that you will hire two workers at a wage of £160, and, depending on which case applies, three workers or five at a wage of £80. It is demand curves like these that are shown in Figure 14.1, which are then added together to get the market demand curve for the input.

Changes in the demand for an input

Having seen that a firm's demand curve for labour depends on its *MRP* curves, we can now explain the reasons why a firm's demand curve, and in turn, the market demand curve, may shift.

- **The demand for the firm's output may change.** Suppose the demand for window cleaning in the suburb increases. Then the price of cleaning will rise, so the *MR* from each house cleaned will rise. In turn, the *MRP* at any number of workers will rise, because it equals the *MR* times the *MP* at that number; higher *MRP* figures lead to higher *MRP* curves and an increase in demand.

- **The prices of other inputs may change**. Suppose the price of fuel rises, so firms use their vans less. This reduces the extra output or *MP* from any extra worker. So the *MRP* at any number of workers falls, because it equals the *MP* at that number times the *MR*; lower *MRP* figures lead to lower *MRP* curves and a decrease in demand.
- **The productivity of an input may change, perhaps because of a new technology**. Suppose sponges are improved, so that windows can be cleaned more quickly. Then each firm will find that all of its *MP* figures increase, because extra workers can now clean more windows. However, with all firms being more productive, the supply of cleaning services will increase and the price will fall, so reducing *MR*. If the rise in *MP* is greater than the fall in *MR*, then the *MRP* figures will rise and the *MRP* curves will shift up, so the demand for labour will increase. If the rise in *MP* is smaller than the fall in *MR*, then the *MRP* figures will fall and the *MRP* curves will shift down, so the demand for labour will decrease.

14.1 Everyday economics

Labour productivity and employment

During 2010, the productivity of labour in the US grew by 3.6%. Although this helped to hold down prices, it was not great news for the labour market, because it was achieved in part by firms managing to produce roughly constant levels of output from fewer workers. However, analysts predicted that there was limited scope for further productivity gains, so that if demand in the economy were to pick up as the recession end, firms would want to hire more workers.

'Productivity jumps at unexpectedly fast clip of 2.6 percent', *National Journal*, 3 February 2011.
'US nonfarm productivity up 2.6 pct in fourth quarter', *Reuters*, 3 February 2011

Comment We have just seen in the text that higher productivity may lead some firms to hire more labour and others to hire less; these news items suggests that, in 2010, a majority of US firms hired less. However, the view that employment will in future rise if productivity remains constant might be optimistic: the danger is that firms abroad might improve their productivity and make it hard for US firms to compete. If any US firms were then to produce less, this would reduce their demand for labour.

Question 14.1 How does the price elasticity of demand for a firm's output affect the likely direction in which its *MRP* curve will shift if the wage rate falls?

14.1 Summary

- If a firm hires one more worker, and uses an unchanged quantity of other inputs, then its extra revenue is called its marginal revenue product of labour. This equals the marginal product of the extra worker multiplied by the marginal revenue of the extra output.
- Suppose the wage rate changes. If a firm uses an unchanged quantity of other inputs, and if other firms ignore the wage rate change, then the firm's *MRP* curve shows its demand curve for labour.
- If those two assumptions are relaxed, then the firm's *MRP* curve will shift if the wage rate changes. Its demand curve for labour will not be given by either *MRP* curve, but it can be derived from them.
- A firm's *MRP* curves for labour and its demand curve for labour shift if there is a change in the demand for its output, or a change in the price of any other input, or a change in the productivity of any input.

14.2 Competitive and monopsonistic labour markets

In this section, we will look at some competitive labour markets and consider why the wage rates paid in them vary so much. We will then look at labour markets that are not competitive, because the assumption that the labour is hired by many different firms does not apply.

But before we do any of that, we must look at the concepts of transfer earnings and economic rent.

Transfer earnings and economic rent

Each part of Figure 14.4 shows the demand and supply curves, *D* and *S*, in the labour market for some particular occupation. The equilibrium quantity is 400 workers hired each week, and each is paid the equilibrium weekly wage of £500.

The supply curve meets the wage axis at a wage of £300. This tells us that if the wage were below £300, no one would want to work in this occupation. If the wage were £300, one worker would. So this first worker would be willing to leave another occupation to work at this one if the wage were only £300. The income needed to keep a worker, or indeed any factor of production, in its present use is called **transfer earnings**. So, for this first worker, the transfer earnings are £300, as shown in part (a) as a purple line.

However, this worker earns £500. The excess between the actual income of any factor of production and its transfer earnings is called its **economic rent**. So this worker has economic rent of £200, as shown by a pink line.

At higher wages, more people will work in this occupation. Part (a) shows, for example, that if the wage were to rise to £400, then 300 workers would. So the 300th worker has transfer earnings of £400, shown by another purple line. This worker also earns £500, and so has an economic rent of £100, shown by another pink line.

Part (a) also shows, for example, that if the wage were to rise to £500, then 400 workers would work in

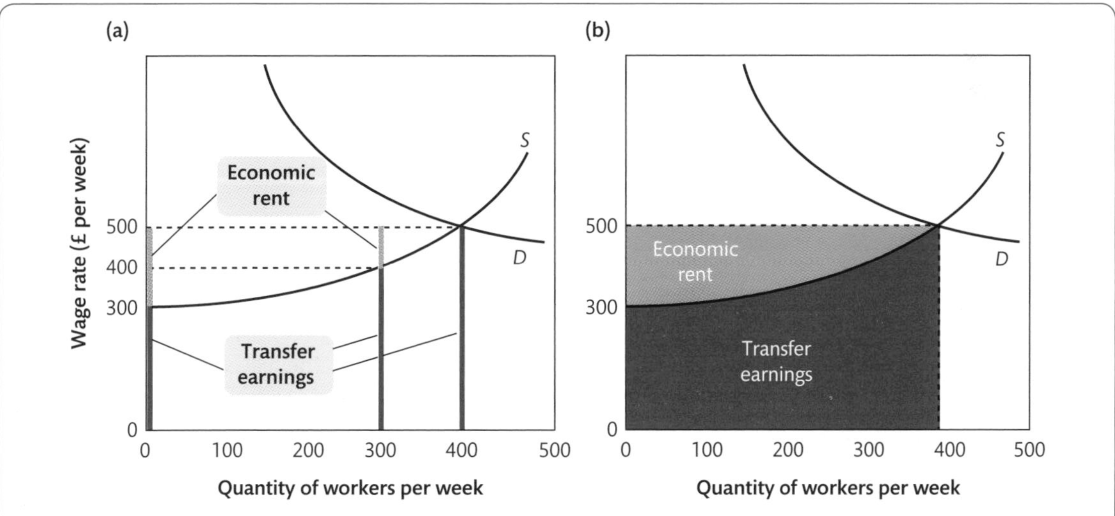

Figure 14.4 **Economic rent and transfer earnings**

All workers in this labour market are paid £500 a week. Part (a) shows that the first worker must be paid £300 to work in this market; so £300 of that worker's wage is transfer earnings and the remaining £200 is economic rent. The 300th worker has transfer earnings of £400, leaving £100 in economic rent. The 400th worker has transfer earnings of £500, so this worker receives no economic rent. Part (b) shows the total transfer earnings and economic rent in the market.

this occupation. However, the 400th worker would not do so for any less, so this worker has transfer earnings of £500, shown by yet another purple line; as there is no difference between this worker's wage and transfer earnings, this worker has no economic rent.

The sloping *S* curve shows that all 400 workers have different transfer earnings and different economic rents. If we put in purple and pink lines for all of them, we would end up with the purple and pink areas as shown in part (b). The total wage bill in this occupation is 400 workers at £500 a week, or £200,000 a week. This sum is represented by the purple area plus the pink area, which together form a rectangle 400 workers long and £500 high. The purple area represents the amount of this sum that is transfer earnings, and the pink area represents the amount that is economic rent.

Question 14.2 Suppose the employer of the 300th worker found out that that worker's transfer earnings were £400. Could the employer reduce the worker's wage to £400 without losing the worker?

Compensating differences in wages

Why do different occupations have very different wages? Why don't people in low-wage occupations move to high-wage ones? This would reduce the supply of labour in low-wage occupations, forcing their wages up, and it would increase the supply in high-wage occupations, forcing wages down.

The 18th-century Scottish economist Adam Smith answered these questions by saying that many high-paid jobs were unpleasant, and to tempt anyone to undertake them, firms had to offer high wages to compensate them for the unpleasantness. Wage differences arising for this reason are called **compensating differences.**

There are many ways in which an occupation can be unpleasant, so that those who do it earn high wages. Here are three of Smith's examples:

- **mining**, because it is dirty and dangerous;
- **butchering**, because it is brutal and messy;
- **innkeeping**, because innkeepers are 'exposed to the brutality of every drunkard'.

Figure 14.5 gives another example. Part (a) shows the market for cleaners on offshore oil rigs and part (b) shows the market for cleaners in an onshore town. Offshore occupations are less pleasant because of the risk, the need to be away from home for long periods, and few social activities in leisure time. No one will work offshore unless the wage is relatively high, so the supply curve in part (a) starts at a wage above the onshore wage, and this supply curve intersects the demand curve at an even higher wage.

Offshore cleaners earn about twice as much as onshore ones, but they have little economic rent. Their earnings are principally the high transfer earnings needed to tempt them to work offshore.

Human capital and training

Smith also noted that there are some jobs for which workers need to be educated with certain skills and knowledge. People will be reluctant to defer their entry into the workforce, or take time away from it, to undertake this education unless these occupations compensate them with high wages. The knowledge and skills that workers acquire through education, and also experience, are called **human capital**.

Figure 14.6 compares two related occupations with very different wages: dentists in part (a) and dental hygienists in part (b). The high wage for dentists arises chiefly because the supply curve starts at a high wage. There are several reasons for this.

- No one would do a five-year dental course unless dentists' wages were to compensate them for that.
- Dentists want a high wage to compensate them for the risk of litigation from dissatisfied patients.
- Dental schools admit only able people, so most dentists could have instead trained for other well-

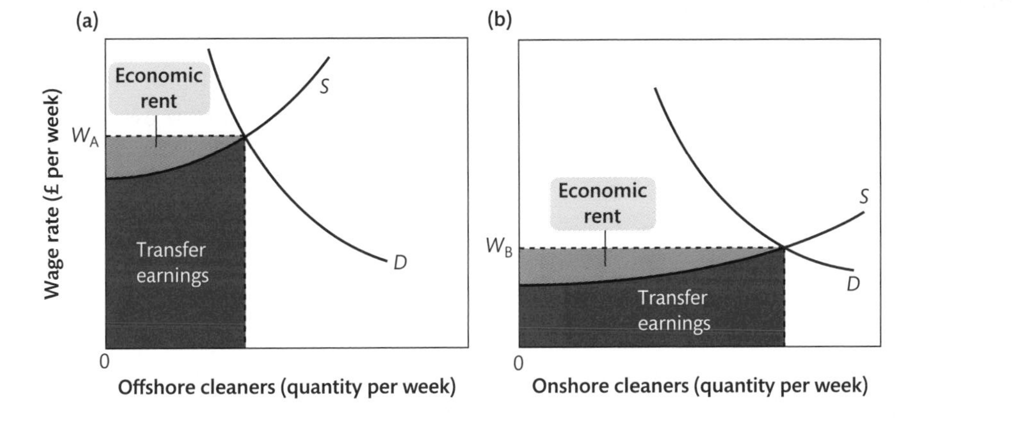

Figure 14.5 **A compensating wage difference arising from unpleasantness**

Part (a) shows the market for an unpleasant job: *S* starts at a high wage because no one will work for less. Part (b) shows the market for a nicer job; *S* starts at a low wage because people will work for a low wage. The wage in part (a), W_A, is much higher than the wage in part (b), W_B, to compensate workers for the unpleasantness. The purple and pink areas show the transfer earnings and the economic rent.

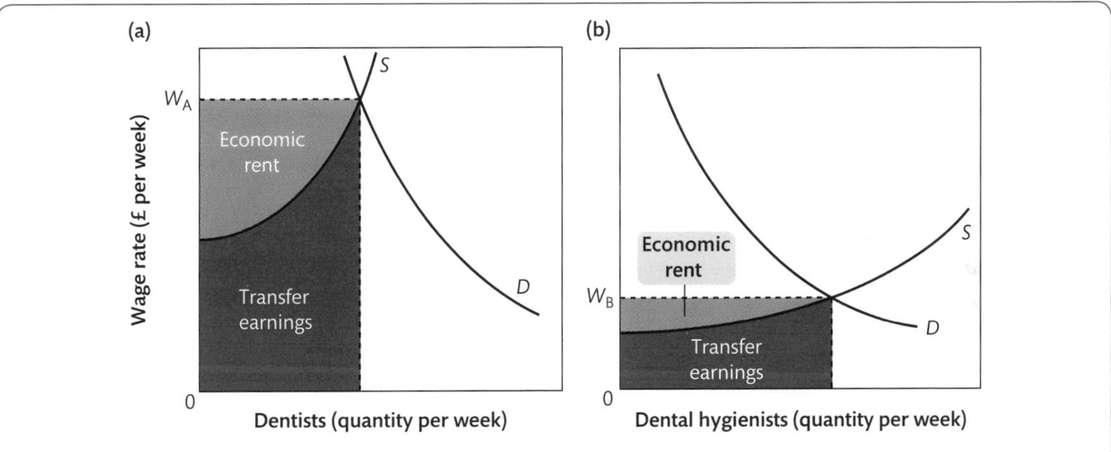

Figure 14.6 **Wage differences arising from several supply-side factors**

Part (a) concerns dentists and part (b) concerns dental hygienists. The lowest wage at which people will be dentists is relatively high, partly to compensate them for their lengthy training and the risk of litigation, and partly because they are able people who could earn high wages in other occupations. So the wage for dentists, W_A, is well above that for hygienists, W_B. Some dentists earn considerable economic rent.

paid careers. So they have to expect high wages to stop them training for other jobs.

Although high transfer earnings are needed to tempt people to be dentists, their high wages mean that some also have much economic rent.

Human capital and experience

In many occupations, people acquire knowledge and skills through experience, and this extra human capital makes them more attractive to employers. So experienced workers often have relatively high wages. Their high wages can be arranged in various ways including the following:

- **pay scales, up which people progress over time**;
- **bonus payments**;
- **responsibility allowances**;
- **promoted posts**.

However, employers may not reward workers for all the human capital they gain by experience. This is because human capital comes in two forms.

- **General human capital.** This is human capital that makes a worker more attractive to all employers. For example, a university lecturer may develop a new line of research that would interest other colleges. Employers need to pay higher wages to people like this to prevent them leaving for other employers who recognize their value and offer them high wages.
- **Firm-specific human capital.** This is human capital that makes a worker more attractive only to their present employer. For example, a city council may employ a guide who learns much about the city, but this may not interest any other employers. Employers do not have to pay higher wages to staff with firm-specific human capital, because other employers do not value it and will not offer them high wages.

Human capital and innate ability

We have defined human capital as knowledge and skills. All skills can be improved with training, but some people are born with **innate ability**, that is the potential to develop a particular skill to a very high level.

Figure 14.7 compares footballers in a high league and a low league. The players in each league may train equally hard, but those in the high league have more innate ability. This leads to the relatively inelastic supply curve for them, as shown in part (a), because no matter how high the wage goes, it is hard to attract many more suitable players because few people have the innate ability required.

Incidentally, innate abilities lead to very high wages only if they produce a product with a high marginal revenue product. This arises with high-league footballers, because people pay high prices to see them.

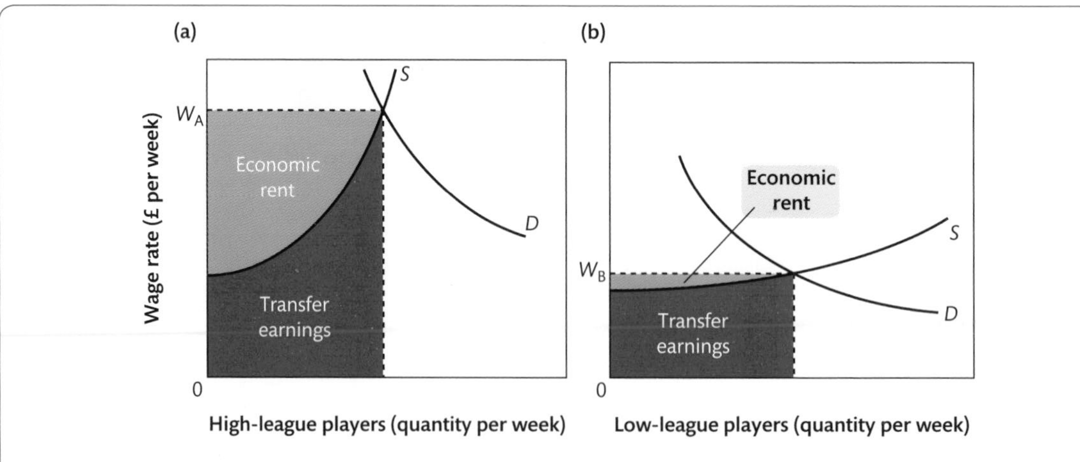

Figure 14.7 **Wage differences arising from differences in demand and innate ability**

The wage for high-league players, shown as W_A in part (a), is much higher than the wage for low-league players, shown as W_B in part (b). High leagues have higher attendances and higher ticket prices, so players have a high *MRP* leading to a high demand curve for them. Also, few people have the innate ability needed for the high league, so supply is inelastic. The earnings in high league include much economic rent.

So they have a high *MRP*, and in turn the demand for them is greater than that in part (b) of Figure 14.7 for players in a low league.

The combination of a higher demand and an inelastic supply gives high-league footballers far higher wages. Much of this is economic rent: it would take an enormous drop in wages to encourage top-league footballers to switch to another occupation, such as playing rugby.

Wage differences caused by demand changes

The wage differences between occupations at which we have looked so far are likely to be permanent. We would always expect onshore cleaners to earn less than offshore cleaners, low-league footballers to earn less than high-league footballers, and dental hygienists to earn less than dentists. But temporary wage differences between occupations can arise if the demand for them changes.

For example, suppose that, currently, the demand and supply of car assembly workers are as shown by D_0 and S_0 in part (a) of Figure 14.8, while the demand and supply of security staff are as shown by D_0 and S_0 in part (b). The current wage of assemblers, WA_0, is similar to that of security staff, WS_0.

But now suppose the demand for car assemblers in part (a) decreases to D_1, perhaps because of growing automation on assembly lines. And suppose that, simultaneously, the demand for security staff increases to D_1 in part (b). The wage for assemblers falls to WA_1, while the wage for security staff rises to WS_1.

This difference may disappear over time. This is because the rise in security staff wages will make some car assemblers keen to leave car plants and work as security staff. In turn, the supply of assemblers will decrease to S_1 in part (a), while the supply of security staff will increase to S_1 in part (b). When these shifts occur, the wages will become equal again at WA_0 and WS_0.

However, while a wage difference that is caused by demand changes may disappear in time, it may not disappear very quickly. In our example, some car assemblers might now wish they were security staff, but they may not find many security jobs near their

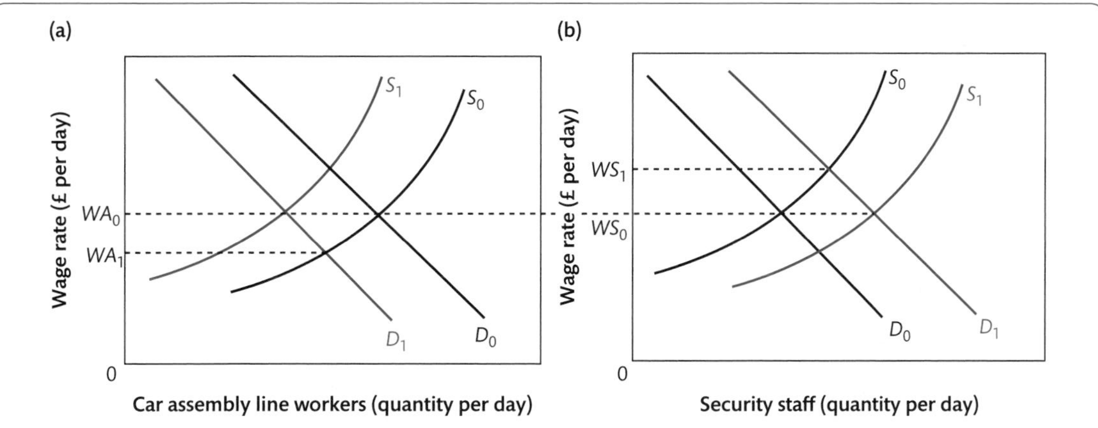

Figure 14.8 **Wage differences arising from changes in demand**

The initial wage for car assemblers in part (a), WA_0, equals the initial wage for security staff in part (b), WS_0. Then the demand for car assemblers decreases and their wages fall to WA_1, while the demand for security staff increases and their wages rise to WS_1. Many car assemblers are tempted to become security staff—but they may not wish to move out of car plant neighbourhoods to find jobs, and older car assemblers may not wish to retrain. But, after some years, when people have time to move and retrain, the supply of car assemblers will fall, while the supply of security staff will rise, and their wages may return to equality at WA_0 and WS_0 once again.

homes, and they may not want to move away from their friends and families. Also, older assemblers may be reluctant to retrain as security staff because they might work in that occupation for only a few years. So the shifts to S_1 in each part may take many years to complete, and meanwhile a wage difference will persist, although it will shrink over time as the supply curves shift.

Monopsonistic labour markets

So far, we have studied competitive labour markets. We can use supply and demand analysis for these markets, because they have many sellers and many buyers.

However, some types of labour are employed by only a few firms, or even by only one. In the UK, for example, National Grid plc is the sole employer of electricity substation maintenance workers and Network Rail is the sole employer of railway track maintenance workers. In a market with only one buyer, that buyer is called a **monopsonist**; a labour market in which all the labour is hired by a monopsonist is a **monopsonistic labour market**.

Unlike the firms we have met so far, a firm that is a monopsonistic hirer of labour is not a price-taker in its labour market. Instead, if it wants extra workers, it must raise the wage to tempt people to transfer from other occupations. So it actually faces the upward-sloping market supply curve of labour for the occupation concerned.

Figure 14.9 concerns a market for a type of labour that is hired by only one firm. This firm faces the market supply curve *S*. *S* shows that if, for example, the firm wants to hire 1,000 workers, then it must pay £20 per hour. If it wants 2,000, that is 1,000 more, then it must raise the wage to £30. This is a rise of £10, or 1,000p, and we can deduce that every time the firm wants just one more worker, it must raise the wage by 1p.

This curve also shows, at each employment level, the **average cost of labour**, *ACL*, to the firm. This is the total cost of labour divided by the number of workers.

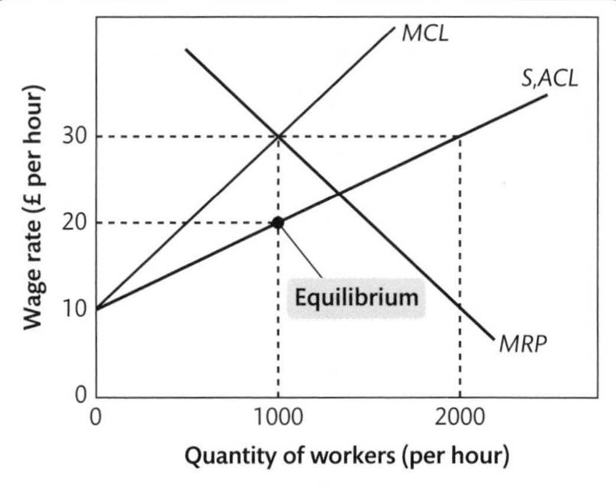

Figure 14.9 **A monopsonistic labour market**

S,ACL shows how many workers wish to work at each wage for the sole employer in this labour market; it also shows the average cost to the firm of hiring each possible number. *MCL* and *MRP* show the marginal cost of labour to the firm, and the marginal revenue product. The firm will hire 1,000 workers, because at any lower number *MRP* exceeds *MCL*. To hire 1,000, *S* shows that the firm must pay £20 an hour, so the equilibrium position is at the black dot.

For example, if the firm hires 1,000 workers at a wage of £20, then its total cost of labour is £20,000; dividing this by 1,000 workers gives an average cost of £20 per worker.

Suppose this firm employs 1,000 workers on £20 an hour, and then wants one extra worker. It will have to raise the wage by 1p to £20.01. It will have to pay this wage to all 1,001 workers, so its wage bill will rise by 1p for all its initial workers as well as by the £20.01 paid to the new worker. So the total wage bill will now be about £20,030, an increase of £30. So the marginal cost of labour here is £30. The curve *MCL* shows the marginal cost of labour to the firm at each employment level.

To find the profit-maximizing number of workers, the firm must also consider the marginal revenue product of labour. Suppose this is as shown by the curve *MRP*. This curve shows the extra revenue that would arise each time an extra worker were employed, assuming the firm uses constant amounts of all other inputs.

The firm will hire extra workers as long as they add more to revenue than they add to its cost, that is as long as *MRP* is above *MCL*. So it will hire 1,000 workers. *S* shows that it must pay £20 an hour to attract this number. So, with the current quantity of other inputs, the firm will settle with 1,000 workers and a wage of £20 an hour, as shown by the black dot. Notice that it settles at a combination of wage and employment that is not on its *MRP* curve. At the employment level of 1,000, the *MRP* of labour is £30 an hour, but each worker is paid less, £20.

14.2 **Summary**

- The wage someone needs to be persuaded to work in a given occupation is called transfer earnings. Most people have an income in excess of their transfer earnings; this excess is called economic rent.
- Some occupations have high wages to compensate people for unpleasant aspects of the job or for the need for lengthy education to acquire the necessary human capital in the form of skills and knowledge.
- Wages are high in some occupations that need an innate ability to master the skills at a high level.
- Wage differences may occur between two occupations if the demand for either or both of them changes. These wage differences cause supply curve shifts that may, in time, end the wage differences.
- A labour market with a single employer is called a monopsonistic labour market and the firm in it is called a monopsonist. A monopsonist faces the upward-sloping market supply curve for the occupation concerned, and it must raise the wage rate it offers whenever it requires more workers.

14.3 A minimum wage, trades unions, and efficiency wages

Some firms actually pay higher wages than those that we would predict on the basis of the analysis given in the last section. In this section, we look at the following three factors that may cause some firms to pay higher wages.

- **Governments may impose a minimum wage**: this may force some firms to pay higher wages.
- **Workers may form trade unions**: sometimes, these can use their power to force wages higher.
- **Some firms may pay efficiency wages**: this means that they pay higher wages voluntarily, to encourage their workers to be efficient.

We will begin by looking briefly at minimum wage legislation and trade unions, and then see how they may affect labour markets in similar ways.

Minimum wage legislation

Many countries have laws about the lowest wage a worker can be paid: the wage laid down is called a **minimum wage**. The UK introduced laws for a National Minimum Wage in 1999. The wages that apply an 2011-12 are as follows:

- **£6.08 an hour for workers aged 21 or over**;
- **£4.98 an hour for workers aged 18-20**;
- **£3.68 an hour for workers aged 16 and 17**.

Trade unions

So far, we have effectively assumed that all workers individually agree their terms and conditions of work with their employers. But sometimes workers in a labour market band together to form an association called a **trade union**. Any given union might list a number of objectives, but the following are the most widespread.

- **To negotiate with employers over wages**. In this chapter, we will focus on this role of unions.
- **To negotiate with employers over working conditions, including training opportunities**.
- **To help individual members in dispute with their employers**. For example, members may want compensation for injuries at work, or believe their employers have broken employment laws.
- **To provide social activities for their members**.
- **To support a political party that they believe will best further their members' interests**.

Over a quarter of workers belong to a trade union. A major reason for this is that if an individual member tries to negotiate with an employer about wages, or any other matter, the employer may be heavy-handed, knowing that it could easily find a replacement if the worker were to resign. But if a union negotiates with the firm, and can threaten to call its members out on strike, then the firm may become more conciliatory.

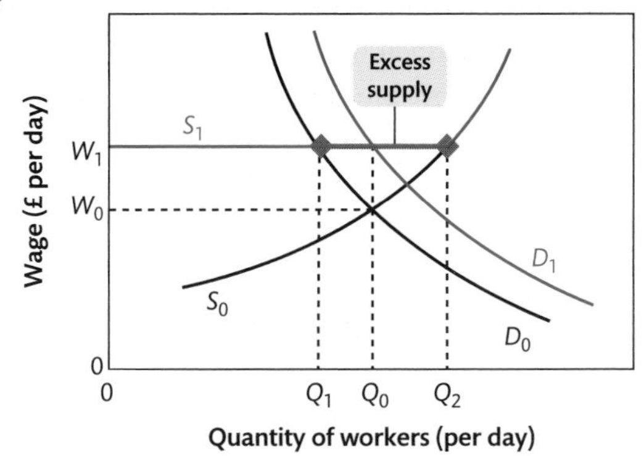

Figure 14.10 **A competitive labour market with a minimum wage or trade union**

The market is initially in equilibrium with wage W_0 and employment Q_0. If the government imposes a minimum wage of W_1, or a union negotiates a wage of W_1, the supply curve becomes the kinked line S_1 and employment falls to Q_1; but now Q_2 people wish to work, so there is an excess supply of labour. A union must try to prevent these unemployed people from offering to work for less than W_1. The union could maintain employment at Q_0, despite the higher wage, if it could somehow increase the demand for labour to D_1.

A minimum wage in a competitive market

The effect of introducing a minimum wage in a competitive labour market is shown in Figure 14.10. Initially, there is no minimum wage and the actual wage is W_0 where the initial supply curve, S_0, intersects the initial demand curve, D_0. And initially Q_0 workers are hired each day.

Now suppose a minimum wage is introduced. If this is set at a level below W_0, then it will have no effect. But we will suppose that it is set at the higher wage W_1. Notice that, at this wage, the number of workers who would be willing to work in the market at this wage is Q_2, as shown by S_0.

As a result of the minimum wage, firms can no longer hire workers at W_0, and now they actually face the kinked supply curve S_1. This shows that the firms can hire as many workers as they want at the minimum wage of W_1, provided that they do not want more than Q_2; if they want more, then they must pay more than W_1, as shown by S_0.

The market will settle where S_1 intersects D_0, with Q_1 workers hired at W_1. So although the wage has risen, employment has fallen. It is the fear of this effect on employment that deters governments S from setting a high minimum wage. Notice that there is now an excess supply of labour, for while at the new wage Q_1 people have jobs, Q_2 people would like a job.

A trade union in a competitive market

We can also use Figure 14.10 to shows the effects of a trade union in a competitive labour market. Suppose that, initially, the union takes no action, so this market settles where the initial demand and supply curves, D_0

and S_0, intersect, with the wage at W_0 per day and Q_0 workers hired each day.

There are many firms in this market. If some workers try to negotiate a wage above W_0 with their own firms, they may fail. Their firms know that if they refuse to pay more, the workers are unlikely to leave because other firms also pay W_0. But suppose the workers form a union, which demands a wage increase from all firms. It could call all the workers out on strike, and so bring the firms to a standstill. So the firms may choose some representatives to negotiate with the union.

Suppose the union and employers eventually agree on a wage of W_1. If all the workers belong to the union, then it has a monopoly supply of labour for the occupation concerned, and no one will work for less than W_1. So the supply curve will again become the kinked curve S_1. This is because firms can hire as many workers as they want at the wage of W_1, provided that they do not want more than Q_2; if they want more, then they must pay more than W_1, as shown by S_0.

The market will settle where S_1 intersects D_0, with Q_1 workers hired at W_1. So although the wage rises, employment falls. And there is now an excess supply of labour, for while at the new wage Q_1 people have jobs, Q_2 people would like a job.

In practice, the extent to which unions can try to raise wages is constrained by several factors.

- **Some workers may not belong to the union**. The smaller the union's membership is, the less worried employers will be about the threat of a strike. Ideally, the union would like all the firms to operate a **closed shop**, in which they would agree to employ only union members, so that the union would have a monopoly supply for the occupation concerned. However, closed shops have been illegal in the UK since 1990.
- **The excess supply of labour creates an alternative pool of labour**. If the union pushes the wage up very far, the excess supply of labour may be very high. Then firms might be able to replace all union members by new employees who agree not to join the union and who will accept a wage below W_1.
- **The fact that wage increases lead to fewer jobs may discourage a union from seeking a substantial wage increase**. However, when a wage rise is negotiated, the union often insists that the firms agree to let employment fall through **natural wastage**, that is when workers retire or leave, and not by forced redundancy.

This third constraint can be further reduced if, at the same time as seeking a wage rise, the union could somehow increase the demand for labour. If, in Figure 14.10, it could raise this to D_1, then the market would settle at the desired wage of W_1 with the same level of employment, Q_0, as before. To try to raise the demand the union could try several approaches. Here are two examples.

- **The union could lobby the government to restrict imports**. Then more products would be produced in the UK, leading to a higher demand for labour.
- **The union might try to agree training schemes that would make workers more productive**. But remember that the demand for labour depends on its marginal revenue product, *MRP*, and that *MRP* equals the marginal product of labour, *MP*, multiplied by the marginal revenue of the firm's output, *MR*. A training scheme might raise *MP*, but it might also lead to a much higher output; this could reduce the price of the output and so lead to a fall in *MR*. So *MRP* and the demand for labour would not necessarily rise.

A minimum wage with a monopsonist

The effect of a minimum wage in a labour market with a monopsonistic employer is shown in Figure 14.11. In each part here, the curves S_0,ACL_0 and MCL_0 apply before a minimum wage is introduced. The firm sets employment at 60 workers a week, where MCL_0 intersects *MRP*, and it pays a wage *of* £400 a week, which is read off S_0,ALC_0 at that employment level.

If a minimum wage is introduced below £400, it will have no effect. But if it is above £400, it may actually *increase* employment. To see why, suppose a minimum wage of £500 is introduced, as shown in part (a). This has two effects.

- **It creates a new supply curve, S_1,ACL_1, with a kink at 80 workers**. The firm can hire up to 80 workers at £500. If it wants any more, it must pay a higher wage, as shown by S_0,ACL_0.
- **It creates a new marginal cost curve, MCL_1, which has two parts**. To the left of the kink in S_1,ACL_1, the firm can hire up to 80 workers at £500, so the marginal cost of labour is always the £500 paid to an extra worker; so MCL_1 here lies along S_1,ACL_1. To the right of the kink, where the firm wants more than 80 workers, it would have to pay more than £500, so it would face the original supply and average cost curve, and so face the original marginal cost curve. So its new marginal cost curve, MCL_1, is in two separate parts, one on each side of the kink in S_1,ACL_1. The two parts are shown dashed and joined by another dashed line to show that they belong to one another.

The firm will hire more workers as long as *MRP* exceeds MCL_1, and this means hiring 80. So the firm has responded to a minimum wage that was above its original wage by hiring 20 more workers. The reason is that, despite the higher wage, the marginal cost of labour between 60 and 80 workers is lower than it was before, and that is because the firm can hire extra workers at the minimum wage of £500, whereas before it had to raise the wage paid to all workers when it wanted any more, and this meant paying a little more to all existing workers as well as paying a new one.

If the minimum wage is raised above £500, and so above the level at which *MRP* intersects the original supply and average cost curve, employment will fall back. Part (b) of Figure 14.11 shows what happens if it is raised to £600 a week. There is then a new supply and average cost curve, S_2,ACL_2, which is initially horizontal at this wage, but is kinked where this horizontal curve meets S_0,ACL_0. To the right of the kink, S_2,ACL_2 follows the original S_0,ACL_0. There is also a new marginal cost curve for labour, MCL_2, which, like MCL_1, is in

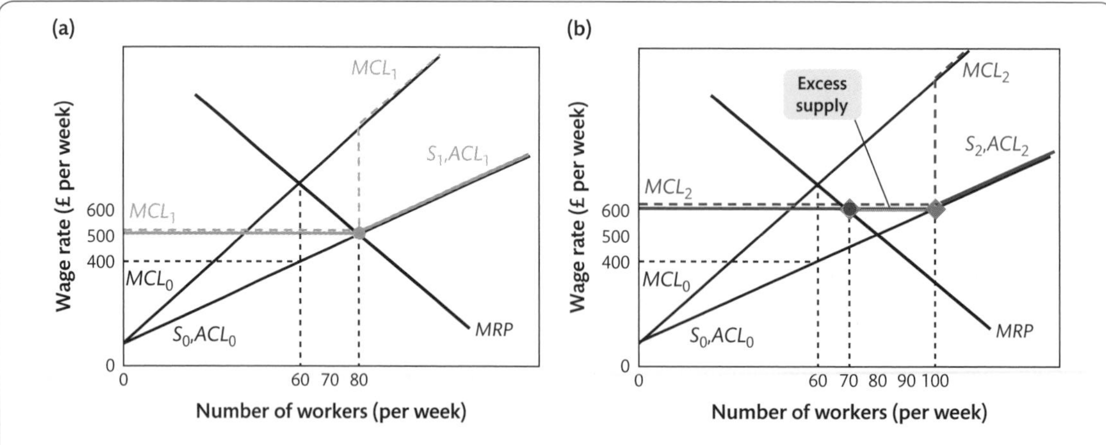

Figure 14.11 **A monopsonistic employer with a minimum wage or trade union**

Each part shows that initially the firm hires 60 workers at £400 a week. Part (a) shows that if the government imposes a minimum wage of £500, or the union negotiates one of £500, then the firm will actually increase its employment to 80 workers. If the minimum or negotiated wage rises above £500, employment will fall back, as in part (b) where the wage is £600 and employment is 70. In each part, the new supply and average cost curve is kinked, the new marginal cost curve has two separate parts, one each side of the kink, and employment is set where *MRP* intersects the new *MCL*. There is an excess supply of labour in part (b).

two separate parts, one each side of the kink. The two parts are dashed, and joined by a dashed line. The firm will select the number of workers where *MRP* intersects MCL_2, here 70. However, 100 workers would like to work at this wage, so there is now an excess supply.

A trade union with a monopsonist

We can also use Figure 14.11 to shows the effects of a trade union in a monopsonistic labour market. Suppose there is initially no union, so the firm hires 60 workers, where *MRP* intersects MCL_0, and it pays a wage of £400, read off S_0,ACL_0 at this level. Now suppose all this firm's workers join a union to form a monopoly supplier of labour. A market with a monopoly supplier and a monopsonistic buyer is called a **bilateral monopoly**.

If the union negotiates a higher wage between £400 and £500, employment rises. For example, part (a) shows what happens if it negotiates a wage of £500. The firm will now face the kinked supply and average cost curve S_1,ACL_1: this shows that it can now hire up to 80 workers at a wage of £500, but if it wants more than 80 workers, it must pay more than £500, as shown by S_0,ACL_0.

As with the minimum wage, this new kinked supply curve leads to the two-part marginal cost curve, MCL_1, and the firm will again hire 80 workers at the negotiated wage of £500. So it has responded to the higher wage by hiring more workers, because the marginal cost of labour between 60 and 80 workers is lower than it was before.

If the union presses for yet higher wages, employment will fall back. Part (b) of Figure 14.11 shows what happens if it presses for £600 a week. The firm will then face a new supply and average cost curve, S_2,ACL_2, which is initially horizontal at this wage, but is kinked where it meets S_0,ACL_0. And associated with this is the two-part marginal cost of labour curve MCL_2.

The firm selects the number of workers where *MRP* intersects MCL_2, here 70. So if the union pushes the wage up from £500 to £600, the firm will respond by hiring 10 fewer workers. And now 100 workers would like to work for it, so there is an excess supply of labour.

Minimum wages and employment

Figure 14.10 shows that, in competitive labour markets, imposing a minimum wage reduces employment. This fear was a major cause of concern before the National Minimum Wage Act was passed in 1998. In the event, analyses of the impact of the National Minimum Wage suggest that it has not reduced employment, despite raising the wages of those whom it affects by about 15% (Centre for Economic Performance, Policy Analysis, 2008, *The National Minimum Wage: The Evidence of its Impact on Jobs and Inequality*).

There are several possible reasons for this result.

- We saw in Figure 14.11 that a minimum wage could increase employment in monopsonistic markets, and increases in employment in these may offset the decreases in competitive markets.
- The minimum wage has been set at a level to affect only a small percentage of the workforce, perhaps 5%, so even if a fifth of these lost their jobs, employment would fall by just 1%.
- Employment levels are affected by many factors, notably the state of the economy, and it is hard to be certain about the effects of one relatively small factor like the minimum wage: so the research findings have to be seen as tentative.
- Hours worked by each worker may have fallen, even if the number of workers has not fallen.
- Perhaps workers have become more productive.
- Perhaps some employers ignore the law and still pay wages below the minimum wage.

Question 14.3 Does the fall in employment caused by a minimum wage in a competitive labour market depend on the elasticity of demand for labour?

Efficiency wages

Consider the competitive labour market shown in part (a) of Figure 14.12. We would expect this market to settle where the demand and supply curves intersect, with 10,000 workers hired at a wage of £400 a week. This wage is shown on the figure as the market wage.

Surprisingly, though, the employers may decide to pay a higher wage. They may do so if they believe the higher wage will increase the productivity or efficiency of their employees. There are several reasons why an employer may believe that a higher wage will raise efficiency.

- **Nutrition**. In poor countries, a higher wage may allow workers to have an adequate diet and in turn work harder.
- **Employee selection**. If individual workers vary, then a firm with a wage above the market wage will attract more applicants and can select from a wider field. Once one employer does this, others may feel obliged to follow.
- **Discouraging shirking**. If employees cannot be frequently monitored to ensure they are efficient, then they may shirk. An employer's main deterrent is to threaten to dismiss any worker who is ever found shirking. This threat may not much concern a worker if all employers pay the market wage, because it may be readily possible to find another job at that wage. But if an employer pays above the market wage, then the employee has an incentive not to shirk, because being fired will result in a job with another employer at the lower market wage. Again, once one employer does this, others may feel obliged to follow, for fear of being left with a workforce of shirkers.

Most of the UK discussion of this topic focuses on shirking, and there may seem to be a fallacy in the argument here. Certainly, if one firm pays a wage above the market wage, then its workers have an incentive not to shirk. But once all firms do so, the incentive seems to disappear, because a dismissed worker would hope to secure a job at another firm that also pays over the market wage.

However, the higher wage *will* still deter shirking, and the reason is illustrated in part (b) of Figure 14.12. This reproduces the supply curve from part (a). Consider, for a moment, a wage of £500. The supply curve shows that if firms were to pay this wage, they could hire 11,000 workers, but unfortunately, many of them might shirk. Although those found shirking could be dismissed, the fear of dismissal is not much of a threat, because every worker in this market who wants a job at this wage has one.

But if employers were to hire fewer than 11,000 people at £500, then the fear of dismissal would become very real, because it might be followed by a period of unemployment. The fewer workers that firms were to hire at this wage, the stronger the threat of dismissal would be, because the fewer jobs there would be available. If firms were to hire just 8,000 people, so that there were an excess supply or unemployment of 3,000 workers, the threat would be so strong that no one would shirk.

At each possible wage, the supply curve shows how many workers would like jobs, and firms would have to hire fewer than that number to make people fear the threat of dismissal so much that no one would shirk. For example, at a wage of £700, 12,000 workers would like jobs, and perhaps no one would shirk if employers were to hire 10,000 to leave an excess supply of 2,000. The excess supply needed to secure non-shirking may be smaller at a wage of £700 than at a wage of £500, because the higher wage makes unemployment even more unappealing.

If we were also to find the wages needed to hire other numbers of non-shirkers, then we could plot the curve labelled the **no shirking constraint**. This shows the number of non-shirkers who could be hired at each wage. This curve is shown in part (b) and reproduced in part (a).

If firms want no shirkers at all, they will set the wage where the no-shirking constraint intersects the demand curve, that is £500, and hire the 8,000 workers at that point. This wage, which is needed to promote efficient working, is above the market wage and is called the **efficiency wage**. Notice that if employers pay an efficiency wage, the market has an excess supply of workers.

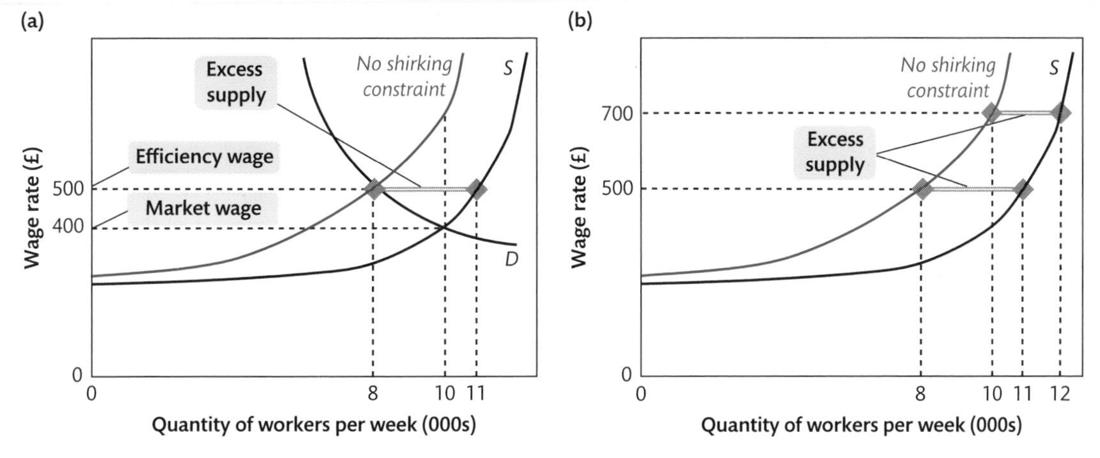

Figure 14.12 **An efficiency wage**

In part (a), *S* shows how many workers wish to work in this labour market at each wage. *D* is the demand for them. The market would clear at a wage of £400 a week with 10,000 workers, but they might shirk. The *No shirking constraint* in part (b) shows, for example, that to have 8,000 or 10,000 workers with no shirking, the wage must be £500 or £700; in each case there would be an excess supply of labour, with shirking deterred by the fear of dismissal and unemployment. The market settles in part (a) where the *No shirking constraint* intersects *D*, at an 'efficiency wage' of £500 and 8,000 workers. There is an excess supply of 3,000 workers.

14.2 Everyday economics

Ireland's see-sawing minimum wage

On 1 February 2011, the Irish government reduced the national minimum wage from €8.65 to €7.65, hoping that this would lead to a rise in employment. It is impossible to say whether this hope would have been realized, because the government soon lost an election and the cut was reversed in 1 July. The cut was naturally unpopular with many people, and poses a risk that some low-paid workers will give up working and prefer to live on state benefits, aggravating the government's financial problems.

14.3 Summary

- If a minimum wage is imposed in a competitive labour market, or if unions negotiate higher wages, then employment will decrease.
- If a minimum wage is imposed in a monopsonistic labour market, or if unions negotiate higher wages, employment will increase, until the new labour supply curve intersects *MRP*, and then decrease.
- Firms may pay efficiency wages, that is wages above the market wage, if they cannot easily monitor their workers. The idea is that the higher wage will lead to an excess supply of labour, in other words unemployment; this makes workers fear dismissal for shirking, so that shirking is deterred.

14.4 Discrimination in labour markets

In our discussions of labour markets, we have not yet considered whether some individuals fare better than others in these markets. In practice, employers may discriminate against certain groups of people. In this section, we will focus on racial and gender discrimination, because these attract the most publicity. But employers may also discriminate, or be believed to do so, against other groups, such as old people, short people, and people of particular religions.

We will look at three ways in which a group of people may be discriminated against:

- **in their right to enter an occupation;**
- **in their efforts to secure employment;**
- **in their efforts to seek promoted positions.**

Discrimination to entry to an occupation

Sometimes, employers will not employ workers of a particular group in a particular occupation. For example, in South Africa's apartheid period from 1948 to 1994, many jobs were closed to black people. And until the 1970s, many jobs in the UK were effectively closed to females, including, for example, most railway jobs.

This type of discrimination makes little sense for profit-maximizing firms. If the firms in a labour market refuse to hire people of a particular group, then the supply of labour to that market is lower than it would otherwise be, so the wage is higher than it would otherwise be, and, in turn, firms make less profit than they would otherwise make. So why might such racial and gender discrimination occur?

- **Racial discrimination**. Suppose a country is ruled by one race. It may wish to raise the income of that race in relation to other races. So it may bar people from other races from entering the better-paid occupations. This reduces the supply of labour to those occupations, forcing up the wage even more—but the race that is allowed to enter the occupation will benefit. The ruling race may also provide poorer education for people from other races, restricting their ability to acquire the human capital needed for many more skilled occupations.
- **Gender discrimination**. Suppose that when there were few females in the labour force, some occupations such as train driving were always done by males. Then time passed and more females entered the labour force and some wanted to drive trains. Employers might have welcomed this extra supply of labour as a way of holding wages down. But trade unions, which then comprised males, might have pressed for a gender bar to prevent the labour supply rising and the wage falling.

Explicit barring of different races and genders from an occupation is generally outlawed in the UK, but there are a few cases in which it is legal.

- **Acting**: race or gender discrimination is legal.
- **Modelling**: race or gender discrimination is legal.
- **Jobs involving a physical or close contact with the opposite sex**: gender discrimination is legal.
- **Places serving drink or food**: race discrimination is legal, but only if it is required for authenticity.

Discrimination against securing employment

Suppose there is no bar to any group entering an occupation. Even so, people in some groups may feel discriminated against when they apply for jobs. At first sight, this seems surprising.

To see why, suppose that one group of people is discriminated against when they apply for jobs in a labour market in which they wish to work. Then they will be unemployed, so there will be an excess supply of labour in the market. This excess supply should, in time, reduce the wage until the excess supply disappears, and then people from groups that are discriminated against should, nevertheless, get jobs, just like people from other groups.

However, discrimination against certain groups could persist in labour markets that have an excess supply when they are in equilibrium. We have seen several reasons why this might occur:

- **minimum wage legislation** (see Figures 14.10–14.11);
- **trade unions negotiating higher wages** (see Figures 14.10–14.11);
- **efficiency wages** (see Figure 14.12).

In these markets, there are always more people seeking work than there are jobs available. So employers can pick and choose among applicants, giving preference to some groups.

This type of discrimination should not always be held solely against employers. For example, suppose an occupation like electricians has, in the past, been predominantly been done by males, but now more females wish to take it up. Employers might in principle be keen to employ females, seeing the increased supply of labour as a downward force on the wages they have to pay.

But suppose the firms' *clients* believe females cannot do this work. Then these clients might prefer firms in which there are no females. So it might be in the commercial interests of each firm to discriminate against females, even though the firms know that females do the job just as well. The root problem here would lie with the public.

Discrimination for identical work

Suppose, now, that people of all groups do enter a given occupation. Sometimes it is alleged that firms pay people of one group more than those of another for doing identical work. However, there are sound economic reasons why firms may not wish to do this. For example, suppose a firm pays male workers £600 a week to do the same job that it pays females £500. The question arises why it would want to employ any males at all and not instead replace them with more females?

One possibility arises in labour markets in which there is an excess supply of labour and in which employers believe males are more productive than females. Here, firms might pay females less than males, thinking that if any females were to leave, they could be replaced by more males who, although being paid more, are believed to be more productive.

Of course, unequal pay for equal work is illegal under both UK and EU law, but it still occurs, and some cases come before the courts every year.

Gender discrimination over senior positions

Table 14.2 presents the average UK hourly earnings of full-time males and females in 20 different occupations. In most occupations, the average male earns more than the average female. It is unlikely that unequal pay for equal work is a major factor, because this is illegal.

The difference between the genders stems chiefly from the fact that each occupation contains a range of jobs with different wages. For example, secondary teachers include heads, deputy heads, heads of departments, teachers with responsibility allowances, and other teachers at different points on a pay scale that they climb over the years. The reason that male teachers on average earn more than females is that males occupy a disproportionate number of the better-paid jobs within teaching. A similar situation arises in many occupations. There are several reasons for this.

- **Prejudice by employers**. This is most likely to arise in occupations in which the labour market settles with an excess supply of labour, so that employers can pick and choose. Many females believe that they are discriminated against by appointing committees, which are mostly male.
- **Career breaks**. Many females take time out to have children and look after young children. So they acquire less human capital through experience than do males.

Table 14.2 Average hourly wages of full-time males and females in selected occupations, UK 2009 (£)

Occupation	Male	Female	F:M
Medical practitioners	38.61	30.32	79%
Lawyers, judges, & coroners	34.04	24.97	73%
Marketing & sales managers	27.45	22.16	81%
Higher education teachers	26.76	23.77	89%
Secondary education teachers	23.55	21.25	90%
Production managers	23.50	20.05	85%
Primary & nursery teachers	22.70	20.71	91%
Police officers (sergeant & below)	18.25	16.50	90%
Nurses	16.66	16.11	97%
Retail & wholesale managers	15.50	11.09	72%
Accounts & wages clerks	13.88	11.53	83%
General office assistants	11.31	10.26	91%
Assemblers & routine operatives	10.14	8.22	81%
Care assistants & home carers	8.88	8.52	96%
Chefs & cooks	8.54	7.99	94%
Food preparation trades	8.51	7.91	93%
Sales & retail assistants	8.28	7.49	90%
Cleaners & domestics	7.43	7.28	98%
Bar staff	6.62	6.20	94%
Kitchen & catering assistants	6.59	7.03	107%

Source: National Statistics Office, *Annual Survey of Hours and Earnings*, Table 14.6a. http://www.statistics.gov.uk/downloads/theme_labour/ashe-2010/2010-occ4.pdf. The wage rates exclude overtime premiums.

- **Less training and development**. If firms believe females are more likely to leave, perhaps to have children, they will be less inclined to give them costly training or a useful wide range of experience. Again, then, females will have less human capital than males.
- **Past differences in education**. In the past, far fewer females than males undertook further education, so among the age group of older workers currently in top positions, fewer females than males acquired human capital in this way.
- **Unequal retirement ages**. Females have often retired at 60 and males at 65. So there are more working males than females in the 60–65 age range, which has many senior positions.
- **Location choice**. If females take time out to look after children and retire earlier, many couples may prefer to live in a location in which the male has the best job opportunity, leaving the female to find the best job she can in the locality.

Occupation differences between genders

There is a further issue in gender differences in pay. Table 14.2 shows that, in 17 of the 20 occupations given there, females earn over 80% as much as men. Yet, taking these 20 groups together, it is possible to show that females on average actually earn little over 77% as much as males. This surprisingly low figure arises because females tend to work less often in high-paid occupations and more often in low-paid occupations. For example, there are over twice as many males as females in the six highest paid occupations in the table, and only about two-thirds as many males as females in the ten lowest paid.

This difference in occupations has an important implication that is often overlooked. In the economy as a whole, full-time females earn about 84% as much as full-time males. Now if, in every occupation in the economy, women on average were to earn the same as men, the average female might still earn only about 93% as much as the average male, simply because females tend to work less frequently in high-paid occupations and more frequently in low-paid ones.

This tendency might arise for several reasons.

- **Physical strength**. Some highly paid jobs may need strength of a level found more often in males than females.
- **Human capital differences**. In the past, females acquired less human capital than males through higher education and work experience. So fewer females may have been qualified for some highly paid occupations.
- **Preferences**. Preferences may differ between the genders over occupation choices, and this could perpetuate some gap in their average wages.

14.3 Everyday economics

Gender pay gaps for new US graduates

A recent report by the National Association of Colleges and Employers shows that, in 2010, female graduates entering the labour force earned on average $36,451, which is 17% less than the $44,159 earned on average by males.

'Female graduates earn 17% less than men', *Msn Money*, 18 May 2011
'Survey: male grads offered more money', *The Herald News*, 19 May 2011

Comment The gap might be partly explained by the types of degree subject chosen; we will see in Chapter 15 how this affects earnings. The only good news for new US female graduates *seemed* to be that a higher percentage of them found jobs—but this might have been because they were more willing to take part-time or temporary work.

14.4 Summary

- Except in a few cases, it is illegal in the UK to bar any race or gender from any type of employment.
- Some employers may discriminate against some groups: this is most likely in labour markets in which union pressure, minimum wage laws, or efficiency wages cause an excess supply of labour.
- It is illegal to pay different genders different wages for the same work; it is also irrational for a profit-maximizing firm to do so, unless it or its clients believe one gender performs better.
- In almost all occupations, females on average earn less than males. This is chiefly because males occupy a disproportionate share of the better paid jobs. Among the reasons for this are that, in the past, fewer females undertook higher education than males, females have tended to retire earlier than males, and females often take career breaks to have children and to look after them while they are young.
- Another reason why females on average earn less than males is that females tend more often to work in low-paid occupations and less often to work in high-paid ones.

In the next chapter we consider the markets for two more types of input: land and capital.

Glossary

Average cost of labour (*ACL*): the total cost of labour divided by the number of workers.

Bilateral monopoly: a market with a monopoly supplier and a monopsonistic buyer.

Closed shop: a situation, illegal in the UK, in which employers agree to employ union members only.

Compensating differences: wage differences that arise when unpleasant occupations offer high wages to tempt people to undertake them.

Competitive labour market: a market in which many households supply labour and many firms hire it.

Derived demand: applies to the demand for all inputs because this demand derives from the demand for the products they help to produce.

Economic rent: the excess between the income of any factor of production and its transfer earnings.

Efficiency wage: the wage needed to promote efficient working; it may exceed the market wage where the quantity of labour supplied equals the quantity demanded.

Firm-specific human capital: human capital that makes workers more attractive only to their present employers.

General human capital: human capital that makes workers more attractive to all employers.

Human capital: the knowledge and skills that workers acquire through education and experience.

Innate ability: the potential some people are born with to develop skills to a very high level.

Marginal cost of labour (*MCL*): the change in the total cost of labour when the number of workers changes by one.

Marginal revenue product (*MRP*): the change in total revenue when the quantity of one variable input is changed by one unit, while the quantity used of all other inputs is held constant.

Minimum wage: the lowest wage that employers are allowed to pay, as laid down in law.

Monopsonist: the term used for the buyer in a market that has only one buyer.

Monopsonistic labour market: a market in which all the labour is hired by a monopsonist.

Natural wastage: a fall in the number of workers resulting from workers retiring or leaving, rather than by forced redundancy.

No shirking constraint: this shows the number of non-shirkers who could be hired at each wage.

Trade union: an association of workers.

Transfer earnings: the income needed to keep any factor of production in its present use.

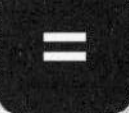

Answers to in-text questions

14.1 If the demand for the product is inelastic, then the rise in output will lead to a large fall in its price, and so in *MR*; so the downward force on *MRP* will be strong. The opposite happens if demand for the product is elastic.

14.2 No. The worker would then leave that firm and seek a similar job with another. So the worker would still have the same occupation, albeit with a different employer. Only if the market wage were to fall below the worker's transfer earnings of £300 would the worker seek a different occupation altogether.

14.3 Yes. If the demand is very inelastic, the minimum wage may raise the wage employers must pay, but it will have little effect on the number of workers they employ. Another reason why the minimum wage seems to have little effect on employment could be that the demand for low-paid jobs like cleaners and shelf stackers is inelastic, because it is hard to replace these workers with other inputs.

? Questions for review

14.1 Suppose you have a job, either full-time or part-time. What would you have to ask yourself in order to find out how whether you were earning any economic rent and, if so, how much?

14.2 Suppose you run a strawberry form, and you can hire as many strawberry-pickers as you want at the current wage. You currently hire extra pickers up to the point at which the wage, or *MCL*, equals the *MRP* of labour. Now suppose there is a big rise in the wage for pickers and you hire fewer, but you end up on a different *MRP* curve. What factors will determine whether it is above or below the original *MRP* curve?

14.3 Suppose you run a firm and some new technology is introduced that enables your workers to produce more. Why might the *MRP* of your workers actually fall, so that you want to hire fewer? And why might their *MRP* instead rise so that you want to hire more?

14.4 Suppose you work for a firm with a large workforce. You hope to persuade your employer to raise your wage. Which of the following might help your case? (**a**) You pay for some evening classes that will help you to work better. (**b**) You learn a great deal about the firm's employees, which makes you adept at organizing them into effective teams. (**c**) You join a trade union.

? Questions for discussion

14.1 Think of some occupations in which employers can readily monitor their workers to check they are not shirking, and therefore need not offer efficiency wages. And think of some occupations in which employers cannot easily monitor their workers, and so may feel the need to offer efficiency wages.

14.2 What factors explain the current tendency for females to work less often than males in high-paid occupations, and to work more often in low-paid occupations?

14.3 To reduce the gender pay gap, what could be done by (**a**) firms, (**b**) the government, (**c**) male workers, (**d**) female workers, and (**e**) people still in education?

✗ Common student errors

In essays on monopsonists, many students make an error in their version of Figure 14.9, because they label the *MRP* curve as *MRP,D*, implying that it is also a demand curve for labour; it is not. For example, at the wage of £20 shown, the firm there hires 1,000 workers, as also shown. If we were mistakenlyto take *MRP* to be the demand curve, we would mistakenly expect it to hire around 1,500.

Also, a student might draw a figure like part (a) of Figure 14.11 and say 'the union is unlikely to seek a wage above £500 because then employment will fall'. This would be true if it had already negotiated a wage of £500. But if it starts with, say, a wage of £400 and employment at 60, it could push for around £700 without driving employment below 60.

15

Land and Capital

Remember from Chapter 14 that the marginal revenue product of labour is the change in a firm's total revenue if it adds one more unit of labour to constant amounts of all other inputs; firms hire more labour if its marginal revenue product exceeds its marginal cost. Also, recall that the income needed to keep a factor of production in its present use is its transfer earnings; any income that it earns above this is its economic rent.

Suppose you run a business and consider buying some new capital that will last for many years: how would decide if this purchase is a good investment? Suppose you own some land with natural resources below it that can be mined: how much of this resource should you extract over the next year, and how much should you leave to extract in future? Suppose you stay in education beyond the school-leaving age: how would you decide if this education were likely to be a good investment?

This chapter shows you how to answer questions like these, by understanding:

- the demand for the many types of input that firms use;
- how firms and other people use the concept of discounting to make investment decisions;
- how firms that own non-renewable natural resources decide the rate at which to extract them;
- the factors that determine when these non-renewable resources will eventually be depleted;
- how children reaching the school-leaving age may decide whether to invest in further education.

15.1 Two types of decision about the use of inputs

Suppose you run a firm that bakes pizzas and delivers them in vans. You will use many inputs, and you must decide how much of each to use. We can divide your decisions into two groups.

The first group of decisions concerns inputs for which you need to think only about the immediate future. This applies to the following inputs.

- **Rented land:** for example, you may decide how much parking space to rent for the next year.
- **Rented or hired capital:** for example, you may decide how much building space to rent for the next year, and how many vans to hire for the next week.
- **Intermediate products:** for example, you may decide how much dough and cheese to buy during the next week.
- **Labour:** for example, you may decide how many cooks and drivers to hire for the next week.

In the last chapter, we saw how you would make your decisions in the case of labour. In this section, we will show how the same approach can be used for all of the other inputs we have just listed.

However, you may also make a second group of decisions for which you need to look further ahead. This would apply to the following inputs:

- **bought capital;**
- **bought land.**

To see why you must look well ahead here, suppose you consider buying a van with a five-year life. Then you must consider how much money it will earn for you over that whole period. We study decisions of this type in the next section.

In later sections, we will study two other types of decision that require people to look well ahead. These are as follows.

- **People who own natural resources:** they must decide how much to extract and sell next year, and how much to keep and extract in future.
- **People who have reached the school-leaving age:** they must decide how much to invest in extra education to acquire extra human capital.

Marginal revenue product analysis

Let's return to rented land, rented or hired capital, intermediate products, and labour. For decisions about how many of these inputs to use, a firm can use the marginal revenue product analysis that we discussed in the case of labour in Chapter 14. The marginal revenue product of any input, *MRP*, is the amount by which a firm's revenue increases if it uses one more unit of that input while using constant amounts of all other inputs. For example, suppose a firm uses one more unit of an input and produces three more units of output, so the marginal product of the input, *MP*, is three, and suppose an extra unit of output adds £10 to the firm's revenue, so the firm's marginal revenue, *MR*, is £10. Then the *MRP* of the input equals its *MP* multiplied by the *MR*, which is £30.

The *MRP* of any input becomes smaller when a firm uses more of it; this is because adding more and more units of that input to fixed amounts of other inputs will add less and less to output. A firm will choose to use the quantity of any input where its *MRP* equals its marginal cost. Let's see why.

- **If it were to choose a quantity where the *MRP* of the input were more than its marginal cost,** then using another unit would add more to the firm's revenue than its costs, so its profit would rise.
- **If it were to choose a quantity where the *MRP* of the input were less than its marginal cost,** then using one fewer unit would reduce the firm's costs more than it reduced its revenue, so its profit would rise.

If the market for the input is competitive, with many buyers and sellers, then we can use a firm's *MRP* figures to derive its demand curve for that input, as we saw in

Figure 14.3. And we can add the demand curves for the input for all the firms that use it to get the market demand curve for the input, as we saw in Figure 14.1. The point at which this curve intersects the market supply curve gives the equilibrium price and quantity.

We will now look at some figures that illustrate some input markets. In each case, the caption to the figure notes that the marginal revenue product for the input equals its marginal product times the marginal revenue from the product it produces.

Rented land

As an example of a market for rented land, Figure 15.1 gives the market for rented arable land, that is land used for crops, in a given region. The supply curve here is very inelastic at high rents because, no matter how high the rent is, there is a limit to how much arable land can be supplied, at least in the short run. In the long run, some land currently used as pasture for animals could be improved and then switched to arable use, albeit at a cost.

The total annual income of the landowners equals the annual rent per hectare, *R*, multiplied by the number of hectares let, *Q*. The figure divides this total income into two parts.

- **Transfer earnings.** This is what the owners of a factor of production must be paid to keep it in its present use. The slope of the supply curve shows that, as the rent rises, more and more landowners will be willing to transfer their land to arable use and let it for that use.
- **Economic rent.** This is the income that the owners of a factor of production receive in excess of their transfer earnings. It is the gap between the rent they actually receive, *R*, and their transfer earnings, as shown by the supply curve.

Rented capital

As an example of a market for rented buildings, Figure 15.2 gives the market for rented office space in a given city. This supply curve is also very inelastic at high rents because, in the short run at least, only a limited amount of office space can be supplied, no matter how high the rent is. In the long run, new offices can be built.

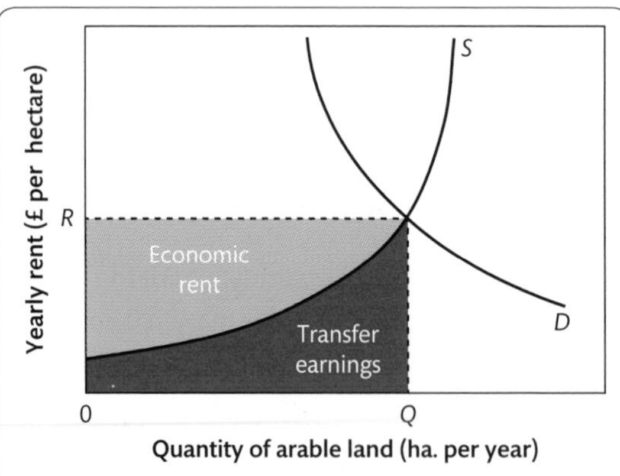

Figure 15.1 **The market for rented arable land in a region**

The demand curve for land for crops depends on the marginal revenue product of the land for firms that use it. This equals the marginal product of the land—the increase in output from using an extra hectare—multiplied by the marginal revenue from an extra unit of output.

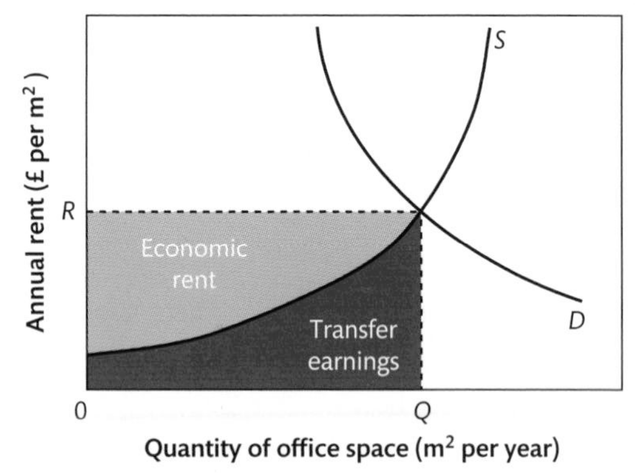

Figure 15.2 **The market for rented office space in a city**

The demand curve for rented office space depends on its marginal revenue product for the firms that use it. This equals the marginal product of the office space—the increase in output from using an extra square metre—times the marginal revenue from an extra unit of output.

The total annual income of the building owners equals the rent, per square metre, *R*, multiplied by the number of square metres let, *Q*. The figure divides this total income into two parts.

- **Transfer earnings.** The slope of the supply curve shows that, as the rent rises, more and more building owners will be willing to transfer their buildings to office use and let it for that use.
- **Economic rent.** This is the gap between the rent that building owners actually receive, *R*, and their transfer earnings as shown by the supply curve.

Hired capital and intermediate products

As an example of the market for a type of hired capital, Figure 15.3 gives the market for rented vans. And as an example of the market for an intermediate product, Figure 15.4 gives the market for yeast, which is used in the production of many products, including bread and beer. In both figures, the supply curve has been drawn to show elastic supply. This is because firms can usually hire out more vans or produce more yeast very readily.

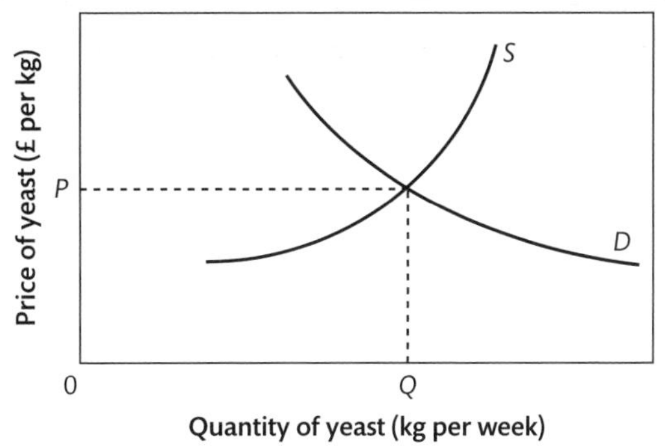

Figure 15.4 **The market for an intermediate product**

The demand curve for yeast depends on its marginal revenue product for the firms that use it. This equals the marginal physical product of yeast—the increase in output from using an extra kg of yeast—multiplied by the marginal revenue from an extra unit of output.

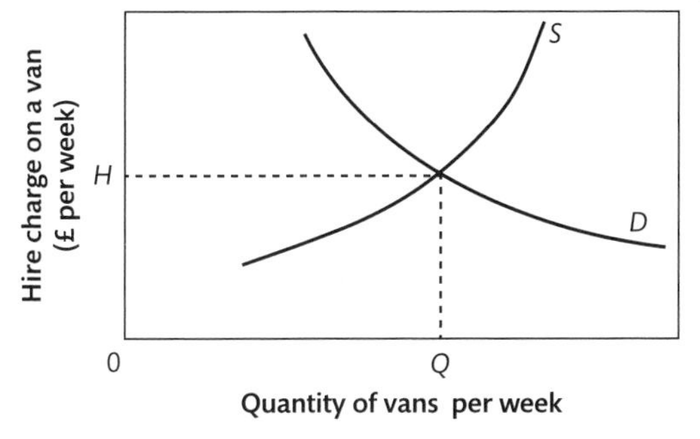

Figure 15.3 **The market for a type of hired capital**

The demand curve for vans depends on the marginal revenue product of vans for the firms that use them. This equals the marginal product of vans—the increase in output from using an extra van—multiplied by the marginal revenue from an extra unit of output.

15.1 Summary

- Firms will rent more buildings or land, or hire more capital, or buy more intermediate products, as long as the marginal revenue product of the input concerned exceeds its marginal cost.
- If the market for an input is competitive, with many buyers and sellers, then the price and quantity of the input are determined by the supply and demand curves for it.
- For people who let land and buildings, transfer earnings are the amounts they must earn before they will let their buildings or land for their present use. Any earnings they get above this are economic rent.

15.2 Investment appraisal

Investment is the purchase of capital, such as plant, buildings, vehicles, and machinery. We will now study **investment appraisal**: this is the theory about how firms should appraise decisions to buy such assets. They can use a similar approach to appraise decisions to buy land.

Decisions to buy capital are more complex than decisions to hire it or rent it. The crucial difference is that if a firm hires or rents an asset for, say, next year, then the firm considers only the hire or rental cost for next year, along with the marginal revenue product that will arise next year from the asset. But when a firm consider buying an asset, it hopes the asset will last for some years; so it must look ahead and consider what may happen over its entire life.

You might think that a decision about buying an asset will depend on only two things:

- **the cost of the asset;**
- **the returns from the asset.** The **returns** are the extra revenue the firm will get each year over its life by owning it, less any extra expenditure on other inputs like labour or intermediate products.

You may also suppose that if the total of all the extra returns exceeds the cost, then the asset should be bought. But an investment decision is not that simple. To see why, suppose you run a business and you consider spending £100,000 on some plant that will last ten years. And suppose your returns from the plant will be £10,400 each year. Then your total returns over the ten years will be £104,000. This is above the £100,000 cost. So the purchase may seem justified.

But maybe you could earn 5% a year simply by lending your money to the government, free from any risk of non-repayment. If so, you could lend your £100,000 next week and have £105,000 in just one year. This would be a much better use of your £100,000 than buying the capital and acquiring just £104,000 over a period of ten years.

So a decision about buying an asset depends also on the interest rate. To understand how such a decision is made, we must look first at the concepts of future values and present values.

Future values

Suppose you have £100 that you can lend to the government risk-free at 5%. If you lend it for one year, then next year you will receive £105, that is a repayment of £100 plus £5 interest. The value on a future date of a sum of money lent risk-free today is called its **future value**: so the future value of your £100 in one year, when lent risk-free at 5%, is £105. We can write this as £100 x 1.05.

But suppose you decide to lend your money for two years. At the end of the first year, you would receive £105, and you could lend all of this for the second year. Then you would receive £110.25, that is a repayment of the £105 you lent for the second year plus interest of 5% on that, which is £5.25. So the future value of £100 lent risk-free today for two years at 5% is £100 x 1.05 x 1.05. We can re-express this as £100 x $(1.05)^2$.

More generally, the future value in *N* years' time of any given sum of money, *S*, lent today at a risk-free interest rate, *i*, can be worked out as follows:

$$\text{The future value of sum } S \text{ equals } S \times (1+i)^N.$$

In our example, *S* was £100, *i* was 5%, that is 5/100 or 0.05, and *N* was two years. So the future value was £100 x $(1.05)^2$, or £110.25.

Present values

We have seen that if you lend £100 risk-free at 5%, its future value in one year will be £105. We can look at this in another way, and say that if you can lend risk-free at 5% and you want to have £105 in one year, then you must lend £100 today.

The sum that must be lent risk-free today to get a given sum in the future is called the **present value** (*PV*) of that given future sum. So the present value of £105 in one year, at an interest rate of 5%, is £100.

We also know that if you lend £100 risk-free today for two years, it will then be worth £110.25. So the present value of £110.25 in two years is also £100.

We can work out these present values as follows:

- *PV* of £105 in one year is £105/(1.05);
- *PV* of £110.05 in two years is £110.25/(1.05)^2.

More generally, if the risk-free interest rate is *i*, then a sum *S* in *N* year's time has a present value, *PV*, given by $PV = S/(1 + i)^N$. But when we use an interest rate to obtain *PV*s, we call it a **discount rate**, *r*. It is better to say:

$$\text{The present value } (pv) \text{ of sum } S \text{ equals } \frac{S}{(1+r)^N}.$$

For example, the present value of £1,000 in five year's time at a discount rate of 5% is 1,000/(1.05)^5, which is £784. This means you could lend £784 today for five years at 5% and end up with £1,000.

An investment example

Now we can study investment appraisal. Let's take a simple example. Suppose you have £400 and you consider buying a hedge trimmer, which will last six years, and then will have no scrap value. You plan in each of the next six summers to hire students to cut people's hedges. You expect that, by the end of each year, your return, that is your revenue net of labour and fuel costs, will be £100. Finally, suppose that the current rate of interest on risk-free loans to the government is 5%. Would the trimmer be a good investment?

The calculations needed are shown in Table 15.1. The middle column sets out the expected returns. The last column gives their *PV*s. For example the *PV* of the return in year 1 is £95.24, which means that if you were to lend £95.24 today at 5%, you would get £100 next year. The *PV* of the return in year 2 is £90.70, which means that if you were to lend £90.70 today, you would get £100 in two years.

Table 15.1 **Appraising the purchase of a machine with a discount rate of 5% (so $r = 0.05$)**

At the end of year	Expected return (£)	*PV* of return (£)
1	100	100/1.05 = 95.24
2	100	100/1.05^2 = 90.70
3	100	100/1.05^3 = 86.38
4	100	100/1.05^4 = 82.27
5	100	100/1.05^5 = 78.35
6	100	100/1.05^6 = 74.62
Total	**600**	**Σ*PV* = 507.57**

With a capital cost, *C*, of £400, the *NPV* of the asset is Σ*PV* - *C*, that is £507.57 - £400, which is £107.57.

The total *PV*, which we call Σ*PV*, is £507.57. This means that if you were to lend £507.57 today, you could get £100 in each of the next six years. It follows that if you lend your £400 at 5%, you will get much less than £100 in each of the next six years. On the other hand, if you spend your £400 on the trimmer, you reckon you *can* get £100 in each of those years. So buying the machine seems much better than lending the money.

Buying the trimmer for £400 seems attractive because you expect it to give you the same returns that you would get by lending only if you lent much more, £507.57. We can express this more formally by saying that it seems worth buying because its cost, *C*, is less than its Σ*PV*, or, in other words, because its Σ*PV* is greater than its cost, *C*, so that Σ*PV* – C is positive. We call an asset's Σ*PV* – C its **net present value**, or *NPV* the *NPV* here is £507.57 - £400, that is £107.57.

This analysis may suggest that any asset is worth buying if its *NPV* is positive, because then it gives higher returns than lending money. But if you ever do undertake this sort of analysis, and you find the asset concerned has a positive *NPV*, think about the following two issues before you buy it.

- **Risk.** We compared the returns on the asset with those on a risk-free loan. But the returns on the asset are uncertain. You can estimate them, but there is a risk your estimates will be wrong. Maybe the demand for hedge-cutting will fall and the price will be lower than you expect. Maybe your student workers will be less productive than you expect. Maybe the wage you need to attract workers, or the price of fuel for the trimmer, will be higher than you expect. If any of these events occurs, your actual returns will be below £100, and the *NPV* will turn out less than you expect, possibly negative. Only buy a risky asset if its *NPV* is large enough to justify the risk.

- **Alternative assets.** In the example, you considered only one asset. There may be other assets you could buy for £400. If so, choose the asset with the highest *NPV*, allowing for risks.

Question 15.1 Suppose you consider investing in an assembly line that will cost £1 million in each of the next three years to build. You estimate the Σ*PV* of the future returns as £3 million. Might you decide this is a sound investment?

Internal rates of return

In our example, the hedge trimmer gave a higher return than lending. But, in that example, the interest rate on risk-free lending was just 5%. If the interest rate had been higher, then lending might have been better than buying the trimmer.

In fact, if the discount rate were 8%, then the Σ*PV* would be £400, so the *NPV* would be £0. In this case, buying the trimmer would be no better than lending, even ignoring risks. So we can say that the expected returns from the trimmer match those from risk-free lending at 8%. The discount rate that would make the *NPV* of an asset zero, and which therefore actually gives a percentage measure of its expected returns, is called its **internal rate of return** or its **marginal efficiency**. Ignoring risk, an asset is worth buying if its internal rate of return exceeds the rate of interest on risk-free loans.

Factors that affect investment

When people consider buying an asset, they may think about it over a period of time and estimate its *NPV* several times, and they may find that their estimated *NPV* changes. Let's see why the asset's *NPV* might rise, making it more tempting.

- **The cost of the asset may fall.** If its *C* falls, then its *NPV*, that is Σ*PV* – *C*, will increase. So firms become more willing to risk buying assets at low prices than they are at high prices, and in turn the demand curves for assets slope downwards.
- **The price of other inputs that will have to be used with the asset may fall.** If so, the asset's expected returns and its *NPV* will both increase.
- **A rise in productivity.** If people can think of ways to make an asset more productive, then its expected returns and *NPV* will both increase.
- **The demand for the product that the asset will help to produce may increase.** If so, the price of the product will rise, so the asset's expected returns and its *NPV* will both increase.
- **The interest rate on risk-free lending may fall.** We have seen that people use this rate to discount the expected future returns of an asset to find its Σ*PV*. If that rate falls and they discount with a lower rate, then the *NPV* will rise. In turn, some projects that were previously unattractive may now be attractive.

This last factor means that we expect a country's total investment in new buildings, plant, vehicles, and machinery to be higher at low interest rates than at high interest rates, as shown in Figure 15.5. The horizontal axis here measures investment, the vertical axis measures interest rates, and the investment demand curve, *I*, shows the level of investment at each interest rate.

Interest rates and project choices

A change in the interest rate not only alters the quantity of assets which firms may buy; it also affects which assets they most want to buy.

This is shown in Table 15.2, which concerns a firm with £300 to spend. It wants to buy either Machine 1, which will last two years, or Machine 2, which will last five years. The table shows the expected returns from

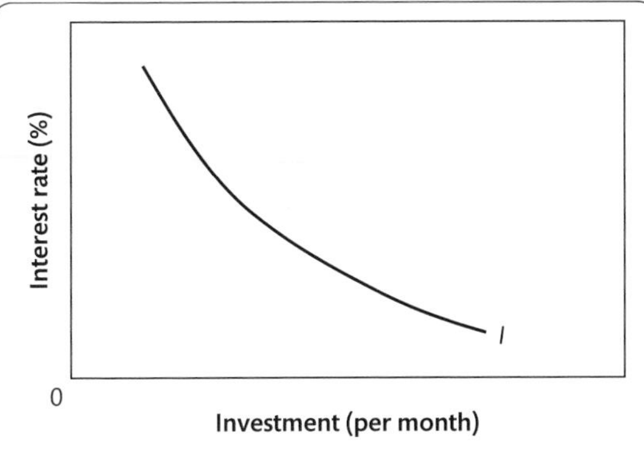

Figure 15.5 **Investment and interest rates**

At high interest rates, high discount rates are used in investment appraisal, so relatively few projects have positive *NPVs*. In turn, investment or purchases of capital are low.

Table 15.2 **The sensitivity of investment appraisal decisions to the discount rate used**

Machine 1 - which has a life of two years

At end of year	Expected return (£)	*PV* of returns if $r = 0.04$ (£)	*PV* of returns if $r = 0.12$ (£)
1	200	192	179
2*	200	185	159
Σ*PV*		**377**	**338**
C		**300**	**300**
NPV		**77**	**38**

Machine 2 - which has a life of five years

At end of year	Expected return (£)	*PV* of returns if $r = 0.04$ (£)	*PV* of returns if $r = 0.12$ (£)
1	100	96	89
2	100	92	80
3	100	89	71
4	100	85	64
5*	50	41	28
Σ*PV*		**403**	**332**
C		**300**	**300**
NPV		**103**	**32**

*The final return includes any scrap value of the machine.

each machine. The final returns include any scrap value from the machine.

Suppose, first, that the interest rate on risk-free loans is just 4%, so the discount rate used is 4%. Then the 2-year machine has an *NPV* of £77, while the 5-year machine has an *NPV* of £103. Both machines seem attractive, but if the firm only wants one, it will take the 5-year machine.

Now suppose the rate on risk-free loans is 12%. Then each machine will have a much lower *NPV*, with £38 for the 2-year machine and £32 for the 5-year machine. Allowing for risks, the firm might buy neither machine, and there would be no surprise that it would do less investment at an interest rate of 12% than at 4%. But suppose it does go ahead and still wants just one machine: this time, it will buy the 2-year machine.

The reason for this switch in preferences is easily seen. When discount rates are high, the *PV* of distant returns becomes very low, and this shifts preferences in favour of projects with shorter lives.

Nominal and real interest rates

So far, we have talked about 'the' interest rate. But we need to distinguish between two types of interest rates. Suppose you can deposit money in a bank, which offers you 5% interest. This interest rate, which is agreed between the borrower and the lender, is called the **nominal interest rate.**

Suppose you place £100 in a deposit and leave it for a year. Then you will have £105. But will you be able to buy 5% more goods and services than you could today? That depends on what happens to prices. There are three possibilities.

- **Prices rise at a rate that is less than the nominal interest rate.** For instance, suppose prices rise over the year by 2%. Then you would need £102 next year to buy what you could buy with £100 today, yet you will have £105. So lending will enable you to buy about 3% more than you could buy today, and so make you about 3% better off.
- **Prices rise at a rate that is more than the nominal interest rate.** For instance, suppose prices rise over

the year by 7%. Then you would need £107 next year to buy what you could buy with £100 today, yet you will have only £105. So lending will enable you to buy about 2% less than you could buy today, and so make you about 2% worse off.

- **Prices rise at the same rate as the nominal interest rate.** If prices rise over the year by 5%, then you would need £105 next year to buy what you could buy with £100 today, and you will have £105. So lending will make you neither better off nor worse off.

The extent to which a loan makes the lender better off, after allowing for inflation, is called the **real interest rate**. In our three cases, the real interest rates were respectively 3%, –2%, and 0%. Likewise, the extent to which buying an asset makes its buyer better off, after allowing for inflation, is called the asset's **real rate of return**.

You can use either type of interest rate in investment appraisal. If you express the expected returns in nominal terms, that is using the actual money value you expect them to have in the future, then you should discount using the nominal interest rate. If you express the expected returns in real terms, that is the value they would have if prices in the future were the same as today, then you should discount using the real interest rate.

Note, though, that it is easy to discover nominal interest rates, perhaps by simply asking a bank. But no one knows what the real interest rate will be over any future period until the end of the period, when the rise in prices can be measured. So people who discount using real interest rates have to use expected real interest rates.

15.1 Everyday economics

New Nissan Jobs in Sunderland

In 2009, the carmaker Nissan announced that its Sunderland factory in north-east England would start producing batteries for electric cars. It expected that 350 new jobs would be created. The plant was in competition for the investment needed with other Nissan factories in Europe.

'Nissan to create hundreds of jobs', *BBC News*, 20 July 2009

'Nissan Sunderland announces £200m electric car investment', *The Northern Echo*, 20 July 2009.

Comment When Nissan appraised investing in a battery-making facility, it considered alternative sites in Europe. Spurred by the need to create jobs in the global recession, the UK government established several initiatives to give the Sunderland site the highest *NPV*. It reduced Nissan's investment costs by offering grants and loan guarantees, and it effectively reduced Nissan's future running costs by setting up a centre for training, research, and development of green technology, so saving Nissan some annual costs of its own for these activities. This intervention was rewarded when, in 2010, Nissan announced that it would build electric cars in Sunderland as well as the batteries, and so create hundreds more jobs.

15.2 Summary

- The annual returns from an investment project are the revenues it will generate, minus the costs of any other inputs needed to use it, and in the last year minus also any scrap value.
- The present value, *PV*, of any return is the sum that could be lent risk-free today to get the same amount as that return on the same future day. The risk-free rate is known as the discount rate.
- A project is worth undertaking if the total *PV* of all its expected returns, ΣPV, exceeds its cost, *C*, by an amount sufficient to justify taking the risk that its actual returns may be less than expected.
- The net present value of a project, *NPV*, equals its ΣPV minus its *C*. So it is worth undertaking if its *NPV* is positive by enough to justify the risk that its actual returns may be less than expected.
- The marginal efficiency, or internal rate of return, on a project indicates what the rate of interest on risk-free loans would have to be for risk-free lending to give equivalent returns.
- A project is worth undertaking if its internal rate of return exceeds the interest rate on risk-free lending by an amount sufficient to justify taking the risk that its actual returns may be less than expected.

- There is less investment in the economy in new capital at high interest rates than at low interest rates.
- When interest rates are high, projects with long lives become relatively less attractive.

15.3 The use of non-renewable natural resources

We have now considered two issues concerning land: decisions by firms to rent land, which we studied in section 15.1, and decisions by firms to buy land, which can be made using the investment appraisal method given in section 15.2.

But in Chapter 1 we saw that economists define land as all the gifts of nature, so we include any resources beneath it that may be extracted and sold, like crude oil and iron ore. These resources can be extracted only once, so we call them non-renewable resources.

The demand for these resources raises no new issues: it depends on their marginal revenue product to the firms that use them. But the supply of these resources raises two new issues, which we will now explore.

- **At what rate should the owners of these resources extract them and deplete them?**
- **What will happen to the market price of these resources over the period between now and the time when they are finally exhausted?**

Two costs for natural resources

To think about these issues, suppose you own a mine with a non-renewable mineral resource. You could choose to extract it all this year, or extract it gradually over several years, or even keep it indefinitely underground. Which choice would you make to maximize your returns from the mine?

Suppose the current market price of the mineral is £120 per tonne, and that each tonne costs £20 to extract. Then you might be tempted to argue as follows: 'Each extra tonne I extract will give me an extra £120 in revenue and cost me an extra £20 to extract, so the extra revenue will exceed the extra cost, so I should extract it all now.'

Yet this could well be the wrong choice. For example, suppose you expect the price of the mineral next year to be £200. Then extracting each tonne now and selling it for £120 would clearly be unwise.

In fact, a simple comparison of the extra £120 revenue and the extra £20 extraction cost is an unsound procedure, because it ignores another very important cost. This cost is the fall in your wealth, in the form of mineral resources, which occurs whenever you sell some. You will actually want the revenue from selling the mineral to compensate you for this loss of wealth, as well as for the extraction cost. And notice that the true value of your loss of wealth depends on what happens to the price of the mineral in future.

Deciding whether or not to extract now

So let's now see how you should decide how much mineral to extract now and in future. You actually need to consider four factors:

- **the current price of the mineral;**
- **the extraction cost of the mineral;**
- **the rate of interest;**
- **the price you expect the mineral to have in future.** In our analysis, we will focus on the price you expect it to have next year.

To see how we allow for these factors, note first that the current price minus the extraction cost is £100 per tonne. So for each tonne you extract now, you effectively acquire £100.

Also, suppose that the rate of interest on risk-free loans to the government is 20%: we take a high rate because it helps to keep the example simple. At this interest rate, you could extract a tonne now and acquire £100, and lend that £100 risk-free to have £120 next year.

Next, consider three possible prices that you might expect the mineral to have next year, and see with each of these prices whether it would be better to extract the mineral now or then.

- **You expect the price next year to be £130; so the price minus the extraction cost will be £110, that is 10% above today's figure of £100.** Here, it is better to extract each tonne now, and lend the money to have £120 next year, because if you leave it in the ground, you would get only £110 by extracting it next year.
- **You expect the price next year to be £140; so the price minus the extraction cost will be £120, that is 20% above today's figure of £100.** Here, you can leave each tonne in the ground now and extract it next year to get £120 then. Or you can extract it now and acquire £100, which you can lend, and so also get £120 next year. So it makes no difference whether you extract the mineral now or next year.
- **You expect the price next year to be £150; so the price minus the extraction cost will be £130, that is 30% above today's figure of £100.** Here, it is better to leave each tonne in the ground now and extract it next year, when you will acquire £130, because if you extract it now, you will acquire only £100, and after lending that at 20%, you will have only £120 next year.

How the price is expected to rise over time

Now let's think about everyone who owns deposits of this mineral, not only you.

- **Suppose every owner expects the price next year to be £130; so the price minus the extraction cost will rise by 10%, that is by less than the rate of interest.** In this case, all mine owners will extract everything this year.
- **Suppose every owner expects the price next year to be £140; so the price minus the extraction cost will rise by 20%, that is equal to the rate of interest.** In this case, all mine owners will be indifferent between extracting the mineral now or next year. Between them, they will no doubt extract something this year, but not everything.
- **Suppose every owner expects the price next year to be £150, so the price minus the extraction cost will rise by 30%, that is by more than the rate of interest.** In this case, all mine owners will extract nothing this year.

We can use this example to draw some general conclusions. In the current year, we do not expect the owners of any non-renewable resource such as oil or coal to extract everything, nor do we expect them to extract nothing. However, we do expect them to extract something between them. This means that they must expect next year's price to be the one that, minus extraction costs, exceeds this year's figure by a percentage equal to the interest rate. Likewise, next year, they will probably extract something, but not everything, so they must then expect the following year's price minus the extraction cost to exceed next year's figure by a percentage equal to the interest rate.

We can apply the same approach to later years, and see that resource owners must expect the price minus the extraction cost to rise *every* year at the same rate as the rate of interest. It follows that the quantities extracted each year over time must be the quantities that lead owners to expect the price to rise like that. This is known as **Hotelling's rule** after the American economist Harold Hotelling who published it in 1931.

Determining the current price

We have seen that the quantity of mineral extracted each year over time causes the expected price minus the extraction cost to rise at the same rate as the interest rate. But what determines the current price, which, in our example, is £120?

Figure 15.6 gives the answer. To keep this figure simple, we assume the mineral will be exhausted in just four more years. Part (a) measures time on the horizontal axis. It calls the current year 'year 0' and shows on the vertical axis that, in this year, the price is £120 and the extraction cost is £20, leaving a gap of £100. It also shows what the prices for the next four years will be under Hotelling's rule.

- **Year 1, £140.** So the price minus the extraction cost will be £120, 20% more than in year 0.
- **Year 2, £164.** So the price minus the extraction cost will be £144, 20% more than in year 1.
- **Year 3, £193.** So the price minus the extraction cost will be £173, 20% more than in year 2.
- **Year 4, £227.** So the price minus the extraction cost will be £207, 20% more than in year 2.

Notice that the black curve plotting these prices in part (a) gets slightly steeper over time. Part (b) shows the demand curve for the mineral, *D*, and uses it to find the quantity that will be sold in each year at these prices. *D* has been drawn slightly curved to give a simple series of 400 tonnes in year 0, 300 in year 1, 200 in year 2, and 100 in year 3. This makes a total of 1,000 tonnes. At the year 4 price of £227, no one will want to buy the mineral: the price, which is just high enough to result in no sales, is called the **choke price**.

Now we can see what determines the current price itself. Suppose there are 1,000 tonnes of mineral left, and consider three possible prices for year 0.

- **Suppose the year 0 price is £120.** Then the price will rise as shown in Figure 15.6, and sales in the next four years will just exhaust the mineral
- **Suppose the year 0 price were above £120.** Then the price each year would be higher than shown.

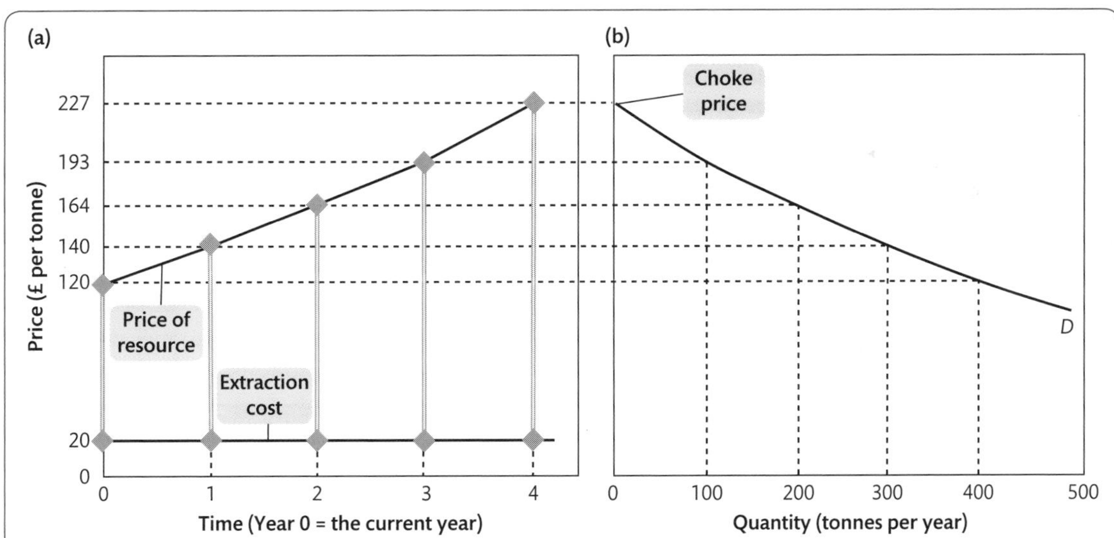

Figure 15.6 **The Hotelling rule**

In the current year 0, there are 1,000 tonnes of a resource left, and the interest rate is 20%. The double lines in part (a) show the price minus the extraction cost: this is £100 in the current year 0, £120 in year 1, and £144, £173, and £207 in year 4. Each year it rises by 20%, the same as the interest rate, as given in the Hotelling rule. Part (b) shows that the quantity bought falls over time; how rapidly it falls depends on the shape of the demand curve, but here it falls steadily by 100 tonnes a year. The price reaches the choke price of £227 in year 4, by when all the remaining 1,000 tonnes have been sold. The price of £120 in the current year 0 is determined so that the last of the 1,000 tonnes will be sold just when the choke price is reached. This allows producers to sell all those 1,000 tonnes at the highest possible prices.

So less would be extracted each year, yet the choke price would arrive sooner. So, when it came, some mineral would be left in the ground. But mines will not set prices so high that buyers disappear before their reserves are exhausted. So they won't set a year 0 price over £120.

- **Suppose the year 0 price were below £120.** Then the price each year would be lower than shown. No doubt every tonne would eventually be sold, but it would be sold for lower prices than those shown. Mines will not want to sell the mineral at prices below the highest they could get, so they will not set a year 0 price below £120.

In short, the current price is the one that leads to a future stream of prices that will sell the entire resource at the highest possible set of prices for which it could just be entirely sold.

Price rises in practice

Our analysis makes it seem that the price of any non-renewable resource should rise smoothly over time in the way shown in Figure 15.6. In practice, there are several reasons why price changes might not be so steady, including the following.

- **Interest rates may change.**
- **The demand for the mineral may change.**
- **New deposits may be found.** This will cause resource owners to revise downwards their expected future prices.
- **Extraction costs may change.** So, even if the gap between the selling price and the extraction cost rises steadily, the total price will not.

Question 15.2 Suppose the mineral owners in our example currently plan this year's output to be the one that will give a price of £120. Then the interest rate rises. On the basis of the Hotelling rule, why will they now decide to produce more this year, and so drive the price below £120?

15.2 Everyday economics

Falling demand for some resources

In the 1970s, many gloomy forecasts were made suggesting that the world would soon run out of some non-renewable resources, including mercury and tin. These forecasts were based on current known reserves and current usage. But the world didn't run out of mercury or tin. Instead, as H. Witcoff, B. Reuben, E. Davis and J. Plotkin have observed (*Industrial Organic Chemicals*, 2nd edn, 1996, p. 568), mercury consumption fell dramatically, partly because more effective alternatives were found for some of its industrial uses; as for tin, new can-making technology displaced its major use in food cans. Indeed, the demand for tin has dropped to the point at which many tin mines in south-west England have closed. The main problem with the forecasts was that they overlooked the Hotelling rule. This rule says that the price of any non-renewable resource will rise over time. This reduces the rate of its use, and also gives a strong incentive for people to devise alternative technologies that avoid using it, as occurred with mercury and tin, or at least use it less. And it is the rising price of non-renewable resources used for energy, principally oil, natural gas, and coal, that is driving the search for alternative energy sources, ranging from nuclear power to wind farms.

15.3 Summary

- When deciding to extract a non-renewable resource, its owners consider two costs: the extraction cost and the cost in the form of the reduction in their wealth when they own less of the resource than before.
- The level of extraction of a resource in any given year will be the level that makes the expected price in the following year, net of extraction costs, greater than the current price minus extraction costs by a percentage that is equal to the rate of interest. This is the Hotelling rule.
- The price of a resource will not actually rise every year by a percentage equal to the current interest rate, because extraction costs, interest rates, and demand may change, and new deposits may be found.

15.4 Investment in human capital

An investment decision for all young people

Section 15.2 looked at decisions by firms to invest in capital such as plant, buildings, vehicles, and machinery. But households also make decisions to invest in capital when they invest in human capital, and you are almost certainly investing in it now. We will now look at decisions about this sort of investment.

At present, the school-leaving age in the UK is 16. It will be raised to 17 in 2013 and to 18 in 2015, but currently people have two choices when they are 16, as follows.

- **Stop studying at 16.** Many people enter the labour force at 16, equipped with the human capital they have already acquired.
- **Continue studying beyond 16.** Many people continue in education, often to degree level, and some even take a postgraduate qualification.

Those who study beyond the age of 16 hope to secure jobs that are more rewarding in terms of income or enjoyment. They hope to secure these more rewarding jobs in two ways.

- **By acquiring extra human capital.** They will acquire this through their extra education.
- **By signalling.** By undertaking extra study, they will signal to employers that they are bright, hard-working, and ambitious.

The decision to study beyond 16 is essentially a decision about an investment, which has two obvious costs:

- **the loss of income that could have been earned by working full-time instead of studying;**
- **direct education costs, such as fees and books;**

However, three items should be subtracted from these costs to get a better idea of the true cost of investing in education:

- **any income from part-time employment while studying;**
- **any scholarships or grants;**
- **the value of any enjoyment from the education process, beyond that which would have been obtained by working full-time instead.**

Suppose someone reckons that the costs of studying for five years in terms of the loss of full-time earnings plus direct costs is £100,000. But suppose, also, that this person earns £15,000 in part-time work while studying, receives grants of £10,000, and obtains £5,000 enjoyment. Then the true sacrifice made purely to acquire human capital will be only just the remaining £70,000 that is not covered by these three items.

Illustrating the benefits and costs

Figure 15.7 illustrates the effects of two choices for someone aged 16. The curve $R_{16\text{-}65}$ shows the future returns this person might secure by leaving school at 16 and at once working full-time until retiring at 65: these returns include earnings plus the value of any pleasure from the work, or minus the value of any displeasure from it. $R_{16\text{-}65}$ slopes upwards because many people gain some human capital through job experience and then attract a higher wage. The total value of these returns is represented by the grey area below $R_{16\text{-}65}$.

But suppose this person instead stays in education until the age of 21, and, for simplicity, suppose this person takes no gap year. The curve $R_{21\text{-}65}$ shows the returns this person might then secure between 21 and 65. This curve has been drawn above $R_{16\text{-}65}$ on the assumption that the human capital acquired through study will lead to a higher returns profile. And $R_{16\text{-}65}$ slopes upwards because earnings may rise over time on account of the acquisition of yet more human capital through experience.

The pink area between $R_{16\text{-}65}$ and $R_{21\text{-}65}$ shows the total value of the extra returns that may result by undertaking more education. This area starts at 21, not 16, because studying until 21 precludes a full-time job until then.

The two grids in the figure show the costs involved in more education. The pink grid shows the full-time

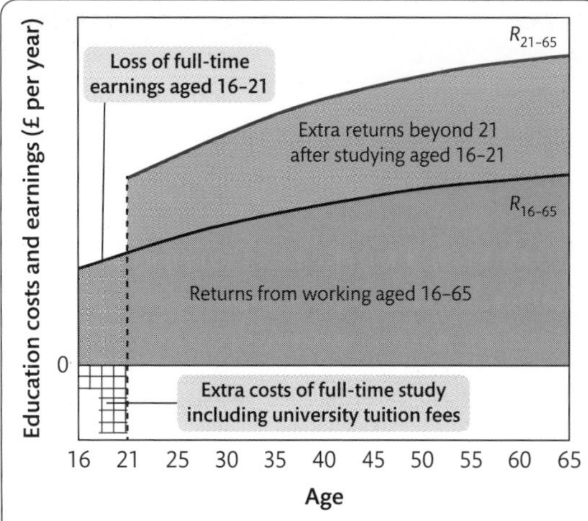

Figure 15.7 **Earnings and study**

R_{16-65} shows the annual returns someone might get working full-time from 16 to 65; the grey area below R_{16-65} represents the total returns. R_{21-65} shows the annual returns that would arise by studying until 21 and working full-time from 21 to 65. The extra returns from 21 to 65 are shaded pink. But studying involves costs: the pink grid shows the full-time earnings that are forgone, and the grey grid shows the direct education costs.

earnings that are sacrificed between 16 and 21 when full-time work is impossible. The purple grid shows the additional direct costs of education, minus any part-time earnings, grants or scholarships, and minus the enjoyment value of the education process. These costs are highest after 18 when university tuition fees are paid.

It may seem that provided that the pink area is larger than the area of these two grids combined, this person should undertake the study. But notice that this person is aged 16 and is making the decision now. The costs will arise in the next five years, while the benefits will begin only after that. This person should, therefore, work out the present value of the costs and the present value of the benefits to make a valid comparison.

Different people aged 16 could draw similar types of graph with very different areas. For example, those aiming to be fund managers would have a much higher R_{21-65} curve than those aiming to be primary school teachers; some people would place very different enjoyment values on the education process and on their chosen careers.

Question 15.3 Suppose the person concerned in Figure 15.7 also expects education from 16 to 21 to lead to a higher pension after 65, because pensions are generally related to pay before retirement. Should this be allowed for in the investment decision?

Extra returns from studying economics

If you want to do some calculations for yourself, you may wonder how much higher your earnings will be with an economics degree compared with entering the labour force at age 18. Table 15.3 shows that, on average, the answer is 41.6% for men and 68.0% for women. Notice that the returns are lower with degrees in any of the other degree subjects covered by the table. Typically, studies like these show that economics graduates on average earn more than most others, aside from those studying medicine, and medical students typically have to study longer to secure their higher incomes.

Table 15.3 **The average extra income of graduates over those who finished education with two or more A levels, 1994–2006**

Degree subject	Men (%)	Women (%)
Arts/humanities	0.4	27.9
Business/ management	38.4	53.2
Economics	**41.6**	**68.0**
Education	12.6	52.5
English	26.9	46.5
Health	39.4	61.8
Languages	11.5	45.5
Law	37.9	60.7
Maths/statistics	34.1	63.9
Science	20.6	40.6
Social science	12.0	35.8

Source: Yu Zhu (Department of Economics, University of Kent) using data from Office for National Statistics, *Labour Force Survey 2007*, for Why Study Economics? (see http://whystudyeconomics.ac.uk/After-you-graduate/)

15.3 Everyday economics

Economics is good for new graduates

The table here concerns 2008–09 and is taken from a study that divides degrees into 62 subject areas. The table covers only the 22 areas in which graduates entering graduate jobs earned above the average wage for graduates as a whole. The table shows the average starting salaries of graduates in these subject areas who entered graduate jobs. It also shows the percentage of graduates in each subject who ended up in non-graduate jobs or unemployed (NG/U). Economics graduates had excellent entry prospects for the labour force. In terms of average earnings, they ranked fifth out of the 62 subject areas, and the percentage who ended up in non-graduate jobs or unemployed was below average. Employers value the skills that economics students acquire during their training. Medical students earned more, but needed more years of training.

'What do graduates do?', HESA 2008–09, The Complete University Guide 2011
'What do graduates earn and do?', HESA 2008–09, The Complete University Guide 2011

Subject	Earnings (£)	NG/U (%)
Dentistry	£30,143	0%
Medicine	£29,146	0%
Chemical Engineering	£27,151	20%
Veterinary Medicine	£25,807	9%
Economics	**£25,637**	**31%**
Middle Eastern & African Studies	£25,004	37%
General Engineering	£24,937	28%
Social Work	£24,630	21%
Mechanical Engineering	£24,337	30%
Civil Engineering	£23,720	27%
Aeronautical & Manufacturing Engineering	£23,478	36%
Librarianship & Information Management	£23,246	39%
Mathematics	£23,160	29%
Physics & Astronomy	£22,946	25%
Electrical & Electronic Engineering	£22,897	33%
Building	£21,979	34%
Nursing	£21,910	4%
Theology & Religious Studies	£21,749	31%
Computer Science	£21,712	39%
Accounting & Finance	£21,551	39%
Geology	£21,182	36%
Business Studies	£21,007	42%
Average	**£20,964**	**35%**

15.4 Summary

- Deciding whether and how much education to have beyond the school-leaving age is a decision about investing in human capital.
- The returns from such an investment are the extra earnings, plus any value from a more enjoyable job.
- The costs are the loss of full-time earnings while studying, plus direct education costs; but against these costs, allowance should be made for any income from part-time earnings, scholarships, or grants, plus the enjoyment value of education beyond that of the jobs that would otherwise have been done.
- Economics graduates secure higher returns than the graduates in most other subjects.

In the next chapter we see how far incomes vary in practice, and see how the government helps the poor.

Glossary

Choke price: the price that is just sufficient to result in no sales.

Discount rate: the interest rate on risk-free loans to the government, which is used to discount future values to find their present values.

Future value: the value on a future date of a sum of money lent risk-free today until that date.

Hotelling's rule: the idea that, over time, the owners of a non-renewable will extract it in a way that leads them to expect the price minus the extraction cost to rise *every* year at the same rate as the interest rate.

Internal rate of return: the discount rate that would make the *NPV* of an asset zero, and so give a percentage measure of its expected returns.

Investment appraisal: the appraisal of decisions to buy capital assets; it can also be applied to decisions to buy land.

Marginal efficiency: another term for the internal rate of return.

Net present value (*NPV*): the total present value of an asset's returns minus its purchase cost.

Nominal interest rate: the interest rate agreed between a borrower and a lender.

Present value (*PV*): the amount that must be lent risk-free today to get a given sum in the future.

Real interest rate: the extent to which a loan makes the lender better off after allowing for inflation.

Real rate of return: the extent to which an investment makes its purchaser better off after allowing for inflation.

Returns: the extra revenue a firm will get each year from buying an asset like capital or land, minus any extra expenditure it will incur on other inputs that are needed in order to use the asset.

Answers to in-text questions

15.1 Yes. We have so far simply compared the *PV* of the returns with the actual value of the cost, assuming the cost arises wholly in the first year. If the cost is spread over more than one year, we must compare the ΣPV of the returns with the ΣPV of the costs. To find the ΣPV of the costs, we add the actual cost in year 1 to the discounted costs of later years, discounting the actual costs of later years in the usual way with the risk-free rate of interest. So the ΣPV of the costs would be less than £3 million and the project might be worth risking.

15.2 A rise in the interest rate means they will adjust the yearly outputs to ensure that the prices expected for future years rise more quickly. If they were to keep this year's price at £120, they would have to have lower outputs in every future year to get faster price rises, and in that case they would reach the choke price before they had exhausted the mineral. But if they were to cut the current price and raise output appropriately, then they would again manage to sell everything before reaching the choke price.

15.3 The higher pension income should be allowed for, but it will mostly arise after 50 years, and discounting over so long gives relatively small *PV*s. For example, someone who expects to receive an extra pension of £10,000 a year over 20 years, that is an extra £200,000 in all, but who expects this extra annual pension to arise in between 50 and 70 years' time, will find that if the discount rate is 5%, the total *PV* is under £11,000.

? Questions for review

Years' ahead:	1	2	3	4	5	6
Discount rate 4%	96	92	89	85	82	79
Discount rate 8%	93	86	79	74	68	63

15.1 The present value of £100 in future years is as shown above, for discount rates of 4% and 8%.

Suppose you consider investing in an asset with an initial capital cost of £500 and estimated returns of £100 over each of the next six years. At which of the two discount rates would your investment definitely not be worth undertaking?

15.2 Use the table in question 15.1 to help you with this question. Suppose you are considering buying two assets, each of which will cost £1,100 today. Asset 1 will bring in returns of £300 a year for each of the next five years. Asset 2 will bring in returns of £700 a year for the next two years. Which would you prefer if the discount rate were 4%? Which would you prefer if the discount rate were 8%?

15.3 Suppose the owners of the deposits of a certain mineral have planned their combined output for the next year. But then they find some new deposits, so they revise their plans. Will they now plan to extract more or less?

15.4 Consider the owners in question 15.3 again. Suppose that, just after they make their plans, demand for the mineral decreases, so again they revise their plans. Will they now plan to extract more or less?

? Questions for discussion

15.1 As the number of people continuing in education beyond age 16 rises, so the supply of people available for occupations that require workers who have acquired human capital in this way will rise. Will this necessarily mean that the wages of these people will fall relative to other wages, so reducing the premium from studying beyond 16?

15.2 What knowledge and skills do you think students of economics acquire that result in employers being willing to pay them more than graduates in most other subjects?

15.3 Suppose the demand for a non-renewable resource is very price inelastic. How would this impact on the rate of extraction by the owners?

Common student errors

If asked to draw a supply and demand curve figure for land, many students draw a vertical supply curve, arguing that no matter how high the rent, no more land can be supplied—except for trivial amounts by reclaiming land from shallow sea. But land has many uses, with different markets and rents, and in most markets the supply curve slopes, because land can be switched between uses. The best case for a vertical supply curve would be the market for land to be used for buildings in a given city.

Students often misrepresent the Hotelling rule as saying that people expect the *selling price* of a non-renewable resource to rise at the same rate as the rate of interest. But the rule applies to the *gap* between the selling price and the extraction cost. As a result, people expect the selling price to rise more slowly than the rate of interest. For example, in Figure 15.6, they expected the selling price to rise from £120 in year 0 to £140 in year 1, a rise of 17%, which is less than the interest rate there of 20%.

16

Governments and the Distribution of Income

Remember from Chapter 1 that one major question in economics is 'For whom are resources used?' Remember from Chapter 13 that private insurers may be reluctant to cover illness and unemployment.

We often hear alarming figures about the number of people who live in poverty. What do we actually mean by poverty? Why do people have very different living standards? How can the government try to help people on low incomes? Why does its help still leave so many people in poverty?

This chapter shows you how to answer questions like these, by understanding:

* how we compare the living standards of people in different households;
* why incomes are unequal and how we measure inequality;
* some theories about why, and how much, governments should try to help people on low incomes;
* the difficulty of defining poverty, and how it is tackled in the UK.

16.1 Measuring the distribution of income

We saw in Chapter 1 that one of the key questions in economics is 'For whom are resources used?' The key issue here is the fact that the quantity of resources that are used to produce goods and services for different people, such as you and me, depends on how many goods and services we buy, and that depends chiefly on our incomes. In this chapter, we will explore the 'For whom?' question by discussing the following issues.

- **How much do incomes vary?**
- **Which types of people have the lowest incomes?**
- **What can be done to help these people?**

This opening section looks at how much incomes vary in the UK. But before we do that, we must consider exactly what incomes we should look at.

Do we compare individuals or households?

The first question is whether we should compare the incomes of different individuals, or of different households. In everyday life, people often compare the incomes of individuals. For example, schoolchildren may compare their pocket money and adults may compare their earnings. But the 'For whom?' question in economics is best answered by comparing households. This question really concerns people's living standards, and that depends on their household incomes, not their individual incomes. For example, a footballer may earn £10 million a year, while his partner and children may have no income of their own. But they will have a far higher standard of living than a typical single working adult.

Comparing actual household incomes

Unfortunately, comparing households raises a problem, which is that they have varying numbers of people. For example, imagine four households that each have a total income of £600 a week, but the compositions of which are as follows:

- a pensioner couple living alone;
- a single mother with children aged 3 and 1;
- a household with four students;
- a working couple with children aged 14, 10, and 6.

It might seem that the best way of comparing the living standards of these households would be to divide the income of £600 in each case by the number of household occupants. But consider two results of this approach.

- It gives the pensioners £300 each and the single mother and her children £200 each. However, toddlers and babies need little money, so the two pensioners probably have a lower standard of living than the mother and her children.
- It gives the students £150 each and the family of five £120 each. However, children need less money than students, so the students probably have a lower living standard than the family.

So statisticians do not compare household incomes divided by the number of occupants. Instead, they compare what they call households' equivalized incomes.

Comparing equivalized incomes

A household's **equivalized income** is the income that it would need in order to enjoy its current standard of living, *if* it were to comprise only a married or cohabiting couple. To work out equivalized incomes, statisticians estimate the relative spending needs of people in different situations. They do this in the UK by using the weights shown in Table 16.1.

To use these weights for a given household, the statisticians first ask if it has at its head a couple or a single

Table 16.1 UK weights used to find equivalized household incomes, and examples for four households with actual incomes of £600 a week

Weights	
Adults if a married or cohabiting couple are heads of household	
The married or cohabiting couple	1.00
First additional adult	0.42
Other adults (each)	0.36
Adults if a single adult is head of household	
The head of household	0.61
First additional adult	0.46
Second additional adult	0.42
Other adults (each)	0.36
Children	
Aged 16–18 (each)	0.36
Aged 13–15 (each)	0.27
Aged 11–12 (each)	0.25
Aged 8–10 (each)	0.23
Aged 5–7 (each)	0.21
Aged 2–4 (each)	0.18
Aged 0-1 (each)	0.09
Examples of weights and equivalized incomes	
Pensioner couple living alone	
Weight 1.00. Equivalized income £600/1.00 = £600.	
Single parent + children aged 3 and 1	
Weight 0.88. Equivalized income £600/0.88 = £682.	
Single head (student) + 3 more students	
Weight 1.85. Equivalized income £600/1.85 = £324.	
Working couple + children aged 14, 10, and 6	
Weight 1.71. Equivalized income £600/1.71 = £513.	

Source: Office of National Statistics, *The Effects of Taxes and Benefits on Household Income 2008/09*, http://www.statistics.gov.uk/articles/nojournal/Taxes_Benefits_0809.pdf

adult. The weight for a couple as head of a household is 1.00, while the weight for a single adult as head is 0.61. This means that if a couple live alone and a single adult lives alone, then for every £1 of income that the couple has, the statisticians reckon the single adult will need 61p to enjoy the same living standard. The single adult needs more than half as much as the couple, because the couple can share many things, such as a TV licence and a kitchen.

In each case, the household would need more money to maintain its living standards if extra people were to live there. For example, suppose the couple produce a baby. The weight for a baby is 0.09, so if the couple are to maintain their previous standard of living, they will need an extra 9p for every £1 they had before.

The bottom part of the table uses these weights to calculate the equivalized incomes of the four households on £600 a week that we met earlier. First, the total weight is found for each household. For example, the retired couple have a weight of 1.00, while the four students have a weight of 0.61 for the head of household, 0.46 for the first additional student, 0.42 for the second, and 0.36 for the third. Their total is 1.85.

Then, each household's equivalized income is found by dividing its actual income by its total weight. This is £600/1.00, or £600, for the pensioners, and £600/1.85, or £324, for the students. The table also shows the equivalized incomes for the single-parent household as £682 and for the large family as £513. What all this means is as follows.

- The living standard for the single mother and her family is the same that a couple would have *if* the couple had an income of £682.
- The living standard for the students is the same that a couple would have *if* the couple had an income of £324.
- The living standard for the family of five is the same that a couple would have *if* the couple had an income of £513.

These equivalized incomes indicate the relative living standards of the people in each household. The student household has the lowest equivalized income, while the single mother's has the highest. So the students have the lowest living standard and the single mother's family has the highest.

The weights used by the statisticians are estimates of different people's needs. If you disagree with some of their weights, then you will disagree with some of their conclusions.

Question 16.1 Suppose the single mother thought the weights for her children should be 0.24 and 0.15. Using these weights, would she still seem to have a higher living standard than the pensioner couple?

Five types of income

Table 16.1 implies that each household has only one income that the statisticians need to equivalize. In fact, for each household, they look at *five* incomes, defined as shown below, and they work out an equivalized figure for each of these five incomes.

- **Its original income.** This is the income that the household gets from earnings, investments, and pensions, excluding any State Pension, which is a pension paid by the government.
- **Its gross income.** This adds in transfers from the government, such as State Pension, Job-seeker's Allowance, and Housing Benefit. A household's gross incomes give a better idea of its living standard than its original income, because it covers all of its income.
- **Its disposable incomes.** This deducts taxes paid directly to the government, mainly income tax and National Insurance contributions. A household's disposable income gives an even better idea of its living standard than its gross income, because it cannot use the income taken by these taxes to buy goods and services.
- **Its post-tax income.** This deducts the amounts spent on other taxes, such as VAT, tobacco, fuel, and alcohol duties. Post-tax incomes give a still better idea of living standards by showing how much households can actually pay to producers.
- **Its final income.** This adds the value of any government services received free of charge, such as education and health care. These services raise living standards, so final incomes give the best idea of living standards.

Showing inequality in a table

When the statisticians compare the equivalized incomes for different households, they find a great deal of inequality. Table 16.2 shows this for four types of income with data for the UK in 2008–09.

To explain the figures in Table 16.2, let's take original incomes as an example. Once the statisticians have estimated each household's equivalized original income, they divide all the households into five groups called quintiles. The bottom quintile contains the fifth of households with the lowest incomes, the second lowest quintile contains the fifth of households with the next lowest incomes, and so on.

The first column in the table shows what share of the country's total original income each quintile has. The poorest quintile naturally has the smallest share, 3%, while the top quintile has the largest, 51%. The other columns show the quintile shares for three more types of income. Let's draw some conclusions from the table.

- **Original incomes.** These are very unequal: the poorest quintile has 3% of the total, while the top quintile has over half. The low figure for the bottom quintile arises because many households with retired or non-working adults have little or no income from earnings, investments, or pensions other than State Pension, and rely chiefly on

Table 16.2 **The shares of different types of income, equivalized households, UK 2008–09 (%)**

Quintile	Original income	Gross income	Disposable income	Post-tax income
Bottom	3	7	7	6
2nd lowest	7	11	12	11
Middle	14	16	16	16
2nd highest	24	23	22	22
Top	51	44	42	44
All	100	100	100	100

Source: Office of National Statistics, *The Effects of Taxes and Benefits on Household Income 2008/09*, http://www.statistics.gov.uk/articles/nojournal/Taxes_Benefits_0809.pdf

state benefits and other transfers from the government.

- **Gross incomes**. These are less unequal than original incomes, because government transfers give most help to the poor.
- **Disposable incomes**. These are slightly less unequal than gross incomes, because income taxes fall most heavily on the rich.
- **Post-tax incomes**. These are slightly more unequal than disposable incomes, because the poor spend a larger fraction of their income, and so spend a larger fraction in taxes like VAT.

It would be useful if Table 16.2 had another column for final incomes, but no such column is published. However, final incomes are much less unequal than the other types of income. This is shown by Table 16.3, which gives figures for the incomes of the average household in each quintile.

This table shows that, in 2008-09, the average top quintile household had an original income of £73,810, which is 15 times more than the £4,970 of the average bottom quintile household. But the average top quintile household had a final income of £53,876, just four times more than the £13,584 of the average bottom quintile household.

Showing inequality in a graph

We can show the degree of inequality of incomes on a graph. The most common type of graph for this purpose is explained in Figure 16.1. The first column of the table there shows that the five quintiles each have one fifth, or 20%, of all the households. The next column shows that the lowest two quintiles have 40% of households between them, the lowest three have 60%, and so on. We call these figures cumulative percentages.

Imagine for a moment that the equivalized incomes of one type were all equal, so that each quintile had 20% of the total. Then the cumulative figures would be as worked out in the next two columns in the table. For example, the lowest two quintiles would have 40% between them. The information from these columns is shown by the five points on a grey line in the graph in part (a), where the horizontal axis measures the cumulative percentage of households and the vertical axis measures the cumulative percentage of income. As this grey line shows what would happen if all incomes were equal, we call it the line of equality.

The next pair of columns work out the cumulative percentage of original incomes in the UK for 2008-09, and the results are plotted as a pink curve in part (b). The final pair of columns work out the cumulative percentage of post-tax incomes in the UK in 2008–09, and the results are plotted as a purple curve in part (c).

Table 16.3 **The effects of taxes and benefits for the average household in each quintile, UK 2008–09, £ per year**

Quintile:	Lowest	2nd lowest	Middle	2nd highest	Top	Top:bottom
Original income	4,970	12,020	23,305	38,321	73,810	15
plus cash benefits	6,431	7,602	5,787	3,609	1,805	
Gross income	11,401	19,622	29,092	41,930	75,615	7
less direct taxes	1,270	2,523	5,046	8,798	18,255	
Disposable income	10,130	17,099	24,047	33,133	57,360	6
less indirect taxes	2,862	3,592	4,316	5,579	7,354	
Post-tax income	7,269	13,507	19,731	27,553	50,006	7
plus benefits in kind	6,315	6,411	5,969	5,000	3,870	
Final income	13,584	19,918	25,699	32,553	53,876	4

Source: Office of National Statistics, *The Effects of Taxes and Benefits on Household Income 2008/09*, http://www.statistics.gov.uk/articles/nojournal/Taxes_Benefits_0809.pdf

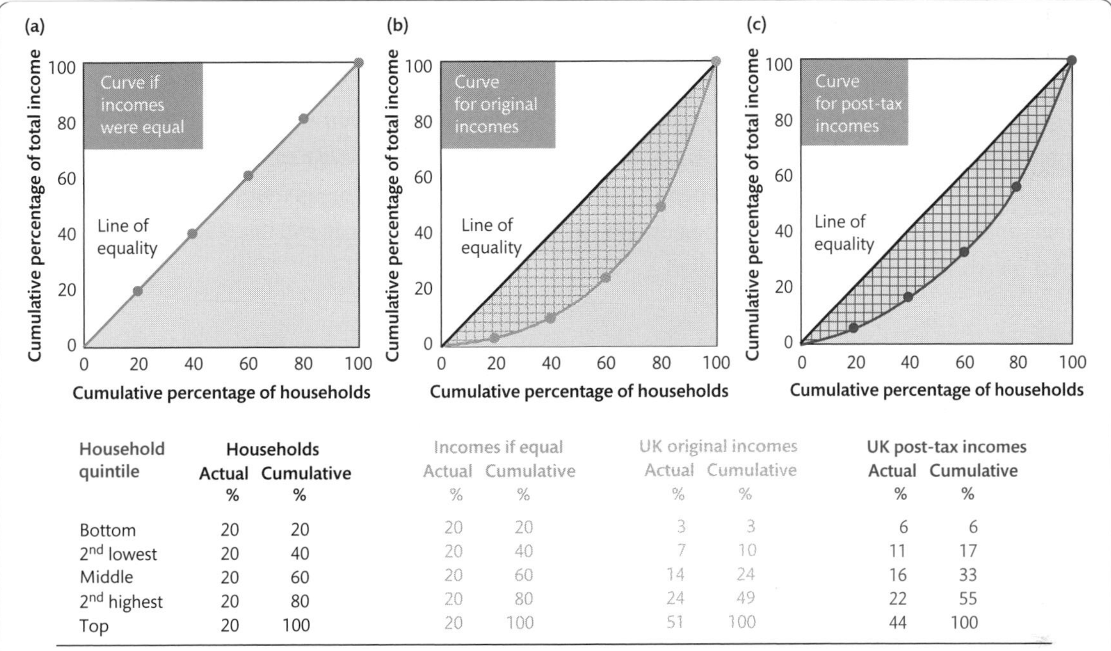

Household quintile	Households Actual %	Households Cumulative %	Incomes if equal Actual %	Incomes if equal Cumulative %	UK original incomes Actual %	UK original incomes Cumulative %	UK post-tax incomes Actual %	UK post-tax incomes Cumulative %
Bottom	20	20	20	20	3	3	6	6
2nd lowest	20	40	20	40	7	10	11	17
Middle	20	60	20	60	14	24	16	33
2nd highest	20	80	20	80	24	49	22	55
Top	20	100	20	100	51	100	44	100

Figure 16.1 **Lorenz curves**

Part (a) shows the cumulative percentage of total income that the quintiles would have if all equivalized incomes were equal. Parts (b) and (c) show the cumulative percentages for the UK's 2008–09 original and post-tax incomes; in each case the area of the grid divided by the area of the grey triangle gives the Gini coefficient, which is 0.52 in part (b) and 0.38 in part (c).

Source: Office of National Statistics, *The Effects of Taxes and Benefits on Household Income 2008/09*, http://www.statistics.gov.uk/articles/nojournal/Taxes_Benefits_0809.pdf

The pink and purple curves are below the line of equality because original incomes and post-tax incomes are unequal, but the purple line is closer to the line of equality than the pink line, because post-tax incomes are less unequal than original incomes.

Lines that relate two cumulative percentages like these are called **Lorenz curves**. This is because they were devised in 1905 by the American economist Max Otto Lorenz.

Measuring inequality

Sometimes, we like to measure inequality. This can be done in various ways, but one way uses Lorenz curves. We have seen in Figure 16.1 that the curve for original incomes is further from the line of equality than the curve for post-tax incomes. So the area between the line of equality and the original income curve, shown by the pink grid in part (b), is larger than the area between the line of equality and the post-tax income curve, shown by the purple grid in part (c).

One measure of inequality is found by dividing the areas of these grids by the area of the grey triangles below the line of equality. The result is 0.52 in part (b), and a smaller 0.38 in the less unequal case of part (c). A measure of inequality based on the area between a Lorenz curve and the line of equality is called a **Gini coefficient**. This is because this measure was devised in 1912 by the Italian Corrado Gini.

A warning about low original incomes

People who look at figures like those shown in Table 16.1 often focus on the original income figures, and then argue that the government should focus on making them less unequal. But governments are chiefly concerned with final incomes, and some of the policies they use to make final incomes less unequal actually make original incomes more unequal.

To see this, consider the UK in 1946, when few people were entitled to a state pension. The government was so concerned about pensioners with low pensions and few investments that it introduced a state pension that covered all workers. Since then, many workers have made little effort over their careers to save or arrange pensions of their own, because they know they will get the State Pension when they retire. So, when they do retire, they have even lower original incomes than they would otherwise have had. But while the State Pension makes original incomes more unequal, it makes final incomes less unequal, and this is what matters.

16.1 Everyday economics

Disposable incomes in the UK are more unequal than in most other similar countries

The chart below gives the Gini coefficients for equivalized disposable household incomes in 24 countries belonging to the Organisation for Economic Co-operation and Development for the mid 2000s. The most unequal countries are on the left. If data on final incomes were available, they would show much less inequality, and the countries would probably be in a slightly different order.

Inequality depends on many factors, but tends to be greatest in countries with many single-parent households, many pensioners, high unemployment, and widely varying levels of education.

Growing Unequal? Income Distribution and Poverty in OECD Countries, OECD, October 2008

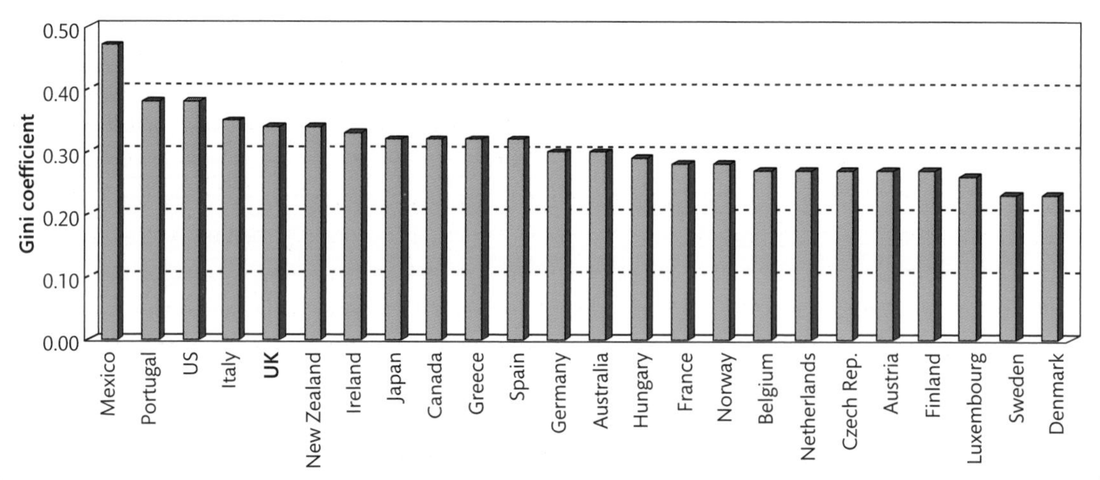

16.1 Summary

- Statistics on income distributions usually refer to households, not individuals.
- Different household compositions are allowed for by using equivalized incomes, not actual incomes.
- A household's equivalized income is the income it would need to have in order to enjoy its current standard of living if it were to comprise just two adults.
- Original incomes, from earnings, investment income, and private pensions, are very unequal. Incomes are less unequal once transfers from the government and tax payments to it are allowed for.

- Final incomes, which allow for the benefits from government services, are even less unequal.
- The inequality of incomes can be shown on a Lorenz curve, and measured with a Gini coefficient.

16.2 Major causes of inequality

We have looked at five different types of income. Each type is unequally distributed, and the root of this inequality lies in the great inequality in original incomes. To see why original incomes are so unequal, we need to see why their three components—earnings, investment income, and private pensions—vary so much.

The inequality of earnings

Earnings vary because people have unequal wages and work varying numbers of hours. The reasons why wage rates vary include the following.

- Some people undertake full-time education after school-leaving age to acquire more human capital, and so secure jobs that pay high wages.
- Some people are more willing to do jobs that pay well because they are unpleasant.
- Some people have more innate ability, which helps them to secure better paid jobs.
- Some people work harder to get promoted to posts with higher wages.
- Some people put more effort into searching for well-paid jobs and moving into them.
- Some people have more luck finding well-paid jobs.

The inequality of incomes from investments

Investment incomes vary because people differ in terms of how much they save, in how much they inherit, in how much they win in gambling and lotteries, and in how well their investments do.

The inequality of private pensions

Many pensioners have no pensions except the State Pension, so their original incomes are far lower than those of other pensioners whose jobs entitled them to occupational pensions.

The importance of the life cycle

Suppose for a moment that all the differences we have just mentioned disappear. So, for example, everyone works the same hours, gets the same education, has the same innate ability, saves the same, inherits the same, has the same access to occupational pensions, and so on.

It might seem that then incomes would be equal. But in fact there would still be a great deal of inequality. This is because different people would be of different ages, and all individuals find that their incomes vary greatly over their lives.

To show this, Table 16.4 concerns the distribution of original incomes between households in an imaginary village where there are 100 single-adult households, the occupants of which do all have the same education, ability, inheritance and so on. The only difference is that they are at different stages of their lives. Maybe your household income will vary something like this if you stay single.

The top part of the table shows that ten of these households have adults aged 18–23: we assume they are in education, with low original incomes of £7,000 from part-time jobs. Ten more households have adults aged 24–29 who earn £25,000 a year. Another 60 households have adults aged 30–65, and they earn progressively higher incomes as they get older because their increasing age and experience help them to get better paid promoted posts.

Table 16.4 **Inequality between 100 households that are identical except for their stages of the life cycle**

Age	No. of households	Household income (£)	Total income (£)
18–23	10	7,000	70,000
24–29	10	25,000	250,000
30–35	10	32,000	320,000
36–41	10	40,000	400,000
42–47	10	50,000	500,000
48–53	10	60,000	600,000
54–59	10	70,000	700,000
60–65	10	80,000	800,000
66–71	8	44,000	352,000
72–77	6	43,000	258,000
78–83	4	42,000	168,000
84–89	2	41,000	82,000
Total	**100**		**4,500,000**

Quintile	Age range	Income range £000s	Quintile's income £000s	Quintile's share of total %
Bottom	18–29	6–22	320,000	7
2nd lowest	30–41	30–34	720,000	16
Middle	66–89	34–37	860,000	19
2nd highest	42–53	45–55	1,100,000	24
Top	54–65	64–72	1,500,000	33

The adults in the 20 remaining households are retired, and have much lower original incomes. We imagine that each of these adults has an occupational pension, plus some income from investments. But as these retirees get older, they sell off some of their investments, so their incomes fall. Sadly, none of the households in this village has anyone aged 90 or above.

The top part of Table 16.4 shows that the total income of the 100 households is £4.5 million. The bottom part notes that the poorest quintile of households are those with the adults aged 18-29; they get just 7% of the total original income. The second lowest quintile is households aged 30-41, followed by those aged 66 and above and those aged 42-53. The top quintile is those aged 54-65, who get 33% of the total original income.

The quintile shares here do not vary as much as those for original incomes in the UK, at which we looked in Table 16.2. But the Table 16.4 shares do vary greatly, so we can see that much inequality in original incomes stems simply from people being at different stages of the life cycle.

Trends in the distribution of income

Table 16.5 gives some information about changes in the distribution of UK original and post-tax incomes since 1986. The Gini coefficients have increased since then, showing that both of these types of income have become more unequal.

Several factors have caused original incomes to become less equal now than in 1986-87. They include the following.

- **Pensioners live longer, so more households have low-income pensioners.**
- **More households have single-parent families.**
- **More households have students instead of workers.**
- **The demand for unskilled labour has fallen faster than its supply, so the wages of unskilled people have fallen in relation to other wages.**
- **Trade union power has been reduced by government legislation, perhaps reducing wages in some low-paid jobs.**

Table 16.5 **Trends in the distribution of original and post-tax incomes, UK**

Quintile	1986-87	1997-98	2008-09
Percentage shares of original incomes			
Bottom	3	2	3
2nd lowest	7	7	7
Middle	16	15	14
2nd highest	26	25	24
Top	49	51	51
Gini coefficient	**0.50**	**0.53**	**0.52**
Percentage shares of post-tax incomes			
Bottom	8	7	6
2nd lowest	12	11	12
Middle	16	16	16
2nd highest	22	22	22
Top	41	44	44
Gini coefficient	**0.35**	**0.38**	**0.38**

Source: Office of National Statistics, *The Effects of Taxes and Benefits on Household Income 2008/09"* http://www.statistics.gov.uk/articles/nojournal/Taxes_Benefits_0809.pdf

- **More people have become self-employed, and their earnings vary even more than wages.**
- **More women now work, so more families have two earners and high incomes.**

Post-tax incomes have become more unequal since 1986–87, chiefly because original incomes have become more unequal. But there are some other reasons including the following.

- **The main government transfers, which we will discuss shortly, have usually been raised each year only in line with prices.** At the same time, wages have generally risen faster than prices, because workers become more productive over time. So households that rely on transfers have fallen further behind those with wage earners.
- **Taxes on profits and investment income have fallen.** This helps households with investments, and they are usually in higher quintiles.

Question 16.2 What effect do you think the introduction of a minimum wage in 1999 might have had on the distribution of original incomes?

16.2 Summary

- The inequality in all types of income stems from unequal original incomes. These are unequal because households have different amounts of earnings, investment income, and private pensions. And much of the difference in these sources of income arises because people are at different stages of their lives.
- The distribution of original and post-tax incomes has become more unequal in the last 25 years for a wide range of reasons. These include pensioners living longer and more single parent families.

16.3 Some theories about redistribution by governments

All governments redistribute some income from the rich to the poor. They do this by levying high taxes on the rich and then using some of the tax revenue to pay cash transfers to the poor. In this section, we look at two reasons why voters may vote for redistribution, and then consider how much redistribution they may want the government to undertake. It is helpful at times to refer to the main reasons why some people have very low original incomes, and these reasons can be put into three broad groups.

- **Adverse events.** Some workers have temporarily low original incomes in periods of sickness and unemployment. Some non-workers, such as mothers who look after children and other carers, may need aid because they have long periods out of work with little or no original income.
- **Low income stages of the life cycle**. In this context, governments chiefly worry about pensioners. Students also have low original incomes, but they can borrow more easily than pensioners because their original incomes should rise in future, enabling them to repay their loans.
- **Low endowments**. Some people have low original incomes because of their inherited endowments. For example, they may suffer permanent ill-health or disability, or have learning difficulties.

Redistribution and the self-interest of voters

The first reason why some voters may vote for the government to redistribute income is a belief that such a policy is in their own interest. For example, some voters are sick, unemployed, or retired, and others know they may become sick or unemployed or expect to live long enough to retire.

However, these voters might wonder if the government needs to try to fix *all* the causes of low original incomes. To answer this, Table 16.6 lists the main causes of low original incomes and explains why all the alternatives to government help are problematic. Admittedly,

Table 16.6 The problems with the alternatives to government help for people with low original incomes

Need for help	Alternative to government help	Problems with the alternative
Adverse events: workers becoming ill	Workers take out insurance against being off with ill-health	Insurance may be hard to get, at least for people whom insurance companies regard as high-risk.
Adverse events: workers becoming unemployed	Workers take out insurance against becoming unemployed	Insurers may be reluctant to sell policies, partly for fear of bankruptcy in a recession, and partly for fear that some people might buy a policy and then try to get laid off and live at the insurer's expense.
Adverse events: non-workers who need aid	There is often no alternative	
Adverse time in the life cycle: students	Students borrow large sums from banks and other lenders	Some students are deterred by the need to repay, especially if they fear not later having a high wage.
Adverse time in the life cycle: retired people	Workers save more during their working years	Workers suffer from myopia, a tendency to underestimate the need to save, and so save too little.
Low endowments	There is often no alternative	

students are helped more with loans from the Student Loans Company than with transfers.

Redistribution as a public good

We have just seen that there may be widespread support for government redistribution from voters who would gain from redistribution now or who know they might gain from it in future. But will it be opposed by rich voters who are likely to pay far more in taxes for redistribution than they could ever get back in benefits from it?

Some rich voters may oppose government redistribution for this reason. However, other rich voters may be **altruistic**, that is concerned about people in need. Even so, altruistic rich people could help the poor simply by giving them voluntary donations, so why might they instead vote for the government to handle redistribution?

To see why, suppose redistribution is left to voluntary donations in a country with 1 million rich people. Each of them might reason like this: 'If I give £1 voluntarily to the poor, then I will gain some pleasure from seeing the poor helped by £1, but I might only gain 10p worth of pleasure, so I will not give away £1 to get 10p return for myself. However, I would be willing for the government to force *all* rich people to give £1 in taxes to help the poor. With this policy, I will still lose £1. But with £1 million given to the poor by the scheme, the gains to the poor will be so big that I will get far more than £1 pleasure from the scheme.'

This analysis implies that redistribution is really a public good. Without a government, rich people might feel that their individual contributions to the poor would have little effect, so they might not make contributions, just as people might not make voluntary contributions for other public goods.

Redistribution and utilitarianism

We have seen that government redistribution may be supported by most people, except the non-altruistic rich. But how much redistribution will voters want to take place? In the case of most voters, this may chiefly depend on their own circumstances, for example on how poor they may be now or believe they might be in future, or on how rich and altruistic they are.

However, some people have suggested principles that they hope will encourage voters to look beyond their own circumstances. In turn, they hope voters will then support more redistribution than they would otherwise support.

The earliest important principle stemmed from the philosophy of utilitarianism, which was developed by two British philosophers, Jeremy Bentham in the 18th century and John Stuart Mill in the 19th century. The utilitarian view of redistribution is based on three key beliefs.

- **All actions should be judged according to how they affect the total level of happiness or utility of society.** So redistribution is justified if the person being taxed loses less utility than the person receiving the transfer gains.
- **All people would get the same utility if they had the same income.** So, for example, anyone on £49 a day might get, say, 1,980 utils a day.
- **All people have a diminishing marginal utility of income.** So anyone whose income rose by £1 from £49 to £50 a day might gain, say, 20 utils a day, to get 2,000 utils a day, but anyone whose income rose by £1 from £50 to £51 would gain less, say 19 utils, to end up with 2,019. The logic of this belief can be seen by imagining the joy an extra £1 would give to a beggar and the insignificance it would have for a millionaire.

Now consider Paul, whose daily income is £49, and Peter, whose daily income is £51. A supporter of utilitarianism would argue that if the government were to take £1 away from Peter each day, and give it to Paul, then Peter would lose 19 utils each day, while Paul would gain 20. So total happiness would rise. Therefore the redistribution is justified.

This approach implies that the government should redistribute income until everyone's final income is exactly the same. If ever one person had a larger income than another, as Peter did here, then total utility would rise if money were taken from the richer and given to the poorer.

Problems with utilitarianism

The utilitarian principle may encourage many people to vote for extensive redistribution. But there are two reasons why few people, if any, would support the aim of equal final incomes.

- We can't be sure that everyone will get the same utility from each income level. Maybe Peter gets more happiness from money than Paul, and would lose more happiness with a cut in income from £51 to £50 than Peter would get with a rise from £49 to £50.
- Suppose the government did set out to leave everyone with the same final income. Then it would really be saying to each worker: 'No matter how hard you work or save in order to secure a high original income, we will ensure that, after allowing for taxes and transfers, you end up with a final income that is not even 1p more than anyone else's.' So there would be no incentive for anyone to work, and income for the country as a whole could fall greatly. In turn, total happiness would plummet.

This second problem means that no government would push redistribution as far as the utilitarian approach suggests. It knows that if it redistributes heavily, it will need high taxes, and this might result in people working less hard, so that the country's total income will fall.

An American economist, Art Laffer, developed this idea. He said that, for any tax, the relationship between the tax rate and the tax revenue is given by a **Laffer curve**. Figure 16.2 shows what a Laffer curve might look like for an income tax in a particular country at a particular point in time. If the government there had no income tax, and so had a 0% tax rate, then it would raise no revenue. If it instead had a tax rate of 100%, then maybe no one would work, so again it would have no tax revenue. But it would raise some revenue at any intermediate tax rates. So the tax revenue must relate to the tax rate in a curve that initially slopes upwards and then slopes downwards, as shown.

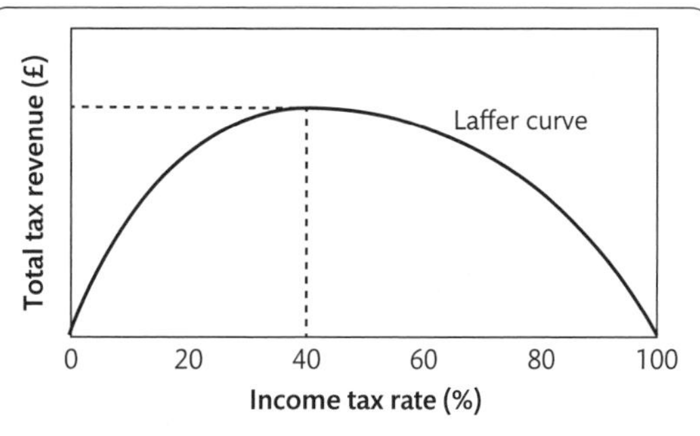

Figure 16.2 **A Laffer curve for an income tax**

Each tax has a Laffer curve. For the income tax shown here, the maximum revenue could be raised if the tax rate were 40%. At higher tax rates, people would work much less; so, even though the tax rate has risen, total income will fall so much that the tax revenue will be lower than at a rate of 40%.

In practice, we are probably on the left-hand part of the Laffer curve for most taxes. So the government probably could raise tax rates and raise more revenue to give to the poor. But the fact that a downward-sloping part must exist makes all governments wary about high tax rates.

Rawls and social justice

In 1971, the American philosopher John Rawls put forward another principle about how much redistribution there should be. He felt that voters disagreed about this issue because their views were coloured by what their current incomes are, or what their future incomes might be. He believed that if voters could forget about their own circumstances, or, in his terms, hide their circumstances behind a *veil of ignorance*, then they might be able to agree on a principle about what amount of redistribution was fair or just.

He imagined that although voters would hide their circumstances behind this veil when they discussed the issue, they would otherwise be very well informed. For example, they would know that some people have very low original incomes and others have high ones. The only thing people would not know, or would at least forget, was whether they are rich or poor.

How much redistribution would these voters want? Rawls argued that their thoughts would be dominated by a fear that they might have the lowest original income of everyone. This fear would make them demand that the government do its best to make the person with the lowest original income as well off as possible. So they would want the government to have redistribution policies that left the poorest person as well off as possible. This means having tax rates that take each tax to the highest point on its Laffer curve. There would be no point raising tax rates beyond that, with a view to helping the poorest person even more, if the higher tax rates were actually to lead to a lower tax revenue, because the government would then actually have to do less redistribution.

The idea of asking people to place their own circumstances behind a veil of ignorance has a widespread appeal. But there is less widespread support for Rawls's specific view about what these ignorant people would agree. For example, people might think that it was most unlikely they would be the poorest person, and they might be willing for the government to do less to help that person if it were to result in a much higher level of incomes for the great majority of people. Even so, Rawls's views have influenced many people who do not fully subscribe to his own conclusion.

Question 16.3 Suppose people were asked for their views on an issue such as granting asylum to people wanting to come to the UK. Why might their views differ if they were to act behind a veil of ignorance about their own situation?

16.3 Summary

- The main causes of low original incomes are adverse events, notably unemployment and illness, adverse stages of the life cycle, notably retirement, and low endowments, such as learning difficulties.
- Some people support government redistribution because they will gain now or may gain in future.
- Altruistic rich people may also support government redistribution: the alternative is voluntary donations to the needy, but few people might make donations, because each individual gift would have negligible effect.
- The utilitarian approach to redistribution says that it should aim to maximize total utility, and this would occur with complete equality, except that high taxes might deter work effort and reduce total income.
- Rawls's approach to redistribution says that it should seek to make the person with the lowest original income as well off as possible. Because high taxes are likely to lead to less work effort and so reduce total income, Rawls's approach also requires redistribution to aim for less than complete equality.

16.4 The meaning of poverty

We have seen reasons why people may not agree on how much government redistribution should take place. But many people would agree with the idea that the government should find out which households have original incomes that would leave them in poverty, and help them to escape from poverty with government transfers.

This raises the question of what level of income should be defined as a poverty line, with those whose income lies below the line being deemed to be in poverty. This question has received a variety of answers, but all have problems. Let's now look at some of the answers. We will divide them into three approaches.

The absolute income approach

The **absolute income approach** to defining poverty states that the poverty line should be defined so that a household is in poverty if it cannot afford to buy some specified items. The problem with this approach is deciding what to put on the list. Here are three possible answers.

- **The items needed merely to survive.** This is the lowest possible poverty line. Few people think that it should be used in a developed economy like the UK, or indeed in any economy.
- **Charles Booth's list.** Booth was a wealthy shipowner who studied poverty in London around 1900. His list allowed for the items needed to survive plus 'reasonable' food, shelter, and clothing. Although the income needed for this list was very low, he found that 30% of Londoners were living below this line at the time.
- **Seebohm Rowntree's list.** Rowntree was a wealthy confectioner in York who also studied poverty there. He made his first study in 1899 with a list that allowed people enough to survive and also to be 'physically efficient'. This meant having food, clothing, shelter, and some other items such as fuel. He found that 28% of York's population lived in poverty. He repeated his studies in 1936 and 1951, each time revising his list to include a few more items, yet poverty had dropped greatly by 1936 and all but disappeared by 1951.

For many years, the US used a related approach to defining poverty called a food ratio method. Studies there in the 1960s found that the poorest families spent around one third of their incomes on food. This gave rise to the poverty line being regarded as equal to the expenditure needed for a nutritionally adequate diet multiplied by three.

For a developed economy in the 21st century, however, the absolute approach is scarcely viable, because poverty at the low levels that the various definitions propose scarcely exists. And there is widespread support for the view that people whose original incomes would take them only modestly over these poverty lines should still be seen as in poverty and therefore entitled to government transfers.

The relative income approach

An alternative approach to defining poverty is the **relative income approach**, which states that a household is in poverty if its income is low relative to other households. This approach is adopted in the EU and the UK, which both define the poverty line as an income level equal to 60% of the income of the median household. The median household is the one that would come halfway if all households were lined up in order of income.

There are two problems with the relative approach.

- **The percentage used, such as 60%, is arbitrary.**
- **The poverty line always moves exactly in step with average incomes, so even if all incomes were to double, the number of people in poverty would stay the same.** To see this, suppose the median income today is £500 a week and the poverty line is £300, so that a family on £250 is in poverty. If all incomes double, this family will have £500 a week, but it will still be in poverty because the

median income will double to £1,000 and the poverty line will double to 60% of that, namely £600.

On the relative income approach, the only way the government can reduce the number of people below the poverty line is to give these people bigger transfers. And it must pay for these by taking larger shares of the income of rich people in tax.

Hybrid approaches

Many people have given definitions of poverty that are neither wholly absolute nor wholly relative. So their poverty lines will rise when incomes rise, unlike an absolute approach, but their poverty lines will not necessarily rise in proportion to income, as happens on a relative approach.

One interesting definition like this is also one of the earliest. It was given by the Scottish economist Adam Smith in 1776. He said poverty was being unable to afford the necessities for survival *plus* 'whatever the custom of the country renders it indecent, for creditable people, even of the lowest order, to be without'.

The problem here is that even if two people were to agree to accept this definition, they would no doubt disagree about what to include. In 1776, Smith felt it was indecent in England for men or women to lack shoes, but in Scotland indecent only for men, and in France indecent for neither. Today, most people would add many more items, such as electricity, running water, and a television. So at least the definition allows for the items included to vary between places and over time.

Many other people have suggested modified versions. For example, the World Bank defines poverty as the inability to acquire the basic goods and services needed to survive with dignity, which is similar to Smith, but it adds that poverty also encompasses low levels of health and education, poor access to clean water and sanitation, inadequate physical security, lack of voice, and insufficient capacity and opportunity to better one's life. Terms like 'survival with dignity' and 'low levels of health and education' will naturally change their nuances as incomes rise, so that more income will be needed to take people out of poverty, but equally a doubling of incomes all round could well reduce the numbers in poverty.

16.2 Everyday economics

Food poverty

Food prices escalated rapidly in 2010–11 for many reasons, including poor harvests of wheat and rice in many parts of the world: for example there were droughts in Argentina and China, and floods in other parts of Australia, India, and Pakistan. The higher prices have little effect on living standards in advanced countries, where food accounts for a small share of household incomes. But in many Asian countries, poor people spend about a half of their income on food. Higher prices lead to malnutrition, hunger, and perhaps starvation.

'Asia's poor suffer as food prices drive inflation', *The Irrawaddy*, 17 February 2011
'Food price spiral: causes and consequences', *Geopolitical Monitor*, 9 February 2011

Comment In developed countries, the food ratio approach to poverty may seem a relic from a former age, but an income equal to three times food spending would be a great improvement to many people elsewhere.

16.4 Summary

- A poverty line is hard to define.
- One approach is to specify an absolute level of income that is needed to buy a specified list of items. But people will disagree about the list, and probably want to extend it as the country becomes richer.
- Another approach, used in the UK and EU, is to specify a relative level of income, such as 60% of the median income. But people may disagree what the percentage should be, and reducing the number of people in poverty is very hard: for example, doubling all incomes will not take anyone out of poverty.
- Alternatively, poverty can be defined in a hybrid way so that the poverty line will rise when average income in a country rises, but the poverty line may not rise in proportion to average incomes.

16.5 Policies to tackle poverty

This final section gives a brief guide to the UK arrangements for government transfers. Before we look at them, note that they are made on two different payments bases.

- **Flat-rate transfers:** here the amount paid to a recipient does not depend on the recipient's other income.
- **Means-tested transfers:** here the amount paid to a recipient does depend on the recipient's other income, and the amount falls to zero if that other income reaches a set level.

The main UK policies were introduced in 1946, following a report by a committee chaired by the economist William Beveridge. This report noted that most poverty arose in households in which adults were unemployed, sick, or old. So let's look first at the benefits offered to these people.

National Insurance

Most people who are old, unemployed, or sick have worked at some stage. The principal policy for helping them when they are not working is the government-run National Insurance scheme. All workers pay contributions into this, topped up by contributions from their employers, and this scheme entitles them to benefits when they are not working, as follows.

- **In unemployment:** a flat-rate Jobseekers' Allowance, whose amount depends on age.
- **In illness or disability:** *either* (a) means-tested Income Support to top up any sick pay from the employer, *or* (b) a flat-rate Employment Support Allowance.
- **If retired:** (a) a flat-rate basic State Pension; *plus* (b) a flat-rate State Second Pension for workers who had no occupational pension and who paid extra into National Insurance; *plus* (c) a means-tested Pension Credit for pensioners with little income other than (a) and (b).

Benefits for those not in National Insurance

Some people who are old, unemployed, or sick have not worked, or at least not enough to qualify for National Insurance benefits. There are benefits available for them.

- **In unemployment:** *either* (a) a means-tested Jobseeker's Allowance, if they are seeking work, *or* (b) means-tested Income Support.
- **In illness or disability:** Employment Support Allowance which is flat-rate if people first claim at an early age, and otherwise means-tested.
- **If retired:** means-tested Pension Credit.

People on low wages

Even people who work can be in poverty if their wages are low. They get some help from having to be paid at least the National Minimum Wage, but they are also entitled to a further benefit.

- **Working Tax Credit:** a means-tested benefit for people aged 25 or more working 30 or more hours a week.

Children

People with children need more income than those without. There are two benefits for them.

- **Child Benefit:** a flat-rate benefit for all children.
- **Child Tax Credit:** a means-tested benefit to which 90% of people with children are entitled.

Housing costs

The benefits paid under all the schemes noted above are the same throughout the UK. However, these benefits are paid at levels which ignore the income that people need for housing costs. This is because housing costs vary greatly in different areas, and to cover these costs there are two additional benefits as follows.

- **Housing Benefit:** a means-tested benefit that depends on local rent levels.
- **Council Tax Benefit:** a means-tested benefit that depends on how much Council Tax is levied by the local authority.

Problems with more generous benefits

In spite of all these policies, some 30% of UK households have disposable incomes below the relative poverty line adopted by the government. Most EU countries have a lower figure. The 30% figure could be cut by making benefits more generous, but this is costly: for example, raising the basic State Pension would mean paying more to many pensioners whose occupational pensions and savings already give them a good lifestyle.

The cheapest way of raising benefits would be to raise the amount of means-tested benefits that the poorest people can claim, and offset the cost of this by withdrawing the benefits faster than at present for those people who have slightly greater means. But this produces two problems.

- **The poverty trap:** this is a situation in which people in poverty find it hard to escape. For example, some working people entitled to means-tested benefits might wish to work more hours to improve their living standards, but if means-tested benefits were withdrawn at a faster rate, they might find that they lose benefits at almost the same rate as their wages rose.
- **The unemployment trap:** this is a situation in which unemployed people find that if they take up a job, their means-tested benefits fall so much that they are little better off. So they prefer to stay unemployed.

Further issues in tackling poverty

There are several further issues that complicate efforts to ease poverty, including the following.

- **Non-claiming.** Many people who are entitled to means-tested benefits never claim them, perhaps through ignorance, illiteracy, or pride.
- **Benefit reliance.** Some people become reliant on benefits and end up on permanently low incomes. To help to stem this in the case of single mothers, the government encourages them to work by helping with childcare costs.
- **Using a relative poverty line.** This means that to reduce the number of people in poverty, their incomes must rise at a faster rate than average incomes.
- **The media focus on numbers in poverty.** Media headlines often focus on the percentage of the population below the poverty line. This may discourage governments from helping those most in need, because helping people who are far below the poverty line get closer to it leaves the number of people in poverty the same, and makes the government seem ineffective. Governments may prefer to give a little help to those who are just below the poverty line, to get them just above it; this reduces the numbers in poverty and makes the government seem to be tackling poverty effectively.
- **Fraud.** It is believed that many people fraudulently claim benefits, and money paid to them reduces the amount available for those in poverty. Along with error, fraud was thought in 2010 to cost over £5 billion a year.

The 2013 reforms: Universal Credit

The UK government intends, over a period of time from 2013, to merge many means-tested benefits for people of working age into a single benefit called Universal Credit. The merged benefits include means-tested Jobseeker's Allowance, Housing Benefit, Child Tax Credit, Working Tax Credit, Income Support, and means-tested Employment Support Allowance. These reforms have several aims.

- **To simplify the system.**
- **To join up the benefits paid to people who are out of work to those paid to people who are working on low pay.** The government can then more easily ensure that working always pays.
- **To tighten the sanctions on unemployed people who refuse work when it is offered to them, perhaps withdrawing all benefits.**

16.5 Summary

- The UK's National Insurance scheme offers benefits to workers if they become unemployed or sick, and when they retire. There are other benefits for people who are not covered by the scheme.
- There are further benefits for people on low wages, people with children, and to help with housing costs.
- Making flat-rate benefits more generous is very costly. It is cheaper to raise the level of means-tested benefits and withdraw them more quickly as incomes rise, but there is then a danger of putting people in a poverty trap or an unemployment trap, in which efforts to help them to help themselves have little effect.
- Many people fail to claim the means-tested benefits to which they are entitled.

In the next chapter we turn from microeconomics to macroeconomics.

abc Glossary

Absolute income approach: defining poverty as being unable to buy a list of specified items.

Altruistic: being concerned about people in need.

Disposable income: a household's gross income minus the taxes it pays directly to the government.

Equivalized income: the income a household would need to have in order to enjoy its current standard of living, if it were to comprise only a married or cohabiting couple.

Final income: a household's post-tax income plus the value of its benefits from government services.

Flat-rate transfer: a benefit for which the amount paid does not depend on the recipient's other income.

Gini coefficient: a measure of inequality derived from a Lorenz curve.

Gross income: a household's original income plus its cash transfers from the government.

Laffer curve: a curve relating the rate set on a tax to the revenue from it.

Lorenz curve: a curve on a graph that relates two cumulative percentages.

Means-tested transfer: a benefit for which the amount paid depends on the recipient's other income, and falls to zero if that income reaches a set level.

Original income: a household's income from earnings, investments, and private pensions.

Post-tax income: a household's disposable income minus its payments of all other taxes.

Poverty trap: a situation in which people find it hard to escape from poverty, because extra earnings are largely offset by lower means-tested benefits.

Relative income approach: defining poverty as having a relatively low income.

Unemployment trap: a situation in which unemployed people find that if they were to take up a job, their means-tested benefits would fall so much that they would be little better off.

Answers to in-text questions

16.1 The weight for her household would be $0.61 + 0.24 + 0.15$, making 1.00, the same as the weight for the couple. So both households would have equivalized incomes of £600/1.00, or £600, indicating the same living standard.

16.2 The minimum wage would (**a**) raise the wages of many people on low wages, and (**b**) cast some low wage people into unemployment, if their employers could not afford the minimum wage. Effect (a) would make original incomes less unequal, and (b) would make them more unequal. In the event, though, there is little evidence that (b) occurred.

16.3 Some people who hold strong views against asylum seekers might moderate their stance if they were to act behind a veil of ignorance, not knowing whether they themselves might be seeking asylum from a foreign tyranny.

? Questions for review

16.1 Use Table 16.1 to estimate the equivalized incomes of the following three households, each of which has an actual income of £1,000 a week: A, a married couple plus an elderly relative; B, a cohabiting couple plus two children aged 2 and 4; C, three unrelated adults.

16.2 Suppose a country has nine households, A–I, whose current disposable weekly incomes are as shown in the first column of the adjacent table. (**a**) Why is the median income £500? (**b**) What will the poverty line be if it is set at 60% of the median income? (**c**) How many households are below the poverty line? (**d**) Suppose the government is comparing the effects of two possible new polices, I and II, which would each leave the median income at £500. Using the figures shown in the table, which policy would help the two poorest citizens the most? (**e**) Which policy would leave the most households in poverty?

Household	Current weekly income (£)	Weekly income with Policy I (£)	Weekly income with Policy II (£)
A	1,100	1,110	1,090
B	800	810	790
C	700	710	690
D	600	610	590
E	500	500	500
F	310	310	290
G	290	310	290
H	200	180	220
I	100	80	140

? Questions for discussion

16.1 Table 16.1 shows that if parents have an 18-year-old child living with them, they are alleged to need just twice as much extra income as they would for a 2-year-old. Would you agree with that assertion?

16.2 If all incomes were to double in the next decade, would you accept that poverty was as serious as it is today?

16.3 Can you think of ways of encouraging people to save more for old age?

16.4 Can you think of ways of encouraging more people to claim their means-tested benefits?

Common student errors

Many students believe that the government should focus its efforts on raising the original incomes of the poorest households. But what matters is their post-tax incomes, or better still their final incomes. As noted in the text, some policies, like state pensions, raise people's post-tax incomes, but probably reduce their original incomes.

Consider a headline such as 'More children in poverty than a decade ago'. Many students overlook the fact that because a relative poverty line is used, the living standards of many children who are in poverty today is higher than the living standards of many children who were not in poverty a decade ago.

Part III

Macroeconomics

17

Introduction to Macroeconomics

Remember from Chapter 1 that macroeconomics is concerned with the economy as a whole, in contrast to microeconomics, which looks at the individual markets in an economy

Every day, the media discuss the state of the economy and what the government is or is not doing about it. The government, in its turn, tries to manage the economy in a way that appeals to voters, in the hope of winning the next election. So what are the issues that most concern voters like you? And how can we illustrate some of the problems on a simple supply and demand curve graph, like the one we used in microeconomics?

This chapter shows you how to answer questions like these, by understanding:

- the three key issues in macroeconomics—economic growth, unemployment, and inflation;
- exactly why economic growth, unemployment, and inflation matter;
- how we measure economic growth, unemployment, and inflation;
- a basic diagram for macroeconomics.

17.1 Three key issues in macroeconomics

We saw in Chapter 1 that microeconomics is concerned with individual markets. When it looks at any market, it chiefly asks what determines the quantity that is traded in that market in any period of time, and what determines the price at which the item in that market is traded. We saw in Chapter 3 and in many later chapters that the main factors that determine prices and quantities are supply and demand.

In contrast, macroeconomics is concerned with the economy as a whole. There are three key issues in macroeconomics, as follows:

- **the rate of economic growth**, which is the rate at which total output is growing over time;
- **the rate of unemployment**, which is the fraction of the labour force who do not have a job;
- **the rate of inflation**, which is the rate at which the general level of prices is rising.

What voters would like governments to secure the following:

- **a high and stable rate of growth in output**;
- **a low and stable rate of unemployment**;
- **a low and stable rate of inflation**.

In this chapter, we will look at output growth, unemployment, and inflation, to see how they are measured and why they matter. We will also see how the UK's economy has performed over many years, and how its recent performance compares with the world's other leading industrial economies. We will also introduce a figure that is basic to macroeconomics.

17.1 Summary

- The chief macroeconomic concerns of voters and governments are achieving a high stable rate of growth, and low stable rates of unemployment and inflation.

17.2 The rate of economic growth

We begin with **economic growth**: this refers to increases in the total quantity of goods and services that are produced in the economy. An economy is growing if this quantity is higher in one period of time, such as a year, than it was in the previous period.

However, although growth eases the economic problem, it may create other serious problems if increased production and consumption impose external costs on the environment and the climate. We discussed externalities in Chapter 13.

Why does growth matter?

Remember from Chapter 1 that 'the economic problem' is that our resources cannot produce nearly as many goods and services as people would like to consume. When an economy grows, then it produces more goods and services, so the economic problem eases a little.

How does growth arise?

To see how growth arises, recall that resources comprise land, labour, and capital. Growth requires some improvement in resources, such as the following.

- **Having additional or better capital**. A country can invest in extra plant, buildings, vehicles, and machinery. It can also use new technologies to invest in new types of capital, which may allow labour and land to be used more productively.

- **Having additional or better labour**. Few countries want to embark on rapid population growth, chiefly for social reasons, but investing in human capital, which is education, will allow the existing workforce to be more productive.
- **Making better or more use of land**. Land is taken as all the free gifts of nature: a country can try to make better use of its natural resources, and also use ones that have been little used before, such as using the tides for generating electricity.

How do we measure growth?

To see how rapidly an economy is growing, we need to measure the total quantity of goods and services that are produced in a period, say a year, and then see how quickly this total quantity is rising. But how can we measure the total quantity of all the different goods and services that are produced in any particular year?

In microeconomics, when we look at the markets for individual products, like eggs, potatoes, and cotton, we can simply measure quantities as the number of eggs, the tonnes of potatoes, and the metres of cotton fibre. But how can we get a single measure for the total quantity of all the different items produced in an economy, when the quantities of these different items are measured in so many different ways? The answer is that we use the monetary value of goods and services.

Ideally, we would include the value of every good and service that is produced. However, it is very difficult to work out the value of the goods and services that households produce for themselves. So economists ignore these and instead look at gross domestic product (GDP), which, as we saw in Chapter 1, attempts to cover all the other goods and services that are produced. Then, to see how rapidly the economy is growing, we can compare the figures of GDP for different years. When we do this, however, we do not use the actual GDP figures for each year. Let's see why, and then see what we do use.

Changes in nominal GDP

Suppose the actual GDP in an economy in 2000 is £600 billion, and that by 2020 it rises by 150% to £1,500 billion, as shown in the first column of Table 17.1. These figures show the actual value of the goods and services produced each year at the prices that applied in that year, and are said to show **GDP at current prices**; another term for GDP at current prices is **nominal GDP**.

So nominal GDP here rises by 150%. However, this doesn't tell us what happens to the quantity of goods and services produced, because we need also to allow for changes in prices. To see why price changes matter, consider three possibilities.

- **The price level stays the same**. In this case, the fact that nominal GDP rises by 150% means that the quantity must have risen by 150%.
- **The price level rises by as much as nominal GDP**, that is by 150%. In this case, the quantity will not have risen at all. The reason nominal GDP rises by 150% is simply that the same quantity is now valued at prices that are 150% more.
- **The price level rises by less than nominal GDP**. In this case, the quantity will have risen, but by less than the rise in nominal GDP. Nominal GDP rises by 150% partly because prices rose and partly because the quantity rose.

Changes in real GDP

We have seen that changes in nominal GDP from one year to another will indicate the change in the quantity of goods and services produced only if prices are stable. In practice, prices are not stable, so to measure changes in the quantity of goods and services we must compare figures for what is called **GDP at constant prices**, or **real GDP**: these figures show what the value of the goods and services produced in each year would have been if prices had been constant at the level that applied at some period of time. This period is called the **reference period** or **base period**.

For example, suppose we take 2008 as the base period, and suppose that prices in 2008 were higher than those in 2000, but lower than those in 2020. Then we can understand the figures for real GDP given in the second column of Table 17.1.

- **Real GDP in 2000**. The goods and services produced in 2000 were worth £600 billion when valued at 2000 prices. But they are worth more if they are valued at the higher prices that applied in 2008. The table shows that their value at these prices is estimated as £750 billion.
- **Real GDP in 2020**. The goods and services produced in 2020 were worth £1,500 billion when valued at 2020 prices. But they are worth less if they are valued at the lower prices that applied in 2008. The table shows their value at these prices is estimated as £1,250 billion.

So we can see that while nominal GDP rose by 150% between 2000 and 2020, much of this rise was accounted for by a rise in prices. If prices had been constant at 2008 levels, then GDP would have risen from £750 million to £1,250 million. This is a rise of 67%, and this figure shows the true rise in the quantity of goods and services produced between 2000 and 2020.

Table 17.1 **Relating changes in nominal GDP, real GDP to the GDP deflator with the reference or base period 2008**

Year	Nominal GDP GDP at current prices (£)	Real GDP GDP at base period prices (£)	GDP deflator Price level as a % of the level in the base period (Index)
2000	600	750	80
2020	1,500	1,250	120
% change	+150%	+67%	+50%

The GDP deflator

Table 17.1 also allows us to work out some information about prices in each year, as follows:

- **Prices in 2000**. The output produced in 2000 was worth £600 million when valued at 2000 prices and £750 million when valued at 2008 prices. So its value at 2000 prices is 80% of its value at 2008 prices. This means that the general level of prices in 2000 was 80% of the level in 2020.
- **Prices in 2020**. The output produced in 2020 was worth £1,500 million when valued at 2020 prices and £1,250 million when valued at 2008 prices. So its value at 2020 prices is 120% of its value at 2008 prices. This means that the general level of prices in 2000 was 120% of the level in 2020.

We can use this information on prices to work out what is called the **GDP deflator**: this is an index that reflects the general level of prices of all the goods and services included in GDP. We set the index at 100 for the base period, here 2008, and say the GDP deflator for that period was 100. Then we say that the GDP deflator was 80 in 2000, when prices were 80% of those in the base period, and 120 in 2020, when prices were 120% of those in the base period. These figures are shown in the last column of Table 17.1. Between 2000 and 2020, the index rose by 50% from 80 to 120, which means prices on average rose by 50%.

Growth in practice

Figure 17.1 gives some information about the growth of output in the UK since 1855. The top part shows the growth rate for each year: these figures show how much higher—or occasionally lower—real GDP was in each year than in the year before. The figures range from 10% in 1940, when real GDP was 10% higher than in 1939, to –10% in 1919, when real GDP was 10% lower than in 1918. The average growth rate since 1855 has been about 2.0%. The most recent year in which real GDP fell was 2009.

The lower part of Figure 17.1 gives an index for real GDP. This sets a figure for real GDP in 1855 as 100. By

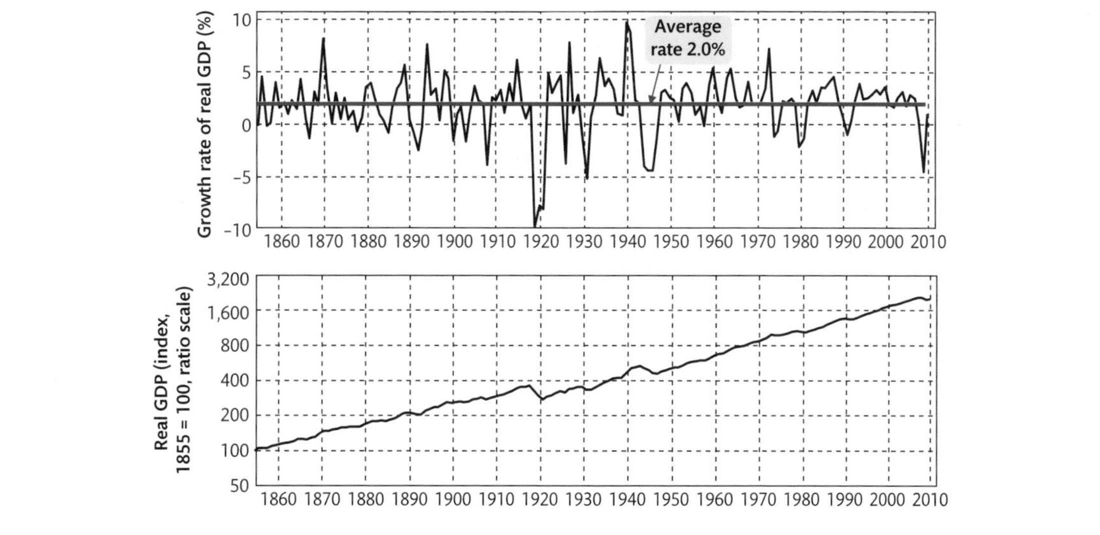

Figure 17.1 **GDP growth in the UK, 1855–2010**

The top figure shows that growth has ranged between 10% and -10% with an average of 2%. The worst years were after the world wars, around 1918 and 1945. The longest period of sustained growth was from 1992 to 2008. The lower figure shows an index of real GDP, with 1855 set at 100. This graph uses a ratio scale, so that each grid line represents a doubling of GDP. GDP doubled between 1855 and 1888, 1888 and 1936, 1936 and 1967, and 1967 and 1999. In 2010, output was about seven times higher than a century earlier.

Sources: B R Mitchell, *British Historical Statistics;* National Statistics, *Economic Trends Annual Supplements* and *UK National Accounts.* The figures are for GDP at factor cost until 1947, and then for GDP at basic prices.

around 2010, the index was almost 20 times higher, showing that almost 20 times as many goods and services were produced. This was the effect of an average growth rate over the 155 years of about 2.0%. But if the average rate had been just a little higher, say 2.4%, then GDP in 2010 would have been very much greater—over double what it was! So, over a long period, small changes in the growth rate make big differences to output, which helps to explain why governments are concerned about growth rates. Indeed, if the UK could sustain its average growth rate of 2.0%, then output would double by the time today's 18-year-olds reach their mid-50s.

Figure 17.2 looks at the average growth rate since 1990 for the world's seven richest developed nations. These nations form a group called G7, because their seven finance ministers have occasional meetings. The UK is one of these nations, and you can see that its growth rate has been a little above that the other countries in this period.

Recessions and business cycles

If you look at the top part of Figure 17.1, you will see that the growth rate fluctuates above and below its long-term average. Moreover, you will see that, from time to time, growth has been negative, which means that output was falling.

The government publishes figures of real GDP for every quarter of the year, that is from January to March, April to June, July to September, and October to December. If output falls for two consecutive quarters, the economy is said to be in **recession**. The economy moved into its most recent recession in 2008, when output fell in the third and fourth quarters; output started to rise again at the end of 2009. The previous recession started way back in 1990, when output fell in the third and fourth quarters; output started to grow again in 1992.

In between recessions, output generally grows and the economy is said to be expanding. The fluctuations in an economy between periods of recession and

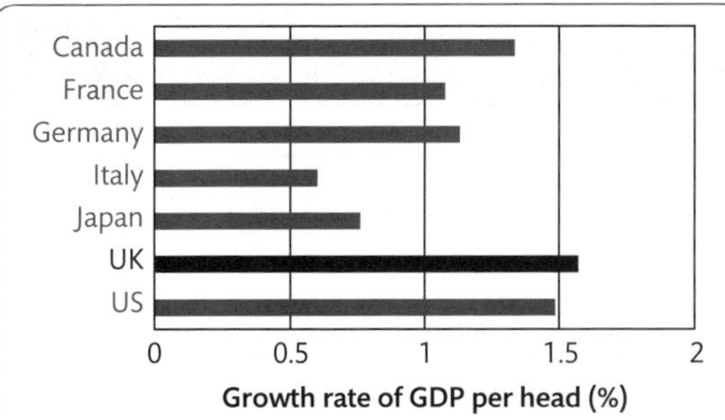

Figure 17.2 **Average growth rate of GDP per head, G7 countries, 1990–2010**

The UK had the highest growth of GDP per head in this period, but growth rates everywhere were at historically low levels.

Source: IMF Online Data.

expansion are called **business cycles**. They are given this name because they chiefly reflect fluctuations in the output of firms, that is businesses. But the word 'cycle' does not mean that there is anything regular about them. Indeed, the period of expansion between the last two recessions lasted for 18 years, an unprecedented length of time for sustained expansion.

When the economy contracts, so that output falls, unemployment always rises, and when the economy expands rapidly, inflation often increases. So, while governments like a high average rate of growth rate, they also like growth to be fairly stable, in the hope that the economy will then avoid recessions and periods of high unemployment, and also avoid periods of very high growth and the risk of high inflation. So growth is linked to both unemployment and inflation, to which we now turn.

17.1 Everyday economics

Two cases of spectacular economic growth

For the global economy, one of the most spectacular events of the last 25 years has been the economic growth in India and China. Between 1985 and 2010, real GDP per head rose more than eightfold in China and more than threefold in India. Between them, these countries have well over a third of the world's population, so this represents a considerable increase in economic well-being. In both countries, growth has been helped by substantial investment by foreign countries, attracted by relatively low wage rates compared with Western economies. But different forces lie behind this trend: until the 1980s, China chose to isolate itself largely from the rest of the world, while India was in principle more open, but had excessive regulations that deterred investment. Since then, China has opened itself and India has pursued deregulation.

Data from International Monetary Fund, online *World Economic Database*, April 2011.

17.2 Summary

- Nominal GDP shows the value of each year's GDP at the current prices of the year concerned. Nominal GDP rises when the quantity of output rises and when the level of prices rises.
- To measure changes in the quantity of output produced, we work out the value that each year's GDP would be if its output were valued at the constant prices that applied in a base or reference period. Changes in these figures show changes in real GDP, that is in the quantity of output.
- We can use figures for real and nominal GDP to work out the GDP deflator, which is an index showing what happens over time to the general level of prices of all the goods and services included in GDP.
- There are occasionally periods of contraction when growth is negative, with periods of expansion in between. An economy is in recession if output falls for two consecutive periods of three months. The fluctuations between one recession and the next are called business cycles.

17.3 The rate of unemployment

The definition of unemployment

We now turn to the second key macroeconomic issue: unemployment. We begin by seeing exactly what economists mean by unemployment.

You may be tempted to think that everyone without a job should be regarded as unemployed. However, economists say that **unemployment** applies only to people who are able, available, and willing to work, but who have no job.

This narrower view means that there are three groups of people without jobs whom we do not regard as unemployed, as follows:

- **people who are not able to work**, such as babies, toddlers, ill people, and very old people;
- **people who are not available for work**, such as schoolchildren and students who are studying;
- **people who are not willing to work**, such as pensioners who are fit enough to work, but prefer not to, and also people who choose to look after their homes and families, perhaps while their partners earn a wage.

The total number of people who are able, available, and willing to work is called the **labour force**. At any moment in time, most of these people are employed, but some are unemployed. The **unemployment rate** is generally regarded as the percentage of the labour force that has no job. However, economists regard people who want to work full-time, but who actually only work part-time, as partly unemployed.

Measuring unemployment

The UK government produces two measures of unemployment. One is based on the number of people claiming Jobseekers' Allowance. We saw in Chapter 16 that this is a benefit paid by the government to unemployed people. However, this measure of unemployment seriously understates the level of unemployment, because there are four groups of unemployed people who are not entitled to Jobseekers' Allowance and who must instead claim other benefits:

- **unemployed people who have left school, but who are aged 16 or 17**;
- **unemployed people aged 60 or over**;
- **unemployed people who have not worked long enough to be entitled to Jobseekers' Allowance;**
- **many part-time workers who want to work full-time**. The part-time earnings of these people are often high enough to disqualify them from Jobseekers' Allowance.

The government's second measure gives a much better idea of the level of unemployment. This measure gets its data from surveys, and it uses an internationally accepted definition of unemployment that covers the following groups:

- **people without a job, who want a job, have sought work in the last four weeks, and are available to start work in the next two weeks**;
- **people who are out of work, have found a job, and are waiting to start in the next two weeks**.

This measure covers the first three groups of people excluded from Jobseekers' Allowance, so it results in higher rates of unemployment. However, although it comes closer to recognizing the full extent of unemployment, it does not cover part-time workers who want to work full-time: indeed, anyone who has worked for as little as one hour in the week during which the survey is conducted is regarded as employed.

Starting and leaving unemployment

There are two groups of people who join the ranks of those who are unemployed, as follows.

- **Those who lose their jobs and intend to stay in the labour force, but have not yet found another job.** This applies to all people who are made redundant, or who are dismissed, or who voluntarily leave their jobs, except for those who intend to leave the workforce, either temporarily, perhaps to look after children, or permanently, perhaps to retire.

- **Those who enter the labour force before finding a job**. This applies to many people entering the labour force for the first time, such as school and college leavers, and to many of those re-entering it, perhaps after a period looking after children.

There are also two groups of people who leave the ranks of those who are unemployed, as follows:

- **those who find a job;**
- **those who choose to leave the labour force**. This may apply, for example, to unemployed people approaching retirement age who eventually decide to give up looking for work.

Why does unemployment matter?

There are three major reasons why unemployment is a problem for an economy.

- **The effect on real GDP**. Unemployment means that less is being produced than would be the case if everyone in the workforce had a job.
- **The effect on the living standards of unemployed people**. The main reason why these people want jobs is to raise their standard of living.
- **Other effects on unemployed people**. Unemployment can lead to social and personal difficulties for those concerned, especially those who are unemployed for long periods. Typically, around a quarter of unemployed people have been unemployed for over a year.

Question 17.1 Can you list some of the personal and social problems faced by unemployed young people?

Unemployment rates in practice

Figure 17.3 gives an idea of unemployment in the UK since 1855. The figures for later years use the government's wider measure, and figures for earlier years have been aligned with these. The average rate over this period was 5.9%. The rate changes as the economy passes through business cycles, and is highest in recessions. Between 1855 and the outbreak of the First World War in 1914, business cycles typically lasted for from five to ten years, so unemployment peaked every five to ten years.

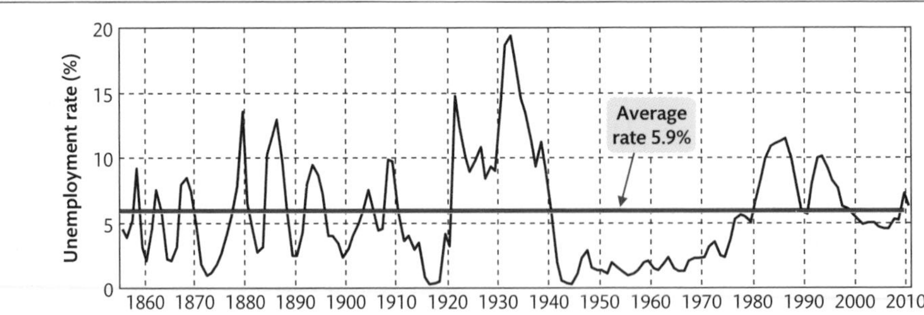

Figure 17.3 **Unemployment in the UK, 1855-2010**

Since 1855, the average rate of unemployment has been 5.9%. Until 1914, the rate rose and fell in a fairly regular—or cyclical—pattern. The rate was high in the Great Depression of the 1920s and 1930s and low in 1940–79. Since then, it has been above average except in 2000–08.

Sources: B R Mitchell, *British Historical Statistics*; OECD *Economic Outlook*; National Statistics, *Annual Abstract of Statistics*. Figures for earlier years were adjusted to reflect later definitions.

Unemployment fell sharply in the First World War, from 1914–18, and then rose to unprecedented levels between 1921 and the start of the Second World War in 1939. The bleakest period, from 1929 to 1939, is called the **Great Depression**. This depression was a worldwide phenomenon and stimulated economists, most notably the British economist John Maynard Keynes, to think about what governments could do to restrain unemployment. Many of the theories in later chapters derive from his work.

Since 1939, unemployment has been relatively low, except from about 1981 to 1996 and in the recent recession. These generally low levels may have been partly a result of fortunate circumstances and partly a result of governments implementing policies recommended by Keynes and those who followed him.

Figure 17.4 shows the average unemployment rate since 1990 for the G7 nations, using the wider international definition. The UK's rate has been a little below most of the others in this period.

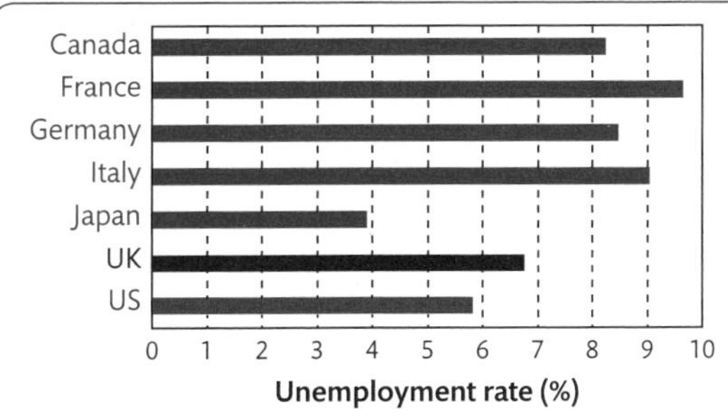

Figure 17.4 **Average unemployment, G7 countries, 1990–2010**

These figures used harmonized definitions of unemployment. The UK has had relatively low unemployment in the last two decades.

Sources: Based on data from Labour force statistics (MEI) under Labour from DECD. Stats Extracts, http://stats.oecd.org.

17.2 Everyday economics

Psychological effects of unemployment

Many studies have shown that the effects of being unemployed extend well beyond having a low income on benefits. For example, a study of young people in Wales found that being out of work caused young people to feel significantly less happy with their health, friendships and family life, in part because they felt ashamed and rejected; they were also more likely to have problems with drugs and alcohol. And the economist Professor Danny Blanchflower has pointed out that the longer someone is unemployed, the worse the psychological effects tend to become; this means that a prolonged recession could lead to a generation whose mental state may make it harder for them to find work in the future.

Undiscovered: The Prince's Trust YouGov Youth Index 2010, Prince's Trust, January 2010
'Scars of unemployment threaten a lost generation', *Wales Online*, 4 January 2010

17.3 Summary

- Unemployment refers to people who are able, available, and willing to work, but who have no jobs.
- Some official UK unemployment figures give underestimates because they are confined to unemployed people who are eligible for Jobseeker's Allowance and claiming it.
- Unemployment pushes output below what it could be, makes unemployed people worse off financially, and causes other social and personal problems.
- Unemployment tends to fluctuate over time, but reached sustained very high levels from 1929 to 1939.

17.4 The rate of inflation

We now look at the third key macroeconomic issue: inflation the **inflation rate**. This refers to the rate at which prices, on average, are rising. Governments and news bulletins treat inflation as having great importance, but how much does it matter?

Does inflation matter?

It is tempting to answer this question as follows:

> 'If prices in the UK rise on average next year by, say, 10%, then we will all buy less each week in December than we bought each week in January. In turn, firms will produce less. So inflation means that fewer resources will be used and people will consume less.'

However, this answer is not very robust. If prices rise next year, then workers may demand higher wages to keep up, and employers can afford to pay higher wages, because they will receive more money for each item they sell. If wages do rise, then maybe people between them will not have to buy less than before.

So, to see why inflation really matters, we need a more robust answer.

The key problem: unexpected inflation

To see why inflation really matters, let's think about you. Suppose that, when you graduate, a firm offers you a job for which you have to sign a one-year contract. The wage offered is £2,000 a month. You tell a friend that £24,000 over the year seems an acceptable wage for you, so you intend to sign the contract.

But your friend urges caution, pointing out that prices rise frequently, so that £2,000 a month at the end of the year will buy you less than £2,000 a month at the beginning. You reply that you know this, and you actually expect prices to rise by 3% over the year. But you still think that £24,000 over the year as a whole is acceptable.

Then your friend points out that prices might suddenly start to rise far more rapidly than the 3% you expect. In that case, £2,000 a month towards the end of the year may buy you very little. You reply that you know that there is this risk, but you think it is a small risk. So you take the job. Now let's see how you feel at the end of the year.

- **Suppose the inflation rate turns out to be 3%, as you expected**. Then you can buy as much over the year as you expected.
- **Suppose the inflation rate turns out to be less than the 3% you expected**. Then you can buy more over the year than you expected.
- **Suppose the inflation rate turns out to be more than the 3% you expected**. Then you can buy less over the year than you expected.

The only case in which you would feel that inflation had been a real problem for you is the last case. So what people are most worried about is not inflation in itself, but the relationship between the actual rate and the rate they expected.

Question 17.2 Suppose the firm that hired you also expected an inflation rate of 3% and expected to raise its prices by 3% over the year to cover its costs, including your wage. Would it face a problem if inflation were more than its expected rate or less?

In our example, the inflation in the second case was not much of a problem, because it was the expected inflation for which you allowed when you signed the contract. Your problems would arise in the third case, when you would face unexpected inflation, for which you had not allowed.

Our example shows how unexpected inflation is a problem for workers. It is also a problem for other groups, including lenders. To see how it is a problem for them, suppose that next vacation you get a job and have £500 left from your earnings at the start of next term. You could spend this money on goods and services, but instead you decide to place it for a year in a bank deposit that guarantees interest at 5% for a year.

Effectively, you lend £500 to the bank. You will earn £25 interest over the year, and by waiting a year you will be able to buy £525 worth of goods and services. Of course, if you expect inflation to be 3%, then you will need £515 in one year's time to buy items that would cost only £500 now. Even so, you will be able to buy more than you could buy now because you will have £525. Now let's see how you feel at the end of the year.

- **Suppose the inflation rate turns out to be 3%, as you expected**. Then you can to buy as much at the end of the year as you expected.
- **Suppose the inflation rate turns out to be less than the 3% you expected**. Then you can buy more at the end of the year than you expected.
- **Suppose the inflation rate turns out to be more than the 3% you expected**. Then you can buy less at the end of the year than you expected.

Again, the only case in which you would feel inflation had been a problem would be the last one in which the rate turned out to be more than you expected.

Unexpected inflation and redistribution

We have seen that unexpected inflation means people making contracts may end up worse off than they expected. But for everyone who ends up worse off, someone else ends up better off. For example, if inflation is very high next year, people who have agreed to work for a given wage or lend for a given interest rate end up worse off than they expected, But their employers and their borrowers end up better off, because the wage and interest they pay is worth less in terms of what it could buy than they expected.

Because unexpected inflation hurts some people and benefits others, it leads to a redistribution of income. This redistribution affects different age groups differently. For example, an unexpected rise in inflation is generally good for younger people and bad for old people. To see why, consider these two groups.

- **People aged 18–40**. These people borrow the most, to finance education and the cost of buying a home. Someone who has borrowed £100,000 may say: 'I will have to work for ten years to repay this.' But if prices and wages rise rapidly, the person may be able to repay more quickly.
- **People aged 40–65**. These people save the most, ahead of retirement. One such person might say: 'I have saved £100,000, which will last me several years in retirement.' But if all prices rise rapidly, then the person may find that £100,000 lasts for a much shorter period.

Unexpected inflation and uncertainty

Unexpected inflation also creates uncertainty. For example, savers may worry about how they can try to make their savings inflation-proof. And firms may respond to the risk of unexpected inflation, and in turn to uncertainty over how much profit they will make, by investing in new capital, by investing less than they would otherwise.

The fear of hyperinflation

If the inflation rate were always fairly low, say below 5%, then the problems discussed above would be modest. But sometimes inflation is much higher, making the problems worse. The highest recorded rate in the UK was 28% in 1975.

There have been far higher inflation rates abroad. A period of very high inflation is called a **hyperinflation**. For the six worst of these, Table 17.2 shows the inflation rates *per day* in the worst month; it also shows that prices doubled very quickly at these times. In hyperinflations, people rush to spend money the moment they receive it, because cash and bank deposits quickly become worthless; also, law and order may break down. Hyperinflations arise when a government allows the quantity of money in its country to grow far faster than the rate at which the quantity of goods and services available to buy is growing.

Table 17.2 **The six most rapid hyperinflations**

Country	Worst month	Daily inflation rate	Time for prices to double
Hungary	July 1946	207%	15.0 hours
Zimbabwe	November 2008	98%	24.7 hours
Yugoslavia	January 1994	65%	1.4 days
Germany	October 1923	21%	3.7 days
Greece	November 1944	18%	4.3 days
China	May 1949	11%	6.7 days

Source: S H Hanke and AKF Kwok, 'On the measurement of zimbabwe's hyperninflation', *Cato journal* 29:2, 2009.

Some problems with expected inflation

Suppose that everyone expects prices to rise by 3% next year and that prices do actually rise by 3%. Then no one will suffer from unexpected inflation. However, even expected inflation can cause problems, as follows.

- **Some people will be in a weak position when they try to get contracts that allow for the expected inflation**. These people include those who depend on benefits from the government, such as the State Pension, and those who could never be expected to threaten to strike, like nurses.
- **Part of the inflation may result from expected increases in import prices**. If import prices rise, even by the same amount as people expect, we will be still able to buy and consume fewer imported goods, such as oil from the Middle East and computers from the Far East.
- **Firms will face costs when they raise their prices**. No matter what the inflation rate is, firms have to prepare new price lists, and firms with slot machines will have to alter them. These costs are called menu costs, because menus are among the items that must be changed.
- **Inflation erodes the value of banknotes and coins**. This might not worry you if inflation is low, but it might if inflation is high. You could then ease the problem by keeping very little cash on you, and going to a cash dispenser every time you want a few pounds, but these visits impose costs on you: these costs are often called shoe-leather costs, because there will be more wear on your shoes, but there are more important costs in the form of the time and effort involved.

Measuring inflation

We saw earlier that statisticians measure changes in the price level of all the goods and services included in GDP with the GDP deflator. But they also produce measures of changes in the level of smaller groups of items.

The two price level measures that attract the highest publicity when they are announced each month both measure changes in the prices of goods and services bought by consumers. These measures are as follows.

- **The retail prices index (RPI)**. This is purely a UK index and was introduced in 1947.
- **The consumer prices index (CPI)**. This is a measure used by all EU countries, and was introduced in the UK in 1996.

The two measures use a very similar methodology. In each case, the statisticians draw up a shopping list of about 650 items, which reflect the wide variety of items bought by households, and they study the prices of these items. The items used are revised annually, to keep the list up to date.

To see how the statisticians proceed, suppose for simplicity that they look only at three products: milk, petrol, and haircuts. And suppose that, in 2000, consumers between them bought 20 litres of milk and 10 litres of petrol for every haircut. Then the statisticians would make a shopping list of, say, one haircut, 20 litres of milk, and 10 litres of petrol, and work out how much this cost in 2000.

Next, they would work out the total cost of this list in other years. For example, if the cost in 2001 were 4% more, they would say prices rose by 4%.

Finally, they would choose a base or reference period. Suppose they choose 2000. Then they will say that the index was 100 for that base period. And in 2001, for example, when prices were 4% higher, they will say the index was 104.

Comparing the RPI and the CPI

The reason for using two similar indexes is that the RPI allows UK price levels today to be compared with UK price levels back to 1947, while the CPI allows inflation in the UK to be compared with inflation in other EU countries. The main differences between the measures are as follows.

- **Small differences in the items included on the list.** For example, only the RPI includes Council Tax, which is levied on the occupiers of all homes, except student-only homes, and only the CPI includes the fees charged by some stockbrokers when they buy or sell shares on behalf of their clients.
- **Some differences in the relative importance of the items on the list**. As well as deciding on what items to include on the lists, the statisticians have to decide on the importance of each item on the CPI and RPI. For example, they have to decide on the relative quantities of milk, petrol, and haircuts to put on the lists. The RPI focuses on typical households, so its list has very small quantities for the items that these households rarely buy, such as the most costly models of car and the cheapest types of clothes. But the CPI sets its quantities in proportion to the total quantities in which they are actually bought.
- **Some differences in the mathematics used**. These mean that the CPI grows a shade more slowly over time than the RPI.

Inflation in practice

In Figure 17.5, the top part plots the UK's inflation rate in each year since 1855, as shown by the GDP deflator, and the lower part plots the price level over the same period. The top part shows that, until the outbreak of the First World War in 1914, inflation was negative as often as it was positive, meaning that the price level fell as often as it rose. So, as shown in the lower part, the actual price level in 1914 was almost the same as in 1855.

The top part of Figure 17.5 shows also that prices fell in between the two World Wars. However, prices have risen in every year since then, and this continuous rise has led to the average rate of inflation over the last 155 years as a whole being 3.2%. Today, prices are about 100 times what they were a century ago, as indicated by the steep rise in prices shown in the lower part.

Figure 17.6 looks at the average inflation rate for consumer prices in the G7 nations since 1996. The UK's rate has typically been similar to that of the other countries except for Japan, where prices have fallen over this period.

17.3 Everyday economics

Zimbabwe's hyperinflation

Zimbabwe provided no official figures for inflation in the Zimbabwe dollar after July 2008, when it said that inflation in the previous year was 231,000,000%. Later in 2008 it introduced a 50 trillion dollar note, and in 2009 a 100 trillion dollar note. Even so, people needed bags of currency for small purchases, savings were rendered worthless, and many people faced starvation. Eventually, people became reluctant to accept the currency at all, and preferred payments in South Africa's rand or US dollars. In 2009, Zimbabwe suspended its currency, and now uses the US dollar. Old 100 trillion dollar notes are available on eBay for a few pounds.

'One hundred trillion Zimbabwean dollars: it's yours for only £20', *New Scotsman*, 5 January 2010
'Zimbabwe inflation second worst in history', *The Telegraph*, 13 November 2008

17.4 Summary

- The main problems with inflation arise when the actual rate differs from the rate that people expected when they made contracts, such as taking a job or lending some money. Some people gain from these differences and other lose, so inflation creates a redistribution of income.
- Even when inflation equals the expected rate, there are some costs, chiefly that some people are in a weak position to ensure that their income rises in line with inflation.
- The UK measures the inflation rate of all products included in GDP with the GDP deflator, and it uses the retail prices index (RPI) and the similar consumer prices index (CPI) to measure inflation in the prices of products bought by consumers. Rises in these indexes reflect rises in the total cost of a shopping list with hundreds of items. The indexes are each set at 100 for a base period.

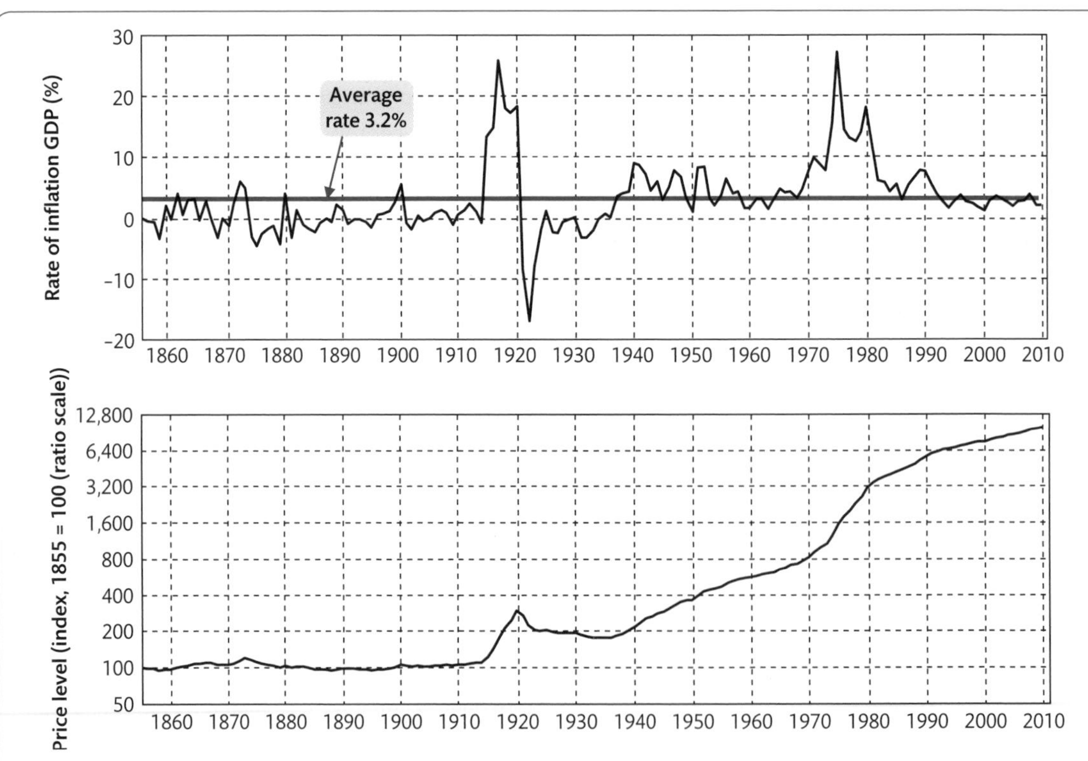

Figure 17.5 **Inflation in the UK 1855–2010**

The top graph shows that price changes have ranged between rises of 30% and falls of -20%, with an average of 3.2%. There was great instability after the First World War. The lower figure shows an index of prices, with 1855 set at 100. This graph uses a ratio scale, so each horizontal grid line indicates a doubling of prices. Until the start of the First World War I in 1914, the top graph shows that prices rose in some years and fell in others, and the bottom graph shows how the price level was then fairly stable. Since 1934, the top graph shows that prices have risen in every year, so the lower graph shows the price level rising. By 2010, it was about 100 times what it was a century earlier in 1910.

Sources: B R Mitchell, *British Historical Statistics;* National Statistics, *Economic Trends Annual Supplements* and *UK National Accounts.* The prices relate to GDP at factor cost before 1948 and to GDP at basic prices since.

17.5 An introduction to macroeconomic theory

We have seen that two of the key issues in macroeconomics are the rate at which output is growing and the rate at which prices are rising. To understand what determines these rates, we need first to see what forces determine the output level and the price level at any moment in time. Only then we can begin to understand why these levels may change.

Note that when we understand what causes the level of output to change, we will also understand what determines the number of workers hired by producers to change. So we will also understand what causes the rate of unemployment to change.

A basic diagram in macroeconomics

Our interest in price and output levels indicates a similarity between macroeconomics and microeconomics. In microeconomics, we are interested in the price and output that arise in individual markets, say for eggs, and we explain the factors that determine the price and output of eggs with a diagram showing the demand and supply curves for eggs. In macroeconomics, we are interested in the overall price level in the economy and the overall level of output or GDP. And we can explain the factors that determine these overall levels with a diagram showing the total, or aggregate, demand in the economy, and the total, or aggregate, supply in the economy.

Such a diagram is shown for a year, 2000, in Figure 17.7. Let's first look at its axes.

- **The vertical axis** measures the overall level of prices. It does this with an index of prices, and as the diagram concerns GDP, the appropriate index is the GDP deflator. In this diagram, the deflator uses 2010 as the reference period.
- **The horizontal axis** measures the total quantity of goods and services. It does this with real GDP. Again, the reference period is taken as 2010, so this axis measures real GDP for 2000 by valuing goods and services at the prices that applied in 2010.

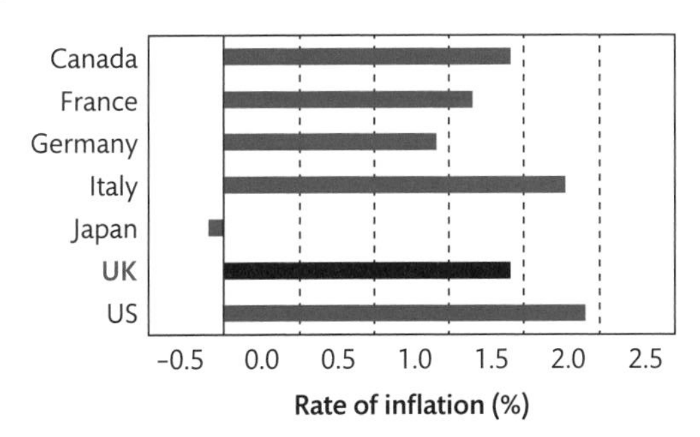

Figure 17.6 **Average inflation, G7 countries, 1996–2010**

These figures relate to consumer prices. The UK rate has been typical of figures in the G7 countries, but note that prices in Japan have fallen over this period.

Sources: Based on data from consumer prices (MEI) under Prices and Purchasing Power Parties from OECD Stats Extracts, http://stats.oecd.org.

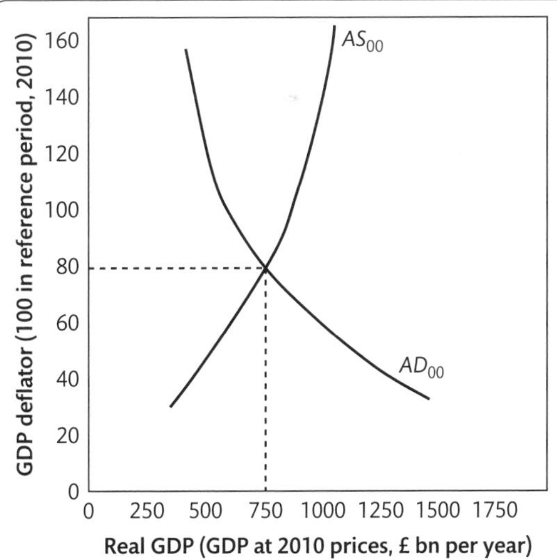

Figure 17.7 **Aggregate demand and aggregate supply**

The curves show, for 2000, the quantity of products suppliers want to sell at each price level and the quantity buyers want to buy. The price level settles at 80, because there would be an excess supply at any higher price level and an excess demand at any lower price level. At this price level, GDP is £750 bn (at 2010 prices).

Figure 17.7 also has two curves, as follows.

- **Aggregate demand**. Aggregate demand is shown by the curve labelled AD_{00}. The subscript means that it relates to the year 2000. AD_{00} shows the total quantity of goods and services that would have been demanded in 2000 at each possible overall price level that could have applied that year. The downward slope of AD_{00} indicates that the lower actual prices had been in 2000, the greater the quantity of goods and services people would have demanded.
- **Aggregate supply**. Aggregate supply is shown by the curve labelled AS_{00}. The subscript means that it relates to the year 2000. AS_{00} shows the total quantity of goods and services that would have been supplied in 2000 at each possible overall price level that could have applied that year. The upward slope of AS_{00} indicates that the higher actual prices had been in 2000, the greater the quantity of goods and services producers would have supplied.

The economy in the figure will have settled in 2000 where the two curves intersect, with the GDP deflator at 80, and real GDP at £750 billion. The price level could not have settled below 80: if it had gone below 80 at any time, it would not have stayed there, because then buyers would have wanted to buy more than suppliers wanted to sell, so the price level would soon have risen. Nor could the price level have settled above 80: if it had gone above 80 at any time, it would not have stayed there, because buyers would have wanted to buy less than suppliers wanted to sell, so the price level would soon have fallen.

So, given these curves, the GDP deflator settled in 2000 at 80, which tells us that prices were 80% of the level that applied in 2010. At that price level of 80, suppliers wanted to sell £750 billion worth of goods and services, at 2010 prices. This exactly matched the amount that buyers wanted to buy. So output or GDP in 2000, was £750 billion, at 2010 prices.

Some predictions from the diagram

We can use this basic diagram to make some predictions. We will do this in Figure 17.8 in which the black curves repeat the situation for 2000 from Figure 17.7. Suppose that, by 2020, producers are willing to sell more goods and services at each possible price level. Then the aggregate supply curve will shift to the right. Perhaps by 2020 it will be as shown by AS_{20} in Figure 17.8. If this is the only curve to shift, then the price level in 2020 will fall to 60, and real GDP will rise to £1,000 billion (at 2010 prices). Conversely, if producers want to supply less in 2020, then aggregate supply will move to the left, causing a rise in prices and a fall in real GDP.

Suppose that, in 2020, producers are actually no more or less willing to sell goods and services than they were in 2000, so that the aggregate supply remains as shown by AS_{00}. But suppose that, by 2020, people become more interested in buying goods and

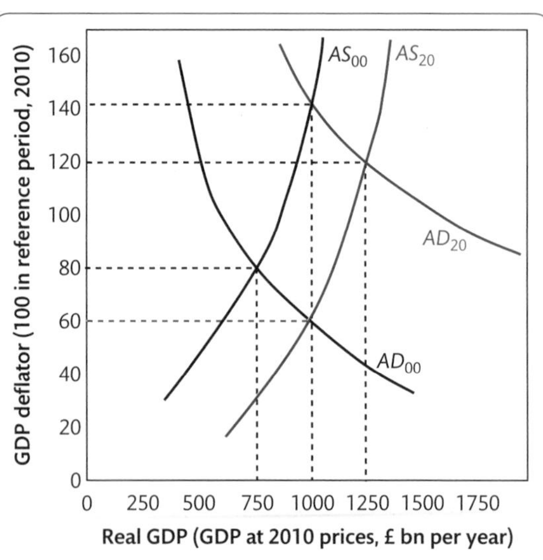

Figure 17.8 **Shifts in aggregate demand and aggregate supply**

If, between 2000 and 2020, aggregate demand and supply shift from AD_{00} and AS_{00} and AD_{20} to AS_{20}, then the price level will rise to 120 and GDP will rise to £1,250 bn (at 2010 prices). If only one curve shifts, GDP in 2020 will be £1,250 bn, and the price level will be 60 or 140 depending on which curve shifts.

services and are willing to buy more at each possible price level. Then the aggregate demand curve will shift to the right. Perhaps in 2020 it will be as shown by AD_{20} in Figure 17.8. If this is the only curve to shift, then the price level will rise to 140, and real GDP will rise to £1,000 billion (at 2010 prices). Conversely, if people want to buy less in 2020, then aggregate demand will shift to the left, causing a fall in prices and a fall in real GDP.

Finally, suppose that in fact both supply and demand rise by 2020, so that in 2020 both AD_{20} and AS_{20} apply. In that case, the price level will be 120, and the quantity will be £1,250 billion (at 2010 prices). So prices will rise by 50% from 2000 and the quantity produced will rise by 67%. So, as drawn, both prices and the quantity will exceed the 2000 levels. Of course, all these results depend on the exact shapes and positions of the two curves in the years concerned.

The curves and prices

Figure 17.7 may seem similar to a microeconomic supply and demand curve diagram for a product like eggs. However, there are some problems with the slopes of the curves in the macroeconomic diagram that do not apply in microeconomic diagrams.

Consider, first, demand curves.

- **Microeconomic demand curves.** With the demand curve for a product like eggs, we can say that if egg prices rise, then people are sure to buy fewer eggs and instead more of other foods. So the demand curve is sure to slope downwards from left to right.
- **Macroeconomic aggregate demand curves.** In Figure 17.7, it may seem equally clear that if the average level of prices shown by the GDP deflator rises, then people will want to buy fewer goods and services altogether. But think: if all prices rise, so that inflation occurs, then workers may negotiate wage rises. So buyers may not have to cut back on their purchases, despite the higher prices. So it is far from clear that the amount people will buy will fall.

Next, consider supply curves.

- **Microeconomic supply curves.** In the case of a supply curve for a product like eggs, we can say that if egg prices rise, then suppliers will find egg production more profitable and will want to produce more. So the supply curve is sure to slope upwards from left to right.
- **Macroeconomic aggregate supply curve.** In Figure 17.7, it may seem equally clear that if the average level of prices shown by the GDP deflator rises, then producers will want to sell more goods and services altogether. But think: if the prices of all items rise, so that inflation occurs, then once again wages may rise, so that production as a whole may not become more profitable. So it is far from clear that the amount producers will want to sell will increase.

As it happens, economists believe that the *AD* curve and *AS* curves probably do generally slope as shown here. But the reasons for these slopes need some careful thought, and this thought is left until Chapter 21.

Difficulties for the government

Later chapters also examine some of the difficulties that governments face when they want to use macroeconomic policies to alter the level of output or prices in the economy. It is worth giving a flavour of some of these difficulties at the outset.

To do this, suppose for example that the government wants to reduce unemployment. Producers will hire more workers only if they want to produce more goods and services. Looking at Figure 17.7, it may seem that one simple way of making them want to produce more would be somehow to shift *AD* to the right, because then the equilibrium level of real GDP or output would rise. And one way of shifting *AD* to the right might be to cut income tax so that people have more purchasing power. But here are just four of the problems that the government would face.

- **Inflation problems**. The rightward shift in *AD* will lead to higher prices, as well as a higher output, and higher prices will conflict with the government's aim of low inflation.
- **Government funding problems**. By cutting taxes, the government itself will have a lower revenue. To maintain its spending levels on services such as healthcare, education, and defence, it will have to replace the lost tax revenue with borrowing. But that has problems for growth, as shown in the next paragraph.
- **Growth problems**. If the government borrows more money, there may be less money available for firms to borrow. So they may cut back on investment, and this will reduce the rate of growth, which conflicts with the government's aim of high growth.
- **Import problems**. When people spend more, they will, among other things, buy more imports. So they will want more foreign currencies, which they will try to buy from the banks. But the extra demand for foreign currencies may drive up their prices, so people will have to pay more pounds for their imports. And, once more, higher prices will conflict with the government's aim of low inflation.

17.5 Summary

- It is possible to use a diagram with an aggregate demand curve and an aggregate supply curve to show the factors that determine the equilibrium levels of output and prices. However, it needs much thought to understand the slopes of these curves, and they are not used again until Chapter 21.
- When a government tries to manage the economy as a whole, it faces the difficulties that the policies that it pursues in order to secure one of its aims may reduce its success with its other aims.

In the next chapter we see how statisticians actually measure GDP, and we look at some other measures related to GDP. We also consider how far real GDP can be used to indicate economic well-being.

abc Glossary

Base period: often a base year, the period for which the value of an index is set at 100.

Business cycle: fluctuations in the rate of growth between one period of contraction and the next.

Consumer prices index (CPI): a price index used in the EU for a wide range of consumer products.

Deflator: the same as a price index.

Economic growth: increases in the total quantity of goods and services produced in the economy over time (measured by changes in real GDP).

GDP at constant prices: the same as real GDP.

GDP at current prices: the same as nominal GDP.

GDP deflator: a price index covering all products included in GDP.

Hyperinflation: a period of very high inflation.

Inflation rate: the rate at which prices, on average, are rising.

Labour force: the total number of people who are able, available, and willing to work.

Nominal GDP: the GDP for a given period, usually a year, measured at the price level that applied in that period.

Price index: a number used to relate the level of prices in a given period, usuallly a year, to the level in a base period, or reference period, the index for which is set at 100.

Real GDP: the GDP for a given period, usually a year, measured at the price level that applied in a reference period.

Recession: a situation in which output falls for at least two consecutive quarters of a year.

Reference period: often a year, the period for which the value of an index is set at 100.

Retail prices index (RPI): a price index used in the UK for a wide range of consumer products.

Unemployment: a term for people who are able, available, and willing to work, but who have no job.

Unemployment rate: the percentage of the labour force that has no job.

Answers to in-text questions

17.1 The everyday economics box on page 369 gives a summary of the main problems highlighted by unemployed young people.

17.2 It would face a problem if inflation were below its expected rate. Suppose prices in general rise only 2%. If the firm raises its prices by 3%, it might lose business to competitors. If it raises its prices by just 2%, its revenue will be less than it expected when it signed the contract with you.

? Questions for review

17.1 Look at Figure 17.1. Ignoring the period from 1915 to 1950, was there ever a fall in output as severe as that experienced in the recent recession?

17.2 Look at Figure 17.3. Ignoring the period from 1915 to 1950, was there ever a level of unemployment as high as that experienced in the recent recession?

17.3 Look at Figures 17.1, 17.3, and 17.5. (**a**) Which of the three key issues, growth, unemployment, and inflation, would have seemed most serious in the late 1950s? (**b**) Which would have seemed most serious in the mid 1970s? (**c**) How well was the economy doing between 2000 and 2008?

17.4 Look at Figures 17.2. Over the period covered, (**a**) which G7 country had the highest average growth, and (**b**) which had the lowest?

17.5 Look at Figure 17.4. Over the period covered, (**a**) which G7 country had the lowest average unemployment, and (**b**) which had the highest?

17.6 Look at Figure 17.6. Over the period covered, (**a**) which G7 country had the lowest inflation, and (**b**) which had the highest?

17.7 Suppose that, in 2000, 2015, and 2030, a country that uses dollars has the nominal GDP shown in the first column of the table below and the GDP deflators shown in the second column. Find real GDP at reference period prices for (**a**) 2010 and (**b**) 2020.

	Nominal GDP (\$ bn)	*GDP deflator (Reference period 2015)*
2000	1,000	92
2015	2,000	100
2030	3,000	123

? Questions for discussion

17.1 Why might it be easier for relatively poor countries like China and India to achieve high growth rates than for relatively rich countries like the UK?

17.2 Are there any problems of being unemployed that are less acute for young people than for older people?

17.3 Can you think of situations this year in which you would regard yourself as unemployed and yet not be included as unemployed in government statistics?

17.4 What do you expect the inflation rate to be next year? Are there any ways in which you might lose or gain if it is different?

Common student errors

A common problem is the meaning of the 'GDP deflator'. The media frequently refer to indexes of consumer prices, but these are found by looking only at representative consumer goods. The GDP deflator relates to the price level of all the goods and services included in GDP. So it allows for the price of consumer products, and for the prices of new capital goods, like lorries, and for the cost of services paid for by the government, like treating people in state hospitals, and also for the prices of products that are sold as exports to foreigners.

18

The National Accounts

Remember from Chapter 1 that economists define gross domestic product, or GDP, as the value of all the goods and services that are produced in an economy, except for those that households produce for themselves. And recall from Chapter 17 that to measure changes in the quantity of goods and services produced from one year to another, we need figures showing each year's GDP at constant prices.

How do statisticians estimate the value of a country's GDP? How does the value of GDP relate to the total income of the country? Suppose you see in the newspaper or on television a comparison of output and income in the UK today with corresponding figures from an earlier year, or with corresponding figures for another country: are these comparisons meaningful?

This chapter shows you how to answer questions like these, by understanding:

* exactly what is meant by the published figures for GDP;
* why there are three different values that can be placed on GDP;
* three methods or approaches that can be used to estimate GDP;
* some measures of a country's total income;
* how to compare output and income over time and across countries.

18.1 What the official UK GDP figures cover

We saw in Chapter 1 that the goods and services produced in an economy are produced by four types of producer:

- **households**;
- **firms**;
- **government departments**;
- **non-profit institutions**.

We also saw that economists define gross domestic product (GDP) as the total value of the goods and services produced in an economy, except those that households produce for themselves. This chapter explains how government statisticians estimate the value of GDP.

However, we must first note two subtle ways in which the definition of GDP used by these statisticians differs from that used by economists. These differences relate to:

- **owner-occupied property**;
- **the underground economy**.

Owner-occupied property

Ideally, the statisticians would like to find the value of all goods and services produced. But to do so they would need to include all household production, and this is hard to value. For example, you may today have already produced some goods and services for yourself, such as washing and preparing breakfast, but we do not know how thorough your washing was or how good your breakfast was, so we cannot value these products.

However, the statisticians can work out the value of one important item that households produce for themselves, and they do include this item in their figures for GDP, even though it is not part of the economist's definition. This item is the accommodation services that owner-occupier households provide for themselves.

The way the statisticians look at this item is to regard each owner-occupying household as a small firm that lets its home to itself. The value of the accommodation that each of these 'firms' provides can be estimated by looking at the rents paid for similar properties that really are let.

The underground economy

To estimate GDP, statisticians need information about producers. But some producers take care not to report their activities to anyone, and they form what is called the **underground economy**, or the **hidden economy**. As the statisticians lack information about these producers, they exclude their output in their estimates of GDP, even though it is included in the economist's definition.

These underground producers can be thought of as unusual types of firm that fall into two groups.

- **Firms the products of which are illegal**. These 'firms' include, for example, people who supply illegal drugs, and people who operate brothels.
- **Firms that seek to avoid taxation**. These 'firms' operate largely in cash, hoping not to be noticed by the tax authorities. They include, for example, many self-employed people, who should be seen as firms, and who get paid in cash for services like cleaning or childcare. They also include firms like some window-cleaning and gardening firms, which get paid in cash and pay their staff wages in cash.

Because these firms operate underground, the size of their production is unknown, but it may be up to 10% of GDP. So GDP as measured by statisticians may omit a sizeable part of production by firms.

Three different values for output

We have talked about GDP as 'the' total value of the output of the producers concerned. In fact, though, we can give three different values to the output of each producer and, in turn, to the total value of their output. These three values arise because of two factors.

- **Taxes on production**: these are taxes that firms have to pay because they are producing products to sell.
- **Subsidies on production**: these are subsidies that the government pays to firms because they are producing products to sell.

Taxes on production fall into two groups.

- **Taxes on products**. With these, the amount that a firm pays depends on how much product it actually sells. Examples include VAT, and also alcohol duty, petrol duty, and tobacco duty, which are collected from firms selling these products.
- **Other taxes on production.** With these, the amount that a firm pays does not depend on how much it sells. The chief example is called business rates: the amount of this tax that a firm pays depends on the value of its land and buildings. Another example is vehicle licence duties: the amount of this that a firm pays depends on the number and type of its vehicles.

Subsidies on production also fall into two groups.

- **Subsidies on products**. With these, the amount that a firm receives depends on how much product it actually sells. The main examples are some subsidies to farms and public transport firms.
- **Other subsidies on production**. With these, the amount that a firm receives does not depend on how much it sells. There are very few subsidies like these, but one example is that some firms are given subsidies to engage in research and development.

To see why these taxes and subsidies mean that the products that a firm sells have three different values, suppose that you run a firm, and suppose that your sales for 2009 resulted in a revenue of £1,070 million. This figure is shown at the top of Table 18.1. The table also shows how we calculate the three different values of your products.

- **Value of sales at market prices**: this is the value measured at the prices that buyers pay, so it is £1,070 million. This is the value of the products to the buyers, because it is the amount that the buyers paid for them.
- **Value of sales at basic prices**: this is the value at market prices, *minus* payments of taxes on products and *plus* receipts from subsidies on products. Table 18.1 supposes that the values of these taxes and subsidies for your firm are £70 million and £20 million, so the value of your firm's sales at basic prices is £1,020 million.
- **Value of sales at factor cost**: this is the value at basic prices, *minus* payments of other taxes on production and *plus* receipts of other subsidies on production. This is the value of a firm's output to the firm itself. Table 18.1 supposes that the values of your firms' other taxes and other subsidies are £30 million and £10 million, so the value of its sales at factor cost is £1,000 million.

Table 18.1 **Three different values that can be placed on the products sold by a firm in 2009**

	£m
Revenue from products sold, equals the value of products sold at market prices	**1,070**
less taxes on products (like VAT)	−70
plus subsidies on products	+20
Value of products sold at basic prices	**1,020**
less other taxes on production (like licence duties on business vehicles)	−30
plus other subsidies on production	+10
Value of products sold at factor cost	**1,000**

These three different measures of the value of products mean that there are also three different measures of GDP, as listed below. Note, though, that each measure excludes products produced by the underground economy, and each also excludes products produced by households for themselves, except for the accommodation services produced by owner-occupiers.

- **GDP at market prices**. This is the total value of the country's output valued at market prices.
- **GDP at basic prices**. This is the total value of the country's output valued at basic prices.
- **GDP at factor cost**. This is the total value of the country's output valued at factor cost.

In the next section, we will see how statisticians estimate these three values.

Question 18.1 From 1948 to 1962, GDP was higher at factor cost than at basic prices. What does this tell us?

18.1 Summary

- Published estimates of GDP cover all products produced by firms, except for firms in the underground or hidden economy, plus all the products produced by non-profit institutions and government departments. The estimates also include the value of housing accommodation provided by owner-occupying households.
- The value of products sold by producers, and the value of GDP, can be calculated at the market prices which buyers pay, or at basic prices by deducting taxes on products and adding subsidies on products, or at factor cost, by also deducting other taxes on production and adding other subsidies on production.

18.2 Three different approaches to estimating GDP

We have seen that the statisticians ignore the underground economy because it is hidden and they have little information about it. Unfortunately, they cannot get wholly accurate figures for the rest of the economy either. So they have to estimate GDP rather than measure it.

Fortunately, though, the statisticians can estimate GDP using three different methods, or approaches. These approaches use data from different sources. The statisticians compare their initial estimates on each approach, and then adjust them to get as close as possible to what they believe GDP really is. The three approaches are as follows:

- **the production approach**;
- **the income approach**;
- **the expenditure approach**.

We will look at each approach in turn.

The production approach and value added

The source used for the production approach is the accounts of producers. The idea is to use these accounts to work out the contribution to GDP of each individual producer, and then to add all of these individual contributions together. To illustrate the idea, consider again your firm. The top line of Table 18.2 repeats the value of your the products you sold at factor cost from Table 18.1, which is the £1,000 million you were left with after allowing for all taxes and subsidies on production.

What is the value of your contribution to GDP at factor cost? It is tempting to say that this is the total of these two items:

- the value, at factor cost, of the products you produced and sold, which is £1,000 million;

- the value of the products that you produced, but did not sell, and instead added to your stocks of finished goods; the word **inventories** is another word for stocks. Table 18.2 gives the value of these goods, which is £20 million.

The table shows that the combined value of these two items is £1,020 million. However, this figure overestimates the value of your firm's production at factor cost, and so it overestimates your firm's contribution to GDP at factor cost. This is because we cannot credit your firm with producing the full value of its output.

To see why, suppose your products include tables that you sell to shops for £200. Your firm does not produce the full value of these tables, because they include intermediate products, like timber, screws, and glue, which you bought off other firms. If we were to include the value of these items as part of your output, and also include them in the output of the timber yard, the screw-maker, and the glue-maker, then we would include them all twice: this is called double counting.

So, to find the value of the production by your firm at factor cost, we start with the value of its output at factor cost and then subtract the value of the intermediate products that it uses in its output. The figure we obtain in this way is called the producer's **value added**, because it shows how much more valuable its output is than the value of the inputs it uses that are produced by others.

Suppose you spent £600 million on intermediate products. And suppose you put £10 million worth of these into your stocks or inventories of them. Then the products you produced used £590 million worth of inputs that were produced by other firms. Table 18.2 shows that if we deduct these £590 million worth of inputs from the value of your output at factor cost, we get £430 million: this is the value of your firm's production at factor cost.

If we instead wanted the value of your production at basic prices, we would add £20 million, because the value of your sales at basic prices was £20 million more than its value at factor cost. And if we wanted your value added at market prices, we would add another £50 million, because the value of your sales at market prices was another £50 million more. These extra amounts arise from taxes and subsidies, and are spelt out in the left-hand column of Table 18.3.

Table 18.2 **A firm's value added at factor cost, 2009**

	£m
Value of the firm's output, at factor cost:	
Value of products sold, at factor cost	1,000
Value of products not sold, but added to inventories of finished goods	20
Total	**1,020**
Value of the intermediate products used in the firm's output:	
Value of intermediate products bought	600
less value of intermediate products not used, but added to inventories of intermediate products	–10
Total	**590**
Value added at factor cost (= 1,020 – 590)	**430**

Table 18.3 **Estimates of a firms value added, and the UK's GDP on the production approach, 2009**

Figures for a firm	£m	Figures for the UK	£ bn
Value added at factor cost	**430**	**Gross value added or GDP factor cost**	**1,241**
Allow for taxes and subsidies on production, except for taxes and subsidies on products	20	Allow for all taxes and subsidies on production, except for taxes and subsidies on products	17
Value added at basic prices	**450**	**Gross value added or GDP at basic prices**	**1,258**
Allow for taxes and subsidies on products	50	Allow for all taxes and subsidies on products	137
Value added at market prices	**500**	**Gross value added or GDP at market prices**	**1,395**

Source for the UK: Office for National Statistics, *United Kingdom Economic Accounts, 2010 Q3*, Tables A1 and A3.

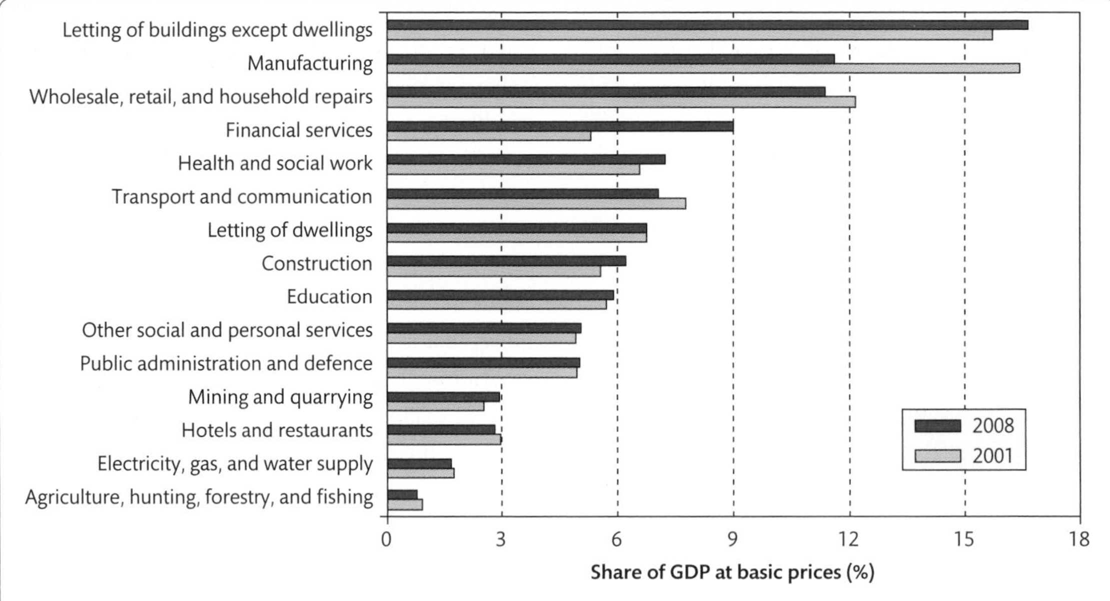

Figure 18.1 **Value added by industry, UK, 2001 and 2008**

Even in this seven-year period, there was a sharp decrease in the share of manufacturing industry. The largest share increase was in financial services.

Source: Office for National Statistics, *United Kingdom National Accounts, 2010 Edition*, Table 2.3.

GDP on the production approach

To estimate GDP on the production approach, the statisticians add up the value added of all producers. The total or gross value added at factor cost in the UK in 2009 was £1,241 billion, as shown at the top of the right-hand column of Table 18.3. The term **gross value added** means the same as GDP, so GDP at factor cost is also £1,241 billion. The statisticians can then estimate gross value added or GDP at basic prices by making the same adjustments for taxes and subsidies that we used for your firm in the left-hand column. GDP in 2009 was £1,258 billion at basic prices and £1,395 billion at market prices.

GDP covers the outputs of many producers who make many products. The statisticians divide these products into several groups, and Figure 18.1 shows the percentage share of each of these groups in total GDP. This figure compares the shares in both 2001 and 2008, to give an idea of how the pattern of production is changing. The most obvious change is a significant decline in manufacturing industry over even that short period. The largest growth was in financial services, which includes banks.

The income approach and operating surpluses

The income approach to estimating GDP refers to what are called operating surpluses. A firm's **operating surplus** is the trading profit it makes from the products that it sells. Table 18.4 shows how to work out a firm's operating surplus, using your firm as an example. The first line on this table recalls that the value at factor cost of the products that your firm sold in 2009 was £1,000 million.

The table then shows that you spent £300 million of this £1,000 million in wages and salaries to your employees; in the accounts, this item is called compensation of employees. You also spent £600 million on intermediate products.

The total of these two costs was £900 million, so it might seem that your operating surplus was the £1,000 million for your sales minus £900 million, which is £100 million. In fact, though, you made more than £100 million profit from the products you sold. This is because not all of the £900 million that you spent was used to make the products that you sold. There are two reasons for this.

- **You spent £10 million on increased inventories of raw materials**. This means that £10 million worth of your intermediate products did not go into anything you made, and certainly did not go into the products you sold.
- **You spent £20 million on increased inventories of finished goods**. This means that some of the intermediate products that you bought, and some of the labour that you hired, were used to produce products that you did not sell, but instead added to inventories.

So, instead of seeing the cost of the products that you sold as £900 million, we should see it as £30 million less, that is £870 million. So for your firm, the operating surplus was £1,000 million minus £870 million, which is £130 million, as shown in Table 18.4.

The reason statisticians use the term 'operating surplus' rather than 'trading profit' is that they include similar figures for all producers, not only firms. The other producers—that is government departments, non-profit institutions, and owner-occupiers—prefer to call any gap between their revenue and their costs an operating surplus rather than a profit. So the term operating surplus can be used for all producers.

Table 18.4 **A firm's operating surplus, 2009**

	£m
Value of the products sold, at factor cost:	**1,000**
Expenditure on products sold:	
Compensation of employees	300
Intermediate products	600
less Increased inventories of intermediate products	−10
less Increased inventories of finished goods	−20
Total	**870**
Operating surplus (= 1,000–870)	**130**

Source: International Bank for Reconstruction and Development The World Bank: World Development Indicators database, and world Bank, 14 April 2001.

GDP on the income approach

If you look at Table 18.4, and add the compensation of your employees, £300 million, to your operating surplus, £130 million, you get £430 million. This is the same as your value added at factor cost, which we worked out in Table 18.2. This may seem a coincidence, but it is not.

To show this, you could replace the numbers in Table 18.2 with any new numbers you like and work out a new figure for the value added at factor cost. You could also slot the new numbers into Table 18.4, put in any new figure for compensation for employees, and then work out the new operating surplus. If you add this to the new compensation to employees, you will find the total is equal to the new value added at factor cost.

The fact that the value added at factor cost for each producer equals its operating surplus plus its compensation to its employees is very useful for the statisticians. This is because it means that the gross value added, or GDP, at factor cost in the country must equal the sum of:

- **the total compensation of all employees; *plus***
- **the total operating surpluses of all producers**.

The income approach to estimating GDP tries to discover the total compensation of all employees and the total operating surpluses of all producers. The statisticians could get data on compensation to employees and operating surpluses from producers' accounts, but they don't do this because they would then be using the same source they use for the production approach. Instead, they ask tax collectors for data, because tax collectors have a lot of information about earnings and surpluses. Of course, some people understate their incomes and surpluses to the tax authorities, and the statisticians make an upwards allowance in their figures to take account of this.

Table 18.5 shows the results for the UK for 2009. You will see that the statisticians divide the country's operating surpluses between three types of company—sometimes called corporations—and other producers. These other producers cover all sole proprietors, partnerships, government departments, non-profit institutions, and owner-occupied households.

Table 18.5 also shows that by allowing for all taxes and subsidies on production, the income approach can also be used to find GDP at market prices.

GDP on the expenditure approach

The third approach to estimating GDP effectively regards all the UK's producers, even including owner-occupied households, as branches of one giant producer. This means that GDP is no longer seen as the sum of the values added by countless separate producers. Instead, it is seen as the value added of this single giant.

Let's see how we can find this producer's value added at market prices for 2009. This is the value of its output at market prices, minus the value of any inputs it used that were produced by other producers.

We first need to find the value of its output in 2009 at market prices. As with any producer, this chiefly comprises the value of what it sold. To estimate the value of its sales, the statisticians first estimate the expenditure made by its five groups of customers, as shown on Table 18.6.

- **Consumption expenditure by households**. This is the total expenditure paid by UK households for consumer goods and services. It even includes the rents that owner-occupier households are assumed to pay themselves.
- **Consumption expenditure by non-profit institutions**. This is the expenditure paid by the people who finance non-profit institutions to cover their running costs.

Table 18.5 **The UK's GDP on the income approach, 2009**

	£bn
Income:	
Compensation of employees	774
Gross operating surplus of:	
government-owned non-financial companies	9
privately owned non-financial companies	234
financial companies	68
other producers	157
GDP (or gross value added) at factor cost	**1,241**
Taxes *less* subsidies on production	155
GDP at market prices (income approach)	**1,395**

Note: Totals subject to rounding errors.
Source: Office for National Statistics, *United Kingdom Economic Accounts, 2010 Q3 edition*, Table A3.

Table 18.6 **The UK's GDP on the expenditure approach, 2009**

	£bn
Expenditure at market prices	
Consumption expenditure by households	874
Consumption expenditure by non-profit institutions	36
Consumption expenditure by general government	327
Gross domestic fixed capital formation	204
Changes in inventories	−16
Acquisition *less* disposals of valuables	1
Exports	391
less Imports	−421
GDP at market prices (expenditure approach)	**1,395**

Source: Office for National Statistics, *United Kingdom Economic Accounts, 2010 Q3 edition*, Table A2.

- **Consumption expenditure by general government**. This is the expenditure paid by the central government and local governments to their departments to cover their running costs.
- **Gross domestic fixed capital formation**. This is the expenditure by all producers on new capital equipment, such as plant, buildings, vehicles, and machinery, which is bought for use in future production.
- **Exports**. This is the expenditure on UK products made by people abroad.

To find the total value of the giant firm's output, we must now add two more items.

- **Changes in inventories**. This covers stocks of finished goods and raw materials. We include the value of these items because they have been produced, even though the finished goods have not yet been sold and the raw materials have not yet been used. Note that, in 2009, stocks fell, so Table 18.6 shows a negative increase here.
- **Acquisition less disposal of valuables**. The output of a country's producers includes some valuable items that may last indefinitely, such as works of art, precious metals, and jewels. The statisticians record all purchases of valuable items separately, and deduct the amount that people receive from selling second-hand items to work out the expenditure on the new items.

Finally, to find the giant producer's value added, we must deduct the value of any inputs it uses that it bought off other producers. Because this giant is the only UK producer, it might seem there can be nothing to subtract, but there is one item.

- **Imports.** These are goods and services bought from people abroad.

Table 18.6 shows the value of all these expenditures in the UK in 2009. Like the other approaches, it ends up with GDP at market prices of £1,395 billion. If we wish, we could deduct the total value of 'other taxes on production', and add in the total value of 'other subsidies on production' to get GDP at basic prices. And we could then deduct the total value of taxes on products and add in the total value of subsidies on products to get GDP at factor cost.

To estimate the expenditure numbers on the expenditure approach, the statisticians don't look at producers' accounts, to see how much they have sold, because this would be using the same source as the production approach. Instead, they conduct surveys of households, non-profit institutions, and firms to estimate how much they spend on goods and services. They also get government spending figures from governments, and figures for exports and imports from a variety of sources.

18.1 Everyday economics

How much decline in manufacturing?

Figure 18.1 shows that the share of manufacturing industry in the UK's output fell from over 16% in 2001 to under 12% in 2008. Similar declines have been observed in many industrialized countries, but statistics on industry output can be misleading. Figure 18.1 reflects the value added of each industry and this is based in part on the *value* of its output, but what matters to consumers is the *quantity* of its output. For example, the figure shows mining and quarrying raising its share of output, but this was entirely because of huge price rises: the quantity of its output actually fell by 38%. And the figure shows the hotel and restaurant industry reducing its share of output, but this was because it restrained its prices: the quantity of its output actually rose by 13%. With manufacturing industry, there are constant improvements in technology that allow it to produce its output at lower prices, so changes in the value of its output, and in turn changes in its value added, can give a misleading idea about changes in the quantity of its output. In fact, although manufacturing industry's share of the value of UK output fell by over a quarter, the quantity of its output fell much less, by just 12%.

18.2 Summary

- For any individual producer, value added is the value of its output minus the value of the intermediate products that it buys from other producers and uses up in its output. The production approach estimates GDP as the value added of all producers added together.
- A producer's value added at factor cost can, in fact, be found also by adding the compensation it pays to its employees to its operating surplus. The income approach estimates GDP at factor cost by adding the total compensation to all employees in the country to the total operating surplus of all producers.
- The expenditure approach estimates GDP at market prices by finding the value of the output of UK producers by adding spending made by other people on their products plus their increases in inventories. Imports are deducted because these are intermediate products supplied to UK producers.

18.3 Measures of national income

We saw in Table 18.5 that the income that people receive from UK producers in the form of compensation to employees, plus the income that they receive from UK producers in the form of operating surpluses, equals GDP at factor cost. We can put this in another way, and say that the people who receive all this income enjoy a total purchasing power that is equal to GDP at factor cost. It follows that the value at market prices of all the goods and services that these people could buy is equal to GDP at market prices.

We can use people's purchasing power as a measure of their income. What we will now consider is whether GDP at market prices equals the total purchasing power or income of UK citizens.

It is tempting to say that GDP at market prices underestimates the income of UK citizens, because in addition to their income from employment and operating surpluses, UK citizens also get income in the form of transfers paid by the government. We looked at these in Chapter 16 and saw that they included items like State Pensions, Jobseekers' Allowance, Child Tax Credits, and Housing Benefit.

However, all the money that the government pays out in transfers, to help the recipients to consume more, has to be financed by taxes, which means that other people can consume less. So these benefits merely take income from some people and give it to others: they do not add a single penny to the total income of UK citizens.

So does GDP at market prices equal the total purchasing power or income of UK citizens at market prices? The answer is 'almost'. But official UK estimates of our income make two small adjustments. These relate to flows of money between UK citizens and people abroad, as follows:

- **net income from abroad**;
- **net current transfers from abroad**.

We must now look at these two items.

Net income from the rest of the world

We have seen that the UK's GDP covers all the compensation to employees, or wages, that are paid by UK producers, along with all the operating surpluses of UK producers. However, some UK citizens receive wages that are not covered by the UK's GDP, because they work abroad for foreign producers and receive wages from them. And some UK citizens receive operating surpluses that are not covered by the UK's GDP, because they receive part of the surpluses of firms abroad, perhaps because they own part of them or even the whole of them, or because they have lent them some money and receive interest from them. Although these sources of income are not covered by the UK's GDP, they are part of the income of UK citizens.

Of course, some of the people employed by UK producers live abroad. And some of the income from the operating surpluses of UK producers is paid to people abroad who own part or all of them, or who have lent them money and get paid interest. So although the wages and operating surpluses paid to these people form part of the UK's GDP, they are not part of the income of UK citizens.

So we can get a truer idea of the income of UK citizens if we add to GDP at market prices what is called net income from abroad: this is the value of the income received by UK citizens from producers abroad, minus the value of the income paid by UK producers to people abroad. The income we then arrive at is called **gross national income** (GNI) at market prices. Table 18.7 shows the effect of this addition in 2009. In that year, as is usually the case, the UK received more income from abroad than it paid abroad, so net income from abroad was positive. The figure was £29 billion, and GNI at market prices was £1,423 billion.

Table 18.7 **The UK's gross national income and gross national disposable income, 2009**

	£bn
Gross domestic product (GDP) at market prices	**1,395**
Net income from abroad	29
Gross national income (GNI) at market prices	**1,423**
less Net current transfers from abroad	–14
Gross national disposable income (GNDI) at market prices	**1.409**

Sources: Office for National Statistics, *United Kingdom Economic Accounts, 2010 Q3 edition*, Table A1, and *United Kingdom National Accounts, 2010 Edition*, Table 1.1.

Net current transfers from abroad

Some people, like the World Bank, take GNI as a final measure of income. But UK statisticians like to make another adjustment by allowing for the receipts of gifts, or current transfers, from abroad. For example, the UK government receives some money from the EU, and some UK citizens receive gifts from friends or organizations abroad.

Of course, the UK government pays some money to the EU and other organizations abroad, and many UK citizens make gifts to friends or organizations abroad. To find our final income, the UK statisticians adjust GNI by the value of net current transfers from abroad: this is the value of current transfers received from abroad minus the value of those paid abroad. The income we then arrive at is called **gross national disposable income** (GNDI) at market prices.

Table 18.7 shows the effect of this addition in 2009. Then, as is always the case, the UK paid more transfers abroad than it received from abroad, so net current transfers were negative. The figure was £14 billion, so GNDI at market prices was £1,409 billion.

It may seem odd to deduct gifts paid before arriving at our final income. To see the issue here, suppose you are lucky enough to have an uncle who gives you £1,000 this year. If someone were to ask the uncle how much his income was this year, he would probably *not* deduct the £1,000. He would most likely say: 'That gift came out of my income, but it did not reduce my income.' But if we were to ask you what your income was this year, you probably would add in the £1,000. Like you, the UK statisticians want to allow for receipts of transfers from abroad as part of the UK's income.

However, it makes no sense to say that gifts received increase income while payments of gifts do not reduce income. To see why, suppose you give a £10 note to a friend who promptly gives it back to you; suppose you do this 1,000 times. If we were to add gifts received to income, but not deduct gifts paid, we would reckon you both got an extra £10,000 income through this exchange of a single note!

Table 18.8 Allowing for capital consumption to get net figures, 2009

	£bn
GDP at market prices	1,395
GNI at market prices	1,423
GNDI at market prices	1,409
each less Capital consumption	−153
NDP at market prices	1,242
NNI at market prices	1,270
NNDI at market prices	1,256

Sources: Office for National Statistics, *United Kingdom Economic Accounts, 2010 Q3 edition*, Table A1, and *United Kingdom National Accounts, 2010 Edition*, Table 1.1.

Allowing for capital consumption

Table 18.8 repeats from Table 18.7 the figures for GDP, GNI, and GNDI at market prices. It then gives a figure for **capital consumption**: this is the value by which the country's stock of capital goods fell during the year, chiefly from the wear and tear that it suffered while being used to produce goods and services. The table then subtracts capital consumption from GDP, GNI, and GNDI in turn. The results are called net domestic product (NDP), net national income (NNI), and net national disposable income (GNDI).

NDP shows the value of goods and services produced, net of the fall in value of the capital goods used to produce them. NNI and NNDI can be seen as measures of a country's income, net of the share of that income that the country's citizens would, if they were prudent, set aside to replace capital goods that are falling in value.

Capital consumption relates to the concept of depreciation, which we met in Chapter 7, but capital consumption is measured in a different way. To see this, suppose a firm buys a machine with a five-year life for £100,000. What is the fall in value of the machine in, say, its third year?

- **Depreciation.** This value is written on the firm's accounts and must follow official rules. For something lasting five years, these rules usually allow depreciation each year as a fifth of the original or historic cost, that is a fifth of £100,000, or £20,000.
- **Capital consumption.** This value is prepared by statisticians to estimate NDP, NNI, and NNDI. They would allow a fifth of the value of a replacement at current prices. Suppose that, because of inflation, this is £110,000, then the machine's capital consumption would be £22,000.

18.3 Summary

- GDP equals the total operating employment income of workers hired by UK producers plus the total surpluses of all UK producers. To get gross national income (GNI), a measure of the income of UK citizens, we add any wages or surpluses received from abroad and deduct any wages or surpluses paid abroad.
- Gross national disposable income (GNDI) is another measure of the income of UK citizens. It adjusts GNI to allow for receipts of gifts or transfers from abroad and payments of gifts or transfers to abroad.
- Net domestic product (NDP), net national income (NNI), and net national disposable income (NNDI) allow for capital consumption, that is the fall in value through wear and tear of the UK's capital goods.

18.4 Comparisons of output and income

We have seen how we can measure a country's output with GDP, and its citizen's total income with GNI or GNDI. Very often, people want to compare output or incomes today with output or incomes in past years, or with output and incomes in other countries. When comparisons like these are made, many issues need to be borne in mind. We will look first at comparisons of output.

Comparisons of output over time

The main issue with comparisons of output over time is to avoid using comparisons of actual or nominal GDP. We discussed this issue in Chapter 17, and we saw that we need to value the output of each year under consideration at the same prices that applied in a base or reference period. Then we will be comparing real GDP, not nominal GDP.

However, we must recall that GDP figures exclude household production, except for the services provided by owner-occupiers, and they also exclude the output of the underground economy. So the total production of goods and services is higher than GDP, and in any particular period of time this total might have grown faster or slower than the production covered by GDP.

Comparisons of output over space

The main issue when comparing GDP in different countries is that they use different currencies. For example, we might want to compare one GDP in pounds with another in euros.

One common way of doing this is to convert the two figures into the same currency using the current exchange rate. However, using exchange rates is not satisfactory. Table 18.9 shows the problem with an example that concerns two countries, Alphaland and Betaland, which use alphas and betas as their currencies.

For simplicity, we assume that these countries produce just one service, haircuts, and one good, mugs. We will also assume that the hourly wage is 2 alphas in Alphaland and 16 betas in Betaland, as shown in the top line of the table.

Suppose that haircuts need half an hour's labour. Then the table shows that the cost of a haircut is 1 alpha in Alphaland and 8 betas in Betaland. Also suppose the main difference between the countries is that Alphaland is a developing country, while Betaland is industrialized. In Alphaland, mugs are made chiefly by hand and need several hours' labour, and cost 10 alphas. In Betaland, mugs are made chiefly by machines and need little labour, and cost 20 betas.

Table 18.9 **Exchange rates and purchasing power parities (PPPs)**

Country	**Alphaland**	**Betaland**
Wage rate per hour	2 alphas	16 betas
Price of a haircut	1 alpha	8 betas
Price of a mug	10 alphas	20 betas
Exchange rate must be:	**1 alpha = 2 betas**	
Price of 2 haircuts + 1 mug	12 alphas	36 betas
Purchasing power parity is:	**1 alpha = 3 betas**	

When these countries trade, they can export and import mugs, but they cannot export and import haircuts. This actually means that the exchange rate must settle at 1 alpha = 2 betas. To see why, consider other possibilities.

- **1 alpha is worth less than 2 betas, say 1 beta.** Then the Betaland mug industry would collapse. Any Betaland citizen who wants a mug could use 10 betas to buy 10 alphas, and use them to import a mug from Alphaland; this is cheaper than buying a Betaland mug for 20 betas. To prevent its mug industry from collapsing, Betaland will want a different exchange rate.
- **1 alpha is worth more than 2 betas, say 3 betas.** Then the Alphaland mug industry would collapse. Any Alphaland citizen who wants a mug could use 6.7 alphas to buy 20 betas, and use them to import a mug from Betaland; this is cheaper than buying an Alphaland mug for 10 alphas. To prevent its mug industry from collapsing, Alphaland will want a different exchange rate.

The exchange rate will have to settle at 1 alpha = 2 betas, because only then will each country find that imported mugs are no cheaper than home-produced mugs. For example, Alphaland citizens could buy a home-produced mug for 10 alphas, or use those alphas to buy 20 betas and spend them on a mug produced in Betaland.

Purchasing power parity

When the exchange rate settles at 1 alpha = 2 betas, you might suppose that 1 alpha will buy as much in Alphaland as 2 betas will buy in Betaland. But suppose that each month consumers in each country want two haircuts and one mug. The total cost of these is 12 alphas in Alphaland and 36 betas in Betaland. So, taking all products into account, including haircuts, which are not imported or exported, 12 alphas have the same purchasing power in Alphaland as 36 betas have in Betaland. So the purchasing power of one alpha is actually the same as the purchasing power of 3 betas. The ratio of the purchasing powers of two currencies is called their **purchasing power parity** (PPP).

In our example, Alphaland was a developing country, but Betaland was industrialized. The exchange rate was 1 alpha = 2 betas, but the purchasing power parity was 1 alpha = 3 betas. Exchange rates generally do underestimate the purchasing power of the currencies of less-developed countries. In turn, using exchange rates to compare their output with other countries underestimates their relative output. We get a more accurate comparison if we convert their currencies using PPPs.

This effect is shown in Figure 18.2 which looks at the shares of world GDP accounted for by the world's 12 largest economies. The pink bars show their shares if their currencies are all converted to a single currency using exchange rates; the purple bars give a better idea by using PPPs. Using PPPs increases the relative output of less-industrialized countries like China and India, and reduces the relative output of more-industrialized countries like the US and Japan.

Economic welfare and welfare

People who compare the income of a country at different points in time, or who compare the incomes of two countries at the same time, often say that they want to compare well-being or welfare across time or space. But there are two sorts of welfare, as follows, and income is far more important to one than it is to the other.

- **Economic welfare**, **or living standards**. This is the ability of people to consume goods and services. Income plays a major part in comparisons of economic welfare.
- **Total welfare.** This is overall well-being and is affected by many factors beyond economic welfare, such as peace, freedom, health, a low crime rate, and a clean environment. Income plays a minor part in comparisons of total welfare.

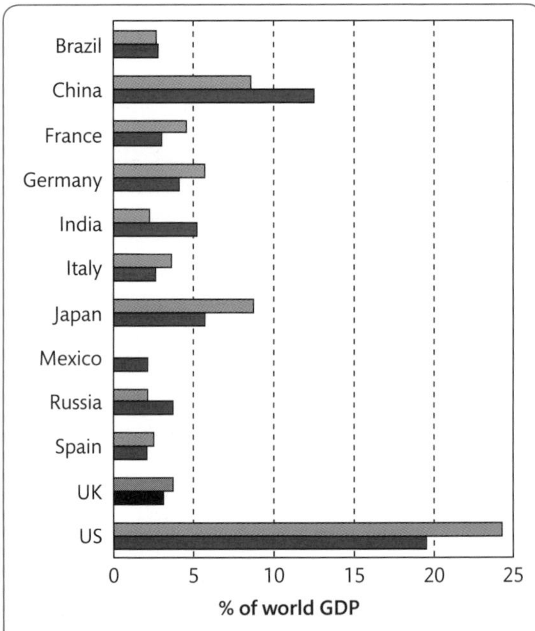

Figure 18.2 **Shares of world GDP in 2009 for 12 countries**

The pink bars show the shares if the various currencies are converted into one currency using exchange rates. The purple bars shows the shares if the conversions are done using the preferred method of purchasing power parities (PPPs). Using PPPs raises the relative output of less industrialized countries, like India and China, and lowers the relative output of more industrialized countries.

Source: World Bank, SiteResources, GDP and PPP.

Comparisons of income: basic points

When people want to use figures for a country's income in different years to compare economic welfare in those different years, there are two basic points they should note.

- **They should compare figures for income at constant prices.** Only then can they compare the quantity of goods and services people can buy.
- **They should compare figures for income per head.** A rise in income will overstate the rise in well-being if the population has grown so that the greater income is shared by more people.

In the UK, however, population growth is modest, so that allowing for it has only a modest effect. In Figure 18.3, the black line shows the growth of real GNDI since 1965. Setting the figure for 1965 as 100, real GNDI reached 282 in 2008. The population did rise a little over this period and the pink line shows the growth in real GNDI per head. Again, setting 1965 as 100, this was 250 by 2008; this is less than 282, but not greatly less.

When people want to use incomes in different countries to compare their economic welfare, there are also two basic points they should note.

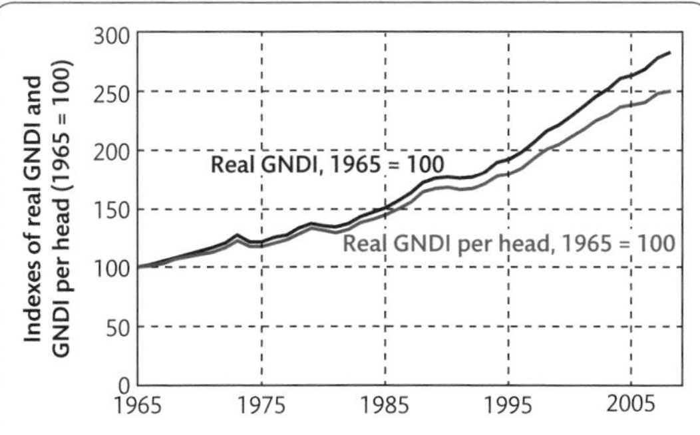

Figure 18.3 **Income growth in the UK, 1965–2008**

A low rate of population growth means that real GNDI per head has grown almost as rapidly as real GNDI.

Sources: National Statistics, *Annual Abstract of Statistics 2002*, Table 5.1, *Annual Abstract of Statistics 2010*, Table 5.1, *Economic Trends Annual Supplement 2006*, Table 2.1A, and *United Kingdom National Accounts 2009*, Table 1.1.

- **They should convert all income figures into a single currency using PPPs.** Otherwise, the gap between less industrialized countries and more-industrialized ones will seem larger than it is.
- **They should use figures for income per head.** The economic welfare of a typical citizen depends on the income of their country and on how many people that income is divided between.

Figure 18.4 show figures for GNI per head in 2009 for the world's 22 most populous countries, converting each country's figures into US dollars using PPPs. The figures ranged from $1,000 in Ethiopia to $47,000 in the US.

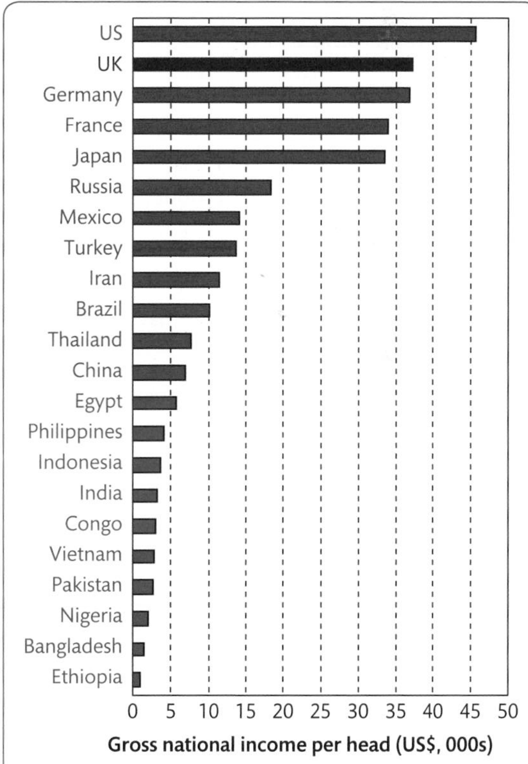

Figure 18.4 **Gross national income per head for the world's 22 most populous countries, 2009**

This chart shows GNI per head in US dollars, with other countries' currencies converted using PPPs.

Sources: World Bank, http://siteresources.worldbank. org/DATASTATISTICS/Resources/GNIPC.pdf.

Comparisons of income: further issues

Quite apart from all these basic points, there are many other issues to bear in mind when using incomes to compare economic welfare or living standards. Many of these issues arise because the largest component of both GNI and GNDI is GDP, and there are two groups of reasons why figures based on GDP can give misleading impressions of well-being.

The first group concerns goods and services that are produced, but not included in GDP, as follows.

- **GDP omits most household production.** Household production of food, clothes, and other products may have been relatively high in the UK's past when people were poorer, and it may be relatively high now in low-income countries. So the economic welfare of the UK in the past, and for poor countries today, might be relatively larger than their income figures suggest.
- **GDP omits production by the underground economy.** The size of this production may vary over time and between countries.

The second group concerns the fact that not all the goods and services produced actually contribute directly to people's economic welfare or living standards. The main points here are as follows.

- **GDP includes investment.** The production of capital, goods generally affects economic welfare more in the future than at the present.
- **GDP includes all government expenditure on goods and services.** Some of these purchases affect current economic welfare more than others: for example, state healthcare has more direct effect than defence.
- **GDP includes exports.** GDP figures include exports, but they are not consumed by UK citizens and so do not affect their well-being.
- **GDP omits leisure.** Leisure can be seen as a type of product that people like to consume, and which they can 'buy' by working fewer hours. But the value of this product is omitted from GDP. If UK citizens enjoy more leisure now than they used to, their well-being may have risen more than income figures suggest. And if people in rich countries have more leisure than people in poor countries, the gap in well-being may be larger than the gap in income suggests.
- **Measures of real GDP struggle with product quality.** Suppose that, over a period of time, computer prices are stable and people buy the same quantity. Then the value added by computer-makers may stay the same. But the computers may have improved greatly in quality and so generate much more economic welfare. Statisticians try to allow for this in the way they work out their figures for changes in real GDP, but it is hard to do so accurately.
- **GDP data may be unreliable.** This particularly applies to estimates of GDP in the UK before 1945, and to estimates of GDP today in many poorer countries. Indeed, in some countries, data on population are also unreliable, so that figures for income per head are doubly unreliable.

Finally, even if the economic welfare of a country has risen, its total welfare may not have risen, and if one country enjoys more economic welfare than another, it may not have more total welfare. This is because so many other factors affect welfare. Indeed, it is possible that the pursuit of high incomes sometimes leads to a poorer environment and so reduces that part of total welfare. The UK is one of a number of countries that is developing a measure of economic well-being that will go beyond GNDI and include factors such as the level of health, the level of education, the degree of inequality and the quality of the environment.

Question 18.2 Suppose a developing country finds that many people who used to produce much of their own food and build rudimentary homes now work in factories and buy all their food and employ builders to build their homes. Other things being equal, will living standards be rising at a faster rate or slower rate than GDP?

18.2 Everyday economics

Comparing consumption in the EU

In 2009, the World Bank estimated that the UK had the eighth highest GDP per head in Europe, after Luxembourg, Norway, Switzerland, the Netherlands, Sweden, Austria, and Denmark. Eurostat, an EU source, also put Ireland Germany, Belgium, and Finland ahead of the UK However, Eurostat also compared consumption per head in each country to try to compare living standards. Here, it allowed not only for consumers' expenditure, as in the national accounts, but also added expenditure by non-profit institutions and expenditure by governments for individuals, chiefly education and health care. This is preferred to using consumers' spending alone, because governments in different countries provide different amounts of individual services. For example, if dental services were paid for by the government in one country and by households in another, then an international comparison of household spending would not compare like with like. On this measure, consumption in the UK was second highest, with only Luxembourg ahead. But most countries with higher GDP and lower consumption had higher investment, so they may have faster growth than the UK.

Gross National Income per Capita 2009, Atlas Method and PPP, World Bank, eurostat, *Statistics in Focus*, 62/2010

18.4 Summary

- Comparisons of GDP and income over time should allow for price changes by using GDP and income figures measured at constant prices. Comparisons of GDP and income between countries should allow for different currencies by converting them into a single currency using PPPs, not using exchange rates.
- Comparisons of income per head give some idea of comparative economic welfare, but many caveats arise because the main component of income is GDP, which has limitations in this context.

In the next chapter we introduce an economic model to explain the factors that determine the level of GDP in an economy. This model is developed in several subsequent chapters.

abc Glossary

Basic prices: the value of a product measured by the sum that buyers pay for it, minus taxes on products and plus subsidies on products.

Capital consumption: the fall in the value of capital owing to wear and tear; it is measured in relation to current replacement prices.

Economic welfare: people's ability to consume goods and services, depending chiefly on their income.

Factor cost: the value of a product measured by the sum that buyers pay for it, minus all taxes on production and plus all subsidies on production.

Gross national disposable income (GNDI): GNI plus current transfers (or gifts) received from abroad minus current transfers paid to people abroad.

Gross national income (GNI): GDP plus income received from producers abroad minus income paid by producers to people abroad.

Gross value added: the total value added by all producers in a country, and so the same as GDP.

Hidden economy: another term for the underground economy.

Inventories: stocks of raw materials or finished products.

Market prices: the value of a product measured by the sum that buyers pay for it.

Operating surplus: for any producer, the revenue at factor cost that it gets from the products it sells minus the cost of producing them.

Other subsidies on production: subsidies on production other than subsidies on products.

Other taxes on production: taxes on production other than taxes on products.

Purchasing power parity (PPP): the ratio of the purchasing powers of two currencies.

Subsidies on production: subsidies that firms receive because they are producing products to sell.

Subsidies on products: subsidies on products for which the amount a firm receives depends on how much it sells.

Taxes on production: taxes that firms have to pay because they are producing products to sell.

Taxes on products: taxes on production for which the amount a firm pays depends on how much it sells.

Total welfare: people's overall well-being, affected by many factors beyond economic welfare.

Underground economy: producers that do not record their activity.

Value added: the difference between the value of a producer's output and the value of the intermediate products that it uses in that output .

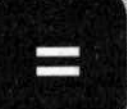

Answers to in-text questions

18.1 It means that 'other subsidies on production' were greater than 'other taxes on production'. The main recipients of the subsidies concerned were the then numerous nationalized industries.

18.2 Living standards will be rising more slowly than GDP, because GDP will omit household production and therefore ignore the fall in household production.

? Questions for review

18.1 The figures below relate to a firm. Find (**a**) the value of its products sold at market prices, basic prices, and factor cost, (**b**) its value added at factor cost, and (**c**) its operating surplus.

	£ m
Compensation of employees	35
Increase in inventory of finished goods	10
Increase in inventory of intermediate products	5
Other subsidies on production	1
Other taxes on production	6
Revenue from products sold	100
Subsidies on products	5
Taxes on products	15
Value of intermediate products bought	50

18.2 The figures below relate to a country. Estimate its GDP at (**a**) factor cost, (**b**) basic prices, and (**c**) market prices.

	£ bn
Compensation of employees	750
Gross operating surplus of companies	350
Gross operating surplus of other producers	150
Other taxes on production	50
Other subsidies on production	10
Subsidies on products	40
Taxes on products	200

18.3 The figures below relate to a country. The spending figures are at market prices. Estimate (**a**) GDP at market prices, (**b**) GNI at market prices, and (**c**) GNDI at market prices.

	£m
Acquisition *less* disposals of valuables	5
Changes in inventories	15
Consumption expenditure by general government	300
Consumption expenditure by households	900
Consumption expenditure by non-profit institutions	30
Current transfers from abroad	30
Current transfers paid abroad	20
Exports	400
Gross domestic fixed capital formation	250
Imports	450
Income from abroad	150
Income paid abroad	110

18.4 What effect would an increase in production by the underground economy have on (**a**) measured GDP, and (**b**) economic welfare?

? Questions for discussion

18.1 Suppose real GNDI per head rises by 15% in the UK in the next five years. Suggest some reasons why this might overstate or understate the true rise in economic welfare. Also, how might the rise in GNDI per head affect other aspects of welfare?

18.2 Suppose GNI per head is the same in two countries, but one has a warmer climate (so that less heating is needed), less crime (so that less law and order spending is needed), and less disease (so that less healthcare spending is needed). How would these affect your views on the relative economic welfare and the relative total welfare of the two countries?

Common student errors

One common confusion is the difference between the value of a producer's output and the value of its production. The value of its production is its value added, and is the difference between the value of its output and the value of any intermediate products it uses up in that production.

Another problem is the plethora of terms used. It is simplest to focus on GDP, a measure of output, and GNI and GNDI, which are measures of income. Each can be valued at market prices, basic prices, or factor cost.

19

GDP and the Multiplier Model

Remember from Chapter 1 that the key flows of money between households and firms can be shown on a diagram called the circular flow of income. Remember from Chapter 17 that macroeconomics studies the economy as a whole, and that it is chiefly interested in output, employment, and the price level.

The level of a country's output, or gross domestic product, is the main factor that determines its citizens' living standards and their level of employment. But what determines the size of its GDP? Can individuals affect GDP by spending more or less? Can governments affect GDP by spending more or less, or by taxing more or less? Can people abroad affect our GDP by exporting more or less to us, or by importing more or less from us? And how sensitive is GDP to the various factors that can affect it?

This chapter shows you how to answer questions like these, by understanding:

* actual injections into the circular flow of income and actual withdrawals from it;
* planned injections into the circular flow of income and planned withdrawals from it;
* how planned injections and planned withdrawals affect the level of output;
* how output is determined in a two-sector economy and why it may change;
* the meaning and value of the multiplier;
* how output is determined in a four-sector economy and why it may change.

19.1 The circular flow of income, injections, and withdrawals

Introduction

This chapter develops a simple model to show the main factors that determine the level of output, or GDP, in a country. We will keep the model simple by saying very little about the price level or interest rates. Effectively, we will assume that the price level and interest rates are constant and can be ignored. In later chapters, we will relax these assumptions, and develop the model given here to show how the price level and interest rates are determined and see how they affect GDP.

To understand the model given here, and later developments of it, we must look first at the flows of money between the different sectors of an economy. In this section, we will look at the *actual* flows. Later, we will look at the *planned* flows, which may be different. For example, you may plan to spend £150 next week, including £30 on a book that you order in a shop, but if the shop can't get a copy, you may actually spend £120.

The circular flow in a two-sector economy

We will look first at the actual flows of income in an economy with only two sectors: households and firms. We discussed these flows back in Chapter 1 and illustrated them on a figure called the circular flow of income. This figure is reproduced in a simplified form in Figure 19.1. The arrows here represent the flows of income in a particular period of time, say a month.

To understand this figure, let's start at the top. Here, there is an arrow flowing from firms to households. This arrow covers two types of payment by firms to households.

- **Wages**: this covers all the compensation paid by firms to their employees.
- **Profits**: these are the trading profits or operating surpluses of firms, and are paid to their owners.

These payments cover the total income that people receive from firms, and we use the symbol Y for this total income. And we saw in Chapter 18 that if we add total wages, or compensation of employees, to total profits, or operating surpluses, we get the value of a country's output of goods and services, that is its gross domestic product, or GDP. So we can also use Y as a symbol for GDP.

All this income belongs to households. It is called their **disposable income**, Y_{DIS}, because they can choose how to dispose of it. The arrow starting at the bottom of the households box shows the two ways in which they can dispose of it.

- **Consumer's expenditure on goods and services**. Income that is spent on consumers' expenditure, C, flows all along the arrow to the firms' box.
- **Saving**. Many households choose not to spend all their income on goods and services and instead save some of it. Income that is saved generally flows to financial markets, but these markets are not shown on this figure. So saving, S, is shown by a grey arrow, which indicates that saving flows out of the circular flow between households and firms. Income that flows out of the circular flow is called a **withdrawal**.

Consumers' expenditure, C, covers firms' costs for producing consumer goods and services. But some firms also produce capital goods such as plant and machinery. These goods are bought by the owners of other firms, and spending on them is called investment, I. The owners of the firms that undertake investment typically raise the funds they need in financial markets. As these markets are not shown on the figure, the grey arrow for investment shows that spending on investment flows into the circular flow between households and firms. Any spending that flows into the circular flow, from outside, is called an **injection**.

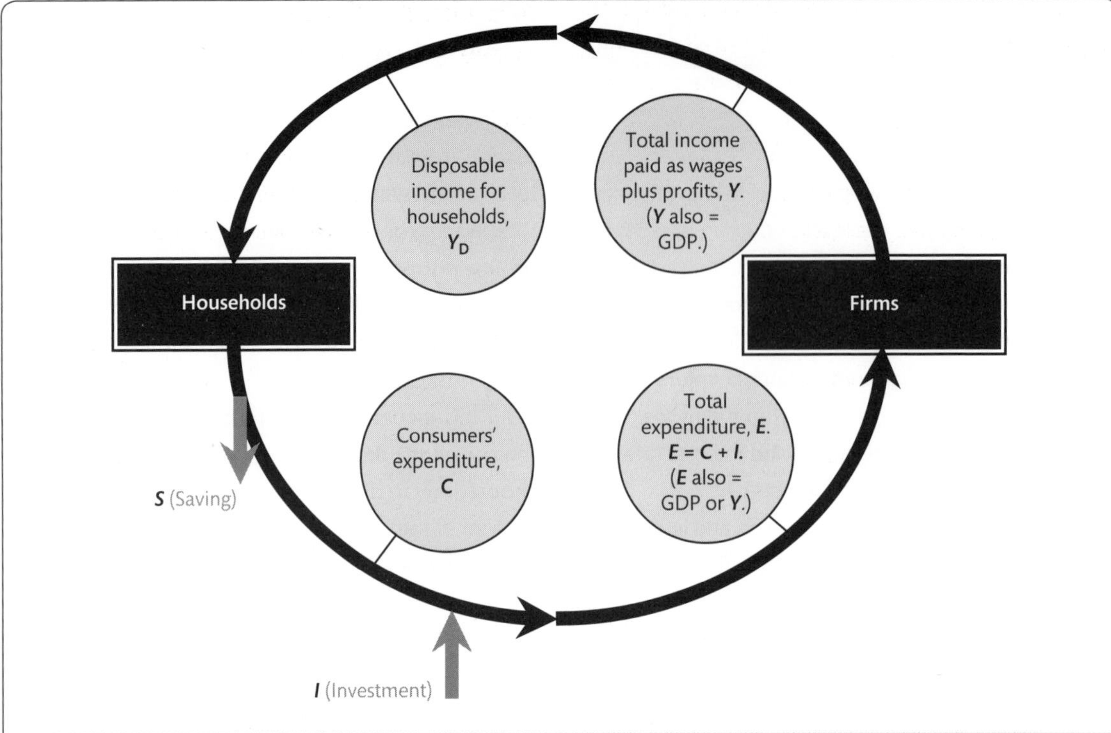

Figure 19.1 **The circular flow of income in a two-sector economy**

The firms' sector receives income when people buy the goods and services that firms produce. Firms pay all this income back to the household sector, much of it as wages to the households that supply employees, and the rest as profits to the households that own the firms. Most of the income that households receive from firms flows back to the firms' sector as consumers' expenditure. But saving is withdrawn from the circular flow, while investment spending is injected into it.

Figure 19.1 shows that the total expenditure on goods and services produced by firms, E, equals $C + I$. E also equals GDP or Y because it equals the value of the goods and services produced by firms.

The equality of actual injections and withdrawals

In any period of time, the amount of income that firms pay into the circular flow equals the amount that they receive from it. To see why, suppose that, one month, firms receive £10 billion and pay £9 billion to households as wages. This will leave them with profits of £1 billion. But profits also get paid to households, so the total sum that firms pay into the circular flow will be £10 billion.

We can put this another way and say that firms receive as much income from the circular flow as they pay into it. This means that once they have paid some income into the circular flow, say £10 billion, then the value of any withdrawals from the circular flow must equal the value of any injections into it; in a two-sector economy, the only withdrawals are saving and the only injections are investment, so they must be equal. For example, if saving were £2 billion, so that consumer spending were £8 billion, then investment would have to be £2 billion to make sure that firms received £10 billion in all.

Investment and stocks

We have assumed so far that the goods and services that firms produce are either consumer goods and services sold to households, or capital goods sold to the owners of other firms. But firms also produce some goods that they do not sell, but instead add to stocks or inventories. It costs firms money to build up stocks, and they get this money from their owners, but we do not add an extra arrow to show this. Instead, we include it in the investment arrow and define **investment** as having two components:

- **expenditure on adding to stocks;**
- **expenditure on new capital goods.**

Much macroeconomic theory hinges on the fact that investment has these two components.

The circular flow in a three-sector economy

Real-world economies have more than two sectors. Figure 19.2 adds in a government sector, which comprises the central government and local governments. This figure allows for additional producers in the form of government departments by including them along with firms. We regard government departments, such as the National Health Service and local education authorities, as selling their products to the governments that finance them. Figure 19.2 then uses three pink arrows to show the three extra income flows that arise in a three-sector economy.

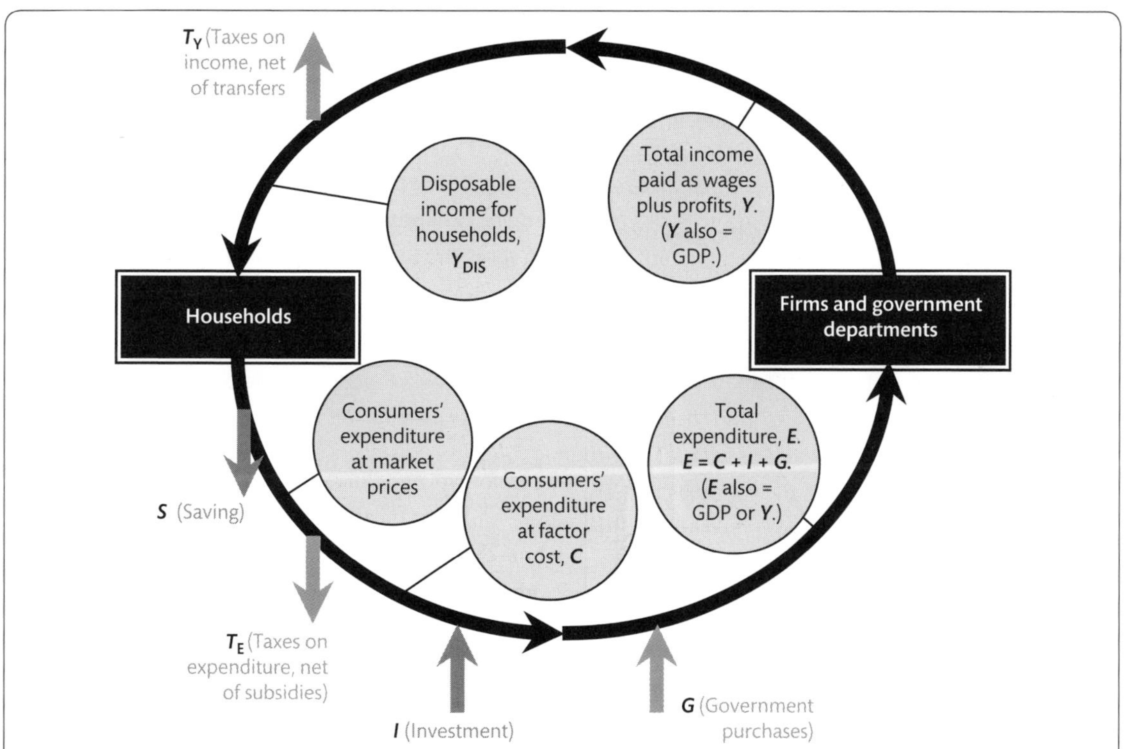

Figure 19.2 **The circular flow of income in a three-sector economy**

Here, goods and services are produced by government departments as well as firms. There are two extra withdrawals from the circular flow. One covers taxes on income, net of income paid out by governments as transfers, such as State Pension. The other covers money taken from consumer spending with taxes on expenditure, net of money added to consumer spending with subsidies. The central government and local governments pay government departments to provide goods and services, and these government purchases from government departments form an extra injection into the circular flow.

- **Household income is taxed**. The income that households can choose how to dispose of is less than the income paid to them as wages and profits, because they have to pay some of this income to the government in taxes on income. Admittedly, the government sector does not only take income away from households; it also pays them some income in transfers like State Pension and Jobseeker's Allowance. However, governments always take more in taxes on income than they pay in transfers, and the arrow T_Y shows how much income is withdrawn from the circular flow with taxes on income, net of any income that is paid as transfers. Disposable income, Y_{DIS}, equals total household income from wages and profits minus T_Y.
- **Consumer spending is taxed**. The amount of disposable income that households spend rather than save is called consumers' expenditure at market prices. Figure 19.2 shows that some of this is taken by the government with taxes on expenditure, such as VAT and alcohol duty. However, the government does not only take money from consumers' spending; it also adds some money with subsidies on products like public transport. But governments always take more in taxes here than they add in subsidies, and the arrow T_E shows how much income is withdrawn from the circular flow with taxes on expenditure, net of any subsidies that are paid in. The value of consumer spending after allowing for these taxes and subsidies is called consumers' expenditure at factor cost. This flows to producers and has the symbol C.
- **Governments purchase goods and services from government departments**. This government expenditure, G, flows to the departments, and is an injection into the circular flow between households and producers.

Figure 19.2 shows that, in a three-sector economy, the total expenditure received by producers equals $C + I + G$, and this in turn equals the value of what they produce, which is GDP, or Y.

Injections and withdrawals in a three-sector economy

Figure 19.2 has two tax arrows, T_Y and T_E. For simplicity, we will use the symbol T to cover all taxes, so $T = T_Y + T_E$. So total withdrawals now equal $S + T$, and total injections now equal $I + G$.

All the income that flows into the firms plus government departments box has to flow out, so these two flows are equal. We can put that another way and say that firms plus government departments must receive as much from the circular flow as they pay into it. That can happen only if total actual withdrawals from the circular flow equal total injections into it, $I + G$. So, in a three-sector economy, actual $S + T$ must equal actual $I + G$.

The circular flow in a four-sector economy

Real-world economies also have a foreign sector. Figure 19.3 uses arrows labelled 'Imports' and 'Exports' to show the two effects of allowing for this sector.

- **Some household income is spent on imports**. Spending on imports, M, is withdrawn from the circular flow of income in the country covered by the figure; instead, it flows abroad.
- **Some products produced by firms are sold as exports**. The expenditure by people abroad on exports, X, flows to the producers in the country covered by the figure, and is an injection into the circular flow income in that country.

Figure 19.3 shows that, in a four-sector economy, the total expenditure received by producers equals $C + I + G + X - M$, and this in turn equals the value of what they produce, which is GDP, or Y.

Injections and withdrawals in a four-sector economy

Figure 19.3 shows that total withdrawals now equal $S + T + M$, where T covers both T_Y and T_E. Total injections equal $I + G + X$. As in the two and three-sector

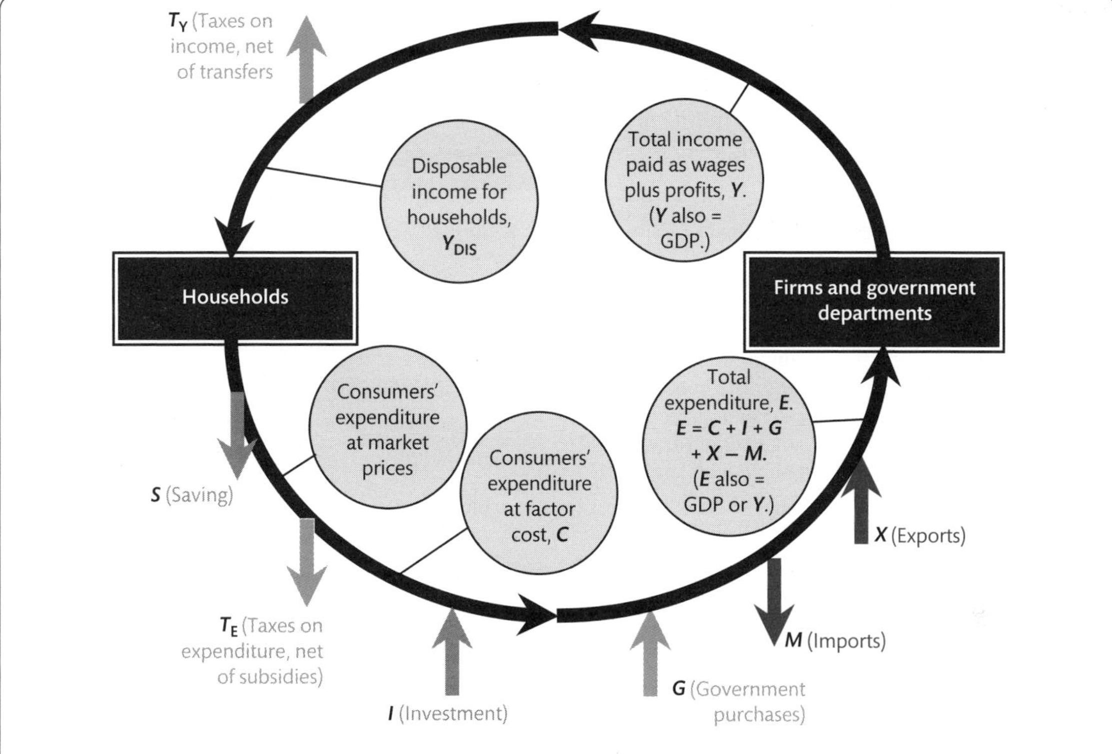

Figure 19.3 **The circular flow of income in a four-sector economy**

Here, some consumers' expenditure is spent on imports and so is withdrawn from the circular flow between households and producers in the country covered by the figure. Money that producers receive from exports is an extra injection into the circular flow. The total value of actual withdrawals, $S + T + M$, equals the total value of actual injections, $I + G + X$.

economies, total withdrawals must equal total injections, because the amount of income flowing into the bottom of the firms plus government department box must equal the amount that flows out at the top. So actual $S + T + M$ must equal actual $I + G + X$.

A summary of withdrawals and injections

We now know that, in all economies, the total actual value of withdrawals must equal the total actual value of injections. This means the following.

- **In a two-sector economy**: $S = I$.
- **In a three-sector economy**: $S + T = I + G$.
- **In a four-sector economy**: $S + T + M = I + G + X$.

Note that, in a two-sector economy, S must equal I because S and I are the only withdrawals and injections. But S need not equal I in a three or four-sector economy.

For instance, take a four-sector economy, and suppose that, one month, S exceeds I. In this case, not all saving is needed in the financial markets to finance investment, so some saving is left over. However, $S + T + M$ equals $I + G + X$, and as S is bigger than I, then the combined value of $T + M$ must be less than the combined value of $G + X$. So perhaps some of the leftover saving is lent to the government, to help it to pay for G at a higher level than T. Or perhaps some is lent to foreigners, to help them to spend more on X than they receive as payments for M.

Non-profit institutions

Economies actually have a fifth sector in the form of non-profit institutions. But macroeconomics ignores this sector because it is relatively small.

19.1 Everyday economics

Government credit rating

The UK government's spending, *G*, is way above its tax revenues, *T*, and it is financing the gap by borrowing. Governments are generally considered safe borrowers, because they can raise taxes to repay their loans. But the UK government is now borrowing so much that some people who lend to it are starting to worry, and in May 2011 a Chinese agency removed the UK from the its lowest risk category. If this sentiment spreads, then the government might be forced to pay higher interest rates, to offset the risk to lenders; alternatively, it might try to reduce the risk by raising taxes and cutting spending on a large scale.

'British government policy of no bailout places large banks at risk of possible credit downgrades', *BBC News*, 24 May 2011.

'UK credit rating downgraded... by China', *BBC News*, 24 May 2011.

19.1 Summary

- Actual withdrawals from the circular flow of income between producers and households equal actual injections into it.
- In a two-sector economy, saving is the only withdrawal and investment is the only injection. Investment includes increases in stocks or inventories, as well as purchases of capital goods.
- In a three-sector economy, taxation is another withdrawal and government purchases are another injection.
- In a four-sector economy, imports are a further withdrawal and exports are a further injection.

19.2 Towards a macroeconomic model for determining GDP

Actual flows and planned flows

To understand the forces that determine a country's GDP, we need to distinguish between actual flows and planned flows of income. The circular flow figures at which we looked earlier concern the *actual* flows in an economy, and they show two key features of these flows.

- **The *actual* expenditure that people pay to producers equals the value of their output, which is GDP or *Y*.**
- ***Actual* injections equal *actual* withdrawals.**

However, we noted earlier that planned flows may differ from actual flows. This means that:

- **the expenditure that people *plan* to pay to producers may not equal the value of their output, which is GDP or *Y*;**
- ***planned* injections may not equal *planned* withdrawals.**

These two conclusions lie at the heart of the macroeconomic model, which we will now develop to explain what determines a country's GDP. This model focuses on the following four flows.

- ***Actual* total expenditure, which equals actual output, GDP**: this is denoted by *Y*.
- ***Planned* total expenditure**: this is denoted by *E*.
- ***Planned* injections**: these are denoted by *J*.
- ***Planned* withdrawals**: these are denoted by *W*.

Notice that the only actual flow we will consider is *Y*. Otherwise, we will use *E*, *J*, and *W* to refer to what people *plan* to do. We will also use *C*, *S*, *I*, *T*, *G*, *X*, and *M* to refer to the consumer spending, saving, investment, government purchases, exports, and imports that people *plan* to make.

The components of *E*, *J*, and *W*

We need to know what we must add up to find *E*, *J*, and *W*. This depends on how many sectors there are. Figures 19.1, 19.2, and 19.3 showed us the components of actual total spending, injections, and withdrawals for economies with two, three, and four sectors. The components of planned total spending, planned injections, and planned withdrawals are the same, as shown below, except that now all the symbols refer to planned flows.

- **In a two-sector economy**:

  $E = C + I \qquad J = I \qquad W = S$

- **In a three-sector economy**:

  $E = C + I + G \qquad J = I + G \qquad W = S + T$

- **In a four-sector economy**:

  $E = C + I + G + X - M \quad J = I + G + X \quad W = S + T + M$

How *E*, *J*, and *W* affect the level of output

The level of a country's output, or *Y*, is ultimately decided by its producers. The output level that these producers will choose depends on *E*, *J*, and *W*. To see both why and how, we will now explore three possible situations, which we will refer to as Case A, Case B, and Case C. In each case, we will take *I* to cover all planned investment, so it includes planned stock increases, as well as planned purchases of capital goods. Also, in each case, we will suppose that producers plan to increase their stocks by £5bn a month.

Case A: *J* is less than *W*, so *E* is less than *Y*

Case A is shown in the first column of Table 19.1. Here, we suppose that, one month, firms and government departments produce £240bn worth of goods and services, so that output, *Y*, is £240bn. In turn, producers pay £240bn worth of income in wages and profits into the circular flow.

But suppose *J* = £25bn and *W* = £35bn. As people plan to withdraw £10bn more from the circular flow than they plan to inject into it, they must plan to spend £10bn less than their income, so *E* = £230bn. So if *J* is less than *W*, *E* is less than *Y*.

The actual output of products in this case, £240bn, is £10bn more than is needed to meet everyone's planned expenditure. Producers will add the £10bn surplus output to their stocks, along with the £5bn worth of goods that they planned to add to their stocks. So producers will actually invest £10bn more

Table 19.1 **How unplanned investment forms the link between *E*, *J*, *W*, and changes in output**

	Case A	**Case B**	**Case C**
Situation in the current month	*Y* = £240n	*Y* = £160bn	*Y* = £200bn
	W = £35bn	*W* = £15bn	*W* = £25bn
	J = £25bn	*J* = £25bn	*J* = £25bn
	So *J* is less than *W*	So *J* is greater than *W*	So *J* equals *W*
	E = £230bn	*E* = £170bn	*E* = £200bn
	So *E* is less than *Y*	So *E* is greater than *Y*	So *E* equals *Y*
Effect on stocks	Stocks rise by £15bn, £10bn more than planned	Stocks fall by £5bn; this is a rise of −£5bn, £10bn less than planned	Stocks rise by £5bn, exactly as planned
Unplanned investment	£10bn	−£10bn	£0bn
Effect on output, *Y*	Producers will reduce *Y*	Producers will increase *Y*	Producers won't alter *Y*

in stocks than they planned, which means there is unplanned investment of £10bn.

If you were a producer here, and your stocks were to rise more than you planned, you would probably decide to produce less in future. Other producers will react in the same way, so output will fall.

Case B: *J* is more than *W*, so *E* is more than *Y*

Case B is shown in the second column of Table 19.1. Here, we suppose that, one month, firms and government departments produce output worth £160bn, so *Y* is £160bn. In turn, producers pay £160bn in wages and profits into the circular flow.

But suppose $J = £25$bn and $W = £15$bn. As people plan to withdraw £10bn less from the circular flow than they plan to inject into it, they must plan to spend £10bn more than their income, so $E = £170$bn. So if *J* is more than *W*, *E* is more than *Y*.

Here, the actual output, £160bn, is £10bn less than is needed to meet everyone's planned expenditure. Yet producers will be reluctant to turn buyers away. Most probably, producers will meet the shortfall in output by cutting their stocks by £5bn instead of raising them by £5bn as they panned. So producers will actually invest £10bn less in stocks than they planned, which means there is unplanned investment of *minus* £10bn.

If you were a producer here, and your stocks were to rise less than you planned, you would probably decide to produce more in future. Other producers will react in the same way, so output will rise.

Case C: *J* equals *W*, so *E* equals *Y*

Case C is shown in the third column of Table 19.1. Here, we suppose that, one month, firms and government departments produce output worth £200bn, so *Y* is £200bn. In turn, producers pay £200bn in wages and profits into the circular flow.

We also suppose that *J* and *W* both equal £25bn. As people plan to inject into the circular flow the same amount as they plan to withdraw from it, they must plan to spend an amount equal to their income, so $E = £200$bn. So, if *J* equals *W*, *E* is equal to *Y*.

Here, the output of £200bn just meets all the planned spending in the economy, including producers' planned stock increases of £5bn. So producers can raise their stocks by this amount and there is no unplanned investment.

If you were a producer here, and your stocks were to rise exactly as much as you planned, you would probably decide to produce the same amount in future. Other producers will react in the same way, so output will stay the same.

We conclude that output will remain the same, and so be in equilibrium, only if $J = W$ so that $E = Y$. We can build on this insight to develop a model that shows the factors that determine the level of output which producers will choose to produce.

Question 19.1 Suppose Case C applies for some months. Then one month, when output is still £200bn and withdrawals are still £25bn, injections fall to £20bn. Will output change next month?

19.2 Summary

- If planned injections are less than planned withdrawals, then planned spending is less than output, and producers produce more than is needed. Stocks will rise more than planned and output will be cut.
- If planned injections are more than planned withdrawals, then planned spending is more than output, and producers produce less than is needed. Stocks will rise less than planned and output will be raised.
- If planned injections equal planned withdrawals, then planned spending equals output, and producers produce just as much as is needed. Stocks will rise just as planned and output will be held constant.

19.3 Equilibrium in a two-sector economy

We have seen that output, *Y*, will be in equilibrium if planned spending, *E*, is equal to *Y*. As it happens, in every economy there is only one level of output at which *E* will be equal to *Y*, so output will not be in equilibrium until it reaches this level.

To find this output level, we must consider what *E* would be at each possible output level. In this section, we consider the level of *E* at different output levels in a two-sector economy, which has only firms and households. Here, $E = C + I$.

Table 19.2 concerns planned consumer spending in this economy. The first line shows four possible levels of output or *Y*: £0bn, £100bn, £200bn, and £300bn a month. In any economy, the value of output equals the value of wages and profits paid by producers, and in a two-sector economy all of this income is available to households as disposable income, Y_{DIS}. So the second line of Table 19.2 shows that, at each output level, Y_{DIS}, would equal output. The third and fourth lines show how, in each case, these households would plan to divide their disposable income between saving, *S*, and consumers' expenditure, *C*.

Notice in Table 19.2 that if output and disposable income in this economy were £0bn per month, then, rather than starve, households would take £25bn from their past savings and spend that. So planned consumer spending, *C*, would be £25bn. Taking money from past savings is called **dissaving**, so dissaving here would be £25bn. We could instead say that saving would be –£25bn.

Suppose output and disposable incomes were to rise by £100bn from £0bn a month to £100bn. Table 19.2 shows that consumers would now plan to spend £100bn, which is £75bn more than they would spend if income were £0bn. They would also plan to save £0bn, which is £25bn more than the –£25bn they would save if income were £0bn. So the fraction of the extra £100bn that they would plan to spend is 0.75, and the fraction they would plan to save is the remaining 0.25.

The marginal propensities to consume and save out of disposable income

The fraction of any rise in disposable income that households plan to spend is called the **marginal propensity to consume out of disposable income**, MPC_{DIS}. The fraction of any rise in disposable income that households plan to save is called the **marginal propensity to save out of disposable income**, MPS_{DIS}. So, in Table 19.2, if disposable income rises from £0bn to £100bn, MPC_{DIS} is 0.75 and MPS_{DIS} is 0.25.

For simplicity, our example will assume that the same fractions apply to any rise in disposable income. So Table 19.2 shows that if disposable income were to rise by another £100bn to £200bn a month, *C* would rise by another £75bn to £175bn a month, while S would rise by another £25bn from £0bn to £25bn. And if disposable income were to rise by another £100bn to £300bn a month, *C* would rise by another £75bn to £250bn a month, and S would rise by another £25bn to £50bn.

Table 19.2 **An example of consumers' expenditure and saving in a two-sector economy**

			£bn	£bn	£bn	£bn
Output or GDP	*Y*		0	100	**200**	300
Disposable income	Y_{DIS}		0	100	**200**	300
Saving	*S*	$MPS_{DIS} = 0.25$	–25	0	**25**	50
Consumers' expenditure	*C*	$MPC_{DIS} = 0.75$	25	100	**175**	250

The consumption and saving functions

The relationship between planned consumers' expenditure, or consumption, and disposable income is called the **consumption function**. The top part of Figure 19.4 plots the consumption function for the example in Table 19.2 with the line, *C*. This graph has disposable income on the horizontal axis and consumption on the vertical axis. The line *C* shows what consumption would be at each possible level of disposable income.

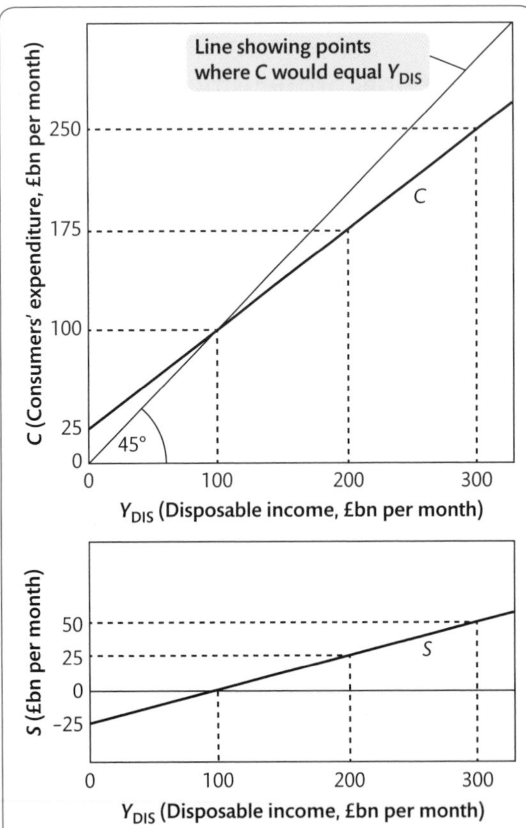

Figure 19.4 **The consumption function, *C*, and saving function, *S***

C and *S* show how households would divide their disposable income between consumer spending and saving at different income levels. At low incomes, they would take money from funds saved previously to help to pay for their spending.

The slope of *C* at any income level equals the MPC_{DIS} at that level. In our example, MPC_{DIS} is always 0.75, so *C* has a constant slope of 0.75 and is therefore a straight line rather than a curve. We can work out its slope at 0.75 because we can see that consumption rises by £75bn whenever disposable income rises by £100bn.

This graph also has a line through the origin with a slope of 45°. If the economy were at any point on this 45° line, then *C* would equal Y_{DIS}. However, the only level of Y_{DIS} at which this economy would end up on the 45° line is the level of Y_{DIS} where the consumption function line intersects it, that is at a Y_{DIS} of £100bn; this line shows that if Y_{DIS} were £100bn, then *C* would also be £100bn.

There is no other level of *Y* at which *C* would equal Y_{DIS}. If Y_{DIS} were less than £100bn, the consumption function line would be above the 45° line. This means that households would spend more than their disposable income: for example, if Y_{DIS} were £0bn, they would dissave £25bn and spend £25bn. If Y_{DIS} were more than £100bn, the consumption function line would be below the 45° line. This means that households would spend less than their disposable income: for example, if Y_{DIS} were £300bn, they would save £50bn and spend £250bn.

The relationship between planned household saving and disposable income is called the **saving function**. The saving function for the example in Table 19.2 is shown by the line *S* in the bottom part of Figure 19.4. This line shows what saving would be at each possible level of disposable income. The slope of the *S* line at any income level equals the MPS_{DIS} at that level. In our example, MPS_{DIS} is always 0.25, so the line has a constant slope of 0.25. We can work out its slope at 0.25 because saving rises by £25bn whenever disposable income rises by £100bn.

Shifts in the consumption function

A country's consumption function shows how much consumption there would be at each possible level of disposable income, assuming everything else stays the same. But other factors sometimes change, and then the consumption function shifts.

This is shown in Figure 19.5. Here, the three points show the combinations of UK disposable income and consumer spending that applied in 1991, 2007, and 2009. Through these points, the figure has lines estimating what the consumption function might have been in each of these years.

You will see that the function shifted upwards between 1991 and 2007, from C_{1991} to C_{2007}, and then shifted down to C_{2009}. The main factors that shift a consumption function are as follows.

- **Changes in wealth**. Other things being equal, the consumption function shifts upwards if wealth rises, because people feel less need to save. Wealth rose between 1991 and 2007, and then fell when the 2007–10 recession reduced property prices and share prices.

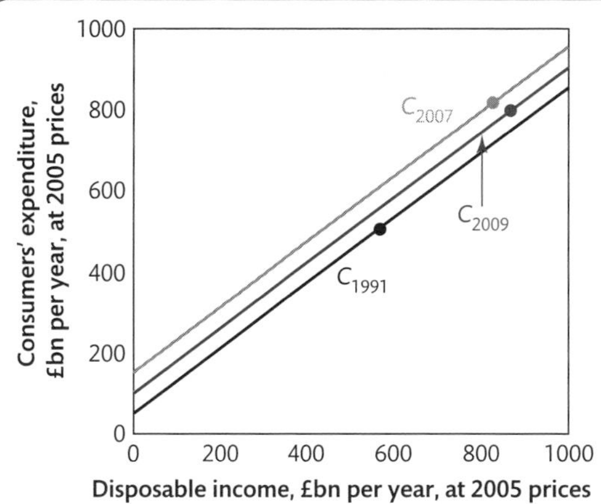

Figure 19.5 **Shifts in the UK consumption function**

The three points show the combinations of UK disposable income and consumer spending in 1991, 2007, and 2009; the three lines estimate the consumption functions for those years. The function usually shifts up over time as wealth rises and people expect sustained growth. The function shifted down in 2009 when wealth fell and people were pessimistic about their future incomes.

Sources: Office for National Statistics, *UK Economic Accounts 2009 Quarter 4*, Tables A7 & A38, and *Economic Trends Annual Supplement 2006*, Table 2.5.

- **Changes in expectations**. Other things being equal, the consumption function shifts upwards if people become more optimistic about the level of their future incomes, and so feel less need to save. The downward shift in the consumption function between 2007 and 2009 arose chiefly because the recession caused people to fear about future employment and income levels.
- **Interest rates**. Other things being equal, lower interest rates cause people to save less and spend more, because saving is less rewarding. Interest rates fell in the 2007–10 recession, and on its own this would have shifted the consumption function up, but this factor was more than offset by falls in wealth and reduced expectations of future incomes.

Note that factors that encourage people to spend more and shift the consumption function upwards also encourage them to save less, and so shift the saving function downwards, and vice versa.

Finding the equilibrium level of output

To find the level of E at each level of Y, we must add planned investment, I, to C. Suppose that I would be £25bn at every level of income, as shown in the fifth line of Table 19.3; the first four lines of this table merely repeat Table 19.2.

It may seem odd to suppose that I would be the same if output and incomes were high as it would be if output and incomes were low. However, I depends greatly on what firms expect to happen in the future. So investment can be high when output is low, if firms expect output to grow and so want much new capital; and investment can be low when output is high, if firms fear that output will fall and so want little new capital. By showing the same level of I at each output, the table says only that I is not necessarily low when output is low, or necessarily high when it is high.

Table 19.3 also shows the level of E, that is $C + I$, at each output level. If Y is £0bn, E is £50bn. If Y is £100bn higher at £100bn, E is £75bn more, at £125bn. The

Table 19.3 **Using a table to find the output level where $J = W$ and $E = Y$ in a two-sector economy**

			£bn	£bn	£bn	£bn
Output or GDP	Y		0	100	**200**	300
Disposable income	Y_{DIS}		0	100	**200**	300
Saving	S	$MPS_{DIS} = 0.25$	–25	0	**25**	50
Consumers' expenditure	C	$MPC_{DIS} = 0.75$	25	100	**175**	250
Investment	I		25	25	**25**	25
Total expenditure	E	$MPE_Y = 0.75$	50	125	**200**	275
Injections	$J = I$		25	25	**25**	25
Withdrawals	$W = S$	$MPW_Y = 0.25$	–25	0	**25**	50

fraction of any rise in Y or GDP that people plan to spend is the **marginal propensity to spend out of GDP,** MPE_Y. Because E here rises by three-quarters as much as any rise in output, MPE_Y is 0.75. The reason that E in this example rises by £75 million when output rises by £100bn is that C rises by £75bn while I remains unchanged.

Table 19.3 also shows the level of J and W at each output. J is constant at £25bn, but W rises by £25bn for each £100bn rise in Y. The fraction of any rise in Y or GDP that people plan to withdraw is the **marginal propensity to withdraw out of GDP,** MPW_Y. As W rises here by a quarter as much as any rise in Y, MPW_Y is 0.25. The reason W rises by £25 million when Y rises by £100bn is that S rises by £25bn.

Let's see what would occur at each level of output.

- $Y =$ **£0bn** or $Y =$ **£100bn** a month: in each of these cases, J would exceed W and E would exceed Y. We have seen that, in such a situation, firms would produce more in future.
- $Y =$ **£200bn**: here, J would equal W and E would equal Y. We have seen that, in this situation, firms would maintain their current output levels.
- $Y =$ **£300bn**: here, J would be less than W and E would be less than Y. We have seen that, in this situation, firms would produce less in future.

In short, if output is below £200bn it will rise, and if it is above £200bn it will fall. So output will eventually settle at £200bn and stay at £200bn, making this the equilibrium level, which we call Y_E.

Showing the equilibrium output on diagrams

Although we can find Y_E using a table, as we have just seen, we can also use diagrams, and economists prefer diagrams because they can then find Y_E more quickly. We can actually use two alternative diagrams, and Figure 19.6 shows both. One diagram concerns E and Y, while the other concerns J and W. Because the two diagrams relate to the same economy, they each give the same equilibrium output, Y_E.

The top part of Figure 19.6 measures Y on the horizontal axis and E on the vertical axis. As in Figure 19.4, there is a 45° line, but this now shows points where Y would equal E. The figure repeats the C line from Figure 19.4, and then adds a curve labelled E to show total planned spending at each output. This simply adds investment of £25bn to consumption. For example: if Y is £100bn, so that C is also £100bn, then E is £125bn.

To find the output where E equals Y, we see where the E line intersects the 45° line. At this point, output is £200bn. This means that *if* output were £200bn a month, E would also be £200bn. At lower outputs, the E line is above the 45° line, so E is higher than Y; for example, if Y is £100bn, E is £125bn. At higher outputs, the E line is below the 45° line, so E is less than Y; for

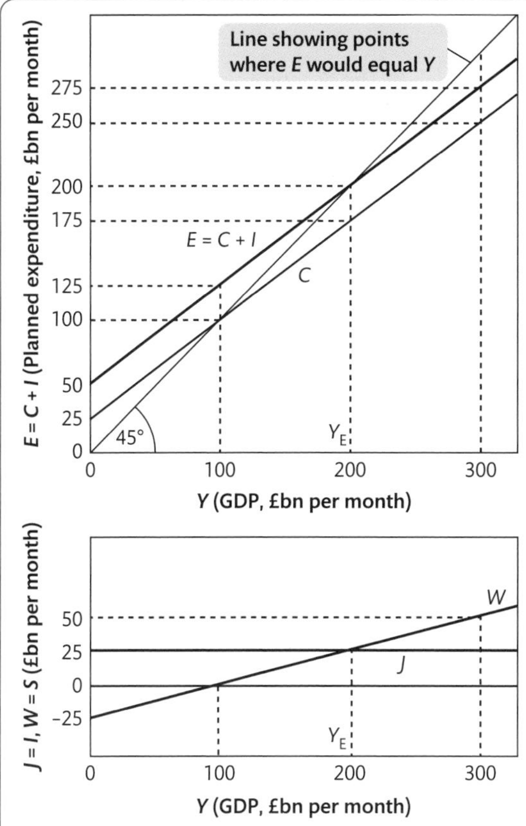

Figure 19.6 **Equilibrium output in a two-sector economy**

Planned spending here is *C* + *I*. The top part shows that the equilibrium output level, Y_E, is the level where planned expenditure would equal *Y*. The bottom part shows that the equilibrium level for *Y* is also the level where planned withdrawals, *W*, would equal planned injections, *J*.

example, if *Y* is £300bn, *E* is £250bn. Output settles at £200bn because it is the only output where *E* = *Y*. So the equilibrium output, Y_E, is £200bn per month.

The bottom part of Figure 19.6 measures *Y* on the horizontal axis and both *W* and *J* on the vertical axis. The horizontal line labelled *J* shows that injections are £25bn at each output level. The sloping line labelled *W* shows withdrawals at each level of output. For example, it shows that if *Y* is £100bn, then *W* are £0bn.

The point at which the two lines intersect shows the level of output where *J* equals *W*, which here is £200bn. At lower outputs, the withdrawals line is below the injections line, so *J* exceeds *W*. At higher outputs, the withdrawals line is above the injections line, so *W* exceeds *J*. Output settles at Y_E, which is £200bn, because it is the only output where injections equal withdrawals.

Autonomous and induced expenditure

In the top part of Figure 19.6, the point at which the *E* line meets the vertical axis shows that if output were £0bn, then planned spending would be £50bn. The planned spending that would arise if output were zero is called **autonomous expenditure**. It has two components as follows

- **The consumer spending that would be planned if output were £0bn**. This spending is called **autonomous consumption**; it would be financed by dissaving. If autonomous consumption were to increase or were to decrease, then the consumption function would shift up or down.
- **Injections**. In a two-sector economy, these come only in the form of investment.

If output rises above £0bn, then *E* rises above the autonomous level of £50bn. This is because a rise in output leads to higher wages and profits, which induce people to consume more. Any planned spending beyond the autonomous level is called **induced expenditure**.

For example, if output was £100bn per month, so that planned spending was £125bn, then planned spending would be £75bn above the autonomous level of £50bn, so induced spending would be £75bn. The amount by which induced expenditure rises when output rises depends on the marginal propensity for expenditure out of output, MPE_Y, which here is 0.75. For example, a rise in output of £100bn from £0bn to £100bn leads to a £75bn rise in planned spending from £50bn to £125bn.

19.3 Summary

- Output is in equilibrium if $E = Y$ and, equivalently, if $J = W$. There is only one output level at which this occurs, so output will eventually settle in equilibrium at this level. We can find this level on diagrams by seeing where the E line intersects the 45° line or where the J line intersects the W line.
- The extent to which consumer expenditure and saving rise when disposable incomes rise are given by the consumption and saving functions, and depend on the marginal propensities to consume and save out of disposable income.
- The planned spending that would arise if output were zero is called autonomous expenditure. All other planned spending is called induced expenditure.

19.4 Changes in output in a two-sector economy

Why the equilibrium output may change

Figure 19.6 illustrated the factors that determine the equilibrium level of output, Y_E, in a two-sector economy. But in any economy, Y_E alters from time to time. It does so in three situations:

- **if the extent to which increases in output induce more expenditure changes;**
- **if injections change;**
- **if autonomous consumption changes, so that the consumption function shifts.**

We will now look at these in turn.

A change in induced expenditure

So far, we have assumed that if output rises by £100bn, so that wages and profits rise by £100bn, then induced consumer spending rises by £75bn. But suppose consumer behaviour changes and that, in future, each £100bn rise in output raises induced consumer spending by £80bn. To see the effects of this on planned spending, E, consider three possible outputs.

- **Y = £0bn**. Here, induced spending would still be £0bn, because induced spending arises only if output is greater than zero. Allowing for autonomous consumption of £25bn and investment of £25bn, total autonomous spending would still be £50bn and E would still be £50bn.
- **Y = £100bn**. Here, induced spending would be £80bn more than if output were £0bn, that is £80bn. Allowing also for autonomous spending of £50bn, E would be £130bn.
- **Y = £200bn**. Here, induced spending would be £80bn more than if output were £100bn, that is £160bn. Allowing also for autonomous spending of £50bn, E would be £210bn.

Figure 19.7 shows the effect on output. For the original position, this figure reproduces in black the E, J and W lines from Figure 19.6 and labels them E_0, W_0, and J. The initial equilibrium output, Y_0, is £200bn per month.

In the top part of the figure, the change in induced expenditure creates a new expenditure curve, E_1. Notice that E_1 is steeper than E_0. Like E_0, the point where E_1 meets the vertical axis shows that autonomous expenditure is £50bn. But if Y is more than £0bn, then, as we have just seen, planned spending will be higher than before. For example, E_1 shows that planned spending would be £130bn if Y were £100bn.

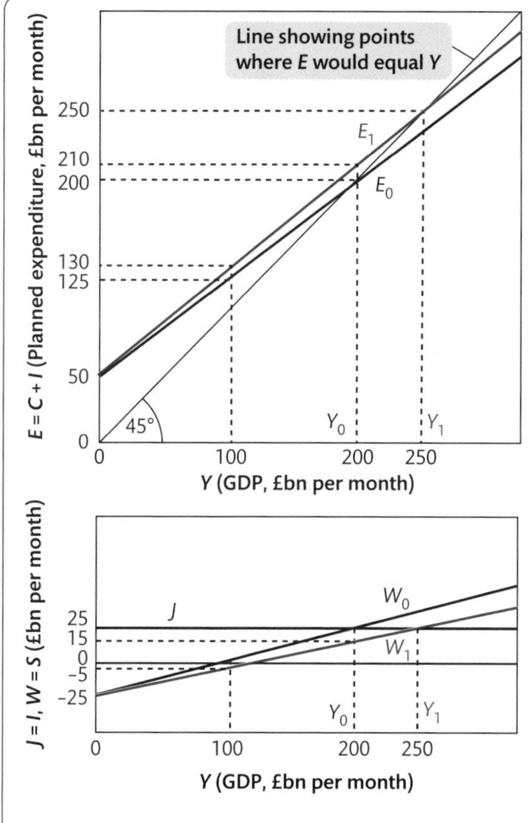

Figure 19.7 **A change in induced spending**

If more of each extra pound of income is spent and less is saved, then *E* pivots upwards and *W* pivots downwards. The equilibrium level of output rises to Y_1.

At the initial output, Y_0, of £200bn, *E* is now £210bn. This means that people want to buy more than firms are producing, so stocks will fall, or at least rise by less than firms want. So firms will raise output until it reaches the new equilibrium level, Y_1, where output will equal spending. This output is £250bn, where E_1 intersects the 45° line to show that *E* equals *Y*.

In the bottom part of Figure 19.7, the change in induced expenditure creates a new withdrawals line, W_1. To understand this line, consider three possible outputs.

- ***Y* = £0bn**. Here, withdrawals would be −£25bn because people would dissave that amount to finance their autonomous consumption of £25bn.
- ***Y* = £100bn**. Here, incomes would be £100m more than if *Y* were £0bn. However, people would now be induced to spend £80bn more, so they would save or withdraw only £20bn more, taking saving from −£25bn to −£5bn.
- ***Y* = £200bn**. Here, incomes would be £100m more than if *Y* were £100bn, but people would be induced to spend £80bn more, so they would save or withdraw only £20bn more, taking saving from −£5bn to £15bn.

At the initial Y_0 of £200bn, withdrawals are now only £15bn, but injections are still £25bn. This gap means that planned spending exceeds output, so stocks will fall, or at least rise less than firms want. So firms will raise output until it reaches the new equilibrium level, Y_1, at which withdrawals equal injections. This output is £250bn, where W_1 intersects the injections line, *J*, to show that withdrawals equal injections. The two parts of Figure 19.6 agree because they look at the same situation in different ways.

A change in injections

In a two-sector economy, injections come only in the form of investment, but the level of investment changes frequently. For example, if firms hear some news that makes them more confident about the future, then they will plan to invest more, so injections will rise.

Figure 19.8 shows the effect. The black lines E_0, J_0 and *W* reproduce *E*, *J* and *W* from Figure 19.6 to give the initial position. The initial equilibrium output, Y_0, is £200bn a month. Now suppose that firms decide to invest £50bn a month instead of £25bn.

In the top part of the figure, this rise in *I* shifts the *E* line up by £25bn from E_0 to E_1. At the initial Y_0 of £200bn, *E* is now £225bn, so people want to buy more than firms are producing and stocks will fall, or at least rise by less than firms want. So firms will raise output until *Y* equals *E*. This new equilibrium output, Y_1, is £300bn per month, where E_1 intersects the 45° line.

In the bottom part of Figure 19.8, the rise in investment shifts the *J* curve up by £25bn from J_0 to J_1. At the

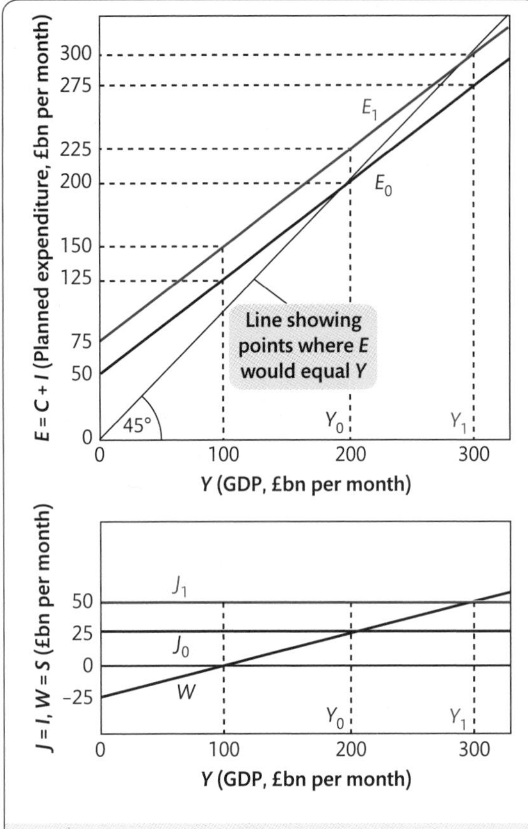

Figure 19.8 **A change in injections**

If injections rise by £25bn, then the E line in the top part and J in the bottom part both rise by £25bn. Output rises by £100bn from Y_0 to Y_1. In this example, output rises by four times as much as injections, so there is a multiplier equal to four.

initial Y_0 of £200bn, injections are now £50bn, but withdrawals are still £25bn. This gap means that planned spending exceeds output, so firms will raise output until W equals J. The new equilibrium output, Y_1, is again £300bn a month, where J_1 intersects W.

A rise in autonomous consumption

So far, we have assumed that autonomous consumption is £25bn. Suppose autonomous consumption rises to £50bn. Then, the consumption function will shift up by £25bn. In turn, $C + I$ will rise by £25bn, so that the planned expenditure line, E, shifts up by £25bn.

The effects are shown in Figure 19.9 where the black lines E_0, J_0 and W reproduce E, J and W from Figure 19.6 to give the initial position. The initial equilibrium output, Y_0, is £200bn a month.

In the top part of the figure, the rise in autonomous consumption shifts the E curve up by £25bn from E_0 to E_1. This is the same shift that we had in Figure 19.8. So Y rises by the same amount, £100bn, to £300bn.

The bottom part of Figure 19.9 shows the effect of a rise in autonomous consumption to £50bn by considering that if Y were £0bn, dissaving would now be £50bn instead of £25bn, so saving and withdrawals would be –£50bn instead of –£25bn. This change shifts the with-

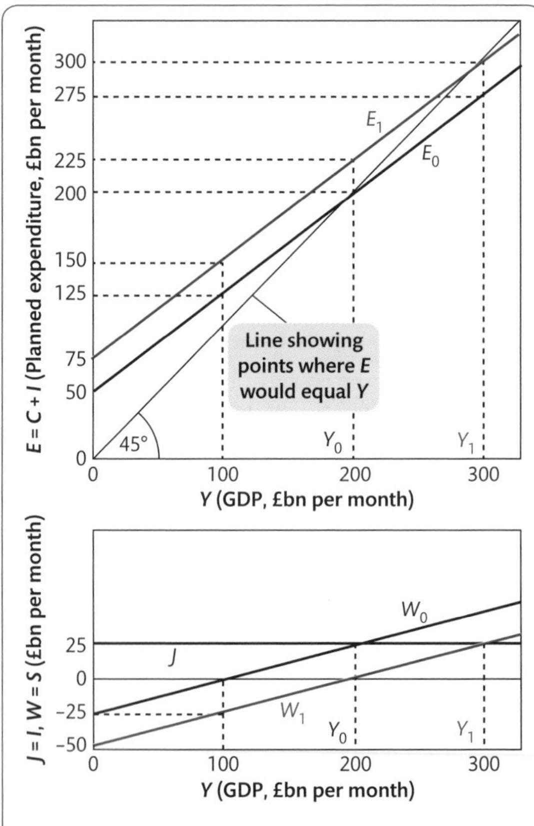

Figure 19.9 **A rise in autonomous consumption**

Recall that E here equals $C + I$. If autonomous consumption rises by £25bn, then the E line shifts up by £25bn. Also, saving falls by £25bn, so the W line shifts down by £25bn. Output rises by £100bn from Y_0 to Y_1. Output here changes by four times as much as the shifts in E and W, so there is a multiplier equal to four.

drawals line down by £25bn from W_0 to W_1. The new equilibrium Y_1, where J intersects W_1, is £300bn.

The multiplier

Figures 19.8 and 19.9 show that if autonomous spending rises by £25bn, whether this is a rise in injections or in autonomous consumption, then output rises by £100bn per month, from £200bn to £300bn. But why does output rise by more than £25bn? After all, in each case, spending and output both started at £200bn and then spending rose by £25bn. So why can't firms bring spending and output back into balance simply by raising output by £25bn to £225bn?

Initially, firms *will* raise output by just £25bn to £225bn. But when they do so, they will pay £25bn more in wages and profits. So then induced spending will rise and, in turn, planned spending will rise above the new output of £225bn. So firms will produce more again, and pay yet more in wages and profits. So induced spending will rise yet again. The whole process will continue until Y and E are equal at £300bn.

So a £25bn rise in autonomous expenditure leads to a £100bn rise in output. The rise in output divided by the rise in autonomous expenditure is called the **multiplier**, so here the multiplier is £100bn/£25bn, which is 4. This multiplier value helps us to work out the effect on output of *any* change in autonomous expenditure. For example, in an economy with a multiplier of 4, a £5bn fall in injections or in autonomous consumption will cause output to fall by four times as much, that is by £20bn. Because the multiplier is so useful, the model given in this chapter is called the multiplier model.

What determines the size of the multiplier?

We have just seen that, in this example, the multiplier is four. What determines its size? To answer this, recall that output was initially in equilibrium at £200bn, with expenditure also £200bn. Then spending rose by £25bn to £225bn, so that people now wanted £25bn more goods and services than firms were producing. So firms initially raised output by £25bn to £225bn. The only reason that they later raised output more was that, as their output expanded, they paid more wages and profits, so that disposable incomes rose; this induced higher consumer spending, so raising total spending again and encouraging yet more rise in output.

The size of the multiplier depends on how much consumer spending, and in turn total spending, will rise when wages and profits rise. In our example, Table 19.3 showed that MPE_Y is 0.75, so the initial rise in output of £25bn caused consumer spending and E to rise by 0.75 times as much, that is just under £19bn.

If MPE_Y had been higher, then there would have been a bigger effect on consumer spending and on E, and the multiplier would be more than 4. So the multiplier depends on MPE_Y, and there is a formula for it as follows.

In any economy, the multiplier $= 1/(1 - MPE_Y)$

In our example, this formula gives the multiplier as $1/(1 - 0.75)$ which is $1/0.25$, or 4.

Of course, any extra wages and profits that are not used to raise consumer spending and E are instead withdrawn. The degree to which income is withdrawn is given by MPW_Y, and the higher this is, the smaller is the multiplier. So there is another formula for the multiplier, as follows.

In any economy, the multiplier $= 1/MPW_Y$

In our example, Table 19.3 shows that MPW_Y is 0.25, so this formula gives the multiplier as $1/0.25$, or 4.

In a two-sector economy, Table 19.3 showed that $MPE_Y = MPC_{DIS}$ and that $MPW_Y = MPS_{DIS}$. So here we can use two more formulae, as follows.

In a two-sector economy, the multiplier also $= 1/(1 - MPC_{DTS})$ and $1/MPS_{DTS}$

Question 19.2 Suppose that, in a two-sector economy, $MPC_{DIS} = 0.80$. What are the values of (**a**) MPS_{DIS}, and (**b**) the multiplier?

Proving the multiplier formulae

Let's prove that the two multiplier formulae for any economy are correct. We will begin with the second formula, $1/MPW_Y$. To prove this, suppose injections change by ΔJ; the Greek letter delta (Δ) is often used for changes. This change in injections will cause the equilibrium level of Y to change, and we call the change ΔY. The value of the multiplier equals $\Delta Y/\Delta J$, and we can prove that this equals $1/MPW_Y$ as follows.

- The change in output, ΔY, will lead to a change in withdrawals, ΔW, equal to $\Delta Y.MPW_Y$. For example, in Figures 19.8 and 19.9, ΔY was £100bn and MPW_Y was 0.25, so ΔW was £25bn.
- In equilibrium, $J = W$. So when Y moves from one equilibrium to another, the change in withdrawals, ΔW, must equal the change in injections, ΔJ. So ΔJ must also equal $\Delta Y.MPW_Y$.
- To find the change in output needed to make $\Delta J = \Delta Y.MPW_Y$, divide both side of this equation by MPW_Y. This tells us that $\Delta J/MPW_Y = \Delta Y$ or, equivalently, that $\Delta Y = \Delta J/MPW_Y$.
- So $\Delta Y = \Delta J/MPW_Y$. If we divide both sides of this equation by ΔJ, we see that $\Delta Y/\Delta J = 1/MPW_Y$. $\Delta Y/\Delta J$ is the multiplier, so we have now proved that it equals $1/MPW_Y$ as in the second formula.

We can now prove the first formula for any economy.

- Remember that, when firms raise Y, and so pay out more wages and profits, the fraction of the extra income withdrawn is MPW_Y, which is 0.25 in our example. The remaining income is spent, so the fraction spent, MPE_Y, is 0.75.
- We can see that $(MPW_Y + MPE_Y) = 1$. If we subtract MPE_Y from each side of this equation, we find that $MPW_Y = (1 - MPE_Y)$.
- So, because the multiplier equals $1/MPW_Y$, it must also equal $1/(1 - MPE_Y)$, as in the first formula.

The paradox of thrift

To end this section, we will use the multiplier model to prove a very surprising result. Suppose that you become thriftier, so that you resolve to save more each month. Then you will indeed save more each month. Or suppose you become less thrifty and resolve to save less each month. Then you will indeed save less each month.

Surprisingly, though, if *everyone* in the country becomes thriftier and decides to save more each month, then between them they will *not* save any more each month. Likewise, if *everyone* decides to be less thrifty, then between them they will *not* save any less each month.

The fact that total saving does not alter if everyone becomes more or less thrifty is called the **paradox of thrift**. And the fact that the outcome if everyone does something is different from what we would predict on the basis of what happens if an individual does it means that we have a situation in which there is what is called a fallacy of composition.

We can check the paradox from Figures 19.7 and 19.9. Suppose we start with curves E_0, W_0, and J, so that output is £200bn and withdrawals and saving are £25bn. If households decide to spend more and save less, then the withdrawals line shifts down and the spending line shifts up. Depending on exactly how much households would plan to save at each output level, the new withdrawals line might pivot, as in Figure 19.7, or be parallel to the old one, as in Figure 19.9.

In each case, output rises, either to £250bn or £300bn, but the total level of withdrawals and saving stays at £25bn. Now suppose that, after some time, households decide to spend less and save more so that the withdrawals and spending curves move back to W_0 and E_0. Output falls back to £200bn, but still saving stays at £25bn!

Why doesn't saving fall if all people become less thrifty and save a smaller fraction of their disposable incomes? It is because they then buy more. So firms produce more and pay more wages and profits, so disposable income rises. So people end up saving a smaller fraction of a larger total income, and the total amount saved each month stays the same.

Likewise, if all people become thriftier and save a larger fraction of their disposable income, they then buy less. So firms produce less and pay fewer wages and profits, so disposable income falls. So people end up saving a larger fraction of a smaller total income, and again the total amount saved each month stays the same.

19.4 Summary

- A country's output changes if there is a change in the extent to which rises in income induce more expenditure.
- A country's output also changes if there is a change in the level of autonomous expenditure, whether autonomous consumption or injections. In each case, output changes by the change in autonomous spending times the multiplier.
- The multiplier in any economy equals (a) $1/MPW_Y$, and (b) $1/(1 - MPE_Y)$, where MPW_Y and MPE_Y are the marginal propensities to spend and withdraw out of GDP. In a two-sector economy, these expressions are equivalent to (a) $1/MPS_{DIS}$, and (b) $1/(1 - MPC_{DIS})$, where MPS_{DIS} and MPC_{DIS} are the marginal propensities to save and consume out of disposable income.
- The paradox of thrift refers to the fact that if everyone increases—or reduces—the fraction of disposable income that they save, then the total amount saved in any period of time is unchanged.

19.5 The multiplier model in a four-sector economy

We now turn to a four-sector economy with a government sector and a foreign sector. We can use an identical analysis to find the equilibrium level of output, as shown in Figure 19.10.

In the top part of this figure, E_0 shows the initial planned spending at each output level, and the 45° line shows points at which E would equal Y. In the lower part, W_0 and J show the initial withdrawals and injections at each output. The equilibrium output is £200bn a month, where E intersects the 45° line, and where W_0 intersects J. At any other output, planned spending would not equal output, and withdrawals would not equal injections, so, as we saw in Table 19.1, output would change.

The only differences between the two-sector case and the four-sector case are that the four-sector case has more components in E, J and W, and that this leads to more complicated formulae for the multiplier. Let's explore this.

Planned spending in a four-sector economy

We saw in section 19.2 that, in a four-sector economy, $E = C + I + G + X - M$. Table 19.4 gives an example to show all the factors that determine E in a four-sector economy at four possible output levels: £0bn, £100bn, £200bn, and £300bn a month. The top part of the table uses six lines to derive C, that is customers' expenditure at factor cost.

- **Wages plus profits**. This always equals output, Y.
- **Taxes on income**. In this example, the amount taken by the government in taxes on income, minus the amount it pays in transfers, is always a fifth of Y, leaving disposable income at four-fifths of Y. So if Y rises by £100bn, taxes net of transfers rise by £20bn, and disposable income Y_{DIS} rises by £80bn. For example, if Y rises from £0bn to £100bn, Y_{DIS} rises

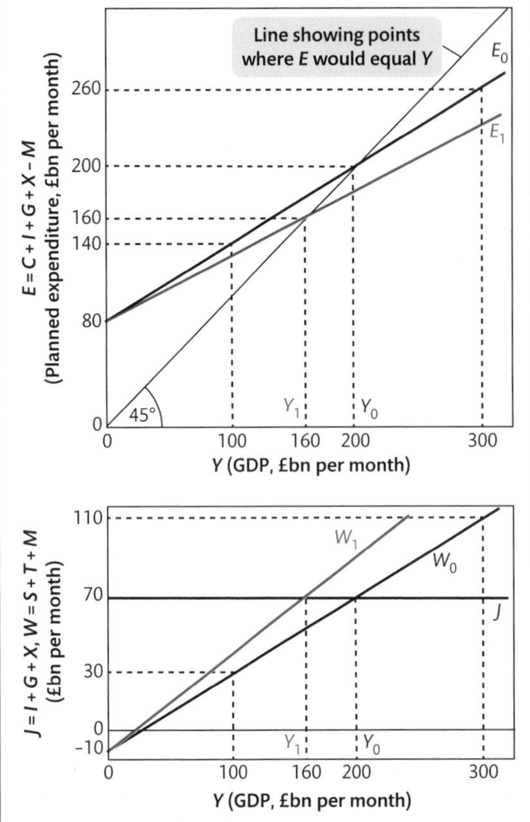

Figure 19.10 **Equilibrium in a four-sector economy, and a change in induced spending**

Output is initially £200bn, where E_0 intersects the 45° line and W_0 intersects J. If people decide to withdraw a larger fraction of any rise in incomes, then the withdrawals line in the bottom part gets steeper, while the spending line in the top part gets flatter. In this example, output falls to £160bn.

from £0bn to £80bn. The fraction of a rise in Y or GDP that governments plan to take in taxes on income net of transfers is the **marginal propensity for taxes on income out of GDP**, $MPTY_Y$, and here it is 0.20.

- **Saving**. In this example, if disposable incomes were £0bn, households would dissave £12bn, or save −£12bn, and spend £12bn at market prices (MP). The table gives the MPS_{DIS} for the example as 0.10, so people would save the fraction 0.10 of any rise in Y_{DIS}. So if Y_{DIS} rises from £0bn to £80bn, planned saving rises by 0.10 × £80bn, that is £8bn, from −£12bn to −£4bn.
- **Consumers' expenditure at market prices**. This equals Y_{DIS} minus saving. As the fraction of a rise in Y_{DIS} that people plan to save is 0.10, the fraction that they plan to spend is the other 0.90, so the marginal propensity to consume out of disposable income, MPC_{DIS}, is 0.90. So if Y_{DIS} rises from £0bn to £80bn, planned consumer spending at market prices rises by 0.90 of this, that is by £72bn, from £12bn to £84bn.
- **Taxes on expenditure**. The government takes some consumer spending for itself with its taxes on expenditure, and it returns much less with its subsidies. In Table 19.4, the government takes with these taxes, net of subsidies, £1bn for every £12bn of spending at market prices. So if output rises from £0bn to £100bn, and consumer spending at market prices rises by £72bn from £12bn to £84bn, these taxes rise by £6bn from £1bn to £7bn. The fraction of a rise in GDP or Y that governments plan to take in taxes on expenditure net of subsidies is the **marginal propensity for taxes on expenditure out of GDP**, $MPTE_Y$; here it is £6bn/£100bn, or 0.06.
- **Consumers' expenditure at factor cost**. Allowing for taxes on expenditure, Table 19.4 shows that if output here rises from £0bn to £100bn, consumer spending at factor cost (FC) rises by £66bn from £11bn to £77bn. The fraction of a rise in GDP or Y that households plan to spend at factor cost is the **marginal propensity to consume out of GDP**, MPC_Y; here, 0.66.

The middle part of Table 19.4 works out E. It repeats from the top part consumer spending at factor cost, C, and then allows for the following.

- **Investment, I**. We saw earlier that investment will not necessarily be low if output is low, or high if output is high. In the table, its value is shown as the same, £25bn, at each output.

Table 19.4 **Using a table to find the output level where $J = W$ and $E = Y$ in a four-sector economy**

			£bn	£bn	£bn	£bn
Output, equals wages plus profits	Y		0	100	**200**	300
Taxes on income	T_Y	$MPTY_Y = 0.20$	0	20	**40**	60
Disposable income	Y_{DIS}		0	80	**160**	240
Saving	S	$MPS_{DIS} = 0.10$	−12	−4	**4**	12
Consumers' expenditure at *MP*	C *at MP*	$MPC_{DIS} = 0.90$	12	84	**156**	228
Taxes on expenditure	T_E	$MPTE_Y = 0.06$	1	7	**13**	19
Consumers' expenditure at *FC*	C *at FC*	$MPC_Y = 0.66$	11	77	**143**	209
Consumers' expenditure at *FC*	C *at FC*	$MPC_Y = 0.66$	11	77	**143**	209
Investment	I		25	25	**25**	25
Government purchases	G		25	25	**25**	25
Exports	X		20	20	**20**	20
Imports	M	$MPM_Y = 0.06$	−1	−7	**−13**	−19
Total expenditure	$E = C + I + G + X - M$	$MPE_Y = 0.60$	80	140	**200**	260
Injections	$J = I + G + X$		70	70	**70**	70
Saving	S	$MPS_Y = 0.08$	−12	−4	**4**	12
Taxes	$T = T_Y + T_E$	$MPT_Y = 0.26$	1	27	**53**	79
Imports	M	$MPM_Y = 0.06$	1	7	**13**	19
Withdrawals	$W = S + T + M$	$MPW_Y = 0.40$	−10	30	**70**	110

- **Government purchases, *G*.** The value of these is set by the government and will not necessarily rise if output rises or fall if output falls. The table shows a value of £25bn at each output.
- **Exports, *X*.** The value of these depends on people abroad and will not necessarily rise if output rises or fall if output falls. The table shows a value of £20bn at each output.
- **Imports, *M*.** Some consumer spending at factor cost is spent on imports, *M*. In the example in Table 19.4, one-eleventh of it is spent on imports. So if output rises from £0 to £100bn, and consumer spending at factor cost rises from £11bn to £77bn, then imports rise from £1bn to £7bn, that is by £6bn. The fraction of a rise in GDP or *Y* that people plan to spend on imports is the **marginal propensity to import out of GDP**, MPM_Y; here it is £6bn/£100bn, or 0.06.

The middle part of Table 19.4 concludes that if *Y* is £0bn, £100bn, £200bn, or £300bn a month, then *E* will be £80bn, £140bn, £200bn, or £260bn. These values are shown by the line E_0 in Figure 19.10.

Equilibrium output

The equilibrium output level of output, Y_E, is the level at which planned spending equals output. The lines for *Y* and *E* in Table 19.4 shows that $E = Y$ only if output level is £200bn, so Y_E is £200bn. This result can also be found using Figure 19.10 because E_0 intersects the 45° line at an output of £200bn.

We know that the equilibrium level of output is also the level at which injections equal withdrawals. To find the output where $J = W$, we must work out what *J* and *W* would be at each output. The bottom part of Table 19.4 does this as follows.

- **Injections.** Section 19.2 showed that, in a four-sector economy, $J = I + G + X$. We can work out from the middle part of Table 19.4 that $I + G + X$

equals £70bn at each output level, and this is recorded in the bottom part of the table.

- **Withdrawals**. Section 19.2 showed that, in a four-sector economy, $W = S + T + M$. The bottom part of Table 19.4 repeats the figures for S from the top part. S rises by £8bn for each £100bn rise in Y. The fraction of a rise in GDP or Y that people plan to save is the **marginal propensity to save out of GDP**, MPS_Y; here it is 0.08. Taxes, T, equal $T_Y + T_E$. T_Y and T_E are each shown in the top part of the table, and the bottom part gives their combined value. T rises by £26bn for each £100bn rise in Y. The fraction of a rise in GDP or Y that governments plan to take in all taxes net of transfers and subsidies is the **marginal propensity for taxes out of GDP**, MPT_Y; here it is 0.26. Finally, the bottom part repeats from the middle part the value of M at each level of output, and recalls that MPM_Y is 0.06.

The last line of Table 19.4 gives the total value of withdrawals, W, at each output. Four lines above the table gives the total value of injections, J. We can see from these lines in the table that $J = W$ if output is £200bn, so this is the equilibrium output, Y_E. This result can also be found using the bottom part of Figure 19.10, where the lines J_0 and W show injections and withdrawals at each output. Injections equal withdrawals at the output of £200bn where these lines intersect.

The multiplier in a four-sector economy

The multiplier in a four-sector economy can be found from the two formulae that apply to any economy.

The multiplier equals $1/(1 - MPE_Y)$

The multiplier equals $1/MPW_Y$

For our example, the middle part of Table 19.4 shows that $MPE_Y = 0.6$, so the first formula gives the multiplier as $1/(1 - 0.6)$, which is $1/0.4$, or 2.5. And the bottom part of the table shows that $MPW_Y = 0.4$, so again the multiplier is $1/0.4$, or 2.5.

Also, we can deduce from the central part of Table 19.4 that $MPE_Y = (MPC_Y - MPM_Y)$, and we can deduce from the bottom part that $MPW_Y = (MPS_Y + MPT_Y + MPM_Y)$. So we can re-express the two formulae as follows:

The multiplier equals $1/(1 - (MPC_Y - MPM_Y))$

The multiplier equals $1/(MPS_Y + MPT_Y + MPM_Y)$

Note that the multiplier in a four-sector economy does *not* also equal $1/(1 - MPC_{DIS})$ because MPC_{DIS} and MPE_Y are different in this case: indeed, in the example in Table 19.4, $MPC_{DIS} = 0.9$ and $MPE_Y = 0.6$.

Changes in output

As in a two-sector economy, the equilibrium output, Y_E, alters in three situations. We will look at these in turn:

- **if the extent to which increases in output induce more expenditure changes;**
- **if injections change;**
- **if autonomous consumption changes, so that the consumption function shifts.**

A change in induced expenditure

We know that, when output rises, wages and profits rise, but consumer spending rises by less than the rise in incomes because a fraction of the extra income is withdrawn from the circular flow. Suppose that this fraction increases. This means that MPW_Y will increase, while MPE_Y will decrease.

These changes could arise because of changes in peoples' plans about any withdrawals, as follows.

- **Saving**: consumers may decide to save larger fractions of any increases in income.
- **Taxes**: governments may decide to set higher tax rates, or to reduce transfers or subsidies.
- **Imports**: consumers may decide to buy more products from producers in other countries.

The fall in MPE_Y will make the planned spending line flatter, while the rise in MPW_Y will make the withdrawals line steeper. Suppose these lines end up as shown in Figure 19.10 by E_1 in the top part and W_1 in the bottom part. Then output will fall to £160bn, where E_1 now equals Y and W_1 equals J.

Question 19.3 If the rate of value added tax is increased, which way will the E line shift? Will output rise or fall? How would this result be derived on the injections and withdrawals figure?

A change in injections

Suppose, instead, that injections change. Suppose they fall by £20bn because of a decrease in investment, government purchases, or exports. Figure 19.11 shows the effects. This figure repeats the black lines from Figure 19.10 to show the initial output of £200bn. Then the fall in injections shifts the spending line in the top part down by £20bn to E_1, and it shifts the injections line in the bottom part down by £20bn to J_1.

Each part shows the equilibrium output falling by £50bn to Y_1 of £150bn. Yet injections fell by just £20bn. So the multiplier is £50bn/£20bn, which is 2.5, as we have just calculated.

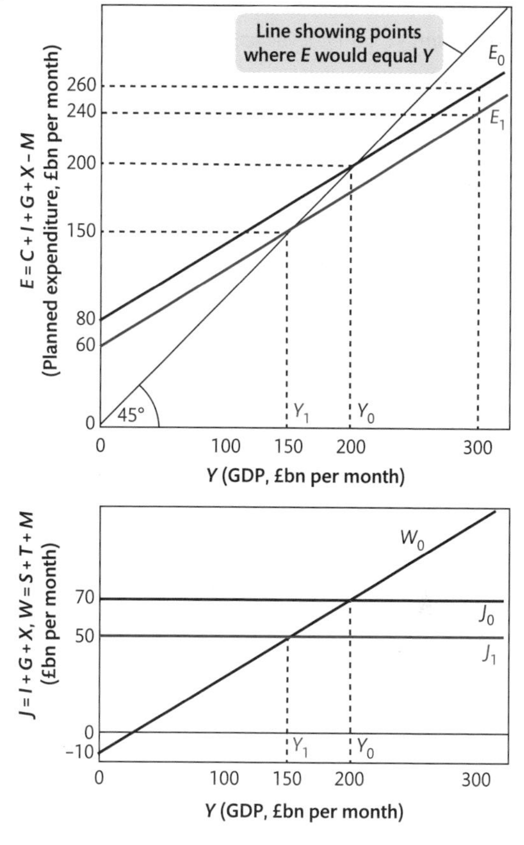

Figure 19.11 **A change in injections**

Output starts at £200bn, where E_0 intersects the 45° line and W intersects J_0. If injections fall by £20bn, then the expenditure and injections lines shift down by £20bn to E_1 and J_1, and equilibrium output falls by £50bn to £150bn. Output falls by 2.5 times as much as injections, as the multiplier here is 2.5.

Question 19.4 If the government spends less on defence, which way will the E line shift? Will output rise or fall? How would this result be derived on the injections and withdrawals figure?

A change in autonomous consumption

We saw in the last section that changes in autonomous consumption shift the consumption function and, in turn, the E line, and also shift the W line. For example, suppose that autonomous consumption falls by £1bn. At each level of output, consumption will be £1bn lower, so the E line will shift down by £1bn; at each level of output, saving will be £1bn higher, so the W line will shift up by £1bn. These shifts are too small to illustrate, but, with a multiplier of 2.5, will reduce output by £2.5bn.

The balanced budget multiplier

We know that if government purchases increase, then injections rise and output rises; we also know that if the government increases its taxes, then withdrawals rise and output falls. Often, if a government decides to spend more, say £25bn more, then it tries to raise £25bn more in taxes to finance its extra spending.

In this case, the expenditure and revenue sides of the government's budget account change by equal amounts, which is a **balanced budget change**.

You might suppose that a balanced budget change will not affect output: it might seem that while a £25bn rise in G will shift E up by £25bn, a £25bn rise in T will make people consume £25bn less, and so shift E back down by £25bn.

In fact, the balanced budget increase will shift E up, causing output to rise. The reason is that if households lose £25bn worth of disposable income each month in higher taxes, then they will save a little less each month, and so manage to cut their consumer spending, C, by less than £25bn. So C will fall less than G rises. So E will rise a little and the E line will shift up a little, and output will rise by the amount of this shift times the multiplier.

We can reach a similar conclusion by thinking about injections and withdrawals. Injections will rise by the full £25bn of the extra G. But withdrawals will rise by the extra £25bn in taxes minus the fall in saving. So the W line will shift up less than the J line, and so output will rise.

The change in the equilibrium output level divided by the balanced budget change that caused it to change is called the **balanced budget multiplier**. For example, if the budget were to rise by £25bn and Y eventually rise by £20bn, then the balanced budget multiplier would be £20bn/£25bn, or 0.8. The size of the balanced budget multiplier depends on which taxes are raised. In some cases, it could even be more than one, but usually it is less.

Question 19.5 Would £100bn more government spending on state pensions have the same effect on output as £100bn more government spending on purchases?

19.5 Summary

- Output is in equilibrium if $E = Y$, where E is given by $C + I + G + X - M$. Equivalently, output is in equilibrium if $J = W$, where J is given by $I + G + X$ and W by $S + T + M$. Output changes if there a change in induced expenditure, or a change in injections, or a change in autonomous consumption.
- A change in injections or autonomous consumption causes output to change by a multiplied amount: the size of the multiplier is given by (a) $1/MPW_Y$, and (b) $1/(1 - MPE_Y)$, where MPW_Y and MPE_Y are the marginal propensities to withdraw and spend out of GDP.
- If government spending and tax revenue rise (or fall) by the same amount, so that there is a balanced budget change for the government, then output will rise (or fall).

19.2 Everyday economics

Job losses in the public sector

Figures issues by the Office for National Statistics showed that more than 130,000 workers for central and local government lost their jobs within the past year. Over half of these were people who had worked in local government. Another 170,000 local government workers were told that their jobs are at risk. Admittedly, there was some rise in private sector jobs, but not enough to offset the fall in public sectors jobs.

'Public sector job cuts top 132,000', *The Guardian*, 16 March 2011
'UK public sector lay-offs accelerate', *Daily Finance*, 17 March 2011

Comment When government workers lose their jobs, the multiplier model argues that their disposable incomes will fall, so they will spend less; then, if everything else stays the same, total consumer spending will fall, so firms will produce less and also shed jobs. In fact, firms were hiring more workers: this suggests that total consumer spending was rising, despite the fall in the income of redundant government workers. But if many more public sector workers are made redundant, consumer spending in future could well fall.

In the next chapter we look at money and banks. This helps us to understand what determines interest rates in an economy. Interest rates play an important role in determining both consumption and investment.

abc Glossary

Autonomous consumption: the consumer spending that would be planned if *Y* were zero.

Autonomous expenditure: the spending that would be planned if *Y* were zero.

Balanced budget change: a change in the government's budget, under which tax revenue and spending rise or fall by identical amounts.

Balanced budget multiplier: the ratio of the change in the equilibrium level of output to the balanced budget change that caused output to change.

Consumption function: the relationship between planned consumers' expenditure and disposable income.

Disposable income: income that households can dispose of by spending or saving; it is measured as total household income minus taxes paid to the government plus transfers from the government.

Dissaving: taking money from past savings.

Induced expenditure: planned spending beyond autonomous expenditure; it is induced by a level of income and GDP that is greater than zero.

Injections: spending that flows into the circular flow, comprising panned investment (including increases in stocks), government purchases, and exports.

Investment: expenditure on adding to stocks or inventories, plus expenditure on new capital goods.

Marginal propensity for taxes on expenditure out of GDP ($MPTE_Y$): the fraction of a rise in GDP or *Y* that governments plan to take in taxes on expenditure, net of subsidies.

Marginal propensity for taxes on GDP (MPT_Y): the fraction of a rise in GDP or *Y* that governments plan to take in all taxes, net of transfers and subsidies; $MPT_Y = MPTY_Y + MPTE_Y$.

Marginal propensity for taxes on income out of GDP ($MPTY_Y$): the fraction of a rise in GDP or *Y* that governments plan to take in taxes on income net of transfers.

Marginal propensity to consume out of disposable income (MPC_{DIS}): the fraction of a rise in disposable income that households plan to spend.

Marginal propensity to consume out of GDP (MPC_Y): the fraction of a rise in GDP or *Y* that households plan to spend on consumer expenditure.

Marginal propensity to import out of GDP (MPM_Y): the fraction of a rise in GDP or *Y* that people plan to spend on imports.

Marginal propensity to save out of disposable income (MPS_{DIS}): the fraction of a rise in disposable income that households plan to save.

Marginal propensity to save out of GDP (MPS_Y): the fraction of a rise in GDP or *Y* that people plan to save.

Marginal propensity to spend out of GDP, (MPE_Y): the fraction of a rise in GDP or *Y* that people plan to spend.

Marginal propensity to withdraw out of GDP (MPW_Y): the fraction of a rise in GDP or *Y* that people plan to withdraw.

Multiplier: the change in output divided by the change in autonomous expenditure that caused output to change; it equals $1/MPW_Y$ and also $1/(1\text{-}MPE_Y)$, where $MPW_Y = (MPS_Y + MPT_Y + MPM_Y)$ and $MPE_Y = (MPC_Y - MPM_Y)$.

Paradox of thrift: the fact that total saving does not alter if everyone becomes more or less thrifty.

Saving function: the relationship between planned consumer saving and disposable income.

Withdrawals: income that flows out of the circular flow, comprising planned saving, taxes (net of transfers and subsidies), and imports.

Answers to in-text questions

19.1 In the month when injections change, J will be less than W, so E will be less than Y. This means that stocks will rise more than planned. So we would expect producers to produce less next month.

19.2 **(a)** In a two-sector economy, income is either used for consumer spending or saved. So if $MPC_{DIS} = 0.80$, meaning that 80% of any rise in income is used for consumer spending, the remaining 20% must be saved, so $MPS_{DIS} = 0.20$. **(b)** The multiplier equals $1/(1 - MPC_{DIS})$, which is $1/(1 - 0.8)$, that is 1/0.2 or 5. The multiplier also equals $1/MPS_{DIS}$, which is 1/0.2 or 5.

19.3 If VAT is increased, people will buy fewer goods and services, so consumer spending at factor cost, C, will fall, in turn reducing E (as $E = C + I + G + X - M$); so the E line shifts down and output falls. On the injections and withdrawals figure, W rises as $W = S + T + M$ and T has risen, so output falls—but note that consumers will no doubt react to the rise in T by slightly reducing S, and this fall in S means W will rise by slightly less than the rise in T.

19.4 Spending on defence is included under government purchases from government departments. So a fall in this spending reduces G, which in turn reduces E (as $E = C + I + G + X - M$) and shifts the E line down, causing output to fall. On the injections and withdrawals figure, J would fall (as $J = I + G + X$) and again the equilibrium output would be lower.

19.5 If state pensions were to rise, some of the increased income may be saved, especially by younger pensioners looking ahead; so C will rise by less than £100 billion. But if government purchases were to rise by £100 billion, G would rise by the full £100 billion, so there would be more effect on E and, in turn, on Y.

Questions for review

19.1 Take a two-sector economy. Suppose that autonomous consumption is 10 per month and that induced consumption is $0.9Y$. So $C = 10 + 0.9Y$, which means that $S = -10 + 0.1Y$. Suppose also that $I = 20$ at all levels of Y, so that $C + I$, or E, equals $30 + 0.9Y$.

(a) What is the total level of autonomous spending?

(b) What are the values of MPC_Y, MPE_Y, MPS_Y, and MPW_Y?

(c) The equilibrium level of output is the one at which $E = Y$. At what level of Y will $30 + 0.9Y = Y$?

(d) What will J and W be at this level?

(e) Use both formulae for the multiplier in any economy to work out its value.

(f) Suppose that autonomous spending falls by 10. By how much will Y fall?

(g) Suppose that autonomous spending stays as it was initially, but induced consumers' expenditure falls to $0.8Y$. What will the new level of Y be? What will the new value of the multiplier be?

19.2 Take a four-sector economy in which $T_Y = 0.1Y$ so that $Y_{DIS} = 0.9Y$. Households split their disposable income of $0.9Y$ so that saving, S, equals $-10 + 0.1Y$, and consumer spending at market prices equals $10 + 0.8Y$. $T_E = 0.1Y$, so consumer spending at factor cost, C, is $10 + 0.7Y$. At all levels of Y, $I = 20$, $G = 30$, and $X = 40$. Finally, $M = 0.1Y$. So E, which equals $C + I + G + X - M$, equals $100 + 0.6Y$. Also, W, which equal $S + T + M$, that is $S + T_Y + T_E + M$, equals $-10 + 0.1Y + 0.1Y + 0.1Y + 0.1Y$, which is $-10 + 0.4Y$.

(a) What is the total level of autonomous spending?

(b) What are the values of MPC_Y, MPE_Y, and MPW_Y?

(c) The equilibrium level of output is the one at which $E = Y$. At what level of Y will $100 + 0.6Y = Y$?

(d) What will J and W be at this level?

(e) Use both formulae for the multiplier in any economy to find its value.

(f) Suppose that autonomous spending rises by 20. By how much will Y rise?

(g) Suppose instead that the country does more trade, and that X rises from 40 to 50 and M rises from $0.1Y$ to $0.2Y$. What is the new equilibrium output?

? Questions for discussion

19.1 Explain which components of *E* and *W* would change if the government were to alter (**a**) its income tax rates, (**b**) its tobacco tax rate, (**c**) Jobseeker's Allowance, (**d**) subsidies on home insulation, and (**e**) its spending on the National Health Service.

19.2 Bearing in mind that the multiplier in a four-sector economy equals $1/MPW_Y$, what changes in household behaviour would lead to the multiplier becoming higher? How could the government encourage these changes, if it wished to do so?

X Common student errors

Students often confuse planned withdrawals and injections with actual withdrawals and injections. The total values of actual withdrawals and actual injections must be equal. The total values of planned withdrawals and planned injections can be unequal; when this happens, total planned expenditure differs from output, and then output will change. Every graph showing withdrawals and injections refers to planned withdrawals and planned injections.

20

Money, Banks, and Interest Rates

How did coins and banknotes evolve? Are bank deposits also money, or are they simply places where money is stored? How safe are banks? Were banks to blame for the 2007 credit crunch? What determines the total amount of money in the country? How is this related to the level of interest rates in the economy? How can the Bank of England alter the money stock and also alter interest rates?

This chapter shows you how to answer questions like these, by understanding:

- how money has developed into the forms we use today;
- the importance of banks and how they work;
- how banks create over 97% of the money that we use;
- the causes and effects of the 2007 credit crunch;
- the factors that determine the stock of money and interest rates in the country;
- how the Bank of England can change the stock of money and interest rates in the country.

20.1 A brief history of money

People who are not economists often imagine that economics is entirely about money, so they might be surprised that we have left a discussion of money until so far in the book. However, we saw in Chapter 1 that economics studies consumption and production. Economists are interested in money only because the quantity of money that there is in a country may affect the levels of production and consumption that take place in it.

In this section, we look at the early development of money. Later sections explain the following:

- **how banks can create money**;
- **how banks operate, and why they got into difficulties in the 2007 credit crunch**;
- **how the total quantity of money in the economy, and also interest rates, can be changed**.

From barter to money

Humans can produce and consume without using any money at all. One way of doing this is to be self-sufficient, so that families or other groups produce for themselves all the food, clothes, and other items that they want to consume. But there are three reasons why humans wish to go beyond self-sufficiency and trade with other people.

- **There are some things people cannot produce for themselves.** For example, people might wish to use minerals that are not locally available, and to consume medicines that they do not have the skills and knowledge to make.
- **Some people are relatively good at making some products.** For example, if one person is skilled at making boats and another at growing crops, then their combined output of boats and crops, and in turn their combined consumption, will be higher if they specialize in producing the products they are good at. But then they must trade in order to be able to consume both products.
- **Mass production often leads to lower costs.** Writing in 1776, Adam Smith gave an example of a pin factory, where ten workers using mass production techniques made 48,000 pins a day; working individually, they would each have made just 10, or 100 in all. However, people who spend their working time mass producing one product must trade with other people to acquire the other products they wish to consume.

Even if people engage in trade, they can still manage without money by using **barter**, which means swapping products. For example, an early tribe might agree to barter some salmon for some cooking pots. But barter has some problems.

- **There must be a double coincidence of wants**. The tribe wishing to swap fish for pots must find another tribe wishing to swap pots for fish.
- **Buying and selling have to occur at the same time**. The tribe wishing to swap salmon for pots cannot choose to dispose of its fish one day and acquire pots on a later day.
- **There could be arguments about relative values**. The two tribes might never previously have swapped salmon and cooking pots, and they may disagree sharply about the relative amounts that would represent a fair exchange.

But suppose that all tribes were willing to accept a particular commodity, say gold, in all transactions. Anything that is generally accepted as a means of payment is called **money**. Using gold as money would remove the problems of barter, as follows.

- **Money would be a medium of exchange.** One tribe could sell salmon for gold to another that wanted to buy them, and buy pots with gold from a different tribe with pots for sale, making a double coincidence of wants unnecessary.

- **Money would be a store of value**. The tribe selling salmon could sell some one day for gold, and then keep the gold until a later date when it wanted to buy pots.
- **Money would be a unit of account or measurement.** People might often buy and sell fish and pots for gold, and acquire a good idea of the value of these products in terms of gold.

In spite of the usefulness of money, it is not used for all transactions, so barter persists today. On a modest level, it is used between friends who might say: 'If you lend me your lecture notes, I will buy you a drink.' On a larger scale, people who buy new cars often pay only partly in money and otherwise trade in their previous cars. And some places have barter exchanges through which people can use the Internet to match up trading partners who meet the need for a double coincidence of wants.

Commodity money

Although barter has never wholly disappeared, the usefulness of money was widely recognized in prehistoric times, and many commodities were used as money. The most persistent is cattle, which are still used among nomadic people in Mongolia. But cattle are useful only for large transactions.

For use in both small and large transactions, the most common items in Europe were metals, chiefly gold, silver, and bronze. Elsewhere, especially in Africa and Asia, the most widespread and persistent item was cowrie shells, the attractive shells of small sea snails, which are washed ashore when the snails die.

In some respects, cowrie shells were better as money than metals. This can be seen by considering five desirable qualities of something to be used as money.

- **Money should be available in small pieces**, to use in small transactions. This applies to cowrie shells. Admittedly, metals can be cut into small pieces, but then there is the problem that the pieces need weighing to everyone's agreement.
- **Money should be durable**, to make it a good store of value. This applies to both shells and metals, although gold and silver are soft and can rub away when used. Cowrie shells may sound fragile, but in fact they are tough.
- **Money should have a stable value**, to make it a good store of value. The value of money falls quickly if the quantity suddenly increases; this was never a problem with shells, but it was sometimes a problem with gold and silver when new deposits were found.
- **Money should be homogeneous**, so that there is no need to spend time checking it for purity. This applies to shells, but not to pieces of metal.
- **Money should be portable**, so that an easily carried amount has a significant purchasing power. This applied both to shells and metals.

Coins

Coins were developed in countries that used metals as money in an attempt to reduce the problems of using metal. The earliest coins were made in Asia Minor around 1,000BC. Coins were made in mints, and were intended to have a specific quantity and quality of a valuable metal. In this way, there should be no need for traders to check the metals being used for weight or purity.

People could take metal to a mint to be made into coins. Usually, the mints charged a fee called **seignorage**. These fees made mints profitable, so the rulers of countries often monopolized them and had their heads shown on the coins.

Although using coins was better than simply using chunks of metal, coins were also problematic. The reasons included the following.

- **Dishonest minters**. A mint might use less of the precious metal than the ruler decreed. Rulers often had savage punishments to deter this.

- **Forgery**. Forgers might circulate similar-looking coins with less of the precious metal.
- **Sweating**. Some people 'sweated' coins by shaking them in a bag and collecting the dust of the metals at the bottom, leaving the coins with less metal than they should have. This was made more difficult in England in the 12th century when its almost pure silver coins were replaced by 'sterling' silver coins that were only 92.5% silver; the other metals used for the remaining 7.5% made the coins harder.
- **Clipping**. Some people clipped the edges of coins. They then collected enough clips to have more coins made, leaving the original coins with less metal than they should have. The idea of grooved edges, like those on the 5p, 10p, £1, and £2 coins, was to make clipping more obvious.
- **Debasement**. Some rulers 'debased' their coins. They got mints to replace existing coins with new ones that had less precious metal, and then used the metal left over to make more coins to spend themselves. When far more coins of the same nominal value, say a pound, chased the same quantity of products, the result was inflation.

Coins in the UK now contain no precious metals. The last coins with gold in them were issued in 1914, and the last with silver in 1947. However, 1p coins made before 1992 were 97% copper, and although copper is not classed as a precious metal, the value of this copper now exceeds 1p!

Banknotes

Wealthy people often had lots of coins, and these could easily be stolen. So, in the 17th century, banks were established with strong rooms, and people could pay to have their coins kept there. In return, they were given a piece of paper on which the banker wrote their name, and promised to repay their money in coins 'on demand'.

Late in the 17th century, banks also issued pieces of paper called **banknotes**, which promised to pay 'the bearer' on demand. So someone might take ten £1 coins to a bank and get a £10 banknote with this promise. This banknote could then be used as money, because everyone would accept it as a medium of exchange, knowing they could take it to the bank and get coins if they wished to do so.

It might seem odd that people who took money in the form of coins to banks for safe keeping were willing to accept in return banknotes, which were simply another form of money. But banknotes were safer than coins for two reasons.

- **They were issued only for large amounts, say £10 or more then, which is worth £1,000 or more today**. So the notes could be used only in large transactions and always attracted the sort of attention that thieves dislike.
- **The notes were numbered, and were generally used quite close to the issuing bank**. So stolen notes could be looked for and reported if used.

From about 1750, almost all banknote issuing in England and Wales has been handled by the Bank of England. Scottish and Northern Irish banks still issue banknotes with their names on, but the amounts they can issue are strictly controlled.

Banknotes are printed on paper that is essentially worthless, yet they were first used when gold and silver coins were in circulation. People accepted banknotes because they could exchange them for coins, or even for gold at the Bank of England. From 1719 until 1931, it was possible to convert notes at a rate of £1 for 29g of gold. This convertibility was suspended only twice, from 1819 to 1821 and from 1914 to 1925, when the demand for gold exceeded the Bank of England's ability to meet it.

Since 1931, Bank of England banknotes have not been convertible into anything except coins with little intrinsic value. Notes and coins together are called **cash**, and account for about 2.3% of the UK's money. The remaining 97.7% is accounted for by bank deposits, which arose following the development of banks in the late 17th and early 18th centuries. We study these in the next section.

20.1 Everyday economics

SwapSity

In March 2010, a 30-year-old entrepreneur named Marta Nowinski set up an online barter site in Ottawa, Canada. People with goods and services to offer can post descriptions, pictures, or videos, and also look at what other people are offering, and arrange swaps if there is something suitable. Then traders negotiate directly. For example, a lawyer might agree to offer legal services in return for a week in someone's holiday cottage, and someone else might offer a baby's crib in return for a used hi-fi. The site has proved so successful that it plans to set up in other Canadian cities.

'Barter and swap', *Ottawa Citizen*, 27 March 2010
'Young entrepreneur spotlight: SwapSity', *Financial Post*, 8 December 2010
SwapSity website, December 2010

Comment This site was helped by the recession, with people being more inclined to try to swap things they no longer wanted instead of throwing them away. A beneficial side-effect is that fewer unused items ended up in landfill.

20.1 Summary

- People can trade without money by using barter, but money avoids the need for a double coincidence of wants, and it acts as a store of value and a unit of account, as well as being a medium of exchange.
- Coins originally contained a standard quantity and quality of valuable metal, but no longer do so. Banknotes used to be convertible into coins with valuable metals, or even gold, but this is no longer the case.

20.2 Bank deposits

Bank deposits as money

Suppose for a moment that a country has only one bank, which is owned by the government, and suppose that its sole function is to issue coins and banknotes. Now consider the total amount of money that the public can spend, which is called the **money stock** or **money supply**: this will equal their holdings of cash, that is their coins plus their banknotes.

Next, suppose some other banks are set up that cannot issue notes. To distinguish the government-owned note-issuing bank from all these other banks, we will call it the 'central bank', and we will call the other banks 'commercial banks'.

The public may place some cash in the commercial banks, partly for safety because all banks have strong rooms, and partly to earn interest. People who place cash in banks have deposits opened there. So someone who places £1,000 cash with a bank has a deposit worth £1,000. People can then reduce their deposits in two ways.

- **They can withdraw part of their deposits in cash**.
- **They can transfer part of their deposits to other people**. This can be done by various means, such as debit cards, cheques, the Internet, and standing orders. Anyone making such a payment ends up with a smaller deposit, while the person receiving the payment ends up with a larger deposit.

This second way means that people can directly use their bank deposits to buy things. So bank deposits are a medium of exchange, and are therefore a form of money. So the introduction of commercial banks means the money stock now equals the cash held by the public plus the bank deposits held by the public.

Handling bank deposits

Suppose that before the commercial banks are set up, the public has £300 million worth of cash, as shown in the top part of Stage (1) of Table 20.1. The money stock also equals £300 million, as shown in the bottom part. Then the commercial banks are set up, and people place £80 million of cash in bank deposits, leaving them holding £220 million worth of cash. This is shown in the top part of Stage (2).

The middle part of this table gives the balance sheet for all the commercial banks combined. Their liabilities show the funds placed with them, and their assets show how they use these funds. In Stage (2), they have acquired £80 million in deposits and have kept all of it in cash. Bank assets in the form of cash are called reserves.

The money stock in Stage (2) equals the public's £220 million holding of cash plus their deposits of £80 million, so it is still £300 million. It may seem odd not to count cash held by the banks as money. But the money stock is the amount that the public can spend, and their spending power, like yours, equals the cash they hold themselves plus their bank deposits.

Imagine you run one of the commercial banks. To handle deposits there, you must act as follows.

- **Pay out cash when your depositors withdraw some**. Then deposits at your bank fall and its reserves fall.
- **Accept cash when your depositors bring in more**. Then deposits at your bank rise and its reserves rise.
- **Handle Internet and other payments between depositors at your bank**. Then you change the numbers against their deposits, but your bank's total deposits and its reserves stay the same.
- **Handle Internet and other payments by your depositors to depositors at other banks**. Suppose a depositor at your bank makes an Internet payment to a depositor at another bank. Then deposits at your bank will fall and deposits at the other bank will rise. Also, the other bank will demand an equal amount of reserves from you, so your reserves will fall and its reserves will rise.
- **Handle Internet and other payments to your depositors from depositors at other banks**. Suppose one of your depositors receives a cheque from a depositor at another bank. Then deposits at your bank will rise and deposits at the other bank will fall. Also, you will demand an equal amount of reserves from the other bank, so your reserves will rise and its reserves will fall.

Table 20.1 **The commercial banks' total liabilities and assets, deposit creation, and money creation**

		Stage (1) *Position with no banks*	**Stage (2)** *The public deposit £80bn cash in banks*	**Stage (3)** *The banks create £720bn of money*	**Stage (4)** *The public deposit £20bn more cash in banks*	**Stage (5)** *The banks create £180bn more money*
Cash held by the public		£300bn	£220bn	£220bn	£200bn	£200bn
Commercial bank liabilities:	Deposits		£80bn	£800bn	£820bn	£1,000bn
Commercial bank assets:	Reserves		£80bn	£80bn	£100bn	£100bn
	Advances & securities		£0bn	£720bn	£720bn	£900bn
Money stock[a]		£300bn	£300bn	£1,020bn	£1,020bn	£1,200bn

a equals cash held by the public plus bank deposits held by the public.

Creating bank deposits

Suppose the commercial banks are at Stage (2) in Table 20.1. Then each individual bank's reserves will fall whenever its depositors withdraw cash or make payments to depositors at other banks; and they will rise whenever its depositors bring in more cash or receive payments from depositors at other banks. So its reserves will change constantly.

However, these rises and falls will largely offset each other, so the total level of a bank's reserves is fairly stable. We will now see how this enables banks to create deposits. And because deposits are a form of money, this means that banks can create money. They can actually create deposits, and so create money, in two ways.

- **By making advances, or loans**. For example, suppose you lend one of your depositors, called Ella, £1,000. All you do is press some keys on your computer and raise the number shown against Ella's deposit by £1,000.
- **By buying securities**. There are several types of security, including shares in companies, which we met in Chapter 7. Suppose Ella sells £500 worth of shares to your bank. All you do is press some keys on your computer and raise her deposit by £500.

Altogether, Ella now has £1,500 more to spend and no one else has any less, so the public between them have £1,500 more. So you have increased the money stock by £1,500.

In Stage (3) of Table 20.1, we suppose that the commercial banks between them create a total of £720 million worth of deposits by making advances and buying securities, taking total deposits from £80 million to £800 billion. So the banks also raise the money stock by £720 billion, from £300 billion to £1,020 billion.

The limits to creating bank deposits

Banks face costs, such as the interest they pay on their deposits, the wages of their staff, and running their buildings. So they must earn an income to cover their costs and, hopefully, make a profit. They earn an income by making advances, on which they charge interest, and by buying securities, which pay dividends and interest. So they like to lend huge sums and buy many securities, all the time creating more money.

What limits the amount of money they can create? To see this, look again at Table 20.1. In Stage (2), the banks had deposits of £80 billion. In a worst-case scenario, their depositors might demand all of this in cash, but that is no problem for the banks because they have cash reserves of £80 billion available. But by Stage (3) deposits have risen to £800 billion, and banks still have cash reserves of just £80 billion.

We define the **reserve ratio** of banks as the ratio of their reserves to their deposits. In Stage (2), it is £80 billion/£80 billion or 100%, but by Stage (3) it has fallen to £80 billion/£800 billion or 10%. So in Stage (3), if only 10% of the deposits are withdrawn in cash, the banks will run out of reserves and be unable to meet any more withdrawals. The more the banks make advances and buy securities, the lower their reserve ratios become, and the more risk they have of running out of reserves. All banks choose to operate with the lowest reserve ratio they think is prudent. Suppose this is 10%: then they will not create any more deposits beyond Stage (3).

Because the amount of money that commercial banks can create is limited by their reserves, they want as many reserves as they can get. They cannot actually create reserves, because these comprise notes and coins, which are issued only by the central bank. But commercial banks can raise the interest rates on their deposits to tempt the public to deposit more cash with them. However, they will do this only if they find that the returns they get from the extra advances and securities cover the interest they must pay on the extra deposits.

Suppose the banks find they can raise their deposit interest rates just a little, and still make a profit by making more advances and buying more securities. Say this interest rate rise attracts £20 billion more cash from the public, as shown in Stage (4) of Table 20.1. The banks now have deposits of £820 billion and reserves of £100 billion. So their reserve ratio is £100 billion/£820 billion, which is above 10%. So they can make more advances and buy more securities, and so expand their deposits by £180 billion when they will reach £1,000 billion. Then their reserve ratio will be back down at 10%. This is what they do in Stage (5).

If we compare Stages (3) and (5), we see that a £20 million rise in their reserves led the banks to raise their deposits by £200 million. The change in deposits divided by the change in reserves is called the **bank deposit multiplier**; here it is £200 million/£20 million, or 10. There is a formula for it as follows:

$$\text{Bank deposit multiplier} = 1/r$$

where r is the reserve ratio that the banks choose. In this example, r is 10%, or 0.1, so $1/r$ equals 10.

The money multiplier

Suppose the situation shown in Stage (5) of Table 20.1 persists for some time. This is repeated in Stage (1) of Table 20.2. This table also includes the **monetary base**, which is defined as publicly held cash plus bank reserves. So, in Stage (1), it is £200 billion plus £100 billion, which is £300 billion.

The monetary base cannot be altered by the commercial banks, because they cannot create cash. Admittedly, they can increase their reserves by tempting the public to hold less cash, but then one component of the monetary base will fall by the same amount as the other component rises. The monetary base can only be altered by the government, as we shall now see, or by the central bank, as we will see later in the chapter.

Suppose, now, that the central bank, which has so far only issued banknotes, opens a deposit for the government. And suppose the government pays £30 billion from its deposit to some members of the public, perhaps pensioners or unemployed people, or government employees. Then the public has £30 billion more in their deposits. Also, their banks can demand £30 billion cash reserves from the government's bank. So the situation moves to Stage (2) of Table 20.2. The money stock and the monetary base have both risen by £30 billion.

The banks' reserve ratio is now £130 billion/£1,030 billion. This is above the 10% they think prudent, so they will make more advances and buy more securities. With £30 billion more reserves, the banks may hope to move to Stage (3A). This will involve making more advances and buying more securities until their deposits reach £1,300 billion. Then, it seems, their reserve ratio will be £130 billion/£1,300 billion, or 10%, as they want. However, the public will not let the banks reach Stage (3A). This is because, as the banks expand from Stage (2), the public will hold more and more deposits. And the public likes

Table 20.2 **The commercial banks and the money multiplier with a cash drain**

		Stage (1) *Starting position*	**Stage (2)** *The public are paid £30bn by the government*	**Stage (3A)** *What would happen if there were no cash drain*	**Stage (3B)** *What does happen because there is a cash drain*
Cash held by the public		£200bn	£200bn	£200bn	£220bn
Commercial bank liabilities:	Deposits	£1,000bn	£1,030bn	£1,300bn	£1,100bn
Commercial bank assets:	Reserves	£100bn	£130bn	£130bn	£110bn
	Advances & securities	£900bn	£900bn	£1,170bn	£990bn
Money stock[a]		£1,200bn	£1,230bn	£1,500bn	£1,320bn
Monetary base[b]		£300bn	£330bn	£330bn	£330bn

a equals cash held by the public plus bank deposits held by the public.
b equals cash held by the public plus bank reserves.

to hold cash and deposits in a fairly constant ratio, so they will also want to hold more and more cash.

So, as the banks increase deposits from Stage (2), they will find that some cash is withdrawn. This will take their reserves below £130 billion, and that means they must expand deposits less dramatically than shown in Stage (3A). The tendency for the public to withdraw cash when their deposits rise is called a **cash drain**.

To see what happens in the end, we must make an assumption about the ratio of cash to deposits that the public want; we call this ratio *d*. In Stage (1), *d* was £200 billion/£1,000 billion or 0.2. Suppose the public always wants *d* to equal 0.2. Also, remember that the banks want a ratio of cash reserves to deposits of 0.1. This means that the public wants twice as much cash as the banks.

It also means that when the banks get £30 billion more reserves, as in Stage (2), the public will withdraw £20 billion in cash; then they will hold £20 billion more cash, leaving the banks with £10 billion more. This is shown in Stage (3B). With just £10 billion more reserves than in Stage (1), that is £110 billion, the banks can expand deposits by only £100 billion to £1,100 billion. However, the money stock rises by more than this £100 billion rise in deposits, because in Stage (3B) the public holds £20 billion more cash than in Stage (1). So the money stock rises by £120 billion.

In Table 20.2, the monetary base rose by £30 million between Stages (1) and (3B), and the money stock rose by £120 million. The change in the money stock divided by the change in the monetary base is called the **money multiplier.** So the money multiplier here is 4. The money multiplier can be found from this formula:

$$\text{Money multiplier} = (1 + d)/(r + d)$$

In Table 20.2, this is $(1 + 0.2)/(0.1 + 0.2)$, which is 1.2/0.3, or 4.

Expansion by a single bank

In Table 20.2, the banks between them acquired £10 billion more reserves between Stages (1) and (3B). With the bank deposit multiplier at 10, they expanded their deposits by ten times as much, or £100 billion, from £1,000 billion to £1,100 billion. But if you ran one bank here, you could not react so dramatically to a rise in your reserves.

To see why, suppose one of your depositors receives £30 million from the government. Then your deposits rise by £30 million, and you get £30 million more reserves from the central bank. Suppose you then expand your advances and securities by £270 million, hoping to raise your deposits by another £270 million, so making a total expansion in your deposits of £300 million.

Let's suppose that you expand both your advances and your securities by £135 million. The people who borrow will spend their loans, and probably most of their purchases will be from depositors at other banks to which you must then give reserves. And you will buy your securities on the stock exchange from a range of sellers, and probably most of them will bank at other banks to which you must then give reserves. So your reserves will fall greatly; indeed, you might even run out of reserves.

So, when your bank acquires extra reserves, it must expand very cautiously, because it will then lose some reserves to the other banks. However, when the other banks get these reserves, then they can expand. And when they expand, you will get some reserves, because some of their depositors will make purchases from some of your depositors, and some of the securities those banks buy will be bought from depositors at your bank. With these extra reserves, you can then expand a little more again. Then you will lose some more reserves to the other banks and they can expand a little more again. In the end, the combined expansion for all the banks combined will be as shown in Table 20.2.

Question 20.1 When a bank makes advances, it knows the borrowers will make many payments to people at other banks, so its reserves will fall. Will its reserves rise when the borrowers make repayments?

20.2 Summary

- People can make Internet and other payments using banks deposits, so bank deposits count as money.
- When depositors at one bank make payments to depositors at another, their bank has to transfer reserves to the bank of the people receiving the payments.
- Banks need a prudent level of reserves to meet demands by their depositors for cash withdrawals, and also to pay reserves to other banks when their depositors make payments to depositors at other banks.
- Banks can create deposits by making advances. They use a computer to increase the number in the deposits of the borrowers. Banks can also create money by buying securities.
- If the banks' reserves rise, they can raise their deposits by a multiplied amount. The value of the bank deposits multiplier equals $1/r$, where r is the ratio in which banks like to hold reserves and deposits.
- The monetary base equals the public's holdings of cash plus bank reserves. Commercial banks cannot change this, but the central bank and the government can.
- If the monetary base changes, the money stock rises by a multiplied amount. The value of the money multiplier equals $(1 + d)/(r + d)$, where d is the ratio in which the public hold cash and deposits.

20.3 Bank liabilities and assets

Commercial banks

This section looks more closely at banks, starting with commercial banks and then looking at central banks. We take the term 'commercial bank' to cover two types of business that handle deposits for the public. One type call themselves banks, like Barclay's Bank, and the other type call themselves building societies, like the Nationwide Building Society. Economists always take them together because they are very much alike, except that building societies lend a larger proportion of their advances to people who want to buy homes.

Bank liabilities

Table 20.3 shows the liabilities in January 2011 for all of the UK's commercial banks combined. Remember that liabilities show the funds that have been made available to the banks. The table begins with the banks' sterling liabilities, which means liabilities denominated in sterling. Most likely you have a deposit at a UK bank denominated in sterling, and this is included here.

The first four lines of Table 20.3 concern deposits, which it divides into four groups, as follows.

- **Sight deposits.** These can be withdrawn in cash, or used for Internet and other payments, on demand without any penalty. Most people with bank deposits have at least one deposit like this, and receive some interest on it.
- **Time deposits.** With these, depositors are meant to give some notice before withdrawing them or using them for Internet and other payments. These deposits earn more interest than sight deposits. In practice, banks often allow people to use them on demand, but then apply a penalty. For example, if

Table 20.3 **Liabilities of all UK banks combined (excluding the Bank of England), January 2011**

	£bn	%
Sterling liabilities		
Deposits		
Sight deposits	1,138	30.8
Time deposits	1,561	42.2
Certificates of deposit (CDs)	199	5.4
Repurchase agreements (Repos)	262	7.1
Miscellaneous liabilities	65	1.7
Capital	473	12.8
Total sterling liabilities	**3,697**	**100.0**
	£bn	**%**
Sterling liabilities	3,697	45.9
Euro liabilities	1,881	23.3
Other currency liabilities	2,480	30.8
Total liabilities	**8,058**	**100.0**

Source: Bank of England, *Monetary and Financial Statistics*, January 2011, Table B1.4.

you have a time deposit and are meant to give a month's notice before using it, but you want to use it today, the bank may allow this, but penalize you by paying you no interest for the last month.

- **Certificates of deposit** (CDs). These are available only for large amounts, such as £50,000. The holder of a CD agrees a term, say a year, and cannot withdraw or spend the deposit until the year is up. However, the holder of a CD can sell it to someone else during the year, so CDs are less inflexible than they sound. CDs receive higher interest than most time deposits.
- **Repurchase agreements** (repos). These are not strictly called deposits, but they are effectively deposits available to people who want to deposit large sums for a short period, usually just a few days. When these people give their money to the bank, they actually buy securities from it, and it agrees to buy the securities back on an agreed date. These people are not paid any interest, but the bank agrees to repurchase the securities at a higher price than the price at which it sold them, and this actually gives repos higher returns than short-term time deposits.

Table 20.3 shows that these types of deposit accounted respectively for 30.8%, 42.2%, 5.4%, and 7.1% of the banks' sterling liabilities. These amounts add up to about 85%. The other 15% of liabilities chiefly comprises what is called capital. This is money that the banks have acquired other than from depositors. For example, it includes money put up by the shareholders who set up the banks and own them, and it includes any profits made in the past that the banks have used to make loans and buy securities.

Table 20.3 ends with the banks' liabilities in other currencies. It is quite possible to approach a UK bank with foreign currency and use this to open a deposit denominated in that currency. The table shows the value of these deposits in terms of sterling by using the current exchange rates. In January 2011, liabilities in sterling accounted for only 45.9% of the banks liabilities; liabilities in euros accounted for another 23.3%, and liabilities in other currencies accounted for the rest.

Bank assets

Table 20.3 shows that, in January 2011, the banks had funds worth £8,058 billion. Table 20.4 shows the assets that the banks acquired with these funds. It begins with the assets denominated in sterling, and divides these into three main groups: reserves; loans and advances; and securities.

Reserves

The first asset shown under reserves in Table 20.4 is cash held in the banks' premises. However, the banks do not keep all their cash reserves on their premises, but instead deposit most at the Bank of England. They do this because these deposits earn interest at an interest rate called the Bank of England's official rate or, more simply, **Bank Rate**. The banks can usually withdraw these deposits in cash on demand.

If the banks' depositors were suddenly to want to withdraw large sums of cash, the banks could use the cash they keep on their premises plus the cash they can withdraw from their deposits at the Bank of England. So the banks regard their reserves as these two items added together, and **reserves** are measured as cash held by banks plus their deposits at the central bank. In January 2011, reserves accounted for 4.1% of sterling assets. Reserves are an example of **liquid assets**: these are assets that are already in cash, or can quickly be made available in cash at a known value.

Table 20.4 Assets of all UK banks combined (excluding the Bank of England), January 2011

	£bn	%
Sterling assets		
Reserves		
Cash held by the banks	9	0.2
Deposits at the Bank of England	143	3.9
Loans and advances		
Market loans	497	13.5
Reverse Repos	248	6.8
Advances	2,068	56.3
Securities		
Bills	28	0.8
Others (bonds and equities)	576	15.7
Miscellaneous	103	2.8
Total sterling assets	**3,672**	**100.0**
	£bn	**%**
Sterling assets	3.672	45.6
Euro assets	1,953	24.2
Other currency assets	2,433	30.2
Total assets	**8,058**	**100.0**

Source: Bank of England, *Monetary and Financial Statistics*, January 2011, Table B1.4.

Loans and advances

The next three assets are types of loan, as follows.

- **Market loans.** These are loans by one bank to another bank. For example, one bank might be short of reserves and borrow from another, which has more reserves than it currently needs. These loans are usually short-term, often just made overnight. The banks that lend them can demand repayment in reserves, so their short-term market loans are very liquid assets.
- **Reverse repos.** Each bank has deposits in the form of repos at many other banks. These are called reverse repos by the banks that hold them as assets. They are short-term, so the banks that hold them will soon be repaid in cash, making them very liquid assets.
- **Advances.** These are loans to anyone other than banks, such as members of the public and businesses. These are very illiquid: if a bank lends someone money for, say, a year, it cannot demand repayment at short notice, and even when the year is up it may fail to get repaid.

Securities

The next two assets shown in Table 20.4 concern securities. There are many types of security, but they fall into three main groups.

- **Bills.** When governments or companies want to borrow money for short periods, typically 13 weeks, they often issue bills and sell them. The people who buy them effectively lend money to the borrowers. The lenders are not paid any interest. However, at repayment time, which is known as maturity, the borrowers repay the lenders more than the lenders initially paid for the bills. Bills can be bought and sold second-hand between the issue date and maturity date. UK government bills are called Treasury bills, and some are issued every week.
- **Bonds.** When governments or companies want to borrow money for periods of many years, they often issue and sell bonds. Most bonds have a face value of £100: this is the price at which they are sold when they are issued. All bonds have an interest rate, or coupon rate. If a bond has, say, a 5% coupon, then

each year the holder is paid 5% of the face value in interest, that is £5. Most bonds have a maturity date on which the holder is repaid the face value, but some have no maturity date and pay interest indefinitely. UK government bonds are called gilts.

Bonds may be bought and sold second-hand, and can trade at prices that are far from their face values. Suppose that, in 2010, interest rates are around 4%. Then people will be willing to pay £100 for a new bond with a face value of £100 and a 4% coupon, to get £4 a year interest. But suppose, in 2020, that interest rates have fallen to around 2%. Then people will be willing to pay £200 to buy this bond second-hand, because they will still get £4 a year in interest, and this is a return of 2% on the second-hand price. So, while the return of the bond is still 4% of its face value, its actual return to the new buyer is 2%. We will refer later to the fact that rises in bond prices mean lower actual returns for new buyers.

- **Equities.** This is another term for shares that we met in Chapter 7. These are issued only by companies, and the buyers become joint owners of the company. Shareholders are paid dividends, which vary over time in line with the company's profits. The shareholders can never demand repayment, but shares can be bought and sold second-hand.

Other assets

The last type of sterling asset shown on Table 20.4 is called miscellaneous assets. The chief ones are the banks' land and buildings.

Table 20.4 ends with the banks' assets in other currencies. Banks make loans and own securities denominated in many other currencies. The table shows the value of these assets in terms of sterling by using the current exchange rates. In January 2011, sterling assets accounted for 45.6% of the banks' total assets. Assets in euros accounted for 24.2%, and assets in other currencies accounted for the rest.

The central bank

We now turn to the UK's central bank, that is the Bank of England. Like any other bank, it takes deposits, makes loans, and buys securities. It is relatively small. In January 2011, when the total assets and liabilities of the commercial banks were £8,058 billion, the assets and liabilities of the Bank of England were just £243 billion.

Despite being small, the Bank of England is important, because it performs some functions that no other banks perform. These include the following.

- **Being the government's bank.** All departments of the central government have deposits at the Bank of England. The Bank can lend to these departments by raising their deposits, just like other banks can lend to their depositors.
- **Being the bankers' bank.** We saw in Table 20.4 that the other banks keep most of their cash reserves in deposits at the Bank of England.
- **Handling clearing between banks.** We saw in the last section that if depositors at one bank make payments to depositors at another bank, then the first bank must give an equivalent amount of cash to the second. Of course, millions of payments are made each day, and the banks can avoid many millions of physical movements of cash by using their deposits at the Bank of England. Suppose Bank A owes Bank B £1 million: then the Bank of England will reduce Bank A's deposit there by £1 million and increase Bank B's by £1 million. This process is called clearing.
- **Issuing bank notes and coins.** If the public wants more cash, they withdraw notes and coins from their banks; then the banks will withdraw more cash from their deposits at the Bank of England. The Bank of England can simply print notes, but it has to buy coins from the Royal Mint.
- **Ensuring banks have adequate reserves.** All banks have low reserves at times like weekends, when the public likes to hold a lot of cash. The Bank of England will help them with loans, as discussed later in section 20.7. This function should not be

confused with loans to banks in serious trouble, for which see the next paragraph.

- **Being the lender of last resort.** Sometimes a bank gets into serious trouble and needs more than a top-up of reserves to survive. The Bank of England is willing to lend large sums to such a bank, if it believes the problems are temporary, to prevent it being unable to meet the demands of its depositors. The Bank supported Northern Rock building society in this way in 2007.
- **Operating monetary policy by changing the money stock and interest rates.** We explore this function in section 20.7 and also in Chapter 26.
- **Managing the exchange rate between sterling and other currencies in line with government policy.** We explore this function in Chapter 28.
- **Supervising the clearing banks to ensure that they act prudently.** In 1997, this function was moved from the Bank of England to the Financial Services Authority. In 2010, it was given to a new branch of the Bank of England called the Prudential Regulatory Authority (PRA).

Most central banks have functions similar to those listed above. Many have one further function, which the Bank of England performed until 1988.

- **Handling borrowing by the government.** In the UK, this function is handled by the Debt Management Office (DMO). When the government needs to borrow money, other than from the Bank of England, the DMO issues Treasury bills and gilts on its behalf. It also handles the repayment of Treasury bills and gilts when they mature.

Question 20.2 We saw in the last section that when the government spends money, bank reserves rise, leading to a multiplier expansion of the money stock. Will there be any offsetting falls in bank reserves if the government borrows the money it needs from the central bank, or borrows the money it needs from the public, or raises the money it needs through taxation?

20.3 Summary

- All banks have liabilities in the form of deposits. Deposits come in the form of sight deposits, time deposits, and certificates of deposits (CDs). Repos are also, effectively, a form of deposit.
- All commercial banks have assets in the form of reserves, which include cash held on their premises and deposits held at the central bank. They also make loans in the form of money market loans to other banks, reverse repos, and advances. And they own securities in the form of bills, bonds, and equities.
- The central bank's functions including being the government's bank and the bankers' bank, clearing, issuing cash, helping banks in difficulty, changing the money stock and interest rates, and regulating commercial banks.

20.4 Financial intermediation

Deficit units and surplus units

We have seen that banks take deposits, make loans, and buy securities. They take deposits from **surplus units**, that is households, businesses, and governments that have some money that they do not need to spend at present. Then the banks actually transfer most of the funds placed on deposit to **deficit units**, which are households, businesses, and governments that have less money than they need to spend at present. The banks lend money to these units, and they also buy securities issued by companies and governments.

By transferring funds from surplus units to deficit units, banks act as **financial intermediaries** between them. The act of transferring is called **financial intermediation**. Banks are generally profitable, and make a profit by demanding higher returns from deficit units than they pay to surplus units. You will be well aware of this if you have borrowed from a bank, because you know that it will charge you a much higher interest rate on your advance than it pays you on a deposit.

This differential in interest rates raises an important question. To see this, suppose for simplicity that banks charge 9% on all loans and pay 1% on all deposits. Then why don't surplus and deficit units deal directly with each other and cut out the banks? If surplus units were to lend directly to deficit units at any rate between 1% and 9%, then both types of unit would seem to be better off than if the loans pass indirectly through banks.

Actually, surplus units often do deal directly with deficit units. For example, they may buy company equities or government bonds, or lend to friends. Nevertheless, substantial transfers are also made through banks, despite the apparently adverse interest rates that each type of unit then gets. These transfers are made because banks offer three advantages that compensate for the adverse rates. We will now look at these advantages.

Maturity transformation

Suppose that, in time, you pay off your student debts and a mortgage, and amass funds worth £50,000. Rather than keep all this in a bank at a low interest rate, you may use some of it to buy securities, or even to lend to some people who need to borrow. But you would not want to use all the £50,000 like this, because you may want to spend some money very soon. So you want some **liquidity**: this means having some assets that are already money, like bank deposits, or which can be easily and quickly converted into a known sum of money.

Compared with funds kept in a sight deposit, funds used to buy securities will give you less liquidity, because you do not know how much you will get by selling them until you actually sell them, and even then it will take a few days for the money paid by the buyer to reach your deposit. Funds used to make loans are even less liquid, because you may not be able to demand quick repayment. It is partly because deposits are much more liquid than securities and loans that surplus units accept relatively low interest rates on deposits.

While surplus units will accept low rates on deposits that can be quickly withdrawn, deficit units often want to borrow for a year or more, and it is partly because banks will lend for such periods that deficit units will pay them relatively high interest rates for lending for such periods. Note, though, that banks end up obliged to repay many deposits on demand while making many advances for quite long periods, and they also buy securities, which cannot be instantly sold. By lending for longer terms than they borrow, banks offer what is called **maturity transformation**. This is risky for the banks: if too many depositors want to withdraw their funds at one time, the banks will be unable to get many loans repaid at once, and they may find security prices tumble if they sell a lot.

Risk transformation

Another problem with transferring all your funds directly to deficit units is that you would probably transfer your funds to a relatively small number of units. It would be very time-consuming to lend small amounts to many different people, and each purchase of securities entails a minimum fee, so that buying small numbers issued by many deficit units would be very costly. However, if you transfer your funds to only a small number of deficit units, you will take a risk that you may be unlucky and find that many are eventually unable to repay you.

If, instead, you place your funds with a bank, your risks are lower. This is partly because banks are skilled at weeding out the riskiest borrowers, and partly because they spread their funds over so many. You can regard any money you have in a bank as split into tiny amounts and spread around the millions of deficit units to whom it lends. If some of these cannot repay, the effect on you will be small; indeed the bank will use its profits to ensure that your deposit is unaffected. The low risk on deposits is another reason why surplus units accept relatively low interest rates on them.

The ability of banks to offer deposits with negligible risks, while still lending to some borrowers who may have some risk, is called **risk transformation**. Of course, banks try to weed out the riskiest borrowers, but they do not always do so, and then their efforts to absorb the losses from their profits may mean there is no profit left for their owners.

Aggregation

Suppose you run a firm and you want to buy £10 million worth of raw materials. You plan to use these raw materials within one month, and then sell the products that use them for enough to cover the cost of the materials plus your other costs.

If you do not have £10 million now to spend on the raw materials, you will want to borrow £10 million for one month. If you try to borrow this directly from deficit units, you might need to contact hundreds to acquire the funds you want; it might even take you a month to raise it. But a bank could lend you a large sum right away, and this ready access to large loans is another reason why deficit units are willing to pay relatively high rates to banks. The ability of banks to combine small amounts from many small deposits and make large loans is called **aggregation**.

How safe is a bank?

We have seen that banks face the following key risks.

- They can cover their costs and make profits only if they lend and buy securities, and then their reserve ratios fall below 100%.
- They essentially lend long and borrow short.
- They have to honour their deposit obligations, even if some borrowers do not repay their loans.

The safety of a bank from the point of view of its depositors depends in part on its reserve ratio. Other things being equal, the higher its reserve ratio, the more it can be relied on to meet demands for cash withdrawals, and to handle payments by its depositors to depositors at other banks to which it must then give reserves.

But measures of the safety of banks often look beyond reserve ratios. Consider Bank A and Bank B in Table 20.5. Each bank has total liabilities and assets of £100 billion, and reserves of £5 billion. So in terms of reserves they may look comparably risky.

Notice, though, that Bank A here has acquired only £6 billion in capital from its owners and past profits, while Bank B has acquired £8 billion. So Bank A has £94 billion worth of deposits to honour and Bank B has only £92 billion worth. So Bank A has a lower reserve ratio, that is a lower ratio of reserves to deposits.

There are also differences in the banks' assets. Different assets vary in risk according to their liquidity. The table gives the generally accepted risk weights for the assets shown.

- **Reserves** carry no risk, and have a weight of 0.0, because they are already available in cash.
- **Government securities** also have a risk of 0.0: they can always be sold, and the government is regarded as a wholly safe borrower because it can always raise taxes to honour its debts.
- **Other securities** have a weight of 1.0, which is the highest level of risk. There is always a risk that the companies that issue them may go bankrupt, leading the securities to be worthless.
- **Mortgages** have a weight of 0.5. These are generally considered moderately safe, because if the borrowers default on their interest or repayment, banks can take possession of their homes and try to sell them to recoup their loans.
- **Other loans** have a weight of 1.0, because there is always a risk of default on the interest and repayment due.

The last two columns of the table work out how the risk value of each bank's assets. To do this, we take

Table 20.5 **Working out capital adequacy ratios**

	Bank A	Bank B		Bank A	Bank B
Liabilities	**£bn**	**£bn**			
Deposits	94	92			
Capital	6	8			
Total	**100**	**100**			
Assets	**£bn**	**£bn**	**Risk weight**	**RWA £bn**	**RWA £bn**
Reserves	5	5	*0.0*	*0*	*0*
Government securities	12	20	*0.0*	*0*	*0*
Other securities	32	25	*1.0*	*32*	*25*
Mortgages	16	22	*0.5*	*8*	*11*
Other loans	35	28	*1.0*	*35*	*28*
Total	**100**	**100**		**75**	*64*
Capital adequacy ratio (CAR):				**6/75 = 8%**	**8/64 = 12.5%**

Note: RWA means risk-weighted assets.

each asset in turn and multiply the amount of the asset by its weight. For example, Bank A has £0 million risk in its assets of government securities, because the £12 billion of these have a zero weight. But it has £8 billion risk in its assets from its mortgages, because the £16 billion in these have a weight of 0.5. The total of these risk-weighted assets is £75 billion for Bank A and £64 billion for Bank B. This means that the total risk of Bank A's assets is higher than the total risk of Bank B's assets.

Which bank would you prefer for your deposit? In the event of many people making simultaneous withdrawals, Bank B has two advantages: it has slightly lower deposits, which we could instead re-express by saying it has more capital, and it has safer assets.

A bank's safety can be measured by its **capital adequacy ratio** (CAR), which is defined as follows:

$$\text{CAR} = \text{Capital/Risk-weighted assets}$$

Bank A's CAR is £6 billion/£75 billion, or 8%, while Bank B's is £8 billion/£64 billion, or 12.5%. Bank B has the higher or safer ratio because its capital is higher and its risk-weighted assets are lower.

Most Western countries agree to require their banks to have a CAR of 10% or more. So Bank A would be breaching the rules while Bank B would be abiding by them. Following the recent credit crunch, the rules are sure to be strengthened.

Shortcomings of CARs

A CAR is by no means a complete measure of bank safety. Consider two banks that happen to have balance sheets identical to Bank B's, so each has a CAR of 12.5%. Yet, on the liabilities side, one bank might have a larger fraction of its deposits in CDs, which cannot suddenly be withdrawn, and in time deposits, where it can prohibit withdrawals without due notice. In contrast, the other might have a larger fraction in sight deposits, where withdrawals can be made on demand. So the second bank could more easily find many depositors wanting to use their deposits for cash withdrawals or spending at the same time.

There could also be differences on the assets side. For example, one bank's 'other securities' might be generally safer, and the borrowers of its 'other loans' might be generally safer. Also, it might have lent most of its mortgages to people whose homes have risen in value since they were bought, so that in the event of default the bank could repossess the homes and sell them for enough to recover the money it lent. In contrast, the other might have lent most of its mortgages to people whose homes have fallen in value, so that in the event of default and repossession, selling the homes would not raise enough to repay the bank.

20.2 **Everyday economics**

ICBC aims to raise its CAR through 2012

Industrial & Commercial Bank of China Ltd (ICBC), the world's most profitable lender, announced in 2010 that it aimed to raise its capital adequacy ratio to 12.4% and to keep it above 12% until 2012, by selling 25bn yuan worth of bonds. This would increase the capital on its balance sheet.

'ICBC aims to raise its capital adequacy ratio through 2012 ', *Bloomberg BusinessWeek*, 1 April 2010.
'ICBC sets higher capital adequacy ratios for 2010–2012', *Reuters*, 4 May 2012

Comment ICBC announced this step in advance, and then took it, to reassure current and potential depositors.

20.4 **Summary**

- Banks offer maturity transformation by having many deposits that can be withdrawn on demand or at short notice, while their loans are longer-term.
- Banks offer risk transformation by making loans that are often risky, while keeping their deposits generally safe. Each deposit is effectively spread across countless borrowers, most of whom will repay.
- Banks offer aggregation, by enabling small sums placed on deposit by many people to be amalgamated to make large loans to business borrowers.
- A bank's riskiness is usually measured by its capital adequacy ratio (CAR), which looks beyond its reserve ratio to see how many of its liabilities are in capital rather than deposits, and how risky its assets are.

20.5 The 2007 credit crunch

The 2007 credit crunch: its causes

A **credit crunch** is a situation in which banks are reluctant to lend, so that it is hard for borrowers to borrow. The 2007 credit crunch was an international one, and this was a result of the international nature of financial intermediation. We have seen that banks make substantial market loans to each other, and they even do this internationally, so that banks in the UK both lend to and borrow from banks around the world. If, for example, US banks suddenly become reluctant to lend, then banks in the UK and elsewhere will find it harder to borrow market loans, and this may make it harder for them to lend in the UK.

The 2007 credit crunch started in the US. A key factor lay in the so-called sub-prime mortgage market, which involved offering mortgages to people with a high risk of default. When banks lend money for mortgages, or any other purpose, they want to be fairly sure of repayment. With most loans, therefore, they look carefully at the creditworthiness of the borrowers. But with mortgages, US banks became very lax and lent huge sums to sub-prime borrowers.

This laxity arose because the banks reckoned that home prices would always rise steadily over time. So, for example, suppose someone approached a bank for a loan of $400,000 to buy a $400,000 home. And suppose this person had an insecure job that meant default was likely. The bank might still have lent, reckoning that if, in a year or two, that person did default, then the bank could repossess the home, and most likely sell it for more than $400,000, so easily recouping its loan.

There was a huge demand for mortgages in the US from 2002 because interest rates were kept very low. The aim of this was to help businesses to invest and so help the economy to grow.

As the US banks lent soaring amounts in mortgages, they needed to raise soaring funds to finance them. Instead of relying wholly on deposits, they also used money market loans and issued bonds linked to the mortgages; a UK bank might buy some of these bonds, and be told that its interest payments and eventual repayment were linked to the mortgages, and so seemingly very safe. These bonds offered attractive returns, but they also passed on some of the risk of default on the mortgages. If a US bank were to find it had lent mortgages to people who could not repay, then it in turn could default on repaying its bonds.

The crunch started in 2007 when US interest rates were increased in an effort to restrain inflation, which was becoming more rapid. The higher rates led many mortgage borrowers to default. They also led to lower property prices, because fewer people now wanted to borrow and buy homes. So when the banks sold off repossessed properties, they often failed to recoup as much money as they had lent. So they faced falling interest income, along with billions of dollars of loans that were not fully repaid.

The 2007 credit crunch: its effects

The chain of events was then roughly as follows.

- Many small and medium-sized US banks that had lent mortgages went out of business, unable to repay the other banks in the US and elsewhere that had lent them market loans and bought their mortgage-linked bonds.
- As these other banks found that many of their market loans to US banks were not repaid, and found many US banks defaulting on the mortgage-linked bonds, they made losses. Often, they were relying on these repayments to acquire reserves, so they ran short of reserves.
- Banks became wary of mortgages everywhere, and often refused to lend to each other to help to fund mortgages; so mortgages became hard to get.
- Moreover, banks became generally more wary about making market loans at all, partly out of a fear that they might be lending to a bank that might eventually be unable to repay, and partly to protect the level of their own reserves.
- To help UK banks with low reserves, the Bank of England lent them huge sums. It also agreed to temporary swaps, whereby it took over the rights to some mortgages lent by banks and gave them other assets instead; this made banks more attractive if they needed money market loans.
- The 'capital' item on banks' balance sheets includes total past profits. When the banks made losses, this item shrank, so their capital fell as, in turn, did their CARs. To make the banks less risky, the government allowed some banks to issue new securities, which it bought. The money from these new securities raised the banks' capital and, in turn, their CARs.
- The banks that had lost money tried to build up their reserve ratios by lending less, so borrowing became harder everywhere.
- The fall in bank lending led to lower investment. This led to lower planned spending, lower output, and higher unemployment, as predicted by the multiplier model, which we studied in Chapter 19.
- The prospects of lower output caused a sharp fall in share prices.
- In response to lower share prices and the threat of bank collapses, the UK government announced in October 2008 that it would set aside £500 billion to help struggling banks.
- In October 2008, several central banks made a sharp cut in interest rates: this included the Bank of England, the European Central Bank (which is central bank for the eurozone), and the Federal

Reserve Board (which is the central bank for the US). It was hoped this would raise planned spending.

Some particular banks attracted especial attention in the crisis. Typically, the banks that suffered most were those that relied least for funds on deposits from the public and most on market loans from other banks. They had borrowed short-term from other banks, and lent longer-term, and relied on a healthy turnover of loans from other banks; when these loans dried up, they were in serious trouble. Some of the major names were as follows.

- **Lehman Brothers.** This US bank collapsed in September 2008; it asked the US government to rescue it, but the government declined to do so.
- **Northern Rock.** This was the UK's fifth largest mortgage supplier and relied heavily on money market loans for funds. When these became hard to get, its depositors became worried that the bank would be unable to repay them, so there were panic withdrawals, which reduced its reserves. It was rescued in October 2007 by the Bank of England acting as lender of last resort, and later taken into government ownership.
- **The Bradford and Bingley Building Society.** This focused on mortgages for people who bought property to let, and many of them defaulted. It also relied heavily on market loans for its funds. It was taken over by the government in 2008, and later its branch network was bought by the Spanish bank Grupo Santander.
- **Lloyds HBOS.** HBOS (Halifax Bank of Scotland) was formed in 2001 by a merger of the UK's largest building society and a major bank. It suffered in the credit crunch and its share price fluctuated widely. It received some lender of last resort help, and then, in September 2008, Lloyds TSB took it over, believing it could return it to profit. But Lloyds had underestimated HBOS's problems, and early in 2009 the merged bank itself had to be rescued by the government, which, by November 2009, owned 43%.
- **Royal Bank of Scotland.** In October 2008, after receiving some lender of last resort support, this bank was rescued by the government, which has made many payments to it and, by 2010, owned 84%.

The 2007 credit crunch: the blame

It is always easy to be wise after the event, but the blame for the crisis has been apportioned among several groups.

- **US mortgage brokers.** They were paid commissions by the banks for finding people who wanted mortgages, so they had an incentive to persuade people to borrow too much and in turn persuade the banks to lend too much.
- **The credit rating agencies (CRAs).** These are businesses, such as Standard & Poor's and Moody's in the US, which give ratings for securities to estimate their riskiness. They failed to spot how risky the mortgage-linked securities were and gave them high ratings; had they spotted the risks, fewer would have been bought and fewer other banks would have been in trouble.
- **US banks.** They underestimated the risks of mortgage lending.
- **Other banks.** No bank can get into serious trouble and claim it has acted with exemplary prudence. The banks that bought mortgage-linked bonds issued by US banks could have been more sceptical of the CRA ratings, because they knew that the CRAs were paid fees by the banks that issued the securities, and so might be tempted to underestimate the risks.
- **Those who pushed for mortgages to have low risk weights in CAR calculations.** These low weights encouraged people to believe that banks with high mortgage lending were relatively safe.
- **The regulators of the banks.** Clearly, the Financial Services Authority in the UK, and equivalent bodies

elsewhere, failed to appreciate how much risk the banks were taking.

20.3 Everyday economics

The credit crunch helps young people

Figures produced by the Office for National Statistics show that the low interest rates introduced in response to the 2007 credit crunch led to savers earning £18bn less interest in 2009 than they would otherwise have earned, while borrowers paid £26bn less interest than they would otherwise have paid. So savers are less wealthy and borrowers more wealthy than they would otherwise be. This has chiefly hurt pensioners, who rely on income from their savings, and helped young people, who are the biggest borrowers.

'Savers lose out to cut in interest rates', *Allen's Accountants*, 8 April 2010
'Bank of England: savers should eat into cash', *Channel4 News*, 27 September 2010
'Savers lose out to cut in interest rates', *Taylor Cocks*, 8 April 2010

Comment Another result of the low rewards to saving is that people now save less, a decision that they may regret in later years when they retire.

20.5 **Summary**

- A credit crunch is a time when it is hard to borrow from banks.
- The root cause of the 2007 credit crunch was that many US banks had lent huge sums in mortgages to people who were liable to default, believing that if they did so, then their homes could be repossessed and sold to repay the loans—but falling property prices meant that many loans could not be fully repaid this way.
- The crisis spread to other banks that had made large market loans to US banks, and to other banks that had bought securities issued by the US banks with interest and repayments linked to mortgages.
- Some UK banks were rescued at high cost by the government.
- In an effort to reduce the risks they took, banks generally lent less, causing falls in spending, with resulting falls in output and increases in unemployment.

20.6 The money market

The money stock and 'the' rate of interest

We have seen that economists define the money stock as all the money available to the public to spend: it equals the cash they hold plus their bank deposits. The UK does not have an official measure of this amount, but it has a close measure called M4. M4 includes all the sterling that UK citizens hold in cash and in UK bank deposits, except for repo deposits. The measure is called M4 to distinguish it from measures introduced earlier called M0, M1, M2, and M3.

In January 2011, M4 was about £1,800 billion. This can be re-expressed as £1.8 trillion. This section explains the factors that determine the size of the money stock and cause it to change over time. We will see that the money stock is determined in what is called the money market by the demand for money and the supply of money.

These two forces also determine what is often called 'the' rate of interest. In practice, there are many different interest rates at any one time; for example, banks charge higher rates to borrowers than they pay to depositors. It is simplest to assume that by 'the' rate of interest, we mean the general or average level, which also allows for the returns on securities. When this level changes, other rates tend to change with it.

Figure 20.1 shows the money market for an economy. It has 'the' rate of interest on the vertical axis and the money stock on the horizontal axis. It also has a money supply curve, *MS*, and a money demand curve, *MD*. *MD* shows how much money the public would want to hold at each possible interest rate, while *MS* shows how much money the banks would like the public to hold at each rate. In this market, the equilibrium position is where the curves intersect, with a money stock, *M*, of £2.4 trillion, and an interest rate, *r*, of 6%.

To understand this figure fully, we will now look more closely at the two curves, and see why the market settles where they intersect.

The demand for money curve

The money demand curve, *MD*, in Figure 20.1 shows how much money the public would want to hold, in cash plus bank deposits, at each possible interest rate, *r*. It may initially seem surprising that the public's demand for money is anything short of infinite, but note that this curve shows how much money they want to *hold* as money, rather than immediately spending.

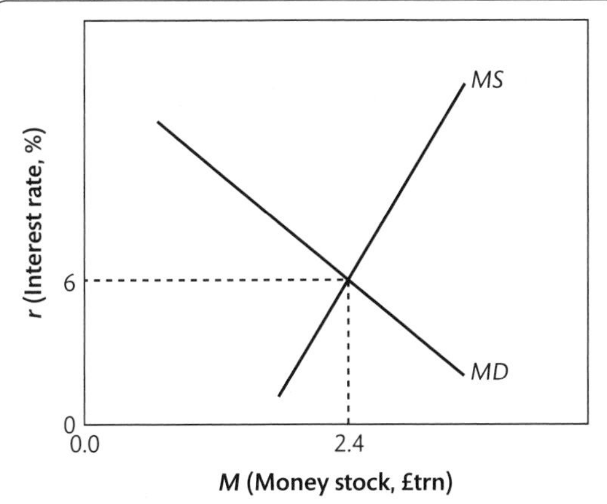

Figure 20.1 The money market

MD shows that the public want to hold more money at a low *r* than at a high *r*. *MS* shows that banks want to create more money at high *r* than at a low *r*. The market equilibrium is where the curves intersect, with *r* at 6% and *M*, the money stock, at £2.4trn.

The demand to hold money is called **liquidity preference**, because money is fully liquid. There are three main reasons why people want to hold some money. This point was first developed by the British economist John Maynard Keynes, who called the reasons 'motives'.

- **The transactions motive.** This motive arises because people do not want to spend all their money as soon as they receive it. For example, many people are paid once a month, but they do not want to spend all their income on payday; this is because they may have bills to pay that will arrive over the next month, and they will also want to spread their shopping out over the month. So they hold some money to spread out their purchases or transactions over the month.

  These employees hold more money for this motive at the beginning of each month than they hold at the end. But each month, while their transactions demand for money falls, their employers need to build up their transactions funds ready to pay the next round of wages. So the total transactions demand in the economy will be stable over the month.
- **The precautionary motive.** This motive arises because people like to hold some money in case an unforeseen crisis occurs, or in case they find an unforeseen bargain.
- **The speculative motive** or **asset motive.** This motive arises with people who have a fund of savings to divide between deposits of money and holdings of securities. Typically, securities have higher returns than deposits, so why would these people ever want to hold savings in money? In Keynes's view, they would hold money only if they expected security prices to fall and choose to move out of securities to avoid capital losses. A more common view today is that these people put most of their savings into securities because these offer higher returns than money, but they also keep some savings in money because securities also have the risk of capital losses.

Several factors affect the total quantity of money demanded.

- **The frequency with which people are paid.** To see this, suppose Wesley earns £1,000 a week, and holds £1,000 for transactions purposes just after being paid, and then reduces this to £0 by the next payday. Then his average holding for transactions purposes is £500. But if instead he were paid £4,000 every four weeks, then he might hold £4,000 for transactions purposes on payday, and then reduce this to £0 by the next payday, so having an average holding £2,000.
- **Incomes.** Suppose Wesley's pay rises from £1,000 every week to £1,200. Then he may on average hold £600 for transactions purposes instead of £500. He may also hold more for precautionary purposes, as he may have higher expectations of what he would do in a crisis and of the bargains that appeal to him.
- **Wealth.** As people become wealthier, so they have more savings. So they may want more money for the speculative or asset motive.
- **Interest rates.** *MD* curves are always drawn sloping downwards because people want to hold less money when the average interest rate is high than when it is low. This is because the gap between the interest rates on deposits and other assets widens when interest rates are high, making deposits less appealing. This especially affects the asset motive because, at high interest rates, holding money in case security prices fall means sacrificing a lot of interest.

Note that if any of the first three factors changes, then the whole *MD* curve will shift left or right. But if interest rates change, the economy moves to a different point on the original curve.

The money supply curve

The money supply curve in Figure 20.1 shows how much money the banks would like the public to hold in cash plus bank deposits. Suppose first that the interest rate if 6%, when *MS* shows that the banks want the public to hold £2.4 trillion.

This sum depends on four factors: the monetary base; how much of it the public holds in cash; how much of it the banks hold in reserves; and the reserve ratio used by the banks. For example, suppose the monetary base is £0.6 trillion, of which the public holds £0.4 trillion in cash and the banks hold £0.2 trillion in reserves. Also, suppose the banks want a reserve ratio of 10%. Then, with reserves of £0.2 trillion, they will want the public to hold deposits worth £2.0 trillion. As the public also has £0.4 trillion in cash, the banks want them to hold £2.4 trillion in all.

The money supply curve will shift to the right if the monetary base expands or if the banks choose to have lower reserve ratios at each possible interest rate. It will shift left if the opposite events occur.

In Figure 20.1, *MS* slopes upwards because the banks would like the public to hold more money at higher interest rates. This is for two reasons.

- **If interest rates rise, banks may risk lower reserve ratios.** Banks may decide a 10% reserve ratio is prudent when interest rates are 6%. But at higher interest rates, the returns on loans and securities will be higher, so the banks may be tempted to risk having a lower reserve ratio. And then they will want to make more loans and buy more securities, and so create more money.
- **If interest rates rise, the public may hold less cash and place more in the banks.** This is because deposits will pay more interest. Suppose a rise in interest rates leads the public to place £1 billion more cash in the banks. With £1 billion more reserves and a 10% reserve ratio, the banks will want deposits to rise by £10 billion. So they will want the money stock to end up £9 billion more than before, with £10 billion more in deposits and £1 billion less in publicly held cash.

Equilibrium in the money market

Figure 20.2 repeats the *MD* and *MS* curves from Figure 20.1. The curves intersect at an interest rate, *r*,

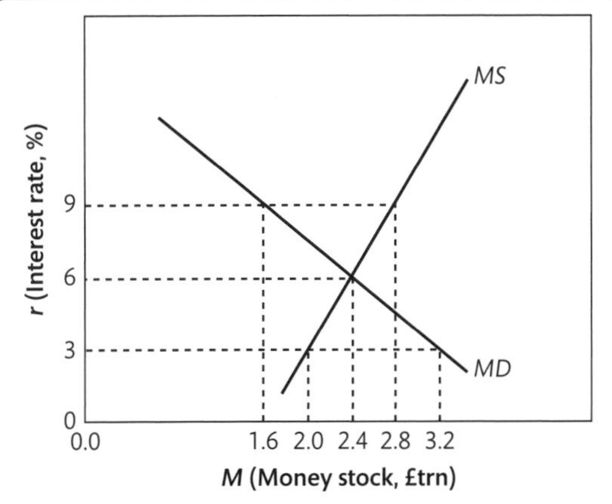

Figure 20.2 **Equilibrium in the money market**

If the interest rate is above equilibrium, say 9%, the public and the banks will buy bonds, raising their prices and reducing their returns; the banks will also reduce the rates on bank loans. So returns in general, measured by *r*, will fall. The opposite happens if the interest rate is below equilibrium at, say, 3%.

of 6%, and at a money stock, *M*, of £2.4 trillion. Let's see why the money market will settle here, making it the equilibrium position.

Suppose first that *r* is above 6%, say 9%. Then *MD* shows that the public wants to hold £1.6 trillion while *MS* shows that the banks want the public to hold £2.8 trillion. Suppose *M* is actually in between. Then the public and the banks will act as follows, and in so doing reduce the interest rates on bonds and bank loans, and so reduce the average rate, *r*.

- **The public.** To reduce the amount of money that they hold, the public will want to buy other assets, like bonds. The increased demand for bonds will raise their prices. Suppose a bond has a fixed income of £5 per year. If the price of this bond rises, then the £5 will be a smaller percentage of its price, so the return or interest rate on the bond for the new buyers will be lower.
- **The banks.** To increase the amount of money they create, the banks will try to lend more by reducing the interest rate on loans. They will also buy more bonds, raising their prices and reducing their returns in the same way as when the public buy bonds.

Now suppose that *r* is below 6%, say 3%. Then *MD* shows that the public wants to hold £3.2 trillion while *MS* shows that the banks want them to hold £2.0 trillion. Suppose *M* is actually in between. Then the public and the banks will act as follows, and in so doing raise the interest rates on bonds and bank loans, and so raise the average rate, *r*.

- **The public.** To increase the amount of money that they hold, the public will want to sell other assets, like bonds. The increased supply of bonds will reduce their prices. Suppose a bond has a fixed income of £5 per year. If the price of this bond falls, then the £5 will be a larger percentage of its price, so the return or interest rate on the bond for the new buyers will be higher.
- **The banks.** To reduce the amount of money they create, the banks will try to lend less by raising the interest rate on loans. The banks will also sell bonds, reducing their prices and raising their returns in the same way as when the public sells bonds.

So we have established that if *r* is above the equilibrium level, here 6%, it will fall, and if it is below that level it will rise. So *r* will end up at 6%, and here *M* will be the £2.4 trillion that is desired by both the public and the banks.

Question 20.3 Suppose the public holds less money than they want, so they sell securities. Every security that is sold by one person must be bought by another, so the total amount of money held will actually remain the same. So how can the public end up holding the amount of money they want, and not still hold less than they want?

Changing the money stock and interest rates

Figure 20.3 shows how the money market equilibrium can change. Initially, the curves MD_0 and MS_0 apply,

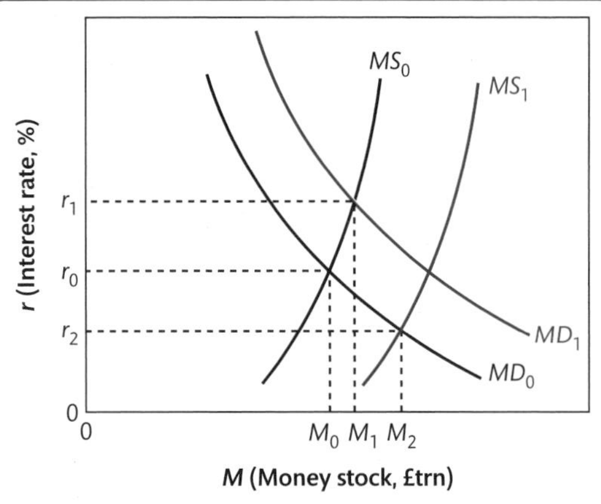

Figure 20.3 **Changes in the money market equilibrium**

An increase in the demand for money shifts the money demand curve right from MD_0 to MD_1, raising the money stock and the interest rate. An increase in the supply of money shifts the money supply curve right from MS_0 to MS_1, raising the money stock, but reducing the interest rate.

and the market is in equilibrium, with interest rate r_0 and money stock M_0.

Now suppose there is an increase in the demand for money that shifts the demand curve right to MD_1. Perhaps some people previously paid weekly are now paid monthly, or wealth or incomes rise. Then the interest rate will rise to r_1 and the money stock will rise to M_1. If opposite events were to occur to shift the demand curve to the left of MD_0, then interest rates and the money stock would fall.

Next suppose that the market is in the initial equilibrium and there is an increase in the supply of money that shifts the supply curve right to MS_1. Perhaps the government or central bank have increased the monetary base, or perhaps the public has decided to hold less cash and place more in the banks, or perhaps the banks have decided to operate with lower reserve ratios. Then the interest rate will fall to r_2 and the money stock will rise to M_2. If opposite events were to occur to shift the supply curve to the left of MS_0, then interest rates would rise and the money stock would fall.

20.6 Summary

- The general level of interest rates and the money stock are determined in the money market.
- In this market, people demand to hold money for transactions purposes, to bridge the period between receiving income and wanting to spend it, and for precautionary purposes, in case of unforeseen crises and bargains, and for speculative or asset purposes, aware that keeping all their savings in securities is risky. The higher the general level of interest rates, the less money people want to hold.
- The banks want to supply more money at high interest rates, partly because the public may then deposit more cash in the banks, and partly because the banks will risk lower reserve ratios.
- The demand for money curve shifts if there are changes in income, wealth, or the frequency with which people are paid. The supply of money curve shifts if the monetary base changes, or if the public decides to hold more or less cash, or if the banks choose to operate with different reserve ratios.

20.7 Intervening in the money market

No country allows its money stock and interest rates to be set by the money market on its own. Instead, either the government or the central bank intervenes. We will suppose here that the central bank intervenes, as in the UK. Various forms of intervention are possible. We will illustrate these in Figure 20.4. Here, the

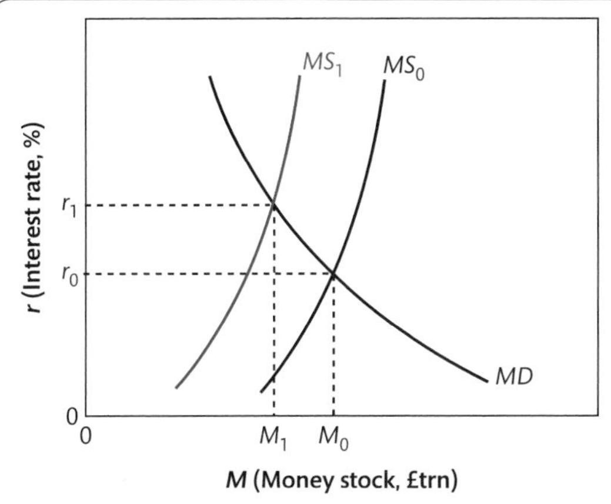

Figure 20.4 **Reducing the money stock and raising interest rates**

To reduce the money stock and raise interest rates, the monetary authorities need to shift the money supply curve left from MS_0 to MS_1. They might require the banks to operate with higher reserve ratios, or use open market sales of securities to reduce the banks' reserves. Either way, the banks have to create less money.

initial demand and supply curves are *MD* and MS_0, and the market is initially in equilibrium, with the interest rate at r_0 and the money stock at M_0.

The central bank can shift the money supply curve to take the market to another point on *MD*. For example, suppose the central bank wants to reduce the money stock to M_1 and so raise the interest rate to r_1. There are two classic ways of doing this.

- **Reserve ratio controls.** The central bank could require commercial banks to adopt a higher reserve ratio than the one they are choosing for themselves. This would reduce their ability to lend and buy securities, and so create money, so the money supply curve would shift left to MS_1, as required.
- **Open market operations** or **monetary base control.** The central bank could sell securities in the markets for them. Usually, it would sell government securities. If it were to sell these to the commercial banks, then they would have to pay it by giving it reserves. If it were to sell them to the public, and they were to make payments from their deposits to the central bank, then their banks would have to give reserves to the central bank. So the monetary base would fall because the banks would have lower reserves. The banks would then have to create less money, so again the money supply curve would shift left to MS_1.

Note that if, in the initial situation, the central bank wished to shift *MS* to the right, it could not use reserve ratio controls: it would be irresponsible to tell the banks to operate with lower reserves than they thought prudent. But it could use open market operations to buy securities. If it were to buy them from the banks, it would give them reserves right away, and if it were to buy them from the public and make payments into their deposits, then the banks would demand reserves from the central bank. Either way, the banks would have more reserves and could then create more money.

In the UK, however, reserve requirements have not been used since the 1980s, and although open market operations are used, they are not the main method. To understand the UK's main method, we must study its reserve arrangements.

The reserve arrangements in the UK

To see how the UK system works, suppose you run a bank. If you run a small bank, you will face no reserve requirements. If you run a big bank, you will have to keep a small deposit called a cash ratio deposit at the Bank of England, which we will simply call the Bank. Cash ratio deposits are so small that we can ignore them, but we will note that big banks get no interest on them, even though the Bank lends the money placed in them to earn an income for itself. The idea here is that this income should cover the costs that the Bank faces when it operates the arrangements that we will now discuss.

Let's return to your bank. You will probably open a deposit at the Bank, quite aside from any cash ratio deposit you may hold there, and place most of your reserves in this deposit. Then the Bank can use this deposit to handle clearing between your bank and other banks.

Each month, the Bank will ask you to set yourself a target for your reserves at the Bank over the next month, and to tell it what the target is. Then three things could happen over the month, as follows.

- **You keep your reserves close to this target.** Then the Bank will pay you interest on all your reserves there at its official Bank Rate.
- **You build up more reserves than your target.** Then you can also keep the excess at the Bank, but you will be paid a little less interest on it.
- **Your reserves threaten to go below your target.** Then, instead of missing your target, you will be expected to borrow more reserves from the Bank at a rate just above Bank Rate.

Suppose, for example, that Bank Rate is 5%. Then the rate on money market loans that banks lend to each other will be close to this. No bank will lend to another for much less, when it can lend at about 5% to the Bank of England. And no bank will borrow from another for much more, when it can borrow at about 5% from the Bank of England. The upshot is that, in normal circumstances, you can always acquire funds at around Bank rate, either from the Bank or with money market loans.

The money supply curve in the UK

As UK banks can generally increase their reserves by borrowing more from the Bank, we need to deepen our understanding of how the UK's money supply curve is derived. To do this, we will make the following three simplifying assumptions.

- Banks create money only by making advances.
- There are only two interest rates in the economy: the Bank Rate on loans between banks, and the rate on banks' advances to households and non-bank firms.
- The total amount of these advances greatly exceeds the total amount that banks borrow from each other, so that we can take 'the' interest rate to be the rate on advances.

Now consider how much your bank would advance if 'the' interest rate, that is the rate on advances, were, say, 7%. This would depend on Bank Rate, as shown by the three following examples.

- **Suppose Bank Rate is 7%.** In this case, you will lend only to borrowers you regard as wholly safe, and so make very few advances. You will not make even slightly risky loans at 7% when you can get 7% safely on your deposit at the Bank, or by lending to other banks.
- **Suppose Bank Rate is 5%.** You will now lend also to borrowers you regard as slightly risky, so you will make more advances. You will not lend at 7% to high-risk borrowers when you can get 5% safely on your deposit at the Bank, or by lending to other banks.
- **Suppose Bank Rate is 3%.** You will now lend to quite risky borrowers and so make even more advances. You can, after all, borrow at about 3% from the Bank, or from other banks, and so by lending at 7%, you should make enough profit on most advances to cover some defaults.

The implication is that, at any given level for 'the' interest rate, such as 7%, the amount you will want to advance depends on Bank Rate: the lower the Bank Rate is, the more you will want to advance. The same applies to other banks. We saw in section 20.2 that banks create money when they make advances, so we can now see that the quantity of money they will want to create is affected by Bank Rate. In turn, the amount they will want people to hold, as shown by the money supply curve, depends on Bank Rate.

In Figure 20.4, points $\boldsymbol{a}_{BR7}$, $\boldsymbol{a}_{BR5}$, and $\boldsymbol{a}_{BR3}$ show how much money the banks between them would like people to hold if 'the' interest rate were 7%, and if Bank Rate were respectively 7%, 5%, or 3%.

Suppose, instead, that 'the' rate on advances were 9%. Then, at each Bank Rate that we considered, the banks would be willing to make more advances by lending to borrowers with greater risk. So the banks would want to create more money. The amounts they would like to create are shown in Figure 20.4 by points $\boldsymbol{b}_{BR7}$, $\boldsymbol{b}_{BR5}$, and $\boldsymbol{b}_{BR3}$, which are to the right of points $\boldsymbol{a}_{BR7}$, $\boldsymbol{a}_{BR5}$, and $\boldsymbol{a}_{BR3}$.

Figure 20.4 has three money supply curves.

- $\boldsymbol{MS}_{BR7}$, which passes through $\boldsymbol{a}_{BR7}$ and $\boldsymbol{b}_{BR7}$. This shows how much money banks would like the public to hold at different levels for 'the' interest rate if Bank Rate were 7%.
- $\boldsymbol{MS}_{BR5}$, which passes through $\boldsymbol{a}_{BR5}$ and $\boldsymbol{b}_{BR5}$. This shows how much money banks would like the public to hold at different levels for 'the' interest rate if Bank Rate were 5%.
- $\boldsymbol{MS}_{BR3}$, which passes through $\boldsymbol{a}_{BR3}$ and $\boldsymbol{b}_{BR3}$. This shows how much money banks would like the public to hold at different levels for 'the' interest rate if Bank Rate were 3%.

Suppose Bank Rate is currently 5%, so that MS_{BR5} applies. Then the money market will settle where this intersects MD with 'the' interest rate at 7% and the money stock at M_0.

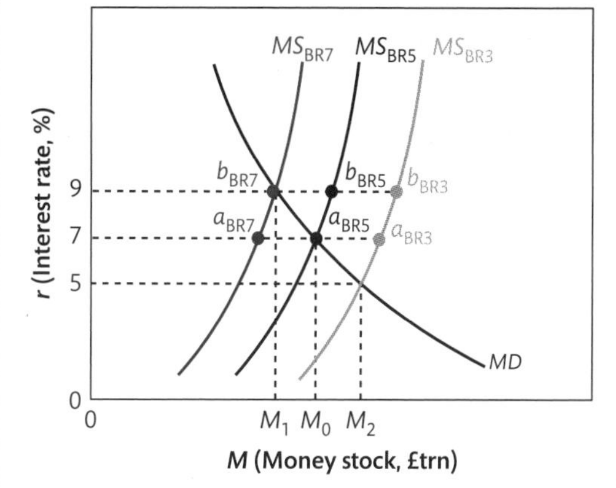

Figure 20.5 **Interest rate control**

The UK money supply curve and money market equilibrium depend on Bank Rate. If Bank Rate is 5%, MS_{BR5} applies and the interest rate is 7% with money stock M_0. A rise in Bank Rate to 7% shifts the money supply curve to MS_{BR7}, raising the interest rate and reducing the money stock to M_1. A fall in Bank Rate to 3% shifts the money supply curve to MS_{BR3}, reducing the interest rate and raising the money stock to M_2.

Interest rate control

We can now see how the Bank of England can alter the money market equilibrium. It does so using a method called **interest rate control**, which means altering Bank Rate. Suppose initially that Bank Rate is 5%, so that, in Figure 20.5, the money supply curve is MS_{BR5}, and the money market is in equilibrium where this intersects MD, with the interest rate at 7% and the money stock at M_0.

If the Bank raises Bank Rate to 7%, the money supply curve shifts left to MS_{BR7}, and equilibrium is where this intersects MD, so the interest rate rises to 9% and the money stock falls to M_1. If the Bank instead cuts Bank Rate to 3%, the money supply curve shifts right to MS_{BR3}, and equilibrium is where this intersects MD, so the interest rate falls to 5% and the money stock rises to M_2.

In practice, the interest rate that banks charge on advances tends to exceed Bank Rate by a fairly constant amount, to cover their risks and also the cost of administering loans. Consequently, when Bank Rate changes, the banks' own lending rates generally change at once by the same amount.

Open market operations in the UK system

In the UK system, the Bank of England uses open market operations in two ways. First, each month it does some open market operations to ensure that the total level of reserves available to the banks is close to the level that prudent banks will want for the current money stock: the Bank does not want banks to have more reserves than they need, because they will place them in the Bank and want it to pay interest on them.

In fact, the Bank generally uses these operations to keep reserves just below the level that prudent banks will want. To make up the shortfall, it then undertakes additional open market operations each week to ensure that the banks end up with the level of reserves they want. These weekly operations rarely involve the traditional type of operations in which a central bank purchases securities. Instead, the Bank makes loans each week in the form of repo deposits at the banks, which can be seen as loans, at Bank Rate. If the banks have too few reserves one week, then it lends more than they must repay from last week; if instead they have too many reserves, then it lends less than they must repay from last week.

Monetary policy and quantitative easing

In Chapter 26, we will see how the Bank makes its decisions over Bank Rate, and we will see how these decisions affect the economy as a whole. We will also look at the recent experience of quantitative easing, which has been called 'open market operations on a grand scale'.

20.7 Summary

- To reduce the money stock, the monetary authorities can reduce the banks' reserves, by using open market sales of securities, or alternatively require the banks to keep higher reserve ratios.
- The authorities can also increase the official interest rate at which the central bank will lend to the banks. This is the main method in the UK, although it is backed up by open market operations.

In the next chapter we look at the price level. And we will develop a model that shows simultaneously how both GDP and the price level are determined.

abc Glossary

Advances: bank loans other than market loans.

Aggregation: the ability of banks to combine small amounts from many small deposits to make large loans.

Asset motive: the desire for savers to hold some savings in money because securities are risky.

Bank deposit multiplier: the ratio of the change in bank deposits to a change in bank reserves.

Banknotes: notes on which banks promise to make a payment to 'the bearer' on demand; the payments were originally in coins of valuable metal.

Bank Rate: the official Bank of England rate that is paid on deposits held there by commercial banks.

Barter: swapping products without using money.

Capital adequacy ratio (CAR): the ratio of a bank's capital to its risk-weighted assets.

Cash: a term used to cover banknotes and coins.

Cash drain: the tendency for the public to withdraw cash from banks when their deposits rise.

Certificates of deposit (CDs): deposits for large amounts that cannot be used before an agreed term, but which can be sold before the term ends.

Credit crunch: a situation in which banks are unwilling to lend, so that it is hard to obtain credit.

Deficit unit: a household, business, or government with less money than it currently needs to spend.

Financial intermediaries: companies, including banks, which undertake financial intermediation.

Financial intermediation: the act of transferring funds from surplus units to deficit units.

Interest rate control: changing the Bank of England's Bank Rate to control the money market.

Liquid asset: cash plus other assets that can be made available quickly in cash at a known value.

Liquidity: having some assets that can be easily and quickly converted into a known sum of money.

Liquidity preference: the demand to hold money.

Market loan: a loan by one bank to another.

Maturity transformation: the fact that banks typically borrow for shorter terms than they lend.

Monetary base: publicly held cash plus bank reserves.

Monetary base control: altering the money stock through open market operations, so-called because this changes the monetary base.

Money: anything that is generally accepted as a means of payment (in practice, cash and bank deposits).

Money multiplier: the ratio of the change in the money stock to a change in the monetary base.

Money stock: the total amount of money the public can spend, equal to their cash plus bank deposits.

Money supply: another term for the money stock.

Open market operations: a term usually used for purchases and sales of securities by the central bank, but also used by the Bank of England for its weekly repo loans of reserves to the banks.

Precautionary motive: the desire to hold money in case of unforeseen crises or bargains.

Repurchase agreements (or repos): agreements to buy securities from a bank and sell them back later at a slightly higher price.

Reserve ratio: the ratio of a bank's reserves to its deposits.

Reserve ratio controls: imposing reserve ratios on the banks, instead of letting banks choose their own.

Reserves: cash held by banks on their premises plus deposits held by banks at the central bank.

Reverse repo: a term used to describe a repo held by a bank that agrees to buy securities from another bank and later sell them back.

Risk transformation: the fact that deposits at banks have little risk, even though loans made by banks may be high risk.

Seignorage: fees charged by mints for making coins when coins included valuable metals.

Sight deposits: deposits that can be withdrawn in cash, or used for Internet and other payments, on demand and without any penalty.

Speculative motive: *see* asset motive.

Surplus unit: a household, business, or government that has some money that it does not need to spend at present.

Time deposits: deposits for which notice is meant to be given before they are withdrawn or used for Internet and other payments; use may be allowed on demand, subject to a penalty of lost interest.

Transactions motive: the desire to hold money because people do not want to spend all their money as soon as they receive it.

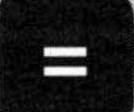

Answers to in-text questions

20.1 To repay a bank loan, a depositor needs to build up his or her deposit. The depositor may bring in cash, which raises the bank's reserves; or the depositor may receive payments from other people, most of whom probably use different banks, and when the payments are made their banks pay reserves to the borrower's bank.

20.2 There is no offsetting fall in reserves with loans from the central bank, which simply presses computer keys to raise the government's deposit; so bank reserves and the money stock rise as discussed in the text. But if the government borrows from the public, or raises taxes, then the public pay it money, so their banks must give reserves to its bank, that is the central bank. As a result, the commercial banks lose just as many reserves as they gain from the government spending, so overall their reserves and the money stock will be unaffected.

20.3 If the public as a whole wants more money, then many people will want to sell securities, so security prices will fall. This will raise the returns on securities as a percentage of their current price, and so raises the general level of interest rates. This, in turn, will reduce the amount of money that people want to hold, and so bring the amount they want to hold into balance with the amount that they do hold.

? Questions for review

20.1 Why are credit cards, debit cards, and store cards not money?

20.2 Suppose the public want a cash to deposit ratio of 2% and the banks want a reserve ratio of 4%. What is the value of the money multiplier?

20.3 Suppose a bond has a face value of £100 and a coupon of 5%. What rate of return will its interest represent to a second-hand buyer if the second-hand price is currently (**a**) £50, (**b**) £100, or (**c**) £125?

20.4 How can a bank increase its capital adequacy ratio?

20.5 Compile a table similar to Table 20.2, in which the Stage (1) figures are the same as Table 20.2, but in which in Stage (2), the public pays £30 million in taxes to the government from their bank deposits. As in Table 20.1, assume that $r = 0.1$ and $d = 0.2$.

20.6 What will happen in the money market if (**a**) investors become more worried that security prices may fall, or (**b**) banks become less worried about the difficulties of securing market loans?

? Questions for discussion

20.1 Why do people accept coins and notes as money when the value of their metal and paper is negligible? And why do they accept bank deposits as money when they are simply numbers in a computer?

20.2 What, if anything, should the UK government have done to prevent the 2007 credit crunch?

20.3 Can you suggest any regulations that could be imposed on the banks to reduce the chance of another credit crunch? Could these controls guarantee there would not be another? Would the controls need to be adopted internationally?

Common student errors

Perhaps the hardest concept to grasp is that bank deposits are simply numbers by people's names that banks can increase simply by pressing keys on a computer. Because these deposits can be spent, they are money, so the banks can literally create money—but note that the banks are not printing notes, which are now a minor form of money.

Some students find it hard to believe that banks do not hold cash of equal amount to the level of their deposits, but Table 20.4 shows that the ratio is very small.

Finally, many students do not pause to think that the demand for money really is the demand to *hold* on to money instead of spending it at once.

Appendix: Output and interest rates—the *IS-LM* model

In Chapter 19, we developed the multiplier model to show the factors that determine GDP. In this chapter, we have developed the money market model to show the factors that determine the interest rate. This appendix develops a model that shows how any event will affect both output and the interest rate. But you can omit this appendix and still understand all later chapters.

The multiplier model

Figure 20.A1 illustrates one of the two figures we used for the multiplier model. The line E_0 shows how much planned spending there would be at each output level: assuming the diagram relates to a four-sector economy, you will recall that planned spending equals $C + I + G + X - M$, that is planned spending by consumers, plus planned investment, plus planned government purchases, plus planned exports, minus planned imports.

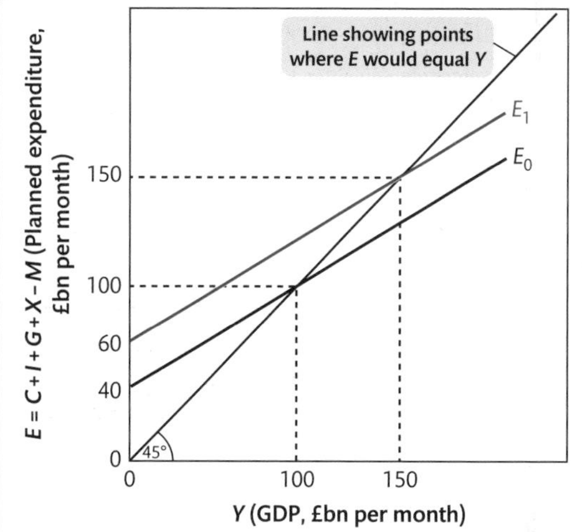

Figure 20.A1 **The multiplier model**

In this example, a shift of £20bn in the planned spending line raises output by £50bn. But this overlooks the fact that, as output rises, incomes and the demand for money will rise, so the interest rate will rise, and that will take planned spending below E_1. So output will actually rise by less than this model predicts.

Output settles at the equilibrium level, which is the level at which output equals planned spending. This level is £100 billion, which we find by seeing where E_0 intersects the 45° line through the origin. To see why this is the equilibrium output, consider what will happen if output, *Y*, is at another level.

- **Y is below £100 billion.** In this case, E_0 is above the 45° line, so *E* exceeds *Y*. So people want to buy more than producers are making. So stocks will fall, or at least rise by less than producers want, and this will encourage them to produce more.
- **Y is above £100 billion.** In this case, E_0 is below the 45° line, so *E* is less than *Y*. So people want to buy less than producers are making. So stocks will rise by more than producers want, and this will encourage them to reduce output.

Now suppose output is at its equilibrium level, and then planned spending rises by £20 billion a month, shifting the spending line up to E_1. The model predicts that output will rise to £150 billion where E_1 intersects the 45° line. So a £20 billion rise in spending leads to a £50 billion rise in output, from which we deduce that the multiplier here is 2½.

However, the model overlooks the fact that the rise in output will lead to a rise in incomes. And we have seen in this chapter that there will then be a rise in the demand for money that will increase the interest rate. This will reduce *C* and *I*, because consumers and firms who need to borrow to finance some of their spending will find loans more costly. So the spending line will end up below E_1, so output will end up less than the £150 billion that the multiplier predicts. We will now develop a new model, which allows for the rise in the interest rate. The new model is called the *IS–LM* model because it is based on two curves: the *IS* curve and the *LM* curve. We will look at these in turn, and then put them together.

Deriving the *IS* curve

The *IS* curve is explained in Figure 20.A2. Suppose the interest rate, *r*, is initially 6% and the spending line is $E(r = 6)$ in the top part, so output is £100 billion where this intersects the 45° line. Now suppose *r* was instead 3% lower or higher, at 3% or 9%. Then borrowing would be less or more costly, so *C* plus *I* would be higher or lower. Suppose *C* plus *I* would be £10 billion more or less. Then the spending line would be as shown by the black lines $E(r = 3)$ or $E(r = 9)$. So output would be £125 billion if *r* were 3% or £75 billion if *r* were 9%.

The bottom part of the figure has a graph that has output on the horizontal axis and the interest rate on the vertical axis. The points ***a***, ***b***, and ***c*** repeat what we found in the top part about the output level at interest rates of 6%, 3%, and 9%. We can plot a curve through these points to show what output would be at each possible interest rate. This curve slopes downwards to show that the lower is the interest rate, the higher is output. This curve is called the *IS* curve.

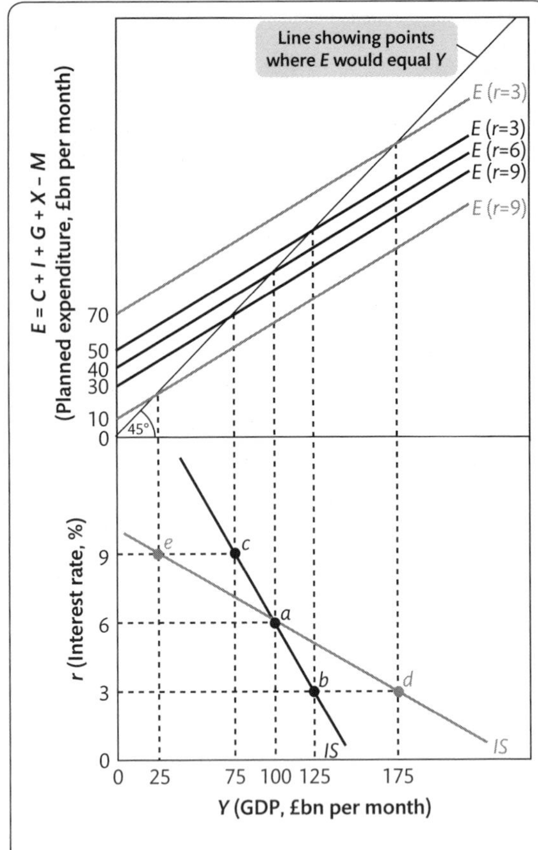

Figure 20.A2 **The *IS* curve**

If 3% changes in *r* shift the *E* line by £10bn, then the relation between *Y* and *r* is as shown by the black *IS* curve. But If they shift *E* by £30bn, then the relationship is as shown by the grey *IS* curve.

Why is the *IS* curve so called?

The *IS* curve is derived by considering the equilibrium level of output. In Figure 20.A2, we did this by using the planned spending line. We could instead have used injections and withdrawals lines. If we had been talking about a two-sector economy, with only households and firms, then the only injections and withdrawals would have been investment, *I*, and saving, *S*. Economists first discussed *IS* curves for a two-sector economy and used the letters *I* and *S* to show that the curve related to the level of output, which, in such an economy, depends on *I* and *S*. We still call the curve the *IS* curve, even for a four-sector economy in which injections include government purchases and exports, and in which withdrawals include taxes and imports.

The interest elasticity of the *IS* curve

In Figure 20.A2, the black spending lines assume that 3% changes in *r* will change *C* plus *I* by £10 billion, and so shift the planned spending line by £10 billion from the initial $E(r = 6)$. But suppose *C* and *I* were more sensitive to changes in interest rates, and changed by £30 billion when *r* changed by 3%. Then the planned spending lines for interest rates of 3% and 9% would be £30 billion away from $E(r = 6)$, as shown by grey $E(r = 3)$ and $E(r = 9)$ lines. So output would be £175 billion or £25 billion. These results are shown in the bottom part by points ***d*** and ***e***. We can draw the grey IS curve through them.

This grey *IS* curve is flatter than the black one, because it concerns a case in which spending and, in turn, output are more responsive to changes in the interest rate. Because output responds more to

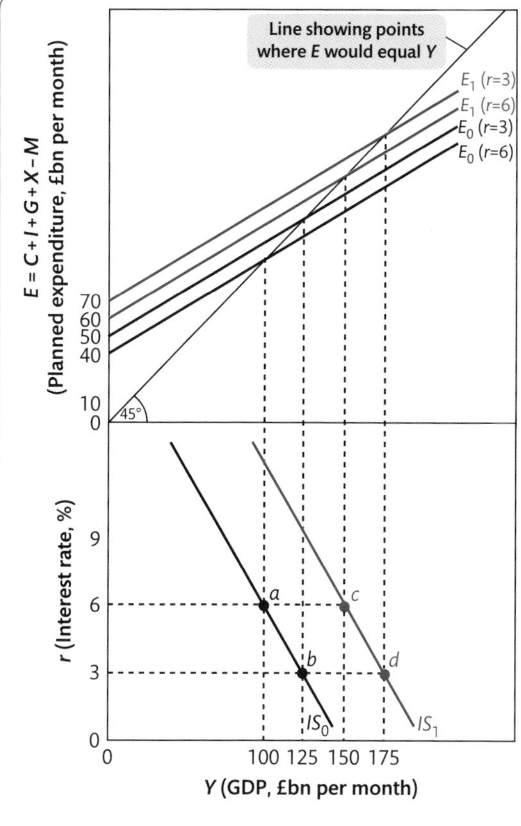

Figure 20.A3 **Shifts in the *IS* curve**

If *E* shifts up because of any factor except a fall in the interest rate, then, at each *r*, *Y* will be greater, so the *IS* curve will shift right.

interest rate changes with this *IS* curve, we say that this curve is more interest elastic.

Shifts in the *IS* curve

Suppose that output is relatively insensitive to interest rate changes, so that the black *IS* curve applies to the economy. The top part of Figure 20.A3 repeats two of the black spending lines we used to derive this, labelled here as $E_0(r = 6)$ and $E_0(r = 3)$. The bottom part repeats the related points ***a*** and ***b***, together with the black *IS* curve drawn through them, labelled here IS_0.

Now suppose something happens that means that, at each possible interest rate, the planned spending line shifts up by £20 billion. Perhaps the government cuts taxes so that *C* rises, or firms become more optimistic so that *I* rises, or the government spends more so that G rises, or exports rise or imports fall. Then the planned spending lines for interest rates of 6% and 3% will shift up to $E_1(r = 6)$ and $E_1(r = 3)$. So, at these interest rates, output will be £150 billion and £175 billion, as noted in the bottom part by points ***c*** and ***d***. Then the *IS* curve will shift right to IS_1, which passes through these new points.

We can conclude that anything that increases planned spending shifts *IS* to the right, except for a fall in the interest rate; a fall in the interest rate would simply take the economy from one point on its *IS* curve to a lower point. Conversely, anything that reduces planned spending, except for a rise in the interest rate, shifts *IS* to the left; a rise in the interest rate would take the economy from one point on its *IS* curve to a higher point.

Deriving the *LM* curve

The *LM* curve is explained in Figure 20.A4. The left-hand part here shows the money market. Suppose that the money supply curve is *MS*. Also, suppose that output, *Y*, is £100 billion a month, and that the money demand curve is the black one labelled $MD(Y = 100)$. This intersects *MS* at 6%, so the interest rate, *r*, is 6%. Now suppose that output rises to £150 billion, so increasing the demand for money to the black $MD(Y = 150)$; then *r* will rise to 11%. Or suppose that output falls to £50 billion, so reducing the demand for money to the black $MD(Y = 50)$; then *r* will fall to 1%.

The right-hand part of the figure has a graph that has output on the horizontal axis and the interest rate on the vertical axis. The points ***a***, ***b***, and ***c*** repeat what we discovered in the left-hand part, namely that if output were £100 billion, £150 billion, or £50 billion, then *r* would be 6%, 11%, or 1%. We can plot a curve through these points to show what *r* would be at each possible output. This curve slopes upwards to show that the higher the output, the higher is the interest rate. This curve is called the *LM* curve.

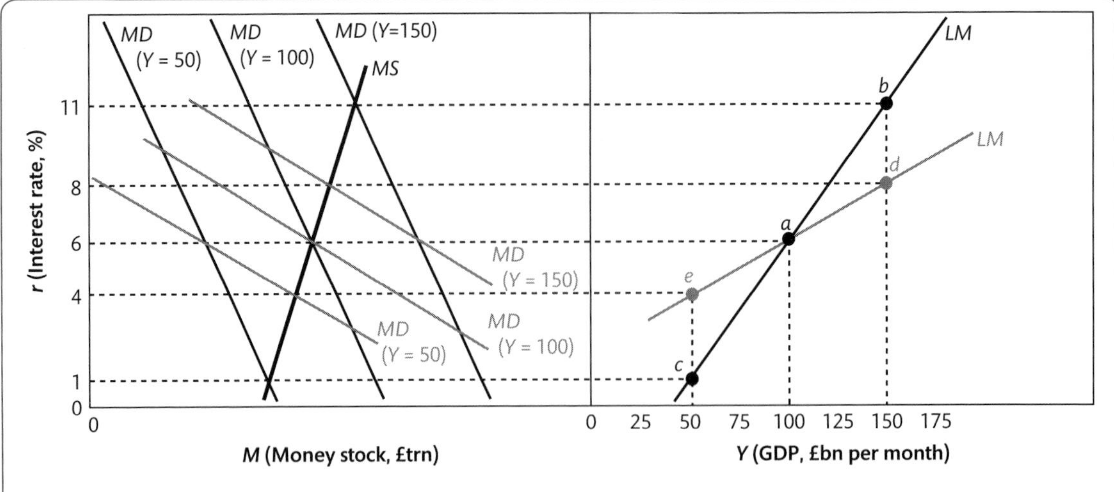

Figure 20.A4 **The *LM* curve**

If money demand is inelastic, and the *MD* at different levels of *Y* is as shown by the black *MD* curves, then *Y* and *r* will be related as on the black *LM* curve. If money demand is elastic and the grey *MD* curves apply, then *Y* and *r* will be related as on the grey *LM* curve.

Why is the *LM* curve so called?

The *LM* curve is derived from the demand and supply of money. People often call the demand for money liquidity preference and use the letter *L* for it. Also, people often use *M* for the money supply. So the name *LM* tells us that the *LM* curve relates to liquidity preference and the money supply.

The interest elasticity of the *LM* curve

In Figure 20.A4, the black money demand curves were relatively interest inelastic. Suppose that the demand for money were interest elastic. Then the demand curves at outputs of £100 billion, £150 billion, and £50 billion might have been as shown by the grey $MD(Y = 100)$, $MD(Y = 150)$, and $MD(Y = 50)$. If you look at the interest rate of 6%, you can see that these curves actually shift as much left or right as the black curves when output changes by £50 billion.

With these curves, an output of £100 billion would still give *r* as 6%, but outputs of £150 billion and £50 billion would give *r* as 8% or 4%. These results are shown in the right-hand part by points ***d*** and ***e***, and a grey *LM* curve is drawn through them. You can see that, in this case, where the money demand is relatively interest elastic, the *LM* curve is flatter or more interest elastic. This is because changes in output are here associated with smaller changes in *r*.

Shifts in the *LM* curve

Suppose the demand for money is relatively inelastic, so the black *LM* curve applies. The left-hand part of Figure 20.A5 repeats two of the black money demand curves that we used to derive it, along with the money supply curve. These curves are labelled here as $MD_0(Y = 100)$, $MD_0(Y = 150)$, and MS_0. The right-hand part repeats points ***a*** and ***b*** with the black *LM* drawn through them, labelled as LM_0.

Now suppose the central bank shifts the money supply curve right to MS_1, perhaps by reducing Bank Rate. Then, at outputs of £100 billion and £150 billion, *r* would now be 3% and 8%, where MS_1 intersects $MD_0(Y = 100)$ and $MD_0(Y = 150)$. These results are recorded in the right-hand part by points ***c*** and ***d***. And the *LM* curve will shift right to LM_1 which passes through these new points.

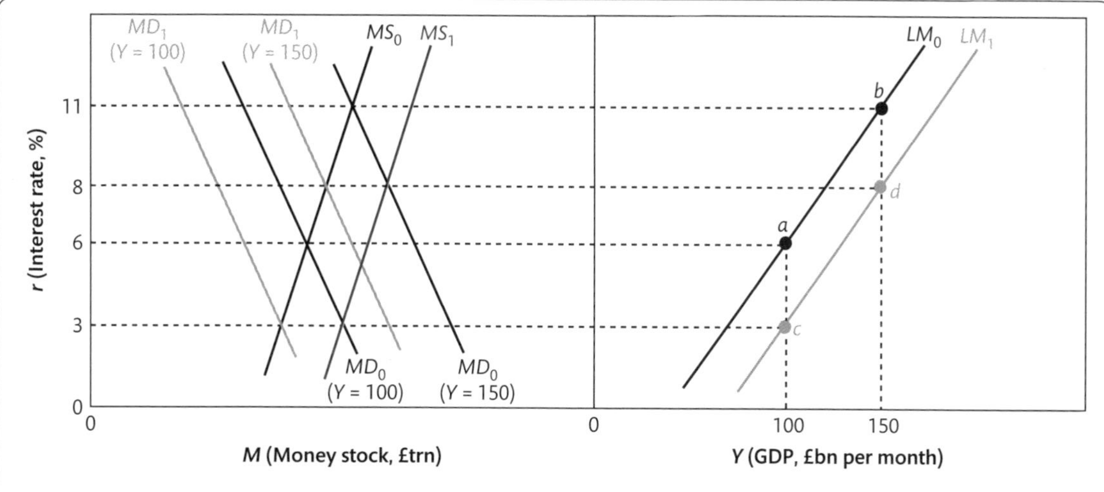

Figure 20.A5 **Shifts in the *LM* curve**

If the money supply curve shifts right, perhaps following a fall in Bank Rate, then each *Y* leads to a lower *r* and the *LM* curve shifts as shown. Also, if at each *Y*, money demand falls, then each *Y* leads to a lower *r*, so again the *LM* curve shifts as shown.

Suppose instead that the money supply curve stays as MS_0, but that something happens that means that at each possible output, the demand for money would be lower. Perhaps people think security prices are likely to rise, so they want to hold more of their savings in securities and less in money. Then, at outputs of £100 billion and £150 billion, the demand for money might now be as shown by $MD_1(Y = 100)$ and $MD_1(Y = 150)$, giving *r* as 3% or 8% respectively, where they intersect MS_0. These results are recorded in the right-hand part by points ***c*** and ***d***. So the *LM* curve would again shift to LM_1.

We can conclude that rightward shifts in *MS* and leftward shifts in *MD* both shift *LM* to the right. Conversely, leftward shifts in *MS* or rightward shifts in *MD* would both shift *LM* to the left.

Putting the *IS* and *LM* curves together

Figure 20.A6 puts the *IS* and *LM* curves together. They intersect at the point where *r* is 6% and *Y* is £100 billion a month, and this is where the economy will settle. So these are the equilibrium values of the interest rate and output, r_E and Y_E. To see why the economy will end up at this point, suppose that it is currently somewhere else, say at the point marked ***j*** with $r = 8\%$ and $Y = £150$ billion.

We know from the *LM* curve that if *Y* is £150 billion, then the interest rate will settle at 11%. So if it is 8% at present, as at ***j***, then it will rapidly rise to 11%, taking

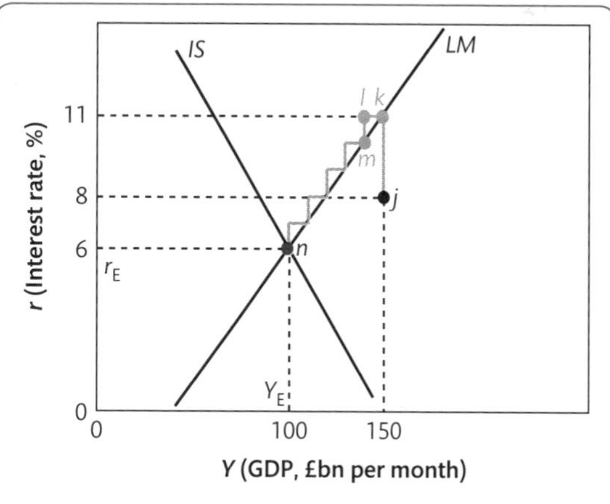

Figure 20.A6 **Equilibrium in the *IS-LM* model**

Suppose the economy has a combination of *Y* and *r* that is not on the *LM* curve, as at ***j***, Then *r* will quickly adjust to take the economy up or down to the *LM* curve, here at ***k***. Then *Y* and *r* continue to adjust to take the economy to the equilibrium, ***n***, where *IS* intersects *LM*.

the economy to point ***k***. Indeed, whenever the economy is below or above *LM*, interest rates will quickly rise of fall to take the economy up or down to *LM*.

At ***k***, *r* is 11%. The *IS* curve tells us that if *r* is 11%, then *Y* will settle well below £100 billion. Now *Y*, or output, can only change slowly, but it will start to fall. And it may soon take the economy to ***l***, which is above *LM*. So *r* will fall a little, returning the economy to *LM*, just below ***l*** at ***m***. So, starting from ***k***, *Y* and *r* fall in turn, and they continue to do so along the path shown in pink until equilibrium is reached at ***n***.

Comparing the *IS*–*LM* and multiplier models

Figure 20.A7 compares the multiplier model and the *IS*–*LM* model. In the bottom part, the initial equilibrium in the *IS*–*LM* model is shown where the initial *IS* curve, IS_0, intersects *LM*. So output is Y_0 and the interest rate is 6%. The initial spending line in the top part is $E_0(r = 6)$, and this intersects the 45° line at Y_0 to show the multiplier model agreeing with *IS*–*LM* that Y_0 is the initial output.

Now suppose that planned spending increases for any reason other than a fall in the interest rate, and that initially the interest rate stays at 6%. The planned spending line in the top part shifts up to $E_1(r = 6)$ and the multiplier model predicts a rise in output to Y_1. The rise in spending shifts *IS* right to IS_1, and this shows that if the interest rate were to stay at 6%, then output would indeed be Y_1.

However, as output starts to rise, incomes and the demand for money increase, so the interest rate increases. The bottom part shows that it increases to 9%, where IS_1 intersects *LM*. It also shows that output ends up at Y_2; this is less than the Y_1 predicted by the multiplier model.

The problem with the multiplier model is that it ignores the fact that an increase in output will increase the interest rate. If it were to allow for this, then it would show that the rise in the interest rate shifts planned spending down. The new spending line must actually be as shown by $E_1(r = 9)$, because this shows the final output as Y_2. But we can draw this line in the correct place only once we have discovered Y_2 from the *IS*–*LM* model. In short, we need the *IS*–*LM* model to give the correct final output, and this model has the further benefit of showing the final interest rate.

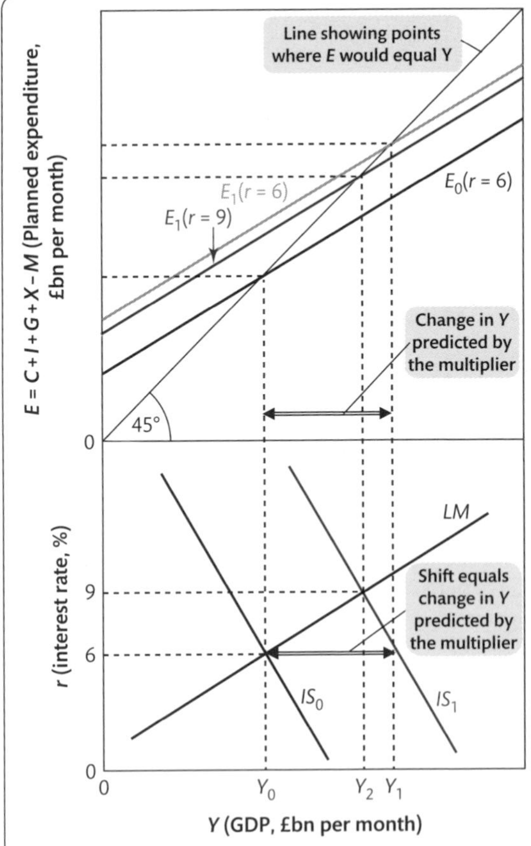

Figure 20.A7 **Comparing the multiplier and *IS*–*LM* models**

Initially *r* equals 6%, *E* is as shown by $E_0(r = 6)$, and output is Y_0. If planned spending increases to $E_1(r = 6)$, the multiplier model predicts that output will rise to Y_1. The *IS*–*LM* model shows that the *IS* curve will shift right by this predicted rise in output, but then *r* will rise to 9%. So output rises only to Y_2 and the spending line must fall to $E_1(r = 9)$.

The effects of shifts in *IS* and *LM* curves

Figure 20.A8 shows some predictions of the *IS*–*LM* model. The economy there starts with IS_0 and LM_0.

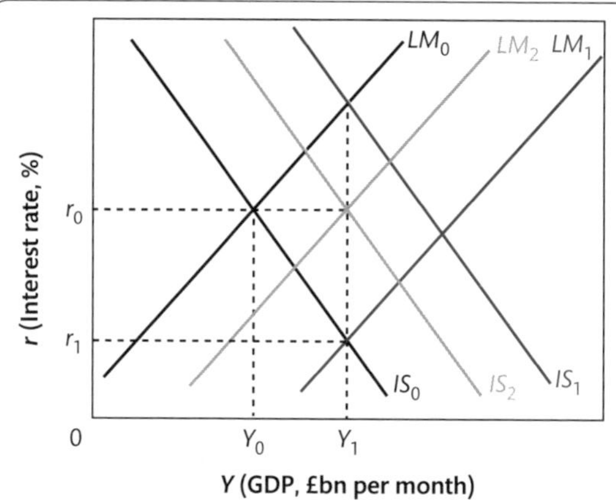

Figure 20.A8 **Monetary and fiscal policies**

To raise output from Y_0 to Y_1, the government could use fiscal expansion, taking *IS* to IS_1; this will also raise *r*. Or it could use monetary expansion, taking *LM* to LM_1; this will reduce *r*. Or it could combine milder expansionary policies that take *IS* to IS_2 and *LM* to LM_2; then *r* will be unchanged.

Then suppose *IS* shifts right, say to IS_2 or IS_1, because planned spending increases for any reason except a fall in the interest rate; then both output and the interest rate will rise. Conversely, a leftward shift in *IS* will reduce both output and the interest rate. Or suppose *LM* shifts right, say to LM_2 or LM_1, either because the Bank of England shifts the money supply curve to the right, or because, at each possible level of output, people want to hold less money; then output will rise and the interest rate will fall. Conversely, a leftward shift in *LM* will reduce output and raise the interest rate.

Monetary and fiscal policy

Often countries try to change the level of output. One way of doing so is called monetary policy, under which the central bank shifts the money supply curve and so shifts *LM*. Another way is called fiscal policy, under which the government alters its taxes or spending in order to change planned spending and so shift the *IS* curve; when it changes its spending, it might change its purchases, or change its transfers and subsidies in order to stimulate changes in planned consumption and investment.

If the central bank or government pursues a policy aimed at increasing output by shifting *LM* or *IS* to the right, then this is called an expansionary policy. If it pursues a policy aimed at reducing output, by shifting *LM* or *IS* to the left, then this is called a contractionary policy.

We can use Figure 20.A8 to show some policy options. For example, suppose the economy starts with IS_0 and LM_0, so the interest rate is r_0 and output is Y_0. And suppose the government wants to raise output to Y_1. Then it could get the central bank to pursue an expansionary monetary policy that takes *LM* to LM_1, or it could itself use an expansionary fiscal policy that takes *IS* to IS_1. Note that the monetary policy will raise the interest rate, while the fiscal policy will reduce it.

The government could instead raise output to Y_1 without altering the interest rate at all, if it combines a milder expansionary monetary policy that takes *LM* to LM_2 with a milder expansionary fiscal policy that takes *IS* to IS_2. Then output will rise to Y_1 while the interest rate remains at r_0.

Sometimes, a government will combine one expansionary policy with one contractionary policy. For example, suppose the economy actually starts with IS_2 and LM_2, so output is Y_1 and the interest rate is r_0. And suppose the government wants to reduce the interest rate to stimulate investment and growth, but also wants to hold output at Y_1. Then it could combine an expansionary monetary policy that takes *LM* to LM_1 with a contractionary fiscal policy that takes *IS* to IS_0, to leave output on Y_1, but with a lower interest rate, r_1.

The power of monetary and fiscal policy

In Figure 20.A8, monetary and fiscal policy had similar effects on output, but in practice one may be stronger than the other. For example, look at Figure 20.A9. Initially, the *IS* curve is IS_0, output is Y_0 and the interest rate is r_0. Suppose the government wants to raise output and uses fiscal policy to shift the *IS* curve to IS_1. If the *LM* curve were relatively interest elastic, like LM_A, then output would rise appreciably to Y_{A1}, and the interest rate would rise modestly to r_{A1}. But if the *LM* curve were instead relatively interest inelastic, like LM_B, then the fiscal policy would have less effect on output, taking it only to Y_{B1}, but more effect on the interest rate, raising it to r_{B1}.

In later chapters, we will see that some economists, called monetarists, have argued that the demand for money is interest inelastic so that, as we saw in Figure 20.A4, the *LM* curve is interest inelastic. On this view, fiscal policy has limited effects on output, but large effects on the interest rate. Other economists, called Keynesians, have argued that the demand for money is interest elastic so that, as we also saw in Figure 20.A4, the *LM* curve is interest elastic. On this view, fiscal policy has large effects on output, but limited effects on the interest rate.

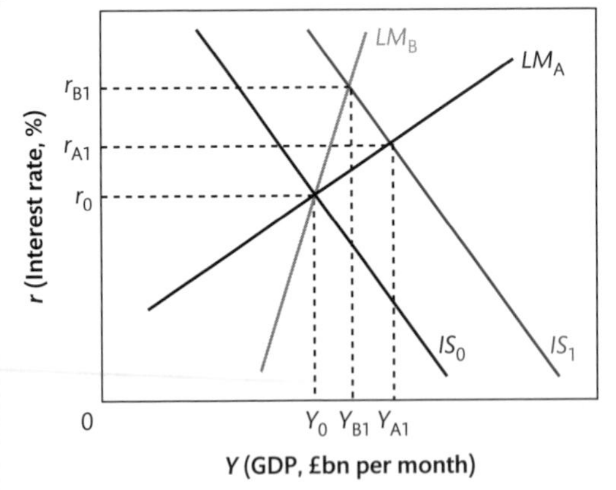

Figure 20.A9 The effects of a change in planned spending depend on the interest elasticity of *LM*

LM_A is more interest elastic than LM_B. Fiscal policy affects *Y* more and *r* less if the more elastic *LM* curve applies.

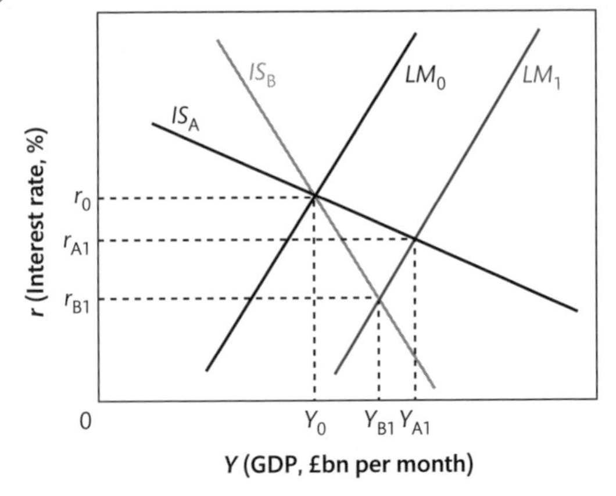

Figure 20.A10 The effects of a change in the money stock depend on the interest elasticity of *IS*

IS_A is more interest elastic than IS_B. Monetary policy affects *Y* more and *r* less if the more elastic *IS* curve applies.

Look also at Figure 20.A10. Initially, the *LM* curve is LM_0, output is Y_0 and the interest rate is r_0. Suppose the central bank wants to raise output and uses monetary policy to shift the *LM* curve to LM_1. If the *IS* curve were relatively interest elastic, like IS_A, then output would rise appreciably to Y_{A1}, and the interest rate would fall modestly to r_{A1}. But if the *IS* curve were relatively interest inelastic, like IS_B, then monetary policy would have less effect on output, taking it only to Y_{B1}, but more effect on the interest rate, reducing it to r_{B1}.

We will see in later chapters that monetarists have argued that consumer spending and investment are very responsive to changes in the interest rate so that, as we saw in Figure 20.A2, the *IS* curve is interest-elastic. On this view, monetary policy has large effects on output, but limited effects on the interest rate. But Keynesians have argued that consumer spending and investment are not very responsive to changes in the interest rate so that, as we also saw in Figure 20.A2, the *IS* curve is interest inelastic. On this view, monetary policy has limited effects on output, but large effects on the interest rate.

20.A **Summary**

- The *IS* curve shows the equilibrium level of output at each possible interest rate. It shifts right or left if planned spending rises or falls for any reason except for a change in the interest rate. The more responsive planned spending is to changes in the interest rate, the more interest elastic is *IS*.
- The *LM* curve shows the equilibrium rate of interest at each possible output. It shifts right or left if the demand for money falls or rises at each level of output, or if the central bank shifts the money supply curve right or left. The more interest elastic is the demand for money, the more interest elastic is *LM*.
- Monetary policy shifts *LM* by shifting the money supply curve. Fiscal policy shifts *IS* by changing taxes or government spending. The policies can be combined in various ways. Fiscal policy has more effect on output if *LM* is interest elastic; monetary policy has more effect on output if *IS* is interest elastic.

21

GDP and Prices: the *AS–AD* model

Remember from Chapter 17 that if the value of output, GDP, rises over time, part of the rise may be due to rises in prices, which we measure with an index called the GDP deflator. To see how much the quantity of output has risen, we use figures for real GDP, which values the goods and services produced over time at constant prices. Remember from Chapter 19 that the equilibrium level of output is the level at which output equals planned expenditure. Finally, recall from Chapter 20 that the equilibrium rate of interest is determined by the supply and demand for money.

Suppose demand in the economy increases. The multiplier model predicts that output will rise. But will prices also rise? And if prices do rise, will the rise in demand chiefly affect output or prices? Again, suppose demand falls and output falls, so that producers want to hire fewer workers. Will they actually hire fewer, so that unemployment rises? Or will wages fall, so that producers eventually hire as many workers as they did initially? Can the government change the level of output and, if so, how?

This chapter shows you how to answer questions like these, by understanding:

- why the assumptions of the multiplier model that prices and interest rates are constant leads to significant shortcomings in that model;
- how the aggregate supply and aggregate demand (*AS–AD*) model overcomes these shortcomings;
- how wages are determined in the national labour market;
- how the price level and real GDP are determined;
- how the *AD–AS* model helps us to understand government economic policies.

21.1 The multiplier model, interest rates, and prices

In Chapter 19, we studied the multiplier model. This gives an explanation of how a country's output or GDP is determined, and it indicates various events that might change GDP. But we noted in that chapter that the multiplier model ignores interest rates and the price level.

In this chapter, we begin by revising the multiplier model. In doing so, we will see that because it ignores interest rates and the price level, it gives an exaggerated idea of the effect on GDP of any event that might change GDP.

We then develop a model that takes interest rates and the price level into account. This model explains how a country's output is determined *and* how its price level is determined. Later chapters use this new model to discuss many issues.

The multiplier model

In Chapter 19, we illustrated the multiplier model with two different diagrams that look at an economy in two different ways. For this chapter, we need to recall only one of these diagrams, and this is shown in Figure 21.1. This figure measures GDP, or *Y*, on the horizontal axis, and it measures planned spending, *E*, on the vertical axis.

Planned spending, *E*, comprises $C + I + G + X - M$, that is planned consumer spending, plus planned investment, plus planned government purchases, plus planned exports, minus planned imports. Now two of these components are affected by interest rates.

- **Planned investment**. High interest rates lead to low *I* because borrowing is more costly.
- **Planned consumption**. High interest rates also lead to low *C*. This is partly because borrowing is more costly. Also, many people with existing loans must pay more interest, so they must spend less on consumption. Moreover, higher interest rates make saving more rewarding, so some people will save more and consume less.

Suppose the average interest rate, *r*, is initially 6%, and that planned spending is as shown by the line $E_0(r = 6)$ in Figure 21.1. This figure also has a 45° line through the origin; this line shows points at which planned spending would equal output. The equilibrium level of output is the level at which $E_0(r = 6)$ intersects the 45° line, that is £125 billion a month. Let's recall why output will settle here by considering two other possibilities.

- ***Y* is below £125 billion**. In this case, $E_0(r = 6)$ is above the 45° line, so *E* exceeds *Y*. So people want to buy more than producers are making. So stocks will fall, or at least rise by less than producers want, and this will encourage them to produce more.

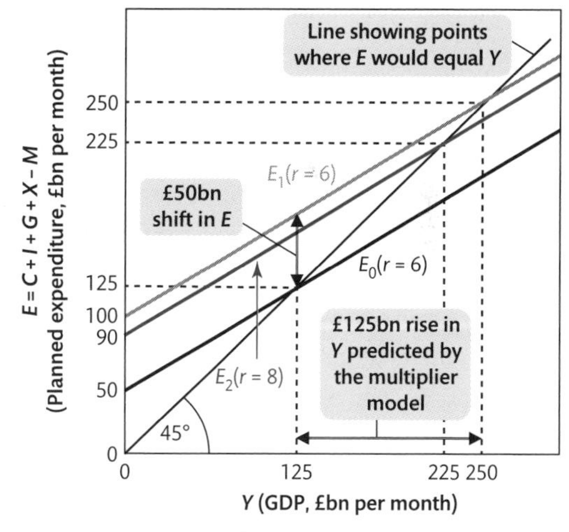

Figure 21.1 **One shortcoming of the multiplier model**

Suppose the interest rate, *r*, is initially 6%, and planned spending is shown by $E_0(r = 6)$. Then planned spending rises by an initial £50m. The multiplier model predicts that the planned spending lines shifts up by £50m, from $E_0(r = 6)$ to $E_1(r = 6)$, raising *Y* to £250bn. But as *Y*, starts to rise, the demand for money increases and so *r* rises, say to 8%. This reduces planned investment and consumption, perhaps taking *E* to $E_2(r = 8)$ and *Y* to £225bn.

- **Y is above £125 billion.** In this case, $E_0(r = 6)$ is below the 45° line, so E is less than Y. So people want to buy less than producers are making. So stocks will rise by more than producers want, and this will encourage them to reduce output.

Interest rates are not constant

To see the problems caused by the multiplier model ignoring interest rates, consider what happens if planned spending rises by £50 billion. We take a huge rise to make the figure clear. The multiplier model assumes that the interest rate will remain unchanged at 6%, and it says the E line will shift up by £50 billion to $E_1(r = 6)$. The model then predicts that Y will in time rise to £250 billion a month, where $E_1(r = 6)$ intersects the 45° line. So the model predicts that Y will rise by £125 billion, that is 2½ times as much as the rise in E. So the multiplier here is 2.5.

In practice, the interest rate, r, will rise when E rises. The reason is that when producers respond to the rise in E by increasing output, they pay more wages and profits, so incomes rise. We saw in Chapter 20 that when incomes rise, then the demand for money rises, so then r rises.

Let's develop Figure 21.1 to allow for this. As Y rises above £125 billion, r will rise. Suppose it ends up at 8%. Then I and C will end up lower than is allowed for in $E_1(r = 6)$, so the final spending line will be below this. Say it is $E_2(r = 8)$. Then output will rise only to £225 billion, where this intersects the 45° line. So output rises by £100 billion, not by £125 billion as predicted by the multiplier model.

Question 21.1 Suppose, in Figure 21.1, that E falls by £10bn from $E_0(r = 6)$. What new level of output would the multiplier predict? Why would output fall less?

So, if we allow that interest rates change when output changes, we find that the planned spending line shifts less than the multiplier model predicts. If you have read the appendix to Chapter 20, then you will have studied the *IS–LM* model, which develops this discussion further. But you do not need to know about that model in order to understand the present chapter.

Prices are not constant

Let's now see why it is unsatisfactory for the multiplier to assume that the price level is constant, when it is not. Suppose, as in Figure 21.1, that the initial planned spending line is $E_0(r = 6)$ and that planned spending then rises by £50 billion. The simple multiplier model says the new spending line will be $E_1(r = 6)$. If we allow for the rise in interest rates, then we have seen that the line will actually be $E_2(r = 8)$.

However, the initial rise in spending will raise prices, and people will then reduce their spending plans. So the planned spending line will actually end up below $E_2(r = 8)$, and output will end up even lower than £225 billion a month. It is because the multiplier model does not show the final effects of a change in spending, that economists prefer the model that we develop in this chapter.

The GDP deflator, nominal GDP, and real GDP

In this chapter, we allow the price level to vary. We will measure it with the GDP deflator, which we met in Chapter 17. This deflator is an index of the prices of all the products included in GDP. It is set at 100 for a period called the base period. For simplicity, we will always take the initial period in our figures as the base period.

As we will allow prices to vary, we must recall two measures of GDP that we also met in Chapter 17.

- **Nominal GDP**. This is the value of the goods and services produced in a period of time, measured at the prices that apply at that time.
- **Real GDP**. This is the value of the goods and services produced in a period of time, measured at the prices that applied in the base period.

We will focus on real GDP: changes in this measure changes in the quantity of goods and services produced, and so measure changes in the quantity that can be consumed, and this is what matters in terms of the economic problem of scarcity. So any figures with GDP will measure real GDP. Also, any figures with planned expenditure will measure real planned expenditure, or real *E*: that is the value of the goods and services that people plan to buy, measured at base period prices.

21.1 **Summary**

- The multiplier model assumes that interest rates do not change when output rises. So it overlooks the fact that if planned spending rises, and output starts to rise, then interest rates will rise. This will reduce investment and consumption, so planned spending will rise by less than at first expected.
- The multiplier model also assumes that prices are constant. So it overlooks the fact that if planned spending rises, and output starts to rise, then prices will rise. Yet the rise in prices will also affect the quantity of goods and services that buyers plan to buy.
- This chapter measures prices using the price index called the GDP deflator, and it refers to real *E* and real GDP; these measure the quantities of goods and services that people plan to buy and that producers produce, all measured at the prices in a base period during which the GDP deflator was 100.

21.2 The multiplier model and the aggregate demand curve

The need to understand aggregate demand

The model that we develop in this chapter, to explain how both the price level and real GDP are determined, is shown in a simplified form in Figure 21.2. This figure has real GDP on the horizontal axis, and the price level or GDP deflator on the vertical axis. It also has two black curves.

- **Aggregate demand curve, AD_0.** This shows the real value, that is the value at base period prices, of the products that people would initially plan to buy at each possible price level.
- **Aggregate supply curve, AS_0.** This shows the real value, that is the value at base period prices, of the products that producers would initially supply at each possible price level.

These curves give the model its name: the *AS–AD* model. The GDP deflator will settle at the level at which these curves intersect. In Figure 21.2, this is at a deflator of 100. To see why the deflator settles here, consider two other possibilities.

- **The deflator is above 100:** then *AS* and *AD* show that producers between them will produce more than people want. So producers' stocks will rise by more than they want; in response, they will produce less and cut their prices.
- **The deflator is below 100:** then *AS* and *AD* show that producers between them will produce less than people want to buy. So their stocks will fall, or at least rise by less than they want; in response, they will produce more and raise their prices.

When the price index reaches equilibrium at 100, producers will produce an output with a real value of £125 billion per month, and buyers will plan to buy the same amount. So real *Y* will settle in equilibrium at £125 billion per month.

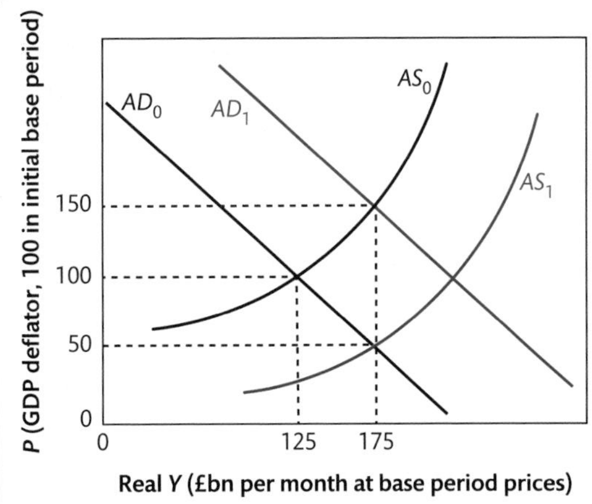

Figure 21.2 **Equilibrium with *AD* and *AS***

At each price level, measured by the GDP deflator, AD_0 shows how much buyers would initially plan to buy, valued at base period prices, and AS_0 shows how much producers would initially produce, valued at base period prices. The price level and real output settle where these curves intersect. If *AD* were to shift to AD_1, both prices and output would rise. But if *AS* were to shift to AS_1, output would rise and prices would fall.

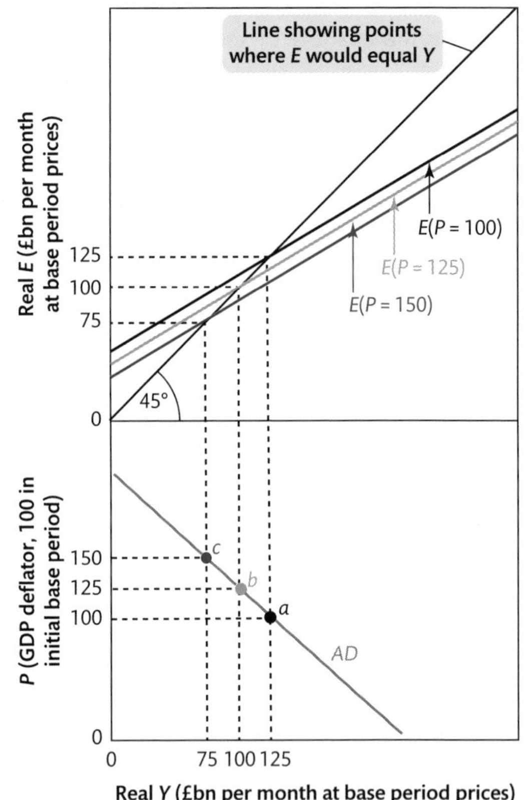

Figure 21.3 **Deriving the *AD* curve**

The *E* lines show the real planned spending that there would be at each real output; at higher prices, people plan to buy fewer products, so real planned spending is lower. *AD* shows the real value of what people would end up demanding at each price level.

This model is very useful, because it shows the forces that determine real output and the price level. Also, we can use it to show that if either curve shifts, then the equilibrium real output and price level will alter. For example, if aggregate demand increases from AD_0 to AD_1, then *Y* will increase to £175 billion, and the price index will increase to 150. If, instead, aggregate supply increases from AS_0 to AS_1, then *Y* will increase to £175 billion, and the price index will decrease to 50.

To make full use of this model, we need to understand the factors that lie behind the two curves, and also the factors that may make them shift. This section looks at the *AD* curve. The next section looks at the *AS* curve and explains why we actually need to consider two different *AS* curves.

Deriving the *AD* curve

We derive the *AD* curve from the multiplier model, as shown in Figure 21.3. The top part here shows the multiplier model, but with the horizontal axis labelled real *Y*, that is real GDP. So this axis shows the value of each possible quantity of output that could be produced if all these quantities were valued at base period prices.

This top part has three planned spending lines.

- ***E*(*P* = 100)** shows the value at base period prices of the products people would plan to buy at each possible real output, if the price level were 100.
- ***E*(*P* = 125)** shows the value at base period prices of the products people would plan to buy at each possible real output, if the price level were 125.
- ***E*(*P* = 150)** shows the value at base period prices of the products people would plan to buy at each possible real output, if the price level were 150.

We assume that, at higher price levels, people would plan to buy fewer products, so the value at base period prices of the products they would plan to buy gets smaller. So $E(P = 150)$ is below $E(P = 125)$, and that is below $E(P = 100)$.

We know that output will settle where $E = Y$, that is where the planned spending line intersects the 45° line. So if the deflator were 100 and $E(P = 100)$ applied, output would be £125 billion a month. So this is the value, at base period prices, of the products people would demand. But if the deflator were 125 or 150, output would be where $E(P = 125)$ or $E(P = 150)$ intersect the 45° line, at £100 billion or £75 billion, and these are the values at base period prices of the products that people would demand.

To derive the *AD* curve, we plot these results in the bottom part of the figure. Like the top part, this part measures real *Y* on the horizontal axis, but it measures the GDP deflator on the vertical axis. We plot the results as follows.

- **If the GDP deflator is 100**, then the real value of what people will demand, that is its value at base year prices, will be £125 billion, as shown by point ***a***.
- **If the GDP deflator is 125**, then the real value of what people will demand, that is its value at base year prices, will be £100 billion, as shown by point ***b***.
- **If the GDP deflator is 150**, then the real value of what people will demand, that is its value at base year prices, will be £75 billion, as shown by point ***c***.

Points ***a***, ***b***, and ***c***, show what real output people would demand at price levels of 100, 125, and 150. We now draw a curve through these points. This is the aggregate demand curve, *AD*, which shows the real output people would plan to buy at each possible price level. In this example, *AD* is straight.

The slope and elasticity of the *AD* curve

The *AD* curve in Figures 21.3 slopes downwards, because we assumed that if prices rise, people will plan to buy less, so the *E* line shifts down. But why would people plan to buy less? You might be tempted to suggest this reason: 'If the price of oil rises, people will buy less oil, so if prices in general rise, they will buy fewer products in total.'

In fact, this reason for higher prices leading people to buy less is flawed. When economists consider the effect of a rise in the price of a product like oil, they assume everything else is unchanged, including nominal incomes. Clearly, if the oil price rises and nominal incomes stay the same, people will buy less oil. Equally, if prices in general rise and nominal incomes are unchanged, people will buy less in total. But if all prices are rising, then nominal incomes must rise too, because most producers will pay higher nominal wages and also make higher nominal profits. Then, with higher nominal incomes, people may not plan to buy less.

However, there are three valid reasons why people will plan to buy fewer products if the price level rises, as listed below. The stronger these reasons are, the more aggregate demand reacts to price changes, so the more price elastic is the *AD* curve.

- **UK prices rise in relation to prices in other countries**. This may increase the real value of imports, *M*, and reduce the real value of exports, *X*, so that real *E*, that is real $C + I + G + X - M$, falls.
- **Many households will face a fall in their real wealth, that is in the purchasing power of their wealth**. This is because the real value of money held in cash or bank deposits will fall, and the real value of bonds will fall. The real consumption, *C*, of these households may fall.
- **The interest rate will rise**. We will see why in a moment. The result will be falls in the real value of both investment, *I*, and consumption, *C*.

Against these reasons, there is another that may actually cause real spending to rise if the price level rises. The point here is that inflation leads to higher nominal incomes, profits, and tax revenues. So households, firms, and governments that have borrowed can now spend a smaller fraction of their income, profits, and tax revenues on interest and, in turn, spend a larger fraction on consumption, government purchases, and investment. But economists think that this rise in real spending will offset very little of the fall that we noted above.

Prices and the interest rate

The effect of rising prices on the interest rate arises in the money market, as shown in Figure 21.4. Like the money market figures in Chapter 20, this has the interest rate, *r*, on the vertical axis, and the quantity of money, *M*, on the horizontal axis. But Chapter 20 assumed the price level was constant, while now we are now allowing it to vary, so Figure 21.4 shows the real quantity of money.

To see what this means, suppose that initially the money stock is £3 trillion. Suppose, too, that the price index is 100, so the real money stock equals the nominal money stock at £3 trillion. Figure 21.4 shows this initial real value at the point where the initial money supply curve, $MS_0(P = 100)$, intersects the money demand curve, *MD*. This intersection also gives the initial interest rate of 6%.

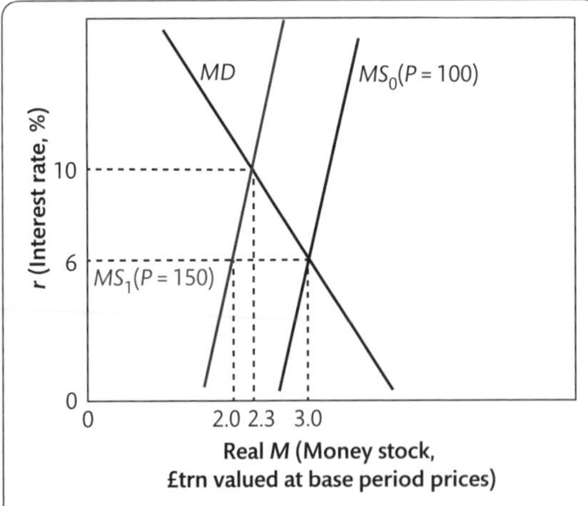

Figure 21.4 **Equilibrium in the money market**

If the price level rises, then the real value of the money stock falls. So in a figure with real *M* on the horizontal axis, the money supply curve shifts left and *r* rises.

Next, suppose that prices rise, and that the price index is now 150. This means that, in the base period, when the index was 100, prices were two-thirds what they are now. Suppose, also, that the banks create the same nominal amount of money as before, that is £3 trillion. The rise in prices means that the products that could be bought with £3 trillion now could have been bought for two-thirds as much money, £2 trillion, in the base period. So £3 trillion today is worth two-thirds as much as it used to be, that is £2 trillion at the base period prices, and this is the real value of the current money stock.

So if prices rise and the nominal money stock stays the same, then the quantity of real money supplied falls. So there is a new money supply curve in Figure 21.4, labelled $MS_1(P = 150)$. This shows that if interest rates were to stay at 6%, so that the banks created the same amount of money in nominal terms as before, then the real money stock would be £2 trillion.

However, the shift in the money supply curve will actually raise the interest rate to 10%, and this will encourage the banks to raise the nominal money enough for the real money stock to rise to the new equilibrium level of £2.3 trillion, where $MS_1(P = 150)$ intersects *MD*.

Question 21.2 In this example, what will the nominal money stock be when the real money stock is £2.3trn?

The key point to note from Figure 21.4 is that the rise in the price level raises *r*, here from 6% to 10%. This reduces real investment, *I*, and real consumption, *C*, and so reduces real *E*, that is $C + I + G + X - M$. This is an important reason why a rise in prices reduces the quantity of products that people plan to buy, so that *AD* slopes downwards.

Shifts in the *AD* curve

We will now use the multiplier model to explain why the *AD* curve may shift. This is done in Figure 21.5 where the two black lines labelled $E_0(P = 100)$ and

$E_0(P = 150)$ repeat two of the lines given in Figure 21.3. They show what E would be initially if the price index were 100 or 150, and they allow us to see that output would be £125 billion or £75 billion a month. The bottom part repeats this information, with points $\boldsymbol{a}_0$ and $\boldsymbol{c}_0$, and these are sufficient for us to derive the initial AD curve, AD_0.

Now suppose something happens that increases the real amount that people plan to spend, that is real $C + I + G + X - M$. Here are some possibilities.

- **C will rise** if the government cuts taxes, or raises transfers, or increases subsidies, or if the money stock increases and interest rates fall, or if consumers become less thrifty.
- ***I* will rise** if firms become more optimistic about the future, or if the money stock increases causing interest rates to fall.
- ***G* will rise** if the government decides to make more purchases.
- ***X* will rise** if foreigners buy more exports.
- ***M* will fall** if people buy fewer imports.

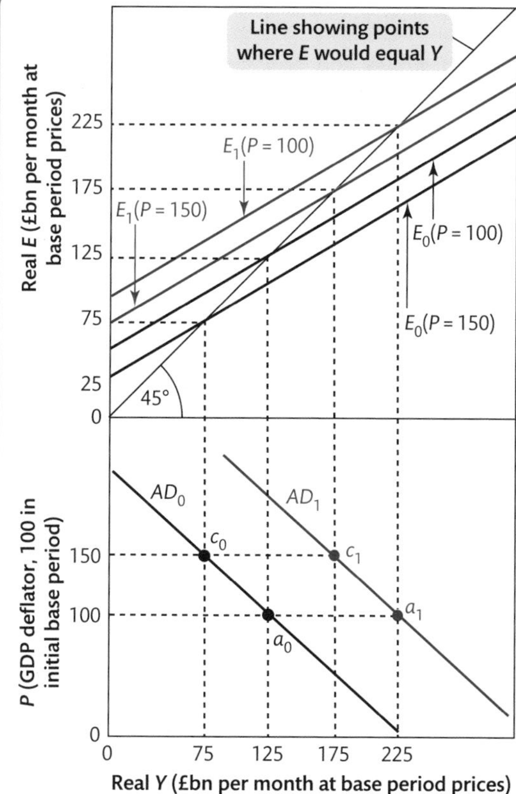

Figure 21.5 **Shifts in the *AD* curve**

The black E curves show what planned spending would initially be at two price levels, 100 and 150. The purple E curves suppose that people now decide to buy more at each of these two price levels. This causes aggregate demand to to shift right from AD_0 to AD_1.

Suppose one of these events occurs, and that if the price index were 100, planned spending would now be as shown on Figure 21.5 by $E_1(P = 100)$. This intersects the 45° line at £225 billion, and point $\boldsymbol{a}_1$ on the lower part shows that if the price index were 100, then Y would be £225 billion per month.

Also, suppose that if the price index were 150, then planned spending would now be as shown by $E_1(P = 150)$. This intersects the 45° line at £175 billion, and point $\boldsymbol{c}_1$ on the lower part shows that if the price index were 150, Y would be £175 billion per month. From $\boldsymbol{a}_1$ and $\boldsymbol{c}_1$, we can trace out the new aggregate demand curve, AD_1, which is to the right of AD_0. So events that increase real $C + I + G + X - M$ shift AD to the right. Figure 21.2 shows how such shifts increase both output and prices. Conversely, of course, events that decrease real $C + I + G + X - M$ shift aggregate demand to the left, and so reduce both output and prices.

Monetary and fiscal policy

Often, governments want to shift aggregate demand. There are various ways in which they can shift it, and these are divided into two groups.

- **Monetary policy.** Here, the government, or the monetary authorities on its behalf, alter the money stock or interest rates; the aim is to alter planned investment and consumption.
- **Fiscal policy.** Here, the government alters its taxes or its spending. Changes in government spending include changes in government purchases, and also

changes in transfers and subsidies intended to alter planned consumption and planned investment.

If the government pursues a policy aimed at shifting *AD* to the right to increase output, then it is said to be pursuing an **expansionary policy**. If it pursues a policy aimed at shifting *AD* to the left, to reduce output, then it is said to be pursuing a **contractionary policy**.

21.1 Everyday economics

The *AS–AD* model and the weather

In 2010, the UK had its coldest December for over 100 years, and this led to output falling, but output recovered again in early 2011.

'Service sector rebounds after snow', *Daily Telegraph*, 4 April 2011
'UK service sector rebounds in January', *Arab News*, 31 March 2011

Comment Bad weather can shift *AS* to the left, simply by making it harder for people to get to work. It can also shift *AD* to the left, because it is harder for people to go shopping. These are only temporary effects, but in late 2010 the fall in output was of particular concern because of fears that the economy's recovery from recession might have been stalling.

21.2 Summary

- The aggregate demand curve, *AD*, shows the real output that buyers plan to buy at each price level.
- *AD* slopes downwards for several reasons, including the facts that a rise in the price index reduces exports and increases imports, that it reduces the real wealth of people who hold money and bonds, and that it reduces the real value of the money stock, so raising interest rates and reducing consumption and investment.

21.3 The national labour market

We have now looked briefly at the *AS-AD* model. We have also derived the *AD* curve from the multiplier model and we have seen why this curve may shift. We now need to discover the forces that determine where the *AS* curve is, and why it may shift. In fact, an economy has two *AS* curves, one that applies in the short run and one that applies in the long run. Both of these are derived from the country's labour market. So, in this section, we look at the labour market.

The labour market diagram

Figure 21.6 shows the diagram for the labour market in a country. This figure has some similarity to the labour market figures that we met in Chapter 14. However, there are some important differences between Figure 21.6 and the figures in Chapter 14. These differences arise because Figure 21.6 is concerned with labour in the economy as a whole, whereas the figures in Chapter 14 concerned markets for specific types of labour. These differences are as follows.

- **The horizontal axis measures the number of workers in the country as a whole, *N*.** It does not show the number in any particular occupation.
- **The supply curve is labelled *ASL*.** This is because it represents the aggregate or total supply of labour in the country.
- **The demand curve is labelled *ADL*.** This is because it represents the aggregate or total demand for labour in the country.
- **There is a third curve, labelled *LF*,** which relates to the labour force. We will explain this shortly.

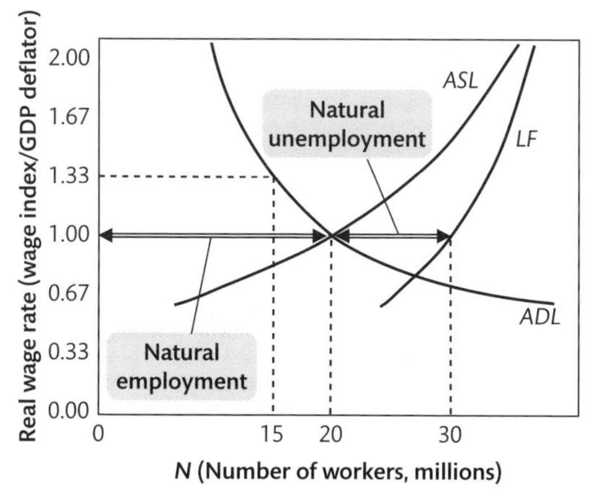

Figure 21.6 **The labour market**

At each real wage, *ADL* show how many workers producers want to hire, and *ASL* show how many workers will accept jobs. At the equilibrium real wage, those working are in natural employment and those not working are in natural unemployment.

- **The vertical axis relates to the average level of wages in the economy**. Because the figure relates to the labour market as a whole, its vertical axis cannot measure the wage of any particular group. We will now see exactly what the vertical axis does measure.

A wage index and real wages

We can convey information about the average level of wages in a country with a wage index. To construct a wage index, we consider the total cost of employing a representative selection of workers of different types for a period of time, say a month. Suppose that employing this group for a month would cost £10 million now, and that it would have cost £9 million a year ago. Then, taking the present month as the base period, we say the wage index is 100 now. And as wages a year ago were on average 90% as high as they are now, the index for a year ago was 90.

We could draw our labour market figures so that their vertical axes measured the wage index, but we don't. This is because workers are not very interested in their actual or nominal wages; they are interested in the quantity of goods and services that they can buy from their wages. We call this the **real wage**, and we measure this on the vertical axis of our labour market figures.

For any given period, we measure the real wage as the wage index for that period divided by the price index for that period, using the GDP deflator for the price index. For example, suppose we take the current period as the base period, so that the wage index is 100 and the price index is 100. Then the wage index divided by the price index is 100/100, or 1.0, so we say that real wages now are represented by the number 1.0. You can see on the figure that the current *ADL* and *ASL* intersect at this real wage level.

Now suppose that wages rise to an index of 133 while prices stay still, so that wages will buy more. Then the real wage will rise and will be 133/100, which is 1.33. Or suppose that prices rise by 50% while wages stay still, so that wages will buy less. Then the real wage will fall and will be 100/150, which is 0.67.

The labour force, *LF*

We will now discuss the curves on Figure 21.6, starting with *LF*. This concerns the labour force. We defined the labour force in Chapter 17 as people who are able, available, and willing to work. *LF* shows how many people who are able to work would actually want to be employed at each possible real wage.

To understand this curve, suppose the country has a population of 70 million, of whom 30 million are too old, too young, or too ill to work. That leaves a maximum possible labour force of 40 million. But not all of these people will want to be employed. Some will prefer to look after their homes, or have a gap year, or retire early. However, we can assume that the number who do want to be employed depends on the real wage. The upward slope of *LF* indicates an assumption that more of these 40 million people will want to be employed if the real wage is high than if it is low.

The aggregate demand for labour, *ADL*

The aggregate demand curve for labour, *ADL*, shows the total number of workers that producers wish to employ at each real wage. It slopes downwards. To see why, suppose the wage index and price index are initially both 100, so the real wage is 1.00. Then the wage index rises to 133 while the price index stays at 100, so the real wage rises to 133/100, or 1.33. Wages are now higher in relation to prices, so production is less profitable. So employers want to produce less; in turn, they demand fewer workers. On *ADL*, employers want 20 million workers at a real wage of 1.00, and 15 million at a real wage of 1.33.

The aggregate supply of labour, *ASL*

The aggregate supply curve of labour, *ASL*, shows the total number of people who will accept jobs at each real wage. It slopes upwards because higher real wages make having a job more attractive.

It may seem odd that *ASL* is to the left of *LF*, because this means that not everyone who wants to work will actually accept a job. For example, suppose the real wage in the figure is 1.00, then 30 million people will want jobs, but only 20 million will be willing to accept jobs. There are two main reasons why this gap arises, although it is very much smaller in practice than it is in the diagram.

- **Some people who want to work will not accept a job until they find what they feel is the right job in the right place**. These people include school leavers, college leavers, mothers who have taken time out of the workforce and want to return, and people who have been made redundant. Unemployment that is caused by delays when people move in and out of jobs is called **frictional unemployment**.
- **Over time, the demand for some types of skilled work falls**. For example, the demand for workers in agriculture and clothes making has fallen in the last decade, leading to many people losing their jobs. In order to find new jobs, many of these redundant workers have had to retrain or move to another area. Meanwhile, they were often unemployed for long periods. Unemployment that results from a fall in the demand for a given type of labour is called **structural unemployment**.

Because everyone in frictional and structural unemployment wants a job, you may suppose that many of them will apply for every job vacancy. In turn, you may suppose that employers will be tempted to cut their wages. However, many of these unemployed people apply only for the few jobs that really appeal to them. Until they get one, they would rather be unemployed than work at a lower wage.

Labour market equilibrium

The labour market will be in equilibrium if the real wage and employment are at the levels at which *ADL* intersects *ASL*. In Figure 21.6 this at a real wage is 1.00 and with 20 million workers employed. To see why this position is the equilibrium, consider two other possibilities.

- **The real wage is above the equilibrium level**. Suppose, for example, that the real wage were 1.33. *ASL* and *ADL* show that, at this wage, far more people would be willing to accept jobs than employers would want to hire. In this case, many people would apply for each vacancy, so employers would tend to reduce their wages.
- **The real wage is below the equilibrium level**. Suppose instead that the real wage were 0.67. *ASL* and *ADL* show that, at this wage, fewer people would be willing to accept jobs than employers would want to hire. In this case, many vacant posts would be unfilled, so employers would tend to raise their wages.

Suppose the labour market reaches equilibrium, with a real wage of 1.00. Then 30 million people would like jobs, and 20 million have one. The 10 million unemployed people are unemployed only because of frictional and structural unemployment; these two sources of unemployment added together give rise to what is called **natural unemployment**. The workers who would have jobs at the equilibrium wage represent what is called **natural employment**. Natural employment and natural unemployment are both marked in Figure 21.6. The figure greatly exaggerates the extent of natural unemployment simply to get a clear gap between *ASL* and *LF*.

The **natural unemployment rate** is the number of people in natural unemployment at the equilibrium wage as a percentage of people in the labour force at that wage, that is the number employed plus the number unemployed. In this example, there are 10 million unemployed at that wage and 20 million employed, so the rate of natural unemployment is 10 million as a percentage of 30 million, or 33%. In practice it is probably closer to 5%, but it does vary over time.

21.2 Everyday economics

Retraining Bosch workers

Bosch has announced that it will close its car part plant in south Wales in 2011, leading to almost 1,000 job losses over the period until then. But it also announced that it will help redundant workers to train to find new employment. Unfortunately, at a time of high unemployment, there are limited options even for people with new skills.

'Redundant Bosch staff offered retraining', *Wales Online*, 11 February 2010
'Mass meeting for redundant Bosch staff in South Wales', *BBC News*, 16 January 2010

Comment Relatively few employers help redundant workers with retraining to help them to get alternative employment. The Welsh Assembly Government also has a scheme call ReAct to support retraining.

21.3 Summary

- The national labour market settles at the real wage where the *ASL* and *ADL* curves intersect, so that the number of workers willing to accept jobs equals the number that employers want to hire.
- The number of people in employment when the labour market is in equilibrium is less than the labour force, that is the number of people who want to work at the equilibrium real wage. Those in work are said to be in natural employment, and those out of work are in natural unemployment.
- Natural unemployment arises because of frictional unemployment, caused by people moving in and out of jobs, and structural unemployment, caused by some people needing to retrain in order to find a job.

21.4 The short-run aggregate supply curve

Two aggregate supply curves, *SAS* and *LAS*

We argued in the last section that if the labour market were not in equilibrium, then the real wage would change until it was. In our example, the equilibrium or natural level of employment was 20 million. So we might expect this number of workers always to be employed. In turn, we might expect the country's producers to want to supply whatever real output those workers could produce, say £125 billion worth of goods and services a month at base period prices.

However, suppose this country's labour market is not currently in equilibrium. Then it might actually take some time for the real wage to reach the equilibrium level, and so for employment to become the national level of 20 million and for output to be £125 billion a month. The reason why this adjustment might take some time is that there are four factors that could cause nominal wages and prices to change slowly, and so in turn cause the real wage to change slowly. These four factors are as follows.

- **Nominal wages may not adjust very quickly, but may instead be sticky, especially downwards.** This would apply if, for example, unions were to oppose wage cuts, and if people were to resist pay cuts that would mean they would, in future, earn less than people who used to earn less than them.
- **Prices, too, may not adjust very quickly, but may also be sticky.** This would apply if, for example, firms had already produced price lists and brochures, or if they had agreed prices in long-term contracts with buyers.
- **Misperceptions by producers.** If demand in the economy falls, individual producers may initially notice only that the demand and prices of their products have fallen, and may not notice that prices in general are falling. We will see shortly how these misperceptions may hold the labour market out of equilibrium.
- **Misperceptions by workers.** If demand in the economy falls, individual workers may initially notice only a fall in their actual, or nominal, wages, and may not notice that prices in general have fallen to reduce the fall in their real wages. We will see shortly how these misperceptions may hold the labour market out of equilibrium.

Because a country's labour market may stay out of equilibrium for some time, the country will actually have two aggregate supply curves, as follows.

- **The short-run aggregate supply curve,** ***SAS*****.** This shows how much producers would want to produce at each possible price level in the current period, when the labour market may not have reached the equilibrium real wage that leads to the natural level of employment.
- **The long-run aggregate supply curve,** ***LAS*****.** This shows how much producers would want to produce at each possible price level in any period, when the labour market has reached the equilibrium real wage that leads to the natural level of employment.

We will study the long-run aggregate supply curve in the next section. In this section, we will now see how the four factors that may prevent the labour market from being currently in equilibrium affect the short-run aggregate supply curve. For simplicity, we will take each factor in turn and, when we take it, we will assume that the other three factors are not at work. We will also consider large changes in the price level to make the effects clearer on the figures.

Sticky wages

Suppose a country's wage and price indexes both equal 100, so the real wage is 1.00, and suppose this is the equilibrium real wage, as shown in the top part of Figure 21.7. Then producers will hire 20 million workers. Suppose, also, that these workers can produce £125 billion worth of output a month. Then point ***b*** in the lower part will be on the short-run aggregate supply curve, showing that producers want to supply this output if the price index is 100.

Suppose the initial aggregate demand curve, AD_0, passes point ***b***, and then aggregate demand falls to AD_1. We would expect prices to fall, and also nominal wages. But suppose nominal wages are sticky downwards and that the wage index stays at 100. Suppose also that the new price index is 50. Then the real wage will rise to 100/50, or 2.00. At this real wage, the top part of Figure 21.7 shows that producers will hire 10 million workers. Suppose these workers can produce

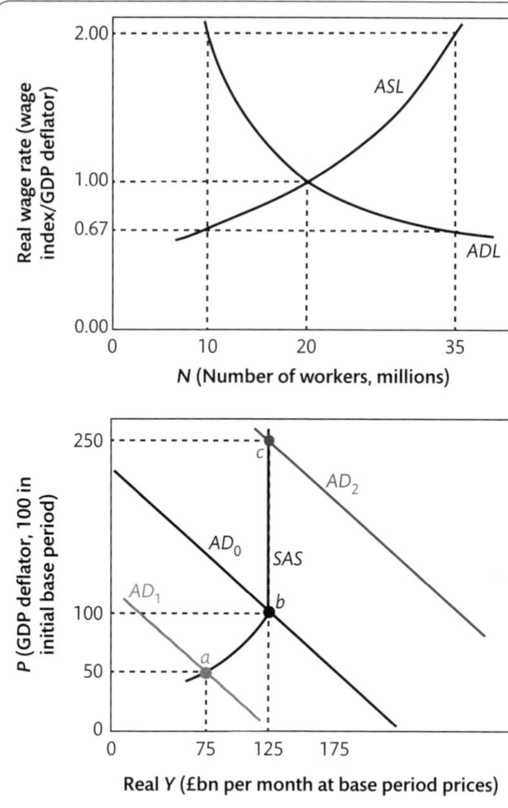

Figure 21.7 **The *SAS* curve with wages that are sticky downwards**

Suppose a fall in aggregate demand from AD_0 to AD_1 reduces the price index to 50 while the wage index sticks at 100. So the real wage rises to 2.00, and producers hire 10 million workers, who supply a real output of, say, £75bn, to give point ***a***. If aggregate demand instead rises from AD_0 to AD_2, and the price index rises but the wage index briefly sticks at 100, then the real wage will fall, causing an excess demand for labour. Suppose the price index rises to 250. Then the wage index will probably rise quickly to 250, to return the real wage to its equilibrium level of 1.00. So producers will hire 20 million workers and produce a real output of £125bn, to give point ***c***.

an output with a real value of £75 billion; this is the value that it would have if the initial base period price level of 100 were still to apply. Then point ***a*** in the lower part will be on the short-run aggregate supply curve, showing that producers want to supply this output if the price index is 50.

Suppose instead that aggregate demand rises to AD_2. We would expect prices and nominal wages to rise. But if nominal wages were sticky upwards, then the wage index might stay at 100. Then the higher price index would reduce the real wage below its initial 1.00, so producers would want to hire more than 20 million workers. However, *ASL* in the top part shows that if the real wage is below 1.00, then fewer than 20 million people will want to work. Most economists think that when the quantity of workers demanded exceeds the quantity supplied, then wages will rise quickly to take the labour market back to equilibrium. So we will assume that any upward stickiness in wages is so short-lived that we can ignore it.

So, suppose the shift in aggregate demand to AD_2 raises the price index to 250. Then the wage index must rise quickly to 250 to return the real wage to its equilibrium value of 1.00. Then employment will stay at 20 million and real output will stay at £125 billion. So point ***c*** in the lower part must be on the short-run aggregate supply curve, showing that producers want to supply this output if the price index is 250.

We can plot a short-run aggregate supply curve through ***a***, ***b***, and ***c***. It becomes vertical at the output that will be produced when the labour market is in equilibrium.

Question 21.3 What shape would *SAS* be at price levels above 100 if wages really were sticky upwards?

Sticky prices

Suppose a country has the same initial equilibrium that applied in Figure 21.7. This is repeated in Figure 21.8. So the price index is 100 and producers want to hire 20 million workers and supply an output of £125 billion a month. This gives point ***b*** on the short-run aggregate supply curve.

Now suppose aggregate demand falls to AD_1. We would expect prices to fall, but suppose all prices are

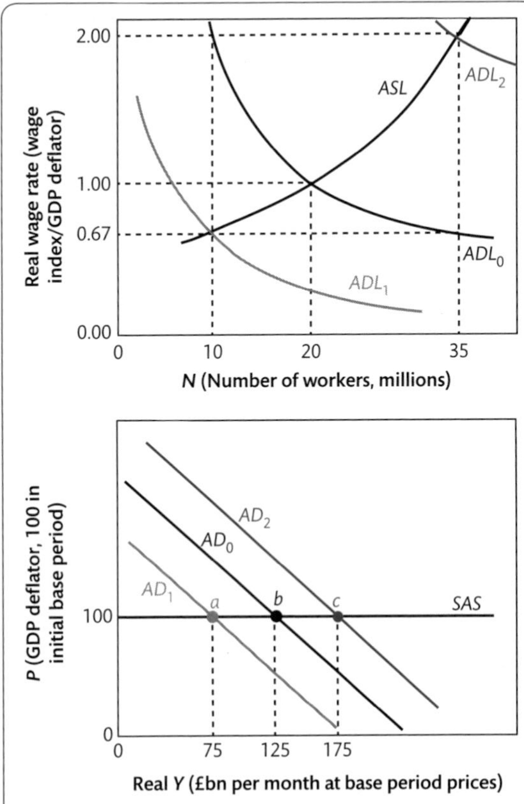

Figure 21.8 **The *SAS* curve with sticky prices**

Suppose aggregate demand falls from AD_0 to AD_1, yet the price index sticks at 100. Then producers react to lower demand by cutting output, so their labour demand falls, say to ADL_1. Equilibrium is restored when the wage index falls to 67, to take the real wage to 0.67. Producers hire 10 million workers whose real output is, say, £75bn; this gives point ***a***. Similar reasoning in reverse gives point ***c***.

sticky downwards, so the price index actually stays at 100. If producers fail to reduce prices in the face of lower demand, they will sell much less, and so want fewer workers. So the demand for labour curve in the top part will shift to the left, say to ADL_1. Assuming there is no wage stickiness, equilibrium will be restored when the wage index falls to 67, to take the real wage to 0.67. Then 10 million workers will be hired whose real output will be, say, £75 billion. So we get another point on the short-run aggregate supply curve in the bottom part, ***a***, showing that producers want to produce this output at the unchanged price index of 100.

Suppose instead that aggregate demand rises to AD_2. We would expect prices to rise, but suppose all prices are sticky upwards, so the price index actually stays at 100. If producers fail to raise prices in the face of higher demand, they will sell much more, and so want more workers. So the demand for labour curve in the top part will shift to the right, say to ADL_2. Equilibrium will be restored when the wage index rises to 200, to take the real wage to 2.00. Then 35 million workers will be hired whose real output will be, say, £175 billion. So we get another point on the short-run aggregate supply curve in the bottom part, ***c***, showing that producers want to produce this output at the unchanged price index of 100.

We can plot the short-run aggregate supply curve through ***a***, ***b***, and ***c***. It is horizontal at the price level at which prices stick.

Misperceptions by producers

Suppose a country starts in the same equilibrium that applied in Figures 21.7 and 21.8. This is repeated in Figure 21.9. So the price index is 100 and producers want to hire 20 million workers and supply an output of £125 billion a month. This gives point ***b*** on the short-run aggregate supply curve.

Now suppose aggregate demand falls to AD_1 and that the price level falls to 75. Then the real wage will rise to 1.33. Assuming there is no wage stickiness, we would expect the wage index to fall quickly to 75 to return the real wage to its equilibrium of 1.00. Then all producers would hire as many workers as before, and produce the same real output of £125 billion.

But suppose each producer mistakenly believes that it is the only producer that has faced a fall in demand. Then each producer will actually produce less and so demand less labour. So the demand for labour curve in the top part will shift left, say to ADL_1. Equilibrium will be restored when the wage index falls to 50, to take the real wage to 50/75, that is 0.67. Here, 10 million workers are hired and produce a real

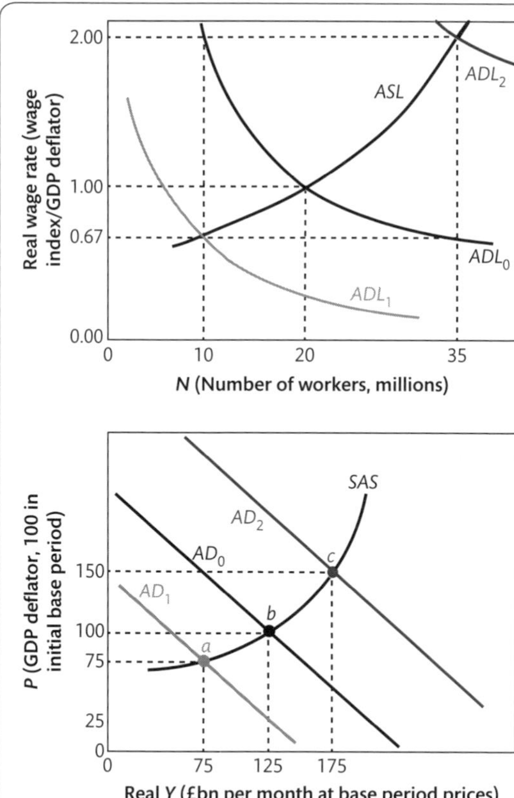

Figure 21.9 **The *SAS* curve with misperceptions by producers**

If aggregate demand falls from AD_0 to AD_1, but each producer thinks only it is facing a fall in demand, then all producers produce less. So the demand for labour falls, say, to ADL_1. Equilibrium is restored when the price index falls to 75 and the wage index falls to 50, giving a real wage to 0.67. Producers then hire 10 million workers who supply a real output of, say, £75bn; this gives point ***a***. Similar reasoning in reverse gives point ***c***.

output of, say, £75 billion. So in the bottom part, point ***a*** will be on the short-run aggregate supply curve, showing that producers want to supply this output at a price index of 75.

Suppose instead that aggregate demand rises to AD_2 and that the price level rises to 150. Then the real wage will fall to 0.67. We would expect the wage index to rise quickly to 150 to return the labour market to the equilibrium real wage of 1.00. Then all producers would hire as many workers as before, and produce the same real output of £125 billion.

But suppose each producer mistakenly believes that it is the only producer that has faced a rise in demand. Then each producer will actually produce more and so demand more labour. So the demand for labour curve in the top part will shift to the right, say to ADL_2. Equilibrium will be restored when the wage index rises to 300, to take the real wage to 300/150, that is 2.00. Here, 35 million workers are hired and produce a real output of, say, £175 billion. So in the bottom part, point **c** will be on the short-run aggregate supply curve, showing that producers want to supply this output at a price index of 150.

We can plot the short-run aggregate supply curve through ***a***, ***b***, and ***c***. It slopes upwards, and it continues beyond the £125 billion that would be produced if the labour market were in equilibrium.

Misperceptions by workers

Suppose a country starts in the same equilibrium that applied in earlier figures. This is repeated in Figure 21.10. So the price index is 100 and producers want to hire 20 million workers and supply an output of £125 billion a month. This gives point ***b*** on the short-run aggregate supply curve.

Now suppose aggregate demand falls to AD_1 and that the price level falls to 33. The real wage will rise to 3.00, but in the absence of wage stickiness, we expect nominal wages to fall quickly to a wage index to 33, to return the labour market to equilibrium with the real wage back at 1.00. So we expect producers still to hire 20 million workers and produce a real output of £125 billion.

But suppose workers mistakenly believe that while nominal wages have fallen, the price level has not; they will notice the fall in their wages at once, but may take time to recognize the fall in the price index. Then workers will believe the real wage has fallen, so fewer will want to accept jobs. This reduces the downward pressure on nominal wages.

Suppose the wage index falls only to 67, so that the real wage rises only to 67/33, or 2.00. The figure

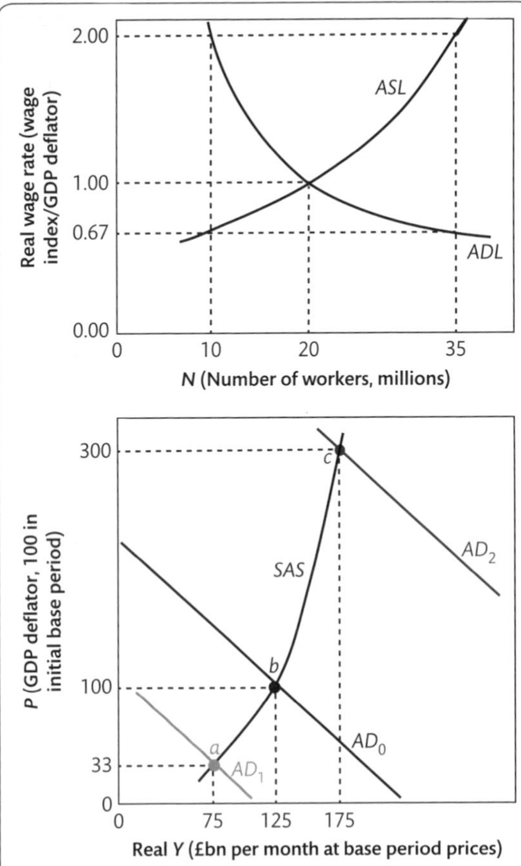

Figure 21.10 **The *SAS* curve with misperceptions by workers**

Suppose aggregate demand falls from AD_0 to AD_1 and that the price level falls to 33. Also, suppose the wage index falls to 67. Then the real wage is 2.00 and producers want to hire 10 million workers. Also, workers misperceive the fall in prices and believe the real wage is 0.67, so 10 million workers will accept jobs. With 10 million people employed, real output is £75bn; this gives point ***a***. Similar reasoning in reverse gives point ***c***.

shows the final equilibrium. At a real wage of 2.00, producers want to hire 10 million workers who will produce a real output of, say, £75 billion. At the same time, workers have not spotted the fall in prices and believe the real wage has fallen from the initial 1.00 to 67/100, or 0.67, so only 10 million want jobs. So there is no pressure in the labour market for any further change in wages. So, at a price level of 33, producers want to supply a real output of £75 billion, so point ***a*** in the bottom part is on the short-run aggregate supply curve.

Suppose instead that aggregate demand rises to AD_1 and that the price level rises to 300. The real wage will fall to 0.33, but we expect nominal wages to rise quickly to a wage index to 300, to return the labour market to the equilibrium real wage of 1.00. So we expect producers still to hire 20 million workers and produce an output of £125 billion.

But suppose workers mistakenly believe that while nominal wages have risen, the price level has not; so they believe that the real wage has risen, and more people want to accept jobs. This reduces the upward pressure on nominal wages. Suppose the wage index rises only to 200, so that the real wage falls only to 200/300, or 0.67. The figure shows the final equilibrium. At a real wage of 0.67, producers want to hire 35 million workers who will produce a real output of, say, £175 billion. At the same time, workers have not spotted the rise in prices and believe the real wage has risen from the initial 1.00 to 200/100, or 2.00, so 35 million want jobs. So there is no pressure in the labour market for any further change in wages. So at a price level of 200, producers want to supply a real output of £175 billion, so point ***c*** in the bottom part is on the short-run aggregate supply curve.

We can plot the short-run aggregate supply curve through ***a***, ***b***, and ***c***. It slopes upwards and continues beyond the £125 billion that would be produced if the labour market were in equilibrium.

Conclusions about the *SAS* curve

We have now seen four reasons why the short-run aggregate supply curve may slope upwards. In practice, not all wages and prices will be sticky, and not all producers and workers will misperceive changes in the price level. But most economists believe that some or all of these factors are sufficiently strong that the short-run aggregate supply curve does slope upwards, rather like the *SAS* curves in Figures 21.9 and 21.10.

21.4 Summary

- The short-run aggregate supply curve, *SAS*, shows the real output that producers would want to produce at each possible price index in the current period, when the labour market may not have reached the equilibrium real wage that leads to the natural level of employment.
- The factors that can cause *SAS* to slope upward are: sticky wages; sticky prices; misperceptions about the current price level by producers; and misperceptions about the current price level by workers.
- This slope of the *SAS* means that, at low prices, output is less than it would be if the labour market were in equilibrium, so unemployment is above the natural level. At high prices, output is more than it would be if the labour market were in equilibrium, so unemployment is below the natural level.

21.5 The long-run aggregate supply curve

The short-run aggregate supply curve shows how much real output will be supplied at each price level if the labour market is not given enough time to reach equilibrium. We will now explore the long-run aggregate supply curve, *LAS*. This shows how much output will be supplied at each price level if the labour market is given enough time to reach equilibrium, which means enough time for any sticky wages and prices to adjust fully, and for any misperceptions by producers and workers to disappear. Figure 21.11 derives a country's *LAS* by considering how much output producers would supply at three different price levels, if in each case the labour market had reached equilibrium.

LAS at a price index of 100

We will assume that the labour market is initially in equilibrium with a real wage of 1.00, as shown in the top part of Figure 21.11. So producers will hire 20 million workers who, we assume, produce a real output worth £125 billion a month.

We will also assume that the initial wage and price indexes are both 100. So in this initial period, the price index is 100 while output is £125 billion. The price and output levels in any period are always determined by the intersection of the current short-run aggregate supply curve and aggregate demand curve, so the initial curves, SAS_0 and AD_0, must intersect at this point, as shown in the bottom part of Figure 21.11. SAS_0 is taken to slope upwards for some or all of the reasons we have just explored.

Now the long-run aggregate supply curve, *LAS*, shows how much producers would supply at each price level if the labour market were in equilibrium. In the initial position in our example, we have said the labour market is in equilibrium, and we have said that the price level is 100 and producers want to supply an output of £125 billion a month. So *LAS* must pass point ***b*** in the lower part of the figure.

The *LAS* with a lower price index

Suppose in Figure 21.11 that aggregate demand falls to AD_1. In the short-run, the economy will move to the point at which AD_1 intersects SAS_0, with a price level of 75 and real output at £75 billion. The fall in output will lead to lower employment. But in time nominal wages will fall and return the labour market to the equilibrium real wage of 1.00. Then producers will again hire 20 million workers to supply a real output of £125 billion a month.

It may seem that the wage index needs to fall only to 75, to take the real wage back to 1.00 at 75/75. But the bottom part of Figure 21.11 shows that when AD_1

applies, the price index must fall to 25 to persuade buyers to buy a real output of £125 billion a month. So, in the end, both the price index and wage index must fall to 25 to take the real wage back to 1.00 at 25/25. So the equilibrium long-run position is a price index of 25 and producers wanting to supply a real output of £125 billion. This is shown by point ***a*** in the bottom part of the figure, and this is another point on *LAS*.

Initially, producers needed a price index of 100 to persuade them to supply a real output of £125 billion a month, as shown by point ***b*** on SAS_0. But point ***a*** shows that when the wage index has fallen to 25, they will need a price index of only 25. So SAS_0 will then no longer apply, and instead, we will be on a new short-run aggregate supply curve, SAS_1, which shows that producers now want to supply a real output of £125 billion a month at a price index of 25.

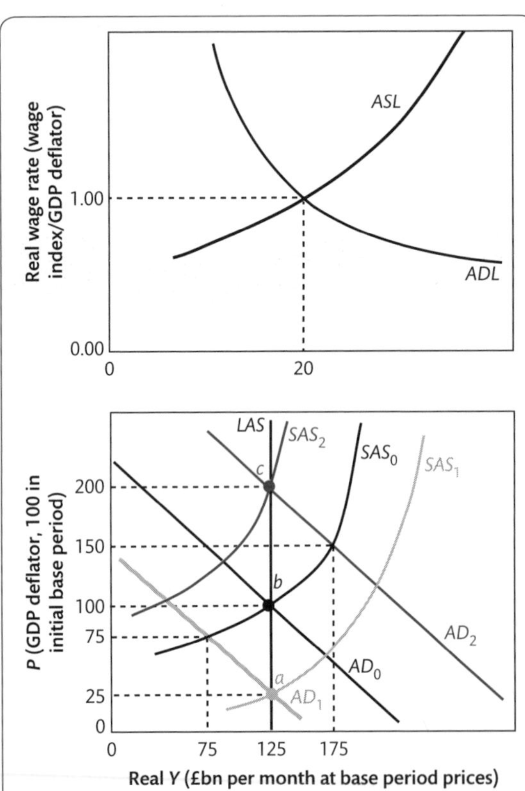

Figure 21.11 **Deriving the *LAS* curve**

In the long run, changes in the price level lead to identical changes in nominal wages, and this returns the real wage to the equilibrium level, here 1.00. So producers always end up hiring 20 million workers and want to supply the real *Y* of £125bn a month that these workers can produce, so *LAS* is vertical at that output. Also in the long run, *SAS* shifts until it intersects *LAS* at the same price level as the current *AD*.

The *LAS* with a higher GDP deflator

Now return to the initial equilibrium and suppose that aggregate demand rises to AD_2. In the short run, the economy will move to the point at which AD_2 intersects SAS_0, with the price level at 150 and real output at £175 billion. The rise in output will lead to higher employment. But in time nominal wages will rise and return the labour market to the equilibrium real wage of 1.00. Then producers will again hire 20 million workers and produce a real output of £125 billion a month.

It may seem that the wage index needs to rise only to 150, to take the real wage back to 1.00 at 150/150. But the bottom part of Figure 21.11 shows that, when AD_2 applies, the price index must rise to 200 to persuade buyers to buy a real output of just £125 billion a month. So both the price index and wage index must rise to 200 to take the real wage back to 1.00 at 200/200. So the equilibrium long-run position is a price index of 200 and producers wanting to supply a real output of real *Y* at £125 billion. This is shown by point ***c*** in the bottom part, and this is another point on *LAS*.

Initially, producers needed a price index of 100 to persuade them to supply a real output of £125 billion a month, as shown by point ***b*** on SAS_0. But point ***c*** shows that when the wage index has risen to 200, they will need a price index of 200. So SAS_0 will then no longer apply, and instead, we will be on a new short-run aggregate supply curve, SAS_2, which shows that producers now want to supply a real output of £125 billion a month at a price index of 200.

The *LAS* curve and long-run equilibrium

With points ***a***, ***b***, and ***c***, in the bottom part of Figure 21.11, we can now derive *LAS*. It is a vertical line at a real *Y* of £125 billion per month. *LAS* is always vertical at the real output that will be supplied when the labour market is in equilibrium with employment at the natural level; this is called the **potential output** level, Y_P. The economy can actually produce more than this, as we have seen, but only temporarily while the labour market out of equilibrium.

The long-run equilibrium output and price level for the economy can be found from the point where *AD* intersects *LAS*. The long-run equilibrium output is always the potential output level, because *LAS* is vertical. Also, in the long run, we have seen that *SAS* will shift until it intersects *LAS* at the same price level as *AD*. We will use this important result frequently in the next section.

21.5 **Summary**

- The long-run aggregate supply curve, *LAS*, shows how much producers would want to produce at each possible price level in any period when the labour market has reached the equilibrium real wage, which is the one that leads to the natural level of employment. In turn, output will be at its potential level.
- *LAS* is vertical because, in the long run, no matter what the price level is, producers want to supply the potential level of output. This is the equilibrium output in the long run, and the equilibrium price level is where *AD* intersects *LAS*. Also in the long run, *SAS* shifts until it intersects *LAS* at the same price level.

21.6 Some implications of the *AS-AD* model

This section looks at some implications of the *AS-AD* model. We look first at the effects of changes in aggregate demand and aggregate supply.

Demand shocks

A shift in aggregate demand is called a **demand shock.** The aggregate demand curve is derived from the multiplier model, and it shifts if there is a change in planned spending. We saw in Figure 21.5 how an increase in planned spending shifts *AD* to the right. Conversely, a decrease in planned spending shifts *AD* to the left.

Figure 21.12 illustrates demand shocks. This figure concerns an economy in which the labour market is initially in equilibrium, so that employment and unemployment are at their natural levels. In turn, output is at its potential level, Y_P. This level is shown by the position of the long-run aggregate supply curve, *LAS*. And because the economy is in equilibrium at this level, the initial aggregate demand curve, AD_0, intersects the

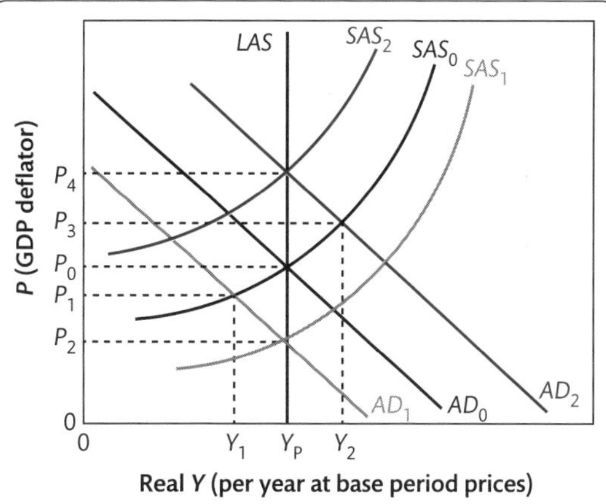

Figure 21.12 **Demand shocks**

If aggregate demand falls from AD_0 to AD_1, then, in the short run, the price level falls to P_1 and output falls to Y_1; in the long run, prices fall further to P_2, output returns to Y_P, and the short-run aggregate supply curve shifts to SAS_1. If aggregate demand rises AD_0 to AD_2, then, in the short run, the price level rises to P_3 and output rises to Y_2; in the long run, prices rise further to P_4, output returns to Y_P, and the short-run aggregate supply curve shifts to SAS_2.

initial short-run aggregate supply curve, SAS_0, at this level, and this intersection gives the initial price level, P_0.

There are two types of demand shock that can disturb this economy, as follows.

- **A decrease in planned spending, which shifts *AD* left to AD_1.** In the short run, the price level falls to P_1 and real output falls to Y_1. As output is now below its potential level, Y_P, the labour market is not in equilibrium, and unemployment is above the natural rate. In the long run, the real wage will fall so that the labour market returns to equilibrium. The fall in wages shifts the short-run aggregate supply curve right to SAS_1. So the price level will fall further, to P_2, but output will return to the potential level, Y_P.
- **An increase in planned spending, which shifts *AD* right to AD_2.** In the short run, the price level rises to P_3 and real output rises to Y_2. As output is now above its potential level, Y_P, the labour market is not in equilibrium, and unemployment is below the natural rate. In the long run, the real wage will rise so that the labour market returns to equilibrium. The rise in wages shifts the short-run aggregate supply curve to the left to SAS_2. So the price level will rise further, to P_4, but output will return to Y_P.

Government responses to demand shocks

We have seen in Figure 21.12 that if there is a demand shock, then, in the long run, the economy will return to its potential output level with output back at the natural rate. Admittedly, the price level will be lower or higher according to which way aggregate demand shifts. However, this long-run adjustment might take some time.

So, suppose aggregate demand shifts to the left to AD_1. Then unemployment rises above its natural level. This is serious partly because it means there are idle resources, and also because of its effect on the lives of those involved. But what could the government do? Rather than wait for the labour market to return to equilibrium, the government might undertake expansionary monetary or fiscal policy to shift aggregate demand back to AD_0, so returning output to its potential level and unemployment to its natural level.

Whether this is needed depends partly on the price elasticity of the short-run aggregate supply curve, because this affects how much the shift in the aggregate demand curve *AD* will reduce output and employment. It also depends on how quickly the economy would return to its long-run equilibrium without government intervention. We discuss this issue in the next chapter, and we will see that economists have different beliefs here, and accordingly disagree about the need for government intervention.

Or suppose aggregate demand shifts to the right to AD_2. The government knows that if it waits for the labour market to return to equilibrium, then the price level will rise. But it might be worried about rising prices and inflation. So, rather than wait for this to happen, it might undertake contractionary monetary or fiscal policy to shift aggregate demand back to AD_0 to eliminate any upward pressure on prices.

Whether this is needed depends partly on the price elasticity of the short-run aggregate supply curve, because this affects how much the shift in the aggregate demand curve will raise prices. It also depends on how anxious the government is about inflation. We discuss this issue in Chapter 23, and again we will see that economists have different beliefs, and so disagree about the need for government intervention.

Supply shocks

Strictly, a **supply shock** is a shift in a country's short-run aggregate supply curve. But, as we shall see, supply shocks are usually accompanied by shifts in the long-run supply curve.

We derived a country's aggregate supply curves from its labour market, and one source of supply shocks is a change in the labour market. Supply shocks like these are illustrated in Figure 21.13. The top part here shows the country's labour market, which starts in equilibrium where the aggregate demand and supply curves for labour, ADL_0 and ASL_0, intersect. The real wage is W_0 and employment is at its natural level N_0.

In turn, output is at its potential level, Y_P, as shown in the bottom part by the initial long-run aggregate supply curve LAS_0. The point where this is intersected by both the aggregate demand curve, *AD*, and the initial short-run aggregate supply curve, SAS_0, gives the initial price level, P_0.

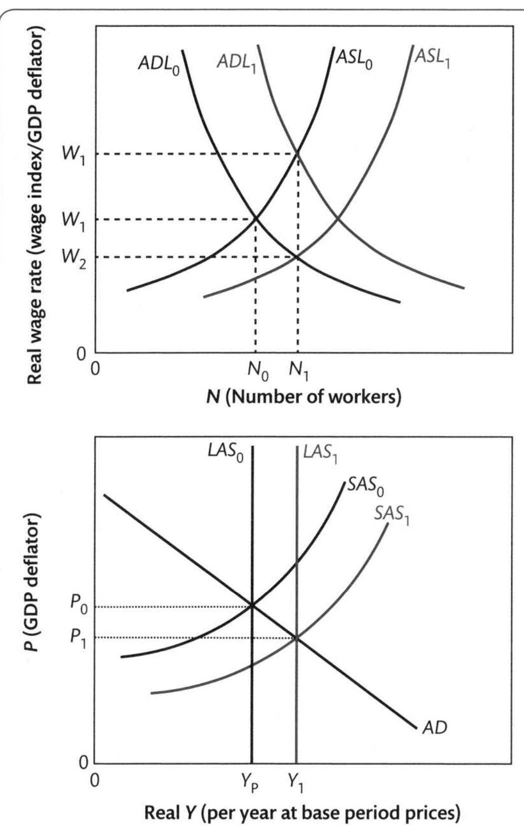

Figure 21.13 **Supply shocks starting in the labour market**

If labour demand shifts right to ADL_1 following a rise in productivity, or if labour supply shifts right to ASL_1 following a rise in the number of people willing to accept jobs at each wage, then equilibrium employment increases to N_1. This increases the real output that producers want to supply, shifting long-run aggregate supply to LAS_1. The short-run aggregate supply curve also shifts right until it intersects LAS_1 at the same price level as does *AD*.

We will now look at the two types of supply shock that can originate in the labour market.

Supply shocks and the demand for labour

Suppose the aggregate demand for labour shifts to the right to ADL_1. It would shift to the right if, at any given real wage, workers were to become more productive and so more profitable to hire. This could happen for several reasons including the following.

- **Technology may improve**.
- **Investment**. Extra capital makes workers more productive. (Note, though, that a loss of capital, as might occur with a war or earthquake, will shift the demand for labour curve to the left.)
- **Improved working practices**.
- **Deregulation**. If the government imposes fewer regulations on firms, new ones may be established and existing ones may expand.

When ADL_1 is reached, the labour market in Figure 21.13 has a new equilibrium position with a higher real wage, W_1, and higher employment, N_1, which increases potential output to Y_1. So the long-run aggregate supply curve shifts right to LAS_1, which is vertical at Y_1. The intersection of LAS_1 with *AD* shows that the shift in *LAS* raises real output in the long run to Y_1, and reduces the price level to P_1. Also, in the long run, the short-run aggregate supply curve shifts to SAS_1, which intersects LAS_1 at the same price level as *AD*.

Supply shocks and the supply of labour

Suppose instead that the supply curve of labour in Figure 21.13 shifts right to ASL_1. It can shift for several reasons including the following.

- **The size of the labour force may increase;** perhaps there is net immigration, or more people leave education than retire, or people take less time out of the labour force to look after young children, or changes in taxes make more people want to work. Note that opposite events would shift the supply of labour curve to the left.

- **People may become less picky about the jobs they will accept;** perhaps the government reduces its transfers to people without jobs, or unemployed people become more willing to retrain or move home in order to find a job. Note that opposite events would shift the supply of labour curve to the left.

When ASL_1 is reached, the labour market in Figure 21.13 has a new equilibrium with a lower real wage, W_2, and higher employment, N_1, which increases potential output to Y_1. Once again, the long-run aggregate supply curve shifts to the right to LAS_1, which is vertical at Y_1. The intersection of LAS_1 with *AD* shows that the shift in *LAS* raises real output to Y_1, and reduces the price level to P_1. Also, in the long run, the short-run aggregate supply curve shifts to SAS_1, which intersects LAS_1 at the same price level as *AD*.

Question 21.4 Suppose the government in the country shown in Figure 21.13 reduced spending on universities so that, in time, the labour force was less well equipped with the skills employers want. Taking the initial position to be shown by the black curves, which curves would shift? What would be the final effect on employment, prices, and output?

21.3 Everyday economics

Women and the Labour Force

Each year, 8 March is International Women's Day. One purpose of this day, and the original purpose, is to mark the role of women in the labour force. In a speech made in Istanbul to mark the date in 2011, the United Nations Secretary-General Ban Ki-moon stressed that, in terms of women's empowerment and gender equality, there are still many more things to do before the world will be fair and harmonious and balanced in terms of gender balance. He mentioned, for example, discrimination in the workplace, and the removal of the glass—or iron—ceiling that many professional women feel limits their promotion and earnings potential. From an economic perspective, such discrimination is counter-productive, because encouraging women to work, and to acquire human capital, and to use their skills to the full, will shift a country's *LAS* curve to the right and lead to higher output.

'Secretary-General, at Global Summit of Women, says his challenge is breaking 'glass ceiling' in United Nations middle management', United Nations press release, 9 May 2011

Other supply shocks

Supply shocks can originate outside the labour market. For example, the short-run aggregate supply curve will shift to the left in cases like these.

- **Natural disasters**. Events such as floods, severe winters, outbreaks of foot-and-mouth disease, and earthquakes all reduce the amount that can be produced. These shocks are generally short-lived, so the short-run supply curve returns to the original position and the economy returns to its original equilibrium.
- **Trade union activity**. There may be strikes that disrupt production temporarily. Also, wages may be pushed above the equilibrium level; but, if this happens, then, in the long run, the labour market should return to equilibrium so that the economy will return to its initial equilibrium.
- **The price of imported inputs like oil, rise**. This has more complex effects, as we shall now see.

Figure 21.14 shows the effects of a rise in the price of imported inputs or raw materials. We assume the economy starts in the equilibrium given by the black curves. The initial output here is labelled Y_0.

A rise in the price of imported inputs makes production less profitable, so the short-run aggregate supply curve shifts to the left to SAS_1, raising the price level to P_1 and reducing output to Y_1. The rise in the price level at once reduces the real wage, say to W_1. But the fall in output has reduced the demand for labour to ADL_1,

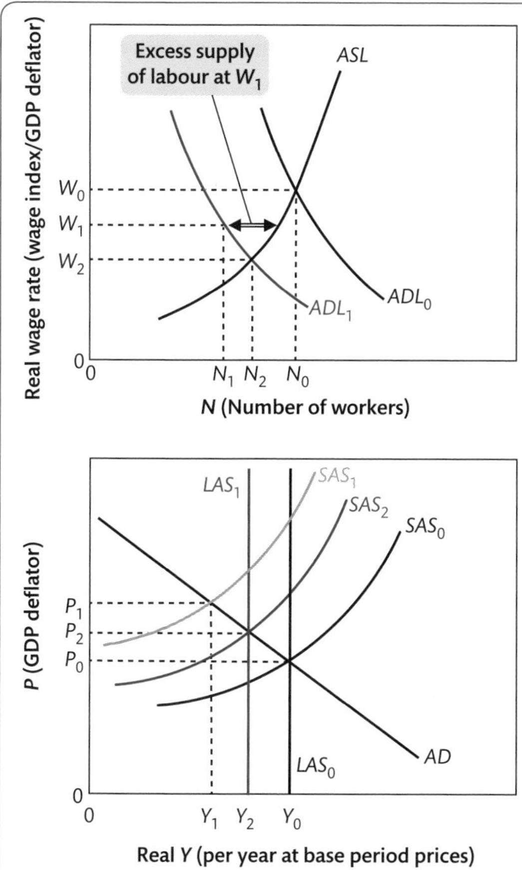

Figure 21.14 **A supply shock from the prices of imported inputs**

If these prices rise, the short-run supply curve shifts left to SAS_1. So output falls to Y_1, which reduces the demand for labour to ADL_1. Also, the price level rises to P_1, reducing the real wage to W_1. At W_1, there is an excess supply of labour, so the real wage falls to W_2 and natural employment falls to N_2, shifting long-run aggregate supply to LAS_1. The fall in the real wage also shifts short-run aggregate supply right to SAS_2. The final effects are to raise prices from P_0 to P_2 and reduce output from Y_0 to Y_2.

and the result is that at W_1, more people want to accept jobs than employers want to hire. So there is an excess supply of labour as marked in the figure.

This excess supply eventually leads to a fall in the real wage that takes the labour market to a new equilibrium position at which the real wage is W_2 and the natural employment level is N_2. The fall in natural employment from N_0 reduces potential output from the initial Y_0 to Y_2, so the long-run aggregate supply curve shifts to LAS_1, which is vertical at this level. The price level and output end up at Y_P and P_2, where LAS_1 intersects *AD*.

The fall in the real wage means that wages fall in relation to prices. This shifts the short-run aggregate supply curve rightwards to SAS_2, so that, like *AD*, it intersects LAS_1 at P_1.

Question 21.5 Suppose there is a rise in the price of imported finished goods such as cars. What sort of shock will this create?

AS-AD theory and the multiplier theory

We first met a model to show what determines the equilibrium of output in Chapter 19. This was the multiplier model. In most of the following chapters, we will refer to the *AS-AD* model instead. So it is worth noting the uses of the multiplier model, and the reasons for preferring the *AS-AD* model.

The multiplier model has two very important uses.

- **It shows the components of planned spending; changes in any of these shift *AD*.** These components are planned consumer spending, investment spending government purchases, exports, and imports. Changes in any of these shift *AD* because *AD* is derived from the planned expenditure line, *E*, in the multiplier model.
- **It shows that if *E* rises, then *AD* will shift right by a multiplied amount.** We saw this in Figure 21.5.

However, the *AS-AD* model has some very important additional uses.

- **It shows that when *E* changes and *AD* shifts by a multiplied amount, then, in the short run, real output will change by less than *AD* shifts.** This is because a change in *AD* leads to a change in prices that reduces the change in real spending.

- **It shows that when *E* changes and *AD* shifts by a multiplied amount, then, in the long run, real output will not change**. Only prices will change.
- **It shows the effect on output and the price level of changes in the demand and supply of labour.**

21.6 Summary

- Demand shocks shift *AD*. In the short run, these shifts in *AD* move the economy along *SAS*, so both output and the price level change. In the long run, these shifts move the economy up or down the vertical *LAS*, and then *SAS* shifts to intersect the new *AD* at the same price level that *LAS* intersects it.
- Supply shocks shift *LAS*, and can originate in the labour market. For example, suppose the demand for labour rises, perhaps because of an increase in labour productivity or in the country's capital stock, or suppose the supply of labour increases, perhaps because the labour force has grown or because more people in it are willing to accept jobs. Each event raises the level of natural employment and so raises the potential output level, shifting *LAS* to the right. Output rises and the price level falls, and *SAS* shifts to pass through the intersection of the new *LAS* with *AD*.
- Supply shocks can originate outside the labour market. For example, a rise in the price of imported inputs shifts *SAS* left, reducing output, raising the price level and reducing the real wage. But the lower output reduces the demand for labour and there is an excess supply of labour. When the labour market returns to equilibrium, with an even lower real wage, *SAS* will shift right a little, but natural employment and potential output will be lower than they were initially, so *LAS* shifts left.
- In the short run, unemployment can be above the natural level. Economists disagree about how long the labour market will take to return to equilibrium, and so disagree about the need for government intervention.

In the next chapter we look closely at what causes unemployment and what might be done to reduce it.

abc Glossary

Aggregate demand curve, *AD*: this shows the real value, that is the value at base period prices, of the goods and services that people would plan to buy at each possible price level.

Aggregate supply curve, *AS*: this shows the real value, that is the value at base period prices, of the goods and services that producers would want to supply at each possible price level. (*See also* long-run aggregate supply curve *and* short-run aggregate supply curve.)

Contractionary policy: a policy designed to reduce output.

Demand shock: a shift in the aggregate demand curve.

Expansionary policy: a policy designed to increase output.

Fiscal policy: a policy under which the government uses its taxes or its own spending to alter the economy.

Frictional unemployment: unemployment caused by delays when people move in and out of jobs.

Long-run aggregate supply curve, *LAS*: this shows how much producers would want to produce at each possible price level in any period when the labour market has reached the equilibrium real wage that leads to the natural level of employment.

Monetary policy: a policy under which the government or monetary authorities use the money stock or interest rates to affect the economy.

Natural employment: the number of workers who would have jobs at the equilibrium wage.

Natural unemployment: frictional unemployment plus structural unemployment.

Natural unemployment rate: the number of people in natural unemployment at the equilibrium wage as a percentage of the labour force at that wage.

Potential output level, Y_P: the real output that is produced when unemployment is at the natural level.

Real wage: the quantity of goods and services that people can buy from their wages.

Short-run aggregate supply curve, *SAS*: this shows how much producers would want to produce at each price level in the current period, when the labour market may not have reached the equilibrium real wage that leads to the natural level of employment.

Structural unemployment: unemployment caused by a fall in the demand for a given type of labour.

Supply shock: a shift in the short-run aggregate supply curve; it is usually accompanied by a shift in the long-run aggregate supply curve.

= Answers to in-text questions

21.1 In this figure, the multiplier is 2.5, so the multiplier model predicts that output would fall by 2.5 × £10 billion, that is £25 billion per month to £100 billion. But as output started to fall, incomes would fall; then money demand would fall and the interest rate would fall. So investment and consumption would rise a little, and the spending line would actually end less than £10 billion below $E_0(r = 6)$. So output would fall by less than £25 billion.

21.2 With the price index at 150, the real money stock is two-thirds the nominal money stock. So a real money stock of £2.3 trillion requires a nominal money stock of £3.45 trillion, because £2.3 trillion is two-thirds of £3.45 trillion.

21.3 It is tempting to suppose that *SAS* must then be a continuous curve rather than having a kink, so that output would continue to rise as prices increased, but this is not so. As the price level rose above 100, the real wage would now fall and fewer people would accept jobs, so output would fall; so *SAS* would slope backwards.

21.4 Like any fall in government spending, this will shift *AD* left, but it has additional effects. As fewer people would have the skills needed by employers, fewer people in the labour force would be able to accept jobs, so the labour supply curve would shift to the left; this would reduce the equilibrium employment level, so *LAS* would shift to the left. So output would fall, but the effect on the price level depends on whether *AD* or *LAS* shifts left more. *SAS* will shift to the left to intersect the new *AD* at the same output and price level as the new *LAS*.

21.5 This would create a demand shock as imports fell and people switched to products produced in the UK.

? Questions for review

21.1 Each of the following events will shift the long-run aggregate supply curve. In each case, say whether it will shift left or right and why, whether real output will rise or fall, whether the GDP deflator will rise or fall, and how the short-run aggregate supply curve will be affected. Take each event separately.

(a) Increasing use of the Internet enables people to find the 'right' job more quickly.

(b) A revised national curriculum for schools eventually raises worker productivity.

(c) A cut in taxes on income encourages many people who previously were outside the labour force to join it.

21.2 Assume the economy starts in long-run equilibrium. Each of the following events will shift the aggregate demand curve. Take each event separately and for each answer the following. (i) Will *AD* shift left or right? (ii) What will happen in the short run to the price level, the real wage, unemployment, and real output? (iii) What will happen to them in the long run? (iv) How will *SAS* be affected? .

(a) The government spends more on the National Health Service.

(b) A rise in taxes on income leads to a fall in consumer spending.

(c) Economic recovery abroad raises the demand for exports.

(d) Firms become more pessimistic about the future outlook for the economy.

? Questions for discussion

21.1 Suppose unemployment is above its natural level, and the government chooses to intervene. But it wants, if it can do so, to keep the price level from rising. Can you suggest any suitable policy or mix of policies?

21.2 The price elasticity of the *AD* curve depends on how sensitive the components of planned spending are to changes in the price level. What factors determine this sensitivity?

21.3 Suppose you decide to take a part-time job and, in turn, increase your spending on consumer goods and services. Although these decisions will have tiny effects on the economy, what will the effects be in terms of the *AS–AD* model?

Common student errors

Some students get confused between the planned expenditure line, *E*, in the multiplier model, and the aggregate demand curve, *AD*, in the *AS–AD* model. The *AD* line is derived from the multiplier model, but the multiplier model assumes prices are constant, while *AD* shows how much people want to buy at each possible price level.

Some students find it odd that unemployment can fall below the natural level, so that employment rises above the equilibrium level in the labour market; it seems that not enough people will want to work at any real wage for this to happen. But we saw in Figures 21.8, 21.9, and 21.10 that this can happen if prices are sticky or if producers or workers have misperceptions.

22

Unemployment

Remember from Chapter 20 that interest rates and the money stock are determined in the money market. And recall from Chapter 21 that employment and unemployment are determined in the labour market, while the output level and the price level are determined in the short run by aggregate demand and short-run aggregate supply, and in the long run by aggregate demand and long-run aggregate supply.

'The only reason for unemployment is that wages are too high for the labour market to clear.' This view may seem consistent with a common theme in economics, which is that in any market with excess supply, the price will fall until the excess supply disappears. But is this an explanation—or even the only explanation—for unemployment? What sorts of people are unemployed and why? What could governments try to do about unemployment? Why do economists disagree about what they should do?

This chapter shows you how to answer questions like these, by understanding:

* how unemployment is defined, and which groups are most affected by it;
* how natural unemployment arises and how it may be reduced;
* how demand-deficient unemployment arises, and why different groups of economists hold differing views about what could or should be done to reduce it.

22.1 Review of unemployment

We have mentioned unemployment in several earlier chapters. In this section, we will look more closely at unemployment itself, and in later sections, we will consider how it may be reduced.

The meaning of unemployment

We saw in Chapter 17 that the term 'unemployment' is not used to cover all those people who have no job. Instead it is confined to people without a job who are able, available, and willing to work. So we exclude three groups of people who have no jobs:

- **people who are not able to work**, such as babies, toddlers, ill people, and very old people;
- **people who are not available for work**, such as schoolchildren and students who are studying;
- **people who are not willing to work**, such as pensioners who are fit enough to work, but prefer not to, and also people who choose to look after their homes and families.

The total number of people who are able, available, and willing to work is called the labour force. At any moment in time, the **unemployment rate** is the percentage of the labour force that has no job.

The problems of unemployment

Unemployment creates three types of problem.

- **It means some resources are unused**. In turn, this means that a country is producing at a point inside its production possibility frontier, and so doing less than it could to tackle the underlying economic problem of scarcity.
- **It affects the living standards of people who are unemployed**. The transfers that these people receive from the government are generally below the wages they would get if they were employed. Admittedly, their reduced income is to some extent offset by more leisure time.
- **It causes personal and social difficulties for people who are unemployed**. These can be especially acute for people who have been unemployed for a long time.

Measuring unemployment

Chapter 17 gave an internationally used measure of unemployment that covers these two groups:

- **people without a job, who want a job, have sought work in the last four weeks, and are available to start work in the next two weeks;**
- **people who are out of work, but have found a job, and are waiting to start it in the next two weeks.**

We will use this measure in this chapter, but note that it understates the true level of unemployment. This is because it regards people who work for just one hour a week as employed. Yet many part-time workers would be willing to work more hours than they do, so in truth they are partly unemployed.

Unemployment and the labour market

Chapter 21 gave a model of the labour market in a country, similar to that shown in Figure 22.1. The curve *LF* here shows how many people would want to be in the labour force at each possible real wage. *LF* slopes upwards because at higher real wages, more people would want to work.

At each possible wage, the number of workers that employers would want to hire is shown by the aggregate demand of labour curve, *ADL*, and the number of people who would actually accept jobs is shown by the aggregate supply of labour curve, *ASL*. If the current real wage were W_E, where these curves intersect, then the market would be in equilibrium, with employment at its

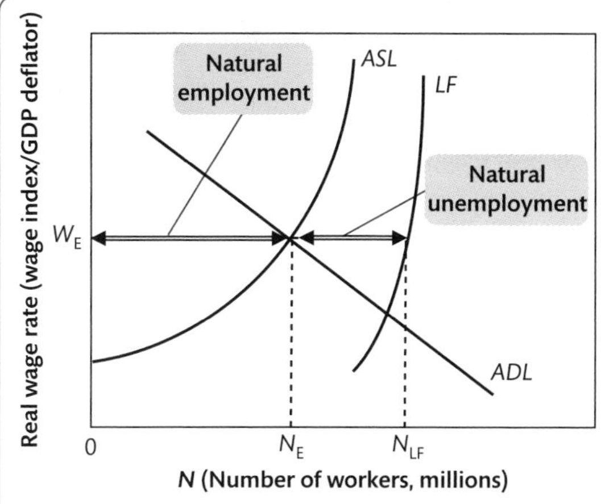

Figure 22.1 **The labour market**

At each real wage, *LF* shows how many people want to work, *ASL* shows how many will accept jobs, and *ADL* shows how many workers employers want to hire. At the equilibrium wage, W_E, some people in the labour force will have jobs and be in natural employment; the rest will be in natural unemployment.

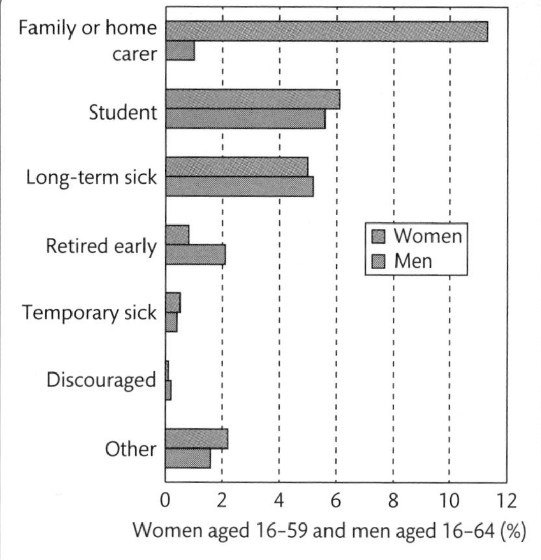

Figure 22.2 **The economically inactive, UK, 2010**

Among people of working age, 11% of women are caring for family and home, but only 1% of men. Some 6% of each gender are students and about 5% are long-term sick.
Source: Office for National Statistics, *Labour Market Statistics, April 2010*, Table 13.

natural level, N_E. But there would still be some natural unemployment, that is frictional and structural unemployment. If the real wage were above W_E, *ADL* shows that employers would hire fewer workers, while *LF* shows that more people would want jobs, so unemployment would be higher.

Economic activity and inactivity

In any country, everyone who wants to be in the labour force at the current real wage, that is everyone who is employed plus everyone defined as unemployed, is called **economically active**. Other people, who do not want to be in the labour force at the current real wage, are called **economically inactive**.

Most UK data about economic activity and inactivity concern people of 'working age', which is defined as being above the school-leaving age of 16 and below the age at which people can claim State Pension, currently 65 for men and 60 for women. For people in this age range, the percentages who were economically active in 2010 were about 82% for men and 74% for women.

Figure 22.2 looks at the 18% of men and 26% of women who were economically inactive, to see why this was so. The main reasons were caring for the family and home, being students, long-term sickness, and retiring early. However, caring accounted for far more women than men, and this is why more women than men were economically inactive. Incidentally, the carers and many others on the figure were no doubt very active in providing valuable services at home, but they are defined as economically inactive because they did not want paid employment.

Another group of economically inactive people is called discouraged workers. These people are able, available, and willing to work, but they have not looked for work in the last four weeks, so they are not defined as unemployed, and are therefore not in the labour force. Instead, they have currently stopped looking for jobs because they think they are unlikely to find any that they will take.

In Figure 22.1, the curve *LF* sloped upwards because every increase in the real wage would tempt some

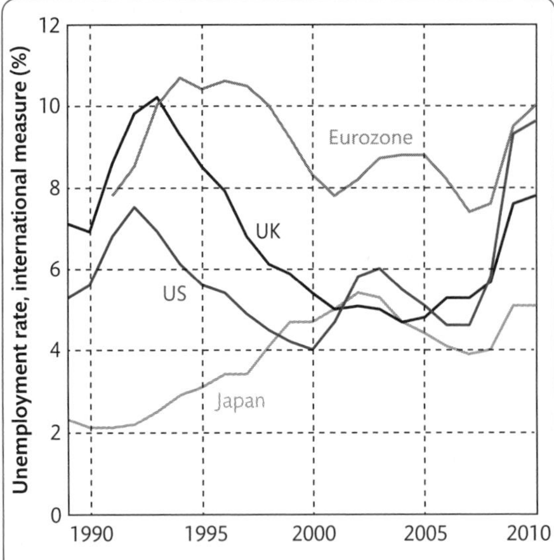

Figure 22.3 **Unemployment in the UK compared with the eurozone, Japan, and the US, 1989–2010**

Since 1989, the UK unemployment rate has been below the eurozone's and above Japan's. The UK rate was above the US rate in the 1990s, but has since been similar.

Source: OECD iLibrary, *Labour Force Statistics, April 2010.*

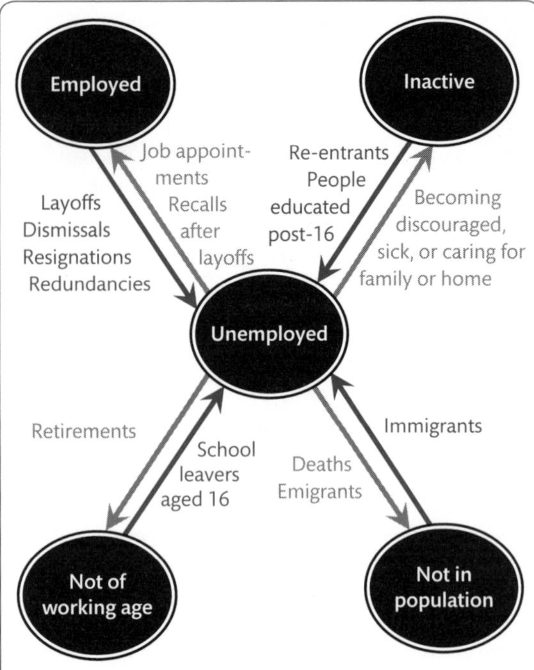

Figure 22.4 **Flows into and out of unemployment**

The arrows show the main flows in and out of unemployment from employment, economic inactivity, being of non-working age, and not being in the population. There are many flows between the other groups. For example, some employed people leave their jobs to care for a family or home, or because they reach retirement age, or because they leave the country's population by immigration or death.

people who were previously economically inactive to join the labour force and look for jobs. For example, some carers might prefer to have jobs and hire other people to do the caring.

Unemployment rates over time

The recent unemployment rates for the UK are plotted on Figure 22.3, and then compared with the rates in the eurozone, Japan, and the US. Notice that, while these rates do not always move up and down at the same time, they have all risen sharply since 2007. However, in 2010, the UK rate was below the rates for the US and the eurozone.

Flows into and out of unemployment

There are constant flows of people joining and leaving the ranks of the unemployed. Figure 22.4 shows how these flows arise between the unemployed and four other groups: the employed; the economically inactive; people whose age moves them into or out of working age; and people who, through migration or death, move into or out of the population.

Question 22.1 How might a full-time student, currently classed as economically inactive, move after graduation to other boxes in Figure 22.4?

Unemployment by age and duration

Unemployment affects different age groups to different extents. This is shown for the UK in Figure 22.5, in which the working age population is divided into four groups. In 2010, unemployment rates ranged from under 5% for people aged 50 or over, to more than 35% for people aged 16 or 17.

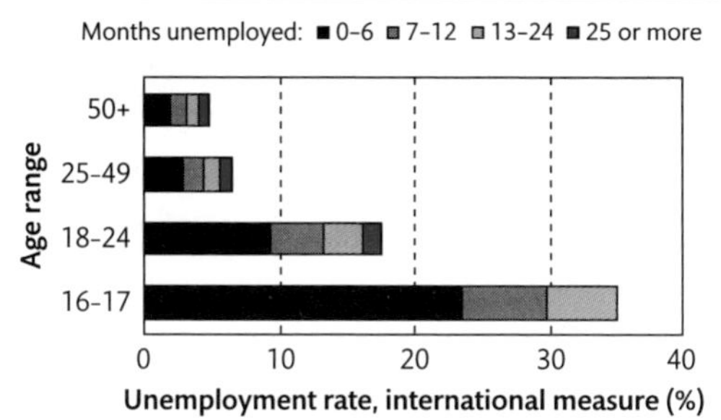

Figure 22.5 **Total unemployment rates by age group, broken down by duration, UK, 2010**

Over a third of economically active people aged 16-17 were unemployed. The percentage was much lower for older groups, but in the 50+ range, one sixth of those who were unemployed had been without work for over two years.

Source: Office for National Statistics, *Labour Market Statistics, April 2010*, Table 9.

Figure 22.5 also shows the proportions in each age group who have been unemployed for different lengths of time. A large proportion of unemployed people in the 50 and over group have been unemployed for more than six months.

Unemployment rates between groups

Data for unemployment in the country as a whole mask differences in the rates between different groups. These differences include the following.

- **Differences between genders**. Unemployment rates tend to be higher for males than females. Early in 2011, the rate for people aged 16 or over was 8.7% for males and 7.2% for females.
- **Differences between ethnic groups**. In the UK, a 2003 Cabinet office report, *Ethnic Minorities and the Labour Market*, found that, on average, ethnic Indians and Chinese often out-perform white British in the labour market, while Pakistani, Bangladeshi, and Black Caribbean groups experience significantly higher unemployment.
- **Differences between educational groups**. In 2009, the UK unemployment rate for people who had left school at the age of 16 or earlier was about 9.4%, compared with 3.2% for people with higher education qualifications.
- **Differences between regions**. Early in 2011, the rate ranged from 6.2% of those aged 16 or over in the East of England to 10.2% in the North East of England.

22.1 Everyday economics

Youth unemployment for Spain's youth

Unemployment in Spain has doubled in recent years and is now the highest unemployment rate among industrialized nations, standing at over 20%. The figure is particularly high for young people aged 16–24 for whom it stands at over 40%.

'Spanish unemployment continues to climb', *Finance Markets*, 4 April 2011
'Spain's official unemployment above 20%, with 43% of young Spaniards jobless', *Merco Press*, 6 April 2011

Comment Spain has traditionally had relatively high unemployment, and its overall rate today is about double the EU average. Its youth unemployment is much worse than elsewhere, although it is over 25% in Greece, Ireland, and Italy. In recent years, many youths were employed on temporary contracts. High youth unemployment for long periods will lead to a major loss of human capital in training and experience.

22.1 Summary

- The labour force comprises all economically active people, that is people who are able, willing, and available to work at the current real wage, whether or not they are actually employed.
- Working age people who are not in the labour force are economically inactive: they may care for a home or family, be sick, be students, be already retired, or be discouraged and have given up searching for jobs.
- Unemployment is lower for older people than younger people, for females than males, for ethnic White British people than most other ethnic groups, and for people with higher education qualifications than those without.

22.2 Natural unemployment

The causes of natural unemployment

We saw in Figure 22.1 that even if the labour market reaches its equilibrium real wage, where the demand and supply curves intersect, there will still be some unemployment called natural unemployment. We will study natural unemployment in this section: it is important because of its effects on those involved, and because it represents scarce resources that are idle.

We saw in Chapter 21 that natural unemployment arises because, even if the labour market were in equilibrium, not everyone who is able, available, and willing to work would accept a job currently on offer. There are two reasons for this.

- **Structural unemployment**. Some unemployed people do not have the right skills for the jobs currently on offer.
- **Frictional unemployment**. Some unemployed people will not accept a job until they find what they feel is the right job in the right place. The reason the gap between the labour force and labour supply curves gets smaller at high wages is that high wages make people less picky.

The rate of natural unemployment

In a discussion of natural unemployment, it would be nice to include good estimates of its size, but its exact size is unknown. This is because, at any point in time, we cannot be sure exactly where the supply and demand curves for labour are, nor where the labour force curve is. So we do not know what the equilibrium real wage is, or how much unemployment there would be if it were to apply. All we know for sure about the labour market at any point in time is the current real wage and the current rate of unemployment, but the real wage may well differ from the equilibrium wage.

However, economists believe that the rate of natural unemployment has varied in the last 50 years. They believe that if the only unemployment had been natural unemployment, then the UK unemployment rate would have been a little over 2% in the 1960s, and would then have risen steadily to 10% or more in the 1980s. Since then, it would have fallen back to, perhaps, 6%.

To see why the natural rate changes, we will consider separately why structural and frictional unemployment may change over time.

Changes in structural unemployment

The level of structural unemployment changes when there are changes in the types of job that firms want workers to do. To see this, suppose the labour market is initially as shown in Figure 22.6 by the curves ADL_0, ASL_0, and *LF*. And suppose the market is initially in equilibrium with the real wage W_0. The level of natural unemployment is shown by the line ***ab*** between ASL_0 and *LF* at this wage.

Now suppose, for example, that manufacturing industries shed jobs while service industries create new ones. And suppose for simplicity that, at each real wage, employers still want to hire the same total number of workers as before, so the demand curve remains at ADL_0.

However, some manufacturing workers will be made redundant because their skills are no longer required. And although new vacancies will arise in service industries, many of these jobs may require skills that the redundant workers do not possess, so they cannot apply for them. So the number of people who will actually accept jobs at each real wage falls, shifting the labour supply curve left to, say, ASL_1. The new equilibrium wage is W_1, and if the market reaches this equilibrium, natural unemployment will be as shown by ***cd***. This is more than the original natural unemployment ***ab***.

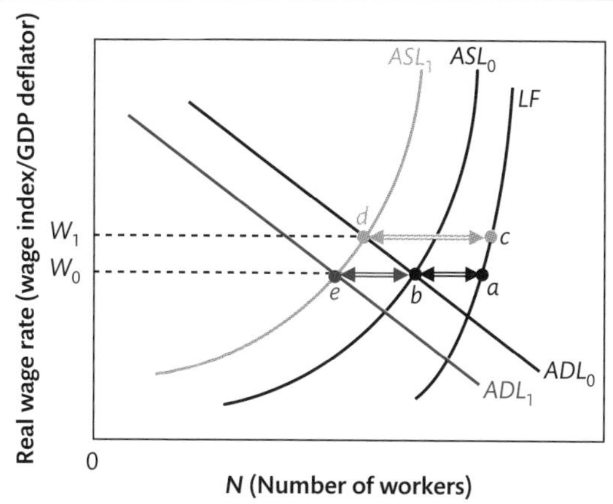

Figure 22.6 **Increases in structural unemployment**

If the demand for some skills falls, while the demand for other skills rises, then labour demand may stay at ADL_0. However, some people who become redundant will lack the skills for the new jobs that are being created, so labour supply shifts to ASL_1 and natural unemployment rises from ***ab*** to ***cd***. If all that happens is a fall in the demand for some skills, then labour demand shifts left, say to ADL_1, and natural unemployment rises even more, to ***ab*** + ***be***.

In time, some redundant workers will retrain while others will retire, to be replaced by a new generation with more up-to-date skills. Then the market supply curve will shift back to the right. But changing skills alone may not be enough to shift it back to ASL_0. Often, the new jobs will be in different places from the where the old ones were lost, so workers may have to relocate as well.

Note that if there had there a fall in the demand for some skills, and no rise in the demand for others, then the market demand curve would also have shifted to the left, say to ADL_1. This would have resulted in a lower real wage than W_1. For simplicity, Figure 22.6 shows the real wage staying at W_0, but natural unemployment would exceed the initial ***ab*** by the amount marked ***be***.

The demand for some skills in the UK has fallen for several reasons, including the following.

- **Some industries have declined, following the introduction of new alternative products.** In the 1960s and 1970s, this applied particularly to cotton and woollen textiles.
- **Some industries have introduced labour-saving technologies.** In the 1960s and 1970s, this applied particularly to agriculture. More recently, it has applied to vehicle manufacture and other industries in which robots have replaced humans.
- **Some industries have declined, following more competition from firms abroad.** In the 1960s and 1970s, this applied particularly to coal mining, shipbuilding, and steel manufacture. More recently, there has been stiff competition from East European and Asian countries, most notably China, which has led to a general shrinkage in the demand for labour in manufacturing industry.
- **North Sea oil.** When North Sea oil came on stream in the 1970s and 1980s, UK citizens needed to buy fewer foreign currencies to pay for imported oil. As a result, the supply of sterling on the foreign exchange markets fell, and the value of sterling rose. This encouraged UK citizens to import more manufactured goods, and it encouraged people abroad to buy fewer UK manufactured goods, and this exacerbated the decline in the UK's manufacturing industry.

The demand for some other skills in the UK has risen for several reasons, including the following.

- **The increased demand for services and hence for service employees.** Examples include tourism, travel, and the financial services industry.
- **The growing use of microchips.** This has led to a rising demand for programmers and other highly skilled workers.

In their efforts to minimize structural unemployment, governments have focused their policies on two issues:

- **producing school and college leavers who possess the new skills that employers want;**
- **encouraging retraining by those unemployed people whose skills are in little demand.**

Changes in frictional unemployment

The level of frictional unemployment is affected by demographic changes and by changes in the benefits paid to unemployed people. To see this, suppose the labour market is initially as shown in Figure 22.7 by the curves ADL_0, ASL_0, and *LF*. And suppose the market is initially in equilibrium with the real wage W_0 and natural unemployment ***ab***.

Now suppose that a demographic change increases the number of people of working age. An example of this occurred in the UK in the 1960s and 1970s, when babies born in the post-Second World War baby boom entered the workforce. The effect is to shift the labour force curve right to LF_1, taking the labour supply curve right to ASL_1. When the market reaches the new equilibrium with wage W_1, natural unemployment will be ***cd***. This is greater than ***ab*** because the gap between the labour force and labour supply curves is greater at low wages.

Return to the initial position in Figure 22.7 and suppose instead that the government pays higher benefits to unemployed people, or makes more generous rules about entitlement to these benefits. These moves will make unemployed people more picky about jobs, so the labour supply curve will shift to the left, say to ASL_2. When the labour market reaches the new equilibrium wage W_2, natural unemployment will be ***ef***, which is greater than ***ab***.

Governments can do little about demographic changes, but they can alter the benefits for unemployed people. Much of their focus in the UK has been to restrain the **replacement ratio**, that is the ratio of these benefits to the general level of wages. Governments have also tightened the rules on eligibility for benefits, making it harder for people to claim these for long periods. Both policies have helped to reduce frictional unemployment since the 1980s.

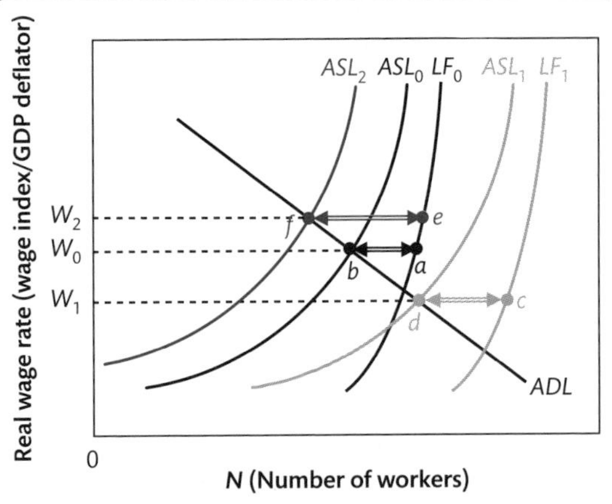

Figure 22.7 **Increases in frictional unemployment**

If the labour force increases, the supply of labour shifts to ASL_1, and natural unemployment rises from ***ab*** to ***cd***. If, instead, a rise in transfers to the unemployed makes them more selective about jobs, labour supply shifts to ASL_2, and natural unemployment rises from ***ab*** to ***ef***.

Equilibrium at a wage above the equilibrium

So far, we have allowed the labour market to settle at the equilibrium wage where the demand and supply curves intersect. However, there are some factors that may force the wage to settle at a higher level, perhaps indefinitely.

If these factors are at work, then the market will settle with more unemployment than natural unemployment. We can show this on Figure 22.7, where the initial labour force, labour supply, and labour demand curves are LF_0, ASL_0, and *ADL*. Initially, the market is in equilibrium with wage W_0, so that the only unemployment is the natural unemployment ***ab***. Now suppose some factor forces the wage to W_2 and holds it there. Then unemployment will increase to ***ef***.

It may seem that the real wage must eventually fall from W_2. However, we saw three reasons in Chapter 14 why the wage in an individual labour market might stay higher than the level at which the supply and demand curves intersect. If these reasons apply to many labour markets, then the same result may apply to the labour market as a whole. The reasons are as follows.

- **Efficiency wages**. Some employers may pay higher wages to get more applicants to choose from when recruiting, or to discourage shirking.

- **Trade unions**. Some employers may pay higher wages if trade union pressure forces them to do so. The higher wages benefit people who have jobs, called **insiders**, but reduce the number of workers employers wish to hire; this is bad for people without jobs, called **outsiders**.
- **A legal minimum wage**. This may force some employers to pay higher wages.

There is not much governments can do about efficiency wages, but since the 1970s they have tried to restrain trade union power, and they have held the minimum wage at modest levels.

Hysteresis—or previous employment

One factor that can affect the level of unemployment that arises if the labour market reaches equilibrium is the past actual rate of employment. This is shown in Figure 22.8, where the initial labour force, labour supply, and labour demand curves are LF_0, ASL_0, and ADL. Suppose the wage is initially in equilibrium at W_0, and that it has not been forced up by efficiency wages, unions, or a minimum wage. So employment is at the natural level N_0.

Now imagine that the economy enters a long recession, so the demand for labour falls and employment decreases. Later, the economy picks up, so the demand for labour increases. Suppose it returns to the original level. Even then, the employment level may not return to N_0 for several reasons, including the following.

- **Discouraged workers**. People who have been unemployed for a long time may be discouraged from looking for jobs, so the labour force curve, and in turn the labour supply curve, will shift left.
- **Human capital problems**. Workers gain human capital from experience and training, and this will apply to those who hold on to their jobs in a recession. In contrast, workers who experience a long spell of unemployment will not gain this human capital, so at the end of the recession they are less attractive to employers and may be unsuitable for many of the vacancies that arise. Once again, the labour supply curve will shift to the left. This problem can be seen as a form of structural unemployment.

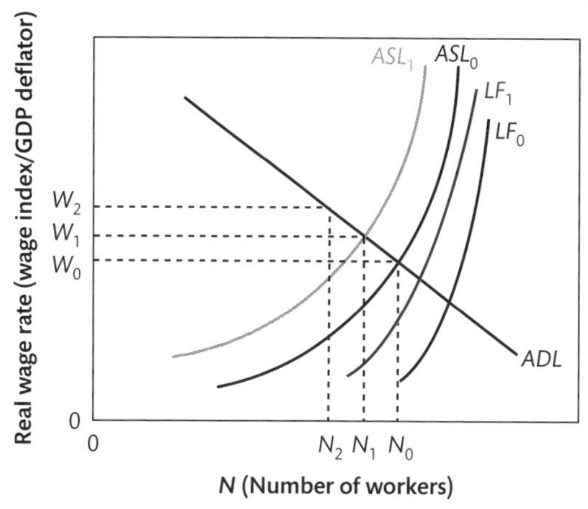

Figure 22.8 **Hysterisis**

The market starts with wage W_0 and employment N_0. If labour demand falls in a recession and later returns to ADL_0, employment may not return to N_0. This is because the labour force and labour supply curves may shift left if some unemployed workers are discouraged or have too little work experience to secure jobs. So employment may be only N_1. If existing workers can force the wage up to W_2, employment may be only N_2.

Suppose these two factors shift the labour force and supply curves to LF_1 and ASL_1. Then the equilibrium wage will be W_1 and employment will recover only as far as N_1. Even then, a third factor may come into play.

- **Insider-outsider issues**. Insiders may be able to capitalize on their attractiveness compared to people who have been unemployed for a long time by negotiating yet higher wages through their unions. Suppose they force the wage up to W_2; then employment will recover only up to N_2.

The possibility that the equilibrium employment level at any point in time may be affected by previous actual levels is called **hysteresis**. This is because the Greek word *hysteresis* means 'coming late', and the fall in the equilibrium level comes after the rise in the actual level. The government could tackle hysteresis by stepping up training programmes for unemployed workers, and by imposing further restraints on union power.

22.2 Summary

- Natural unemployment comprises structural and frictional unemployment. Its rate is uncertain but fluctuates over time, and may currently be around 6%.
- The wage rate could be held above the equilibrium level by efficiency wages, minimum wage laws, and trade unions. In this case, the equilibrium rate of unemployment will exceed the natural rate.
- The equilibrium rate of employment may be affected by previous actual levels owing to hysteresis. For example, previous high levels may reduce the labour supply by discouraged and inexperienced workers.

22.3 Demand-deficient unemployment: the classical view

We now turn from natural unemployment to the additional unemployment that arises if a recession takes the labour market away from equilibrium. We can illustrate this in Figure 22.9. This concerns a labour market that is initially in equilibrium where the initial demand and supply curves, ADL_0 and ASL, intersect, with wage W_0 and employment N_0.

Then aggregate demand in the economy falls. This leads to a fall in the price level and so to a rise in the real wage above W_0, say to W_1. At this real wage, producers will hire only N_1 workers, while ASL shows that many more people want jobs, so there is an excess supply of labour. In principle, nominal wages might then quickly fall to return the real wage to W_0 and employment to N_0. However, we saw four reasons in Chapter 21 why employment may stay below N_0 for some time, and Figure 22.9 illustrates two of them.

- **Nominal wages may be sticky downwards.** In this case, the real wage may stick at W_1, and this will hold the number of workers that employers want to hire at N_1.
- **Some prices may be sticky when aggregate demand falls.** Some firms may not initially reduce their prices. So these firms will not actually see any rise in their labour costs in relation to their output prices. But because they are not reducing their prices, they must react to the lower demand solely by cutting output. Then they will demand less

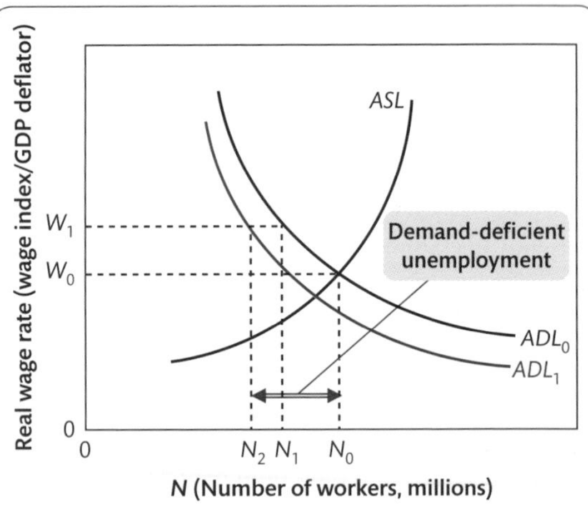

Figure 22.9 **Demand-deficient unemployment**

In a recession, many prices fall, so the real wage rises to W_1; this in itself causes employment to fall to N_1. Also, some firms may maintain their former prices and simply reduce output. These firms would then want to hire less labour even if the real wage did not rise. So the demand for labour shifts to ADL_1 and employment falls to N_2.

labour, so the labour demand curve shifts left to, say, ADL_1.

The combined effect of these events is to reduce employment from N_0 to N_2. The extra unemployment that arises when a recession takes the labour market away from equilibrium is called **demand-deficient unemployment.**

Chapter 21 also showed that a fall in aggregate demand could raise unemployment if workers and producers were initially to misperceive the effects of the fall in demand. For simplicity, we will assume here that these misperceptions are short-lived and we will focus on the events shown in Figure 22.9.

For this labour market to return to equilibrium, and so for the demand-deficient unemployment to disappear, it is necessary for sticky prices to fall, so that labour demand returns to ADL_0, and it is necessary for sticky money wages to fall, to return the real wage to W_0. Only then will employment return to N_0. In practice, sticky prices may take some time to fall enough, and sticky wages may take even longer. So, instead of waiting for some time while prices and wages fall enough to remove the demand-deficient unemployment, we may ask what, if anything, the government should do to reduce it faster.

On this issue, economists hold differing views. These disagreements have a long history, but we can usefully begin with the Great Depression of 1929–39. Until then, as we saw back in Figure 17.3, unemployment had fluctuated sharply, but was never persistently high.

In this section, we will look at the view that was widely held when the Great Depression set in: this is called the classical view. In the next section, we will look at two later views, which evolved in the following years: these are the Keynesian and monetarist views. In Chapter 23, we will see how all of these views about government policies towards unemployment later evolved to allow for the fact that governments also want to restrain inflation.

It should be stressed that while these views represent three schools of thought, there are still disagreements within each school. Also, many economists believe that more than one school has useful insights, while other economists have alternative views, which we have no time to explore.

Classical economics

The term 'classical economics' applies to a school of thought that derives from the 18th-century British economist Adam Smith and several 19th-century economists. These economists believed that most markets worked reasonably well when left alone, so they were wary about government intervention. In the case of the labour market, they believed that, until the 1930s, unemployment had never persisted at high levels because wages were sufficiently flexible to return the real wage to equilibrium fairly soon after a recession set in. So, they argued, governments need not take steps to reduce unemployment.

Figure 22.10 represents this view. The economy is initially in long-run equilibrium where the aggregate demand curve, AD_0, intersects the long-run aggregate supply curve, *LAS*. So output is at the potential level Y_P, and the price level is P_0. The initial short-run aggregate supply curve SAS_0 intersects AD_0 at the same price level.

Then a recession occurs and aggregate demand shifts to AD_1. So prices fall to P_1, output falls to Y_1, and demand-deficient unemployment arises. But wage flexibility soon returns the labour market to equilibrium with employment back at its original level, and then output returns to Y_P. The economy ends up where AD_1 intersects *LAS*, and the lower wages shift the short-run aggregate supply curve to the right to SAS_1 to pass the same point; the only permanent change is a fall in the price level to P_2.

The classical view and monetary policy

Suppose a country's labour market is in equilibrium, so its only unemployment is natural unemployment. Its government might be tempted to increase aggregate

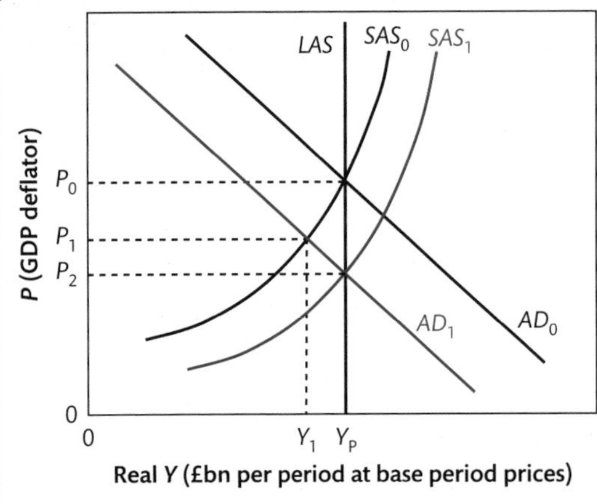

Figure 22.10 **Recessions and the classical view**

A fall in aggregate demand from AD_0 to AD_1 reduces the price level to P_1 and output to Y_1. Lower output reduces employment and raises unemployment. But wages soon fall to return the labour market to equilibrium with the same employment as before, returning output to Y_0. However, lower wages also shift the short-run aggregate supply curve to SAS_1, so the price level will be lower than it started at P_2.

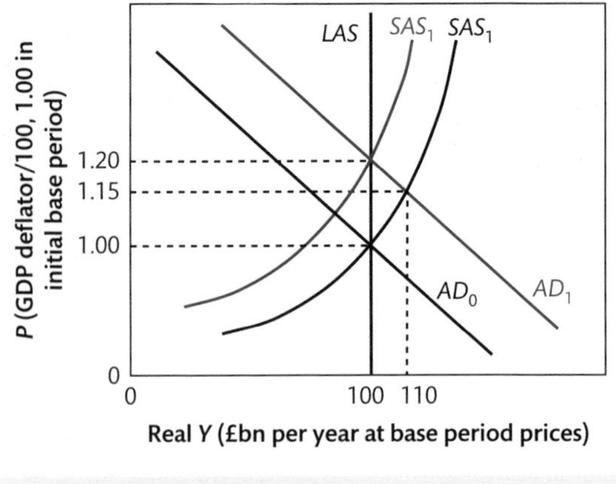

Figure 22.11 **The classical dichotomy**

A rise in aggregate demand from AD_0 to AD_1 raises the price level and also raises output. Higher output means that employment rises, so unemployment falls. But wages soon rise to return the labour market to equilibrium with the same employment as before, so output returns to its original level. However, the high wages shift the short-run aggregate supply curve to SAS_1, so the price level rises yet further.

demand in an effort to raise output and so reduce unemployment even further. However, the classical economists' belief in wage flexibility meant that they were opposed to governments doing this. We will now use Figure 22.11 to see why they opposed using monetary policy for this purpose.

Suppose the economy initially has the black curves shown in Figure 22.11, and that the initial year is the base period. This figure makes one departure from others we have had in that the price level, *P*, is not measured by the GDP deflator, but is measured as the deflator divided by 100. So in the base year it is 1.00, and real output is £100 billion.

Now suppose the government increases the money stock to reduce interest rates. So consumer spending and investment rise and aggregate demand shifts to AD_1. Then the price level rises to 1.15 and output rises to £110 billion a year, so unemployment falls below the natural level that would arise if the labour market were in equilibrium. But wage flexibility means that wages will soon rise enough to return the labour market to equilibrium with unemployment back at its natural level, and so return real output to £100 billion a year. The higher wages shift the short-run aggregate supply curve to the left to SAS_1, and the final equilibrium is where AD_1 intersects both this and *LAS*. The only lasting effect is that prices rise to 1.20.

This conclusion is called the **classical dichotomy** or the **neutrality of money**. These terms mean that changes in the money stock, which is measured in nominal terms, have no lasting effects on variables that are measured in real terms, such as real output or unemployment.

The quantity theory of money

The classical view of money went beyond this, in what is called the quantity theory of money. To understand this theory, it is necessary to see that nominal GDP is always equal to *PY*, where *P* is the price level measured as the GDP deflator divided by 100, and *Y* is real GDP. For example, consider both the initial and final years in Figure 22.11.

- **Initial year**: *P* was 1.00. This means the GDP deflator was 100. When the GDP deflator is 100, nominal GDP is the same as real GDP, that is *Y*, which was £100 billion. So nominal GDP equalled *PY*, that is $1.00 \times$ £100 billion.
- **Final year**: compared with the initial year, real GDP, *Y*, was the same at £100 billion, but the price level, *P*, was 20% higher at 1.20. So nominal GDP must have been 20% higher at £120 billion. This equalled *PY*, that is $1.20 \times$ £100 billion.

Suppose the nominal money stock, *M*, was initially £50 billion. Then, in that initial year when nominal GDP was £100 billion, each £1 of money was on average used twice to buy the products that comprise GDP. The number of times that money is used on average in a period to purchase items included in GDP is called the **velocity of circulation**, *V*, so here *V* was 2 per year.

Notice that *MV* equals £100 billion, that is nominal GDP. *MV* always equals nominal GDP because of the way we define the terms. We can check this in the final year when nominal GDP was £120 billion. Let's assume *V* was still 2. Then there must have been £60 billion worth of money changing hands twice buying the products included in GDP. So nominal GDP equalled *MV* with *M* at £60 billion and *V* at 2.

In any period, then, nominal GDP equals both *PY* and *MV*. This means it is always the case that:

$$MV = PY$$

This is true, simply because of the way the terms are defined. However, the classical economists also asserted that *V* is constant. This means that people do not sometimes want to hold little money and spend what comes in quickly, and at other times to hold large amounts and spend what comes in slowly. Now if $MV = PY$, and also *V* is constant, then *PY* is proportional to *M*. In our example, we assumed *V* was constant, and we saw that while *M* rose by 20% from £50 billion to £60 billion, nominal GDP or *PY* also rose by 20%, from £100 billion to £120 billion.

The classical economists also believed that because of wage flexibility, real GDP, *Y*, never strayed for long from its potential level given by *LAS*, which in our case was £100 billion. So they regarded *Y*, too, as effectively constant and believed that *P* is proportional to *M*; this theory is called the **quantity theory of money**. In our example, *M* rose by 20% and so did *P*. This theory goes beyond the classical dichotomy, which says that that an increase in *M* has no effect on any real variables such as output and employment, to say that its effect on prices is to raise them in exact proportion to the rise in *M*.

The classical view and fiscal policy

We used Figure 22.11 to show why classical economists were wary about using monetary policy to raise demand in an effort to reduce unemployment below its natural rate. The same figure can be used to show why they were just as wary of fiscal policies, such as raising government purchases or cutting taxes to raise consumption. If these policies were used to shift aggregate demand to the right, then output would rise and unemployment would fall below the natural level. But again the labour market would soon return employment and output to their original levels, and the only effect would be a rise in prices.

There was another worry with fiscal policy. If the government spent more on purchases or on transfers, how would this be financed? If it raised taxes, it was feared that consumer spending might fall nearly as much as government spending rose. If it borrowed, it was feared that fewer funds would be available for other borrowers, so investment and consumption would fall.

22.3 Summary

- If wages or prices are sticky, or if employers of workers have misperceptions, then a recession will lead to a period in which the labour market is out of equilibrium, with demand-deficient unemployment.
- Economists generally accept that prices may not be sticky for long, and that misperceptions may not last for long. So if demand-deficient unemployment persists, sticky wages are the most likely cause.
- Classical economists believed that wages were not very sticky, so they expected the labour market to return to equilibrium soon after a recession. So they saw no need for government intervention.
- Classical economists argued that, in the long run, expansionary monetary or fiscal policies raised prices, but not output. The quantity theory of money holds that prices are proportional to the money stock.

22.4 Demand-deficient unemployment: Keynesians and monetarists

The Keynesian view

The classical view was challenged during the Great Depression by the British economist John Maynard Keynes. He argued that the persistent demand-deficient unemployment showed that wages were not flexible enough for the problem to disappear without government intervention. He suggested two main reasons for sticky wages.

- **Workers' concern about their wages relative to those paid in other occupations**. Workers will resist wage cuts that reduce their wages relative to those paid in other occupations.
- **Trade unions**. Unions will resist employers who want to cut the nominal wages of their current workers, or who want to recruit new workers at wages below those paid to current workers.

Keynes also argued that even if nominal wages were to fall in a recession, there might be little effect on employment. This was chiefly because falling wages might lead to falling prices; if prices started to fall, then people might expect them to continue to fall, and then they might defer some consumption, especially of durable goods. This would cause a further fall in real spending.

So if a fall in aggregate demand caused a recession, Keynes argued that the government should use an expansionary policy to raise demand and output. He appreciated that such a policy might raise prices as well as output; but he pointed out that a rise in prices would reduce real wages and so result in producers hiring more workers. He said the government could use either monetary policy or fiscal policy, but he argued that fiscal policy would be more effective. We will now explain why he thought this.

Keynes and monetary policy

It was Keynes who put forward the model of the money market that we studied in Chapter 20. Suppose the money market is initially in equilibrium as shown in Figure 22.12, at the point where the initial money supply and demand curves, MS_0 and MD_0, intersect. So the interest rate is r_0 and the money stock is M_0.

Then suppose the authorities shift the money supply curve to MS_1. The model says interest rates will fall to r_1. This should lead to more investment and consumption, so raising aggregate demand. This will increase real output and reduce unemployment.

However, Keynes argued that although increases in the money stock would increase output and reduce

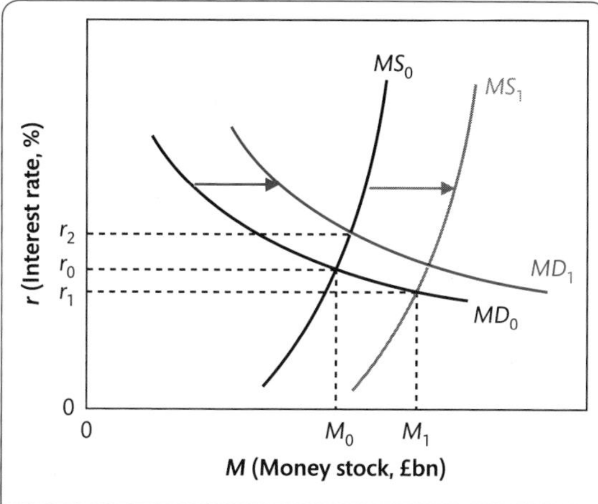

Figure 22.12 **A Keynesian view of the money market**

On this view, money demand is interest elastic. So the interest rate is little affected by a shift in the money supply curve, or by a shift in the money demand curve.

unemployment, the effect might be small. His arguments included the following.

- **The demand for money may be interest elastic.** This applies in Figure 22.12, where a large shift in the money supply curve has only a modest effect on interest rates. In turn, there might be little effect on investment or consumption. In the Great Depression, interest rates were very low, and at these low levels Keynes believed that money demand might be highly interest elastic, so that shifts in the money supply curve would have hardly any effect on the interest rate.
- **Consumer spending depends chiefly on incomes.** Keynes argued that consumer spending depended chiefly on incomes, so even if interest rates were to fall, consumer spending might not rise much.
- **Investment is affected by 'animal spirits'.** Keynes argued that investment decisions depend chiefly on producers' expectations or 'animal spirits' about future output. If they have bad 'animal spirits' about the future, and expect a recession to continue, then investment might not rise much, even if interest rates were to fall.

These three points suggest that if there is an increase in the money stock, *M*, then there might be little change in aggregate demand. In turn, there might be little change in the price level, *P*, or in real output, *Y*. Yet we know that $MV = PY$, where *V* is the velocity of circulation. So if a rise in *M* has little effect on *P* or *Y*, then it follows that the rise in *M* must be largely offset by a fall in *V*.

We can deduce from Figure 22.12 that this is what happens. The monetary expansion raises the amount of money that people hold substantially from M_0 to M_1. So if people hold more money, and if output rises little, then the velocity of circulation must be lower.

Keynes and fiscal policy

Keynes argued that fiscal policy would have more effect than monetary policy. He argued for spending on 'public works', such as roads and state schools, paid for by the government. But he did not want these works to be financed through taxes, because the tax rises would cut consumer spending by nearly as much as government spending rose, leading to little increase in aggregate demand. We saw this in Chapter 19 when we studied the balanced budget multiplier.

Instead, Keynes argued that the government should finance the public works with loans. And he claimed that, owing to the multiplier effect, the rise in demand should greatly raise output and incomes and greatly reduce unemployment. The rise in incomes would lead to higher tax revenues, and the fall in unemployment would reduce government transfers to the unemployed. As a result, the government could readily afford the interest and repayment costs of the loans.

This argument led to the view that governments should undertake **demand management**: this means trying to offset the rises and falls in aggregate demand that occur over a business cycle. The idea is for a government to raise demand when it is too low by having a budget deficit, that is by spending more than it raises in taxes, and to reduce demand when it is too high by having a budget surplus, that is by spending less than it raises in taxes.

The effect of deficit finance on employment and output appeared manifest in the Second World War, when high public spending on defence, admittedly coupled with conscription, almost eliminated unemployment. Technically, the government raised most of the finance through taxes, but it offered people post-war credits, which entitled them to have some taxes repaid later; so the finance could be seen in part as compulsory lending to the government.

Question 22.2 Suppose the government simply borrows money and pays people to dig holes and fill them in again. Will this reduce unemployment and increase output?

Keynesians versus monetarists

Until the 1970s, few people doubted that demand management on Keynesian lines worked: if you look back at Figure 17.3, you will see how unemployment in the UK was always low between the 1940s and the 1970s. The same applied in many other countries. The major issue was whether monetary or fiscal policy was the more effective tool to use. If you studied the appendix to Chapter 20, you will have already met this controversy. Many economists believed that both policies could be effective, but two groups evolved, monetarists and Keynesians, who tended to champion one over the other.

The key differences between these groups were over the interest elasticity of demand for money and over the effect of interest rates changes on planned investment and consumption, and so on aggregate demand.

Like Keynes, the Keynesians argued that the demand for money was interest elastic, as shown in Figure 22.12. They also argued that changes in interest rates had little effect on aggregate demand. So they reached the following conclusions.

- **Monetary policy is weak**: policies that shift the money supply curve to the right, say from MS_0 to MS_1 in Figure 22.12, so increasing the money stock, will reduce interest rates very little from r_0 to r_1; any fall in interest rates that does occur will have little effect on aggregate demand.
- **Fiscal policy is strong**: policies to increase government spending, or to increase consumer spending through tax cuts, will at once shift aggregate demand and raise output. Admittedly, when incomes rise, the demand for money will rise, say from MD_0 to MD_1 in Figure 22.12, so raising the interest rate from r_0 to r_2; that will reduce consumption or investment. But the interest rate rise will be small, and any rise that does occur will have little effect on consumption or investment.

The monetarists argued that the demand for money was interest inelastic, as shown in Figure 22.13. They also argued that changes in interest rates had significant effects on aggregate demand. So they reached these conclusions.

- **Monetary policy is strong**: policies that shift the money supply curve to the right, say from MS_0 to MS_1 in Figure 22.13, so increasing the money stock, will reduce interest rates greatly from r_0 to r_1. And any fall in interest rates has a significant effect on aggregate demand.

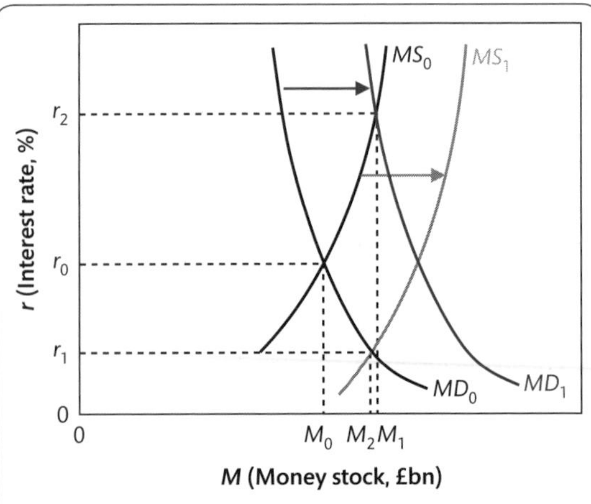

Figure 22.13 **A monetarist view of the money market**

On this view, money demand is interest inelastic. So the interest rate is much affected by a shift in the money supply curve, and by a shift in the money demand curve.

- **Fiscal policy is weak**: policies to increase government spending, or to increase consumer spending through tax cuts, might shift aggregate demand at once. But then, as soon as incomes start to rise, the demand for money will rise, say from MD_0 to MD_1 in Figure 22.13. This will cause a large rise in the interest rate, from r_0 to r_2, and this will lead to a significant fall in consumption and investment that could offset much of the initial rise in government spending or consumption.

However, monetarists believed that tax cuts might not increase consumer spending much in the first place: it is true that disposable incomes will rise, but they argued that consumers base their spending decisions not only on their current disposable income, but also on the disposable income they expect to have in future. So, for example, if they think a tax cut is only temporary, they might think that it will have little effect on their disposable incomes over the long term, and so might not spend much more now.

It may seem that the monetarist–Keynesian debate could be readily resolved by establishing the interest-elasticity of the demand for money and by establishing how much spending responds to changes in interest rates. But it is hard to estimate how much money people would hold, or how much they would spend, if interest rates were different from what they are. Also, the situation could vary over time and between countries.

The monetarist position is chiefly associated with the American economist Milton Friedman. It might be wondered why he thought monetary policy was effective, because interest rates were held low during the Great Depression with seemingly little effect. His response was to cite research that he did with Anna Schwartz. This indicated that, in the US at least, the Depression was largely caused by a sharp fall in the money stock, which resulted from bank failures; he blamed the US central bank, the Federal Reserve, for not having done more to offset this fall. His claim was later accepted by the Federal Reserve, which added in 2002 that, thanks to him, it would not make the same mistake again.

Developments in macroeconomic thinking

Most economists accept that, in the long run, the labour market will arrive at equilibrium with employment at the natural level, so that output will be at its potential level. So these economists agree with the classical theory that, in the long run, neither fiscal policy nor monetary policy can alter output and unemployment. They also accept that the quantity theory of money applies in the long run, in that changes in the money stock eventually have no effect on real output.

However, these economists also argue that the labour market might take several years to return to equilibrium. So they believe there is a case for using monetary or fiscal policies, or both, to manage demand in order to manage output and employment.

Incidentally, some other economists, who call themselves 'Post Keynesian' in the belief that their ideas are rooted in Keynes's ideas, argue that if the labour market is out of equilibrium, then it might never on its own return to equilibrium. So they are even more supportive of demand management policies.

We have already mentioned that the use of monetary and fiscal policies from the 1940s to the 1970s seemed largely successful at holding unemployment at low levels. But all was not well on another front: inflation. If you look back at Figure 17.5, you will see that there was no sustained inflation in the UK between 1855 and 1940, except around the First World War. But after the Second World War, when demand management policies were implemented, prices began to rise constantly. And in the 1970s, the inflation rate accelerated.

Economists then studied the causes of inflation, and considered whether governments could restrain inflation and unemployment simultaneously. That is what we will study in the next chapter, and we will see how the inflation problem modified people's views of economic policy and led to 'new' classical, 'new' monetarist and 'new' Keynesian views. We will return to monetary and fiscal policy also in several later chapters, including Chapter 28, where we will see how the power of these policies is affected by international flows of money.

Policy in the 2007–10 recession

We will see in the next chapter that, from the 1970s, governments became cautious about using either monetary or fiscal expansion in recessions, fearing that any increases in aggregate demand would make inflation worse. However, caution was thrown to the winds at the onset of the 2007–10 recession, when Bank Rate was held at 0.5%, much lower than the 2% of the 1930s, and the government ran up a huge deficit.

22.2 Everyday economics

UK unemployment highest for 17 years

Recent figures show that, on the international measure, unemployment in the UK rose above 2½ million in the period November 2010 to January 2011 to reach the highest level since 1994, with 8% of the workforce out of work. Unemployment had fallen a little earlier in 2010, but rose later, partly because the government's spending cuts began to take effect. With more cuts on the way, the short-term outlook is bleak.

'UK unemployment rises to 2.53 million', *The Guardian*, 16 March 2011

'UK unemployment total hits 17-year high', *BBC News*, 16 March 2011

Comment The government's sole consolation seemed to be that, while unemployment rose on the international definition, the number of people claiming Jobseeker's Allowance actually fell. But, as we saw in Chapter 17, this is a poorer measure of unemployment than the international one.

22.4 Summary

- Keynes argued that if the labour market were not in equilibrium, then it might take a long time to return, so governments should try to raise demand when it was low. This view led to a widespread view that governments should manage demand, and so also try to reduce demand when it was high. Keynes also argued that fiscal policies would be more effective than monetary policies.
- Monetarists argued that monetary policy has more effect than fiscal policy.
- From the 1970s, governments became cautious about raising demand when it is low, for fear of aggravating inflation, but monetary and fiscal policies were used aggressively in the 2007–10 recession.

In the next chapter we study inflation and explore the problems that arise when governments try to restrain unemployment and inflation simultaneously.

abc Glossary

Classical dichotomy: the view that changes in the money stock, which is measured in nominal terms, have no lasting effects on variables measured in real terms, such as real output or unemployment.

Demand-deficient unemployment: the extra unemployment that arises when a recession takes the labour market away from equilibrium

Demand management: using government policies to try to offset the rises and falls in aggregate demand that occur over a business cycle.

Economically active: someone who is able, available, and willing to work.

Economically inactive: someone who is not able, available, or willing to work.

Hysteresis: the possibility that the equilibrium employment level at a point in time may be affected by previous actual unemployment levels.

Insiders: people with jobs.

Neutrality of money: another term for the classical dichotomy.

Outsiders: people without jobs.

Quantity theory of money: the theory that the price level, *P*, is proportional to the nominal money stock, *M*; this follows from the relationship $MV = PY$, in which *V* is the velocity of circulation and *Y* is real GDP, if it is assumed that changes in *M* do not affect *V* or *Y*.

Replacement ratio: the ratio of the benefits paid to the unemployed to the general level of wages.

Unemployment rate: the percentage of the labour force that has no job.

Velocity of circulation: the number of times that money, on average, is used in any period to purchase items included in GDP.

Answers to in-text questions

22.1 The student might have been given a job offer before graduation and move at once into employment, or become unemployed, or emigrate (or die) and no longer be in the population. Also, a mature student who happened to reach retirement age on the day of graduation would move out of working age. Mature students who are already of retirement stage are not counted in the workforce, so they would in the 'not of working age' box both before and after graduation.

22.2 Yes. Those paid to do the work would get jobs, and when they spent their earnings, they would create jobs for others. This tongue-in-cheek suggestion is often attributed to Keynes, but his actual tongue-in-cheek suggestion was for the government to hire workers to bury banknotes in old coal mines and fill them in. Then private firms would hire workers to dig them up. All of this would create employment. However, Keynes added that 'it would be more sensible to build houses and the like'.

? Questions for review

22.1 Refer to the curves shown in a labour market diagram to suggest the effects that the following might have on employment. **(a)** An increase in the country's capital stock that led to firms replacing labour with machines. **(b)** Growing use of computer software to match unemployed people to vacant jobs. **(c)** An increase in the school-leaving age.

22.2 This chapter has considered classical economists, Keynesians, and monetarists. **(a)** Which of these three would oppose government efforts to reduce unemployment? **(b)** Which would choose monetary policy to reduce unemployment? **(c)** Which would choose fiscal policy to reduce unemployment? **(d)** Which of them thinks aggregate demand is not very sensitive to interest rate changes?

? Questions for discussion

22.1 Structural unemployment results when the demand for some skills falls. Suggest some skills for which demand might fall and others for which it might rise. Do you think young people allow for future demand changes of this type when training and choosing their first jobs?

22.2 Suppose unemployed workers attempt to get jobs by offering to accept advertised vacancies for less than the wage rates offered. Will this lead to a fall in the real wage and a fall in unemployment?

Common student errors

The most confusing concepts here arise from some commonly used definitions. Sometimes, people use the term 'full employment' for the natural employment level that applies when the labour market is in equilibrium; this overlooks the fact that there will then still be natural unemployment. And sometimes people use the term 'voluntary employment' for natural unemployment, because the people concerned are not accepting job offers. But redundant workers with outdated skills, and college leavers looking for reasonable jobs, might feel that the term 'voluntary unemployment' is misleading. This book avoids the terms full employment and voluntary unemployment.

23

Inflation and Unemployment

Remember from Chapter 21 that the point at which a country's short-run aggregate supply curve intersects its aggregate demand curve shows the short-run equilibrium position for its price level and output. If this output happens to be the level at which the country's long-run aggregate supply curve is vertical, then the price and output levels are also in long-run equilibrium, with output at its potential level; when output is at this level, the labour market will be in equilibrium, with employment and unemployment at their natural levels.

'If the government increases aggregate demand, in an effort to increase output and reduce unemployment, then prices will rise. So it is impossible to reduce unemployment without causing inflation.' Is this true? What does cause inflation? Does it get worse if unemployment falls? What can governments do about it? And why do economists disagree about what they should do about it?

This chapter shows you how to answer questions like these, by understanding:

* the relationship between inflation and unemployment;
* short-run and long-run Phillips curves;
* how expected inflation affects actual inflation;
* how supply and demand shocks affect inflation;
* why economists have differing views about what could or should be done to reduce inflation.

23.1 Inflation and the Phillips curve

The term 'inflation' means rises in the general level of prices in a country. We saw in Chapter 17 that the main problems with inflation are as follows.

- **Some people gain and some people lose, especially if the actual rate of inflation differs from the expected rate.** This leads to a redistribution of income.
- **Inflation creates uncertainty.**
- **There is a possibility of hyperinflation.**
- **Firms face costs when they change their prices.**
- **Inflation erodes the value of cash.**

These problems mean that governments are keen to restrain inflation. But before we discuss how they can do so, we must see how inflation can arise. We must also see how the rate of inflation may be affected by the rate of unemployment.

Inflation can arise in two ways, as follows:

- **cost-push inflation**;
- **demand-pull inflation.**

We will begin by explaining these, using the *AD–AS* model, which we met in Chapter 21. This model shows how a country's price level, as measured by the GDP deflator, is determined.

Cost-push inflation

Figure 23.1 illustrates cost-push inflation for a country whose initial aggregate demand and short-run aggregate supply curves are AD_0 and SAS_0. Their intersection gives its initial price and output levels P_0, and Y_P. This output is also the potential level because the long-run aggregate supply curve, *LAS*, is vertical here. As output is at its potential level, the labour market must be in equilibrium with the natural level of employment.

Now suppose that some cost increases create a supply shock. Perhaps workers negotiate higher nominal wages. Then the short-run aggregate supply curve shifts to SAS_1, and the price level rises to P_1 while output falls to Y_1, so employers hire fewer workers and unemployment rises.

If the government ignores this shock, then, in the long run, unemployment will lead to lower nominal wages, and most economists believe the real wage rate will fall until employment returns to its natural level. Also, the lower nominal wages will return the short-run aggregate supply to SAS_0, taking output and the price level back to Y_P and P_0, so there is no lasting rise in the price level.

But suppose the government reacts to the supply shock with monetary or fiscal expansion, to return output more quickly to its original level. It will shift

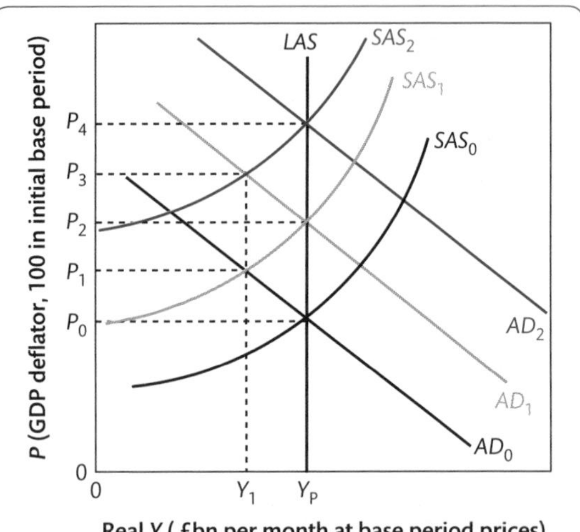

Figure 23.1 **Cost-push inflation**

Suppose a rise in costs shifts aggregate supply to SAS_1, and the government responds to the fall in output by raising aggregate demand to AD_1; then the price level will rise to P_2. If there is a later shift in *SAS* to SAS_2, and in *AD* to AD_2, prices will rise again to P_4. If this process continues, there is cost-push inflation.

aggregate demand to AD_1, returning output to Y_P, and employment to its natural level. The price level will rise again to P_2, and then stop rising.

The only way in which cost increases can lead to sustained inflation is if costs persistently rise and if the government persistently tries to return output to its potential level. For example, if further cost increases shift the short-run aggregate supply curve to SAS_2, taking the price level to P_3 and output back to Y_1, and if the government reacts by raising demand to AD_2, then output will return to Y_P and the price level will rise again to P_4. Inflation caused by persistent cost increases combined with government action to offset any falls in output, is called **cost-push inflation.**

Demand-pull inflation

Demand-pull inflation is explained in Figure 23.2. Suppose the country initially faces the same initial black curves as in Figure 23.1, so the price level is P_0 and output is Y_P.

Now suppose aggregate demand increases to AD_1. Perhaps firms become more optimistic so that investment rises. The price level rises to P_1 and output rises to Y_1. The rise in output above the potential level means that employers hire more workers, so unemployment falls below the natural rate, and the labour market is out of equilibrium.

In time, nominal wages rise. This will return the labour market to equilibrium and shift the short-run aggregate supply to SAS_1, so that output returns to Y_P. The price level will rise again to P_2 and then stop rising.

The only way in which demand increases can lead to sustained inflation is if aggregate demand rises persistently and the labour market always returns to equilibrium. For example, suppose a further demand increase shifts aggregate demand to AD_2, taking the price level to P_3 and output to Y_1. Again unemployment will fall below the natural rate, so nominal wages will soon rise, shifting short-run aggregate supply to SAS_2. This will return output to Y_P, but raise the price level to P_4.

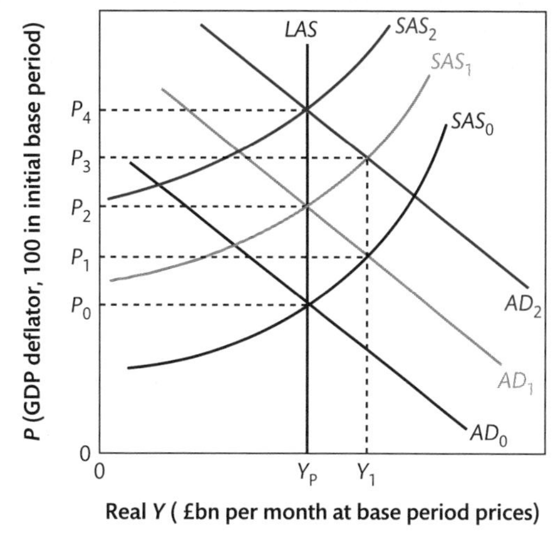

Figure 23.2 **Demand-pull inflation**

Suppose a rise in demand shifts aggregate demand to AD_1, so output rises above the potential level and unemployment falls below the natural level. In time wages rise to return the labour market to equilibrium, so short-run aggregate supply shifts to SAS_1, taking prices to P_2. If there is a later shift in AD to AD_2, causing a shift in SAS to SAS_2, prices will rise again to P_4. If this process continues, there is demand-pull inflation.

Inflation caused by successive increases in aggregate demand is called **demand-pull inflation.**

Phillips's observations

We must now explore the relationship between inflation and unemployment. To do this, we will begin with a discovery published in 1958 by a New Zealand economist, William Phillips, who was working in the UK. This discovery concerned unemployment as well as inflation, and the rest of this chapter also considers them both.

For each year from 1861 to 1957, Phillips looked at the average rate of unemployment and at the amount by which nominal or money wages rose. He found that, in most years, the relationship between unemployment and wages increases was close to that shown by the curve in Figure 23.3. This figure plots

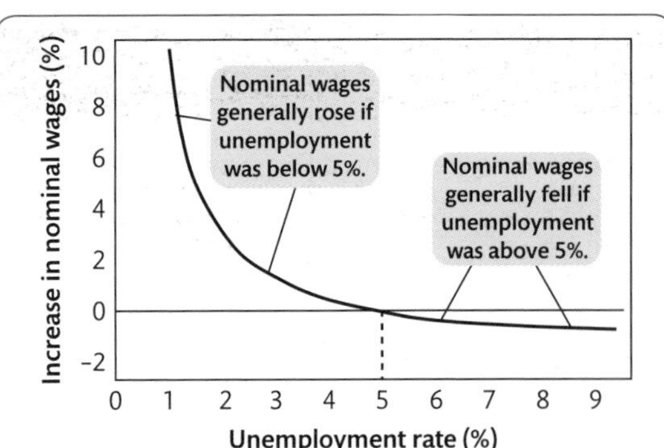

Figure 23.3 **Phillips's original curve**

In most years between 1861 and 1957, the relationship between the rate of unemployment and the rate at which nominal wages increased was at a point quite close to this curved line.

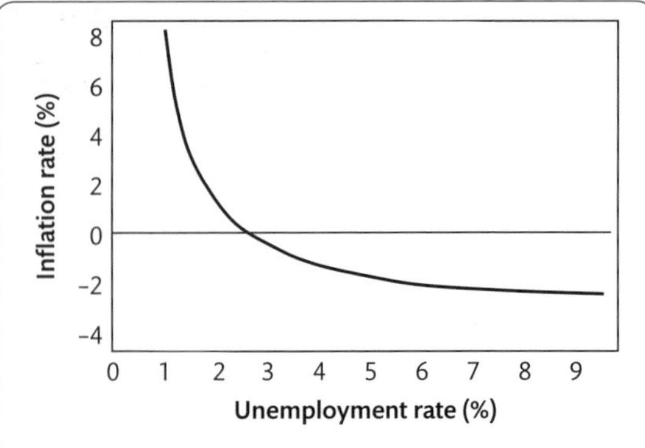

Figure 23.4 **The original idea of the Phillips curve**

It was assumed that the relationship between the rate of unemployment and the rate at which prices increased would generally be at a point quite close to a curve like this.

the unemployment rate on the horizontal axis and the rate of wage increases on the vertical axis. The curve shows that in years when unemployment was around 5%, nominal wages changed little. But nominal wages generally fell in years when unemployment was above 5% and rose in years when it was below 5%. Indeed, the lower the unemployment rate, the more nominal wages tended to rise.

The Phillips curve

Shortly after Phillips published his work, other people plotted a similar-looking curve like that shown in Figure 23.4. This also has the unemployment rate on the horizontal axis, but its vertical axis shows the rate of price inflation, not wage increases. A curve that relates price inflation to unemployment is called a **Phillips curve,** even though Phillips's curve did not do so.

If you compare Figures 23.3 and 23.4, you will see that prices rise by less than wages at each level of unemployment. This occurs because, over time, productivity rises, so the economy produces more and workers can buy more; in order for them to be able to buy more, nominal wages must rise at a faster rate than prices.

It was found that other countries had similar curves. These curves suggested that if a government managed to reduce unemployment by using monetary or fiscal policies, then it would move its country leftwards along the curve and create higher inflation. In other words, it seemed that there was a trade-off: a government could reduce unemployment or reduce inflation, but it could not do both at the same time.

Although the data used for these curves covered about a century, not everyone accepted that there was a trade-off. Some economists, notably Milton Friedman, used the analysis given in Chapter 22 to argue that, in the long run, the labour market always settles with unemployment at the natural rate, and that price rises then depend on how fast the money stock is growing.

This argument did not attract much support at the time, because in the century after 1861 inflation was so closely related to unemployment, as shown in the Phillips curves. But this close relationship disappeared in the late 1960s, when both inflation and unemployment rose sharply at the same time.

In fact, the Phillips curve shifted. Figure 23.5 shows with black dots the combinations of UK unemployment and inflation for the years between 1953 and 1966. These dots suggest that, in those years, the Phillips curve stayed close to the one shown in black. Then the curve shifted away from the origin through the grey

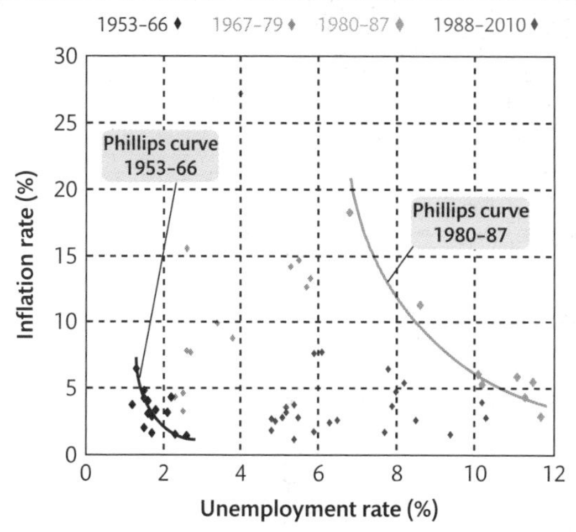

Figure 23.5 **The shifting Phillips curve**

In each year from 1953 to 1966, the short-run Phillips curve was close to the black curve shown here. The curve then moved away from the origin, and between 1980 and 1987 it was close to the pink curve shown. Since then, it has been closer to the origin, but it has moved erratically. In 2010, for example, unemployment was 8.0% and inflation was 4.8%.

dots, reaching the position shown by the pink dots and the pink curve in the years 1980–87. Since then, it has shifted erratically through the purple dots, always being in between the 1953–66 and the 1980–87 curves.

In the next two sections, we will explain what determines the position of the Phillips curve and also see why it stayed put for so long and then leaped about!

23.1 Summary

- Sustained inflation requires either sustained increases in costs, combined with government policies to offset any falls in output, or sustained increases in aggregate demand.
- From the 1850s to the 1960s, there seemed to be a fairly stable relationship between unemployment and inflation, which suggested that policies to reduce unemployment would increase inflation in a fairly predictable way. Since the 1960s, the relationship has been unstable.

23.2 The short-run and long-run Phillips curves

In this section, we will look more closely at the relationship between inflation and unemployment. To do so, we actually need to derive and use two types of Phillips curve.

- **A short-run Phillips curve.** This shows the relationship between unemployment and the inflation rate in the short run, before the labour market has time to reach equilibrium after any disturbance. This means that unemployment may not be at the natural rate and that output may not be at the potential level.
- **A long-run Phillips curve.** This shows the relationship between unemployment and the inflation rate in the long run, when the labour market has had time to reach equilibrium after any disturbance. So unemployment is at the natural rate and output is at the potential level.

We will use the Greek letter π for the inflation rate. Also, for simplicity, we will ignore the possibility of improvements in productivity.

The short run and expectations

To derive a short-run Phillips curve, we need to explore the relationship between inflation and unemployment in the short run, when the labour market does not have time to return to equilibrium after a disturbance. The relationship depends very much on the nominal wages agreed between employers and workers. We will suppose that they agree these wages at the start of each year. The wages that they agree depend very much on what rate of inflation they expect in that year. We will consider two possibilities, one in which they expect no inflation and one in which they expect some.

In each case, we will assume there is no supply shock during the year, so that aggregate supply does not unexpectedly shift. We will consider the effects of supply shocks in the next section.

Expected inflation is zero

Figure 23.6 illustrates a case in which no inflation is expected. Suppose the labour market starts in equilibrium, so that unemployment is at its natural rate, U_N. Then the initial aggregate demand curve, AD_0, will intersect the short-run aggregate supply curve, SAS, at the potential output level, Y_P, as shown in the top part of the figure. We will assume the price index is 100.

Suppose that, at the start of one year, people expect no shift in aggregate demand, and so expect no rise in prices, so the expected rate of inflation, π_{EXP}, is zero. And suppose employers and workers then agree to keep nominal wages unchanged over the year. Now consider three scenarios for what might happen in the year.

- **Scenario 1: as expected, aggregate demand is unchanged**. Then AD_0 will still apply. So the price level will stay at P_0, so there is zero inflation. Also, output is unchanged at Y_P, so unemployment stays at U_N, Therefore the combination of unemployment and inflation over the year will be as shown by point ***a*** in the bottom part.
- **Scenario 2: unexpectedly, aggregate demand increases**. Maybe there is a surge in exports or the government increases its purchases, so aggregate demand shifts to the right to AD_1. Then the price level will rise by 3% to 103. Also, output will rise to Y_1. So unemployment will fall, say to U_1 shown in the bottom part. So, in that part, the economy would be at point ***b***.
- **Scenario 3: unexpectedly, aggregate demand decreases**. Maybe there is a surge in imports or the government reduces its purchases, so aggregate demand shifts left to AD_2. Then the price level will fall by 3% to 97. Also, output will fall to Y_2. So unemployment will rise, say to U_2 shown in the bottom part. So, in that part, the economy would be at point ***c***.

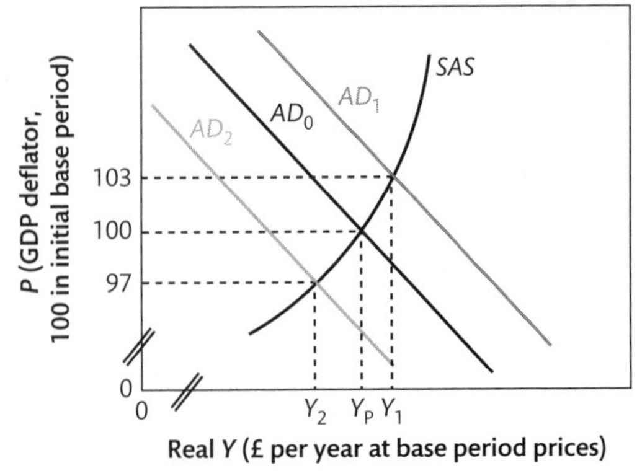

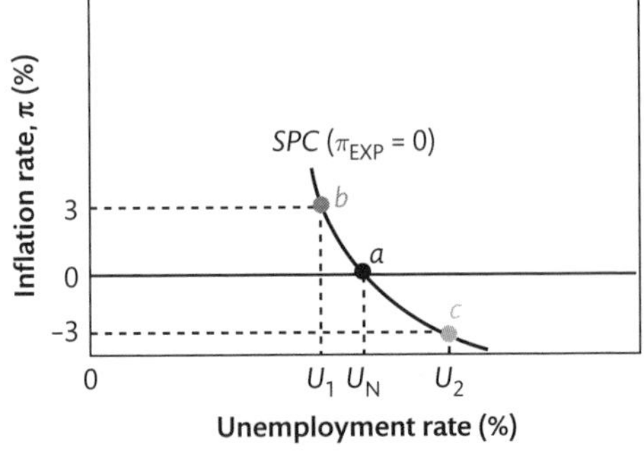

Figure 23.6 **The short-run Phillips curve if $\pi_{EXP} = 0$**

Here, people expect no shift in aggregate demand. If there is no supply shock, and if demand does stay at AD_0, inflation is 0% and unemployment is U_N. But if demand actually rises to AD_1, inflation is 3% and unemployment is U_1; if instead demand actually falls to AD_2, inflation is –3% and unemployment is U_2. These results give the short-run Phillips curve $SPC(\pi_{EXP} = 0)$.

So if $\pi_{EXP} = 0$, then, the relationship between unemployment and inflation for the year ahead will be as shown by a curve that passes through ***a***, ***b***, and ***c***. We label this curve short-run Phillips curve $SPC(\pi_{EXP} = 0)$. Notice that it shows that inflation will actually equal the expected rate of zero if the unemployment rate ends up at U_N.

Expected inflation is positive

Figure 23.7 derives a short-run Phillips curve in a case in which π_{EXP} is not zero. We assume again that the labour market starts in equilibrium, so unemployment is at its natural rate, U_N. So the initial aggregate demand curve, AD_0, intersects the initial short-run aggregate supply curve, SAS_0, at the potential output level, Y_P. We also assume again that the initial price index is 100.

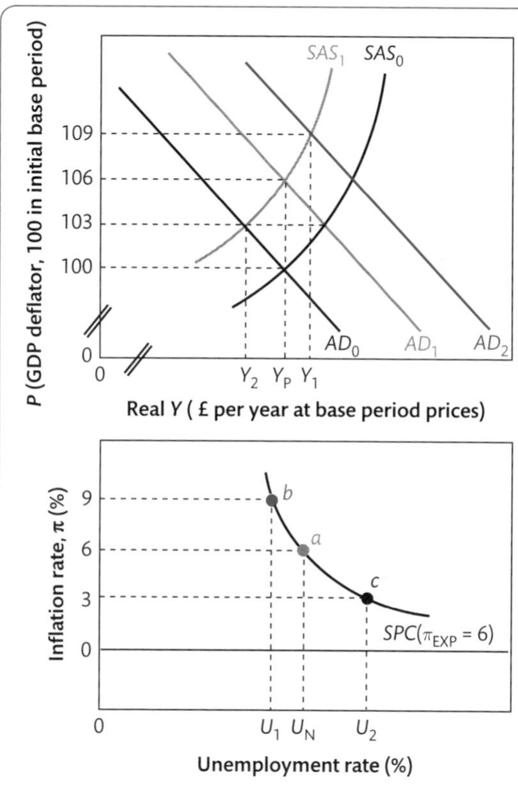

Figure 23.7 **The short-run Phillips curve if $\pi_{EXP} = 6$**

People expect aggregate demand to shift from AD_0 to AD_1. Workers and employers agree higher nominal wages that will keep the labour market in equilibrium at the initial real wage. The wage rises shift aggregate supply to SAS_1, so people expect 6% inflation. The combinations of unemployment and inflation that will actually arise depend on what actually happens to demand and, assuming there is no supply shock, are shown by the short-run Phillips curve $SPC(\pi_{EXP} = 6)$.

Suppose that, at the start of one year, people expect aggregate demand to rise to AD_1. If this is all that happens, they will expect prices to rise to 103. But workers will want a rise in nominal wages to prevent their real wage from falling. This means they actually want a rise in nominal wages, which will shift *SAS* to SAS_1: then output will stay at Y_P, which means the labour market will stay in equilibrium with unemployment at U_N and the real wage at its original level.

When people allow for this shift in short-run aggregate supply as well as the expected shift in aggregate demand, they will expect prices to rise by 6% to 106. So $\pi_{EXP} = 6$. Now consider three possible scenarios for the year.

- **Scenario 1: aggregate demand increases by the expected amount**. Then AD_1 will apply. So the price level will rise to 106, and output will stay at the potential level, so the unemployment rate will stay at the natural rate U_N. So, in the bottom part, the economy will be at point ***a***.
- **Scenario 2: aggregate demand increases more than is expected**. Suppose aggregate demand shifts to the right to AD_2. Then the price level will rise by 9% to 109, where AD_2 intersects SAS_1. Also, output will rise to Y_1, so that unemployment will fall, say to U_1 shown in the bottom part. So, in that part, the economy would be at point ***b***.
- **Scenario 3: aggregate demand increases less than expected**. For simplicity, suppose there is no increase after all, so that aggregate demand remains as shown by AD_0. Then the price level will rise by 3% to 103, where AD_0 intersects SAS_1. Also, output will fall to Y_2, so that unemployment will rise, say to U_2 shown in the bottom part. So, in that part, the economy would be at point ***c***.

The short-run Phillips curve here passes through ***a***, ***b***, and ***c***. Remember, though, that we assumed people expected prices to rise by 6%, so we label it $SPC(\pi_{EXP} = 6)$. Notice that it shows that inflation will equal the expected rate of 6% if the unemployment rate is U_N.

The long-run Phillips curve

A long-run Phillips curve shows the relationship between unemployment and the inflation rate that will apply in the long run, when the labour market has time to return to equilibrium after any disturbance. This means that unemployment must be at the natural rate, U_N. As this is the only possible unemployment rate, the long-run Phillips curve, *LPC*, must be a vertical line through U_N, as shown in Figure 23.8. But what determines the rate of inflation?

To answer this, recall from Chapter 22 the relationship $MV = PY$ in which *M* is the money stock, *V* is the velocity of circulation, *P* is the price level, and *Y* is real output. We saw that this relationship must always be true, because in any period the nominal value of GDP must equal both *MV* and *PY*.

Now consider the classical economists. They believed employment was always close to its natural level, and they also believed *V* is constant. So if one year *Y* were constant, they would say that the rate of increase in prices must equal the rate at which the money stock increases. For example, if *M* increases by 4%, then *P* must rise by 4%, so that inflation will be 4%.

Suppose instead that workers become more productive, perhaps because the country acquires more capital for them to work with. Then, even if unemployment were to remain at the natural rate, *Y* would increase. In this case, the relationship $MV = PY$ means that if *V* is constant, then *P* will rise by less than *M*. For example, if *M* increases by 4% and *Y* increases by 3%, then prices will increase by about 1%. More generally, the inflation rate will approximately equal the rate of growth in *M* minus the rate of growth in *Y*.

Monetarists and Keynesians do not accept that *V* is completely constant. But they do agree that the major factors that determine the rate of inflation in the long run are the rate of growth in the money stock and the rate of growth of real output.

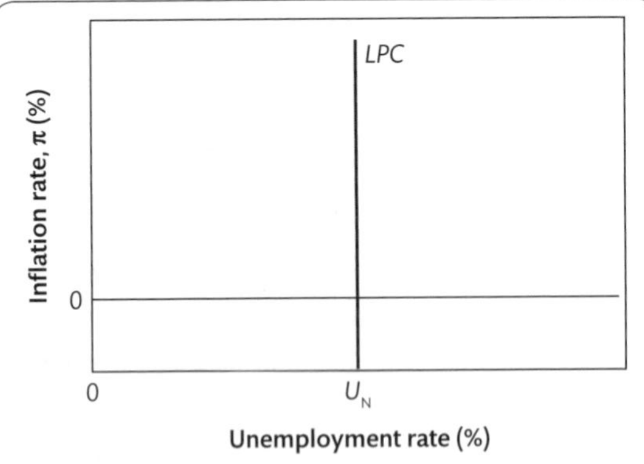

Figure 23.8 **The long-run Phillips curve**

In the long-run, the labour market is always in equilibrium, so unemployment is always at the natural rate U_N. The rate of inflation that arises in the long run depends on what happens in the economy to the rate of growth of the money stock and the rate of growth of real output.

Question 23.1 Suppose that increases in *M* generally lead to falls in *V*. Will this make the effects of *M* on prices greater or smaller than if *V* were constant?

23.2 Summary

- The short-run Phillips curve shows the relationship between unemployment and inflation when the labour market is not given time to return to equilibrium after a disturbance. It slopes downwards, and its position depends on the natural unemployment rate and on the expected rate of inflation.
- The long-run Phillips curve shows the relationship between unemployment and inflation when the labour market is given time to return to equilibrium. It is vertical at the natural unemployment rate.
- In the long run, the inflation rate depends chiefly on the growth rates of the money stock and output.

23.3 Shifts in Phillips curves

We saw in Figure 23.5 that the UK was on one fairly stable sloping Phillips curve from 1953 to 1966, and on another from 1980 to 1987. As these curves sloped, they were actually short-run Phillips curves. But why did the short-run Phillips curve shift away from the origin after 1966, and why has it tended to shift back since 1987?

In this section, we will explore in turn the four main factors that can cause short-run Phillips curves to shift. We will also see that some of these factors can cause the long-run Phillips curve to shift as well. These factors are:

- **changes in the expected rate of inflation;**
- **supply shocks from changed labour demand;**
- **supply shocks from changed labour supply;**
- **supply shocks arising outside the labour market.**

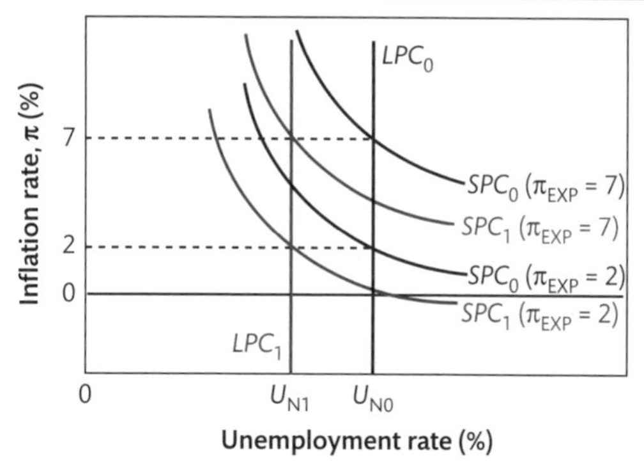

Figure 23.9 **Phillips curves and changes in the labour market**

If there is a rise in the demand for labour, or if people become less picky about jobs, then the natural rate of unemployment falls, say from U_{N0} to U_{N1}. This shifts the long-run Phillips curve to the left, along with the short-run curve for any expected inflation rate, such as 2% or 7%.

Phillips curves and expected inflation

If the rate of inflation that people expect changes, then the short-run Phillips curve will shift. We can see this by looking back at Figures 23.6 and 23.7. These showed where a country's short-run curve would be if there was no supply shock. For example, if expected inflation was 0%, as in Figure 23.6, the short-run curve would show 0% inflation at the natural rate of unemployment. If expected inflation rose to 6%, as in Figure 23.7, then the short-run curve would shift up to show 6% inflation at the natural rate of unemployment.

Changes in the expected rate of inflation have no effect on the long-run Phillips curve: this is vertical at the natural rate of unemployment, no matter how much or how little inflation is expected.

Phillips curves and the demand for labour

We saw in Chapter 21, there are four main reasons why labour demand may increase:

- **improved technology;**
- **investment in extra capital;**
- **improved working practices;**
- **deregulation.**

When any of these occurs, the labour market moves to a new equilibrium with a higher real wage. This encourages a larger proportion of the labour force to accept jobs, so the natural rate of unemployment falls. Suppose it falls from U_{N0} to U_{N1}, as shown in Figure 23.9. Then the long-run Phillips curve shifts to the left from LPC_0, which is vertical at U_{N0}, to LPC_1, which is vertical at U_{N1}.

There are also new short-run Phillips curves. For example, if the expected rate of inflation were 2% or 7%, the initial curves would be $SPC_0(\pi_{EXP} = 2)$ and $SPC_0(\pi_{EXP} = 7)$, which respectively show inflation rates of 2% and 7% at U_{N0}. But with the rise in natural unemployment, they would be $SPC_1(\pi_{EXP} = 2)$ and $SPC_1(\pi_{EXP} = 7)$, which show inflation rates of 2% and 7% at U_{N1}.

The aggregate demand for labour can also decrease, and this shifts the long-run and short-run Phillips curves to the right. The main reasons why the demand for labour would decrease are as follows:

- **Loss of capital.** This could occur because, for example, of a war or an earthquake.
- **More regulation**. This might deter businesses.

Phillips curves and the supply of labour

We saw in Chapter 21 that there are two main reasons why labour supply may increase:

- **people may become less picky about the jobs they will accept;**
- **the size of the labour force may increase;**

Suppose that benefits to unemployed people are cut so they become less picky about which jobs to accept. Then the proportion of the labour force who will accept jobs will increase, and this will reduce the natural rate of unemployment. So the long-run and short-run Phillips curves will shift to the left, exactly as shown in Figure 23.9.

The effects of an increase in the labour force are less clear-cut. This will lead to an increase in the supply of labour, so it will certainly result in more people being employed. But as the labour force is larger, there may not be an increase in the percentage of the labour force that is employed. So the percentage of the labour force that is unemployed when the labour market reaches a new equilibrium, that is the natural rate of unemployment, could be higher, lower, or the same as before. In turn, the Phillips curves could shift to the right, or the left, or stay put.

Phillips curves and other supply shocks

We saw in Chapter 21 that supply shocks can occur even if labour demand and supply remain constant. We also saw that there are three main other types of supply shock, as follows:

- **natural disasters;**
- **trade union activity;**
- **changes in the prices of imported inputs.**

Figure 23.10 shows the effect of a natural disaster. The top part repeats all the curves shown in the top part of Figure 23.6. These curves include the short-run aggregate supply curve, labelled SAS_0, which applies if there is no supply shock.

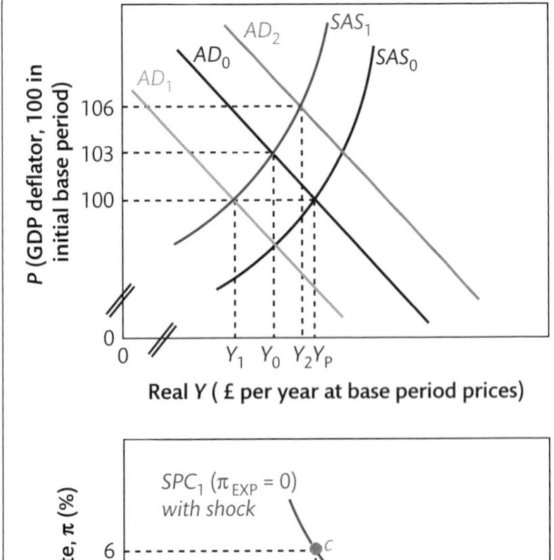

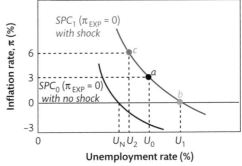

Figure 23.10 **The effect on the short-run Phillips curve of a supply shock from a natural disaster**

People expect no aggregate demand to stay at AD_0, and so expect zero inflation. The outcomes for unemployment and inflation depend on what happens to aggregate supply and aggregate demand. If there is no supply shock, the outcomes fall on $SPC(\pi_E = 0)$. If there is a disaster that shifts the short-run aggregate supply curve to SAS_1, the outcomes fall on $SPC(\pi_E = 0)$. So a disaster will shift the short-run Phillips curve upwards.

The bottom part of Figure 23.10 repeats the short-run Phillips curve $SPC_0(\pi_{EXP} = 0)$ that we derived in Figure 23.6. This shows the possible outcomes for unemployment and inflation in the year ahead if there is no supply shock, and if people expect aggregate demand to remain unchanged at AD_0, and so expect inflation to be zero. This curve shows that inflation will be zero if unemployment is at the natural rate, U_N.

But suppose, during this year, there are bad floods that hamper production. This will shift the short-run aggregate supply curve left to SAS_1. Let's now see what would happen to unemployment and inflation at the three possible levels of aggregate demand shown on the figure, AD_0, AD_1, and AD_2.

- $\boldsymbol{AD_0}$. Here, the price level will rise from 100 to 103, so there is inflation of 3%. Output will fall below Y_P to Y_0, so unemployment will rise above U_N, say to U_0. This gives point ***a*** in the bottom part.
- $\boldsymbol{AD_1}$. Here, the price level will stay at 100, so there is inflation of 0%. Output will fall below Y_P to Y_1, so unemployment will rise above U_N, say to U_1. This gives point ***b*** in the bottom part.
- $\boldsymbol{AD_2}$. Here, the price level will rise from 100 to 106, so there is inflation of 6%. Output will fall below Y_P to Y_2, so unemployment will rise above U_N, say to U_2. This gives point ***c*** in the bottom part.

The result is that even though people expected inflation of zero, there is a new short-run Phillips curve, labelled $SPC_1(\pi_{EXP} = 0)$, which passes through points ***a***, ***b***, and ***c***. You will see that, at the natural unemployment rate, U_N, this curve is well above the expected rate of 0%. In a similar way, the short-run Phillips curve for any other expected rate of inflation will shift upwards.

Assuming these floods were temporary, the short-run Phillips curves will soon return to their original positions. The same will apply if unions temporarily disrupt production with strikes, or if they secure wage rises that temporarily take the real wage above the equilibrium level. However, prolonged trade union activity could lead to people expecting inflation to exceed zero in future years, leading to persistently higher short-run Philips curves.

A rise in the price of imported inputs can have different and permanent effects. This is because, as we saw in Figure 21.14, it could reduce the demand for labour and so raise the natural rate of unemployment. If this were to happen, then the long-run Phillips curve would shift to the right, and the short-run curves would shift away from the origin.

Phillips curves shifts between 1967 and 1979

The UK's short-run and long-run Phillips curves shifted away from the origin between 1967 and 1979 for several reasons, including the following.

- **People expected the government to try to hold unemployment below the natural rate.** As a result, people expected prices to rise. We will return to this issue in the next section.
- **Increases in oil prices**. In 1960, an inter-governmental body called the Organization of the Petroleum Exporting Countries (OPEC) was established, and soon included the world's major oil producing countries, which were mostly Middle Eastern. In 1973, OPEC became a cartel, which set prices, and over the next seven years crude oil prices rose tenfold. All oil-importing nations suffered a series of severe supply shocks. OPEC's influence waned after 1980 because new oil fields opened in Alaska, Canada, the Gulf of Mexico, and the North Sea, and the relevant governments do not belong to OPEC.
- **Trade union militancy**. It is difficult to measure the effect of trade union militancy on the Phillips curves, and strikes may be a response to price rises as well as a cause. However, if we take days lost through strikes as a measure of militancy, the number quadrupled from an average of around 35

million a year in the 1960s to 130 million in the 1970s. This was partly because new legislation increased protection for workers. Also, many industries were nationalized monopolies, and governments often succumbed to pressure when these faced strikes, and that encouraged more strikes.

The combination of ever rising oil prices and union militancy led to **stagflation**, that is high inflation and high unemployment at the same time.

Phillips curves shifts from 1988

Several factors explain why the UK's short-run and long-run Phillips curves have tended to shift back towards the origin after 1988. Four factors have worked directly on the curves, as follows.

- **Oil prices fell**. Oil prices fell sharply in the 1980s and stayed low in the 1990s.
- **Trade union power fell**. Trade unions became less able to force wages up, partly because firms sometimes responded to higher wages by shifting production to low-wage countries, and partly because many firms became more anxious to restrain wages. For example, many nationalized monopolies were privatized into competitive environments, and many other firms faced growing international competition. The average number of working days lost each year to strikes between 2001 and 2010 was under 7 million.
- **Credible inflation targets**. We return to this issue in the next section. The idea is that, since 1992, governments have announced low target rates for inflation, and if people believe the government is serious in intent, then the rate of inflation that they expect will fall.
- **There are more skilled jobs and fewer unskilled jobs**. So governments have discouraged people from leaving school at age 16, and encouraged unemployed workers to retrain. This has reduced structural unemployment and, in turn, natural unemployment, so shifting the long-run and short-run Phillips curves towards the origin.

In addition, two factors have increased the supply of labour. This has restrained the rate at which nominal wages grow, and so reduced inflationary pressure. These factors are as follows.

- **Changes in government benefits**. Governments now give more practical help to unemployed people to find jobs, and give less generous transfers if they do not try hard to find jobs.
- **Migrant workers**. Many East European countries joined the EU in 2004, and migrant workers have increased the supply of labour.

We look further at the recent Phillips curve experience at the end of the chapter.

23.1 Everyday economics

US concern with expected inflation

'Participants expected that the boost to headline inflation from recent increases in energy and other commodity prices would be transitory and that underlying inflation trends would be little affected as long as commodity prices did not continue to rise rapidly and longer-term inflation expectations remained stable. However, a significant increase in longer-term inflation expectations could contribute to excessive wage and price inflation, which would be costly to eradicate. Accordingly, participants considered it important to pay close attention to the evolution not only of headline and core inflation, but also of inflation expectations.'

Minutes of the Federal Open Market Committee (FOMC), 15 March 2011

Comment The FOMC meets eight times a year to give advice on economic conditions to the US Federal Reserve Board. The minutes of this meeting illustrate its concern with expectations of inflation, and also the difficulty of predicting whether people's expectations will change.

23.3 Summary

- The short-run Phillips curve shifts upwards or downwards when the expected inflation rate rises or falls.
- All Phillips curves shift towards the origin if the demand for labour or the supply of labour increase, except perhaps if labour supply rises because the labour force has risen. Decreases in the demand and supply of labour have opposite effects.
- The short-run Phillips curve shifts away from the origin if there is a temporary supply shock from a natural disaster or trade union activity. A shock from higher import price can lead to a permanent shift of the long-run Phillips curve to the right and of the short-run curves away from the origin.

23.4 The new monetarist and new classical views

Chapter 25 explored the classical, monetarist, and Keynesian views on policies for unemployment. We now explore the modifications to these views that were made after the 1970s when inflation began to accelerate.

Monetarists and inflation

Chapter 24 explained that monetarists believe monetary policy has more effect than fiscal policy on aggregate demand, and so on unemployment. Monetarists still agree with that. But the rising inflation in the 1970s led Milton Friedman and other monetarists to a new view on government policy. This advises governments not to use either type of policy to alter aggregate demand.

The origins of this new view can be seen back in Figure 17.3. Although unemployment was always low between 1945 and the 1960s, it was not stable. So governments tried to raise demand when unemployment was high and to restrain demand when unemployment was low and inflationary pressures were growing. In the UK, this approach was called 'stop-go.'

The new monetarist view gives three main reasons for opposing the use of demand management policies to alter unemployment.

- **Real wages adjust quite quickly.** Monetarists believe that if unemployment ever exceeds the natural rate, it will return fairly quickly, so demand management is hardly needed.
- **Policies have lags that limit their effectiveness, and may cause perverse effects.** Suppose unemployment is above the natural rate, and the government want to hasten its return with expansionary policies. In practice, the government might not act until unemployment has risen for some time. And when it does implement expansionary policies, there may be a lag before their full effect on aggregate demand is felt. These lags mean that, by the time the policies come into full effect, the help they are meant to give may no longer be needed. Indeed, it may sometimes happen that, by this time, what is needed is a reduction of demand to restrain inflation.
- **Governments may try to hold unemployment below the natural rate: if so, this will lead to accelerating inflation**. We will now use the Phillips curve to explain this.

Accelerating inflation

To explain accelerating inflation, we need to think about how people form their expectations of the rate of inflation in any year. This is because their expectations affect the short-run Phillips curve, as we saw in Figures 23.6 and 23.7. Let's suppose that people use **adaptive expectations**: this means they form their expectations about the future on what has occurred in the past.

To see how adaptive expectations can lead to accelerating inflation, we will take a very simple version of them: we will assume that, each year, people expect inflation in the year ahead to be at the same rate that it was in the past year. We will also assume that there are no supply shocks.

Suppose that, last year, there was no inflation, so people expect zero inflation in the year ahead, which we call year 0. Then, in year 0, the economy will end up somewhere on the short-run Phillips curve $SPC_0(\pi_{EXP} = 0)$ shown in the lower part of Figure 23.11. Point ***a*** on this curve shows that the actual rate of inflation will equal the expected zero rate if unemployment turns out to be at the natural rate, U_N. The long-run Phillips curve is vertical at this level.

Let's also suppose that in year 0 the economy does end up at ***a***. With unemployment at the natural rate, output must be at its potential level, Y_P. So the economy must be in equilibrium at point ***a*** in the top part, where the initial aggregate demand and supply curves, AD_0, SAS_0, and LAS, all intersect. The price level is taken as 100.

Now consider year 1. As there was no inflation in year 0, people still expect none in year 1, so the economy will again end up on $SPC_0(\pi_{EXP} = 0)$. But suppose that, in year 1, the government wants to reduce unemployment below U_N, so it increases aggregate demand to AD_1. This takes the economy to point ***b*** in the top part, raising prices by 2% to 102 and raising output above Y_P to Y_1. So unemployment falls, say to U_1 in the bottom part, taking the economy to point ***b*** there also.

As inflation was 2% in year 1, we suppose that people will expect inflation to be 2% in year 2, so they expect a price level of about 104. So employers and workers will negotiate wage increases that will leave the labour market in equilibrium, and output at the potential level, if the price level is 104. These wage rises will shift short-run aggregate supply to SAS_1, which intersects AD_1 at Y_P and at a price level of 104.

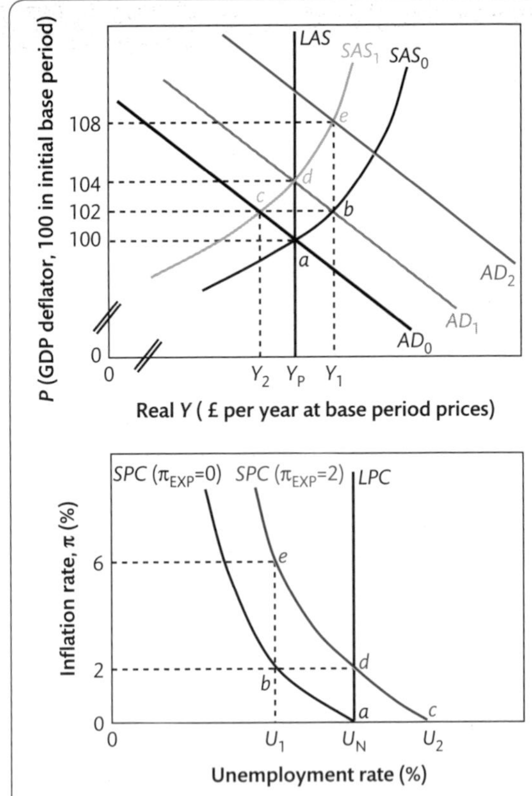

Figure 23.11 **A new monetarist view of accelerating inflation**

The economy has the black curves in year 0, so output is Y_P and unemployment is U_N. To reduce unemployment to U_1, the government raises aggregate demand in year 1 to AD_1. Prices rise by 2%, and adaptive expectations lead people to expect 2% inflation in year 2, so wage rises are then agreed that shift aggregate supply to SAS_1; also, the short-run Phillips curve shifts up. To hold unemployment at U_1, the government must raise demand again to AD_2, raising prices by about 6% to 108. So holding unemployment below U_N causes accelerating inflation.

The expected inflation of 2% shifts the short-run Phillips curve to $SPC(\pi_{EXP} = 2)$; this shows that inflation will equal the expected 2% if unemployment is U_N. Whereabouts on this curve the economy ends up in year 2 depends on the government. Consider three possibilities.

- **Alarmed by the inflation in year 1, the government returns aggregate demand to AD_0.** This takes the economy to point ***c*** in the top part. The price level stays at 102, so there is no inflation. But output is below Y_P, so unemployment is above U_N, say U_2 in the bottom part, so the economy goes to point ***c*** there too.
- **To avoid unemployment rising above U_N, the government maintains aggregate demand at AD_1.** This takes the economy to point ***d*** in the top part. The price level rises by 2% from 102 to 104, so inflation is 2%. Also output is Y_P, so unemployment is U_N in the bottom part, so the economy goes to point ***d*** there too.
- **To hold unemployment at U_1, the government increases aggregate demand to AD_2.** This takes the economy to point ***e*** in the top part. The price level rises by 6% from 102 to 108, so inflation is 6%. Also, output is held at Y_1, so in the bottom part unemployment is held at U_1, so the economy goes to point ***e*** there too.

So the economy started in year 0 with unemployment at the natural rate and inflation at zero. The government reduced unemployment in year 1 to U_1, and this led to inflation of 2%. And if the government holds unemployment at U_1 in year 2, there will be inflation of 6%. The conclusion is that efforts to maintain unemployment below the natural rate lead to accelerating inflation.

Because efforts to hold unemployment below the natural rate U_N lead to accelerating inflation, U_N itself is also called the **non-accelerating inflation rate of unemployment**, NAIRU. The idea that governments cannot hold unemployment below U_N and have a stable rate of inflation was put forward separately by Milton Friedman and another American economist Edmund Phelps.

The *k*% rule

Although Friedman did not advocate using monetary policy for demand management, he had strong views about monetary policy. These hinged on the relationship $MV = PY$. Friedman believed that the velocity of circulation, V, was quite stable, so that PY always changes in proportion to changes in the money stock, M.

He actually advised governments to increase the money stock each year at the average rate by which real output, Y, grows over time; he called this rate k, and his suggestion is called the ***k*% rule.** To see how this rule works, suppose k is 3%. Then following the rule means that M will rise by 3% a year. So if V is indeed stable, MV will rise by 3% a year, and as $MV = PY$, so PY must rise by 3% a year. So in an average year, when Y rises by 3%, P will be stable. Admittedly, P will rise a little in years when Y grows by less than 3%, and fall a little in years when Y grows by more than 3%, but there will be no sustained inflation.

Friedman knew that there might be times when a government would like to offset a demand shock by using monetary policy to make an appropriate shift in aggregate demand. But lags mean that these shifts might actually prove destabilizing, so he felt it would be better to stick to the *k*% rule.

This rule is now rarely advocated, partly because it is accepted that V is not as stable as Friedman believed. However, his idea of having a rule stimulated discussions that have led to other rules, which we will discuss below.

Another legacy of the new monetarist view is a general acceptance that unemployment cannot be held below the natural rate without accelerating inflation. This means that efforts to reduce the number of unemployed people often focus on reducing the natural rate. We saw several policies for this in Chapter 22, including:

- **trying to ensure that school and college leavers possess the skills that employers want;**
- **encouraging retraining by those unemployed people whose skills are in little demand;**
- **restraining trade union power;**
- **holding the minimum wage at modest levels.**

The new classical view

The new classical view stems from the classical view that we discussed in the last chapter, and it shares the belief that the labour market will return to equilibrium very quickly after any disturbance. In this respect, it can be seen as an extreme form of monetarism. Also, it sees no need for governments to act if unemployment rises above the natural rate, because it will rapidly fall back.

However, the new classical view has some other policy implications. These result from a new approach to expectations about future inflation, which we will now study. This approach was first suggested by the American economist John Muth in the 1960s, but it became better known following work in the 1970s by his compatriot Robert Lucas.

Rational expectations

In our discussion of the monetarist view, we assumed that people's expectations about future inflation are based entirely on what has happened in the past. The new classical view assumes that people instead form what are called **rational expectations**: this means that their expectations have the following two features:

- **people take account of all information;**
- **on average, people's forecasts are correct.**

Let's illustrate this with respect to your forecasts of inflation. Suppose inflation has been 1% for several years and then, during this year, the government announces that next year it will cut taxes, spend more, and raise the money stock. Will you forecast 1% for next year, just because past inflation has been 1%? Probably not. You will probably forecast higher inflation.

But will your forecast be right? Almost certainly not. One problem is that your ability to make accurate forecasts will be modest: after all, even economic experts and people in the financial markets with billions of pounds at stake make errors. However, suppose you found over time that your forecasts were generally too low, then you would adjust your forecasts upwards a little, and vice versa. So it is reasonable to expect that on average your forecasts, and other people's, are correct. Even so, forecasts for any given year could still be wrong, perhaps wildly so if an unexpected shock were to occur during the year.

Policy implications of rational expectations

Figure 23.12 gives an example to illustrate the policy implications of rational expectations. In this example, we assume that the black curves apply in year 0. So,

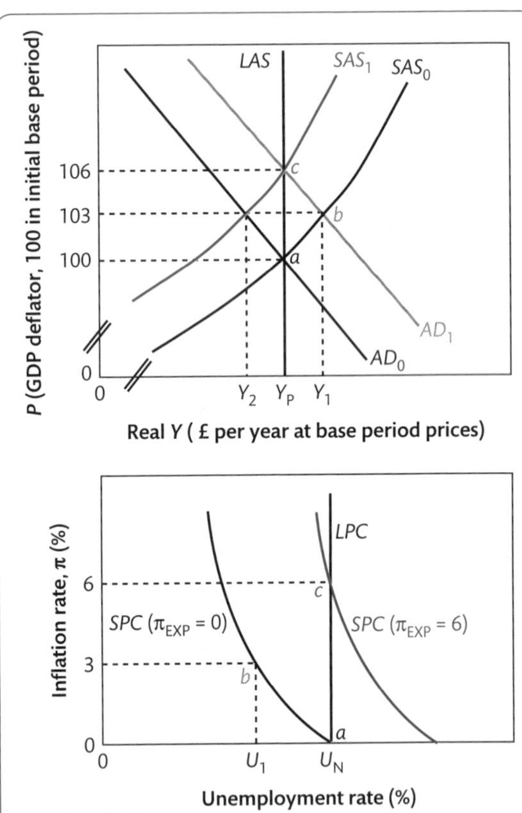

Figure 23.12 **A new classical view of inflation**

The economy has the black curves in year 0 and is at the points marked ***a***. Then demand rises. If the rise is unexpected, the economy goes to the points marked ***b***; if it is expected, the economy goes to the points marked ***c***. Either way there is inflation, but only the unexpected rise affects output and employment; the new classical view says this effect will be brief, as the labour market will soon return to equilibrium.

in the top part, the economy is at point ***a***, with output at the potential level Y_P and the price level at 100. And in the bottom part, the short-run Phillips curve $SPC(\pi_{EXP} = 0)$ applies, which means that people expect no inflation in year 0. The economy will then also be at point ***a*** on this curve, because with output at the potential level, unemployment will be at the natural rate U_N.

Now suppose aggregate demand increases in year 1 to AD_1, and consider two possible scenarios.

- **The increase in demand was unexpected**. In this case, we will assume that employers and workers did not expect any rise in prices in year 1, so they did not agree any wage increases at the start of the year. This means that, in the top part, the economy stays on SAS_0 and go to point ***b***. So output rises above Y_P, taking unemployment below U_N, say to U_1 in the bottom part, taking the economy to ***b*** there also. Admittedly, the new classical view predicts that output and employment will soon return to Y_P and U_N.
- **The increase in demand was expected**. Then employers and workers will expect AD_1 to apply in year 1, and will negotiate wage increases at the start of the year that will leave the labour market in equilibrium with unemployment at U_N and output at Y_P. These wage increases shift the short-run aggregate supply curve to SAS_1, so people expect inflation of 6% and the short-run Phillips curve will be $SPC(\pi_{EXP} = 6)$. The outcome will be as shown by point ***c*** in each part.

There are three implications of this analysis.

- **Expected changes in demand do not affect output or employment**. So governments that wish to affect output and unemployment should not announce their policies in advance.
- **Unexpected changes in demand have only short-term effects on output and unemployment**. The labour market will quickly return to equilibrium with unemployment at the natural rate and output at the potential level.
- **Both expected and unexpected changes in demand affect the rate of inflation.**

If the new classical view is correct, so that expected changes in demand really do affect inflation, but not output, then there is an important implication. This is that if the government announces that it will reduce demand next year, then it can reduce the rate of inflation, while leaving workers and employers to negotiate whatever wage rates are needed to keep employment at its natural level, and so keep output at its potential level.

A government may be able to go further. Suppose it wants to have inflation at 2%, and announces that it will manage aggregate demand to secure this target rate. If its policy has **credibility**, that is if people believe that it will manage demand as it says, then employers and workers will negotiate wage rises that ensure inflation is 2%, while keeping employment at its natural level and output at its potential level. People will not agree higher wage rises that take inflation above 2% if they know the government will then reduce demand, so taking employment below its natural level. But if the government fails to manage demand as promised, perhaps only once, then it may not be believed again, and future policy announcements may have little effect on future wage agreements or, in turn, future inflation.

Reducing UK inflation in the 1980s

In 1979, the UK government announced its intention to reduce demand to reduce inflation. The country then moved quickly down the pink Phillips curve in Figure 23.5 and the inflation rate fell from 18% in 1980 to 4% in 1984. Initially, unemployment rose sharply, and some economists argued that this disproved the new classical view, which assumes that workers and employers agree wages that will keep employment close to its natural level. Other economists argued that workers and employers might have agreed wages that were too high for this because they did not believe that government would reduce demand sufficiently to meet its inflation target. Perhaps they agreed appropriate wages only when they realized that the government would indeed do so.

Question 23.2 Other things being equal, would a low target rate for inflation of, say, 2% be more credible if unemployment were high or if it were low?

23.4 Summary

- The new monetarist view opposes demand management policies on the grounds that lags reduce their effectiveness and may even lead to perverse effects; also, the labour market always returns fairly quickly to equilibrium. Efforts to hold unemployment below the natural rate cause accelerating inflation through adaptive expectations. Inflation can be controlled by having a rule for money stock growth.
- The new classical view argues that people form rational expectations, so that demand management policies affect demand and employment only if they are unexpected; even then the effects are brief because the labour market always returns quickly to equilibrium. Inflation can be controlled by stating that demand will be managed to secure a target rate, but this works only if the policy is credible.

23.5 The new Keynesian view and the Taylor rule

The need for a new Keynesian view

The new Keynesian view evolved in the 1990s. It shares the original Keynesian view that an economy can have a long recession with unemployment above the natural rate, unless the government uses monetary or fiscal policy to raise aggregate demand.

This belief raises the question of why the labour market can settle for long periods with unemployment above the natural rate. Economists generally believe that most markets 'work' in the sense of reaching equilibrium positions reasonably quickly, and the new classical view says the same applies to labour markets. The new Keynesians wanted to provide some microeconomic foundations for their belief that labour markets might not work smoothly like that.

Their answers fall into three main groups, as follows, which we look at in turn.

- **Some labour markets never reach equilibrium.**
- **Some wages are sticky downwards.**
- **There are some price rigidities.**

Labour markets that don't reach equilibrium

We explored the possibility that some individual labour markets settle with wages that are above the equilibrium level in Chapter 14. We saw that the following factors can cause this to happen:

- **efficiency wages;**
- **trade unions;**
- **minimum wage laws.**

If a significant number of individual labour markets end up with wages above the equilibrium level, then it seems reasonable to suppose that the same applies to the labour market as a whole.

Some money wages are sticky downwards

Suppose you run a firm and face a fall in demand. In a new classical world, you will at once cut your prices and reduce your output. So you will want to hire less labour, and will then offer lower wage rates. But we saw in Chapter 24 Keynes's reasons for thinking your wages might prove sticky.

- **Workers' concern about their wages relative to those paid in other occupations.** Your workers will resist wage cuts that reduce their wages relative to those paid in other occupations.
- **Trade unions.** Unions will resist you cutting the nominal wages of your existing workers, and they will also oppose you recruiting new workers at lower wages than your existing workers.

New Keynesians have added further arguments.

- **Wage contracts.** You will probably make contracts with your workers, often for a year or more ahead. This is at least partly because they will probably prefer stable wages to wages that constantly fluctuate in line with changes in the demand for the products they make. This means you cannot reduce your wages immediately after every fall in demand. It also means that when you make the next wage agreement, you may focus on what you think will happen to the demand for your product in future, not on its current state, and not seek the equilibrium wage for the current level of demand.
- **Workers' concern about their wages relative to those paid to other people in the same occupation.** Suppose all the firms in your industry adjust their wages once a year, but on different dates: some at the end of January; some at the end of April; some at the end of July; and some at the end of October. Then suppose aggregate demand falls in January and you are an end-of-January firm. Your workers will be among the first to face a request for lower wages, and one reason they may resist is that their wages will then fall in relation to those of people in the same occupation who work for other firms and whose wages will be cut later.

Institutional and practical price rigidities

New Keynesians argue that many prices are sticky as well as wages, and this aggravates the problem of a recession for unemployment. A moment ago, we supposed you ran a firm and faced a fall in demand. We supposed that you would react by reducing your prices and your output. The fall in output resulted in you wanting to hire less labour.

But suppose you are reluctant to cut prices. In that case, your prices will be higher than we supposed there, so your sales will be lower. So you will want to hire even less labour. This will take the labour market further from equilibrium and prolong the time needed for it to return.

In practice, some firms will not have sticky prices. This is the case with perfect competitors, who must always take the going market price. If a fall in demand reduces the market price, any firm that lags behind the others in cutting its own price will lose its entire sales. But because relatively few firms are perfect competitors, this is not a serious critique of this element of the new Keynesian view.

To see why other firms may have sticky prices, let's consider why your firm may not reduce its prices. Here are some possible reasons.

- **Menu costs.** Changing your prices may mean producing new price lists and catalogues—and menus if you happen to run a restaurant. It also involves working out what the new prices should be. These costs may seem modest, but in practice demand constantly fluctuates a little, and reacting to every change would be costly.
- **Customers prefer stable prices.** Suppose you run one of two clubs in a town. You decide to vary your prices in line with changing demand, even changing your prices in response to changes in the number of people queuing to come in. The other club has stable prices. Consumers might prefer the stable one, because they then know the cost in

advance. You might do better business if your prices were less flexible.

- **Price psychology.** Some firms hold their prices at a significant level, say £99.99, even if current demand would justify a slightly higher price. So they will not reduce the price if demand falls.
- **Consumers may judge quality by prices.** So if you react to a fall in demand by cutting your price, then your sales might fall even further.

New Keynesians and rational expectations

We have now seen why new Keynesians see a need for demand management policies. When they devise their policies, they accept the idea that people form rational expectations. So, like new classical economists, they believe that unexpected changes in demand have more impact on output and employment than expected ones. And they believe that wage negotiations will be responsive to credible announcements about inflation targets, although wage stickiness means that these negotiations will not return the labour market quickly to equilibrium after a disturbance.

A Taylor rule

New Keynesians see more a role for monetary policy and less a role for fiscal policy than the original Keynesians. This is because, from the 1970s, the UK government no longer set a fixed exchange rate for sterling against the dollar, and we will see in Chapter 28 why this strengthened monetary policy and weakened fiscal policy. Regarding monetary policy, new Keynesians generally advocate a rule that is named after the American economist John Taylor, who suggested it.

A **Taylor rule** says the central bank should have a target rate for inflation, and then adjust interest rates according to how far inflation is from the target and how far output is from its potential level. For example, suppose inflation is above target. Then if output is above its potential level, so that unemployment is below the natural rate, the bank should raise interest rates to reduce aggregate demand. But if output is below its potential level, so that unemployment is above the natural rate, then the bank should raise interest rates only if it is chiefly concerned by the high inflation, and it should reduce interest rates if it is chiefly concerned about the high unemployment.

Figures 23.13 and 23.14 show how this rule would operate in the presence of shocks. In each case, we assume in the top part that, in the initial year, year 0,

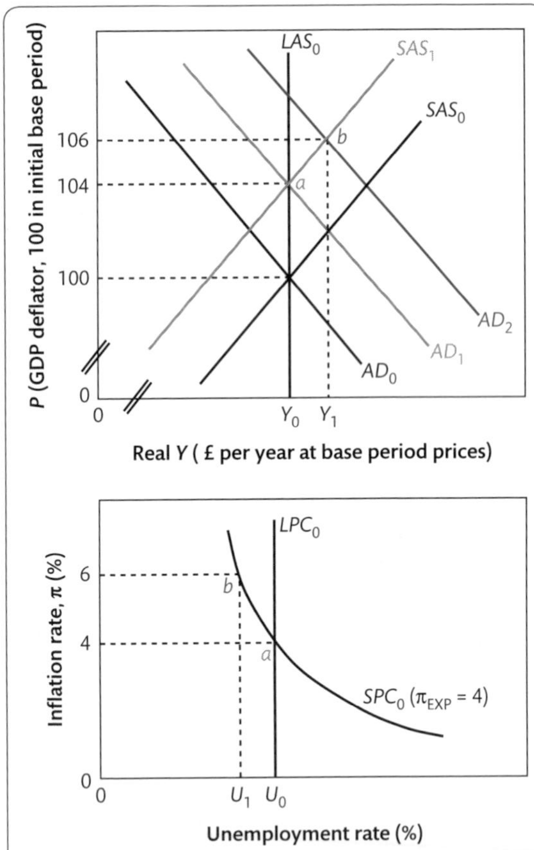

Figure 23.13 **A Taylor rule and a demand shock**

If aggregate demand in year 1 shifts to AD_2, not AD_1 as expected, then the economy moves towards point ***b***, instead of ***a***, with inflation above the 4% target, output above the potential level of Y_0, and unemployment below U_N. A central bank following a Taylor rule will raise interest rates and shift demand to AD_1, taking the economy to ***a***.

the economy is in equilibrium where the initial aggregate demand and supply curves, AD_0, SAS_0, and LAS_0 all intersect. So the output, Y_0, is the potential output, and the price level is 100. Also, unemployment is at the natural rate, labelled U_0 in the lower part.

We also assume that the government sets a credible inflation target of 4% for year 1, and that people expect this rate. So the initial short-run Phillips curve, $SPC_0(\pi_{EXP} = 4)$, has 4% inflation at U_0. Finally, we assume that people expect demand in year 1 to be AD_1, and agree wages so that if there are no shocks, supply will be given by SAS_1. Then the price level will rise by the expected 4% to 104, and output will remain at its potential level leaving unemployment at the natural rate. So the year 1 position will be as shown by point ***a*** in each part.

The Taylor rule and a demand shock

Now suppose there is a demand shock in year 1 that shifts the aggregate demand curve to AD_2 shown in Figure 23.13. The economy will move towards point ***b*** in the top part, where SAS_1 intersects AD_2, with a price level of 106 and output Y_1, and towards ***b*** in the bottom part, which shows 6% inflation and a fall in unemployment.

However, if the central bank follows a Taylor rule, it will see that inflation is rising above target and that output is rising above the potential level, so that unemployment is falling below the natural rate. So it will raise interest rates to reduce aggregate demand to AD_1; then, in year 1, the economy will actually end up at ***a*** in each part as intended.

The Taylor rule and a supply shock

Suppose instead there is a supply shock in year 1. Perhaps the government increases its transfers to unemployed people so that the supply of labour falls. We saw in Figure 21.14 of Chapter 21 that this will shift both the short-run and long-run aggregate supply curves to the left. The top part of Figure 23.14 shows them shifting to SAS_2 and LAS_1. And we can deduce from the analysis of Figure 23.9 that the fall in the supply of labour will also shift the Phillips curves to the right, as shown by $SPC_1(\pi_{EXP} = 4)$ and LPC_1 in the bottom part, where U_1 is the new natural rate.

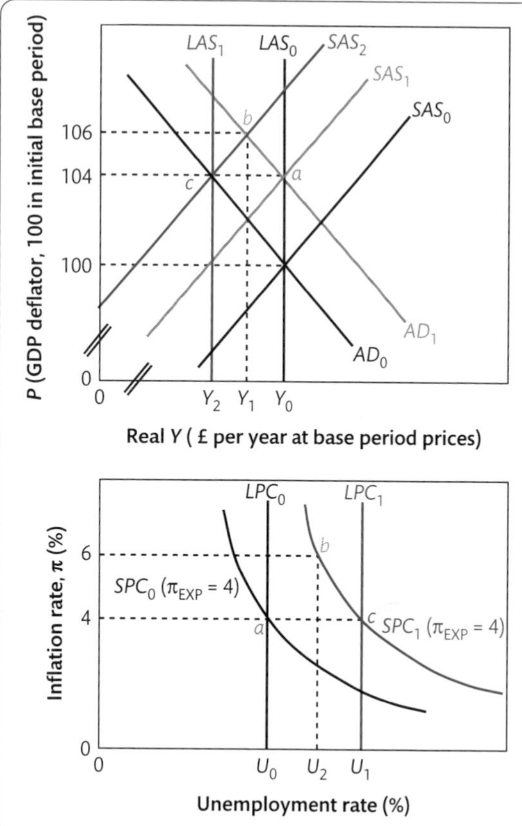

Figure 23.14 **A Taylor rule and a supply shock**

If the aggregate supply curves in year 1 are SAS_2 and LAS_1, not SAS_1 and LAS_0 as expected, then the Phillips curves shift to LPC_1 and SPC_1. The economy moves towards point ***b***, instead of ***a***, with inflation above the 4% target, output above the new potential level, Y_2, and unemployment below the new natural rate, U_1. A central bank following a Taylor rule will shift demand to AD_1, taking the economy to ***c***.

The economy will move towards point ***b*** in the top part, where SAS_2 intersects AD_1, with a price level of 106 and so with inflation above target at 6%. If the central bank follows a Taylor rule, it will raise interest rates and shift aggregate demand to AD_0, leaving the price level on target at 104, and taking output and unemployment to Y_2 and U_1, as shown by the points marked ***c***. It may seem perverse to raise interest rates when output falls, but this makes sense because, at ***b*** in the top part, output would be above the new potential level, Y_2; at ***b*** in the bottom part, unemployment at U_2 would be below the new natural rate, U_1.

A Taylor rule is more interesting with a temporary supply shock, such as a bad winter, that shifts only the short-run supply curve. If only this curve had shifted in the top part of Figure 23.14, the economy would still move towards point ***b***, with inflation exceeding the target. But the potential level of output would be unchanged at Y_0, so output would be falling below this.

If the central bank wanted to follow a Taylor rule in this case, the excess inflation would point to a rise in interest rates, while output falling below the potential level would point to a fall in interest rates. Most probably the central bank would leave interest rates little altered, and wait for the short-run aggregate supply curve to shift back.

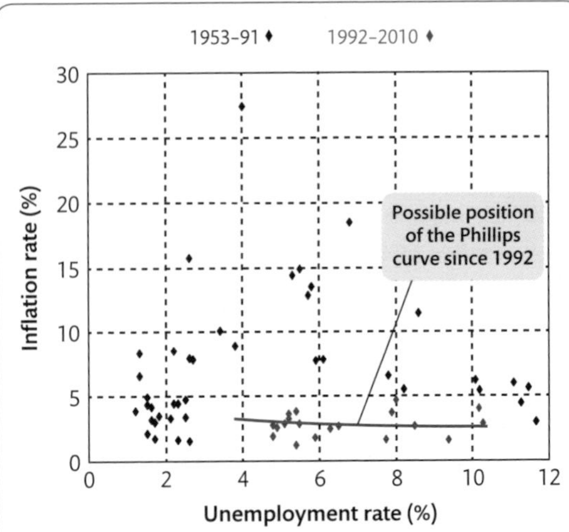

Figure 23.15 **The flat Phillips curve**

The traditional interpretation of post-1953 data is that in each year the economy was on a sloping short-run Phillips curve, which often shifted because of changes in expectations, changes in the natural unemployment rate, and other supply shocks. But from 1992 the economy may have been on a virtually flat short-run Phillips curve; this will have shifted left or right when the natural unemployment rate changed, but these shifts in a flat curve would not show up well on a graph. It may also have shifted up and down a little after any small changes in expectations or small supply shocks.

A flat Phillips curve?

If you look back to Figure 23.5, you will see that it suggests that the economy has a sloping short-run Phillips curve. This was fairly stable between 1953 and 1966, and then moved erratically away from the origin until 1980. It was then stable until 1987, since when it to have moved erratically back towards the origin. There are two reasons why it might have moved towards the origin.

- **Expected inflation may have fallen**. Figures 23.6 and 23.7 show why this would shift the short-run Phillips curve.
- **The natural rate of unemployment may have fallen**. Figures 23.9 and 23.10 show why this would shift the short-run Phillips curve.

However, there is another interpretation that can be given to on the short-run Phillips curve since about 1992, as shown in Figure 23.15, which is that it may have become flat. It may still shift left and right in reaction to supply shocks, but such moves in a flat curve do not mean much and do not show up. It would also shift up and down if expectations changed, but perhaps they haven't changed very much.

There are several reasons why the Phillips curve may have become flat, so that inflation is fairly stable, no matter how much unemployment fluctuates. These reasons include the following.

- **Inflation targeting**. Suppose the government wants a credible inflation target of 3%. Then demand must be adjusted to keep inflation at 3%, no matter how much unemployment varies
- **Globalization**. Growing international competition means that UK producers of tradable goods cannot easily raise their prices when demand is high and unemployment is low.
- **Mobility of labour**. UK workers may be reluctant to push for high wage rises when demand is high, for

fear that they could lose their jobs to workers from other countries, especially EU countries, who would work for less.

UK economic policy in the 2007–10 recession

Between 1992 and 2007, UK governments can be seen as following policies related to those of the new Keynesians. So monetary policy focused on inflation targets, even if it did not follow a precise Taylor rule. The general aim was to set interest rates so that, in two years' time, inflation would be within a target range; this meant that if inflation were currently above target, but was expected to fall to the target without any change in interest rates, interest rates would be left alone.

Also, in line with a belief that wages and perhaps prices are sticky, the government was willing to spend more than it raised in taxes, and so run a budget deficit in periods of relatively low aggregate demand, while it would run a budget surplus in periods of relatively high aggregate demand. But there was generally an aim of adhering to a 'golden rule' whereby, over any business cycle, the total level of government borrowing would not exceed its total expenditure on investment in capital assets.

But the response to the 2007–10 recession suggests an abandonment of this cautious approach. The Bank of England's base rate was held at a historically low level of 0.5%, and the government ran up a huge deficit. We look at this in more detail in Chapter 26.

23.2 Everyday economics

The ECB and a Taylor rule?

After holding its benchmark interest rate at 1.00% for almost two years, the European Central Bank raised its main interest rate to 1.25% on 13 April 2011. It was concerned that inflation in the eurozone had gone above the 2.0% target set by eurozone countries to 2.6%.

'ECB raises key interest rate to 1.25% to stem faster inflation', *Bloomberg*, 7 April 2011.
'ECB raises interest rate to 1.25%', *Global Pensions*, 7 April 2011.

Comment The ECB reduced its key benchmark rate to 1.00% in May 2009 to help to soften the impact of the recession in the eurozone. In April 2011, eurozone output was still below its potential level, but inflation went above its target. In this situation, advocates of a Taylor rule say a central bank should raise interest rates only if it is more concerned about the inflation than output, which the ECB clearly was. But many eurozone countries were more concerned about unemployment than inflation.

23.5 Summary

- The new Keynesian view argues that price and wage stickiness prevent the labour market from returning quickly to equilibrium after a disturbance, so it favours demand management policies.
- The new Keynesians also accept that money is neutral in the long run.
- They propose a Taylor rule, under which the money stock would be reduced, so that interest rates would be increased, if inflation were to go above a target rate or if output were to go above its potential level, and vice versa.
- In recent years, it is possible that the UK's short-run Phillips curve has become fairly flat.

In the next chapter we look at business cycles, to see why economies alternate between periods of low demand, which threatens high unemployment, and periods of high demand, which threatens high inflation.

Glossary

Adaptive expectations: expectations of the future that are based on what occurred in the past.

Cost-push inflation: inflation caused by a series of cost increases that are combined with government policies to offset any fall in output.

Credibility: a term used when people believe the government will follow a pre-announced policy.

Demand-pull inflation: inflation caused by successive increases in aggregate demand.

***k*% rule:** a rule under which the money stock would be raised at k% per year, where k is the average rate by which real output grows.

Long-run Phillips curve: this shows the relationship between unemployment and the inflation rate when the labour market has had time to reach equilibrium after any disturbance.

Non-accelerating inflation rate of unemployment (NAIRU): another term for the natural rate, U_N, and used because holding unemployment below U_N causes accelerating inflation.

Phillips curve: a curve that relates price inflation to unemployment

Rational expectations: expectations of the future that take account of all information and which are on average correct.

Short-run Phillips curve: this shows the relationship between unemployment and the inflation rate before the labour market has had time to reach equilibrium after any disturbance.

Stagflation: having high inflation and high unemployment at the same time.

Taylor rule: a rule that the central bank should have a target rate for inflation, and adjust interest rates according to how far inflation is from the target and how far output is from its potential level.

Answers to in-text questions

23.1 Smaller. The more V falls, the less is the effect of a rise in M on MV, and so the smaller is its effect on PY.

23.2 It would be more credible if unemployment were low. If unemployment were high, then people might expect the government to lose its nerve about reducing demand if inflationary pressures increased.

Questions for review

23.1 At the start of the current year in an economy, unemployment is at its natural rate, U_N, which is 5%, and people expect inflation of 2% during the year.

(a) At what unemployment rate does the long-run Phillips curve, *LPC*, intersect the horizontal axis?

(b) What inflation rate does the current short-run Phillips curve, *SPC*, have at U_N?

(c) During the year, aggregate demand rises. What will happen to the short-run Phillips curve for next year if people form adaptive expectations?

(d) Can we say what will happen to the short-run Phillips curve for next year if people form rational expectations?

(e) What, if anything, will happen to the short-run Phillips curve for the current year if there is a prolonged strike in a key industry?

23.2 Suppose an economy starts at the point at which its *AD*, *SAS*, and *LAS* curves all intersect, so that output is at the potential level. Then there is an unexpected decrease in aggregate demand that threatens to increase unemployment. What advice might be given to the government by the following?

(a) An economist with new classical views.

(b) An economist with new monetarist views.

(c) An economist with new Keynesian views.

Questions for discussion

23.1 Suppose you run a country's central bank. Suppose, too, that inflation is above target, while output is below its potential level, so that unemployment is above its natural rate. How will you decide what to do about interest rates?

23.2 The Bank of England is very wary that inflationary pressures will increase as the country pulls out of recession. What factors could cause these pressures? What policy would you recommend, on the basis of the views given in this chapter?

✗ Common student errors

It is easy to confuse the monetarist views outlined in the last chapter with the new monetarist views here. Rising inflation in the 1970s led monetarists away from advocating the use of monetary policy to raise demand in recessions for fear of aggravating inflation; instead they adopted a new monetarist position that would principally leave labour market adjustments to sort out unemployment.

It is also easy to confuse the Keynesian views given in the last chapter with the new Keynesian views here. Rising inflation in the 1970s led Keynesians to become more cautious about using fiscal or monetary policy in recessions. But they still believe wages and prices are sticky, and new Keynesians would advocate both fiscal policy and increasing the money stock when conditions so required, as in a Taylor rule.

24

Business Cycles

Remember from Chapter 17 that an economy has business cycles, with output fluctuating between periods of expansion and recession, so that unemployment also fluctuates. Recall from Chapter 21 that, in the long run, when the labour market reaches equilibrium, output will also be in equilibrium at its potential level.

Since the 19th century, incomes and living standards in the UK have risen greatly. But output and incomes have not expanded steadily. Sometimes, in recessions, they have fallen; at other times, they have grown very rapidly. Why does the economy expand in such an unsteady or cyclical fashion? Is this entirely the result of shocks, or might growth be unstable even if there were no shocks? Does the economy pull itself out of recessions, or is it essential for the government to intervene?

This chapter shows you how to answer questions like these, by understanding:

* the nature of business cycles and why they matter;
* differing views among economists on the causes of business cycles;
* why cycles might persist even if there are no future shocks;
* the meaning of technology shocks and real business cycles;
* why an economy has an automatic tendency to reduce the effect of demand shocks.

24.1 The nature of business cycles

The meaning of business cycles

In Chapter 21, we developed the aggregate supply and demand model to explain what determines real output in any given period of time. But we did not consider what happens to the path of real output as time passes.

Over time, real output generally increases, but sometimes it contracts. Figure 24.1 shows this in a stylized way. The wavy line here shows the actual path of real output or real GDP, and we can note four terms in relation to this path.

- **Expansion:** this applies when real output rises, as it does on the black parts of the wavy line.
- **Contraction:** this applies when real output falls, as it does on the grey parts of the wavy line.
- **Peak:** this arises when an expansion ends. Each peak is followed by a contraction.
- **Trough:** this arises when a contraction ends. Each trough is followed by an expansion.

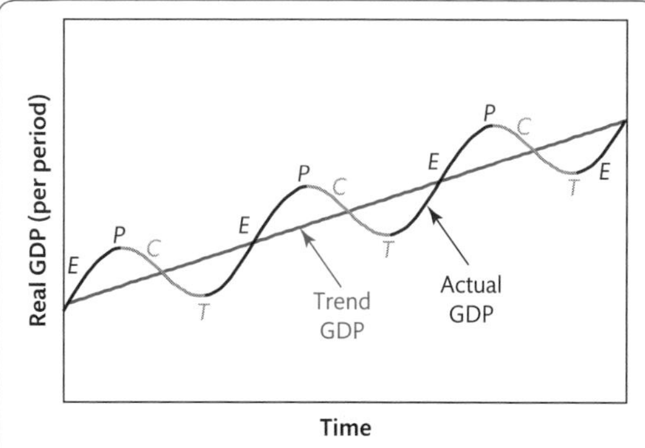

Figure 24.1 **Business cycles**

GDP tends to move in cycles, around a rising trend. There are alternate periods of expansion (*E*), shown in black, and contraction (*C*), shown in grey. These are separated by peaks (*P*) and troughs (*T*).

Figure 24.1 also has a purple line labelled **trend GDP**: this shows the path that GDP would have followed if it had grown by the same total amount over time, but had grown steadily rather than erratically. The fluctuations in real GDP around its rising trend are called **business cycles.** A complete cycle can be seen as the period from one peak to another, or from one trough to another.

Recent UK fluctuations

In practice, real GDP does not move in the regular wave-like way shown in Figure 24.1. Figure 24.2 shows the UK experience since 1975, using figures for each quarter of each year. The actual path of GDP is shown in the top part, with GDP given as an index that has 2005 as the reference period. This path seems fairly stable, but look at the middle part of the figure. This shows the growth rate in each quarter. Growth has been very unsteady, and even negative in many quarters.

If growth is negative for two or more consecutive quarters, so that there is a contraction for two or more quarters, the economy is said to be in **recession.** There were recessions as follows:

- **1975**, in quarters 2 and 3;
- **1980–81**, from 1980 quarter 1 to 1981 quarter 1;
- **1990–91**, from 1990 quarter 3 to 1991 quarter 3;
- **2008–09**, from 2008 quarter 2 to 2009 quarter 3.

When a recession occurs, unemployment rises, and it stays high until output expands significantly. The bottom part of Figure 24.2 shows unemployment since 1975, and you can see how it started to rise in 1975, 1980, 1990, and 2008.

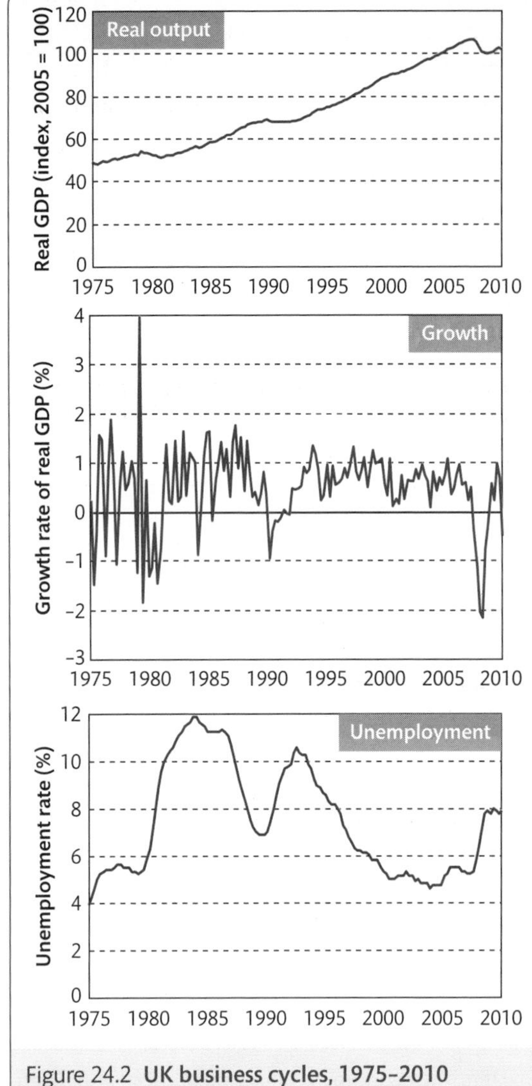

Figure 24.2 **UK business cycles, 1975–2010**

The top part shows output, and gives a misleading impression of stable growth. The middle part shows how wildly growth rates fluctuated when measured on a quarterly basis. The bottom shows also wide fluctuations in unemployment.

Source: Office of National Statistics Inline Data sets.

Trend GDP and potential GDP

Figure 24.3 repeats the actual and trend GDP lines from Figure 24.1, and adds another line showing potential GDP. The potential GDP line is a little above the trend line. This is because actual GDP is more

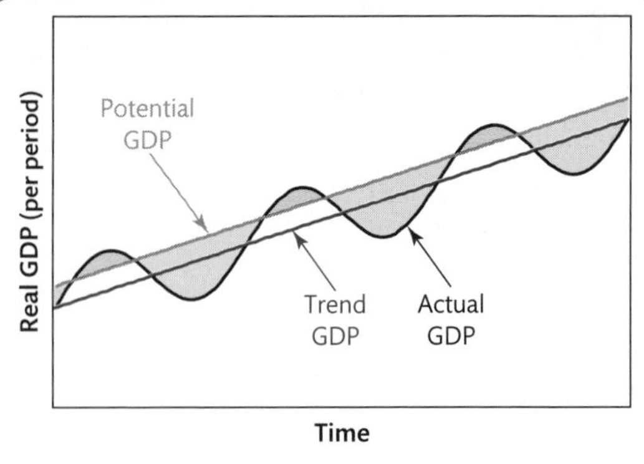

Figure 24.3 **Output and business cycles**

Potential GDP exceeds trend GDP, so actual GDP is below potential GDP more often than it is above. The lost output when it is below, shown by the grey areas, is more than the extra output when it is above, shown by the pink areas.

often below potential GDP than above, so the trend for GDP is below its potential level. The reason for this is that when output rises above its potential level, then unemployment is below the natural level, and we expect wages to rise quickly to return unemployment to the natural level and output to the potential level. In contrast, when output falls below its potential level, then unemployment is above the natural level, and we expect wages to fall less quickly to return unemployment to the natural level and output to the potential level. So, if events that take output above and below its potential level occur with equal frequency and severity, then we should expect the economy to spend less time above potential output than it spends below it.

Why the unstable path of GDP is of concern

The fact that GDP follows an unstable path is a matter of concern for three main reasons.

- **Loss of output**. Suppose, in Figure 24.3, that output had risen steadily along the potential GDP line instead of unsteadily along the actual GDP wave. Then, in most years, output would have been higher than it actually was, and this 'lost' output is shown by areas shaded grey. Admittedly, in other years, output would have been lower than it actually was, and the 'extra' output is shown by areas shaded pink. But the pink areas are smaller than the grey ones, so growth along the potential GDP line would have led to higher living standards, on average, over the period.

- **Unemployment**. At any time when output is below the potential level, unemployment rises above the natural level; this causes problems for the unemployed people involved.
- **Inflation**. At any time when output is above the potential level, unemployment falls below the natural level, or non-accelerating inflation rate of unemployment (NAIRU), so inflation accelerates.

Differing views about business cycles

Economists have varying views on why economies grow in an erratic way, and we will explore these views in the following sections. These views actually agree that if an economy were growing steadily along the potential output line shown in Figure 24.3, then it could be knocked off its steady path by various shocks. But the views differ in the shocks they consider most likely to affect output significantly.

Most economists also agree that, after a shock, output will in time return to the potential output path, when real wages have adjusted to return unemployment to the natural level. So, if an economy were to display neat cycles like those in Figures 24.1 and 24.3, then it would be a result of it facing alternating upward and downward shocks of similar size.

24.1 Everyday economics

Misleading statistics

Employment in the US fell by more than 130,000 in July 2010. This was about twice the number that economists had expected, and US share prices fell when the figures were released. Despite the fall in employment, the official US unemployment rate remained at 9.5%. This was because many people gave up looking for work, so the workforce shrank at the same rate as employment.

'US employment falls at twice rate predicted by economists', *Independent.ie*, 7 August 2011
'US economy lost 131,000 jobs in July', *World Socialist*, 7 August 2010

Comment This shows how the unemployment rate may not accurately measure the number of people who want to work and yet fail to find jobs.

24.1 Summary

- Output grows in an erratic cyclical way around a rising trend. Cycles comprise periods of expansion and contraction separated by peaks and troughs. The trend path of GDP is below the path that GDP would take if it were always at the potential level.
- The erratic nature of the path that GDP follows matters partly because, on average, output is below the potential level, so some output is 'lost'. Also, inflation accelerates when unemployment falls below the natural rate or NAIRU, while unemployment is of more concern when it is above the natural rate.
- Economists generally agree that GDP follows an erratic path because the economy is subject to shocks of various sorts. But they disagree about which type of shocks they think are most important.

24.2 The classical, monetarist, and Keynesian views

This section looks at classical, monetarist, and Keynesian views of business cycles.

Trade cycles and classical economists

No estimates of GDP were produced at the time of the 19th-century classical economists. But they knew that output grew erratically, because unemployment fluctuated. They used the term 'trade cycles' for the fluctuations in employment and economic activity, and they generally attributed these cycles to occasional shocks.

However, one feature of these cycles seemed to demand particular attention, and this was that the 19th-century cycles exhibited a fairly regular pattern, and lasted from seven to eleven years. You can most easily appreciate this by looking back at Figure 17.3 (on page 368); there, you will see how unemployment fluctuated between 1855 and 1910 in a fairly regular way.

The best-known effort to explain this fairly regular nature of the cycles was put forward in 1875 by the British economist William Jevons. He suggested that the cause might the activity of sunspots. These spots tend to fluctuate in size in cycles of about a decade, and he thought they might affect the weather. So they might cause periodic runs of good crops, which increased real output, and periodic runs of poor crops, which reduced it. Some people still argue that there is a link between sunspots and crop yields, but no one now attributes business cycles to them.

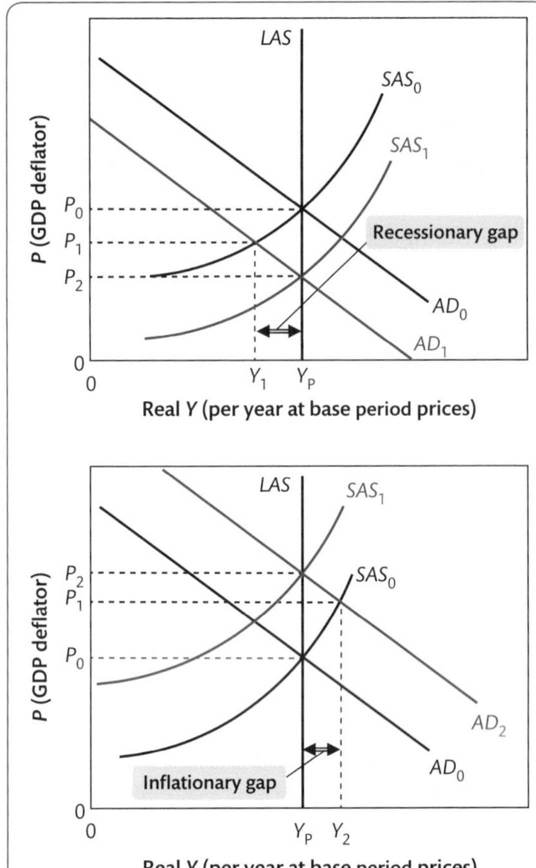

Figure 24.4 **Demand shocks and output**

In the short run, a negative demand shock reduces output and creates a recessionary gap, as shown in the top part, while a positive demand shock increases output and creates an inflationary gap, as shown in the bottom part. In the long run, real wages adjust to shift the short-run aggregate supply curve and return output to the potential level Y_P.

Monetarists and Keynesians: agreements

The monetarist and Keynesian views on business cycles both accepted that output departs at times from its potential level because of demand shocks. This is shown in the two parts of Figure 24.4. In each part, output is initially at its potential level, Y_P, where the aggregate demand and supply curves, AD_0, SAS_0, and *LAS*, all intersect. As output is at the potential level, unemployment must be at its natural rate.

In the top part, there is now a fall in aggregate demand to AD_1, and output falls to a trough level, Y_1. When output is below its potential level, the gap between them is called a **recessionary gap.** The fall in output takes unemployment above its natural rate, so in time nominal wages will fall and encourage producers to produce more. The short-run aggregate supply curve will then shift to the right to SAS_1, to return output to its potential level, Y_P, where SAS_1 intersects both AD_1 and LAS. Note that the price level falls from its initial level, P_0, to P_2.

In the bottom part of Figure 24.4, aggregate demand rises to AD_2, and output rises to a peak level, Y_2. When output is above its potential level, the gap between them is called an **inflationary gap.** The rise in output takes unemployment below its natural rate, so in time nominal wages will rise and encourage producers to produce less. The short-run aggregate supply curve will then shift to the left to SAS_1, returning output to its potential level, Y_P, where SAS_1 intersects both AD_2 and LAS. Note that the price level rises from its initial level, from, P_0 to P_2.

Monetarists and Keynesians: disagreements

There are two major differences between the monetarist and Keynesian views. One difference concerns how long the labour market will take to return to equilibrium, especially in a recession, when wages need to fall. Monetarists believed wages are more flexible than Keynesians believed. So monetarists thought recessions would sort themselves out more quickly, with less need for governments to try to raise demand.

The other difference is why aggregate demand may change in the first place. To explain this difference, we will consider why aggregate demand may increase. We will also use Figure 24.5: each part of this shows the money market, where the initial supply and demand curves are MS_0 and MD_0, and the initial equilibrium money stock and interest rate are MS_0 and r_0.

The monetarists argued that the demand for money is interest inelastic, as in the top part of Figure 24.5. They also argued that changes in interest rates have significant effects on planned consumption and investment and so, in turn, on aggregate demand. So they reached the following conclusions.

- ***AD* is much affected by changes in planned spending caused by changes in the money stock**. For example, suppose the money supply curve in the top part of Figure 24.5 shifts right to MS_1. Then the

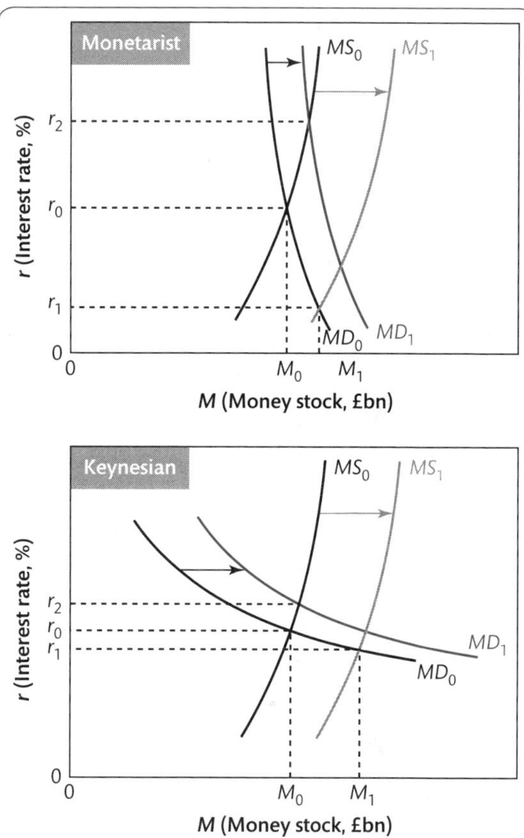

Figure 24.5 **Views about demand shocks**

On the monetarist view, money demand is interest inelastic. So a shift in the money supply curve causes a large change in the interest rate, and so causes large changes in investment and consumption, and, in turn, aggregate demand. But any other cause of a rise in aggregate demand will be largely offset because, as output starts to rise, the demand for money rises and the interest rate rises, causing falls in consumption and investment. On the Keynesian view, money demand is interest elastic. So a shift in the money supply curve has little effect on the interest rate and so has little effect on aggregate demand. But any other cause of a change in aggregate demand has an appreciable effect. Admittedly, as output starts to rise, the demand for money rises, so the interest rate rises, but this rise will be small and so cause little offsetting fall in consumption and investment.

money stock will increase to M_1, and the interest rate will fall appreciably to r_1; and because planned investment and consumption are sensitive to interest rate changes, aggregate demand will increase appreciably.

- ***AD* is little affected by changes in planned spending brought about by other causes.** For example, suppose the government cuts taxes, which leads to a rise in consumption or investment, or suppose there is an increase in government purchases or exports, or a fall in imports. Then aggregate demand will indeed increase, so that output starts to rise. But then incomes will start to rise, raising the demand for money, say to MD_1 in the top part of Figure 24.4. Then the interest rate will rise appreciably to r_2, and that will appreciably reduce consumption and investment. These reductions will offset much of the initial rise in aggregate demand, taking it back close to where it started.

The Keynesians argued that the demand for money is interest elastic, as in the bottom part of Figure 24.5. They also argued that changes in interest rates have little effect on consumption and investment and so, in turn, on aggregate demand. So they reached the following conclusions.

- ***AD* is little affected by changes in planned spending cause by changes in the money stock.** For example, suppose the money supply curve in the bottom part of Figure 24.4 shifts to the right to MS_1. Then the money stock will increase to M_1, but the interest rate will fall only slightly to r_1; and because planned investment and consumption are insensitive to interest rate changes, aggregate demand will increase only slightly.
- ***AD* is much affected by changes in planned spending brought about by other causes.** For example, suppose the government cuts taxes, which leads to a rise in consumption or investment, or suppose there is an increase in government purchases or exports, or a fall in imports. Then output will start to rise, and so will incomes, so the demand for money will increase, say to MD_1 in the bottom part of Figure 24.5. This will raise the interest rate to r_2 and so reduce consumption or investment. But the interest rate rise will be small, and any rise that does occur will have little effect on consumption or investment and so offset very little of the initial rise in aggregate demand.

The importance of investment

Although the Keynesians argued that a wide range of demand shocks can cause changes in output, they also argued that the most common cause of instability is changes in the level of planned investment. This raises two questions.

- **What determines the level of investment?**
- **How do changes in investment relate to cycles?**

The Keynesians argued that any firm's decision on whether to undertake a particular investment project depends chiefly on its expected returns. But what determines a firm's expectations? Keynes suggested that all firms might initially assume that they will continue to face the current level of demand, and then consider if demand might change. If firms adopt this approach, then their investment decisions may ultimately depend on their instincts or optimism, or, as Keynes put it, their 'animal spirits'.

We will now develop a model to relate changes in investment to business cycles. For simplicity, this model is based on the multiplier theory, and it assumes that when firms make their investment decisions, they always expect the current level of demand to persist, and do not consider if demand might change.

Time periods and replacement investment

In this model, we will divide time into periods, say quarters of a year, and we will assume that, on the first day of each period, firms decide how much investment they will do during that period. We will also assume that each firm believes there is an ideal, or

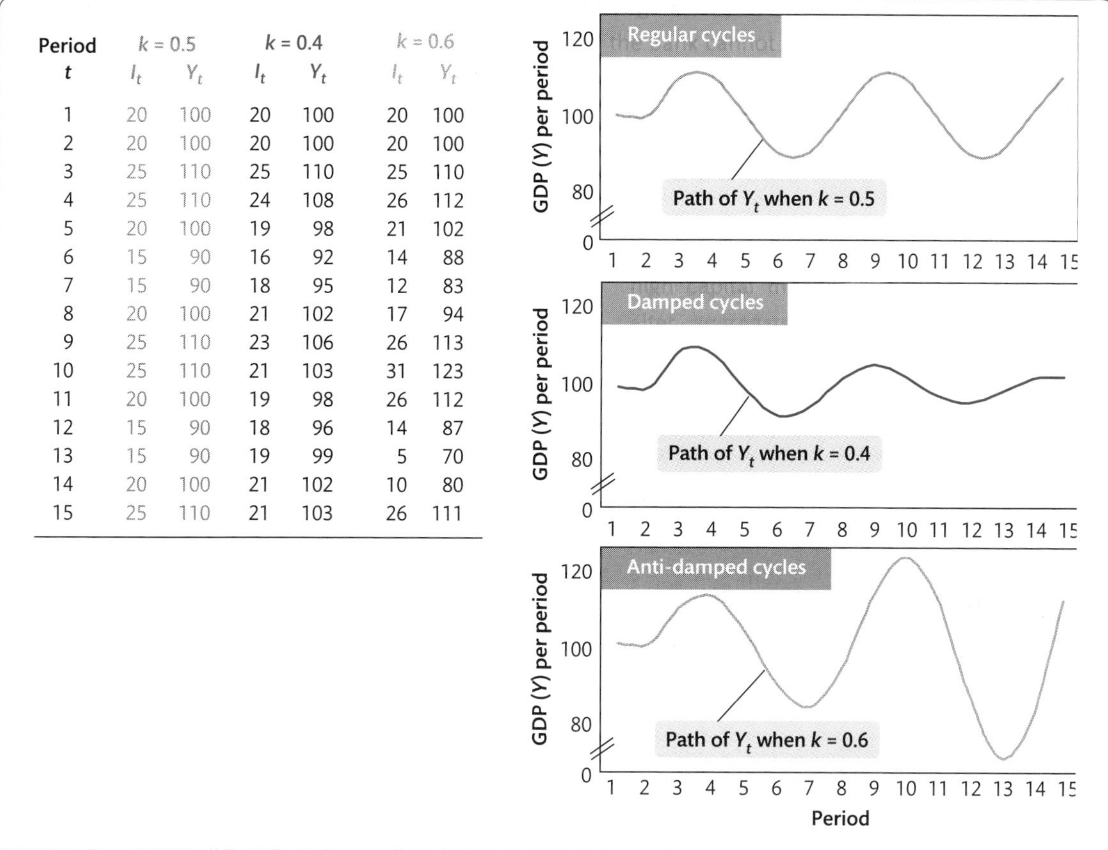

Period	k = 0.5		k = 0.4		k = 0.6	
t	I_t	Y_t	I_t	Y_t	I_t	Y_t
1	20	100	20	100	20	100
2	20	100	20	100	20	100
3	25	110	25	110	25	110
4	25	110	24	108	26	112
5	20	100	19	98	21	102
6	15	90	16	92	14	88
7	15	90	18	95	12	83
8	20	100	21	102	17	94
9	25	110	23	106	26	113
10	25	110	21	103	31	123
11	20	100	19	98	26	112
12	15	90	18	96	14	87
13	15	90	19	99	5	70
14	20	100	21	102	10	80
15	25	110	21	103	26	111

Figure 24.6 **The accelerator model of cycles**

The table and the graphs show how a one-off change in I_t in period 3 leads to cycles. These cycles are regular if $k = 0.5$, damped if $k = 0.4$, and anti-damped if $k = 0.6$. Note that in each period from period 4, investment is given by $I_t = 20 + k(Y_{t-1} - Y_{t-2})$. Also, the multiplier is 2, so that output always changes by twice as much as investment changes.

optimum, ratio between the value of its capital and the value of its output.

Suppose that, for the economy as a whole, the optimum ratio for capital to output, k, is 0.5, and suppose that output is constant at 100 for several periods. Then firms will want a constant capital stock of 50. However, even though they want a constant capital stock, they will still do some investment each period, because they will need to replace capital when it wears out. Suppose that, in each period, they want to do replacement investment of 20. Then, in each period, investment will be 20 and output will be 100. This is what happens in periods 1 and 2 in the example in Figure 24.6. You can see this in the table there in the columns headed $k = 0.5$.

The effects of a shock in just one period

Now consider period 3. We are assuming that firms always expect demand in any period about to start to be the same as demand in the last period. So because output was 100 in period 2, they expect it to be 100 in period 3. So we would ordinarily expect them simply to do only replacement investment of 20 in period 3. But in order to disturb the system, we will assume that, for this one period only, they form different plans. Maybe new technology is introduced, so they want to scrap some outdated capital worth 5 as well as replace worn out capital worth 20. So they plan to do investment of 25, while still leaving their capital stock at 50. We will assume the multiplier is 2, so the rise of investment by 5 to 25 raises output by 10 to 110.

Now consider period 4. Firms will expect output to be 110, as it was in period 3. So they will want a capital stock of 0.5 times 110, which is 55. So in period 4, as well as replacing 20 worth of capital that wears out, they will want an extra 5 to increase their capital stock from 50 to 55. As investment stays at 55, output stays at 110.

Now consider period 5. Firms will expect output to be 110, as it was in period 4. So they will think their current capital stock of 55 is ideal. So they will want to do only replacement investment of 20. As a result of this fall of 5 in investment, output falls by 10 to 100.

We can actually work out the amount of investment firms will do in any period, *t*, from period 4 on by using this formula:

$$I_t = 20 + 0.5(Y_{t-1} - Y_{t-2})$$

where Y_{t-1} and Y_{t-2} are the values of output in the previous period and the one before that. For period 4, this formula gives $I_t = 20 + 0.5(110 - 100)$, which is 25, as we have just seen. For period 5, the formula gives $I_t = 20 + 0.5(110 - 110)$, which is 20, as we have also just seen.

The columns headed $k = 0.5$ in Figure 24.6 work out investment in each period from period 4 using this formula, and they use the multiplier of 2 to show how much output changes in each period in response to the changes in investment. The first graph in the figure shows how these output figures change over time: you can see that the only disturbance, the introduction of new technology in period 3, leads here to persistent **regular cycles**.

In fact, regular cycles would be something of a fluke. The table in Figure 24.6 has extra columns and extra graphs that show that if, in this example, *k* were 0.4, then the cycles would get smaller in time, that is **damped**, while if *k* were 0.6, they would get larger, that is **anti-damped**.

Question 24.1 Even if *k* were equal to 0.6, why could the cycles not lead to output forever rising and falling to higher peaks and lower troughs?

No one argues that this model gives a full description of investment decisions, or that it gives a full explanation of how output changes over time. In particular, firms may not always expect the output that they produced in the last period to persist into the next period. Nevertheless, firms' expectations of the future probably are influenced by recent output levels, so the model may give a part explanation of their investment decisions. In turn, it offers a plausible reason for supposing that a one-off shock could cause some fluctuations in output rather than a one-off change.

In this model, a rise in output leads to a rise in investment, and a rise in investment leads to a rise in output: so the model is called the **accelerator model**. This description makes it sound as if the model predicts that a shock like the one we had must cause ever-increasing output, but in our example the result was cycles.

24.2 Summary

- Classical economists attributed cycles to shocks, perhaps from runs of good crops and bad crops.
- Monetarists attributed cycles chiefly to demand shocks that are caused by changes in the money stock, while Keynesians attributed them chiefly to demand shocks that are caused by any other factors.
- The accelerator model of business cycles offers an explanation of how a single demand shock can lead to a whole series of cycles, not just to a one-off change in output. The model assumes that each firm plans its investment for the period about to start so that it will have its optimum ratio of capital to output, if output in that period turns out to be at the same level as it was in the previous period.
- Depending on the average capital-output ratio in the economy, the cycles caused by a shock might be regular or of equal size, or they might be damped or anti-damped and get smaller or larger over time.

24.3 The new Keynesian and new classical views

This section looks at new views of business cycles. It focuses on the new Keynesian and new classical views, because these differ most from the relevant older views that we explored in the last section.

The new Keynesian view

The new Keynesian view departs from the Keynesian view in two respects: it is more willing to accept monetary shocks as a source of demand shocks, and it incorporates rational expectations for inflation. Figure 24.7 illustrates this view. The current year is year 0, and output is at its potential level, Y_P, where the aggregate demand and supply curves, AD_0, SAS_0, and LAS, all intersect. As output is at the potential level, unemployment must be at its natural rate.

Suppose that people expect aggregate demand in year 1 to be as shown by AD_1. If wages were highly flexible, then workers and employers would negotiate wages for year 1 that took the short-run aggregate supply curve to SAS_1. Then, if aggregate demand turned out to be AD_1 as expected, output would remain at Y_P, so that employment would remain at the natural rate, and the price level would rise by 6% to 106.

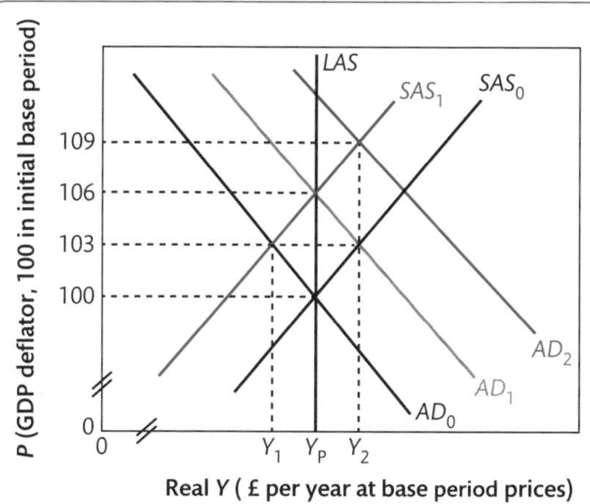

Figure 24.7 **Output variations with rational expectations**

In year 0, the economy has the black curves, with output at Y_P and the price level at 100. For year 1, people expect aggregate demand to be AD_1, so wages may be negotiated that will take short-run aggregate supply to SAS_1. If aggregate demand is indeed AD_1, output will stay at Y_P with prices at 106. But if there is an unexpected demand shock taking aggregate demand to, say, AD_0 or AD_2, then output will be Y_1 or Y_2, not Y_P.

However, as we saw in Chapter 23, new Keynesians do not believe that wages are highly flexible. So employers and workers may not make wage agreements that lead to SAS_1 applying in year 1. So, even if demand is AD_1, as expected, output might differ from Y_P. However, we will suppose here for simplicity that the wage rates negotiated for year 1 do lead to SAS_1 in year 1.

Then, if aggregate demand turns out to be AD_1, as expected, output will be Y_P. However, if aggregate demand is unexpectedly lower or higher, say AD_0 or AD_2, then output will be Y_1 or Y_2. In turn, employment will be below or above the natural level, and this will put downward or upward pressure on wages. But new Keynesians expect wages to adjust slowly, especially downwards. So even if there are no more demand shocks, it could take some years for output to return to Y_P.

So new Keynesians conclude that demand shocks can take output away from Y_P for long periods, as observed in business cycles. They also believe that if a demand shock does take output away from Y_P, then the government should use monetary or fiscal policies to try to return it to Y_P.

One new classical view: repeated shocks

New classical economists differ from new Keynesians in believing that wages adjust quickly, so that the unemployment rate never differs from the natural rate for long. We can return to Figure 24.7 to show the implications of this belief. Again, we assume that AD_0, LAS, and SAS_0 apply in year 0, so that output is Y_P and the price level is 100. We will also assume that people expect aggregate demand in year 1 to be AD_1. So, with highly flexible wages, employers and workers will definitely negotiate wages for year 1 that take the short-run aggregate supply curve to SAS_1. So if aggregate demand turns out to be AD_1 as expected, then output will be Y_P.

The only way in which the economy can deviate from Y_P in year 1 is if there is an unexpected demand shock. As new classical economists are extreme monetarists who believe that monetary shocks are the most powerful, let's suppose in year 1 that the money stock rises by less than was expected, so that demand is less than expected. Suppose, for simplicity, that demand remains at AD_0: then output will fall to Y_1 and the price level will be 103. Or suppose instead that, in year 1, the money stock rises by more than was expected, so demand is higher than expected, say as shown by AD_2: then output will rise to Y_2 and the price level will be 109.

However, while output might differ from Y_P in year 1, the new classical view supposes that a completely fresh set of wage contracts is made each year. So, no matter what happens in year 1, the wages agreed for year 2 will be based on the expected demand in year 2, and will shift the short-run aggregate supply curve to whatever position is needed to take the economy to Y_P in that year, if demand in year 2 turns out as expected. The only way in which output will differ from Y_P in year 2 is if another unexpected demand shock then occurs.

So this new classical view suggests that it is most unlikely that output would ever stay below Y_P for a long period, or rise above it for a long period; it would do so only in the unlikely case of a run of unexpected downward or upward demand shocks. Yet, in practice, economies often do have output above or below Y_P for long periods, and this fact raises a question mark about the validity of this new classical view.

Some new classical economists try to defend this view by adding extra features to the model to show why output might take some time to return to Y_P after a shock, despite flexible wages. Other new classical economists have proposed a quite different explanation of business cycles to which we now turn.

Another new classical view: the RBC theory

Like other new classical economists, the proponents of this alternative theory believe that wages are highly flexible, and in our discussion we will suppose for simplicity that they are so flexible that the labour market is always in equilibrium, with employment at the natural level.

This theory argues as follows.

- **Business cycles occur when output fluctuates.**
- **Output fluctuates only because of fluctuations in aggregate supply.**
- **Aggregate supply fluctuates only because of fluctuations in the demand for labour.**

Now the demand for labour depends chiefly on real factors, such as productivity. And it is because this business cycle theory sees output fluctuations as chiefly caused by changes in real factors, not by changes in the money stock that are measured in nominal terms, that it is called **real business cycle theory** (RBC theory).

To explain RBC theory, consider Figure 24.8. The top part here shows a country's labour market for the year just starting. RBC theory believes that the supply of labour is elastic, as shown by *ASL* here. The demand curve for labour, ADL_0, shows the demand for labour that employers expect to apply in this year.

If the demand for labour turns out as expected, so that ADL_0 applies, the equilibrium position will be with N_0 workers hired at a wage of W_0. N_0 is the natural employment level. These N_0 workers will produce the potential output, Y_0. This is shown by the vertical aggregate supply curve AS_0 in the bottom part. In RBC theory, we assume wages are so flexible that output can never depart from the potential level, so we have no sloping short-run aggregate supply curve. Y_0 is at the point where the aggregate demand curve, AD_0, intersects AS_0.

Labour demand shocks

Now suppose that, in the year, there is actually a shock which results in labour demand being higher than employers expected. Perhaps there is a positive technology shock, which means that technological progress is more than expected. Then, at each possible real wage,

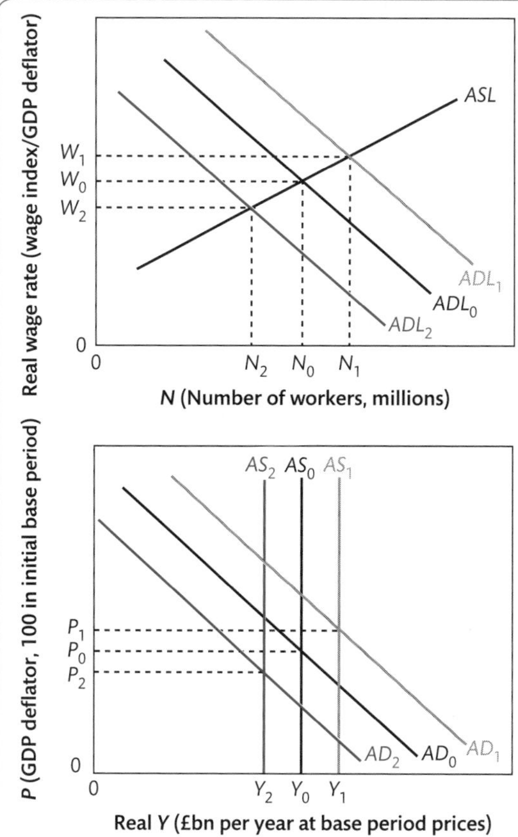

Figure 24.8 **Real business cycle theory**

Labour demand is expected to be ALD_0, but there may be a shock that takes it to ALD_1 or ALD_2. If the supply of labour is elastic, the shock will have large effects on employment and lead to large shifts in aggregate supply, taking output to Y_1 or Y_2. If the labour demand shock was caused by a technology shock, then aggregate demand would shift to AD_1 or AD_2; this would affect the price level, but not output.

employers will want to hire more workers than they initially expected, so the demand for labour will be higher than ADL_0 at, say ADL_1. So the labour market will be in equilibrium with N_1 workers, taking output to a new potential level, say, Y_1 in the lower part, and shifting aggregate supply to the right to AS_1.

Or suppose that, in the year, there is a shock that results in labour demand being lower than employers expected. Perhaps there is a negative technology shock, so that technological progress is less than expected, or perhaps there is bad weather or tighter laws about worker safety. Then, at each possible real wage, employers will want to hire fewer workers than they initially expected, so the demand for labour will be lower than ADL_0 at, say, ADL_2. Incidentally, we saw back in Figure 21.14 (on page 491) that the demand for labour would also fall if there was an increase in the price of imported raw materials such as oil. Then the labour market would be in equilibrium with N_2 workers, taking output to a new potential level, say Y_2 in the lower part, and shifting aggregate supply to the left to AS_2.

If the labour demand shocks were the result of technology shocks, then aggregate demand would also be affected. This is because a positive technology shock stimulates investment, while a negative productivity shock depresses it. So aggregate demand might end up at AD_1 with a positive technology shock and at AD_2 with a negative one. These aggregate demand shifts would not affect output in this model, because the aggregate supply curve is always vertical, so output will still be Y_1 or Y_2. But the shifts in aggregate demand will affect the price level, which will be P_1 with the positive shock and P_2 with the negative shock.

So RBC concludes that cyclical variations in output and employment are due to labour demand shocks, and most particularly to technology shocks.

Question 24.2 Suppose in Figure 24.8 that the technology shocks affected aggregate supply, but not aggregate demand. How would the final price levels differ from those shown?

Elastic labour supply in the RBC model

Our description of the RBC in Figure 24.8 assumed that labour supply was elastic. Suppose it had been very inelastic. Then the fluctuations in labour demand caused by technology shocks would have had little effect on employment and hence little effect on output.

Many people believe that labour supply is inelastic. After all, you may plan to work a roughly constant number of hours a week over your career, irrespective of any erratic increases in your real wage caused by erratic technological progress.

So RBC theory has to justify its assumption that labour supply is elastic. It does this by saying that people's decisions about their working hours do not depend only on their current wages, but also depend on their current wages in relation to their wages in other periods.

To get a feel for this, suppose you need to earn £1,600 next August, and suppose a local firm offers a wage of £10 an hour. You might decide to work 40 hours in each of the first four weeks of August. But suppose instead the firm needs extra labour in the middle two weeks of August and offers £16 an hour then, but offers only £10 in the other two weeks. Then you might decide to work 50 hours in each of the middle two weeks, and not work in the other two. In each case, the firm offers £10 an hour in the first week, but your decision over how many hours to work that week looks beyond the £10 wage for that week.

Now let's consider what happens when you leave college. You may expect real wages to rise on average at 2% a year over your working life, because of technological progress. Will you choose to work relatively little in the early years, when work is less worthwhile, and more in later years when work is more worthwhile?

It is unlikely that you will make this choice. Instead, you will probably be one of many people who ignore this issue and work roughly the same hours each year. But RBC says that if real wages were above expected in some years, then *some* people might work longer hours in those years, while the going was good; and if real wages were below expected in other years, then *some* people might take more leisure while work was less rewarding. If enough people behave like this, then the labour supply curve could be elastic, as in Figure 24.8.

Further comments about the RBC theory

There are four more points to make about RBC theory. First, it requires technological growth to be sometimes above average and sometimes below. And it needs both 'good times' and 'bad times' to last some years when they come, to explain why troughs and peaks last some time. There is some evidence that this is so.

Secondly, it says that because the labour market is always in equilibrium, any unemployment is a result of people's choices and need not concern the government.

Thirdly, although aggregate demand fluctuates in this model, it does so only because of the variations in technological progress; it is not aggregate demand fluctuations that cause the cycles.

Fourthly, the RBC model has been around for some 30 years. Most economists think it is interesting, and think there might be something in it, but very few think it gives the only reason, or indeed the main reason, for business cycles.

24.3 Summary

- The new Keynesian view of business cycles is that they are caused by demand shocks, even perhaps ones resulting from changes in the money stock. Sticky wages mean that output may take a long time to return to the potential level, Y_P, after a shock, unless the government intervenes.
- New classical economists argue that wage flexibility will quickly return output to Y_P after any shock. Some of them argue that output will stay away from Y_P for long periods, as occurs in business cycles, only if there are repeated demand shocks.
- Other new classical economists adopt the real business cycle theory, RBC, in which cycles result from supply shocks in labour demand, especially ones caused by technology shocks, when technology increases faster or slower than expected.
- For the RBC theory to explain large changes in output, the supply of labour must be elastic, but many economists believe the supply is inelastic and so do not regard technology shocks a major cause of cycles.

24.4 An automatic stabilizer

The meaning of an automatic stabilizer

We have seen that most views of business cycles regard fluctuations in aggregate demand as the main cause. These fluctuations are of concern to governments, because they lead to recessionary gaps, when output is below its potential level and unemployment is above its natural rate, and they also lead to inflationary gaps, when output is above its potential level and prices rise sharply.

However, if there is an inflationary or deflationary gap, the government does not have to intervene. This is because there are two forces that will tend to return output eventually to its potential level. These forces are as follows.

- **Changes in wages**: we saw in Chapter 21 that a fall in aggregate demand takes unemployment above the natural rate, so in time wages will fall and short-run aggregate supply will shift to the right. The opposite happens if aggregate demand rises.
- **Changes in the exchange rate**: we will see in Chapter 28 that a fall in aggregate demand tends to reduce the value of the pound against other currencies, so in time exports rise and imports fall, shifting aggregate demand some way back to the right. The opposite occurs when aggregate demand increases.

So if there is a recessionary or inflationary gap, a government has two choices: it can wait for these two forces to return output to its potential level, or it can use monetary or fiscal policies to alter aggregate demand and so return output to its potential level. Either way, it is of some comfort to the government to know that its mere existence introduces an **automatic stabilizer**, that is a mechanism related to taxes and government spending that automatically reduces the extent to which output changes when there is a demand shock, and so reduces the size of any subsequent gap. We will now explain this stabilizer.

Automatic stabilizing of demand shocks

Figure 24.9 explains automatic stabilization. Suppose for a moment that there is no government, and that aggregate demand is initially AD_0, so that output is at its potential level, Y_P, where AD_0 intersects both *LAS* and *SAS*. And suppose that, over time, demand fluctuates between the low level AD_1 and the high level AD_2, so that output fluctuates between Y_1 and Y_2.

Now return to the initial level of demand AD_0, and suppose a government is introduced that levies a range of taxes. And suppose that it uses some of its tax revenue to pay transfers to people in need, including the unemployed and the low paid, and that it spends the rest of its revenue on purchases of goods and services. As its tax revenue exceeds its

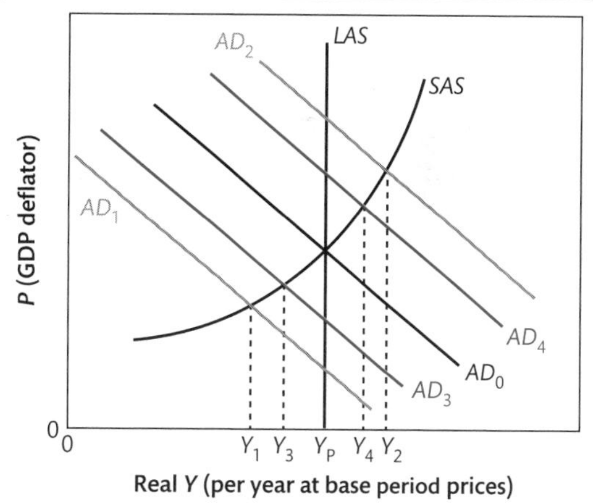

Figure 24.9 **Automatic stabilizer effects with demand shocks**

With no government, demand shocks shift demand between AD_1 and AD_2, so short-run output ranges from Y_1 to Y_2. Then a government is introduced that, at low incomes, has low taxes and high transfers, so encouraging consumption, and at high incomes has low transfers and high taxes, so restraining consumption. The result is that aggregate demand shifts less, say between AD_3 and AD_4, and output varies less, between Y_3 and Y_4.

transfers, total disposable income will fall and so will consumption. But suppose the fall in consumption is exactly offset by the government purchases, so that aggregate demand stays at AD_0.

Next, suppose there is a demand shock that would previously have reduced aggregate demand to AD_1. This time, as output and incomes start to fall, the government's tax revenues fall; also, its transfers rise, because more people will be unemployed and on low pay. The fall in taxes and the rise in transfers stimulate consumer spending, putting some upward pressure on aggregate demand. So demand may actually fall only as far as AD_3.

Or suppose there is a demand shock that would previously have raised aggregate demand to AD_2. This time, as output and incomes start to rise, the government's tax revenues rise; also, its transfers fall because fewer people will be unemployed or on low pay. The rise in taxes and the fall in transfers dampen consumer spending, putting some downward pressure on aggregate demand. So demand may actually rise only as far as AD_4.

So the mere existence of the government, along with a system of taxes and transfers, means that output would fluctuate between Y_3 and Y_4 rather than Y_1 and Y_2. Incidentally, if the government's revenue just covers its spending when aggregate demand is AD_0, the lower taxes and higher transfers when demand is AD_3 mean the government will then run a deficit. And the higher taxes and lower transfers when demand is AD_4 mean the government will then run a surplus.

Strengthening the automatic stabilizer

This analysis suggests that the government could reduce fluctuations in output still more by taxing people more heavily when their incomes are high, and by paying more generous transfers to people who are unemployed or on low pay. However, governments are reluctant to take these two steps, because they fear they might reduce the supply of labour and so reduce the level of potential output. The reasons for this fear are as follows:

- **higher taxes on the rich might reduce their incentive to work long hours;**
- **higher transfers to the unemployed might reduce their incentive to accept some jobs that might be offered to them.**

The automatic stabilizer and supply shocks

Unfortunately, this automatic stabilizer mechanism is of no help with supply shocks that shift the long-run aggregate supply curve. This is shown on Figure 24.10. The economy here initially has the aggregate demand curve AD_0 and the long-run aggregate supply curve LAS_0, and output is Y_0 and the price level is P_0.

Then long-run aggregate supply shifts left to LAS_1. If there were no automatic stabilizer effect, output would fall to Y_1 and the price level would rise to P_1. The automatic stabilizer effect means that the fall in output

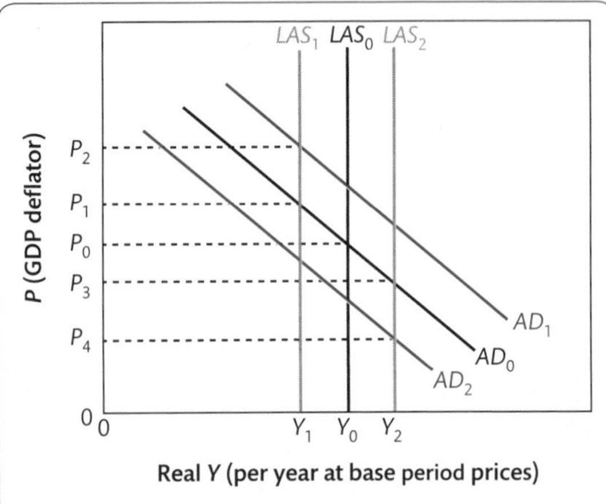

Figure 24.10 **The automatic stabilizer and supply shocks**

Suppose supply shocks shift long-run aggregate supply between LAS_0 and LAS_1. If there is no government, then output ranges between Y_1 and Y_2. If there is a government that, at Y_1, has low taxes and high transfers, then it will raise consumption and shift demand to AD_1; and if at Y_2 it has low transfers and high taxes, it will reduce consumption and shift demand to AD_2. Output will still range between Y_1 and Y_2, but prices will fluctuate more, between P_2 and P_4 instead of P_1 and P_3.

makes demand higher than it would otherwise be, say AD_1, but output still falls to Y_1 while the price level rises even further, to P_2.

Or suppose long-run aggregate supply shifts to the right to LAS_2. If there were no automatic stabilizer effect, output would rise to Y_2 and the price level would fall to P_3. The automatic stabilizer effect means that the rise in output makes demand lower than it would otherwise be, say AD_2, but output still rises to Y_2, while the price level falls even further, to P_4.

24.2 Everyday economics

A note of caution about austerity

The US economist Joseph Stiglitz has argued that, at a time when output is low, governments in Europe which reduce their spending risk a fall in output and a rise in unemployment. Governments are spending less to try to bring their deficits below 3% of GDP, but he says this is essentially an arbitrary number.

'Fears grow of double-dip slump after US home sales plummet', *The Guardian*, 24 August 2010
'Stiglitz: European economy at risk of double-dip recession', *Finance Freedom Success*, 25 August 2010

Comment Joseph Stiglitz won the 2001 Nobel Prize for economics, and his argument is sound. However, governments could rightly add that if their deficits were very big when aggregate demand is low, then the people who lend to them may begin to fear that the governments will be unable to repay them. As a response, lenders may suddenly demand high interest rates or even refuse to lend anything.

24.4 Summary

- Government taxation and spending policies automatically reduce the effect of changes in aggregate demand on output. When a fall in demand reduces incomes, tax revenues fall and transfers rise, so putting upward pressure on aggregate demand. When a rise in demand raises incomes, tax revenues rise and transfers fall, so putting downward pressure on aggregate demand.
- Government taxation and spending policies have no effect on changes in output that are caused by shocks in long-run aggregate supply, and make the effects of those shocks on prices more marked.

In the next chapter we look at economic growth, that is the rate at which the potential level of real GDP increases over time.

abc Glossary

Accelerator model: a model in which a rise in output leads to a rise in investment, and in which a rise in investment leads to a rise in output.

Anti-damped cycles: cycles that get larger over time.

Automatic stabilizer: a mechanism related to taxes and government spending that automatically reduces the impact of demand shocks on output.

Business cycles: the fluctuations in real GDP around its rising trend.

Contraction: a period during which real output decreases.

Damped cycles: cycles that get smaller over time.

Expansion: a period during which real output increases.

Inflationary gap: the gap between actual and potential output when actual output is the higher.

Peak: when real output moves from expansion to contraction.

Real business cycle theory: a theory in which cycles are caused by something real, chiefly technology shocks.

Recession: a period during which growth of real GDP is negative for two or more consecutive quarters.

Recessionary gap: the gap between actual and potential output when actual output is the lower.

Regular cycles: a series of cycles of equal size.

Trend GDP: the path that GDP would have followed over time if it had grown by the same total amount, but had grown steadily rather than erratically.

Trough: when real output moves from contraction to expansion.

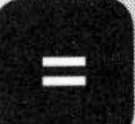

Answers to in-text questions

24.1 Output would be restricted to a ceiling value equal to the maximum that could be produced if all resources were used to full capacity. And investment could never be less than zero, which actually gives a minimum value for output of 60.

24.2 If *AS* were to shift to AS_1 and *AD* were to stay at AD_0, then the price level would fall, whereas in the figure it rises if *AD* also shifts to AD_1. And if *AS* were to shift to AS_2 and *AD* were to stay at AD_0, then the price level would rise, whereas in the figure it falls if *AD* also shifts to AD_2.

? Questions for review

24.1 Suppose the central bank increases interest rates sharply. What would the following views expect to happen to output and unemployment?

(a) The monetarist view.

(b) The Keynesian view.

(c) The new Keynesian view.

(d) The new classical view.

24.2 Suppose there is an unexpected development of a diesel engine that uses less fuel. What might the following views expect to happen to output in the short run?

(a) The monetarist view.

(b) The Keynesian view.

(c) The new Keynesian view.

(d) RBC theory.

? Questions for discussion

24.1 Suppose that, in a certain country, the capital output ratio is such that the accelerator model would predict regular cycles. Would firms learn from their experiences in the first few cycles after a demand shock to modify the way they plan their investment?

24.2 To what extent do you believe the arguments of RBC explain business cycles? How elastic do you believe the aggregate supply of labour might be?

Common student errors

The main errors in this topic arise from two misleading terms. One is 'business cycle theories'. It is easy to suppose that these theories must explain how a single shock can lead to a series of regular cycles, like those shown in Figure 24.1, but the only theory that shows how one event could do this is the accelerator model. The other theories merely say how shocks can alter output, so successive shocks are needed for a series of cycles.

The other confusing term is 'automatic stabilizer'. It is easy to suppose that anything that is given this name must help to return output to its potential level after a shock, but the automatic stabilizer discussed in this chapter doesn't: it merely reduces the effect of a demand shock on output. The text explains that the only automatic features that will help to return output to its potential level are adjustments in the real wage and the exchange rate.

25

Economic Growth

Remember from Chapter 17 that we measure economic growth by using figures for real GDP: these show how much a country's output or GDP would have changed over time if prices had been constant. And recall from Chapter 18 that the income of a country's citizens is almost identical to the value of the country's GDP.

In the 20th century, the UK's output rose on average by about 2% a year while its population rose by about 0.5%, leaving output and income per head to rise by about 1.5%. Output and income per head rose in most other countries too. What are the benefits of growth? How serious are its costs? Why do some countries have faster growth rates and higher incomes than others? Can income per head continue to rise during the lifetime of today's young people, or will the world run out of resources? And will the continued growth in the world's population eventually lead to ever falling incomes?

This chapter shows you how to answer questions like these, by understanding:

- what factors cause economic growth;
- the chief benefits and costs of economic growth;
- what factors may cause a temporary rise in a country's growth rate;
- why growth rates differ between countries;
- differing views about what factors may cause a permanent rise in a country's growth rate.

25.1 Economic growth and growth accounting

Recent growth in G7 countries

Economic growth occurs when the quantity of goods and services that are produced increases. Changes in this quantity are measured by changes in real GDP, and they are important because they affect living standards, that is economic welfare.

However, changes in real GDP can give very misleading impressions about changes in economic welfare in periods when the population changes. For example, if real GDP rises by 10% over a period when the population also rises by 10%, then living standards will not rise. For this reason, discussions of economic welfare and living standards generally focus on real GDP per head.

Figure 25.1 compares the growth experience of six of the G7 countries since 1971. It shows the average growth rate of GDP per head for each country in each decade. The UK's growth rate fell slightly over this period, but its relative position improved because the other countries' growth rates fell more.

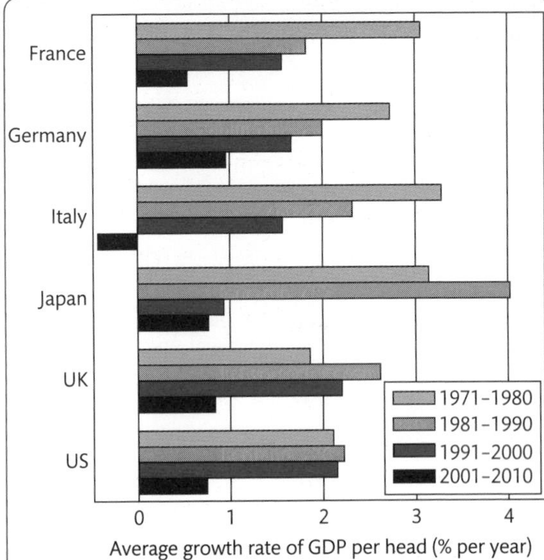

Figure 25.1 **Average growth rates per head in recent decades for six G7 countries**

In the 1970s, the UK's growth rate lagged behind other major industrial countries. More recently it has grown faster than most, although this is chiefly because the growth rates in the other countries have fallen sharply.

Source: European Commission, *Statistical Annex of European Economy*, Autumn 2010. Figures for Germany apply only to West Germany up to 1991.

The rule of 72

Figure 25.1 shows that GDP per head generally grows between 1% and 3% a year. These low figures may make growth seem of limited interest, but over a period of time, small figures have a big effect. We can illustrate this by using the mathematical **rule of 72**, which says that if a variable grows at a given rate of x% per year, then it will double in approximately $72/x$ years.

Suppose you leave college aged 22 and hope to work for 48 years until you are 70. If real GDP per head grows at an average of 3% a year in that period, then this rule says that real incomes will double in 72/3, or 24 years, and then double again in the next 24, to be four times what they are today. If GDP per head instead grows at an average of only 1½%, then real incomes will take 48 years merely to double. So living standards over the next 48 years as a whole will be hugely affected by a small change in the growth rate.

Growth accounting

Growth accounting is a statistical exercise that tries to see how different factors contribute to growth. Because goods and services are produced by resources of capital, labour, and land (or natural resources), growth accounting naturally shows that output increases when the following occur.

- **There is more physical capital.** This occurs as a result of investment in plant, buildings, vehicles, and machinery.

- **There is more labour.** This occurs if more people join the workforce, or if people who are already in the workforce work more hours.
- **There is more human capital.** This occurs if there is more education and work experience.
- **More natural resources are used.** This occurs if, for example, more use is made of wind power or if new oil reserves are exploited.

However, growth accounting finds that the rate at which output grows is faster than the rate at which the quantity of resources used increases. This shows that, as time passes, people use resources more productively. The relationship between the quantity of a country's output and the quantity of inputs that it uses is called **total factor productivity**. This may be increased in several ways, including the following.

- **Government policies:** for example, a fall in government regulation may allow firms to make better use of the available resources.
- **Management and organization:** an improvement in these may allow resources to be better used.
- **Technological progress:** the invention and use of new production methods may allow more output to be produced from the same quantity of inputs.
- **Economies of scale:** these might allow output to grow more quickly than the total resources used.

The main aims of this chapter are to outline some theories about how the rate of growth is affected by the various factors that we have just mentioned, and to see what advice these theories offer to governments who want faster growth. But first we will see what benefits growth may bring to society, and also what costs it may impose.

25.1 Summary

- We use real GDP to measure economic growth, and real GDP per head is often used as a guide to living standards.
- Economic growth arises when, in relation to population, there is more physical capital, more human capital a larger labour force, and more use of 'land' or natural resources. Economic growth also arises when resources are used more productively, perhaps through technological change, or with better government policies and management, or more exploiting of economies of scale.

25.2 The benefits and costs of economic growth

A rise in GDP per head is generally taken to indicate a rise in economic welfare. However, its effect on economic welfare depends on three issues, which we will discuss in this section. These issues are as follows:

- **the extent to which the rise in GDP has actually led to an increase in the output of goods and services that directly benefit consumers;**
- **the extent to which households benefit from having extra products;**
- **the costs that are involved in raising real GDP.**

Real GDP and products for consumers

Suppose for simplicity that the population is constant, and that real GDP rises by 5%. This means that 5% more products are produced, but there are several reasons why the output that benefits consumers might not rise by 5% per head. We discussed these reasons in Chapter 18 and summarize them below.

- **GDP includes investment.** If investment grows faster than 5%, then some other components of GDP, perhaps including consumption, will grow more slowly.

- **GDP includes all government purchases of goods and services.** Some of these purchases directly affect living standards, such as healthcare and state schools, but others do not, such as new warships and tanks. If spending on the second group grows faster than 5%, then some other components of GDP, perhaps including consumption, will grow more slowly.
- **GDP includes exports.** Exports are consumed abroad, and if they grow faster than 5%, then some other components of GDP, perhaps including consumption, will grow more slowly.
- **GDP omits most household production.** Households produce for themselves many of the goods and services they consume. If real GDP rises by 5%, but household output rises by less, then total consumption rises by less than 5%.
- **GDP omits production by the underground economy.** If real GDP rises by 5%, but the output of the underground economy rises by less, then total consumption rises by less than 5%.
- **GDP omits leisure.** Households consume leisure as well as other products, and as time passes, working hours fall so that workers consume more leisure. But suppose leisure rises by 1% when real consumer spending rises by 5%. Then any measure of total consumption that includes leisure would rise by less than 5%.
- **Real GDP struggles with product quality.** Even if the quantity of goods and services produced stayed the same, living standards would rise if their quality improved. The statisticians try to allow for improvements in product quality when they calculate their figures for changes in real GDP, but it is hard for them to be accurate.

The benefits of economic growth

Consumption per head in the UK has grown enormously since the Industrial Revolution, and this has brought some clear benefits, as follows.

- **A reduction in absolute poverty.** Poverty, in the absolute sense of not having enough to meet any of the absolute poverty lines that we met in Chapter 16, has almost wholly disappeared.
- **Help with tackling relative poverty.** Growth makes it possible to help the relatively poor without hurting the relatively rich.
- **Less drudgery and pain.** For example, people no longer have to sweep carpets by hand, do all their washing by hand, and constantly stoke up coal fires to keep themselves warm. And people have access to much better healthcare.
- **More access to some products.** For example, people have far more access to travel, education, and information.
- **Better products.** For example, people can enjoy products such as colour television compared with black-and-white television, or even no television, and mobile phones compared with landlines or even no phones.
- **More leisure.** People have taken part of their increased consumption in the form of leisure, and enjoy improved recreational facilities.

The costs of economic growth

Although these benefits have greatly improved economic welfare, economic growth comes at a cost, and growth is worthwhile only if its benefits exceed its costs. One cost is that the money spent investing in new capital, to increase output in future, could instead be spent on more consumption today. There is an issue of redistribution over time here: increased investment restrains economic welfare now, but it increases economic welfare in future.

There are further costs to economic growth. To understand these, recall from Chapter 18 that economic welfare is only one of many factors that affect welfare as a whole. Economic growth may adversely affect some of the other factors in a variety of ways including the following.

- **More pollution of the atmosphere,** some of it widely believed to contribute to adverse climate change. Of course, government policy can help to reduce this, and recall from Chapter 13 that the optimum amount of pollution is not zero.

- **More pollution of the sea and the ground,** from hazardous items disposed of in rivers or landfill waste sites, and from non-biodegradable items like plastic bags disposed of as litter.
- **More noise and visual pollution,** for example from machinery and vehicles, and from factories, pylons, wind farms, and quarries.
- **More congestion,** for example at tourist sites and on roads.
- **Redundant skills.** Technological progress reduces the demand for some skills, so many people have to retrain during their working lives. For example, video presentations may, in future, reduce the need for lecturers.
- **Faster depletion of non-renewable resources.** Any debate of this controversial issue should appreciate that, as we saw in Chapter 15, the price of these resources rises over time, and this encourages the development of new technologies that reduce or avoid their use.
- **An increase in crime?** In principle, crime might be fuelled by new consumer durables that can be stolen, and by new products like video games, which may encourage some people to be violent. However, the British Crime Survey suggests that while crime nearly doubled between 1981 and 1995, it has since fallen below the 1981 level.
- **A broken society?** Some people allege that family life has deteriorated in recent decades. If so, might this be because people have pursued higher incomes at the expense of high-quality personal relationships?

Economists have differing views about the net benefit of economic growth. Some challenge the view that countries become happier when they are richer: these economists often argue that making everyone richer does not make them happier because all they really care about is how rich they are compared to other people. Other economists dispute this, but most agree that the marginal utility of income declines as income increases, so that the net benefits of growth may decline as more growth occurs.

25.1 Everyday economics

The views of a 'happiness tsar'

Professor Richard Layard at the London School of Economics has written extensively on happiness, and advised governments about it, leading to him being dubbed the happiness tsar. In his book *Happiness: Lessons from a New Science* (Penguin, 2006) he says that despite Western economies growing richer over the last 50 years, the evidence suggests that their citizens are no happier; indeed, once people reach subsistence, making them happier is difficult. Of course, it is hard to be sure how accurate the measures of happiness used in the evidence are—but increases in income doubtless bring diminishing marginal utility, and this makes it ever more important to consider other factors that affect welfare as a whole, such as freedom, families, and communities.

25.2 Summary

- Rising GDP may not lead to an equivalent rise in the real spending that benefits households. Instead, much of the extra output may be used for investment, exports, and government purchases of limited benefit. Also leisure and production by households and the underground economy may rise more slowly than GDP.
- Economic growth reduces absolute poverty and makes relative poverty easier to tackle. It has led to more leisure and less drudgery and pain, and it allows consumers access to new and better products.
- Economic growth also has costs. These include pollution of the atmosphere, ground, and sea, noise and aural pollution, litter, congestion, redundant skills, and pressure on non-renewable resources. Some people argue that growth also fuels crime and a broken society.

25.3 The neoclassical theory of economic growth

The need for a model

In this section, we develop a model to show the factors that affect an economy's rate of growth. As growth concerns increases in GDP, it might seem that we could simply develop the *AS–AD* model, which shows how GDP is determined.

However, the main purpose of the *AS–AD* model is to explain why actual output might differ from potential output. Growth theory is not interested in this. Instead, it considers why potential output grows, and it ignores the fact that, at any point in time, actual output may often be a few percentage points away from the current potential output.

We saw in Chapter 21 that potential output depends on the level of natural employment. It also depends on how productive workers are, so any model of growth must allow for changes in productivity. The model given here was developed in the 1940s and 1950s by several economists, most notably the American, Robert Solow. The model is called the neoclassical model because, like the classical economists that we mentioned in Chapter 22, it is not interested in differences between actual output and potential output.

Assumptions

To keep the model simple, we will make the following assumptions throughout.

- **The economy has only two sectors, households and firms.** So, as we saw in Table 19.3 (on page 412), output, *Y*, equals disposable income; in turn, *Y* equals consumption plus saving, that is $C + S$. Also, the only injection is investment, *I*, and the only withdrawal is saving, *S*.
- **Actual output always equals potential output;** so output is always in equilibrium. This means that injections always equal withdrawals, so $I = S$.

Initially, we will make some further assumptions, as follows. We will relax these assumptions later.

- **The total population is constant, and the percentage that is economically active is constant, so the number of workers is constant.**
- **The fraction of income that is saved is constant.**
- **The hours worked by workers are constant.**
- **Workers have a constant level of human capital.**
- **Technology is constant.**

The basic diagram

The diagram used in this model is shown in Figure 25.2. All the variables used here have small letters, such as *s*, *i*, and *y*. This is because they do not show total saving, investment, or output. Instead, they show saving per worker, investment per worker, and output per worker.

The horizontal axis measures the value of the physical capital available per worker, *k*; physical capital comprises plant, buildings, vehicles, and machinery. The vertical axis measures the value of the output or GDP per worker in a year. The more capital each worker has, the more each can produce. This is shown by the upward-sloping curve *pf*, which stands for production function. For example, if the capital per worker rises from k_1 to k_2, then the output per worker rises from y_1 to y_2.

The curve *pf* gets flatter as *k* increases. This reflects the law of diminishing marginal returns, which we met in Chapter 8. This law implies that if a constant number of workers is given more and more capital, then their output will increase by progressively smaller amounts.

In a two-sector' economy, output equals income, so *pf* also shows the income per worker at each level of *k*. We are assuming that a constant fraction of income is saved, and we will assume that the saving per worker at

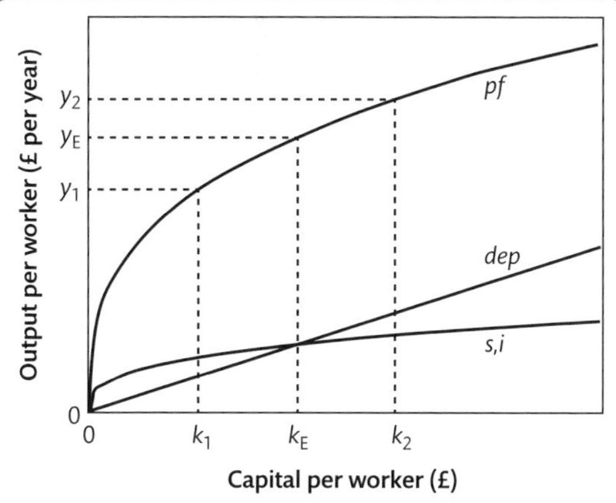

Figure 25.2 **Equilibrium capital and output per worker, and a one-off increase in the workforce**

The equilibrium capital and output per worker are k_E and y_E: if capital per worker is lower, investment exceeds depreciation and capital increases, and vice versa. A one-off increase in the workforce initially reduces capital and output per worker, say to k_1 and y_1. But the capital stock and output per worker will eventually return to equilibrium.

each level of k is shown by the curve s; the height of this curve is a constant fraction of the height of pf. Because investment equals saving, this curve also shows the investment per worker, so we label it s,i.

The significance of depreciation

Each year, some capital wears out through use and must be replaced. The investment needed each year to cover this depreciation is shown by the line *dep*. This line slopes upwards. To see why, compare two possible levels of capital per worker, k_1 and k_2. At k_2 there is more capital per worker, so there is more capital to wear out. So it will need more investment to maintain the capital per worker at k_2 than to maintain it at k_1.

At any level of k where there is a gap between the i and *dep* lines, the level of capital per worker will soon change. To see this, consider two levels of k.

- $\boldsymbol{k_1}$. Here investment, i, exceeds depreciation, *dep*, so there is **capital accumulation**, that is a growing capital stock. This accumulation leads to more capital per worker, that is **capital deepening**. So the capital per worker will increase above k_1.
- $\boldsymbol{k_2}$. Here depreciation, *dep*, exceeds investment, i, so investment is too small to do all the replacement needed to maintain the current level of capital per worker, so the capital per worker will decrease below k_2.

So this model concludes that if i is more than *dep*, then k will increase, while if i is less than *dep*, then k will decrease. This means that k must end up at the equilibrium level shown as k_E, where $i = dep$; here, output per worker is y_E a year. And when output per worker reaches this equilibrium level, it will stay there, so there will then be no growth.

It may seem that this economy will only ever grow if k is less than k_E and increases to k_E. But let's now relax some of our assumptions to see if we can find other possible sources of growth.

A one-off increase in the workforce

Suppose there is a one-off increase in the workforce. Perhaps the percentage of the population that is economically active rises, or perhaps the population increases because there are more births than deaths, or there is immigration.

We can use Figure 25.2 to see the effects. Suppose the economy starts in equilibrium with capital and output per worker at k_E and y_E. And suppose the workforce has a one-off increase. When the extra people start working, there will not instantly be more capital, so capital per worker will fall, say to k_1, and output per worker will fall to y_1.

At k_1 investment exceeds depreciation. So there is capital accumulation, and capital and output per worker will rise. However, they will stop rising when i equals *dep*, that is at k_E and y_E; it might take some years to reach this point, but there will be no more growth after that. The capital accumulation here is called **capital widening**, because it is needed to return the capital per worker to the initial level when the workforce increases.

Although output per worker returns to y_E, there would be benefits if the workforce were to grow because the economic activity rate grew. In this case, there would be more workers in relation to the population as a whole: so although output per worker would end up the same, output per head of population would rise.

A sustained population increase

Suppose, instead, that the population starts to rise continuously. This situation is shown in Figure 25.3. Initially, the economy faces the black curves and is in equilibrium with capital and output per worker as shown by k_0 and y_0.

Then the population starts to grow, say at a constant rate. So the workforce will grow every year, and capital widening investment will be needed every year, in addition to depreciation, to maintain the capital per worker at any given level. We show this extra investment by adding capital widening to depreciation in the line *dep* + *cw*. The gap between this line and *dep* increases, the larger is *k*, because then more extra capital is needed to keep the capital per worker at a constant level when the workforce rises.

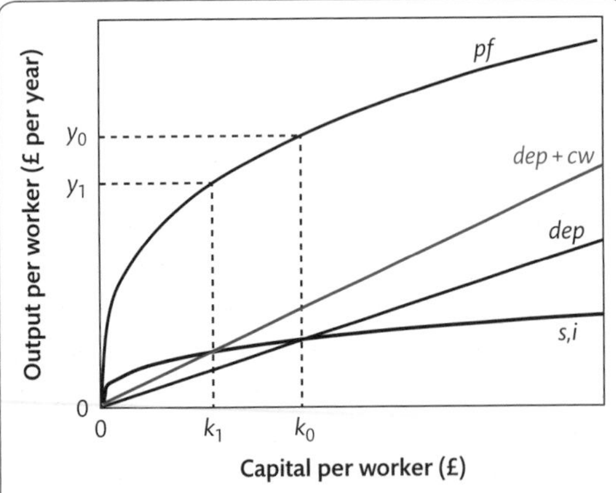

Figure 25.3 **An ever-rising population**

The economy starts at k_0 and y_0. Then the population and workforce start to rise constantly. Maintaining the capital stock per worker at any given level now means allowing for capital widening as well as depreciation, as shown by *dep* + *cw*. Capital and output per worker end up at k_1 and y_1.

At the initial capital per worker, k_0, investment per worker, *i*, is less than *dep* + *cw*. So the capital per worker falls to a new equilibrium value, k_1, where *s,i* intersects *dep* + *cw*, and this reduces the equilibrium output per worker to y_1. So an ever-rising population permanently reduces output per worker. If you compare the situations at y_1 in Figures 25.2 and 25.3, you will see that, in each case, investment per worker exceeds depreciation—but in Figure 25.3 this does not increase the capital per worker, because the ever-rising number of workers requires continued capital widening.

Although output per worker in Figure 25.3 will remain at y_1, the economy's GDP will grow, because the population and workforce are growing. For example, if output per worker is constant, but the workforce rises by 1% a year, then GDP will rise by 1% a year. So here is a possible explanation of sustained growth in GDP, although not of GDP per head of population.

Figure 25.3 paints a negative picture of population growth because it reduces output per head. But in section 25.5 we will look again at population growth and see it in a more positive light.

Higher saving and investment

Figure 25.4 shows the effects of an increase in the saving ratio, that is the fraction of incomes that people save and so invest. The economy initially faces the black curves and is in equilibrium at k_0 and y_0. Then the saving ratio increases, to shift the saving and investment curve up to s_1,i_1. At the initial capital per worker, k_0, investment now exceeds depreciation, so there will be capital deepening. Capital per worker will rise to k_1 where investment equals the higher depreciation that arises with a larger capital stock, and output per worker will rise to y_1. But when output reaches its new higher level, it will stay there, and so there will be no sustained growth.

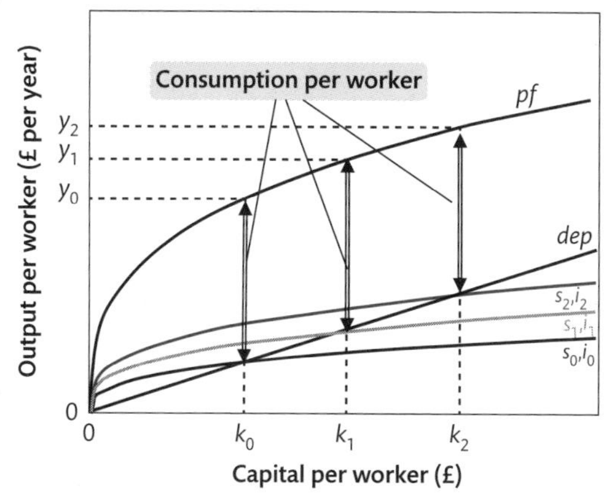

Figure 25.4 **A rise in the saving ratio**

If the fraction of income saved and invested rises, the *s,i* curve shifts up, so capital and output per worker rise. The optimal saving ratio is shown by s_1,i_1: this results in the highest possible consumption per worker, albeit by a small margin.

An optimum saving ratio

The ultimate aim of growth in this economy will be higher consumption. It might seem that the best strategy is to have ever higher saving ratios, and so ever higher capital and output per worker. But a higher output and income per worker may not lead to higher consumption per worker if a higher fraction of the higher income is saved.

Recall that *pf* shows the income per worker as well as the output per worker. So the gap between the *pf* and *s,i* curves shows consumption per worker. Figure 25.4 shows the consumption per worker that will arise if s_0,i_0 applies, and capital per worker is k_0, and also if s_1,i_1 applies, so that capital per worker is k_1.

Actually, s_1,i_1 has been carefully drawn to show the *s,i* curve that leads to the maximum level of consumption that can arise in this example. If the saving ratio rises again, say to give curve s_2,i_2, then the capital per worker will rise to k_2 and the output per worker will rise to y_2. But the gap between *pf* and s_2,i_2 at k_2 is smaller than the gap between *pf* and s_1,i_1 at k_1. The saving ratio reflected in s_1,i_1 is called the **golden rule** ratio because it maximizes consumption.

One-off shifts in the production function

Sometimes, there is a one-off upward shift in the production function. This arises when, for any given level of capital per worker, there is a one-off increase in the output per worker. This can happen for any of the following reasons.

- **Workers work longer hours**. Then, using the same amount of capital, they will produce more.
- **Workers acquire more human capital**. For example, an increase in the school-leaving age might increase the average human capital of the workforce and allow it to produce more from the same quantity of physical capital.
- **Technology may have a one-off change**. This will occur if new inputs are developed and used, or if better ways are found for using existing inputs. In either case, if workers are given the same amount of physical capital as before in terms of value, they will be able to produce more with it. Technological change that makes workers more productive is called **labour-augmenting technological progress**.

Figure 25.5 shows the effects of a one-off shift in the production function. The economy initially faces the black curves and is in equilibrium at k_0 and y_0. Then the production function shifts up to pf_1. So at each level of *k*, output and incomes are higher than before.

Assuming people now save the same fraction as before of their higher incomes, the saving and investment line shifts to s_1,i_1. At the initial capital per worker, k_0, investment now exceeds depreciation, so capital per worker will rise to k_1 where s_1,i_1 intersects *dep*. So the one-off shift leads to a higher output per worker, y_2, but it does not lead to sustained growth.

Sustained growth

Figure 25.5 showed that one-off increases in working hours, human capital, or technological progress increase output per worker, but they do not lead to

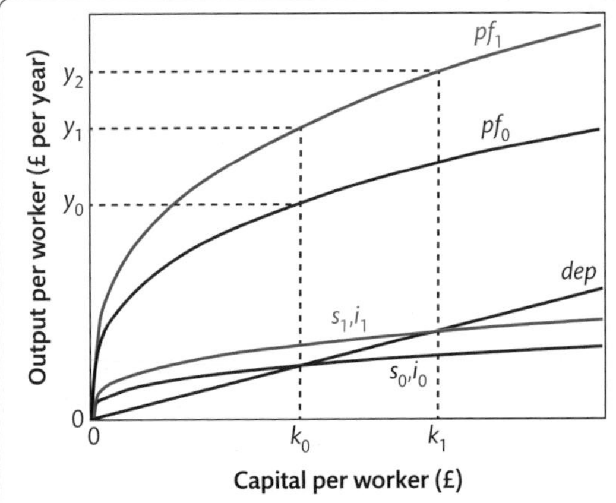

Figure 25.5 **One-off changes in working hours, human capital, or technology**

If workers work more hours, or acquire more human capital, or technology improves, the production function shifts to pf_1. With capital per worker at k_0, output per worker rises to y_1. But the s,i line shifts to s_1,i_1, so investment exceeds depreciation; so capital per worker rises to k_1 taking output per worker to y_2.

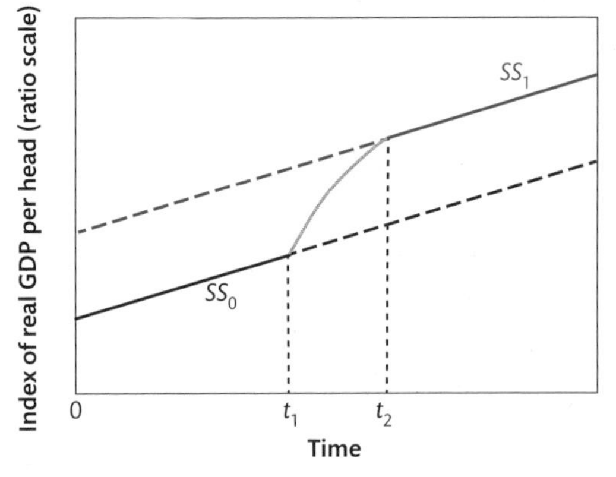

Figure 25.6 **A disturbance in the growth rate**

Until t_1, GDP per head grows along SS_0 at a steady rate that depends on the rate of technological change. At t_1, there is a shock, such as a rise in the percentage of the population who work, or in the saving ratio, or in working hours, or in human capital, and output per head grows rapidly along the pink curve. After t_2, output grows along SS_1 at the original rate that applied on SS_0. The shock raised GDP per head permanently, but raised the growth rate only temporarily.

sustained growth in GDP. However, continual increases in working hours, human capital, or technological progress would continually shift the production function upwards and so would lead to sustained growth in output per worker.

In practice, working hours are limited by the fact that there are only 24 hours a day, and increasing human capital through training is limited by the fact that people have only limited life spans. But technology can and does increase continually, and it is only this that leads to sustained growth of output per worker, and so of real GDP per head.

Sustained growth is illustrated in Figure 25.6, which has time on the horizontal axis and real GDP per head of population on the vertical axis. If technology improves at a constant rate, then output per head rises at a constant rate, and the economy is said to be in a steady state. The line SS_0 shows a steady state that lasts until time t_1.

Now suppose that, at time t_1, there is an increase in the percentage of the population who join the workforce, or in the saving ratio, or in the hours that workers work, or in human capital. Then there will be a rise in output per head, as we have seen earlier. When this rise has finished, at time t_2, GDP per head will resume growing, because of technological progress, at the original constant rate, following the path shown by SS_1.

Figure 25.6 illustrates a limitation of neoclassical growth theory. This theory says the sustained growth in output per head that is shown by SS_0 and SS_1 will occur only if there is sustained technological change; it says nothing about the factors that determine the rate of technological change. So the growth rate is determined by factors that lie outside the model, or are exogenous to it; so this theory is called an **exogenous growth theory**. Section 25.5 looks at some later models that do try to explain the actual rate of growth. But the next section looks at some applications of the neoclassical model.

Question 25.1 Return to the equilibrium position in Figure 25.2. Suppose that, over time, capital is made more durable, so depreciation per year falls and the depreciation line *dep* pivots clockwise to become flatter. Will this lead to sustained growth?

25.3 Summary

- In the neoclassical growth model, capital per worker is in equilibrium when investment per worker equals depreciation per worker. The equilibrium output per worker can be read off the production function at this level of capital per worker.
- Various factors can cause a one-off rise in the output per worker, without leading to sustained growth. These include one-off rises in the saving ratio, or in working hours, or in human capital, or in technological change.
- If the population starts to rise continually, output per worker falls. Thereafter, the rising population will lead to sustained growth in GDP, but it will not lead to any growth in GDP per head of population.
- Sustained growth in GDP per head requires sustained technological progress. The neoclassical growth model does not explain the factors that lead to this. As these factors are exogenous to the model, it is called an exogenous theory of economic growth.

25.4 Applications of neoclassical growth theory

This section uses the neoclassical growth model to explore some further aspects of economic growth.

The Malthusian trap

Some early classical economists held a very pessimistic view of growth. The most notable exposition of this view was in an essay published in 1798 by a British scholar Thomas Malthus.

As we presented the neoclassical model, the key inputs were labour and capital, but in Malthus's day they were labour and farming land. To illustrate his view, Figure 25.7 has land per worker on the horizontal axis. The line pf_0 shows output per worker for different levels of land per worker.

Malthus argued that if output per head and income per head were ever to rise above the subsistence level, then people would have more children, because of 'the passion between the sexes'. The resulting rise in the population would return output and income per head to the subsistence level.

Suppose the subsistence income is y_{SUB} per worker, as shown on the vertical axis in Figure 25.7. And suppose the economy currently has the production function pf_0, along with l_0 land per worker, so that output per worker is y_{SUB}. As people have only enough income to live on, there is no saving or investment, and the line s_0,i_0 shows that saving and investment would

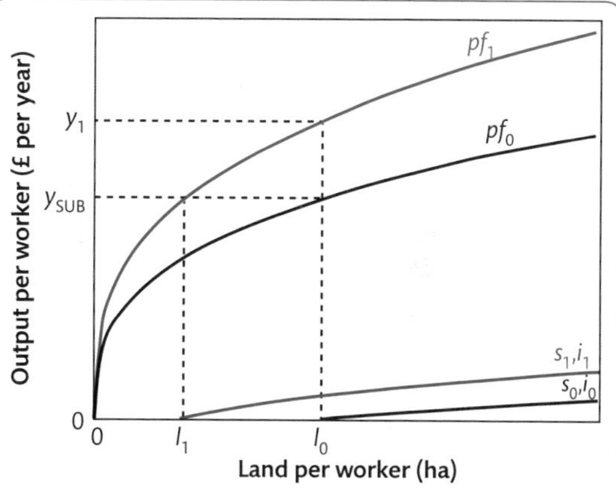

Figure 25.7 **The Malthusian trap**

Initially, there is l_0 land per worker and output per worker is at the subsistence level, y_{SUB}. There no saving or investment. If productivity increases, output per head at first rises to y_1, but then the population rises; Malthus claims that land per worker will eventually fall to l_1, taking output per worker back to y_{SUB}.

occur only at higher incomes. As there is currently no investment, there is no capital to depreciate.

Now suppose there is technological progress: maybe a better system of rotating crops between fields is introduced. Then the production function shifts up to pf_1. Initially, with l_0 land per worker, output per worker rises to y_1. But incomes are now above subsistence, so people have more children. In a few years, these children grow up to become workers, and then land per worker falls. It will do so until it reaches l_1, when output per worker returns to the subsistence level y_{SUB} and people stop having more children.

Malthus predicted that the world's population, or at least most of it, would always be trapped at subsistence incomes, an idea called the **Malthusian trap**. As it happens, Malthus was wrong. In most countries, technology has persistently grown faster than populations, so output per head has risen.

The limits to growth

Malthus is a distant figure whose predictions have proved wrong, so far anyway, but his views are still influential. Many people worry about the world's resources, especially when the world's population is increasing at between 1% and 2% a year. Resources can be divided into those that are renewable, like timber, and those that are not, like oil. Inevitably, concern focuses on the non-renewable ones. Could living standards continue to rise, or even be maintained, if the world's population continued to grow? Or will population growth eventually reduce all our living standards?

The answer is that living standards could continue to rise despite the population growth, although we cannot guarantee that they will rise for ever. And while it might seem obvious that it would help if population growth were slower, section 25.5 will show that population growth brings some benefits.

The key to rising living standards is technological progress. This has many aspects. Consider for example what it could achieve with oil.

- **Technology can increase the usable stock of oil**, by allowing it to be extracted from more difficult places.
- **Technology can reduce the need for oil**, by improving the efficiency with which it is used.
- **Technology can develop alternatives to oil**, such as wind power, wave power, and hydrogen cars.

The potential for technological change to reduce dependence on resources is reflected in the fact that, for most of the 20th century, the price of most natural resources fell in relation to average wage rates. This happened despite the huge growth of population and incomes per head.

We cannot guarantee that technological change will last indefinitely, but the recent past gives some reason for optimism in the future. Over the past 50 years, the world's population has more than doubled, yet living standards for most people have risen in that period.

Convergence and catch-up

An interesting and optimistic implication of the neoclassical growth theory is shown in Figure 25.8. This concerns two countries, one rich and developed, and the other poor and undeveloped. We will make four assumptions, as follows.

- **The rich country has a higher production function, pf_R, than the poor country, pf_P.** This is because the richer country has more advanced technology and more human capital.
- **Each country has a stable population.** So its capital per worker will rise if its investment exceeds its depreciation, which is shown by the line *dep*.
- **The proportion of income saved and invested in each country is the same.** So the height of the *s,i* lines, s_R,i_R and s_P,i_P, as a fraction of the height of the relevant *pf* is the same.
- **Each country starts with the equilibrium capital per worker, where its *i,s* curve intersects *dep*.** So the capital per worker is k_R in the rich country and k_P in the poor country, and the production functions show that the income per worker is y_R in the rich country and y_P in the poor country.

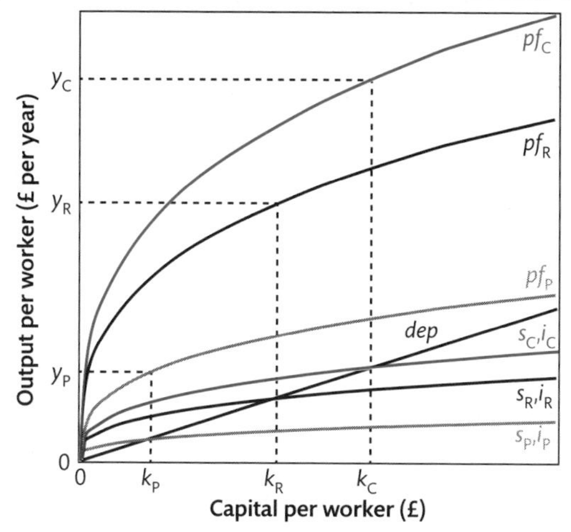

Figure 25.8 **Convergence**

A poor country has less human capital and poorer technology than a rich one, and starts at k_P and y_P compared with k_R and y_R. But its technology may increase faster as it copies from the rich country. If the poor country also catches up on human capital, the economies may in time converge at k_C and y_C.

Over time, technological progress will shift up the *pf* curves. The rich country's *pf* is likely to shift more slowly, because this can shift up only when new technologies are discovered. In contrast, the poor country's *pf* can shift up rapidly by adopting the technology that is already known and used in richer countries, a process called **technology transfer**. So the poor country should grow faster.

In time, poor countries may catch rich ones up. At a distant time in our example, the rich country's *pf* may have shifted the modest distance up to pf_C, while the poor country's may have moved more rapidly to that same line. The subscript C stands for converged, and associated with the converged *pf* is a converged saving and investment line s_C,i_C.

A tendency for income per head in poor countries to catch up the income per head in rich ones is called **convergence**, and it does sometimes occur. For example, since the 1980s, India, China, and some other formerly poor East Asian countries have grown greatly. And within the developed world, the richest countries such as the US and Switzerland have tended to grow the slowest.

But other poor countries, notably many in Africa, have not tended to converge. There are many reasons why convergence may not always happen, or at least not quickly. They include the following.

- **Some countries have rapid population growth.** Figure 25.3 showed that population growth reduces the equilibrium output per worker.
- **The production function depends also on human capital.** So a poor country needs to catch up on education and experience as well as technology, and this could be a long, drawn-out process.
- **Technology may be protected by patents.** A poor country may be unable to pay patent holders the fees they charge for using their technology.
- **Countries may have different saving ratios.** Even if pf_C were to apply to all countries, a country that saves and invests a lower fraction of its income than shown by s_C,i_C will have a saving and investment curve below s_C,i_C and so end up with less capital than k_C and a lower output per worker than y_C. A country that saves and invests more will end up with more capital and a higher output.
- **Some countries have excessive regulation.** It is often claimed that India's development was restrained until the 1980s by excessive regulation and bureaucracy.
- **Some countries are not very open to the world economy.** China had a very insular outlook until the 1980s. This restricted the inflow of technology from abroad. It also reduced the potential for trade to raise living standards, which we will discuss in Chapter 27.
- **Some countries have political instability.** This deters the investment in the extra capital that is needed for growth.

A further point to note is that, in some countries, the proportion of the population in the labour force is low. So, even if convergence were to give two countries equal capital and output per worker, say y_C in Figure 25.8, their outputs per head of population would differ if different proportions of their populations were in the labour force.

A widening income gap

There is a pessimistic point to make alongside the optimistic possibility of convergence. Some of the world's poorest countries still have virtually subsistence levels of income. So they can have little saving and investment, which means they can hardly increase their capital per worker or, in turn, their incomes per head. But incomes per head elsewhere continue to rise. So there is an ever-increasing gap between the incomes in these countries and incomes elsewhere.

Policies for growth

The neoclassical model implies that there are several ways in which a country's government could try to increase output per worker.

- **Encouraging people to save and invest more.** This should be pursued only if the saving ratio is below the golden rule. It might be pursued by having lower taxes on the income that people get on their saving, by having lower interest rates, by having subsidies or tax breaks on investment, and by promoting competition between firms.
- **Trying to increase human capital.** For example, the government might spend more on education and on retraining workers with dated skills.
- **Encouraging more people to join the workforce.** This aim might be pursued by altering the tax and transfer system.

But while these policies will lead to higher growth for a while, the neoclassical model says that sustained growth can be achieved only by having technological change. This can be stimulated with various policies, including the following.

- **Stimulating the research and development (R&D) that leads to progress by the invention and development of new production techniques.** Firms may be discouraged from doing R&D if their new ideas could at once be copied by competitors who did not have to spend money doing the R&D themselves. Governments can help to overcome this problem by giving firms legal protection with patents. Indeed, it is likely that one reason why the Industrial Revolution started in Britain was that, by the 18th century, it had developed the most effective patent laws.
- **Stimulating basic research.** Firms may always be reluctant to do basic research with no immediate prospect of commercial use. But such research often proves in time to be useful. Governments can pay bodies such as universities to do it.
- **Stimulating investment in the new physical capital that is needed for new production techniques.** This is called **embodied technological change**.
- **Stimulating the use of new ideas in management and organization.** This is called **disembodied technological change**.

25.4 Summary

- Malthus argued that population growth would always trap most people on subsistence incomes. In fact, technology has grown faster than populations, and living standards for most people continue to rise.
- Technological progress can be quicker in poor countries than rich ones, because poor countries can copy the rich ones. So incomes per head may converge in time. This happens sometimes, but not always. Some poor countries are hindered by population growth, political instability, and few funds to invest.
- The only way of having permanently higher growth rates is to have permanently faster technological change. Governments can help here by supporting research and development.

25.5 Endogenous growth theory

The neoclassical growth theory that we have studied so far says that sustained growth in output per head requires sustained technological change. But it says nothing about the factors that determine the rate of technological change. So the actual rate of growth depends on factors that are exogenous to the theory, making it an exogenous growth theory.

Since the 1980s, many economists have tried to develop models of growth that include the factors that determine the growth rate. So these factors lie inside their models, or are endogenous to them, and that means that each of their models is an **endogenous growth theory**.

There are several endogenous growth models, and there is much active work in this field. This section merely gives a flavour of two strands of thought, both closely associated with the American economist Paul Romer.

Growth and ideas

The first strand of thought begins by asking why there may be sustained technological progress. A key insight here is that technological progress requires ideas. For example, people have had ideas for new types of capital, like wheels, printing presses, steam engines, plastics, and microchips, and also ideas for new processes, like assembly lines and self-service checkouts.

Sustained technological progress requires a sustained flow of ideas, and most ideas require a great deal of research and development (R&D). So how can we encourage firms to spend large sums on R&D? Firms face the problem that ideas are non-rival, which means that they can be used simultaneously by many people. For example, a car maker might spend huge sums developing a better type of hydrogen engine, only to find it used almost immediately by other car makers.

This problem forms a case for governments to promote R&D. Sometimes they subsidize it. And often they allow firms to protect their ideas with patents and copyrights. This protection does not mean that a firm's ideas cannot be copied, but it means that its ideas can be used by others only in return for a fee. So firms that have good ideas will get a profit from their R&D spending.

The need for more and more new ideas

We saw in Figure 25.1 that the UK economy has grown fairly steadily at around 2% for the last 40 years. You might suppose that steady growth like this requires a fairly steady stream of ideas. In fact, a steady stream of ideas is not sufficient, as we will now see using Table 25.1.

This table concerns an economy in which the index of GDP per head in year 1 is 100.0. Suppose, for simplicity, that people want GDP per head to grow by 10% each year. Then the index for real GDP per head must be 110.0 in year 2, 121.0 in year 3, 133.1 in year 4, and so on. So the index must grow by 10.0 between year 1 and year 2, by 11.0 between year 2 and year 3, and by 12.1 between year 3 and year 4. So if GDP per head is to grow at a steady rate, then it must actually rise by a greater absolute amount each year.

Suppose that each year's GDP per head depends on how many ideas have been had in times past before the start of the year, and suppose that 10 ideas are needed for each point on the index. So at the start of year 1, 1,000 ideas must have been had beforehand so

Table 25.1 **The need for new ideas if GDP per head is to grow at a constant rate, here 10% per year**

Year	Index of real GDP per head	Growth of GDP per head index from year before	Stock of ideas at start of year	New ideas needed during the year
1	100.0		1,000	100
2	110.0	10.0	1,100	110
3	121.0	11.0	1,210	121
4	133.1	12.1	1,331	

that the index can be 100.0 that year. We can then work out how many ideas are needed in later years.

- **For the index to be 110.0 in year 2,** there must have been 1,100 ideas before the start of year 2; this is 100 more than at the start of year 1, so there must be 100 ideas in year 1.
- **For the index to be 121.0 in year 3,** there must have been 1,210 ideas before the start of year 3; this is 110 more than at the start of year 2, so there must be 110 ideas in year 2.
- **For the index to be 133.1 in year 4,** there must have been 1,331 ideas before the start of year 4; this is 121 more than at the start of year 3, so there must be 121 ideas in year 3.

This example shows that if GDP per head is to grow at a constant rate, and so by a greater absolute amount each year, then new ideas are needed at an increasing rate, 100 in year 1, 110 in year 2, 121 in year 3, and so on.

Obtaining more and more ideas

In this model, the growth rate depends on the rate at which new ideas occur. It may seem impossible for an economy, or even the world, to have ideas at faster and faster rates for ever. So it may seem that growth must eventually slow down. However, two ways in which ideas might arise at faster rates have been suggested.

- **As the number of ideas that have been had in the past increases, people may find it easier to have new ideas.** If this were so, then a constant number of R&D workers would have more ideas each year. However, there is little evidence to support this suggestion. Indeed, it might be that people have the obvious ideas first, so that having new and less obvious ideas in future requires ever more and more effort.
- **More and more people could be allocated to R&D.** This would help more ideas to be had each year, but it would not be easy if the world's population were constant, because using more people for R&D would mean using fewer to produce goods and services. But if the world's population growth continues, then more people can used for both R&D and production.

So population growth might be the key to sustained economic growth. Indeed, perhaps it is no coincidence that the world's population and output per head have both risen so much since the Industrial Revolution. Perhaps the population explosion helped the growth of output per head?

This conclusion leads to a more optimistic view of population growth than arose in section 25.3. There, we saw that population growth reduces output per head in a situation in which technology is static. Now we see that this drawback of population growth may be handsomely offset by its helping technology to improve indefinitely.

The concept behind $y = Ak$ growth theories

A second strand of endogenous growth theory argues that increases in the physical capital per worker shift the production function upwards. Figure 25.9 illustrates this. Here, the economy initially faces the production function pf_0 and has capital per worker of k_0. So output per worker is y_0 and the economy is at the point marked ***a***.

Now suppose that for some reason capital per worker increases to k_1. The neoclassical theory predicts that output per worker will rise to y_1, which we read off pf_0. However, there is a group of endogenous growth theories that argue that if the capital stock rises, then the production function will shift up above pf_0, say to pf_1. So with capital per worker at k_1, the economy will end up at point ***b***.

These theories do not merely say that the production function will shift up. They say that it will shift up by exactly enough to leave the origin, ***a***, and ***b*** on a straight line. And if capital per worker rose again, say to k_2, then the production function would shift up again to pf_2, which is exactly enough to take the economy to ***c***, which is also on the same straight line.

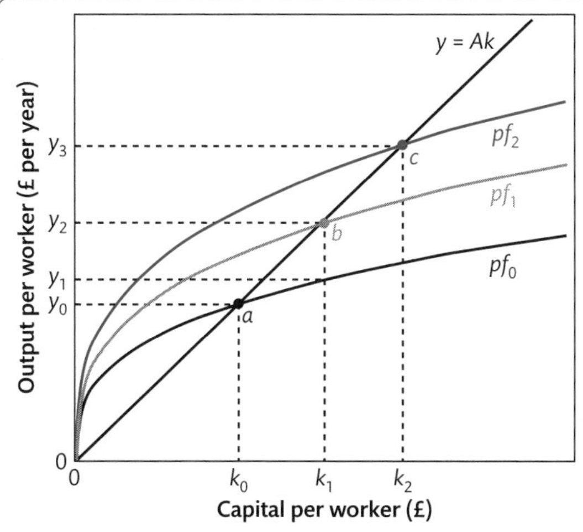

Figure 25.9 **The $y = Ak$ line**

The economy starts with production function pf_0 and capital per worker k_0, so output per worker is y_0 and the economy is at ***a***. A group of endogenous growth theories argue that if the capital per worker rises to k_1, and then to k_2, the production function will shift to pf_1 and then to pf_2, taking the economy to ***b*** and then to ***c***. ***a***, ***b***, and ***c*** lie on the straight line $y = Ak$, so that output per worker is proportional to capital per worker.

The fact that this line is straight means that output per worker ends up being proportional to capital per worker. For example, k_2 is actually double k_0, and this leads to y_2 being double y_0.

We call this straight line $y = Ak$, where y is output per worker, k is capital per worker, and A is a constant. Growth theories that refer to a straight line like this, and so regard output per worker as being proportional to capital per worker, are called **$y = Ak$ models**.

We must now explain why these theories believe a rise in capital per worker shifts the production function, and then see what they believe determines the growth rate.

Why the production function may shift

Various suggestions have been made about why a rise in capital per worker may shift the production function, including the following.

- **Learning by doing.** The firms that acquired the extra capital between k_0 and k_1 in Figure 25.9 now produce in a more capital-intensive way, and over time their workers will acquire new experience and skills, which will increase their human capital. This rise in human capital will shift the production function up.
- **Creating a pool of extra human capital.** The firms in which workers have acquired extra human capital create a pool of human capital that can then be used by other firms if they recruit any of those workers. Then the new skills pass to their workers, so human capital rises again, shifting the production function up.
- **Creating a pool of ideas.** The firms that expanded may have faced new challenges and have had new ideas that other firms can use, because ideas are non-rival. These ideas may allow other firms to improve their own technology or the human capital of their own workers, so shifting the production function up.
- **Helping other firms make technological progress.** If the firms that acquire extra capital can in time reduce their prices or develop better products, then this will benefit any other firms that use their products. This might help those firms to make technological progress, shifting the production function up.

The growth rate in $y = Ak$ models

Figure 25.10 illustrates what the $y = Ak$ models believe determines the growth rate. This figure repeats $y = Ak$ from Figure 25.9. This line shows the output per worker for each level of capital per worker, and so it also shows the income per worker for each level of capital per worker. Assuming, as in the neoclassical model, that a constant proportion of income is saved and invested, then saving and investment per worker will be shown by a sloping straight line, say *s,i*.

The figure also shows the depreciation per worker with the line *dep*. As before, this slopes upwards because there is more capital to depreciate when

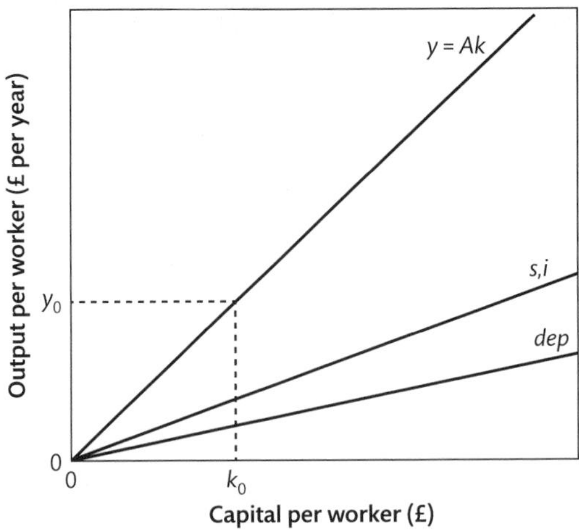

Figure 25.10 **Growth rate in $y = Ak$ models**

The line $y = Ak$ shows output per worker, and in turn income per worker, at each level of k. The line *s,i* shows saving and investment per worker. If, as shown, this is steeper than the depreciation line, d, then at any level of k such as k_0, capital deepening will occur, leading to sustained growth.

the capital stock is high. As drawn, *s,i* is steeper than *dep*.

Suppose capital per worker is initially k_0. Here, investment per worker exceeds depreciation, so capital per worker will rise and output per worker will rise. But no matter how high capital per worker gets, investment will exceed depreciation because *s,i* is always above *dep*, so capital per worker and output per worker will continue to rise. So $y = Ak$ models offer an explanation for sustained growth.

Note that if *s,i* were a little flatter, and coincided with *dep*, then at k_0 investment would equal depreciation. So capital per worker would not rise and there would be zero growth.

Question 25.2 What would happen if output per worker were initially k_0, and the saving and investment line was flatter than the depreciation line?

We can now derive a formula for growth. As output per worker is related to capital per worker by $y = Ak$, it follows that the change in output per worker between one period of time and another, Δy, is related to the change in the capital stock per worker, Δk, as follows:

$$\Delta y = A.\Delta k$$

Δk depends on two factors.

- **The amount of saving and investment per worker.** We take this to be a constant fraction of income, s, so investment equals sy.
- **Depreciation per worker.** Depreciation is proportional to the amount of capital. And, in $y = Ak$ models, output is also proportional to the amount of capital. This means that depreciation must be proportional to output. We call this proportion d. So depreciation per worker equals dy.

It follows that the change in the capital stock per worker equals $sy - dy$, which is $(s - d)y$. So:

$$\Delta y = A(s - d)y.$$

Dividing each side of this by y gives:

$$\Delta y/y = A(s - d).$$

The left-hand side of this equation shows the growth in output per worker as a fraction of total output per worker, that is the growth rate, g. So these endogenous models conclude that:

$$g = A(s - d).$$

Policy implication of the $y = Ak$ theories

The main policy implication of the $y = Ak$ models is that if people can be encouraged to save and invest a higher fraction of their income, so that s increases, then the growth rate, g, will increase permanently. In contrast, Figure 25.4 showed that, in the neoclassical model, a higher saving ratio will raise the growth rate only temporarily.

The validity of the $y = Ak$ models

Most economists are somewhat sceptical about the $y = Ak$ models. However, one piece of support for them may come from the fact that growth rates often vary widely between countries that are at similar stages of development. It is hard to explain this using the neoclassical model, but $y = Ak$ models offer an explanation in cases in which the countries have different saving ratios.

A problem for the $y = Ak$ models is that increases in capital per worker must shift the production function up by just enough to keep the economy on the $y = Ak$ line, as in Figure 25.9. If they shift the production function more, then output per worker will rise more than proportionately to capital per worker, and this is never observed. If they shift it less, then output per worker will rise less than proportionately to capital per worker, as assumed in the neoclassical model.

25.5 **Summary**

- Endogenous growth models include the factors that determine the rate of growth.
- One type of model focuses on the idea that a sustained growth rate needs ideas to occur at an accelerating rate. This might be helped if the world population continues to grow.
- Another type of model suggests that output per worker, y, is related to capital per worker, k, by the equation $y = Ak$, where A is a constant. These models suggest that the growth rate depends on the proportion of income that is saved and invested, along with the amount of depreciation that occurs.

25.2 **Everyday economics**

Beyond population growth

Virtually all demographic projections expect the number of humans on earth to reach a maximum in this century, which may lead to a slowing of ideas and so in technology growth. Many forces could offset this change: the effective number of people with whom each individual can share ideas could grow through more intense integration; rising levels of human capital per head could make the average individual better at discovering and sharing ideas; and the fraction of the available human capital that is devoted to producing and sharing ideas could go up. So it is quite possible that technology growth could continue for the foreseeable future and even increase, even if growth in the stock of ideas is no longer to be supported by population growth.

Charles I. Jones & Paul M. Romer, 'The new Kaldor facts: ideas, institutions, population, and human capital', *American Economic Journal: Macroeconomics*, January 2010, Vol. 2 No. 1.

Comment A further population issue in many countries, including the UK, is that the population is aging, so that the proportion aged between 16 and 65 is shrinking. To keep living standards growing, there may have to be a higher retirement age as well as technological progress.

In the next chapter we bring together our discussions on unemployment, inflation, business cycles, and growth, and use them to discuss the government's macroeconomic policies.

abc Glossary

Capital accumulation: a growth in the capital stock.

Capital deepening: capital accumulation that results in more capital per worker.

Capital widening: capital accumulation that is needed to keep the capital per worker at its original level when the workforce increases.

Convergence: a tendency for the income per head in poor countries to catch up with the income per head in rich countries.

Disembodied technological change: the use of new ideas in management and organization.

Embodied technological change: investment in the physical capital needed for new production techniques.

Endogenous growth theory: a theory of growth that offers an explanation of the actual growth rate, as the relevant factors lie inside the model.

Exogenous growth theory: a theory of growth that offers no explanation of the actual growth rate, as the relevant factors lie outside the model.

Golden rule: the saving ratio that maximizes consumption.

Growth accounting: a statistical exercise that tries to see how different factors contribute to growth.

Labour-augmenting technological progress: technological change that makes workers more productive.

Malthusian trap: the idea that the world's population, or at least most of it, will always be trapped at subsistence incomes.

Rule of 72: the fact that if a variable grows at a given rate of x% per year, then it will double in approximately $72/x$ years.

Technology transfer: adopting the technology that is already known and used in other countries.

Total factor productivity: the relationship between the quantity of a country's output and the quantity of inputs that it uses.

$y = Ak$ models: growth theories in which output per worker, y, is proportional to capital per worker, k.

= Answers to in-text questions

25.1 Assuming the increased durability is a one-off change, capital per worker will increase to where s,i intersects the new depreciation line, and output per worker will rise. But there will be no sustained growth after that.

25.2 In this case, investment per worker would be less than depreciation, so the capital per worker would fall, leading to a sustained fall in output, or negative growth. Presumably people would eventually decide to invest a larger proportion of their incomes to arrest this fall in output: otherwise incomes would eventually be zero!

? Questions for review

25.1 Countries A and B have different production functions, so that, with any common level of physical capital per worker, output per worker would be higher in A. Why might their production functions differ like this?

25.2 Countries C and D have identical production functions. There is currently no technological progress, and each country has the equilibrium amount of capital per worker. But C has the higher output per worker. Why might this be so?

25.3 Countries E and F have identical production functions and there is currently no technological progress. But E is growing while F is not. Why might this be the case?

25.4 Suppose that increases in capital per worker do shift the production function up. But suppose they do not shift it up enough to raise output per worker in proportion to capital per worker. Would this give a growth model the results of which were identical to the neoclassical model?

? Questions for discussion

25.1 Do you believe that there are any social problems that have been aggravated by economic growth? If so, could society change in a way that permitted future growth without these problems getting worse? Could growth even help to ease these problems?

25.2 Consider the advantages and disadvantages of sustained growth in the world's population on the future of living standards. How might the living standards of different countries grow at different rates, depending on their population growth rates?

Common student errors

The chief errors made in growth theory arise from not grasping two of its most surprising results. One of these results, which arises in the neoclassical growth model, is that sustained growth in living standards will occur only if there is sustained technological progress; in contrast, an increase in the saving ratio will increase the growth rate only temporarily. The other result, which arises in endogenous growth theory, is that ideas need to come in ever-growing numbers for constant growth—and this might be helped if the world's population continues to grow.

26

Monetary, Fiscal, and Supply-side Policies

Remember from Chapter 20 that changes in Bank Rate affect the money stock and interest rates generally, and recall from Chapter 21 that, in the long run, output is in equilibrium at the potential level, which is the level produced when the labour market is in equilibrium with unemployment at its natural rate.

Everyone likes to complain about the way in which the government manages the economy. But suppose you became Chancellor, how would you react to the situation you inherited? Also, would you announce in advance how you would react when conditions changed in the future? How would you instruct the Bank of England to operate monetary policy? How worried would you be about the government's deficit and its debt? Would you try to manage aggregate supply as well as aggregate demand, and, if so, how?

This chapter shows you how to answer questions like these, by understanding:

- output gaps;
- rules versus discretion;
- monetary policy targets and instruments;
- the transmission mechanism of Bank Rate decisions and quantitative easing;
- the problems of government deficits and debts;
- supply-side policies.

26.1 Macroeconomic policy: appraising the current situation

Becoming Chancellor of the Exchequer

Macroeconomic policy concerns us all, because it affects economic growth, unemployment, and inflation, and it involves interest rates, taxes, and government spending. However, we will begin this chapter by looking at it from the perspective of the Chancellor of the Exchequer, who is in charge of it. And we will add a twist, and suppose that, on some future date, when the economic situation may be very different from what it is now, you become Chancellor, even perhaps the first female one.

If you have studied economics for a year or so, then you will have had more formal training in economics than most Chancellors. But you know that this training is just a beginning, so you may be pleased to be met at the Treasury by a team of highly qualified economic advisers.

However, one problem with these advisers is that their views may vary. Some may be new monetarists, some new classicists, some new Keynesians, and some Post Keynesians; some may adopt other views that we have not had time to mention; and some may believe that all schools of economic thought have important insights.

The current economic situation

The first topic that you will discuss with these advisers will be the relationship between the current equilibrium level of output, Y_E, and the potential level of output, Y_P. But before we discuss this here, let's recall two features of Y_P.

- **Y_P is the output at which the long-run aggregate supply curve LAS_0 is a vertical line.** This is shown in each part of Figure 26.1.
- **Y_P is the output at which unemployment would be at its natural rate.** Equivalently, the unemployment rate would equal NAIRU, that is the rate at which the inflation rate will not change.

Now the equilibrium level of output is determined by the current aggregate demand curve, AD_0, and the current short-run aggregate supply curve, SAS_0. Depending on where these curves intersect, there are three possible relationships between Y_E, and Y_P, as shown in the three parts of Figure 26.1. These possibilities are as follows.

- **Y_E equals Y_P**, as in case (a). This rarely occurs.
- **Y_E is below Y_P**, as in case (b). When Y_E is below Y_P, the gap between them is called a recessionary gap, or a negative output gap, and unemployment is above the natural rate.
- **Y_E is above Y_P**, as in case (c). When Y_E exceeds Y_P, the gap between them is called an inflationary gap, or a positive output gap, and it threatens accelerating inflation.

Your views on the policies that you might adopt will depend on which of these three situations applies. To see this, we will look at these situations in turn, and we will also refer to four types of policy to shift aggregate demand.

- **Expansionary monetary policies**: these involve raising the money stock and reducing interest rates to shift *AD* to the right.
- **Contractionary monetary policies**: these involve reducing the money stock and raising interest rates to shift *AD* to the left.
- **Expansionary fiscal policies**: these involve tax cuts or more government spending to shift *AD* to the right.
- **Contractionary fiscal policies**: these involve tax rises or less government spending to shift *AD* to the left.

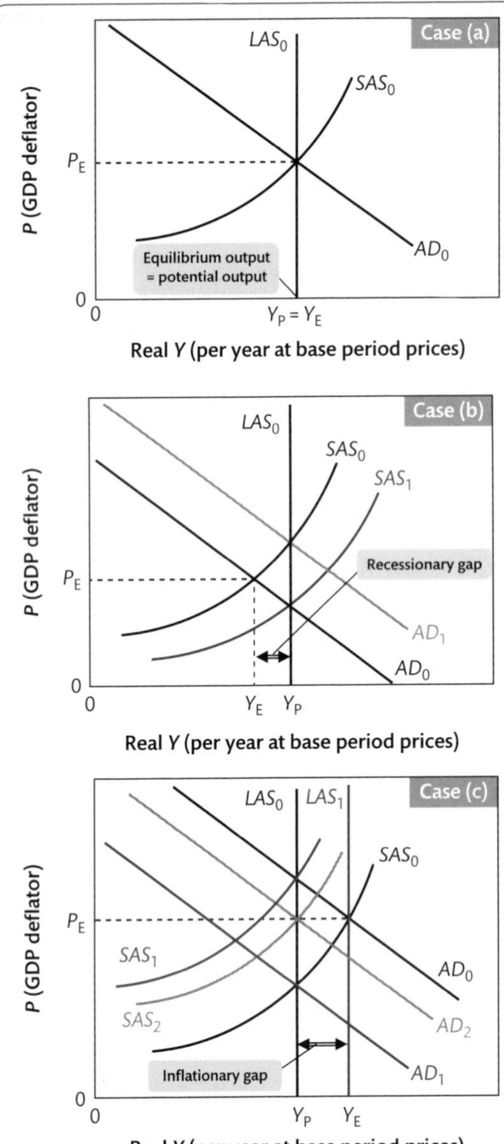

Figure 26.1 **Equilibrium and potential output**

In case (a), Y_E equals Y_P. In case (b), Y_E is below Y_P, so unemployment is above the natural rate or NAIRU, but it would fall if flexible wages shifted short-run aggregate supply to SAS_1, or if aggregate demand was shifted to AD_1. In case (c), Y_E is above Y_P, so unemployment is below NAIRU, and flexible wages would add to inflationary pressure by shifting aggregate supply to SAS_1. Inflation could be restrained if aggregate demand was shifted to AD_1, or shifted only to AD_2, but with a credible target of zero inflation that shifted short-run aggregate supply to SAS_2; alternatively, supply-side policies might shift long-run aggregate supply to LAS_1.

Case (a): output is equal to potential output

If Y_E equals Y_P, as case (b) in Figure 26.1, then you might think it best to take no action. After all, an expansionary policy would raise output above Y_P and so take unemployment below NAIRU, causing inflation to accelerate, and a contractionary policy would reduce output below Y_P, so that unemployment would rise above the natural rate.

But suppose you think the growth rate is too low. You would like to increase the money stock in order to reduce interest rates and stimulate investment, but you know this will cause inflation to accelerate, partly because the unemployment rate will fall below NAIRU, and partly because a higher money stock will increase the rate of inflation that people expect.

However, you could try to combine an expansionary monetary policy with a contractionary fiscal policy in a very careful way so that their effects on aggregate demand exactly cancelled out. Then AD_0 would still apply, leaving output unchanged at Y_P. But the expansionary monetary policy would reduce interest rates.

Case (b): output is less than potential output

If Y_E is below Y_P, as shown in case (b) in Figure 26.1, your main concern will be unemployment. Here are two ways in which you might respond.

- **Wait for wages to fall and shift short-run aggregate supply to SAS_1, so removing the recessionary gap**. New classical and new monetarist advisers would advise this, believing it will happen quite quickly. New Keynesians and Post Keynesians would oppose it, believing it will happen slowly, or maybe not at all.
- **Apply an expansionary monetary or fiscal policy to shift aggregate demand to AD_1, so removing the recessionary gap**. New Keynesian and

Post Keynesian advisers would advise this, so that wages would not have to fall.

In the light of this advice, you might not want to rely on wage flexibility, in case it does turn out to be slow. But if you adopt an expansionary policy, you must be alert to three concerns.

- **Inflation concerns**. By raising demand, you will raise the price level. This might in turn raise people's expectations about future inflation and so create inflationary pressure.
- **Budget concerns**. An expansionary fiscal policy requires higher government spending or lower taxes. Either way, the result is likely to be a budget deficit, that is a gap between the government's spending and its tax revenue that it must finance with loans. We will look at deficits and their problems later in the chapter.
- **Growth concerns**. An expansionary fiscal policy initially has no effect on interest rates, but as incomes start to rise, the demand for money increases, so interest rates rise and this hurts investment and growth. In contrast, an expansionary monetary policy at once reduces interest rates; and while the subsequent rise in incomes and the demand for money will put some upward pressure on interest rates, they will end up lower than they started, stimulating investment and growth. So if growth is a major issue, you may focus on monetary expansion.

Case (c): output is above potential output

If Y_E is above Y_P, as shown in case (c) in Figure 26.1, your main concern will be accelerating inflation. Here are four ways in which you could respond.

- **Wait for wages to rise and shift short-run aggregate supply to SAS_1, so removing the inflationary gap**. The snag with this anti-inflation policy is that it actually means letting the price level rise above the initial level P_E.
- **Apply a contractionary monetary, or fiscal policy to shift aggregate demand to the left to AD_1, so removing the inflationary gap**. In this case, the price level will actually fall.
- **Announce that you want zero inflation and that you will use monetary policy to shift aggregate demand to AD_2, which intersects LAS_0 at the current price level**. The hope is that if employers and workers believe your announcements, then they will agree wages that will shift short-run aggregate supply to SAS_2. Then the economy will settle where this intersects both AD_2 and LAS_0, so output will and up at Y_P and the price level will stay at P_E, so that there is indeed no inflation.
- **Try to shift long-run aggregate supply to the right to LAS_1, so removing the inflationary gap**. A policy to shift long-run aggregate supply is called a **supply-side policy**. We will discuss supply-side policies later in the chapter and see that, although they are appealing, they are hard to apply and slow to work.

Many advisers would suggest that you to use two or more of these responses. If you include a contractionary policy, you must be alert to two concerns.

- **Unemployment concerns**. If you reduce aggregate demand, unemployment will rise. Admittedly, output is initially above Y_P, so that unemployment is below NAIRU and causing inflationary pressure, so higher unemployment is reasonable from an economic perspective. But you will get adverse headlines in the media.
- **Growth concerns**. A contractionary fiscal policy initially has no effect on interest rates, but as incomes fall, the demand for money falls, so interest rates fall and this promotes investment and growth. In contrast, a contractionary monetary policy at once raises interest rates; while the subsequent fall in incomes and the demand for money

will put some downward pressure on interest rates, they will end up higher than they started, harming interest rates and growth. So if growth is a major issue, you should avoid a contractionary monetary policy.

Discretionary policies versus rules policies

Even when you have tackled the current economic situation, you know the economy will face shocks in the future. You can react to these in two ways.

- **By using discretionary policies**: in this case, you will look at each shock as it happens and choose whatever policy seems right at the time.
- **By using rules policies**: in this case, you will announce in advance how you will respond to future shocks of various types.

You may think that discretionary polices sound best, so that you can fine-tune them according to the current situation. But many economists would prefer you to use rules policies, for these reasons.

- **Discretionary policies and elections**. Chancellors want their political party to win the next election. So, shortly before an election, they may want to cut interest rates or taxes, or raise government spending, even if the current state of the economy makes this unwise. They may also reduce aggregate demand after an election, sending the economy into a modest downturn, and then boost demand shortly before the next election, hoping that, by election day, output will be rising and unemployment will be falling, while inflation will be under control. So politicians who adopt discretionary policies may abuse them by creating **political business cycles**, that is business cycles that relate to election times.
- **Discretionary fiscal policy and time lags**. Fiscal policy involves changes in tax rates and government spending. But these changes often need the approval of Parliament, so they can be changed only in a Budget, which is usually held once a year, or in a special 'minibudget'. Even when the changes are approved, it may be some time before they are put in place and have any effect. So economists are wary about using discretionary fiscal policy, although many supported it in the major recession in 2008.
- **Discretionary monetary policy and expectations**. Monetary policy centres on the Bank of England's Bank Rate: this can be changed without recourse to Parliament, so monetary policy can be used quickly to nudge aggregate demand. However, we saw in Chapter 23 that most schools of thought advocate using a rule for monetary policy, such as a Taylor rule; with this, the Bank of England would have a target rate of inflation, and if the actual rate were to go above target, then it would generally raise Bank Rate enough to cause a fall in aggregate demand that would bring inflation back to the target level. If the Bank were to follow a rule like this, then people would expect it to secure a low rate of inflation, and low expectations help to keep inflation under control. But if Bank Rate were instead altered on a discretionary basis, then the power of a rule to hold expectations down would be lost.

Issues for discussion

In the following sections, we will look more closely at monetary policy, fiscal policy, and supply-side policies. Finally, we will consider the problems for economic policy in the UK since 2010.

However, this chapter largely ignores one important aspect of monetary and fiscal policies. This is that they can affect transactions between the UK and other countries, and in turn affect the exchange rate between sterling and other currencies. These effects strongly influence the views of Chancellors about monetary and fiscal policies. We consider these issues in Chapter 28.

26.1 **Summary**

- Governments can react to recessionary gaps by waiting for wages to fall or with expansionary policies.
- Governments can react to inflationary gaps with contractionary policies, or with credible announcements about restraining inflation, or with supply-side policies that shift long-run aggregate supply.
- Governments can react to shocks on a discretionary basis, choosing whatever policies seem best at the time, or on a rules basis, announcing ahead how they will react to different types of shock.
- Discretionary polices have drawbacks: these include the possibility of governments using discretionary policies to create political business cycles, the lags involved if discretionary fiscal policies are used, and the problem of restraining inflationary expectations if discretionary monetary policies are used.

26.2 Monetary policy: targets, instruments, and central banks

This section looks briefly at five issues concerning monetary policy, as follows.

- **What targets should monetary policy pursue?**
- **What instruments can a central bank use to conduct monetary policy?**
- **How far should the government allow the central bank to take monetary policy decisions?**
- **How does the Bank of England make decisions?**
- **What happens in the eurozone and the US?**

Monetary policy targets

Although monetary policy can be used to tackle inflationary or recessionary gaps, the chief aim of monetary policy until the 1970s was simply to hold interest rates at low levels. This made sense because unemployment and inflation were generally low, as we saw in Figures 17.3 and 17.5 (on pages 368 and 374), and the government wanted low interest rates to promote investment and growth.

However, by the 1970s, inflation had accelerated, reaching 28% in 1975. Many people argued that, in the pursuit of low interest rates, the money stock had been allowed to grow too rapidly. Since the 1970s, the chief aim of monetary policy has been to restrain inflation.

For some years, governments set target rates of growth for the money stock, M. This approach was based on the relationship $MV = PY$, where V is the velocity of circulation, P is the price level, and Y is real output. It was thought that V was fairly stable, while Y can change only slowly, so changes in P should depend chiefly on changes in M.

However, targeting the growth rate for M fell from favour. This was because the relationship between changes in P and the growth of M proved to be very erratic, and that was chiefly because V is not very stable. To take a recent example, V in the UK fell by over a third between 2005 and 2010.

So, in 1992, the UK moved from targeting the money stock to targeting inflation itself. Most other developed nations now do likewise. This strategy broadly accords with the idea behind the Taylor rule, which we met in Chapter 23.

However, the UK's approach differs from a Taylor rule in that the aim is not to try to keep the current inflation rate at the target rate. Instead, it tries to ensure that the rate in two years' time will be at the target rate. So monetary policy could be tightened at a time when the inflation rate was below target, if it were expected to rise above target in two years' time. The logic here is that monetary policy takes time to have its full effects.

On the other hand, the UK's approach does follow a Taylor rule in looking beyond inflation to support the government's objectives for growth and employment. So, if unemployment is very high or growth is very low, then monetary policy might be eased, even if that threatened to take inflation above target in two years' time.

Targeting policies also need to consider the effect of changes in interest rates on the relationship between the value of sterling and other currencies. We will explore this issue in Chapter 28.

Instruments of monetary control

We saw in Chapter 20 that there are four main instruments of monetary control that a central bank like the Bank of England can use to alter the money stock and general level of interest rates.

- **Imposing reserve ratio controls on the commercial banks**. The UK has not used this instrument since the 1980s. This is because banks have many types of asset and liability, and it is hard to devise effective controls in a complex world.
- **Interest rate control**. This is the Bank of England's main instrument. It involves changing its official interest rate known as Bank Rate.
- **Open-market operations**. With this instrument, the central bank chiefly buys or sells government securities in the open market, and so alters the reserves of the commercial banks. The Bank of England uses this instrument to back up interest rate control and quantitative easing.
- **Quantitative easing**. We will explore this instrument in the next section.

The monetary policy role of the central bank

Until 1998, monetary policy in the UK was entirely the responsibility of the government. It set the targets, it chose the instruments to use, and it decided when to use them. The Bank of England's role was essentially restricted to applying the instruments as and when required.

In 1998, the Bank of England was given more freedom and is now called an independent central bank. Many other countries have also moved towards having independent banks. However, although becoming independent has given the central banks more responsibility, it has not made them free from control. Governments can still set the targets, and they can always remove any independence their central banks currently have.

The UK government's chief role in monetary policy is to set the inflation target that the Bank of England should pursue, while also considering the government's objectives for growth and employment. Since 2004, the inflation target has been set as an inflation rate in two years' time of 2% per year, as measured by the consumer prices index (CPI), which we met in Chapter 17.

The Bank cannot achieve 2% exactly, because the economy faces constant shocks and because any actions the Bank takes in response to those shocks need time to have their effect. So the Bank is actually asked to achieve a rate between 1% and 3%. If it fails, it must write an open letter to the Chancellor saying why, and how it intends to bring inflation back into that range.

Given that inflation has problems, which we discussed in Chapter 17, you may wonder why the government sets a target inflation rate of 2%, rather than 0%. There are two reasons.

- **To help real wages to fall when this is needed**. Whenever unemployment exceeds the natural rate, real wages must fall in order for it to return to the natural rate. However, workers resist falls in nominal wages, so the easiest way for real wages to fall is to keep nominal wages constant and let prices rise slightly.
- **To reduce the risk of having falling prices**. A target above 0% reduces the risk that the price level might fall. Falling price levels are best avoided because they encourage people to spend less, while they

wait for prices to fall further, and may therefore send the country into recession.

The case for making the Bank independent is that if the government takes day-to-day decisions, then it will be affected by electoral considerations, whereas if the Bank takes them, it will not. There are two reasons why it is best for decisions to be taken by a body with no interest in elections.

- **Long-term economic health**. Electoral considerations may lead governments to take decisions that put their short-term popularity ahead of the long-term interests of the economy.
- **Credibility**. If people know that interest rates are set by the government, and that it will be reluctant to have high interest rates, especially before an election, then its announcements about inflation targets may lack credibility.

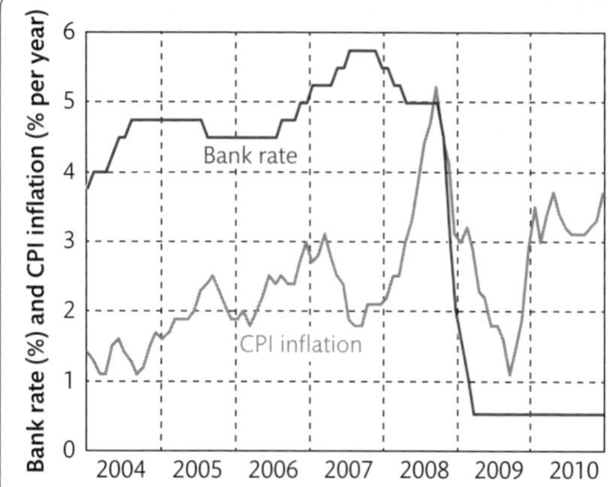

Figure 26.2 **Bank Rate and CPI inflation, 2004–10**

CPI inflation was held within the 1–3% target range for most of 2004–07. Bank Rate was raised in 2007 when forecasts suggested inflation would rise; Bank Rate was cut in 2008 when forecasts suggested inflation would fall.

Sources: For CPI, Office for National Statistics online data; for Bank Rate, Bank of England Statistical Interactive Database.

Decision-making at the Bank of England

The Bank of England relies chiefly on changes in Bank Rate to try to meet its inflation target. The government requires its decisions about Bank Rate to be made by what is called the Monetary Policy Committee (MPC). This has nine members. Five of them come from the Bank of England itself, including its governor, currently Sir Mervyn King, as chairman. The other four are appointed by the Chancellor, and are usually economists with academic backgrounds.

The MPC has a two-day meeting early each month. This meeting is attended by a Treasury official who reports on the government's current economic thinking, but who cannot vote about Bank Rate. The Bank Rate decision is announced at 12 noon on the second day. The minutes of the meetings are published and show how each member voted. The Bank also publishes a quarterly inflation report, which explains the factors that have affected Bank Rate decisions.

Figure 26.2 shows the MPC's monthly decisions about Bank Rate since 2004, and also the rise in the CPI over the year before each decision. There are four main points to note.

- **From 2004–07**: inflation was held within the 1–3% range.
- **In 2007**: inflation fell, but Bank Rate was raised because forecasts suggested that inflation would rise, which it did in 2008.
- **In 2008**: Bank Rate was cut, even though inflation was above 3%, because forecasts suggested that inflation would fall in 2009, which it did.
- **In 2010**: Bank Rate was held at 0.5%, even though inflation was above 3%, chiefly to help to reduce unemployment; so another government aim affected the Bank Rate decisions.

The European Central Bank in the eurozone

This section concludes with a brief look at the central banks in charge of two of the world's major currencies: the euro and the US dollar.

The European Central Bank (ECB) in Frankfurt was established in 1998 and is the central bank for the 17 EU countries that use the euro. Its primary goal, set by the 17 members, is to keep inflation in the eurozone just under 2%. The ECB is also expected to support employment and growth, but only if doing so will not threaten inflation.

Monetary policy is formulated by the ECB's Governing Council: this meets twice a month, but it takes policy decisions only at its first meeting. The Council comprises the six members of the ECB's Governing Board, who must be approved by the 17 participating governments, plus the governors of the 17 central banks in the participating countries: these central banks now have no monetary policy functions of their own. The ECB's constitution prevents the Governing Council from taking direct instructions from the EU or from any government.

The ECB uses open market operations, reserve ratio requirements, and interest rate control. Commercial banks in the eurozone actually hold their deposit reserves at the central banks of their own countries, not at the ECB, and they also make short-term loans to and from those central banks using what are called standing facilities. But the ECB sets the required reserve ratios and the interest rates on standing facilities.

The Federal Reserve System in the US

The functions of a central bank in the United States are handled by the Federal Reserve System, or the Fed, which was created in 1913. The Fed comprises 12 regional Federal Reserve Banks and a Board of Governors in Washington. The Governors are appointed by the President.

The regional banks handle the system's banking activities by holding deposits for the government and for the commercial banks. But monetary policy is handled by the Federal Open Market Committee (FOMC). This comprises the seven members of the Board, the President of the New York Reserve Bank, and the Presidents of four other Reserve Banks on a rotating basis.

The FOMC generally meets eight times a year. Its chief instrument is open market operations, although it can also use what is called the discount rate, which is the US equivalent of Bank Rate, along with reserve ratio requirements, and it has recently undertaken quantitative easing. The FOMC is not given targets by the US government, but, like the Bank of England, it pursues low inflation, while being mindful of the need to restrain unemployment and promote growth.

We saw in Chapter 20 how the low interest rates set by the Fed from 2002, and the subsequent rises a few years later, were a major contributor to the recent recession.

26.1 Everyday economics

Different policies

In April 2011, UK inflation was above 4%, well over the Bank of England's 1–3% target. Meanwhile, in the eurozone, inflation was only 2.6%, and so much closer to the ECB's 2% target. But the Bank of England held Bank Rate at 0.5% while the ECB raised its equivalent rate from a record low of 1% to 1.25%.

'Citigroup, Nomura change BOE rate forecasts after signal on growth concern', *Bloomberg*, 20 April 2011
'King holds his nerve as eurozone rates raised', *Business Scotsman*, 8 April 2011

Comment The key difference between the Bank of England and the ECB is that the remits given to them make it easier for the Bank than the ECB to maintain low interest rates in a recession if inflation is above target. But some MPC members wanted a rise in the UK rate, while some eurozone countries opposed the rise in the rate there.

26.2 Summary

- Monetary policy in the UK chiefly pursues an inflation target, but also bears unemployment and growth in mind. The current UK inflation target is a rate between 1% and 3%.
- The main instrument of monetary control is Base Rate, which is set monthly by the Bank of England's Monetary Policy Committee (MPC).

Open-market operations and quantitative easing are also used.

- The European Central Bank (ECB) in the eurozone, and the Federal Reserve System (the Fed) in the US, have broadly similar aims, but they rely rather more on open market operations.

26.3 Monetary policy transmission and quantitative easing

Economists call the way in which monetary policy instruments affect the economy the **monetary policy transmission mechanism**. We saw in the last section that the chief aim of monetary policy is to restrain inflation, and this section explores the transmission mechanism between changes in Bank Rate and inflation. It then looks at quantitative easing.

Bank rate changes and aggregate demand

To explain how Bank Rate changes affect inflation, let's suppose that Bank Rate is raised in order to restrain inflation. The main reason that the Bank Rate rise will put downward pressure on prices is that it will reduce aggregate demand. The Bank Rate rise will actually reduce aggregate demand in five different ways, as follows.

- **It increases other nominal interest rates**. This is because the commercial banks must now pay higher interest rates on loans they make from the Bank of England; so, as we saw in Figure 20.5 (on page 455), the money supply curve shifts to the left and nominal interest rates generally rise. Then households and firms borrow less, so that consumer spending and investment fall.
- **It reduces the expected rate of inflation**. Suppose the Bank Rate rise is taken as a credible signal that the Bank intends to reduce the rate of inflation. Then households and firms will expect real interest rates, that is interest rates after allowing for inflation, to rise by more than the rise in nominal interest rates. This will further reduce their willingness to borrow, and so further reduce consumer spending and investment.
- **It reduces wealth**. We have seen that the Bank Rate rise increases the interest rates on loans. This makes savers more keen to lend their funds and so less keen to buy securities. So the demand for securities falls and their prices fall. Also, the higher interest rates reduce the demand for mortgages, so home prices fall. So people who own securities and homes become less wealthy. This may encourage them to save more and so consume less.
- **It reduces the amount by which people expect output and incomes to rise in future**. Households may initially have expected a large rise in incomes and so felt little need to save. They now expect a smaller rise in incomes, so they may plan to save more and, as a result, plan to consume less. Firms may initially have expected a large rise in output and so planned to invest a lot. They now expect a smaller rise in output and therefore plan to invest less.
- **It increases the value of sterling**. Among the interest rates that rise after a rise in Bank Rate are the rates paid on sterling bank deposits. This tempts people with deposits in other currencies to convert their currencies into sterling and keep their funds in sterling deposits. So the demand for sterling increases, raising its value relative to other

currencies. Suppose the value of £1 rises from €1.20 to €1.40. Then a UK export priced at £100 will cost eurozone citizens €140 instead of €120, so exports will fall. At the same time, though, the price of a euro will fall from £0.83 to £0.71. So a product made in the eurozone and priced at €100 will cost UK consumers £71 instead of £83, so consumers will buy more imports. Lower exports and higher imports will both reduce aggregate demand.

Bank rate changes and inflation

We have now seen how a rise in Bank Rate can put downward pressure on prices and inflation by reducing aggregate demand. But a Bank Rate rise has two further effects that may also reduce inflationary pressure, as follows.

- **It may lead to more moderate wage increases.** If a rise in Bank Rate leads workers and employers to expect lower inflation, then they may agree more moderate wage increases. This will make it easier for firms to restrain their prices.
- **It will reduce the sterling prices of imports.** We have just seen that a rise in Bank Rate will reduce the sterling prices paid for imports, in our example from £83 to £71. This fall in prices will help to reduce inflationary pressure.

We have now seen how a change in Bank Rate affects inflation. But two questions remain.

- **How long does it take for a change in Bank Rate to affect the rate of inflation?** The Bank reckons that if it were to change Bank Rate for one year, and then return it to the original level, inflation would not change much during the first year, but the full effect of the Bank Rate change on inflation would be felt by the end of the next year.
- **How much does Bank Rate have to rise for one year to reduce inflation by 1% after the next year?** The Bank reckons that it is about 3%.

Question 26.1 What effect might a rise in interest rates have on consumption by households that are currently lending money rather than borrowing money?

The need for quantitative easing

In 2008, a recession began, and unemployment rose sharply. The Bank of England expected inflation to go well below the 2% target. It therefore reduced Bank Rate, hoping that this would trigger the reverse of the events we have just described, and so increase inflationary pressure and bring inflation up to its 2% target.

However, in spite of holding Bank Rate close to zero at 0.5%, inflation went below 1%. So the Bank adopted an additional strategy called **quantitative easing**: this means taking direct action to increase the money stock. Like open market operations, quantitative easing involves buying securities, but it differs from traditional open market operations in three ways.

- **The Bank buys securities directly from financial and non-financial firms, not in the open market.**
- **The Bank buys company bonds as well as government bonds.**
- **The Bank buys securities on a grand scale; between March 2009 and February 2010, it bought £200 billion worth.**

Quantitative easing and the money market

Figure 26.3 shows the effects of quantitative easing. Assume that Bank Rate is 0.5% and that this has led to the money supply curve, MS_0. This intersects the money demand curve, MD, at the money stock M_0 and an interest rate of r_0, which we take to be the average rate in the economy.

To increase inflationary pressure, the Bank wants to shift the money supply curve to the right, so reducing

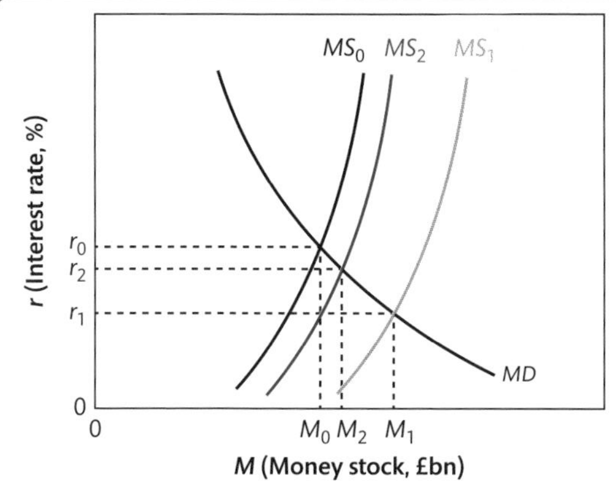

Figure 26.3 **Quantitative easing**

With Bank Rate close to zero, the money supply curve is MS_0 and the interest rate is r_0. By buying securities and increasing banks' reserves, the Bank hopes the money supply curve will shift to MS_1, taking the interest rate to r_1. But it may shift only as far as MS_2, taking the interest rate only to r_2.

the interest rate and increasing spending. But it cannot shift the money supply curve much by cutting Bank Rate, because that is close to zero. Instead, it buys securities. This has two effects on the banks of the people who sell securities:

- **it increases their liabilities**, because the deposits of the sellers have risen;
- **it increases their reserves by an equal amount**, because they can demand reserves from the Bank of England, which paid their depositors.

With extra reserves, these banks can create more money, so the Bank hoped the money supply curve would shift a long way to the right, say to MS_1, reducing the interest rate appreciably to r_1. However, the commercial banks were already able to borrow reserves from the Bank at about 0.5% and they wanted to create money only to the extent shown by MS_0. They clearly had little desire to lend more, so with their extra reserves they did not shift the money supply curve very far, say only to MS_2, taking the interest rate only to r_2.

Fortunately, a fall in interest rates is not the only route by which quantitative easing may increase spending, and so increase inflationary pressure. The other routes including the following.

- **By buying securities directly from non-financial firms, the Bank supplied funds to firms that wanted to invest, but which struggled to get loans from banks.**
- **By buying securities directly from non-financial firms, the Bank showed that it was willing to provide them with funds.** It hoped this would force the commercial banks to cut the interest rates on their loans to remain active lenders.
- **By buying securities, the Bank increased security prices, making people with securities wealthier.** It hoped these people would then spend more.

26.3 **Summary**

- A change in Bank Rate affects aggregate demand, and in turn inflationary pressure, in five ways: it causes other nominal interest rates to change; it changes the expected rate of inflation and so changes expected real interest rates; it changes wealth; it changes the output and incomes that people expect; and it changes the value of sterling.
- A change in Bank Rate also affects inflationary pressure because changed expectations of inflation affect wage agreements, and changes in the value of sterling affect the prices of imports in terms of sterling.
- With quantitative easing, the Bank of England buys securities directly from firms. The banks of these firms then acquire extra reserves so they can create more money, but they may not create much more.
- However, quantitative easing may raise spending in other ways, for example by injecting funds directly to firms that need them, and by raising security prices so that people become wealthier.

26.4 Fiscal policy: budgets and deficits

We now turn to fiscal policy, when the government changes in its own spending or its taxes to affect the economy. We will look first at the main components of government spending and revenue. We will then consider how different types of government spending should be financed: this will enable us to derive a rule for fiscal policy.

Government revenue and spending

The main components of government expenditure and revenue in the UK are shown in Table 26.1, along with their 2009–10 values. This table covers the central government in Westminster along with all the devolved and local governments.

The left-hand part of the table lists the main spending functions in order of importance. The largest two, healthcare and education, accounted for 31.1% of all government spending. Three of the next five items are transfer payments, such as State Pensions, which accounted for 24.5%. No other single item accounted for much over 5%.

The bottom two lines on the left-hand part show that 89.8% of the total expenditure was called current

Table 26.1 **The main UK government expenditure functions and revenue sources, 2009–10**

Expenditure function	£bn	% of total	Revenue source	£bn	% of total
Health	119.8	17.9	Personal income tax	141.9	21.2
Education	88.3	13.2	NI contributions	96.6	14.4
State Pensions	82.3	12.3	VAT	84.7	12.7
Family benefits, income support, tax credits	49.4	7.4	Corporation tax	35.8	5.3
Defence	34.0	5.1	Fuel duty	26.2	3.9
Housing & housing development	33.2	5.0	Council tax	25.3	3.8
Incapacity, disability, & injury benefits	32.3	4.8	Business rates	23.4	3.5
Police, courts, & prisons	31.7	4.7	Alcohol taxes	9.2	1.4
Debt interest	31.4	4.7	Tobacco tax	8.8	1.3
Personal social services	30.2	4.5	Stamp duties	7.9	1.2
Public transport & roads	23.1	3.4	Motor vehicle duties	5.4	0.8
Industry	22.5	3.4	Capital gains tax	2.4	0.4
Recreation, sport, culture, & broadcasting	14.1	2.1	Inheritance tax	2.4	0.4
Government and foreign affairs	12.1	1.8	Insurance premium tax	2.3	0.3
Waste & environment	11.4	1.7	Air passenger duty	1.9	0.3
Other	42.7	8.1	Other	15.8	2.4
Total expenditure	**669.5**	**100.0**	**Total taxes**	**490.0**	**73.2**
Of which			Interest and profits	23.0	3.4
Current expenditure	601.0	89.8	Borrowing	156.5	23.4
Capital expenditure	68.5	10.2	**Total revenue**	**669.5**	**100.0**

Sources: HM Treasury, *Public Finances Databank*, 2011, and HM Treasury, *Public Expenditure Statistical Analyses (PESA)*, 2010.

expenditure: this actually refers to recurrent or recurring spending, on items like wages, energy, and supplies. The other 10.2% of spending was capital expenditure: this is spending on new capital, like buildings, vehicles, and equipment.

The total expenditure was £669.5 billion, so the government had to raise £669.5 billion in revenue. The right-hand part of the table shows, at the bottom, that £490 billion of this revenue came from taxes, while £23 billion came from interest on loans made by governments and from profits made by firms that they own. These sources left a shortfall, or deficit, of £156.5 billion, which the government had to meet with borrowing.

The right-hand part of the table also shows the main taxes in order of importance. Income tax, National Insurance contributions, and VAT raised 48.3% of government revenue. Other major taxes include the corporation tax on company profits, and council tax and business rates, which are levied on homes and business properties.

Equity over time

Suppose that output is at its potential level, so the government does not want total spending to change. But suppose the government decides to spend more itself. Then an equal amount of other spending in the economy must be forgone.

The type of spending that will be forgone actually depends on how the government finances its increased spending. Many economists argue that it should finance increases in its current and capital spending in different ways, so that the forgone spending affects different groups of people at different times. They believe this is needed to secure equity, that is fairness. Let's see why.

- **Current expenditure**. Suppose the government increases its current spending this year by paying doctors £100 million more to work longer hours. The benefits of this will be felt only by people this year, so it seems fair that only they should be affected by the £100 million worth of other spending that must be forgone. The government can achieve this by raising taxes this year by enough to reduce the consumption of these people by a total of £100 million.
- **Capital expenditure**. Suppose the government increases its capital spending by buying £100 million worth of extra medical equipment. The benefits of this will be felt by people over the whole lifetime of the equipment, say ten years. So it would seem unfair to finance this with taxes that aim to reduce consumption this year by £100 million, because then the only people affected by the forgone spending would be this year's consumers. It would seem fairer for the effects to be felt by people over the next ten years. The government can achieve this by borrowing £100 million, and by raising interest rates by enough to reduce investment by firms by £100 million. Then everyone over the next ten years will be affected because firms will have £100 million less capital to use producing goods and services for them than they would otherwise have had.

A basic principle for government finance

Suppose the government decides to finance its current government spending with taxes and its capital spending with loans. Then we can use a very simple example to show how much it must borrow each year. We will make these assumptions:

- **The government's only capital spending occurs on 1 July each year when it buys one new ambulance with a ten-year life**. This means that it will always own ten ambulances, although they will all have different ages.
- **On each 1 July, the government borrows £100,000 for the new ambulance that it buys that day, and it agrees to repay £10,000 of this loan on 1 July in each of the following ten years**. This means it will make the last repayment on the day the ambulance concerned ends its life.

These assumptions mean that, on 1 July each year, the government makes the final repayment on the ambulance that it bought ten years ago, to coincide with the day when that ambulance ends its life. It also repays £10,000 on each of the nine ambulances it has bought in the last nine years. So each 1 July, it will borrow £100,000 for its new ambulance, and repay a total of £100,000 on other ambulances. This means that the total amount of its outstanding loans, that is its total debt, remains unaltered over time.

So any government that adopts this approach will actually have a constant debt if the only investment it does is to replace assets when they wear out. But its debt will increase if it ever buys extra capital, which is called making net investment. Table 26.1 shows that the UK government's investment spending in 2009–10 was £68.5 billion. But £19.3 billion of this was actually used to replace assets the lives of which were ending, so net investment was only £49.2 billion. So, if the UK government had followed this approach, it would have increased its debt by just £49.2 billion.

A rule for fiscal policy

If you were Chancellor, you might find the principle just outlined appealing. So you might plan over the next year to increase your debt by only enough for purchases of extra capital. In practice, however, you would almost certainly end up increasing your debt by a different amount. To see why, suppose output is currently at its potential level, and consider what will happen to your borrowing over the next year if aggregate demand changes. Consider two possibilities.

- **Aggregate demand falls, taking output below its potential level**. In this case, output and incomes fall, so your tax receipts fall; also your spending rises, because you will pay more in transfers to people who are unemployed or low paid. Your lower tax receipts and higher spending will virtually force you to borrow more than you planned. Your only options will be to raise some taxes or to cut some government spending, but both of these will reduce aggregate demand; yet output is already below potential.
- **Aggregate demand rises, taking output above its potential level**. In this case, output and incomes rise, so your tax receipts rise; also, your spending falls, because you will pay less in transfers to people who are unemployed or low paid. Your higher tax receipts and lower spending will virtually force you to borrow less than you planned. Your only options will be to cut some taxes or to raise some government spending, but both of these will raise aggregate demand; yet output is already above potential.

So you might instead adopt a rule for fiscal policy in which you would borrow more than you need for net investment when output is below potential, and borrow less than you need for net investment when output is above potential. But, over any business cycle as a whole, you might try to borrow the same total amount as you need for your total net investment.

However, even this rule has a problem. To see why, suppose you adopt it in a year when output is at its potential level, and then output rises. According to the rule, you should now borrow less than you need for your extra capital, so that you can borrow more than you need for extra capital when the next recession comes. But how much less should you borrow now? You cannot answer that, because you don't know when the next recession will come, or how bad it will be.

The UK's Labour government of 1997–2010 committed itself to this rule and called it the golden rule. But when the 2008 recession came, it was clear that it had borrowed too much since the last recession. However, if no recession had occurred for many more years, then it might have been seen as having followed the rule after all.

The coalition government elected in 2010 no longer calls this rule a golden rule. But it seems to have adopted it, because it is aiming by 2015 to create a situation in which, over each future cycle, total borrowing will equal total net investment.

Cyclical and structural deficits

Figure 26.4 explores the UK government's deficit, that is the amount of its borrowing, from 1990 to 2010, with forecasts up to 2015. The purple line shows the output gap, that is the gap between actual output and potential output. This gap is negative in recessions when actual output is below potential output. The grey line shows the government's actual deficit or borrowing. This is always highest in recessions, when tax yields are low and transfers are high.

The black line shows what each year's deficit would have been if output had always been at its potential level so that unemployment had always been at its natural rate: this is called the **cyclically adjusted deficit** or **structural deficit**. This line shows that the government would actually still have run big deficits in the periods of recession, but its deficits would have been less unstable.

The pink line shows the government's net investment. If the government had stuck to the fiscal rule that we have outlined throughout this period, then the average level of the cyclically adjusted deficit would have equalled the average level of the government's net investment. In fact, this deficit averaged about 3.0% of output, while net investment averaged about 1.3%. So, over a full cycle from, say, 1993 to 2009, the government's borrowing was well in excess of its net investment.

Crowding out

Suppose the government wants to increase its capital spending and finance it with extra borrowing. Then aggregate demand will increase, so output and incomes will rise. This will raise the demand for money and so raise interest rates, which will reduce investment by firms, offsetting some of the rise in aggregate demand. The tendency for loan financed government spending to reduce investment is called **crowding out**. The government can avoid this by simultaneously expanding the money stock so that the interest rate won't rise, but the government must then be aware that there will be no fall in investment to offset any of the rise in aggregate demand that results from its extra capital spending.

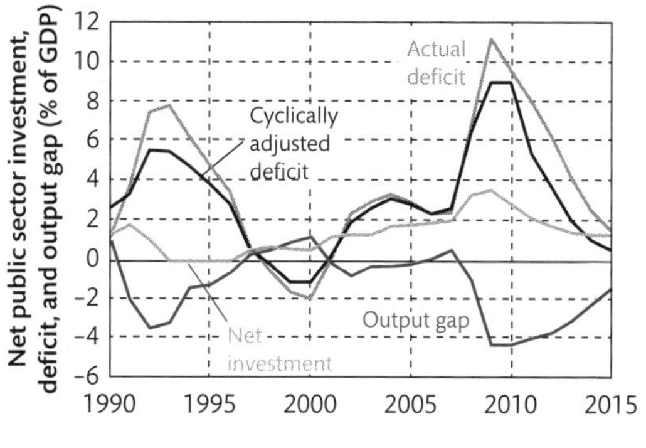

Figure 26.4 **The UK and the golden rule, 1990–2015**

Over a complete business cycle, many governments aim to borrow only as much as they spend on net investment. So, on average, the deficit allowing for cyclical factors should equal net investment. But on average, in this period, the cyclically adjusted deficit was more than twice the size of net investment.

Source: HM Treasury, *Public Finances Databank*, 2011.

26.4 Summary

- The largest components of government expenditure are healthcare, education, and transfer payments. The largest taxes are income tax, VAT, and National Insurance contributions.
- To try to secure equity over time, a government may adopt a fiscal rule under which, over any complete cycle, its total borrowing will equal its total net investment. However, it will doubtless allow its borrowing to exceed its net investment in years when output is below its potential level, and vice versa.
- Financing government spending with loans will lead to some crowding out of investment by firms.

26.5 Fiscal policy: government debt

We have seen that there is a case for a government to finance its capital spending by loans. This means that its debt will rise each year by an amount equal to its net investment for the year. However, government debt raises three important issues, and we will discuss them in this section. For simplicity, we will suppose that governments always borrow by selling new bonds.

The burden of government debt

One issue raised by government debt is that if a government sells bonds today, then in the future it will have to pay interest on them and repay them. It will meet these costs by raising taxes in the future. So people often claim that issuing government bonds today will impose a burden on future citizens, and they claim that this is unfair.

To explore these claims, suppose the government buys some new ambulances and finances them by selling some new bonds. Then it will have to raise taxes during the lifetime of those bonds, and this will indeed be a burden for future UK taxpayers.

However, the debt may not be a burden for future UK citizens as a whole. The interest payments and the repayments will all be made to whoever owns the bonds at the relevant times. If all the owners were UK citizens, then the government would simply raise taxes on UK taxpayers and pay money to the UK bondholders, so UK citizens as a whole would be no worse off.

In contrast, if some of the bonds were owned by non-UK citizens, then UK citizens as a whole would be worse off. So, while government debt is always a burden to taxpayers, it is a burden to UK citizens as a whole only on bonds held by non-UK citizens.

But is the burden of debt on taxpayers unfair? This depends on the life of the ambulances and the repayment or maturity date of the bonds. Suppose the ambulances last ten years and the bonds mature over those ten years. Then the bonds will place a burden on taxpayers over those ten years, but this seems fair because the burden concerns ambulances, which are available to them. But if the bonds matured later, then after ten years they would lead to a burden on taxpayers for ambulances that no longer exist, and this would seem unfair. So it seems fairest to finance net government investment with bonds that will mature over the lifetimes of the assets concerned.

Concerns with the level of government debt

Most economists believe governments should set limits on their borrowing. Otherwise, various worries may arise: these worries depend on who lends to the government.

One possibility is the central bank. Suppose the government sells some new bonds to the central bank and uses the money it receives to buy some new offices. Then the office builders will have larger bank deposits, and their banks will demand reserves from the central bank, because it is the government's bank. When the commercial banks get more reserves, they can create more money, as we saw in Chapter 20. This will lead to inflationary pressure.

To avoid this inflationary pressure, most governments borrow chiefly from the public or from the commercial banks. But a government that set no limits on its total borrowing from them would raise the following concerns.

- **Poor scrutiny of government investment projects.** A government that sets no limit to its borrowing may not ask how much benefit its investment projects will bring before it undertakes them.
- **Concerns with economic growth.** The more money a government borrows and spends, the more it raises output and incomes, so raising the

demand for money and in turn raising interest rates to crowd out investment by firms. This may not reduce the growth rate if the government spends the money on projects like new research laboratories, which will help growth, but it will reduce the growth rate if the money is spent on projects like prisons, which do not help growth.

- **Doubts about whether the government will be able to honour the interest and repayments of its bonds**. If these doubts arise, then people who buy government bonds may demand high coupon rates in return for taking the risk, and so make it harder for the government to honour its debt.
- **Concerns with fiscal policy**. If a recession sets in, the government may want to raise demand with fiscal policy, by borrowing more and using the loans to cut taxes or spend more. But if its debt is already high, it may feel unable to borrow more, and so it cannot have fiscal expansion.

How government debt can increase

Because high debt raises concerns, many governments try to limit their debt. Often they try to limit it as a percentage of the country's output or income. For example, the 1997–2010 Labour government tried to hold its net debt—that is the value of what it owed to other people minus what other people owed to it—below 40% of output. The idea of setting a limit related to output is that if output grows each year, then so can debt, and this means that the government can fund some net investment each year with borrowing. But the amount of borrowing a government can do is restrained by the limit that it sets, and by the rate of economic growth.

This is shown in the three cases in Table 26.2. In each case, we suppose that output, *Y*, is £100 billion in year 1. In case (a), we suppose that the government wants its debt on 1 January each year to equal 40% of the output in the year ahead, so on 1 January in year 1 it can have a debt of £40 billion. Now suppose that output grows at 3% per year. Then the table shows the output for the next two years, along with the permitted debt on 1 January each year at 40% of these outputs. The rise in the debt each year shows how much net investment the government can finance from loans. It turns out here to be 1.2% of output each year.

But suppose the government wants more net investment, say 2.4% of output each year. And suppose it

Table 26.2 **Growth rates and government debt**

Year	Output, *Y* (£bn)	Ratio of debt to *Y* (%)	Debt on 1 Jan (£bn)	Rise in debt (£bn)	Rise in debt (% of *Y*)
			Case (a): Growth rate 3%, debt to output ratio 40%		
1	100.00	40.00	40.00	1.20	1.2
2	103.00	40.00	41.20	1.24	1.2
3	106.09	40.00	42.44	1.27	1.2
			Case (b): Growth rate 6%, debt to output ratio 40%		
1	100.00	40.00	40.00	2.40	2.4
2	106.00	40.00	42.40	2.54	2.4
3	112.36	40.00	44.94	2.70	2.4
			Case (c): Growth rate 3%, debt to output ratio 80%		
1	100.00	80.00	80.00	2.40	2.4
2	103.00	80.00	82.40	2.47	2.4
3	106.09	80.00	84.87	2.55	2.4

wants to finance this by borrowing, but does not want its debt to grow in relation to output. There are only two ways of achieving this.

- **Higher output growth**. This is shown in case (b) of Table 26.2, where we assume growth is 6% rather than 3%, but the debt limit is still 40% of output. The table shows that the debt here can rise by 2.4% of GDP each year, not 1.2%.
- **A higher ratio of debt to output**. This is shown in case (c), where we return to growth at 3%, but now have a debt limit of 80% of output rather than 40%. The table shows that here, too, the debt can rise by 2.4% of GDP each year.

26.5 **Summary**

- Government debt is a burden for taxpayers, and also a burden to a country's citizens as a whole on any debt held by non-residents. The burden on taxpayers is generally felt fair, provided that the loans used to fund each different government capital project mature by the end of the lifetime of that project.
- High borrowing may aggravate inflation, encourage poor scrutiny of government projects, crowd out much investment by firms, raise fears that the government cannot meet its interest and repayment obligations, and prevent a government from tackling a recession with higher spending and lower taxes.
- Governments often try to limit their debts as a percentage of output. This limits how much net investment they can finance by loans.

26.6 Supply-side policies

Two broad types of supply-side policy

We have now studied monetary and fiscal policies, which aim to shift aggregate demand. But, in the long run, output settles where the aggregate demand curve intersects the vertical long-run supply curve. So if output is to rise in the long run, this curve must shift to the right. Since the 1980s, many countries have used supply-side policies, which aim to secure just such a shift.

The long-run aggregate supply curve is vertical at the potential output level. This is the output level that will be produced when the labour market is in equilibrium. Accordingly, there are two types of supply-side policy at which we look briefly in this section. These types are as follows:

- **policies that aim to increase the total hours of labour that will be hired when the labour market is in equilibrium, so that more output will be produced**;
- **policies that aim to increase the output that can be produced even if hours don't change**.

The quantity of labour and income tax

One way in which governments can try to increase the amount of labour that will be hired is to reduce the income tax rates. To explain this, we will use Figure 26.5, which concerns the labour market in a country that initially has no income tax. At each real wage, the demand curve *ADL* shows how many workers employers want to hire, the labour force curve LF_0 shows how many people would initially like jobs, and the supply curve ASL_0 shows how many people would actually accept jobs.

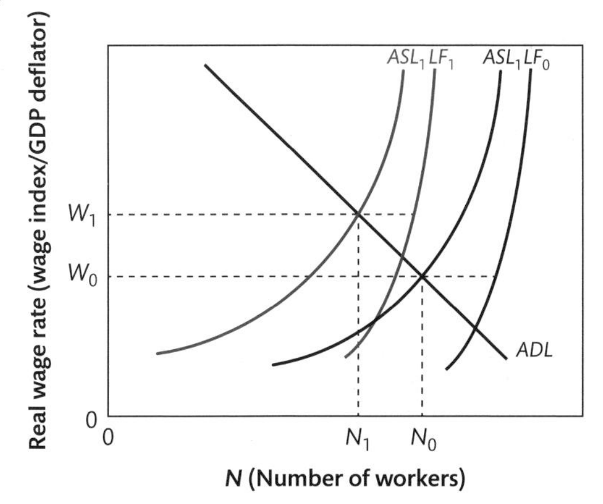

Figure 26.5 **Income taxation**

Introducing an income tax may discourage people from working, shifting the labour force and labour supply curves left to LF_1 and ASL_1, and reducing employment from N_0 to N_1. If so, a lowering of income tax rates should raise employment.

The gap between the labour force curve and the labour supply curve arises because, at each wage, there will be some natural unemployment; we saw in Chapter 21 that this arises because some unemployed people will be waiting for job offers they will accept and some will possess skills that are no longer required. The initial equilibrium is where ASL_0 intersects *ADL*, at a real wage of W_0 and a quantity of N_0 workers. Potential output for a period of, say, a month, is the output that can be produced by these N_0 workers in a month.

Now suppose the government imposes an income tax on labour. Many economists believe that, as a result, fewer people will want jobs at each wage, and fewer will accept jobs at each wage. So they expect the labour force and labour supply curves to shift to the left, say to LF_1 and ASL_1. Then the market will reach a new equilibrium with fewer workers employed, N_1, so that potential output will fall. People who believe this argue that, as the UK has an income tax, the government should reduce income tax rates, and try to shift the labour force and labour supply curves to the right, to increase the equilibrium number of workers.

This argument is often extended to the hours that people work. Even if income taxes had no effect on how many people wanted jobs or accepted them, they might encourage people with jobs to work fewer hours, so the output they could produce would fall. Recent UK governments have accepted this argument, and since 1979 they have, for example, reduced the top rate of income tax from 83% to 50%.

But some economists believe that introducing an income tax will shift the labour force and labour supply curves to the right, not the left. For example, some older workers might stay in the workforce longer, because the tax reduces the amount they can save each year for retirement; and some younger people might work more hours to repay debts like mortgages and student loans. If an income tax does raise potential output, then cutting income tax rates would reduce it.

The quantity of labour and other policies

Governments can try to increase the amount of labour that will be hired in other ways. These include the following.

- **Reduce non-wage labour costs**. In addition to wages, employers face non-wage labour costs such as pension contributions, National Insurance contributions, payments to people on maternity leave, and redundancy payments to people who they lay off. Figure 26.6 shows the effect of these costs in a labour market. Suppose there are initially no such costs, and employment is N_0 where *ADL* intersects *ASL*. Now *ADL* actually shows the number of workers that employers would want to hire at each possible total cost per worker to them. If non-wage costs are introduced that account for a quarter of total labour costs, then employers will actually pay to workers only three-quarters of their total labour costs, as shown by ADL_{NNC}, where NNC means net of non-wage costs. This is the curve that interests workers, and employment will fall to N_1 where it intersects *ASL*. Workers now receive W_1, but

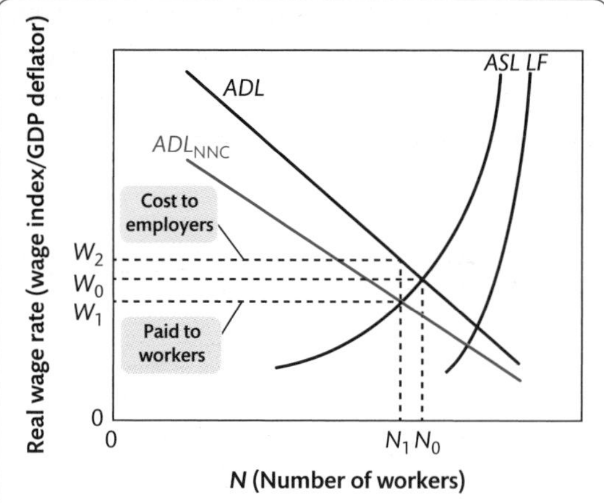

Figure 26.6 **Non-wage costs**

If the only labour costs faced by employers are wages, employment is N_0. But suppose non-wage costs arise that equal a quarter of labour costs. Then only three-quarters of labour costs are paid to employees, as shown by ADL_{NNC}. Employment falls to N_1. Each worker receives W_1, but costs the employer W_2.

employers face a total cost per worker of W_2. Any fall in non-wage costs would shift ADL_{NNC} upwards and increase employment. The main recent government efforts here have been to promote less-generous pension schemes that need smaller contributions from employers.

- **Reduce the benefits paid to people who are unemployed, and tighten the eligibility rules.** This might encourage people who are looking for jobs to be less picky. Then the supply of labour will increase so the number of people hired will rise. The main recent government efforts here have focused on tightening the rules for single mothers and unemployed youths.
- **Encourage unemployed workers with outdated skills to retrain.** This will increase the supply of labour and lead to more workers being hired.
- **Reduce the power of trade unions.** Some people believe that unions can force the wage above the level where the supply and demand curves for labour intersect, and so create a higher equilibrium wage. This will reduce the number of workers hired and so reduce potential output. Since the 1980s, governments have tried to reduce or restrain union power to limit any such tendency that may occur.
- **Increase the demand for labour by encouraging new firms to set up and create jobs.** Governments can offer help to new firms, and they can also try to reduce the myriad regulations that their owners need to meet.
- **Help unemployed people to move to areas with jobs.** Some unemployed people live in local authority homes; there may be suitable jobs for them in distant areas, but they would face long waits for local authority homes in those areas. The government is trying to reduce this problem.

Increasing output per labour hour

There are many ways in which a government can try to increase the output per labour hour, so that potential output would rise even if employment stayed the same. They include the following.

- **Increase human capital in new entrants to the workforce to make the workforce more productive.** One recent policy is the decision gradually to raise the school-leaving age.
- **Stimulate technological progress.** This also makes workers more productive. The government can encourage firms to undertake research and development (R&D) with tax concessions and subsidies, and with patent and copyright laws that increase the returns firms can get from their discoveries and innovations.
- **Encourage firms to invest in plant, buildings, vehicles, and machinery, so that workers have more physical capital.** This could be done by using monetary policy to reduce interest rates, but this might raise the expected inflation rate, making it harder to restrain the actual inflation rate. It might also be done by reducing the rates of tax levied on firms' profits; this would encourage investment by making it more rewarding to the

owners of the firms that do it. Incidentally, globalization is giving more firms the chance to invest in different countries, and governments across the world are in a form of competition to set low profits tax rates.

- **Promote competition to stimulate efficiency and so raise output per worker**. We looked at policies to promote competition in Chapter 12.
- **Deregulation**. Governments have tried to reduce regulations generally, to make it easier for firms to become more productive. Governments have also given a stimulus to some industries by reducing the regulations that applied specifically to them, in order to promote competition and efficiency. Major examples include bus companies, which were allowed to compete on individual bus routes only from 1985, and building societies, which were allowed to compete effectively against banks only from 1986.
- **Making government departments more efficient**. A large fraction of output is produced by government departments. Governments have stimulated their efficiency by contracting much of their work to competing private firms. For example, rubbish collection, road repairs, hospital cleaning, and prisons are now often supplied by private industry.
- **Nationalization or privatization**. In the 1940s, the UK government nationalized many firms, that is took them into public ownership; it believed this would lead to better management and higher productivity. However, this policy later fell from favour, and since 1980 most nationalized industries have been privatized in the belief that this would be better.

26.2 **Everyday economics**

Green energy and supply-side policies

A survey by Centrica, the UK's biggest domestic energy supplier, finds that most young people support low-carbon technology, but that too few A level students and undergraduates are interested in careers in science, technology, and energy for the UK to have the resources needed to make the most of the potential low-carbon energy sources such as wind, solar, and tidal power. The survey urges the government to look at the supply of workers with the necessary skills.

'Resistance to IT education will hinder green energy development, *Computing.co.uk*, 18 August 2010
'School leavers "not interested" in engineering career', *The Telegraph*, 15 August 2010

Comment The government may try to encourage more young people to acquire human capital in the form of science skills. Alternatively, it may leave a shortage of such workers to increase wages to levels that will hopefully tempt more young people. The government may also be concerned about the supply of physical capital, because there is a danger that demand will exceed supply if aging coal-fired and old nuclear power stations are not soon replaced by new nuclear and renewable sources.

26.6 **Summary**

- Some supply-side policies aim to increase the quantity of hours that will be worked when the labour market is in equilibrium. This might be done by reducing income tax rates, reducing non-wage labour costs, reducing benefits to unemployed people, encouraging unemployed workers to retrain, reducing trade union power, helping new firms to start, and helping unemployed people move to areas with jobs.
- Other supply-side policies aim to increase the output per labour hour. This might be done by increasing human capital, stimulating technological progress, encouraging firms to invest in more physical capital, promoting competition, deregulation, and promoting efficiency in government departments.

26.7 Macroeconomic policy for the UK: 2010–15

A quandary

We began this chapter by supposing you become Chancellor on some future date, and that your first act is to see whether there is an output gap. If there were, you might use monetary and fiscal policies, and perhaps also supply-side policies.

But suppose you had become Chancellor in 2010. We saw back in Figure 26.4 that there was then a recessionary gap. Now consider the policy choices that we have suggested in earlier sections for handling a recessionary gap.

- **Wait for wages to fall, so returning unemployment to its natural rate and output to its potential level.** You might not want to rely on this, because the recessionary gap was large, so it could take a long time.
- **Pursue a more expansionary monetary policy.** You would find this almost impossible. We saw in Figure 26.2 how the Bank of England had already set Bank Rate at virtually zero. It had also undertaken extensive quantitative easing.
- **Pursue a more expansionary fiscal policy.** You might not want to do this, because it would mean cutting taxes or increasing government spending; that would increase the government's deficit, and we saw in Figure 26.4 that this was already about 10% of GDP, which was actually the highest since the Second World War.
- **Pursue a supply-side policy to raise output.** You might not want to do this because, in the short run, shifting *LAS* to the right would actually make the recessionary gap bigger.

Question 26.2 What effect would supply-side policy have in the long run?

So what did the new 2010 government do? It actually opted to make the fiscal policy it had inherited *less* expansionary, by reducing government spending and raising taxes, even though this is the opposite of what is needed in a recession. To see why it did this, we must look at what it regarded as the most serious economic problem: the level of the government's debt.

The growing government debt problem

The debt problem is illustrated in Figure 26.7, which covers the period from 1990. The pink line here shows government spending as a percentage of GDP, and the purple line shows government revenue from taxes, interest, and profits.

These two lines may look fairly close, but the gap between them, that is the government's need to borrow, is shown by the grey line. This shows that the government had to borrow in most years. However, we have seen a case for borrowing to finance net investment, and we have also seen that borrowing will not necessarily increase the government's debt as a

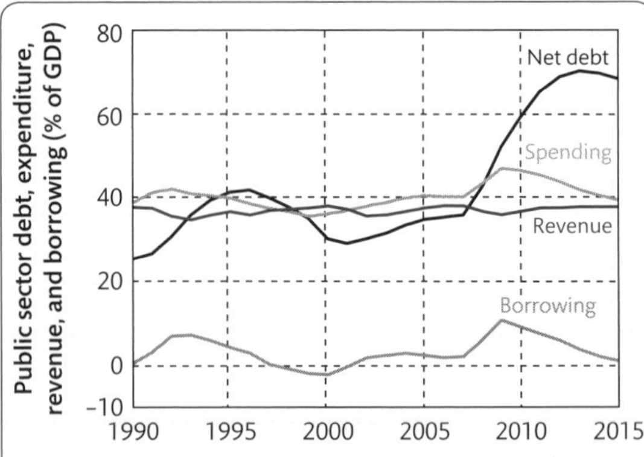

Figure 26.7 **The UK's public sector debt, 1990–2015**

The pink expenditure line and the revenue line may seem fairly close, but the gap, which shows how much borrowing is needed, was generally positive, as shown by the grey line. When borrowing is relatively high for a few consecutive years, as in the early 1990s and after 2007, debt increases rapidly. (Figures after 2010 are forecasts.)

Source: HM Treasury *Public Finances Databank*, 2011.

percentage of GDP. And the black line shows that the government's debt was indeed fairly stable until the 2008 recession.

This recession had forced the then government to borrow more, because it led to more spending on transfers and to lower tax revenues; the government had increased its borrowing needs yet further by trying to offset the recession by raising demand with a temporary cut in VAT and extra spending. The rise in borrowing quickly raised the net debt from under 40% of GDP towards 70%.

The big problem for the new 2010 government problem was that if it were to let the deficit persist much longer, then the ratio of debt to GDP would rapidly rise further. Then lenders might doubt if the government could pay the interest on its loans and repay them in due course, so lenders might demand higher interest rates in return for taking the risk. This would raise government spending even more. So the government cut spending and increased taxes. Other governments might have postponed these actions for a while, but no one would have postponed them for very long.

Table 26.3 **Government deficits, debts and unemployment, eurozone countries and UK, 2010**

Country	Gross debt (% of GDP)	Deficit (% of GDP)	Unemployment (%)
Austria	72	4.6	4.4
Belgium	97	4.1	8.3
Cyprus	61	5.3	6.5
Finland	48	2.5	8.4
France	82	7.0	9.7
Germany	83	3.3	6.9
Greece	143	10.5	12.6
Ireland	96	32.4	13.7
Italy	119	4.6	8.4
Luxembourg	18	1.7	4.5
Malta	68	3.6	6.8
Netherlands	63	5.4	4.5
Portugal	93	9.1	11.0
Slovakia	41	7.9	14.4
Slovenia	38	5.6	7.3
Spain	60	9.2	20.1
UK	**80**	**10.4**	**7.8**

Source: Eurostat.

The eurozone dimension

As the recession was international, you might wonder what was happening elsewhere, especially in the nearby eurozone. Table 26.3 compares the 2010 situations of the eurozone countries with that of the UK. The debt figures here refer to governments' gross debts, that is the amount they owe without any deduction for what is owed to them. In seven eurozone countries, the ratio of gross debt to GDP was higher than it was in the UK. These countries were Belgium, France, Germany, Greece, Ireland, Italy, and Portugal, and you might suppose that lenders would prefer to lend to the UK than to them.

However, lenders do not just consider the current debt ratios: they also look ahead. They are wary of countries where the ratio of the deficit to GDP is high, because that will tend to increase the debt ratios. Table 26.3 shows that all those seven countries had lower deficit ratios than the UK, except Greece and Ireland. Lenders are also wary of countries with high unemployment, because it will take the countries a long time to secure low unemployment, so there may be low taxes and high transfers for a long time. Table 26.3 shows that all those seven countries had higher unemployment than the UK except Germany.

As it happens, lenders did become wary of lending to Greece, Ireland, and Portugal, and they had to turn embarrassingly to other governments and the International Monetary Fund to borrow the funds they needed. The UK's position was much better than that of Greece and Ireland, and a little better than that of Portugal, but lenders were keeping a wary eye, and the government was keen to reduce the deficit and debt ratios.

EU rules for deficits and debts

Many governments set rules for their deficits and debts, and the EU also has rules for its members. These rules originated in the Maastricht Treaty of 1992, which paved the way for the creation of the euro. A major concern was that it would be absurd for the ECB to harmonize monetary policy in the eurozone if individual countries had fiscal policies that were pulling in different directions.

The Maastricht Treaty required countries to try to keep their deficits below 3% of GDP, and their gross debts below 60% of GDP, before the euro was introduced. The 1997 Growth and Stability Pact required countries to follow these rules afterwards, unless they had mitigating circumstances.

Although the UK has not joined the euro, it did sign the Maastricht Treaty. However, the EU cannot do much to the UK or any other country that breaks the rules. If a country's deficit exceeds the limit, the EU has an Excessive Deficit Procedure (EDP), which initially offers 'recommendations' to reduce borrowing, and the UK has received these. The EDP then issues instructions, with the ultimate step of a fine of up to 0.5% of GDP, but this applies only to eurozone countries and has never been used.

Many countries have breached the rules. And when France and Germany broke the rules in 2005, they insisted that the Pact be suspended. It was later reinstated with the same 3% and 60% limits, but with more generous mitigating circumstances. These included considering also the level of debt, the stage in the cycle, and spending on defence, education, foreign aid, research, and German reunification.

The UK's recent policy

The UK government has set itself a target of reducing the ratio of debt to GDP by 2015. To get anywhere near achieving this, it has had to raise taxes and reduce government spending. However, it is focusing on spending cuts, because spending had recently risen rapidly, as Figure 26.8 shows.

This figure divides spending into major groups, of which social protection is chiefly transfers, and economic affairs are chiefly support to industry. You can see that spending as a percentage of GDP rose in most

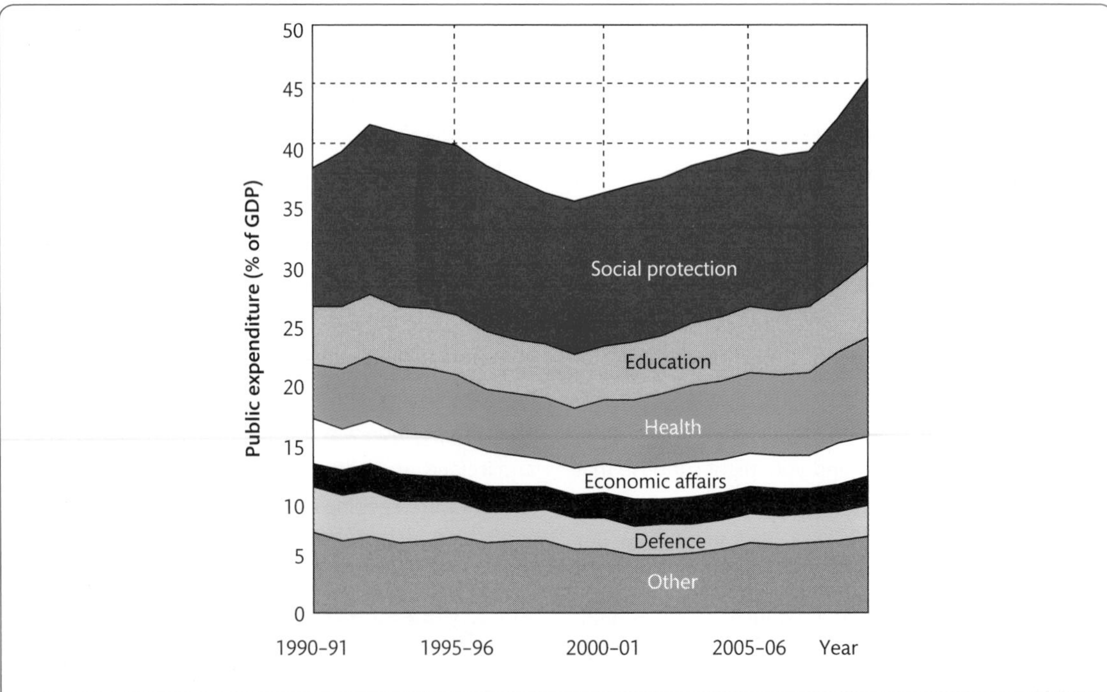

Figure 26.8 **Government spending by function, UK 1990-91 to 2009-10**

After 2000, spending on most broad groups of functions rose in relation to GDP.

Source: HM Treasury, *Public Expenditure Statistical Analyses (PESA)* 2010.

groups in the years after 2000. The biggest rise came in healthcare, which share rose from 5.3% to 8.5%; however, cuts in this are very unpopular with voters, so the government has actually concentrated on cutting transfers.

The government has also raised some taxes, chiefly VAT, and it has made some changes in income tax. It is allowing people to earn more income before they pay any tax, and it is adopting the former government's plan to raise the marginal tax rate on the highest incomes from 40% to 50%.

There a supply-side argument for increasing the amount people can earn before they pay tax. The point here is that many unemployed people are only offered jobs with wages that are so low that, once they have paid income tax, they will be little better off than being unemployed, so they choose to remain in frictional unemployment. If these jobs were to attract less income tax, these people might be encouraged to accept them.

On the other hand, some people worry about the supply-side implications of the 50% rate on high incomes. If people on these incomes face a higher marginal rate, and so have to pay more tax on each extra pound they earn, then may regard extra effort as not worthwhile and work less, or else move abroad.

The government's tightening fiscal policy will prolong the time its takes for unemployment to fall to its natural level. The government is caught between this problem and the risks of a huge debt. Even with its chosen policies, its forecast shown in Figure 26.7 suggests that its net debt will not be much below 70% of GDP by 2015. These forecasts are prepared by a new independent Office for Budget Responsibility rather than the Treasury, to avoid the charge that they have been massaged for political reasons.

There is probably never a really good time to become Chancellor, but 2010 was a worse time than most. If you do become Chancellor one day, you will hope for a better situation.

26.7 Summary

- Although the UK economy was in recession in 2010, it was not possible to reduce interest rates any more to make monetary policy more expansionary. And the government's deficit and debt were so high that it actually made fiscal policy less expansionary, not more expansionary.
- The government focused more on cutting spending than raising taxes, because expenditure had risen sharply in the previous few years.
- Countries with high deficits and debts, and with high unemployment that makes it hard to reduce their deficits and debt, may face high interest rates if lenders regard them as risky borrowers.

In the next chapter we consider why countries trade with each other and also how much trade they do.

abc Glossary

Crowding out: the tendency for government spending financed by borrowing to reduce investment by firms.

Cyclically adjusted deficit: another term for the structural deficit.

Discretionary policies: when governments look at each shock as it happens and choose whatever policy seems right at the time.

Monetary policy transmission mechanism: how monetary policy instruments affect the economy.

Political business cycles: cycles created by governments which adopt discretionary policies that are related to election times.

Quantitative easing: when the central bank takes direct action to increase the money stock; it involves buying securities from firms.

Rules policies: when governments say in advance how they will respond to various types of shock.

Structural deficit: the deficit that a government would have if output were at its potential level.

Supply-side policy: a policy to shift long-run aggregate supply.

Answers to in-text questions

26.1 Their consumption might be little affected. Higher interest rates will raise their incomes, which may encourage them to consume more, but at the same time higher interest rates will make saving more appealing, which may encourage them to consume less.

26.2 In the long run, output settles where aggregate demand intersects long-run aggregate supply, so the more supply-side policies shift *LAS*, the higher output will be. Also, wages should adjust to shift the short-run aggregate supply curve until it intersects aggregate demand at the same point as *LAS* intersects it.

? Questions for review

26.1 **(a)** In what circumstances might the Bank of England leave interest rates unaltered even though the inflation rate is increasing? **(b)** In what circumstances do you think that it might decide to sell the securities which it has bought in a period of quantitative easing?

26.2 If the Bank of England were to raise Bank Rate, would it expect much effect on inflation within a year?

26.3 A government aims over a business cycle to raise its debt by the same amount as it spends on net investment. **(a)** In what circumstances might it increase its current spending by £10 billion and also reduce taxes? **(b)** In what circumstances might it reduce its capital spending even though the central bank has recently increased interest rates? **(c)** In what circumstances might it leave its spending unaltered, but raise taxes even though the central bank has recently decreased interest rates?

26.4 **(a)** In what circumstances might quantitative easing have little effect on interest rates? **(b)** In what circumstances would a government that limited its debt to a fixed percentage of GDP have to reduce its net investment? **(c)** In what circumstances would a reduction in income tax rates have little effect on labour supply?

? Questions for discussion

26.1 Do you think that, because the Bank of England is independent, the government can really claim no responsibility when the Bank increases interest rates?

26.2 What changes, if any, would you make to the government's current macroeconomic policies if you were Chancellor?

26.3 If employers perceive a shortage in some types of skill, say engineers, should the government try to encourage more young people to become engineers, and, if so how? Or should it assume that engineers' wages will rise, so encouraging more people to train as engineers?

Common student errors

Some students are persuaded by media pundits to think ill of Chancellors who do not manage simultaneously to achieve low unemployment, low inflation, low interest rates, and low taxes along with high growth and high public spending. Hopefully, this chapter has persuaded you that the Chancellor has a challenging task and could hardly achieve all that, even in an ideal world with no shocks.

27

International Trade

Remember from Chapter 2 that a country's production possibility frontier shows the various patterns of output that it is possible for it to produce, assuming there is full employment and full efficiency.

This book was printed in Italy. As you read it, let's imagine that you are eating an apple grown in South Africa, wearing a top made in India, and have just ridden on a bus made in Germany. Why does the UK import these items from other countries when they could be produced here? And why does the UK export items like chemicals and financial services to other countries that could produce them themselves? Do consumers gain from trade? Does anyone lose from it? Why do countries often impose tariffs and other barriers to reduce trade? Why does the EU want to remove all barriers within the EU?

This chapter shows you how to answer questions like these, by understanding:

- how differences in relative costs—or comparative advantages—allow countries to benefit from trade;
- how differences in preferences and economies of scale allow countries to benefit from trade;
- the varied arguments made for tariffs and other trade barriers;
- why many countries join free trade areas, or customs unions, or the EU;
- how countries across the world have tried to increase their trade in recent years.

27.1 Trade and free trade

The UK trades with other nations on a vast scale. Almost 30% of the products produced in the UK are exported, and just over 30% of the products sold in the UK are imported. Table 27.1 divides the many different products that are traded into broad categories, along with their 2009 values.

Moreover, the UK trades with every continent and almost every nation. Table 27.2 gives some details of this. But although the UK trades with many countries, you could work out from this table that about half of its trade takes place within the EU.

Table 27.1 **UK international trade by product group, 2009**

Product group	Exports (£bn)	Imports (£bn)
Goods		
Food, drink, and tobacco	15	33
Lumber, pulp, fibres, and ores	5	7
Timber, paper, textiles, and metals	25	36
Crude oil and oil products	25	28
Coal, gas, and electricity	2	7
Medicines and toiletries	25	17
Chemical and plastics	22	22
Mechanical goods	29	24
Electrical goods	24	45
Vehicles and transport equipment	26	38
Clothing and footwear	4	17
Scientific and photographic goods	8	8
Other goods	17	27
Services		
Transport and communications	27	23
Travel	19	31
Financial services	52	13
Business services	58	38
Other services	6	7
Total	**388**	**420**

Source: Office for National Statistics, *Annual Abstract of Statistics 2010*, Tables 19.2, 19.3, and 19.9.

Trade between nations has occurred ever since nations came into being. One reason for this trade is that people in one nation sometimes want to consume something that their nation cannot supply. In ancient Britain, for example, long before the Roman

Table 27.2 **UK international trade by continent and major trading parties, 2009**

Geographical area	Exports (£bn)	Imports (£bn)
Europe		
Belgium	14	7
France	25	29
Germany	35	48
Ireland	24	17
Italy	13	17
Netherlands	27	26
Spain	15	19
Rest of EU	36	43
Norway	5	17
Russia	4	6
Switzerland	11	8
Turkey	3	6
Rest of Europe	6	3
Americas		
Canada	6	6
United States	67	43
Rest of Americas	11	11
Asia		
China	8	25
Hong Kong	6	9
India	5	7
Japan	8	10
Rest of Asia	36	31
Africa	15	14
Australasia	8	6
Total	**388**	**420**

Source: Office for National Statistics, *United Kingdom Balance of Payments, 2010*, Table 9.1.

Conquest of AD 43, the Celts imported wine, ivory, and silver.

UK citizens still buy from foreign producers many other products that cannot readily be produced here. These include goods such as gold, pineapples, and silk. They also include services, such as travel to sun-drenched beaches and places of religious importance, and licence fees paid to use foreign inventions protected by patents.

However, most of the products imported into the UK could be produced here, and most of the products that the UK exports could be produced in the countries in which they are sold. So why is there so much international trade in products that nations could supply for themselves? We will explain why in sections 27.2 and 27.3.

Trade barriers

Just as trade between nations has occurred since they came into being, so have official barriers to reduce trade. The most common barriers have always been **tariffs**, which are taxes on imported products. Many early tariffs were imposed chiefly to raise revenue rather than to reduce trade, but they did reduce it; admittedly, the reduction was often offset a little by smugglers who evaded the tariffs.

However, from the 16th to the 18th centuries, most European countries levied large tariffs in a deliberate attempt to reduce trade. This was because they accepted a doctrine called mercantilism. At that time, as we saw in Chapter 20, money comprised coins with precious metals, and the supporters of mercantilism disliked the fact that paying for imports led to precious metals leaving the country. They believed that this would make the country poorer, although we now know that a fall in the money stock would lead to a fall in prices, which would increase exports and help to bring precious metals back.

Mercantilism appealed to producers, because import barriers meant they faced less competition and could make more profit. And it appealed to governments, which liked the revenue from tariffs.

The free trade movement

In the late 18th century, economists began to argue that there would be widespread benefits if countries were to engage in **free trade**, which means that governments would impose no tariffs or other barriers on trade. Adam Smith was an early advocate of free trade, but its most notable exponent was the British economist, David Ricardo: his theory, published in 1817, remains the basis for most later trade theories.

However, any moves towards free trade were widely opposed in the 19th century. For example, in 1846, the UK government repealed the Corn Laws, which had imposed tariffs on imported corn, and the arrival of cheap imported corn so angered landowners that the Prime Minister, Sir Robert Peel, resigned, and his party, the Tories, split.

Few other countries abolished any tariffs in the 19th century, so tariffs were still widespread in the early 20th century. They were often increased during the Great Depression as each country tried to protect its workers from foreign competition.

Nevertheless, Ricardo's insights remained for everyone to see, and the second half of the 20th century witnessed great strides towards global free trade. This, along with ever-falling transport costs and easy internet information about products around the world, has done much to further the globalization of the world economy.

Section 27.4 looks at the effects of tariffs and other trade barriers. We also mention the numerous arguments by which people have tried to justify them, and sometimes still do.

Section 27.5 explains how trade barriers have been reduced. It looks at the EU, which tries to remove all barriers between its member countries, and at the World Trade Organization, which tries to reduce barriers between 153 countries.

27.1 Summary

- Almost a third of products produced in the UK are exported, and almost a third of products purchased in the UK are imported. Half of UK trade is made within the EU, and half with other countries.
- Governments have often imposed barriers that reduce trade, most notably tariffs on imports. But for well over 200 years economists have advocated free trade, and in the last 50 years great progress towards it has been made by removing trade barriers.

27.2 Trade theory when countries use only one input

The meaning of comparative advantages

We now look at Ricardo's theory to explain how countries can benefit from international trade. For simplicity, his theory makes four key assumptions.

- **There are only two countries**—we will assume they are the UK and Sri Lanka.
- **These countries produce only two goods**—we will assume they are DVDs and tops.
- **These two countries use only one input**—labour.
- **All industries are in perfect competition**—so, as we saw in Chapter 9, the prices of DVDs and tops in the UK will equal their marginal costs here, and their prices in Sri Lanka will equal their marginal costs there.

To explain the theory, we will assume that, in a single day, a UK worker could produce 3 DVDs or 1 top, while a Sri Lankan worker could produce 1 DVD or 4 tops. These figures are shown in Table 27.3. We will also suppose that there is initially no trade between the UK and Sri Lanka.

Now suppose that each country wants 1 more DVD per day. Then the UK must switch a worker from tops to DVDs for ⅓ of a day, and so forgo ⅓ of a top; so the opportunity cost of a DVD here is ⅓ of a top. But Sri Lanka must switch a worker from tops to DVDs for a whole day, and so forgo 4 tops; so the opportunity cost of a DVD there is 4 tops.

Suppose, instead, that each country wants 1 more top per day. Then the UK must switch a worker from DVDs to tops for a whole day, and so forgo 3 DVDs; so the opportunity cost of a top here is 3 DVDs. But Sri Lanka must switch a worker from DVDs to tops for just ¼ of a day, and so forgo ¼ of a DVD, so the opportunity cost of a top there is ¼ of a DVD.

The table gives all these opportunity costs, and we can use them to explain two definitions.

- **Absolute advantage:** a country has an absolute advantage in a product if it needs less labour to

Table 27.3 **Example of comparative advantages where each country has one absolute advantage**

	UK	Sri Lanka
One worker in a day can make:	3 DVDs *or* 1 top	1 DVD *or* 4 tops
Opportunity cost of 1 DVD:	⅓ top	4 tops
Opportunity cost of 1 top:	3 DVDs	¼ DVD
Absolute advantage:	DVDs	Tops
Comparative advantage:	DVDs	Tops
Price of a DVD/ price of a top:	⅓	4

make it. So, in this example, the UK has an absolute advantage in DVDs and Sri Lanka has one in tops.

- **Comparative advantage:** a country has a comparative advantage in a product if it has a lower opportunity cost for it. So, in this example, the UK has a comparative advantage in DVDs and Sri Lanka has one in tops.

Finally, note that in the UK it costs the same—one day's wages here—to make 3 extra DVDs or 1 extra top, so the price of a DVD here will equal ⅓ of the price of a top. And in Sri Lanka, it costs the same—one day's wages there—to make 1 extra DVD or 4 extra tops, so the price of a DVD there will equal 4 times the price of a top. The table notes these results.

Gains from trade when each country has an absolute advantage in one of the products

We will now show how each country in this example can benefit by shifting resources into the product in which it has a comparative advantage, and then trading.

- **The UK**. Suppose the UK shifts one worker a day from tops to DVDs, so each day it produces 3 more DVDs and 1 fewer top. And suppose it sells 1 of the extra DVDs each day as an export to Sri Lanka; there, the price of a DVD is 4 times that of a top, so each day the UK can use the money from its exported DVD to buy 4 Sri Lankan tops. Altogether, each day it produces 1 fewer top, but buys 4 tops from Sri Lanka to have 3 more tops overall, and it keeps 2 of its extra DVDs to have 2 more DVDs overall. In short, it can consume more DVDs and more tops.
- **Sri Lanka**. Suppose Sri Lanka shifts one worker a day from DVDs to tops, so each day it produces 4 more tops and 1 fewer DVD. And suppose it sells 1 of the extra tops each day as an export to the UK; here, the price of a DVD is a third that of a top, so each day Sri Lanka can use the money from its exported top to buy 3 UK DVDs. Altogether, each day it produces 1 fewer DVD, but buys 3 DVDs from the UK, to have 2 more DVDs overall, and it keeps 3 of its extra tops to have 3 more tops overall. So it, too, can consume more DVDs and more tops.

Gains from trade when one country has an absolute advantage in both products

In the example in Table 27.3, each country could produce one product with less labour than the other, giving it an absolute advantage in that product. But suppose that one country could produce both products with less labour, giving it an absolute advantage in both products. Could it benefit by trading with a less efficient country? And could the less-efficient country gain from trade, or would no one buy its products as they always need more labour, which is the only input?

We can use Ricardo's theory to show that both countries could still benefit from trade. To see this, we will make just one change to our example, and suppose that now one worker in the UK can produce 18 DVDs or 6 tops a day. But in Sri Lanka, one worker can still produce 1 DVD or 4 tops. So, as noted in Table 27.4, the UK has an absolute advantage in both products.

Table 27.4 **Example of comparative advantages where one country has two absolute advantages**

	UK	Sri Lanka
One worker in a day can make:	18 DVDs *or* 6 tops	1 DVD *or* 4 tops
Opportunity cost of 1 DVD:	⅓ top	4 tops
Opportunity cost of 1 top:	3 DVDs	¼ DVD
Absolute advantages:	DVDs *and* tops	None
Comparative advantage:	DVDs	Tops
Price of a DVD/ price of a top:	⅓	4

The UK also has a comparative advantage in DVDs. To produce one more, it must now shift a worker for 1⁄18 of a day and so forgo ⅓ of a top, but Sri Lanka must still shift a worker for a whole day and so forgo 4 tops. However, Sri Lanka still has a comparative advantage in tops. To produce one more it must still shift a worker for ¼ of a day and so forgo ¼ of a DVD; but the UK must now shift a worker for ⅙ of a day, and so forgo 3 DVDs.

In the UK, it now costs the same to make 18 extra DVDs or 6 extra tops, so the price of a DVD will still be ⅓ of the price of a top. And the price ratio for DVDs to tops in Sri Lanka will still be 4.

Trade will again benefit each country, as follows.

- **The UK**: it can, for example, shift a worker for ⅙ of a day from tops to DVDs, producing 1 fewer top and 3 more DVDs. It can export 1 DVD to Sri Lanka and trade it for 4 tops. So altogether it can consume 2 more DVDs and 3 more tops.
- **Sri Lanka**: it can, for example, shift a worker for a whole day from DVDs to tops, producing 1 fewer DVD and 4 more tops. It can export 1 top to the UK and trade it for 3 DVDs. So altogether it can consume 2 more DVDs and 3 more tops.

Table 27.5 **Example where there are absolute advantages, but no comparative advantages**

	UK	Sri Lanka
One worker in a day can make:	4 DVDs *or* 6 tops	2 DVDs *or* 3 tops
Opportunity cost of 1 DVD:	1½ tops	1½ tops
Opportunity cost of 1 top:	⅔ DVD	⅔ DVD
Absolute advantages:	DVDs *and* tops	None
Comparative advantage:	None	None
Price of a DVD/ price of a top:	1½	1½

A case with no gains from trade

In Ricardo's theory, the only situation in which countries could not benefit from shifting resources and trading is if neither had a comparative advantage in either product. We can see this from the example in Table 27.5. Here, in a day, a UK worker can produce 4 DVDs or 6 tops, while a Sri Lankan worker can produce 2 DVDs or 3 tops.

In this example, the opportunity costs are the same in each country. For example, by shifting a worker for a day from tops to DVDs, the UK would gain 4 DVDs, but forgo 6 tops, so each extra DVD requires it to forgo 1½ tops. And by shifting a worker for a day from tops to DVDs, Sri Lanka would gain 2 DVDs, but forgo 3 tops, so it too finds that each extra DVD requires it to forgo 1½ tops. It is easy to work out also that, for tops, each country faces an opportunity cost of ⅔ of a DVD.

With the same opportunity costs for DVDs, neither country has a comparative advantage in them. And with the same opportunity cost for tops, neither has a comparative advantage in them.

Finally, note that each country requires the same resources to produce 1 DVD or 1½ tops—a quarter of a day's labour in the UK, and half a day's labour in Sri Lanka. So, in each country, the price of a DVD will be 1½ that of a top.

We can now readily see that neither country can gain from trade. For example, suppose the UK shifts one worker a day from tops to DVDs, so each day it produces 4 more DVDs and 6 fewer tops. Then suppose it sells all 4 of the extra DVDs each day as exports to Sri Lanka; there, the price of a DVD is 1½ times that of a top, so the UK can use the money from its exports to buy 6 Sri Lankan tops each day. So it has produced 6 fewer tops and 4 more DVDs, but it has exported all 4 of its extra DVDs and been able to buy only 6 tops. So it has gained no extra consumption.

Question 27.1 Why would Sir Lanka not gain from shifting one worker a day from DVDs to tops?

Conclusions from Ricardo's theory

Ricardo's theory has two main conclusions.

- **Suppose countries have comparative advantages in different products**: then both can benefit from shifting labour between products and trading. This applies no matter which country happens to have any absolute advantages.
- **Suppose countries have no comparative advantages in any product**: then neither country can benefit from shifting labour and trading.

Because the benefits from trade arise only when there are comparative advantages, this theory is called comparative advantage theory. But notice that even when countries do have comparative advantages, so that opening up trade allows each country to consume more of each product, some individuals are likely to be worse off.

For example, if trade opens up between the UK and Sri Lanka in the case shown in Table 27.3, then UK top makers and Sri Lankan DVD makers will face a fall in demand. So the owners of firms in these industries will make lower profits, and some of their firms may go out of business. Also, these industries will now hire fewer workers, so they will pay lower wages; so the workers who continue to work in them will be paid less, and other workers will be laid off and have to retrain before they can work in the other industry.

Limitations of simple Ricardian theory

One limitation of this theory is that it assumes that there is only one input, labour; in practice, there are many inputs. Another limitation is that it does not explain how many resources each country will shift. However, it suggests that if the UK can gain by shifting one worker from tops to DVDs, then it should shift all its workers into DVDs and produce only DVDs; and it suggests that if Sri Lanka can gain by shifting one worker from DVDs to tops, then it should shift all its workers into tops and produce only tops.

The next section develops trade theory to overcome these two limitations. It then shows that, even if they do trade, the UK will probably still produce some tops, while Sri Lanka will probably still produce some DVDs.

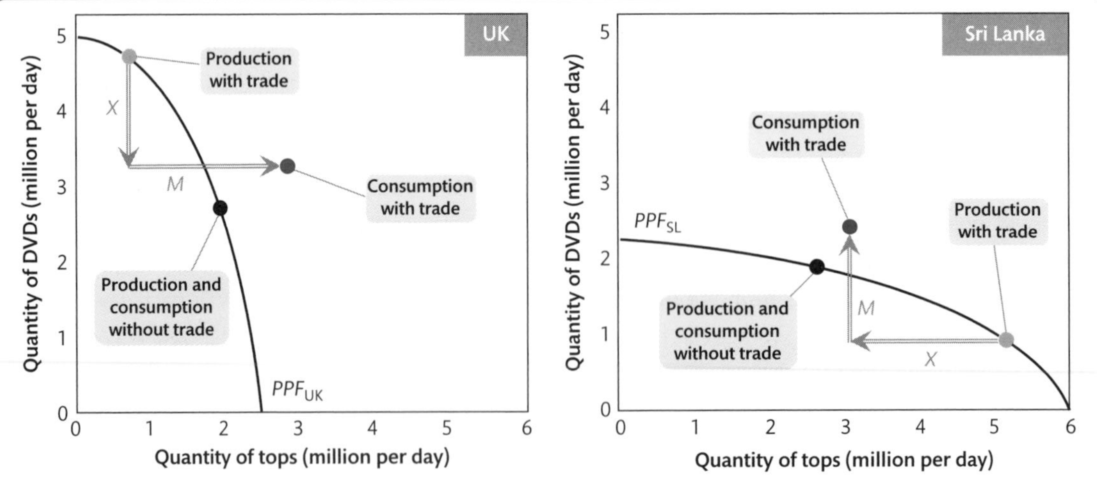

Figure 27.1 **Production and consumption changes with trade**

Without trade, each country produces and consumes the combination of tops and DVDs shown by its black spot. With trade, the UK shifts some resources from tops to DVDs, while Sri Lanka shifts some resources the other way; so each country produces at its pink spot. But each country's exports (*X*) and imports (*M*) mean it consumes the combination of products at its purple spot.

27.2 Summary

- If two countries do no trade and have different relative costs for producing two products, then each has a comparative advantage in one product. Each country could consume more of both products if it were to put more resources into the product for which it has this advantage and then trade with the other country.
- A country has an absolute advantage in a product if it needs less labour than the other country to produce it. The gains from trade occur if each country has an absolute advantage in one product, or if one has an absolute advantage in both products.
- If the relative costs of producing two products are the same in two countries, then neither has a comparative advantage in either product, and there will be no gains from shifting resources.
- Although trade may benefit countries as a whole, some individuals will lose when trade is opened up.

27.3 Trade theory when countries use many inputs

Production possibility frontiers and comparative advantages

We will now develop our example by assuming that the two countries use many inputs to produce their products, not only labour. This will help us to see how far countries that trade end up specializing in producing one product or the other.

To make this development, we must consider each country's production possibility frontier, or *PPF*. We saw in Chapter 2 that a country's frontier shows the various output patterns that it could produce if it were to employ all of its resources with full efficiency. Suppose the frontiers for the UK and Sri Lanka are as shown by PPF_{UK} and PPF_{SL} in Figure 27.1.

As drawn, the frontiers have different shapes, and we will consider why this may be so later. But both frontiers are steep at their right-hand ends. To see why, suppose that a country was at that end, producing only tops, and that it then wanted to produce some DVDs too. It would shift out of tops the resources that were of little use for tops, but of much use for DVDs; so its top output would fall only a little, while its DVD output would rise a lot.

However, the frontiers are fairly flat at their left ends. If a country was at that end, producing only DVDs, and then wanted to produce some tops too, it would shift out of DVDs the resources that were of little use for DVDs, but of much use for tops. So it would lose few DVDs, but gain many tops.

Suppose there is initially no trade and that each country is producing at the black spot marked on its frontier. As there is no trade, this combination of products that a country produces is also the combination that its citizens must consume: nothing that is being produced is being exported to be consumed abroad, and nothing that is being consumed is being produced abroad and imported.

At the black spots, PPF_{UK} is steeper than PPF_{SL}. This means the UK would have to forgo fewer tops to produce an extra DVD, so it has a comparative advantage in DVDs. But Sri Lanka would have to forgo fewer DVDs to produce an extra top, so it has a comparative advantage in tops.

For example, suppose that, with a small shift in resources, the UK could produce 3 more DVDs and 1 fewer top, or instead 3 fewer DVDs and 1 more top. Then the opportunity cost of producing an extra DVD is ⅓ of a top, and the opportunity cost of producing an extra top is 3 DVDs. Also, the price of a DVD will be ⅓ the price of a top.

And suppose that, with a small shift in resources, Sri Lanka could produce 4 more tops and 1 fewer DVD, or instead 4 fewer tops and 1 more DVD. Then the opportunity cost of producing an extra top is ¼ of a DVD, and the opportunity cost of producing an extra DVD is 4 tops. Also, the price of a top will be ¼ the price of a DVD.

The gains from trade

As each country has a comparative advantage, we can now show that each would benefit from trade.

- **The UK**. Suppose it produced 3 more DVDs and 1 fewer top each day. Then it could sell 1 of the extra DVDs each day to Sri Lanka, and as the price of a top there is ¼ the price of a DVD, it could buy 4 Sri Lankan tops. Altogether, it would have 2 more DVDs and 3 more tops to consume each day.
- **Sri Lanka**. Suppose it produced 4 more tops and 1 fewer DVD each day. Then it could sell 1 of the extra tops each day to the UK, and as the price of a DVD here is ⅓ the price of a top, it could buy 3 UK DVDs. Altogether, it would have 3 more tops and 2 more DVDs to consume each day.

The extent of specialization

Each country could gain yet more by shifting yet more resources. But how many more should each shift? The answer is that they should shift resources until they reach spots like the pink ones at which their frontiers have the same slope. Here, each country must give up the same number of tops to produce one more DVD, and the same number of DVDs to produce one more top. This means there are no comparative advantages here. So, as we saw with Table 27.5, the countries will gain nothing if they shift any more resources.

So each country will produce each day the combination of products at its pink spot. But each day the UK will export some DVDs, which Sri Lanka will import, and Sri Lanka will export some tops, which the UK will import. The amount of trade will depend on supply and demand. Suppose each country does the amount of exports, *X*, and imports, *M*, that are shown by the grey arrows; then each country will consume each day the combination of products at its purple spot. So each country in this example ends up consuming more of both products than it would do at the black spot without trade. Sometimes a country ends up consuming more of one product and less of the other, but it will always consume at a point outside its *PPF* that it could not reach before.

The *PPF*s here differ in shape. There are several factors that explain why the pattern of products that different countries could produce is different. These include the following.

- **Land or natural resources**: these affect a country's possible output of crops and minerals. You may be eating an apple from South Africa because its land produces apples at this time of year while UK land does not.
- **Capital to labour ratios**: a country like the UK has a relatively high ratio of capital to labour and is well placed for producing capital-intensive products like DVDs, but not for producing labour-intensive products like clothes. This is why you may be wearing a top made in India.
- **Human capital**: countries with highly trained and skilled workforces are better placed for producing products that need human capital. This is why the UK exports some medicines and financial services which require the human capital that UK workers possess.
- **Efficiency**: some industries are very productive just because they are highly efficient, perhaps, for example, because they are very competitive.

Differences in preferences

Suppose two countries have identically shaped production possibility frontiers. Even so, they could still benefit from trade. This would happen if their consumers had different preferences. Figure 27.2 shows a case in which two countries A and B have identical production possibility frontiers. Suppose they initially do no trade and are at the black spots. Country A's black spot is towards the right of its frontier, which implies that its consumers have a large preference for product X on the horizontal axis, while country B's black spot is towards the left of its frontier, which implies that its consumers have a large preference for product Y on the vertical axis.

At these spots, the frontiers have different slopes: country A, with the steeper slope, has a comparative advantage in Y, while country B with the flatter slope has a comparative advantage in X. Each country could benefit by shifting resources into the product in which it has a comparative advantage, until the slopes are the same, as at the pink spots. It could then do the exports and imports shown and end up consuming more of each product, as at the purple spots.

Economies of scale and intra-industry trade

The trade theory we have developed here explains a lot of trade. For example, the UK imports more food than it exports partly because less densely populated countries have relatively more agricultural land; it imports more clothes than it exports because clothes require a low ratio of capital to labour and the UK has a high one. And it exports more chemicals and financial services than it imports because it has many people with the human capital required to produce them.

But in many industries, the UK's exports are similar in value to its imports. For example, it exports Vauxhalls and Wharfedale loudspeakers, and imports Fiats and Sony loudspeakers. Trade within industries is called **intra-industry trade**, and it may often occur even if, without trade, there would be no comparative advantages.

The explanation lies in economies of scale. For example, it would be very costly for every country to

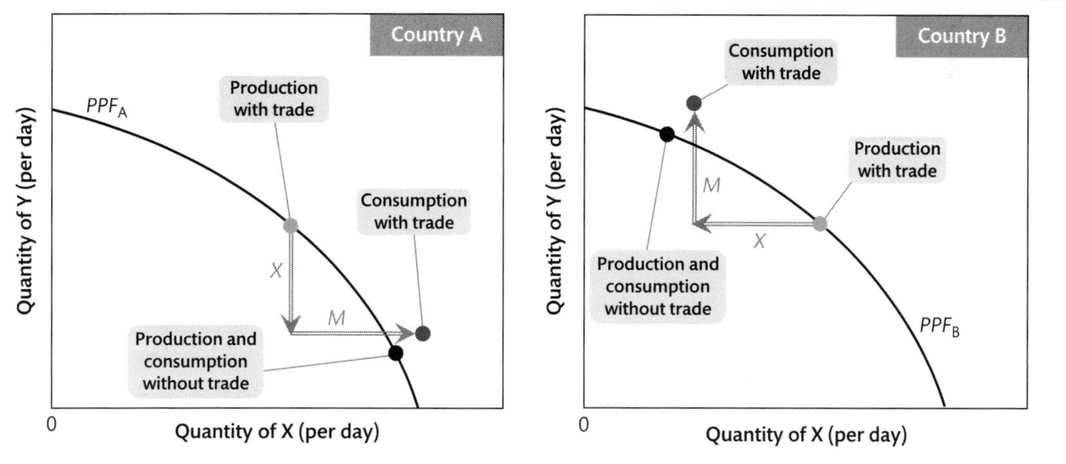

Figure 27.2 **Trade and different consumer preferences**

Trade will benefit countries with identical production possibility frontiers if their consumers have different preferences. Here, consumers in Country A have stronger preferences for product X, and weaker preferences for product Y, than occurs in Country B. Without trade, the countries will be at the black spots where the frontiers have different slopes, which means that relative costs are different. Each country could end up consuming at the purple spot outside its frontier if they engage in the specialization and trade shown.

try to produce every conceivable type of car or loudspeaker. The effect of economies of scale is shown in the example in Figure 27.3.

Here, two countries, C and D, produce service buses and luxury coaches. Each industry has economies of scale. PPF_C and PPF_D show that if each country were to divide its resources equally between the two types of vehicle, then each month it could produce 400 buses or 300 coaches. But if it were to put all its resources into one type of vehicle, so doubling the resources used for it, its output would more than double to either 1,000 buses or 800 coaches.

We will suppose that if there is no trade, then each country will produce 400 buses and 300 coaches, as shown by its black spot. Here, the frontiers have identical slopes, so there are no comparative advantages. But the countries would gain with trade if, somehow, this were to result in one, say C, producing only coaches, leaving the other, D, to produce only buses. Then they would produce at opposite ends of the frontiers, as shown by the pink spots; with the exports and imports shown, each could now have more buses than before, 500, and also more coaches, 400.

Losers from trade

We have now seen several cases in which trade can benefit each country by raising its total consumption. But, as we noted at the end of the last section, some individuals lose when trade is opened up. This is because some industries will expand and others contract. The owners of firms in the contracting industry will earn lower profits, and some of their firms may go out of business. Also, these industries will lay some workers off and pay lower wages to those who remain.

Because we have shown each country ending up producing at a pink spot on its production possibility frontier, we have actually assumed that, in the end, there is again full employment. So we have effectively assumed that that all laid-off workers eventually find new jobs. But they may have low incomes while they retrain, and even then some of them may earn less than before.

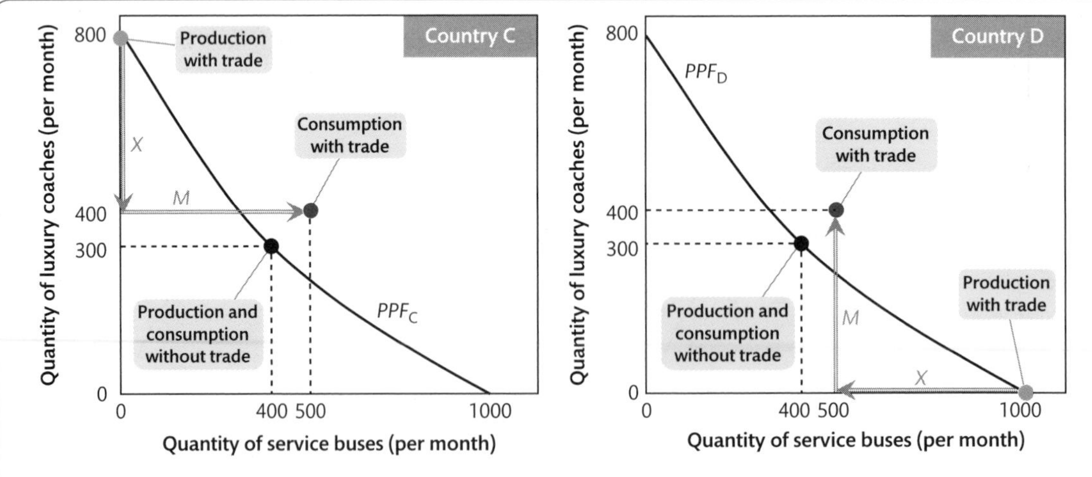

Figure 27.3 **Intra-industry trade and economies of scale**

There are economies of scale in the production of service buses and luxury coaches. Without trade, each country would be at the black spot; here the slopes are the same and there are no comparative advantages. But if each country were to specialize in one product, total output would increase, and the countries could end up consuming more of both products, as at the purple spots.

27.1 Everyday economics

Boost to UK exports

Figures released by the Office of National Statistics show that, in February 2011, the value of goods exported by UK firms reached a record high of £6.8bn. However, it was well below the value of goods imported, which stood at £7.8bn.

'Exports hit record high as UK trade deficit falls', *Belfast Telegraph*, 13 April 2011
'UK exporters are doing sterling work', *The Guardian*, 12 April 2011

Comment The UK generally has a deficit in its trade in goods and a surplus in its trade in services. But the value of all exports and imports change constantly, in part at least because of constant changes in countries' relative costs.

27.3 Summary

- As countries use many inputs, it is useful to illustrate the causes and effects of trade with production possibility frontiers. If, in the absence of trade, countries would be at positions with different slopes, then comparative advantages will exist, so specialization and trade will be beneficial to both countries.
- Countries that open up trade will shift resources into the industries in which they hold comparative advantages, but only until relative costs are the same in each country. Each country will export some of the output of the industry in which its production has increased, and import some of the other product.
- Comparative advantages in the pre-trade position may arise because of differences in the countries' land and natural resources, or their capital-labour ratios, or human capital, or even in consumer preferences.
- Intra-industry trade, under which countries trade very similar products, arises because of economies of scale.
- Some individuals lose out whenever trade is opened up.

27.4 Government intervention with trade

We have so far ignored any possible barriers to trade. And we have seen that all countries gain from free trade, that is trade without barriers. Nevertheless, countries have often moved away from free trade by imposing tariffs or non-tariff barriers on imports; these barriers generally reduce imports rather than prevent them. In this section, we will look first at the effects of tariffs, which are perhaps the most common barrier; then we will mention some non-tariff barriers; and then we will explore some of the arguments that are made for these barriers.

Some countries also move away from free trade in exports, and we will look briefly at this also.

Tariffs and the importance of country size

The effects of tariffs on the country that imposes them depend in part on its size. To see why, suppose there is initially free trade in tea, and then both Panama and the US impose a tariff on tea. Their consumers will now pay more for tea, so the demand for tea on world markets will fall.

However, the fall in the purchases by Panama's consumers will have little effect on the world market, so we can assume the world price will stay the same. In contrast, the fall in the purchases by the more numerous US consumers may well drive down the world price of tea. So we need to consider small and large countries separately.

The effects of tariffs by a small country

Figure 27.4 shows the effects of a tariff imposed on a product by a small country. In each part of the figure, the supply and demand curves, *S* and *D*, relate to the country's own producers and consumers. If there were actually no trade, then the price would be where these curves intersect. However, we will assume that the price in the rest of the world, P_R, is lower than this. So, if there is free trade, the situation will be as shown in the left-hand part. The country's producers cannot charge any more than P_R, so they will produce only Q_{S0}. But the country's consumers will buy Q_{D0}, and imports will fill the gap between Q_{S0} and Q_{S0}.

We saw back in Figure 5.1 in Chapter 5 (on page 88) that the gap between the price consumers are willing to pay and the price they do pay is a gain to them called consumer surplus; it is shown here by a dark grey triangle. We also saw that the gap between the price that producers are willing to accept and the price they receive is a gain to them called producer surplus; it is shown here by a light grey triangle. The total surplus from this product in this country is the combined area of these two triangles.

Now suppose this country imposes a tariff that raises the price of imports to consumers to P_{R+T}, as shown in the right-hand part. Consumers then buy less, Q_{D1}, and their consumer surplus falls to the smaller dark grey triangle. However, at this higher price, the country's producers can now sell more, Q_{S1}, and their producer surplus rises to the larger light grey triangle. With less consumption, but more production, imports fall.

The combined consumer surplus plus producer surplus is now smaller, and the total shrinkage is shown by the areas marked 1, 2, and 3. However, the true loss from imposing the tariff is less than areas 1 + 2 + 3. This is because area 3 also shows the revenue from the tariff: the height of this area is the tariff per unit imported, that is P_{R+T} minus P_R, and its length is the number of units imported. This revenue can be spent by the government on services that

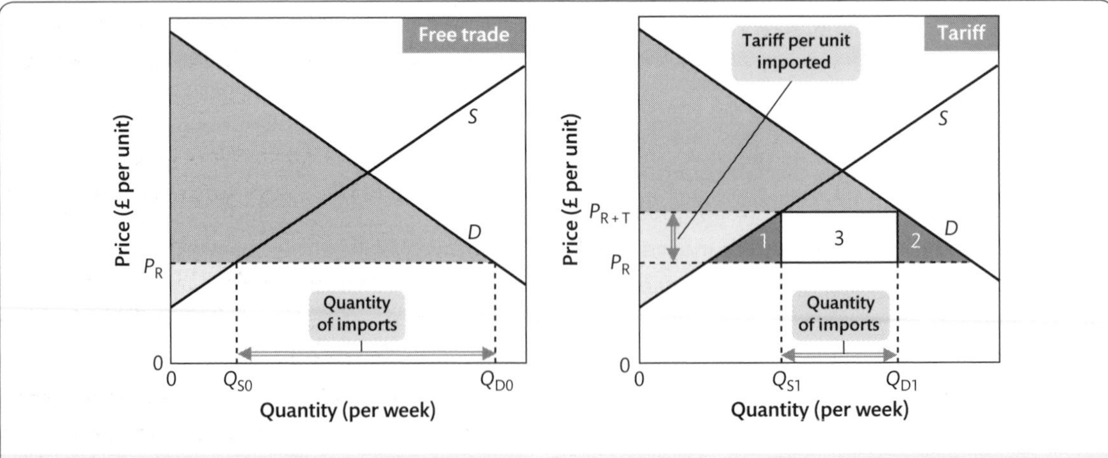

Figure 27.4 **A tariff imposed by a small country**

The left part shows in dark grey the consumer surplus and in light grey the producer surplus that arise in a country with free trade in a product where some demand is met by imports. The right part shows the effects of a tariff: consumer surplus falls, producer surplus rises, and their combined value shrinks by areas 1 + 2 + 3. However, area 3 represents the tariff revenue, which can be spent for the benefit of citizens. The net loss to citizens from the tariff is areas 1 + 2.

benefit citizens, or used to reduce other taxes that these citizens pay, so their final welfare loss actually equals areas 1 + 2.

The effects of tariffs by a large country

The effects of a tariff imposed by a large country are shown in Figure 27.5. The left-hand part shows the free trade position, in which we take the world price to be P_0. So the consumer surplus and producer surplus are as shown in dark grey and light grey.

The middle part shows the effects of a small tariff that reduces consumption a little and drives the world price down a little to P_1. The right-hand part shows the effects of a large tariff that reduces consumption more and drives the world price down to P_2. So the price paid by consumers is P_{1+T} in the middle part and P_{2+T} in the right-hand part.

In each case, the fall in consumer surplus plus producer surplus, compared with free trade, is shown by areas 1 + 2 + 3. Also, in each case, the revenue from the tariff is areas 3 + 4; notice that the tariff revenue per unit is more than the gap between P_0 and the new consumer price, because the price paid to foreign producers is below P_0.

So the final loss to this country is areas 1 + 2 + 3 minus areas 3 + 4, that is areas 1 + 2 – 4. Areas 1 and 2 are losses caused by the higher price paid by consumers; area 4 is a gain caused by the fact that the price paid to other countries has been driven down.

In the middle part of Figure 27.5, area 1 + 2 is less than area 4, so the loss, that is areas 1 + 2 – 4, is actually negative, and of course a negative loss is really a gain. So this country can gain with a tariff. Other countries will remain better off than with no trade, but not as well off as they were with free trade, because they now receive less for their exports.

But a large country that imposes a tariff should be careful. If it raises the tariff too much, then it will find as in the right-hand part that area 1 + 2 is bigger than area 4, so it will be worse off than with free trade; its problem is that while it has driven the world price down even more, it is now importing so little that this is of little benefit. It could face an additional loss if other large countries were to retaliate with tariffs on its exports. In short, a large country may be worse off with tariffs than with free trade.

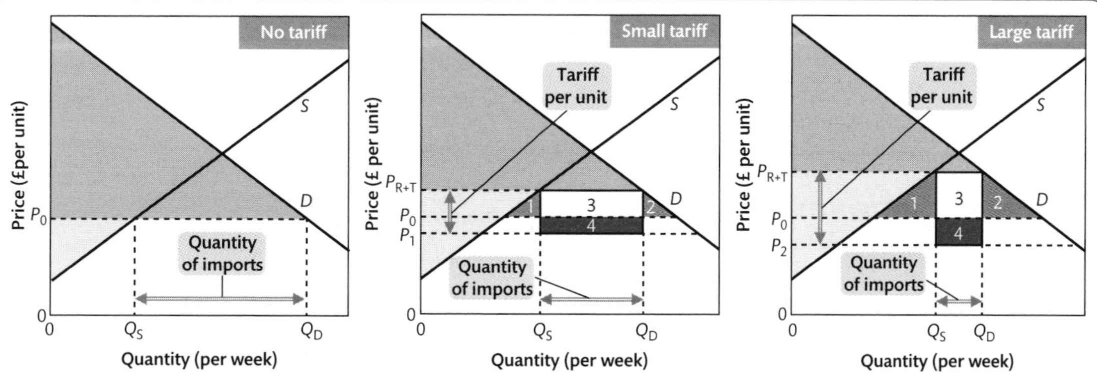

Figure 27.5 **Tariffs with a large country**

A large country's tariff may drive down the price charged by exporting countries from P_0 to P_1 in the middle part, with a small tariff, or to P_2 in the right part with a large one. Each time the total of consumer plus producer surplus falls by areas 1 + 2 + 3, but the tariff revenue is areas 3 + 4, so the net loss is areas 1 + 2 - 4. In the middle part, area 4 is bigger than areas 1 + 2, so there is actually a net gain. There is a net loss on the right where area 4 is smaller than areas 1 + 2.

Non-tariff barriers to imports

There are several other ways in which a government can reduce imports, including the following.

- **Quotas**: a country may limit the quantity of a product that can be imported. It can do this by requiring importers to obtain a licence for each shipment and by limiting the amount of licences it will issue. For example, the EU limits some food imports from outside the EU.
- **Foreign exchange controls**: a country may limit the amount of foreign currency that people can buy in order to purchase imports. The UK had such controls until 1979, and most other EU countries had them for some years after that.
- **Government department procurement policies**: these departments may be instructed to buy products like vehicles that are produced in their own country rather than imports.
- **Domestic content laws**: for example, until the 1990s, Australia restricted imports of tobacco by requiring all cigarettes made there to include at least 57% Australian tobacco.
- **Technical barriers**: a country might require all products to meet a standard that favours its own producers. For example, a country might ban food imports from another country that has had an outbreak of foot-and-mouth disease for far longer than necessary.
- **Subsidizing firms that make substitutes for imports**. For example, the EU subsidizes farmers so that it is harder for farms outside the EU to sell products within the EU.

Arguments for imposing trade barriers

Given the benefits from free trade, it may be wondered what arguments a country might use to restrict it. There are many, including the following.

- **To benefit from a fall in the price that is paid to other countries for their exports**. We saw in Figure 27.5 that a large country can reduce the price it pays to a foreign country. It could do the same with other import barriers, but it must always be wary about retaliation by other large countries.
- **To nurture infant industries**. A country may have a new industry with a comparative disadvantage, but believe that if the industry can be protected from imports, then it will in time develop a comparative advantage. This argument can justify protection for only a limited period. And while it is sometimes valid, there is a danger that the protection will simply encourage inefficiency, so that the industry never becomes competitive.
- **To soften the fall of declining industries**. If a country has an industry, such as coal mining in the UK, which is declining owing to foreign countries developing comparative advantages, it may protect it from imports to reduce the human cost in terms of job losses. But if this protection becomes permanent, then consumers will be permanently denied the full advantages of trade.
- **To protect industries from competition from low-wage countries**. This protection will certainly help industries that face competition from imports. However, we have seen that consumers benefit when countries open up trade in products for which there are differences in relative costs. This result applies whatever their relative wage rates are, and this is why we did not have to mention their relative wages rates at any point in the discussion. If trade is reduced to help industries that face competition from low-wage countries, then the benefits of trade to consumers will be reduced.
- **To help the balance of payments**. A country may spend more on imports than it earns on exports. This applies to the UK, as we saw in Tables 27.1 and 27.2. This trade deficit can cause problems, which we will explore in the next chapter. But import barriers are a risky way of tackling a deficit, because

they may encourage other countries to retaliate, which will reduce exports.

- **To promote self-sufficiency**. This was a particularly common reason given for protecting UK agriculture after the First World War, when the dangers of the UK relying on imports that were brought by ships that could be sunk had been exposed. It is also an argument often used to protect industries making armaments.
- **To protect industries from dumping**. Dumping occurs when a country's exporters sell exports at prices below their true costs, perhaps because they receive subsidies. Suppose one country engages in dumping steel. Then steel producers in other countries may want to have their industries protected by import barriers. If the dumping is expected to be temporary, then it may well be right to protect those producers from collapse, but if the dumping is expected to be permanent, then it may instead be best to allow consumers to enjoy low-priced imports.
- **To retaliate against trade barriers imposed by other countries**. If a large country retaliates to barriers imposed on its exports by other countries, then it may make its citizens better off than they would be without retaliation. But they would generally be even better off if negotiations between the countries were to remove all the barriers.
- **To save jobs**. Relative production costs are subject to constant change, so free trade means that countries sometimes find their comparative advantages and disadvantages changing. In turn, some industries expand and create more jobs, while others contract and create fewer jobs. Industries in which jobs are being lost may ask for protection with import barriers, but, while understandable, this will reduce the benefits from trade for consumers. And, in time, job losses should anyway be offset by new posts in the expanding industries.
- **For broad environmental reasons**. For example, many countries restrict trade in ivory, fur, and other animal products, and also try to restrict timber imports from countries that do not operate sustainable forest policies. Restrictions may also be placed on imports from countries with lax environmental standards which, aside from harming the environment, may keep their costs below those in countries with higher standards.
- **For political reasons**. For example, there are currently widespread barriers on trade with Iran.
- **To ban goods deemed harmful**. For example, many countries ban the import of certain drugs, and some ban the import of the Bible.

Intervention with exports

While many countries have moved away from the free trade position by restricting imports, some have interfered with exports. They have done so in contrasting ways, including the following.

- **Export subsidies**. If a country wants to help infant industries or declining industries, or indeed any other industries, it may sometimes help them to compete in world markets with subsidies. But subsidies cost governments money, so they generally prefer other methods of help, notably protecting these industries from imports with tariffs, which raise money.
- **Lax regulations**. A country might help its exporters to have relatively low costs, for example by allowing them to operate with poor safety standards, low pension contributions, and poor environmental standards.
- **Export restrictions**. The most notable example of this arose in the 1970s with OPEC, the Organization of the Petroleum Exporting Countries. These countries controlled most of the world supply of oil at the time and the demand for their oil as a whole was inelastic. By forming a cartel and forcing the price above the free trade price, they were able to earn more money from their exports, and so buy more imports, while reducing their exports of oil.

27.3 Summary

- A small country cannot gain from imposing a tariff. A large country may gain, because the tariff reduces its imports and so reduces world demand, so the world price of its remaining imports will be lower than before. But it could still end up worse off than with free trade, especially if other large countries were to retaliate.
- There are many types of non-tariff barrier to imports including quotas, foreign exchange controls, government department procurement policies, and domestic content laws.
- Aside from the benefits to large countries of reducing world prices, many other arguments are used to support trade barriers: perhaps the most persuasive are protecting infant industries, promoting self-sufficiency in key products, reducing trade in harmful products, and political and environmental issues.
- Barriers designed to protect firms from competing imports made in low-wage countries do not benefit consumers.

27.5 Breaking down trade barriers

We have seen that major barriers to trade were imposed in the 16th–18th centuries in line with the doctrine of mercantilism. Although economists championed free trade from the 18th century, barriers persisted. Indeed, they increased in the Great Depression during which countries tried to protect employment by reducing imports. For example, the US had an average tariff rate above 50%.

Admittedly, as we saw in the last section, there may be some arguments for barriers, but by 1945 it was widely accepted that all consumers would gain from major moves towards free trade. Even so, removing the barriers has been a long process. It would have been much quicker if individual countries had simply removed their own barriers and let others do the same. But countries were reluctant to act alone for two reasons.

The first reason applies to all countries. Suppose a country acts alone and removes its barriers on an import, as the UK did with corn back in 1846. Millions of UK consumers gained, but each gained only a little, so they supported the move quietly. At the same time, thousands of UK corn producers each lost a lot, so they opposed the move loudly. It would have been easier for the government if other countries had agreed to remove their barriers on UK exports at the same time. Then some other UK producers would have gained a lot, and so given the government their loud support.

The second reason applies between large countries. Consider two large countries, A and B, which have both imposed tariffs on each other, but which still do some trade. And suppose each country's consumers are £600 billion a year better off with this trade than they would be with no trade. This is shown in the top left-hand box of Figure 27.6.

Now suppose each country knows that if there were free trade with no tariffs, then its consumers would be £700 billion better off, as in the bottom right-hand box. Even so, neither country will act alone to abolish its tariffs. To see why, consider A.

A knows that as long as B has tariffs and it has tariffs itself, then it gains £600 billion. It also knows that its own tariffs drive down the price of its imports from B. So if it were to act alone and abolish its tariffs it would be worse off, and gain perhaps only £500 billion from trade, while B would be better off and gain perhaps £800 billion, as in the top right-hand box. So if B keeps its tariff, it is best for A to do the same.

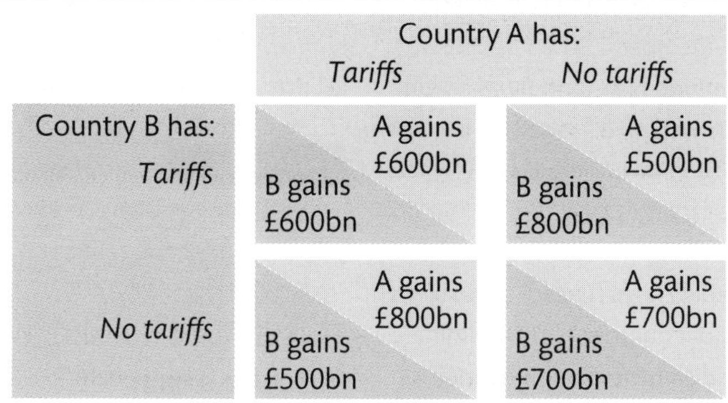

Figure 27.6 **Gains from trade**

Countries A and B would each gain £700bn if they had free trade rather than no trade. But each says 'if the other has no tariffs, we would gain even more, £800bn, if we had some; and if the other has tariffs, we would gain £500bn if we had none and £600bn if we had some'. So, if they act alone, each will have tariffs and gain £600bn. To secure free trade, they must make an agreement.

But suppose B sets a good example and abolishes its tariffs, hoping A will follow suit. Then A will reckon that if it were to follow suit, it would gain £700 billion, as in the bottom right-hand box. However, if it keeps its tariffs and drives down the price of imports from B, it might gain £800 billion while B might gain just £500 billion, as in the bottom left-hand box. So A will still keep its tariffs.

In short, whatever B does, it is best for A to keep its tariffs. Likewise, you can deduce from the figure that whatever A does, it is best for B to keep its tariffs. So, if the countries act alone, each will keep its tariffs and gain just £600 billion, even though each could gain £700 billion if they were both to remove their tariffs. If you studied Chapter 11, you will recognize this situation as an example of the prisoners' dilemma. The only way in which the tariffs will be removed and allow consumers to gain £700 billion instead of £600 billion is if the countries agree to remove them simultaneously.

For these reasons, then, tariff reduction generally needs international action, and this action comes in two main forms which we will now discuss:

- **preferential trading areas**;
- **multinational agreements**.

Free trade areas and customs unions

The most basic type of preferential trading area is a **free trade area**: this is a group of countries that aim to eliminate tariffs between them, while keeping independent tariffs against other countries. There are several of these in various stages of development, including the following.

- **The Association of Southeast Asian Nations Free Trade Area (called the ASEAN Free Trade Association, or AFTA)**. This has ten members, of which Indonesia, the Philippines, and Vietnam are the most populous.
- **The North American Free Trade Association (NAFTA)**. This comprises Canada, Mexico, and the US.
- **Asia-Pacific Economic Cooperation (APEC)**. This promotes free trade and has 21 members including many members of ATFA, all members of NAFTA, and China, Japan, Russia, and Taiwan.
- **Mercosur**. This comprises Argentina, Brazil, Paraguay, and Uruguay; it also has several associate South American countries.

The fact that members may have different tariffs on non-members can cause intriguing effects. For example, suppose member A sets a higher tariff than member B on products from a non-member C. Then people in A can escape their government's high tariff by importing indirectly through B. They will pay B's lower tariff when the imports arrive there, and pay nothing more when the imports continue their journey to A.

To avoid this, countries may instead form another type of preferential trading area called a **customs union**, in which a group of countries aim to eliminate tariffs between them *and* to have common tariffs on other countries. The EU is a customs union. Mercosur aspires to become one.

Trade creation and trade diversion

When a country joins a free trade area or a customs union, its trade is affected in two ways.

- **Trade creation**. This means that a country does more trade once it joins. To see why, suppose the cost of making a good is £8 in country A, £6 in a nearby customs union, and £10 in the rest of the world. And suppose country A has a 50% tariff on all imports, so its consumers will have to pay £9 for imports from the union and £15 for imports from elsewhere. Then they will buy no imports. But if country A joins the union and removes its tariffs on imports from there, then its consumers will buy the import from the union because they can now buy it for just £6. So some trade will be created.
- **Trade diversion**. This means that a country will divert some trade once it joins a customs union or free trade area. To see why, suppose the cost of making a good is £10 in country A, £8 in a nearby union, and £6 in the rest of the world. And suppose country A has a 50% tariff on all imports, so its consumers will have to pay £12 for imports from the union and £9 for imports from elsewhere; then they will import from elsewhere. But if country A joins the union, and removes its tariff on imports from there, then its consumers will divert their purchases and buy the import from the union, because this will now cost them £8.

Trade creation and trade diversion contribute to the high level of trade between the UK and the rest of the EU that we noted in Table 27.2.

Question 27.2 Can you spot why economists regard trade diversion as less desirable than trade creation?

The EU and the single European market

We have seen that the EU is a customs union. It was founded in 1957 with six members, and was initially called the European Economic Community (EEC). It now has 27 members. Table 27.6, shows the dates at which different countries joined and also some other key dates in EU history.

Table 27.6 **The 27 EU members—as of 2011—and key dates in the evolution of the EU**

1957: **Belgium, France, West Germany, Italy, Luxembourg,** and the **Netherlands** sign the Treaty of Rome. This creates the European Economic Community (EEC) as a customs union.

1973: **Denmark,** the **UK,** and **Ireland** join the EEC.

1981: **Greece** joins the EEC.

1986: **Portugal** and **Spain** join the EEC.

1986: The Single European Act is signed. This promotes a single market by allowing most future Directives needed to create a single market to be adopted with majority support rather than unanimous support.

1990: West Germany is reunited with East Germany.

1992: The Maastricht Treaty re-establishes the EEC as the European Union (EU) from 1993, and paves the way for a common currency by stating the criteria that countries aiming to join the euro must meet.

1995: **Austria, Finland,** and **Sweden** join the EU.

2002: The euro is introduced and is used by 16 members, plus Estonia from 2011, as shown on Table 26.3, plus Estonia from 2011.

2004: **Cyprus**, the **Czech Republic, Estonia, Hungary, Latvia, Lithuania, Malta, Poland, Slovakia,** and **Slovenia** join the EU.

2007: **Bulgaria** and **Romania** join the EU.

However, the EU has always aimed to go beyond a customs union. Given the benefits of free trade, a customs union has several limitations, as follows.

- **There may be non-trade barriers.** These may protect inefficient businesses and, in some industries, prevent firms from expanding sufficiently to take full advantage of the possibilities of economies of scale.
- **There may be barriers to the movement of labour and finance.** These may prevent labour going where it is most productive, and prevent investors investing in the projects with the highest returns. Barriers to the movement of labour include one country not recognizing qualifications earned in another, or having poorer social security.

Many EU members have long aspired to remove all non-trade barriers and barriers to the movement of labour and capital. This would create a **single market** in which firms compete just as they do in a single country. To create such a single market, the EU would have to harmonize hundreds of regulations and have largely common taxes, and all EU members would have to use the euro.

The EU has not yet reached this position, but it is progressing towards it. The Single European Act of 1986 was a big step, because this allowed the EU to issue many Directives that would promote a single market if they secured the support of merely majority of EU members; previously they had needed unanimous support. The EU estimates that, over the period 1992–2006, its progress towards a single market had great benefits including the following.

- **Increasing the EU's GDP by 2.2%.** In 2006 alone, this was worth about £300 for every EU citizen.
- **Increasing consumer choice and reducing prices,** for example with air travel and phone calls.
- **Creating 2.75 million jobs.**
- **Making it easier to live and study abroad.**

Multinational agreements: the GATT

Aside from forming preferential trading areas, countries can try to free up trade with multinational agreements. This approach began in 1947 in Geneva. There, 23 countries began a round of talks that led to substantial cuts in the tariffs on goods. Their agreement was called the General Agreement on Tariffs and Trade (GATT).

There were seven later rounds of GATT negotiations, mostly named after the place where they began and their dates they began. These were as follows: Annecy (France) 1949; Torquay (UK) 1950–51; Geneva II 1956; Dillon 1960–61 (Douglas Dillon was the US Treasury Secretary who initiated this round); Kennedy 1964–67 (named after US President John F. Kennedy); Tokyo 1973–79; and Uruguay 1986–93.

By the time of the Tokyo round, over 100 countries were involved and the discussion went beyond tariffs to non-tariff barriers. The Uruguay round made even further inroads into non-tariff barriers, and also covered trade in services. It also obliged signatories who were developing nations to begin removing their import barriers.

The World Trade Organization

The Uruguay round also agreed for the GATT to be replaced in 1995 by a permanent body called the World Trade Organization (WTO). This has 153 members and so covers the bulk of world trade.

The WTO has overseen a number of agreements, but the only wide round of talks it has started is the 2001 Doha (Qatar) round. This has not yet reached any settlement. Its lack of conclusion arises partly because the WTO now has so many members, and partly because this round is focusing on tricky issues that earlier GAT rounds either ignored or left unresolved; these include the environment and more access by developing countries into the markets of developed countries. A major sticking point is the way in which the EU and Japan subsidize and protect agriculture.

It has been suggested that the GATT and the WTO have helped the average level of tariffs on goods fall from over 40% in 1945 to under 4% today. And there should be no slipping back, because countries agree not to raise their tariffs, and not to raise any non-tariff barriers, unless the changes are agreed with other WTO countries.

If a WTO member is believed to be breaking any GATT or WTO agreement, then it can be referred to the WTO. And if the WTO accepts that its rules have been broken, then it can allow other countries to retaliate against the offender. In practice, countries that have been found to breach the rules have always come back into line rather than face retaliation.

27.2 Everyday economics

WTO orders EU to lift high-tech tariffs

The WTO has ordered the EU to remove tariffs on $11bn worth of high-tech goods, following complaints by the US, Japan, and Taiwan. The complaint hinged on a WTO rule that there should be no tariffs on a wide range of 'high-tech' electronic goods. The EU had imposed tariffs of up to 14% on flat-panel computer screens, and printers that also scan, fax, or copy, arguing that these were old-fashioned consumer goods, not high-tech. If the EU fails to remove the tariffs, then the WTO will allow the US, Japan, and Taiwan to impose tariffs on goods made in the EU.

'WTO orders EU to lift tech tariffs', *Wall Street Journal*, 17 August 2010
'WTO dispute ruling high tech products', *EurActiv*, 17 August 2010

Comment The WTO would allow retaliation on $11bn worth of EU exports, which could, for example, cover all EU exports of cars, pharmaceuticals, and cheese.

27.5 Summary

- Countries may find it easier to reduce trade barriers collectively than unilaterally.
- A free trade area is a group of countries with no internal tariffs, but with independent external tariffs.
- A customs union is a group of countries with no internal tariffs and with common external tariffs.
- The EU has gone beyond a customs union with major moves towards a single market in which there would be no non-trade barriers and no barriers to the movement of labour or finance.
- The General Agreement on Tariffs and Trade (GATT) and its successor, the World Trade Organization (WTO), have made great progress in reducing tariffs between over 150 countries.

In the next chapter we consider payments between countries and exchange rates between currencies.

abc Glossary

Absolute advantage: a country has an absolute advantage in a product if it needs less labour than another country to make it.

Comparative advantage: a country has a comparative advantage in a product if it has a lower opportunity cost for it than another country.

Customs union: a group of countries with no internal tariffs and with common external tariffs.

Dumping: when a country sells exports at prices below their true costs, perhaps because its firms receive subsidies.

Free trade: a situation with no barriers to trade.

Free trade area: a group of countries with no internal tariffs but with independent external tariffs.

Intra-industry trade: trade within industries.

Single market: a customs union the members of which also remove all non-trade barriers and barriers to movements of labour and finance between them.

Tariff: a tax on an imported product.

Trade creation: the new trade done by a country joining a free trade area or customs union, created by the removal of tariffs between it and other members.

Trade diversion: the trade that a country joining a free trade area or customs union has with other members, but previously had with non-members.

Answers to in-text questions

27.1 If Sri Lanka shifts one worker a day from DVDs to tops, it produces 3 more tops and 2 fewer DVDs. Say it exports all 3 extra tops each day to the UK; there, the price of a DVD is 1½ times that of a top, so Sri Lanka can use the money from its exports to buy 2 UK DVDs each day. So it has produced 2 fewer DVDs and 3 more tops, but it has exported all 3 extra tops to buy only 2 DVDs. So it gains no extra consumption.

27.2 With trade creation, production of a product switches from the new member to another union member that has lower production costs. With trade creation, production switches from a non-union member to a union member that actually has higher production costs.

Questions for review

27.1 Alphaland and Betaland use only labour as an input, and produce only cloth and potatoes. They do not trade, and a week's labour can produce the below outputs.

	Alphaland	Betaland
Cloth	20 m^2	15 m^2
Potatoes	1 tonne	3 tonnes

(a) For each product, say which country has the absolute advantage.

(b) For each country, what is the opportunity cost of each product?

(c) For each product, which country has the comparative advantage?

(d) Explain briefly how each country could shift some labour and gain from trade.

27.2 Suppose that the figures in question 27.1 were the same, except that one week's labour in Alphaland could produce 10 tonnes of potatoes instead of 1 tonne. What would the answers to question 27.1 have been?

27.3 Why might two countries that have identical production possibility frontiers benefit from trade?

27.4 **(a)** If a single country were to impose a tariff, could it be better off?

(b) If a country or group of countries were to restrict exports, could it or they be better off?

Questions for discussion

27.1 Think of some products you have bought recently that were made abroad, aside from those suggested in the chapter opener. Was each of these imported because the country that supplied it has a comparative advantage? If so, why does it have one?

27.2 Suppose the EU wants a fully single market with common taxes, regulations, and a common currency in all countries. Would this inevitably mean effectively forming a single country and so having political union?

Common student errors

One error is to claim that trade theory proves that trade benefits everyone: it certainly shows that countries as a whole benefit from trade, but it also shows that opening up trade means that some industries contract, so their profits fall and some of their workers lose their jobs, so some people may well end up worse off.

Another error is to suppose that trade theory proves that countries can never benefit by imposing tariffs: in fact, the theory shows how a large country may benefit from tariffs, or indeed other import barriers, and that some country groups like OPEC can benefit from restricting exports.

Finally, it is tempting to say 'countries trade when they have comparative advantages in different products'. But look at Figure 27.1: the countries there end up producing at the pink spots where they have identical relative costs, so neither country has a comparative advantage in either product. Likewise the UK has similar relative costs in different products to most of its trading partners. It is sharper to say 'countries trade when, if they did not trade, they would have comparative advantages in different products'; in Figure 27.1, for example, they would be at the black spots where they have different relative costs.

28

International Finance

Remember from Chapter 26 that a government may wish to use monetary or fiscal policy if output is not at its potential level. And remember from Chapter 20 that if the government pays sterling to the public, bank reserves rise so the money stock rises; if the public pay sterling to the government, the opposite happens.

The balance of payments is often mentioned on the news, but what does it mean? Does it matter? The exchange rate between sterling and other currencies changes frequently; indeed, if you take a foreign holiday, the rate may change adversely between the day you leave and buy foreign currencies, and the day you return and sell what you have left. Why do exchange rates fluctuate? Does it matter if they do? Do international payments affect the government's ability to try to maintain output at its potential level and to restrain inflation? Should the UK give up the pound and use the euro?

This chapter shows you how to answer questions like these, by understanding:

- what we mean by the balance of payments;
- the forces that determine the exchange rate between the pound and other currencies;
- how international payments affect the government's ability to use monetary and fiscal policy;
- the arguments about whether the UK should use the euro.

28.1 The balance of payments accounts

This chapter is concerned with payments between the UK and other countries. It has five sections, and these explore the following five questions.

- **What do these international payments cover, how large are they, and why do they matter?**
- **What determines the exchange rates between the various currencies used in these payments?**
- **How do exchange rates relate to prices and interest rates?**
- **How do international payments affect the use of monetary and fiscal policy by the government?**
- **What might the UK gain, and what might it lose, if it decided to use the euro instead of sterling?**

The balance of payments account

Government statisticians try to record the value in pounds of all the payments between the UK and abroad. Among these payments are those made when UK citizens acquire foreign assets, and those made when foreigners acquire UK assets.

Table 28.1 gives a summary of the records for 2010. Payments into the UK are recorded in the column headed 'Credits', and these payments are given positive values. Payments out of the UK are recorded in the column headed 'Debits', and these payments are given negative values.

The column headed 'Balance' shows the gap between the credits and the debits for each item on the table. A positive balance for an item shows that credits were bigger than debits, and this is called a surplus; a negative balance shows that credits were smaller than debits, and this is called a deficit. A table like this, which gives the balance for international payments, is called the **balance of payments account**.

The balance of payments current account

The balance of payments account begins with a 'current account'. This covers the following.

- **Trade in goods**. Credits here are payments to UK firms for exported goods. Debits are payments to foreign firms for imported goods. The UK almost always has a large deficit here.
- **Trade in services**. Credits here are payments to UK firms for exported services. Debits are payments to foreign firms for imported services. The UK almost always has a large surplus here.
- **Wage income**. Credits here are wages paid to UK citizens by employers located abroad. Debits are

Table 28.1 **UK balance of payments, 2010**

	Credits (£bn)	Debits (£bn)	Balance (£bn)
Current account			
Trade in goods	265	−363	−98
Trade in services	163	−113	50
Wage income	1	−2	−1
Investment income	170	−137	33
Current transfers	14	−34	−20
Current balance			**−36**
Capital & financial account			
Capital transfers	6	−3	3
Direct investment	28	−16	12
Portfolio investment	87	−76	10
Loans and deposits	224	−241	−17
Financial derivatives			26
Reserves			−6
Capital & financial balance			**28**
Errors and omissions			**8**
Overall balance			**0**

Source: Office for National Statistics, *Statistical Bulletin, Balance of Payments*, 4th quarter 2010 and annual 2010.

wages paid to foreigners by employers in the UK. The UK generally has a small deficit here.

- **Investment income**. Credits here are receipts of interest, profits, and dividends by UK citizens who own the whole or part of foreign firms, or who have lent money abroad. Debits are similar payments to foreigners from the UK. The UK generally has a large surplus here.
- **Current transfers**. Credits here cover most gifts received by the UK from abroad. These include most payments to the UK by the EU and foreign governments, taxes paid to the UK by foreign tax-payers, and most private gifts from foreign citizens. Debits cover similar, but usually larger, payments paid to foreign countries from the UK.

The news media are chiefly interested in two figures that can be found from the current account of the balance of payments, as follows.

- The **balance of trade**: this is the balance for the trade in goods and services combined. We can work out from Table 28.1 that the balance of trade in 2010 was –£98 billion plus £50 billion, which gives a combined deficit of –£48 billion. The UK generally has a balance of trade deficit.
- The **current balance**: this is the overall balance for the current account. Table 28.1 shows that in 2010 it was a deficit of –£36 billion. The UK has had a current deficit in each year since 1986.

The capital and financial account

The next part of the balance of payments is the 'capital and financial account'. The credits here cover the money received from foreigners who acquire UK assets, minus the money paid to foreigners who dispose of UK assets. The debits cover the money spent by UK citizens who acquire foreign assets, minus the money received by UK citizens who dispose of foreign assets.

The six items on the capital and financial account concern different types of asset. We will take these in turn, although we will leave the first item, capital transfers, until last.

- **Direct investment**. This covers assets in the form of the ownership of 10% or more of a business. For example, a Chinese firm buying a UK car plant adds to credits here.
- **Portfolio investment**. This covers assets in the form of securities, other than any bought for direct investment. For example, a UK citizen buying shares in Fiat adds to debits here.
- **Loans and deposits**. Credits here cover new loans by foreigners to the UK, minus any existing loans that are repaid to them. Credits also cover money placed by foreigners in deposits in the UK, minus any withdrawals. Table 28.1 shows a figure for 2010 of £224 billion; this means foreigners paid £224 billion more to the UK than they took from it. Debits cover new loans by UK citizens abroad, minus any existing loans that are repaid to them. Debits also cover money placed by UK citizens in deposits abroad, minus any withdrawals. Table 28.1 shows a figure for 2010 of –£241 billion, this means UK citizens paid £241 billion more abroad than they took from abroad.
- **Financial derivatives**. This item covers payments made for various types of financial contract. The statisticians just give a balance here. In 2010 it was positive at £26 billion, so, on these contracts more money flowed into the UK than flowed out.
- **Reserves**. The UK government owns some gold and foreign currencies, which it calls reserves. Table 28.1 just gives the balance of spending on reserves in 2010. This was –£6 billion, which means that the government spent £6 billion more on buying reserves than it received from selling reserves. So, very confusingly, this negative sign means that its reserves actually rose!

These five items all record payments made when people acquire or dispose of assets in different countries from their own. But sometimes people make payments concerning assets without acquiring any, and sometimes people acquire assets in other countries without making any payments. The capital transfers item captures these cases, and it includes the following.

- **EU capital grants**. For example, the EU may give a grant for a new road in the UK. The money flowing in is a credit, but the EU does not own the road.
- **Waiving debt**. For example, the UK government may waive the debt on a £1 million loan it has made to a foreign country. Although no money changes hands, the accounts assume that the loan is actually repaid, which raises credits under loans and investment by £1 million, and they assume that the government then sends £1 million back as a gift, which adds £1 million to debits under capital transfers.
- **Migration**. Suppose you borrow £1 million from a UK bank, buy a UK firm, and then emigrate. At this time, no money changes hands. However, the accounts add a £1 million debit under loans and deposits, because the UK bank is now lending £1 million to a foreigner, and they add a £1 million credit in capital transfers, because a £1 million UK asset has been transferred to a foreign owner.

Table 28.1 gives the 2010 net balance for the capital and financial accounts as £28 billion. This is positive: so, overall, foreign citizens acquired more assets in the UK than UK citizens acquired abroad. This is usually the case.

Capital flows and capital mobility

In Table 28.1, the only item that uses the word 'capital' is capital transfers. However, economists use the term **capital flows** to cover all the items on the capital and financial accounts. The ease with which people can make these flows between countries is called **capital mobility**. Until the 1980s, most governments restricted these flows, but capital mobility is now very high.

Notice that many capital flows concern funds used for buying securities, making deposits, or making loans. Relatively few capital flows are concerned with purchases of capital as we have defined it in the rest of this book, namely goods such as plant, buildings, vehicles, and machinery.

Why the payments always balance

The statisticians are unable to record every item in the balance of payments accurately, and Table 28.1 gives a net figure for errors and omissions of £8 billion. Taken with a current deficit of –£36 billion and a capital and financial surplus of £28 billion, this gives an overall balance of £0 billion. The balance always is zero, and this is simply because every transaction between a UK citizen and abroad actually gives rise to two offsetting entries in the accounts.

To see this, suppose you use the Internet to buy a €60 good from a French firm, and suppose the exchange rate is £1 = €1.20, so this good is worth £50. Clearly, you add a £50 debit to trade in goods, but you actually also add a £50 credit. Exactly how you do this depends on how you pay for your purchase. Here are just four possibilities.

- **You borrow €60 from a French bank**: then that bank makes a €60 loan to a UK citizen, so £50 is added to credits under loans and deposits.
- **You pay £50 to a French bank and ask it for €60**: then that French bank acquires £50, which it may well place in a deposit in the UK, so again £50 is added to credits under loans and deposits.
- **You might have a deposit in a French bank and use €60 from it**: then your withdrawal will reduce debits under loans and deposits by £50.
- **You ask your UK bank for €60**: then your bank may well find these euros by withdrawing them from a deposit it has at a French bank, so again debits under loans and deposits fall by £50.

Does the balance of payments matter?

We have just seen that the balance of payments must always balance, yet the media often refer to a balance of payments deficit. By this, they usually mean a balance of trade deficit or a current account deficit. Do either of these deficits matter?

To answer this, consider first a current deficit. Because the balance of payments must balance, a current deficit must be offset by a surplus on the capital and financing account. So more money flows in from foreign citizens acquiring assets here than flows out from UK citizens acquiring assets abroad. Effectively, the UK is borrowing from abroad. This matters if the total debt owed by the UK to foreign countries is growing faster than the UK's GDP: in that case, the UK will in future have to spend a larger proportion of its GDP paying interest on this debt and on repaying it.

Next consider a balance of trade deficit. This occurs when actual exports, which we will call X, are smaller than actual imports, which we will call M. So the trade balance ($X - M$) is negative. To see if this deficit matters, suppose first that the balances for wage income, investment income, and current transfers are zero. Then the current account deficit equals ($X - M$), and this in turn shows how much has to be borrowed from abroad on the capital and financing account.

Now recall from Chapter 19 that, in a four-sector economy, actual withdrawals equal actual injections. So:

$$I + G + X = S + T + M$$

where I, G, S, and T refer to the actual figures for investment, government purchases, saving, and taxes. We can rearrange this equation as follows:

$$(X - M) = (S - I) + (T - G)$$

So if there is a balance of trade deficit, and the left-hand side is negative, then the right-hand side must also be negative. So either S is less than I, or T is less than G, or both. This means that the borrowing from abroad, which offsets the trade deficit, is effectively financing gaps between I and S, or G and T, or both. Whether this borrowing matters depends, once again, on how fast the debt to foreign countries is growing in relation to GDP.

But remember that we assumed that the balances for wage income, investment income, and current transfers were all zero. In practice, the UK always has a net surplus on these items taken together. This means that the current deficit is always less than the trade deficit. In turn, borrowing from abroad is always smaller than the trade deficit.

28.1 Summary

- The UK's balance of payments accounts record payments between the UK and abroad. They include payments for foreign assets acquired by UK citizens, and payments for UK assets acquired by foreigners.
- The balance of payments current account covers exports and imports, wages for people with foreign employers, interest, profits and dividends for people with assets in foreign countries, and current transfers or gifts. The capital and financial account covers capital transfers, direct investment, portfolio investment, loans, and deposits.
- Allowing for errors and omissions, the overall deficit or surplus on the current account is matched by an offsetting surplus or deficit on the capital and financial account. This leaves an overall balance of zero.
- A capital and financial account surplus means the country is increasing its debt to foreign countries.

28.2 How exchange rates are determined

Using foreign currencies

Let's return to your Internet purchase of a French good priced at €60. Most likely you only own pounds and the supplier wants euros, so somewhere your pounds must be exchanged for euros. There are many currency exchanges, including banks, and banks will probably be used in this case. You could pay in pounds, and leave the exporter to exchange the pounds for euros at its bank. Or you could ask your bank to exchange some of your pounds for euros and use those.

Suppose the current actual exchange rate, which we call the **nominal exchange rate**, is £1 = €1.20. Then the deal will cost you £50. But what determines this exchange rate? Before we answer that, we must note five important points.

- **Currency exchanges are regarded as buying and selling currencies in a market**. This market is called the **foreign exchange market**.
- **There are separate exchange rates between sterling and each other currency**. As an example, this section will focus on the exchange rate between sterling and the euro.
- **For each currency there are two exchange rates, one for people buying it and a slightly lower one for people selling it**. The reason is that currency exchanges need to hold large amounts of many different currencies in sight deposits, ready to sell them to anyone who wants to buy them. These deposits earn little interest, and the exchanges could earn more income by lending their funds or by using them to buy securities. They want a profit on their foreign exchange deals to compensate them for the low interest on these deposits. However, the gaps between the two exchange rates are modest, and we will ignore them in what follows.
- **Exchange rates are set by the exchanges.**
- **For any pair of currencies, say pounds and euros, all exchanges set the same exchange rate at any moment in time.**

Question 28.1 What would happen if, at the same time, Bank A set a rate of £1 = €1.25 and Bank B set £1 = €1.15?

The market for a currency

Currency exchanges alter their exchange rates frequently, so we will look at the rate that applies for a brief period of one minute. During this minute, many people will come to the exchanges, some supplying pounds that they want to use to buy euros, and some demanding pounds for which they will pay in euros. Between them, these people will no doubt want foreign currencies to handle transactions of all of the types that are covered by Table 28.1.

The exchange rate for £1 in terms of euros is effectively the price of £1 in euros. So the exchange rate, or price, during this minute, will be determined by the supply and demand for pounds during this minute. This is shown in Figure 28.1. Here, the horizontal axis measures the quantity of pounds during the minute, and the vertical axis measures the price of £1 in euros.

At each possible exchange rate, the demand curve, *D*, shows how many pounds would be demanded over the minute by people selling euros, and the supply curve, S_0, shows how many pounds would be supplied over the minute by people buying euros. These curves intersect at point ***a***, at a price of £1 = €1.20. This point shows the quantity of pounds that will be supplied and demanded, and the price the exchanges will set. Let's see why they will not set any other price.

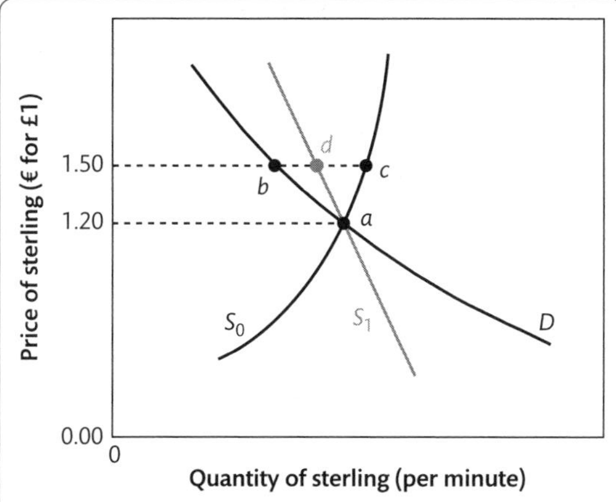

Figure 28.1 **The price of sterling in euros**

The demand curve for sterling slopes downwards. The supply curve may slope upwards, like S_0, but it could slope backwards like S_1 if the demand for most imports was inelastic.

- **If they set a lower price**: then the quantity of pounds demanded would exceed the quantity supplied, so they might run out of pounds.
- **If they set a higher price**: then the quantity of pounds supplied would exceed the quantity demanded. This means the quantity of euros demanded would exceed the quantity supplied, so they might run out of euros.

The shape of the demand and supply curves

The demand curve for pounds must slope downwards, as shown in Figure 28.1. To see why, consider a UK good that is priced at £100. With the exchange rate of £1 = €1.20, this good costs eurozone residents €120.

But suppose the exchange rate rose, say to £1 = €1.50. Then this good would cost eurozone residents €150. So they would buy fewer units of it, and would therefore spend fewer pounds on it. This would apply to all products, so eurozone residents would demand fewer pounds at this exchange rate, as shown by point ***b*** in Figure 28.1.

The supply curve for pounds doubtless slopes upwards, as shown by S_0 in Figure 28.1, but in prinicple it might not. To see why consider a eurozone good that is priced at €120. With the exchange rate of £1 = €1.20, this good costs UK residents £100.

But suppose the exchange rate rises, say to £1 = €1.50. Then the good will cost UK residents £80, so they will buy more units of it. However, the euros they need for each unit will now cost them only £80 instead of £100. So will they actually supply more pounds or fewer pounds?

This depends on the elasticity of demand for the good. If its demand was elastic, then UK citizens would buy many more units and so supply more pounds, as at point ***c*** Figure 28.1. If its demand was inelastic, they would buy only a few more units and so supply fewer pounds, as at point ***d***.

In practice, the demand for some UK imports is inelastic, but it is elastic for most. So the supply curve of pounds slopes upwards like S_0, which passes point ***c***. But if the demand for imports were mostly inelastic, then the supply curve would slope backwards like S_1, which passes point ***d***.

The causes of changes in demand and supply

Exchange rates change continually because the supply and demand for currencies change continually. We know that people demand and supply pounds for many types of transaction, and this means that the supply and demand can shift for a whole raft of reasons.

We will consider first the main events that cause the demand for pounds to increase. Opposite events cause it to decrease.

- **A rise in incomes abroad**. This will increase the demand by foreign citizens for UK exports, and so increase the demand for pounds.
- **A general rise in the prices of products produced abroad, or a general fall in the prices of products produced in the UK**. These events will increase the

demand by foreign citizens for UK exports, and so increase the demand for pounds.

- **A rise in UK interest rates or a fall in foreign rates.** These events will tempt people with bank deposits in foreign currencies to switch to deposits in sterling, so increasing the demand for pounds.
- **News that suggests improved prospects for UK industry.** This will tempt foreign citizens to buy securities issued by UK companies, so increasing the demand for pounds.
- **An expected rise in the value of sterling.** This will tempt speculators to switch from deposits of foreign currencies to deposits of sterling, which they hope will rise in value, and this will increase the demand for pounds.

We will consider next the main events that cause the supply of pounds to increase. Opposite events will cause it to decrease.

- **A rise in UK incomes.** This will increase the demand by UK citizens for imports, so they will increase the supply of pounds as they buy more foreign currencies.
- **A general fall in the prices of products produced abroad, or a general rise in the prices of products produced in the UK.** These events will increase the demand by UK citizens for imports, and so increase the supply of pounds.
- **A fall in UK interest rates or a rise in foreign rates.** These events will tempt people with bank deposits in sterling to switch to deposits in foreign currencies, so increasing the supply of pounds as they buy more foreign currencies.
- **News that suggests improved prospects for industry abroad.** This will tempt UK citizens to buy securities issued by foreign companies, so increasing the supply of pounds as they buy more foreign currencies.
- **An expected fall in the value of sterling.** This will tempt speculators to switch from deposits of sterling, which might fall in value, to deposits in foreign currencies. This will increase the supply of pounds as they buy more foreign currencies.

These are only the main reasons why the demand and supply of currencies may change. There are many other possibilities. For example, a foreign government might demand pounds in order to buy arms made in the UK. Or UK citizens might decide to help a foreign country, and so supply pounds.

The effects of changes in demand and supply

The effects of changes in demand and supply are shown in Figure 28.2. Here, the initial demand and supply curves are D_0 and S_0, and they give an initial exchange rate of £1 = €1.20. But suppose demand increases to D_1 or supply decreases to S_1. Then the pound will rise in value to €1.50. A rise in the value of a currency on the foreign exchange markets is called an **appreciation**. Or suppose supply increases to S_2 or that demand decreases to D_2. Then the pound will fall in value to €1.00. A fall in the value of a currency on the foreign exchange markets is called a **depreciation**.

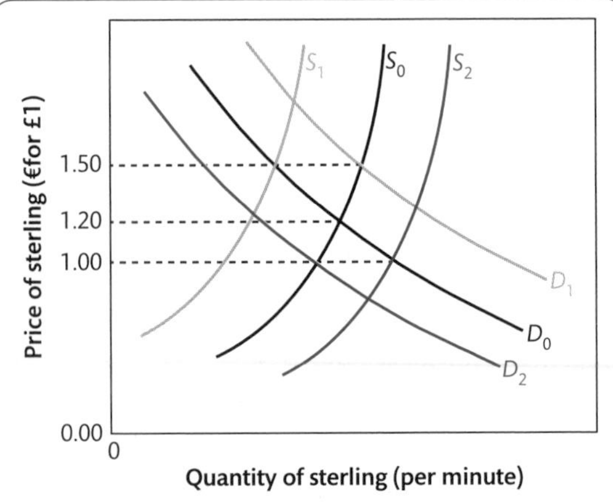

Figure 28.2 **Currency appreciation and depreciation**

Sterling will appreciate if the demand for it increases, or if the supply decreases, and it will depreciate if the supply of it increases or if the demand decreases.

Exchange rate regimes

Sometimes, governments intervene in the foreign exchange markets to affect the value of their currencies. Governments can adopt various approaches to this sort of intervention, or, as economists put it, they can adopt different exchange rate regimes, as follows.

- **A fixed exchange rate.** Here, a government fixes the value of its currency against another. For example, Hong Kong fixes the HK dollar at 12.8 US cents. If the supply of HK dollars falls, or if the demand rises, so that exchanges might raise their value, the Hong Kong authorities increase the supply of HK dollars by selling some for foreign currencies, which they then place in their reserves of foreign currencies. If the supply of HK dollars rises, or if the demand falls, so that exchanges might reduce their value, the authorities increase the demand for HK dollars by using some of the foreign currencies in their reserves to buy some.

  A fixed exchange rate has a problem, which is that when there is downward pressure on a country's currency, its government must use some of its reserves of foreign currencies to buy some, and it must continue to do so until the pressure eases. If the pressure persists, it may run out of reserves and have to let the exchange rate fall, unless it is lent some more foreign currencies. The International Monetary Fund sometimes makes such loans. Hong Kong is not concerned about this problem because it has huge reserves.

- **Adjustable peg.** This is like a fixed exchange rate except that a country will reduce, or devalue, the value of its currency if its reserves run low. Most developed countries adopted this regime after 1945, pegging their currencies to the US dollar, which the US in turn pegged at $35 per ounce of gold. Sterling was devalued against the dollar in 1949 and 1967. The UK and many other countries abandoned this regime in the 1970s because huge oil price rises forced them to spend more on imports. Then the supplies of their currencies on exchange markets rose greatly and it became impossible to peg their values.

- **Managed float.** Here, a country generally lets the value of its currency fluctuate in line with market forces, but occasionally intervenes. For example, China sometimes sells its currency, the yuan, for foreign currencies in order to hold the yuan's value down and so keep its exports highly competitive. The UK adopted this regime after 1973, but management became harder in the 1980s when capital controls ended.

- **A floating exchange rate.** Here, a government lets the value of its currency fluctuate in line with market forces, with no intervention. This is effectively the regime that most countries now adopt, including the UK. Indeed, it is has had little option since it abandoned capital flows in the 1980s. For example, if the demand for sterling fell and the UK government tried to prevent its value falling, then it would have to use some of the foreign currencies in its reserves to buy sterling. But its reserves are limited, so people would doubt whether it could prevent the fall. So people would exchange huge amounts of sterling for more stable currencies, which would make it impossible to prevent a fall.

  However, a floating exchange rate has two problems. One is that depreciations threaten inflation, because people have to use more of their currency to buy imports, while appreciations threaten unemployment, by encouraging the country's citizens to buy imports instead of products made in their own country, and by encouraging citizens abroad to buy fewer of the country's exports. The other problem is that floating exchange rates also create uncertainty for firms that undertake exports and imports, so they may do less trade, so reducing the benefits to consumers from trade.

- **Exchange rate band.** This is when a country aims to keep the value of its currency within a broad band of one or more others. The UK did actually move from a floating exchange rate into an exchange rate band from 1990 to 1992, when it joined an arrangement that the EU operated at the time called the Exchange Rate Mechanism (ERM). The idea of the ERM was to encourage stability between the currencies of the countries that hoped to join the euro. But by 1992, it was widely believed that the UK could not keep within its band and that the pound would soon fall in value. So speculators sold billions of pounds. Unable to buy them all, the government left the band on 16 September. This was called Black Wednesday because it was humiliating for the government, but the subsequent floating regime led to a fall in sterling that helped to pave the way for rising exports and sustained growth until 2008.

28.2 Summary

- The actual or nominal exchange rate between one currency and another is set in the foreign exchange market and depends on the supply and demand for the currencies concerned. Exchange rates generally move continually in line with shifts in supply and demand.
- A government can choose to have a fixed exchange rate for its currency, but must then itself demand or supply its currency to whatever extent is needed to keep its value stable. It will need large reserves of foreign currencies with which to buy its currency if the demand for it by other people is low.
- Most countries, including the UK, effectively adopt a floating exchange rate regime, and their governments do not intervene in the value of their currencies.

28.3 Looking behind the exchange rates

We now know that exchange rates are determined by the supply and demand for currencies. Now the supply and demand arise chiefly when people trade or make capital flows. So we will now look at trade and capital flows to see how they are related to exchange rates.

Exports, imports, and the law of one price

To understand the relationship between exchange rates and trade, we must look first at the so-called law of one price. We will explain this by considering a product, wheat, and two of the countries where it is produced, the UK and the US.

The **law of one price** is a theory that the prices that producers in different countries set for a product will all be the same, if they are expressed in a single currency at the current exchange rate. So if, for example, UK wheat producers have a price of £100 a tonne, then the law says that the price of US wheat in the UK must also be £100. This means that if US producers have a price of, say, \$150 a tonne, then the exchange rate must be £1 = \$1.50, which makes \$150 equal to £100. We can express this law with the following equation:

$$\text{Exchange rate of \$ per£} = \frac{\text{Price of basket in the US}}{\text{Priceof basket in the UK}}$$

The logic here is that if the exchange rate did not equal this value, then one set of producers would have to alter their price until it did. To see this, consider two other possible exchange rates.

- **£1 is worth more than \$1.50, say \$2.00**. Then UK consumers will not buy any UK wheat at £100 as they can import US wheat at £75; and US consumers will not import any UK wheat at $200, but will buy US wheat at $150. So UK producers will be forced to reduce their price.

- **£1 is worth less than $1.50, say $1.00**. Then US consumers will not buy any US wheat at $150, as they can import UK wheat at $100; and UK consumers will not import any US wheat at £150, but will buy UK wheat at £100. So US producers will be forced to reduce their price.

In practice, exchange rates do not adjust so that all products sell at one price. To see this, we need to divide products into two broad groups.

- **Non-tradables**. International trade is hard with some products, and the prices that their producers set can differ between countries, at the current exchange rate, without trade occurring to drive any of them out of business. This applies, for example, to milk, which is too perishable for trade, and to concrete, for which high transport costs prohibits trade. It also applies to services like meals out and haircuts, because no consumers will undertake costly international travel simply because, at the current exchange rate, the price is lower in another country.
- **Tradables**. The prices of tradable products like cars and TVs should be broadly similar at current exchange rates, although small differences can persist because of transport costs. Also, product prices do not change every time the supply and demand for currencies to be used in capital flows causes actual exchange rates to change.

Purchasing power parity theory

Suppose the law of one price did apply to all products. Then the total price of any particular basket of products would be the same in each country, if the prices were expressed in one currency at the current exchange rates. **Purchasing power parity theory** (PPP theory) is a theory that this will happen. In the case of our two countries, the UK and the US, we can express the exchange rate predicted by this theory in the following formula:

$$\text{Exchange rate of \$ per £} = \frac{\text{Price of basket in the US}}{\text{Price of basket in the UK}}$$

For example, if a basket of products costs $3,000 in the US and £2,000 in the UK, then PPP theory predicts that the exchange rate will be £1 = $1.50, because this makes the two prices equal.

We can use PPP theory to show how exchange rates are affected by inflation rates. Suppose inflation in the UK is faster than in the US, and in five years the prices of the baskets are $4,000 in the US and £4,000 in the UK. Then the value of the pound predicted by PPP theory will fall from its previous level of £1 = $1.50 to £1 = $1. Notice that the basket initially cost ⅔ as many pounds as dollars, but it eventually cost the same number of pounds as dollars. It was this ⅓ rise in the relative cost in pounds that reduced the value of £1 predicted by PPP theory by ⅓ from $1.50 to $1.00.

In fact, actual exchange rates do not exactly equal the rates predicted by PPP theory. This is because, as we have seen, the law of one price does not apply universally. However, the gap between the two rates is often modest. Figure 28.3 gives an example of this by comparing the two exchange rates between sterling and US dollars over the last 20 years.

Interest rate parity

We will now see how exchange rates and capital flows and are related. Consider a US citizen, Chuck, who has $300 that he wants to put in a deposit for a year. He considers two options: one is to place them in a dollar deposit, and the other is to use them to buy pounds at the current exchange rate of, say, £1 = $1.50, and then place £200 in a sterling deposit. To choose between these options, Chuck must consider two issues.

- **The interest rates on both types of deposit**. We will assume throughout that the interest rate on dollar deposits is 5%, so with one of these Chuck would earn $15 interest over the year and end up with $315.

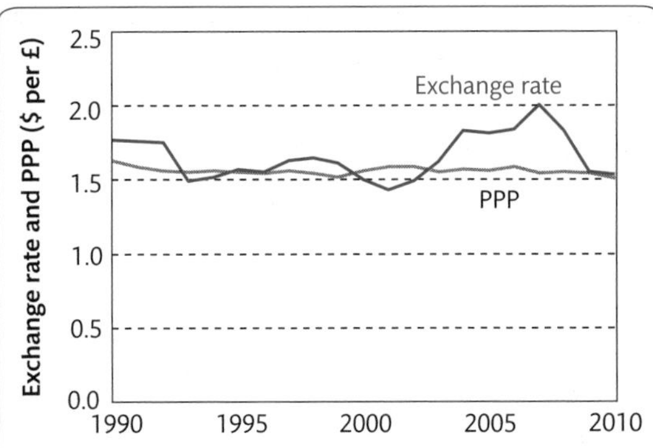

Figure 28.3 **Purchasing power parity and exchange rates for the US dollar and sterling, 1990–2010**

The actual exchange rate has mostly been above the PPP rate.

Source: OECD, *Main Economic Indicators*.

- **What might happen to the exchange rate over the next year**. We will assume that Chuck's views about this are widely shared.

We will now show how the UK interest rate must be related to the US rate and these widely shared views. To see this, consider three possibilities.

- **People expect the pound to appreciate over the year to £1 = $1.53**. In this case, UK interest rates must be 3%. Then Chuck's £200 deposit would earn £6 interest, giving him a total of £206 at the end of the year, and he would expect to exchange this for $315 (that is 206 × 1.53). If UK interest rates were any higher, UK deposits would be more attractive than US ones and UK banks would be swamped by depositors, so they would reduce their interest rate to 3%.
- **People expect the pound to stay put over the year at £1 = $1.50**. In this case, UK interest rates must equal the US rate of 5%. Then Chuck's £200 would earn £10 interest, giving him a total of £210 at the end of the year, and he would expect to exchange this for $315 (that is 210 × 1.50). If UK interest rates were higher, then UK deposits would be more attractive than US deposits, and UK banks would be swamped by depositors and would reduce their rate; if UK rates were lower, UK deposits would be less attractive than US deposits and UK banks would attract few deposits and would raise their rate.
- **People expect the pound to depreciate over the year to £1 = $1.47**. In this case, UK interest rates must be 7%. Then Chuck's £200 would earn £14 interest, giving him a total of £214 at the end of the year, and he would expect to exchange this for $315 (that is 214 × 1.47). If UK interest rates were lower, UK deposits would be less attractive than US ones, so UK banks would attract few deposits and would raise their rate to 7%.

This example explains the reasoning behind a theory called **interest rate parity**: this says that the expected returns from deposits in different countries, allowing for both interest rates and expected changes in exchange rates, must be the same. So if sterling is expected to rise against the dollar, then sterling deposits must have lower interest rates than dollar deposits, and vice versa.

This theory extends beyond deposits to say that the expected returns on all assets in a country must reflect the risks of those assets, and also the risk that the country's currency might fall in value. So if two countries have different interest rates on similar assets, then investors must fear that one currency will depreciate against the other.

Real exchange rates

So far we have discussed actual or nominal exchange rates. But sometimes economists refer to real exchange rates. These concern a basket of products, often those that are used in a country's CPI calculations. The **real exchange rate** is defined as the rate at which the basket of products produced in one country can be traded with a similar basket produced in another country.

Table 28.2 shows what this means for a case with two countries, the UK and the US. We will suppose that, in year 1, a basket of these products is priced at £2,000 by UK producers and at $4,000 by US producers. And we will suppose that, by a later year 2, the UK has had more inflation, so the price of a basket produced in the UK has risen to £3,000, while the price of a basket produced in the US has risen to $4,500.

Consider what would happen if purchasing power parity (PPP) applied. In year 1, the nominal exchange rate would be £1 = $2; then, in the UK, the price of baskets produced in each country would be £2,000. In year 2, the nominal exchange rate would be £1 = £1.50; then, in the UK, the price of baskets produced in each country would be £3,000. So in each year people could trade one UK basket for one US basket. This means that, in each year, the real exchange rate would be 1.00. In fact, if PPP always applied, real exchange rates would always equal 1.00.

But we know that actual exchange rates usually differ from PPP rates. Let's assume that, in year 1, the actual value of the pound was below the PPP rate of $2.00, and was $1.60, while in year 2 the actual rate was above the PPP rate of $1.50 at $1.80. Then the table shows that, in year 1, the price in the UK of a basket produced in the US was £2,500. So a basket produced in the UK, which was priced at £2,000, had only 0.80 the price of a US basket, and the real exchange rate was 0.80. In year 2, the price in the UK of a basket produced in the US was £2,500. So a basket produced in the UK, which was priced at £3,000, had 1.20 the price of a US basket, and the real exchange rate was 1.20.

The real exchange rate, *rer*, is related to the nominal exchange rate, *ner*, by this formula:

$$rer = ner \times \frac{\text{Price of UK basket}}{\text{Price of US basket}}$$

So in year 1 the *rer* is 1.6 x 2,000/4,000, or 0.8, and in year 2 the *rer* is 1.8 x 3,000/4,500, or 1.2.

A rise in the real exchange rate for sterling means UK products have risen in value against those of other countries. So UK citizens can buy more imports for a given quantity of exports. However, a rise in the real exchange rate also makes UK products less competitive in terms of price, so it encourages UK citizens to buy more imports and it deters foreign citizens from buying UK exports. Conversely, a fall in the real exchange rate makes UK products more competitive in terms of price, so it deters imports and helps exports.

Table 28.2 **Real exchange rates**

	Year 1	Year 2
Price of basket produced in UK:	£2,000	£3,000
Price of basket produced in US:	$4,000	$4,500
What would happen with PPP		
The nominal exchange rate would settle so that £1 buys:	$2.00	$1.50
So price in UK of UK basket:	£2,000	£3,000
And price in UK of US basket:	£2,000	£3,000
So the real exchange rate is:	**1.00**	**1.00**
What might happen without PPP		
Suppose the nominal exchange rate settles so that £1 buys:	$1.60	$1.80
So price in UK of UK basket:	£2,000	£3,000
And price in UK of US basket:	£2,500	£2,500
So the real exchange rate is	**0.80**	**1.20**

28.1 **Everyday economics**

Is the euro overvalued?

US travellers to the eurozone typically find that, at current exchange rates, the prices of hotels and meals are well above US prices, so the euro seems overvalued, and some people expect it to fall. However, if we allow for VAT, we find that prices are similar to the US, and there are three reasons why the euro may actually appreciate against the dollar. First, the products that affect exchange rates are those traded internationally, and the eurozone has a balance of trade surplus. Secondly, major exporting countries like China have even larger surpluses and may want to buy euros to invest in a major market. Thirdly, countries with foreign exchange reserves largely in dollars may prefer to diversify into euros.

'Is the euro overvalued?', *The Star Online*, 27 March 2010
'Is the euro overvalued?', *Project Syndicate*, 29 March 2010

Comment The euro's actual exchange rates have tended to exceed its PPP exchange rates, but this analysis by Professor Martin Feldstein from Harvard University suggests that the euro is unlikely soon to plummet.

28.3 Summary

- Purchasing power parity theory builds on the law of one price to say that exchange rates will settle so that the prices at which any particular basket of products sells in any two countries will be the same, if the prices are expressed in one currency at the current exchange rate.
- In practice, exchange rates differ from those predicted by this theory, partly because some products are not tradable, so that their prices can differ between countries. However, exchange rates are related to those predicted by this theory.
- Interest rate parity theory argues that the expected returns from similar assets in different countries, including bank deposits, must be equal once expected changes in exchange rates are allowed for.
- The real exchange rate is the rate at which a basket of products produced in one country can be traded with a similar basket produced in another country. If a country's real exchange rate increases, its imports will rise and its exports will fall.

28.4 International finance and demand management

We know that countries often use monetary and fiscal policies to alter aggregate demand. So each country needs to know how its demand management policies may be affected by international payments. The effects actually depend greatly on its choice of exchange rate regime and on whether it restricts capital flows. We will now consider the effects in the case of the UK, which for nearly 20 years has had a floating exchange rate and high capital mobility. But what we say about demand management in the UK applies to most other developed countries and to the eurozone, because they also have floating exchange rates and highly mobile capital.

We will begin by supposing that the economy has a recessionary gap, as shown in the right-hand part of Figure 28.4. Here, actual output is Y_0, where the short-run aggregate supply curve, *SAS*, intersects the initial aggregate demand, AD_0. But Y_0 is below potential output, Y_P, which is, as always, at the level of the long-run aggregate supply curve, *LAS*.

The left-hand part of the figure shows the money market. The initial interest rate is r_0 where the initial money supply and demand curves, MD_0 and MS_0, intersect. We will assume that the same rate also applies abroad; this actually means that people do not expect sterling's value to change.

Monetary policy

Let's suppose that the government asks the Bank of England to tackle the recessionary gap with an expansionary monetary policy. Most likely the Bank will cut Bank Rate, and this will shift the real money supply curve in Figure 28.4 to the right to MS_1. Suppose the Bank holds the curve there. Then the following sequence of events will occur.

- **The interest rate will fall to r_1, and this raises consumer spending, C, and investment, *I*.** So aggregate demand shifts to the right, say to AD_1. So output starts to rise towards Y_1.
- **The lower interest rate also leads to capital outflows, so the nominal exchange rate falls.** According to interest rate parity, it must fall until

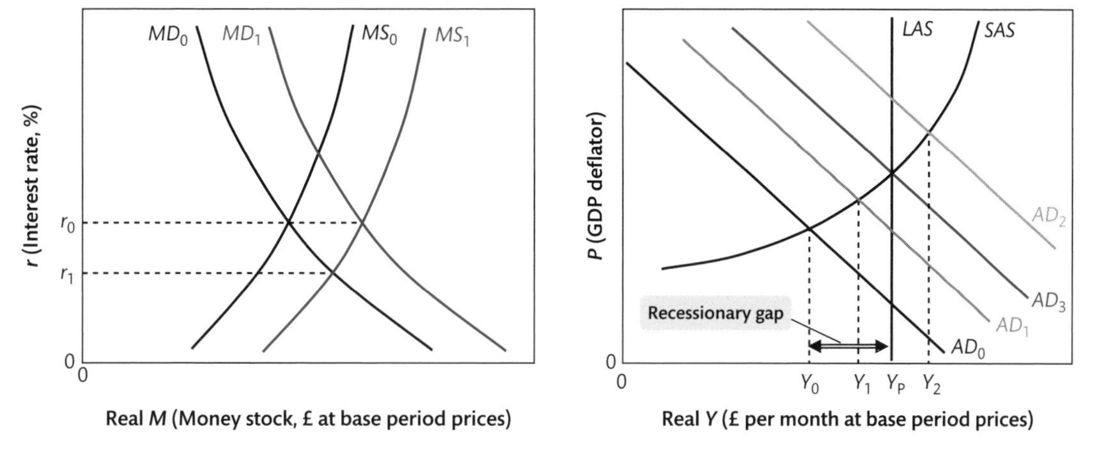

Figure 28.4 **Monetary policy and a recessionary gap with a floating exchange rate**

A fall in Bank Rate shifts the money supply curve right and reduces the interest rate, so consumption and investment rise, taking demand to AD_1. Also, the exchange rate falls, raising exports and cutting imports, taking demand to AD_2. As output rises, the demand for money rises, raising the interest rate: it ends up at its initial level if people expect no more changes in the exchange rate. Then consumption and investment return to their initial levels, taking demand to AD_3 and output to Y_P.

people believe that it will later rise by enough to offset the fact that the UK's interest rate is now below the level of r_0 that applies elsewhere.

- **The fall in the nominal exchange rate increases exports, *X*, and decreases imports, *M*.** So aggregate demand shifts further to the right, say to AD_2. So it seems that output will rise to Y_2, which, as drawn, is above Y_P.
- **As output starts to rise, the demand for money rises, so the interest rate rises.**

This interest rate rise offsets much of the impact of the initial interest rate fall, and it causes most variables, including the nominal exchange rate, to move back towards their original values. However, if the Bank holds the money supply curve at its new position, MS_1, then the final outcome cannot be the same as the initial position. The final outcome actually depends on what views people hold about the value of sterling that is given by the new exchange rate, as follows.

- **First view: people expect sterling to stay at its new value.** In this case, interest rate parity means the UK interest rate must again equal the rate abroad, which is r_0. So money demand must end up at MD_1, which intersects MS_1 at r_0. So money demand ends up higher than it started. This means that output and incomes must be higher than they were initially, and that in turn means that aggregate demand must be higher. However, as the UK interest rate returns to r_0, so *C* and *I* return to their initial levels, and this means that the rise in aggregate demand must be entirely the result of a rise in *X* and a fall in *M*. This means that the exchange rate must end up lower than it started. In Figure 28.4, aggregate demand ends up at AD_3 to take output to Y_P as desired. If aggregate demand is any lower, then Bank Rate should be reduced further.
- **Second view: people expect that, at some future date, sterling will appreciate from its new value.** In this case, interest rate parity means that the UK interest rate must end up below the rate abroad of r_0; people will accept a low UK rate in return for the expected rise in sterling. As the interest rate will end

up below r_0, money demand must end up less than MD_1, and this means that output and incomes must end up less than Y_P. In turn, aggregate demand must be less than AD_3, so the exchange rate must have fallen less than in it did in the first view; this is because the expected appreciation of sterling makes people with funds less keen to move out of sterling.

Note that, in both views, the key result is that monetary policy can be used to change output.

Fiscal policy

Now suppose that the government tackles the recessionary gap with fiscal policy: perhaps it cuts taxes to raise consumer spending, *C*, and also increases government purchases, *G*. The effects are shown in Figure 28.5, where the initial black curves are repeated from Figure 28.4. The fiscal policy causes the following sequence of events.

- **The rise in *C* and *G* shift aggregate demand say to AD_1.** So output starts to rise towards Y_P. As it does, the demand for money starts to rise towards MD_1. So the interest rate rises above r_0.
- **The higher interest rate causes a capital inflow to the UK, and so raises the nominal exchange rate.** Incidentally, output may initially rise very little, causing only a small rise in the demand for money and so only a small rise in the interest rate. But this could cause a large capital inflow and so, in turn, a large rise in the nominal exchange rate.
- **The rise in the exchange rate reduces *X* and raises *M*.** So aggregate demand falls below AD_1.

To see what the final outcome may be, we will consider two views as before. In each case, the key to understanding the final outcome is to realize that there can be no equilibrium until the capital inflow stops, because until it does stop the exchange rate will continue to rise, leading to further changes in *X*, *M*, and aggregate demand.

- **First view: people expect sterling to stay at its new value.** In this case, for the capital inflow to stop, the UK interest rate must end up back at r_0, which is the level we take to apply elsewhere. In Figure 28.5, this

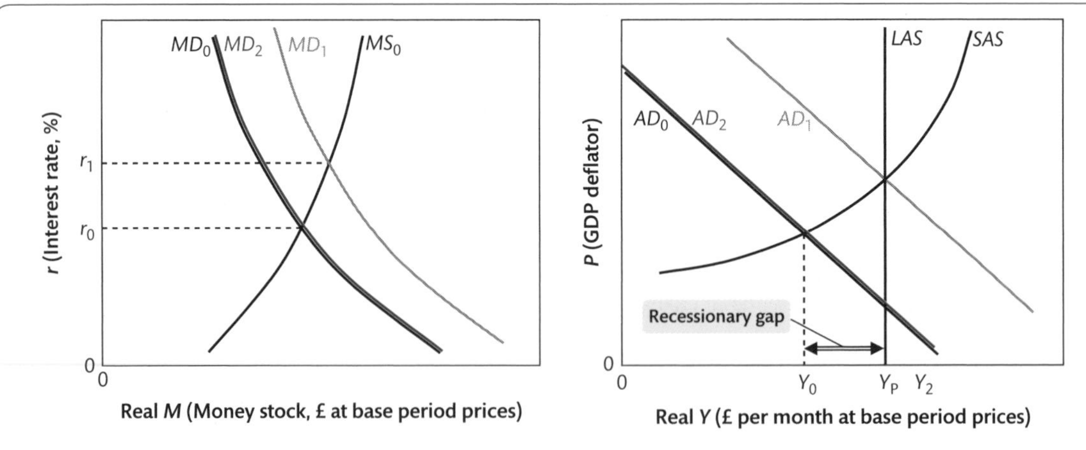

Figure 28.5 **Fiscal policy and a recessionary gap with a floating exchange rate**

A cut in taxes raises consumption and this, along with higher government purchases, shifts demand to AD_1. But as output starts to rise, the demand for money starts to rise and the interest rate rises causing capital inflows. This raises the exchange rate, reducing exports and increasing imports, reducing demand again. If people end up expecting no more changes in the exchange rate, then the interest rate returns to its initial level, and this means that the demand for money must be at its original level, and in turn that means that aggregate demand and output must be back at their initial levels.

means money demand must fall to MD_2 which intersects MS_1 at r_0. Note that MD_2 coincides with MD_0, and this means that output and incomes must return to the original Y_0. That in turn means aggregate demand must fall back to AD_2 which coincides with AD_0. Note that as the capital inflow comes to an end, the nominal exchange rate will drop back. But it will not return to its original level. It must end up higher to ensure that there is a fall in X and a rise in M that will offset the initial rise in C and G to return aggregate demand to its initial level.

- **Second view: people expect that, at some future date, sterling will depreciate from its new value.** Here, the interest rate will not return to its initial level, r_0. This is because people will want a higher UK interest rate than the r_0 that applies elsewhere in return for the expected fall in sterling. As the interest rate ends up above r_0, the demand for money must be more than MD_0. Accordingly, output and incomes must end up above Y_0, so aggregate demand must be above AD_0. This means that the nominal exchange rate must drop back more than it did in the first view, so that the rises in C and G are not wholly offset by changes in X and M. The exchange rate rise is less here because people with funds are less keen to move into sterling.

The key result here is that, with the first view, fiscal policy has no effect on output, although the composition of aggregate demand changes, with the initial effects on C and G offset by effects on X and M. With the second view, fiscal policy is likely to have only a modest effect on output, and the initial changes in C and G are not wholly offset by changes in X and M.

Overshooting

In our analysis of monetary expansion, we saw that it initially caused the nominal exchange rate to fall; then the exchange rate rose again, but to a lower level than where it started. Likewise, we saw that the attempted fiscal expansion initially caused the nominal exchange rate to rise; then the nominal exchange rate dropped back, but to a higher level than that at which it started. When a variable reacts to a shock by initially going beyond its new equilibrium level, there is said to be **overshooting**. Figure 28.6 shows how the exchange rate between sterling and another currency, such as the euro, will change over time in response to each type of expansionary policy.

Question 28.2 Suppose at time t in Figure 28.6 there were **(a)** a monetary contraction, or **(b)** a fiscal contraction. What paths would the exchange rate take over time?

Combining monetary and fiscal policy

Figure 28.4 showed how monetary policy led to a rise in exports and a fall in imports, which then increased demand and output. But suppose the government would prefer a rise in consumers' expenditure and government purchases. Then it could combine a monetary expansion with a fiscal expansion. The former would raise exports and cut imports and so raise output. The latter might not affect demand and output at all, as we saw in Figure 28.5. But it would raise

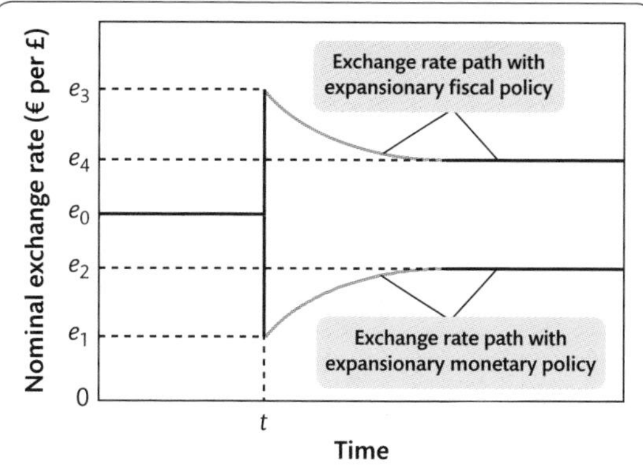

Figure 28.6 **An overshooting exchange rate**

The initial exchange rate for sterling against the euro is e_0. Monetary expansion at time t reduces the rate to e_1, but it later rises back to e_2; fiscal expansion at time t raises the rate to e_3, but it later drops back to e_4. Overshooting occurs in each case, as shown by the pink parts of each path.

consumers' expenditure and government purchases, and offset that with a fall in exports and a rise in imports.

Responses to demand shocks

Let's now suppose that the economy starts with output at the potential level Y_P. So, as shown in Figure 28.7, the initial aggregate demand and short-run aggregate supply curves, AD_0 and SAS_0, intersect at Y_P. Now suppose that any component of aggregate demand falls, so that aggregate demand shifts to the left to AD_1, causing output to fall towards Y_1. As output falls, unemployment rises, so there will be downward pressure on wages. This will shift the short-run aggregate supply curve to the right to help to increase output and employment.

A floating exchange gives further help. As output falls, so the demand for money falls and the interest rate falls, and this reduces the nominal exchange rate. So exports rise and imports fall, shifting aggregate demand to the right. If short-run aggregate supply shifts to SAS_1, and aggregate demand shifts to AD_2, then output will return to Y_P without any use of monetary or fiscal policy.

The government might simply wait for these factors to return output to Y_P. But it could implement policies to speed things up, as follows.

- **Monetary policy**. It could reduce Bank Rate and so reduce interest rates further, causing a bigger fall in the exchange rate, and so bigger changes in exports and imports.
- **Fiscal policy**. It could cut taxes and raise government purchases. If it were to act as soon as the shock occurs it might even hold aggregate demand at AD_0, despite the fall in whichever component of demand causes the shock. In this case, there would be no fall in the interest rate or exchange rate, and so no rise in exports or fall in imports. Instead, aggregate demand would be held at AD_0 by higher consumer spending and government purchases. This result preserves a clear role for fiscal policy in demand management.

With either policy, however, and especially with fiscal policy, there is a risk that time lags could result in the effect on aggregate demand taking place after output had returned to Y_P. If so, the policies would increase demand when it was not needed, and then create an inflationary gap.

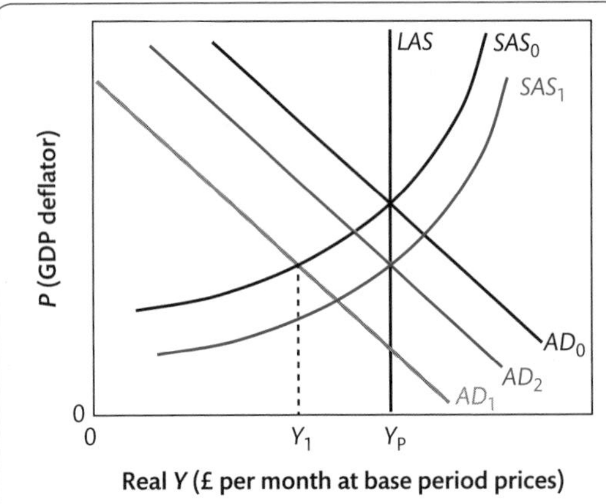

Figure 28.7 **A demand shock and a floating exchange rate**

The shock reduces output to Y_1. The resulting unemployment reduces wages and shifts short-run aggregate supply to SAS_1. Also the demand for money falls, reducing the interest rate and in turn the nominal exchange rate. So exports rise and imports fall, shifting demand to AD_1.

Policies with fixed exchange rates

We noted at the start of this section that the effects of international payments on demand management policies depend on a country's choice of exchange rate regime and capital mobility. To see this, consider for example the possibility of combining a fixed exchange rate with high capital mobility.

- **Fiscal policy**. Suppose the government raises its purchases, G, or cuts taxes to raise consumption, C. Then aggregate demand rises, and so in turn do output, incomes, the demand for money, and the interest rate. We would normally expect the higher interest rate to cause some fall in *C* and investment, *I*, that would offset some of the initial rise in aggregate demand. However, the interest rate rise will lead to capital inflows and so put upward pressure on sterling. To maintain the fixed value of sterling, the government must sell sterling for foreign currencies; in other words, it must buy foreign currencies. Then, as with any other government spending, the banks will gain reserves, so the money supply curve will shift to the right. The government must do this until the interest rate returns to its initial level to stop capital inflows, and this means there will be no fall in *C* and *I* to offset any of the initial rise in aggregate demand. So fiscal policy acts powerfully on aggregate demand and output.

- **Monetary policy**. Suppose the Bank of England cuts Bank Rate to shift the money supply curve to the right, aiming to reduce the interest rate and so raise aggregate demand. The fall in the interest rate will cause capital outflows and put downward pressure on sterling. To keep the value of sterling fixed, the government must buy some sterling. It will pay for this sterling by selling some of its reserves of foreign currencies. When people use sterling to buy these foreign currencies, their banks lose reserves, so the money supply curve shifts back to the left; and the downward pressure on sterling will persist until it returns to its original position and so returns the interest rate to the original level to stop the capital outflows. Because the Bank cannot cause a lasting shift in the money supply curve, monetary policy cannot be used to alter aggregate demand or output.

28.4 Summary

- If a country has a floating exchange rate and high capital mobility, monetary policy will alter aggregate demand and output. For example, a lower Bank Rate initially reduces the interest rate, *r*, so *C* and *I* rise. But the exchange rate falls, so *X* rises and *M* falls. In time, higher output raises the demand for money, so *r*, *C*, and *I* may return to their original levels, but the changes in *X* and *M* ensure a rise in output.
- In contrast, fiscal policy may not be able to change aggregate demand and output. For example, tax cuts to raise *C* combined with a rise in *G* will initially increase output; then in turn money demand rises, *r* rises, the exchange rate rises, *X* falls, and *M* rises, so aggregate demand falls back. In time, the changes in *X* and *M* may fully offset those in *C* and *G*, returning output to its original level.
- Both fiscal policy and monetary policy can be used to tackle demand shocks.
- With fixed exchange rates and capital mobility, fiscal policy can alter output, but monetary policy cannot.

28.5 Should the UK use sterling or the euro?

Most countries allow their currencies to float, or else independently determine fixed exchange rates for them. Sometimes, however, a group of countries form a **monetary union**, in which they agree on fixed exchange rates between their currencies and try to maintain those rates. Sometimes a group of countries goes even further to form a **currency union**, in which they share a single currency and, perhaps, a central bank.

Many currency unions are dominated by a single large country: for example the US dollar is used in several much smaller countries including Panama, Ecuador and, more recently, Zimbabwe. Likewise sterling is used in several small countries including Gibraltar and the Falkland Islands.

The eurozone is another currency union. It has 17 member countries with no dominant member, and it has its own central bank, the European Central Bank. This section explores the arguments for and against a country joining a currency union, as would apply to the UK joining the eurozone.

Advantages of joining a currency union

The main advantages for a country joining a currency union are as follows.

- **It promotes competition and efficiency between members**. If all UK products were priced in euros, it would be easier to compare their prices with competing eurozone products. This should encourage producers to be more efficient.
- **International traders no longer face the risks that arise when currency values can change**. So there may be more international trade, which will benefit consumers.
- **It removes the cost of exchanging currencies for international transactions**. Every time you buy a product made elsewhere in the eurozone, part of what you pay goes to a currency exchange, and this would be avoided if the UK were to join.
- **It may reduce inflation**. This point applies chiefly to eurozone members with a history of high inflation and government reluctance to raise interest rates enough to reduce inflation. Joining the euro with its independent central bank has reduced their inflation. However, the UK has low inflation, so this point is not strong in its case.

Finally, we should note that some people support the EU's currency union in the hope that it will lead to a political union at some future date.

Disadvantages of joining a currency union

If a country joins a currency union, then it can no longer operate its own monetary policy, because the interest rate and the money stock will be determined by the union for the union. Eurozone countries also have limited scope for fiscal policy, because there are limits on the deficits and debt levels that their governments are allowed. However, the UK may not be too concerned about how much freedom it would lose over fiscal policy if it were to join the eurozone, because it has already signed up to the limits, and there is not much the eurozone can do to countries that break them.

On the other hand, there are several reasons why the UK might be concerned about its inability to operate its own monetary policy if it were to join the eurozone. They include the following.

- **Some members might have recessionary gaps, while others have inflationary gaps**. In this case, there is no single monetary policy that will suit everyone and there might instead be a neutral monetary policy. So a member with a recessionary gap might be stuck with it until its wages fall sufficiently to remove it; yet, if it were outside the union, it could have an expansionary monetary policy and also allow its currency to depreciate to reduce imports and raise exports.
- **Factors that cause shocks may affect members differently, so that ideally each would have a different policy response**. For example, an oil price shock would greatly affect most eurozone countries, so the eurozone might react with an expansionary monetary policy. But the shock will not affect the UK much, because it exports almost

as much oil as it imports. So it might not want any change in monetary policy.

- **Mortgages**. A high proportion of UK households are owner-occupiers, many of whom have mortgages with variable interest rates. So changes in interest rates may affect consumer spending, and in turn demand and output, more in the UK than elsewhere in the eurozone.

Another problem for the UK of joining the eurozone would be a greater obligation to make large and costly loans to countries in difficulty. For example, in 2010 and 2011, many eurozone countries had to help Greece, Ireland, and Portugal, as we saw in Chapter 26. Without this help, those countries might have had to leave the eurozone, in order to stimulate their economies by having low interest rates and letting their currencies depreciate. Their eurozone partners did not want them to leave, fearing that this might threaten the future of the euro. In 2010, the eurozone set up a European Financial Stability Facility (EFSF) to organize loans to members in difficulty.

Finally, some opponents of the UK joining the euro fear that it will lead to political union. And politicians, mindful of the humiliation of Black Wednesday, are very cautious about any monetary links with the EU.

An optimal currency area

We will now explore the conditions under which the advantages of joining a currency union are likely to outweigh the disadvantages, focusing on the UK and the eurozone. When a large geographical area is better off with a single currency than with more than one, it is called an **optimal currency area**.

We have seen that the chief advantages of the UK joining the eurozone would be more competition, removing the cost of exchanging currencies, and removing uncertainty. The more trade there is between the UK and the eurozone, the bigger these benefits will be. Interestingly, the UK does relatively less trade with eurozone countries than most eurozone countries do with the others; admittedly, it might well do more trade with them if it were to join.

We have also seen that the main disadvantage of the UK joining the eurozone is that it would be unable to pursue its own individual policies if its economy were in a different position from the others. This disadvantage is likely to be of least concern if the following conditions are met.

- **Wages are flexible**. In this case, a recessionary gap would disappear quickly through falling wages, with no need for a lower exchange rate or for expansionary monetary or fiscal policies. UK legislation to restrict the power of trade unions may actually make wages here relatively flexible; even so, it might not feel that its wages are flexible enough to want to join the eurozone.
- **Labour is highly mobile geographically**. Then, if UK unemployment was high, and wages in fact proved fairly sticky, people could go and work elsewhere. But within the eurozone, different languages and cultures restrict mobility between countries, and many people dislike moving in order to find jobs.
- **Members tend to have similar output gaps over time, so that a uniform policy will suit them all**. Many people worry that the UK's gaps differ over time from those in the eurozone as a whole. Certainly its gaps are not as close to the eurozone as some members, but they are closer than others. For example, Figure 28.8 shows that, since 1992, the UK's gaps have been closer to those of the eurozone than Ireland's gaps, although not as close as France's gaps. However, even if the UK's gaps were to become very close to those of the eurozone for many years, there would always be a worry that one day they might diverge.

It is unclear from these arguments whether joining the euro would be in the UK's interest, and UK governments are wary. One further issue is how durable the euro will prove. If it weathers the next few years with no members leaving, then it will have proved more robust than some cynics expected, and that may strengthen the chances of the UK joining at some future date.

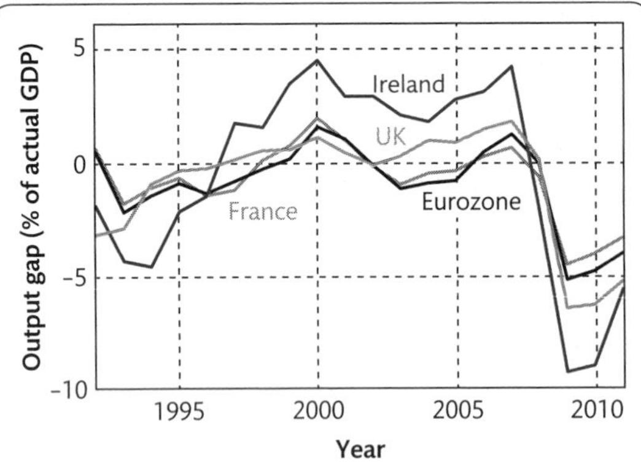

Figure 28.8 **Some EU output gaps, 1992–2011**

Output gaps in the eurozone as a whole are shown by the black line. Some members, like France have had similar gaps, but others, like Ireland, have not. The UK's gaps have been closer than Ireland's but not as close as France's.

Source: OECD Economic Outlook.

28.2 Everyday economics

Ireland has €67.5 billion bailout

Ireland's government has been loaned €67.5 billion, two-thirds of it coming from EU countries and one-third from the International Monetary Fund. Some €35 billion will be used to support Ireland's banks and the rest to help its government to meet its budget deficit.

'Details of Ireland's €85 billion bail-out agreed', *Slugger O'Toole*, 28 November 2010
'Ireland bailout: main points', *The Telegraph, 29* November 2010

Comment Ireland's government deficit had escalated rapidly to 30% of GDP, partly because the government paid huge sums to rescue its banks, which were very hard hit by the recession. And that was because property prices in Ireland, which had rocketed in the previous 20 years, plummeted, so the banks could not fully recoup loans to mortgage borrowers who defaulted by repossessing their homes and selling them off. Ireland also had the problem that, as a member of the eurozone, it could not tackle its high unemployment by monetary expansion or by depreciating its currency. And it has to raise taxes and cut government spending to reduce its deficit in line with EU limits, so that it is experiencing fiscal contraction.

28.5 Summary

- Joining a currency union such as the euro has several advantages, including increased efficiency because of more competition, removing fees for currency exchange, and ending uncertainty over exchange rates.
- The key disadvantages of joining a union are that a member cannot operate its own monetary policy, and may have limited freedom over its use of fiscal policy. These disadvantages are smallest if the country has inflationary and recessionary gaps at similar times and extents as the union as a whole, and if it has flexible wages, and if its labour is mobile between it and the union.

abc Glossary

Adjustable peg: this is like a fixed exchange rate except that a country is willing to alter the rate if there is a persistent drain on its reserves.

Appreciation: a rise in the value of a currency on the foreign exchange markets.

Balance of payments account: an account that gives the balance for international payments.

Balance of trade: the balance for international trade in goods and services combined.

Capital flows: all payments covered by the capital and financial accounts of the balance of payments.

Capital mobility: the ease with which people can make capital flows between countries.

Currency union: a monetary union with a single currency and, perhaps, a single central bank.

Current balance: the overall balance for the current account of the balance of payments.

Depreciation: a fall in the value of a currency on the foreign exchange markets.

Exchange rate band: when a country aims to keep the value of its currency within a broad band of one or more other currencies.

Fixed exchange rate: when a government fixes the exchange rate of its currency against another.

Floating exchange rate: when a government allows the value of its currency to fluctuate in line with market forces, never buying it or selling it.

Foreign exchange market: the market in which currency exchanges buy and sell currencies.

Interest rate parity: a theory that the expected returns from deposits, or from any other similar assets, must be the same in all countries; these returns allow for the interest paid on the assets and for any expected changes in exchange rates.

Law of one price: a theory that the prices at which a product sells in different countries will all be the same if they are expressed in one currency at the current exchange rates.

Managed float: this is like a floating exchange rate except that a country intervenes occasionally.

Monetary union: when countries fix the exchange rates between them and try to maintain those rates.

Nominal exchange rate: the actual rate of exchange.

Optimal currency area: when a large geographical area is better off with one currency than with more than one.

Overshooting: when a variable reacts to a shock by initially going beyond its new equilibrium level.

Purchasing power parity theory: a theory that exchange rates settle so that the prices at which any particular basket of products sells in any two countries will be equal, if the prices are expressed in one currency at the current exchange rate.

Real exchange rate: the rate at which a basket of products produced in one country can be traded with a similar basket produced in another country.

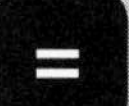

Answers to in-text questions

28.1 Anyone could make a profit here using a process called arbitrage. They could take £1 to Bank A and ask for €1.25, then take that to Bank B and ask for £1.09 (that is the value of €1.25 at its exchange rate). They would want to do this with all their pounds. To stop running out of euros, Bank A would have to give fewer for each pound, say €1.20, and to stop running out of pounds, Bank B would want more euros for each, say €1.20.

28.2 **(a)** Monetary contraction is the opposite of monetary expansion, so the exchange rate rises and then falls back a little, with a path like the upper one in Figure 28.6. **(b)** Fiscal contraction is the opposite of fiscal expansion, so the exchange rate falls and then rises back a little, with a path like the lower one in Figure 28.6.

? Questions for review

28.1 For each of the following events, which items on the balance of payments would be affected?

(a) You paint a portrait of a student from overseas who pays you £500 from an account in the UK.

(b) You donate £50 from your bank account to a foreign charity, which exchanges it for the currency used in its own country.

(c) Prior to a gap year in Australia, you ask your UK bank to use £1,000 in your deposit to buy some Australian dollars and to place these in a new deposit, which you open at an Australian bank.

28.2 What will happen to the price of sterling in euros in the following cases?

(a) A German firm buys a UK hotel group.

(b) Inflation is higher in the UK than in the eurozone.

(c) An item on today's news makes people think sterling will fall in value.

28.3 Explain briefly how, in a country with an inflationary gap and a floating exchange rate, monetary policy might successfully remove the gap.

28.4 Explain briefly how, in a country with an inflationary gap and a floating exchange rate, fiscal policy might have no effect on the gap.

? Questions for discussion

28.1 When China buys reserves to hold down the value of the yuan, it also raises the value of other currencies against the yuan. What does China gain and lose from its policy? What does the UK gain and lose?

28.2 Suppose you were Chancellor of the Exchequer. Would you join the euro now? If so, why? If not, explain whether this is because you think the time is not right or because you think it will never be right.

Common student errors

It is sometimes argued that a country like the UK, with a floating exchange rate, abandons all influence over the value of its currency. It certainly makes little or no use of reserves to do so, but Figure 28.6 shows that it can still alter its exchange rates with monetary and fiscal policies.

Also, it is sometimes claimed that there is no place for fiscal policy in a country with a floating exchange rate. But the text shows that fiscal policy will affect output if people believe that the country's currency will later change from its new value, so that the interest rate does not return to its original level.

Fiscal policy can also be used with monetary policy to ensure that consumer spending and government spending cause output to change rather than exports and imports. And it can be used to offset a demand shock, if it is used promptly.

Index

Bold black type is used for the key terms which appear in the end-of-chapter glossaries; it is also used to indicate the pages of the relevant golssary entries. **Bold purple** type is used to indicate pages where these key terms are first explained in the text.

A

B

C

D

E

F

H

M

N

P

Q

R

T

U

V

W

Z